| **Interest, Principal, Rate, and Time Formulas** | Interest | $I = PRT$ | Time | Time in years $= \dfrac{I}{PR}$ |
|---|---|---|---|---|
| | Principal | $P = \dfrac{I}{RT}$ | | Time in days $= \dfrac{I}{PR} \times 360$ |
| | Rate | $R = \dfrac{I}{PT}$ | | |

---

**Maturity Value**

The *maturity value*, $M$, of a principal of $P$ dollars at a rate of interest $R$ for $T$ years is either

$$M = P + I$$

or, since $I = PRT$,

$$M = P(1 + RT).$$

---

**Present Value at Simple Interest**

The *present value at simple interest*, $P$, of a future value $M$ at a rate of interest $R$ for a time $T$ is

$$P = \frac{M}{1 + RT}.$$

---

**Simple Interest and Simple Discount**

| Variables Used for Simple Interest | Variables Used for Simple Discount |
|---|---|
| $I$ = Interest | $B$ = Discount |
| $P$ = Principal (Face value) | $P$ = Proceeds |
| $R$ = Rate of interest | $D$ = Discount rate |
| $T$ = Time in years, or Fraction of a year | $T$ = Time in years, or Fraction of a year |
| $M$ = Maturity value | $M$ = Maturity value |

| | Simple Interest | Simple Discount |
|---|---|---|
| Face value | Stated on note, or $P = \dfrac{M}{1 + RT}$ | Same as maturity value, or $M = \dfrac{P}{1 - DT}$ |
| Interest charge | $I = PRT$ | $B = M \cdot D \cdot T$ |
| Maturity value | $M = P + I$ or $M = P(1 + RT)$ | Same as face value, or $M = \dfrac{P}{1 - DT}$ |
| Amount received by borrower | Face value or principal | Proceeds: $P = M - B$ or $P = M(1 - DT)$ |
| Identifying phrases | Interest at a certain rate. Maturity value greater than face value | Discounted at a certain rate. Proceeds. Maturity value equal to face value |
| Annual interest rate | Same as stated rate, $R$ | Greater than stated rate, $D$ |

# MATHEMATICS FOR BUSINESS

# MATHEMATICS FOR
# BUSINESS

SIXTH EDITION

**Stanley A. Salzman**
*American River College*

**Charles D. Miller**

**Gary Clendenen**
*University of Texas—Tyler*

 **ADDISON-WESLEY**

An imprint of Addison Wesley Longman, Inc.

Reading, Massachusetts • Menlo Park, California • New York • Harlow, England
Don Mills, Ontario • Sydney • Mexico City • Madrid • Amsterdam

Publisher: Greg Tobin

Editorial Project Manager: Christine O'Brien

Production Supervisor: Rebecca Malone

Cover and Text Design: Susan Carsten

Cover Photo: Ron Chapple/FPG International

Senior Marketing Manager: Andrew Fisher

Manufacturing Supervisor: Ralph Mattivello

Prepress Services Buyer: Caroline Fell

Project Management, Composition, and Prepress Services: University Graphics, Inc.

Illustrations: Tech-Graphics Corp.


**Library of Congress Cataloging-in-Publication Data**

Salzman, Stanley A.
   Mathematics for business / Stanley A. Salzman, Charles D. Miller,
Gary Clendenen.—6th ed.
     p.  cm.
   Includes index.
   ISBN 0-321-01598-3
   1. Business mathematics.   I. Miller, Charles David, 1942–    .
II. Clendenen, Gary.   III. Title.
HF5691.S26   1998
650′.01′513—dc21                       97-21401
                                           CIP

1 2 3 4 5 6 7 8 9 10—DOC—00999897

# Contents

# Part 2    Accounting Mathematics

# Part 3    Mathematics of Retailing

## Part 4    Mathematics of Finance

# Part 5    Advanced Accounting

# Appendixes

# Preface

The sixth edition of *Mathematics for Business* provides solid, practical, and up-to-date coverage of those topics students must master to attain success in business today. The text has an increased focus on current issues in society that directly affect students including taxes, mutual funds, IRAs, debt, and inflation. The globalization of society is introduced through examples and exercises. Over 50% of the exercises have been rewritten, and they have all been carefully checked for accuracy. There is a greater emphasis on application problems than ever before.

## Features

***Clippings and Charts*** A new selection of clippings and charts from various news media appear within chapter sections and are tied to examples within the section. This is a constant reminder to the student of the relevance and application of the various topics.

***Scientific Calculator Solutions*** New in this edition, scientific calculators are introduced in Appendix A, and calculator approaches to solving the problems, each marked with an icon, are shown throughout the text.

***Financial Calculators*** For the first time in this edition, coverage of financial calculators is included. They are illustrated in Appendix A, which also includes exercises that may be solved by students using the financial calculator of their choice.

***Graded Application Exercises*** Also new for this edition, application exercises increase in difficulty level. Each even-numbered application exercise is the same type of problem as the preceding odd-numbered exercise. This allows the student to solve an odd-numbered exercise, check the answer in the answer section, and then solve the following even-numbered exercise.

***Numerous Exercises*** Mastering business mathematics requires working many exercises, so we have included more than 3,400 in the sixth edition. They range from simple drill problems to real life application exercises that require several steps to solve. All problems have been independently checked to ensure accuracy.

***Supplementary Exercises*** Sets of supplementary exercises to help students review and synthesize difficult concepts appear in Chapter 3 (Percent).

***Writing Exercises*** Designed to help students better understand and relate the concepts within a section, these exercises require a short written answer. They often include references to a specific learning objective to help students formulate an answer.

*Pretests*  A Pretest in business mathematics is included in the text's introduction. This helps students and instructors identify individual and class strengths and weaknesses.

*Problem Solving Hints*  These hints provide helpful suggestions to the student and are located throughout the text.

*Chapter Review Material*  Each chapter ends with a Quick Review, Summary Exercises, and Chapter Review Exercises, which together serve to reinforce students' understanding of the chapter topics.

# New Content Highlights

The calculator section in Chapter 1 (Operations with Fractions) has been moved to Appendix A where there are sections on scientific and financial calculators. Chapters 1 and 2 (Basic Mathematics) review the basics of fractions and algebra and contain numerous drill problems.

Extensive changes to the drill and application exercises have been made in Chapter 3 (Percent). This chapter alone contains over 300 exercises, most of which are application problems. The wide selection of application problems offers the instructor the chance to work on the reading and comprehension skills of students while reviewing the concepts of percent.

The material in Chapter 4 (Banking Services) has been updated to reflect current banking trends and practices. Banking charges and credit card deposit slips are the latest available, and the reconciliation form has been simplified to reflect current industry changes.

In Chapters 5 and 6 (Payroll, Taxes), all wages and salaries have been updated along with FICA, Medicare, and tax-withholding rates. Chapter 7 (Risk Management) has been updated to include current insurance coverages and rates. Estimating inventory value using the retail method has been added to Chapter 10 (Markdown and Inventory Control).

The concept of inflation, the time value of money, future and present value, and consumer price indexes were added to Chapter 11 (Simple Interest), and Chapter 13 (Compound Interest). Chapter 14 (Annuities and Sinking Funds) includes the important topic of retirement accounts.

Chapter 15 (Business and Consumer Loans) was extensively revised and now includes sections on Personal Property Loans and Real Estate Loans.

Important topics such as paying off credit card balances when due to avoid high interest charges and loan consolidation to reduce payments have also been added to the chapter.

Chapter 17 (Financial Statements and Ratios) uses the actual financial statements of the Coca-Cola Company. Students learn how to study and analyze the financial statements of a real company whose products they probably use. Additions to Chapter 18 (Securities and Profit Distribution) include definitions and applications of mutual funds and the Dow Jones Industrial Average. The difference between population and mean is now included in Chapter 19 (Business Statistics).

## Supplements

***Instructor's Resource Guide and Solutions Manual*** (ISBN 0-321-02417-6) An extensive instructor's manual contains teaching tips, pretests in basic mathematics and business mathematics, six different test forms for each chapter (two are multiple choice), additional test items, two final examinations, answers to all test materials and solutions to selected even-numbered exercises in the textbook.

***Student's Solutions Manual*** (ISBN 0-321-02416-8) This contains solutions to selected odd-numbered exercises in the text.

***Electronic Calculator Workbook*** (ISBN 0-673-38902-2) The *Electronic Calculator Workbook with Business Applications* by Rita Evans Bowtell, Bakersfield College, may be used with this textbook in a standard course, or may become the central text of an electronic calculator-based course.

**The Test Generator/Editor with QuizMaster** is a computerized test generator that allows instructors to select test questions by objective or section, or to use a ready-made test for each chapter. The software is algorithm driven so that regenerated number values maintain problem types and provide many test items in both multiple-choice and open-response formats for one or more test forms. The **editor** allows instructors to modify existing questions or to create their own including graphics and accurate math symbols. Tests created with Test Generator/Editor can be used with QuizMaster, which records student scores on a single computer or network as they take tests, and prints reports for students, classes, or courses. Test Generator/Editor and QuizMaster are available in IBM (DOS program, will run on Windows) and Macintosh formats.

**Videotape Series and Telecourse** (available through Intelecom at 1-800-LRN-BY-TV) The Southern California Consortium has produced a videotape series called *By the Numbers*, based on *Mathematics for Business*. The series has been aired on the Public Broadcasting System (PBS). Your school can offer a telecourse using *Mathematics for Business* and the teleguide for *By the Numbers*, or the videotapes can be used for a traditional lecture course.

## Acknowledgments

We would like to thank the many users of the fifth edition for their insightful observations and suggestions for improving this book. We also wish to express our appreciation and thanks to the following reviewers for their contributions:

> Ruth Ann Briggs, *Detroit College of Business*
> Linda Bruenjes, *Bay State College*

Richard A. Buck, *Harrisburg Area Community College*

Lea Campbell, *Lamar University*

Bobbie D. Corbett, *Northern Virginia Community College*

N. Eric Ellis, *Essex Community College*

Fran Ford, *Virginia Western Community College*

Diane Hendrickson, *Becker College*

Jan Hoeweler, *Cincinnati State Technical and Community College*

Larry Hollar, *Catawba Valley Community College*

Howard Hunnius, *John Tyler Community College*

Jagmohan Kapoor, *University of Maryland Baltimore County*

Dawn Kindel, *Newbury College*

Theodore Lai, *Hudson County Community College*

Marjorie Lapham, *Quinsigamond Community College*

Michel Marette, *Northern Virginia Community College*

John Mastiani, *El Paso Community College*

A. Ally Mishal, *Stark State College of Technology*

Bonnie D. Phillips, *Casper College*

Pat Reinardy, *Chippewa Valley Community College*

Thomas J. Ryan, *Madison Area Technical College*

Ellen Sawyer, *College of DuPage*

Ned Schillow, *Lehigh Carbon Community College*

Lawrence J. Skane, *Catonsville Community College*

Francis C. Widmer, *Tidewater Community College*

Our appreciation also goes to Jeff Suzuki and Robert Martin for their careful work checking all the exercises and examples in the book. We also would like to express our gratitude to our colleagues at American River College and the University of Texas at Tyler who have helped us immeasurably with their support and encouragement.

Also, special thanks and appreciation go to Sheri Minkner and Judy Martinez for their neat and accurate manuscript typing and to Larry and Cyndi Clendenen for their help in checking the manuscript for errors.

At Addison-Wesley, we would like to thank Christine O'Brien and Rebecca Malone. We also thank Meg Arnosti, Sandy Gormley, and Ginny Guerrant. These very talented and focused people made sure that all the elements of this project came together in superb fashion.

Stanley A. Salzman

Gary Clendenen

# Introduction to Students

## Success in Business Mathematics

With a growing need for record keeping, establishing budgets, and understanding finance, taxation, and investment opportunities, mathematics has become a greater part of our daily lives. This text applies mathematics to daily business experience. Your success in future business courses and pursuits will be enhanced by the knowledge and skills you will learn in this course.

Studying business mathematics is different than studying subjects such as English or history. The key to success is regular practice. This should not be surprising. After all, can you learn to ski or to play a musical instrument without a lot of regular practice? The same is true for learning mathematics. Working problems nearly every day is the key to becoming successful. Here are suggestions to help you succeed in business mathematics.

**1. Pay attention in class to what your instructor says and does, and make careful notes.** Note the problems the instructor works on the board and copy the complete solutions. Keep these notes separate from your homework to avoid confusion.

**2. Don't hesitate to ask questions in class.** It is not a sign of weakness, but of strength. There are always other students with the same question who are too shy to ask.

**3. Determine whether tutoring is available and know how to get help when needed.** Use the instructor's office hours and contact the instructor for suggestions and direction.

**4. Before you start on your homework assignment, rework the problems the instructor worked in class.** This will reinforce what you have learned. Many students say, "I understand it perfectly when you do it, but I get stuck when I try to work the problem."

**5. Read your text carefully.** Many students read only enough to get by, usually only the examples. Reading the complete section will help you to be successful with the homework problems. As you read the text, work the example problems and check the answers. This will test your understanding of what you have read. Pay special attention to highlighted statements and those labeled "Note" and "Problem-Solving Hint."

**6. Do your homework assignment only after reading the text and reviewing your notes from class.** Estimate the answer before you begin working the problem in the text. Check your work before looking at the answers in the back of the book. If you get a problem wrong and are unable to see why, mark that problem and ask your instructor.

**7. Work as neatly as you can using a *pencil* and organize your work carefully.** Write your symbols clearly, and make sure the problems are clearly separated from each other.

**8. After you have completed a homework assignment, look over the text again.** Try to decide what the main ideas are in the lesson. Often they are clearly highlighted or boxed in the text.

**9. Keep any quizzes and tests that are returned to you for studying for future tests and the final exam.** These quizzes and tests indicate what your instructor considers most important. Be sure to correct any test problems that you missed. Write all quiz and test scores on the front page of your notebook.

**10. Don't worry if you do not understand a new topic right away.** As you read more about it and work through the problems, you will gain understanding. No one understands each topic completely right from the start.

## Pretest in Business Mathematics

This pretest measures your business mathematics skills at the beginning of the course. The solutions to each of these problems are to be found in this book on the given page.

**(page 2)**    **1.** Convert to an improper fraction: $8\frac{3}{4}$

**(page 3)**    **2.** Convert to a mixed number: $\frac{23}{3}$

**(page 7)**    **3.** Find the least common denominator of the fractions $\frac{5}{12}$, $\frac{7}{18}$, and $\frac{11}{20}$.

**(page 8)**    **4.** Mixed numbers—add: $34\frac{1}{2} + 23\frac{3}{4} + 34\frac{1}{2} + 23\frac{3}{4}$

**(page 9)**    **5.** Common fractions—subtract: $\frac{17}{18} - \frac{20}{27}$

**(page 9)**    **6.** Mixed numbers—subtract:    $36\frac{2}{9}$

$- 27\frac{5}{6}$

(page 14)    **7.** Mixed numbers—multiply: $5\dfrac{5}{8} \times 4\dfrac{1}{6}$

(page 15)    **8.** Common fractions—divide: $\dfrac{25}{36} \div \dfrac{15}{18}$

(page 17)    **9.** Convert the decimal 0.028 to a fraction.

(page 30)    **10.** Solve $y + 12.3 = 20.5$ for $y$.

(page 34)    **11.** Solve $5r - 2 = 2(r + 5)$ for $r$.

(page 45)    **12.** Solve for $T$ in the formula $M = P(1 + RT)$

(page 52)    **13.** Find $x$ in the proportion: $\dfrac{4}{9} = \dfrac{36}{x}$

(page 62)    **14.** Express as a percent: 0.7

(page 63)    **15.** Express as a decimal: 142%

(page 68)    **16.** Solve for part: 1.2% of 180 is _____.

(page 74)    **17.** Solve for base: 135 is 15% of _____.

(page 74)    **18.** The 5% sales tax collected by Famous Footwear was $780. What was the amount of total sales?

(page 87)    **19.** The price of a home sold by real estate agent Kim Crosby this year is $121,000, which is 10% more than last year's value. Find the value of the home last year.

(page 90)    **20.** After a dealer deducted 10% from the price of a pair of skis, your friend paid $135. What was the original price of the skis?

(page 177)    **21.** Suppose that during a certain quarter Leslie's Pool Supplies has collected $2,765.42 from its employees for FICA tax, $638.17 for medicare tax, and $3,572.86 in federal withholding tax. Compute the total amount due to the Internal Revenue Service from Leslie's Pool Supplies.

(page 200)    **22.** Find the taxes on each of the following pieces of property. Assessed valuations and tax rates are given.
(a) $58,975; 8.4%   (b) $875,400; $7.82 per $100
(c) $129,600; $64.21 per $1,000   (d) $221,750; 94 mills

(page 211)    **23.** Brad Beltram is single, has no dependents, and had an adjusted gross income of $19,238 last year. He had deductions of $1,352 for other taxes, $2,616 for mortgage interest, and $317 for charity. Find his taxable income and his income tax.

(page 229)    **24.** Barbara Weaks owns a commercial building valued at $380,000. Her fire insurance policy (with an 80% coinsurance clause) has a face value of $285,000. The building suffers a fire loss of $72,000. Find the amount of the loss that the insurance company will pay and the amount that Weaks must pay.

**(page 271)**    **25.** The Home Depot is offered a series discount of 20/10 on a worm drive circular saw with a list price of $150. Find the net cost after the series discount.

**(page 286)**    **26.** An invoice received by Oaks Hardware for $840 is dated July 1 and offers terms of 2/10, n/30. If the invoice is paid on July 8 and the shipping and insurance charges, which were "FOB shipping point," are $18.70, find the total amount due.

**(page 309)**    **27.** The manager of Kitchen Things purchased a pastry tool manufactured in France for $10 and will sell it for $15. Find the percent of markup based on cost.

**(page 325)**    **28.** An athletic shoe manufacturer makes a walking shoe at a cost of $16.80 per pair. Based on past experience 10% of the shoes will be defective and must be sold as irregulars for $24 per pair. If the manufacturer produces 1,000 pairs of the shoes and desires a markup of 100% on cost, find the selling price per pair.

**(page 350)**    **29.** Suppose Olympic Sports and Leisure made the following purchases of the Explorer External Frame backpack during the year.

| | |
|---|---|
| Beginning inventory | 20 backpacks at $70 |
| January | 50 backpacks at $80 |
| March | 100 backpacks at $90 |
| July | 60 backpacks at $85 |
| October | 40 backpacks at $75 |

At the end of the year there are 75 backpacks in inventory. Use the weighted average method to find the inventory value.

**(page 367)**    **30.** Jeff Guerrant took out a loan for $9,000 for 9 months for a used truck and had an interest charge of $540. What was the interest rate?

**(page 426)**    **31.** On February 27, Andrews Lincoln-Mercury receives a 150-day note with a face value of $3,500 at 8% interest per year. On March 27, the firm discounts the note at the bank. Find the proceeds if the discount rate is 12%. (Use ordinary or banker's interest.)

**(page 441)**    **32.** A savings account at Northstar Bank in Canada pays 7% per year compounded semiannually. If you initially deposit $2,500, (a) find the compound amount after 2 years and (b) find the compound interest.

**(page 498)**    **33.** KidsToys, Inc. sold $100,000 worth of bonds that must be paid off in 8 years. They now must set up a sinking fund to accumulate the necessary $100,000 to pay off their debt. Find the amount of each payment going into a sinking fund if the payments are made at the end of each year, and the fund earns 10% compounded annually.

**(page 551)**    **34.** George Willis arranged for a client to receive a $75,000 loan for 25 years at 8% to purchase a summer cabin. Annual insurance and taxes on the property are $654 and $1,329 respectively. Find the monthly payment.

**(page 581)**   **35.** City Saturn purchased an electronic smog analyzer for $9,000. Using the sum-of-the-years'-digits method of depreciation, find the first and second years' depreciation if the analyzer has an estimated life of 4 years and no salvage value.

**(page 589)**   **36.** A boat dock with a life of 10 years is installed on April 12 at a cost of $18,000. If the double-declining-balance method is used, find the depreciation for the first partial year and the next full year.

**(page 619)**   **37.** Write each of the following items as a percent of net sales.

| | | | |
|---|---|---|---|
| Gross sales | $209,000 | Salaries and wages | $11,000 |
| Returns | $9,000 | Rent | $6,000 |
| Cost of goods sold | $145,000 | Advertising | $11,000 |

**(page 658)**   **38.** Due to a steep drop in the price of oil, Alamo Energy paid no dividend last year. The company has done much better this year and the board of directors has set aside $175,000 for the payment of dividends. The company has outstanding 12,500 shares of cumulative preferred stock having par value of $50, with an 8% dividend. The company also has 40,000 shares of common stock. What dividend will be paid to the owners of each type of stock?

**(page 681)**   **39.** Laura Cameron, Jay Davis, and Donna Friedman opened a tool rental business. Cameron contributed $250,000 to the opening of the business, which will be operated by Davis and Friedman. The partners agree that Cameron will first receive a 10% return on her investment before any further division of profits. Additional profits will be divided in the ratio $1:2:2$. Find the amount that each partner would receive from a profit of $75,000.

**(page 724)**   **40.** The diameter of a part coming out of a machining process is measured regularly. The diameters vary some as shown in the frequency table. Find the (a) mean, (b) median, and (c) mode.

| Diameter (inches) | Frequency |
|---|---|
| 0.720–0.729 | 3 |
| 0.730–0.739 | 12 |
| 0.740–0.749 | 8 |
| 0.750–0.759 | 9 |
| 0.760–0.769 | 2 |

**Answers: 1.** $\dfrac{35}{4}$ **2.** $7\dfrac{2}{3}$ **3.** 180 **4.** $116\dfrac{1}{2}$ **5.** $\dfrac{11}{54}$ **6.** $8\dfrac{7}{18}$

**7.** $23\dfrac{7}{16}$ **8.** $\dfrac{5}{6}$ **9.** $\dfrac{7}{250}$ **10.** 8.2 **11.** 4 **12.** $T = \dfrac{M-P}{PR}$ **13.** 81 **14.** 70%

**15.** 1.42 **16.** 2.160 **17.** 900 **18.** $15,600 **19.** $110,000 **20.** $150

**21.** $10,380.04 **22. (a)** $4,953.90 **(b)** $68,456.28 **(c)** $8,321.62 **(d)** $20,844.50

**23.** $12,403; $1,860.45 **24.** $67,500; $4,500 **25.** $108 **26.** $841.90

**27.** 50% **28.** $34.67 **29.** $6,249.75 **30.** 8% **31.** $3,469.59

**32. (a)** $2,868.81 **(b)** $368.81 **33.** $8,744.40 **34.** $744.25 **35.** $3,600; $2,700

**36.** $2,700; $3,060 **37.** 104.5%; 4.5%; 72.5%; 5.5%; 3%; 5.5% **38.** $8; $1.88

**39.** $35,000; $20,000; $20,000 **40.(a)** 0.743 **(b)** 0.7445 **(c)** 0.7345

# Index of Applications

This index includes many of the business and consumer applications used in discussions, examples, and exercises throughout the text.

# Operations with Fractions

Businesses use mathematics every day: to calculate employee payrolls, find the interest on loans, determine the markups on items to be sold, maintain the firm's financial records, or to find the amount of taxes owed.

It is important to understand the fundamentals of mathematics, so that the more advanced problems in business mathematics can be solved. The first chapter reviews fractions, Chapter 2 looks briefly at basic equations and formulas, and Chapter 3 discusses percent. The rest of the chapters apply these mathematical skills to the many areas of business.

## 1.1 Addition and Subtraction of Fractions

**OBJECTIVES**

1. *Learn the basic terminology of fractions.*
2. *Convert mixed numbers to improper fractions.*
3. *Write fractions in lowest terms.*
4. *Use the rules for divisibility.*
5. *Add or subtract like fractions.*
6. *Find the least common denominator.*
7. *Add unlike fractions.*
8. *Add mixed numbers.*
9. *Subtract unlike fractions.*
10. *Subtract mixed numbers.*

**OBJECTIVE** 1 *Learn the basic terminology of fractions.* A **fraction** represents parts of a whole. Fractions are written as one number over another, with a line between the two numbers, as in the following.

$$\frac{5}{8} \qquad \frac{1}{4} \qquad \frac{9}{7} \qquad \frac{13}{10}$$

1

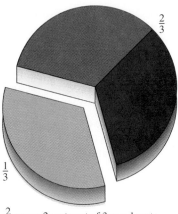

$\frac{2}{3}$ means 2 parts out of 3 equal parts

FIGURE **1.1**

The number above the line is called the **numerator**, and the number below the line is called the **denominator**. In the fraction $\frac{2}{3}$, for example, the numerator is 2 and the denominator is 3. The denominator tells the number of equal parts into which the whole is divided and the numerator tells how many (the number) of these parts are needed. For example, $\frac{2}{3}$ is "2 parts out of 3 equal parts." (See Figure 1.1.)

If the numerator of the fraction is smaller than the denominator, the fraction is a **proper fraction**. Examples of proper fractions include $\frac{2}{3}, \frac{3}{4}, \frac{15}{16}$, and $\frac{1}{8}$. A fraction with a numerator greater than or equal to the denominator is an **improper fraction**. Examples of improper fractions include $\frac{17}{8}, \frac{19}{12}, \frac{11}{2}$, and $\frac{5}{5}$. A proper fraction has a value less than 1, while an improper fraction has a value greater than or equal to 1.

To write a whole number as a fraction, place the whole number over 1; for example,

$$7 = \frac{7}{1} \quad \text{and} \quad 12 = \frac{12}{1}.$$

**OBJECTIVE** **2** *Convert mixed numbers to improper fractions.*     The sum of a fraction and a whole number is called a **mixed number**. Examples of mixed numbers include $2\frac{2}{3}, 3\frac{5}{8}$, and $9\frac{5}{6}$. The mixed number $2\frac{2}{3}$ is a short way of writing $2 + \frac{2}{3}$. A mixed number can be converted to an improper fraction. For example, to convert the mixed number $4\frac{5}{8}$ to an improper fraction, first multiply the denominator of the fraction part, 8, by the whole number part, 4. This gives $4 \times 8 = 32$. Then add the product (32) to the numerator (in this case, 5). This gives $32 + 5 = 37$. This sum is the numerator of the new improper fraction. The denominator stays the same.

$$4\frac{5}{8} = \frac{37}{8} \longleftarrow (4 \times 8) + 5$$

**EXAMPLE 1** *Converting Mixed Numbers to Improper Fractions*

Convert $8\frac{3}{4}$ to an improper fraction.

**SOLUTION**   First multiply 4 by 8, then add 3. This gives $(4 \times 8) + 3 = 32 + 3 = 35$. The parentheses are used to show that 4 and 8 are multiplied first.

$$8\frac{3}{4} = \frac{35}{4} \longleftarrow (4 \times 8) + 3$$

∎

Convert an improper fraction to a mixed number by dividing the numerator of the improper fraction by the denominator. The quotient is the whole number part of the mixed number, and the remainder is used as the numerator of the fraction part. The denominator stays the same.

| **EXAMPLE 2**  *Converting Improper Fractions to Mixed Numbers*

Convert $\frac{23}{3}$ to a mixed number.

**SOLUTION**   Divide 23 by 3.

$$\begin{array}{r} 7 \\ 3\overline{)23} \\ \underline{21} \\ 2 \end{array}$$

The whole number part is the quotient 7. The remainder 2 is used as the numerator of the fraction part. Keep 3 as the denominator.

$$\frac{23}{3} = 7\frac{2}{3}$$

∎

**OBJECTIVE** **3**  ***Write fractions in lowest terms.***      If no number except 1 divides without remainder into both numerator and denominator of a fraction, the fraction is in **lowest terms**. For example, only 1 divides without remainder into both 2 and 3, so that $\frac{2}{3}$ is in lowest terms. In the same way, $\frac{1}{9}$, $\frac{4}{11}$, $\frac{12}{17}$, $\frac{8}{9}$, and $\frac{11}{15}$ are all in lowest terms. The fraction $\frac{15}{25}$ is *not* in lowest terms, however, because both 15 and 25 may be divided by 5. Write $\frac{15}{25}$ in lowest terms by dividing numerator and denominator by 5.

$$\frac{15}{25} = \frac{15 \div 5}{25 \div 5} = \frac{3}{5}$$

| **EXAMPLE 3**  *Writing Fractions in Lowest Terms*

Write the following in lowest terms.

**(a)** $\dfrac{30}{42}$     **(b)** $\dfrac{33}{39}$

**SOLUTION**   Look for the largest number that can be divided into both numerator and denominator.

**(a)** Both 30 and 42 can be divided by 6.

$$\frac{30}{42} = \frac{30 \div 6}{42 \div 6} = \frac{5}{7}$$

**(b)** Divide by 3.

$$\frac{33}{39} = \frac{33 \div 3}{39 \div 3} = \frac{11}{13}$$ ∎

**OBJECTIVE 4** *Use the rules for divisibility.* Deciding which numbers will divide into another number without remainder is sometimes difficult. The following **rules for divisibility** can help.

---

A number can be divided by:

**2,** if the last digit is 0, 2, 4, 6, or 8;

**3,** if the sum of the digits is divisible by 3;

**4,** if the last two digits are divisible by 4;

**5,** if the last digit is 0 or 5;

**6,** if the number is even and the sum of the digits is divisible by 3;

**8,** if the last three digits are divisible by 8;

**9,** if the sum of the digits is divisible by 9;

**10,** if the last digit is 0.

---

| **EXAMPLE 4** *Using Rules for Divisibility*

Determine whether the following statements are true.

**(a)** 892 is divisible by 4.

**(b)** 231 is divisible by 3.

**SOLUTION**

**(a)** The number 892 is divisible by 4, since the last two digits form a number divisible by 4.

$$\underset{\underset{\longrightarrow 92 \text{ is divisible by 4.}}{\rule{0.4em}{0pt}}}{8\underline{92}}$$

**(b)** See if 231 is divisible by 3 by adding the digits of the number.

$$2 + 3 + 1 = \underset{\underset{\longrightarrow 6 \text{ is divisible by 3.}}{\rule{0.4em}{0pt}}}{6}$$

Since 6 is divisible by 3, the given number is divisible by 3. (Be careful: testing for divisibility by adding the digits works only for 3 and 9.) ∎

**NOTE** The rules for divisibility only help to identify which numbers divide evenly into a larger number. The division must actually be done in order to find the number of times one number divides into another. ∎

**OBJECTIVE 5** *Add or subtract like fractions.* Fractions with the same denominator are called **like fractions**. Such fractions have a **common denominator**. For example,

$\frac{3}{4}$ and $\frac{1}{4}$ are like fractions and 4 is the common denominator, but $\frac{4}{7}$ and $\frac{4}{9}$ are not like fractions. Add or subtract like fractions by adding or subtracting the numerators and then placing the result over the common denominator. The answer can then be written in lowest terms, if necessary.

### EXAMPLE 5 *Adding Like Fractions*

Add or subtract the following fractions.

**(a)** $\dfrac{3}{4} + \dfrac{1}{4} + \dfrac{5}{4}$   **(b)** $\dfrac{13}{25} - \dfrac{7}{25}$

**SOLUTION**   The fractions in both parts of this example are like fractions. Add or subtract the numerators and place the result over the common denominator. Write as a mixed number in lowest terms, as necessary.

**(a)** $\dfrac{3}{4} + \dfrac{1}{4} + \dfrac{5}{4} = \dfrac{3 + 1 + 5}{4} = \dfrac{9}{4} = 2\dfrac{1}{4}$

**(b)** $\dfrac{13}{25} - \dfrac{7}{25} = \dfrac{13 - 7}{25} = \dfrac{6}{25}$                            ∎

**OBJECTIVE** **6** *Find the least common denominator.*    Fractions having different denominators are called **unlike fractions**. Add unlike fractions by first converting them to like fractions which have a common denominator.

The **least common denominator (LCD)** for two or more fractions is the smallest whole number that can be divided, without remainder, by all the denominators of the fractions. For example, the least common denominator of the fractions $\frac{3}{4}$, $\frac{5}{6}$, and $\frac{1}{2}$ is 12, since 12 is the smallest number that can be divided by 4, 6, and 2.

Notice that in the cabinet specifications from American Landmark Cabinetry, the fractions shown in the Shelf End Base drawing are **like fractions**, $23\frac{3}{16}$, $10\frac{9}{16}$, and $11\frac{3}{16}$. However, in the drawing of the Shelf End Peninsula Base, the fractions are unlike fractions, $22\frac{7}{16}$, $11\frac{3}{32}$, and $11\frac{5}{8}$.

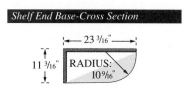

Detailed cross-section of SEB.

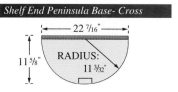

Detailed cross-section of SEPB.

There are two ways to find the least common denominator.

***Inspection.***   Check to see if the least common denominator can be found by inspection. For example, the least common denominator of $\frac{1}{3}$ and $\frac{1}{4}$ is 12, since 12 is the smallest number into which 3 and 4 both divide with remainder zero. This method works best when the denominators involved are small.

***Method of Prime Numbers.***   If you cannot find the least common denominator by inspection, use the method of prime numbers, as shown in the next example.

> A **prime number** is a number that can be divided without remainder only by itself and by 1. Prime numbers are 2, 3, 5, 7, 11, 13, 17, and so on.

**NOTE**   All prime numbers other than 2 are odd numbers. All odd numbers however, are not prime numbers. The number 1 is not a prime number.   ■

## EXAMPLE 6   *Finding the Least Common Denominator*

Use the method of prime numbers to find the least common denominator of the fractions $\frac{5}{12}$, $\frac{7}{18}$, and $\frac{11}{20}$.

**SOLUTION**   First write down the three denominators.

$$12 \quad 18 \quad 20$$

Begin by trying to divide the three denominators by the smallest prime number, 2. Write each quotient directly above the given denominator. (This way of writing the division process is just a handy way of writing the separate problems $2\overline{)12}$, $2\overline{)18}$, and $2\overline{)20}$.)

$$
\begin{array}{c}
6 \quad\; 9 \quad 10 \\
\hline
2\,\lfloor 12 \quad 18 \quad 20
\end{array}
$$

Two of the new quotients, 6 and 10, can still be divided by 2, so perform the division again. Since 9 cannot be divided by 2, just bring up the 9.

$$
\begin{array}{ccc}
3 & 9 & 5 \qquad \text{Just bring 9 up.} \\
\hline
2\,\lfloor\ 6 & 9 & 10 \\
\hline
2\,\lfloor 12 & 18 & 20
\end{array}
$$

None of the new quotients in the top row can be divided by 2, so try the next prime number, 3. The number 9 can be divided twice by 3 as shown on the left.

$$
\begin{array}{ccc}
 & 1 \quad 1 \quad 5 \\
3\,\lfloor 1 & 3 & 5 \\
\hline
3\,\lfloor 3 & 9 & 5 \\
\hline
2\,\lfloor 6 & 9 & 10 \\
\hline
2\,\lfloor 12 & 18 & 20
\end{array}
\qquad
\begin{array}{ccc}
 & 1 \quad 1 \quad 1 \\
5\,\lfloor 1 & 1 & 5 \\
\hline
3\,\lfloor 1 & 3 & 5 \\
\hline
3\,\lfloor 3 & 9 & 5 \\
\hline
2\,\lfloor 6 & 9 & 10 \\
\hline
2\,\lfloor 12 & 18 & 20
\end{array}
$$

Since none of the new quotients in the top row can be divided by 3, try the next prime number, 5. The number 5 can be used only once, as shown on the right. Now that the top row contains only 1s, find the least common denominator by multiplying the prime numbers in the left column.

$$2 \times 2 \times 3 \times 3 \times 5 = 180$$

The least common denominator is 180.   ■

**NOTE**  It is not necessary to start with the smallest prime number as shown in Example 6. In fact, no matter which prime number we start with, we will still get the same least common denominator.  ∎

**OBJECTIVE** **7** *Add unlike fractions.*     Add unlike fractions by rewriting the fractions with a common denominator. Since Example 6 shows that 180 is the least common denominator for $\frac{5}{12}$, $\frac{7}{18}$, and $\frac{11}{20}$, these three fractions can be added if each fraction is first written with a denominator of 180.

$$\frac{5}{12} = \frac{}{180} \qquad \frac{7}{18} = \frac{}{180} \qquad \frac{11}{20} = \frac{}{180}$$

Rewrite these fractions with a common denominator by first dividing the common denominator by the denominator of the original fractions.

$$180 \div 12 = 15 \qquad 180 \div 18 = 10 \qquad 180 \div 20 = 9$$

Next, multiply each quotient by the original numerator.

$$15 \times 5 = 75 \qquad 10 \times 7 = 70 \qquad 9 \times 11 = 99$$

Finally, rewrite the fractions.

$$\frac{5}{12} = \frac{75}{180} \qquad \frac{7}{18} = \frac{70}{180} \qquad \frac{11}{20} = \frac{99}{180}$$

Now add the fractions.

$$\frac{5}{12} + \frac{7}{18} + \frac{11}{20} = \frac{75}{180} + \frac{70}{180} + \frac{99}{180} = \frac{75 + 70 + 99}{180} = \frac{244}{180} = 1\frac{64}{180} = 1\frac{16}{45}$$

| **EXAMPLE 7**  *Adding Unlike Fractions*

Add the following fractions.

**(a)** $\dfrac{3}{4} + \dfrac{1}{2} + \dfrac{5}{8}$     **(b)** $\dfrac{9}{10} + \dfrac{4}{5} + \dfrac{3}{8}$

**SOLUTION**

**(a)**  Inspection shows that the least common denominator is 8. Rewrite the fractions so they each have a denominator of 8. Then add.

$$\frac{3}{4} + \frac{1}{2} + \frac{5}{8} = \frac{6}{8} + \frac{4}{8} + \frac{5}{8} = \frac{6 + 4 + 5}{8} = \frac{15}{8} = 1\frac{7}{8}$$

**(b)**  The method of prime numbers shows that the least common denominator is 40. Rewrite the fractions so they each have a denominator of 40. Then add.

$$\frac{9}{10} + \frac{4}{5} + \frac{3}{8} = \frac{36}{40} + \frac{32}{40} + \frac{15}{40} = \frac{36 + 32 + 15}{40} = \frac{83}{40} = 2\frac{3}{40} \qquad ∎$$

All calculator solutions are shown using a scientific calculator. The calculator solution to Example 7(b) uses the fraction key on the scientific calculator.

$$9 \boxed{a^{b}\!/_{c}}\ 10 \boxed{+}\ 4 \boxed{a^{b}\!/_{c}}\ 5 \boxed{+}\ 3 \boxed{a^{b}\!/_{c}}\ 8 \boxed{=}\ 2\frac{3}{40}$$

For a review of scientific calculators, see Appendix A, Calculator Basics.

**OBJECTIVE  8  *Add mixed numbers.***    Add two mixed numbers by first adding the whole number parts. Then add the fraction parts and combine the two sums.

**EXAMPLE 8  *Adding Mixed Numbers***

A rubber gasket must extend around all four edges (perimeter) of the dishwasher panel shown below before it is installed. Find the length of gasket material needed.

◄ DISHWASHER
PANEL (veneer
both sides)
COMES IN:
White Melamine (Special Order)
Oak Melamine (Special Order)
Light Oak (Special Order)
Medium Oak (Special Order)
Dark Oak (Special Order)
Pickled Oak (Special Order)

Add $34\frac{1}{2}$ inches and $23\frac{3}{4}$ inches and $34\frac{1}{2}$ inches and $23\frac{3}{4}$ inches.

**SOLUTION**

$$34\frac{1}{2} = 34\frac{2}{4}$$
$$23\frac{3}{4} = 23\frac{3}{4}$$
$$34\frac{1}{2} = 34\frac{2}{4}$$
$$+\ 23\frac{3}{4} = 23\frac{3}{4}$$

$$\frac{10}{4} = 2\frac{2}{4}$$

$$114\frac{10}{4} = 114 + 2\frac{2}{4} = 116\frac{2}{4} = 116\frac{1}{2}\ \text{inches} \quad\blacksquare$$

**NOTE**  When adding mixed numbers, first add the fraction parts, then add the whole number parts. Then combine the two answers.

**OBJECTIVE  9  *Subtract unlike fractions.***    If the fractions to be subtracted have different denominators, first find the least common denominator. For example, to subtract

$\frac{1}{3}$ from $\frac{5}{8}$, first find the least common denominator, 24. Now write each fraction with a denominator of 24 and subtract.

$$\frac{5}{8} - \frac{1}{3} = \frac{15}{24} - \frac{8}{24} = \frac{15 - 8}{24} = \frac{7}{24}$$

**EXAMPLE 9**  *Subtracting Fractions*

Subtract the following fractions.

**(a)** $\dfrac{3}{4} - \dfrac{5}{9}$    **(b)** $\dfrac{17}{18} - \dfrac{20}{27}$

**SOLUTION**    Find the common denominator and then subtract.

**(a)** $\dfrac{3}{4} - \dfrac{5}{9} = \dfrac{27}{36} - \dfrac{20}{36} = \dfrac{7}{36}$    **(b)** $\dfrac{17}{18} - \dfrac{20}{27} = \dfrac{51}{54} - \dfrac{40}{54} = \dfrac{11}{54}$    ∎

**OBJECTIVE** **10** *Subtract mixed numbers.*    Subtract two mixed numbers by changing the mixed numbers, if necessary, so that the fraction parts have a common denominator. Then subtract the fraction parts and the whole number parts separately. For example, subtract $3\frac{1}{12}$ from $8\frac{5}{8}$ by first finding the least common denominator, 24. Then rewrite the problem.

$$8\frac{5}{8} = 8\frac{15}{24}$$
$$-3\frac{1}{12} = 3\frac{2}{24}$$

Now subtract the fraction parts and subtract the whole number parts.

$$8\frac{15}{24}$$
$$-3\frac{2}{24}$$
$$5\frac{13}{24}$$

— Subtract fractions.
— Subtract whole numbers.

The following example shows how to subtract when **borrowing** is needed.

**EXAMPLE 10**  *Subtracting with Borrowing*

Subtract $27\frac{5}{6}$ from $36\frac{2}{9}$.

**SOLUTION**    Start by rewriting the problem with a common denominator.

$$36\frac{2}{9} = 36\frac{4}{18}$$
$$-27\frac{5}{6} = 27\frac{15}{18}$$

Subtracting $\frac{15}{18}$ from $\frac{4}{18}$ requires borrowing 1 from 36.

$$36\frac{4}{18} = 35 + 1 + \frac{4}{18}$$

$$= 35 + \frac{18}{18} + \frac{4}{18} \qquad 1 = \frac{18}{18}$$

$$= 35\frac{22}{18}$$

$$\begin{array}{r} 35\frac{22}{18} \\ -\ 27\frac{15}{18} \\ \hline 8\frac{7}{18} \end{array}$$

■

Rewrite the problem as shown at the right. Check by adding $8\frac{7}{18}$ and $27\frac{5}{6}$. The answer should be $36\frac{2}{9}$.

**CALCULATOR APPROACH TO EXAMPLE 10**

*The calculator solution to this example uses the fraction key.

36 $\boxed{a^b\!/_c}$ 2 $\boxed{a^b\!/_c}$ 9 $\boxed{-}$ 27 $\boxed{a^b\!/_c}$ 5 $\boxed{a^b\!/_c}$ 6 $\boxed{=}$ $8\frac{7}{18}$

## 1.1 EXERCISES

*Convert each of the following mixed numbers to an improper fraction.*

**1.** $2\frac{1}{2}$      **2.** $1\frac{3}{4}$      **3.** $4\frac{1}{4}$      **4.** $2\frac{8}{11}$

**5.** $22\frac{7}{8}$      **6.** $15\frac{2}{3}$      **7.** $12\frac{5}{8}$      **8.** $17\frac{5}{8}$

*Write each of the following fractions in lowest terms. Use the divisibility rules as needed.*

**9.** $\frac{6}{8}$      **10.** $\frac{12}{16}$      **11.** $\frac{40}{75}$      **12.** $\frac{36}{42}$

**13.** $\frac{63}{70}$      **14.** $\frac{27}{45}$      **15.** $\frac{120}{150}$      **16.** $\frac{24}{64}$

**17.** $\frac{132}{144}$      **18.** $\frac{40}{96}$      **19.** $\frac{96}{180}$      **20.** $\frac{32}{128}$

*Convert each of the following improper fractions to a mixed number and write it in lowest terms.*

**21.** $\frac{18}{7}$      **22.** $\frac{17}{8}$      **23.** $\frac{76}{20}$      **24.** $\frac{42}{15}$

**25.** $\frac{14}{11}$      **26.** $\frac{55}{8}$      **27.** $\frac{21}{15}$      **28.** $\frac{85}{52}$

*NOTE All calculator solutions use a scientific calculator. Refer to Appendix A for scientific and financial calculator basics.

**29.** $\dfrac{124}{64}$     **30.** $\dfrac{190}{35}$     **31.** $\dfrac{81}{32}$     **32.** $\dfrac{360}{64}$

 **33.** Define in your own words what a mixed number is. Give three examples of mixed numbers. (See Objective 2.)

**34.** There were eight rules of divisibility given. Write the three rules that are most useful to you. (See Objective 4.)

*Add each of the following and reduce to lowest terms.*

**35.** $\dfrac{5}{9} + \dfrac{1}{9}$     **36.** $\dfrac{5}{8} + \dfrac{1}{8}$     **37.** $\dfrac{7}{10} + \dfrac{3}{20}$     **38.** $\dfrac{3}{8} + \dfrac{1}{4}$

**39.** $\dfrac{7}{12} + \dfrac{8}{15}$     **40.** $\dfrac{5}{8} + \dfrac{7}{12}$     **41.** $\dfrac{9}{11} + \dfrac{1}{22}$     **42.** $\dfrac{5}{6} + \dfrac{7}{9}$

**43.** $\dfrac{3}{4} + \dfrac{5}{9} + \dfrac{1}{3}$     **44.** $\dfrac{1}{4} + \dfrac{1}{8} + \dfrac{1}{12}$     **45.** $\dfrac{5}{6} + \dfrac{3}{4} + \dfrac{5}{8}$     **46.** $\dfrac{7}{10} + \dfrac{8}{15} + \dfrac{5}{6}$

**47.** $\begin{array}{r} 19\frac{5}{7} \\ + 38\frac{1}{7} \\ \hline \end{array}$     **48.** $\begin{array}{r} 56\frac{1}{4} \\ + 27\frac{3}{8} \\ \hline \end{array}$     **49.** $\begin{array}{r} 51\frac{1}{4} \\ + 29\frac{1}{2} \\ \hline \end{array}$     **50.** $\begin{array}{r} 38\frac{5}{6} \\ 29\frac{1}{3} \\ + 47\frac{1}{2} \\ \hline \end{array}$

**51.** $\begin{array}{r} 28\frac{1}{4} \\ 23\frac{3}{5} \\ + 19\frac{9}{10} \\ \hline \end{array}$     **52.** $\begin{array}{r} 16\frac{7}{10} \\ 26\frac{1}{5} \\ + 8\frac{3}{8} \\ \hline \end{array}$     **53.** $\begin{array}{r} 89\frac{5}{9} \\ 10\frac{1}{3} \\ + 87\frac{1}{9} \\ \hline \end{array}$     **54.** $\begin{array}{r} 74\frac{1}{5} \\ 58\frac{3}{7} \\ + 21\frac{3}{10} \\ \hline \end{array}$

*Subtract each of the following and reduce to lowest terms.*

**55.** $\dfrac{7}{8} - \dfrac{3}{8}$     **56.** $\dfrac{11}{12} - \dfrac{5}{12}$     **57.** $\dfrac{2}{3} - \dfrac{1}{6}$     **58.** $\dfrac{7}{8} - \dfrac{1}{2}$

**59.** $\dfrac{5}{12} - \dfrac{1}{16}$     **60.** $\dfrac{5}{6} - \dfrac{7}{9}$     **61.** $\dfrac{3}{4} - \dfrac{5}{12}$     **62.** $\dfrac{5}{7} - \dfrac{1}{3}$

**63.** $\begin{array}{r} 18\frac{2}{3} \\ - 7\frac{1}{4} \\ \hline \end{array}$     **64.** $\begin{array}{r} 25\frac{13}{24} \\ - 18\frac{5}{12} \\ \hline \end{array}$     **65.** $\begin{array}{r} 9\frac{7}{8} \\ - 6\frac{5}{12} \\ \hline \end{array}$     **66.** $\begin{array}{r} 24\frac{5}{6} \\ - 18\frac{5}{9} \\ \hline \end{array}$

**67.** $\begin{array}{r} 71\frac{3}{8} \\ - 62\frac{1}{3} \\ \hline \end{array}$     **68.** $\begin{array}{r} 19\frac{5}{6} \\ - 12\frac{3}{4} \\ \hline \end{array}$     **69.** $\begin{array}{r} 19 \\ - 12\frac{3}{4} \\ \hline \end{array}$     **70.** $\begin{array}{r} 374 \\ - 211\frac{5}{6} \\ \hline \end{array}$

 **71.** Prime numbers are used to find the least common denominator. Give the definition of a prime number in your own words. (See Objective 6.)

**72.** Can you add or subtract fractions without using the least common denominator? Describe how you would do this.

**73.** Where are fractions used in everyday life? Think in terms of business applications, hobbies, and vacations. Give three examples.

**74.** When subtracting mixed numbers explain when you need to borrow. Use an example to explain how to borrow.

*Solve each of the following application problems.*

**75.** When installing cabinets, Robin Strang must be certain that the proper type and size of mounting hardware is used. Find the total length of the bolt below.

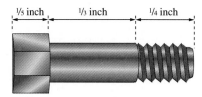

**76.** A wetlands reserve has four sides which measure $1\frac{7}{8}$ mile, $\frac{1}{2}$ mile, $1\frac{2}{3}$ mile, and $\frac{1}{3}$ mile. What is the total distance around the wetlands reserve?

**77.** John Blazer paid $\frac{1}{8}$ of a debt in January, $\frac{1}{3}$ in February, $\frac{1}{4}$ in March, and $\frac{1}{12}$ in April. What fraction of the debt was paid in these 4 months?

**78.** Kristin Petty wants to open a day-care center and has saved $\frac{2}{5}$ of the amount needed for start-up costs. If she saves another $\frac{1}{8}$ of the amount needed and then $\frac{1}{6}$ more, find the total portion of the start-up costs she has saved.

**79.** Find the diameter of the hole in the mounting bracket pictured below.

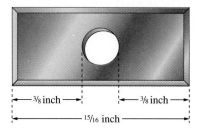

**80.** A hydraulic jack contains $\frac{7}{8}$ gallon of hydraulic fluid. A cracked seal resulted in a loss of $\frac{1}{6}$ gallon of fluid in the morning and another $\frac{1}{3}$ gallon in the afternoon. Find the amount of fluid remaining.

**81.** To complete a custom accessory order for a customer, Stephen West of the Home Depot must find the number of inches of brass trim needed to go around the four sides of the lamp base plate shown below. Find the length of brass trim needed.

**82.** On a recent vacation to Canada, Hernando Ramirez drove for $5\frac{1}{2}$ hours on the first day, $6\frac{1}{4}$ hours on the second day, $3\frac{3}{4}$ hours on the third day, and 7 hours on the fourth day. How many hours did he drive altogether?

**83.** Meg Malde-Arnosti owns $83\frac{5}{8}$ acres of land in Mexico, $76\frac{3}{4}$ acres in the United States, and $182\frac{1}{3}$ acres in Canada. Find the total number of acres that she owns in these three countries.

**84.** Last month Lim's Wholesale Vegetable Market sold $3\frac{1}{4}$ tons of broccoli, $2\frac{3}{8}$ tons of spinach, $7\frac{1}{2}$ tons of corn, and $1\frac{5}{16}$ tons of turnips. Find the total number of tons of these vegetables sold by the firm last month.

**85.** Comet Auto Supply sold $16\frac{1}{2}$ cases of generic brand oil last week, $12\frac{1}{8}$ cases of Havoline Oil, $8\frac{3}{4}$ cases of Valvoline Oil, and $12\frac{5}{8}$ cases of Castrol Oil. Find the number of cases of oil that Comet Auto Supply sold during the week.

**86.** Goldi's Resort decided to expand by buying a piece of property next to the resort. The property is irregularly shaped, with five sides. The lengths of the five sides are $146\frac{1}{2}$ feet, $98\frac{3}{4}$ feet, $196\frac{2}{3}$ feet, $76\frac{5}{8}$ feet, and $100\frac{7}{8}$ feet. Find the total distance around the piece of property.

**87.** In order to sample a shipment of grain, an inspector took $1\frac{5}{8}$ bushels from one part of a load, $3\frac{1}{4}$ bushels from a second part, $2\frac{3}{8}$ bushels from a third part, and $3\frac{1}{3}$ bushels from a fourth. Find the total number of bushels inspected.

**88.** Pam Harder worked 40 hours during one week. She worked $8\frac{1}{4}$ hours on Monday, $6\frac{1}{6}$ hours on Tuesday, $7\frac{2}{3}$ hours on Wednesday, and $8\frac{3}{4}$ hours on Thursday. How many hours did she work on Friday?

**89.** Eboni Perkins bought four shares of stock. The prices for three of the shares were $\$71\frac{3}{8}$, $\$18\frac{1}{2}$, and $\$143\frac{5}{8}$. Find the price of the fourth share if she paid a total of $\$352\frac{1}{8}$.

**90.** A contractor has a truck loaded with $9\frac{5}{8}$ cubic yards of peatmoss. The driver gives out $1\frac{1}{2}$ cubic yards at the first stop and $2\frac{3}{4}$ cubic yards at the second stop. At a third stop, the landscaper delivers $3\frac{5}{12}$ cubic yards. How much peatmoss is then left in the truck?

## 1.2 Multiplication and Division of Fractions

**OBJECTIVES**

**1** *Multiply fractions.*

**2** *Divide fractions.*

**3** *Convert decimals to fractions.*

**4** *Round decimals.*

**5** *Convert fractions to decimals.*

Multiply two fractions by first multiplying the numerator (forming a new numerator) and then multiplying the denominators (forming a new denominator). Write the answer in lowest terms. For example, multiply $\frac{2}{3}$ and $\frac{5}{8}$.

$$\frac{2}{3} \times \frac{5}{8} = \frac{2 \times 5}{3 \times 8} = \frac{10}{24} = \frac{5}{12} \quad \text{(in lowest terms)}$$

Multiply numerators. / Multiply denominators.

**OBJECTIVE** **1** *Multiply fractions.*     This problem can be simplified by using **cancellation**, a modification of the method of writing fractions in lowest terms. If a number divides evenly into a numerator and a denominator without remainder, then divide (cancel).

$$\frac{\overset{1}{\cancel{2}}}{3} \times \frac{5}{\underset{4}{\cancel{8}}} = \frac{1 \times 5}{3 \times 4} = \frac{5}{12} \qquad \text{Divide 2 into both 2 and 8.}$$

**EXAMPLE 1** *Multiplying Common Fractions*

Multiply the following fractions.

**(a)** $\dfrac{6}{11} \times \dfrac{7}{8}$     **(b)** $\dfrac{35}{12} \times \dfrac{32}{25}$

**SOLUTION**     Use cancellation in both of these problems.

**(a)** $\dfrac{\overset{3}{\cancel{6}}}{11} \times \dfrac{7}{\underset{4}{\cancel{8}}} = \dfrac{3 \times 7}{11 \times 4} = \dfrac{21}{44}$     2 was divided into both 6 and 8.

**(b)** $\dfrac{\overset{7}{\cancel{35}}}{\underset{3}{\cancel{12}}} \times \dfrac{\overset{8}{\cancel{32}}}{\underset{5}{\cancel{25}}} = \dfrac{7 \times 8}{3 \times 5} = \dfrac{56}{15} = 3\dfrac{11}{15}$     4 was divided into both 12 and 32, while 5 was divided into both 35 and 25.

**NOTE** When cancelling, be certain that a numerator and a denominator are both divided by the same number. ∎

To multiply mixed numbers, change the mixed numbers to improper fractions, then multiply. For example, multiply $6\frac{1}{4}$ and $2\frac{2}{3}$.

$$6\frac{1}{4} \times 2\frac{2}{3} = \frac{25}{4} \times \frac{8}{3} = \frac{25}{\underset{1}{\cancel{4}}} \times \frac{\overset{2}{\cancel{8}}}{3} = \frac{25 \times 2}{1 \times 3} = \frac{50}{3} = 16\frac{2}{3}$$

**EXAMPLE 2** *Multiplying Mixed Numbers*

Multiply the following.

**(a)** $5\dfrac{5}{8} \times 4\dfrac{1}{6}$     **(b)** $1\dfrac{3}{5} \times 3\dfrac{1}{3}$

**SOLUTION**

**(a)** $\dfrac{\overset{15}{\cancel{45}}}{8} \times \dfrac{25}{\underset{2}{\cancel{6}}} = \dfrac{15 \times 25}{8 \times 2} = \dfrac{375}{16} = 23\dfrac{7}{16}$

**(b)** $\dfrac{8}{\underset{1}{\cancel{5}}} \times \dfrac{\overset{2}{\cancel{10}}}{3} = \dfrac{8 \times 2}{1 \times 3} = \dfrac{16}{3} = 5\dfrac{1}{3}$

∎

CALCULATOR APPROACH
TO EXAMPLE 2

The calculator solution to Example 2(b) uses the fraction key.

$$1 \boxed{a^b/_c} \, 3 \boxed{a^b/_c} \, 5 \boxed{\times} \, 3 \boxed{a^b/_c} \, 1 \boxed{a^b/_c} \, 3 \boxed{=} \, 5\frac{1}{3}$$

**OBJECTIVE** **2** *Divide fractions.*     Divide two fractions by inverting and multiplying by the second fraction. (Invert the second fraction by exchanging the numerator and denominator.)

| **EXAMPLE 3** *Dividing Common Fractions*

Divide.

**(a)** $\dfrac{25}{36} \div \dfrac{15}{18}$     **(b)** $\dfrac{21}{8} \div \dfrac{14}{16}$

**SOLUTION**     Invert the second fraction and multiply.

**(a)** $\dfrac{25}{36} \div \dfrac{15}{18} = \dfrac{\overset{5}{\cancel{25}}}{\underset{2}{\cancel{36}}} \times \dfrac{\overset{1}{\cancel{18}}}{\underset{3}{\cancel{15}}} = \dfrac{5 \times 1}{2 \times 3} = \dfrac{5}{6}$

**(b)** $\dfrac{21}{8} \div \dfrac{14}{16} = \dfrac{\overset{3}{\cancel{21}}}{\underset{1}{\cancel{8}}} \times \dfrac{\overset{2}{\cancel{16}}}{\underset{2}{\cancel{14}}} = \dfrac{3 \times \overset{1}{\cancel{2}}}{1 \times \cancel{2}} = 3$     ■

**NOTE**   The second fraction (divisor) is inverted when dividing by a fraction. Cancellation is done *only after inverting*.   ■

Divide mixed numbers by changing all mixed numbers to improper fractions, as follows.

$$3\frac{5}{9} \div 2\frac{2}{5} = \frac{32}{9} \div \frac{12}{5} = \frac{\overset{8}{\cancel{32}}}{9} \times \frac{5}{\underset{3}{\cancel{12}}} = \frac{8 \times 5}{9 \times 3} = \frac{40}{27} = 1\frac{13}{27}$$

Multiply or divide by a whole number by first writing the whole number as a fraction over 1.

$$3\frac{3}{4} \times 16 = 3\frac{3}{4} \times \frac{16}{1} \qquad \text{whole number over 1}$$

$$= \frac{15}{4} \times \frac{16}{1}$$

$$= \frac{15}{\underset{1}{\cancel{4}}} \times \frac{\overset{4}{\cancel{16}}}{1} = 15 \times 4 = 60$$

Also:

$$2\frac{2}{5} \div 3 = \frac{12}{5} \div \frac{3}{1} = \frac{\overset{4}{\cancel{12}}}{5} \times \frac{1}{\underset{1}{\cancel{3}}} = \frac{4 \times 1}{5 \times 1} = \frac{4}{5}$$

**EXAMPLE 4** *Multiplying a Whole Number by a Mixed Number*

Bill Monroe earns $12 per hour. On Saturday he is paid time and a half. How much does he earn per hour on Saturday?

**SOLUTION**   Multiply the regular rate by $1\frac{1}{2}$, or $\frac{3}{2}$.

$$12 \times \frac{3}{2} = \frac{\overset{6}{\cancel{12}}}{1} \times \frac{3}{\underset{1}{\cancel{2}}} = \frac{6 \times 3}{1 \times 1} = \frac{18}{1} = 18$$

Monroe earns $18 per hour when he is paid time and a half.   ∎

---

**CALCULATOR APPROACH TO EXAMPLE 4**

Use the fraction key to solve this example.

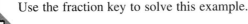

12 $\boxed{\times}$ 1 $\boxed{a^{b/c}}$ 1 $\boxed{a^{b/c}}$ 2 $\boxed{=}$ 18

---

**OBJECTIVE 3** *Convert decimals to fractions.*   A **decimal number** is really a fraction with a denominator that is a power of ten such as 10, 100, or 1,000. The digits written to the right of the decimal point have place values as shown in Figure 1.2.

Convert a decimal to a fraction by thinking of the decimal as being written in words. For example, think of 0.47 as "forty-seven hundredths." Then write this in fraction form.

$$0.47 = \frac{47}{100}$$

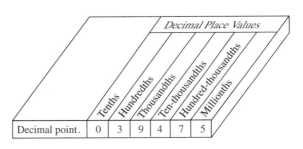

FIGURE 1.2

In the same way, 0.3, read as "three tenths," is written in fraction form as follows.

$$0.3 = \frac{3}{10}$$

Also, 0.963, read "nine hundred sixty-three thousandths," is written $\frac{963}{1,000}$.

**EXAMPLE 5** *Converting Decimals to Fractions*

Convert the following decimals to fractions.

**(a)** 0.75    **(b)** 0.028

**SOLUTION**

**(a)** 0.75 is read as "seventy-five hundredths."

$$0.75 = \frac{75}{100} = \frac{3}{4}$$

Here $\frac{75}{100}$ is written in lowest terms as $\frac{3}{4}$.

**(b)** 0.028 is read as "twenty-eight thousandths," and the resulting fraction is written in lowest terms.

$$0.028 = \frac{28}{1,000} = \frac{7}{250}$$ ∎

**OBJECTIVE** **4** *Round decimals.*    It is important to be able to round decimals. For example, the 7-Eleven Store is selling candy mints 2 for $0.25 but you only want to buy one mint. The price of one mint is $0.25 ÷ 2, which is $0.125. Since you cannot pay part of a cent, the store rounds the price to $0.13 for one mint.

Use the following steps for rounding decimals.

### ROUNDING DECIMALS

***Step 1.*** Find the place to which the rounding is being done. Draw a line **after** that place to show that you are cutting off the rest of the digits.

***Step 2A.*** Look **only** at the **first** digit you are cutting off. If the first digit is **5 or more**, increase by one the digit in the place to which you are rounding.

***Step 2B.*** If the first digit to the right of the line is **4 or less**, do not change the digit in the place to which you are rounding.

***Step 3.*** Drop all digits to the right of the place to which you have rounded.

**NOTE** Do not move the decimal point when rounding.  ∎

| EXAMPLE 6    *Rounding to the Nearest Tenth*

Round 98.5892 to the nearest tenth.

**SOLUTION**

***Step 1***    Locate the tenths digit and draw a line to the right of it.

$$98.5\,|\,892$$

↑ ⌞⎯⎯ tenths digit

The tenths digit is 5.

***Step 2***    Locate the digit just to the right of the line.

$$98.5\,|\,892$$

⌞⎯⎯ just to the right of the line

The digit just to the right of the line is 8.

***Step 3***    If the digit found in Step 2 is 4 or less, leave the digit of Step 1 alone. If the digit found in Step 2 is 5 or more, increase the digit of Step 1 by 1. The digit found in Step 2 is 8, so 98.5892 rounded to the nearest tenth is 98.6.

∎

| EXAMPLE 7    *Rounding to the Nearest Thousandth*

Round 0.008572 to the nearest thousandth.

**SOLUTION**    Locate the thousandths digit and draw a line.

$$0.008\,|\,572$$

↑ ⌞⎯⎯ thousandths digit

Since the digit to the right of the line is 5, increase the thousandths digit by 1; so that 0.008572 rounded to the nearest thousandth is 0.009.    ∎

| EXAMPLE 8    *Rounding Decimals*

Round 24.6483 to the nearest:

**(a)** thousandth

**(b)** hundredth

**(c)** tenth

**SOLUTION**    Use the method described.

**(a)**  24.6483 to the nearest thousandth is 24.648

**(b)**  24.6483 to the nearest hundredth is 24.65

**(c)**  24.6483 to the nearest tenth is 24.6    ∎

**PROBLEM-SOLVING HINT**   The answer to part (c) in Example 8 may be surprising because of the answer in (b). However, **always round a number by going back to the original number, and not to some number that was rounded from the original number.**   ■

**OBJECTIVE** **5** *Convert fractions to decimals.*     To convert a fraction to a decimal, divide the numerator of the fraction by the denominator. Place a decimal point after the numerator and attach additional zeros, one at a time, to the right of the decimal point as the division is performed. Keep going until the division ends or until the desired degree of precision is reached. As a general rule, divide until the quotient has one more digit than the desired degree of precision, then round from the last digit. **The result is the decimal equivalent to the fraction.**

For example, to convert $\frac{1}{8}$ to a decimal, divide 1 by 8.

$$8\,\overline{\smash{)}\,1.}$$

Since 8 will not divide into 1, place a 0 to the right of the decimal point. Now 8 divides into 10 once, with a remainder of 2.

$$
\begin{array}{r}
0.1 \\
8\,\overline{\smash{)}\,1.0} \\
\underline{8} \\
2
\end{array}
$$

Be sure to move the decimal point up.

Continue placing 0s to the right of the decimal point and continue dividing. The division now gives a remainder of 0.

$$
\begin{array}{r}
0.125 \\
8\,\overline{\smash{)}\,1.000} \\
\underline{8} \\
20 \\
\underline{16} \\
40 \\
\underline{40} \\
0
\end{array}
$$

Keep attaching zeros.

remainder of 0

Therefore, $\frac{1}{8} = 0.125$.

**NOTE**   The decimal answer, 0.125, was not rounded; instead, the division was continued until there was no remainder. In most problems the answer will be rounded to the required accuracy.   ■

**EXAMPLE 9**   *Rounding a Repeating Decimal*

Convert $\frac{2}{3}$ to a decimal. Round to the nearest ten-thousandth.

**SOLUTION**   Divide 2 by 3.

$$
\begin{array}{r}
0.66666 \\
3\overline{\smash{\big)}\,2.00000} \\
\underline{1\ 8}\phantom{0000} \\
20\phantom{000} \\
\underline{18}\phantom{000} \\
20\phantom{00} \\
\underline{18}\phantom{00} \\
20\phantom{0} \\
\underline{18}\phantom{0} \\
20 \\
\underline{18} \\
2
\end{array}
$$

This division results in a **repeating decimal**, which is often indicated by placing a bar over the digit or digits that repeat. The answer could be written as follows.

$$0.\overline{6} \qquad \text{or} \qquad 0.6\overline{6} \qquad \text{or} \qquad 0.666\overline{6}$$

However, rounded to the nearest ten-thousandth:

$$\frac{2}{3} = 0.6667$$

◾

---

**CALCULATOR APPROACH TO EXAMPLE 9**

The calculator solution to the example is

$$2 \boxed{\div} 3 \boxed{=} \quad 0.666666667.$$

---

**Decimal equivalents.** Some of the more common decimal equivalents of fractions are listed below. These decimals appear from least to greatest value and are

**Decimal Equivalents**

| | | |
|---|---|---|
| $\frac{1}{16} = 0.0625$ | $\frac{1}{4} = 0.25$ | $\frac{5}{8} = 0.625$ |
| $\frac{1}{9} = 0.1111$ | $\frac{5}{16} = 0.3125$ | $\frac{2}{3} = 0.6667$ |
| $\frac{1}{8} = 0.125$ | $\frac{1}{3} = 0.3333$ | $\frac{11}{16} = 0.6875$ |
| $\frac{1}{7} = 0.1429$ | $\frac{3}{8} = 0.375$ | $\frac{3}{4} = 0.75$ |
| $\frac{1}{6} = 0.1667$ | $\frac{7}{16} = 0.4375$ | $\frac{13}{16} = 0.8125$ |
| $\frac{3}{16} = 0.1875$ | $\frac{1}{2} = 0.5$ | $\frac{5}{6} = 0.8333$ |
| $\frac{1}{5} = 0.2$ | $\frac{9}{16} = 0.5625$ | $\frac{7}{8} = 0.875$ |

rounded to the nearest ten-thousandth. Sometimes decimals must be carried out further to give greater accuracy, while at other times they are not carried out as far and are rounded sooner.

## 1.2   EXERCISES

*Multiply each of the following and write in lowest terms.*

**1.** $\dfrac{2}{3} \times \dfrac{3}{4}$

**2.** $\dfrac{3}{4} \times \dfrac{1}{3}$

**3.** $\dfrac{6}{7} \times \dfrac{2}{3}$

**4.** $1\dfrac{1}{4} \times 3\dfrac{1}{2}$

**5.** $1\dfrac{2}{3} \times 2\dfrac{7}{10}$

**6.** $6 \times 4\dfrac{2}{3}$

**7.** $4\dfrac{3}{5} \times 15$

**8.** $\dfrac{3}{4} \times \dfrac{8}{9} \times 2\dfrac{1}{2}$

**9.** $\dfrac{5}{9} \times 2\dfrac{1}{4} \times 3\dfrac{2}{3}$

**10.** $\dfrac{2}{3} \times \dfrac{9}{8} \times 3\dfrac{1}{4}$

**11.** $12 \times 2\dfrac{1}{2} \times 3$

**12.** $18 \times 1\dfrac{2}{3} \times 2$

*Divide each of the following and write in lowest terms.*

**13.** $\dfrac{1}{2} \div \dfrac{2}{3}$

**14.** $\dfrac{5}{8} \div \dfrac{3}{16}$

**15.** $\dfrac{7}{12} \div \dfrac{14}{15}$

**16.** $\dfrac{7}{8} \div \dfrac{3}{4}$

**17.** $\dfrac{15}{16} \div \dfrac{5}{8}$

**18.** $\dfrac{12}{11} \div \dfrac{3}{22}$

**19.** $2\dfrac{1}{2} \div 3\dfrac{3}{4}$

**20.** $6\dfrac{1}{2} \div \dfrac{1}{2}$

**21.** $3\dfrac{1}{8} \div \dfrac{15}{16}$

**22.** $5\dfrac{1}{2} \div 4$

**23.** $6 \div 1\dfrac{1}{4}$

**24.** $3 \div 1\dfrac{1}{4}$

 **25.** Write in your own words the rule for multiplying fractions. Make up an example problem of your own showing how this works. (See Objective 1.)

 **26.** A useful shortcut when multiplying fractions involves dividing a numerator and a denominator before multiplying. This is often called cancellation. Describe how this works and give an example. (See Objective 1.)

*Find the total price for each of the following purchases of stock. It is common for the price of a share of stock to be given as a mixed number.*

**27.** 80 shares of Mattel at $25\dfrac{7}{8}$ per share

**28.** 20 shares of Bank of America at $41\dfrac{1}{8}$ per share

**29.** 24 shares of Merck at $55\dfrac{7}{8}$ per share

**30.** 48 shares of Home Depot at $45\dfrac{3}{4}$ per share

**31.** 32 shares of Ford Motor at $57\dfrac{1}{8}$ per share

**32.** 56 shares of McDonald's at $47\dfrac{3}{8}$ per share

*Convert each of the following decimals to fractions and reduce to lowest terms.*

**33.** 0.5            **34.** 0.6            **35.** 0.24           **36.** 0.72

**37.** 0.81           **38.** 0.012          **39.** 0.875          **40.** 0.375

**41.** 0.0375         **42.** 0.8125         **43.** 0.1875         **44.** 0.3125

*Round each of the following decimals to the nearest tenth and to the nearest hundredth.*

**45.** 32.605         **46.** 672.537        **47.** 0.0837         **48.** 2.548

**49.** 8.643          **50.** 86.472         **51.** 58.956         **52.** 8.065

*Convert each of the following fractions to decimals. Round the answer to the nearest thousandth if necessary.*

**53.** $\dfrac{1}{2}$     **54.** $\dfrac{7}{8}$     **55.** $\dfrac{5}{8}$     **56.** $\dfrac{5}{6}$

**57.** $\dfrac{1}{6}$     **58.** $\dfrac{2}{3}$     **59.** $\dfrac{13}{16}$     **60.** $\dfrac{19}{50}$

**61.** $\dfrac{22}{25}$     **62.** $\dfrac{1}{3}$     **63.** $\dfrac{1}{99}$     **64.** $\dfrac{73}{93}$

✐ **65.** A classmate of yours is confused about how to convert a decimal to a fraction. Write an explanation of this for your classmate including changing the fraction to lowest terms. (See Objective 3.)

✐ **66.** Explain how to convert a fraction to a decimal. Be sure to mention rounding in your explanation. (See Objective 5.)

✐ **67.** Explain in your own words the difference between hundreds and hundredths. (See Objective 3.)

✐ **68.** Write the directions for rounding a money answer to the nearest cent.

*Solve each of the following application problems.*

**69.** Shirley Cicero wants to make 8 stuffed dolls to sell at the craft fair. Each doll needs $1\frac{5}{8}$ yards of material. How many yards does she need?

**70.** Vonne Thomas worked $36\frac{1}{2}$ hours at $9 per hour. How much money did she make?

**71.** Dawn Cassinelli bought some stock in Telex Chile for $$8\frac{3}{8}$ per share. If she paid $5,025 for the stock, how many shares did she buy?

**72.** Ms. Nishimoto bought 12 shares of stock at $$18\frac{3}{4}$ per share, 24 shares at $$36\frac{3}{8}$ per share, and 16 shares at $$74\frac{1}{8}$ per share. Her broker charged her a commission of $12. Find the total amount that she paid.

**73.** Each home of a certain design needs $109\frac{1}{2}$ yards of prefinished baseboard. How many homes can be fitted with baseboards if there are 1,314 yards of baseboard available?

**74.** For one acre of crop, $7\frac{1}{2}$ gallons of fertilizer must be applied. How many acres can be fertilized with 1,200 gallons of fertilizer?

**75.** An insect spray manufactured by Dutch Chemicals, Incorporated, is mixed with $1\frac{3}{4}$ ounces of chemical per gallon of water. How many ounces of chemical are needed for $12\frac{1}{2}$ gallons of water?

**76.** Each home in a new development requires $37\frac{3}{4}$ pounds of roofing nails. How many pounds of roofing nails are needed for 36 homes?

**77.** On average, a photographer uses $12\frac{3}{4}$ rolls of film at a wedding and $7\frac{1}{8}$ rolls of film at a retirement party. Find the total number of rolls needed for 28 weddings and 16 retirement parties.

**78.** One necklace can be completed in $6\frac{1}{2}$ minutes, while a bracelet takes $3\frac{1}{8}$ minutes. Find the total time that it takes to complete 36 necklaces and 22 bracelets.

**79.** A water tank contains 35 gallons when it is $\frac{5}{8}$ full. How much water will it hold when it is full?

**80.** The fuel gauge on a piece of earth-moving equipment shows $\frac{3}{4}$ full when there are 156 gallons of fuel in the tank. Find the number of gallons in the tank when it is full.

# Chapter 1 Quick Review

| TOPIC | APPROACH | EXAMPLE |
|---|---|---|
| **1.1 Identifying types of fractions** | Proper: Numerator smaller than denominator. | $\dfrac{2}{3}, \dfrac{3}{4}, \dfrac{15}{16}, \dfrac{1}{8}$ |
| | Improper: Numerator equal to or greater than denominator. | $\dfrac{17}{8}, \dfrac{19}{12}, \dfrac{11}{2}, \dfrac{5}{3}, \dfrac{4}{4}$ |
| | Mixed: Whole number plus proper fraction. | $2\dfrac{2}{3}, 3\dfrac{5}{8}, 9\dfrac{5}{6}$ |
| **1.1 Converting fractions** | Mixed to improper: Multiply denominator by whole number and add numerator. | $7\dfrac{2}{3} = \dfrac{23}{3}$ |
| | Improper to mixed: Divide numerator by denominator and place remainder over denominator. | $\dfrac{17}{5} = 3\dfrac{2}{5}$ |
| **1.1 Writing fractions in lowest terms** | Divide numerator and denominator by the same number. | $\dfrac{30}{42} = \dfrac{30 \div 6}{42 \div 6} = \dfrac{5}{7}$ |
| **1.1 Adding like fractions** | Add numerators and reduce to lowest terms. | $\dfrac{3}{4} + \dfrac{1}{4} + \dfrac{5}{4} = \dfrac{3 + 1 + 5}{4}$ $= \dfrac{9}{4} = 2\dfrac{1}{4}$ |
| **1.1 Finding a least common denominator (LCD)** | Inspection method: Look to see if the LCD can be found. | $\dfrac{1}{3} + \dfrac{1}{4} + \dfrac{1}{10}$ |

|  |  |  |
|---|---|---|
| | Method of prime numbers: Divide by prime numbers to find LCD. | $$\begin{array}{c|ccc} & 1 & 1 & 1 \\ 5 & 1 & 1 & 5 \\ 3 & 3 & 1 & 5 \\ 2 & 3 & 2 & 5 \\ 2 & 3 & 4 & 10 \end{array}$$ |
| | Multiply the prime numbers. | $2 \times 2 \times 3 \times 5 = 60$ LCD |

| **1.1** | **Adding unlike fractions** | | |
|---|---|---|---|
| | | 1. Find the LCD. | $\dfrac{1}{3} + \dfrac{1}{4} + \dfrac{1}{10}$; LCD $= 60$ |
| | | 2. Rewrite fractions with LCD. | $\dfrac{1}{3} = \dfrac{20}{60}, \dfrac{1}{4} = \dfrac{15}{60}, \dfrac{1}{10} = \dfrac{6}{60}$ |
| | | 3. Add numerators, placing answer over LCD. | $\dfrac{20 + 15 + 6}{60} = \dfrac{41}{60}$ |

| **1.1** | **Adding mixed numbers** | | |
|---|---|---|---|
| | | 1. Add fractions. | |
| | | 2. Add whole numbers. | $9\dfrac{2}{3} = 9\dfrac{8}{12}$ |
| | | 3. Combine sums of whole numbers and fractions and simplify answer. | $+ 6\dfrac{3}{4} = 6\dfrac{9}{12}$ |
| | | | $15\dfrac{17}{12} = 16\dfrac{5}{12}$ |

| **1.1** | **Subtracting fractions** | | |
|---|---|---|---|
| | | 1. Find the LCD. | $\dfrac{5}{8} - \dfrac{1}{3} = \dfrac{15}{24} - \dfrac{8}{24}$ |
| | | 2. Subtract numerator of number being subtracted. | |
| | | 3. Write difference over LCD. | $= \dfrac{15 - 8}{24} = \dfrac{7}{24}$ |

| **1.1** | **Subtracting mixed numbers** | | |
|---|---|---|---|
| | | 1. Subtract fractions, borrowing if necessary. | $8\dfrac{5}{8} = 8\dfrac{15}{24}$ |
| | | 2. Subtract whole numbers. | $- 3\dfrac{1}{12} = 3\dfrac{2}{24}$ |
| | | 3. Combine the differences of whole numbers and fractions. | $5\dfrac{13}{24}$ |

| **1.2** | **Multiplying proper fractions** | | |
|---|---|---|---|
| | | Multiply numerators and denominators, cancelling if possible. | $\dfrac{6}{11} \times \dfrac{7}{8} = \dfrac{\overset{3}{\cancel{6}}}{11} \times \dfrac{7}{\underset{4}{\cancel{8}}} = \dfrac{21}{44}$ |

**1.2  Multiplying mixed numbers**

1. Change mixed numbers to improper fractions, cancelling if possible.
2. Multiply as proper fractions.

$$1\frac{3}{5} \times 3\frac{1}{3} = \frac{8}{\cancel{5}_1} \times \frac{\cancel{10}^2}{3}$$

$$= \frac{8}{1} \times \frac{2}{3}$$

$$= \frac{16}{3} = 5\frac{1}{3}$$

**1.2  Dividing proper fractions**

Invert the divisor and multiply.

$$\frac{25}{36} \div \frac{15}{18} = \frac{\cancel{25}^5}{\cancel{36}_2} \times \frac{\cancel{18}^1}{\cancel{15}_3}$$

$$= \frac{5}{2} \times \frac{1}{3} = \frac{5}{6}$$

**1.2  Dividing mixed numbers**

1. Change mixed numbers to improper fractions.
2. Invert the divisor, cancelling if possible.
3. Multiply.

$$3\frac{5}{9} \div 2\frac{2}{5} = \frac{32}{9} \div \frac{12}{5}$$

$$= \frac{\cancel{32}^8}{9} \times \frac{5}{\cancel{12}_3}$$

$$= \frac{40}{27} = 1\frac{13}{27}$$

**1.2  Converting decimals to fractions**

Think of the decimal as being written in words, then write it in fraction form. Reduce to lowest terms.

To convert 0.47 to a fraction, think of 0.47 as "forty-seven-hundredths," then write it as $\frac{47}{100}$.

**1.2  Rounding decimals**

Round 0.073265 to the nearest ten-thousandth.

$$0.0732\,|\,65$$
↑
ten-thousandth position

Since the digit to the right of the line is 6, increase the ten-thousandths digit by 1: 0.073265 rounds to 0.0733.

**1.2    Converting fractions to decimals**

Divide the numerator by the denominator. Round if necessary.

Convert $\frac{1}{8}$ to a decimal.

$$8\overline{)1.000} = 0.125$$

with long division:
0.125
8)1.000
    8
    ‾‾
    20
    16
    ‾‾
    40
    40
    ‾‾
     0

# Chapter 1 Review Exercises

*Write each of the following fractions in lowest terms. [1.1]*

**1.** $\dfrac{12}{20}$    **2.** $\dfrac{32}{64}$    **3.** $\dfrac{27}{81}$    **4.** $\dfrac{147}{294}$

**5.** $\dfrac{63}{70}$    **6.** $\dfrac{84}{132}$    **7.** $\dfrac{24}{1,200}$    **8.** $\dfrac{375}{1,000}$

*Convert each of the following improper fractions to mixed numbers and write in lowest terms. [1.1]*

**9.** $\dfrac{36}{5}$    **10.** $\dfrac{56}{12}$    **11.** $\dfrac{38}{24}$    **12.** $\dfrac{55}{7}$

**13.** $\dfrac{120}{45}$    **14.** $\dfrac{196}{24}$    **15.** $\dfrac{258}{32}$    **16.** $\dfrac{194}{64}$

*Solve each of the following problems and write in lowest terms. [1.1]*

**17.** $\dfrac{5}{12} + \dfrac{5}{24}$    **18.** $\dfrac{1}{5} + \dfrac{3}{10} + \dfrac{3}{8}$    **19.** $\dfrac{2}{3} - \dfrac{1}{6}$    **20.** $\dfrac{3}{4} - \dfrac{2}{3}$

**21.**
$$25\frac{1}{6}$$
$$+\, 46\frac{2}{3}$$
___

**22.**
$$18\frac{3}{5}$$
$$47\frac{7}{10}$$
$$+\, 25\frac{8}{15}$$
___

**23.**
$$6\frac{7}{12}$$
$$-\, 2\frac{1}{3}$$
___

**24.**
$$92\frac{5}{16}$$
$$-\, 11\frac{1}{4}$$
___

*Solve each of the following application problems. [1.1]*

**25.** The National Food Company sold $2\frac{2}{3}$ pounds of wheat bran, $6\frac{1}{8}$ pounds of oat bran, $15\frac{1}{2}$ pounds of wheat flour, and $10\frac{1}{6}$ pounds of flaked coconut. Find the total weight of the products sold.

**26.** Brad Beltram studied $15\frac{1}{8}$ hours over the weekend. If he studied $6\frac{1}{2}$ hours on Saturday, find the number of hours he studied on Sunday.

**27.** Desiree Ramirez worked $5\frac{1}{2}$ hours on Wednesday, $6\frac{1}{4}$ hours on Thursday, $3\frac{3}{4}$ hours on Friday, and 7 hours on Saturday. How many hours did she work altogether?

**28.** Sandy Cubelic, pastry chef, used $23\frac{1}{2}$ pounds of powdered sugar for one recipe, $34\frac{3}{4}$ pounds of powdered sugar for another recipe, and $17\frac{5}{8}$ pounds of powdered sugar for a third recipe. If Cubelic started with two 50-pound sacks of powdered sugar, find the amount of powdered sugar remaining.

**29.** Three sides of Sheri Minkner's kiwi ranch are $202\frac{1}{8}$ feet, $370\frac{3}{4}$ feet, and $274\frac{1}{2}$ feet. If the distance around the ranch is $1,166\frac{7}{8}$ feet, find the length of the fourth side.

**30.** The Catering Crew served $12\frac{2}{3}$ pounds of American cheese, $16\frac{1}{8}$ pounds of jack cheese, $15\frac{1}{2}$ pounds of sharp cheddar cheese, and $10\frac{1}{6}$ pounds of meunster cheese at a catered event. Find the total weight of the cheese served.

*Solve each problem and reduce to lowest terms. [1.2]*

**31.** $\dfrac{3}{4} \times \dfrac{7}{8}$  **32.** $\dfrac{1}{3} \times \dfrac{7}{8} \times \dfrac{3}{5}$  **33.** $\dfrac{5}{6} \div \dfrac{1}{2}$  **34.** $10 \div \dfrac{5}{8}$

**35.** $5\dfrac{7}{8} \times 2\dfrac{1}{3}$  **36.** $3\dfrac{3}{4} \div \dfrac{27}{16}$  **37.** $12\dfrac{1}{2} \times 1\dfrac{2}{3}$  **38.** $12\dfrac{1}{3} \div 2$

*Solve each of the following application problems. [1.2]*

**39.** How many athletic bags can be made from $78\frac{3}{4}$ yards of material if each bag requires $4\frac{3}{8}$ yards?

**40.** The directions on a can of fabric glue say to apply $3\frac{1}{2}$ ounces of glue per square yard. How many ounces are needed for $43\frac{5}{9}$ square yards?

**41.** The area of a piece of land is $63\frac{3}{4}$ acres. One-third of the land is sold. What is the area of the land that is left?

**42.** Kaci Salmon bought 25 shares of Korea Equity stock for $\$8\frac{3}{8}$ per share and 16 shares of Snyder Oil stock for $\$12\frac{1}{4}$ per share. How much did she pay altogether?

**43.** As the owner of an apartment complex you are remodeling, you have found that each apartment unit requires $62\frac{1}{2}$ square yards of carpet. Find the number of apartment units that can be carpeted with 6,750 square yards of carpet.

**44.** Play It Now Sports Center has decided to divide $\frac{2}{3}$ of the company's profit sharing funds evenly among the 8 store managers. What fraction of the total amount will each receive?

*Convert each of the following decimals to a fraction and reduce to lowest terms. [1.2]*

**45.** 0.75  **46.** 0.625  **47.** 0.93  **48.** 0.005

*Round each of the following decimals to the nearest tenth and to the nearest hundredth. [1.2]*

**49.** 34.324

**50.** 861.545

**51.** 0.3549

**52.** 8.025

**53.** 6.965

**54.** 0.428

**55.** 0.955

**56.** 71.249

*Convert each of the following fractions to a decimal. Round to the nearest thousandth. [1.2]*

**57.** $\dfrac{7}{8}$

**58.** $\dfrac{1}{9}$

**59.** $\dfrac{5}{6}$

**60.** $\dfrac{7}{16}$

# Chapter 1 Summary Exercise

Walt Hardin, a full-time accounting professor and experienced stock trader, had been following the stock price of Roadmaster Industries, Incorporated. The price of the stock had been just slightly over $1 per share. (Some of the lower priced stocks will sell for fractions of a dollar as small as 16ths, 32nds, and occasionally 64ths.) On January 29, Hardin purchased 1,000 shares of Roadmaster Industries at $1$\frac{1}{32}$ per share and agreed to pay a purchase commission of $90. The price of Roadmaster Industries showed increases in value over the next two weeks and Hardin phoned his stock broker with an order to sell the stock on February 13 at $1$\frac{5}{8}$ per share agreeing to a sales commission of $90.

**(a)** Find the purchase price of the stock excluding the commission.

**(b)** Find the purchase price of the stock including the commission.

**(c)** Find the selling price of the stock excluding the commission.

**(d)** Find the amount Hardin received after deducting the commission.

**(e)** How much profit did Hardin make on the investment?

# 2

# Equations and Formulas

Both equations and formulas occur again and again throughout business mathematics. For example, formulas are used for finding markup, interest, depreciation, and in other important areas of business. This chapter discusses various ways of solving basic equations and working with formulas.

## 2.1 Solving Equations

### OBJECTIVES

1. *Learn the basic terminology of equations.*
2. *Use basic rules to solve equations.*
3. *Combine similar terms in equations.*
4. *Use the distributive property to simplify equations.*

An **equation** is a statement that says two expressions are equal. For example, the equation

$$x + 5 = 9$$

says that the expression $x + 5$ and 9 are equal. In dealing with an equation certain terminology is used.

**OBJECTIVE 1** ***Learn the basic terminology of equations.*** The letter $x$ is called a **variable**—a letter that represents a number. The variable $x$, as well as the numbers 5 and 9, are called terms. A **term** is a single letter, a single number, or the product of a number and one or more letters. Different terms are separated from one another by $+$ or $-$ signs. The expression $x + 5$ is called the **left side** of the equation while 9 is the **right side**. A **solution** to the equation is any number which can replace the variable and result in a true statement. The solution for this equation is the number 4, since the replacement of the variable $x$ with the number 4 results in a true statement.

$$x + 5 = 9$$

$$4 + 5 = 9 \quad \text{Let } x = 4.$$

$$9 = 9 \quad \text{True.}$$

**29**

The preceding check is an example of **substitution**: the variable $x$ was replaced with 4.

**OBJECTIVE** **2** *Use basic rules to solve equations.*    In solving equations, the object is to find numbers that can be used to replace the variable so that the equation is a true statement. This is accomplished by changing the equation so that all the terms containing a variable are on one side of the equation and all the numbers are on the other side. Since an equation states that two expressions are equal, as long as both sides of the equation are changed in the same way the resulting expressions remain equal. The rules for solving equations follow.

**Addition Rule.** The same number may be added or subtracted on both sides of an equation.

**Multiplication Rule.** Both sides of an equation may be multiplied or divided by the same nonzero number.

**NOTE**   Remember, what you do to one side of an equation must also be done to the other side.   ■

**EXAMPLE 1** *Solving Equations Using Addition*

Solve $x - 9 = 15$.

**SOLUTION**   To solve this equation, $x$ must be alone on one side of the equal sign, and all numbers collected on the other side. To change the $x - 9$ to $x$, perform the opposite operation to "undo" what was done. The opposite of subtraction is addition, so add 9 to both sides.

$$x - 9 = 15$$
$$x - 9 + 9 = 15 + 9 \qquad \text{Add 9 on both sides.}$$
$$x + 0 = 24$$
$$x = 24$$

To check this answer, substitute 24 for $x$ in the original equation.

$$x - 9 = 15 \qquad \text{Original equation.}$$
$$24 - 9 = 15 \qquad \text{Let } x = 24.$$
$$15 = 15 \qquad \text{True.}$$

The answer, 24, checks.   ■

**EXAMPLE 2** *Solving Equations Using Subtraction*

Solve $y + 12.3 = 20.5$.

**SOLUTION**   To isolate $y$ on the left side, do the opposite of adding 12.3, which is *subtracting* 12.3.

$$y + 12.3 = 20.5$$

$$y + 12.3 - 12.3 = 20.5 - 12.3 \qquad \text{Subtract 12.3 from both sides.}$$

$$y + 0 = 8.2$$

$$y = 8.2$$

Check the answer by substituting 8.2 for $y$ in the original equation.

$$y + 12.3 = 8.2 + 12.3 = 20.5$$

The answer checks. ∎

In formulas, the product of a number and a variable is often written without any special symbol for multiplication. As an example, the product of 5 and $p$ could be written as $5p$, instead of $5 \times p$. The number 5 in the term $5p$ is the **coefficient** of $p$. Also, $\frac{1}{2}$ is the coefficient of $z$ in the term $\frac{1}{2}z$, and the coefficient of $s$ is 1 since $s = 1 \cdot s$.

### EXAMPLE 3  *Solving Equations Using Division*

Solve $5p = 60$.

**SOLUTION**  The term $5p$ indicates the product of 5 and $p$. Since the opposite of multiplication is division, solve the equation by *dividing* both sides by 5.

$$5p = 60$$

$$\frac{5p}{5} = \frac{60}{5} \qquad \text{Divide both sides by 5.}$$

$$p = 12$$

Check by substituting 12 for $p$ in the original equation. ∎

### EXAMPLE 4  *Solving Equations Using Multiplication*

Solve $\dfrac{r}{8} = 13$.

**SOLUTION**  The bar in $\frac{r}{8}$ means to divide ($r \div 8 = 13$), so solve the equation by multiplying both sides by 8. (The opposite of division is multiplication.) As in the following solution, it is common to use a dot to indicate multiplication.

$$\frac{r}{8} = 13$$

$$\frac{r}{8} \cdot 8 = 13 \cdot 8 \qquad \text{Multiply both sides by 8.}$$

$$\frac{r}{\cancel{8}} \cdot \cancel{8} = 104$$

$$r = 104$$ ∎

Example 5 shows how to solve an equation using a reciprocal. To get the **reciprocal** of a nonzero fraction, exchange the numerator and the denominator. For example, the reciprocal of $\frac{7}{9}$ is $\frac{9}{7}$. The product of two reciprocals is 1:

$$\frac{\overset{1}{\cancel{7}}}{\underset{1}{\cancel{9}}} \cdot \frac{\overset{1}{\cancel{9}}}{\underset{1}{\cancel{7}}} = 1.$$

| **EXAMPLE 5**  *Solving Equations Using Reciprocals*

Solve $\frac{3}{4}z = 9$.

**SOLUTION**    Solve this equation by multiplying both sides by $\frac{4}{3}$, the reciprocal of $\frac{3}{4}$. This process will give just $1z$, or $z$, on the left.

$$\frac{3}{4}z = 9$$

$$\frac{4}{3} \cdot \frac{3}{4}z = \frac{4}{3} \cdot 9 \qquad \text{\small Multiply both sides by } \frac{4}{3}.$$

$$z = 12 \qquad\qquad\qquad\qquad\qquad\qquad ∎$$

The equation in Example 6 requires two steps to solve.

| **EXAMPLE 6**  *Solving Equations Involving Several Steps*

Solve $2m + 5 = 17$.

**SOLUTION**    To solve equations that require more than one step, first isolate the terms involving the unknown (or variable) on one side of the equation and constants (or numbers) on the other side by using addition and subtraction.

$$2m + 5 = 17$$

$$2m + 5 - 5 = 17 - 5 \qquad \text{\small Subtract 5 from both sides.}$$

$$2m = 12$$

Now divide both sides by 2.

$$\frac{2m}{2} = \frac{12}{2} \qquad \text{\small Divide by 2.}$$

$$m = 6$$

As before, check by substituting 6 for $m$ in the original equation.    ∎

**NOTE**    The unknown can be on either side of the equal sign. $6 = m$ is the same as $m = 6$. The number is the solution when the equation has the variable on the left *or* the right.    ∎

**OBJECTIVE** **3** *Combine similar terms in equations.* Some equations have more than one term with the same variable. Terms with the same variables can be *combined* by adding or subtracting the coefficients, as shown.

$$8x + 2x = 10x$$

$$11y - 3y = 8y$$

$$12p - 5p + 2p = 9p$$

$$2z + z = 2z + 1z = 3z$$

**NOTE** Since multiplying by 1 does not change the value of a quantity, $1 \cdot z$ is the same as $z$. ■

**EXAMPLE 7** *Combining Similar Terms*

Solve $9z - 3z + 2z = 50$.

**SOLUTION** Start by combining terms on the left: $9z - 3z + 2z = 6z + 2z = 8z$. This gives the simplified equation:

$$8z = 50$$

$$\frac{8z}{8} = \frac{50}{8} \qquad \text{Divide by 8.}$$

$$z = 6\frac{1}{4} \text{ or } 6.25$$

■

**OBJECTIVE** **4** *Use the distributive property to simplify equations.* Some of the more advanced formulas used later in this book involve a coefficient in front of parentheses. These formulas often require the use of the **distributive property**, by which a number on the outside of a parentheses can be multiplied times each term inside the parentheses, as shown here.

$$a(b + c) = ab + ac$$

The following diagram may help in remembering the distributive property.

$$a(b + c) = ab + ac$$

The *a* is *distributed* over the *b* and the *c*, as in the following examples.

$$2(m + 7) = 2m + 2 \cdot 7 = 2m + 14$$

$$8(k - 5) = 8k - 8 \cdot 5 = 8k - 40$$

**EXAMPLE 8** *Solving Equations Using the Distributive Property*

Solve $6(p - 2) = 30$.

**SOLUTION**   First use the distributive property on the left to remove the parentheses.

$$6(p - 2) = 30$$

$$6p - 12 = 30$$

Add 12 to both sides, then divide.

$$6p - 12 + 12 = 30 + 12$$

$$6p = 42$$

$$\frac{6p}{6} = \frac{42}{6} \qquad \text{Divide by 6.}$$

$$p = 7 \qquad\qquad\qquad \blacksquare$$

Use the following steps to solve an equation.

## SOLVING EQUATIONS

**Step 1.**   Remove all parentheses on both sides of the equation using the distributive property.

**Step 2.**   Combine all similar terms on both sides of the equation.

**Step 3.**   Add to or subtract from both sides whatever is needed to produce a term with the variable on one side and a number on the other side.

**Step 4.**   Multiply or divide the variable term by whatever is needed to produce a term with a coefficient of 1. Multiply or divide the number term on the other side by the same quantity.

**EXAMPLE 9**   *Solving Equations Involving Several Steps*

Solve $5r - 2 = 2(r + 5)$.

**SOLUTION**

$$5r - 2 = 2(r + 5)$$

$$5r - 2 = 2r + 10 \qquad \text{Use distributive property on the right.}$$

$$5r - 2 + 2 = 2r + 10 + 2 \qquad \text{Add 2 to both sides to get all numbers on the right side.}$$

$$5r = 2r + 12$$

$$5r - 2r = 2r + 12 - 2r \qquad \text{Subtract } 2r \text{ from both sides to get all variables on the left side.}$$

$$5r - 2r = 12 \qquad \text{Combine similar terms on the left.}$$

$$3r = 12$$

$$\frac{3r}{3} = \frac{12}{3} \qquad \text{Divide both sides by 3 to get 1 as a coefficient.}$$

$$r = 4 \qquad\qquad \blacksquare$$

> **Problem-Solving Hint** Be sure to check the answer in the *original* equation and not in any other step. ∎

## 2.1 Exercises

*Solve each equation. Check each answer.*

**1.** $z + 12 = 42$

**2.** $s + 9 = 26.3$

**3.** $m - 10 = 17$

**4.** $a - 7 = 3$

**5.** $14 = c + 8$

**6.** $7 = m - 3$

**7.** $10k = 42$

**8.** $7s = 84$

**9.** $12q = 144$

**10.** $8z = 136$

**11.** $60 = 30m$

**12.** $94 = 2z$

**13.** $3.8t = 7.98$

**14.** $13.2 = 1.1p$

**15.** $4.72 = 0.8r$

**16.** $3.9a = 15.6$

**17.** $3.92w = 3.136$

**18.** $2.773m = 3.3276$

**19.** $0.0002x = 0.08$

**20.** $0.0324 = 0.0135y$

**21.** $\dfrac{s}{7} = 42$

**22.** $\dfrac{m}{5} = 6$

**23.** $\dfrac{r}{7} = 1$

**24.** $\dfrac{c}{7} = 2$

**25.** $\dfrac{2}{3}b = 8$

**26.** $22 = \dfrac{5}{4}s$

**27.** $35 = \dfrac{7}{5}t$

**28.** $\dfrac{7}{3}s = 21$

**29.** $2x = \dfrac{5}{3}$

**30.** $4y = \dfrac{1}{3}$

**31.** $3p = \dfrac{5}{12}$

**32.** $\dfrac{3}{4} = 9a$

**33.** $7b + 9 = 37$

**34.** $3m + 5 = 17$

**35.** $4y - 2 = 30$

**36.** $9p - 7 = 11$

**37.** $4x + 5 = 12$

**38.** $7p + 11 = 13$

**39.** $3t + \dfrac{1}{5} = 4$

**40.** $5z + \dfrac{2}{3} = 2$

**41.** $7q - \dfrac{2}{3} = 4$

**42.** $7a - \dfrac{5}{4} = \dfrac{9}{4}$

**43.** $5.2z - 4 = 1.2$

**44.** $3.6m + 2 = 6.32$

**45.** $27.85 = 3 + 7.1p$

**46.** $0.9 = 4t - 3.5$

**47.** $7m + 4m - 5m = 78$

**48.** $13r - 7r + 3r = 81$

**49.** $2s + s + 3s = 12$

**50.** $3.5k + k + k = 11.55$

**51.** $5y + 2 = 3(y + 4)$

**52.** $4z + 2 = 2(z + 2)$

**53.** $3(m - 4) = m + 2$

**54.** $s + 8 = 3(s - 6)$

**55.** $4(y + 8) = 3(y + 14)$

**56.** $7(z - 5) = 4(z + 8)$

**57.** $\dfrac{3}{4}s + \dfrac{1}{5}s = \dfrac{4}{5}$

**58.** $\dfrac{3}{4}q - \dfrac{1}{9} = \dfrac{1}{3} + \dfrac{1}{4}q$

**59.** $\dfrac{3}{8}y + \dfrac{1}{4} = \dfrac{9}{8}y - \dfrac{1}{4}$

**60.** $3(2p - 1) = 4(2.2 - p)$

**61.** $2(y + 1) = 4(4 - 2.5y)$

**62.** $9.1765y + 0.3284y = 6.65343$

**63.** $0.7452(3k - 1) = 3.94956$

**64.** $0.3255(1 + 7.5s) = 6.67275$

**65.** $1.2(2 + 3r) = 0.8(2r + 5)$

**66.** Explain why all terms with a variable should be placed on one side of the equation, and all terms without a variable should be placed on the opposite side when solving an equation.

**67.** A student obtains the equation $6x = 5x$ after applying several steps correctly. The student then divides both sides by $x$ and obtains the result $6 = 5$ and gives "no solution" as the answer. Is this correct? If not, state why not and give the correct solution. (See Objective 3.)

## 2.2  Applications of Equations

**OBJECTIVES**

1. *Translate phrases into mathematical expressions.*
2. *Write equations from given information.*
3. *Solve applied problems.*

Most problems in business are expressed in words. Before these problems can be solved, they must be converted into mathematical language.

**OBJECTIVE** 1 *Translate phrases into mathematical expressions.*     Applied problems tend to have certain phrases that occur again and again. The key to solving such problems is to correctly translate these phrases into mathematical expressions. The next few examples illustrate this process.

**EXAMPLE 1**  *Translating Phrases into Expressions*

Write the following verbal expressions as mathematical expressions. Use $x$ to represent the unknown. (Other letters could be used to represent this unknown quantity.)

| Verbal Expression | Mathematical Expression | Comments |
|---|---|---|
| (a) **7 plus a number** | $7 + x$ | $x$ represents the number and "plus" means addition |
| (b) **Add 20 to a number** | $x + 20$ | $x$ represents the number to which 20 is added |
| (c) **The sum of a number and 12** | $x + 12$ | "sum" indicates addition |
| (d) **6 more than a number** | $x + 6$ | "more than" indicates addition |

■

**EXAMPLE 2**  *Translating Phrases Involving Subtraction*

Write each of the following verbal expressions as a mathematical expression. Use $y$ as a variable.

| | Verbal Expression | Mathematical Expression | Comments |
|---|---|---|---|
| **(a)** | **5.5 less than a number** | $y - 5.5$ | "less than" indicates subtraction |
| **(b)** | **A number decreased by $12\frac{1}{4}$** | $y - 12\frac{1}{4}$ | "decreased" indicates subtraction |
| **(c)** | **Eight fewer than a number** | $y - 8$ | "fewer than" indicates subtraction |
| **(d)** | **Eighteen minus a number** | $18 - y$ | "minus" indicates subtraction |

■

| EXAMPLE 3 | *Translating Phrases Involving Multiplication and Division* |

Write the following verbal expressions as mathematical expressions. Use $z$ as the variable.

| | Verbal Expression | Mathematical Expression | Comments |
|---|---|---|---|
| **(a)** | **The product of a number and 7.5** | $7.5z$ | "product" indicates multiplication |
| **(b)** | **Ten times a number** | $10z$ | "times" indicates multiplication |
| **(c)** | **One-fourth of a number** | $\frac{1}{4}z$ | "of" indicates multiplication |
| **(d)** | **The quotient of a number and 9** | $\dfrac{z}{9}$ | "quotient" indicates division |
| **(e)** | **The sum of 6 and a number, multiplied by 8.3** | $8.3(6 + z)$ | multiplying a sum requires parentheses |

■

**NOTE** When adding or ~~subtracting~~ multiplying, the order of the variable and the number doesn't matter. For example:

$$3 + x = x + 3 \quad \text{and} \quad 5 \cdot y = y \cdot 5 \quad ■$$

Now that statements have been translated into mathematical expressions, you can use this knowledge to solve problems. The following steps represent a systematic approach to solving applied problems.

## SOLVING APPLIED PROBLEMS

*Step 1.* **First, read the problem very carefully.** Reread the problem to make sure that its meaning is clear.

*Step 2.* Identify the unknown and give it a variable name such as $x$. If possible, write other unknowns in terms of the same variable.

*Step 3.* Use the given information to write an equation describing the relationship given in the problem.

*Step 4.* Solve the equation.

*Step 5.* Answer the question asked in the problem.

*Step 6.* Check the solution using the original words of the problem.

**NOTE**  The third step is often the hardest. To write an equation from the information given in the problem, convert the facts stated in words into mathematical expressions. This converted mathematical expression, or equation, is called the *mathematical model* of the situation described in the original words.  ■

**OBJECTIVE** **2** *Write equations from given information.*    Since equal mathematical expressions represent the same number, any words that mean *equals* or *same* translate into an =. The = sign produces an equation which can be solved.

**EXAMPLE 4** *Solving Number Problems*

Translate "the product of 5, and a number decreased by 8, is 100" into an equation. Use *y* as the variable. Solve the equation.

**SOLUTION**   Translate as follows.

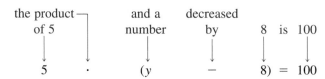

Simplify and complete the solution of the equation.

$$5 \cdot (y - 8) = 100$$

$$5y - 40 = 100 \qquad \text{Apply the distributive property.}$$

$$5y = 140 \qquad \text{Add 40 to both sides.}$$

$$y = 28 \qquad \text{Divide by 5.} \qquad ■$$

**OBJECTIVE** **3** *Solve applied problems.*

**EXAMPLE 5** *Solving Applied Number Problems*

At a business meeting there were 25 more women than men. The total number of people at the meeting was 139. Find the number of men.

**SOLUTION**

$$x = \text{number of men}$$

$$x + 25 = \text{number of women (There were 25 more women than men.)}$$

$$139 = \text{total number of people at the meeting}$$

Now, use this information to write an equation.

| the<br>total | is | the number<br>of men | plus | the number<br>of women |
|:---:|:---:|:---:|:---:|:---:|
| ↓ | ↓ | ↓ | ↓ | ↓ |
| 139 | = | $x$ | + | $x + 25$ |

Solve the equation.

$$139 = 2x + 25$$

$$139 - 25 = 2x + 25 - 25 \qquad \text{Subtract 25.}$$

$$114 = 2x$$

$$57 = x \qquad \text{Divide by 2.}$$

There were 57 men at the meeting. Also, there were $57 + 25 = 82$ women at the meeting. Check this answer in the words of the original problem: 82 women is 25 more than 57 men, and $82 + 57 = 139$. ■

## EXAMPLE 6 *Solving Number and Cost Problems*

The Eastside Nursery ordered 27 trees. Some of the trees were elms, costing $17 each, while the rest of the trees were maples at $11 each. The total cost of the trees was $375. Find the number of elms and the number of maples.

SOLUTION   Let $x$ represent the number of elm trees, then $(27 - x)$ is the number of maples. The total cost of the elm trees is $17x$ and the total cost of the maples is $11(27 - x)$. A table can be very helpful in identifying the knowns and unknowns.

|  | Number<br>of Trees | Cost<br>per Tree | Total Cost |
|:---:|:---:|:---:|:---:|
| **Elms** | $x$ | $17 | $17x$ |
| **Maples** | $(27 - x)$ | $11 | $11(27 - x)$ |
| **Totals** | 27 | | 375 |

The information in the table is used to get the following equation.

$$\text{Cost of elms} + \text{Cost of maples} = \text{Total cost}$$

$$17x + 11(27 - x) \quad = 375$$

Now solve this equation. First use the distributive property.

$$17x + 297 - 11x = 375$$

$$6x + 297 = 375 \qquad \text{Combine terms.}$$

$$6x = 78 \qquad \text{Subtract 297 from each side.}$$

$$x = 13 \qquad \text{Divide each side by 6.}$$

There were 13 elm trees and 27 − 13, or 14, maple trees. Check this answer.

$$\text{Cost of elms} + \text{Cost of maples} = \text{Total cost}$$

$$17(13) + 11(14) \qquad = 375$$

$$221 + 154 \qquad\qquad = 375$$

$$375 \qquad\qquad = 375$$

The answer checks.                                                             ■

### EXAMPLE 7  *Solving Investment Problems*

Laurie Zimms has $15,000 to invest. She places a portion of the funds in a passbook account and $3,000 more than twice this amount in a retirement account. How much is put into the passbook account? How much is placed in the retirement account?

**SOLUTION**    Let $z$ represent the amount invested in the passbook account. To find the amount invested in the retirement account, translate as follows.

| 3,000 | more than | 2 times the amount |
|-------|-----------|--------------------|
| ↓ | ↓ | ↓ |
| 3,000 | + | $2z$ |

Since the sum of the two investments must be $15,000, an equation can be formed as follows.

| Amount invested in passbook | + | Amount invested in retirement account | = | Total amount invested |
|-----------------------------|---|---------------------------------------|---|-----------------------|
| $z$ | + | $(3{,}000 + 2z)$ | = | $15,000 |

Now solve the equation.

$$z + (3{,}000 + 2z) = 15{,}000$$

$$3z + 3{,}000 = 15{,}000$$

$$3z = 12{,}000 \qquad \text{Subtract 3000.}$$

$$z = 4{,}000 \qquad \text{Divide by 3.}$$

The amount invested in the passbook account is $z$, or $4,000. The amount invested in the retirement account is $3{,}000 + 2z$ or $3{,}000 + 2(4{,}000) = \$11{,}000$.    ■

## 2.2  EXERCISES

*Write the following as mathematical expressions. Use x as the variable.*

**1.** 16 plus a number

**2.** the sum of a number and 4

**3.** a number added to 8

**4.** 7 added to a number

**5.** 4 less than a number

**6.** 12 fewer than a number

**7.** a number decreased by $\frac{1}{3}$

**8.** subtract a number from 5.4

9. triple a number

10. the product of a number and 9

11. three fifths of a number

12. double a number

13. the quotient of 9 and a number

14. the quotient of a number and 11

15. 16 divided by a number

16. a number divided by 4

17. the product of 2.1 and the sum of 4 plus a number

18. the quantity of a number plus 4, divided by 9

19. 7 times the difference of a number and 3

20. the difference of a number and 2, multiplied by 7

*Write mathematical expressions for each of the following.*

21. Find the cost of 3,000 bearings at $x$ dollars each.

22. Find the cost of $x$ police cars at $19,200 each.

23. The demand forecast for next month is 472 tons. Find the amount that should be ordered if inventory is $x$ tons.

24. Eighty-three of the $x$ employees have computers. How many do not have computers?

25. A company has 73 employees of whom $x$ are union. How many employees are nonunion?

26. The inventory of a small card shop is valued at $73,000. The value of the greeting cards is $x$. Find the value of the rest of the inventory.

27. A market paid $172 for $x$ crates of berries. Find the cost of one crate of berries.

28. A lodge paid $1,853 for tickets for its $x$ members to visit the state capitol. Find the cost of one ticket.

29. Robin has 21 books on computers. She donates $x$ of them to the school library. How many does she have left?

30. A video rental store is $x$ years old. How old will it be in 8 years?

*Solve the following application problems. Steps 1–6 are repeated here for your convenience— use them.*

## SOLVING APPLIED PROBLEMS

***Step 1.*** Read the problem carefully.

***Step 2.*** Identify the unknown and choose a variable to represent it. If possible, write any other unknowns in terms of the same variable.

***Step 3.*** Translate the problem into an equation.

***Step 4.*** Solve the equation.

***Step 5.*** Answer the question asked in the problem.

***Step 6.*** Check your solution using the original words of the problem.

**31.** Four subtracted from 6 times a number is 22. Find the number.

**32.** Fifty-four equals 5 plus 7 times a number. Find the number.

**33.** Eight times the sum of a number plus 4 equals 48. Find the number.

**34.** Seven times the difference of a number minus 2 equals 24.5. Find the number.

**35.** When 6 is added to a number, the result is 7 times the number. Find the number.

**36.** If 6 is subtracted from three times a number, the result is 4 more than the number. Find the number.

**37.** When 5 times a number is added to twice the number, the result is 10. Find the number.

**38.** If 7 times a number is subtracted from 11 times the number, the result is 9. Find the number.

**39.** Jean Watson sold $1,500 more in one week than did the other salesperson. Given that the total sales for the two was $6,800, find Ms. Watson's sales.

**40.** A pharmacist found that at the end of the day she had 12 more prescriptions for antibiotics than she had for tranquilizers. She had 84 prescriptions altogether for these two types of drugs. How many did she have for tranquilizers?

**41.** At one company, 15 more people work in the production department than work in the packaging department. The total number of people in the two departments is 277. Find the number of people in the production department.

**42.** Twenty-one students went on a student exchange program to Guadalajara, Mexico. There were 11 more women than men. Find the number of women.

**43.** An automobile is on sale for $18,450 which is $\frac{9}{10}$ of its original price. Find the original price.

**44.** Because of handling and freight charges, Western Oil Equipment charges $\frac{5}{4}$ of the list price for an item shipped to Indonesia. Find the list price of an item that was charged at $725.

**45.** A contractor built 105 homes last year, some economy models and some deluxe models. The number of economy models was $\frac{3}{2}$ the number of deluxe models. Find the number of each type of home that was built.

**46.** The Regency Culinary School spent $18,000 on advertising using radio and newspaper. The amount spent on newspaper advertising was $\frac{5}{4}$ that spent on radio advertising. Find the amount spent on each type of advertising.

**47.** KLRS radio station spent $10,500 on salaries one month. The amount spent on announcers was $\frac{3}{5}$ that amount spent on all other employees. Find the amount spent on announcers and on all other employees.

**48.** An engineer is studying a busy intersection. In one hour, the number of cars going north/south was $\frac{3}{4}$ of those going east/west, and the total number of cars was 1,400. Find the number of cars going north/south and east/west.

**49.** A building can be used either for retail stores or for offices. The owner wants to receive a total annual rent of $67,500, with $3\frac{1}{2}$ times as much rent coming from retail stores as from offices. How much rent will come from offices? How much from retail stores?

**50.** Karen has a piece of material that is 106 inches long. She wishes to cut it into two pieces so that one piece is 12 inches longer than the other. What should be the length of each piece?

**51.** There are 63 people employed at Dewey's Department Store. New workers receive $6 per hour while experienced workers receive $9 per hour. If the company spends a total of $483 per hour in wages, find the number of each type of worker the company employs.

**52.** Jumbo Market makes $0.05 on a head of lettuce and $0.04 on a bunch of carrots. Last week, a total of 12,900 heads of lettuce and bunches of carrots were sold, with a total profit of $587. How many heads of lettuce and how many bunches of carrots were sold?

**53.** Profits on Nissan Altimas and Sentras average $1,200 and $850 respectively at one dealership. If the total profit in a month in which they sold 120 of these models was $130,350, find the number of each sold.

**54.** One month, revenue from the 95 repairs at an auto repair shop totaled $10,020. The average charges for repairs on personal and commercial vehicles were $125 and $90 respectively. Find the number of each type of vehicle repaired.

**55.** Are the problems in this section difficult for you? Explain why or why not. If they are not difficult, explain two things you would recommend to a classmate who is having difficulty.

**56.** Write out the steps necessary to solve an applied problem. (See Objective 3.)

## 2.3 Formulas

### OBJECTIVES

**1**  *Evaluate formulas for given values of the variables.*

**2**  *Solve formulas for a specific variable.*

**3**  *Use standard business formulas to solve word problems.*

**4**  *Evaluate formulas containing exponents.*

Many of the most useful rules and procedures in business are given as **formulas**, or equations, showing the relationship between different variables such as:

$$\text{Interest} = \text{Principal} \times \text{Rate} \times \text{Time}$$

**OBJECTIVE 1** *Evaluate formulas for given values of the variables.*    A formula can take up too much space and be hard to remember, when written out in words. As a result, it is common to use letters as variables for the words in a formula. Many times the first letter in each word of a formula is used, to make it easier to remember the formula. By this method, the formula for simple interest is written as follows.

$$I = PRT$$

By using letters to express the relationship between interest, principal, rate, and time we have generalized the relationship so that any value can be substituted into the formula. Once three values are substituted into the formula, we can then find the value of the remaining variable.

**NOTE** The variable $T$ is always expressed as a fraction of a year in $I = PRT$. ∎

**EXAMPLE 1** *Finding Interest*

Use the formula $I = PRT$ and find $I$ if $P = 7,000$, $R = 0.07$, and $T = 2$ (years).

**SOLUTION** Substitute 7,000 for $P$, 0.07 for $R$, and 2 for $T$ in the formula $I = PRT$. (Remember that writing $P$, $R$, and $T$ together as $PRT$ indicates the product of the three letters.)

$$I = PRT$$

$$I = 7,000(0.07)(2)$$

Multiply on the right to get the solution.

$$I = 980$$ ∎

**EXAMPLE 2** *Finding Principal*

Use the formula $I = PRT$ and find $T$ if $P = \$4,000$, $I = \$720$, and $R = 0.09$.

**SOLUTION** Substitute the given numbers for the letters of the formula.

$$I = PRT$$

$$720 = 4,000(0.09)T$$

On the right, $4,000(0.09) = 360$.

$$720 = 360T$$

To find $T$, divide both sides of this equation by 360.

$$\frac{720}{360} = \frac{360T}{360}$$

$$2 = T$$ ∎

**OBJECTIVE** **2** *Solve formulas for a specific variable.* In Example 2 we found the value of $T$ when given the values of $P$, $I$, and $R$. If several problems of this type must be solved, it may be better to rewrite the formula $I = PRT$ so that $T$ is alone on one side of the equation. Do this with the rules of equations given earlier. Since $T$ is multiplied by $PR$, get $T$ alone by dividing both sides of the equation by $PR$.

$$I = PRT$$

$$\frac{I}{PR} = \frac{PRT}{PR} \qquad \text{Divide by } PR.$$

$$\frac{I}{PR} = \frac{\cancel{PR}T}{\cancel{PR}}$$

$$\frac{I}{PR} = T$$

This process of rearranging a formula is sometimes called *solving a formula for a specific variable*.

**EXAMPLE 3** *Solving for a Specific Variable*

Solve for $T$ in the formula $M = P(1 + RT)$.

**SOLUTION** This formula expresses the maturity value *(M)* of an initial amount of money *(P)* invested at a specified rate *(R)* for a certain period of time *(T)*.

Start by using the distributive property on the right side.

$$M = P(1 + RT)$$
$$M = P + PRT$$

Now subtract $P$ from both sides.

$$M - P = P + PRT - P$$
$$M - P = PRT$$

Divide each side by $PR$.

$$\frac{M - P}{PR} = \frac{\cancel{P}\cancel{P}T}{\cancel{P}\cancel{R}}$$

$$\frac{M - P}{PR} = T$$

The original formula is now solved for $T$. ∎

**EXAMPLE 4** *Solving for a Specific Variable*

An employee earns $7.89 per hour plus $0.45 for each circuit board she assembles. **(a)** Write an equation for her total income *(T)* in terms of hours *(H)* and number of circuit boards assembled *(C)*. **(b)** Solve for the variable $C$. **(c)** Use this to find the number of circuit boards she must assemble in a 40 hour week in order to earn $450.

**SOLUTION**

**(a)** Her total earnings is the sum of her hourly wage times the number of hours plus the amount for each circuit board times the number of circuit boards assembled.

**(b)**
$$T = 7.89H + 0.45C$$

$$T - 7.89H = 7.89H + 0.45C - 7.89H \qquad \text{Subtract } 7.89H.$$

$$T - 7.89H = 0.45C$$

$$\frac{T - 7.89H}{0.45} = \frac{0.45C}{0.45} \qquad \text{Divide by } 0.45.$$

$$C = \frac{T - 7.89H}{0.45}$$

**(c)** Substitute $450 in place of $T$ and 40 in place of $H$.

$$C = \frac{450 - 7.89(40)}{0.45}$$

$$C = \frac{134.40}{0.45}$$

$$C = 298.666\ldots$$

She must assemble 299 circuit boards.    ■

CALCULATOR APPROACH
TO EXAMPLE 2

The calculator solution to this example uses chain calculations and the order of operations.

OBJECTIVE **3** *Use standard business formulas to solve word problems.*    In the following two examples, applied problems that use some common business formulas are solved. (These formulas are discussed in more detail later in the book.)

## EXAMPLE 5  *Finding Gross Sales*

Find the gross sales from selling 480 fishing lures at $1.42 each.

SOLUTION    The formula for gross sales is

$$G = NP.$$

For this formula, $N$ is the number of items sold and $P$ is the price per item. To find the gross sales from selling 480 fishing lures at $1.42 each, use the formula as shown.

$$G = NP$$

$$G = 480(\$1.42)$$

$$G = \$681.60$$

The gross sales will be $681.60.    ■

## EXAMPLE 6  *Finding Selling Price*

Find the selling price if the cost of an item is $5.15 and its markup is $2.11.

SOLUTION    The selling price of an item is found by adding the cost of the item and the markup.

$$S = C + M$$

The variable $C$ is the cost of the item, and $M$ is the markup (an amount added to cover expenses and profit). If an item costs $5.15, and has a markup of $2.11, the selling price would be found as shown.

$$S = \$5.15 + \$2.11$$
$$S = \$7.26$$

The selling price is $7.26.     ∎

**OBJECTIVE** **4** *Evaluate formulas containing exponents.*     Exponents are used to show repeated multiplication of some quantity. For example,

$$x \cdot x = x^2$$

Exponent —— number of times quantity is multiplied

Base —— quantity being multiplied

Similarly, $z \cdot z \cdot z = z^3$   and   $5 \cdot 5 \cdot 5 \cdot 5 = 5^4$ which is 625.

**EXAMPLE 7** *Finding Monthly Sales*

Trinity Sporting Goods has found that monthly sales can be approximated using

$$\text{Sales} = 40 + 1.6 \times (\text{advertising})^2$$

as long as advertising is less than $4,000. All of the figures in the equation above are in thousands. Estimate sales for a month with $3,500 in advertising.

**SOLUTION**     Place 3.5 in the equation for the number of thousands of dollars of advertising and find sales.

$$\text{Sales} = 40 + 1.6(3.5)^2$$
$$\text{Sales} = 40 + 1.6(12.25)$$
$$\text{Sales} = 40 + 19.6$$
$$\text{Sales} = 59.6$$

Sales are projected to be $59,600 for the month.     ∎

## 2.3 EXERCISES

*In the following exercises a formula is given, along with the values of all but one of the variables in the formula. Find the value of the variable that is not given. Round to the nearest hundredth, if applicable.*

**1.** $I = PRT$; $P = 2,800$, $R = 0.09$, $T = 2$

**2.** $S = C + M$; $C = 275$, $M = 49$

**3.** $G = NP$; $N = 840$, $P = 3.79$

**4.** $M = P(1 + RT)$; $P = 420$, $R = 0.07$, $T = 2\frac{1}{2}$

**5.** $R = \dfrac{D}{1 - DT}$; $D = 0.05$, $T = 4$

**6.** $\dfrac{I}{PR} = T$; $P = 100$, $R = 0.02$, $T = 500$

**7.** $P = 2L + 2W$; $P = 40$, $W = 6$

**8.** $P = 2L + 2W$; $P = 340$, $L = 70$

**9.** $P = \dfrac{I}{RT}$; $T = 3$, $I = 540$, $P = 2,250$

**10.** $M = P(1 + RT)$; $R = 0.15$, $T = 2$, $M = 481$

**11.** $y = ax^2$; $a = 4$, $x = 12$

**12.** $F = \dfrac{GMm}{r^2}$; $G = 1$, $M = 3$, $m = 1$, $r = 2$

**13.** $M = P(1 + i)^n$; $P = 640$, $i = 0.02$, $n = 8$

**14.** $M = P(1 + i)^n$; $M = \$2,400$, $i = 0.05$, $n = 4$

**15.** $E = mc^2$; $m = 7.5$, $c = 1$

**16.** $x = \dfrac{1}{2}at^2$; $t = 5$, $x = 150$

**17.** $A = \dfrac{1}{2}(b + B)h$; $A = 105$, $b = 19$, $B = 11$

**18.** $A = \dfrac{1}{2}(b + B)h$; $A = 70$, $b = 15$, $B = 20$

**19.** $P = \dfrac{S}{1 + RT}$; $S = 24,600$, $R = 0.06$, $T = \dfrac{5}{12}$

**20.** $P = \dfrac{S}{1 + RT}$; $S = 23,815$, $R = 0.09$, $T = \dfrac{11}{12}$

*Solve each formula for the indicated variable.*

**21.** $A = LW$; for $W$

**22.** $d = rt$; for $r$

**23.** $V = LWH$; for $H$

**24.** $I = PRT$; for $R$

**25.** $M = P(1 + i)^n$; for $P$

**26.** $R(1 - DT) = D$; for $R$

**27.** $P = \dfrac{A}{1 + i}$; for $i$

**28.** $M = P(1 + RT)$; for $R$

**29.** $P = M(1 - DT)$; for $D$

**30.** $P = \dfrac{M}{1 + RT}$; for $R$

**31.** $A = \dfrac{1}{2}(b + B)h$; for $h$

**32.** $P = 2L + 2W$; for $L$

**33.** $M = Pe^{ni}$; for $P$

**34.** $S = R\left[\dfrac{(1 + i)^n - 1}{i}\right]$; for $R$

*Solve the following application problems.*

**35.** Anthony's Wharf Seafood Restaurant buys 400 pounds of shrimp for a special party for a total of $3,800. Find the cost per pound.

**36.** A small business owner purchased 8 computers at a total cost of $18,000. Find the cost per computer.

**37.** Thompson Cleaning Service bought 8 vacuum cleaners and 19 drums of cleaning solvent for $3,403. Each vacuum cleaner costs $176. Find the cost of a drum of solvent.

**38.** Lake Boating bought 5 small boats and 3 large boats for $14,878. A small boat costs $1,742. Find the cost of a large boat.

**39.** An employee of Wilson's Department Store is paid a weekly salary given by the formula $S = 160 + 0.03x$, where $x$ is the total sales of the employee for the week. Find the salary of employees having the following weekly sales. (a) $1,152 (b) $1,796 (c) $2,314

**40.** A principal ($P$) of $3,500 invested over an unknown amount of time ($T$) at rate 9.5% ($R = 0.095$) yields $748.13 in interest ($I$). Use $I = PRT$ to find the time rounded to the nearest hundredth of a year.

**41.** An unknown principal ($P$) invested at 8% ($R = 0.08$) for $1\frac{3}{4}$ years yields a maturity value ($M$) of $1,368. Use $M = P(1 + RT)$ to find the principal.

**42.** The Bridal Shop has net sales of $33,000 and a return of $\frac{1}{12}$ of gross sales. If net sales equal gross sales minus returns, find the gross sales.

**43.** One store sets markup at $\frac{3}{4}$ of its cost for the item. Find the cost of an item if the selling price is $84.

**44.** The bookstore at Ironwood Community College has a markup that is $\frac{1}{4}$ its cost on a book. Find the cost to the bookstore of a book selling for $20.

**45.** Last year, the expenses at the Taco Mary Restaurant were $\frac{5}{6}$ of the revenue. The profit (the difference between revenue and expenses) was $15,000. Find the revenue.

**46.** Computerworld has expenses that run $\frac{15}{16}$ of revenue. Profit (the difference between revenue and expenses) was $9,000. Find the revenue.

**47.** Find the interest if principal of $5,200 is invested at $7\frac{1}{2}\%$ for one year. ($I = PRT$)

**48.** Ben Cross loaned $8,000 to his uncle for 4 years and received $1,920 in interest. Find the interest rate. ($I = PRT$)

**49.** Terry Twitty made a $22,000 loan so that Melissa Graves could start an auto parts business. The loan was for 2 years, and interest was $5,720. Find the rate of interest. ($I = PRT$)

**50.** Fred Tausz loaned $39,000 to Anne Topsy. The loan was at 7% (or 0.07), with interest of $13,650. Find the time for the loan. ($I = PRT$)

**51.** Jackie Williams loaned $18,200 to Colleen Sullivan. The two agreed on an interest rate of 11% (or 0.11), with interest of $8,008. Find the time for the loan. ($I = PRT$)

**52.** Mary Scott invests $1,000 at 8% (or 0.08) for 5 years. How much did Mary have in her account at the end of 5 years? [$M = P(1 + RT)$]

**53.** John Wood had $4,560 in his account after 2 years. If the account paid 7% (or 0.07) interest, how much did John initially deposit in his account. [$M = P(1 + RT)$]

**54.** Jan Rice borrowed $2,800 from her uncle to help her start a hair salon. She repaid $3,472 exactly 3 years later. Find the interest rate. [$M = P(1 + RT)$]

**55.** Bill Abel paid a maturity value of $5,989.50 on a 3 year note with annual interest of 10%. Use $M = P(1 + i)$," where $n$ is the number of years in this problem, to solve for the amount borrowed.

**56.** June Smith won $5,000 in a church lottery and placed it in a mutual fund yielding 12% (hopefully) for 20 years. Use $M = P(1 + i)$," where $n$ is the number of years in this problem to solve for the maturity value.

**57.** Write a step-by-step explanation of the procedure you would use to solve the equation $A = P + PRT$ for $R$. (See Objective 2.)

**58.** Formulas are used in business, physics, biology, chemistry, engineering, and many other places. Why do you think formulas are so commonly used? (See Objective 1.)

## 2.4    Ratios and Proportions

### OBJECTIVES

**1**  Define a ratio.

**2**  Set up a proportion.

**3**  Solve a proportion for unknown values.

**4**  Use proportions to solve problems.

**OBJECTIVE** ■ *Define a ratio.*    A **ratio** is a quotient of two quantities. It can be used to compare the quantities. The ratio of the number $a$ to the number $b$ is written in any of the following ways.

$$a \text{ to } b \qquad a:b \qquad \text{or} \qquad \frac{a}{b}$$

This last way of writing a ratio is most common in algebra, while $a:b$ is perhaps most common in business. Both quantities in a ratio should be in the same units if possible, i.e. cents to cents or dollars to dollars, not dollars to cents.

### EXAMPLE 1    *Writing Ratios from Words*

Write a ratio in the form $\frac{a}{b}$ for each word phrase. (Notice in each phrase that the number mentioned first always gives the numerator.)

### SOLUTION

**(a)**  The ratio of 5 hours to 3 hours is $\frac{5}{3}$.

**(b)**  To find the ratio of 5 hours to 3 days, first convert 3 days to hours. There are 24 hours in 1 day so 3 days = $3 \cdot 24 = 72$ hours. Then the ratio of 5 hours to 3 days is the quotient of 5 hours and 72 hours.

$$\frac{5}{72}$$

**(c)**  The ratio of $700,000 in sales to $950,000 in sales is written this way.

$$\frac{\$700,000}{\$950,000}$$

Write this ratio in lowest terms.

$$\frac{\$700,000}{\$950,000} = \frac{14}{19} \qquad\qquad ■$$

**NOTE**  In the ratios of Example 1, the quantities were changed so that they had the same units (hours to hours, dollars to dollars).  ■

**OBJECTIVE** ■ *Set up a proportion.*    A ratio is used to compare two numbers or amounts. A **proportion** says that two ratios are equal, as in the following example.

$$\frac{3}{4} \;\times\; \frac{15}{20}$$

This proportion says that the ratios $\frac{3}{4}$ and $\frac{15}{20}$ are equal.

To see if a proportion is true, use the method of **cross products** as shown.

The proportion

$$\frac{a}{b} = \frac{c}{d}$$

is true if the cross products $b \cdot c$ and $a \cdot d$ are equal, that is, if $ad = bc$.

**EXAMPLE 2** *Determining True Proportions*

Decide if the following proportions are true.

**(a)** $\dfrac{4}{7} = \dfrac{20}{35}$  **(b)** $\dfrac{5\frac{1}{2}}{4.2} = \dfrac{66}{57}$

**SOLUTION**

**(a)** Find each cross product.

$$\frac{4}{7} \times \frac{20}{35}$$

$$4 \cdot 35 = 7 \cdot 20$$

$$140 = 140$$

Since the cross products are equal, the proportion is true.

**(b)** Find each cross product.

$$\frac{5\frac{1}{2}}{4.2} = \frac{66}{57}$$

$$5\frac{1}{2} \cdot 57 = 66 \cdot 4.2$$

$$5.5 \cdot 57 = 277.2$$

$$313.5 = 277.2$$

This proportion is false because 313.5 does not equal 277.2.  ■

**NOTE** The numbers in a proportion need not be whole numbers.  ■

We might mention that the method of cross products is just a shortcut version of solving an equation. To see how, start with the proportion

$$\frac{a}{b} = \frac{c}{d}$$

and multiply both sides by the product of the denominators (*bd*).

$$bd \cdot \frac{a}{b} = bd \cdot \frac{c}{d}$$

$$ad = bc$$

The expressions *ad* and *bc* are the cross products, and this solution shows that they are equal.

**OBJECTIVE 3** *Solve a proportion for unknown values.*     Four numbers are used in a proportion. If any three of these numbers are known, the fourth can be found.

**EXAMPLE 3** *Finding Unknown Values in a Proportion*

Find the unknown in each proportion.

**(a)** $\dfrac{4}{9} = \dfrac{36}{x}$    **(b)** $\dfrac{3.4}{12} = \dfrac{z}{96}$

**SOLUTION**

**(a)** Set the cross products equal to one another, then solve the resulting equation.

$$4 \cdot x = 936$$

$$4x = 324$$

$$\frac{4x}{4} = \frac{324}{4} \qquad \text{Divide by 4.}$$

$$x = 81$$

**(b)** Set the cross products equal to one another.

$$3.4 \cdot 96 = 12 \cdot z$$

$$326.4 = 12z$$

$$\frac{326.4}{12} = \frac{12z}{12} \qquad \text{Divide by 12.}$$

$$27.2 = z \qquad\qquad\qquad ■$$

**OBJECTIVE 4** *Use proportions to solve problems.*     Proportions are used in many practical applications, as Example 4 shows.

**EXAMPLE 4** *Solving Applications*

A hospital charges a patient $7.80 for 12 capsules. How much should it charge for 18 capsules?

SOLUTION   Let $x$ be the cost of 18 capsules. Set up a proportion: one ratio in the proportion can involve the number of capsules, while the other ratio can use the costs. Make sure that corresponding numbers appear in the numerator and the denominator. Use this pattern.

$$\frac{\text{capsules}}{\text{capsules}} = \frac{\text{cost}}{\text{cost}}$$

Now substitute the given information.

$$\frac{12}{18} = \frac{7.80}{x}$$

Use cross products to solve the proportion.

$$12x = 18(7.80)$$
$$12x = 140.40$$
$$x = 11.70$$

The 18 capsules should cost $11.70.   ∎

## EXAMPLE 5  *Solving Applications*

A firm in Hong Kong and one in Thailand agree to jointly develop a controller chip to be sold to North American auto manufacturers. They agree to split the development costs in a ratio of 8:3 (Hong Kong firm to Thailand firm), resulting in a cost of $9,400,000 to the Hong Kong firm. Find the cost to the Thailand firm.

SOLUTION   Let $x$ represent the cost to the Thailand firm, then

$$\frac{8}{3} = \frac{9,400,000}{x}$$
$$8x = 3 \cdot 9,400,000 \qquad \text{Cross multiply.}$$
$$8x = 28,200,000$$
$$x = 3,525,000 \qquad \text{Divide by 8.}$$

The Thailand firm's share of the costs is $3,525,000.   ∎

## EXAMPLE 6  *Solving Applications*

Bill Thomas wishes to estimate the amount of timber on some forested land that he owns. One value he needs to estimate is the average height of the trees. One morning, Thomas notices that his own 6 foot body casts an 8 foot shadow at the same time that a typical tree casts a 34 foot shadow. Find the height of the tree.

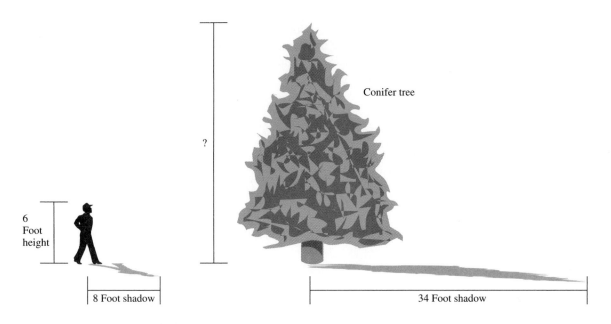

**SOLUTION**  Set up a proportion in which the height of the tree is given the variable name $x$.

$$\frac{6}{8} = \frac{x}{34}$$

$$6 \cdot 34 = 8 \cdot x \qquad \text{Cross multiply.}$$

$$204 = \frac{8 \cdot x}{8} \qquad \text{Divide by 8.}$$

$$x = 25.5 \text{ feet}$$

The height of the tree is 25.5 feet. ∎

## 2.4  EXERCISES

*Write the following ratios. Write each ratio in lowest terms.*

**1.** 750 feet to 90 feet

**2.** 80 yards to 120 yards

**3.** 70 meters to 180 meters

**4.** 40 miles to 200 miles

**5.** 8 men to 6 women

**6.** 12 feet to 1 inch

**7.** 30 kilometers to 8 meters

**8.** 30 inches to 5 yards

**9.** 90 dollars to 40 cents

**10.** 148 minutes to 4 hours

**11.** 4 dollars to 10 quarters

**12.** 35 dimes to 6 dollars

**13.** 20 hours to 5 days

**14.** 6 days to 9 hours

**15.** $0.80 to $3

**16.** $1.20 to $0.75

**17.** $3.24 to $0.72

**18.** $3.57 to $0.42

*Decide whether the following proportions are true or false.*

**19.** $\dfrac{2}{5} = \dfrac{8}{20}$

**20.** $\dfrac{9}{10} = \dfrac{18}{20}$

**21.** $\dfrac{84}{48} = \dfrac{14}{8}$

**22.** $\dfrac{12}{18} = \dfrac{8}{12}$    **23.** $\dfrac{7}{10} = \dfrac{82}{120}$    **24.** $\dfrac{17}{19} = \dfrac{72}{84}$

**25.** $\dfrac{19}{32} = \dfrac{33}{77}$    **26.** $\dfrac{19}{30} = \dfrac{57}{90}$    **27.** $\dfrac{110}{18} = \dfrac{160}{27}$

**28.** $\dfrac{46}{17} = \dfrac{212}{95}$    **29.** $\dfrac{32}{75} = \dfrac{61}{108}$    **30.** $\dfrac{28}{75} = \dfrac{224}{600}$

**31.** $\dfrac{7.6}{10} = \dfrac{76}{100}$    **32.** $\dfrac{95}{64} = \dfrac{320}{217}$    **33.** $\dfrac{2\frac{1}{4}}{5} = \dfrac{9}{20}$

**34.** $\dfrac{\frac{3}{4}}{80} = \dfrac{\frac{9}{8}}{120}$    **35.** $\dfrac{4\frac{1}{5}}{6\frac{1}{8}} = \dfrac{27}{41}$    **36.** $\dfrac{1\frac{1}{2}}{12} = \dfrac{5\frac{1}{4}}{42}$

**37.** $\dfrac{8.15}{2.03} = \dfrac{61.125}{15.225}$    **38.** $\dfrac{423.88}{17.119} = \dfrac{330.6264}{13.35282}$

*Solve each of the following proportions.*

**39.** $\dfrac{y}{32} = \dfrac{3}{8}$    **40.** $\dfrac{33}{11} = \dfrac{x}{13}$    **41.** $\dfrac{5}{7} = \dfrac{175}{r}$

**42.** $\dfrac{16}{41} = \dfrac{112}{t}$    **43.** $\dfrac{63}{s} = \dfrac{3}{5}$    **44.** $\dfrac{260}{390} = \dfrac{x}{3}$

**45.** $\dfrac{1}{2} = \dfrac{r}{7}$    **46.** $\dfrac{2}{3} = \dfrac{5}{s}$    **47.** $\dfrac{\frac{3}{4}}{6} = \dfrac{3}{x}$

**48.** $\dfrac{3}{x} = \dfrac{11}{9}$    **49.** $\dfrac{12}{p} = \dfrac{23.571}{15.714}$    **50.** $\dfrac{86.112}{57.408} = \dfrac{k}{15}$

**51.** Explain the difference between ratio and proportion. (See Objective 2.)

**52.** Which rules of algebra allow us to cross multiply when working with proportions? (See Objective 2.)

*Solve each of the following application problems.*

**53.** A chemical mixture requires 2 parts acid to 7 parts alcohol. Find the amount of alcohol needed to mix with 600 gallons of acid.

**54.** A 170-pound person has about 30 trillion blood cells. Estimate the number of blood cells in a 140-pound person to the nearest tenth of a trillion.

**55.** On average, about 5,000 people die every 6 months from earthquakes. How many would you expect to die in 30 months?

**56.** A 450-pound circus tiger eats 15 pounds of meat per day. How many pounds of meat would you expect a 360-pound tiger to eat per day?

**57.** If 22 children's dresses cost $176, find the cost of 12 dresses.

**58.** Jose paid $199,500 for a 7-unit apartment house. Find the cost for a 16-unit apartment house.

**59.** Fifteen yards of material are needed for 5 dresses. How much material is needed for 12 dresses?

**60.** Suppose that 7 sacks of fertilizer cover 3,325 square feet of lawn. Find the number of sacks needed for 7,125 square feet.

**61.** The distance between two cities on a road map is 2 inches. Actually, the cities are 120 miles apart. The distance between two other cities is 17 inches. How far apart are these cities?

**62.** The charge to move a load of freight 750 miles is $90. Find the charge to move the freight 1,200 miles.

**63.** To ride a bus 80 miles costs $15. Find the charge to ride 180 miles.

**64.** Hite and Clark are partners who agree to divide any profits in the ratio $4:7$. Find Clark's profit if Hite gets $8,000.

**65.** Suppose two partners agree to divide their profits in the ratio $5:8$. If the first partner receives $15,000 in profits, how much does the second partner get?

**66.** The owner of a factory has always kept the ratio of salespeople to production employees at $2:7$. If she currently has 24 salespeople, how many production employees are there?

**67.** Small songbirds migrate at 20 miles per hour whereas ducks migrate at 59 miles per hour. How far would ducks migrate in the amount of time it takes the songbirds to migrate 500 miles?

**68.** Indonesia has an area of 741,101 square miles and is made up of 13,677 islands. Assume the United States, with an area of 3,618,770 square miles, were similarly broken up into islands. How many islands would there be (to the nearest whole number)?

**69.** Seven-eighths of an iceberg is below the water since icebergs are made up of fresh water which is not as dense as sea water. Find the amount of an iceberg that is under water if the amount above water has a volume of 500,000 cubic meters.

**70.** An auto plant produces 3 red sports models for every 7 blue family models. Find the number of red sports models produced if the plant produces 868 blue family models.

# Chapter 2 Quick Review

| TOPIC | APPROACH | EXAMPLE |
|---|---|---|
| **2.1  Solving equations** | 1. Remove all parentheses on both sides of the equation using the distributive property. | $12(y + 2) = 84$ |
|  | 2. Combine all similar terms on both sides of the equation. | $12y + 24 = 84$ |
|  | 3. Add to or subtract from both sides whatever is needed to produce a term with the variable on one side and a number on the other side. | $12y + 24 - 24 = 84 - 24$ |
|  | 4. Multiply or divide the variable term by whatever is needed to produce a term with a coefficient of 1. Multiply or divide the number term on the other side by the same quantity. | $12y = 60$ $y = 5$ |

**2.2** **Translating phrases** | Use mathematical symbols to represent verbal expressions. | 2 plus a number: $2 + x$
5 less than a number: $x - 5$

---

**2.3** **Solving applied problems**

1. Read the problem carefully.
2. Choose a variable to represent the unknown. If possible, write any other unknowns in terms of the same variable.
3. Write an equation describing the relationship among the quantities.
4. Solve the equation.
5. Answer the problem.
6. Check solution.

A committee had 7 fewer men than women. The total number of people on the committee was 19. Find the number of women.

Let $x$ represent the number of women.

$$x + (x - 7) = 19$$
$$2x - 7 = 19$$
$$2x = 26$$
$$x = 13 \text{ women}$$

---

**2.3** **Evaluating formulas for given values of the variable** | Substitute numerical values for variables and evaluate.

Use the formula $M = P(1 + RT)$ to find $M$ if $P = \$8,500$, $R = 0.09$, and $T = 4$.

$$M = 8,500(1 + 0.09 \cdot 4)$$
$$M = 8,500(1.36)$$
$$M = \$11,560$$

---

**2.3** **Solving formulas for specific variables** | Use the rules for solving equations.

Solve $M = P + PRT$ for $T$.

$$M - P = PRT$$
$$\frac{M - P}{PR} = T$$

---

**2.3** **Working with exponents** | Use the definition of an exponent.

Find $6^4$.

$$6^4 = 6 \cdot 6 \cdot 6 \cdot 6$$
$$= 1,296$$

---

**2.4** **Solving a proportion for a missing part** | Use the principle of cross products and solve the resulting equation.

$$\frac{a}{b} = \frac{c}{d} \text{ if } a \cdot d = b \cdot c.$$

Find $x$ in the proportion.

$$\frac{5}{x} = \frac{35}{63}$$
$$5 \cdot 63 = 35x$$
$$315 = 35x$$
$$9 = x$$

| 2.4 | **Using proportions to solve problems** | Set up the proportion, use the principle of cross products, and solve the resulting equation. | A video store charges $12 to rent 5 tapes. How much does it charge for 8 tapes? |
|---|---|---|---|

$$\frac{\$12}{5} = \frac{x}{8}$$

$$\$12 \cdot 8 = 5 \cdot x$$

$$\$96 = 5x$$

$$\$19.20 = x$$

# Chapter 2 Review Exercises

*Solve each equation [2.1]*

1. $y + 12 = 28.5$

2. $z - 4 = 13\frac{1}{4}$

3. $3t + 9 = 21$

4. $4t - 6 = 15$

5. $\frac{s}{6} = 42$

6. $\frac{5z}{8} = 85$

7. $\frac{m}{4} - 5 = 9$

8. $5(x - 3) = 3(x + 4)$

9. $6y = 2y + 28$

10. $3r - 7 = 2(4 - 3r)$

11. $0.15(2x - 3) = 5.85$

12. $0.6(y - 3) = 0.1y$

*Write a mathematical expression. Use x as the variable. [2.2]*

13. 5 times a number

14. $\frac{1}{2}$ times a number

15. 6 times a number is added to the number

16. 5 times a number is decreased by 11

17. The sum of 3 times a number and 7

*Solve the following application problems. [2.2]*

18. The inventory at a bike shop in bankruptcy was valued at $42,360. What value does it have if the bankruptcy trustee assumes that it can only be sold at $\frac{7}{10}$ of this amount?

19. A furniture store has found that profits ($P$) are related to advertising ($A$) according to $P = 2.775A + 4.5$ where all figures are in thousands of dollars.

How much must they spend on advertising in order to obtain a quarterly profit of $60,000?

**20.** Phone and water bills together cost a company $540 for March. If the phone cost 4 times as much as the water, how much was each utility?

**21.** Five more than $\frac{1}{4}$ of the employees of a company have 25 years or more of service. If 24 employees have 25 or more years of service, how many employees does the company have?

**22.** The local movie theater sold 100 tickets for $390. If children's tickets cost $3 and adult tickets $6, how many of each were sold?

*For each problem, use the formula to find the value of the variable that is not given.* [2.3]

**23.** $I = PRT$; $I = \$960$, $R = 0.12$, $T = 2$

**24.** $M = P(1 + RT)$; $M = \$3,770$, $R = 0.04$, $T = 4$

**25.** $M = P(1 + i)^n$; $M = \$14,526.80$, $i = 0.1$, $n = 6$

*Solve each equation for the variable indicated.* [2.3]

**26.** $M = P(1 + RT)$; for $T$

**27.** $C = \dfrac{5}{9}(F - 32)$; for $F$

**28.** $R = \dfrac{D}{1 - DT}$; for $T$

*Write the following ratios.* [2.4]

**29.** 40 feet to 10 yards

**30.** 9 days to 12 hours

**31.** $5,000 to $250

**32.** 3 years to 15 months

**33.** 2 dollars to 75 cents

*Solve the following proportions.* [2.4]

**34.** $\dfrac{3}{x} = \dfrac{93}{124}$

**35.** $\dfrac{5}{y} = \dfrac{20}{27}$

**36.** $\dfrac{3}{8} = \dfrac{z}{12}$

**37.** $\dfrac{5}{9} = \dfrac{15}{t}$

**38.** $\dfrac{20}{r} = \dfrac{60}{72}$

*Solve the following application problems.* [2.4]

**39.** The ratio of defective to total microprocessor chips at one plant has averaged $2:100$. Find the number of defects in a batch of 12,500 chips.

**40.** Bud Jones can produce 200 parts in a 6-hour shift. How many can he produce in a 40-hour work week? (Round your answer.)

**41.** Gas costs $1.40 per gallon. If Joe fills his tank with 12.5 gallons, how much does the gas cost?

**42.** John proofreads 7 pages in 12 minutes. How many pages does he proofread in 3 hours?

**43.** A company spends three times as much on training as it does on company cars. If $19,000 is spent on cars, how much is spent on training?

**44.** If 8 shirts cost $223.20, how much would 5 shirts cost?

**45.** If 4 video cassettes cost $75, how many did Kim buy if she received $31.25 in change from her $500 check?

# Chapter 2 Summary Exercise

The average selling price of a book at The Book Barn is $10.60. Typically, 70% of this amount goes to pay for the cost of the book which includes shipping and handling. Monthly expenses at The Book Barn are:

| | |
|---|---|
| Salaries (including owner's salary) | $2,800 |
| Rent | $2,200 |
| Utilities | $ 250 |
| Supplies (other than books) | $ 200 |
| Other | $ 650 |

---

*These definitions may help you:*

Gross Revenue is the total of all revenue from all sales.

Breakeven is the point at which total revenue equals cost of goods sold plus total expenses.

Profit or net profit is the amount left over after all expenses have been paid.

Percents are parts out of 100, so that 70% is 70 parts out of 100 parts.

---

**(a)** Find the total monthly expenses.

**(b)** Write an equation for monthly net profit. Net profit is gross revenue from the sale of books (use $N$ for the number of books sold in a month) less monthly expenses.

**(c)** How many books must they sell to break even (round up to next whole number)?

**(d)** What happens if they don't break even one month?

**(e)** How many books must they sell to reach a profit of $2,500 in one month?

# Percent

Percents are widely used in business and everyday life. For example, interest rates on automobile loans, home loans, and other installment loans are almost always given as percents. Advertisers often claim that their products perform a certain "percent better" than other products or cost some "percent less." Stores often advertise sale items as being a certain "percent off" the regular price. In business, marketing costs, damage, and theft may be expressed as a percent of sales; profit as a percent of investment; and labor as a percent of production costs. Current numbers about inflation, recession, and unemployment are also reported as percents. This chapter discusses the various types of percent problems that will be used throughout this text.

## 3.1    Writing Decimals and Fractions as Percents

**OBJECTIVES**

**1**   *Write a decimal as a percent.*

**2**   *Write a fraction as a percent.*

**3**   *Write a percent as a decimal.*

**4**   *Write a percent as a fraction.*

**5**   *Write a fractional percent as a decimal.*

Percents represent parts of a whole, just as fractions or decimals do. **Percents** are *hundredths* or parts of a hundred. "One percent" means one of one hundred parts. Percents are written with a percent sign, %. For example, 25% refers to 25 parts out of 100 equal parts $\left(\frac{25}{100}\right)$, just as 50% refers to 50 out of 100 equal parts $\left(\frac{50}{100}\right)$, and 100% refers to all 100 of the 100 equal parts $\left(\frac{100}{100}\right)$. Therefore, 100% is equal to the whole item. If a percent is larger than 100% (for example 150%), more than one item has been divided into 100 equal parts, and 150 of the parts are being considered $\left(\frac{150}{100}\right)$.

**OBJECTIVE** **1** ***Write a decimal as a percent.***    Write a decimal as a percent by moving the decimal point two places to the right and attaching a % sign.

For example, write 0.75 as a percent by moving the decimal point two places to the right and attaching a % sign, giving 75% as the result.

|  *Decimal* | *Percent* |
|---|---|
| 0.75 (0.75.) | 75% ← attach percent sign |

└── 2 places to the right

| **EXAMPLE 1** *Changing Decimals to Percents*

When completing some market research you must express your findings as percents. Write the following decimals as percents.

**(a)** 0.25    **(b)** 0.38    **(c)** 0.65

**SOLUTION**    Move the decimal point two places to the right and attach a percent sign.

**(a)** 25%    **(b)** 38%    **(c)** 65%    ∎

If there is nothing in the hundredths position, place zeros to the right of the number to hold the hundredths position. For example, the decimal 0.5 is expressed as 50%, and the number 1.2 is 120%.

$$0.5 = 0.50.\% = 50\% \qquad 1.2 = 1.20.\% = 120\%$$

└── attach zero           └── attach zero

| **EXAMPLE 2** *Writing Decimals as Percents*

Write the following decimals as percents.

**(a)** 0.7    **(b)** 1.3    **(c)** 0.1    **(d)** 3

**SOLUTION**    It is necessary to attach zeros to these decimals.

**(a)** 70%    **(b)** 130%    **(c)** 10%    **(d)** 300%    ∎

If the decimal extends farther than the hundredths position, the resulting percent includes decimal parts of whole percents.

| **EXAMPLE 3** *Writing Decimals as Percents*

Write the following decimals as percents.

**(a)** 0.857    **(b)** 0.0057    **(c)** 0.0025

**SOLUTION**

**(a)** 85.7%    **(b)** 0.57%    **(c)** 0.25%    ∎

**NOTE** In Example 3 both (b) and (c) are less than 1%; they are decimal parts of 1%.    ∎

**OBJECTIVE** **2** ***Write a fraction as a percent.***    There are two ways to write a fraction as a percent. One way is to first convert the fraction to a decimal, as explained in Section

1.2. For example, to express the fraction $\frac{2}{5}$ as a percent, write $\frac{2}{5}$ as a decimal by dividing 2 by 5. Then write the decimal as a percent.

| Fraction | Decimal | Percent |
|:---:|:---:|:---:|
| $\dfrac{2}{5}$ | 0.4 | 40% |

## EXAMPLE 4 *Writing Fractions as Percents*

An advertising account representative is given the following data in fraction form and must change the data to percent.

**(a)** $\frac{1}{4}$ **(b)** $\frac{3}{5}$ **(c)** $\frac{7}{8}$

**SOLUTION** First write each fraction as a decimal. Then write the decimal as a percent.

**(a)** $\frac{1}{4} = 0.25 = 25\%$ **(b)** $\frac{3}{5} = 0.6 = 60\%$ **(c)** $\frac{7}{8} = 0.875 = 87.5\%$ ■

A second way to write a fraction as a percent is to multiply the fraction by 100%. For example, write the fraction $\frac{2}{5}$ as a percent by multiplying $\frac{2}{5}$ by 100%.

$$\frac{2}{5} = \frac{2}{5} \times 100\% = \frac{200\%}{5} = 40\%$$

## EXAMPLE 5 *Writing Fractions as Percents*

Write the following fractions as percents.

**(a)** $\frac{3}{4}$ **(b)** $\frac{1}{3}$ **(c)** $\frac{5}{8}$

**SOLUTION** Write these fractions as percents by multiplying each by 100%.

**(a)** $\frac{3}{4} \times 100\% = 75\%$ **(b)** $\frac{1}{3} \times 100\% = 33.3\%$ (rounded)
**(c)** $\frac{5}{8} \times 100\% = 62.5\ \%$ ■

**NOTE** When writing the fraction $\frac{1}{3}$ as a percent it is often expressed as $33\frac{1}{3}\%$. It is expressed this way because $\frac{1}{3} \times 100\% = 33\frac{1}{3}\%$. Also, $\frac{2}{3}$ is expressed as $66\frac{2}{3}\%$ ($\frac{2}{3} \times 100\% = 66\frac{2}{3}\%$). ■

**OBJECTIVE** **3** *Write a percent as a decimal.* Write a percent as a decimal by moving the decimal point two places to the left and dropping the percent sign. For example, 50% becomes 0.50 or 0.5, 100% becomes 1, and 352% becomes 3.52.

## EXAMPLE 6 *Writing Percents as Decimals*

To calculate some insurance claims an insurance agent must change the following percents to decimals.

**(a)** 25% **(b)** 142% **(c)** $37\frac{1}{2}\%$
                                    (Hint: $37\frac{1}{2}\% = 37.5\%$)

**SOLUTION** Move the decimal point two places to the left and drop the percent sign.

**(a)** 0.25 **(b)** 1.42 **(c)** 0.375 ■

**NOTE** In Example 6(c) change $37\frac{1}{2}\%$ to 37.5%. It is usually best to change fractional percents to the decimal form and then change the percent to a decimal. ∎

**OBJECTIVE 4** *Write a percent as a fraction.* Write a percent as a fraction by first changing the percent to a decimal.

**Technology Usage in the Office**

| Technology Type | Percent who Use It |
|---|---|
| Fax machine | 96% |
| Computer | 82% |
| Modems | 83% |
| CD—ROM | 51% |
| On—Line Bulletin board | 22% |
| Laptop computers | 18% |
| Internet | 14% |
| Portable fax | 4% |

*Source: Today's Realtor*, Jan. 96, p. 15.

**EXAMPLE 7** *Writing Percents as Fractions*

The information at the side shows the use of technology in today's business office. Write the following percents as fractions.

**(a)** 96% **(b)** 22% **(c)** 4%

**SOLUTION** First write each percent as a decimal and then write each decimal as a fraction in lowest terms.

**(a)** $96\% = 0.96 = \dfrac{96}{100} = \dfrac{24}{25}$ **(b)** $22\% = 0.22 = \dfrac{22}{100} = \dfrac{11}{50}$

**(c)** $4\% = 0.04 = \dfrac{4}{100} = \dfrac{1}{25}$ ∎

**OBJECTIVE 5** *Write a fractional percent as a decimal.* A fractional percent such as $\frac{1}{4}\%$ has a value less than 1%. In fact, $\frac{1}{4}\%$ is equal to $\frac{1}{4}$ of 1%. Write a fractional percent as a decimal by first changing the fraction to a decimal, leaving the percent sign. For example, first write $\frac{1}{2}\%$ as 0.5%. Then write 0.5% as a decimal by moving the decimal point two places to the left and dropping the percent sign.

$$\frac{1}{2}\% = 0.5\% = 0.005$$

written as decimal with percent sign remaining

**EXAMPLE 8** *Writing Fractional Percents as Decimals*

Write each of the following fractional percents as decimals.

**(a)** $\frac{1}{5}\%$ **(b)** $\frac{3}{4}\%$ **(c)** $1\frac{1}{8}\%$

**SOLUTION** Begin by writing the fraction as a decimal.

**(a)** $\frac{1}{5}\% = 0.2\% = 0.002$ **(b)** $\frac{3}{4}\% = 0.75\% = 0.0075$

**(c)** $1\frac{1}{8}\% = 1.125\% = 0.01125$ ∎

TABLE 3.1   **Common Fractions and Their Equivalent Percents**

$$\frac{1}{100} = 1\%$$     $$\frac{1}{8} = 12\frac{1}{2}\%$$     $$\frac{3}{8} = 37\frac{1}{2}\%$$     $$\frac{5}{6} = 83\frac{1}{3}\%$$

$$\frac{1}{50} = 2\%$$     $$\frac{1}{7} = 14\frac{2}{7}\%$$     $$\frac{2}{5} = 40\%$$     $$\frac{7}{8} = 87\frac{1}{2}\%$$

$$\frac{1}{25} = 4\%$$     $$\frac{1}{6} = 16\frac{2}{3}\%$$     $$\frac{1}{2} = 50\%$$     $$1 = 100\%$$

$$\frac{1}{20} = 5\%$$     $$\frac{3}{16} = 18\frac{3}{4}\%$$     $$\frac{3}{5} = 60\%$$     $$1\frac{1}{4} = 125\%$$

$$\frac{1}{16} = 6\frac{1}{4}\%$$     $$\frac{1}{5} = 20\%$$     $$\frac{5}{8} = 62\frac{1}{2}\%$$     $$1\frac{1}{2} = 150\%$$

$$\frac{1}{12} = 8\frac{1}{3}\%$$     $$\frac{1}{4} = 25\%$$     $$\frac{3}{4} = 75\%$$     $$1\frac{3}{4} = 175\%$$

$$\frac{1}{10} = 10\%$$     $$\frac{1}{3} = 33\frac{1}{3}\%$$     $$\frac{4}{5} = 80\%$$     $$2 = 200\%$$

$$\frac{1}{9} = 11\frac{1}{9}\%$$

Table 3.1 shows many fractions and their percent equivalents. It is often helpful to memorize those which are most commonly used.

## 3.1 EXERCISES

*Write the following decimals as percents.*

**1.** 0.5          **2.** 0.25          **3.** 0.72          **4.** 0.86

**5.** 1.4          **6.** 3.017          **7.** 0.375          **8.** 0.875

**9.** 3.751          **10.** 7.8          **11.** 0.0025          **12.** 0.0008

**13.** 0.0015          **14.** 0.221          **15.** 7.12          **16.** 5.5

*Write the following fractions as percents.*

**17.** $\dfrac{1}{4}$          **18.** $\dfrac{5}{8}$          **19.** $\dfrac{1}{10}$          **20.** $\dfrac{1}{20}$

**21.** $\dfrac{3}{5}$          **22.** $\dfrac{3}{4}$          **23.** $\dfrac{3}{8}$          **24.** $\dfrac{4}{5}$

**25.** $\dfrac{1}{8}$          **26.** $\dfrac{13}{20}$          **27.** $\dfrac{1}{200}$          **28.** $\dfrac{1}{400}$

**29.** $\dfrac{7}{8}$          **30.** $\dfrac{1}{100}$          **31.** $\dfrac{3}{50}$          **32.** $\dfrac{4}{25}$

*Write the following percents as decimals.*

**33.** 15%          **34.** 32%          **35.** 75%          **36.** 65%

**37.** 0.6%         **38.** 0.5%         **39.** 0.25%        **40.** 0.125%

**41.** 210%         **42.** 150%         **43.** 200.6%       **44.** 475.6%

**45.** 350.8%       **46.** 135.6%       **47.** 0.07%        **48.** 0.05%

**49.** Fractions, decimals, and percents are all used to describe a part of something. The use of percent is much more common than fractions and decimals. Why do you suppose this is true?

**50.** List three uses of percent that are or will be part of your life. Consider the activities of working, shopping, saving, and planning for the future.

**51.** To change a fraction to a percent you must first change the fraction to a decimal. Why is this true? (See Objective 2.)

**52.** The fractional percent $\frac{1}{2}\%$ is equal to 0.005. Explain each step as you change $\frac{1}{2}\%$ to its decimal equivalent. (See Objective 4.)

*Determine the fraction, decimal, or percent equivalents for each of the following, as necessary. Write fractions in lowest terms.*

|  | **Fraction** | **Decimal** | **Percent** |
|---|---|---|---|
| **53.** | $\frac{3}{4}$ | _____ | _____ |
| **54.** | $\frac{1}{50}$ | _____ | _____ |
| **55.** | _____ | _____ | 15% |
| **56.** | _____ | _____ | 87.5% |
| **57.** | _____ | 0.25 | _____ |
| **58.** | _____ | 0.35 | _____ |
| **59.** | $6\frac{1}{8}$ | _____ | _____ |
| **60.** | $3\frac{1}{2}$ | _____ | _____ |
| **61.** | _____ | 7.25 | _____ |
| **62.** | $1\frac{3}{4}$ | _____ | _____ |
| **63.** | _____ | 0.0025 | _____ |
| **64.** | _____ | 0.00125 | _____ |
| **65.** | $\frac{1}{3}$ | _____ | _____ |
| **66.** | _____ | _____ | $4\frac{1}{4}\%$ |
| **67.** | _____ | _____ | $\frac{3}{4}\%$ |

| | Fraction | Decimal | Percent |
|---|---|---|---|
| 68. | _____ | _____ | 12.5% |
| 69. | _____ | 0.025 | _____ |
| 70. | _____ | 2.5 | _____ |
| 71. | _____ | _____ | 375% |
| 72. | _____ | _____ | 1038.35% |
| 73. | _____ | 23.82 | _____ |
| 74. | $4\frac{3}{8}$ | _____ | _____ |
| 75. | _____ | _____ | $37\frac{1}{2}\%$ |
| 76. | _____ | _____ | $6\frac{3}{4}\%$ |

## 3.2  Finding the Part

### OBJECTIVES

**1**  *Identify the three elements of a percent problem.*

**2**  *Use the percent formula.*

**3**  *Apply the percent formula to a business problem.*

**4**  *Recognize the terms associated with base, rate, and part.*

**5**  *Use the basic percent equation.*

**OBJECTIVE 1** *Identify the three elements of a percent problem.*    Problems in percent have three main quantities. Usually two of these quantities are given and the third must be found. The three key quantities in a percent problem are as follows.

> **Base.** The whole or total, the starting point, or that to which something is being compared.
>
> **Rate.** A number followed by "%" or "percent."
>
> **Part.** The result of multiplying the base and the rate. Part is always part of the base.

**NOTE**  Percent and part are different quantities. The stated percent in a given problem is always the rate. The part is the product of the base and the rate. It is a portion of the base, as sales tax is a portion of the total sales and as the number of sports utility vehicles is a portion of the total number of motor vehicles. This makes part a number and it never appears with "percent" or "%" following it.  ■

**OBJECTIVE 2** *Use the percent formula.*    The above three quantities are related by the basic **percent formula**.

***Percent Formula***

Part = Base × Rate   or   $P = B \times R$   or   $P = BR$

A real estate agent finds a buyer for a $120,000 home and will earn a 6% commission. Find 6% of $120,000 by using $P = BR$, with $B = \$120,000$ and $R = 6\%$ (the rate). The rate must be changed to a decimal before multiplying.

$$P = BR$$

$$P = \$120,000 \times 6\%$$

$$P = \$120,000 \times 0.06$$

$$P = \$7,200$$

Finally, 6% of $120,000 = $7,200.

### EXAMPLE 1  *Solving for Part*

Solve for part ($P$) using $P = B \times R$.

**(a)** 4% of 50      **(b)** 1.2% of 180

**(c)** 140% of 225      **(d)** $\frac{1}{4}$% of 560

(Hint: $\frac{1}{4}\% = 0.25\%$)

### SOLUTION

**(a)**  $B \times R$  $= P$
    $50 \times 0.04 = 2$

**(b)**  $B \times R$  $= P$
    $180 \times 0.012 = 2.16$

**(c)**  $B \times R = P$
    $225 \times 1.4 = 315$

**(d)**  $B \times R$  $= P$
    $560 \times 0.0025 = 1.4$    ∎

**OBJECTIVE 3** *Apply the percent formula to a business problem.*     Calculating *sales tax* is an excellent example of finding part. States, counties, and cities often collect taxes on sales to the consumer. The sales tax is a percent of the sale. This percent varies from as low as 3% in some states to 8% or more in other states. The percent formula is used for finding sales tax.

$$P \quad = \quad B \quad \times \quad R$$
Sales tax = Sales × Sales tax rate

### EXAMPLE 2  *Calculating Sales Tax*

Racy Feed and Pet Supply sold $284.50 worth of merchandise. If the sales tax was 4%, find the sales tax and the total cost including the tax.

### SOLUTION
The amount of sales, $284.50, is the starting point or base, and 4% is the rate. Since the tax is a *part* of total sales, use the formula $P = BR$ to find the part.

$$P = BR$$
$$P = \$284.50 \times 4\%$$
$$P = \$284.50 \times 0.04$$
$$P = \$11.38$$

The tax, or part, was $11.38.

To find the total amount of sales and tax, the amount of sales, $284.50, is added to the sales tax, $11.38.

The total sales and tax is $295.88 ($284.50 + $11.38). ■

**NOTE** An alternative approach to finding the sales and tax would be to multiply $284.50 by 104% (100% sales + 4% sales tax) to get $284.50 × 104% = $295.88. ■

CALCULATOR APPROACH TO EXAMPLE 2

*The calculator solution to this example is

284.5 $\boxed{\times}$ 104 $\boxed{\%}$ $\boxed{=}$ 295.88.

## EXAMPLE 3 *Finding Part*

Pay 'N' Save Stores employ 600 people, with $35\frac{1}{2}\%$ being part-time student help. How many students does Pay 'N' Save employ?

**SOLUTION** The total number of employees, 600, is the starting point, or base. The rate, $35\frac{1}{2}\%$, is the portion of the total number of employees who are students. Since the number of students employed is a part of the total, find the number of students employed by using the formula to find part.

$$P = BR$$
$$P = 600 \times 35\frac{1}{2}\%$$
$$P = 600 \times 0.355$$
$$P = 213$$

Pay 'N' Save Stores has 213 part-time student employees. ■

**OBJECTIVE** **4** *Recognize the terms associated with base, rate, and part.* Percent problems have certain similarities. For example, some phrases are associated with the base in the problem. Other phrases lead to the part, while "%" or "percent" following a number identifies the rate. Table 3.2 helps distinguish between the base and the part.

*NOTE: All calculator solutions use a scientific calculator. Refer to Appendix A for scientific and financial calculator basics.

TABLE 3.2    **Distinguishing the Base from the Part**

| Usually the Base | Usually the Part |
| --- | --- |
| Sales | Sales tax |
| Investment | Return |
| Savings | Interest |
| Value of bonds | Interest |
| Retail price | Discount |
| Last year's anything | Increase or decrease |
| Value of real estate | Rents |
| Old salary | Raise |
| Total sales | Commission |
| Value of stocks | Dividends |
| Earnings | Expenditures |
| Original | Change |

Most percent problems can be written in the following form.

_____ % of _____ is _____

**OBJECTIVE 5** *Use the basic percent equation.*    This is known as the **basic percent equation**, several examples of which follow.

5% of the automobiles are red.
4.2% of the workers are unemployed.
28% of the income is income tax.
75% of the students are full-time.

When expressed in this standard form, the elements in the percent problem appear in the following order.

$$
\begin{array}{ccccc}
R & \times & B & & P \\
\text{Rate} & \times & \text{Base} & = & \text{Part} \\
\downarrow & \downarrow & \downarrow & \downarrow & \downarrow \\
\_\_\_\_ \% & \text{of} & \_\_\_\_ & \text{is} & \_\_\_\_
\end{array}
$$

**NOTE** Rate is identified by "%" (the percent sign); the word "of" means "×" (multiplication); the *multiplicand*, or number being multiplied, is the base; the word "is" means "=" (equals); and the product, or answer, is part of the base.    ■

**EXAMPLE 4** *Identifying the Elements in Percent Problems*

Identify the elements given in the following percent problems and determine which element must be found.

(a) During a recent sale, Stockdale Marine offered a 15% discount on all new recreation equipment. Find the discount on a jet ski originally priced at $2,895.

**SOLUTION** First arrange this problem using the basic percent equation.

$$R \times B = P$$

_____ % of _____ is _____

% of price is discount

15% of $2,895 = discount

$R \times B = P$

0.15 × $2,895 = P

0.15 × $2,895 = $434.25 discount

At this point, check that rate is given, base is given, and part must be found. To find the discount, multiply 0.15 by $2,895.

The discount is $434.25.

(b) Round Table Pizza spends an amount equal to 5.8% of its sales on advertising. If sales for the month were $12,500, find the amount spent on advertising.

**SOLUTION** Use the basic percent equation.

$$R \times B = P$$

_____ % of _____ is _____

% of sales is advertising

5.8% of $12,500 = advertising

$R \times B = P$

Rate is given as 5.8%, base (sales) is $12,500, and part (advertising) must be found. Find the amount spent on advertising by multiplying 0.058 and $12,500.

$$0.058 \times \$12,500 = P$$

$$0.058 \times \$12,500 = \$725$$

The amount spent on advertising is $725. ■

# 3.2 EXERCISES

*Solve for part in each of the following. Round to the nearest hundredth.*

1. 10% of 520 adults
2. 15% of 1,500 tires
3. 22.5% of $1,086
4. 20.5% of $1,500
5. 4% of 120 feet
6. 125% of 2,000 products
7. 175% of 5,820 miles
8. 15% of 75 cases
9. 35% of 520 crates
10. 400% of 3,008 cars
11. 118% of 125.8 yards
12. 6% of 128 gallons

**13.** $90\frac{1}{2}$% of $5,930

**14.** $7\frac{1}{2}$% of $150

**15.** 0.5% of $1,300

**16.** 0.75% of 180,000 calls

**17.** List the three elements in a percent problem and tell how you can identify each of the elements. (See Objective 1.)

**18.** There are words and phrases that are usually associated with base and part. Give three examples of words that usually identify base and the accompanying word for the part. (See Objective 4.)

*Solve for part in each of the following application problems. Round to the nearest cent unless otherwise indicated.*

**19.** Arnold Parker works part-time, earns $110 per week, and has 18% of this amount withheld for taxes, Social Security, and medicare. Find the amount withheld.

**20.** Kay LaBarre needs 64 credits to graduate. If she has already completed 75% of the credits, find the number of credits completed.

**21.** A collection agency specializing in collecting past-due child support charges $25 as an application fee plus 20% of the amount collected. What is the total charge for collecting $3,100 of past-due child support?

**22.** Caralee Woods has $123,000 invested in her advertising business and finds that she is earning 12% per year on her investment. How much money is she earning per year on the investment?

**23.** The Point of Purchase Advertising Institute says that 55% of all supermarket shoppers have a written list of their needs. If there are 3,680 shoppers per day entering the supermarket that you manage, what number of shoppers would you expect to have a written shopping list?

**24.** A bar of Ivory Soap is $99\frac{44}{100}$% pure. If the bar of soap weighs 9 ounces, how many ounces are pure? (Round to the nearest hundredth.)

**25.** The Yale University marching band has 250 members. If 18.4% of the band members are senior class students, find the number of students who are seniors.

**26.** A U.S. Food and Drug Administration (FDA) biologist found that canned tuna is "relatively clean." Extraneous matter was found in 5% of the 1,600 cans of tuna tested. How many cans of tuna contained extraneous matter?

**27.** In Cuba there are 3.8 million people in the labor force. If 61% of the labor force is male, find (a) the percent who are female and (b) the number of workers who are male.

**28.** In the United States there are 132 million people in the labor force. If 54% of the labor force is male, find (a) the percent of the labor force who are female and (b) the number of workers who are male.

**29.** Erin Kelly owns a coffee stand and must pay $5\frac{1}{2}$% sales tax on her total sales of $11,500. Find the amount of tax she must pay.

**30.** The Bank of Tokyo pays $3\frac{3}{4}$% interest per year. What is the annual interest on an account of $4,130?

**31.** Marketing Intelligence Service says that there were 15,401 new products introduced last year. If 86% of the products introduced last year failed to reach their business objectives, find the number of products that did reach their objectives. (Round to the nearest whole number.)

**32.** A family of four with a monthly income of $2,900 spends 90% of its earnings and saves the balance. Find (a) the monthly savings and (b) the annual savings of this family.

**33.** The average industry-wide profit on all new cars and vans is 6.7% of the dealer's cost. If a new Plymouth Voyager costs the dealer $18,700, find the selling price of the van after the dealer has added the profit to the cost.

**34.** The Saturn automobile dealers use a one price, no haggle selling policy. Saturn dealers average 13% profit on new car sales. If a dealer pays $13,600 for a Saturn SC, find the selling price after adding the profit to the dealers cost.

**35.** As the owner of a copy and print shop, you must collect $6\frac{1}{2}$% of the amount of each sale for sales tax. If sales for the month are $48,680, find the combined amount of sales and tax.

**36.** A Polaris Vac-Sweep 380 is priced at $559 and allows a $125 trade-in rebate for an old unit. If sales tax of $7\frac{3}{4}$% is charged on the price of the new Polaris unit before the trade-in rebate, find the total cost to the customer after receiving the trade-in rebate.

**37.** J & K Mustang has increased its sales of auto parts by $32\frac{1}{2}$% over the last year. If the sale of parts last year amounted to $385,200, find the volume of parts sold this year.

**38.** The value of Brookefield stock rose 6.25% from yesterday's $80 per share. Find the value of the stock after the increase. (Do not round.)

**39.** Diane Bolton of Herrick and Company Realtors sold a home for $165,500. The commission was 6% of the sale price; however, Bolton receives only 60% of the commission while 40% remains with her broker. Find the amount of commission received by Bolton.

**40.** Rick Wilson has an 82% ownership in a company called Puppets and Clowns. If the company has a value of $49,200 and Wilson receives an income of 30% of the value of his ownership, find the amount of his income.

## 3.3     Finding the Base

### OBJECTIVES

**1**  Use the basic percent equation to solve for base.

**2**  Find the amount of sales when taxes and rate of tax are known.

**3**  Find the amount of investment when expense and rate of expense are known.

**4**  Find base when rate and part are for different quantities.

**OBJECTIVE 1** *Use the basic percent equation to solve for base.*    In some problems, the rate and part are given and the base must be found. For example, suppose that a couple, interested in purchasing a home, can make a monthly payment of $770 which is 28% of their monthly income. To find their monthly income, use the rate (28%) and part ($770) to find the base by using the basic percent equation, Rate × Base = Part. The key word here, indicating that their monthly income is the base, is "of."

$$R \times B = P$$

$$28\% \text{ of } \underline{\qquad} = \$770$$

$$0.28 \times B = 770$$

Now divide both sides by 0.28, as explained in Chapter 2.

$$\frac{0.28B}{0.28} = \frac{770}{0.28}$$

$$B = \frac{770}{0.28}$$

$$B = 2{,}750$$

Their monthly income is $2,750.

### EXAMPLE 1 *Solving for Base*

Solve for base using the basic percent equation.

(a)  8 is 4% of _____     (b)  135 is 15% of _____

(c)  1.25 is 25% of _____

SOLUTION

(a)     $8 = 4\% \text{ of }$ _____

$8 = 4\% \times B$

$8 = 0.04B$

$\dfrac{8}{0.04} = \dfrac{0.04B}{0.04}$

$B = \dfrac{8}{0.04} = 200$

(b)  $135 = 15\% \text{ of }$ _____

$135 = 15\% \times B$

$135 = 0.15B$

$\dfrac{135}{0.15} = \dfrac{0.15B}{0.15}$

$B = \dfrac{135}{0.15} = 900$

(c)  $1.25 = 25\% \text{ of }$ _____

$1.25 = 25\% \times B$

$1.25 = 0.25B$

$\dfrac{1.25}{0.25} = \dfrac{0.25B}{0.25}$

$B = \dfrac{1.25}{0.25} = 5$

**OBJECTIVE 2** *Find the amount of sales when taxes and rate of tax are known.*     A common business application of percent involves sales tax and the sales tax rate.

### EXAMPLE 2 *Finding Sales When Sales Tax Is Given*

The 5% sales tax collected by Famous Footwear was $780. What was the amount of total sales?

SOLUTION    Here the rate of tax collection is 5% and taxes collected are a part of total sales. The rate is 5% and the part is $780. Use the percent equation.

$$R \times B = P$$

$$5\% \text{ of } \underline{\hspace{1.5cm}} = \$780$$

$$0.05B = \$780$$

$$\frac{0.05B}{0.05} = \frac{\$780}{0.05}$$

$$B = \frac{\$780}{0.05} = \$15,600$$

The total sales of the company were $15,600.  ■

Calculator Approach to Example 2

In the calculator solution, the percent key may be used when dividing.

780  ÷  5  %  =  15600

**Problem-Solving Hint** Consider whether your answer is reasonable. A common error in a base problem is to confuse the base and part. For example, if the taxes, $780, had been mistakenly used as the base, the resulting answer would have been $39 ($780 × 5%). Obviously, $39 is not a reasonable amount for total sales given $780 as sales tax.  ■

**Objective** **3** *Find the amount of investment when expense and rate of expense are known.*     The amount of an investment is the base. When the amount of expenses and the rate of expenses are known, the percent equation may be used to find the amount of the investment.

**Example 3** *Finding the Amount of an Investment*

The yearly maintenance cost of the campus gymnasium is $1\frac{1}{2}\%$ of its value. If maintenance amounts to $31,500 per year, what is the value of the building?

**Solution**    To find the total value of the building, which is the base, use the percent equation.

$$R \times B = P$$

$$1\frac{1}{2}\% \text{ of } \underline{\hspace{1.5cm}} = \$31,500$$

$$0.015B = \$31,500$$

$$\frac{0.015B}{0.015} = \frac{\$31,500}{0.015}$$

$$B = \frac{\$31,500}{0.015} = \$2,100,000$$

The total value of the building is $2,100,000.   ■

**NOTE**   When working with a fraction of a percent, it is best to change the fraction to a decimal. In Example 3, $1\frac{1}{2}$% was changed to 1.5% which equals 0.015.   ■

**OBJECTIVE** **4** *Find the base when rate and part are for different quantities.*     The rate used and the part given in a problem do not always refer to the same quantity. Always pay careful attention to reading and understanding a problem.

**EXAMPLE 4**   *Finding Base When Rate and Part Are for Different Quantities*

United Hospital finds that 25% of its employees are women and 180 are men. Find the total number of employees.

**SOLUTION**     The rate given, 25%, refers to women employees, while 180, the part, is the number of men. A rate of 75% (100% of all employees $-$25% women employees) must be used to solve for the total number of employees, which is the base. Use the percent equation.

$$R \quad \times \quad B \quad = P$$
$$75\% \text{ of } \underline{\hspace{1cm}} = 180$$
$$0.75B = 180$$
$$\frac{\cancel{0.75}B}{\cancel{0.75}} = \frac{180}{0.75}$$
$$B = \frac{180}{0.75} = 240$$

The total number of employees is 240.   ■

## 3.3   EXERCISES

*Solve for base in each of the following. Round to the nearest hundredth.*

**1.** 530 trucks is 20% of _____ trucks.

**2.** 240 letters is 80% of _____ letters.

**3.** 75 miles is 40% of _____ miles.

**4.** 64 envelopes is 16% of _____ envelopes.

**5.** 110 books is 5.5% of _____ books.

**6.** $850 is $4\frac{1}{4}$% of _____.

**7.** 18 hats is 0.75% of _____ hats.

**8.** 23 workers is 0.5% of _____ workers.

**9.** 33 rolls is 0.15% of _____ rolls.

**10.** 54,600 boxes is 60% of _____ boxes.

**11.** 50 doors is 0.25% of _____ doors.

**12.** 39 bottles is 0.78% of _____ bottles.

**13.** $33,870 is $37\frac{1}{2}$% of _____.

**14.** $8,500 is $27\frac{1}{2}$% of _____.

**15.** 20% of _____ sacks is 350 sacks.

**16.** 16% of _____ is $45.

**17.** 375 crates is 0.12% of _____ crates.

**18.** 3.5 quarts is 0.07% of _____ quarts.

**19.** 0.5% of _____ homes is 327 homes.

**20.** 6.5 barrels is 0.05% of _____ barrels.

**21.** 12 audits is 0.03% of _____ audits.

**22.** 8 banks is 0.04% of _____ banks.

**23.** The basic percent formula is $P = B \times R$. Show how to find the formula to solve for $B$ (base). (See Objective 1.)

**24.** A problem includes amount of sales, sales tax, and a sales tax rate. Explain how you could identify the base, rate, and part in this problem. (See Objective 2.)

*Solve for base in each of the following application problems. Round to the nearest hundredth, unless otherwise noted.*

**25.** A group of graduating hotel management students included 62 people who signed up for internship at a hotel. If this group represented 66% of the graduating class, find the size of the graduating class. (Round to the nearest whole number.)

**26.** In a large metropolitan area 81% of the employed population is enrolled in a health maintenance organization (HMO). If 700,650 employees are enrolled, find the total number of people in the employed population.

**27.** This semester there are 1,785 married students on campus. If this figure represents 23% of the total enrollment, what is the total enrollment? (Round to the nearest whole number.)

**28.** Registered voters make up 13.8% of the county population. If there are 345,000 registered voters in the county, find the total population in the county.

**29.** Liz Covello found a home for Suzanne and Walter Roig that will require a monthly loan payment of $840. If the lender insists that the buyer's monthly payment not exceed 30% of the buyer's monthly income, find the minimum monthly income required by the lender.

**30.** Byron Hopkins spends 22% of his income on housing, 24% on food, 8% on clothing, 15% on transportation, 11% on education, and 7% on recreation, and saves the balance. If his savings amount to $154 per month, what are his monthly earnings?

**31.** Fleet Financial Group has offered to purchase the 19% of its own stock that it does not already own. If the price of this purchase is $190 million, find the total value of the company.

**32.** In analyzing the success of real estate license applicants, the state finds that 58.3% of those examined received a passing mark. If the records show that 8,370 new licenses were issued, what was the number of applicants? (Round to the nearest whole number.)

**33.** Chrysler Corporation raised the base price on its hot-selling Jeep Grand Cherokee by $500 or 2.21%. Find the price of a Jeep Grand Cherokee after the increase. (Round to the nearest dollar.)

**34.** The price of a drill press manufactured by a Malaysian tool company was raised by $250 or 1.93%. Find the price of the drill press after the price increase. (Round to the nearest dollar.)

**35.** An Atlantic City casino advertises that it gives a 97.4% payback on slot machines, and the balance is retained by the casino. If the amount retained by the casino in one day is $4,823, find the total amount played on the slot machines.

**36.** A casino hotel in Barbados states that 45% of its rooms are for nonsmokers. If the resort allows smoking in 484 rooms, find the total number of rooms.

# SUPPLEMENTARY EXERCISES: BASE AND PART

*Solve for base or part as indicated in the following application problems.*

1. Sara Lee Corporation, owning businesses in pastry, pantyhose, and underwear, has laid off 9,000 employees worldwide. If the layoffs amounted to 6% of Sara Lee's workforce, find the total number of employees before the layoffs.

2. Chemical Banking Corporation gave $338 million worth of mortgage loans to minorities last year. If this represented 18.6% of all their mortgages, find the total value of all mortgages that they originated last year. (Round to the nearest tenth of a million.)

3. A building is valued at $423,750 and is insured for 68% of its value. Find the amount of insurance coverage.

4. In a recent survey of 1,100 employers, it was found that 84% offer only one health plan to employees. How many of these employers offer only one health plan?

5. The Chevy Camaro was introduced in 1967. Sales that year were 220,917, which was 46.2% of the number of Ford Mustangs sold in the same year. Find the number of Mustangs sold in 1967. (Round to the nearest whole number.)

6. Unemployment reported by the Bureau of Labor Statistics states that the number of unemployed people is 8.9 million or 7.1% of all workers. What is the size of the employable population? (Round to the nearest tenth of a million.)

7. The total sales of frozen yogurt were $594 million in the past twelve months. If 15.8% of the sales were private label brands, find the amount of sales that were private label brands. (Round to the nearest tenth of a million.)

8. Häagen-Dazs vanilla ice cream has 270 calories per serving. If 60% of these calories come from fat, find the number of calories coming from fat.

9. Julie Ward has 8.5% of her earnings deposited into the credit union. If this amounts to $131.75 per month, find her annual earnings.

10. The Northridge PTA received $79.75 in annual interest on its bank account. If the bank paid $5\frac{1}{2}$% interest per year, how much money was in the account?

11. A survey at an intersection found that of 2,200 drivers, 38% were wearing seat belts. How many drivers in the survey were wearing seat belts?

12. At a recent health fair 32% of the people tested were found to have high blood cholesterol levels. If 350 people were tested, find the number having high blood cholesterol.

13. International Chemical Laboratories, Inc., stock soared $7.25—a 46% increase in value. Find the value of the stock after the increase. (Round to the nearest dollar.)

14. Roper Corporation stock rose $11—a 29% increase in value. Find the value of the stock after the increase. (Round to the nearest dollar.)

## 3.4    Finding the Rate

### OBJECTIVES

1    *Use the percent equation to solve for rate.*

2    *Find the rate of return when the amount of the return and the investment are known.*

**3** Solve for the percent remaining when the total amount and amount used are given.

**4** Find the percent of change.

In the third type of percent problem, the part and base are given and the rate must be found. The rate is identified by the "%" sign, or "percent." For example, what percent of 32 is 8? Use the percent equation as shown next.

**OBJECTIVE 1** *Use the percent equation to solve for rate.*

$$R \times B = P$$

$$\underline{\hspace{2cm}} \% \text{ of } 32 = 8$$

$$R \times 32 = 8$$

$$32R = 8$$

Now divide both sides by 32.

$$\frac{\cancel{32}R}{\cancel{32}} = \frac{8}{32}$$

$$R = \frac{8}{32} = 0.25 = 25\%$$

Finally, 8 is 25% of 32, or 25% of 32 is 8.

**NOTE** When solving for rate the resulting decimal answer must be changed to a percent.   ■

**EXAMPLE 1** *Solving for Rate*

Solve for rate.

**(a)** 13 is what percent of 52?

**(b)** What percent of 500 is 100?

**(c)** 54 is what percent of 12?

**SOLUTION**

**(a)** 13 is $\underline{\hspace{2cm}}$ % of 52

$$\underline{\hspace{2cm}} \% \text{ of } 52 = 13$$

$$52R = 13$$

$$\frac{\cancel{52}R}{\cancel{52}} = \frac{13}{52}$$

$$R = \frac{13}{52} = 0.25 = 25\%$$

**(b)**  100 is _____ % of 500

$$\text{_____ \% of } 500 = 100$$

$$500R = 100$$

$$\frac{500R}{500} = \frac{100}{500}$$

$$R = \frac{100}{500} = 0.2 = 20\%$$

**(c)**  54 is _____ % of 12

$$\text{_____ \% of } 12 = 54$$

$$12R = 54$$

$$\frac{12R}{12} = \frac{54}{12}$$

$$R = \frac{54}{12} = 4.5 = 450\%$$   ∎

**OBJECTIVE 2** *Find the rate of return when the amount of the return and the investment are known.*    It is often necessary to find the rate of return when the amount of the return and investment are known.

### EXAMPLE 2  *Finding the Rate of Return*

The accounting office of J. Susan Hessney and Associates invested $3,420 in a new computer. As a result of having the equipment, the company had additional income of $960. Find the rate of return.

**SOLUTION**    The amount of investment, $3,420, is the base, and the return, $960, is the part. The return is a part of the total investment. Start with $R \times B = P$.

$$\text{_____ \% of } \$3,420 = \$960$$

$$R \times \$3,420 = \$960$$

$$\$3,420R = \$960$$

$$\frac{3,420R}{3,420} = \frac{960}{3,420}$$

$$R = \frac{960}{3,420} = 0.2807 = 28.1\% \qquad \text{rounded to the nearest tenth of a percent} \quad ∎$$

**NOTE**   The rate in Example 2 had to be rounded. The rules for rounding percents are identical to the rules for rounding discussed in Chapter 1. Change the decimal answer to percent and round as indicated. Here, 28.07% rounds to the nearest tenth as 28.1%.   ∎

**OBJECTIVE** **3** *Solve for the percent remaining when the total amount and amount used are given.* When the total amount of something and the amount used are known, it is common to solve for the percent remaining.

| **EXAMPLE 3** *Solving for the Percent Remaining*

A roof is expected to last 12 years before it needs replacement. If the roof is 10 years old, what percent of the roof's life remains? Round to the nearest tenth of a percent.

**SOLUTION** The total life of the roof, 12 years, is the base. Subtract the amount of life already used, 10 years, from the total life, 12 years, to find the number of years remaining.

$$12 \text{ yrs. (total life)} - 10 \text{ yrs. (life used)} = 2 \text{ yrs. (life remaining)}$$

Use the equation $R \times B = P$ to find the solution.

$$\underline{\hspace{2cm}} \% \text{ of } 12 \text{ is } 2$$

$$R \times 12 = 2$$

$$12R = 2$$

$$\frac{\cancel{12}R}{\cancel{12}} = \frac{2}{12}$$

$$R = \frac{2}{12} = \frac{1}{6} = 0.166 \ldots = 16.7\% \qquad \text{rounded to the nearest tenth of a percent}$$

If the age of the roof (10 years) had been used as part, the resulting answer, 83.3% (rounded), would be the percent of life used. Find the percent of remaining life by subtracting 83.3% from 100%. The result, 16.7% (the same answer), would be the percent of life remaining. ■

**NOTE** Remember that the base is always 100%. ■

**OBJECTIVE** **4** *Find the percent of change.* A common business problem is to find the percent of change in amounts involved in operating a business, such as sales and returns and to determine the percent of gain or loss of an investment.

| **EXAMPLE 4** *Finding the Percent of Increase*

Laura Stowe purchased stock in Snowboard Technology for $9,300 and sold it for $10,416. What percent of her original investment was her gain?

**SOLUTION** The original purchase price or investment, $9,300, is the base. Profit (sale price − cost) is the part.

$$\$10,416 \text{ (sale price)} - \$9,300 \text{ (cost)} = \$1,116 \text{ (profit)}$$

Use the basic percent equation as follows.

$$\text{_____ \% of } \$9,300 = \$1,116$$

$$R \times \$9,300 = \$1,116$$

$$\$9,300R = \$1,116$$

$$\frac{9,300R}{9,300} = \frac{1,116}{9,300}$$

$$R = \frac{1,116}{9,300} = 0.12 = 12\%$$ ∎

**PROBLEM-SOLVING HINT**    Remember, to find the percent of increase, the first step is to determine the amount of increase. The base is *always* the original amount, or last year's or last month's amount, and the amount of increase is the part.

## EXAMPLE 5    *Finding the Percent of Decrease*

The Canadian dollar fell to 66.5 U.S. cents this year from 70 U.S. cents last year. Find the percent of decrease.

**SOLUTION**    The base is always the previous period (in this example, last year) which is 70 U.S. cents. Subtract the value this year, 66.5 U.S. cents, from the value last year, 70 U.S. cents, to find the decrease in value.

$$70(\text{last year}) - 66.5(\text{this year}) = 3.5(\text{decrease in value})$$

Use the basic percent equation.

$$\text{_____ \% of } 70 = 3.5$$

$$R \times 70 = 3.5$$

$$70R = 3.5$$

$$\frac{70R}{70} = \frac{3.5}{70}$$

$$R = \frac{3.5}{70} = 0.05 = 5\%$$ ∎

**CALCULATOR APPROACH TO EXAMPLE 5**

The calculator solution to this example is to subtract to find the difference and then divide.

$$70 \boxed{-} \ 66.5 \boxed{=} \ \boxed{\div} \ 70 \boxed{=} \ 0.05$$

PROBLEM-SOLVING HINT   To find the percent of decrease, the first step is to determine the amount of decrease. The amount of decrease is the part in the problem and the base is *always* the original amount or last year's, last month's, or last week's amount.   ∎

## 3.4  EXERCISES

*Solve for rate in each of the following. Round to the nearest tenth of a percent.*

**1.** _____ % of 1,380 clients is 552 clients.

**2.** _____ % of 624 jeeps is 156 jeeps.

**3.** 312 sales is _____ % of 208 sales.

**4.** 144 desks is _____ % of 300 desks.

**5.** _____ % of 78.57 ounces is 22.2 ounces.

**6.** _____ % of 728 miles is 509.6 miles.

**7.** 73.1 quarts is _____ % of 786.8 quarts.

**8.** $310.75 is _____ % of $124.30.

**9.** _____ % of $27 is $1.36.

**10.** _____ % of 850 liters is 3.4 liters.

**11.** 46 shirts is _____ % of 780 shirts.

**12.** 5.2 vats is _____ % of 28.4 vats.

**13.** _____ % of 2 acres is 2.05 acres.

**14.** _____ % of $5 is $0.04.

**15.** 13,830 books is _____ % of 78,400 books.

**16.** _____ % of 73 cases is 350.4 cases.

**17.** _____ % of $330 is $91.74.

**18.** _____ % of 752 employees is 470 employees.

**19.** The basic percent formula is $P = B \times R$. Show how to use the formula to solve for $R$ (rate). (See Objective 1.)

**20.** A problem includes last year's sales, this year's sales, and asks for the percent of increase. Explain how you would identify the base, rate, and part in this problem. (See Objective 4.)

*Solve for rate in each of the following application problems. Round to the nearest tenth of a percent.*

**21.** Theresa Piselli of Insurance Direct reports that office income last month was $265,800 while advertising expenses were $14,884.80. What percent of last months income was spent on advertising?

**22.** American Medical Response, a Boston-based ambulance company, will lay off 140 of its 275 local employees. Find the percent of the employees to be laid off.

**23.** A coronary bypass operation costs $41,000. If Medicare will pay the hospital $27,000 toward this cost, find the percent of the cost paid by Medicare.

**24.** There are 55,000 words in Webster's Dictionary, but most educated people can identify only 20,000 of these words. What percent of the words in the dictionary can these people identify?

**25.** Advertising expenditures for the Radisson Hotel are as follows.

| | | | |
|---|---|---|---|
| Newspaper | $2,250 | Television | $1,425 |
| Radio | $954 | Yellow Pages | $1,605 |
| Outdoor | $1,950 | Miscellaneous | $2,775 |

What percent of the total advertising expenditures is spent on radio advertising?

**26.** Barbara's Antiquery says that of its 3,800 items in inventory, 3,344 are just plain junk, while the rest are antiques. What percent of the total inventory is antiques?

27. This year the Ford Motor Company is hoping to sell 60,000 cars in Japan. The company goal is to achieve annual sales of 200,000 cars by the year 2000. Find the percent of increase needed to achieve this goal.

28. Students were charged $1,449 for tuition this quarter. If the tuition was $1,228 last quarter, find the percent of increase.

29. The price of Toys ''R'' Us stock fell from $33.125 to close at $30.125. Find the percent of decrease.

30. In the past five years, the cost of generating electricity from the sun has been brought down from 24 cents per kilowatt hour to 8 cents (less than the newest nuclear power plants). Find the percent of decrease.

## SUPPLEMENTARY EXERCISES: RATE, BASE, AND PART

*Solve for rate, base, or part as indicated in the following. Round rates to the nearest tenth of a percent.*

1. Last year 20 million Americans visited chiropractors. If 3% of these chiropractic patients were referred by a medical doctor, find the number of patients who were referred to chiropractors by medical doctors.

2. When larger firms (over 1,000 employees) were surveyed, it was found that 27% of the firms offered only one health plan to employees. If 1,800 firms were surveyed, find the number offering only one health plan.

3. In a test by Consumer Reports, 6 of the 123 cans of tuna that it analyzed contained more than the 30 microgram intake limit of mercury. What percent of the cans contained this level of mercury?

4. Scientists tell us that there are 9,600 species of birds and that 1,000 of these species are in danger of extinction. What percent of the bird species are in danger of extinction?

5. According to industry figures there are 44,500 hotels and motels in America. Economy hotels and motels account for 38% of this total. Find the number of economy hotels and motels.

6. There are 50,000 licensed chiropractors in the nation. If 30% of these chiropractors belong to the American Chiropractic Association (ACA), find the number of chiropractors in the ACA.

7. Ford Motor Company hopes to have annual sales of 200,000 cars in Japan by the year 2000. If this will amount to only 4% of the annual automobile sales in Japan, find the total number of cars sold annually in Japan.

8. There are 1,200 new car dealers in the U.S. who are using some form of one price selling—abandoning haggling in favor of a discounted but nonnegotiable price. If these dealers represent 8% of the total number of new car dealers, find the number of dealers in the U.S.

9. A fax machine priced at $398 is marked down 7% to promote the new model. If the sales tax is also 7%, find the cost of the fax machine including sales tax.

10. College students are offered a 6% discount on a dictionary that sells for $18.50. If the sales tax is 6%, find the cost of the dictionary including the sales tax.

11. Americans are eating more fish. This year the average American will eat $15\frac{1}{2}$ pounds compared to only $12\frac{1}{2}$ pounds per year a decade ago. Find the percent of increase.

12. If there are 9,600 species of birds worldwide and the population of 6,500 of these species are in decline, what percent of the bird species are declining in population?

13. In the past year 51,156 airline workers have lost their jobs through layoffs. If this was a 9.8% reduction in the number of workers, find the number of workers after the layoffs.

14. According to the National Association of Realtors the median national sales price of a house was down 1.4%, or $1,390 from last month. Find the median national sales price this month. (Round to the nearest dollar.)

15. According to a recent report, a person owes more than $30,000 to 15 different credit card companies. If his payment on this debt amounts to $1,220 each month and $298 of this is interest, what percent of his payment is interest?

16. Machine tool orders rose $10.5 million last month from $359.8 million the month before. Find the percent of increase.

*The number of existing single-family homes sold in four regions of the country in the same month of two separate years are shown in the table below.*

**Existing Home Sales**

| Region | Last Year | This Year |
|--------|-----------|-----------|
| Northeast | 32,000 | 36,000 |
| Midwest | 65,000 | 66,300 |
| South | 82,000 | 77,500 |
| West | 54,000 | 49,600 |

*Use the table above to answer Exercises 17–20.*

17. Find the percent of increase in sales in the northeastern region.

18. Find the percent of increase in sales in the midwestern region.

19. What is the percent of decrease in sales in the southern region?

20. What is the percent of decrease in sales in the western region?

21. Of the total candy bars contained in a vending machine, 240 bars have been sold. If 25% of the bars have been sold, find the total number of candy bars that were in the machine.

22. If the sales tax rate is 6% and the sales tax collected is $478.20, find the total sales.

23. Lou and Sheri Minkner established a budget allowing 25 percent for rent, 30 percent for food, 8 percent for clothing, 20 percent for travel and recreation, and the remainder for savings. Lou takes home $1,950 per month, and Sheri takes home $28,500 per year. How much will the couple save in a year?

24. Campbell Soup sells 80% of the canned soup sold in this country. The total market for canned soup is worth $843 million. What is the value of the Campbell soup sold in a year?

25. According to the Federal Emergency Management Agency (FEMA) there are 11 million buildings at risk of flooding. The agency finds that only 2.6 million of these are currently insured for flooding. Find the percent that are insured.

26. A Hotpoint refrigerator has a capacity of 11.5 cubic feet in the refrigerator and 5.5 cubic feet in the freezer. What percent of the total capacity is the capacity of the freezer?

27. Automobile accidents involving side-impact collision resulted in 9,000 deaths last year. If automobiles were manufactured to meet a ''side-impact standard'' it is estimated that 63.8% of these deaths would have been prevented. How many deaths would have been prevented?

28. The average price of a new home rose 4.2%. If the average price of a new home was $131,500, find the average price after the increase.

29. Early sales of the Ford Mustang in Japan have amounted to 500 cars. If the Ford Motor Company expects to sell 2,500 Mustangs in Japan this year, what percent of the expected sales have already been made?

30. Instead of laying off workers, a company cut all employees hours from 40 hours a week to 30 hours a week. What was the percent cut in employee hours?

  **Increase and Decrease Problems**

**OBJECTIVES**

1  *Learn to identify an increase or a decrease problem.*

2  *Apply the basic diagram for increase problems.*

3  *Use an equation to solve increase problems.*

4  *Apply the basic diagram for decrease problems.*

5  *Use an equation to solve decrease problems.*

Businesses commonly look at how amounts change, either up or down. For example, a manager might need to know the percent by which sales have increased, or the percent by which costs have decreased, while a consumer might need to know the percent by which the price of an item has changed. Identify these **increase** and **decrease** problems as follows.

OBJECTIVE  1  *Learn to identify an increase or a decrease problem.*

**Increase Problem**—The part equals the base (100%) plus some portion of the base, resulting in a new value. Phrases such as ''after an increase of,'' ''more than,'' or ''greater than'' often indicate an increase problem. The basic formula for an increase problem is

$$\text{Original} + \text{Increase} = \text{New value}$$

> **Decrease Problem**—The part equals the base (100%) minus some portion of the base, resulting in a new value. Phrases such as "after a decrease of," "less than," or "after a reduction of" often indicate a decrease problem. The basic formula for a decrease problem is
>
> $$\text{Original} - \text{Decrease} = \text{New value}$$

**NOTE** Base is always the original amount and both increase and decrease problems are base problems. Base is always 100%. ∎

| **EXAMPLE 1** *Using a Diagram to Understand an Increase Problem*

The price of a home sold by real estate agent Kim Crosby this year is $121,000, which is 10% more than last year's value. Find the value of the home last year.

**SOLUTION**    Use a diagram to help solve this problem. Since base is the starting point, or that to which something is compared, the base here is last year's sales. Call base 100% and remember that

$$\text{Original} + \text{Increase} = \text{New Value}.$$

**OBJECTIVE** **2** *Apply the basic diagram for increase problems.*

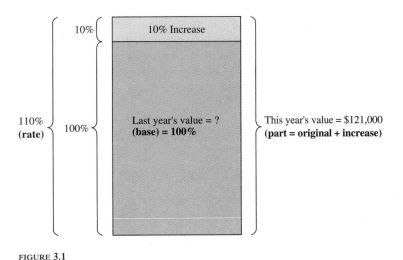

FIGURE 3.1

**OBJECTIVE** **3** *Use an equation to solve increase problems.*    As shown in Figure 3.1, the 10% increase is based on last year's value (which is unknown) and not on this year's value of $121,000. This year's value is the result of adding 10% of last year's value to the amount of last year's value. Therefore, this year's value is all of last year's value (100%) plus 10% (100% + 10% = 110%). Solve with the increase formula, using $B$ to represent base.

$$\text{Original} + \text{Increase} = \text{New value}$$

$$\text{Last year's value} + 10\% \text{ of last year's value} = \text{This year's value}$$

$$100\% \times B + 10\% \times B = \$121,000$$

$$110\% \times B = \$121,000$$

$$1.1B = \$121,000$$

$$\frac{\cancel{1.1}B}{\cancel{1.1}} = \frac{\$121,000}{1.1}$$

$$B = \frac{\$121,000}{1.1}$$

$$B = \$110,000 \qquad \text{last year's value}$$

Check the answer by taking 10% of last year's value and adding it to last year's value.

$$
\begin{array}{ll}
\$110,000 & \text{last year's value} \\
\underline{+\quad 11,000} & \text{(10\% of \$110,000)} \\
\$121,000 & \text{this year's value}
\end{array}
$$  ∎

**PROBLEM-SOLVING HINT**   The common error in solving an increase problem is thinking that the base is given and that the solution can be found by solving for part. Remember that the number given in Example 1, $121,000, is the result of having added 10% of the base to the base (100% + 10% = 110%). In fact, the $121,000 is the part, and base must be found.   ∎

Example 2 shows how to solve a problem with two increases.

**EXAMPLE 2** *Finding Base After Two Increases*

At Builder's Doors, production last year was 20% more than the year before. This year's production is 93,600 doors, which is 20% more than last year's. Find the number of doors produced two years ago.

**SOLUTION**   The two 20% increases cannot be added together because these increases are from two different years, with two separate bases. The problem must be solved in two steps. First, use a diagram to find last year's production.

From Figure 3.2, last year's production plus 20% of last year's production equals this year's production. Use the formula on the facing page.

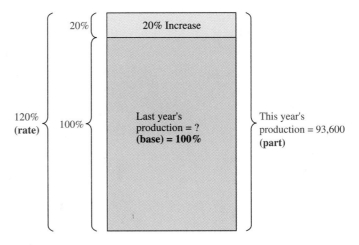

FIGURE 3.2

$$100\% \times B + 20\% \times B = 93{,}600$$

$$120\% \times B = 93{,}600$$

$$1.2B = 93{,}600$$

$$\frac{\cancel{1.2}B}{\cancel{1.2}} = \frac{93{,}600}{1.2}$$

$$B = \frac{93{,}600}{1.2}$$

$$B = 78{,}000 \qquad \text{last year's production}$$

Production last year was 78,000 units. Production for the preceding year (two years ago) must now be found (Figure 3.3). Use another diagram.

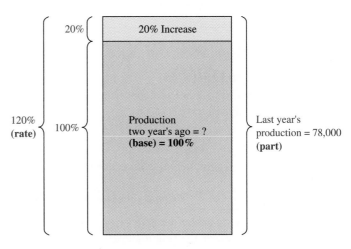

FIGURE 3.3

Thus, production two years ago + 20% of production two years ago = last year's production. In the following solution $b$ is used since $B$ was used before.

$$100\% \times b + 20\% \times b = 78{,}000$$

$$120\% \times b = 78{,}000$$

$$1.2b = 78{,}000$$

$$\frac{\cancel{1.2}b}{\cancel{1.2}} = \frac{78{,}000}{1.2}$$

$$b = \frac{78{,}000}{1.2}$$

$$b = 65{,}000 \qquad \text{production two years ago}$$

Check the answer.

| | |
|---|---|
| 65,000 | production two years ago |
| + 13,000 | 20% increase |
| 78,000 | production last year |
| + 15,600 | 20% increase |
| 93,600 | production this year |

■

**CALCULATOR APPROACH TO EXAMPLE 2**

The calculator solution to this example divides in a series.

93600 $\div$ 1.2 $\div$ 1.2 $=$ 65000

**PROBLEM-SOLVING HINT**    It is important to realize that the two 20% increases cannot be added together to equal one increase of 40%. Each 20% increase is calculated on a different base.

**OBJECTIVE 4**    *Apply the basic diagram for decrease problems.*

**EXAMPLE 3**    *Using a Diagram to Understand a Decrease Problem*

After a dealer deducted 10% from the price of a pair of skis, your friend paid $135. What was the original price of the skis?

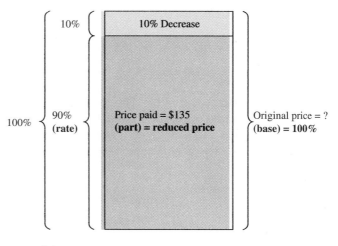

FIGURE 3.4

**SOLUTION**    Use a diagram again and remember that the base is the starting point—in this case, the original price. As always, the base is 100%. Use the decrease formula.

**OBJECTIVE 5**    *Use an equation to solve decrease problems.*    As Figure 3.4 shows, 10% was deducted from the original price. The result equals the price paid, which is 90% of the original price.

Be careful in finding the rate: 10% cannot be used because the original price to which 10% was applied is not given. The rate 90% (the difference, 100% − 10% = 90%) must be used since 90% of the original price is the resulting $135 price paid. Now find the original price.

$$\text{Original} - \text{Decrease} = \text{New value}$$

$$\text{Original price} - 10\% \text{ of the original price} = \text{Price paid}$$

$$100\% \times B - 10\% \times B = \$135$$

$$90\% \times B = \$135$$

$$0.9B = \$135$$

$$\frac{\cancel{0.9}B}{\cancel{0.9}} = \frac{\$135}{0.9}$$

$$B = \frac{\$135}{0.9}$$

$$B = \$150 \qquad \text{original price}$$

Check the answer.

|  |  |
|---|---|
| $150 | original price |
| −    15 | 10% discount |
| $135 | price paid |

■

**PROBLEM-SOLVING HINT**   The common mistake made in Example 3 is thinking that the reduced price, $135 is the base. The original price is the base while the reduced price, $135, is a result of subtracting 10% from the base. The reduced price is the part or 90% *of the base* (100% − 10% = 90%).   ■

## 3.5   EXERCISES

*Solve for base in each of the following. Round to the nearest cent.*

| | Part (after increase) | Rate of Increase |
|---|---|---|
| **1.** | $320 | 25% |
| **2.** | $660 | 20% |
| **3.** | $30.70 | 10% |
| **4.** | $10.09 | 5% |

*Solve for base in each of the following. Round to the nearest cent.*

| | Part (after decrease) | Rate of Decrease |
|---|---|---|
| **5.** | $18 | 10% |
| **6.** | $1,760 | 12% |
| **7.** | $598.15 | 30% |
| **8.** | $98.38 | 15% |

 **9.** Certain words or word phrases help to identify an increase problem. Discuss how you will identify an increase problem. (See Objective 1.)

 **10.** Certain words or word phrases help to identify a decrease problem. Discuss how you will identify a decrease problem. (See Objective 1.)

*Solve each of the following application problems. Read each carefully to determine which are increase or decrease problems and work accordingly. Round to the nearest cent, when necessary.*

**11.** Patricia Quinlin of Country Realtors just listed a home for $165,550. If this is 10% more than what the home sold for last year, find last year's selling price.

**12.** John Chavez Auto Stereos sold an auto stereo for $337.92, a loss of 12% of the dealer's original cost. Find the original cost.

13. The top ten films at the movie theaters had sales of $94 million over one holiday weekend. If this was an increase of 9% over last year's sales, find the amount of last year's sales. (Round to the nearest tenth of a million.)

14. Emma Price bought a steering wheel lock for her pickup truck for $34.64 including $6\frac{1}{4}$% sales tax. (a) How much of the $34.64 was for the lock, and (b) how much was the sales tax?

15. In a recent test of an automobile antilock braking system (ABS) on wet pavement, the stopping distance was 114 feet. If this was 28.75% less than the distance needed to stop the same automobile without the ABS, find the distance needed to stop without the antilock braking system.

16. Katie Reynolds installed an electronic alarm and several simple auto-theft devices in her car. As a result her auto insurance policy premium was reduced by 5.2% to $1,147 per year. Find the amount of her insurance premium before installing these devices. (Round to the nearest cent.)

17. Mail Boxes, Etc. collects 8% state sales tax on all sales. If total sales including tax are $3,423.60, find the amount of tax.

18. In 1997 the population of Rio Linda was 10% more than it was in 1996. If the population was 26,620 in 1998, which was 10% more than in 1997, find the population in 1996.

19. Christy Lawrence, owner of Walpaper Plus, says that her sales have increased exactly 20% per year for the last 2 years. Her sales this year are $170,035.20. Find her sales two years ago.

20. Existing home sales last year in the major Texas real estate markets totaled 113,764. If this was 7.3% more than the previous year, find the number of home sales in the previous year. (Round to the nearest whole number.)

21. The cost of nursing home care in the United States will jump nearly 12% to $66 billion next year. Find the cost of nursing home care this year. (Round to the nearest tenth of a billion.)

22. R. H. Macy and Company (Macy's) reported annual sales of $6.18 billion. If this was a 2% drop in sales from a year earlier, find the previous year's sales. (Round to the nearest hundredth of a billion.)

23. In a 3-day public sale of Jackson County surplus equipment, the first day brought $5,750 in sales and the second day brought $4,186 in sales, with 28% of the original equipment left to be sold on the third day. Find the value of equipment left to sell.

24. After spending $3,450 for tuition and $4,350 for dormitory fees, Donald Cole finds that 35% of his original savings remains. Find the amount of his savings that remains.

25. Appliance Parts Incorporated has an inventory this year of 36,504 items which is 6.4% fewer items than last year. Find last year's inventory.

26. If an owner quickly sold her condominium for $86,330, which was a loss of 11% of the original purchase price, how much had the owner paid originally?

27. Even though wheat prices are rising during the planting season, farmers have planted only 50.2 million acres of winter wheat varieties. If this is 2% fewer acres than last year, find the number of acres planted last year. (Round to the nearest tenth of a million.)

28. Department stores and specialty chains sold 4.1 million leather jackets and coats this year. If this is a 38% drop in sales from last year, find last year's sales. (Round to the nearest tenth of a million.)

**29.** In 1997 the student enrollment at American River College was 8% more than it was in 1996. If the enrollment was 23,328 students in 1998, which was 8% more than it was in 1997, find the student enrollment in 1996.

**30.** Students at the state universities are outraged. The annual university fees were 30% more last year than they were the year before. If the fees are $2,704 per year this year, which is 30% more than they were last year, find the annual student fees 2 years ago.

**31.** The sales of Ben and Jerry's frozen yogurt during a one year period were $44.1 million. If this was an increase of 39.4% over the previous year, find the sales of frozen yogurt in the previous year. (Round to the nearest tenth of a million.)

**32.** Chemical Banking Corporation, the nation's fourth largest bank, made 52% more loans to minorities this year than last year. If the number of loans to minorities this year is 2,660, find the number of loans made to minorities last year.

**33.** New home sales this year in the Sacramento area were 14% fewer than last year. If the number of new homes sold this year was 5,645, find the number of new homes sold last year. (Round to the nearest whole number.)

**34.** The median price for a new home in the Sacramento area is $148,950—down 2.5% from last year. Find the median price for a new home last year. (Round to the nearest dollar.)

# Chapter 3 Quick Review

| TOPIC | APPROACH | EXAMPLE |
|---|---|---|
| **3.1 Writing a decimal as a percent** | Move the decimal point two places to the right and attach a % sign. | $0.75 \ (0.75,) = 75\%$ |
| **3.1 Writing a fraction as a percent** | First change the fraction to a decimal, then write the decimal as a percent. | $\dfrac{2}{5} = 0.4$ <br> $0.4 \ (0.40,) = 40\%$ |
| **3.1 Writing a percent as a decimal** | Move the decimal point two places to the left and drop the % sign. | $50\% \ (0.50.\%) = 0.5$ |
| **3.1 Writing a percent as a fraction** | First change the percent to a decimal. Then write the decimal as a fraction in lowest terms. | $15\% \ (0.15.\%) = 0.15$ <br> $= \dfrac{15}{100} = \dfrac{3}{20}$ |
| **3.1 Writing a fractional percent as a decimal** | First change the fraction to a decimal leaving the % sign, then move the decimal point two places to the left and drop the % sign. | $\dfrac{1}{2}\% = 0.5\%$ <br> $0.5\% = 0.00.5$ |

| 3.2 | Solving for part using the percent formula | Part $=$ Base $\times$ Rate<br><br>$P = B \times R$<br><br>$P = BR$<br><br>_____ % of _____ is _____ | A company offered a 15% discount on all sales. Find the discount on sales of $1,850.<br><br>_____ % of <u>sales</u> is discount<br><br>15% of $1,850 $=$ discount<br><br>$R \times B = P$<br><br>$0.15 \times \$1,850 = P$<br><br>$0.15 \times \$1,850 = \$277.50$ discount |

| 3.3 | Using the basic percent equation to solve for base | Remember that base is the starting point, reference point, all of something, or 100%.<br><br>Rate $\times$ Base $=$ Part<br><br>_____ % $\times$ _____ is _____ | If the sales tax rate is 4%, find the sales if the sales tax is $18.<br><br>$R \times B = P$<br><br>$4\% \times \underline{\quad} = \$18$<br><br>$0.04 \, B = \$18$<br><br>$\dfrac{\cancel{0.04}B}{\cancel{0.04}} = \dfrac{\$18}{0.04}$<br><br>$B = \dfrac{18}{0.04}$<br><br>$= \$450$ sales |

| 3.4 | Using the basic percent equation to solve for rate | Remember that rate is a percent and is followed by a % sign.<br><br>Rate $\times$ Base $=$ Part<br><br>_____ % $\times$ _____ is _____ | The return is $307.80 on an investment of $3,420. Find the rate of return.<br><br>$R \times B = P$<br><br>_____ % of $3,420 is $307.80<br><br>$R \times \$3,420 = \$307.80$<br><br>$\$3,420R = \$307.80$<br><br>$\dfrac{\cancel{3,420}R}{\cancel{3,420}} = \dfrac{307.80}{3,420}$<br><br>$= 0.09$<br><br>$R = 9\%$ |

**3.4   Finding the percent of change**

Calculate the change (increase or decrease), which is the part. Base is the amount before the change.

Use $R = \dfrac{P}{B}$

Production rose from 3,820 units to 5,157 units. Find the percent of increase.

5,157 − 3,820 = 1,337 increase

$$R = \frac{1,337}{3,820} = 0.35 = 35\%$$

**3.5   Drawing a diagram and using an equation to solve an increase problem**

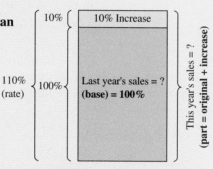

Solve for base given rate (110%) and part (after increase).

This years sales are $121,000, which is 10% more than last year's sales. Find last year's sales.

Original + Increase = New value

$100\% \times B + 10\% \times B =$ $121,000

$1B + 0.1B = \$121,000$

$1.1B = \$121,000$

$$B = \frac{\$121,000}{1.1}$$

$= \$110,000$ last year's sales

**3.5   Drawing a diagram and using an equation to solve a decrease problem**

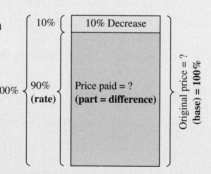

Solve for base given rate (90%) and part (after decrease).

After a deduction of 10% from the price, a customer paid $135. Find the original price.

Original − Decrease = New value

$100\% \times B - 10\% \times B =$ $135

$1B - 0.1B = \$135$

$0.9B = \$135$

$$B = \frac{\$135}{0.9}$$

$B = \$150$ original price

# Chapter 3 Review Exercises

*Solve each of the following. [3.1–3.4]*

**1.** 21 customers is 15% of what number of customers?

**2.** What is 2% of 350 trucks?

**3.** 33 shippers is 3% of what number of shippers?

**4.** 36 accounts is what percent of 1,440 accounts?

**5.** What is $\frac{1}{4}$% of $1,500?

**6.** Find the fractional equivalent of 16%.

**7.** 24 loads is $2\frac{1}{2}$% of how many loads?

**8.** Change 62.5% to its fractional equivalent.

**9.** $282.20 is what percent of $3,320?

**10.** What is the fractional equivalent of $\frac{1}{2}$%?

*Solve each of the following application problems, reading each carefully to determine whether base, part, or rate is being asked for. Also, check to see which are increase or decrease problems, and work accordingly. (Round to the nearest cent or tenth of a percent, as necessary.)*

**11.** One share of stock in Telefonos de Mexico sells for $35.75 and pays a 4% dividend. Find the dividend per share. [3.2]

**12.** A supervisor at Barrett Manufacturing finds that rejects amount to 1,120 units per month. If this amounts to 0.5% of total monthly production, find the total monthly production. [3.3]

**13.** The number of middle managers at Empire Lumber Suppliers this year is 120% of last year's 35 middle managers. Find the number of middle managers this year. [3.2]

**14.** Americans who are 65 years of age or older make up 12.7% of the total population. If there are 31.5 million Americans in this group, find the total U.S. population. (Round to the nearest tenth of a million.) [3.3]

**15.** Gabberts Furniture, with a monthly advertising budget of $3,400, decides to set up a media budget. They plan to spend 22% for television, 38% for newspaper, 14% for outdoor signs, 15% for radio, and the remainder for bumper stickers. (a) What percent of the total budget do they plan to spend on bumper stickers? (b) How much do they plan to spend on bumper stickers for the entire year? [3.2]

**16.** The government is offering a $25,000 bonus to federal employees for retiring early. After taxes and other deductions the employee will receive only $17,000. What percent of the bonus will the employee actually receive? [3.4]

**17.** A video camcorder is marked "reduced 35%, now only $942.50." Find the original price of the video camcorder. [3.5]

**18.** Last year's backpack sales were 10% more than they were the year before. This year's sales are 1,452 units, which is 10% more than last year. Find the number of backpacks sold 2 years ago. [3.5]

**19.** The number of industrial accidents this month fell to 989 accidents from 1,276 accidents last month. Find the percent of decrease. (Round to the nearest tenth of a percent.) [3.4]

**20.** The number of residential housing permits issued in the U.S. this year is predicted to be 1.38 million. If this is an increase of 15% over last year, find the number of permits issued last year. [3.3]

**21.** The number of apartment unit vacancies was predicted to be 2,112 while the actual number of vacancies was 2,640. The actual number was what percent of the predicted number of vacancies? [3.4]

**22.** Most shampoos contain 75% to 90% water. If a 16-ounce bottle of shampoo contains 78% water, find the number of ounces of water in the 16-ounce bottle. (Round to the nearest tenth of an ounce.) [3.2]

**23.** Bookstore sales of the *Physicians Desk Reference*, which contains prescription drug information, rose 13.7% this year. If sales this year were 111,150 copies, find last year's sales. (Round to the nearest whole number.) [3.5]

**24.** After deducting 11.8% of total sales as her commission, George Ann Hornor, a salesperson for Marx Toy Company, deposited $35,138.88 to the company account. Find the total amount of her sales. [3.5]

**25.** Navistar International Corporation, the heavy-duty truck maker, will lay off 499 of the plant's 2,100 workers. Find the percent to be laid off. [3.4]

**26.** Doctors in Argentina report that 240,000 Argentines will have plastic surgery this year. If the population of the entire country is 33 million, what percent of the Argentines will have plastic surgery this year? [3.4]

**27.** Beef consumption in the U.S. is at a five-year high. Of the total meat expenditures, 49 percent of every dollar consumers spend is for beef. If expenditures for meat during one week were $108,780,220, find the amount spent on beef. [3.2]

**28.** Tupperware, which was built on parties in peoples' homes where sellers demonstrated the use of plastic containers, is part of Premark International, Incorporated. Last year, Tupperware products accounted for 39% of Premarks $3.5 billion in sales. Find the amount of the Tupperware sales. [3.2]

**29.** The whooping crane, which is the tallest bird (5 feet) in North America, now has a population of 155 after dropping to near extinction in 1941, when there were only 15 birds. Find the percent of increase in the number of whooping cranes since 1941. [3.4]

**30.** The Small Business Administration (SBA) guaranteed 55,600 loans this year compared with 36,000 loans last year. Find the percent of increase in the number of loans guaranteed. [3.4]

**31.** The number of business failures this year were 64,031 compared to 64,743 business failures last year. Find the percent of decrease. [3.4]

**32.** The number of Canadian tourists traveling to Florida this year has decreased 25% since 1990, when a record 2.4 million visited the ''Sunshine State.'' Find the number of Canadian tourists visiting Florida this year. [3.2]

**33.** At Chrysler, light-truck sales (minivans, pickups, and sport utility vehicles) were up 21% last month from the same month last year. If sales this year were 111,026 units, find the number of units sold last year. (Round to the nearest whole number.) [3.5]

34. General Motors light-truck sales were up 2% last month from the same month last year. If sales this year were 151,477 units, find the number of units sold last year. (Round to the nearest whole number.) [3.5]

35. This year NBC is getting $300,000 for a 30-second advertising spot during the World Series Game. If this is an increase of 25% over NBA All-Star Game ads, find the cost of an All-Star Game advertisement.

36. Navistar International Corporation will cut daily production of class 8 trucks— those that can haul more than 33,000 pounds—by 26%, reducing daily production to 72 units. Find the daily production before the cutback. (Round to the nearest whole number.) [3.5]

# Chapter 3 Summary Exercise

Many people collect baseball cards as a hobby, some collect them as an investment, and a few people support themselves through college by buying and selling cards. A 1952 Jackie Robinson card recently sold for $4,675. (The one pictured here is from 1953.)

In the past year some cards have gone up in value while others have gone down.

JACKIE ROBINSON

*Source:* National Baseball Library and Archive, Cooperstown, New York.

*Find the card price last year, the percent change from last year, or the card price this year as necessary. Round dollar amounts to the nearest half dollar.*

**The Ups and Downs of Last Year**

| Rookie Card | Card Price Last Year* | Card Price This Year* | % Change from Last Year |
|---|---|---|---|
| **Frank Thomas** | $4.50 | _____ | +33% |
| **Cal Ripken, Jr.** | $65.00 | $65.00 | _____ |
| **Dave Justice** | _____ | $3.00 | −25% |
| **Nolan Ryan** | $1,200.00 | _____ | +35% |
| **Ken Griffey, Jr.** | _____ | $5.00 | −45% |
| **José Canseco** | $10.00 | $3.50 | _____ |
| **Will Clark** | $15.00 | _____ | −33% |
| **Mark McGwire** | _____ | $4.00 | −67% |

*Average prices for rookie cards.

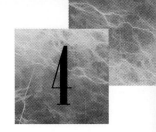

# Banking Services

Modern banks and savings institutions today offer so many services that they have become more than places to deposit savings and take out loans. These financial institutions now offer a wide range of services to individuals and business customers. Today, many types of savings and checking accounts are offered, as well as services such as computerized home and business banking, automated teller machines (ATMs), credit cards, debit cards, investment securities services, and even payroll services for the business owner.

Most of the innovations in modern banking today are the result of electronic technology. While tradition keeps us writing and depositing checks, the growing use of direct deposits, ATM cards, debit cards, and home and business banking, all known as *electronic banking* will become the common practice.

This chapter examines checking accounts and check registers, and how to use them. It also discusses business checking account services, the depositing of credit card transactions, and bank reconciliation (balancing the checking account).

## 4.1 Checking Accounts and Check Registers

**Checking Facts**

- **3 of every 4 families have a checking account.**
- **On average we write about 20 checks each month.**
- **Checks became common after World War II.**
- **Today 60 billion checks are processed each year.**

*Source: The Wall Street Journal,* Guide to Understanding Personal Finance, 1992, pp. 8–9. *Source: Consumer Reports,* March 1996, p. 11.

**OBJECTIVES**

1. *Identify the parts of a check.*
2. *Know the types of checking accounts.*
3. *Find the monthly service charges.*
4. *Identify the parts of a deposit slip.*
5. *Identify the parts of a check stub.*
6. *Complete the parts of a check register.*

The overwhelming majority of all business transactions today involve checks. Goods are purchased by check, and bills are paid by check. A small business may write several hundred checks each month and take in several thousand, while large businesses can take in several million checks in a month. This heavy reliance on checks makes it important for all people in business to have a good understanding of checks and checking accounts. The various parts of a check are explained in Figure 4.1.

**OBJECTIVE 1** *Identify the parts of a check.*

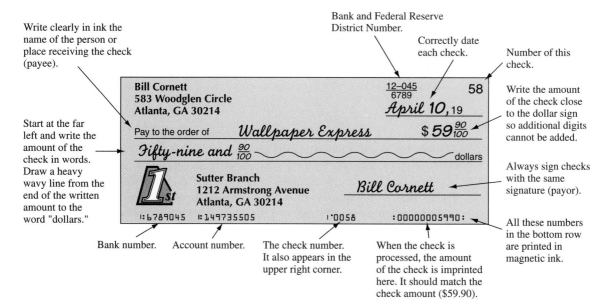

FIGURE 4.1

**OBJECTIVE 2** ***Know the types of checking accounts.***    Two main types of checking accounts are available.

**Personal checking accounts** are used by individuals. The bank supplies printed checks (normally charging a check-printing fee) for the customer to use. Some banks offer the checking account at no charge to the customer but most require that a minimum monthly balance remain in the checking account. If the minimum balance is not maintained during any month, a service charge is applied to the account. Today, the **flat fee checking account** is common. For a fixed charge per month, the bank supplies the checking account, check printing, a bank charge card, and a host of other services. Interest paid on checking account balances is common with personal checking accounts. These accounts are offered by savings and loan associations, credit unions, and banks, and are available to individuals as well as a few business customers. These accounts often require much higher minimum balances than regular accounts.

**Business checking accounts** often receive more services than do personal accounts. For example, banks often arrange to receive payments on debts due to business firms. The bank automatically credits the amount to the business account.

A popular service available to personal and business customers is the **automated teller machine (ATM)**. Offered by many banks, savings and loans, and credit unions, an ATM allows customers to perform a great number of transactions on a 24-hour basis. The customer can make cash withdrawals and deposits, transfer funds from one account to another (including the paying of credit card accounts or other loans), and make account-balance inquiries. In addition, through several networking arrangements, the customer may make purchases and receive cash advances from hundreds, and in some cases thousands, of participating businesses nationally, and often worldwide.

**NOTE** Students traveling on exchange trips in foreign countries can often get cash in the local currency using their ATM cards.  ■

These ATM cards are **debit cards**, *not* credit cards. When you use your debit card at a **point of sale terminal** the amount of your purchase is instantly subtracted from your account and credit is given to the seller's account. When you use a credit card you usually sign a receipt, however, when using a debit card you enter your **personal identification number (PIN)**, (your special code) to authorize the transition.

**NOTE** When using the ATM card remember to keep receipts so that the transaction can be subtracted from your bank balance. Be certain to subtract any charge made for using the ATM card.  ■

**OBJECTIVE** **3** *Find the monthly service charges.*     Service charges for business checking accounts are based on the average balance for the period covered by the statement. This average balance determines the **maintenance charge per month**, to which a **per debit charge** (per check charge) is added. The charges generally apply regardless of the amount of account activity. Some typical bank charges for a business checking account appear in Table 4.1.

**EXAMPLE 1** *Finding the Checking Account Service Charge*

Find the monthly service charge for the following business accounts.

**(a)** Pittsburgh Glass, 38 checks written, average balance $833

**SOLUTION**     From Table 4.1, an account having an average balance between $500 and $1,999 will have a maintenance charge of $7.50 for the month. In addition, there is a per debit (check) charge of $0.20. Since 38 checks were written during the month, the monthly service charge is calculated as follows.

$$\$7.50 + 38(\$0.20) = \$7.50 + \$7.60 = \$15.10$$

TABLE 4.1   **Typical Bank Charges for a Business Checking Account**

| Average Balance | Maintenance Charge Per Month | Per Check Charge |
|---|---|---|
| Less than $500 | $12.00 | $0.20 |
| $500–$1,999 | $7.50 | $0.20 |
| $2,000–$4,999 | $5.00 | $0.10 |
| $5,000 or more | $0 | $0 |

**(b)** Fargo Western Auto, 87 checks written, average balance $2,367

$OLUTION   Since the average balance is between $2,000 and $4,999, the maintenance charge for the month is $5.00, to which a $0.10 per debit (check) charge is added. The monthly service charge is $5.00 + 87($0.10) = $5.00 + $8.70 = $13.70.  ∎

CALCULATOR APPROACH
TO EXAMPLE 1

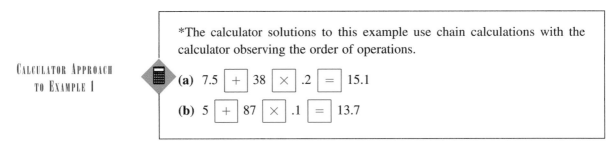

*The calculator solutions to this example use chain calculations with the calculator observing the order of operations.

**(a)** 7.5 $+$ 38 $\times$ .2 $=$ 15.1

**(b)** 5 $+$ 87 $\times$ .1 $=$ 13.7

**OBJECTIVE 4** *Identify the parts of a deposit slip.*      Money, either cash or checks, is placed into a checking account with a **deposit slip** or **deposit ticket** such as the one in Figure 4.2. The account number is written at the bottom of the slip in magnetic ink. The slip contains blanks in which are entered any cash (either currency or coins), as well as checks that are to be deposited.

When a check is deposited, it should have ''for deposit only'' and either the depositor's signature or the company stamp placed on the back within 1.5 inches of the vertical top edge. In this way, if a check is lost or stolen on the way to the bank, it will be worthless to anyone finding it. Such an endorsement, which limits the ability to cash a check, is called a **restricted endorsement**. An example of a restricted endorsement is shown in Figure 4.3, along with two other types of endorsements. The most common endorsement by individuals is the **blank endorsement**,

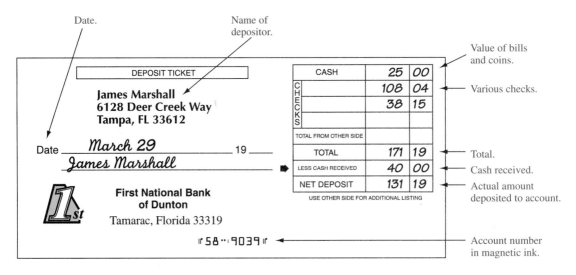

FIGURE 4.2

*NOTE: All calculator solutions use a scientific calculator. Refer to Appendix A for scientific and financial calculator basics.

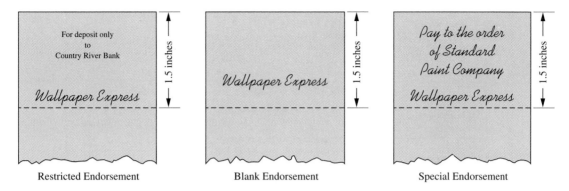

Restricted Endorsement          Blank Endorsement          Special Endorsement

FIGURE **4.3**

where only the name of the person being paid is signed. This endorsement should be used only at the moment of cashing a check. The **special endorsement**, used to pass on the check to someone else, might be used to pay a bill on another account.

After the check is endorsed, it is normally cashed or deposited at a bank. The payee is either given cash or receives a credit in their account for the amount of the check. The check is then routed to a Federal Reserve Bank which forwards the check to the payers bank. After going through this procedure, known as **processing**, the check is then **canceled** and returned to the payer. The check will now have additional processing information on its back as shown below on Figure 4.4.

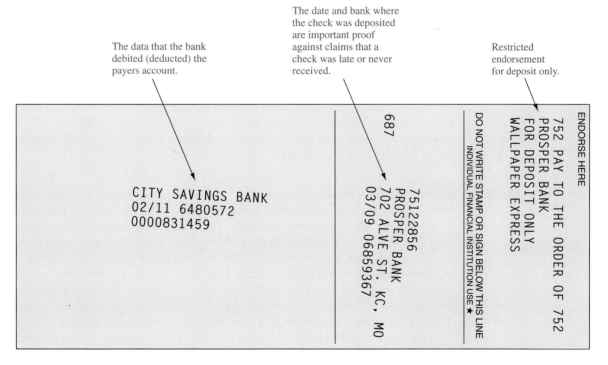

FIGURE **4.4**

COUNTRY
RIVER BANK
Checking Account Deposit Slip

WALLPAPER EXPRESS
1515 Sunrise Blvd.
Fayetteville, GA 30214

For Bank Use Only
Cash Count

| 4 | x | 100 | 400 |
| 7 | x | 50 | 350 |
| 32 | x | 20 | 640 |
| 11 | x | 10 | 110 |
| 7 | x | 5 | 35 |
| | x | 2 | |
| 33 | x | 1 | 33 |
| | x | | |
| Total | | | 1,568 |

Deposited for credit in the above account

11/26
Date

21048461
Account Number

Please list all items on the back of this
deposit slip and enter the total deposit here.

Total Deposit

$ 3,467 29

NOTICE: The Bank may place a hold for uncollected funds on an item you deposit. You will be notified if a
hold is placed and when the funds will be available for withdrawal. Please refer to our Hold Policy brochure.

⑆121000086⑆ 021048461⑈4444

Please list each check separately
Specify by number the bank on which each check is drawn

| Description | Dollars | Coins |
|---|---|---|
| Currency | 1,568 | 00 |
| Coin | 135 | 00 |
| Checks—List Below | | |
| 1  90 - 7030/1 | 38 | 18 |
| 2  11 - 8 | 462 | 53 |
| 3  119 | 79 | 24 |
| 4  2208 | 57 | 14 |
| 5  514 | 118 | 32 |
| 6  111 | 68 | 76 |
| 7  35/8 | 25 | 14 |
| 8  721 | 9 | 05 |
| 9  76 - 218 | 188 | 29 |
| 10  4421 | 8 | 56 |
| 11  119 | 220 | 15 |
| 12  218 | 79 | 86 |
| 13  90 - 725 | 26 | 19 |
| 14  90 - 725 | 18 | 74 |
| 15  71 - 668 | 134 | 55 |
| 16  119 | 156 | 24 |
| 17  721 | 73 | 35 |
| 18 | | |
| 19 | | |
| 20 | | |
| 21 | | |
| 22 | | |
| 23 | | |
| 24 | | |
| 25 | | |
| TOTAL | 3,467 | 29 |

Please enter total on front of this slip

FIGURE 4.5

A two-sided commercial deposit slip is shown in Figure 4.5. Notice that much
more space is given for an itemized list of customers' checks that are being deposited
to the business account. Many financial institutions require that the bank and federal
reserve district numbers be shown in the description column of the deposit slip.
These numbers appear in the upper right-hand corner of the check and are identified
in the sample check on page 102.

**OBJECTIVE 5** *Identify the parts of a check stub.* A record must be kept of every deposit
made and every check written. Business firms normally do this with one **check stub**
for each check. These stubs provide room to list the date, the person or firm to whom
the check will be paid, and the purpose of the check. Also, the stub provides space
to record the balance in the account after the last check was written (called the
**balance brought forward**, abbreviated Bal. Bro't. For'd., on the stub), and any
money deposited since the last check was written. The balance brought forward and
amount deposited are added to provide the current balance in the checking account.
The amount of the current check is then subtracted, and a new balance is found.
This balance forward from the bottom of the stub should be written on the next stub.
Figure 4.6 shows a typical check stub.

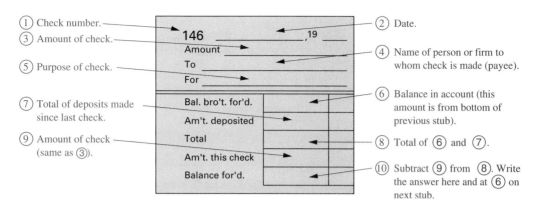

FIGURE 4.6

**EXAMPLE 2**    *Completing a Check Stub*

Check number 2724 is made out on June 8 to Lillburn Utilities as payment for water and power. Assume that the check is for $182.15, that the balance brought forward is $4,245.36, and that deposits of $337.71 and $193.17 have been made since the last check was written. Complete the check stub as shown in Figure 4.7.

**SOLUTION**

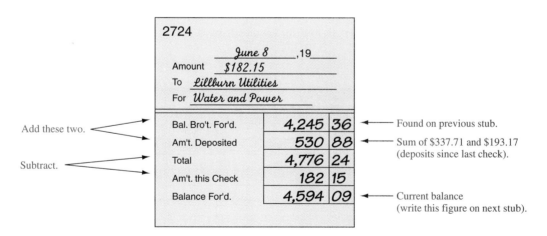

FIGURE 4.7

Banks offer many styles of checkbooks. Notice that the following two styles shown in Figure 4.8 offer two stubs and may be used for payrolls. The stub next to the check can be used as the employee's record of earnings and deductions. The second style provides space on the check itself for listing a group of invoices or bills that are being paid with that same check.

FIGURE **4.8**

*Source:* Reprinted by permission of Deluxe Corporation.

OBJECTIVE **6** *Complete the parts of a check register.*    Some depositors prefer a check register to the check stubs, while others use both. The **check register** shows at a glance the checks written and deposits made, as seen in Figure 4.9. The column headed ✔ is used to check off each check after it is received back from the bank.

| CHECK NO. | DATE | CHECK ISSUED TO | AMOUNT OF CHECK | | V | DATE OF DEP | AMOUNT OF DEPOSIT | | BALANCE | |
|---|---|---|---|---|---|---|---|---|---|---|
| | | BALANCE BROUGHT FORWARD → | | | | | | | 3,518 | 72 |
| 1435 | 5/8 | SWAN BROTHERS | 378 | 93 | | | | | 3,139 | 79 |
| 1436 | 5/8 | CLASS ACTS | 25 | 14 | | | | | 3,114 | 65 |
| 1437 | 5/9 | MIRROR LIGHTING | 519 | 65 | | | | | 2,595 | 00 |
| | | DEPOSIT | | | | 5/10 | 3,821 | 17 | 6,416 | 17 |
| 1438 | 5/10 | WOODLAKE AUDITORIUM | 750 | 00 | | | | | 5,666 | 17 |
| | | DEPOSIT | | | | 5/12 | 500 | 00 | 6,166 | 17 |
| 1439 | 5/12 | RICK'S CLOWNS | 170 | 80 | | | | | 5,995 | 37 |
| 1440 | 5/14 | Y.M.C.A. | 219 | 17 | | | | | 5,776 | 20 |
| ATM | 5/14 | ATM (cash) | 120 | 00 | | | | | 5,656 | 20 |
| | | DEPOSIT | | | | 5/15 | 326 | 15 | 5,982 | 35 |
| 1441 | 5/16 | STAGE DOOR PLAYHOUSE | 825 | 00 | | | | | 5,157 | 35 |
| 1442 | 5/17 | GILBERT ECKERN | 1,785 | 00 | | | | | 3,372 | 35 |
| | | DEPOSIT | | | | 5/19 | 1,580 | 25 | 4,952 | 60 |
| | | | | | | | | | | |

FIGURE **4.9**

**NOTE** ATM transactions for cash withdrawals and purchases must be entered on check stubs or in the check register. The transaction amount and the charge for each transaction must then be subtracted to maintain an accurate balance. ■

## 4.1 EXERCISES

*Use Table 4.1 to find the monthly checking account service charge for the following business accounts.*

1. Wallpaper Express, 49 checks, average balance $1,915
2. Mandarin Restaurant, 76 checks, average balance $3,318
3. Pest-X, 40 checks, average balance $491
4. Hobby House, 17 checks, average balance $118
5. Mak's Smog and Tune, 48 checks, average balance $1,763
6. Property Management Co., 287 checks, average balance $7,838
7. Software and More, 72 checks, average balance $516
8. Mart & Bottle, 74 checks, average balance $875

*Use the following information to complete the stubs.*

| Date | To | For | Amount | Bal. Bro't. For'd. | Deposits |
|------|-----|-----|--------|--------------------|----------|
| 9. Feb. 11 | Victoria Beltrano | travel | $380.71 | $3,971.28 | $79.26 |
| 10. Apr. 6 | Charles Hickman | consulting service | $850.00 | $2,973.09 | $1,853.24 |
| 11. Dec. 4 | Enid Power | utilities | $37.52 | $1,126.73 | — |

**9.**

```
85
_____ , 19 ____
Amount _____
To _____
For _____

Bal. Bro't. For'd.  |    |   |
Am't. Deposited     |    |   |
Total               |    |   |
Am't. this Check    |    |   |
Balance For'd.      |    |   |
```

**10.**

```
12
_____ , 19 ____
Amount _____
To _____
For _____

Bal. Bro't. For'd.  |    |   |
Am't. Deposited     |    |   |
Total               |    |   |
Am't. this Check    |    |   |
Balance For'd.      |    |   |
```

**11.**

```
73
_____ , 19 ____
Amount _____
To _____
For _____

Bal. Bro't. For'd.  |    |   |
Am't. Deposited     |    |   |
Total               |    |   |
Am't. this Check    |    |   |
Balance For'd.      |    |   |
```

12. List and explain at least six parts of a check. Draw a sketch showing where these parts appear on a check. (See Objective 1.)

13. Explain to a friend at least two advantages and two possible disadvantages of using an ATM card. Do this in writing.

**14.** Write an explanation for a friend of two types of check endorsements. Describe where these endorsements must be placed.

 **15.** Explain in your own words the factors that determine the service charges on a business checking account. (See Objective 3.)

*Complete the following check stubs for Wallpaper Express. The balance brought forward for stub 7283 is $7,223.69.*

Checks Written

| Number | Date | To | For | Amount |
|--------|------|----|----|--------|
| 7283 | May 3 | Beth Kaufman, Inc. | Wall Border | $1,250.80 |
| 7284 | May 8 | County Clerk | License | $39.12 |
| 7285 | May 12 | M-C Tool | Inventory Supplies | $356.28 |

Deposits Made

| Date | Amount |
|------|--------|
| May 5 | $752.18 |
| May 7 | $23.32 |
| May 10 | $1,025.45 |

**16.**

| 7283 | |
|------|--|
| _____ , 19 ____ | |
| Amount _____ | |
| To _____ | |
| For _____ | |

| Bal. Bro't. For'd. | |
| Am't. Deposited | |
| Total | |
| Am't. this Check | |
| Balance For'd. | |

**17.**

| 7284 | |
|------|--|
| _____ , 19 ____ | |
| Amount _____ | |
| To _____ | |
| For _____ | |

| Bal. Bro't. For'd. | |
| Am't. Deposited | |
| Total | |
| Am't. this Check | |
| Balance For'd. | |

**18.**

| 7285 | |
|------|--|
| _____ , 19 ____ | |
| Amount _____ | |
| To _____ | |
| For _____ | |

| Bal. Bro't. For'd. | |
| Am't. Deposited | |
| Total | |
| Am't. this Check | |
| Balance For'd. | |

*Complete the balance column in the following check registers after each check or deposit transaction.*

**19.**

| CHECK NO. | DATE | CHECK ISSUED TO | AMOUNT OF CHECK | ✓ | DATE OF DEP. | AMOUNT OF DEPOSIT | BALANCE |
|-----------|------|------------------|-----------------|---|--------------|-------------------|---------|
| | | | | | BALANCE BROUGHT FORWARD → | | 1,629 | 86 |
| 861 | 7/3 | AHWAHNEE HOTEL | 250 | 45 | | | | |
| 862 | 7/5 | WILLOW CREEK | 149 | 00 | | | | |
| 863 | 7/5 | VOID | | | | | | |
| | | DEPOSIT | | | | 7/7 | 117 | 73 | |
| 864 | 7/9 | DEL CAMPO HIGH SCHOOL | 69 | 80 | | | | |
| | | DEPOSIT | | | | 7/10 | 329 | 86 | |
| | | DEPOSIT | | | | 7/12 | 418 | 30 | |
| 865 | 7/14 | BIG 5 SPORTING GOODS | 109 | 76 | | | | |
| 866 | 7/14 | DR. YATES | 614 | 12 | | | | |
| 867 | 7/16 | GREYHOUND | 32 | 18 | | | | |
| | | DEPOSIT | | | | 7/16 | 520 | 95 | |

**20.**

| CHECK NO. | DATE | CHECK ISSUED TO | AMOUNT OF CHECK | | ✓ | DATE OF DEP. | AMOUNT OF DEPOSIT | | BALANCE | |
|---|---|---|---|---|---|---|---|---|---|---|
| | | | | | | BALANCE BROUGHT FORWARD → | | | 832 | 15 |
| 1121 | 3/17 | WORLDBOOK INC. | 257 | 29 | | | | | | |
| 1122 | 3/18 | CURRY VILLAGE | 190 | 50 | | | | | | |
| | | DEPOSIT | | | | 3/19 | 78 | 29 | | |
| | | DEPOSIT | | | | 3/21 | 157 | 42 | | |
| 1123 | 3/22 | SAN JUAN DISTRICT | 38 | 76 | | | | | | |
| 1124 | 3/23 | MACY'S GOURMET | 175 | 88 | | | | | | |
| | | DEPOSIT | | | | 3/23 | 379 | 28 | | |
| 1125 | 3/24 | CLASS VIDEO | 197 | 20 | | | | | | |
| 1126 | 3/24 | WATER WORLD | 25 | 10 | | | | | | |
| 1127 | 3/25 | BEL AIR MARKET | 75 | 00 | | | | | | |
| | | DEPOSIT | | | | 3/28 | 722 | 35 | | |
| | | | | | | | | | | |

**21.**

| CHECK NO. | DATE | CHECK ISSUED TO | AMOUNT OF CHECK | | ✓ | DATE OF DEP. | AMOUNT OF DEPOSIT | | BALANCE | |
|---|---|---|---|---|---|---|---|---|---|---|
| | | | | | | BALANCE BROUGHT FORWARD → | | | 3,852 | 48 |
| 2308 | 12/6 | Village Printing | 143 | 16 | | | | | | |
| 2309 | 12/7 | Water and Power | 118 | 40 | | | | | | |
| | | Deposit | | | | 12/8 | 286 | 32 | | |
| | 12/10 | ATM (cash) | 80 | 00 | | | | | | |
| 2310 | 12/11 | Clare Lynch Suppliers | 986 | 22 | | | | | | |
| 2311 | 12/11 | Account Temps | 375 | 50 | | | | | | |
| | | Deposit | | | | 12/14 | 1,201 | 82 | | |
| 2312 | 12/14 | Central Chevrolet | 735 | 68 | | | | | | |
| 2313 | 12/15 | Miller Mining | 223 | 94 | | | | | | |
| | | Deposit | | | | 12/17 | 498 | 01 | | |
| 2314 | 12/18 | Federal Parcel | 78 | 24 | | | | | | |
| | | | | | | | | | | |

**22.**

| CHECK NO. | DATE | CHECK ISSUED TO | AMOUNT OF CHECK | | ✓ | DATE OF DEP. | AMOUNT OF DEPOSIT | | BALANCE | |
|---|---|---|---|---|---|---|---|---|---|---|
| | | | | | | BALANCE BROUGHT FORWARD → | | | 8,284 | 18 |
| 1917 | 6/4 | Valley Electric | 188 | 18 | | | | | | |
| 1918 | 6/5 | Harrold Ford | 433 | 56 | | | | | | |
| 1919 | 6/5 | Sheila Jones (photography) | 138 | 17 | | | | | | |
| | | Deposit | | | | 6/6 | 453 | 28 | | |
| | | Deposit | | | | 6/8 | 1,475 | 69 | | |
| 1920 | 6/9 | U.S. Rentals | 335 | 82 | | | | | | |
| 1921 | 6/11 | Quick Turn Merchandise | 573 | 27 | | | | | | |
| | 6/11 | ATM (gas) | 16 | 35 | | | | | | |
| 1922 | 6/14 | Broadly Plumbing | 195 | 15 | | | | | | |
| | | Deposit | | | | 6/16 | 635 | 85 | | |
| 1923 | 6/16 | National Dues (F.F.A.) | 317 | 20 | | | | | | |
| | | | | | | | | | | |

## 4.2   Checking Services and Depositing Credit Card Transactions

### OBJECTIVES

**1**   *Identify bank services available to customers.*

**2**   *Understand interest-paying checking plans.*

**3**   *Deposit credit card transactions.*

**4**   *Calculate the discount fee on credit card deposits.*

Most business checking account charges are based on either the average balance or minimum balance in the account, together with specific charges for each service performed by the bank. Following are explanations of some of the more common services provided by banks, along with the typical charges. (These charges may vary from bank to bank.)

OBJECTIVE **1**   *Identify bank services available to customers.*   An **overdraft** occurs when checks are written for which there are **nonsufficient funds (NSF)** in the checking account and when the customer has no overdraft protection. (This may also be referred to as *bouncing a check*.) A typical charge is $10 to $30 per check. The same charges occur when a check is returned because it was improperly completed.

**ATM** cards are used as **debit cards** when making point-of-sale purchases. The fee for purchases varies from $0.10 per transaction to $1.00 per month for unlimited transactions. When used at the ATM machine there is usually no fee at your bank branch, a fee as high as $2.00 at other banks, and an international fee as high as $5.00.

**Overdraft protection** is given when an account balance is insufficient to cover the amount of a check and an overdraft occurs. This is a special line of credit and the bank automatically transfers money to your account to cover the check. The bank then charges you interest on the full amount transferred. In the long run, overdraft protection can save you aggravation and money.

A **returned deposit item** is a check which was deposited and then returned to the bank, usually because of lack of funds in the account of the person or firm writing the check ($5.00 per item).

A **stop payment order** is a request to the bank that it not honor a check which the depositor has written ($15.00 per request).

A **cashier's check** is a check written by the financial institution itself. It therefore has the full faith and backing of the institution ($5.00).

A **money order** is an instrument which is purchased and is often used in place of cash. It is sometimes required by the payee instead of a personal or business check ($4.00).

**Noncustomer check cashing** is sometimes offered to an individual who does not have an account with the institution ($5.00).

A **notary service** (official certification of a signature on a document) is often given free to customers. This is a service which is required on certain business documents. To a noncustomer there is usually a charge ($10.00).

**Telephone transfer** of funds allows the customer to make fund transfers by telephone ($2.00 per transfer after the third transfer each month).

**OBJECTIVE 2** *Understand interest-paying checking plans.* Federal banking regulations now allow both personal and business interest-paying checking plans. Some of the plans combine two accounts—a savings account and a checking account—while others are simply checking accounts which pay interest on the average daily balance.

A **NOW account** is technically a savings account with special withdrawal privileges. For all practical purposes, it functions as a checking account that pays interest. Instead of writing a check, however, the customer writes a "negotiable order of withdrawal" (NOW), which looks and works like a check.

NOW accounts were introduced by a savings bank in Massachusetts in the early 1970s. In the mid '70s, Congress used the New England states as a testing ground to determine whether federal banking laws should be revised to allow NOW accounts or other types of interest-bearing checking accounts nationwide. The test was a success and helped change the 1933 law against paying interest on checking accounts.

**Credit union share draft accounts** are offered to members by many credit unions. Share drafts look like checks and are used in the same ways checks are used. Members of credit unions can write share drafts against their credit union shares (savings). The major difference between share drafts and personal checks is that share drafts usually are not returned to members after they have been processed and paid, while regular checks are usually returned to the customer by the bank.

**OBJECTIVE 3** *Deposit credit card transactions.* Credit cards are used in a very large number of today's retail purchases. These credit card sales are deposited into a business checking account with a **merchant batch header ticket** such as the one in Figure 4.10 in Example 1. This form is used with VISA or MasterCard credit card deposits. Notice that the form lists both sales slips and credit slips (refunds). Entries in each of these categories are totaled, and the total credits are subtracted from the total sales to give the net amount of deposit.

The merchant batch header ticket is a triplicate form and the bank copy along with the charge slips, credit slips, and a printed calculator tape showing the itemized deposits and credits is deposited in the business checking account.

**Card craze**

- **Total bank credit cards in circulation in the U.S.: 460 million.**
- **Number of bankcard issuers: 9,000.**
- **Top 10 issuers' share of the market: 55%.**
- **Average balance: $1,828 per card, $3,019 per family.**
- **Accounts 30 or more days past due: 4.33%.**
- **Average interest rate: 17.98%; fewer than one card in five has a rate under 16.5%.**

*Source: Consumer Reports,* Jan. 1996, p. 31.

| EXAMPLE 1 *Determining Deposits with Credit Card Transactions*

Wallpaper Express had the following credit card sales and refunds on wallpaper and accessories. Complete a merchant batch header ticket.

| Sales | | Refunds (Credit) |
|---|---|---|
| $12.31 | $44.31 | $13.83 |
| $38.18 | $78.80 | $25.19 |
| $65.29 | $63.14 | $78.56 |
| $178.22 | $11.92 | |

4577044

4425 0138 739 846

**WALLPAPER EXPRESS**

121000086 02104

MERCHANT BATCH HEADER TICKET

| TYPE | NUMBER | AMOUNT |
| | | DOLLARS | CENTS |
| SALES SLIPS | 8 | 492 | 17 |
| LESS CREDIT SLIPS | 3 | 117 | 58 |
| GROSS AMOUNT | | 374 | 59 |

DATE
MONTH DAY YEAR
**Deposit Date**

CIRCLE GROSS AMOUNT IF
CREDITS ARE GREATER THAN SALES.

x *Maria Gaona*

MERCHANT AUTHORIZED SIGNATURE

The enclosed slips are transmitted for processing in accordance with merchant agreement and received subject to audit.

- IMPRINT FOR IDENTIFICATION BEFORE DEPOSITING
- INCLUDE ADDING MACHINE TAPE FOR ALL BATCHES

MasterCard.    VISA®

PRINT YOUR CHARACTERS LIKE THIS

1 2 3 4 5 6 7 8 9 0

MERCHANT COPY

FIGURE 4.10

**SOLUTION**    All credit slips and sales slips must be totaled. The number of each of these and the totals are written at the right. The total sales slips are $492.17, and the credit slips total $117.58. The difference is the net deposit; here $374.59 is the net deposit. The completed merchant batch header ticket is shown in Figure 4.10.    ■

**OBJECTIVE 4**  *Calculate the discount fee on credit card deposits.*    The bank collects a fee (a percent of sales) from the merchant and also an interest charge from the card user on all accounts not paid in full at the first billing. Although credit card transactions are deposited frequently by a business, the bank calculates the discount fee on the net amount of the credit card deposits since the last bank statement date. The fee paid by the merchant varies from 2% to 5% of the sales slip amount and is determined by the type of processing used (electronic or manual), the dollar volume of credit card usage by the merchant, and the average amount of the sale at the merchant's store. All credit card deposits for the month are added, and the fee is subtracted from the total at the statement date.

**EXAMPLE 2**  *Finding the Discount and the Credit Given on a Credit Card Deposit*

If the deposit in Example 1 represented total credit card deposits for the month, find the fee charged and the credit given to the merchant at the statement date if Wallpaper Express pays a 3% fee.

**SOLUTION**    Since the total credit card deposit for Wallpaper Express is $374.59 and the fee is 3%, the discount charged is

$$\$374.59 \times 0.03(3\%) = \$11.24 \text{ discount charge}$$

Out of a deposit of $374.59, the merchant will receive a credit of

$$\$374.59 - \$11.24 = \$363.35.$$    ■

CALCULATOR APPROACH
TO EXAMPLE 2

The calculator solution to this example uses chain calculation with the calculator observing the order of operations.

$$374.59 \boxed{-} 374.59 \boxed{\times} .03 \boxed{=} 363.3523$$

## 4.2 EXERCISES

*For each of the following businesses, find (a) the total charges, (b) the total credits, (c) the amount of the net deposit, (d) the amount of the discount charged at the statement date, and (e) the amount of credit given after the fee is subtracted.*

1. John Young owns The Cellular Center. The shop sells new and used cellular phones and accessories and does a major portion of its business in adjustments and repairs. The following credit card sales and credits took place during a recent period. The bank charges a 5% discount.

| Sales | | Credits |
|---|---|---|
| $14.86 | $76.15 | $43.15 |
| $49.70 | $226.17 | $17.06 |
| $183.60 | $63.95 | |
| $238.75 | $111.10 | |
| $18.36 | $77.86 | |
| $52.08 | $132.62 | |

2. Amber Tune Up and Brake accepts travel and leisure cards from customers for auto repairs and the sale of parts. The following credit card transactions occurred during a recent period. The bank charges a 4% discount.

| Sales | | Credits |
|---|---|---|
| $66.68 | $18.95 | $62.16 |
| $119.63 | $496.28 | $106.62 |
| $53.86 | $21.85 | $38.91 |
| $178.62 | $242.78 | |
| $219.78 | $176.93 | |

**3.** Bayside Jeepers does most of its business on a cash basis or through its own credit department, although it does honor major bank charge cards. In a recent period, the business had the following credit card charges and credits. The bank charges a 4% discount.

| Sales | | | Credits |
|---|---|---|---|
| $25.18 | $77.51 | $14.73 | $38.15 |
| $15.73 | $357.18 | $106.78 | $106.86 |
| $138.97 | $72.73 | $88.34 | $44.38 |
| $58.73 | $29.68 | $72.21 | |
| $255.18 | $15.76 | $262.73 | |

**4.** Industrial Supply had the following credit card transactions during a recent period. The bank charges a $4\frac{1}{2}$% discount.

| Sales | | Credits |
|---|---|---|
| $42.60 | $29.50 | $22.10 |
| $38.25 | $72.85 | $14.67 |
| $16.60 | $19.30 | $30.30 |
| $52.40 | $6.75 | |
| $14.38 | $88.98 | |

**5.** Elizabeth Linton Photography had the following credit card transactions during a recent period. The bank charges a 3% discount.

| Sales | | Credits |
|---|---|---|
| $118.68 | $235.82 | $15.36 |
| $7.84 | $98.56 | $57.47 |
| $33.18 | $318.72 | |
| $50.76 | $116.35 | |
| $12.72 | $23.78 | |
| $9.36 | $38.95 | |

**6.** David Fleming owns Campus Bicycle Shop near a college campus. The shop sells new and used bicycle parts, and does a major portion of its business in adjustments and repairs. The following credit card charges and credits took place during a recent period. The bank charges a 5% discount.

|  | Sales | Credits |
|---|---|---|
| $16.40 | $184.16 | $23.17 |
| $18.98 | $137.61 | $7.26 |
| $6.76 | $24.69 | $14.53 |
| $11.75 | $86.17 |  |
| $29.63 |  |  |

**7.** List and describe in your own words four services offered to business checking account customers. (See Objective 1.)

**8.** The merchant accepting a credit card from a customer must pay a fee of 2% to 5% of the transaction amount. Why is the merchant willing to do this? Who really pays this fee?

## 4.3   Reconciliation

### OBJECTIVES

**1**   *Reconcile a bank statement with the checkbook.*

**2**   *List outstanding checks.*

**3**   *Find the adjusted bank balance or current balance.*

**4**   *Use the T-account form of reconciliation.*

Each month, banks send their checking account customers a **bank statement**. This bank statement shows all deposits made during the period covered by the statement, as well as all checks paid by the bank and any automated teller machine (ATM) transactions. Bank charges for the month covered by the statement are also listed. This is especially important with a business checking account because the bank charge normally varies from month to month. On occasion, a customer's check that was deposited must be returned due to **nonsufficient funds (NSF)** in the account. This is identified as a **returned check** and the amount of the check must be subtracted from the checkbook balance along with any other charges. The business must then resolve this matter with the writer of the bad check.

**NOTE**   Reconciling the bank statement is an important step in maintaining accurate checking account records and in helping to avoid writing checks for which there are nonsufficient funds. In addition to nonsufficient funds charges, which can be costly, a certain amount of irresponsibility is associated with the person or business who writes "bad checks."   ■

**OBJECTIVE** **1** *Reconcile a bank statement with the checkbook.*     Many businesses have automatic deposits from customers and other sources made to their accounts. These amounts must be added to the checkbook balance. When the bank statement is received, it is very important to verify its accuracy. In addition, it is a good time to check the accuracy of the check register, making certain that all checks written have been listed and subtracted and that all deposits have been added to the checking account balance. This process of checking the bank statement and the check register is called **reconciliation**.

Reconciliation is best done using the forms usually printed on the back of the bank statement. A sample bank statement is shown in Figure 4.11, and an example of the reconciliation process follows. The codes on the bank statement indicate the following: RC means Returned Check, SC means Service Charge, IC means Interest Credit, ATM means Automated Teller Machine.

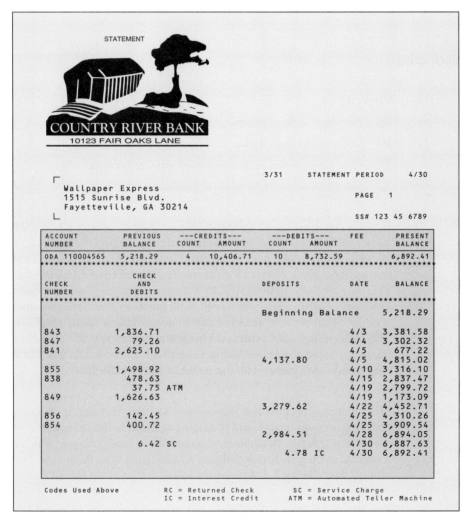

FIGURE 4.11

| EXAMPLE 1 | *Reconciling a Checking Account* |

Wallpaper Express received its bank statement. The statement shows a balance of $6,892.41, after a bank service charge of $6.42 and an interest credit of $4.78. Wallpaper Express's checkbook now shows a balance of $7,576.38. Reconcile the account using the following steps (illustrated in Figure 4.12).

SOLUTION

| Checks Outstanding | | |
|---|---|---|
| Number | Amount | |
| 846 | $ 42 | 73 |
| 852 | 598 | 71 |
| 853 | 68 | 12 |
| 857 | 79 | 80 |
| 858 | 160 | 30 |
| | | |
| | | |
| | | |
| Total | $ 949 | 66 |

**Compare the list of checks paid by the bank with your records. List and total the checks not yet paid.**

(1) Enter new balance from bank statement:   $ 6,892.41

(2) List any deposits made by you and not yet recorded by the bank:
   + 892.41
   + 739.58
   +
   +

(3) Add all numbers from lines above. Total:   8,524.40
(4) Write total of checks outstanding:   − 949.66

(5) Subtract (4) from (3). This is adjusted bank balance:   $ 7,574.74

**To reconcile your records:**

(6) List your checkbook balance:   $ 7,576.38

(7) Write the total of any fees or charges deducted by the bank and not yet subtracted by you from your checkbook:   − 6.42

8) Subtract line (7) from line (6):   7,569.96

New balance of your account; these numbers should be the same.

(9) Enter interest credit: (Add to your checkbook)   + 4.78

(10) Add line (9) to line (8): Adjusted checkbook balance:   $ 7,574.74

FIGURE 4.12

**OBJECTIVE 2** *List outstanding checks.*   Compare the list of checks on the bank statement with the list of checks written by the firm. Checks that have been written by the firm but do not yet appear on the bank statement were not paid by the bank as of the date of the statement. These unpaid checks are called **checks outstanding**. The firm finds that the following checks are outstanding.

| Number | Amount | Number | Amount |
|---|---|---|---|
| 846 | $42.73 | 857 | $79.80 |
| 852 | $598.71 | 858 | $160.30 |
| 853 | $68.12 | | |

After listing the outstanding checks in the space provided on the form, total them. The total is $949.66.

The following steps are used to reconcile the checking account of Wallpaper Express.

## RECONCILING A CHECKING ACCOUNT

**Step 1.** Enter the new balance from the front of the bank statement. As given, the new balance is $6,892.41. Write this number in the space provided on the reconcilement form.

**Step 2.** List any deposits made that have not yet been recorded by the bank (deposits in transit). Suppose that Wallpaper Express has deposits of $892.41 and $739.58 that are not yet recorded. These numbers are written at step 2 on the form.

**Step 3.** All the numbers from steps 1 and 2 are added. Here the total is $8,524.40.

**Step 4.** Write down the total of outstanding checks. The total is $949.66.

**Step 5.** Subtract the total in step 4 from the number in step 3. The result here is $7,574.74, called the **adjusted bank balance** or the **current balance**. This number should represent the current checking account balance.

**OBJECTIVE** **3** *Find the adjusted bank balance or current balance.*     Now look at the firm's own records.

**Step 6.** List the firm's checkbook balance. As mentioned before, the checkbook balance for Wallpaper Express is $7,576.38. This number is entered on line 6.

**Step 7.** Enter any charges not yet deducted. The check charge here is $6.42. Since there are no other fees or charges, enter $6.42 on line 7.

**Step 8.** Subtract the charges on line 7 from the checkbook balance on line 6 to get $7,569.96.

**Step 9.** Enter the interest credit on line 9. The interest credit here is $4.78. (This amount is interest paid on the money in the account.)

**Step 10.** Add the interest on line 9 to get $7,574.74, the same result as in step 5.

Since the result from step 10 is the same as the result from step 5, the account is **balanced** (reconciled). The correct current balance in the account is $7,574.74. ∎

**OBJECTIVE** **4** *Use the T-account form of reconciliation.* Many business people and accountants prefer a *T-account form* for bank reconciliation. With this method, the bank statement is written on the left and the checkbook balance is written on the right. Adjustments are made to either the bank balance or the checkbook balance, depending on which side was unaware of the transaction or charge. T-account reconciliation uses the format in Figure 4.13. The adjusted balances must agree, with the result showing the actual amount remaining in the account.

Bank Reconciliation

| Bank statement balance | $ | Checkbook balance | $ |
|---|---|---|---|
| Add: | | Add: | |
| 1) Add all deposits not yet recorded. | | 1) Add all miscellaneous credits, collections, and interest. | |
| Less: | | Less: | |
| 2) Subtract all outstanding checks. | | 2) Subtract previously deposited overdrafts and bank charges. | |
| Adjusted balance | $ _____ | Adjusted balance | $ _____ |

FIGURE 4.13

**EXAMPLE 2** *Using the T-Account Form*

The bank statement of Hazel Nut Gifts shows a balance of $4,385.88. Checks outstanding are $292.70, $75.16, and $636.55; deposits not yet recorded are $483.11 and $89.95. Also appearing are a service charge of $7.90, a check printing charge of $9.20, a returned check for $94.25, and an interest credit of $10.06. The checkbook now shows a balance of $4,055.82. Use the T-method to reconcile the checking account.

**SOLUTION** The reconciliation is shown in Figure 4.14

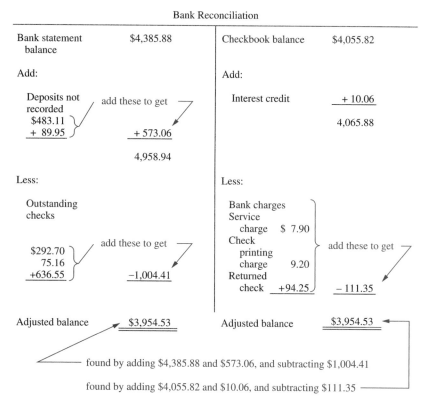

FIGURE 4.14

There are several typical reasons why checking accounts do not balance.

## WHY THE CHECKING ACCOUNT DOES NOT BALANCE

- Forgetting to enter a check in the check register.
- Forgetting to enter a deposit in the check register.
- Transposing numbers (writing 961 as 916, for example).
- Addition or subtraction errors.
- Forgetting to subtract one of the bank service fees such as those charged using your debit card or for ATM use.
- The bank may have charged the customer an amount different from the check amount.
- The check may be altered or forged.

## EXAMPLE 3  *Reconciling a Checking Account*

A checking account register is shown in Figure 4.15. A ✔ on the register indicates that the check appeared on the previous month's bank statement. Reconcile the account with a bank statement shown in Figure 4.16. (Codes on the statement have the following meaning: RC, Returned Check; SC, Service Charge; IC, Interest Credit; ATM, Automated Teller Machine.)

**SOLUTION**   Follow the instructions on the form in Figure 4.13. The completed reconciliation is shown in T-form in Figure 4.17.   ∎

| CHECK NO. | DATE | CHECK ISSUED TO | AMOUNT OF CHECK | | √ | DATE OF DEP | AMOUNT OF DEPOSIT | | BALANCE | |
|---|---|---|---|---|---|---|---|---|---|---|
| | | | | | | | BALANCE BROUGHT FORWARD → | | 2,782 | 95 |
| 721 | $^7/_{11}$ | MILLER'S OUTPOST | 138 | 50 | ✓ | | | | 2,644 | 45 |
| 722 | $^7/_{12}$ | BARBER ADVERTISING | 73 | 08 | | | | | 2,571 | 37 |
| 723 | $^7/_{18}$ | WAYSIDE LUMBER | 318 | 62 | ✓ | | | | 2,252 | 75 |
| | | DEPOSIT | | | | $^7/_{20}$ | 1,060 | 37 | 3,313 | 12 |
| 724 | $^7/_{25}$ | I.R.S. | 836 | 15 | | | | | 2,476 | 97 |
| 725 | $^7/_{26}$ | JOHN LESSOR | 450 | 00 | | | | | 2,026 | 97 |
| 726 | $^7/_{28}$ | CHRIS BATCHELOR | 67 | 80 | | | | | 1,959 | 17 |
| 727 | $^8/_2$ | T.V.A. | 59 | 25 | | | | | 1,899 | 92 |
| 728 | $^8/_3$ | CARMICHAEL OFFICE | 97 | 37 | | | | | 1,802 | 55 |
| | | DEPOSIT | | | | $^8/_4$ | 795 | 45 | 2,598 | 00 |
| | $^8/_5$ | ATM (cash) | 80 | 00 | | | | | 2,518 | 00 |

FIGURE 4.15

**Bank Statement**

| Check Number | Checks and Debits | | Deposits | Date | Balance |
|---|---|---|---|---|---|
| | | | | 7/20 | 2,325.83 |
| 722 | 73.08 | | | 7/22 | 2,252.75 |
| | | | 1,060.37 | 7/24 | 3,313.12 |
| 724 | 836.15 | | | 7/28 | 2,476.97 |
| 725 | 450.00 | 49.07RC | | 7/30 | 1,977.90 |
| 727 | 59.25 | | 3.22IC | 8/4 | 1,921.87 |
| | | 80.00ATM | | 8/5 | 1,841.87 |
| | | 7.60SC | | 8/5 | 1,834.27 |

FIGURE 4.16

Bank Reconciliation

| | | | | |
|---|---|---|---|---|
| Bank statement balance | $1,834.27 | | Checkbook balance | $2,518.00 |
| Add: | | | Add: | |
| Deposits not recorded | + 795.45 | | Interest credit (IC) | +3.22 |
| | 2,629.72 | | | 2,521.22 |
| Less: | | | Less: | |
| Outstanding checks | | | Bank charges Returned check (RC) | $49.07 |
| $67.80 +97.37 | −165.17 | | Service charge (SC) +7.60 | −56.67 |
| Adjusted balance | $2,464.55 | | Adjusted balance | $2,464.55 |

FIGURE 4.17

## 4.3 EXERCISES

*Find the current balance for each of the following accounts.*

| | Balance from Bank Statement | Checks Outstanding | | Deposits Not Yet Recorded |
|---|---|---|---|---|
| 1. | $3,681.52 | $78.91 $328.58 | $218.34 | $753.19 $419.62 |
| 2. | $8,765.42 | $831.50 $37.81 | $574.36 $75.14 | $76.55 $88.74 |
| 3. | $7,911.42 | $52.38 $95.42 | $528.02 $76.50 | $492.80 $38.72 |
| 4. | $9,343.65 | $840.71 $78.68 | $665.73 $87.00 | $971.64 $3,382.71 |
| 5. | $19,523.20 | $6,853.60 $795.77 | $340.00 $22.85 | $6,724.93 $78.81 |
| 6. | $32,489.50 | $3,589.70 $263.15 | $18,702.15 $7,269.78 | $7,110.65 $2,218.63 |

*Use the steps given in Example 1 and Figure 4.12 to reconcile the following accounts.*

|  | 7. | | 8. | |
| --- | --- | --- | --- | --- |
| Balance from bank statement | | $6,875.09 | | $4,721.30 |
| Checks outstanding (check number is given first) | 421 | $371.52 | 21 | $82.74 |
| | 424 | $429.07 | 29 | $69.08 |
| | 427 | $883.69 | 30 | $124.73 |
| | 429 | $35.62 | 32 | $51.20 |
| Deposits not yet recorded | | $701.56 | | $758.06 |
| | | $421.78 | | $32.51 |
| | | $689.35 | | $298.06 |
| Bank charge | | $8.75 | | $2.00 |
| Interest credit | | $10.71 | | $9.58 |
| Checkbook balance | | $6,965.92 | | $5,474.60 |

*Use the T-account form, Figure 4.13, to reconcile the following accounts.*

9. The checkbook of Dottie Fogel Furnishings shows a balance of $7,779. When the bank statement is received, it shows a balance of $6,237.44, a returned check amounting to $246.70, a service charge of $15.60 and a check printing charge of $18.50. There are unrecorded deposits of $1,442.44 and $479.50, and checks outstanding of $146.36, $91.52, $43.78, and $379.52.

10. Charles Hickman received a bank statement showing a balance of $1,248.63, a returned check amounting to $35.17, a service charge of $7.70, and an interest credit of $2.51. Checks outstanding are $380, $36.66, $15.29, and $143.18; deposits not yet recorded are $478.18 and $359.12. The checkbook shows a balance of $1,551.16. Reconcile the checking account.

11. The bank statement of Kris Wright Interiors showed a bank balance of $4,074.65, a returned check amounting to $168.40, a service charge of $7.08, and an interest credit of $10.18. There were unrecorded deposits of $907.82 and $1,784.15, and checks outstanding of $642.55, $1,082.98, $73.25, and $471.83. The checkbook shows a balance of $4,661.31.

12. The bank statement of Don Cole Sports shows a balance of $1,270.08. The checkbook balance showed $1,626.63. There were unrecorded deposits of $370.64 and $219.38 and outstanding checks of $38.18, $185.10, $14.75, and $90.14. Check printing charges were $8.50; the service charge was $3.80; there was a returned check of $83.85, and an interest credit of $1.45.

13. Explain in your own words the significance of writing a bad check. What might the cost be in dollars? What are the other consequences? (See Objective 1.)

14. As a business person, what happens when you receive a bad check? What are the financial costs to the business? What are you likely to do regarding this customer? (See Objective 1.)

15. Briefly describe the importance of reconciling a checking account. What are the benefits derived from keeping good checking records? (See Objective 2.)

16. Suppose your checking account will not balance. Name four types of errors that you will look for in trying to correct this problem.

*Reconcile the following checking accounts. Compare the items appearing on the bank state-
ment to the check register. A ✔ indicates that the check appeared on the previous month's
statement. (Codes indicate the following: RC means Returned Check, SC means Service
Charge, CP means Check Printing Charge, IC means Interest Credit, ATM means Automated
Teller Machine.)*

**17.**

| CHECK NO. | DATE | CHECK ISSUED TO | AMOUNT OF CHECK | | ✓ | DATE OF DEP | AMOUNT OF DEPOSIT | | BALANCE | |
|---|---|---|---|---|---|---|---|---|---|---|
| | | | BALANCE BROUGHT FORWARD → | | | | | | 7,682 | 07 |
| 662 | 3/3 | Action Packing Supplies | 451 | 16 | | | | | 7,230 | 91 |
| 663 | 3/3 | Crown Paper | 954 | 29 | √ | | | | 6,276 | 62 |
| 664 | 3/5 | ATM CASH | 80 | 00 | √ | | | | 6,196 | 62 |
| | | Deposit | | | | 3/7 | 913 | 28 | 7,109 | 90 |
| 665 | 3/10 | Fairless Water District | 72 | 37 | | | | | 7,037 | 53 |
| 666 | 3/12 | Audia Temporary | 340 | 88 | | | | | 6,696 | 65 |
| 667 | 3/13 | Lionel Toys | 618 | 65 | | | | | 6,078 | |
| 668 | 3/14 | Fairless Hills Power | 100 | 50 | | | | | 5,977 | 50 |
| | | Deposit | | | | 3/16 | 450 | 18 | 6,427 | 68 |
| | | Deposit | | | | 3/18 | 163 | 55 | 6,591 | 23 |
| 669 | 3/20 | Hunt Roofing | 238 | 50 | | | | | 6,352 | 73 |
| 670 | 3/22 | Standard Brands | 315 | 62 | | | | | 6,037 | 11 |
| 671 | 3/23 | Pennye Saver Products | 67 | 29 | | | | | 5,969 | 82 |
| | | Deposit | | | | 3/24 | 830 | 75 | 6,800 | 57 |
| | | | | | | | | | | |

Bank Statement

| Check Number | Checks and Debits | | Deposits | Date | Balance |
|---|---|---|---|---|---|
| | | | | 3/5 | 6,647.78 |
| | | | 913.28 | 3/7 | 7,561.06 |
| 662 | 451.16 | | | 3/11 | 7,109.90 |
| 666 | 340.88 | 82.15RC | 450.18 | 3/16 | 7,137.05 |
| 665 | 72.37 | | 22.48IC | 3/20 | 7,087.16 |
| 667 | 618.65 | | 163.55 | 3/22 | 6,632.06 |
| 669 | 238.50 | 12.70SC | | 3/26 | 6,380.86 |

**18.**

| CHECK NO. | DATE | CHECK ISSUED TO | AMOUNT OF CHECK | | ✓ | DATE OF DEP | AMOUNT OF DEPOSIT | | BALANCE | |
|---|---|---|---|---|---|---|---|---|---|---|
| | | | BALANCE BROUGHT FORWARD → | | | | | | 6,669 | 34 |
| 760 | 2/8 | FLOORS TO GO | 248 | 96 | | | | | 6,420 | 38 |
| 762 | 2/9 | HEALTHWAYS DIST. | 125 | 63 | | | | | 6,294 | 75 |
| | | DEPOSIT | | | | 2/11 | 618 | 34 | 6,913 | 09 |
| 763 | 2/12 | FRANCHISE TAX | 770 | 41 | √ | | | | 6,142 | 68 |
| 764 | 2/14 | FOOTHILL REPAIR | 22 | 86 | √ | | | | 6,119 | 82 |
| 765 | 2/15 | YELLOW PAGES | 91 | 24 | | | | | 6,028 | 58 |
| | | DEPOSIT | | | | 2/17 | 826 | 03 | 6,854 | 61 |
| 766 | 2/17 | MORNING HERALD | 71 | 59 | | | | | 6,783 | 02 |
| 767 | 2/18 | SAN JUAN ELECTRIC | 63 | 24 | | | | | 6,719 | 78 |
| ATM | 2/22 | ATM GAS | 15 | 26 | | | | | 6,704 | 52 |
| 769 | 2/23 | WEST CONSTRUCTION | 405 | 07 | | | | | 6,299 | 45 |
| 770 | 2/24 | RENT | 525 | 00 | | | | | 5,774 | 45 |
| | | DEPOSIT | | | | 2/26 | 220 | 16 | 5,994 | 61 |
| 771 | 2/28 | CAPITAL ALARM | 135 | 76 | | | | | 5,858 | 85 |

Bank Statement

| Check Number | Checks and Debits | | Deposits | Date | Balance |
|---|---|---|---|---|---|
| | | | | 2/14 | 5,876.07 |
| 765 | 91.24 | | 618.34 | 2/16 | 6,403.17 |
| 760 | 248.96 | | 826.03 | 2/17 | 6,980.24 |
| | | 60.00ATM | | 2/19 | 6,920.24 |
| 762 | 137.22 | | | 2/21 | 6,783.02 |
| | | 198.17RC | | 2/22 | 6,584.85 |
| 768 | 15.26 | | 8.12IC | 2/24 | 6,577.71 |
| 769 | 405.07 | 4.85CP | | 2/26 | 6,167.79 |
| | | 6.28SC | | 2/27 | 6,161.51 |
| 770 | 525.00 | | | 2/28 | 5,636.51 |

# Chapter 4 Quick Review

| TOPIC | APPROACH | EXAMPLE |
|---|---|---|
| **4.1 Checking account service charges** | There is usually a checking account maintenance charge and often a per check charge. | Find the monthly checking account service charge for a business with 36 checks and transactions, given a monthly maintenance charge of $7.50 and a $0.20 per check charge. <br> $7.50 + 36($0.20) = $7.50 + $7.20 = $14.70 monthly service charge |
| **4.2 Banking services offered** | The checking account customer must be aware of various banking services. | ATM services <br> Overdraft protection <br> Stop payment order <br> Cashier's check <br> Money order <br> Noncustomer check cashing <br> Notary service <br> Telephone transfer |

**4.2  Depositing credit card transactions**

Subtract credit card refunds from total credit card sales to find the net deposit. Then subtract the discount charge from this total.

| Sales | | Credits |
|---|---|---|
| $28.15 | $78.59 | $21.86 |
| $36.92 | $63.82 | $19.62 |

(a) Find total sales.
$28.15 + $36.92 + $78.59 + $63.82 = $207.48

(b) Find total credits.
$21.86 + $19.62 = $41.48

(c) Find net deposit.
$207.48 − $41.48 = $166

(d) Given a 3% fee, find the amount of the charge.
$166 × 0.03 = $4.98

(e) Find the amount of credit given to the business.
$166 − $4.98 = $161.02

**4.3  Reconciliation of a checking account**

A checking account customer must periodically verify checking account records with those of the bank or financial institution. The bank statement is used for this.

Verify all checks, deposits, service charges, and interest. The checkbook balance and bank balance must be the same for the account to reconcile, or balance.

# Chapter 4 Review Exercises

*Use Table 4.1 on page 103 to find the monthly checking account service charge for the following accounts. [4.1]*

1. The Foster Bakery, 36 checks, average balance $1,275

2. Sangi Market, 35 checks, average balance $485

3. Old English Chimney Sweep, 52 checks, average balance $3,017

*Complete the following three check stubs for Jack Armstrong International Trucking Company. The balance brought forward for stub 1561 is $16,409.82. Find the balance forward at the bottom of each stub. [4.1]*

Checks Written

| Number | Date | To | For | Amount |
|--------|------|-----|-----|--------|
| 1561 | Aug. 6 | Fuel Depot | Fuel | $6,892.12 |
| 1562 | Aug. 8 | First Bank | Payment | $1,258.36 |
| 1563 | Aug. 14 | Security Service | Guard dogs | $416.14 |

*Deposits made: $1,572 on Aug. 7, $10,000 on Aug. 10.*

**4.**

1561

_____ 19 ____

Amount _____
To _____
For _____

| Bal. Bro't. For'd. | | |
| Am't. Deposited | | |
| Total | | |
| Am't. this Check | | |
| Balance For'd. | *9,517* | *70* |

**5.**

1562

_____ 19 ____

Amount _____
To _____
For _____

| Bal. Bro't. For'd. | | |
| Am't. Deposited | | |
| Total | | |
| Am't. this Check | | |
| Balance For'd. | *9,831* | *34* |

**6.**

1563

_____ 19 ____

Amount _____
To _____
For _____

| Bal. Bro't. For'd. | | |
| Am't. Deposited | | |
| Total | | |
| Am't. this Check | | |
| Balance For'd. | *19,415* | *20* |

*Cordova Electrical Supply accepts credit cards from customers for parts and supplies. The following credit card transactions occurred during a recent period. [4.2]*

| Sales | | Credits |
|-------|-------|---------|
| $66.68 | $18.95 | $62.16 |
| $119.63 | $496.28 | $106.62 |
| $53.86 | $21.85 | $38.91 |
| $178.62 | $242.78 | |
| $219.78 | $176.93 | |

**7.** Find the total charges for the store.

**8.** What is the total amount of the credit?

9. Find the amount of the net deposit when these credit card transactions are deposited.

10. If the bank charges the retailer a 4% discount charge, find the amount of the discount charge at the statement date.

11. Find the amount of credit given to Cordova Electrical Supply after the fee is subtracted.

*Solve the following application problems.*

12. Kelly Melcher Drilling received a bank statement showing a balance of $4,964.52, a returned check amounting to $140.68, a service charge of $30.84, and an interest credit of $10.04. Checks outstanding are $1,520, $146.64, $31.16, and $572.76; deposits not yet recorded are $1,912.72 and $1,436.48. The checkbook shows a balance of $6,204.64. Use Figure 4.12 to reconcile the checking account. [4.3]

13. The bank statement of Superior Bushings showed a bank balance of $8,149.30, a returned check amounting to $336.80, a service charge of $14.16, and an interest credit of $20.36. There were unrecorded deposits of $1,815.64 and $3,568.30, and checks outstanding of $1,285.10, $2,165.96, $146.50, and $943.66. The checkbook shows a balance of $9,322.62. Use Figure 4.13 to reconcile the checking account. [4.3]

14. Use Figure 4.13 and the following check register and bank statement to reconcile the checking account. Compare the items appearing on the bank statement to the check register. A ✔ indicates that the check appeared on the previous month's statement. (Codes indicate the following: RC means Returned Check, SC means Service Charge, CP means Check Printing Charge, IC means Interest Credit, ATM means Automated Teller Machine.) [4.3]

| CHECK NO. | DATE | CHECK ISSUED TO | AMOUNT OF CHECK | | ✔ | DATE OF DEP | AMOUNT OF DEPOSIT | | BALANCE | |
|---|---|---|---|---|---|---|---|---|---|---|
| | | | | | | | BALANCE BROUGHT FORWARD → | | 1,876 | 93 |
| 318 | 9/6 | MUIR TRAVEL | 76 | 18 | ✔ | | | | 1,800 | 75 |
| 319 | 9/6 | NORTH COAST TOURS | 322 | 40 | | | | | 1,478 | 35 |
| 320 | 9/8 | AMES PHOTO | 41 | 12 | ✔ | | | | 1,437 | 23 |
| | | DEPOSIT | | | | 9/10 | 851 | 62 | 2,288 | 85 |
| 321 | 9/14 | AMERICAN FLYERS | 970 | 40 | | | | | 1,318 | 45 |
| 322 | 9/15 | REVERE INTER. | 386 | 92 | | | | | 931 | 53 |
| | | DEPOSIT | | | | 9/18 | 995 | 20 | 1,926 | 73 |
| 324 | 9/20 | IDAHO EDISON | 68 | 17 | | | | | 1,858 | 56 |
| 325 | 9/20 | WESSON SUPPLY | 195 | 76 | | | | | 1,662 | 80 |
| 326 | 9/22 | PARKER PACKERS | 348 | 33 | | | | | 1,314 | 47 |
| 327 | 9/23 | FREEZE DRY SUPPLY | 215 | 84 | | | | | 1,098 | 63 |
| 328 | 9/24 | COUNTY WATER | 169 | 56 | | | | | 929 | 07 |
| | | DEPOSIT | | | | 9/28 | 418 | 35 | 1,347 | 42 |

Bank Statement

| Check Number | Checks and Debits | | Deposits | Date | Balance |
|---|---|---|---|---|---|
| | | | | 9/9 | 1,759.63 |
| | | | 851.62 | 9/10 | 2,611.25 |
| 321 | 970.40 | | | 9/15 | 1,640.85 |
| 319 | 322.40 | | | 9/18 | 1,318.45 |
| 322 | 386.92 | 78.93RC | 995.20 | 9/20 | 1,847.80 |
| 325 | 195.76 | | 6.52IC | 9/23 | 1,658.56 |
| 326 | 348.33 | 7.80SC | | 9/25 | 1,302.43 |

# Chapter 4 Summary Exercise

Shafali Patel owns a retail store specializing in imported women's clothing, authentic traditional fabrics, and women's accessories from India. Many of her customers use credit cards for their purchases and her credit card sales in a recent month amounted to $6,438.50. During the same period Ms. Patel had $336.81 in credits and she pays a credit card fee of $3\frac{1}{2}$%.

When receiving her bank statement the balance was $4,228.34. The checks outstanding were found to be $758.14, $38.37, $1,671.88, $120.13, $2,264.75, $78.11, $3,662.73, $816.25, and $400. Ms. Patel had both her credit card deposit and bank deposits of $458.23, $771.18, $235.71, $1,278.55, $663.52, and $1,475.39 that were not recorded.

(a) Find the gross deposit when the credit card sales and credits are deposited.

(b) Find the amount of the credit given to Ms. Patel after the fee is subtracted.

(c) What is the total of the checks outstanding?

(d) Find the total of the deposits that were not recorded.

(e) Find the current balance in Ms. Patel's checking account.

# 5

# Payroll

Preparing the payroll is one of the most important jobs in any office. Payroll records must be accurate, and the payroll must be prepared on time so that the necessary checks can be written. The first step in preparing the payroll is to determine the **gross earnings** (the total amount earned) for each employee. There are many methods used to find gross earnings and several of these are discussed in this chapter. A number of **deductions** may be subtracted from gross earnings to find **net pay**, the amount actually received by the employee. These various deductions also will be discussed in this chapter. Finally, the employer must keep records to maintain an efficient business and to satisfy legal requirements.

## 5.1 Gross Earnings (Wages and Salaries)

### OBJECTIVES

1. *Use hourly rate to calculate gross earnings.*
2. *Use time-and-a-half rate for over 40 hours to find overtime earnings.*
3. *Use overtime premium method of calculating gross earnings.*
4. *Find overtime earnings using time-and-a-half rate for over 8 hours of work per day.*
5. *Understand double time, shift differential, and split-shift premiums.*
6. *Find equivalent earnings for different pay periods.*
7. *Find gross earnings when overtime is paid to salaried employees.*

Several methods are used for finding an employee's pay. Two of these methods, salaries and wages, are discussed in this section; two additional methods, piecework and commission, will be discussed in the next two sections.

In many businesses, the first step in preparing the payroll is to look at the **time card** maintained for each employee. An example of a time card is shown in Figure 5.1. The card includes the dates of the pay period; the employee's name and other personal information; the days, times, and hours worked; the total number of hours worked; and a signature verification by the employee as to the accuracy of the card. While the card in Figure 5.1 is filled in by hand, many companies use a time clock that automatically stamps the days, dates, and times on the card. The information on

SEMI-MONTHLY OR TWO WEEKLY

# PAYROLL CARD

NO TIME CLOCK REQUIRED

EMPL. NO. 1375 CARD NO. ____

FULL NAME EBONI PERKINS AGE (IF UNDER 18) ____

ADDRESS 1900 EAST LAKE SOCIAL SECURITY NO. 545-06-3189

DATE EMPLOYED ____ POSITION ____ RATE $ 9.80

PAY PERIOD STARTING 7/23 ENDING 7/27 19__

| DATE | REGULAR TIME | | | | | OVER TIME | | |
|---|---|---|---|---|---|---|---|---|
| | IN | OUT | IN | OUT | DAILY TOTALS | IN | OUT | DAILY TOTALS |
| 7/23 | 8:00 | 11:50 | 12:20 | 4:30 | 8 | 4:30 | 6:30 | 2 |
| 7/24 | 7:58 | 12:00 | 12:30 | 4:30 | 8 | 5:00 | 7:30 | 2.5 |
| 7/25 | 8:00 | 12:00 | 12:30 | 4:32 | 8 | | | |
| 7/26 | 7:56 | 12:05 | 12:35 | 4:30 | 8 | 4:30 | 5:00 | 0.5 |
| 7/27 | 8:01 | 12:00 | 1:00 | 5:00 | 8 | | | |
| APPROVED BY DCR FOREMAN | | | | TOTAL REGULAR TIME | 40 | TOTAL OVER TIME | | 5 |

REGULAR DAYS WORKED 5 @ 8 HRS. @ 9.80 EARNINGS $ 392.00

ADDITIONAL COMPENSATION:
VALUE OF MEALS, LODGING, GIFTS, ETC. AMOUNT $ ____

COMMISSIONS, FEES, BONUSES, GOODS, ETC. OT 5 @ $ 14.70 AMOUNT $ 73.50

OTHER REMUNERATIONS (KIND) $ ____

DEDUCTIONS: TOTAL EARNINGS $465.50

STATE DISAB. OR UNEMPL. TAX @____% $____

FEDERAL SOCIAL SECURITY TAX @____% $____

FEDERAL WITHHOLDING TAX____ $____

STATE WITHHOLDING TAX____ $____

OTHER DEDUCT.____ $____

CASH ADVANCED____ $____

TOTAL DEDUCTIONS (TO RIGHT) $____

NET PAY $____

I CERTIFY THE FOREGOING TO BE A CORRECT ACCOUNT OF THE TIME WORKED AND WAGES RECEIVED:

SIGNATURE ____ DATE PAID ____

4K402 REDIFORM®

FIGURE 5.1

these cards is then transferred to a **payroll ledger** (a chart showing all payroll information), as shown in Example 1.

**OBJECTIVE** **1** *Use hourly rate to calculate gross earnings.*    Eboni Perkins, whose time card is shown in Figure 5.1, is paid an **hourly wage** of $9.80 (see the time card). Her **gross earnings** would be calculated with the formula

Gross earnings = Number of hours worked × Rate per hour.

For example, if Perkins works 7 hours at $9.80 per hour, her gross earnings would be

Gross earnings = 7 × $9.80 = $68.60.

**EXAMPLE 1** *Completing a Payroll Ledger*

Meg Holden is doing the payroll for two employees, Abruzzo and Williams. The first thing she must do is complete a payroll ledger.

| Employee | Hours Worked | | | | | | | Total Hours | Rate | Gross Earnings |
|---|---|---|---|---|---|---|---|---|---|---|
| | S | M | T | W | Th | F | S | | | |
| Abruzzo, S. | — | 2 | 4 | 8 | 6 | 3 | — | | $8.43 | |
| Williams, N. | — | 3.5 | 3 | 7 | 6.75 | 7 | — | | $6.08 | |

**SOLUTION**    The first step is to find the total number of hours worked by each person.

Abruzzo: 2 + 4 + 8 + 6 + 3 = 23 hours

Williams: 3.5 + 3 + 7 + 6.75 + 7 = 27.25 hours

To find the gross earnings, multiply the number of hours worked and the rate per hour.

Abruzzo, S.: 23 × $8.43 = $193.89

Williams, N.: 27.25 × $6.08 = $165.68

The payroll ledger can now be completed.

| Employee | Hours Worked | | | | | | | Total Hours | Rate | Gross Earnings |
|---|---|---|---|---|---|---|---|---|---|---|
| | S | M | T | W | Th | F | S | | | |
| Abruzzo, S. | — | 2 | 4 | 8 | 6 | 3 | — | 23 | $8.43 | $193.89 |
| Williams, N. | — | 3.5 | 3 | 7 | 6.75 | 7 | — | 27.25 | $6.08 | $165.68 |

■

OBJECTIVE **2** *Use time-and-a-half rate for over 40 hours to find overtime earnings.* The **Fair Labor Standards Act**, which covers the majority of full-time employees in this country, was passed by Congress in 1938. It establishes minimum hourly wages, overtime pay, and other labor standards for workers. This law does not cover all employees. Those specifically excluded from coverage are business executives and administrators; commission salespeople; professionals such as doctors, lawyers, and teachers; employees of small retail businesses; and many seasonal agricultural workers. The law states that **overtime** (a higher than usual hourly rate) must be paid for all hours worked in excess of 40 per week. A great number of companies not covered by the Fair Labor Standards Act have voluntarily followed the practice of paying a **time-and-a-half rate** ($1\frac{1}{2}$ times the normal rate) for any work over 40 hours per week. With the time-and-a-half rate, gross earnings are found by the formula

Gross earnings =
Earnings at regular rate + Earnings at time-and-a-half rate.

| EXAMPLE 2 *Completing a Payroll Ledger with Overtime*

Complete the following payroll ledger

| | Hours Worked | | | | | | | Total Hours | | Reg. Rate | Gross Earnings | | |
|---|---|---|---|---|---|---|---|---|---|---|---|---|---|
| Employee | S | M | T | W | Th | F | S | Reg. | O.T. | | Reg. | O.T. | Total |
| Hicks, V. | 6 | 9 | 8.25 | 8 | 9 | 4.5 | — | | | $7.90 | | | |
| Blake, D. | — | 10 | 6.75 | 9 | 6.25 | 10 | 4.25 | | | $9.48 | | | |

SOLUTION First find the total number of hours worked.

Hicks: 6 + 9 + 8.25 + 8 + 9 + 4.5 = 44.75 hours

Blake: 10 + 6.75 + 9 + 6.25 + 10 + 4.25 = 46.25 hours

Both employees worked more than 40 hours. Gross earnings at the regular rate can now be found as discussed previously. Hicks earned 40 × $7.90 = $316 at the regular rate, and Blake earned 40 × $9.48 = $379.20 at the regular rate. To find overtime earnings, first find the number of overtime hours worked by each employee.

Hicks: 44.75 − 40 = 4.75 overtime hours

Blake: 46.25 − 40 = 6.25 overtime hours

The regular rate given for each employee can be used to find the time-and-a-half rate.

$$\text{Hicks: } 1\frac{1}{2} \times \$7.90 = \$11.85$$

$$\text{Blake: } 1\frac{1}{2} \times \$9.48 = \$14.22$$

Now find the overtime earnings.

Hicks: 4.75 hours × $11.85 per hour = $56.29    (rounded to the nearest cent)

Blake: 6.25 hours × $14.22 per hour = $88.88    (rounded)

The ledger can now be completed.

| Employee | Hours Worked | | | | | | | Total Hours | | Reg. Rate | Gross Earnings | | |
|---|---|---|---|---|---|---|---|---|---|---|---|---|---|
| | S | M | T | W | Th | F | S | Reg. | O.T. | | Reg. | O.T. | Total |
| **Hicks, V.** | 6 | 9 | 8.25 | 8 | 9 | 4.5 | — | 40 | 4.75 | $7.90 | $316 | $56.29 | $372.29 |
| **Blake, D.** | — | 10 | 6.75 | 9 | 6.25 | 10 | 4.25 | 40 | 6.25 | $9.48 | $379.20 | $88.88 | $468.08 |

■

**OBJECTIVE 3** *Use overtime premium method of calculating gross earnings.*    Gross earnings with overtime is sometimes calculated with the **overtime premium method** (sometimes called the **overtime excess method**). With this method, which produces the same result as the method just described, the total hours at the regular rate are added to the overtime hours at one half of the regular rate to arrive at gross earnings.

Total hours × Regular rate = Straight-time earnings

$$+ \text{ Overtime hours} \times \frac{1}{2} \text{ regular rate} = \text{Overtime premium (Overtime excess)}$$

= Gross earnings

**EXAMPLE 3** *Using the Overtime Premium Method*

This week Sharon Cosgrove worked 40 regular hours and 12 overtime hours. Her regular rate of pay is $12.38 per hour. Find her total gross pay using the overtime premium method.

**SOLUTION**    The total number of hours worked by Cosgrove is 52(40 + 12) and her overtime premium is $6.19 ($\frac{1}{2}$ × $12.38).

52 hours × **$12.38** = $643.76    regular-rate earnings

12 overtime hours × **$6.19** = $\underline{\phantom{0}\$74.28}$    overtime

$718.04    gross earnings    ■

**CALCULATOR APPROACH
TO EXAMPLE 3**

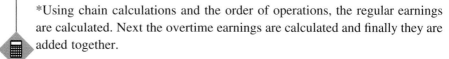

*Using chain calculations and the order of operations, the regular earnings are calculated. Next the overtime earnings are calculated and finally they are added together.

52 $\boxed{\times}$ 12.38 $\boxed{+}$ 12 $\boxed{\times}$ 12.38 $\boxed{\times}$ .5 $\boxed{=}$ 718.04

**NOTE**  Some companies prefer the overtime premium method since it readily identifies the extra cost of overtime labor and can be seen easily. Quite often, excessive use of overtime indicates inefficiencies in management.  ■

**OBJECTIVE  4**  *Find overtime earnings using time-and-a-half rate for over 8 hours of work per day.*   Some companies pay the time-and-a-half rate for all time worked over 8 hours in any one day, no matter how many hours are worked in a week. This *daily overtime* is shown in the next example.

**EXAMPLE 4**  *Finding Overtime Each Day*

Rodger Klas worked 10 hours on Monday, 5 on Tuesday, 7 on Wednesday, and 12 on Thursday. His regular rate of pay is $10.10. Find his gross earnings for the week if everything over 8 hours in one day is overtime.

|       | S | M | T | W | Th | F | S | Total Hours |
|-------|---|---|---|---|----|---|---|-------------|
| **Reg.** | — | 8 | 5 | 7 | 8  | — | — | 28 |
| **O.T.** | — | 2 | — | — | 4  | — | — | 6 |

**SOLUTION**   Klas worked more than 8 hours on both Monday and Thursday. On Monday, he had $10 - 8 = 2$ hours of overtime, with $12 - 8 = 4$ hours of overtime on Thursday. For the week, he earned $2 + 4 = 6$ hours of overtime. His regular hours are 8 on Monday, 5 on Tuesday, 7 on Wednesday, and 8 on Thursday, or

$$8 + 5 + 7 + 8 = 28$$

hours at the regular rate. His hourly earnings are $10.10, giving

$$28 \times \$10.10 = \$282.80$$

at the regular rate. If the regular rate is $10.10, the time-and-a-half rate is

$$\$10.10 \times 1\frac{1}{2} = \$15.15.$$

*NOTE: All calculator solutions use a scientific calculator. Refer to Appendix A for scientific and financial calculator basics.

He earned time and a half for 6 hours.

$$6 \times \$15.15 = \$90.90$$

Gross earnings are found by adding regular earnings and overtime earnings.

$$\$282.80 + \$90.90 = \$373.70 \qquad \blacksquare$$

**NOTE** There are many careers that require unusual schedules and do not pay overtime for over 40 hours worked in one week or over 8 hours worked in one day. An obvious example is the work schedule of a firefighter where the employee may work 24 hours and then get 48 hours off.   ■

**OBJECTIVE 5** *Understand double time, shift differential, and split-shift premiums.*   In addition to premiums paid for overtime, other **premium payment** plans include **double time** for holidays and, in some industries, Saturdays and Sundays. A **shift-differential** is often given to compensate employees for working less desirable hours. For example, an additional amount per hour or per shift might be paid to swing shift (4 P.M. to midnight) and graveyard shift (midnight to 8:00 A.M.) employees.

Restaurant employees and telephone operators often receive a **split-shift premium**. The employees' hours are staggered so that the employees are on the job only during the busiest times. For example, an employee may work 4 hours, be off 4 hours, then work 4 hours. The employee is paid a premium because of this less desirable schedule.

Some employers offer **compensatory time**, or **comp time**, for overtime hours worked. Instead of receiving additional money, an employee is given time off from the regular work schedule as compensation for overtime hours already worked. Quite often, the compensatory time is given at $1\frac{1}{2}$ times the overtime hours worked. For example, 12 hours might be given as compensation for 8 hours of previously worked overtime. Occasionally an employee is given a choice of overtime pay or comp time. Many companies reserve the use of compensatory time for their supervisors or managerial employees. Also, compensatory time is very common in government agencies.

**OBJECTIVE 6** *Find equivalent earnings for different pay periods.*   The second common method of finding gross earnings uses a **salary**, an amount given as so much per **pay period** (time between pay checks). Common pay periods are weekly, biweekly, semimonthly, and monthly, see Table 5.1 below.

TABLE 5.1   **Common Pay Periods**

| | |
|---|---|
| **Monthly** | **12 paychecks each year** |
| **Semimonthly** | **Twice each month; 24 paychecks each year** |
| **Biweekly** | **Every two weeks; 26 paychecks each year** |
| **Weekly** | **52 paychecks each year** |

**NOTE** One person's salary might be a certain amount per month, while someone else might earn a certain amount every two weeks. Many people receive an annual salary, divided among shorter pay periods. ■

**Big Bucks: The Ten Highest Paying Jobs in America**

| | Median Salaries |
|---|---|
| Physician | $148,000 |
| Dentist | 93,000 |
| Lobbyist | 91,300 |
| Management consultant | 61,900 |
| Lawyer | 60,500 |
| Electrical engineer | 59,100 |
| School principal | 57,300 |
| Aeronautical engineer | 56,700 |
| Airline pilot | 56,500 |
| Civil engineer | 55,800 |

*Sources: Money* magazine, Bureau of Labor Statistics, American Medical Association, American Dental Association.

The average annual earnings of those in the ten highest paying careers in America are shown to the side.

**EXAMPLE 5** *Determining Equivalent Salaries*

You are a career counselor and want to compare the earnings of four clients for which you have helped find jobs. John Cross receives a weekly salary of $273, Jo Ann Smith a biweekly salary of $1,686, Fontaine Evalado a semimonthly salary of $736, and Larry Sifford a monthly salary of $1,818. For each worker, find the following: (a) earnings per year, (b) earnings per month, and (c) earnings per week.

**SOLUTION**

John Cross
**(a)** $273 × **52** = $14,196 per year
**(b)** $14,196 ÷ **12** = $1,183 per month
**(c)** $273 per week

Jo Ann Smith
**(a)** $1,686 × **26** = $43,836 per year (biweekly = 26 per year)
**(b)** $43,836 ÷ **12** = $3,653 per month
**(c)** $1,686 ÷ **2** = $843 per week

Fontaine Evalado
**(a)** $736 × **24** = $17,664 per year
**(b)** $736 × **2** = $1,472 per month
**(c)** $17,664 ÷ **52** = $339.69

Larry Sifford
**(a)** $1,818 × **12** = $21,816 per year
**(b)** $1,818 per month
**(c)** $21,816 ÷ **52** = $419.54 ■

**OBJECTIVE** **7** *Find gross earnings when overtime is paid to salaried employees.* A salary is paid for the performance of a certain job, without keeping track of the number of hours worked. However, the Fair Labor Standards Act requires that certain salaried positions receive additional compensation for overtime. Just as with wage earners, the salaried employee is often paid time and a half for all hours worked over the normal number of hours per week.

## EXAMPLE 6  *Finding Overtime for Salaried Employees*

Della Daniel is paid $648 a week as an executive assistant. If her normal work week is 40 hours, and she is paid time and a half for all overtime, find her gross earnings for a week in which she works 46 hours.

**SOLUTION**    The executive assistant's salary has an hourly equivalent of

$$\frac{\$648}{40 \text{ hours}} = \$16.20 \text{ per hour.}$$

Since she must be paid overtime at the rate of $1\frac{1}{2}$ times her regular pay, she will get $24.30 per hour ($1\frac{1}{2} \times \$16.20$) for overtime. Her gross earnings for the week are calculated as follows.

$$
\begin{array}{ll}
\text{Salary for 40 hours} = \$648.00 & \text{regular-rate earnings} \\
\text{Overtime for 6 hours (6} \times \$24.30) = \underline{\quad 145.80} & \text{overtime} \\
\$793.80 & \text{gross earnings}
\end{array}
$$

**CALCULATOR APPROACH TO EXAMPLE 6**

The calculator solution to this example is

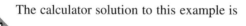

648 $+$ 648 $\div$ 40 $\times$ 1.5 $\times$ 6 $=$ 793.8.

## EXAMPLE 7  *Finding Gross Earnings with Overtime*

A conference coordinator is paid a salary of $432 per week. If his regular work week is 36 hours, find his gross earnings for a week in which he works 46 hours. All overtime hours are paid at time and a half.

**SOLUTION**    The coordinator's salary has an hourly equivalent of

$$\frac{\$432}{36 \text{ hours}} = \$12 \text{ per hour.}$$

Since he is paid $1\frac{1}{2}$ times the regular rate per hour, he will receive $18 per hour ($1\frac{1}{2} \times \$12$) for overtime. His gross earnings for the week are found as follows.

$$
\begin{array}{ll}
\text{Salary for 36 hours} = \$432 & \text{regular-rate earnings} \\
\text{Overtime for 10 hours (10} \times \$18) = \underline{\quad 180} & \text{overtime} \\
\$612 & \text{gross earnings}
\end{array}
$$

## 5.1 EXERCISES

*Find the number of regular hours and overtime hours (any hours over 40) for each of the following employees. Then calculate the overtime rate (time and a half) for each employee.*

| | Employee | S | M | T | W | Th | F | S | Reg. Hrs. | O.T. Hrs. | Reg. Rate | O.T. Rate |
|---|---|---|---|---|---|---|---|---|---|---|---|---|
| 1. | Bishop, K. | — | 6 | 5 | 8 | 10 | 7 | 4 | | | $7.40 | |
| 2. | Twomey, J. | — | 6.5 | 9 | 7.5 | 8 | 9.5 | 7 | | | $8.24 | |
| 3. | McKee, J. | 3 | 4.75 | 8.5 | 8 | 8.5 | 6 | — | | | $6.52 | |
| 4. | Eberz, L. | 8.5 | 9 | 7 | 8 | 9.75 | 9 | — | | | $8.10 | |
| 5. | Pott, A. | — | 9 | 8 | 8.75 | 9 | 10.5 | — | | | $11.48 | |
| 6. | Fuqua, B. | — | 8 | 8 | 9 | 7.25 | 6 | 7 | | | $9.80 | |

*Find the earnings at the regular rate, the earnings at the overtime rate, and the gross earnings for each of the employees in problems 1–6.*

7. Bishop, K.
8. Twomey, J.
9. McKee, J.
10. Eberz, L.
11. Pott, A.
12. Fuqua, B.

*Complete the following partial payroll ledger by finding the overtime rate at time and a half, the amount of earnings at regular pay, the amount at overtime pay, and the total gross wages for each employee.*

| | Employee | Total Hours | | Reg. Rate | O.T. Rate | Gross Earnings | | |
|---|---|---|---|---|---|---|---|---|
| | | Reg. | O.T. | | | Reg. | O.T. | Total |
| 13. | Walsh, G. | 38.25 | — | $8.10 | | | | |
| 14. | Clark, D. | 37.5 | — | $9.90 | | | | |
| 15. | Stingly, J. | 40 | 4.5 | $7.20 | | | | |

| | | Total Hours | | Reg. Rate | O.T. Rate | Gross Earnings | | |
|-----|-----------|------|------|-----------|-----------|------|------|-------|
| | **Employee** | **Reg.** | **O.T.** | | | **Reg.** | **O.T.** | **Total** |
| 16. | Lange, D. | 40 | 6.75 | $6.06 | | | | |
| 17. | White, C. | 40 | 4.25 | $9.18 | | | | |
| 18. | Tracey, N. | 40 | 5 | $7.10 | | | | |

*Some companies use the overtime premium method to determine gross earnings. Use this method to complete the following partial payroll ledger. Overtime is paid at time-and-a-half rate for all hours over 40.*

| | | Hours Worked | | | | | | | Total Hours | Reg. Rate | O.T. Hours | O.T. Pre-mium | Gross Earnings | | |
|-----|-----------|------|-------|-------|-----|------|------|---|-------------|-----------|------------|---------------|------|------|-------|
| | **Employee** | **S** | **M** | **T** | **W** | **Th** | **F** | **S** | **Total Hours** | **Reg. Rate** | **O.T. Hours** | **O.T. Pre-mium** | **Reg.** | **O.T.** | **Total** |
| 19. | Wilson, G. | 10 | 9 | 8 | 5 | 12 | 7 | — | | $6.80 | | | | | |
| 20. | Lavin, A. | 7.5 | 10.25 | 5 | 9.5 | 8.25 | 10 | — | | $6.10 | | | | | |
| 21. | Howell, K. | — | 12 | 11.75 | 8 | 7.5 | 11 | — | | $8.60 | | | | | |
| 22. | Sakari, J. | — | 5.25 | 8.75 | 10 | 12 | 10.5 | 7 | | $7.50 | | | | | |
| 23. | Kelley, R. | — | 10.5 | 8.75 | 9.5 | 11.5 | 10 | — | | $10.20 | | | | | |
| 24. | Firavich, S. | 8.5 | 7 | 9.75 | — | 10.5 | 12 | — | | $6.90 | | | | | |

*Some companies pay overtime for all time worked over 8 hours in a given day. Use this method to complete the following payroll ledger. Overtime is paid at time-and-a-half rate.*

| | | Hours Worked | | | | | | | Total Hours | | Reg. Rate | O.T. Rate | Gross Earnings | | |
|-----|-----------|------|------|------|------|------|------|---|------|------|-----------|-----------|------|------|-------|
| | **Employee** | **S** | **M** | **T** | **W** | **Th** | **F** | **S** | **Reg.** | **O.T.** | **Reg. Rate** | **O.T. Rate** | **Reg.** | **O.T.** | **Total** |
| 25. | Merill, K. | — | 10 | 9 | 11 | 6 | 5 | — | | | $5.54 | | | | |
| 26. | Keen, C. | — | 9 | 8.25 | 7.5 | 8.5 | 10 | — | | | $5.40 | | | | |

| | Employee | | | Hours Worked | | | | | Total Hours | | Reg. Rate | O.T. Rate | Gross Earnings | | |
|---|---|---|---|---|---|---|---|---|---|---|---|---|---|---|---|
| | | S | M | T | W | Th | F | S | Reg. | O.T. | | | Reg. | O.T. | Total |
| 27 | Cooper, D. | 9 | 7.5 | 8 | — | 10.75 | 8 | — | | | $6.70 | | | | |
| 28. | Russel, G. | — | 9 | 10 | 8 | 6 | 9.75 | — | | | $8.60 | | | | |
| 29. | Taylor, O. | — | 9.5 | 8.5 | 7.75 | 8 | 9.5 | — | | | $10.20 | | | | |
| 30. | Lerner, M. | 6 | 8 | 6.5 | 8.75 | — | 10.25 | — | | | $7.20 | | | | |

**31.** Explain in your own words what premium payment plans are. Select a premium payment plan and describe it. (See Objective 5.)

**32.** If you were given a choice of overtime pay or compensatory time, which would you choose? Why? (See Objective 5.)

*Find the equivalent earnings for each of the following salaries as indicated.*

| | | | Earnings | | |
|---|---|---|---|---|---|
| | Weekly | Biweekly | Semimonthly | Monthly | Annual |
| 33. | $248 | —— | —— | —— | —— |
| 34. | —— | —— | $480 | —— | —— |
| 35. | —— | $852 | —— | —— | —— |
| 36. | —— | —— | —— | $1,150 | —— |
| 37. | —— | —— | $1,087.50 | —— | —— |
| 38. | $436 | —— | —— | —— | —— |
| 39. | —— | —— | —— | $2,680 | —— |
| 40. | —— | $768 | —— | —— | —— |
| 41. | —— | —— | —— | —— | $21,580 |
| 42. | —— | —— | —— | —— | $26,100 |

*Find the weekly gross earnings for the following people who are on salary and are paid time and a half for overtime. (Hint: Round hourly equivalents and overtime amounts to the nearest cent.)*

| | Employee | Regular Hours per Week | Weekly Salary | Hours Worked | Weekly Gross Earnings |
|---|---|---|---|---|---|
| 43. | Roberts, E. | 40 | $520 | 56 | —— |
| 44. | Glenn, D. | 40 | $360 | 42 | —— |

| Employee | Regular Hours per Week | Weekly Salary | Hours Worked | Weekly Gross Earnings |
|---|---|---|---|---|
| 45. Lewin, J. | 45 | $418 | 50 | _____ |
| 46. Gray, D. | 38 | $340 | 40 | _____ |
| 47. Camp, J. | 32 | $450 | 44 | _____ |
| 48. Sypniewski, D. | 30 | $484 | 45 | _____ |

*Solve each of the following application problems. (Hint: Round hourly equivalents, regular rates, and overtime rates to the nearest cent.)*

49. Last week, Regina Hasner worked 48 hours at Blockbuster Video. Find her gross earnings for the week if she is paid $7.40 per hour and earns time and a half for all hours over 40.

50. Joane Ong is an accounts payable clerk and is paid $9.50 per hour for straight time, and time and a half for all hours over 40 worked in a week. Find her gross earnings for a week in which she worked 52 hours.

51. James Northington, a bookstore employee, earns $7.80 per hour and is paid time and a half for all time over 8 hours worked on a given day. Find his gross earnings for a week in which he worked the following hours: Monday, 9.5; Tuesday, 7; Wednesday, 10.75; Thursday, 4.5; and Friday, 8.75.

52. Ben Rakusin is a tree trimmer and worked 10 hours on Monday, 9.75 hours on Tuesday, 5.5 hours on Wednesday, 12 hours on Thursday, and 7.25 hours on Friday. His regular rate of pay is $9.50 an hour, with time and a half paid for all hours over 8 worked on a given day. Find his gross earnings for the week.

53. Anne Felsted is paid $648 a week as an escrow officer at a bank. Her normal work week is 40 hours. She is paid time and a half for overtime. Find her gross earnings for a week in which she worked 46 hours.

54. An employee at Valley Feed Stores is paid $298 for a normal work week of 35 hours. If she is paid time and a half for overtime, find her gross earnings for a week in which she worked 48 hours.

55. Charles Dawkins, manager of the Cellular Phone Center, is paid a salary of $638 per week, has a normal work week of 40 hours, and is paid time and a half for overtime. Find his gross earnings in a week in which he worked 52 hours.

56. Frank Capek, senior vice-president of Countrywide Mortgage, worked 54 hours this week. If he is paid a weekly salary of $800, and has a normal work week of 45 hours, find his gross earnings for the week. He is paid time and a half for all overtime.

57. An employee earns $420 weekly. Find the equivalent earnings if paid (a) biweekly, (b) semimonthly, (c) monthly, and (d) annually.

58. Angelica Canales is a plant supervisor and is paid $42,900 annually. Find the equivalent earnings if this amount is paid (a) weekly, (b) biweekly, (c) semimonthly, and (d) monthly.

59. Semimonthly pay periods result in 24 paychecks per year. Biweekly pay periods result in 26 paychecks per year. Which of these pay periods gives three checks in two months of the year? Will it always be the same two months? Explain.

60. How would you budget your money if you were paid just once a month instead of each week? Which would you prefer: a monthly pay period or a weekly pay period?

## 5.2   Gross Earnings (Commission)

### OBJECTIVES

**1** *Find gross earnings using commission rate × sales (P = R × B).*

**2** *Determine commission using a variable commission rate.*

**3** *Use salary and commission rate to find gross earnings.*

**4** *Use a drawing account and quota to find gross earnings.*

**5** *Determine override as part of gross earnings.*

Many people in sales and marketing are paid on **commission**, usually a fixed percent of sales. This is an incentive system of compensation and the commissions are designed to produce maximum employee output, since pay is directly dependent on sales. This section discusses all of the common types of sales commissions.

**OBJECTIVE 1** *Find gross earnings using commission rate × sales (P = R × B).*     With a **straight commission**, the salesperson is paid a fixed percent of sales. Gross earnings are found by the following formula.

$$P \quad = \quad R \quad \times \quad B$$
$$\text{Gross earnings} = \text{Commission rate} \times \text{Amount of sales}$$

#### EXAMPLE 1   *Determining Earnings Using Commission*

A real estate broker is paid a 6% commission. Find the commission on a house selling for $118,500.

**SOLUTION**   The broker would receive

$$6\% \times \$118,500 = 0.06 \times \$118,500 = \$7,110$$

for selling the house.                                                            ■

#### EXAMPLE 2   *Subtracting Returns When Using Commissions*

Julie Campbell, a textbook sales representative, had sales of $8,295 with returns of $950. If her commission rate is 14%, find her gross earnings.

**SOLUTION**   The returns must first be subtracted from gross sales, and the difference, net sales, multiplied by the commission rate.

$$\text{Gross earnings} = (\$8,295 - \$950) \times 14\%$$
$$= \$7,345 \times 0.14$$
$$= \$1,028.30$$                                                    ■

**PROBLEM-SOLVING HINT**   Before calculating the commission, all items returned are first subtracted from the amount of sales. The company will not pay a commission on sales that are not completed.   ■

**OBJECTIVE 2** *Determine commission using a variable commission rate.* The **sliding-scale** or **variable commission** plan is a method of pay designed to retain top producing salespeople. With these plans, a higher rate of commission is paid as sales get larger and larger.

| EXAMPLE 3  *Finding Earnings Using Variable Commission*

A salesperson at Farmer Bob's Produce is paid as follows.

| Sales | Rate |
|-------|------|
| Up to $10,000 | 6% |
| $10,001–$20,000 | 8% |
| $20,001 and up | 9% |

Find the gross earnings of a salesperson selling $32,768 worth of produce.

**SOLUTION**    Use the three commission rates as follows.

$32,768 (total sales)
$- \underline{10,000}$ (first $10,000)    $10,000 at 6%    =    $600.00
$22,768
$- \underline{10,000}$ (next $10,000)    $10,000 at 8%    =    $800.00
$\underline{12,768}$ (over $20,000)    $\underline{12,768 \text{ at } 9\%}$    $= \underline{\$1,149.12}$
                                     $32,768 total sales    =    $2,549.12 total commissions

The salesperson earned gross pay of $2,549.12.    ■

---

**CALCULATOR APPROACH TO EXAMPLE 3**

The first thing to do is find the commission at the highest rate and *place* it in memory.

( 32768 − 20000 ) × 9 % = STO

Next, find the commission at the second highest rate and *add* this to memory.

( 20000 − 10000 ) × 8 % = + RCL = STO

Finally, find the commission at the lowest rate and *add* it to memory. The result is the total commission.

10000 × 6 % = + RCL = 2549.12

---

**OBJECTIVE 3** *Use salary and commission rate to find gross earnings.* With a **salary plus commission**, the salesperson is paid a fixed sum per pay period, plus a commission on all sales. This method of payment is commonly used by large retail stores. Gross earnings with salary plus commission are found by the following formula.

Gross earnings =

Fixed amount per pay period + Amount earned on commission

Many salespeople favor this method of determining gross earnings. It is especially attractive to the beginning salesperson who lacks selling experience and personal self-confidence. While providing an incentive, it offers the security of a guaranteed income to cover basic living costs.

## EXAMPLE 4 *Adding Commission to a Salary*

Stacy Trash is paid $225 per week by the Potters Exchange, plus 3% on all sales. Find her gross earnings for a week in which her sales were $7,250.

**SOLUTION**    Use the formula in the box.

$$\text{Gross earnings} = \text{Fixed earnings} + \text{Commission}$$
$$= \$225 + (0.03 \times \$7,250)$$
$$= \$225 + \$217.50$$
$$= \$442.50 \qquad \blacksquare$$

**OBJECTIVE 4** *Use a drawing account and quota to find gross earnings.*    The fixed amount of earnings is often a **draw** or loan against future commissions. A **drawing account** is set up with the amounts drawn repaid with future commissions. This is a loan against future commissions but offers the salesperson the assurance of a fixed sum per pay period. The salesperson must repay the drawing account as commissions are earned.

## EXAMPLE 5 *Subtracting a Draw from Commission*

Richard Stratten, a computer sales representative, has sales of $38,560 for the month and is paid a 7% commission rate. He had draws of $750 for the month. Find his gross earnings after repaying the drawing account.

**SOLUTION**        
$$\text{Gross earnings} = \text{Commissions} - \text{Draw}$$
$$= (0.07 \times \$38,560) - \$750$$
$$= \$2,699.20 - \$750$$
$$= \$1,949.20 \qquad \blacksquare$$

**NOTE**  Commission earning plans are a strong deterrent to attracting new salespeople. It is for this reason that many companies offer the salary plus commission and the draw plans to help attract new employees.    ■

A *sales quota* is often established for salespeople. The quota is the minimum amount of sales expected from the employee. If the salesperson continually falls short of the sales quota, termination may result. Normally, however, the salesperson is rewarded for passing the sales quota with a bonus or commission. This plan is called a **quota bonus** system.

**EXAMPLE 6** *Using the Quota Bonus System*

David Shea is a sales representative for a mountain bike manufacturer. During a recent week he had sales of $18,780 and was paid a commission of 8% after meeting the sales quota of $5,000. Find his gross earnings.

**SOLUTION**

$$\text{Gross earnings} = \text{Commission rate} \times (\text{Sales} - \text{Quota})$$
$$= 0.08 \times (\$18,780 - \$5,000)$$
$$= 0.08 \times \$13,780$$
$$= \$1,102.40 \qquad \blacksquare$$

**OBJECTIVE 5** *Determine override as part of gross earnings.* Sales supervisors and department heads of retail stores are often paid a commission based on the total sales of their staff or department. This payment, for the efforts of others, rewards the supervisor or department head for doing a good job in training and maintaining a sales staff. This commission is called an **override**. Calculate it like any other commission, but use the total department sales.

**EXAMPLE 7** *Finding Gross Earnings with Commission and Override*

Roller Blades and More pays their managers a salary plus commission and override. Find the gross earnings for a manager given the following.

| | | | |
|---|---|---|---|
| **Personal sales** | $4,386 | **Personal returns** | $118 |
| **Store sales** | $11,865 | **Store returns** | $562 |
| **Salary** | $375 | **Personal quota** | $2,500 |
| **Commission rate** | 4% | **Override rate** | 1% |

**SOLUTION** First, find the manager's commission on personal sales.

$$\text{Personal sales} - \text{Returns} - \text{Quota} = \text{Personal commission sales}$$
$$\$4,386 \quad - \quad \$118 \; - \; \$2,500 = \$1,768$$
$$\text{Personal commission} = 0.04 \times \$1,768$$
$$= \$70.72$$

Now find the override on store sales.

$$\text{Store sales} - \text{Returns} = \text{Override commission sales}$$
$$\$11,865 \quad - \quad \$562 \; = \$11,303$$
$$\text{Override commission} = 0.01 \times \$11,303$$
$$= \$113.03$$

Calculate gross earnings as follows.

$$\text{Gross earnings} = \text{Salary} + \text{Commission} + \text{Override}$$
$$= \$375 + \$70.72 + \$113.03$$
$$= \$558.75 \qquad \blacksquare$$

The approach here is to first find the manager's commission on personal sales and *place* it in memory.

| ( | 4386 | − | 118 | − | 2500 | ) | × | 4 | % | = | STO |

Next, find the override on store sales and *add* it to memory.

| ( | 11865 | − | 562 | ) | × | 1 | % | = | + | RCL | = | STO |

**CALCULATOR APPROACH TO EXAMPLE 7**

Finally, *add* the salary to the commission and override in memory. The result is the gross earnings.

| 375 | + | RCL | = | 558.75 |

## 5.2  EXERCISES

*Find the gross earnings for each of the following salespeople.*

| | Employee | Total Sales | Returns and Allowances | Rate of Commission |
|---|---|---|---|---|
| 1. | Johnson, B. | $2,810 | $208 | 8% |
| 2. | Gilbert, D. | $5,734 | $415 | 5% |
| 3. | Cutrer, L. | $2,875 | $64 | 15% |
| 4. | Freeman, K. | $2,603 | $76 | 18% |
| 5. | Brown, K. | $25,658 | $4,083 | 9% |
| 6. | Dramatinos, M. | $18,765 | $386 | 8% |
| 7. | Dobbins, G. | $45,618 | $2,281 | 1% |
| 8. | Phares, H. | $34,183 | $1,169 | 2% |

*Bayside Janitorial Supply pays its salespeople the following commission.*

| | |
|---|---|
| $7,500 in sales | 6% |
| Next $7,500 in sales | 8% |
| over $15,000 | 10% |

*Find the gross earnings for each of the following employees (top of next page).*

| Employee | Total Sales | | Employee | Total Sales |
|---|---|---|---|---|
| 9. Warrener, G. | $18,550 | | 10. Pasco, S. | $17,640 |
| 11. Prentiss, C. | $10,480 | | 12. Maria, P. | $16,250 |
| 13. Sanchez, J. | $11,225 | | 14. Fisher, L. | $22,650 |
| 15. Butter, M. | $25,860 | | 16. Manly, C. | $23,340 |

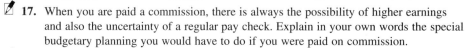

17. When you are paid a commission, there is always the possibility of higher earnings and also the uncertainty of a regular pay check. Explain in your own words the special budgetary planning you would have to do if you were paid on commission.

18. A variable commission plan is often referred to as an incentive within an incentive. Explain why this might be an accurate description of a variable commission plan. (See Objective 2.)

*Complete the following commission payroll to find gross earnings.*

| | Employee | Gross Sales | Sales Returns | Net Quota | Commission Sales | Commission Rate | Gross Commission | Salary | Gross Earnings |
|---|---|---|---|---|---|---|---|---|---|
| 19. | Carlton, B. | $3,980 | $180 | — | | 5% | | $340 | |
| 20. | Williams, L. | $10,218 | $1,120 | $1,000 | | 7% | | — | |
| 21. | Lott, D. | $6,380 | $295 | $2,000 | | 6% | | — | |
| 22. | Farrell, S. | $3,270 | $420 | — | | 7% | | $280 | |
| 23. | Chen, C. | $12,420 | $390 | $2,500 | | 3% | | — | |
| 24. | Ng, B. | $10,680 | $490 | $1,500 | | 6% | | — | |
| 25. | Jidobu, B. | $4,215 | $318 | $1,000 | | 5% | | $210 | |
| 26. | Kroeger, T. | $3,850 | $310 | $1,400 | | 6% | | $350 | |

*Solve each of the following application problems.*

27. Vicky Valerin is a sales representative for CITCO Chemical Supplies. She is paid a 10% commission rate, and has had a draw of $250 this week. If her sales are $8,270 this week, find her gross earnings after repaying the drawing account.

28. Karima Layton has sales of $82,280 for the month and is paid a 7% commission rate. She has had draws totaling $1,200 for the month. Find her gross earnings after repaying the drawing account.

29. Clare Lynch, a salesperson for Electro Tech, has sales of $235,700 this month and is paid a 2% commission by her office. She also receives a salary of $1,500 each month. Find her gross earnings for the month.

30. Jim Snelling, an account representative for Ad-Art is paid a 3% commission rate and a salary of $300 each week. If his sales are $28,720 this week, find his gross earnings for the week.

31. John Chavez is a commission salesperson for Fastener Manufacturing which allows him to draw $800 per month. His commission is 6% of the first $6,000 in sales, 8% of the next $16,000, and 15% of all sales over $22,000. If his sales for the month were $27,700, find (a) his total commission and (b) the earnings due at the end of the month after repaying the drawing account balance of $800.

32. Andrea Abriani is a sales representative for Hi Side Greeting Card Company. She is paid a monthly draw of $650. Her commission is 10% of the first $2,000 in sales, 12% of the next $4,000, and 20% of all sales over $6,000. If her sales for the month were $8,750, find (a) her total commission and (b) the gross earnings due at the end of the month after repaying the drawing account.

33. The manager of Toys For Tots is paid a salary plus commission and an override. Find his gross earnings given the following.

| | | | |
|---|---|---|---|
| **Personal sales** | **$2,825** | **Personal returns** | **$84** |
| **Department sales** | **$8,656** | **Department returns** | **$317** |
| **Salary** | **$200** | **Personal quota** | **$1,000** |
| **Commission rate** | **5%** | **Override** | **$1\frac{1}{2}\%$** |

34. The sales manager for A & A Appliance is paid a salary plus commission and an override. Find her gross earnings given the following.

| | | | |
|---|---|---|---|
| **Personal sales** | **$5,856** | **Personal returns** | **$185** |
| **Store sales** | **$19,622** | **Store returns** | **$358** |
| **Salary** | **$250** | **Personal quota** | **$3,000** |
| **Commission rate** | **3%** | **Override** | **2%** |

## 5.3    Gross Earnings (Piecework)

**OBJECTIVES**

**1** *Find the gross earnings for piecework.*

**2** *Find the gross earnings for differential piecework.*

**3** *Determine chargebacks and dockings.*

**4** *Find overtime earnings for piecework.*

The salaries and wages discussed in Section 5.1 are called **time rates**, since they depend only on the amount of time an employee was actually on the job. Commission earnings in Section 5.2 and the piecework methods discussed in this section are called **incentive rates**. These gross earnings are based on production and pay an employee for actual performance on the job.

**OBJECTIVE** **1** *Find the gross earnings for piecework.* A **piecework rate** pays an employee so much per item produced. Gross earnings are found using the following formula.

$$\text{Gross earnings} = \text{Number of items} \times \text{Pay per item}$$

For example, a cabinet finisher who finishes 23 cabinets and is paid a piecework rate of $4 per cabinet would have total gross earnings of

$$\text{Gross earnings} = \$4 \times 23 = \$92.$$

**EXAMPLE 1** *Finding Gross Earnings for Piecework*

Selina Gaisy was paid $0.73 for sewing a jacket collar, $0.87 for a sleeve with a cuff, and $0.99 for a lapel. One week she sewed 318 jacket collars, 112 sleeves with cuffs, and 37 lapels. Find her gross earnings.

**SOLUTION** Multiply the rate per item by the number of that type of item.

| Item | Number | Rate | Total |
|------|--------|------|-------|
| Jacket collars | 318 | × $0.73 = | $232.14 |
| Sleeves with cuffs | 112 | × $0.87 = | $97.44 |
| Lapels | 37 | × $0.99 = | $36.63 |

The gross earnings can be found by adding the three totals. $232.14 + $97.44 + $36.63 = $366.21. ∎

**OBJECTIVE** **2** *Find the gross earnings for differential piecework.* A **straight-piecework** plan, such as in Example 1, is perhaps the oldest of all incentive payment plans. It is used in many manufacturing and production jobs such as fine jewelry finishing, agricultural and farm work, garment manufacturing, and in the building trades for structural framing, roofing, and floor laying. While many workers prefer working under a piecework plan, there are just as many who dislike it. Labor unions and other employee organizations, senior employees, and others claim that piecework plans result in unsafe work habits and poor quality workmanship.

Companies still using piecework have often made various modifications and changes to the straight piece rate plan. Many of these modified plans incorporate quotas which must be met and then offer an additional **premium rate** for each item produced beyond the quota. These plans offer an added incentive within an incentive. For example, in the **differential-piecework** plan the rate paid per item depends on the number of items produced.

| EXAMPLE 2 | *Using Differential Piecework*

Metro Electric pays assemblers as follows.

| 1–100 units | $2.10 each |
| 101–150 units | $2.25 each |
| 151 or more units | $2.40 each |

Find the gross earnings of an employee producing 214 items.

**SOLUTION**    The gross earnings of a worker producing 214 items would be found as follows.

$$
\begin{array}{ll}
214 \ (\text{total units}) \\
\underline{-\ 100} \ (\text{first 100 units}) & \quad 100 \text{ units at } \$2.10 \text{ each } = \$210.00 \\
114 \\
\underline{-\ 50} \ (\text{next 50 units}) & \quad 50 \text{ units at } \$2.25 \text{ each } = \$112.50 \\
64 \ (\text{number over 150}) & \quad \underline{64} \text{ units at } \$2.40 \text{ each } = \underline{\$153.60} \\
& \quad 214 \text{ total units } \ \ = \$476.10
\end{array}
$$

The gross earnings are $476.10.    ■

**NOTE**    With differential piecework, the highest amount paid only applies to the last units produced. In Example 2, $2.10 is paid for units 1–100, $2.25 is paid for units 101–150, and $2.40 is only paid on those units beyond unit 150, which in this case is 64 units.    ■

**OBJECTIVE 3** *Determine chargebacks and dockings.*    While companies are often pleased to reward employees with premium rates for surpassing quotas, management is equally concerned with unacceptable quality and unusable production. Ruined items may produce a total loss of material and labor; correctable flaws require additional handling, resulting in added costs and decreased profits. To discourage carelessness and mistakes, many companies require the employee to share in the cost of the spoiled item. These penalties, called **chargebacks** or **dockings**, are normally at a lower rate than the employee receives for producing that piece. This lower rate is used because a small amount of production error is expected.

| EXAMPLE 3 | *Understanding and Using Chargebacks*

In Example 2, suppose the company had a chargeback of $1.50 per spoiled item and the employee had spoiled 14 items. Find the gross earnings after the chargeback.

**SOLUTION**    Gross earnings are found by subtracting the chargeback from piece rate earnings.

$$
\begin{aligned}
\text{Gross earnings} &= \text{piecework earnings} - (\text{spoiled items} \times \text{chargeback rate}) \\
&= \$476.10 - (14 \text{ items} \times \$1.50) \\
&= \$476.10 - \$21 \\
&= \$455.10
\end{aligned}
$$

■

Piecework and differential-piecework rates are frequently modified to include some guaranteed hourly rate of pay. Often this is necessary to meet minimum wage laws. To satisfy the law, the employer may either pay minimum wage or piecework earnings, whichever is higher.

**EXAMPLE 1**  *Finding Earnings with a Guaranteed Hourly Wage*

A production worker is paid $8.40 an hour for an 8-hour day, or $0.95 per casting, whichever is higher. Find the weekly earnings for an employee having the following production.

| | | |
|---|---|---|
| Monday | 85 | castings |
| Tuesday | 70 | castings |
| Wednesday | 88 | castings |
| Thursday | 68 | castings |
| Friday | 82 | castings |

**SOLUTION**  The hourly earnings for an 8-hour day are $67.20 (8 × $8.40). If the piecework earnings for the day are less than this amount, the hourly earnings will be paid.

| | | | |
|---|---|---|---|
| Monday | 85 × $0.95 = | $80.75 | piece rate |
| Tuesday | 70 × $0.95 = | $67.20 | hourly (piece rate is $66.50) |
| Wednesday | 88 × $0.95 = | $83.60 | piece rate |
| Thursday | 68 × $0.95 = | $67.20 | hourly (piece rate is $64.60) |
| Friday | 82 × $0.95 = | $77.90 | piece rate |
| | | $376.65 | weekly earnings |

**NOTE**  Since the piecework earnings on Tuesday and Thursday are below the minimum, the hourly rate is paid on those days.  ∎

**OBJECTIVE 4**  *Find overtime earnings for piecework.*    Piecework employees, just as other workers, are paid time and a half for overtime. The overtime rate may be computed as $1\frac{1}{2}$ times the hourly rate, but most often, the overtime rate is $1\frac{1}{2}$ times the regular rate per piece.

**EXAMPLE 5**  *Determining Earnings with Overtime Piecework*

A worker is paid $0.46 per electrical panel wired. During one week she produces 530 items on regular time and 110 items during overtime hours. Find her gross earnings for the week if time and a half per piece is paid for overtime.

**SOLUTION**    Gross earnings = Earnings at regular piece rate
$$+ \text{ Earnings at overtime piece rate}$$
$$= 530 \times \$0.46 + 110 \times \left(1\frac{1}{2} \times \$0.46\right)$$
$$= \$243.80 + \$75.90$$
$$= \$319.70$$

CALCULATOR APPROACH
TO EXAMPLE 5

The calculator solution to this example uses parentheses to first calculate the overtime piece rate.

530 ×ˣ .46 + 110 ×ˣ ( 1.5 × .46 ) = 319.7

## 5.3 EXERCISES

*Complete the following payroll ledger for Pet Salt Products. Employees are paid a straight piece rate. Rates per unit vary depending on worker skills involved.*

| | Employee | M | T | W | T | F | Total Pieces | Rate per Unit | Gross Earnings |
|---|---|---|---|---|---|---|---|---|---|
| 1. | Polstra, R. | 75 | 62 | 86 | 55 | 48 | | $0.78 | |
| 2. | Carlton, B. | 120 | 108 | 89 | 130 | 95 | | $0.87 | |
| 3. | Young, C. | 98 | 86 | 79 | 108 | 80 | | $0.75 | |
| 4. | McIntosh, R. | 67 | 54 | 72 | 83 | 59 | | $0.72 | |
| 5. | Todd, R. | 118 | 124 | 143 | 132 | 148 | | $0.68 | |
| 6. | Eckern, G. | 157 | 148 | 169 | 145 | 178 | | $0.59 | |
| 7. | Anderson, N. | 125 | 118 | 115 | 132 | 98 | | $0.46 | |
| 8. | Duerr, D. | 76 | 68 | 85 | 72 | 96 | | $0.86 | |
| 9. | Parker, R. | 149 | 135 | 118 | 125 | 143 | | $0.78 | |
| 10. | Pearson, D. | 96 | 84 | 115 | 102 | 96 | | $0.72 | |

Column header spanning M–F: **Units Produced**

*Employees at the Almond Growers Exchange are paid as follows.*

| 1–100 cases | $0.18 |
| 101–200 cases | $0.19 |
| 201–300 cases | $0.20 |
| 301 cases and up | $0.21 |

*Find the gross earnings for each of the following employees (top of next page).*

| Employee | Number of Cases | | Employee | Number of Cases |
|---|---|---|---|---|
| 11. Navell, C. | 370 | | 12. Stagg, S. | 452 |
| 13. Smith, J. | 618 | | 14. McCarthy, S. | 640 |
| 15. Sullivan, G. | 422 | | 16. O'Callaghan, J. | 566 |

*Suppose that production workers at Classic Old Tyme Radio Shows are paid as follows for labeling and packaging CDs.*

| 1–500 CDs | $0.10 each |
|---|---|
| 501–700 CDs | $0.12 each |
| 701–1,000 CDs | $0.14 each |
| over 1,000 CDs | $0.16 each |

*Find the gross earnings for each of the following employees.*

| Employee | Number of CD's | | Employee | Number of CD's |
|---|---|---|---|---|
| 17. Manly, R. | 829 | | 18. Goodwin, T. | 926 |
| 19. Stephenson, K. | 1,182 | | 20. Chin, L. | 1,380 |
| 21. Waipo, T. | 1,250 | | 22. Roseborough, M. | 1,408 |

*Find the gross earnings for each of the following employees. Each has an 8-hour workday and is paid $0.75 for each unit of production or the hourly rate, whichever is greater.*

| | Employee | Units Produced | | | | | Hourly Rate | Gross Earnings |
|---|---|---|---|---|---|---|---|---|
| | | M | T | W | T | F | | |
| 23. | Foster, B. | 66 | 75 | 58 | 72 | 68 | $6.18 | |
| 24. | Arcade, A. | 62 | 58 | 49 | 60 | 51 | $5.20 | |
| 25. | Pieri, Y. | 65 | 60 | 71 | 78 | 64 | $5.80 | |
| 26. | Dal Porto, J. | 72 | 70 | 62 | 88 | 82 | $6.50 | |
| 27. | Zurcher, S. | 50 | 56 | 48 | 62 | 45 | $4.50 | |

| | | Units Produced | | | | | Hourly Rate | Gross Earnings |
|---|---|---|---|---|---|---|---|---|
| | Employee | M | T | W | T | F | | |
| 28. | Frase, E. | 63 | 57 | 67 | 75 | 70 | $5.70 | |
| 29. | Pantera, A. | 73 | 62 | 78 | 64 | 81 | $6.30 | |
| 30. | Enos, C. | 60 | 55 | 59 | 68 | 66 | $5.40 | |

*Find the gross earnings for each of the following employees. Overtime is $1\frac{1}{2}$ times the normal per piece rate. Rejected units are charged at the chargeback rate.*

| | | Units Produced | | Rejected Units | Rate per Unit | Chargeback per Unit | Gross Earnings |
|---|---|---|---|---|---|---|---|
| | Employee | Reg. | O.T. | | | | |
| 31. | Miller, J. | 510 | 74 | 20 | $0.72 | $0.38 | |
| 32. | Kavanagh, M. | 380 | 26 | 6 | $0.69 | $0.56 | |
| 33. | Boghoussian, A. | 493 | 74 | 34 | $0.86 | $0.46 | |
| 34. | Carlson, K. | 508 | 38 | 16 | $0.59 | $0.42 | |
| 35. | Balbi, G. | 286 | 38 | 4 | $0.95 | $0.82 | |
| 36. | Fukano, H. | 315 | 64 | 35 | $0.74 | $0.65 | |
| 37. | Hughes, G. | 403 | 72 | 15 | $0.68 | $0.45 | |
| 38. | Dos Reis, A. | 452 | 12 | 6 | $0.59 | $0.50 | |

39. Wages and salaries are known as time rates while commissions are called incentive rates of pay. Explain in your own words the difference between these payment methods.

40. Describe what a chargeback or docking is for rejected units. Why do you think that the chargeback per unit is usually less than the rate paid per unit? (See Objective 3.)

*Solve each of the follow application problems.*

41. Earl Karn is paid $3.75 for each vacuum cleaner assembled, is charged $1.25 for each rejection, and is paid time and a half for overtime production. Find his gross earnings

for the week when he assembles 118 vacuum cleaners at the regular rate, 26 vacuums at the overtime rate, and has 7 chargebacks.

**42.** John Davis decorates cakes at the French Meadow Bakery, for which he is paid $2.42 each. He is charged $1.40 per rejection and is paid time and a half for all overtime production. Find his gross earnings when production for the week is 128 cakes at the regular rate and 19 cakes at the overtime rate. He has a total of 5 chargebacks.

**43.** Robert Andrews is paid $1.35 per alternator installed, is charged $0.85 for each rejection, and is paid time and a half for overtime production. Find his gross earnings for the week when he installs 310 alternators at the regular rate, 110 alternators at the overtime rate, and has 20 chargebacks.

**44.** Cindy Perez sews lace on dance costumes, for which she is paid $1.18 each. She is charged $0.90 per rejection and is paid time and a half for all overtime production. Find her gross earnings when production for the week is 138 costumes at the regular rate and 28 costumes at the overtime rate. She has a total of 9 chargebacks.

**45.** Erica Gheen inspects and packages keyboards. She is paid $0.65 per unit and is charged $0.25 for each rejection. Find her gross earnings for the week given the following production.

|  | M | T | W | T | F | Totals |
|---|---|---|---|---|---|---|
| **Production** | 128 | 97 | 109 | 136 | 112 |  |
| **Chargebacks** | 4 | 2 | 7 | 5 | 3 |  |

**46.** George Parr checks and ships customer orders for Feathers and Stream Sportswear. He receives $0.35 per package and is charged $0.12 for each rejection. Find his gross earnings for the week given the following production.

|  | M | T | W | T | F | Totals |
|---|---|---|---|---|---|---|
| **Production** | 178 | 165 | 186 | 171 | 174 |  |
| **Chargebacks** | 5 | 3 | 2 | 7 | 4 |  |

## 5.4    Social Security, Medicare, and Other Taxes

**OBJECTIVES**

**1** *Understand FICA.*

**2** *Find the maximum FICA tax paid by an employee in one year.*

**3** *Understand medicare tax.*

**4** *Find FICA tax and medicare tax.*

**5** *Determine the FICA tax and the medicare tax paid by a self-employed person.*

**6** *Find state disability insurance deductions.*

Finding gross earnings is only the first step in preparing a payroll. The employer must then subtract all required deductions from gross earnings. For most employees, these deductions include social security tax, medicare tax, federal income tax withholding, and state tax withholding. Other deductions may include state disability insurance, union dues, retirement, vacation pay, credit union savings or loan payments, purchase of bonds, uniform expenses, group insurance plans, and charitable contributions. Subtracting these deductions from gross earnings results in **net pay**, the amount the employee receives.

**OBJECTIVE** **1** *Understand FICA.*     The **Federal Insurance Contributions ACT (FICA)** was passed into law in the 1930s during the middle of the Great Depression. This plan, now called **social security**, was originally designed to give monthly benefits to retired workers and their survivors. Also included today are death benefits and medicare payments. As the numbers of people receiving benefits has increased along with the individual benefit amounts, people paying into social security have had to pay a larger amount of earnings into this fund each year. From 1937 through 1950 an employee paid 1% of income into social security, up to a maximum of $30 per year. This amount has increased over the years until an employee in 1996 paid 6.2% of income to FICA and 1.45% to medicare which together can total $4,800 or more per year.

For many years both the social security tax rate and the medicare tax rate were combined, however since 1991 these tax rates have been expressed individually. Table 5.2 shows the tax rates and the maximum earnings on which social security and medicare taxes are paid by the employee. The employer pays the same rate as the employee matching dollar for dollar all employee contributions. Self-employed people pay double the rate paid by those who are employees.

Congress sets the tax rates and the maximum employee earnings subject to both social security tax and medicare tax. Because these tax rates change, we will use

TABLE 5.2  **Maximum Earnings on Which Social Security and Medicare Taxes Are Paid**

| | Social Security Tax | | Medicare Tax | |
|---|---|---|---|---|
| **Year** | **Social Security Tax Rate** | **Employee Earnings Subject to the Tax** | **Medicare Tax Rate** | **Employee Earnings Subject to the Tax** |
| 1991 | 6.2% | $53,400 | 1.45% | $125,000 |
| 1992 | 6.2% | $55,500 | 1.45% | $130,200 |
| 1993 | 6.2% | $57,600 | 1.45% | $135,000 |
| 1994 | 6.2% | $59,600 | 1.45% | all |
| 1995 | 6.2% | $61,200 | 1.45% | all |
| 1996 | 6.2% | $62,700 | 1.45% | all |
| 1997 | 6.2% | $65,400 | 1.45% | all |
| ⋮ | ⋮ | ⋮ | ⋮ | ⋮ |

Form Approved
OMB No. 0960-0466 [ ] SP

**Request for Earnings and Benefit Estimate Statement**

[ ] Please check this box if you want to get your statement in Spanish instead of English.

Please print or type your answers. When you have completed the form, fold it and mail it to us.

1. Name shown on your Social Security card:

First Name ______ Middle Initial ______

Last Name Only ______

2. Your Social Security number as shown on your card:

☐☐☐-☐☐-☐☐☐☐

3. Your date of birth ______ Month ______ Day ______ Year

4. Other Social Security numbers you have used:

☐☐☐-☐☐-☐☐☐☐

☐☐☐-☐☐-☐☐☐☐

5. Your sex: [ ] Male [ ] Female

6. Other names you have used *(including a maiden name)*:

______

______

**For items 7 and 9 show only earnings covered by Social Security.** Do NOT include wages from State, local or Federal Government employment that are NOT covered for Social Security or that are covered ONLY by Medicare.

7. Show your actual earnings (wages and/or net self-employment income) for last year and your estimated earnings for this year.

A. Last year's actual earnings: *(Dollars Only)*

$ ☐☐☐,☐☐☐.00

B. This year's estimated earnings: *(Dollars Only)*

$ ☐☐☐,☐☐☐.00

8. Show the age at which you plan to stop working.

☐☐ *(Show only one age)*

9. Below, show the average yearly amount (not your total future lifetime earnings) that you think you will earn between now and when you plan to stop working. Include cost-of-living, performance or scheduled pay increases or bonuses.

If you expect to earn significantly more or less in the future due to promotions, job changes, part-time work, or an absence from the work force, enter the amount that most closely reflects your future average yearly earnings.

**If you don't expect any significant changes, show the same amount you are earning now (the amount in 7B).**

Future average yearly earnings: *(Dollars Only)*

$ ☐☐☐,☐☐☐.00

10. Address where you want us to send the statement.

Name ______

Street Address (Include Apt. No., P.O. Box, or Rural Route) ______

City ______ State ______ Zip Code ______

**Notice:**
I am asking for information about my own Social Security record or the record of a person I am authorized to represent. I understand that when requesting information on a deceased person, I must include proof of death and relationship or appointment. I further understand that if I deliberately request information under false pretenses, I may be guilty of a Federal crime and could be fined and/or imprisoned. I authorize you to use a contractor to send the statement of earnings and benefit estimates to the person named in item 10.

**Please sign your name (Do Not Print)**

Date ______ (Area Code) Daytime Telephone No. ______

Form SSA-7004-SM(4-95) Destroy prior editions

Printed on recycled paper

FIGURE 5.2

6.5% of the first \$66,000 that the employee earns in a year for social security tax. For medicare tax, we will use 1.5% of everything that the employee earns in a year. These figures are used in all examples and exercises in this chapter.

Each employee whether a citizen or not must have a social security card. Most post offices have application forms for the cards. All money set aside for an individual is credited to his or her account according to the social security number. Mistakes are rare, but they do occur. For this reason, every employee should submit a **Request for Earnings and Benefit Estimate Statement** every 2 years or so, by filling out a form like the one in Figure 5.2. There is a limit of about 3 years, after which errors may not be corrected. To obtain one of the forms and other information about social security you may phone (800) 772-1213.

**OBJECTIVE 2** ***Find the maximum FICA tax paid by an employee in one year.*** Remember that social security tax is paid on only the first \$66,000 of gross earnings in our examples. An employee earning \$66,000 during the first 10 months of a year would pay no more social security tax on additional earnings that year. The maximum social security tax to be paid by an employee is $\$66,000 \times 6.5\% = \$66,000 \times 0.065 = \$4,290$.

NOTE  Only 7% of income earners are affected by the social security maximum.  ■

OBJECTIVE **3** *Understand medicare tax.*    Medicare tax is paid on all earnings in our examples. The total earnings are multiplied by 1.5%.

OBJECTIVE **4** *Find FICA tax and medicare tax.*    When finding the amounts to be withheld for social security tax and medicare tax, the employer must use the current rates.

EXAMPLE 1 **Finding FICA Tax and Medicare Tax**

Find the social security tax and the medicare tax for the following gross earnings.

**(a)** Hurwitz; $342.16     **(b)** Christofferson; $418.28

SOLUTION

**(a)** The social security tax is found by multiplying gross earnings by 6.5%.

$$\$342.16 \times 6.5\% = \$342.16 \times 0.065 = \$22.24 \text{ (rounded)}$$

Medicare tax is found by multiplying gross earnings by 1.5%.

$$\$342.16 \times 1.5\% = \$342.16 \times 0.015 = \$5.13 \text{ (rounded)}$$

**(b)** Social security tax is

$$\$418.28 \times 6.5\% = \$418.28 \times 0.065 = \$27.19 \text{ (rounded)}.$$

Medicare tax is

$$\$418.28 \times 1.5\% = \$418.28 \times 0.015 = \$6.27 \text{ (rounded)}.$$  ■

EXAMPLE 2 **Finding FICA Tax**

Cindy Herring has earned $62,791.08 so far this year. Her gross earnings for the current pay period are $4,842.08. Find her social security tax.

SOLUTION   Social security tax is paid on only the first $66,000 earned in a year. Herring has already earned $62,791.08. Subtract $62,791.08 from $66,000, to find that she has to pay social security tax on only $3,208.92 of her earnings for the rest of the year.

|  |  |
|---|---|
| $66,000.00 | maximum earnings subject to tax |
| − $62,791.08 | earnings to date |
| $3,208.92 | earnings on which tax is due |

The social security tax on $3,208.92 is $208.58 ($3,208.92 × 6.5%). Therefore, Herring pays $208.58 for the current pay period and no additional social security tax for the rest of the year.  ■

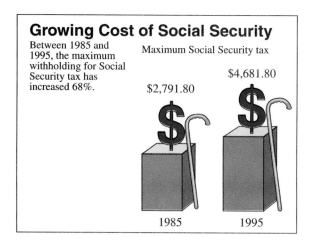

**Growing Cost of Social Security**

Between 1985 and 1995, the maximum withholding for Social Security tax has increased 68%.

Maximum Social Security tax

$2,791.80     $4,681.80

1985     1995

*Source:* USA TODAY research.

The graph above shows how the maximum social security tax amount has grown since 1985. Recall that the maximum amount paid by any employee from 1937 through 1950 was $30 in any one year.

**OBJECTIVE 5** *Determine the FICA tax and the medicare tax paid by a self-employed person.* People who are self-employed pay higher social security tax and higher medicare tax than people who work for others. There is no employer to match the employee contribution so the self-employed person pays a rate that is double that of the employee. In our examples the self-employed person pays 13% (6.5% × 2) of gross earnings for social security tax and 3% (1.5% × 2) of gross earnings for medicare tax.

**EXAMPLE 3** *Finding FICA and Medicare Tax for the Self-Employed*

Find the social security tax and the medicare tax paid by Lino Torres, a self-employed gardener, who earned $20,680 this year.

**SOLUTION**     Social security tax = $20,680 × 13% = $20,680 × 0.13
                    = $2,688.40

            Medicare tax = $20,680 × 3% = $20,680 × 0.03
                    = $620.40     ∎

**NOTE** All employers and those who are self-employed should use the current tax rates for both social security and medicare. These can always be found in **Circular E, Employee's Tax Guide** which is available from the Internal Revenue Service. ∎

**OBJECTIVE 6** *Find state disability insurance deductions.* Many states have a state disability insurance program that is paid for by employees. If disabled, the employee would receive weekly benefits. A typical state program defines "disability" as "any illness or injury incurred on or off the job, either physical or mental, including pregnancy, childbirth or related condition, that prevents you from doing your regular work.'' The employee processes the claim after obtaining certification from a doctor or other qualified examiner. Weekly disability benefits are determined by the highest quarter's earnings within the past year of employment.

A typical state program also requires the qualifying employee to pay an **SDI (state disability insurance) deduction** of 1% of the first $31,800 earned each year. There are no payments on earnings above this amount. Some states have similar programs, but their insurance is placed with private insurance companies rather than with the state.

### EXAMPLE 4  *Finding State Disability Insurance Deductions*

Find the state disability deduction for an employee at Comet Auto Parts with gross earnings of $418 this pay period. The SDI rate is 1%, and the employee has not earned $31,800 this year.

**SOLUTION**    The state disability deduction is $4.18 ($418 × 1%).    ∎

### EXAMPLE 5  *Finding State Disability Insurance Deductions*

Milo Lacy has earned $30,620 so far this year. Find the SDI deduction if gross earnings this pay period are $3,096. Use an SDI rate of 1% on the first $31,800.

**SOLUTION**    The SDI deduction will be taken on $1,180 of the current gross earnings.

$$\begin{array}{r} \$31,800 \\ - \ \$30,620 \\ \hline \$ \ \ 1,180 \end{array}$$    earnings this year subject to SDI

The SDI deduction is $11.80 ($1,180 × 1%).    ∎

**NOTE**    Always be aware of the current rates and the maximum annual earning amounts against which FICA, Medicare, and SDI payroll deductions may be taken. Those involved in payroll work must always be up to date on federal and state laws and practices.    ∎

## 5.4  EXERCISES

*Find the social security tax and the medicare tax for each of the following amounts of gross earnings. Assume a 6.5% FICA rate and a 1.5% medicare tax rate.*

1. $215.82
2. $305.48
3. $840.77
4. $458.21
5. $368.51
6. $533.47
7. $916.23
8. $675.71

*Find the social security tax for each of the following employees for the current pay period. Assume a 6.5% FICA rate up to a maximum of $66,000.*

| Employee | Gross Earnings this Year (so far) | Earnings Current Pay Period |
|---|---|---|
| 9.  Copley, T. | $63,871.24 | $3,218.36 |
| 10.  Andrews, R. | $64,818.93 | $2,700.00 |
| 11.  Crowe, V. | $61,721.59 | $5,780.00 |
| 12.  Horwitz, D. | $64,018.67 | $2,162.34 |
| 13.  Odjakjian, G. | $65,819.75 | $516.92 |
| 14.  Beckenstein, J. | $63,992.06 | $3,273.81 |

*Find the regular earnings, overtime earnings, gross earnings, social security tax, medicare tax, and state disability insurance deduction for each of the following employees. Assume time and a half is paid for any hours over a 40-hour week. Assume a 6.5% FICA rate, a 1.5% medicare rate, a state disability rate of 1% and that no one has earned more than the FICA or SDI maximum at the end of the current pay period.*

| Employee | Hours Worked | Regular Rate |
|---|---|---|
| 15.  Levinson, H. | 45.5 | $9.22 |
| 16.  Clouse, R. | 47.75 | $7.52 |
| 17.  McCarthy, K. | 44 | $10.30 |
| 18.  Escabl, R. | 45 | $6.58 |
| 19.  Cavaliere, C. | 45 | $5.10 |
| 20.  Taggart, G. | 47 | $11.68 |
| 21.  Yates, D. | 46.75 | $6.24 |
| 22.  Bartelson, A. | 48.25 | $7.40 |

*Solve each of the following application problems. Assume that the FICA rate is 6.5%, the medicare rate is 1.5%, the SDI rate is 1%, and earnings will not exceed $31,800.*

23. Kaci Salmon worked 43.5 hours last week at Circuit City. She is paid $8.58 per hour, plus time and a half for overtime. Find her (a) social security tax and (b) medicare tax for the week.

24. Erik Dolison receives 7% commission on all sales. His sales on Monday of last week were $1,412.20, with $1,928.42 on Tuesday, $598.14 on Wednesday, $1,051.12 on Thursday, and $958.72 on Friday. Find his (a) social security tax and (b) medicare tax for the week.

25. Lisa Wunderle is paid an 8% commission on sales. During a recent pay period, she had sales of $19,482 and returns and allowances of $193. Find the amount of her (a) social security tax, (b) medicare tax, and (c) state disability for this pay period.

**26.** Mr. Lupe De La Torre is a salesperson for a Hong Kong manufacturer of sporting goods and is paid $350 per week plus a commission of 2% on sales. His sales last week were $17,240. Find the amount of (a) his social security tax, (b) his medicare tax, and (c) his state disability for the pay period.

*The following problems refer to self-employed individuals. These people pay social security tax of 13% and medicare tax of 3%. Find the taxes on each of the following gross incomes.*

**27.** Lanisha Easter, owner of a music store, earned $30,786.34

**28.** Kara Shimizu, interior decorator, earned $18,226.52

**29.** Shannon Farrell, accountant, earned $34,817.16

**30.** Ken Albers, surveyor, earned $48,007.14

**31.** Grace Yates, shop owner, earned $23,384.50

**32.** Janet Kellen, commission salesperson, earned $52,748.32

**33.** A young person who has just received her first pay check is puzzled by the amounts that have been deducted from gross earnings. Briefly explain both the FICA and medicare deductions to this person. (See Objectives 1–4.)

**34.** Describe the difference between the FICA paid by an employee and that paid by a self-employed person. Why does this difference exist? (See Objective 5.)

## 5.5   Income Tax Withholding

### OBJECTIVES

**1**   *Understand the Employee's Withholding Allowance Certificate (Form W-4).*

**2**   *Find the federal withholding tax from tables.*

**3**   *Find the federal tax using the percentage method.*

**4**   *Find the state withholding tax from tables.*

**5**   *Find net pay when given gross wages, taxes, and other deductions.*

The **personal income tax** is the largest single source of money for the federal government. The law requires that the bulk of this tax owed by an individual be paid periodically, as the income is earned. For this reason, employers must deduct money from the gross earnings of almost every employee. These deductions, called **income tax withholdings**, are sent periodically to the Internal Revenue Service and credited to the accounts of the employees. The amount of money withheld depends on the employee's marital status, the number of withholding allowances claimed, and the amount of gross earnings.

***Marital Status.***   Generally, the withholding tax for a married person is less than the withholding tax for a single person making the same income.

**OBJECTIVE 1** ***Understand the Employees Withholding Allowance Certificate (Form W-4).***

Form **W-4**
Department of the Treasury
Internal Revenue Service

**Employee's Withholding Allowance Certificate**

▶ **For Privacy Act and Paperwork Reduction Act Notice, see reverse.**

OMB No. 1545-0010

1 Type or print your first name and middle initial | Last name | 2 Your social security number

Home address (number and street or rural route) | 3 ☐ Single ☐ Married ☐ Married, but withhold at higher Single rate.
**Note:** *If married, but legally separated, or spouse is a nonresident alien, check the Single box.*

City or town, state, and ZIP code | 4 If your last name differs from that on your social security card, check here and call 1-800-772-1213 for a new card . . . . . ▶ ☐

5 Total number of allowances you are claiming (from line G above or from the worksheets on page 2 if they apply) . | 5

6 Additional amount, if any, you want withheld from each paycheck . . . . . . . . . . . . . . . | 6 $

7 I claim exemption from withholding for 1996 and I certify that I meet **BOTH** of the following conditions for exemption:
- Last year I had a right to a refund of **ALL** Federal income tax withheld because I had **NO** tax liability; **AND**
- This year I expect a refund of **ALL** Federal income tax withheld because I expect to have **NO** tax liability.

If you meet both conditions, enter "EXEMPT" here . . . . . . . . . . . . . . . ▶ | 7

Under penalties of perjury, I certify that I am entitled to the number of withholding allowances claimed on this certificate or entitled to claim exempt status.

**Employee's signature** ▶ **Date** ▶ , 19

8 Employer's name and address (Employer: Complete 8 and 10 only if sending to the IRS) | 9 Office code (optional) | 10 Employer identification number

Cat. No. 10220Q

FIGURE 5.3

***The Number of Withholding Allowances Claimed by the Employee.*** Each employee must file with the employer a W-4 form as shown in Figure 5.3. On this form the employee states the number of withholding allowances being claimed along with additional information, so that the employer can withhold the proper amount for income tax.

A W-4 form is usually completed at the time of employment. A married person with three children will normally claim five allowances (one each for the employee and spouse, plus one for each child). However, when both spouses are employed, each may claim himself or herself. The number of allowances may be raised if an employee has been receiving a refund of withholding taxes, or the number may be lowered if the employee has had a balance due in previous tax years. The W-4 form has instructions to help determine the proper number of allowances. Some people enjoy receiving a tax refund when filing their income tax return, so they claim fewer allowances, having more withheld from each check. Other individuals would rather receive more of their income each pay period, so they claim the maximum number of allowances to which they are entitled. The exact number of allowances *must* be claimed when the income tax return is filed.

**OBJECTIVE 2** ***Find the federal withholding tax from tables.*** The withholding tax is found on the basis of the gross earnings per pay period. Income tax withholding is applied to all earnings, unlike social security tax. Generally, the higher a person's gross earnings, the more withholding tax is paid.

There are two methods that employers use to determine the amount of federal

## SINGLE Persons—WEEKLY Payroll Period

| If the wages are— | | And the number of withholding allowances claimed is— | | | | | | | | | | |
|---|---|---|---|---|---|---|---|---|---|---|---|---|
| At least | But less than | 0 | 1 | 2 | 3 | 4 | 5 | 6 | 7 | 8 | 9 | 10 |
| | | The amount of income tax to be withheld is— | | | | | | | | | | |
| 300 | 310 | 38 | 31 | 24 | 17 | 9 | 2 | 0 | 0 | 0 | 0 | 0 |
| 310 | 320 | 40 | 33 | 25 | 18 | 11 | 4 | 0 | 0 | 0 | 0 | 0 |
| 320 | 330 | 41 | 34 | 27 | 20 | 12 | 5 | 0 | 0 | 0 | 0 | 0 |
| 330 | 340 | 43 | 36 | 28 | 21 | 14 | 7 | 0 | 0 | 0 | 0 | 0 |
| 340 | 350 | 44 | 37 | 30 | 23 | 15 | 8 | 1 | 0 | 0 | 0 | 0 |
| 350 | 360 | 46 | 39 | 31 | 24 | 17 | 10 | 2 | 0 | 0 | 0 | 0 |
| 360 | 370 | 47 | 40 | 33 | 26 | 18 | 11 | 4 | 0 | 0 | 0 | 0 |
| 370 | 380 | 49 | 42 | 34 | 27 | 20 | 13 | 5 | 0 | 0 | 0 | 0 |
| 380 | 390 | 50 | 43 | 36 | 29 | 21 | 14 | 7 | 0 | 0 | 0 | 0 |
| 390 | 400 | 52 | 45 | 37 | 30 | 23 | 16 | 8 | 1 | 0 | 0 | 0 |
| 400 | 410 | 53 | 46 | 39 | 32 | 24 | 17 | 10 | 3 | 0 | 0 | 0 |
| 410 | 420 | 55 | 48 | 40 | 33 | 26 | 19 | 11 | 4 | 0 | 0 | 0 |
| 420 | 430 | 56 | 49 | 42 | 35 | 27 | 20 | 13 | 6 | 0 | 0 | 0 |
| 430 | 440 | 58 | 51 | 43 | 36 | 29 | 22 | 14 | 7 | 0 | 0 | 0 |
| 440 | 450 | 59 | 52 | 45 | 38 | 30 | 23 | 16 | 9 | 2 | 0 | 0 |
| 450 | 460 | 61 | 54 | 46 | 39 | 32 | 25 | 17 | 10 | 3 | 0 | 0 |
| 460 | 470 | 62 | 55 | 48 | 41 | 33 | 26 | 19 | 12 | 5 | 0 | 0 |
| 470 | 480 | 64 | 57 | 49 | 42 | 35 | 28 | 20 | 13 | 6 | 0 | 0 |
| 480 | 490 | 66 | 58 | 51 | 44 | 36 | 29 | 22 | 15 | 8 | 0 | 0 |
| 490 | 500 | 69 | 60 | 52 | 45 | 38 | 31 | 23 | 16 | 9 | 2 | 0 |
| 500 | 510 | 72 | 61 | 54 | 47 | 39 | 32 | 25 | 18 | 11 | 3 | 0 |
| 510 | 520 | 75 | 63 | 55 | 48 | 41 | 34 | 26 | 19 | 12 | 5 | 0 |
| 520 | 530 | 78 | 64 | 57 | 50 | 42 | 35 | 28 | 21 | 14 | 6 | 0 |
| 530 | 540 | 80 | 67 | 58 | 51 | 44 | 37 | 29 | 22 | 15 | 8 | 1 |
| 540 | 550 | 83 | 70 | 60 | 53 | 45 | 38 | 31 | 24 | 17 | 9 | 2 |
| 550 | 560 | 86 | 73 | 61 | 54 | 47 | 40 | 32 | 25 | 18 | 11 | 4 |
| 560 | 570 | 89 | 75 | 63 | 56 | 48 | 41 | 34 | 27 | 20 | 12 | 5 |
| 570 | 580 | 92 | 78 | 65 | 57 | 50 | 43 | 35 | 28 | 21 | 14 | 7 |
| 580 | 590 | 94 | 81 | 68 | 59 | 51 | 44 | 37 | 30 | 23 | 15 | 8 |
| 590 | 600 | 97 | 84 | 70 | 60 | 53 | 46 | 38 | 31 | 24 | 17 | 10 |

FIGURE 5.4

withholding tax to deduct from paychecks: the **wage bracket method** and the **percentage method**.

The Internal Revenue Service supplies withholding tax tables to be used with the wage bracket method. These tables are extensive and cover weekly, biweekly, monthly, and daily pay periods. Figures 5.4 and 5.5 show samples of the withholding tables. Figure 5.4 is for single persons paid weekly, and Figure 5.5 is for married persons paid monthly. Methods of using these tables are shown in the following examples.

**EXAMPLE 1** *Finding Federal Withholding Using the Wage Bracket Method*

Kathi Callahan is single and claims no withholding allowances. (Some employees do this to receive a refund from the government or to avoid owing taxes at the end of the year. The proper number will be used when filing her income tax return.) Use the wage bracket method to find her withholding tax if her weekly gross earnings are $553.75.

**SOLUTION**    Use the table in Figure 5.4 for single persons–weekly payroll period. The given earnings are found in the row "at least $550 but less than $560." Go across this row to the column headed "0" (for no withholding allowances). From the table, the withholding is $86.    ∎

## MARRIED Persons—MONTHLY Payroll Period

| If the wages are— | | And the number of withholding allowances claimed is— | | | | | | | | | | |
|---|---|---|---|---|---|---|---|---|---|---|---|---|
| At least | But less than | 0 | 1 | 2 | 3 | 4 | 5 | 6 | 7 | 8 | 9 | 10 |
| | | The amount of income tax to be withheld is— | | | | | | | | | | |
| 1,440 | 1,480 | 133 | 102 | 71 | 39 | 8 | 0 | 0 | 0 | 0 | 0 | 0 |
| 1,480 | 1,520 | 139 | 108 | 77 | 45 | 14 | 0 | 0 | 0 | 0 | 0 | 0 |
| 1,520 | 1,560 | 145 | 114 | 83 | 51 | 20 | 0 | 0 | 0 | 0 | 0 | 0 |
| 1,560 | 1,600 | 151 | 120 | 89 | 57 | 26 | 0 | 0 | 0 | 0 | 0 | 0 |
| 1,600 | 1,640 | 157 | 126 | 95 | 63 | 32 | 1 | 0 | 0 | 0 | 0 | 0 |
| 1,640 | 1,680 | 163 | 132 | 101 | 69 | 38 | 7 | 0 | 0 | 0 | 0 | 0 |
| 1,680 | 1,720 | 169 | 138 | 107 | 75 | 44 | 13 | 0 | 0 | 0 | 0 | 0 |
| 1,720 | 1,760 | 175 | 144 | 113 | 81 | 50 | 19 | 0 | 0 | 0 | 0 | 0 |
| 1,760 | 1,800 | 181 | 150 | 119 | 87 | 56 | 25 | 0 | 0 | 0 | 0 | 0 |
| 1,800 | 1,840 | 187 | 156 | 125 | 93 | 62 | 31 | 0 | 0 | 0 | 0 | 0 |
| 1,840 | 1,880 | 193 | 162 | 131 | 99 | 68 | 37 | 6 | 0 | 0 | 0 | 0 |
| 1,880 | 1,920 | 199 | 168 | 137 | 105 | 74 | 43 | 12 | 0 | 0 | 0 | 0 |
| 1,920 | 1,960 | 205 | 174 | 143 | 111 | 80 | 49 | 18 | 0 | 0 | 0 | 0 |
| 1,960 | 2,000 | 211 | 180 | 149 | 117 | 86 | 55 | 24 | 0 | 0 | 0 | 0 |
| 2,000 | 2,040 | 217 | 186 | 155 | 123 | 92 | 61 | 30 | 0 | 0 | 0 | 0 |
| 2,040 | 2,080 | 223 | 192 | 161 | 129 | 98 | 67 | 36 | 4 | 0 | 0 | 0 |
| 2,080 | 2,120 | 229 | 198 | 167 | 135 | 104 | 73 | 42 | 10 | 0 | 0 | 0 |
| 2,120 | 2,160 | 235 | 204 | 173 | 141 | 110 | 79 | 48 | 16 | 0 | 0 | 0 |
| 2,160 | 2,200 | 241 | 210 | 179 | 147 | 116 | 85 | 54 | 22 | 0 | 0 | 0 |
| 2,200 | 2,240 | 247 | 216 | 185 | 153 | 122 | 91 | 60 | 28 | 0 | 0 | 0 |
| 2,240 | 2,280 | 253 | 222 | 191 | 159 | 128 | 97 | 66 | 34 | 3 | 0 | 0 |
| 2,280 | 2,320 | 259 | 228 | 197 | 165 | 134 | 103 | 72 | 40 | 9 | 0 | 0 |
| 2,320 | 2,360 | 265 | 234 | 203 | 171 | 140 | 109 | 78 | 46 | 15 | 0 | 0 |
| 2,360 | 2,400 | 271 | 240 | 209 | 177 | 146 | 115 | 84 | 52 | 21 | 0 | 0 |
| 2,400 | 2,440 | 277 | 246 | 215 | 183 | 152 | 121 | 90 | 58 | 27 | 0 | 0 |
| 2,440 | 2,480 | 283 | 252 | 221 | 189 | 158 | 127 | 96 | 64 | 33 | 2 | 0 |
| 2,480 | 2,520 | 289 | 258 | 227 | 195 | 164 | 133 | 102 | 70 | 39 | 8 | 0 |
| 2,520 | 2,560 | 295 | 264 | 233 | 201 | 170 | 139 | 108 | 76 | 45 | 14 | 0 |
| 2,560 | 2,600 | 301 | 270 | 239 | 207 | 176 | 145 | 114 | 82 | 51 | 20 | 0 |

FIGURE 5.5

| EXAMPLE 2   *Using the Wage Bracket Method for Federal Withholding*

Richard Gonsalves is married, claims three withholding allowances, and has monthly gross earnings of $2,354.18. Find his withholding tax using the wage bracket method.

SOLUTION   Use the table in Figure 5.5 for Married Persons-Monthly Payroll Period. Look down the two left columns, and find the range that includes Gonsalves' gross earnings: "at least $2,320 but less than $2,360." Read across the table to the column headed "3" (for the three withholding allowances). The withholding tax is $177. Had Gonsalves claimed six withholding allowances, his withholding tax would have been only $84.   ∎

OBJECTIVE **3** *Find the federal tax using the percentage method.*   Many companies today prefer to use the *percentage method* to determine federal withholding tax. The percentage method does not require the several pages of tables needed with the wage bracket method and is more easily adapted to computer applications in the processing of payrolls. Instead, the table shown in Figure 5.6 is used.

| Payroll Period | One withholding allowance |
|---|---|
| Weekly ........................................................... | $48.08 |
| Biweekly ........................................................ | 96.16 |
| Semimonthly ................................................. | 104.17 |
| Monthly ........................................................ | 208.33 |
| Quarterly ...................................................... | 625.00 |
| Semiannually ............................................... | 1,250.00 |
| Annually ....................................................... | 2,500.00 |
| Daily or miscellaneous (each day of the payroll period) ........................................ | 9.62 |

## Tables for Percentage Method of Withholding

### TABLE 1—WEEKLY Payroll Period

**(a) SINGLE person** (including head of household)—

If the amount of wages (after subtracting withholding allowances) is:  The amount of income tax to withhold is:

Not over $50 . . . . .  $0

| Over— | But not over— | | of excess over— |
|---|---|---|---|
| $50 | —$476 . . . | 15% | —$50 |
| $476 | —$999 . . . | $63.90 plus 28% | —$476 |
| $999 | —$2,295 . . . | $210.34 plus 31% | —$999 |
| $2,295 | —$4,960 . . . | $612.10 plus 36% | —$2,295 |
| $4,960 . | . . . . . | $1,571.50 plus 39.6% | —$4,960 |

**(b) MARRIED person—**

If the amount of wages (after subtracting withholding allowances) is:  The amount of income tax to withhold is:

Not over $123 . . . . .  $0

| Over— | But not over— | | of excess over— |
|---|---|---|---|
| $123 | —$828 . . . | 15% | —$123 |
| $828 | —$1,664 . . . | $105.75 plus 28% | —$828 |
| $1,664 | —$2,839 . . . | $339.83 plus 31% | —$1,664 |
| $2,839 | —$5,011 . . . | $704.08 plus 36% | —$2,839 |
| $5,011 | . . . . . | $1,486.00 plus 39.6% | —$5,011 |

### TABLE 2—BIWEEKLY Payroll Period

**(a) SINGLE person** (including head of household)—

If the amount of wages (after subtracting withholding allowances) is:  The amount of income tax to withhold is:

Not over $100 . . . . .  $0

| Over— | But not over— | | of excess over— |
|---|---|---|---|
| $100 | —$952 . . . | 15% | —$100 |
| $952 | —$1,998 . . | $127.80 plus 28% | —$952 |
| $1,998 | —$4,590 . . . | $420.68 plus 31% | —$1,998 |
| $4,590 | —$9,919 . . . | $1,224.20 plus 36% | —$4,590 |
| $9,919 . | . . . . . | $3,142.64 plus 39.6% | —$9,919 |

**(b) MARRIED person—**

If the amount of wages (after subtracting withholding allowances) is:  The amount of income tax to withhold is:

Not over $246 . . . . .  $0

| Over— | But not over— | | of excess over— |
|---|---|---|---|
| $246 | —$1,656 . . . | 15% | —$246 |
| $1,656 | —$3,329 . . . | $211.50 plus 28% | —$1,656 |
| $3,329 | —$5,679 . . . | $679.94 plus 28% | —$3,329 |
| $5,679 | —$10,021 . . . | $1,408.44 plus 36% | —$5,679 |
| $10,021 . | . . . . . | $2,971.56 plus 39.6% | —$10,021 |

### TABLE 3—SEMIMONTHLY Payroll Period

**(a) SINGLE person** (including head of household)—

If the amount of wages (after subtracting withholding allowances) is:  The amount of income tax to withhold is:

Not over $108 . . . . .  $0

| Over— | But not over— | | of excess over— |
|---|---|---|---|
| $108 | —$1,031 . . | 15% | —$108 |
| $1,031 | —$2,165 . . | $138.45 plus 28% | —$1,031 |
| $2,165 | —$4,973 . . | $455.97 plus 31% | —$2,165 |
| $4,973 | —$10,746 . . | $1,326.45 plus 36% | —$4,973 |
| $10,746 | . . . . . | $3,404.73 plus 39.6% | —$10,746 |

**(b) MARRIED person—**

If the amount of wages (after subtracting withholding allowances) is:  The amount of income tax to withhold is:

Not over $267 . . . . .  $0

| Over— | But not over— | | of excess over— |
|---|---|---|---|
| $267 | —$1,794 . . . | 15% | —$267 |
| $1,794 | —$3,606 . . . | $229.05 plus 28% | —$1,794 |
| $3,606 | —$6,152 . . . | $736.41 plus 31% | —$3,606 |
| $6,152 | —$10,856 . . | $1,525.67 plus 36% | —$6,152 |
| $10,856 . | . . . . . | $3,219.11 plus 39.6% | —$10,856 |

### TABLE 4—MONTHLY Payroll Period

**(a) SINGLE person** (including head of household)—

If the amount of wages (after subtracting withholding allowances) is:  The amount of income tax to withhold is:

Not over $217 . . . . .  $0

| Over— | But not over— | | of excess over— |
|---|---|---|---|
| $217 | —$2,063 . . | 15% | —$217 |
| $2,063 | —$4,329 . . | $276.90 plus 28% | —$2,063 |
| $4,329 | —$9,946 . . | $911.38 plus 31% | —$4,329 |
| $9,946 | —$21,492 . . | $2,652.65 plus 36% | —$9,946 |
| $21,492 | . . . . . | $6,809.21 plus 39.6% | —$21,492 |

**(b) MARRIED person—**

If the amount of wages (after subtracting withholding allowances) is:  The amount of income tax to withhold is:

Not over $533 . . . . .  $0

| Over— | But not over— | | of excess over— |
|---|---|---|---|
| $533 | —$3,588 . . . | 15% | —$533 |
| $3,588 | —$7,213 . . . | $458.25 plus 28% | —$3,588 |
| $7,213 | —$12,304 . . | $1,473.25 plus 31% | —$7,213 |
| $12,304 | —$21,713 . . | $3,051.46 plus 36% | —$12,304 |
| $21,713 . | . . . . . | $6,438.70 plus 39.6% | —$21,713 |

FIGURE 5.6

## EXAMPLE 3 *Finding Federal Withholding Using the Percentage Method*

Jamal Story is married, claims four withholding allowances, and has weekly gross earnings of $1,080. Use the percentage method to find his withholding tax.

### SOLUTION

**Step 1**   Find the withholding allowance for *one* on the weekly payroll period in Figure 5.6. The amount is $48.08. Since Story claims four allowances, multiply the one withholding allowance $48.08, by his number of withholding allowances (4).

$$\$48.08 \times 4 = \$192.32$$

**Step 2**   Subtract the amount in step 1 from gross earnings.

$$\$1,080 - \$192.32 = \$887.68$$

**Step 3**   Find the "married person weekly" section of the percentage method withholding table. Since $887.68 is over $828 but not over $1,664, an amount of $105.75 is added to 28% of the excess over $828.

$$\$887.68 - \$828 = \$59.68 \text{ (excess over \$828)}$$

$$\$59.68 \times 28\% = \$59.68 \times 0.28 = \$16.71$$

$$\$105.75 + \$16.71 = \$122.46 \text{ withholding tax} \qquad \blacksquare$$

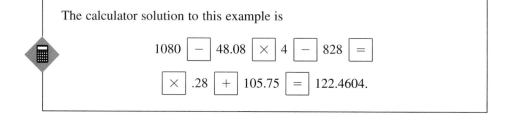

CALCULATOR APPROACH TO EXAMPLE 3

The calculator solution to this example is

1080 − 48.08 × 4 − 828 =

× .28 + 105.75 = 122.4604.

**NOTE**   The amount of withholding tax found using the wage bracket method can vary slightly from the amount of withholding tax found using the percentage method. Any differences would be eliminated when the income tax return is filed.   ■

**OBJECTIVE 4** *Find the state withholding tax from tables.*   Many states and some cities also have an income tax or **state withholding** tax collected by withholding from the gross earnings of the employee. The state or city supplies tables similar to the one in Figure 5.7.

## EXAMPLE 4 *Finding State Withholding Tax*

Adam Strong is single and has weekly gross earnings of $418.50. Find his state withholding tax.

```
                    STATE WITHHOLDING SCHEDULE
                      WEEKLY PAYROLL PERIOD
               ==================================

         SINGLE PERSONS                         MARRIED PERSONS

   IF THE TAXABLE      THE COMPUTED        IF THE TAXABLE      THE COMPUTED
     INCOME IS...        TAX IS...           INCOME IS...        TAX IS...
  ---------------   ---------------      ---------------   ---------------
  OVER    BUT NOT   AMOUNT    MINUS      OVER    BUT NOT   AMOUNT    MINUS
            OVER    TIMES                          OVER    TIMES
    0       65...   1%  -      .00         0      130...   1%  -      .00
   65      113...   2%  -      .65       130      227...   2%  -     1.30
  113      162...   3%  -     1.77       227      324...   3%  -     3.57
  162      211...   4%  -     3.41       324      422...   4%  -     6.81
  211      260...   5%  -     5.51       422      520...   5%  -    11.02
  260      309...   6%  -     8.12       520      618...   6%  -    16.23
  309      357...   7%  -    11.21       618      714...   7%  -    22.43
  357      406...   8%  -    14.77       714      812...   8%  -    29.53
  406      455...   9%  -    18.84       812      909...   9%  -    37.68
  455      503...  10%  -    23.42       909    1,007...  10%  -    46.74
  503  AND  OVER   11%  -    28.38     1,007  AND  OVER   11%  -    56.88
```

FIGURE 5.7

**Solution**    Use the left-hand table of Figure 5.7 for single persons. Earnings of $418.50 are found in the row "over 406 but not over 455." The withholding can be found by multiplying 9% by the amount of earnings and then subtracting $18.84.

$$9\% \times \$418.50 = 0.09 \times \$418.50 = \$37.67 \text{ (rounded)}$$

$$\$37.67 - \$18.84 = \$18.83 \text{ state withholding tax}$$    ■

**OBJECTIVE 5** *Find net pay when given gross wages, taxes, and other deductions.*    It is common for employees to request additional deductions, such as union dues and credit union payments. The final amount of pay received by the employee, called the **net pay**, is given by the formula

> Net pay = Gross earnings − FICA tax (social security) − Medicare tax − Federal withholding tax − State withholding tax − Other deductions

**EXAMPLE 5** *Determining Net Pay After Deductions*

Beth Kaufman is married and claims three withholding allowances. Her weekly gross earnings are $489.64. Her union dues are $20. Find her net pay using the percentage method.

**SOLUTION**    First find FICA (social security) tax, which is $31.83, then medicare, $7.34. Federal withholding tax is $33.36 and state withholding is $13.46. Total deductions are

| | |
|---:|---|
| $31.83 | FICA tax (6.5%) |
| $7.34 | medicare tax (1.5%) |
| $33.36 | federal withholding |
| $13.46 | state withholding |
| + $20.00 | union dues |
| $105.99 | total deductions |

Find net pay by subtracting total deductions from gross earnings.

| | |
|---:|---|
| $489.64 | gross earnings |
| − $105.99 | total deductions |
| $383.65 | net pay |

Kaufman will receive a check for $383.65.    ∎

An employee's contribution to social security and medicare must be matched by the employer.

## 5.5  EXERCISES

*Find the federal withholding tax for each of the following employees. Use the wage bracket method.*

| | Employee | Gross Earnings | Married? | Withholding Allowances |
|---|---|---|---|---|
| 1. | Barman, E. | $2,333.18 monthly | yes | 3 |
| 2. | Salas, D. | $385.16 weekly | no | 2 |
| 3. | Reynolds, C. | $449.38 weekly | no | 0 |
| 4. | Mooney, L. | $1,475.37 monthly | yes | 1 |
| 5. | Whaley, K. | $2,229.83 monthly | yes | 5 |
| 6. | Yoshi, S. | $1,810.42 monthly | yes | 4 |
| 7. | Crammer, K. | $2,387.92 monthly | yes | 6 |
| 8. | Keller, J. | $332.14 weekly | no | 1 |
| 9. | Crowe, K. | $1,598.14 monthly | yes | 4 |
| 10 | Bessenbacher, S. | $479.08 weekly | no | 0 |

*Use the state withholding schedule to find the state withholding tax for each of the following employees.*

| Employee | Gross Weekly Earnings | Married? |
|---|---|---|
| 11. Ryan, A. | $126.50 | no |
| 12. Devaney, S. | $192.93 | yes |
| 13. Steinbacker, K. | $426.82 | no |
| 14. Lee, L. | $531.45 | yes |
| 15. O'Brien, M. | $352.29 | yes |
| 16. Stratton, R. | $573.41 | no |

*Use the percentage method of withholding to find federal withholding tax, a 6.5% FICA rate to find FICA tax, and a 1.5% rate to find medicare tax for each of the following employees. Then find the net pay for each employee. The number of withholding allowances and the marital status are listed after each employee's name. Assume that no employee has earned over $66,000 so far this year.*

| Employee | Gross Earnings |
|---|---|
| 17. Stagg, 5, M | $417.58 weekly |
| 18. Karia, 2, S | $2,356.21 monthly |
| 19. Walrath, 1, S | $1,532.18 monthly |
| 20. Kavanaugh, 2, M | $347 weekly |
| 21. Sakari, 4, M | $2,385.74 semimonthly |
| 22. Grummitt, 1, S | $621.34 weekly |
| 23. Green, 6, M | $3,942.12 monthly |
| 24. Parker, 5, M | $400 weekly |
| 25. Mandler, 3, S | $710.56 biweekly |
| 26. Scott, 2, S | $3,998.17 monthly |
| 27. Mills, 1, S | $715.34 weekly |
| 28. McCarthy, 4, M | $2,705.20 biweekly |
| 29. Wilson, 3, M | $5,312.59 monthly |
| 30. Deal, 2, M | $948.75 semimonthly |
| 31. Coop, 2, S | $431.25 weekly |
| 32. Beltram, 1, S | $3,285.20 monthly |

33. In your present or past job, which deductions were subtracted from gross earnings to arrive at net pay? Which was the largest deduction?

🖎 **34.** If you were an employer, would you prefer to use the wage bracket method or the percentage method to determine federal withholding tax? Why? (See Objectives 2 and 3.)

*Use the percentage method of withholding, an FICA rate of 6.5%, a medicare rate of 1.5%, an SDI rate of 1%, and the state withholding schedule in the following application problems.*

**35.** Adam Bryer, a marketing representative, has weekly earnings of $783. He is married and claims four withholding allowances. His deductions include FICA, medicare, federal withholding, state disability insurance, state withholding, union dues of $15.50, and credit union savings of $100. Find his net pay for a week in February.

**36.** Ann Buesing has earnings of $588 in one week of March. She is single and claims four withholding allowances. Her deductions include FICA, medicare, federal withholding, state disability insurance, state withholding, a United Way contribution of $10, and a savings bond of $50. Find her net pay for the week.

**37.** The top salesperson for Educational Resources is paid a salary of $410 per week plus 7% of all sales over $5,000. She is single and claims two withholding allowances. Her deductions include FICA, medicare, federal withholding, state disability, disability insurance, state withholding, credit union savings of $50, a Salvation Army contribution of $10, and dues of $15 to the National Association of Professional Saleswomen. Find her net pay for a week in April during which she has sales of $11,284 with returns and allowances of $424.50.

**38.** George Duda, an account executive for a travel agency specializing in travel to South America is paid on a variable commission, is married, and claims four withholding allowances. He receives 2% of the first $20,000 in sales, 3% of the next $10,000 in sales, and 5% of all sales over $30,000. This week he has sales of $38,740 and the following deductions: FICA, medicare, federal withholding, state disability insurance, state withholding, a retirement contribution of $23.83, a savings bond of $37.50, and charitable contributions of $14. Find his net pay after subtracting all of the deductions.

**39.** Sheri Minkner, a commission sales representative for Alternate Heating Company, is paid a monthly salary of $4,200 plus a bonus of 1.5% on monthly sales. She is married and claims three withholding allowances. Her deductions include FICA, medicare, federal withholding, state disability insurance, credit union savings of $150, charitable contributions of $25, and a savings bond of $50. Find her net pay for a month in which she receives a bonus on sales of $42,618. The state in which Minkner works has no state income tax.

**40.** River Raft Adventures pays its manager Lisa DeMol a monthly salary of $2,880 plus a commission of 0.8% based on total monthly sales volume. In the month of May, River Raft Adventures has total sales of $86,280. DeMol is married and claims five withholding allowances. Her deductions include FICA, medicare, federal withholding, state disability insurance, state withholding of $159.30, credit union payment of $300, March of Dimes contributions of $20, and savings bonds of $250. Find her net pay after subtracting all of the deductions.

**5.6   Payroll Records and Quarterly Returns**

**OBJECTIVES**

> **1**  *Understand payroll records kept by employers.*
>
> **2**  *Calculate employer's matching social security and medicare contributions.*
>
> **3**  *Find the quarterly amount due the Internal Revenue Service.*
>
> **4**  *Identify the form used by employers to file a quarterly tax return.*
>
> **5**  *Find the amount of Federal Unemployment Tax due.*

Employers keep payroll records for many reasons. Individual payroll records for each employee are used to keep track of social security tax, medicare tax, federal and state withholding, and many other items. The amounts withheld from employee earnings are sent periodically to the proper agency; most are paid entirely by the employee and others are matched by the employer. Usually these records are filed quarterly. These quarters and the filing dates are shown in Table 5.3.

**OBJECTIVE 1** *Understand payroll records kept by employers.*    The payroll ledger, discussed in Section 5.1, was a record of the number of hours worked by all of the employees for a certain time period. The Employee's Earnings Record shown in Figure 5.8 details quarterly totals for an individual employee. This record shows the gross earnings, deduction amounts, and net pay for each pay period during the quarter.

**OBJECTIVE 2** *Calculate employer's matching social security and medicare contributions.* The employer must check the earnings of each employee to make sure that the FICA, medicare, and the Federal Unemployment Tax Act (FUTA) (discussed in this section) cutoff points are not passed. Since the employer must also give an end-of-year wage and tax statement (Form W-2) to each employee, the records are also used as the source of this information. In addition, accurate payroll records are important because the employer is required by law to match the employee's social security and medicare contributions.

TABLE 5.3   **Filing Schedules for Employee Withholding**

| Quarter | Ending | Due Date |
|---|---|---|
| **January–February–March** | **March 31** | **April 30** |
| **April–May–June** | **June 30** | **July 31** |
| **July–August–September** | **September 30** | **October 31** |
| **October–November–December** | **December 31** | **January 31** |

| NAME *Lisa Kamins* | | | | | | CLOCK NUMBER *114* | | DEPT *Production* | M | 3 | RECORD OF PAY CHANGES | |
|---|---|---|---|---|---|---|---|---|---|---|---|---|
| | | | | | | | | | MARITAL STATUS | NO. OF EXEMPT | *1/1/9___* | *7.20* |
| STREET *407 Glen Oak Dr.* | | | | | | SOC.SEC. NUMBER *349 - 62 - 0156* | | | ☐ M. ☒ F. | | | |
| CITY *Forth Worth, Texas* | | | | | | PHONE NO. *482 -6319* | | DATE STARTED DATE LEFT | | | | |

| TIME WORKED | DATE PAY PERIOD ENDING | YEAR *199___* | | TIME WORKED | | | | ENCIRCLE QUARTERS ① 2 3 4 | GROSS PAYROLL | F.W.T. | SOC. SEC. | MEDI | S.W.T. | U.D. | D. INS. | CHECK NO. | ← DEDUCTION AMOUNTS | |
|---|---|---|---|---|---|---|---|---|---|---|---|---|---|---|---|---|---|---|
| | | SUN | M | TU | W | TH | F | SAT | | | | DEDUCTIONS | | | | | NET PAY | |
| | | BROUGHT FORWARD → | | | | | | | | | | | | | | | | |
| | 1/7 | | 8 | 8 | 7 | 8 | 10 | | 298⁸⁰ | 18⁰⁰ | 19⁴² | 4⁴⁸ | 13⁸⁰ | 5⁰⁰ | 18⁰⁰ | 1186 | 220¹⁰ | 1 |
| | 1/14 | | 8 | 8 | 8 | 8 | 8 | | 288⁰⁰ | 16⁰⁰ | 18⁷² | 4³² | 13⁴⁰ | 5⁰⁰ | 18⁰⁰ | 1295 | 212⁵⁶ | 2 |
| | 1/21 | | 8 | 10 | 8 | 9 | 8 | 4 | 363⁶⁰ | 28⁰⁰ | 23⁶³ | 5⁴⁵ | 15⁰⁶ | 5⁰⁰ | 18⁰⁰ | 1378 | 268⁴⁶ | 3 |
| | 1/28 | | 8 | 8 | 8 | 8 | 8 | | 288⁰⁰ | 16⁰⁰ | 18⁷² | 4³² | 13⁴⁰ | 5⁰⁰ | 18⁰⁰ | 1498 | 212⁵⁶ | 4 |
| | 2/4 | | 8 | 8 | 6 | 8 | 8 | 2 | 288⁰⁰ | 16⁰⁰ | 18⁷² | 4³² | 13⁴⁰ | 5⁰⁰ | 18⁰⁰ | 1601 | 212⁵⁶ | 5 |
| | 2/11 | | 8 | 8 | 8 | 8 | 8 | | 288⁰⁰ | 16⁰⁰ | 18⁷² | 4³² | 13⁴⁰ | 5⁰⁰ | 18⁰⁰ | 1738 | 212⁵⁶ | 6 |
| | 2/18 | | 8 | 8 | 8 | 8 | 8 | | 288⁰⁰ | 16⁰⁰ | 18⁷² | 4³² | 13⁴⁰ | 5⁰⁰ | 18⁰⁰ | 1856 | 212⁵⁶ | 7 |
| | 2/25 | | 10 | 8 | 10 | 6 | 6 | 5 | 342⁰⁰ | 25⁰⁰ | 22²³ | 5¹³ | 14⁷⁰ | 5⁰⁰ | 18⁰⁰ | 2023 | 251⁹⁴ | 8 |
| | 3/3 | | 8 | 8 | 8 | 8 | 8 | | 288⁰⁰ | 16⁰⁰ | 18⁷² | 4³² | 13⁴⁰ | 5⁰⁰ | 18⁰⁰ | 2186 | 212⁵⁶ | 9 |
| | 3/10 | | 8 | 7 | 8 | 9 | 10 | | 309⁶⁰ | 19⁰⁰ | 20¹² | 4⁶⁴ | 13⁹⁰ | 5⁰⁰ | 18⁰⁰ | 2316 | 228⁹⁴ | 10 |
| | 3/17 | | 8 | 8 | 8 | 8 | 8 | | 288⁰⁰ | 16⁰⁰ | 18⁷² | 4³² | 13⁴⁰ | 5⁰⁰ | 18⁰⁰ | 2479 | 212⁵⁶ | 11 |
| | 3/24 | | 10 | 8 | 10 | 8 | 8 | | 391⁰⁰ | 33⁰⁰ | 25⁴² | 5⁸⁷ | 16⁶⁰ | 5⁰⁰ | 18⁰⁰ | 2632 | 287¹¹ | 12 |
| | 3/31 | | 8 | 8 | 8 | 9 | 8 | 4 | 403⁷⁵ | 34⁰⁰ | 26²⁴ | 6⁰⁶ | 17⁰⁶ | 5⁰⁰ | 18⁰⁰ | 2801 | 297³⁹ | 13 |
| | | | | | | | | | | | | | | | | | | 14 |
| | | | | | | | | | | | | | | | | | | 15 |
| | | | | | | | | | | | | | | | | | | 16 |
| | QTR. | | | | | | | | 4124⁷⁵ | 269⁰⁰ | 268¹⁰ | 61⁸⁷ | 184⁹² | 65⁰⁰ | 234⁸⁰ | | 3,041⁸⁶ | |
| | TO DATE | | | | | | | | | | | | | | | | | |

FIGURE 5.8

**OBJECTIVE 3** *Find the quarterly amount due the Internal Revenue Service.* An employee's contribution to social security and medicare must be matched by the employer.

**EXAMPLE 1** *Finding the Amount of FICA and Medicare Tax Due*

If the employees at Fair Oaks Garage pay a total of $789.10 in social security tax, and $182.10 in medicare tax, how much must the employer send to the Internal Revenue Service?

**SOLUTION** The employer must match this and send a total of $971.20 ($789.10 + $182.10 from employees) + $971.20 (from employer) = $1,942.40 to the government. ■

**NOTE** In addition to the employee's social security tax and a matching amount paid by the employer, the employer must also send the amount withheld for income tax to the Internal Revenue Service on a quarterly basis. ■

| EXAMPLE 2 | *Finding the Employers Amount Due the IRS* |

Suppose that during a certain quarter Leslie's Pool Supplies has collected $2,765.42 from its employees for FICA tax, $638.17 for medicare tax, and $3,572.86 in federal withholding tax. Compute the total amount due to the Internal Revenue Service from Leslie's Pool Supplies.

**SOLUTION**

| | |
|---|---|
| $2,765.42 | collected from employees for FICA tax |
| $2,765.42 | equal amount paid by employer |
| $638.17 | collected from employees for medicare tax |
| $638.17 | equal amount paid by employer |
| $3,572.86 | federal withholding tax |
| $10,380.04 | total due to Internal Revenue Service |

The firm must send $10,380.04 to the Internal Revenue Service.     ■

**CALCULATOR APPROACH TO EXAMPLE 2**

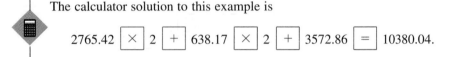

The calculator solution to this example is

2765.42 ⊠ × ⊠ 2 ⊠ + ⊠ 638.17 ⊠ × ⊠ 2 ⊠ + ⊠ 3572.86 ⊠ = ⊠ 10380.04.

**OBJECTIVE 4** *Identify the form used by employers to file a quarterly tax return.*     At the end of each quarter, employers must file **Form 941**, the **Employer's Quarterly Federal Tax Return**. This form reports the amount of income tax withheld by the employer, and the amount of social security taxes and medicare taxes due.

A copy of Form 941 is shown in Figure 5.9. The right column (lines 1 through 16) itemizes total employee wages and earnings, and the income, FICA, and medicare taxes due.

The "Net taxes" (line 13) must equal line (17(d)) "Total liability for quarter." This lower portion of Form 941 (line 17) divides the quarter into its three months and the amount of the tax liability (employee and employer) are entered on the line of the proper month in that quarter. The withheld income tax and employee and employer FICA and medicare taxes must be deposited with an authorized financial institution or a Federal Reserve Bank or branch. The amount of taxes owed determines how often these deposits must be made. If the amount of taxes owed by an employer is less than $500 at the end of a quarter, the money does not have to be deposited, but is sent directly to the IRS. Funds can be deposited using the Federal Tax Deposit Coupon Form 8109, shown in Figure 5.10. This form is filed, along with the proper amount of money, at an authorized financial institution, which then forwards the money to the U.S. Treasury.

**OBJECTIVE 5** *Find the amount of Federal Unemployment Tax due.*     The **Federal Unemployment Tax Act (FUTA)** requires employers to pay an additional tax. This

Form **941**
(Rev. April 199 )
Department of the Treasury
Internal Revenue Service (1)  41.41

**Employer's Quarterly Federal Tax Return**
▶ See separate instructions for information on completing this return.
Please type or print.

OMB No. 1545-0029

Enter state code for state in which deposits made . ▶ ☐ (see page 2 of instructions).

*Shirley Cicero*
*Desktop Publishing Company*
*P.O. Box 505*
*Carmichael, MO 63834*

| | |
|---|---|
| T | |
| FF | |
| FD | |
| FP | |
| I | |
| T | |

If address is different from prior return, check here ▶ ☐   IRS Use

1 1 1 1 1 1 1 1 1 1  2  3 3 3 3 3 3  4 4 4
5 5 5   6   7   8 8 8 8 8   9 9 9   10 10 10 10 10 10 10 10

If you do not have to file returns in the future, check here ▶ ☐ and enter date final wages paid ▶
If you are a seasonal employer, see **Seasonal employers** on page 2 and check here (see instructions) ▶ ☐

| | | | | |
|---|---|---|---|---|
| 1 | Number of employees (except household) employed in the pay period that includes March 12th ▶ | | | 9 |
| 2 | Total wages and tips subject to withholding, plus other compensation . . . . . . . | 2 | 46,228 | |
| 3 | Total income tax withheld from wages, tips, and sick pay . . . . . . . . . . | 3 | 5815 | |
| 4 | Adjustment of withheld income tax for preceding quarters of calendar year . . . . . | 4 | | |
| 5 | Adjusted total of income tax withheld (line 3 as adjusted by line 4—see instructions) | 5 | 5815 | |
| 6a | Taxable social security wages . . . . . . $ 46,228 × 12.4% (.124) = | 6a | 5732 | 27 |
| b | Taxable social security tips . . . . . . $ × 12.4% (.124) = | 6b | | |
| 7 | Taxable Medicare wages and tips . . . . . $ 46,228 × 2.9% (.029) = | 7 | 1340 | 61 |
| 8 | Total social security and Medicare taxes (add lines 6a, 6b, and 7). Check here if wages are not subject to social security and/or Medicare tax . . . . . . . . . . ▶ ☐ | 8 | 7072 | 88 |
| 9 | Adjustment of social security and Medicare taxes (see instructions for required explanation) Sick Pay $_____ ± Fractions of Cents $_____ ± Other $_____ = | 9 | | |
| 10 | Adjusted total of social security and Medicare taxes (line 8 as adjusted by line 9—see instructions) | 10 | 7072 | 88 |
| 11 | **Total taxes** (add lines 5 and 10) . . . . . . . . . . . . . . . . | 11 | 12,887 | 88 |
| 12 | Advance earned income credit (EIC) payments made to employees, if any . . . . . . | 12 | | |
| 13 | Net taxes (subtract line 12 from line 11). **This should equal line 17, column (d) below** (or line D of Schedule B (Form 941)) . . . . . . . . . . . . . . . . . . | 13 | 12,887 | 88 |
| 14 | Total deposits for quarter, including overpayment applied from a prior quarter . . . . . | 14 | 12,887 | 88 |
| 15 | **Balance due** (subtract line 14 from line 13). Pay to Internal Revenue Service . . . . . | 15 | ∅ | |

Income Tax

Social Security and Medicare

16 **Overpayment,** if line 14 is more than line 13, enter excess here ▶ $_____
and check if to be:  ☐ Applied to next return  **OR**  ☐ Refunded.
• **All filers:** If line 13 is less than $500, you need not complete line 17 or Schedule B.
• **Semiweekly depositors:** Complete Schedule B and check here . . . . . . . . ▶ ☐
• **Monthly depositors:** Complete line 17, columns (a) through (d) and check here . . . . ▶ ☐

| 17 | Monthly Summary of Federal Tax Liability. | | | |
|---|---|---|---|---|
| | **(a)** First month liability | **(b)** Second month liability | **(c)** Third month liability | **(d)** Total liability for quarter |
| | $3810.30 | $4707.10 | $4370.88 | $12,887.88 |

**Sign Here**
Under penalties of perjury, I declare that I have examined this return, including accompanying schedules and statements, and to the best of my knowledge and belief, it is true, correct, and complete.
Signature ▶ *S Cicero*   Print Your Name and Title ▶ *Cicero - Pres*   Date ▶ *4/15*

For Paperwork Reduction Act Notice, see page 1 of separate instructions.   Cat. No. 17001Z   Form **941** (Rev. 4-9 )

FIGURE 5.9

**unemployment insurance tax**, paid entirely by employers, is used to pay unemployment benefits to an individual who has become unemployed and is unable to find work.

In general, all employers who paid wages of $1,000 or more in a calendar quarter or had one or more employees for some part of a day in any 20 different weeks must

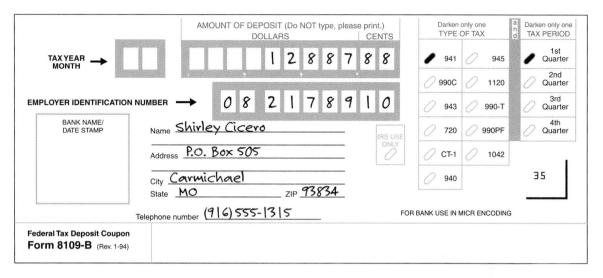

FIGURE 5.10

file an *Employer's Annual Federal Unemployment (FUTA) Tax Return*. This federal return must be filed each January for the preceding year. The FUTA tax that must be paid by the employer is 6.2% of the first $7,000 in earnings for that year for each employee. Most states have unemployment taxes (SUTA) paid by the employer for which the employer is given credit on the FUTA return.

The credit given cannot exceed 5.4%, so the minimum amount due for FUTA is 0.8% (6.2% − 5.4%). States normally require quarterly payment of the unemployment tax. As soon as an employee reaches earnings of $7,000, no additional unemployment tax must be paid.

If an employer has a history of few layoffs, an individual state may drop the unemployment tax rate below 5.4%. On the other hand, an employer with high labor turnover may have to pay the higher unemployment tax rate.

## EXAMPLE 3  *Finding the Amount of Unemployment Tax Due*

Jennifer Eddy earns $2,400 each quarter. Find the following amounts: (a) Eddy's earnings in the third quarter of the year that are subject to unemployment tax and (b) the amount of unemployment tax due on third quarter earnings. (Assume a tax rate of 6.2%.)

### SOLUTION

**(a)** Since earnings in the first two quarters are $4,800 (2 × $2,400), the earnings subject to unemployment taxes in the third quarter are $2,200 ($7,000 − $4,800).

**(b)** The federal unemployment tax due is $136.40 (0.062 × $2,200).  ∎

# 5.6 EXERCISES

*Find the total combined amount of social security and medicare tax (employees' contribution plus employer's contribution) for each of the following firms. Use a FICA rate of 6.5%, a medicare tax rate of 1.5%, and assume no employee has earned over $60,000 so far this year.*

| | Firm | Total Employee Earnings |
|---|---|---|
| 1. | Fowler's Nursery | $7,412.72 |
| 2. | Norm's Cel Phones | $8,866.24 |
| 3. | Adin Feed and Fuel | $17,462.80 |
| 4. | Leisure Outdoor Furniture | $15,324.15 |
| 5. | Computers Plus | $14,131.59 |
| 6. | Owl Drugstore | $21,281.60 |
| 7. | Plescia Produce | $62,476.56 |
| 8. | Crescent Foundry | $122,819.50 |

*Calculate the total amount due from each of the following firms. Use a FICA rate of 6.5% and a medicare tax rate of 1.5%.*

| | Firm | Total Employee Earnings | Total Withholding for Income Tax |
|---|---|---|---|
| 9. | Atlasta Ranch | $4,945.30 | $498.71 |
| 10. | McIntosh Meats | $9,384.50 | $2,370.56 |
| 11. | Childlike Publishers | $32,121.85 | $8,215.08 |
| 12. | Mart & Bottle | $20,255.60 | $4,436.80 |
| 13. | Todd Consultants | $37,271.39 | $7,128.64 |
| 14. | Mail Boxes Etc. | $10,158.24 | $2,768.62 |
| 15. | Tony Balony's | $34,547.86 | $12,628.19 |
| 16. | Oaks Hardware | $21,394.77 | $5,671.30 |

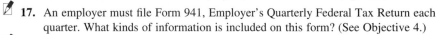 17. An employer must file Form 941, Employer's Quarterly Federal Tax Return each quarter. What kinds of information is included on this form? (See Objective 4.)

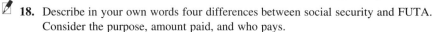 18. Describe in your own words four differences between social security and FUTA. Consider the purpose, amount paid, and who pays.

*Solve the following application problems. Assume no employee has earned over $60,000 so far this year. Use a FICA rate of 6.5% and a medicare tax rate of 1.5%.*

19. Total employee earnings at Capital Landscape are $21,928.10. Find the combined total amount of FICA and medicare taxes sent to the IRS by the employer.

20. Biondi Paving has a payroll of $13,650.30. How much FICA and medicare taxes should be sent to the IRS?

**21.** The AM-PM Mart has an employee payroll of $5,103.26. During the same time period, $1,109.27 was withheld as income tax. Find the total amount due to the IRS.

**22.** The payroll at the Oak Mill Florist is $22,607.72. During the same pay period, $3,898.14 was withheld as income tax. Find the total amount that must be sent to the IRS.

*Assume a FUTA rate of 6.2% of the first $7,000 in earnings in each of the following.*

**23.** An employee earns $3,280 in the first quarter of the year, $2,600 in the second quarter, and $3,156 in the third quarter. Find (a) the amount of earnings subject to unemployment tax in the third quarter and (b) the amount of unemployment tax due on third quarter earnings.

**24.** Terry White earns $910 per month. Find (a) the amount of earnings subject to unemployment tax in the third quarter and (b) the amount of unemployment tax due on fourth quarter earnings.

**25.** Emma Price is paid $1,800 per month. Find (a) the amount of earnings subject to unemployment tax in the second quarter and (b) the amount of unemployment tax due on second quarter earnings.

**26.** Michael Booth received $4,820 in earnings in the first quarter of the year. His earnings in the second quarter are $3,815. Find (a) the amount of his earnings subject to FUTA in the second quarter and (b) the amount of tax due in the second quarter.

# Chapter 5 Quick Review

| TOPIC | APPROACH | EXAMPLE |
|---|---|---|
| **5.1 Gross earnings** | Gross earnings = Hours worked × Rate per hour | 40 hours at $6.30 per hour<br>Gross earnings = 40 × $6.30 = $252 |
| **5.1 Gross earnings with overtime** | First, find regular earnings. Then, determine overtime pay at overtime rate. Finally, add regular and overtime earnings. | 40 hours at $6.30 per hour; 10 hours at time and a half.<br>Gross earnings = (40 × $6.30) + (10 × $6.30 × $1\frac{1}{2}$) = $252 + $94.50 = $346.50 |

**5.1 Common pay periods**

| Pay Period | Payckecks per Year |
|---|---|
| Monthly | 12 |
| Semimonthly | 24 |
| Biweekly | 26 |
| Weekly | 52 |

Find the earnings equivalent of $1,400 per month for other pay periods.

$$\text{Semimonthly} = \frac{1,400}{2}$$
$$= \$700$$

$$\text{Biweekly} = \frac{1,400 \times 12}{26}$$
$$= \$646.15$$

$$\text{Weekly} = \frac{1,400 \times 12}{52}$$
$$= \$323.08$$

**5.1 Overtime for salaried employees**

First, find the equivalent hourly rate. Next, multiply the rate by the overtime hours by $1\frac{1}{2}$. Finally, add overtime earnings to salary.

Salary is $324 per week for 36 hours. Find earnings for 46 hours.

$324 \div 36 = \$9.00$ per hour

$\$9.00 \times 10 \times 1\frac{1}{2} = \$135$ overtime

$\$324 + \$135 = \$459$

**5.2 Straight commission**

Gross earnings =
Commission rate $\times$ Amount of sales

Sales of $25,800; commission rate is 5%.

$0.05 \times \$25,800 = \$1,290$

**5.2 Variable commission**

Commission rate varies at different sales levels.

Up to $10,000, 6%; $10,001–$20,000, 8%; $20,001 and up, 9%. Find the commission on sales of $32,768.

| | | |
|---|---|---|
| (first $10,000) | $0.06 \times \$10,000 =$ | $600.00 |
| (next $10,000) | $0.08 \times \$10,000 =$ | $800.00 |
| (amount over $20,000) | $0.09 \times \underline{\$12,768} =$ | $\underline{\$1,149.12}$ |
| | Totals  $32,768 | $2,549.12 |

**5.2 Salary and commission**

Gross earnings =
Fixed earnings + Commission

Salary, $250 per week; commission rate, 3%. Find gross earnings on sales of $6,848.

Gross earnings
$$= \$250 + (0.03 \times 6,848)$$
$$= \$250 + \$205.44$$
$$= \$455.44$$

| | | | |
|---|---|---|---|
| **5.2** | **Commissions with a drawing account** | Gross earnings = $$\text{Commission} - \text{Draw}$$ | Sales for month, \$28,560; commission rate, 7%; draw, \$750 for month. Find gross earnings.<br><br>Gross earnings<br>$= (0.07 \times \$28{,}560) - \$750$<br>$= \$1{,}999.20 - \$750$<br>$= \$1{,}249.20$ |
| **5.2** | **Commissions with a quota bonus** | Gross earnings = $$\text{Commission rate} \times (\text{sales} - \text{quota})$$ | Sales for week, \$14,370; commission rate, 10% after meeting the sales quota of \$4,000. Find gross earnings.<br><br>Gross earnings<br>$= 0.1 \times (\$14{,}370 - \$4{,}000)$<br>$= 0.1 \times \$10{,}370$<br>$= \$1{,}037$ |
| **5.3** | **Gross earnings for piecework** | Gross earnings = Number of items $\times$ Payment per item | Items produced, 175; payment per item, \$0.65. Find gross earnings.<br><br>$175 \times \$0.65 = \$113.75$ |
| **5.3** | **Gross earnings for differential piecework** | The rate paid per item produced varies with level of production. | 1–100 items, \$0.75 each; 101–150 items, \$0.90; 151 or more items, \$1.04. Find gross earnings for 214 items.<br><br>(first 100 units) $\quad 100 \times \$0.75 = \quad \$75.00$<br>(next 50 units) $\qquad 50 \times \$0.90 = \quad \$45.00$<br>(number over 150) $\quad \underline{64} \times \$1.04 = \quad \underline{\$66.56}$<br>Total $214 \qquad\qquad\qquad\qquad \$186.56$ |
| **5.3** | **Gross earnings with piece rate and chargebacks** | Find piece rate earnings; then calculate chargebacks and subtract them from piece rate earnings to find gross earnings. | Items produced, 318; piece rate, \$0.75; spoiled items, 26; chargeback, \$0.60. Find gross earnings.<br><br>$318 \times \$0.75 = \$238.50$<br>$26 \times \$0.60 = \$15.60$<br>$\$238.50 - \$15.60 = \$222.90$ |

| | | |
|---|---|---|
| **5.3 Overtime earnings on piecework** | Gross earnings = Earnings at regular rate + Earnings at overtime rate | Items produced on regular time, 530; items produced on overtime, 110; piece rate, $0.34. Find gross earnings |

Gross earnings

$$= 530 \times \$0.34$$

$$+ 110 \left( 1\frac{1}{2} \times \$0.34 \right)$$

$$= \$180.20 + \$56.10$$

$$= \$236.30$$

| | | |
|---|---|---|
| **5.4 FICA; social security tax** | The gross earnings are multiplied by the rate. When the maximum earnings are reached, no additional FICA is withheld that year. | Gross earnings, $458; social security tax rate, 6.5%; find social security tax.<br><br>$\$458 \times 0.065 = \$29.77$ |
| **5.4 Medicare tax** | The gross earnings are multiplied by the tax rate. When the maximum earnings are reached, no additional medicare tax is withheld that year. | Gross earnings, $458, medicare tax rate, 1.5%, find medicare tax.<br><br>$\$458 \times 0.015 = \$6.87$ |
| **5.4 State disability insurance deductions** | Multiply the gross earnings by the SDI tax rate. When maximum earnings are reached, no additional taxes are paid in that year. | Gross earnings, $3,210; SDI tax rate 1%; find SDI tax.<br><br>$\$3,210 \times 0.01 = \$32.10$ |
| **5.5 Federal withholding tax** | Tax is paid on total earnings. No maximum as with FICA. | Single employee with 3 allowances; weekly earnings of $526; find the federal withholding tax. Using wage bracket amount "at least $520, but less than $530," withholding is $50. With the percentage method withholding is |

$$\$526 - (\$48.08 \times 3) = \$381.76$$
$$\$381.76 - \$50 = \$331.76$$
$$\$331.76 \times 0.15 = \ \ \$49.76$$

| 5.5 | State withholding tax | Tax is paid on total earnings. No maximum as with FICA. | Married employee with weekly earnings of $392; find the state withholding tax. Use the "married" table for earnings "over 324, but not over 422."<br><br>$(4\% \times \$392) - \$6.81$<br>$\qquad = \$15.68 - \$6.81$<br>$\qquad = \$8.87$ |
|---|---|---|---|
| 5.6 | Quarterly report, Form 941 | Filed each quarter; FICA and federal withholding are sent to the IRS. (FICA + medicare) × 2 (employer) + federal withholding tax | If quarterly FICA withheld from employees is $5,269, medicare tax is $1,581, and federal withholding tax is $14,780, find the total due the IRS.<br><br>$(\$5,269 + \$1,581) \times 2$<br>$+ \$14,780 = \$28,480$ |
| 5.6 | Federal Unemployment Tax (FUTA) | FUTA is paid by the employer on the first $7,000 of earnings each year for each employee. | An employee earned $3,850 in the first quarter of a year. Find the amount of unemployment tax using a 6.2% tax rate.<br><br>$\$3,850 \times 6.2\% = \$238.70$ |

# Chapter 5 Review Exercises

*Complete the following partial payroll ledger. Find the total gross earnings for each employee. Time and a half is paid on all hours over 40 in one week. [5.1]*

| | Employee | Hours Worked | Reg. Hours | O.T. Hours | Reg. Rate | Gross Earnings |
|---|---|---|---|---|---|---|
| 1. | Carter, M. | 48.5 | | | $9.14 | |
| 2. | Ackerly, T. | 48 | | | $8.50 | |
| 3. | Mandler, S. | 38.25 | | | $7.40 | |
| 4. | Rosenthal, L. | 57.25 | | | $6.80 | |

*Find the equivalent earnings for each of the following salaries as indicated. [5.1]*

| | Weekly | Biweekly | Semimonthly | Monthly | Annually |
|---|---|---|---|---|---|
| 5. | $410.80 | _____ | _____ | _____ | _____ |
| 6. | _____ | $1,060 | _____ | _____ | _____ |
| 7. | _____ | _____ | _____ | _____ | $18,000 |
| 8. | _____ | _____ | $875 | _____ | _____ |

*Find the weekly gross earnings for the following people who are on salary and are paid time and a half for overtime. [5.1]*

| | Employee | Regular Hours per Week | Weekly Salary | Hours Worked | Weekly Gross Earnings |
|---|---|---|---|---|---|
| 9. | Uldall, E. | 40 | $640 | 45 | _____ |
| 10. | Donovan-Dickerson, K. | 36 | $342 | 42 | _____ |

*Find the gross earnings for each of the following salespeople. [5.2]*

| | Employee | Total Sales | Returns | Rate of Commission |
|---|---|---|---|---|
| 11. | Gillette, P. | $32,170 | $2,308 | 7% |
| 12. | McRill, G. | $21,960 | $755 | 8% |

*Solve each of the following application problems.*

**13.** Twenty Minute Lube and Oil pays its employees $1.25 for an oil change, $1.50 for each car lubed, and $2.50 if a car gets both an oil change and a lube. This week Andre Herrebout changed the oil in 63 cars, lubed 46 cars, and gave an oil change and lube to 38 cars. Find his gross pay for the week. [5.3]

**14.** At an electronics factory in Mexicali, Mexico, assemblers are paid as follows: 1–20 units in a week, $4.50 each; 21–30 units, $5.50 each; and more than 30 units, $7 each. Adrian Ortega assembled 28 units in one week. Find his gross pay. [5.3]

**15.** Lee Ann Fisher receives a commission of 6% for selling a $115,000 house. Half the commission goes to the broker, and half of the remainder to another salesperson. Fisher gets the rest. Find the amount she receives. [5.3]

*Use the following information for Exercises 16 and 17. [5.2]*

*Employees at Appliance Giant are paid a commission on the following schedule.*

| | |
|---|---|
| First $2,000 in sales | 6% |
| Next $2,000 in sales | 8% |
| Sales over $4,000 | 10% |

**16.** Find the gross earnings for an employee with total sales of $5,850.

**17.** Find the gross earnings for an employee with total sales of $7,200.

**18.** Pat Rowell ties bows on Christmas wreaths and is paid $0.12 for each bow tied. She is charged $0.09 for each rejection and is paid time and a half for overtime production. Find her gross earnings for a week when she produces 1,850 at the regular rate, 285 at the overtime rate, and has 92 rejections. [5.3]

*Use the following information for Exercises 19 and 20. [5.4]*

*An employee is paid a salary of $6,250 per month. If the FICA rate is 6.5% on the first $66,000 of earnings and the medicare tax rate is 1.5% on all earnings, how much will the employee pay in (a) FICA tax and (b) medicare tax during the following months?*

**19.** October

**20.** November

*Find the federal withholding tax using the wage bracket method for each of the following employees. [5.5]*

**21.** Ortega: 4 withholding allowances, single, $408.75 weekly earnings

**22.** Pieri: 2 withholding allowances, married, $1,920.80 monthly earnings

**23.** Hill: 3 withholding allowances, married, $2,208.79 monthly earnings

**24.** Chang: 3 withholding allowances, single, $570.32 weekly earnings

**25.** Leyton: 6 withholding allowances, married, $2,580.76 monthly earnings

**26.** Tewell: 2 withholding allowances, single, $595.50 weekly earnings

*Find the net pay for each of the following employees after FICA, medicare, federal withholding tax, state disability, and other deductions have been made. Assume that no one has earned over $66,000 so far this year. Assume a FICA rate of 6.5%, medicare rate of 1.5%, and a state disability rate of 1%. Use the percentage method of withholding. [5.5]*

**27.** Precilo: $1,852.75 monthly earnings, 1 withholding allowance, single, $37.80 in other deductions

**28.** Colley: $522.11 weekly earnings, 4 withholding allowances, married, state withholding of $15.34, credit union savings of $20, educational television contribution of $7.50

**29.** Harper: $677.92 weekly earnings, 6 withholding allowances, married, state withholding of $22.18, union dues of $14, charitable contribution of $15

*Solve the following application problems. Assume no employee has earned over $66,000 so far this year. Use a FICA rate of 6.5% and a rate of 1.5% for medicare. [5.6]*

**30.** Total employee earnings for Round Table Pizza are $12,720.15. Find the total amount of FICA and medicare taxes sent to the IRS by the employer.

**31.** San Juan Electric has an employee payroll of $29,185.17. During the same period $4,921 was withheld as income tax. Find the total amount due the IRS.

*Solve the following application problems.*

**32.** A salesperson is paid $452 per week plus a commission of 2% on all sales. The salesperson sold $712 worth of goods on Monday, $523 on Tuesday, $1,002 on Wednesday, $391 on Thursday, and $609 on Friday. Returns and allowances for the week were $114. Find the employee's (a) social security tax (6.5%), (b) medicare tax (1.5%), and (c) state disability insurance (1%) for the week. [5.3 and 5.4]

**33.** Kara Gourley earned $64,998.73 so far this year until last week. Last week she earned $2,190.15. Find her (a) FICA tax and (b) medicare tax for last week's earnings.

**34.** The employees of Miracle Floor Covering paid a total of $1,496.11 in social security tax last month, $345.30 in medicare tax, and $1,768.43 in federal withholding tax. Find the total amount that the employer must send to the Internal Revenue Service.

*For Exercises 35 and 36, find (a) the social security tax and (b) the medicare tax for each of the following self-employed people. Use a FICA tax rate of 13% and a medicare tax rate of 3%. [5.4]*

**35.** Kyle: $23,417.21

**36.** Trearty: $34.539.04

*Assume a FUTA rate of 6.2% on the first $7,000 in earnings in each of the following. [5.6]*

**37.** An employee earns $2,875 in the first quarter of the year, $3,212 in the second quarter, and $2,942 in the third quarter. Find (a) the amount of earnings subject to unemployment tax in the third quarter and (b) the amount of unemployment tax due on third quarter earnings.

**38.** Amy Berk earns $810 per month. Find (a) the amount of earnings subject to unemployment tax in the third quarter and (b) the amount of unemployment tax due on third quarter earnings.

# Chapter 5 Summary Exercise

Sheila Avery, the manager of a Blockbuster Video, receives an annual salary of $29,120 which is paid weekly. Her normal workweek is 40 hours and she is paid time and a half for all overtime. She is single and claims one withholding allowance. Her deductions include FICA, medicare, federal withholding, state disability insurance, state withholding, credit union payments of $125, retirement deductions of $75, association dues of $12, and a Diabetes Association contribution of $15. Find each of the following for a week in which she works 52 hours.

(a) Regular weekly earnings.

(b) Overtime earnings.

(c) Total gross earnings.

(d) FICA.

(e) Medicare.

(f) Federal withholding.

(g) State disability.

(h) State withholding.

(i) Net pay.

# 6 Taxes

There is one thing on which almost everyone agrees. "Taxes are too high." But, taxes are a fact of life. In the early part of this century, Justice Oliver Wendell Holmes, Jr., of the United States Supreme Court said, "taxes are the price we pay to live in a civilized society." Tax dollars pay for education, health services, national defense, streets and highways, parks and recreation facilities, police and fire protection, public assistance for the poor, libraries, and even street lights. As government provides more services, taxes go up.

There are basically three forms of taxation: taxes on sales, property, and income. This chapter examines the basics of taxation and discusses the calculations necessary to work with each type of tax.

## 6.1 Sales Tax

### OBJECTIVES

1. *Understand how sales tax is determined.*
2. *Find the amount of sales tax and the total sale.*
3. *Find the selling price when the sales tax is known.*
4. *Find the amount of the sale when the total price is known.*
5. *Define excise tax.*
6. *Find the total cost including sales tax and excise tax.*

Most states and a large number of counties and cities have a tax on sales. This tax, called **sales tax**, is paid on the amount of retail sales. Normally calculated as a percent of the retail price, this tax varies from area to area. For instance, since food is considered a basic necessity, most states do not tax the majority of food items purchased in a grocery store. The same food items, however, may be taxed when purchased in a restaurant.

**OBJECTIVE 1** *Understand how sales tax is determined.* Many small retail stores use a tax table to compute sales tax. The sales clerk looks up the tax on the sales tax table and enters the amount into the cash register.

Today many stores have cash register systems that keep track of taxable items and automatically calculate the necessary tax. Sales tax tables from a typical state appear in Table 6.1. Table 6.2 shows the 1996 sales tax rate in each state, the District of Columbia, and New York City.

TABLE 6.1  $7\frac{3}{4}\%$ Sales Tax Collection Schedule

| Up to and Including | Tax |
|---|---|
| $0.06 | $0.00 |
| 0.19 | 0.01 |
| 0.32 | 0.02 |
| 0.45 | 0.03 |
| 0.58 | 0.04 |
| 0.70 | 0.05 |
| 0.83 | 0.06 |
| 0.96 | 0.07 |
| 1.09 | 0.08 |
| 1.22 | 0.09 |
| 1.35 | 0.10 |
| 1.48 | 0.11 |
| 1.61 | 0.12 |
| 1.74 | 0.13 |
| 1.87 | 0.14 |
| 1.99 | 0.15 |
| 2.12 | 0.16 |
| 2.25 | 0.17 |
| 2.38 | 0.18 |
| 2.51 | 0.19 |

TABLE 6.2  **1996 Sales Tax Rates**

|  |  |
|---|---|
| **Alabama** (plus city and/or county tax where applicable) | 4% |
| **Alaska** (local tax where applicable) | 0% |
| **Arizona** | 5% |
| **Arkansas** (plus local tax where applicable) | $4\frac{1}{2}\%$ |
| **California** (plus $\frac{1}{2}\%$ or more local tax where applicable) | $7\frac{1}{4}\%$ |
| **Colorado** | 3% |
| **Connecticut** | 6% |
| **Delaware** | 0% |
| **District of Columbia** | $5\frac{3}{4}\%$ |
| **Florida** (plus local tax where applicable) | 6% |
| **Georgia** (plus local tax where applicable) | 4% |
| **Hawaii** | 4% |
| **Idaho** | 5% |
| **Illinois** | $6\frac{1}{4}\%$ |
| **Indiana** | 5% |
| **Iowa** (plus local tax where applicable) | 5% |
| **Kansas** | 4.9% |
| **Kentucky** | 6% |
| **Louisiana** | 4% |
| **Maine** | 6% |
| **Maryland** | 5% |
| **Massachusetts** | 5% |
| **Michigan** | 6% |
| **Minnesota** | $6\frac{1}{2}\%$ |
| **Mississippi** | 7% |
| **Missouri** (plus local tax where applicable) | 4.225% |
| **Montana** | 0% |
| **Nebraska** (plus local tax where applicable) | 5% |
| **Nevada** (plus local tax where applicable) | $4\frac{1}{4}\%$ |
| **New Hampshire** | 0% |
| **New Jersey** | 6% |
| **New Mexico** | 5% |
| **New York City** (includes 4% state tax) | $8\frac{1}{4}\%$ |
| **New York (State)** (plus city or county tax where applicable) | 4% |
| **North Carolina** (plus local tax where applicable) | 3% |
| **North Dakota** (plus local tax where applicable) | 5% |
| **Ohio** (plus local tax where applicable) | 5% |
| **Oklahoma** (plus local tax where applicable) | $4\frac{1}{2}\%$ |
| **Oregon** | 0% |
| **Pennsylvania** (plus local tax where applicable) | 6% |
| **Rhode Island** | 7% |
| **South Carolina** | 5% |
| **South Dakota** (plus local tax where applicable) | 4% |
| **Tennessee** (plus city or county tax where applicable) | 6% |
| **Texas** (plus local tax where applicable) | $6\frac{1}{4}\%$ |
| **Utah** (plus county and local taxes where applicable) | $4\frac{7}{8}\%$ |
| **Vermont** | 5% |
| **Virginia** | $4\frac{1}{2}\%$ |
| **Washington** (plus local tax where applicable) | $6\frac{1}{2}\%$ |
| **West Virginia** | 6% |
| **Wisconsin** (plus local tax where applicable) | 5% |
| **Wyoming** (plus local tax where applicable) | 4% |

The basic percent equation is used to solve sales tax problems. The amount of the sale is the base, the sales tax rate is the rate, and the amount of sales tax is the part.

$$\text{Sales tax} = \text{Amount of Sale} \times \text{Sales tax rate}$$
$$P = B \times R$$

**OBJECTIVE** **2** *Find the amount of sales tax and the total sale.* A common calculation in business is to find the amount of sales tax and the total amount of the sale including tax.

**EXAMPLE 1** *Finding Sales Tax and the Total Sale*

A customer at Crown Software makes a purchase of $29.49. Sales tax in the state is 4%. Find (a) the amount of sales tax and (b) the total amount collected from the customer.

**SOLUTION**

(a) The amount of sales tax (part) is found by multiplying the sales tax rate (rate) by the amount of the sale (base). Use the percent equation to find the sales tax.

$$P = BR$$
$$P = \$29.49 \times 4\%$$
$$P = \$29.49 \times 0.04 = \$1.18 \text{ rounded}$$

Sales tax is $1.18.

(b) Add to find the total amount collected from the customer.

$29.49 (amount of sale) + $1.18 (sales tax) = $30.67 (total sale including tax)

∎

---

**CALCULATOR APPROACH TO EXAMPLE 1**

*The calculator solution to this example uses the percent add-on.

29.49 \[ + \] 4 \[ % \] \[ = \] 30.67

---

**OBJECTIVE** **3** *Find the selling price when the sales tax is known.* If the amount of sales tax and the sales tax rate are known, it is possible to determine the selling price.

**NOTE** Several states do not have any sales tax. Many counties and cities impose a tax on sales to raise additional revenue which is then used locally. ∎

---

*NOTE: All calculator solutions use a scientific calculator. Refer to Appendix A for scientific and financial calculator basics.

**EXAMPLE 2** *Finding the Price When Sales Tax Is Known*

Sales tax on a Murray 5–horsepower Ultra Push Mower is $16.14. If the sales tax rate is 6%, find the price of the mower.

**SOLUTION** Since sales tax (part) is found by multiplying the sales tax rate (rate) by the amount of the sale (base), the amount of sale is found using the percent equation and solving for base.

$$P = BR$$
$$\$16.14 = B \times 6\%$$
$$\$16.14 = 0.06B$$
$$\frac{\$16.14}{0.06} = \frac{0.06B}{0.06}$$
$$\$269 = B$$

The mower sells for $269. ■

**OBJECTIVE 4** *Find the amount of the sale when the total price is known.* When the total price including sales tax and the sales tax rate are known, the sale amount can be found as shown in the next example.

**EXAMPLE 3** *Determining the Sale Amount When Total Price Is Known*

The total cost of some preschool equipment is $610.56, which includes the sales tax of 6%. Find the price of the equipment before the sales tax.

**SOLUTION** First, remember that the amount of sale + sales tax = total. Then, use the percent equation to find the amount of the sale (base).

$$B + (6\%)B = \$610.56$$
$$1B + 0.06B = \$610.56$$
$$1.06B = \$610.56$$
$$B = \frac{610.56}{1.06}$$
$$B = \$576$$

The amount of the sale is $576.

To check this answer, multiply the amount of the sale ($576) by the tax rate (6%) to find the tax. Then, add the tax to the amount of the sale to find the total amount.

$$BR = P$$
$$\$576 \times 6\% = P$$
$$\$576 \times 0.06 = \$34.56 \quad \text{amount of sales tax}$$

Now add.

$$\$576 \text{ (sale)} + \$34.56 \text{ (tax)} = \$610.56 \text{ total sale}$$ ∎

**OBJECTIVE 5** *Define excise tax.*     An **excise tax** or **luxury tax** is charged on certain items by the federal, state, or local government. The tax is similar to sales tax since it is paid by or passed on to the consumer of goods and services. Excise taxes are charged on gasoline, tires, and on such services as telephone, entertainment, air transportation, luxury cars, and business licenses.

Excise taxes are either a percent of the sale price of an item or a fixed amount for each unit sold. Table 6.3 shows the current federal excise taxes charged on several items.

**OBJECTIVE 6** *Find the total cost including sales tax and excise tax.*

**EXAMPLE 4** *Finding the Total Cost with Sales and Excise Taxes*

A tire for a John Deere backhoe weighs 76 pounds and sells for $680. Find the total cost of the tire including 7% sales tax and excise tax of $4.50 plus 30¢ per each pound over 70 pounds.

**SOLUTION**     First, find the sales tax using the percent equation.

$$BR = P$$

$$\$680 \times 7\% = P$$

$$\$680 \times 0.07 = \$47.60 \qquad \text{amount of sales tax}$$

TABLE 6.3   **Federal Excise Taxes**

| Product or Service | Rate | Product or Service | Rate |
|---|---|---|---|
| **Telephone service** | **3%** | **Tires (by weight)** | |
| **Teletypewriter service** | **3%** | under 40 pounds | No tax |
| **Air transportation** | **10%** | 40–69 pounds | 15¢/pound over 40 |
| **International air travel** | **$6.00/person** | 70–89 pounds | $4.50 plus 30¢/pound over 70 |
| **Air freight** | **6.25%** | **90 pounds and more** | $10.50 plus 50¢/pound over 90 |
| **Coal** | | **Truck and trailer, chassis and bodies** | 12% |
| underground (lower amount) | **$1.10/ton or 4.4%** | | |
| surface (lower amount) | **55¢/ton or 4.4%** | **Inland waterways fuel** | 24.3¢/gallon |
| **Fishing rods** | **10%** | **Ship passenger tax** | $3.00 per passenger |
| **Bows and arrows** | **11%** | **Luxury cars (amount over $34,000)** | 10% |
| **Gasoline** | **18.3¢/gallon** | | |
| **Diesel fuel** | **24.3¢/gallon** | | |
| **Aviation fuel** | **43¢/gallon** | | |

*Source:* Publication 510, I.R.S., Excise Taxes for 1996.

Next, find the excise tax.

$$\$4.50 + (76 - 70)(\$0.30) = \text{excise tax}$$

$$\$4.50 + (6 \times \$0.30) = \text{excise tax}$$

$$\$4.50 + \$1.80 = \$6.30 \qquad \text{excise tax}$$

Now find the total cost.

$$\text{Amount of sale} + \text{Sales tax} + \text{Excise tax} = \text{Total cost}$$

$$\$680 \text{ (tire)} + \$47.60 \text{ (sales tax)} + \$6.30 \text{ (excise tax)} = \$733.90 \text{ (total cost)}$$

The total cost of the tire is $733.90    ∎

**CALCULATOR APPROACH TO EXAMPLE 4**

To solve this example using a calculator, the parentheses set aside the excise tax calculation and allow excise tax to be added in the chain calculation.

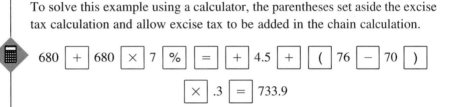

**NOTE** Excise taxes are added to the price in addition to sales tax. The excise tax is calculated on the amount of the sale before sales tax is added.    ∎

## 6.1 EXERCISES

*Find (a) the amount of sales tax, (b) the amount of excise tax, and (c) the total sale price including taxes in each of the following problems.*

| | Sale Price | Sales Tax Rate | Excise Tax Rate |
|---|---|---|---|
| 1. | $15.00 | 6% | 10% |
| 2. | $83.00 | 5% | 8% |
| 3. | $47.70 | $4\frac{1}{2}\%$ | 3% |
| 4. | $21.15 | $8\frac{1}{4}\%$ | 12% |
| 5. | $173.50 | 5% | 9¢/gallon; 165 gallons |
| 6. | $216.75 | 3% | 14¢/gallon; 190 gallons |
| 7. | $822.18 | 7% | 12% |
| 8. | $648.52 | 4% | 10% |
| 9. | $29,400.00 | $6\frac{1}{4}\%$ | $3.00 per person; 168 people |
| 10. | $57,552.00 | $4\frac{1}{2}\%$ | $3.00 per person; 218 people |

*Find the sale price and total price when given the amount of tax and the sales tax rate. Round to the nearest cent.*

| | Amount of Sales Tax | Sales Tax Rate |
|---|---|---|
| 11. | $2.29 | 5% |
| 12. | $0.80 | 7% |
| 13. | $6.30 | 4% |
| 14. | $21.84 | 8% |
| 15. | $21.45 | $6\frac{1}{2}\%$ |
| 16. | $58.00 | $7\frac{1}{4}\%$ |
| 17. | $63.84 | 5% |
| 18. | $22.32 | 4% |

*Find the amount of the sale before sales tax was added and the amount of sales tax in each of the following. Round to the nearest cent.*

| | Total Sale | Sales Tax Rate |
|---|---|---|
| 19. | $34.24 | 7% |
| 20. | $167.88 | 5% |
| 21. | $551.52 | 6% |
| 22. | $312.66 | $5\frac{1}{2}\%$ |
| 23. | $20.60 | $4\frac{1}{4}\%$ |
| 24. | $85.28 | 4% |
| 25. | $333.90 | 6% |
| 26. | $1,352.01 | 3% |
| 27. | $2,945.76 | 7% |
| 28. | $4,469.64 | 5% |

29. What is the sales tax rate where you live? Is there a different tax rate in a county or city near you? Explain why this difference exists.

30. List three items that you, your family, or your employer purchased within the last year on which an excise tax was paid. (See Objective 5.)

*Solve each of the following application problems.*

31. The retail price of an archery set (bow and arrows) is $119.80. If sales tax is 6% and the excise tax is 11%, find (a) the amount of the sales tax, (b) the amount of the excise tax, and (c) the total sale including sales tax and excise tax.

32. Mid-State Trucking pays $28,756.80 for a truck chassis. If sales tax is 7% and excise tax is 12%, find (a) the amount of the sales tax, (b) the amount of the excise tax, and (c) the total price including sales tax and excise tax.

33. The sales tax on a mountain bike is $17.10. If the sales tax rate is $4\frac{1}{2}\%$, find the sale price of the mountain bike.

**34.** Sales tax on a used car was $348. If the tax rate was 8%, find the sale price of the used car.

**35.** The price of a Toshiba laptop computer is $2,639.40 including a 6% sales tax. Find the amount of the sale price.

**36.** K-Ron's Hobbies charges $321.36 including 3% sales tax for a radio controlled glider. Find the price of the glider without tax.

**37.** Total sales for one day at Club Sunset were $1,285.44 including the 4% sales tax charged on all purchases. Find the amount that is sales tax.

**38.** The Tropical Fish Place has total receipts for the day of $875.43. If this includes $6\frac{1}{2}$% sales tax on all sales, find the amount that is sales tax.

**39.** At the close of business one day, Mike Roche, a new employee, totaled the amount in the cash register and found $1,908. He multiplied this sum by the sales tax rate of 6% to find the amount of sales tax due. Is this procedure correct? Find (a) the correct amount of sales tax and (b) the amount of error made by Roche.

**40.** Santiago Rowland has total daily receipts of $1,856. His lounge manager multiplies this total by 5.5%, the tax rate in the area. Is this procedure correct? Find (a) the correct amount of sales tax and (b) the amount of error made by the manager.

**41.** Auburn Tire offers a 74-pound truck tire for $182 plus tax. If sales tax is $7\frac{1}{2}$% and excise tax is $4.50 plus 30¢ per pound over 70 pounds, find the total cost including tax.

**42.** Jack Anderson purchased a set of 8 truck tires at a cost of $390 each. Each tire weighs 52 pounds, sales tax is 6%, and excise tax is 15¢ per pound over 40 pounds for each tire. Find the total cost to Anderson.

**43.** Bob Towers Travels pays $33,850 for a chartered international flight. Sales tax is $7\frac{1}{2}$% and excise tax is $6 per person. If 240 people make the flight, find the total cost including tax.

**44.** Ticket sales for an international flight are $26,970 before taxes. If sales tax is 5.5% and excise tax is $6 per person, find the total sales including tax if there are 128 passengers.

## 6.2    Property Tax

### OBJECTIVES

**1** *Understand fair market value and find assessed valuation.*

**2** *Use the tax rate formula.*

**3** *Use the formula for property tax.*

**4** *Express tax rates in percent, dollars per $100, dollars per $1,000, and mills.*

**5** *Find taxes given the assessed valuation and the tax rate.*

**6** *Find the assessed valuation given the tax rate and the tax.*

**7** *Find the tax rate given the assessed valuation and the tax.*

In virtually every area of the nation, the owners of **real property** (such as buildings and land) must pay a property tax on their property. In many areas **personal property** (such as mobile homes, furnishings, appliances, motor homes, trailers, boats, and other non-real estate items) is also taxed. Some areas handle these two taxes separately, while others combine them. The money raised by this property tax is used to provide services in the local community, such as police and fire protection, roads, schools, and parks.

**OBJECTIVE 1** *Understand fair market value and find assessed valuation.*     To find the amount of this tax, each piece of real property in an area must be **assessed**. In this process, a local official, called the assessor, makes an estimate of the **fair market value** of the property, the price for which the property could reasonably be expected to be sold. The **assessed valuation** of the property is then found by multiplying the fair market value by a certain percent called the **assessment rate**. The percent that is used varies drastically from state to state, but normally remains constant within a state.

In some states, assessed valuation is 25% of fair market value, while in other states, the assessed valuation is 40% to 60% or even 100% of fair market value. Occasionally, different rates will be used for homes and for businesses. In theory, this step is unnecessary in calculating property tax. However, using an assessed valuation that is a percent of fair market value has become an accepted practice over the years.

| EXAMPLE 1   *Determining the Assessed Value of Property*

Find the assessed valuation for the following pieces of property.

**(a)** fair market value, $112,000; assessment rate (percent), 25%

**(b)** fair market value, $1,382,500; assessment rate (percent), 60%

**SOLUTION**     Multiply the fair market value by the assessment rate.

**(a)** $112,000 × 0.25 = $28,000 assessed valuation

**(b)** $1,382,500 × 0.60 = $829,500 assessed valuation     ■

**OBJECTIVE 2** *Use the tax rate formula.*     After calculating the assessed valuation of all the taxable property in an area, and determining the amount of money needed to provide the necessary services (the budget), the agency responsible for levying the tax announces the annual **property tax rate**.

This tax rate is determined by the following formula.

$$R = \frac{P}{B}$$

$$\text{Tax rate} = \frac{\text{Total tax amount needed}}{\text{Total assessed value}}$$

| EXAMPLE 2 *Finding the Tax Rate*

Find the tax rate for the following park districts in River County.

**(a)** total tax amount needed, $368,400; total assessed value, $7,368,000

**(b)** total tax amount needed, $633,750; total assessed value, $28,800,000

SOLUTION   Divide the total tax amount needed by the total assessed value.

**(a)** $368,400 ÷ $7,368,000 = 0.05 = 5% tax rate

**(b)** $633,750 ÷ $28,800,000 = 0.022 = 2.2% tax rate  ∎

OBJECTIVE **3** *Use the formula for property tax.*   Property tax rates are expressed in different ways in different parts of the country. However, property tax is always found with the formula

$$P \;=\; R \times B$$
$$\text{Tax} = \text{Tax rate} \times \text{Assessed valuation}$$

OBJECTIVE **4** *Express tax rates in percent, dollars per $100, dollars per $1,000, and mills.*

*Percent.*   Some areas express tax rates as a percent of assessed valuation. The tax on a piece of property with an assessed valuation of $74,000 at a tax rate of 9.42% (9.42% = 0.0942) would be

$$\text{Tax} = 0.0942 \times \$74,000 = \$6,970.80.$$

*Dollars Per $100.*   In other areas, the rate is expressed as a number of dollars per $100 of assessed valuation. For example, the rate might be expressed as $11.42 per $100 of assessed valuation. Assuming a tax rate of $11.42 per $100, find the tax on a piece of land having an assessed valuation of $18,000 as follows. First, move the decimal point two places left to find the number of hundreds in $18,000.

$18,000 = 180$ hundreds      Move the decimal two places to the left.

Then, find the tax.

$$\text{Tax} = \text{Tax rate} \times \text{Number of hundreds of valuation}$$
$$= \;\$11.42 \;\times\; 180 = \$2,055.60$$

*Dollars Per $1,000.*   In other areas, the tax rate is expressed as a number of dollars per $1,000 of assessed valuation. If the tax rate is $98.12 per $1,000, a piece of property having an assessed valuation of $197,000 would be taxed as follows.

$197,000 = 197$ thousands      Move the decimal three places to the left.

$$\text{Tax} = \$98.12 \times 197 = \$19,329.64$$

*Mills.*   Finally, some areas express tax rates in mills (a **mill** is one-tenth of a cent, or one-thousandth of a dollar). For example, a tax rate might be expressed as 46

TABLE 6.4    **Writing Tax Rates in Four Systems**

| Percent | Per $100 | Per $1,000 | In Mills |
|---------|----------|------------|----------|
| 12.52% | $12.52 | $125.20 | 125.2 |
| 3.2% | $3.20 | $32.00 | 32 |
| 9.87% | $9.87 | $98.70 | 98.7 |

mills per dollar (or $0.046 per dollar). The tax on a property having an assessed valuation of $81,000, at a tax rate of 46 mills, is

$$\text{Tax} = (0.046) \times \$81,000 \qquad \text{46 mills} = \$0.046$$
$$= \$3,726.$$

Table 6.4 shows the same tax rates written in the four different systems. Although expressed differently, they are equivalent tax rates.

**NOTE**    The number of decimal places used and rounding practices in tax rates vary among taxing jurisdictions. A common practice is to round *up* the last digit used. In Table 6.4 rounding 125.2 mills and 98.7 mills to whole mills would result in 126 mills and 99 mills, respectively.    ■

**OBJECTIVE 5** *Find taxes given the assessed valuation and the tax rate.*    Property taxes are found by multiplying the tax rate by the assessed valuation. Use the formula for finding property tax.

**EXAMPLE 3** *Finding the Property Tax*

Find the taxes on each of the following pieces of property. Assessed valuations and tax rates are given.

**(a)** $58,975; 8.4%          **(b)** $875,400; $7.82 per $100

**(c)** $129,600; $64.21 per $1,000          **(d)** $221,750; 94 mills

**SOLUTION**    Multiply tax rate by the assessed valuation.

**(a)** 8.4% = 0.084

$$\text{Tax} = \text{Tax rate} \times \text{Assessed valuation}$$
$$\text{Tax} = 0.084 \times \$58,975 = \$4,953.90$$

**(b)** $875,400 = 8,754 hundreds

$$\text{Tax} = \$7.82 \times 8,754 = \$68,456.28$$

**(c)** $129,600 = 129.6 thousands

$$\text{Tax} = \$64.21 \times 129.6 = \$8,321.62$$

**(d)** 94 mills = $0.094

$$\text{Tax} = 0.094 \times \$221,750 = \$20,844.50$$    ■

**N**OTE Some states offer certain tax exemptions which will reduce the amount of property tax due. One type of exemption is the Homeowner's Tax Exemption which allows a specific amount of tax exemption to a person who owns and occupies a home or condominium as a personal residence. ■

The graph below shows the percent of income paid on all types of taxes by people in major countries of the world. The United States (U.S.) still enjoys the lowest taxes among industrialized nations. Note that total taxes in France are approximately 48% while total taxes in the United States are approximately 31%.

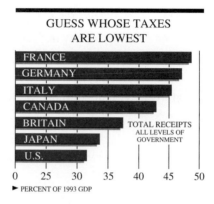

*Source:* Reprinted from Jan. 23, 1995 issue of *Business Week* by special permission, copyright © 1995 by McGraw-Hill, Inc.

**O**BJECTIVE **6** *Find the assessed valuation given the tax rate and the tax.* The tax formula can also be used to find the assessed valuation when given the amount of tax and the tax rate.

**E**XAMPLE 4 *Finding the Assessed Valuation*

The taxes on a car wash in Boden County are $1,024. If the tax rate is $3.00 per $100, find the assessed valuation.

**S**OLUTION Use the formula for finding tax.

$$\text{Tax} = \text{Tax rate} \times \text{Assessed valuation}$$

$$\$1,024 = \$3.00 \times \text{Assessed valuation}$$

$$\frac{1,024}{3} = \text{Assessed valuation}$$

$$341.33 \text{ hundreds} = \text{Assessed valuation}$$

The assessed valuation is $34,133 (341.33 × 100). ■

CALCULATOR APPROACH
TO EXAMPLE 4

The calculator solution to this example is

1024 $\boxed{\div}$ 3 $\boxed{=}$ $\boxed{\times}$ 100 $\boxed{=}$ 34133.

**OBJECTIVE** **7** *Find the tax rate given the assessed valuation and the tax.*    The tax rate may be found by using the tax formula when the assessed valuation and the amount of tax are given.

EXAMPLE 5 *Finding the Tax Rate Given Assessed Valuation and Tax*

A commercial property in Suffolk County has an assessed valuation of $46,700 and an annual property tax of $3,000.28. Find the tax rate per $1,000.

SOLUTION    Use the formula for finding tax.

$$\text{Tax} = \text{Tax rate} \times \text{Assessed valuation}$$

The assessed valuation is 46.7 thousands ($46,700 ÷ 1,000).

$$\$3,000.28 = \text{Tax rate} \times 46.7$$

$$\frac{3,000.28}{46.7} = \text{Tax rate}$$

$$\$64.25 = \text{Tax rate per } \$1,000$$

The tax rate per $1,000 is $64.25.    ∎

## 6.2  EXERCISES

*Find the assessed valuation for each of the following pieces of property.*

| | Fair Market Value | Rate of Assessment |
|---|---|---|
| 1. | $32,000 | 35% |
| 2. | $218,500 | 70% |
| 3. | $182,500 | 60% |
| 4. | $98,200 | 42% |
| 5. | $1,300,500 | 25% |
| 6. | $2,450,000 | 80% |

*Find the tax rate for the following. Write the tax rate as a percent rounded to the nearest tenth.*

| | Total Tax Amount Needed | Total Assessed Value |
|---|---|---|
| 7. | $625,000 | $5,200,000 |
| 8. | $322,500 | $4,300,000 |
| 9. | $1,580,000 | $19,750,000 |
| 10. | $2,175,000 | $54,375,000 |
| 11. | $1,224,000 | $40,800,000 |
| 12. | $2,941,500 | $81,700,000 |

*Complete the following list comparing tax rates.*

| | Percent | Per $100 | Per $1,000 | In Mills |
|---|---|---|---|---|
| 13. | (a) _____ % | (b) _____ | (c) _____ | 56 |
| 14. | (a) _____ % | $4.93 | (b) _____ | (c) _____ |
| 15. | 2.41% | (a) _____ | (b) _____ | (c) _____ |
| 16. | 7.42% | (a) _____ | (b) _____ | (c) _____ |
| 17. | (a) _____ % | $7.08 | (b) _____ | (c) _____ |
| 18. | (a) _____ % | (b) _____ | $28 | (c) _____ |

 19. What is the difference between fair market value and assessed value? How is the assessment rate used when finding the assessed value? (See Objective 1.)

 20. Describe two circumstances where you would want to be able to calculate taxes, given the assessed valuation and the tax rate.

*Find the tax for each of the following.*

| | Assessed Valuation | Tax Rate |
|---|---|---|
| 21. | $86,200 | $6.80 per $100 |
| 22. | $41,300 | $46.40 per $1,000 |
| 23. | $685,400 | 6.93% |
| 24. | $128,200 | 42 mills |
| 25. | $7,500 | $12.20 per $100 |
| 26. | $38,250 | $89.70 per $1,000 |

*Find the missing quantity.*

| | Assessed Valuation | Tax Rate | Tax |
|---|---|---|---|
| 27. | $98,500 | _____ % | $5,713 |
| 28. | _____ | $7.18 per $100 | $15,652.40 |
| 29. | $73,800 | 85 mills | _____ |
| 30. | _____ | $48.18 per $1,000 | $1,903.11 |
| 31. | $152,680 | _____ per $100 | $8,015.70 |
| 32. | $435,500 | 37.6 mills | _____ |
| 33. | _____ | 4.3% | $10,182.40 |
| 34. | $96,200 | _____ per $1,000 | $3,367 |

*Solve each of the following application problems.*

**35.** Kali Barnum owns the real estate on which she operates her business, Flowers For You. The property has a fair market value of $242,000, property in the area is assessed at 28% of market value, and the property tax is $2,134.44. Find the tax rate as a percent.

**36.** Al Espinal owns a 6-unit apartment building with a fair market value of $192,600. Property in the area is assessed at 40% of market value and the property tax is $4,237.20. Find the tax rate as a percent.

**37.** A new FM radio station broadcasts from a building having a fair market value of $334,400. The building is in an area where property is assessed at 25% of market value and the tax rate is $75.30 per $1,000 of assessed value. Find the property tax.

**38.** The Consumer's Cooperative owns property with a fair market value of $785,200. The property is located in a county that assesses at 80% of market value. Find the property tax if the tax rate is $14.30 per $1,000 of assessed value.

**39.** Downtown Office Park has a fair market value of $5,700,000. Property is assessed in the area at 25% of market value. The tax rate is $14.10 per $100 of assessed valuation. Find the property tax.

**40.** Gilstrap's Five and Dime has property with a fair market value of $148,500. The property is located in an area that is assessed at 25% of market value. The tax rate is $8.26 per $100. Find the property tax paid.

**41.** In one county, property is assessed at 40% of market value, with a tax rate of 32.1 mills. In a second county, property is assessed at 24% of market value with a tax rate of 50.2 mills. Feathers Custom Wood Products is trying to decide where to place a building with a fair market value of $95,000. (a) Which county would charge the lower property tax? (b) Find the annual amount saved.

**42.** Property taxes vary from one county to the next. In one county, property is assessed at 30% of market value, with a tax rate of 45.6 mills. In a second county, property is assessed at 48% of market value, with a tax rate of 29.3 mills. Misty Arce is trying to decide where to build her $140,000 dream house. (a) Which county would charge the lower property tax? (b) Find the annual amount saved.

**43.** Last year the property tax on an executive's estate was $4,625, and the tax rate was $12.50 per $1,000. After a reassessment this year, the assessed value was increased by

$25,000 and the property tax due is $5,350. Find the percent of increase in the tax rate. Round to the nearest tenth of a percent. Hint: Do not round until the final answer.

**44.** Last year the property tax on a warehouse was $3,042, and the tax rate was $3.60 per $100. After a reassessment this year, the assessed value was increased by $10,500 and the property tax due is $3,705. Find the percent of increase in the tax rate. Round to the nearest tenth of a percent.

**45.** A prime commercial corner lot was assessed at $45,000, and the tax was $1,327.50. The following year the property tax increased to $1,353.75 while the tax rate decreased by $0.10 per $100. Find the amount of increase in the assessed value of the commercial lot.

**46.** An investment property was assessed at $240,000, and the tax was $5,400. The following year the property tax increased to $5,805, while the tax rate decreased by $1.00 per $1,000. Find the amount of increase in the assessed value of the property.

## 6.3    Personal Income Tax

### OBJECTIVES

**1**   *Know the four steps that determine tax liability.*

**2**   *Identify information needed to find adjusted gross income.*

**3**   *Determine adjusted gross income.*

**4**   *Know the standard deduction amounts.*

**5**   *Recall the tax rates.*

**6**   *List possible deductions to find taxable income.*

**7**   *Calculate income tax.*

**8**   *Determine a refund or balance due the Internal Revenue Service.*

**9**   *Prepare a 1040A and a Schedule 1 Federal Tax Form.*

The federal government, most states, many local governments, and some cities use income tax as a source of revenue. However, for most people the federal income tax is the largest tax expense.

As shown in Figure 6.1, the individual income tax provides the largest single source of income to the federal government.

Instructions provided with the tax forms have to cover the situation of every possible taxpayer, from students who earn very little money to professional people, such as lawyers and doctors, who often have complicated financial affairs. For this reason, many people take their tax returns to a professional tax preparer. But even tax preparers do not solve all the problems of the taxpayer—the taxpayer still must supply all the necessary information. Tax preparers only insert the figures in the correct places on the correct forms and then do the necessary calculations.

**OBJECTIVE 1** *Know the four steps that determine tax liability.*   There are four basic steps in finding a person's total tax liability. If a taxpayer understands these steps and does

**Federal Income and Outlays**

**Income:**

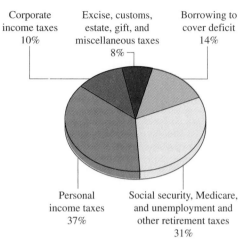

Corporate income taxes 10%

Excise, customs, estate, gift, and miscellaneous taxes 8%

Borrowing to cover deficit 14%

Personal income taxes 37%

Social security, Medicare, and unemployment and other retirement taxes 31%

**Outlays:**

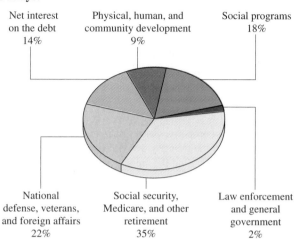

Net interest on the debt 14%

Physical, human, and community development 9%

Social programs 18%

National defense, veterans, and foreign affairs 22%

Social security, Medicare, and other retirement 35%

Law enforcement and general government 2%

FIGURE 6.1

not have involved tax questions, he or she should be able to fill out the federal tax return in a fairly short time.

> ### PREPARING YOUR INCOME TAX RETURN
>
> ***Step 1.*** Find the adjusted gross income (AGI) for the year.
>
> ***Step 2.*** Find the taxable income.
>
> ***Step 3.*** Find the tax.
>
> ***Step 4.*** Check to see if a refund is due, or if more money is owed to the government.

**OBJECTIVE 2** *Identify information needed to find adjusted gross income.* These steps are explained in order. The first step is to find the **adjusted gross income** for the year by collecting all the **W-2 forms** that were provided by employers during the year. A W-2 form is shown in Figure 6.2. The form shows the total amount of money paid to the employee by the employer, and also shows the total amount that was withheld from the employee's paycheck and sent, in his or her name, to the IRS. Add all the amounts paid to the employee.

Next, collect any **1099 forms** that may have been received. These informational forms, copies of which go to the IRS, show miscellaneous income received, such as interest on checking or savings accounts, as well as stock dividends. A sample 1099 form is shown in Figure 6.3. Also, include any tips or other employee compensation, and enter the total on the correct line of the income tax form.

| a Control number | 22222 | Void ☐ | For Official Use Only ▶ OMB No. 1545-0008 | | |
|---|---|---|---|---|---|

| b Employer's identification number 94-1287319 | 1 Wages, tips, other compensation $ 24,738.41 | 2 Federal income tax withheld $ 3,275.68 |
|---|---|---|
| c Employer's name, address, and ZIP code | 3 Social security wages $ 24,738.41 | 4 Social security tax withheld $ 1,533.78 |

Towne Books
1568 Liberty Heights Avenue
Baltimore, MD 21230

| | 5 Medicare wages and tips $ 24,738.41 | 6 Medicare tax withheld $ 358.71 |
|---|---|---|
| | 7 Social security tips | 8 Allocated tips |

| d Employee's social security number 418-23-0152 | 9 Advance EIC payment | 10 Dependent care benefits |
|---|---|---|
| e Employee's name (first, middle initial, last) | 11 Nonqualified plans | 12 Benefits included in box 1 |

Patricia Rowell
2136 Old Road
Towson, MD 21285

| | 13 See Instrs. for box 13 | 14 Other |
|---|---|---|

15 Statutory employee ☐  Deceased ☐  Pension plan ☐  Legal rep. ☐  Hshld. emp. ☐  Subtotal ☐  Deferred compensation ☐

f Employee's address and ZIP code

| 16 State MD | Employer's state I.D. No. 600-5076 | 17 State wages, tips, etc. | 18 State income tax | 19 Locality name | 20 Local wages, tips, etc. | 21 Local income tax |
|---|---|---|---|---|---|---|
| | | | | | | |

Form **W-2** Wage and Tax Statement

41-1628061

Department of the Treasury—Internal Revenue Service
For Paperwork Reduction Act Notice, see separate instructions.

Copy A For Social Security Administration

FIGURE 6.2

---

| 9292 | ☐ VOID | ☐ CORRECTED |
|---|---|---|

| PAYER'S name, street address, city, state, and ZIP code | Payer's RTN (optional) | OMB No. 1545-0112 | |
|---|---|---|---|
| Employees Credit Union 2572 Brookhaven Drive Dundalk, MD 21222 | | Form **1099-INT** | **Interest Income** |

| PAYER'S Federal identification number 95-0598071 | RECIPIENT'S identification number 418-23-0152 | 1 Interest income not included in box 3 $    $ 427.82 | | Copy A For Internal Revenue Service Center |
|---|---|---|---|---|
| RECIPIENT'S name Patricia Rowell | | 2 Early withdrawal penalty $ | 3 Interest on U.S. Savings Bonds and Treas. obligations $ | File with Form 1096. |
| Street address (including apt. no.) 2136 Old Road | | 4 Federal income tax withheld $ | | For Paperwork Reduction Act Notice and instructions for completing this form, see **Instructions for Forms 1099, 1098, 5498, and W-2G.** |
| City, state, and ZIP code Towson, MD 21285 | | 5 Foreign tax paid $ | 6 Foreign country or U.S. possession | |
| Account number (optional) | 2nd TIN Not. ☐ | $ | | |

Form **1099-INT**    41-1628061

Department of the Treasury - Internal Revenue Service

FIGURE 6.3

**OBJECTIVE 3** *Determine adjusted gross income.*   Using the information from the W-2 and 1099 forms, and adding any dividends, capital gains, unemployment compensation, tips, or other employee compensation, enter the total on the correct line of the income tax form. Subtract any adjustments to income, such as an **Individual Retirement Account (IRA)** or alimony payments. An IRA is a retirement plan which allows contributions to be deducted from income. The result is the **adjusted gross income**.

Adjusted gross income is found with the following formula.

$$\text{Adjusted gross income} = \text{Total income} - \text{Total adjustments}$$

**EXAMPLE 1** *Finding Adjusted Gross Income (AGI)*

Patricia Rowell earned $24,738.41 last year from Towne Books as assistant manager and $427.82 in interest from her credit union (see her W-2 and 1099 forms). She had $1,500 in IRA contributions. Find her adjusted gross income.

**SOLUTION**   Add the income from her job ($24,738.41) and the interest ($427.82). Then subtract the IRA contributions.

$$\$24,738.41 + \$427.82 - \$1,500 = \$23,666.23 \qquad \blacksquare$$

**NOTE**   When filing your income tax a copy of all W-2 Forms is sent to the Internal Revenue service along with the completed tax forms. However, the IRS does not require the taxpayer to send copies of 1099 Forms to them.   ■

**OBJECTIVE 4** *Know the standard deduction amounts.*   Most people are almost finished at this point. If deductions for medical expenses, interest, and so on are not to be itemized, and if there are no further adjustments, then the **standard deduction** amount must be determined and subtracted from the adjusted gross income. The most current standard deduction amounts are shown as follows.

- $4,000 for single people
- $6,700 for married people filing jointly and qualifying widow(er)s
- $3,350 for married people filing separately
- $5,900 for head of a household

Additional standard deductions are given for taxpayers and dependents who are blind or 65 years of age or older.

Now, only one step remains before the tax owed is found: determine the number of **personal exemptions**. An exemption is taken for the head of the household and for each of his or her dependents, including spouse and children. For example, a married person with a spouse and three children would be allowed to claim five exemptions. The taxpayer is allowed a $2,550 reduction in gross income for each exemption. After subtracting $2,550 per exemption from the adjusted gross income, the result, **taxable income**, is multiplied by the proper tax rate to determine taxes due.

TABLE 6.5   **Tax Rate Schedule**

**Single**

| Over— | But not over— | Tax is– | of the amount over— |
|---:|---:|:---|---:|
| $0 | $23,350 | ........ 15% | $0 |
| 23,350 | 56,550 | $3,502.50 + 28% | 23,350 |
| 56,550 | 117,950 | 12,798.50 + 31% | 56,550 |
| 117,950 | 256,500 | 31,832.50 + 36% | 117,950 |
| 256,500 | ..... | 81,710.50 + 39.6% | 256,500 |

**Married Filing Jointly or Qualifying Widow(er)**

| Over— | But not over— | Tax is— | of the amount over— |
|---:|---:|:---|---:|
| $0 | $39,000 | ........ 15% | $0 |
| 39,000 | 94,250 | $5,850.00 + 28% | 39,000 |
| 94,250 | 143,600 | 21,320.00 + 31% | 94,250 |
| 143,600 | 256,500 | 36,618.50 + 36% | 143,600 |
| 256,500 | ..... | 77,262.50 + 39.6% | 256,500 |

**Married Filing Separately**

| Over— | But not over— | Tax is— | of the amount over— |
|---:|---:|:---|---:|
| $0 | $19,500 | ........ 15% | $0 |
| 19,500 | 47,125 | $2,925.00 + 28% | 19,500 |
| 47,125 | 71,800 | 10,660.00 + 31% | 47,125 |
| 71,800 | 128,250 | 18,309.25 + 36% | 71,800 |
| 128,250 | ..... | 38,631.25 + 39.6% | 128,250 |

**Head of Household**

| Over— | But not over— | Tax is— | of the amount over— |
|---:|---:|:---|---:|
| $0 | $31,250 | ........ 15% | $0 |
| 31,250 | 80,750 | $4,687.50 + 28% | 31,250 |
| 80,750 | 130,800 | 18,547.50 + 31% | 80,750 |
| 130,800 | 256,500 | 34,063.00 + 36% | 130,800 |
| 256,500 | ..... | 79,315.00 + 39.6% | 256,500 |

**OBJECTIVE 5**  *Recall the tax rates.*    Most recently individual income tax rates have been either 15%, 28%, 31%, 36%, or 39.6%, depending on the amount of taxable income and the taxpayer's filing status. Table 6.5, the tax rate schedule, shows the individual tax rates for each filing status.

**EXAMPLE 2**  *Finding Taxable Income and the Income Tax Amount*

Find the taxable income and the tax for each of the following people.

(a)  Liz Covello, single, 1 exemption, adjusted gross income, $21,835

(b)  The Zagorins, married, filing jointly, 5 exemptions, adjusted gross income, $64,308

**SOLUTION**

(a)  Taxable income is $15,285 ($21,835 − $4,000 standard deduction − $2,550 for one exemption). Since the total adjusted gross income is below $23,350, the 15% tax rate applies. The tax is calculated as follows.

$$15\% \times \$15,285 = \$2,292.75$$

The tax is $2,292.75.

**(b)** Taxable income is $44,858 ($64,308 − $6,700 standard deduction − $12,750 for five exemptions). ''Married filing jointly'' tax is:

$$15\% \times \$39,000 = \$5,850.00$$
$$28\% \times \$5,858 \ (\$44,858 - \$39,000) = \underline{\$1,640.24}$$
$$\text{Total } \$7,490.24$$

The tax is $7,490.24. ∎

**PROBLEM-SOLVING HINT** When taxable income goes beyond the 15% tax rate amount, do not make the mistake of using the 28% tax rate on the entire amount of taxable income. For example, for a single person having a taxable income greater than $23,350, a tax rate of 15% is used for the first $23,350 and a tax rate of 28% is used *only* on the amount *over* $23,350 up to the next bracket. ∎

**OBJECTIVE 6** *List possible deductions to find taxable income.* A **tax deduction** is any expense that the IRS will allow the taxpayer to subtract from adjusted gross income. To be of benefit, itemized deductions must exceed the automatic standard deduction allowed by the IRS. Usually, taxpayers will benefit from itemized deductions when they take out a loan in order to purchase a home and are allowed to deduct the interest on the loan.

The 20% of the American population who do itemize all their deductions must go through one additional step before subtracting exemptions to determine taxable income: all deductions must be listed. The most common deductions are given here.

*Medical and Dental Expenses.* Not all such expenses may be deductible. In general, only amounts in excess of 7.5% of the adjusted gross income may be deducted. For most people, however, this restriction limits medical deductions to catastrophic illnesses.

The medical and dental payments you may possibly deduct include all visits to medical doctors, dentists, chiropractors, and therapists, all medical examinations and treatments, nursing help, hospital care, ambulance service, a mileage deduction for travel to and from medical services and those medical and dental insurance premiums paid by the taxpayer. Expenses reimbursed by insurance companies cannot be deducted.

*Taxes.* State and local income taxes, real estate taxes, and personal property taxes may be deducted. You may not deduct federal income tax, gasoline taxes, social security or medicare taxes or any sales taxes.

*Interest.* Home mortgage interest on the taxpayer's principle residence and a qualified second home is deductible. Other interest charges (including credit card interest) may not be deducted.

*Contributions.* Contributions to most charities may be deducted.

*Miscellaneous Deductions.* Miscellaneous expenses are only deductible to the extent that the total amount of such deductions exceeds 2% of the taxpayer's adjusted gross income. These deductions include union dues, qualified education expenses, income tax preparation fees, tax preparation books or computer software, appraisal fees for tax purposes, legal fees for tax planning or tax litigation, and safe deposit box rental fees.

**NOTE** When itemizing deductions, the gain in deductions is not the total of all itemized deductions but the difference between the standard deduction amount and the total itemized deductions. ■

**OBJECTIVE 7** *Calculate income tax.*    After determining the taxable income, the amount of income tax must be found.

The amount of income tax is found using the following formula.

$$\text{Income tax} = \text{Taxable income} \times \text{Tax rate}$$

**EXAMPLE 3** *Using Itemized Deductions to Find Taxable Income and Income Tax*

Brad Beltram is single, has no dependents, and had an adjusted gross income of $19,238 last year. He had deductions of $1,352 for other taxes, $2,616 for mortgage interest, and $317 for charity. Find his taxable income and his income tax.

**SOLUTION** First find the total of all deductions.

$$\text{Deductions} = \$1,352 + \$2,616 + \$317 = \$4,285$$

Since Beltram is single, and the standard deduction is $4,000, the larger itemized deduction amount, $4,285, is taken. Now find his taxable income.

$$\text{Taxable income} = \$19,238 - \$4,285 - \$2,550 = \$12,403$$

Finally, income tax is determined.

$$15\% \times \$12,403 = \$1,860.45$$

His tax is $1,860.45. ■

**NOTE** In preparing personal income tax, refer to current Internal Revenue Service publications, and always use the current tax rates. ■

**OBJECTIVE 8** *Determine a refund or balance due the Internal Revenue Service.*    After calculating the proper tax, determine whether a refund will come from the government. Look again at the W-2 forms to find out how much already has been paid toward the tax bill. These forms show the total amount the employer has withheld and sent to the government. (Usually, no money is withheld for amounts on 1099 forms.) If the amount withheld is greater than the tax owed, the taxpayer is entitled to a refund. If the amount withheld is less than the tax owed, the taxpayer must send the difference along with the tax return.

**EXAMPLE 4** *Determining Tax Due or a Tax Refund*

Gale Klein had $375.20 per month withheld for federal income tax from her checks last year. She is single and has taxable income of $24,056 for the year. Does she get a refund? If so, how much?

**SOLUTION**    Klein had $375.20 \times 12 = \$4,502.40$ withheld from her checks last year. The tax due on taxable income of \$24,056 is \$3,700.18; therefore, she will receive a refund in the amount of

$$\$4,502.40 - \$3,700.18 = \$802.22.$$ ∎

**PROBLEM-SOLVING HINT**    Be certain that the proper income tax form is used when filing your individual income tax. The 1040 EZ Form is used by many students but you must be single to use this form. If you have over \$400 in interest or any adjustments to income, a 1040A Form is used. In order to itemize deductions the taxpayer must use a 1040 Form. There are additional considerations and restrictions that determine whether the 1040 EZ, 1040A, or 1040 forms should be used.    ∎

**OBJECTIVE 9**    *Prepare a 1040A and a Schedule 1 Federal Tax Form.*    The next example shows how to complete an income tax return using Form 1040A and a Schedule 1 (Form 1040).

**EXAMPLE 5**    *Preparing a 1040A and a Schedule 1*

Patricia Rowell is single and claims one exemption. Her income appears on the W-2 and 1099 forms on page 207. Rowell contributes \$1,500 to an IRA. Since she has interest income over \$400 but does not itemize her deductions she may use Form 1040A and must also file a Schedule 1 (Form 1040A). Complete her income tax return (Figures 6.4–6.6).

**CALCULATOR APPROACH TO EXAMPLE 5**

First, find the adjusted gross income.

$$24738 \;\boxed{+}\; 428 \;\boxed{-}\; 1500 \;\boxed{=}\;$$

Next, subtract the standard deduction and the personal exemption.

$$\boxed{-} \; 4000 \; \boxed{-} \; 2550 \; \boxed{=}$$

Now, multiply by the tax rate to find the amount of tax and store this in memory.

$$\boxed{\times} \; .15 \; \boxed{=} \; \boxed{\text{STO}}$$

Finally, subtract the amount of tax from the amount withheld to find the amount of refund.

$$3276 \; \boxed{-} \; \boxed{\text{RCL}} \; \boxed{=} \; 708.6$$

**NOTE**    When completing income tax forms and calculations, notice that all amounts may be rounded to the nearest dollar.    ∎

Form

# 1040A (X)

Department of the Treasury—Internal Revenue Service

**U.S. Individual Income Tax Return**

199

IRS Use Only—Do not write or staple in this space.

**Label** (See page 15.) Use the IRS label. Otherwise, please print in ALL CAPITAL LETTERS.

OMB No. 1545-0085

L A B E L

H E R E

| Your first name | Init. | Last name |
|---|---|---|
| Patricia | | Rowell |

Your social security number

4 1 8 2 3 0 1 5 2

| If a joint return, spouse's first name | Init. | Last name |
|---|---|---|

Spouse's social security number

Home address (number and street). If you have a P.O. box, see page 15. | Apt. no.

2136 Old Road

City, town or post office. If you have a foreign address, see page 15. | State | ZIP code

Towson, | M D | 2 1 2 5 8+

**For Privacy Act and Paperwork Reduction Act Notice, see page 9.**

**Presidential Election Campaign Fund** (See page 15.)

| | Yes | No |
|---|---|---|
| Do you want $3 to go to this fund? | | X |
| If a joint return, does your spouse want $3 to go to this fund? | | |

**Note:** Checking "Yes" will not change your tax or reduce your refund.

1 ☒ Single

2 ☐ Married filing joint return (even if only one had income)

3 ☐ Married filing separate return. Enter spouse's social security number above and full name here. ▶ _____

4 ☐ Head of household (with qualifying person). (See page 16.) If the qualifying person is a child but not your dependent, enter this child's name here. ▶ _____

5 ☐ Qualifying widow(er) with dependent child (year spouse died ▶ 19    ). (See page 16.)

6a ☒ **Yourself.** If your parent (or someone else) can claim you as a dependent on his or her tax return, **do not** check box 6a.

b ☐ Spouse

No. of boxes checked on lines 6a and 6b | 1

c **Dependents.** If more than six dependents, see page 17.

| (1) First name    Last name | (2) Dependent's social security number. If born in Dec. 1996, see page 18. | (3) Dependent's relationship to you | (4) No. of months lived in your home in 1996 |
|---|---|---|---|
| | | | |
| | | | |
| | | | |
| | | | |
| | | | |
| | | | |

No. of your children on line 6c who:
• lived with you
• did not live with you due to divorce or separation (see page 18)

Dependents on 6c not entered above

d Total number of exemptions claimed . . . . . . . . . . . . ▶

Add numbers entered in boxes above | 1

7 Wages, salaries, tips, etc. This should be shown in box 1 of your W-2 form(s). Attach Form(s) W-2. | 7 $ 2 4 7 3 8

8a **Taxable** interest income. If over $400, attach Schedule 1. | 8a $ 4 2 8

b **Tax-exempt** interest. DO NOT include on line 8a. | 8b $

9 Dividends. If over $400, attach Schedule 1. | 9 $

10a Total IRA distributions. 10a $ | 10b Taxable amount (see page 20). | 10b $

11a Total pensions and annuities. 11a $ | 11b Taxable amount (see page 20). | 11b $

12 Unemployment compensation. | 12 $

13a Social security benefits. 13a $ | 13b Taxable amount (see page 22). | 13b $

14 Add lines 7 through 13b (far right column). This is your **total income.** ▶ | 14 $ 2 5 1 6 6

15a Your IRA deduction (see page 22). | 15a $ 1 5 0 0

b Spouse's IRA deduction (see page 22). | 15b $

c Add lines 15a and 15b. These are your **total adjustments.** | 15c $ 1 5 0 0

16 Subtract line 15c from line 14. This is your **adjusted gross income.** If under $28,495 (under $9,500 if a child did not live with you), see the instructions for line 29c on page 29. ▶ | 16 $ 2 3 6 6 6

Attach Copy B of W-2 and 1099-R here.

Cat. No. 11327A | **1996 Form 1040A page 1**

FIGURE 6.4

| | | |
|---|---|---|
| **17** | Enter the amount from line 16. | **17** $ 2 3 6 6 6 |

**18a** Check if:  ☐ **You** were 65 or older  ☐ Blind  ☐ **Spouse** was 65 or older  ☐ Blind  Enter number of boxes checked ▶ 18a  0

**b** If you are married filing separately and your spouse itemizes deductions, see page 26 and check here . . . . . . . . . . . . . . . . . . ▶ 18b  ☐

**19** Enter the **standard deduction** for your filing status. **But** see page 26 if you checked any box on line 18a or b **OR** someone can claim you as a dependent.
- Single—4,000    • Married filing jointly or Qualifying widow(er)—6,700
- Head of household—5,900    • Married filing separately—3,350
**19** $ 4 0 0 0

**20** Subtract line 19 from line 17. If line 19 is more than line 17, enter 0.  **20** $ 1 9 6 6 6

**21** Multiply $2,550 by the total number of exemptions claimed on line 6d.  **21** $ 2 5 5 0

**22** Subtract line 21 from line 20. If line 21 is more than line 20, enter 0. This is your **taxable income.** **If you want the IRS to figure your tax, see page 26.** ▶  **22** $ 1 7 1 1 6

**23** Find the tax on the amount on line 22 (see page 26).  **23** $ 2 5 6 7

**24a** Credit for child and dependent care expenses. Attach Schedule 2.  **24a** $

**b** Credit for the elderly or the disabled. Attach Schedule 3.  **24b** $

**c** Add lines 24a and 24b. These are your **total credits.**  **24c** $

**25** Subtract line 24c from line 23. If line 24c is more than line 23, enter 0.  **25** $ 2 5 6 7

**26** Advance earned income credit payments from Form(s) W-2.  **26** $

**27** Household employment taxes. Attach Schedule H.  **27** $

**28** Add lines 25, 26, and 27. This is your **total tax.** ▶  **28** $

**29a** Total Federal income tax withheld from Forms W-2 and 1099.  **29a** $ 3 2 7 6

**b** 1996 estimated tax payments and amount applied from 1995 return.  **29b** $

**c** **Earned income credit.** Attach Schedule EIC if you have a qualifying child.  **29c** $

Nontaxable earned income: amount ▶ $ _____ and type ▶ _____

**d** Add lines 29a, 29b, and 29c (do not include nontaxable earned income). These are your **total payments.** ▶  **29d** $ 3 2 7 6

**30** If line 29d is more than line 28, subtract line 28 from line 29d. This is the amount you **overpaid.**  **30** $ 7 0 9

**31a** Amount of line 30 you want **refunded to you.** If you want it sent directly to your bank account, see page 35 and fill in 31b, c, and d.  **31a** $ 7 0 9

**b** Routing number _____

**c** Type: ☐ Checking  ☐ Savings

**d** Account number _____

**32** Amount of line 30 you want **applied to your 1997 estimated tax. 32** $

**33** If line 28 is more than line 29d, subtract line 29d from line 28. This is the **amount you owe.** For details on how to pay, including what to write on your payment, see page 36.  **33** $

**34** Estimated tax penalty (see page 36).  **34** $

**Sign here**

Under penalties of perjury, I declare that I have examined this return and accompanying schedules and statements, and to the best of my knowledge and belief, they are true, correct, and accurately list all amounts and sources of income I received during the tax year. Declaration of preparer (other than the taxpayer) is based on all information of which the preparer has any knowledge.

| Your signature | Date | Your occupation |
|---|---|---|
| *Patricia Rowell* | 4/15 | Assistant Manager |

Keep a copy of this return for your records.

| Spouse's signature. If joint return, BOTH must sign. | Date | Spouse's occupation |
|---|---|---|

**Paid preparer's use only**

| Preparer's signature ▶ | Date | Check if self-employed ☐ | Preparer's SSN |
|---|---|---|---|
| Firm's name (or yours if self-employed) and address ▶ | | | EIN _____ |
| | | | ZIP code _____ |

**1996 Form 1040A page 2**

FIGURE 6.5

**214**

**Schedule 1**

(Form 1040A)

(X)

Department of the Treasury—Internal Revenue Service

**Interest and Dividend Income for Form 1040A Filers**

**199**

OMB No. 1545-0085

| Name(s) shown on Form 1040A: First and initial(s) | Last | Your social security number |
|---|---|---|
| Patricia Rowell | | 4 1 8 2 3 0 1 5 2 |

## Part I  Interest Income  (See pages 19 and 50.)

**Note:** *If you received a Form 1099–INT, Form 1099–OID, or substitute statement from a brokerage firm, enter the firm's name and the total interest shown on that form.*

1  List name of payer. If any interest is from a seller-financed mortgage and the buyer used the property as a personal residence, see page 50 and list this interest first. Also, show that buyer's social security number and address.

Amount

Employee Credit Union  1  $  428

$

$

$

$

$

$

$

$

$

$

$

2  Add the amounts on line 1.  2  $  428

3  Excludable interest on series EE U.S. savings bonds issued after 1989 from Form 8815, line 14. You **must** attach Form 8815 to Form 1040A.  3  $

4  Subtract line 3 from line 2. Enter the result here and on Form 1040A, line 8a.  4  $  428

## Part II  Dividend Income  (See pages 20 and 50.)

**Note:** *If you received a Form 1099–DIV or substitute statement from a brokerage firm, enter the firm's name and the total dividends shown on that form.*

5  List name of payer

Amount

5  $

$

$

$

$

$

$

$

$

$

$

$

6  Add the amounts on line 5. Enter the total here and on Form 1040A, line 9.  6  $

For Paperwork Reduction Act Notice, see Form 1040A instructions.  Cat. No. 12075R  **1996 Schedule 1 (Form 1040A)**

FIGURE 6.6

## 6.3 EXERCISES

*Find the adjusted gross income for each of the following.*

| | Name | Income from Jobs | Interest | Misc. Income | Dividend Income | Adjustments to Income |
|---|---|---|---|---|---|---|
| 1. | R. Garrett | $18,610 | $74 | $1,936 | $115 | $135 |
| 2. | C. Manly | $38,156 | $285 | $73 | $542 | $317 |
| 3. | The Hanks | $21,380 | $625 | $139 | $184 | $618 |
| 4. | The Papoffs | $33,650 | $722 | $375 | $218 | $473 |
| 5. | The Brashers | $38,643 | $95 | $188 | $105 | $0 |
| 6. | The Ameens | $41,379 | $1,147 | $536 | $186 | $2,258 |

*Find the amount of taxable income and the tax for each of the following. Use the tax rate schedule. The letter following the name indicates marital status, and all married people are filing jointly.*

| | Name | Number of Exemptions | Adjusted Gross Income | Total Deductions |
|---|---|---|---|---|
| 7. | E. Gragg, S | 1 | $20,300 | $1,985 |
| 8. | P. Phelps, S | 1 | $15,615 | $3,182 |
| 9. | The Cooks, M | 3 | $28,751 | $4,968 |
| 10. | The Loveridges, M | 7 | $32,532 | $7,672 |
| 11. | The Lanes, M | 5 | $61,800 | $4,509 |
| 12. | T. Taybe, S | 1 | $29,322 | $4,976 |
| 13. | R. Bowtell, S | 1 | $40,350 | $3,885 |
| 14. | K. Whaley, S | 1 | $39,502 | $4,365 |
| 15. | N. Weggener, S | 1 | $68,574 | $2,793 |
| 16. | The Printices, M | 5 | $119,378 | $7,253 |
| 17. | The Albers, M | 2 | $52,613 | $7,681 |
| 18. | The Reents, M | 8 | $68,544 | $6,753 |

*Find the amount of any refund or tax due for the following people. The letter following the name indicates marital status. Assume a 52-week year and that married people are filing jointly.*

| | Name | Taxable Income | Federal Income Tax Withheld from Checks |
|---|---|---|---|
| 19. | Powell, L., S | $13,378 | $243.10 monthly |
| 20. | Woo, C., S | $27,204 | $347.80 monthly |

| Name | Taxable Income | Federal Income Tax Withheld from Checks |
|------|----------------|------------------------------------------|
| 21. Pender, B., S | $23,552 | $72.18 weekly |
| 22. The Fungs, M | $39,238 | $119.27 weekly |
| 23. The Todds, M | $21,786 | $208.52 monthly |
| 24. The Fords, M | $45,436 | $128.35 weekly |

25. List four sources of income for which an individual might receive W-2 and 1099 forms. Which form would commonly be received for each? (See Objective 3.)

26. List four possible tax deductions and explain the effect that a tax deduction will have on taxable income and on income tax due. (See Objective 6.)

*Find the tax in each of the following application problems.*

27. The Werners had an adjusted gross income of $45,378 last year. They had deductions of $482 for state income tax, $187 for city income tax, $472 for property tax, $3,208 in mortgage interest, and $324 in contributions. They file a joint return and claim 5 exemptions.

28. Diane Bolton had an adjusted gross income of $34,975 last year. She had deductions of $971 for state income tax, $564 for property tax, $2,747 in mortgage interest, and $235 in contributions. Bolton claims one exemption and files as a single person.

29. Helen Dale, filing as a single person and claiming one exemption, had an adjusted gross income of $31,998. Her deductions amounted to $3,255.

30. The Slausons had an adjusted gross income of $36,116 last year. They had deductions of $1,078 for state income tax, $253 for city income tax, $879 for property tax, $5,218 in mortgage interest, and $386 in contributions. They claim 3 exemptions and file a joint return.

31. Valerie Hunter, a full time college student and a single person, had wages from three part-time jobs amounting to $1,385; $2,653; and $1,838. She had interest of $137, no adjustments to income and no itemized deductions. Since her parents claim her as an exemption, Hunter must claim zero exemptions. Hunter is allowed the standard deduction.

32. Tyrone Goodwin, a single person, had wages from three part-time jobs while attending college full time. Wages amounted to $974; $2,793; and $3,210. He had interest of $96, no adjustments to income, and no itemized deductions. Goodwin must claim zero exemptions since his parents still claim him as a tax exemption. Goodwin is allowed the standard deduction.

33. The Rusks had wages of $68,645, dividends of $385, interest of $672, and adjustments to income of $1,058 last year. They had deductions of $877 for state income tax, $342 for city income tax, $786 for property tax, $8,180 in mortgage interest, and $186 in contributions. They claim 5 exemptions and file a joint return.

34. John Walker had wages of $32,364, other income of $2,892, dividends of $240, interest of $315, and an IRA contribution of $750 last year. He had deductions of $1,163 for state income tax, $1,268 for property tax, $1,826 in mortgage interest, and $540 in contributions. Walker claims one exemption and files as a single person.

**35.** John and Vicki Karsten had combined wages and salaries of $45,428, other income of $5,283, dividend income of $324, and interest income of $668. They have adjustments to income of $2,484. Their itemized deductions are $7,615 in mortgage interest, $729 in state income tax, $1,185 in real estate taxes, and $1,219 in charitable contributions. The Karstens filed a joint return and claimed 6 exemptions.

**36.** Judy Lewis had wages and salaries of $43,846, other income of $1,682, dividend income of $478, and interest income of $986. She has an adjustment to income of $1,452. Her itemized deductions are $4,615 in mortgage interest, $1,136 in state income tax, $856 in real estate taxes, and $835 in charitable contributions. Lewis claims one exemption and is a single person.

# Chapter 6 Quick Review

| TOPIC | APPROACH | EXAMPLE |
|---|---|---|
| **6.1 Finding sales tax** | Collected by states, and some counties and cities. Use $P = BR$, where $P$ is the sales tax, $B$ is the amount of the sale, and $R$ is the sales tax rate. | Sales tax of 5% is charged on a sale of $173.15. Find the amount of sales tax and the total sale including tax. $$P = \$173.15 \times 0.05 = \$8.66$$ $$\$173.15 \text{ sale} + \$8.66 \text{ tax} = \$181.81 \text{ total sale}$$ |
| **6.1 Finding selling price when the sales tax is known** | Use the basic percent equation. $$P = B \times R$$ Sales tax = Selling price $\times$ Tax rate | Sales tax is $4.59; sales tax rate is 6%. Find the amount of the sale. $$\$4.59 = B \times 0.06$$ $$\frac{\$4.59}{0.06} = B$$ $$\$76.50 = B \text{ selling price}$$ |
| **6.1 Finding the amount of the sale when the total price is known** | Use the percent equation and remember Amount of sale + Sales tax = Total. | Total price including tax, $128.96; sales tax, 4%. Find the amount of the sale. $$B + (0.04)\,B = \$128.96$$ $$1.04\,B = \$128.96$$ $$B = \frac{\$128.96}{1.04} = \$124$$ |

**6.1 Excise tax (luxury tax)**

A tax charged on certain items by the federal, state, or local government. It may be either a percent of the sale price or a certain amount per item.

A tire weighs 50 pounds and sells for $118; sales tax rate is 7%; excise tax is 15¢ per pound over 40 pounds. Find the total cost.

$118.00 tire
$\phantom{+}$ 8.26 sales tax (0.07 × $118)
$+$ 1.50 excise tax (0.15(50 − 40))
$\overline{\phantom{+}}$ $127.76 total cost

---

**6.2 Fair market value and assessed valuation**

Multiply the market value of the property by the assessment rate (a local assessed percent) to arrive at the assessed valuation.

The assessment rate is 30%; fair market value is $115,000. Find the assessed valuation.

0.3 × $115,000 = $34,500

---

**6.2 Tax rate**

The tax rate formula is

$$\text{Tax rate} = \frac{\text{Total tax amount needed}}{\text{Total assessed value}}.$$

Tax amount needed $245,664; total assessed value, $3,070,800. Find the tax rate.

$$\frac{245,664}{3,070,800} = 0.08$$

---

**6.2 Expressing tax rates in different forms and finding tax**

1. Percent—multiply assessed valuation by rate.
2. Dollars per $100—move decimal 2 places to left in assessed valuation and multiply.
3. Dollars per $1,000—move decimal 3 places to left in assessed valuation and multiply.
4. Mills—move decimal 3 places to the left in rate and multiply by assessed valuation.

Assessed value, $90,000; Tax rate, 2.5%.

$90,000 × 0.025 = $2,250

Tax rate, $2.50 per $100

900 × $2.50 = $2,250

Tax rate, $25 per $1,000

90 × $25 = $2,250

Tax rate, 25 mills

90,000 × $0.025 = $2,250

---

**6.3 Adjusted gross income**

Adjusted gross income includes wages, salaries, tips, dividends, and interest.

Salary, $32,540; interest income, $875; dividends, $315. Find adjusted gross income.

$32,540 + $875 + $315 = $33,730

| | | | |
|---|---|---|---|
| **6.3** | **Standard deduction amounts** | The majority of taxpayers use the standard deduction allowed by the IRS. | $4,000 for single people<br>$6,700 for married people filing jointly<br>$3,350 for married people filing separately<br>$5,900 for head of household |
| **6.3** | **Taxable income** | The larger of either the total of itemized deductions or the standard deduction is subtracted from adjusted gross income along with $2,550 for each personal exemption. | Adjusted gross income, $18,200; single taxpayer; itemized deductions total $2,830; find taxable income. Standard deduction is $4,000; larger than $2,850 itemized deduction.<br><br>Taxable income = $18,200 − $4,000 − $2,550 = $11,650 |
| **6.3** | **Tax rates** | There are 5 tax rates: 15%, 28%, 31%, 36%, and 39.6%. | Single 15%; over $23,250, 28%; over $56,550, 31%; over $117,950, 36%; over $256,500, 39.6%.<br><br>Married filing jointly or qualifying widow(er)s 15%; over $39,000, 28%; over $94,250, 31%; over $143,600, 36%; over $256,500, 39.6%.<br><br>Married filing separately 15%; over $19,500, 28%; over $47,125, 31%; over $71,800, 36%; over $128,250, 39.6%.<br><br>Head of household 15%; over $31,250, 28%; over $80,750, 31%; over $130,800, 36%; over $256,500, 39.6%. |

**6.3 Tax due or refund**

If the total amount withheld by employers is greater than the tax owed, a refund results. If the tax owed is the greater amount, a balance is due.

Tax owed, $1,253; tax withheld, $113 per month for 12 months. Find balance due or refund.

$113 × 12 = $1,356 withheld

$1,356 withheld − $1,253 owed = $103 refund

# Chapter 6 Review Exercises

*Find the amount of the sales tax, the excise tax, and the total sale price including taxes in each of the following problems. [6.1]*

| | Sale Price | Sales Tax Rate | Excise Tax Rate |
|---|---|---|---|
| 1. | $472.10 | 5% | 10% |
| 2. | $91.68 | 4% | 11% |
| 3. | $16,500 | 5% | $6.00 per person; 110 people |
| 4. | $345.96 | 7% | 18.3¢/gallon; 285 gallons |

*Find the sale price when given the amount of tax and the sales tax rate. [6.1]*

| | Amount of Sales Tax | Sales Tax Rate |
|---|---|---|
| 5. | $34.02 | 6% |
| 6. | $7.10 | 5% |
| 7. | $19.60 | 7% |
| 8. | $15.75 | $4\frac{1}{2}$% |

*Find the amount of the sale before sales tax was added in each of the following. [6.1]*

| | Total Sale | Sales Tax Rate |
|---|---|---|
| 9. | $348.82 | 7% |
| 10. | $180.20 | 6% |
| 11. | $292.95 | 5% |
| 12. | $430.56 | 4% |

*Complete the following list comparing tax rates. Do not round. [6.2]*

| | Percent | Per $100 | Per $1,000 | In Mills |
|---|---|---|---|---|
| 13. | _____ % | $4.06 | _____ | _____ |
| 14. | _____ % | _____ | _____ | 27 |
| 15. | 1.27% | _____ | _____ | _____ |
| 16. | _____ % | _____ | $19.50 | _____ |

*Find the missing quantity. [6.2]*

| | Assessed Valuation | Tax Rate | Tax |
|---|---|---|---|
| 17. | $426,000 | 32 mills | _____ |
| 18. | $98,200 | _____ per $1,000 | $1,816.70 |
| 19. | _____ | 3.5% | $1,627.50 |
| 20. | $140,500 | _____ % | $3,934 |
| 21. | _____ | $3.80 per $100 | $3,655.60 |
| 22. | $103,600 | 27 mills | _____ |

*Find the taxable income and the tax for each of the following. The letter following the name indicates the marital status. All married people are filing jointly. [6.3]*

| Name | Number of Exemptions | Adjusted Gross Income | Total Deductions |
|---|---|---|---|
| 23. R. Wright, S | 1 | $31,914 | $2,486 |
| 24. The Bridges, M | 5 | $58,721 | $7,230 |
| 25. B. Sullivan, M | 3 | $42,662 | $8,040 |
| 26. R. Tewell, S | 1 | $48,752 | $3,695 |

*Solve each of the following application problems.*

**27.** The Oak Glen Park District budgets on the basis that it will collect $1,978,000. If the total assessed value of the property in the city is $90,550,000, find the tax rate as a percent rounded to the nearest tenth. [6.1]

**28.** Total receipts for the day at the Toy Circus are $3,442.88. If this includes 6% sales tax, find the amount of the sales tax. [6.1]

**29.** A shopping center has a fair market value of $2,608,300. Property in the area is assessed at 28% of fair market value, with a tax rate of $21.50 per $1,000. Find the annual property tax. [6.2]

*Find the tax owed in each of the following application problems. [6.3]*

**30.** The Jidobus, married and filing a joint return, have an adjusted gross income of $63,280, 6 exemptions, and deductions of $4,662.

**31.** Tim McCleary had an adjusted gross income of $31,560 last year. He had deductions of $817 for state income tax, $875 for property tax, $1,495 in mortgage interest, and $343 in contributions. McCleary claims 1 exemption and files as a single person.

**32.** Heather and Stephen Hall had total wages and salaries of $59,750, other income of $852, and interest income of $2,880. They are allowed an adjustment to income of $2,450. Their itemized deductions are $4,218 in mortgage interest, $471 in state income taxes, and $1,040 in charitable contributions. The Halls are filing a joint return and claim 4 exemptions.

| Name | Taxable Income | Federal Income Tax Withheld from Checks |
|------|---------------|----------------------------------------|
| **33. The Whites, M** | $54,780 | $158.50 weekly |
| **34. Lagera, T., S** | $33,825 | $533.20 monthly |
| **35. Rosa, D., S** | $28,315 | $135.40 weekly |
| **36. The Schmidts, M** | $37,480 | $417.80 monthly |

# Summary Exercise

Jack Armstrong, owner of All American Truck Stop, is considering two separate locations along the interstate, Anderson and Bentonville. The two locations are about 200 miles apart, and while offering similar business potential there are differences in land acquisition costs, building costs, and most importantly property taxes. Armstrong feels that he needs 11 acres of land and buildings, and improvements that will total 90,000 square feet. The land and building costs and property tax information are as follows.

| | Anderson | Bentonville |
|------|----------|-------------|
| **Land cost (per square foot)** | $0.40 | $0.35 |
| **Building and improvement cost (per square foot)** | $32.80 | $36.90 |
| **Assessment rate** | 25% | 20% |
| **Tax rate** | 32 mills | $2.95 per $100 |

Knowing that there are 43,560 square feet in an acre and that the total cost of land improvements will be used as fair market value in both locations, Jack Armstrong needs to answer the following questions to help him in his decision.

**(a)** What is the cost of the land and improvements in each location?

**(b)** Find the assessed valuation of the land and improvements in each location.

**(c)** Find the annual property tax in each location.

**(d)** What is the total cost including land, building, and property taxes over a ten-year period in each location?

**(e)** On the basis of cost over a ten-year period, which location should Armstrong select?

**(f)** Are there other nonfinancial considerations that might influence your choice of location? Name three or four additional considerations.

# Risk Management

People buy insurance to protect against risk. In the event that some undesirable event occurs, **peril insurance** provides financial compensation. Perils which are insurable include illness, death, fire, flood, theft, automobile collision, property damage, and personal liability. A person or business buying the insurance, the **insured** or **policyholder**, pays a relatively small amount of money—called the **premium**—to provide protection against a large loss. If the undesirable event occurs, the insurance company, the **insurer** or **carrier**, pays the insured for the loss up to the **face value** or stated amount of the policy.

Insurance is based on the idea that many pay into a fund while a few draw out of the fund. For example, a business may pay a fire insurance premium of a few hundred dollars for several years without ever having a fire loss. However, should a fire occur, the loss may result in many thousands of dollars being paid to the business.

This chapter looks first at business insurance, including fire and liability coverage; next, motor vehicle insurance is discussed; then, the many types of life insurance policies are examined. Nonforfeiture options and settlement options are covered in the last section of the chapter.

## 7.1 Business Insurance

**OBJECTIVES**

1. *Define the terms: policy, face value, and premium.*
2. *Identify the factors that determine the premium.*
3. *Find the annual premium for fire insurance given rating and property values.*
4. *Calculate short-term rates and cancellations.*
5. *Calculate prorated insurance premium cancellations.*
6. *Use the coinsurance formula to solve problems.*
7. *Find the insurance liability when there are multiple carriers.*
8. *Find liability of multiple carriers when coinsurance requirement is not met.*
9. *List additional risks against which a business may be insured.*

225

TABLE 7.1 **Annual Rates for Each $100 of Fire Insurance**

| | Building Rating | | | | | |
|---|---|---|---|---|---|---|
| | A | | B | | C | |
| **Territorial Rating** | **Building** | **Contents** | **Building** | **Contents** | **Building** | **Contents** |
| 1 | $0.25 | $0.32 | $0.36 | $0.49 | $0.45 | $0.60 |
| 2 | $0.30 | $0.44 | $0.45 | $0.55 | $0.54 | $0.75 |
| 3 | $0.37 | $0.46 | $0.54 | $0.60 | $0.63 | $0.80 |
| 4 | $0.50 | $0.52 | $0.75 | $0.77 | $0.84 | $0.90 |
| 5 | $0.62 | $0.58 | $0.92 | $0.99 | $1.14 | $1.05 |

There is only a slight chance that any particular building will suffer fire damage during a given year. However, if such fire damage were to occur, the financial loss could be very large. To protect against this small chance of a large loss, people pay an amount equal to a small percent of the value of their property to a fire insurance company. The company collects money from a large number of property owners, then pays for expenses due to fire damage for those few buildings which are damaged.

OBJECTIVE **1** *Define the terms: policy, face value, and premium.*      The contract between the owner of a building and a fire insurance company is called a **policy**. The amount of insurance provided by the company is called the **face value of the policy**. The charge for the policy is called the **premium**.

OBJECTIVE **2** *Identify the factors that determine the premium.*      The amount of premium charged by the insurance company depends on several factors, such as the type of construction of the building, the contents and use of the building, the location of the building, and the type of available fire protection. Wood frame buildings are generally more likely to be damaged by fire, and thus require a larger premium than masonry buildings. Categories are assigned to building types by insurance company employees called **underwriters**. These categories are usually named by letters, such as A, B, C, and so on. Underwriters also assign ratings, called territorial ratings, to each area served which describe the quality of fire protection in the area. While fire insurance rates vary from state to state, the rates in Table 7.1 are typical.

OBJECTIVE **3** *Find the annual premium for fire insurance given rating and property values.*      The annual premium rate for fire insurance is expressed as a certain amount for each one hundred dollars in value. The basic percent equation is used to find the annual insurance premium. The value of the building in hundreds of dollars is the base, the insurance premium per $100 of fire insurance is the rate, and the annual insurance premium is the part.

$$
\begin{array}{ccccc}
\text{Annual Premium} & = & \text{Building Value} & \times & \text{Insurance Premium} \\
 & & \text{(per \$100)} & & \text{(per \$100)} \\
P & = & B & \times & R
\end{array}
$$

## EXAMPLE 1  *Finding the Annual Fire Insurance Premium*

Mail Boxes Etc. is in a building having a rating class of B. The territory is rated 3. Find the annual premium to insure a building worth $242,000 with contents valued at $62,000.

**SOLUTION**  From Table 7.1, the rates per $100 for a class B building in area 3 are $0.54 for the building and $0.60 for the contents. The premium for the building is found as follows.

$$\text{Value of building} = \$242{,}000 = 2{,}420 \text{ hundreds}$$

$$\text{Rate for building (from table)} = \$0.54$$

$$
\begin{aligned}
\text{Premium for building} &= \text{Value (in hundreds)} \times \text{Rate} \\
&= 2{,}420 \times \$0.54 \\
&= \$1{,}306.80
\end{aligned}
$$

The premium for the contents can be found in the same way.

$$\text{Value of contents} = \$62{,}000 = 620 \text{ hundreds}$$

$$\text{Rate for contents} = \$0.60 \text{ (from table)}$$

$$
\begin{aligned}
\text{Premium for contents} &= \text{Value (in hundreds)} \times \text{Rate} \\
&= 620 \times \$0.60 \\
&= \$372
\end{aligned}
$$

$$
\begin{aligned}
\text{Total premium} &= \$1{,}306.80 \text{ (building)} + \$372 \text{ (contents)} \\
&= \$1{,}678.80 \text{ (building and contents)} \\
&= \$1{,}679 \text{ (rounded)} \quad\blacksquare
\end{aligned}
$$

**NOTE**  Fire insurance premiums are rounded to the nearest dollar.  ∎

**OBJECTIVE** **4** *Calculate short-term rates and cancellations.*  Insurance is sometimes purchased for part of a year, perhaps even for just a few months. Perhaps only a short period of time remains on a lease. Also, if a business is sold or the owner wishes to change insurance carriers during the period of a policy, the existing policy must be canceled. In each of these cases, the insurance company will charge a **short-term** or **cancellation rate**. When the short-term rate is used, a penalty results.

As shown in Table 7.2, one month's insurance costs 18% of an annual premium while one month is only $8\frac{1}{3}$% of a year $(1 \div 12 = 0.083333)$. The premium for a

TABLE 7.2 **Short-Term Rate Schedule**

| Time in Months | Percent of Annual Premium | Time in Months | Percent of Annual Premium |
|:---:|:---:|:---:|:---:|
| 1 | 18% | 7 | 75% |
| 2 | 35% | 8 | 80% |
| 3 | 45% | 9 | 85% |
| 4 | 55% | 10 | 90% |
| 5 | 65% | 11 | 95% |
| 6 | 70% | 12 | 100% |

six-month policy or a policy canceled after six months costs 70% of the annual premium.

**EXAMPLE 2** *Determining Short-Term Rates*

Bob Garrett sold his Irving, Texas grocery store. Because of the sale he canceled his fire insurance after four months. If the annual premium was $4,680, use the short-term rate schedule (see Table 7.2) to find the amount of refund to the insured.

**SOLUTION** The short-term rate for four months is 55% of the annual premium.

$4,680 (annual premium) $\times$ 0.55 = $2,574 (premium for four months)

The refund is found by subtracting the four-month premium from the annual premium.

$4,680 (annual premium) $-$ $2,574 (four-month premium)

= $2,106 (refund) ∎

**OBJECTIVE 5** *Calculate prorated insurance premium cancellations.* Occasionally an insurance company may cancel an insurance policy. This is normally the result of fraud on the part of the insured or any violation of the insurance agreement with the insurance company.

When the insurance company initiates a policy cancellation, the insured is not penalized as with the short-term or cancellation rate. Instead, the insured is charged only for the exact amount of time that the insurance was in force. It is normal for this proration to be to the exact day. Here, we will prorate on a monthly basis, which results in the insured paying only for the number of months that the insurance was provided.

**EXAMPLE 3** *Calculating Prorated Insurance Cancellations*

Your Creations Art Supplies had a fire insurance policy with an annual premium of $2,832. Because the insured was in violation of fire codes, the insurance company canceled the policy after seven months and prorated the premium. Find (a) the amount of the premium retained by the company and (b) the amount of refund to the insured.

SOLUTION     Since the cancellation is after seven months, the insured is charged for $\frac{7}{12}$ of the year.

**(a)** The amount of the premium retained by the company is found by multiplying the annual premium by $\frac{7}{12}$.

$$\$2,832 \text{ (annual premium)} \times \tfrac{7}{12} = \$1,652 \text{ (premium for seven months)}$$

**(b)** The refund is found by subtracting the premium for seven months from the annual premium.

$$\$2,832 \text{ (annual premium)} - \$1,652 \text{ (seven-month premium)} = \$1,180 \text{ (refund)}$$

The refund is equal to $\frac{5}{12}$ of the annual premium.     ■

**OBJECTIVE** **6** *Use the coinsurance formula to solve problems.*     Most fires damage only a portion of a building and its contents. Since complete destruction of a building is rare, many owners save money by buying insurance for only a portion of the value of the building and contents. Realizing this, insurance companies place a **coinsurance clause** in fire insurance policies. With coinsurance, part of the risk of fire, under certain conditions, is assumed by the business firm taking out the insurance. For example, an 80% coinsurance clause provides that for full protection, the amount of insurance taken out must be at least 80% of the replacement cost of the building and contents insured.

If the amount of insurance is less than 80% of the replacement cost, the insurance company pays only a portion of any loss. For example, if a business firm took out insurance with a face value of only 40% of the replacement cost of the building insured and then had a loss, the insurance company would pay only half the loss, since 40% is half of 80%.

Use the following formula to find the portion of a loss that will be paid by the insurance company.

*Coinsurance Formula*

Amount insurance companies will pay (assuming 80% coinsurance)

$$= \text{Amount of loss} \times \frac{\text{Amount of policy}}{80\% \text{ of replacement cost}}$$

NOTE    The company will never pay more than the face value of the policy, nor will the company pay more than the amount of the loss.    ■

**EXAMPLE 1** *Using the Coinsurance Formula*

Barbara Weaks owns a commercial building valued at $380,000. Her fire insurance policy (with an 80% coinsurance clause) has a face value of $285,000. The building suffers a fire loss of $72,000. Find the amount of the loss that the insurance company will pay and the amount that Weaks must pay.

SOLUTION     The policy should have been for at least 80% of the value of the building, or

$$0.80 \times \$380,000 = \$304,000.$$

Since the face value of the policy is less than 80% of the value of the building, the company will pay only a portion of the loss. Use the coinsurance formula.

$$\text{Amount insurance company pays} = \$72,000 \times \frac{\$285,000}{\$304,000} = \$67,500$$

The company will pay $67,500 toward the loss, and Weaks must pay the additional $4,500 ($72,000 − $67,500).    ■

**CALCULATOR APPROACH
TO EXAMPLE 4**

*The calculator solution to this example uses chain calculations and parentheses to set off the denominator. The result is then subtracted from the fire loss.

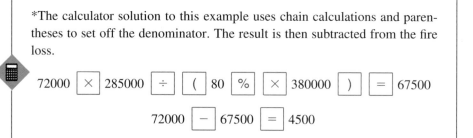

### EXAMPLE 5    *Finding the Amount of Loss Paid by the Insurance Company*

A Swedish investment group owns a warehouse valued at $3,450,000. The company has a fire insurance policy with a face value of $2,950,000. The policy has an 80% coinsurance feature. If the firm has a fire loss of $233,500, find the part of the loss paid by the insurance company.

**SOLUTION**    The value of the warehouse is $3,450,000. Take 80% of this value.

$$0.80 \times \$3,450,000 = \$2,760,000$$

The business has a fire insurance policy with a face value of more than 80% of the value of the store. Therefore, the insurance company will pay the entire $233,500 loss.    ■

**OBJECTIVE  7  *Find the insurance liability when there are multiple carriers.***    A business may have fire insurance policies with several companies at the same time. Perhaps additional insurance coverage was purchased over a period of time, as new additions were made to a factory or building complex. Or perhaps the value of the building is so high that no one insurance company wants to take the entire risk by itself, so several companies each agree to take a portion of the insurance coverage and thereby share the risk. In either event, the insurance coverage is divided among **multiple carriers**. When an insurance claim is made against multiple carriers, each insurance company pays its fractional portion of the total claim on the property.

*NOTE: All calculator solutions use a scientific calculator. Refer to Appendix A for scientific and financial calculator basics.

| **EXAMPLE 6** *Understanding Multiple Carrier Insurance*

World Recycling Conglomerate (WRC) has an insured loss of $980,000 while having insurance coverage greater than its coinsurance requirement. The insurance is divided among Company A with $5,900,000 coverage, Company B with $4,425,000 coverage, and Company C with $1,475,000 coverage. Find the amount of the loss paid by each of the insurance companies.

**SOLUTION** Start by finding the total face value of all three policies.

$$\$5,900,000 + \$4,425,000 + \$1,475,000 = \$11,800,000 \text{ total face value}$$

$$\$5,900,000 \qquad \text{Company A pays } \frac{\$5,900,000}{\$11,800,000} = \frac{1}{2} \text{ of the loss}$$

$$\$4,425,000 \qquad \text{Company B pays } \frac{\$4,425,000}{\$11,800,000} = \frac{3}{8} \text{ of the loss}$$

$$\underline{+ \ \$1,475,000} \qquad \text{Company C pays } \frac{\$1,475,000}{\$11,800,000} = \frac{1}{8} \text{ of the loss}$$

$$\$11,800,000 \text{ total face value}$$

Since the insured loss is $980,000 the amount paid by each of the multiple carriers is

$$\text{Company A} \qquad \frac{1}{2} \times \$980,000 = \$490,000$$

$$\text{Company B} \qquad \frac{3}{8} \times \$980,000 = \$367,500$$

$$\text{Company C} \qquad \frac{1}{8} \times \$980,000 = \underline{\$122,500}$$

$$\text{Total loss } = \$980,000 \qquad ■$$

**OBJECTIVE** **8** *Find liability of multiple carriers when coinsurance requirement is not met.* If the coinsurance requirement is not met, the total amount of the loss paid by the insurance coverage is found, and then the amount that each of the carriers pays is found by the method shown in Example 7.

| **EXAMPLE 7** *Finding Liability of Multiple Carriers When Coinsurance Requirements Are Not Met*

The Carpet Solution warehouse is valued at $2,000,000 and is insured under an 80% coinsurance clause for $1,200,000. $800,000 of the insurance is placed with Company A and $400,000 with Company B. If the warehouse suffers a loss of $200,000, find (a) the part of any loss that is covered, (b) the amount of the loss the insurance companies will pay, (c) each insurance company's payment after the $200,000 loss, and (d) the amount paid by the insured.

## SOLUTION

**(a)** First, find the amount of insurance needed to satisfy the 80% coinsurance clause.

$$0.80 \times \$2,000,000 = \$1,600,000$$

Since the face value of the policy ($1,200,000) is less than 80% ($1,600,000), the insurance company will only pay a portion of the loss.

$$\text{Part insurance company pays} = \frac{\$1,200,000}{\$1,600,000}$$

**(b)** Use the coinsurance formula to find the amount of the loss that the insurance companies will pay.

$$\text{Amount insurance companies pay} = \$200,000 \times \frac{\$1,200,000}{\$1,600,000} = \$150,000.$$

**(c)** The total face value of the insurance is $1,200,000. Since the amount of the loss that the insurance companies will pay is $150,000, the amount paid by each of the multiple carriers is as follows.

$$\frac{\$800,000}{\$1,200,000} \times \$150,000 = \$100,000 \qquad \text{Company A}$$

$$\frac{\$400,000}{\$1,200,000} \times \$150,000 = \frac{\$50,000}{\$150,000} \qquad \begin{array}{l}\text{Company B}\\ \text{amount of loss paid}\end{array}$$

**(d)** The Carpet Solution must pay $50,000, the difference between the loss and the amount paid by the insurance companies.  ∎

**OBJECTIVE** **9** *List additional risks against which a business may be insured.*     There are many types of insurance coverage that a business might want. One of the most common is liability coverage, which protects against monetary awards from personal-injury lawsuits caused by the business; another common coverage protects property against damage caused by windstorm, hail, or fire. Homeowners usually buy a **homeowner's policy**, which protects against these losses and many others, including all credit cards and automated teller cards, business property brought home, and medical costs for guests who are injured. Other policies are designed for condominium owners, rental property owners, and apartment dwellers. Many types of additional coverage are available to give complete and comprehensive insurance coverage.

A **business owner's package policy**, known in the insurance industry as a special multiperils policy or **SMP**, typically includes coverage of the following:

- replacement cost for the building and contents;
- contents coverage that provides for a 25% peak season increase;
- business property that is in transit or temporarily away from the premises;
- money, securities, accounts receivable, and other valuable papers up to $1,000;

- loss of income, that includes rents and interruption of business for up to 12 months;
- liability and medical coverage resulting from personal injury, advertising injury, and medical malpractice.

In addition to coverage of these standard risks, a list of optional coverages is also available. The businessperson may select those which he or she feels are necessary. A few of these are:

- replacement cost coverage on exterior signs;
- replacement cost coverage for glass;
- minicomputer coverage;
- coverage for loss of refrigeration;
- professional liability coverage for barbers, beauticians, pharmacists, hearing aid sellers, morticians, optometrists, and veterinarians;
- coverage for non-owned and hired automobiles;
- liquor liability coverage.

In addition to the many coverages for business property and personal liability, the employer may be required to provide **worker's compensation insurance** for employees, which provides payments to an employee who is unable to work due to a job-related injury or illness.

An employer may pay the entire premium or part of the premium for employee health insurance, dental insurance, and group life insurance. Most often these **group insurance plans** offer slightly reduced premiums to those participating in the plan. Participation in group insurance plans is sometimes an incentive for remaining with an employer, since changing jobs may eliminate participation in the group insurance plan.

## 7.1 EXERCISES

*Find the total annual premium for fire insurance for each of the following. Round to the nearest dollar. Use Table 7.1.*

|     | Territorial Rating | Building Classification | Building Value | Contents Value |
| --- | --- | --- | --- | --- |
| 1.  | 4 | C | $200,000 | $80,000 |
| 2.  | 3 | A | $90,000 | $50,000 |
| 3.  | 1 | C | $142,500 | $76,000 |
| 4.  | 3 | C | $220,500 | $105,000 |
| 5.  | 5 | B | $782,600 | $212,000 |
| 6.  | 2 | B | $345,700 | $174,500 |
| 7.  | 5 | C | $583,200 | $221,400 |
| 8.  | 4 | A | $850,500 | $425,800 |

*Find the amount of refund to the insured using the Short-Term Rate Schedule (Table 7.2).*

|      | Annual Premium | Months in Force |
|------|----------------|-----------------|
| 9.   | $1,080         | 9               |
| 10.  | $1,448         | 1               |
| 11.  | $763           | 6               |
| 12.  | $964           | 2               |
| 13.  | $1,507         | 3               |
| 14.  | $1,866         | 10              |
| 15.  | $4,860         | 11              |
| 16.  | $2,250         | 5               |

*Find (a) the amount of premium retained by the company and (b) the amount of refund to the insured using proration.*

|      | Annual Premium | Months in Force |
|------|----------------|-----------------|
| 17.  | $1,350         | 10              |
| 18.  | $1,632         | 7               |
| 19.  | $1,872         | 5               |
| 20.  | $876           | 11              |
| 21.  | $5,308         | 6               |
| 22.  | $3,192         | 3               |

*Find the amount of each of the following losses that will be paid by the insurance company. Assume that each policy includes an 80% coinsurance clause.*

|      | Value of Building | Face Value of Policy | Amount of Loss |
|------|-------------------|----------------------|----------------|
| 23.  | $250,000          | $225,000             | $17,800        |
| 24.  | $780,000          | $680,000             | $10,400        |
| 25.  | $78,500           | $47,500              | $1,500         |
| 26.  | $750,000          | $500,000             | $56,000        |
| 27.  | $218,500          | $195,000             | $36,500        |
| 28.  | $124,800          | $80,000              | $25,000        |
| 29.  | $147,850          | $100,000             | $14,850        |
| 30.  | $285,000          | $150,000             | $18,500        |

*Find the amount paid by each insurance company in the following problems involving multiple carriers. Assume that the coinsurance requirement is met. Round all answers to the nearest dollar.*

| | Insurance Loss | Companies and Coverage | |
|---|---|---|---|
| **31.** | $80,000 | Company A | $750,000 |
| | | Company B | $250,000 |
| **32.** | $360,000 | Company 1 | $1,200,000 |
| | | Company 2 | $800,000 |
| **33.** | $650,000 | Company 1 | $1,350,000 |
| | | Company 2 | $1,200,000 |
| | | Company 3 | $450,000 |
| **34.** | $1,600,000 | Company A | $4,800,000 |
| | | Company B | $800,000 |
| | | Company C | $2,400,000 |

*Find (a) the amount of the loss paid by the insurance companies, (b) each insurance company's payment, and (c) the amount paid by the insured in each of the following problems involving coinsurance and multiple carriers. Assume an 80% coinsurance clause and round all answers to the nearest dollar.*

| | Property Value | Insurance Loss | Companies and Coverage | |
|---|---|---|---|---|
| **35.** | $100,000 | $40,000 | Company A | $40,000 |
| | | | Company B | $20,000 |
| **36.** | $160,000 | $70,000 | Company A | $90,000 |
| | | | Company B | $30,000 |
| **37.** | $250,000 | $20,000 | Company 1 | $75,000 |
| | | | Company 2 | $50,000 |
| **38.** | $480,000 | $100,000 | Company 1 | $180,000 |
| | | | Company 2 | $60,000 |

*Find the annual fire insurance premium for each of the following application problems. Round to the nearest dollar. Use Table 7.1.*

**39.** Lisa Fuller owns a class C building worth $238,000. Contents are valued at $178,000. The territorial rating is 2.

**40.** Dave's Auto Body and Paint owns a class A building worth $143,000. Contents are worth $78,500. The territorial rating is 5.

**41.** The Nutrition Center owns a building worth $375,000. The contents are worth $98,500. The building is class B and the territorial rating is 3.

**42.** Wheelchair Whitney, Numismatist, owns a building rated C with a territorial rating of 4. The building is worth $210,000 and the contents are worth $1,364,000.

*Find the amount of refund to the insured using the Short-Term Rate Schedule (Table 7.2) in each of the following.*

**43.** Re Max Realty pays an annual fire insurance premium of $2,350. They transfer insurance companies after four months.

**44.** Postal Printers pays an annual fire insurance premium of $1,960. The business is sold and insurance canceled after six months.

**45.** Minkner Ranch Supply cancels their fire insurance after nine months. Their annual premium is $2,750.

**46.** Martinez Horse Stables pays an annual fire insurance premium of $3,960. They change insurance companies after two months.

*Find (a) the amount of premium retained by the company and (b) the amount of refund to the insured using proration.*

**47.** West Construction pays an annual fire insurance premium of $2,670. The insurance company cancels the policy after five months.

**48.** The Sports Center has had their fire insurance canceled after ten months. Their annual premium is $3,380.

**49.** As the result of a recent claim, Buy-Rite Drug Store has had their fire insurance policy canceled after seven months. Their annual premium is $1,944.

**50.** Java City Coffee pays an annual fire insurance premium of $4,270. The insurance company cancels the policy after three months.

**51.** Describe three factors that determine the premium charged for fire insurance. (See Objective 2.)

**52.** Explain the coinsurance clause and describe how coinsurance works. (See Objective 6.)

*In each of the following application problems, find the amount of the loss paid by (a) the insurance company and (b) the insured. Assume an 80% coinsurance requirement.*

**53.** Indonesian Gift Shop has a value of $395,000. The shop is insured for $280,000. Fire loss is $22,500.

**54.** Flashpoint Welding Supplies owns a building valued at $540,000 and insured for $308,000. Fire loss is $34,000.

**55.** The main office of the Salvation Army suffers a loss from a fire of $45,000. The building is valued at $550,000 and insured for $300,000.

**56.** Cyndy Perez owns a duplex valued at $96,000 and insured for $64,000. Fire loss is $8,000.

**57.** Explain in your own words multiple carrier insurance. Give two reasons for dividing insurance among multiple carriers. (See Objective 7.)

**58.** Several types of insurance coverage beyond basic fire coverage are included in a homeowner's policy. List and explain three losses that would be covered. (See Objective 9.)

*In each of the following, find the amount paid by each of the multiple carriers. Assume that the coinsurance requirement has been met and round to the nearest dollar.*

**59.** Valley Crop Dusting had a fire loss of $76,000. They had insurance coverage as follows: Company A, $100,000; Company B, $200,000; and Company C, $140,000.

**60.** Camp Curry Stable had a fire loss of $548,000. They had insurance as follows: Company 1, $600,000; Company 2, $400,000; and Company 3, $300,000.

*In each of the following application problems, find (a) the amount that the insured would receive and (b) the amount that each of the insurance companies would pay. Round to the nearest dollar.*

**61.** The John L. Sullivan Chevrolet Dealership is valued at $4,000,000, and the fire insurance policies contain an 80% coinsurance clause. The fire policies include $1,800,000 with Company A and $600,000 with Company B. The dealership suffers a $500,000 fire loss.

**62.** The fire insurance policies on the Global Manufacturing Company contain an 80% coinsurance clause and the warehouse is valued at $2,400,000. Fire policies on the warehouse are $900,000 with Company A and $300,000 with Company B. Global Manufacturing has a fire loss of $800,000.

**63.** Jack Pritchard's Steak House is valued at $360,000. The fire policies are $100,000 with Company 1, $50,000 with Company 2, and $30,000 with Company 3, while each contains an 80% coinsurance clause. There is a fire at the steakhouse causing a $120,000 loss.

**64.** The main foundry of Delta Steel is appraised at $5,500,000. Fire insurance policies on the plant are $1,500,000 with Company 1, $1,000,000 with Company 2, and $800,000 with Company 3. The policies contain an 80% coinsurance clause and the foundry suffers a $1,200,000 fire loss.

## 7.2 Motor Vehicle Insurance

### OBJECTIVES

**1** *Describe the factors that affect the cost of motor vehicle insurance.*

**2** *Define liability insurance and determine the premium.*

**3** *Define property damage insurance and determine the premium.*

**4** *Describe comprehensive and collision insurance and determine the premium.*

**5** *Define no-fault insurance and uninsured motorist.*

**6** *Apply youthful operator factors.*

**7** *Calculate a motor vehicle insurance premium.*

**8** *Find the amounts paid by the insurance company and the insured.*

OBJECTIVE **1** ***Describe the factors that affect the cost of motor vehicle insurance.***    The cost of repairing a motor vehicle after an accident now averages between $2,900 and \$3,200. Businesses and individuals buy motor vehicle insurance to protect against the possible high cost of an accident. The cost of this insurance, the **premium**, is determined by people called **actuaries**, who classify accidents according to location, age and sex of the drivers, and other factors. Insurance companies use these results to determine the premiums. For example, there are more accidents in heavily populated cities than in rural areas. Certain makes and models of automobiles are stolen more often than others. Young male drivers (16–25 years of age) are involved in many more accidents than they should be, considering their proportion of the population. The more expensive a vehicle and the newer a vehicle, the more it costs to repair. These are several of the factors that determine the cost of insurance.

**NOTE** The combination of a youthful driver and an expensive car can result in very large premiums for a 21-year-old male driver of a Corvette. ■

The various types of automobile insurance are discussed in this section.

**OBJECTIVE 2** *Define liability insurance and determine the premium.*

*Liability or Bodily Injury Insurance.* **Liability** or **body injury insurance** protects the insured in case he or she injures someone with a car. The amount of liability insurance is expressed as two numbers with a slash between them, such as 15/30. The 15/30 means that the insurance company will pay up to \$15,000 for injury to one person, and a maximum of \$30,000 for all persons injured in the same accident. Table 7.3 shows typical premium rates for various amounts of liability coverage.

*Medical Insurance.* Included in the cost of the liability insurance is **medical insurance** provided to the driver and passengers of a vehicle in case of injury. For example, the column of the table headed ''15/30'' shows that the insured can also receive reimbursement for up to \$1,000 of his or her own medical expenses in an accident.

For purposes of setting premiums, insurance companies divide the nation into territories, as many as thirty or more. These territories are established on the basis of population, the number of motor vehicles, and the number of accidents and other claims within the territory. Four territories are shown in Table 7.3. All tables in this section show annual premiums.

**EXAMPLE 1** *Finding the Liability and Medical Premium*

Dawn Owen, owner of Stone Oak Landscape, is in territory 2 and wants 100/300 liability coverage. Find the amount of the premium for this coverage and the amount of medical coverage included.

**SOLUTION** Look up territory 2 in Table 7.3 and 100/300 coverage to find a premium of \$196, which includes \$5,000 of medical coverage. ■

**OBJECTIVE 3** *Define property damage insurance and determine the premium.*

*Property Damage Insurance.* **Property damage insurance** pays for damages caused to the property of others. Table 7.4 shows the premiums for property damage

TABLE 7.3  **Liability (Bodily Injury) and Medical Insurance**

| | Annual Premiums for the Indicated Coverage | | | | |
|---|---|---|---|---|---|
| Territory | 15/30 $1,000 | 25/50 $2,000 | 50/100 $3,000 | 100/300 $5,000 | 250/500 $10,000 |
| 1 | $207 | $222 | $253 | $282 | $308 |
| 2 | 148 | 156 | 168 | 196 | 198 |
| 3 | 310 | 314 | 375 | 398 | 459 |
| 4 | 216 | 218 | 253 | 284 | 310 |

insurance. The coverage amount is the maximum amount that the insurance company will pay. If a claim for damages exceeds this maximum amount, the insured must pay the excess.

## EXAMPLE 2  *Finding the Premium for Property Damage*

Find the premium if Dawn Owen, in territory 2, wants property damage coverage of $50,000.

**SOLUTION**    Property damage coverage of $50,000 in territory 2 requires a premium of $76, as Table 7.4 shows.     ∎

**OBJECTIVE 4** *Describe comprehensive and collision insurance and determine the premium.*

*Comprehensive Insurance.*    **Comprehensive insurance** pays for damage to the insured's vehicle caused by fire, theft, vandalism, falling trees, and other such events.

*Collision Insurance.*    **Collision insurance** pays for repairs to the insured's vehicle in case of an accident. Collision insurance often includes a **deductible**. The de-

TABLE 7.4  **Property Damage Insurance**

| | Property Damage | | | |
|---|---|---|---|---|
| Territory | $10,000 | $25,000 | $50,000 | $100,000 |
| 1 | $88 | $93 | $97 | $103 |
| 2 | 64 | 69 | 76 | 84 |
| 3 | 129 | 134 | 145 | 158 |
| 4 | 86 | 101 | 112 | 124 |

TABLE 7.5    **Comprehensive and Collision Insurance**

| Territory | Age Group | Comprehensive Symbol 6 | Comprehensive Symbol 7 | Comprehensive Symbol 8 | Collision ($250 Deductible) Symbol 6 | Collision ($250 Deductible) Symbol 7 | Collision ($250 Deductible) Symbol 8 |
|---|---|---|---|---|---|---|---|
| 1 | 1 | $58 | $64 | $90 | $153 | $165 | $184 |
|   | 2,3 | 50 | 56 | 82 | 135 | 147 | 171 |
|   | 4,5 | 44 | 52 | 76 | 116 | 128 | 147 |
|   | 6 | 34 | 44 | 64 | 92 | 110 | 128 |
| 2 | 1 | $26 | $28 | $40 | $89 | $95 | $104 |
|   | 2,3 | 22 | 24 | 36 | 80 | 86 | 98 |
|   | 4,5 | 20 | 24 | 34 | 71 | 77 | 86 |
|   | 6 | 16 | 20 | 28 | 60 | 68 | 77 |
| 3 | 1 | $70 | $78 | $108 | $145 | $157 | $174 |
|   | 2,3 | 60 | 66 | 90 | 128 | 139 | 162 |
|   | 4,5 | 52 | 64 | 92 | 111 | 122 | 139 |
|   | 6 | 42 | 52 | 78 | 88 | 105 | 122 |
| 4 | 1 | $42 | $46 | $66 | $97 | $104 | $124 |
|   | 2,3 | 36 | 40 | 58 | 87 | 94 | 107 |
|   | 4,5 | 32 | 38 | 54 | 77 | 84 | 94 |
|   | 6 | 26 | 32 | 46 | 64 | 74 | 84 |

ductible is paid by the insured in the event of a claim, with the insurance company paying all amounts above the deductible. Common deductible amounts are $100, $250, and in some cases $500 or $1,000. For example, if the cost of repairing damage caused by an accident is $1,045 and the deductible amount is $250, the insured pays $250, and the insurance company pays $795 ($1,045 − $250 = $795).

**NOTE** The higher the deductible amount, the lower the cost of the collision coverage—the insured shares a greater portion of the risk as the deductible amount increases. ■

Table 7.5 shows some typical rates for comprehensive and collision insurance. Rates are determined not only by territories, but also by Age Group and Symbol. Here, age group refers to the age of the vehicle, not the driver. Age group 1 is a new vehicle to one year of age and age group 6 is a vehicle six years of age or older. The symbol is determined by the cost of the vehicle.

**NOTE** A Ford Escort might be a symbol 6 and a Lincoln Continental might be a symbol 8. The collision coverage in Table 7.5 is for $250 deductible coverage. ■

Nissan Maxima $3,605

Ford Contour GL $3,188

Mitsubishi Gallant $3,121

Ford Taurus GL $2,814

Chevrolet Lumina $2,629

Volkswagon Passat GLX $2,390

Toyota Camry LE $2,328

Chrysler Cirrus LX $2,276

Volvo 850 $2,131

Mazda Millenia $2,031

Suburu Legacy L $1,966

Chevrolet Cavelier $1,795

Saab 900 S $1,734

Honda Accord $1,433

## EXAMPLE 3 *Finding the Comprehensive and Collision Premium*

Dawn Owen, owner of Stone Oak Landscapes, is in territory 2, and has a minivan which is two years old and has a symbol of 8. Use Table 7.5 to find the annual premium for (a) comprehensive coverage and (b) collision coverage.

### SOLUTION

**(a)** The annual premium for comprehensive coverage is $36.

**(b)** The annual premium for collision coverage is $98. ■

The cost of repairing 14 different midsize cars after a 5 mile per hour crash is shown at the side. These repair costs may affect the rates for collision coverage on the various models.

**OBJECTIVE** **5** *Define no-fault insurance and uninsured motorist.*

*No-Fault Insurance.* With **no-fault insurance**, the insured is reimbursed for medical expenses and all costs associated with an accident by his or her own insurance company, no matter who caused the accident. Any damages for pain and suffering are eliminated except in cases of permanent injury or death. Insurance companies argue that no-fault insurance removes lawyers and the courts, and results in easier and less expensive settlements. On the other hand, some trial lawyers and consumer groups contend that no-fault insurance leaves accident victims unable to recover all of their damages and unprotected from the abuses of some insurance companies.

*Uninsured Motorist Insurance.* In the states that do not have no-fault insurance a driver must be concerned about an accident with an uninsured driver. Drivers in these states need **uninsured motorist insurance**, which protects the vehicle owner in a collision with a vehicle that is not insured. Some insurance companies offer **underinsured motorist insurance**, which provides protection in the event that there is a collision with a vehicle that is underinsured. Typical costs for uninsured motorist insurance are shown in Table 7.6.

TABLE 7.6 **Uninsured Motorist Insurance**

| Territory | Basic Limit |
|-----------|-------------|
| 1 | $66 |
| 2 | 44 |
| 3 | 76 |
| 4 | 70 |

| EXAMPLE 4 *Determining the Premium for Uninsured Motorist Coverage*

Dawn Owen, living in territory 2, wants uninsured motorist coverage. Find the premium in Table 7.6.

**SOLUTION** The annual premium for uninsured motorist coverage in territory 2 is $44. ∎

**OBJECTIVE 6** *Apply youthful operator factors.* The graph below shows why most insurance companies distinguish between **youthful** and **adult operators**. Although the age at which a driver becomes an adult varies from company to company, drivers

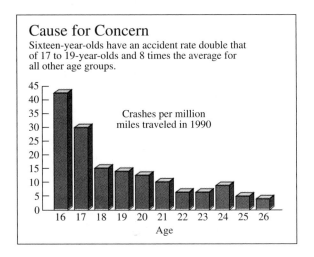

*Source:* Insurance Institute for Highway Safety.

of age 25 or less are usually considered youthful drivers and drivers over 25 are considered adults. Due to the higher proportion of accidents in the 25-and-under bracket, insurance companies add an additional amount to the insurance premium. In Table 7.7, there are two categories of youthful drivers, age 20 or less, and age 21–25. Consideration is also given to the youthful operator who has had driver's training. Some companies give discounts to youthful drivers who are "good students" (a "B" average or better). To use the youthful operator table, first determine the premium for all coverage desired and then multiply this premium by the appropriate youthful operator factor to find the total premium.

**OBJECTIVE 7** *Calculate a motor vehicle insurance premium.* The total annual insurance premium is found by adding the costs of each type of insurance coverage.

| EXAMPLE 5 *Using the Youthful Operator Factor*

James Ito lives in territory 4, is 22 years old, has had driver's training, and drives a 5-year-old car with a symbol of 7. He wants a 25/50 liability policy, $10,000 property

TABLE 7.7   **Youthful Operator Factor**

| Age | With Driver's Training | Without Driver's Training |
|---|---|---|
| 20 or less | 1.55 | 1.75 |
| 21–25 | 1.15 | 1.40 |

damage coverage, a comprehensive and collision policy, and uninsured motorist coverage. Find his annual insurance premium.

**SOLUTION**   As shown in Table 7.3, his annual premium for 25/50 liability insurance is $218. In Table 7.4, his annual premium for $10,000 property damage coverage is $86. In Table 7.5, comprehensive insurance costs $38 and the premium for collision is $84. Uninsured motorist insurance from Table 7.6 is $70. The youthful operator factor for a 22 year old with driver's training from Table 7.7 is 1.15. First add the premiums from the various tables.

$$\$218 + \$86 + \$38 + \$84 + \$70 = \$496$$

Then multiply by the youthful operator factor of 1.15, found in Table 7.7.

$$\text{Total premium} = \$496 \times 1.15 = \$570.40 \qquad \blacksquare$$

**CALCULATOR APPROACH TO EXAMPLE 5**

The calculator solution to this example uses parentheses and chain calculations.

( 218 + 86 + 38 + 84 + 70 ) × 1.15 = 570.4

**OBJECTIVE 8** *Find the amounts paid by the insurance company and the insured.*   The cost of increasing insurance coverage limits is usually quite small. For example, in Table 7.3 the additional cost of increasing liability coverage in territory 1 from 50/100 to 100/300 is only $29 per year ($282 − $253). Medical coverage would also be increased.

**NOTE**   Since the insurance company pays only to the maximum amount of insurance coverage and with the driver liable for all additional amounts, many people pay an additional premium for increased coverage.   ■

**EXAMPLE 6**   *Finding the Amounts Paid by the Insurance Company and the Insured*

Kevin Connors has 25/50 liability limits, $25,000 property damage limits, and $250 deductible collision insurance. While on vacation he was at fault in an accident which caused $5,800 damage to his car, $3,380 in damage to another car, and resulted in severe injuries to the other driver and her passenger. A subsequent lawsuit for injuries resulted in a judgment of $45,000 and $35,000, respectively, to the other parties. Find the amounts that the insurance company will pay for (a) repairing Connors' car, (b) repairing the other car, and (c) paying the court judgment resulting from the lawsuit. (d) How much will Connors have to pay to the injured parties?

### SOLUTION

(a) The insurance company will pay $5,550 ($5,800 − $250 deductible) to repair Connors' car.

(b) Repairs on the other car will be paid to the property damage limits; here, the total repairs of $3,380 are paid.

(c) Since more than one person was injured, the insurance company pays the limit of $50,000 ($25,000 to each of the two injured parties).

(d) Connors is liable for $30,000 ($80,000 − $50,000), the amount awarded over the insurance limits.  ■

Additional factors may affect the annual premium for motor vehicle insurance, such as whether the vehicle is used for pleasure, as transportation to and from work or for business purposes, how far the vehicle is driven each year, whether the youthful driver is male or female, the marital status of the male youthful driver, the past driving record of the driver, and whether the driver has more than one car insured with the insurance company. Quite often, discounts are given to nonsmokers and good students. There are also discounts for automobiles equipped with air bags and antilock braking systems. Many insurance companies charge an annual **policy fee**, which covers the cost of processing the policy each year.

**NOTE**  Many insurance companies give discounts on insurance premiums. You must be certain that you receive any discounts to which you are entitled. The chart below shows the number of states requiring various discounts on insurance premiums.  ■

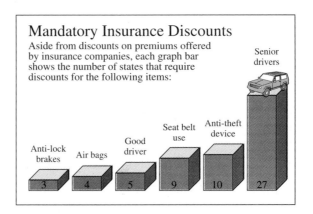

*Source:* CNA Insurance Companies (includes 50 states plus D.C., Puerto Rico, Virgin Islands).

# 7.2 EXERCISES

*Find the annual premium for each of the following people.*

| Name | Territory | Age | Driver Training | Liability | Property Damage | Comprehensive Collision Age Group | Symbol | Uninsured Motorist |
|------|-----------|-----|-----------------|-----------|-----------------|-----------------------------------|--------|--------------------|
| 1. Horton | 4 | 28 | — | 25/50 | $25,000 | 4 | 8 | no |
| 2. Arons | 3 | 21 | yes | 15/30 | $50,000 | 3 | 7 | yes |
| 3. Harper | 1 | 40 | — | 15/30 | $25,000 | 2 | 6 | yes |
| 4. Lew | 4 | 19 | no | 25/50 | $10,000 | 6 | 8 | yes |
| 5. Carter | 1 | 35 | — | 100/300 | $25,000 | 5 | 6 | no |
| 6. Tao | 2 | 24 | yes | 100/300 | $50,000 | 5 | 7 | yes |
| 7. Baeta | 4 | 52 | — | 250/500 | $50,000 | 1 | 8 | yes |
| 8. Gualco | 1 | 31 | — | 250/500 | $50,000 | none | none | no |
| 9. Harrison | 3 | 44 | — | 50/100 | $25,000 | 5 | 6 | yes |
| 10. Ballinger | 2 | 17 | yes | 15/30 | $10,000 | 4 | 8 | yes |
| 11. Green | 2 | 43 | — | 100/300 | $100,000 | 6 | 6 | no |
| 12. Rodriquez | 3 | 60 | — | 50/100 | $100,000 | 5 | 7 | yes |

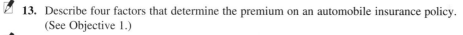 13. Describe four factors that determine the premium on an automobile insurance policy. (See Objective 1.)

14. Explain the difference between comprehensive insurance and collision insurance. (See Objective 4.)

*Solve each of the following application problems.*

15. Susan Reynolds is 24 years old, has had driver's training, lives in territory 1, and drives a 1-year-old car with a symbol of 7. She wants 50/100 liability limits, $25,000 property damage limits, comprehensive and collision insurance, and uninsured motorist coverage. Find her annual insurance premium.

16. David Bolton is 53 years old, lives in territory 3, and drives a 2-year-old car with a symbol of 7. He wants 250/500 liability limits, $100,000 property damage limits, comprehensive and collision insurance, and uninsured motorist coverage. Find his annual insurance premium.

17. Matt Van Natta is 17 years old, has not had driver's training, lives in territory 3, and just purchased a new pickup truck with a symbol of 7. He wants 15/30 liability limits, $25,000 property damage limits, comprehensive and collision insurance, and uninsured motorist coverage. Find his annual insurance premium.

18. Sadie Simms lives in territory 3 and drives a new car with a symbol of 7. She wants 250/500 liability limits, $50,000 property damage limits, comprehensive and collision insurance, and uninsured motorist coverage. She is 45 years old. Find her annual insurance premium.

19. Suppose your bodily injury policy has limits of 15/30 and you injure a person on a bicycle. The judge awards damages of $18,500 to the cyclist. (a) How much will the company pay and (b) how much will you pay?

20. Your best friend causes injury in a car accident to three people and they receive damages of $20,000 each. She has a policy with bodily injury limits of 50/100. (a) How much will the company pay to each person? (b) How much must your friend pay?

21. A reckless driver caused Leslie Silva to collide with a car in another lane. Silva had 50/100 liability limits, $25,000 property damage limits, and collision coverage with a $250 deductible. Silva's car had damage of $1,878, while the other car suffered $6,936 in damage. The resulting lawsuit gave injury awards of $60,000 and $55,000, respectively, to the two people in the other car. Find the amount that the insurance company will pay for (a) repairing Silva's car, (b) repairing the other car, and (c) personal injury damages. (d) How much must Silva pay beyond her insurance coverage, including the collision deductible?

22. Bob Armstrong was driving a dangerous vehicle at excessive speed and crashed into another car. Armstrong had 15/30 liability limits, $10,000 property damage limits, and collision coverage with a $250 deductible. Damage to Armstrong's car was $2,980; the other car, with a value of $22,800, was totaled. The results of a lawsuit awarded $75,000 and $45,000, respectively, in damages for personal injury to the two people in the other car. Find the amount that the insurance company will pay for (a) repairing Armstrong's car, (b) repairing the other car, and (c) personal injury damages. (d) How much must Armstrong pay beyond his insurance coverage?

23. An employee for Safeco Security was driving to a job when a ladder fell from the truck into the path of an oncoming car. Damage to the car was $10,250. Both the driver and the passenger suffered injuries and were given court awards of $20,000 and $40,000, respectively. The security company had 25/50 liability insurance limits and $10,000 property damage limits. (a) Find the total amount paid by the insurance company for both property damage and liability and (b) find the total amount beyond the insurance limits for which the business owner was liable.

24. A trailer-mounted concrete mixer being towed by a contractor broke loose on the beltway and caused a serious accident involving a car and three occupants. Damage to the car was $10,807. The driver and two passengers were given court awards for personal injury of $25,000, $35,000, and $38,000, respectively. The contractor had 25/50 liability insurance limits and $10,000 property damage limits. Find (a) the total amount paid by the insurance company for both property damage and liability, and (b) the total amount beyond the insurance limits for which the contractor was liable.

25. Explain why insurance companies charge a higher premium on auto insurance sold to a youthful operator. Do you think that this higher premium is a good idea or not? (See Objective 6.)

26. Property damage pays for damage caused by you to the property of others. Since the average cost of a new car today is over $20,000, what amount of property damage coverage would you recommend to a friend who owns her own business? Why is this your recommendation?

## 7.3   Life Insurance

**OBJECTIVES**

1. *List reasons for purchasing life insurance.*

2. *Define term, whole life, limited payment, and endowment life insurance policies.*

3. *Understand universal life and variable life policies.*

4. Find the annual premium for life insurance.

5. Use premium factors with different modes of premium payment.

6. Describe discounts, conditions, and additional coverage.

7. Understand nonforteiture options.

8. Calculate income under various settlement options.

**OBJECTIVE** 1 ***List reasons for purchasing life insurance.***    Individuals buy life insurance for a variety of reasons. Most often the insured wants to provide for the needs of others in the event of early death or disability. Parents may want to guarantee that their children will have enough money for college, even if the parents die. Also, some types of life insurance provide paybacks upon retirement, paybacks that allow a retired person to live better than he or she might otherwise live. Insurance money can also be used to pay off mortgages. According to the *World Almanac and Book of Facts*, the average amount of life insurance per household in the United States today is $112,400.

Life insurance is perhaps even more important for a person in business, particularly for an owner or partner in a small business. A business often takes a number of years to grow and may be the owner's main asset. The unexpected death of the owner might leave the business without proper guidance and control, so that the business might suffer drastically before it can be sold. Life insurance on the partners in a business supplies the surviving partner with the necessary money to buy out a deceased partner's interest in the partnership.

**OBJECTIVE** 2 ***Define term, whole life, limited payment, and endowment life insurance policies.***    There are several types of life insurance policies available. The most common types are the following.

***Term Insurance.***    **Term insurance** provides protection for a fixed length of time, such as one year, five years, or ten years. At the end of the fixed period of time, the policy can usually be renewed for an additional period of time at a higher premium. Some term policies provide that on the expiration of the term stated in the policy, the insurance can be converted to one of the following types of insurance. Term insurance, the least expensive of the types of insurance listed, accounts for 20% of all policies and gives the greatest amount of life insurance coverage for the premium dollar. At the expiration of a term insurance policy, however, the insured receives nothing from the insurance company except a request to buy more insurance.

***Decreasing Term Insurance.***    **Decreasing term insurance** is a modification of term insurance where the insured pays a fixed premium until age 60 or 65, with the amount of life insurance decreasing periodically. This policy is designed to fit the ages and stages of life as life insurance needs change. For the person just starting out, it gives more protection for less money. A typical policy, costing $11 per month, is shown in Table 7.8. Decreasing term insurance is commonly available to employees of large companies as a fringe benefit, paid for by either the employee or the employer or both. Most mortgage insurance policies are this type. The amount of life insurance coverage decreases as the amount of the mortgage is reduced.

TABLE 7.8  **A Typical Decreasing Term Insurance Policy**

| Age | Amount of Life Insurance |
|---|---|
| Under 29 | $40,000 |
| 30–34 | 35,000 |
| 35–39 | 30,000 |
| 40–44 | 25,000 |
| 45–49 | 18,000 |
| 50–54 | 11,000 |
| 55–59 | 7,000 |
| 60–66 | 4,000 |
| 67 and over | 0 |

**Nation's Top Killers**

The 10 leading causes of death in the United States, ranked according to the number of lives lost in 1992:

1. **Heart disease**
2. **Cancer**
3. **Stroke**
4. **Lung disease**
5. **Accidents**
6. **Pneumonia and influenza**
7. **Diabetes**
8. **AIDS**
9. **Suicide**
10. **Homicide**

*Source:* Centers for Disease Control and Prevention.

*Whole Life Insurance.*    **Whole life insurance** (also called **straight life** or **ordinary life insurance**) combines life insurance protection with savings. The insured pays a constant premium until death or until retirement, whichever occurs sooner. Upon retirement, monthly payments may be made by the company to the insured until his or her death.

Whole life insurance builds up **cash value**, or money used to pay retirement benefits to the insured. Also, these cash values can be borrowed by the insured at favorable interest rates. Cash value accumulation is guaranteed by the company. The rate of interest used to calculate cash values by the company is very conservative. For this reason many consumer finance experts recommend the purchase of term insurance, with the difference in premiums between term insurance and whole life invested in a good no-load mutual fund or money market fund.

NOTE    Many people plan to save the additional money they would have paid for whole life insurance, but they neglect to do so. The advantage of whole life insurance is that regular payments are required. Remember also that term insurance has no cash value where whole life does.    ■

Life expectancy in the United States is now close to 76 years of age. The leading causes of death in the nation are shown to the side.

Two recent developments in the life insurance industry provide the life insurance coverage of term insurance (high coverage per premium dollar) plus a tax-deferred way to accumulate assets and earn interest at money market rates.

OBJECTIVE **3** *Understand universal life and variable life policies.*

*Universal Life Insurance.*    Unlike traditional whole life insurance policies, **universal life insurance** allows the insured to vary the amount of premium depending on the changing needs of the insured. The younger insured with limited funds may want maximum insurance protection for the family. At a later date, the insured may want to begin actively building assets and may increase the premium to build cash value for retirement benefits. Universal life insurance is sensitive to interest rate changes. The portion of the premium going into retirement benefits receives money market interest rates and is usually guaranteed a minimum rate of return regardless of what happens to market rates. The result is that the insured profits from higher interest rates but is also protected if interest rates drop below the guaranteed rate. It is hoped that the returns will be greater than those given to ordinary life policyholders.

***Variable Life Insurance.*** **Variable life insurance** provides both death benefits and cash values that vary with the performance of a portfolio (group) of investments chosen by the insured. This type of policy is offered to encourage sales of the life insurance industry's main product—whole life insurance. It allows you to allocate your premiums among one or more separate investments which offer varying degrees of risk and reward—stocks, bonds, combinations of both, or accounts that provide for guarantees of interest and principal. Typical policies available today allow you to switch investments from one fund to another twice each year.

**NOTE** The above features coupled with some tax benefits have resulted in the variable life policy accounting for 25% and 35% respectively of the new policies sold in recent years by two of the largest life insurance companies. ■

***Limited Payment Life Insurance.*** **Limited payment life insurance** is similar to ordinary life, except that premiums are paid for only a certain fixed number of years, such as 20 years. For this reason, this insurance is often called "20-pay life," representing payments of 20 years. The premium for limited payment life is higher than for ordinary life policies. Limited payment life is commonly used by athletes, actors, and others whose income is likely to be high for several years and then decline.

***Endowment Policies.*** An **endowment policy** is the most expensive type of policy. These policies guarantee payment of a fixed amount of money to a given individual, whether or not the insured lives. Endowment policies might be taken out by parents to guarantee a sum of money for their children's college education. Because of the high premiums, this is one of the least popular types of policies today.

It is not always easy to decide on the best type of policy. While term insurance gives the greatest amount of insurance for each premium dollar, it pays only when the insured dies. Ordinary life insurance provides less coverage for each premium dollar in the event of death, however, it does provide a return to the insured at retirement. The only certain method for determining which policy will give the best return is for the insured to know when he or she will die, and this is not possible.

The Commissioners 1980 Standard Ordinary Table of Mortality (shown in Table 7.9) shows the number of deaths per 1,000 and the remaining life expectancy in years for both males and females among the people in the United States having life insurance. Insurance companies use this **mortality table** to evaluate their life insurance reserves, from which benefits are paid. This table is updated periodically with the most recent one shown here.

TABLE 7.9 **Commissioners 1980 Standard Ordinary Table of Mortality Showing the Life Expectancy of Men and Women at Various Ages**

| | Males | | Females | | | Males | | Females | |
|---|---|---|---|---|---|---|---|---|---|
| Age | Deaths per 1,000 | Expectation of Life (Years) | Deaths per 1,000 | Expectation of Life (Years) | Age | Deaths per 1,000 | Expectation of Life (Years) | Deaths per 1,000 | Expectation of Life (Years) |
| 0 | 4.18 | 70.83 | 2.89 | 75.83 | 25 | 1.77 | 47.84 | 1.16 | 42.34 |
| 1 | 1.07 | 70.13 | 0.87 | 75.04 | 26 | 1.73 | 46.93 | 1.19 | 51.40 |
| 2 | 0.99 | 69.20 | 0.81 | 74.11 | 27 | 1.71 | 46.01 | 1.22 | 50.46 |
| 3 | 0.98 | 68.27 | 0.79 | 73.17 | 28 | 1.70 | 45.09 | 1.26 | 49.52 |
| 4 | 0.95 | 67.34 | 0.77 | 72.23 | 29 | 1.71 | 44.16 | 1.30 | 48.59 |
| 5 | 0.90 | 66.40 | 0.76 | 71.28 | 30 | 1.73 | 43.24 | 1.35 | 47.65 |
| 6 | 0.86 | 65.46 | 0.73 | 70.34 | 31 | 1.78 | 42.31 | 1.40 | 46.71 |
| 7 | 0.80 | 64.52 | 0.72 | 69.39 | 32 | 1.83 | 41.38 | 1.45 | 45.78 |
| 8 | 0.76 | 63.57 | 0.70 | 68.44 | 33 | 1.91 | 40.46 | 1.50 | 44.84 |
| 9 | 0.74 | 62.62 | 0.69 | 67.48 | 34 | 2.00 | 39.54 | 1.58 | 43.91 |
| 10 | 0.73 | 61.66 | 0.68 | 66.53 | 35 | 2.11 | 38.61 | 1.65 | 42.98 |
| 11 | 0.77 | 60.71 | 0.69 | 65.58 | 36 | 2.24 | 37.69 | 1.76 | 42.05 |
| 12 | 0.85 | 59.75 | 0.72 | 64.62 | 37 | 2.40 | 36.78 | 1.89 | 41.12 |
| 13 | 0.99 | 58.80 | 0.75 | 63.67 | 38 | 2.58 | 35.87 | 2.04 | 40.20 |
| 14 | 1.15 | 57.86 | 0.80 | 62.71 | 39 | 2.79 | 34.96 | 2.22 | 39.28 |
| 15 | 1.33 | 56.93 | 0.85 | 61.76 | 40 | 3.02 | 34.05 | 2.42 | 38.36 |
| 16 | 1.51 | 56.00 | 0.90 | 60.82 | 41 | 3.29 | 33.16 | 2.64 | 37.46 |
| 17 | 1.67 | 55.09 | 0.95 | 59.87 | 42 | 3.46 | 32.26 | 2.87 | 36.55 |
| 18 | 1.78 | 54.18 | 0.98 | 58.93 | 43 | 3.87 | 31.38 | 3.09 | 35.66 |
| 19 | 1.86 | 53.27 | 1.02 | 57.98 | 44 | 4.19 | 30.50 | 3.32 | 34.77 |
| 20 | 1.90 | 52.37 | 1.05 | 57.04 | 45 | 4.55 | 29.62 | 3.56 | 33.88 |
| 21 | 1.91 | 51.47 | 1.07 | 56.10 | 46 | 4.92 | 28.76 | 3.80 | 33.00 |
| 22 | 1.89 | 50.57 | 1.09 | 55.16 | 47 | 5.32 | 27.90 | 4.05 | 32.12 |
| 23 | 1.86 | 49.66 | 1.11 | 54.22 | 48 | 5.74 | 27.04 | 4.33 | 31.25 |
| 24 | 1.82 | 48.75 | 1.14 | 53.28 | 49 | 6.21 | 26.20 | 4.63 | 30.39 |

OBJECTIVE **4** *Find the annual premium for life insurance.* Calculation of life insurance rates and premiums uses fairly involved mathematics and is done by *actuaries*. The results of such calculations are published in the tables of premiums. A typical table is shown in Table 7.10 (on page 252).

NOTE Life expectancy for women is greater than for men, so a women pays a lower life insurance premium than does a man of the same age. Find the insurance premium

TABLE 7.9  *(continued)* **Commissioners 1980 Standard Ordinary Table of Mortality Showing the Life Expectancy of Men and Women at Various Ages**

| Age | Males Deaths per 1,000 | Males Expectation of Life (Years) | Females Deaths per 1,000 | Females Expectation of Life (Years) | Age | Males Deaths per 1,000 | Males Expectation of Life (Years) | Females Deaths per 1,000 | Females Expectation of Life (Years) |
|-----|-----|-----|-----|-----|-----|-----|-----|-----|-----|
| 50 | 6.71 | 25.36 | 4.96 | 29.53 | 75 | 64.19 | 8.31 | 38.24 | 10.32 |
| 51 | 7.30 | 24.52 | 5.31 | 28.67 | 76 | 70.53 | 7.84 | 42.97 | 9.71 |
| 52 | 7.96 | 23.70 | 5.70 | 27.82 | 77 | 77.12 | 7.40 | 48.04 | 9.12 |
| 53 | 8.71 | 22.89 | 6.15 | 26.98 | 78 | 83.90 | 6.97 | 53.45 | 8.55 |
| 54 | 9.56 | 22.08 | 6.60 | 26.14 | 79 | 91.05 | 6.57 | 59.35 | 8.01 |
| 55 | 10.47 | 21.29 | 7.09 | 25.31 | 80 | 98.84 | 6.18 | 65.99 | 7.48 |
| 56 | 11.46 | 20.51 | 7.57 | 24.49 | 81 | 107.48 | 5.80 | 73.60 | 6.98 |
| 57 | 12.49 | 19.74 | 8.03 | 23.67 | 82 | 117.25 | 5.44 | 82.40 | 6.49 |
| 58 | 13.59 | 18.99 | 8.47 | 22.86 | 83 | 128.26 | 5.09 | 92.53 | 6.03 |
| 59 | 14.77 | 18.24 | 8.94 | 22.05 | 84 | 140.25 | 4.77 | 103.81 | 5.59 |
| 60 | 16.08 | 17.51 | 9.47 | 21.25 | 85 | 152.95 | 4.46 | 116.10 | 5.18 |
| 61 | 17.54 | 16.79 | 10.13 | 20.44 | 86 | 166.09 | 4.18 | 129.29 | 4.80 |
| 62 | 19.19 | 16.08 | 10.96 | 19.65 | 87 | 179.55 | 3.91 | 143.32 | 4.43 |
| 63 | 21.06 | 15.38 | 12.02 | 18.86 | 88 | 193.27 | 3.66 | 158.18 | 4.09 |
| 64 | 23.14 | 14.70 | 13.25 | 18.08 | 89 | 207.29 | 3.41 | 173.94 | 3.77 |
| 65 | 25.42 | 14.04 | 14.59 | 17.32 | 90 | 221.77 | 3.18 | 190.75 | 3.45 |
| 66 | 27.85 | 13.39 | 16.00 | 16.57 | 91 | 236.98 | 2.94 | 208.87 | 3.15 |
| 67 | 30.44 | 12.76 | 17.43 | 15.83 | 92 | 253.45 | 2.70 | 228.81 | 2.85 |
| 68 | 33.19 | 12.14 | 18.84 | 15.10 | 93 | 272.11 | 2.44 | 251.51 | 2.55 |
| 69 | 36.17 | 11.54 | 20.36 | 14.38 | 94 | 295.90 | 2.17 | 279.31 | 2.24 |
| 70 | 39.51 | 10.96 | 22.11 | 13.67 | 95 | 329.96 | 1.87 | 317.32 | 1.91 |
| 71 | 43.30 | 10.39 | 24.23 | 12.97 | 96 | 384.55 | 1.54 | 375.74 | 1.56 |
| 72 | 47.65 | 9.84 | 26.87 | 12.28 | 97 | 480.20 | 1.20 | 474.97 | 1.21 |
| 73 | 52.64 | 9.30 | 30.11 | 11.60 | 98 | 657.98 | 0.84 | 655.85 | 0.84 |
| 74 | 58.19 | 8.79 | 33.93 | 10.95 | | | | | |

*Source:* American Council of Life Insurance, *Life Insurance Fact Book* (Washington, D.C., 1995).

for a women by subtracting five years from her age before using the table of premiums.  ■

The premium for a life insurance policy is found with the following formula.

Premium = Number of thousands × Rate per $1,000

TABLE 7.10    **Annual Premium Rate\* per $1,000 of Life Insurance**

| Age | Renewable Term | Whole Life | Universal Life | 20-Pay Life |
|-----|----------------|------------|----------------|-------------|
| 20 | 2.28 | 4.07 | 3.48 | 12.30 |
| 21 | 2.33 | 4.26 | 3.85 | 12.95 |
| 22 | 2.39 | 4.37 | 4.10 | 13.72 |
| 23 | 2.43 | 4.45 | 4.56 | 14.28 |
| 24 | 2.52 | 4.68 | 4.80 | 15.95 |
| 25 | 2.58 | 5.06 | 5.11 | 16.60 |
| 30 | 2.97 | 5.66 | 6.08 | 18.78 |
| 35 | 3.41 | 7.68 | 7.45 | 21.60 |
| 40 | 4.15 | 12.67 | 10.62 | 24.26 |
| 45 | 4.92 | 19.86 | 15.24 | 28.16 |
| 50 | | 26.23 | 21.46 | 32.59 |
| 55 | | 31.75 | 28.38 | 38.63 |
| 60 | | 38.42 | 36.72 | 45.74 |

\*For women, subtract five years from the actual age. For example, rates for a 30-year-old woman are shown for age 25 in the table.

## EXAMPLE 1    *Finding the Life Insurance Premium*

Judith Allen, owner of Canadian Book Sales, is 40 years old and wants to buy a life insurance policy with a face value of $50,000. Use Table 7.10 to find her annual premium for (a) a renewable term policy, (b) a whole life policy, (c) a universal life policy, and (d) a 20-pay life plan.

**SOLUTION**    Use Table 7.10 and the life insurance premium formula. Since the table gives rates per $1,000 of face value, first find the number of thousands in $50,000.

$$50,000 = 50 \text{ thousands}$$

(a) The rate per $1,000 for a 40-year-old woman (use $40 - 5 = 35$ age) for a renewable term plan is $3.41. The total annual premium is thus

$$50 \times \$3.41 = \$170.50.$$

(b) For a whole life policy, the rate is $7.68 per $1,000, for a total annual premium of

$$50 \times \$7.68 = \$384.$$

This premium is higher than for renewable term insurance, since whole life insurance builds up cash values, unlike term insurance.

(c) The rate for a universal life policy is $7.45 per $1,000 for an annual premium of

$$50 \times \$7.45 = \$372.50.$$

TABLE 7.11  **Premium Factors**

| Mode of Payment | Premium Factor |
| --- | --- |
| **Semiannually** | **0.51** |
| **Quarterly** | **0.26** |
| **Monthly** | **0.0908** |

This premium is higher than for renewable term but less than the premium for whole life insurance.

**(d)** For 20-pay life, the rate per $1,000 is $21.60 for an annual premium of

$$50 \times \$21.60 = \$1,080.$$

Allen would pay $1,080 annually for 20 years, at which time the plan is paid up. She then has insurance protection until retirement, with retirement income thereafter.    ■

**OBJECTIVE** **5** *Use premium factors with different modes of premium payment.*    The annual life insurance premium is not always paid in one single payment. Many companies give the insured the option of paying the premium semiannually, quarterly, or monthly. For this convenience, the policyholder pays an additional amount, determined by a **premium factor**. Table 7.11 shows typical premium factors.

**EXAMPLE 2**  *Using a Premium Factor*

The annual insurance premium for Kathy Jordan is $1,017. Use Table 7.11 to find the amount of the premium and the total annual cost if she pays at the following periods.

**(a)** semiannually    **(b)** quarterly    **(c)** monthly

**SOLUTION**

**(a)** The semiannual premium factor is 0.51. So, her premium is

$$\$1,017 \times 0.51 = \$518.67. \quad \text{semiannual premium}$$

The total annual cost is $1,037.34 ($518.67 × 2).

**(b)** Since the quarterly premium factor is 0.26, her quarterly premium is

$$\$1,017 \times 0.26 = \$264.42. \quad \text{quarterly premium}$$

The total annual cost is $1,057.68 ($264.42 × 4).

**(c)** The monthly premium factor is 0.0908, making the monthly premium

$$\$1,017 \times 0.0908 = \$92.34. \quad \text{monthly premium}$$

The total annual cost is $1,108.08 ($92.34 × 12).    ■

**OBJECTIVE** **6** *Describe discounts, conditions, and additional coverage.*    Many companies today offer a **nonsmokers discount** because they feel that nonsmokers are better insurance risks. Normally, not having smoked for 12 months qualifies one as a nonsmoker. Most policies also contain a **suicide clause**. This clause states that suicide is not covered, usually for the first two years of the policy.

Additional coverage is often available for small increases in the premium. The **accidental death benefit** coverage will pay an additional death benefit if the insured dies as the result of an accident. An optional benefit known as **waiver of premium** allows the life insurance policy to remain in force without payment of premium when the insured becomes disabled. A **guaranteed conversion privilege** lets the insured convert term insurance to any type of whole life or universal life insurance without physical examination. **Companion** or **spouse insurance** allows an insured to add a companion or spouse to a policy, and results in both being insured.

**OBJECTIVE** **7** *Understand nonforfeiture options.*    Most insurance, such as fire, motor vehicle, and even term life insurance, protects against a specific hazardous event. The insured or the heirs of the insured collect only if the event takes place. Life insurance is different; the insured often receives benefits while living. These benefits build over the life of the policy and are available even if the insured stops paying premiums and cancels the policy. The benefits available upon cancellation are called **nonforfeiture options**. The life insurance company invests the premium dollars remaining after death benefits and operating expenses are paid. The invested money plus interest become the cash values of the insurance policyholders.

Cash value which has accrued to the insured may be received in one of several forms when the policy is canceled.

*Cash Settlement Option.*    The policyholder may decide on a **cash settlement option** when canceling the insurance policy. Often the insured borrows against the cash value, leaving the policy in force as an alternative to canceling the policy.

*Paid-up Insurance.*    The cash value of the policy may be used to buy **paid-up insurance** for a smaller policy amount. This paid-up insurance remains in force for the life of the insured.

*Extended Term Insurance.*    With this option, the insured purchases insurance of the same face value for a specific period of time. The duration of this **extended term insurance** depends on the amount of the cash value of the insured's policy.

Typical nonforfeiture options for a policy issued at age 25 appear in Table 7.12.

**EXAMPLE 3** *Determining Nonforfeiture Options*

Lois Stevens purchased an $80,000 whole life insurance policy when she was 25 years old and has paid on the policy for 20 years. Determine the following values for her policy: (a) cash value, (b) the amount of paid-up insurance which she could receive, and (c) the time period for which she could have extended term insurance.

**SOLUTION**

(a)  The cash value found in Table 7.12 under whole life for 20 years is $283 per $1,000 of insurance. The cash value of her policy is

$$\$283 \times 80 \text{ (number of \$1,000s)} = \$22,640.$$

TABLE 7.12   **Nonforfeiture Options per $1,000/Policy Issued at Age 25**

| Years in Force | Whole Life | | | | 20-Pay Life | | | | Universal Life |
| | Cash Value | Paid-up Ins. | Ext. Term | | Cash Value | Paid-up Ins. | Ext. Term | | Cash Value |
| | | | Years | Days | | | Years | Days | |
|---|---|---|---|---|---|---|---|---|---|
| 3* | $5 | $16 | 1 | 192 | $29 | $93 | 11 | 18 | $40 |
| 5 | 28 | 84 | 10 | 190 | 70 | 228 | 20 | 96 | 96 |
| 10 | 96 | 258 | 18 | 112 | 187 | 554 | 29 | 115 | 310 |
| 15 | 169 | 415 | 20 | 312 | 339 | 789 | 33 | 215 | 680 |
| 20 | 283 | 579 | 23 | 315 | 491 | 1,000 | Life | Life | 1,125 |
| 25 | 394 | 637 | 25 | 130 | 506 | 1,000 | | | 1,495 |
| 30 | 491 | 698 | 26 | 210 | 523 | 1,000 | — | — | 1,968 |

*Normally, there is no cash value accrued in the first two years. The cash value of universal life is an estimate of the value, not a guarantee, and will vary depending on the performance of the portfolio of investments chosen by the insured.

**(b)** Again, from Table 7.12, the amount of paid-up insurance which she could receive is $579 per $1,000, or

$$\$579 \times 80 = \$46,320 \text{ paid-up insurance.}$$

This coverage would remain in force until her death without paying any additional premium.

**(c)** The time period for which she could have extended term insurance of the same amount, $80,000, is 23 years and 315 days.  ∎

There are two types of insurance companies—**mutual companies** and **stock companies**. The policyholders are the owners in a mutual company, with the policies called **participating policies**. The owners (policyholders) share in any profits of the company; the profits are paid in the form of dividends. If the company prospers, the policyholders receive a dividend or refund of premium. In a stock company, the stockholders are the owners of the company, with the policies called **nonparticipating policies**. If the company prospers, the stockholders, not the policyholders, receive a dividend. The distinction is important in determining the **net cost of insurance policies**.

**OBJECTIVE 8** *Calculate income under various settlement options.*   At the death of a life insurance policyholder, the **beneficiary**, the individual chosen by the insured to receive benefits upon death, has several **settlement options** when choosing how the death benefits are to be received. In many cases the beneficiary elects to receive a single lump sum payment of the face value of the policy. In other cases, the beneficiary allows the life insurance company to invest the face value and to pay the beneficiary the proceeds and interest over a period of time in the form of an **annuity**. The more common options available follow.

***Fixed Amount Annuity.***    A **fixed amount annuity** may be paid each month. The monthly payments continue, including interest, until all the proceeds are used up.

***Fixed Period Annuity.***    The beneficiary may prefer the payments of a **fixed period annuity**. The insurance company determines the amount that may be paid monthly, for example, for ten years. The payment continues for exactly that period of time, even if the beneficiary dies.

***Payments for Life.***    **Payments for life** is another option. Based upon the age and sex of the beneficiary, the insurance company calculates an amount to be paid to the beneficiary for as long as he or she lives.

***Payments for Life with a Guaranteed Number of Years.***    A last option is **payments for life with a guaranteed numbers of years**. Here, if the beneficiary dies before receiving the benefits for the guaranteed time period, the payments continue to the beneficiaries' heirs until the guarantee is satisfied. The guarantees usually range from 5 to 25 years.

Table 7.13 shows the monthly income per $1,000 of insurance coverage under various settlement options.

**EXAMPLE 1** *Finding Settlement Options*

Chris Bowler is the beneficiary of a $40,000 life insurance policy. Find (a) the monthly payment if he decides to receive payments for 18 years and (b) the number of years payments will continue if he selects a monthly payment of $300.

**SOLUTION**

**(a)** The monthly payment from Table 7.13 for 18 years is $6.07 per $1,000 of face value. The monthly payment he receives is

$$\$6.07 \times 40 \text{ (thousands)} = \$242.80.$$

TABLE 7.13    **Monthly Payments per $1,000 of Face Value**

| Options 1 and 2: Fixed Amount or Fixed Number of Years | | Options 3 and 4: Income for Life | | | | |
|---|---|---|---|---|---|---|
| | | Age when Payments Begin | | | Life with 10 Years Certain | Life with 15 Years Certain |
| Years | Amount | Male | Female | Life Annuity | | |
| 10 | $9.78 | 50 | 55 | $4.63 | $4.49 | $4.38 |
| 12 | 8.46 | 55 | 60 | 5.36 | 5.16 | 4.78 |
| 14 | 7.63 | 60 | 65 | 5.94 | 5.73 | 4.91 |
| 16 | 6.91 | 65 | 70 | 6.93 | 6.51 | 5.34 |
| 18 | 6.07 | 70 | 75 | 7.86 | 6.93 | 6.28 |
| 20 | 5.78 | | | | | |

**(b)** A monthly payment of $300 is equivalent to

$$\frac{\$300}{40 \text{ (thousands)}} = \$7.50 \text{ per } \$1,000 \text{ face value.}$$

Reading the amount column under Options 1 and 2, find $7.63 (closest to $7.50). The $300 payment will continue a little over 14 years.  ■

### EXAMPLE 5  *Finding Settlement Options*

Clarence Hanks, 60 years of age, is the beneficiary of a $20,000 life insurance policy. Find (a) his monthly payment from a life annuity and (b) his monthly payment from a life annuity with 15 years certain.

### SOLUTION

**(a)** Under Options 3 and 4, in Table 7.13, look up male, age 60. Look across to the life annuity column, to find $5.94. His monthly payment for life is

$$\$5.94 \times 20 \text{ (thousands)} = \$118.80.$$

**(b)** The monthly payment from a life annuity with 15 years certain is

$$\$4.91 \times 20 \text{ (thousands)} = \$98.20.$$  ■

## 7.3  EXERCISES

*Find the annual premium, the semiannual premium, the quarterly premium, and the monthly premium for each of the following. (Note: Subtract five years for females.) Use Tables 7.10 and 7.11.*

| | Face Value of Policy | Age of Insured | Sex of Insured | Type of Policy |
|---|---|---|---|---|
| 1. | $30,000 | 30 | M | renewable term |
| 2. | $60,000 | 23 | M | whole life |
| 3. | $40,000 | 55 | F | 20-pay life |
| 4. | $80,000 | 40 | F | universal life |
| 5. | $90,000 | 35 | F | whole life |
| 6. | $60,000 | 45 | F | renewable term |
| 7. | $10,000 | 25 | M | universal life |
| 8. | $10,000 | 22 | M | 20-pay life |
| 9. | $50,000 | 26 | F | renewable term |
| 10. | $40,000 | 29 | F | 20-pay life |
| 11. | $70,000 | 50 | M | whole life |
| 12. | $60,000 | 35 | M | renewable term |
| 13. | $100,000 | 60 | F | whole life |
| 14. | $100,000 | 27 | F | universal life |

15. Explain the advantages and disadvantages of buying renewable term life insurance. Would you buy renewable term life insurance for yourself? Why or why not? (See Objective 1.)

16. If you were the beneficiary of a $40,000 life insurance policy, what settlement option would you choose? Why? (See Objective 8.)

*Find the nonforfeiture values of the following policies. The policies were issued at age 25. Use Table 7.12.*

|     | Years in Force | Type of Policy | Face Value | Nonforfeiture Option |
| --- | --- | --- | --- | --- |
| 17. | 10 | universal life | $50,000 | cash value |
| 18. | 15 | universal life | $75,000 | cash value |
| 19. | 30 | 20-pay life | $30,000 | paid-up insurance |
| 20. | 15 | whole life | $35,000 | extended term |
| 21. | 30 | universal life | $100,000 | cash value |
| 22. | 15 | 20-pay life | $25,000 | paid-up insurance |
| 23. | 20 | whole life | $100,000 | extended term |
| 24. | 10 | whole life | $40,000 | extended term |

*Find the monthly payment or period of payment under the following policy settlement options. Use Table 7.13.*

|     | Beneficiary Age | Sex | Face Value | Settlement Option | Monthly Payment Years | Amount |
| --- | --- | --- | --- | --- | --- | --- |
| 25. | 55 | M | $50,000 | Fixed amount per month | 20 | _____ |
| 26. | 65 | F | $75,000 | Life-10-years certain | 10 | _____ |
| 27. | 65 | M | $10,000 | Fixed number of years | _____ | $60.70 |
| 28. | 60 | M | $40,000 | Fixed number of years | _____ | $338.40 |
| 29. | 70 | F | $30,000 | Life-15-years certain | 15 | _____ |
| 30. | 60 | F | $100,000 | Fixed amount per month | 10 | _____ |

*Solve each of the following application problems.*

31. Linda Davis buys a $50,000 whole life policy at age 40. Her son Matthew is the beneficiary, and will collect the face value of the policy. (a) Find the annual premium. (b) How much will Matthew get if his mother dies after paying premiums for 9 years?

32. Cindy Chen buys a $100,000, 20-pay life policy at age 45. Her son Bryan is the beneficiary, and will collect the face value of the policy. (a) Find the annual premium. (b) How much will Bryan get if his mother dies after paying premiums for 12 years?

33. Midland Machine Company feels that it would suffer considerable hardship if the firm's head dispatcher died suddenly. Therefore, the firm takes out a $100,000 policy on the dispatcher's life. The dispatcher is a 40-year-old woman, and the company buys a renewable term policy. Find the semiannual premium.

34. City Cellular purchased a $70,000 whole life policy on the finance manager's life. If the finance manager is a 35-year-old man, find the quarterly premium.

35. Henry Hernandez takes out a 20-pay life policy with a face value of $75,000. He is 50 years old. Find the monthly premium.

36. Fred Love, a 40-year-old man, purchases a universal life policy with a face value of $40,000. Find the monthly premium.

37. The annual premium for a whole life policy is $648. Using premium factors, find (a) the semiannual premium, (b) the quarterly premium, (c) the monthly premium, and (d) the total annual cost of each of the plans.

38. A 20-pay life policy has an annual premium of $1,806. Use premium factors to find (a) the semiannual premium, (b) the quarterly premium, (c) the monthly premium, and (d) the total annual cost of each of the plans.

39. Catherine Konradt purchased a $20,000 whole life policy 20 years ago when she was 25 years old. Use the table of nonforfeiture options (Table 7.12) to determine the (a) cash value, (b) the amount of paid-up insurance which she could receive, and (c) the time period for which she could have paid-up insurance.

40. Lee Hardesty purchased a 20-pay life policy 15 years ago when he was 25 years old. The face value of the policy is $80,000. Find the following values using the nonforfeiture options table (Table 7.12): (a) cash value, (b) the amount of paid-up insurance which he could have, and (c) the time period for which he could have paid-up term insurance.

41. The face value of a universal life policy purchased by Patty Gillette is $100,000. She purchased the policy 25 years ago when she was 25 years of age. Use the nonforfeiture options table (Table 7.12) to find the cash value of the policy today.

42. When he was 25 years old, Chuck Manly purchased a $40,000 whole life policy. Now that 30 years have passed Manly wants to know the options available when canceling his policy. Use the nonforfeiture options table (Table 7.12) to find the (a) cash value, (b) the amount of paid-up insurance he could have, and (c) the time period for which he could have paid-up term insurance.

43. Ryan Polstra is the beneficiary of a $25,000 life insurance policy. Polstra is 50 years of age and is considering the various settlement options available. Use Table 7.13 to find (a) the monthly payment if he selects payments for 12 years, (b) the number of years he will receive payments of $145 per month, (c) the monthly payment from a life annuity, and (d) the amount he would receive monthly if he chooses a life annuity with 15 years certain.

44. Jenn Luan is the beneficiary of a $30,000 life insurance policy. Luan is 65 years of age and is considering the various settlement options available. Use Table 7.13 to find (a) the monthly payment she would receive if she selects a fixed amount for 10 years, (b) the number of years she can receive $225 per month, (c) the amount she can receive per month as a life annuity, and (d) the monthly amount she could receive as a life annuity with 10 years certain.

45. James Marcotte is the beneficiary of a $50,000 life insurance policy. Marcotte is 60 years of age and is considering the various settlement options available. Use Table 7.13 to find (a) the monthly payment he would receive if he selects a fixed amount for

16 years, (b) the number of years he can receive $305 per month, (c) the amount he can receive per month as a life annuity, and (d) the monthly amount he could receive as a life annuity with 10 years certain.

46. Meghan Anderson is the beneficiary of a $70,000 life insurance policy. Anderson is 60 years of age and is considering the various settlement options available. Use Table 7.13 to find (a) the monthly payment she would receive if she selects a fixed amount for 18 years, (b) the number of years she can receive $405 per month, (c) the amount she can receive as a life annuity, and (d) the monthly amount she could receive as a life annuity with 10 years certain.

🖉 47. The greatest advantage of a renewable term policy is that you get the most coverage for your premium dollar. However, renewable term provides no cash value for retirement. Explain how you would provide for retirement to offset this disadvantage of a renewable term life policy. (See Objective 2.)

🖉 48. The additional charge for paying an insurance premium semiannually, quarterly, or monthly is determined by a premium factor. Would you select other than the single premium payment? Why or why not? How could you justify the additional charge (premium factor)? (See Objective 5.)

# Chapter 7 Quick Review

| TOPIC | APPROACH | EXAMPLE |
|---|---|---|
| **7.1 Annual premium for fire insurance** | Use the building and territorial rating in Table 7.1 to find the premiums per $100 for the building and for the contents. Add the two premiums. | Building value, $80,000, contents, $35,000; territorial rating, 4; building rating, B. Find the annual premium.<br><br>Building<br>$800 \times \$0.75 = \$600$<br><br>Contents:<br>$350 \times \$0.77 = \$269.50$<br><br>Total premium:<br>$\$600 + \$269.50 = \$869.50$ |
| **7.1 Short-term rates and cancellations** | Annual premium is multiplied by the short-term rate. Use Table 7.2. | Annual premium is $2,320. Short-term rate for 9 months is 85%. Premium for 9 months is<br><br>$\$2,320 \times 0.85 = \$1,972$<br>$\$2,320 - \$1,972 = \$348$ |

| 7.1 | **Calculate prorated insurance premium cancellations** | Multiply annual premium by a fraction with months of insurance in force as numerator and 12 as denominator. | Annual premium, $1,620; policy canceled after four months. Find refund. Premium for four months is |
|---|---|---|---|

$$\$1,620 \times \frac{4}{12} = \$540.$$

$1,620 - $540 = $1,080 refund.

| 7.1 | **Coinsurance formula** | Part of the risk is taken by the insured. An 80% coinsurance clause is common. | Building value, $125,000; policy amount, $75,000; loss, $40,000; 80% coinsurance clause. Find the amount of loss paid by insurance company. |
|---|---|---|---|

Loss paid by insurance company =

$$\text{Amount of loss} \times \frac{\text{Policy amount}}{80\% \text{ of replacement cost}}$$

$$\$40,000 \times \frac{\$75,000}{\$100,000} =$$

$30,000   amount insurance company pays

| 7.1 | **Multiple carriers** | Several companies insure the same property to limit their risk; each company pays its fractional portion of any claim. | Insured loss, $500,000; Insurance is Company A with $1,000,000; Company B with $750,000; Company C with $250,000; find the amount of loss paid by each company. |
|---|---|---|---|

$$
\begin{array}{r}
\$1,000,000 \\
750,000 \\
+\quad 250,000 \\
\hline
\$2,000,000 \text{ Total insurance}
\end{array}
$$

Company A

$$\frac{\$1,000,000}{\$2,000,000} \times \$500,000 =$$
$250,000

Company B

$$\frac{\$750,000}{\$2,000,000} \times \$500,000 =$$
$187,500

Company C

$$\frac{\$250,000}{\$2,000,000} \times \$500,000 =$$
$62,500

**7.2   Annual auto insurance premium**

Most drivers are legally required to purchase automobile insurance. The premium is determined by the types of coverage selected, the type of car, geographic territory, past driving record, and other factors.

Determine the premium: territory, 3; liability, 50/100; property damage, $50,000; comprehensive and collision, 3-year-old car with a symbol of 8; uninsured motorist coverage; driver, age 23 with driver's training.

$$\begin{array}{rl} \$375 & \text{liability (Table 7.3)} \\ 145 & \text{property damage (Table 7.4)} \\ 90 & \text{comprehensive (Table 7.5)} \\ 162 & \text{collision (Table 7.5)} \\ +\ \ 76 & \text{uninsured motorist (Table 7.6)} \\ \hline \$848 & \times\ 1.15\ \text{youthful operator factor} \\ & =\ \$975.20 \end{array}$$

**7.2   Amount paid by insurance company and by insured**

Company pays up to maximum amount of insurance coverage; insured pays balance.

Policy terms: Liability, 15/30; property damage, $10,000; collision, $250 deductible. Accident caused $2,850 damage to insured's car; $3,850 to other car; injury liability of $20,000 and $25,000, respectively. Company pays $2,600 ($2,850 − $250) to repair insured's car; company pays $3,850 to repair other car ($10,000 limit); company pays $30,000 for two injured people ($15,000 each); insured pays $15,000 ($45,000 − $30,000), amount over limit.

**7.3   Annual life insurance premium**

There are several types of life policies. Use Table 7.10 and multiply by the number of $1,000s of coverage. Subtract five years from the age of females.
Premium = Number of thousands × Rate per $1,000

Find the premiums on a $50,000 policy for a 30-year-old male.

**(a)** Renewable Term
    50 × $2.97 = $148.50
**(b)** Whole Life
    50 × $5.66 = $283
**(c)** Universal Life
    50 × $6.08 = $304
**(d)** 20-Pay Life
    50 × $18.78 = $939

| 7.3 | **Premium factors** | If not paid annually, life insurance premiums may be paid semiannually, quarterly, or monthly. The annual premium is multiplied by the premium factor to determine the premium amount. Use Table 7.11. | The annual life insurance premium is $740. Use Table 7.11 to find the semiannual, quarterly, and monthly premium. |

**(a)** Semiannual
$740 × 0.51 = $377.40
**(b)** Quarterly
$740 × 0.26 = $192.40
**(c)** Monthly
$740 × 0.0908 = $67.19

| 7.3 | **Nonforfeiture options** | Upon cancellation of a policy the insured may receive a cash settlement, paid-up insurance, or extended term insurance as a nonforfeiture option. Use Table 7.12. | Insurance is a $40,000, 20-pay life policy; in force for 10 years; issued at age 25. |

**(a)** Cash value =
$187 × 40 = $7,480
**(b)** Paid-up insurance =
$554 × 40 = $22,160
**(c)** Extended term insurance period is 29 years, 115 days.

| 7.3 | **Settlement options** | Upon the death of the insured, the beneficiary often has choices as to how the money may be received. These range from all cash to various types of payment arrangements. Use Table 7.13. | $30,000 policy; female beneficiary, age 60. Find monthly payments for: |

**(a)** 16 years;
$30 × $6.91 = $207.30
**(b)** life annuity;
$30 × $5.36 = $160.80
**(c)** life with 15 years certain.
$30 × $4.78 = $143.40
**(d)** For how many years would $200 a month be paid?

$$\frac{\$200}{30} = \$6.67 \text{ per } \$1,000$$

$6.67 is closest to $6.91; a little more than 16 years.

# Chapter 7 Review Exercises

Find the total annual premium for fire insurance for each of the following. Use Table 7.1. [7.1]

| | Territorial Rating | Building Classification | Building Value | Contents Value |
|---|---|---|---|---|
| 1. | 2 | C | $210,000 | $186,000 |
| 2. | 4 | B | $418,000 | $240,000 |
| 3. | 3 | A | $80,000 | $30,000 |
| 4. | 1 | B | $193,000 | $68,000 |

Find the amount of refund to the insured using the Short-Term Rate Schedule (Table 7.2). [7.1]

| | Annual Premium | Months in Force |
|---|---|---|
| 5. | $1,274 | 6 |
| 6. | $956 | 3 |
| 7. | $1,486 | 9 |
| 8. | $2,878 | 5 |

Find (a) the amount of premium retained by the company and (b) the amount of refund to the insured using proration. [7.1]

| | Annual Premium | Months in Force |
|---|---|---|
| 9. | $1,230 | 4 |
| 10. | $2,136 | 8 |
| 11. | $1,476 | 10 |
| 12. | $2,784 | 2 |

Find the amount of each of the following losses that will be paid by the insurance company. Assume that each policy includes an 80% coinsurance clause. [7.1]

| | Value of Building | Face Value of Policy | Amount of Loss |
|---|---|---|---|
| 13. | $456,000 | $320,000 | $45,000 |
| 14. | $277,500 | $165,000 | $97,800 |
| 15. | $186,700 | $120,000 | $3,400 |
| 16. | $325,000 | $220,000 | $42,200 |

*Find the annual motor vehicle insurance premium for the following people. [7.2]*

| Name | Territory | Age | Driver Training | Liability | Property Damage | Comprehensive Collision Age Group | Symbol | Uninsured Motorist |
|------|-----------|-----|-----------------|-----------|-----------------|-----------------------------------|--------|--------------------|
| 17. Reser | 3 | 53 | — | 100/300 | $100,000 | 4 | 7 | no |
| 18. Elmo | 2 | 20 | yes | 50/100 | $50,000 | 5 | 6 | yes |
| 19. Verano | 1 | 24 | no | 25/50 | $25,000 | 2 | 8 | yes |
| 20. Wilson | 4 | 29 | — | 250/500 | $100,000 | 1 | 6 | yes |

*Find the annual premium for each of the following life insurance policies. [7.3]*

21. Carolyn Phelps: 20-pay life; $70,000 face value; age 55

22. Ralph Todd: renewable term; $50,000 face value; age 45

23. Gilbert Eckern: whole life; $30,000 face value; age 23

24. Ellen Ramos: universal life; $40,000 face value; age 29

*Solve the following application problems.*

25. Camblin Steel Company had a fire loss of $240,000. They had insurance coverage as follows: company A, $1,800,000; company B, $1,200,000; company C, $600,000. Find the amount paid by each of the multiple carriers assuming that the coinsurance clause had been met. Round to the nearest dollar. [7.1]

26. The headquarters building of Western States Life is valued at $820,000, and the fire insurance policies contain an 80% coinsurance clause. The policies include $350,000 with company 1 and $200,000 with company 2. The Western building suffered a $150,000 fire loss. Find (a) the amount that Western would receive after the loss and (b) the amount of loss paid by each insurance company. Round to the nearest dollar. [7.1]

27. Your cousin who has a bodily injury policy with limits of 25/50 injures a bicycle rider. The judge awards damages of $34,000 to the injured cyclist. (a) How much will the company pay and (b) how much will your cousin pay? [7.2]

28. Three people are injured in an automobile accident and receive $15,000 each in damages. The driver has bodily injury insurance of 50/100. (a) How much will the company pay to each person and (b) how much must the driver pay? [7.2]

29. Some scaffolding falls off a truck and into the path of a car, resulting in serious damage and injury. The car had damage of $16,800, while the driver and passenger of the car were given court awards of $25,000 and $35,000, respectively. The driver of the truck had 15/30 liability insurance limits and $10,000 property damage limits. Find (a) the total amount paid by the insurance company for both property damage and liability and (b) the total amount beyond the insurance limits for which the driver was liable. [7.2]

**30.** The annual premium for a whole life policy is $970. Use premium factors to find (a) the semiannual premium, (b) the quarterly premium, (c) the monthly premium, and (d) the total annual cost for each of the plans. [7.3]

**31.** Lisa DeMol purchased a universal life policy 20 years ago when she was 25 years old. The face value of the policy is $60,000. Find the cash value of the policy using the nonforfeiture options table (Table 7.12). [7.3]

**32.** Glenn Lewis purchased a $40,000 whole life policy 20 years ago when he was 25 years old. Use Table 7.12 to determine (a) the cash value, (b) the amount of paid-up insurance he could receive, and (c) the time period for which he could have paid-up term insurance. [7.3]

**33.** Jim Jordan is the beneficiary of an $80,000 life insurance policy. Jordan is 60 years old and is considering the various settlement options available. Use Table 7.13 to find (a) the monthly payment he would receive if he selects a fixed payment for 16 years, (b) the number of years he can receive $675 per month, (c) the amount he can receive as a life annuity, and (d) the monthly amount he could receive as a life annuity with 15 years certain. [7.3]

**34.** Ann-Marie Sargent is the beneficiary of a $40,000 life insurance policy. Sargent is 55 years old and is considering the various settlement options available. Use Table 7.13 to find (a) the monthly payment she would receive if she selects a fixed payment for 20 years, (b) the number of years she can receive $245 per month, (c) the amount she can receive as a life annuity, and (d) the monthly amount she could receive as a life annuity with 10 years certain. [7.3]

# Chapter 7 Summary Exercise

Childcare Playground Toys imports parts from Thailand and Malaysia and assembles quality built playground equipment and riding toys. Planning ahead, the company set aside $41,700 to pay fire insurance premiums on the company property and a semiannual life insurance premium for the president which were both due in the same month. Find each of the following.

**(a)** The building occupied by the company is a class B building worth $1,730,000. The contents are worth $3,502,000 and the territorial rating is 4. Find the annual insurance premium.

**(b)** The president of Childcare Playground Toys is a 45-year-old woman and the company is buying a $175,000, renewable term life insurance policy on the president's life. Find the semiannual premium.

**(c)** Find the total amount needed to pay the fire insurance premium and the semiannual life insurance premium.

**(d)** How much more than the amount needed had the company set aside to pay these expenses?

# Mathematics
# of Buying

Retail businesses make a profit by purchasing items and then selling them for more than they cost. There are several steps in this process: **manufacturers** buy raw materials and component parts and assemble them into products which can be sold to other manufacturers or wholesalers. The **wholesaler**, often called a "middleman," buys from manufacturers or other wholesalers and sells to the retailer. **Retailers** sell directly to the ultimate user, the **consumer**.

Documents called **invoices** help businesses keep track of sales, while various types of **discounts** help them buy products at lower costs to increase profits. This chapter looks at the mathematics needed for working with invoices and discounts—the **mathematics of buying**.

## 8.1 Invoices and Trade Discounts

**OBJECTIVES**

1. *Complete an invoice.*
2. *Understand common shipping terms.*
3. *Identify invoice abbreviations.*
4. *Calculate net cost and trade discounts.*
5. *Differentiate between single and series discounts.*
6. *Calculate series discounts.*
7. *Use complements to calculate series discounts.*
8. *Use a table to find the net cost equivalent of series discounts.*

An **invoice** is a printed record of a purchase and sale. For the seller it is a **sales invoice** and records a sale; for the buyer it is a **purchase invoice** and records a purchase. The invoice identifies the seller and the buyer, includes a description of the items purchased, the quantity purchased, the unit price of each item, the **extension total** (the number of items purchased times the price per unit), any discounts, the shipping and insurance charges, and the **invoice total** (the sum of all the extension totals).

**THE O'BRIEN CORPORATION**
FULLER-O'BRIEN PAINTS • NASON AUTOMOTIVE FINISHES

PLEASE REMIT TO
THE O'BRIEN CORPORATION
PO BOX 44715
SAN FRANCISCO, CA 94144-4715

**FULLER O'BRIEN** PAINTS

SHIP TO

PLEASE REFER TO THIS DOCUMENT NUMBER ON ALL CORRESPONDENCE ▶

ORIGINAL
TW06469

SOLD TO

OAKS HARDWARE

10136 FAIR OAKS BLVD

FAIR OAKS CA 95628-7110

| CUSTOMER NUMBER | SELLING UNIT | SHIPPING UNIT | MKT. CLASS | INVOICE DATE |
|---|---|---|---|---|
| 6205520 | 12263 | 12120 | 13 | 03/11 |

| BATCH | JOB/CONTRACT | PURCHASE ORDER NUMBER | | |
|---|---|---|---|---|
| CARO70BT · | | | | |

| DATE SHIPPED | ZN-PS/P | ZN-PS/S | ZN-PS/0 | PC-0 | TX | INV. |
|---|---|---|---|---|---|---|
| 03/10 | 01-1 | 01-1 | | | R | |

**TERMS**

2%10TH PROX NET EOM

| PRODUCT | SIZE | U/M | P A | P S | T X | DESCRIPTION | UNITS SHIPPED | UNIT PRICE | AMOUNT |
|---|---|---|---|---|---|---|---|---|---|
| 1 00066492 | 005 | EA | | | R | WTHR KNG LTX H&T BASE 2 H 87 | 1 | 84.00 | 84.00 |
| 1 00063136 | 001 | GL | | | R | LTX FLOOR EN SATIN | 1 | 16.56 | 16.56 |
| 1 00022023 | 001 | EA | | | R | EXT ALKYD WOOD PRIMER WHI | 2 | 13.05 | 26.10 |
| 1 00060291 | 001 | EA | | | R | LIQUID VELVET LATEX BASE | 8 | 12.47 | 99.76 |
| 1 00020210 | 001 | EA | | | R | ACRY WALL FIN PASTEL TINT | 6 | 12.84 | 77.04 |
| | | | | | | | | SUB TOTAL | 303.46 |

In the event this account becomes past due beyond normal terms, I (we) agree to pay a service charge of one and one-half percent (1½%) per month (18% annual rate) to reimburse The O'Brien Corporation for the additional costs and expenses it will incur, and in the event court suit is necessary, I (we) also agree to pay reasonable attorney fees.

**ALL CLAIMS MUST BE MADE WITHIN 30 DAYS OF INVOICE DATE.
GOODS MAY NOT BE RETURNED WITHOUT PRIOR APPROVAL**

| TAX% | TAX AMOUNT | FREIGHT | TOTAL INVOICE |
|---|---|---|---|
| | | | 303.46 |

PLEASE PAY THIS AMOUNT ——— ▲

**FIGURE 8.1**

*Source:* Reprinted by permission of The O'Brien Corporation.

**OBJECTIVE** **1** *Complete an invoice.* The document in Figure 8.1 serves as a sales invoice for The O'Brien Corporation and as a purchase invoice for Oaks Hardware. The numbers in the ''units shipped'' column multiplied by the ''unit price'' give the ''amount,'' or extension total, for each item. The **total invoice amount** is the sum of the extension totals.

Trade and cash discounts, discussed later in this section, are never applied to shipping and insurance charges. For this reason shipping and insurance charges are often not included in the invoice total, and the purchaser must add them to the invoice total to find the total amount due.

**OBJECTIVE** ▌2▐ *Understand common shipping terms.*     A common shipping term appearing on invoices is **FOB (free on board)**, followed by the words **shipping point** or **destination**. The term ''FOB—shipping point'' means that the *buyer* pays for shipping and that ownership of the merchandise passes to the purchaser when the merchandise is given to the shipper. The term ''FOB—destination'' means that the *seller* pays the shipping charges and retains ownership until the goods reach the destination. This distinction is important in the event that the merchandise is lost or damaged during shipment.

The shipping term **COD** means **cash on delivery**. Here the shipper makes delivery to the purchaser on the receipt of enough cash to pay for the goods. A shipping term used when goods are moved by ship is ''**FAS**,'' which means **free alongside ship**. Here the goods are delivered to the dock with all freight charges to that point paid by the shipper.

**OBJECTIVE** ▌3▐ *Identify invoice abbreviations.*     A number of abbreviations are used on invoices to identify measurements, quantities of merchandise, shipping terms, and additional discounts. Those most commonly used are shown in Table 8.1. (Some of these measurements are from the metric system. These measurements often appear on invoices for imported goods.)

TABLE 8.1   **Common Invoice Abbreviations**

| | | | |
|---|---|---|---|
| **ea.** | = **each** | **drm.** | = **drum** |
| **doz.** | = **dozen** | **cs.** | = **case** |
| **gro.** | = **gross (144 items)** | **bx.** | = **box** |
| **gr. gro.** | = **great gross (12 gross)** | **sk.** | = **sack** |
| **qt.** | = **quart** | **pr.** | = **pair** |
| **gal.** | = **gallon (4 quarts)** | **C** | = **Roman numeral for 100** |
| **bbl.** | = **barrel ($31\frac{1}{2}$ gallons)** | **M** | = **Roman numeral for 1,000** |
| **ml** | = **milliliter** | **cwt.** | = **per hundred weight** |
| **cl** | = **centiliter** | **cpm.** | = **cost per thousand** |
| **L** | = **liter** | **@** | = **at** |
| **in.** | = **inch** | **lb.** | = **pound** |
| **ft.** | = **foot** | **oz.** | = **ounce** |
| **yd.** | = **yard** | **g** | = **gram** |
| **mm** | = **millimeter** | **kg** | = **kilogram** |
| **cm** | = **centimeter** | **FOB** | = **free on board** |
| **m** | = **meter** | **ROG** | = **receipt-of-goods** |
| **km** | = **kilometer** | **EOM** | = **end-of-month** |
| **ct.** | = **crate** | **ex. or x** | = **extra dating** |
| **cart.** | = **carton** | **COD** | = **cash on delivery** |
| **ctn.** | = **carton** | **FAS** | = **free alongside ship** |

**OBJECTIVE** **4** *Calculate net cost and trade discounts.*     **Trade discounts** are offered to businesses or individuals who buy an item that is to be sold or used to produce an item that will then be sold. Normally, the seller prices an item at its **list price** (the suggested price at which the item is to be sold to the public). Then the seller gives a trade discount that is subtracted from the list price to get the **net cost** (the amount to be paid by the buyer). Find the net cost by using the following formula.

$$\text{Net cost} = \text{List price} - \text{Trade discount} \qquad \text{or} \qquad \begin{array}{r} \text{List price} \\ -\,\text{Trade discount} \\ \hline \text{Net cost} \end{array}$$

**EXAMPLE 1** *Calculating a Single Trade Discount*

The list price of a solar-powered calculator is $12.80, with a trade discount of 25%. Find the net cost.

**SOLUTION**   First find the amount of the trade discount by taking 25% of $12.80.

$$R \;\times\; B \qquad\qquad\qquad = \quad P$$
$$25\% \times \$12.80 = 0.25 \times \$12.80 = \$3.20$$

Find the net cost by subtracting $3.20 from the list price of $12.80.

$$\$12.80 \text{ (list price)} - \$3.20 \text{ (trade discount)} = \$9.60 \text{ (net cost)}$$

The net cost of the calculator is $9.60.                                    ∎

**OBJECTIVE** **5** *Differentiate between single and series discounts.*     In Example 1 a **single discount** of 25% was offered. Another type of discount combines two or more discounts into a **series** or **chain discount**. A series discount written as 20/10 means that a 20% discount is subtracted from the list price, and *from this difference* another 10% discount is subtracted.

Discounts are sometimes added to or subtracted from a series discount. For example, another discount of 5% could be added to the series discount 20/10, for a new series discount of 20/10/5.

**REASONS THAT TRADE DISCOUNTS MAY CHANGE**

*Price changes* may cause trade discounts to be raised or lowered.

As the *quantity purchased* increases, the discount offered may increase.

The buyer's position in *marketing channels* may determine the amount of discount offered (a wholesaler would receive a larger discount than the succeeding retailer).

*Geographic location* may influence the trade discount. An additional discount may be offered to increase sales in one particular area.

*Seasonal fluctuations* in sales may influence the trade discounts offered.

*Competition* from other companies may cause raising or lowering of trade discounts.

**OBJECTIVE** **6** *Calculate series discounts.* Three methods can be used to calculate a series discount and the net cost. The first of these is by *using discounts separately.*

| **EXAMPLE 2** *Calculating Series Trade Discounts*

The Home Depot is offered a series discount of 20/10 on a worm drive circular saw with a list price of $150. Find the net cost after the series discount.

**SOLUTION** First multiply the decimal equivalent of 20% (0.2) by $150. Then subtract the product ($30) from $150, getting $120. Then multiply the decimal equivalent of the second discount, 10% (0.1), by $120. Subtract the product ($12) from $120, getting $108, the net cost. Write this calculation as

$150 list price      Discount: 20/10
$\underline{-\ \ 30}$ (0.2 × $150) ⟵⎯⎯⎯⎯⎯⎯⎯⎯⎯⎯⎤
$120                                     │
$\underline{-\ \ 12}$ (0.1 × $120) ⟵⎯⎯⎯⎯⎯⎯⎯⎯⎯⎯⎯⎯⎯⎯⎯⎯⎯⎯⎯⎯⎯⎯⎯⎤
$108 net cost ■

After the first discount, each discount is applied to the balance remaining after the preceding discount or discounts have been subtracted. This method demonstrates how trade discounts are applied but is usually *not* the preferred method for finding the invoice amount, because it involves too many steps.

**NOTE** **Single discounts in a series are never added together**; for example, a series discount of 20/10 is *not the same* as a discount of 30%. ■

---

**CALCULATOR APPROACH**
**TO EXAMPLE 2**

*On many calculators you can subtract the discount percents from the list price in a series calculation.

150 │−│ 20 │%│ │−│ 10 │%│ │=│ 108

---

**OBJECTIVE** **7** *Use complements to calculate series discounts.*

*Using Complements.* To use this method of finding the net cost, first find the **complement** (with respect to 1, or 100%) of each single discount. The complement is the number which must be added to a given discount to get 1 or 100%. The complement of 20% is 80% since 20% + 80% = 100%. The complement of 40% is 60%.

Discounts with fractions are occasionally used. The complement (with respect to 1) of $22\frac{1}{2}\%$ is $77\frac{1}{2}\%$ or 0.775 ($22\frac{1}{2}\% = 22.5\% = 0.225$). When a fractional discount such as $16\frac{2}{3}\%$ is used, the complement (with respect to 1) of 0.1666 is not

---

*NOTE: All calculator solutions use a scientific calculator. Refer to Appendix A for scientific and financial calculator basics.

TABLE 8.2 **Typical Complements with Respect to 1**

| Discount | Decimal Equivalent | Complement with Respect to 1 |
|----------|--------------------|------------------------------|
| 10% | 0.1 | 0.9 |
| $12\frac{1}{2}$% | 0.125 | 0.875 |
| 15% | 0.15 | 0.85 |
| 25% | 0.25 | 0.75 |
| 30% | 0.3 | 0.7 |
| $33\frac{1}{3}$% | $0.333\overline{3}$ ($\frac{1}{3}$) | $0.666\overline{6}$ ($\frac{2}{3}$) |
| 35% | 0.35 | 0.65 |
| 50% | 0.5 | 0.5 |

exact, but a repeating decimal, and if used can cause errors. In this case the fraction $\frac{5}{6}$ is used as the complement. Since $16\frac{2}{3}$% equals $\frac{1}{6}$, the complement (with respect to 1) is $\frac{5}{6}$. Use of the fraction equivalents of these repeating decimals will result in fewer errors. Other typical complements (with respect to 1) are shown in Table 8.2.

The complement of the discount is the portion actually paid. For example,

10% discount means 90% paid;

25% discount means 75% paid;

$33\dfrac{1}{3}$% discount means $66\dfrac{2}{3}$% $\left(\dfrac{2}{3}\right)$ paid;

50% discount means 50% paid.

Multiply the complements of the single discounts together to get the **net cost equivalent** or **percent paid**. Then multiply the net cost equivalent (percent paid) by the list price to obtain the net cost, as shown in the formula.

$$\text{Percent paid} \times \text{List price} = \text{Net cost}$$
$$R \quad \times \quad B \quad = \quad P$$

**EXAMPLE 3** *Using Complements to Solve Series Discounts*

The Home Depot is offered a series discount of 20/10 on a worm drive circular saw with a list price of $150. Find the net cost after the series discount and the amount of the discount.

**SOLUTION** For a series discount of 20/10, the complements (with respect to 1) of 20% and 10% are 0.8 and 0.9. Multiplying the complements together gives 0.8 × 0.9 = 0.72, the net cost equivalent. (In other words, a series discount of 20/10 is the same as paying 72% of the list price.) To find the net cost, multiply 0.72 by the list price of $150, which gives $108 as the net cost. Write this calculation as follows.

$$20/10 \longleftarrow \text{series discount}$$

$$0.8 \times 0.9 = 0.72 \qquad \text{net cost equivalent}$$
$$\text{(percent paid)}$$

complements with
respect to 1

Use the formula Percent paid × List price = Net cost.

$$R \ \times \ B \ = \ P$$

$$0.72 \times \$150 = \$108 \qquad \text{net cost}$$

Find the amount of the discount by subtracting the net cost from the list price.

$$\$150 \text{ (list price)} - \$108 \text{ (net cost)} = \$42 \text{ (amount of discount)} \qquad \blacksquare$$

### EXAMPLE 4  *Using Complements to Solve Series Discounts*

The list price of some building materials is $250. Find the net cost if a series discount of 20/10/10 is offered.

**SOLUTION**   Start by finding the complements with respect to 1 of each discount.

$$20/10/10 \qquad \text{series discount}$$

$$0.8 \times 0.9 \times 0.9 = 0.648 \qquad \text{net cost equivalent}$$
$$\text{(percent paid)}$$

complements with
respect to 1

Using the formula Percent paid × List price = Net cost.

$$R \ \times \ B \ = \ P$$

$$0.648 \times \$250 = \$162 \qquad \text{net cost} \qquad \blacksquare$$

**CALCULATOR APPROACH TO EXAMPLE 4**

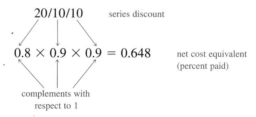

For the calculator solution to this example, first multiply the complements of the discounts. Then multiply by the list price.

.8 ⊠ .9 ⊠ .9 ⊟ 0.648 ⊠ 250 ⊟ 162

**PROBLEM-SOLVING HINT**   Never round the net cost equivalent. If a repeating decimal results, use the fraction equivalent. In Example 4, if the net cost equivalent had been rounded to 0.65, the resulting net cost would have been $162.50 (0.65 × $250). This error of $0.50 demonstrates the importance of not rounding the net cost equivalent.∎

TABLE 8.3 **Net Cost Equivalents of Series Discounts**

|        | 5%       | 10%     | 15%      | 20%    | 25%      | 30%     | 35%      | 40%    |
|--------|----------|---------|----------|--------|----------|---------|----------|--------|
| 5      | 0.9025   | 0.855   | 0.8075   | 0.76   | 0.7125   | 0.665   | 0.6175   | 0.57   |
| 10     | 0.855    | 0.81    | 0.765    | 0.72   | 0.675    | 0.63    | 0.585    | 0.54   |
| 10/5   | 0.81225  | 0.7695  | 0.72675  | 0.684  | 0.64125  | 0.5985  | 0.55575  | 0.513  |
| 10/10  | 0.7695   | 0.729   | 0.6885   | 0.648  | 0.6075   | 0.567   | 0.5265   | 0.486  |
| 15     | 0.8075   | 0.765   | 0.7225   | 0.68   | 0.6375   | 0.595   | 0.5525   | 0.51   |
| 15/10  | 0.72675  | 0.6885  | 0.65025  | 0.612  | 0.57375  | 0.5355  | 0.49725  | 0.459  |
| 20     | 0.76     | 0.72    | 0.68     | 0.64   | 0.6      | 0.56    | 0.52     | 0.48   |
| 20/15  | 0.646    | 0.612   | 0.578    | 0.544  | 0.51     | 0.476   | 0.442    | 0.408  |
| 25     | 0.7125   | 0.675   | 0.6375   | 0.6    | 0.5625   | 0.525   | 0.4875   | 0.45   |
| 25/20  | 0.57     | 0.54    | 0.51     | 0.48   | 0.45     | 0.42    | 0.39     | 0.36   |
| 25/25  | 0.534375 | 0.50625 | 0.478125 | 0.45   | 0.421875 | 0.39375 | 0.365625 | 0.3375 |
| 30     | 0.665    | 0.63    | 0.595    | 0.56   | 0.525    | 0.49    | 0.455    | 0.42   |
| 40     | 0.57     | 0.54    | 0.51     | 0.48   | 0.45     | 0.42    | 0.39     | 0.36   |

**OBJECTIVE 8** *Use a table to find the net cost equivalent of series discounts.*

***Using a Table.*** People working with series discounts daily often use a *table of net cost equivalents* for various series discounts. For example, to use Table 8.3 for a series discount of 20/10/10, find the number located to the right of 10/10 and below 20%. The number is 0.648, the net cost equivalent for a discount of 20/10/10. Multiply this number by the list price to get the net cost.

The order of the discounts in the series makes no difference. A 10/20 series is the same as a 20/10 series, and a 15/10/20 is identical to a 20/15/10. This is true because changing the order in which numbers are multiplied does not change the answer. The net cost equivalent (percent paid) found using Table 8.3 and the list price are multiplied to find the net cost.

**EXAMPLE 5** *Using a Table of Net Cost Equivalents*

Use Table 8.3 to find the net cost equivalent for the following series discounts.

**(a)** 10/20    **(b)** 10/10/40    **(c)** 25/20/10    **(d)** 35/20/15

**SOLUTION**
**(a)** 0.72    **(b)** 0.486    **(c)** 0.54    **(d)** 0.442 ■

**NOTE** Do not round any of the net cost equivalents. Doing so will cause an error in the net cost. ■

# 8.1 EXERCISES

*What do each of the following abbreviations stand for?*

**1.** ft.                                **2.** mm

**3.** sk.                                **4.** qt.

**5.** gr. gro.                           **6.** kg

**7.** cs.                                **8.** gro.

**9.** drm.                              **10.** yd.

**11.** cpm.                             **12.** bbl.

**13.** gal.                             **14.** cwt.

**15.** COD                             **16.** FOB

**17.** Compute each of the following extension totals, find the invoice total, and the total amount due.

## J&K'S MUSTANG PARTS
### New and Used

Sold to: Dave's Auto Body & Paint
4443-B Auburn Blvd.
Sacramento, CA

Date:        July 17
Order No.:   100603
Shipped by:  Emery
Terms:       Net

| Quantity | Order No. / Description | Unit Price | Extension Total |
|----------|------------------------|------------|-----------------|
| 24       | filler tube gaskets    | $2.25 ea.  | _____ |
| 12 pr.   | taillight lens gaskets | $4.75 pr.  | _____ |
| 6 pr.    | taillight bezels to body | $10.80 pr. | _____ |
| 2 gr.    | door panel fasteners   | $14.20 gr. | _____ |
| 18       | bumper bolt kits       | $16.25 ea. | _____ |

| | | |
|---|---|---|
| | Invoice Total | _____ |
| | Shipping and Insurance | $23.75 |
| | Total Amount Due | _____ |

**18.** Compute each of the following extension totals, find the invoice total, and the total amount due.

INTERSTATE SUPPLY

| Sold to: | New England Trucking | Date: | February 19 |
| | 66 East Lane | Order No.: | 796152 |
| | Portland, Maine | Shipped by: | UPS |
| | | Terms: | Net |

| Quantity | Order No./ Description | Unit Price | Extension Total |
|----------|------------------------|------------|-----------------|
| 6 doz. | driver log books | $ 37.80 doz. | _____ |
| 3 gro. | imprinted pencils | $ 12.60 gro. | _____ |
| 9 doz. | sets of dispatch forms | $ 14.04 doz. | _____ |
| 8 | water pumps | $106.12 ea. | _____ |
| 53 pr. | mud guards | $ 68.12 pr. | _____ |

| | | |
|--|--|--|
| | Invoice Total | _____ |
| | Shipping and Insurance | $ 37.45 |
| | Total Amount Due | _____ |

**19.** Explain the difference between "FOB shipping point" and "FOB destination." (See Objective 2.)

**20.** Name six items that appear on an invoice. Try to do this without looking at an invoice. (See Objective 1.)

*Using complements (with respect to 1) of the single discounts, find the net cost equivalent for each of the following discounts. Use Table 8.3 for the first four problems.*

| | | |
|--|--|--|
| **21.** 10/20 | **22.** 10/10 | **23.** 15/5 |
| **24.** 10/25/20 | **25.** 10/16$\frac{2}{3}$ | **26.** 40/20/10 |
| **27.** 30/42$\frac{1}{2}$ | **28.** 20/20/20 | **29.** 20/30/5 |
| **30.** 50/20/10/5 | **31.** 20/20/10 | **32.** 25/10/20/10 |

*Find the net cost for each of the following. Round to the nearest cent.*

**33.** $510 less 15/20            **34.** $90 less 10/20

**35.** $6.50 less 10/5            **36.** $860 less 20/40

**37.** $950 less 30/20

**38.** $8.80 less 40/10/20

**39.** $450 less 10/5

**40.** $15.70 less 5/10/20

**41.** $25 less 30/32$\frac{1}{2}$

**42.** $590 less 10/12$\frac{1}{2}$/10

**43.** $1,250 less 20/20/20

**44.** $1,410 less 10/20/5

**45.** Explain the difference between a single trade discount and a series or chain trade discount. (See Objectives 4 and 5.)

**46.** Identify and explain four reasons that might cause series trade discounts to change. (See Objective 5.)

**47.** Explain what a complement (with respect to 1 or 100%) is. Give an example. (See Objective 7.)

**48.** Using complements, explain how to find the net cost equivalent of a 25/20 series discount. Explain why a 25/10/10 series discount is not the same as a 25/20 series discount. (See Objective 7.)

*Solve each of the following application problems in trade discount. Round to the nearest cent.*

**49.** The list price of an innerspring sleeper couch is $698. If the series discount offered is 10/10/25, what is the net amount after trade discounts?

**50.** Roger Wheatley, a Restorative Nurse Assistant (RNA), finds that the list price of one dozen adjustable walkers is $1,680. Find the cost per walker if a series discount of 40/25 is offered.

**51.** Oaks Hardware purchases an extension ladder list priced at $120. It is available at either a 10/15/10 discount or a 20/15 discount. (a) Which discount gives the lower price? (b) Find the difference.

**52.** The list price of an aluminum tripod is $65. It is available at either a 15/10/10 discount or a 15/20 discount. (a) Which discount gives the lower price? (b) Find the difference.

**53.** Brazilian Chemical Supply offers a series discount of 20/20/10 on all bulk purchases. If a 35,000-gallon tank (bulk) of industrial solvent is list priced at $28,500, what is the net cost after trade discounts?

**54.** How much will Rachel Leach, a sporting goods store buyer, pay for 3 dozen soccer balls if the list price is $180 per dozen and a series discount of 10/25/30 is offered?

**55.** Kaci Salmon, an automotive mechanics student, is offered mechanic's net prices on all purchases at Gilbert Tool Supply. If mechanic's net prices mean a 20/10 discount, how much will Salmon spend on a Black and Decker drill that is list priced at $47?

**56.** The Office Depot offers a series trade discount of 30/20 to its regular customers. Chris Hutchinson, a new man in the billing department, understood the 30/20 terms to mean 50% and computed this trade discount on a list price of $5,440. How much difference did this error make in the amount of the invoice?

**57.** The AAA Foto and Copy Shop purchases stickers at a list price of $135 per 1,000. If they receive a trade discount of 40/33$\frac{1}{3}$, find the net cost of 3,500 stickers.

**58.** One brand of file folders is list priced at $6.60 per dozen. A wholesale stationer offers a trade discount of 10/5/15 on the folders. Find the net cost of 5$\frac{1}{2}$ dozen folders.

**59.** The list price of brass deadbolts is $9.95. A retailer has a choice of two suppliers, one offering a discount of 10/25/15 and the other offering a discount of 20/15/10. If the retailer purchases 4 dozen deadbolts, find (a) the total cost of the less expensive supplier and (b) the amount saved by selecting the lower price.

**60.** Cindy Herring has a choice of two suppliers of fiber optics for her business. Tyler Supplies offers a 20/10/25 discount on a list price of $5.70 per unit. Irving Optics offers a 30/20 series discount on a list price of $5.40 per unit. (a) Which supplier gives her the lower price? (b) How much does she save if she buys 12,500 units from the lower priced supplier? (Hint: Do not round.)

## 8.2    Single Discount Equivalents

**OBJECTIVES**

**1** *Express a series discount as an equivalent single discount rate.*

**2** *Find net cost by multiplying list price by the complements of single discounts.*

**3** *Find the list price if given the series discount and the net cost.*

**4** *Determine a single trade discount rate.*

**5** *Find the trade discount that must be added to match a competitor's price.*

**OBJECTIVE 1** *Express a series discount as an equivalent single discount rate.*    Series or chain discount rates must often be expressed as a single discount rate. Find a **single discount equivalent to a series discount** by multiplying the complements (with respect to 1 or 100%) of the individual discounts. As in the previous section, the result is the net cost equivalent. Then, subtract the net cost equivalent from 1. The result is the single discount (expressed as a decimal) that is equivalent to the series discount. The single discount decimal value should then be changed to a percent.

$$\text{Single discount equivalent} = 1 - \text{Net cost equivalent}$$

**EXAMPLE 1** *Finding a Single Discount Equivalent*

If Petco offered a 20/10 discount on pet grooming supplies, what would the single discount equivalent be?

**SOLUTION**    Find the net cost equivalent (percent paid).

20/10

$0.8 \times 0.9 = 0.72$    net cost equivalent

Subtract the net cost equivalent from 1.

1.00 (base) − 0.72 (remains) = 0.28 or 28% was discounted.

The single discount equivalent of a 20/10 series discount is 28%.    ∎

This method may also be used with the table of Net Cost Equivalents of Series Discounts (Table 8.3). For example, the table shows 0.72 as the net cost equivalent for the series discount 20/10. The single discount is therefore 28% (1.00 − 0.72 = 0.28 = 28%).

**OBJECTIVE** **2** *Find net cost by multiplying list price by the complements of single discounts.*     The net cost can also be found by multiplying the list price by the complements of each of the single discounts in a series, as shown in Example 2.

| EXAMPLE 2 *Finding the Net Cost Using Complements*

The list price of an oak entertainment center is $970. Find the net price if trade discounts of 20/15/27½ are offered.

**SOLUTION**

$$\text{Net Cost} = \text{List price} \times \text{Complements of individual discounts}$$

$$\text{Net cost} = \$970 \times 0.8 \times 0.85 \times 0.725$$

$$20/15/27\frac{1}{2}$$

Net cost = $478.21     ∎

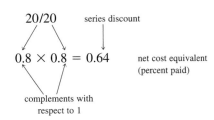

**CALCULATOR APPROACH
TO EXAMPLE 2**

For the calculator solution, enter the list price and multiply by the complements to find the net price.

970 $\boxed{\times}$ .8 $\boxed{\times}$ .85 $\boxed{\times}$ .725 $\boxed{=}$ 478.21

**OBJECTIVE** **3** *Find the list price if given the series discount and the net cost.*     Sometimes the net cost after trade discounts is known along with the series discount, and the list price must be found.

| EXAMPLE 3 *Solving for List Price*

Find the list price of a handmade rug from Pakistan that has a net cost of $544 after trade discounts of 20/20.

**SOLUTION**     Use a net cost equivalent, along with knowledge of percent. Start by finding the percent paid, using complements.

20/20     series discount

$$0.8 \times 0.8 = 0.64$$     net cost equivalent
(percent paid)

complements with
respect to 1

As the work shows, 0.64 or 64% of the list price, or $544, was paid. Use the basic percent equation to find the list price.

$$R \times B = P$$

$$0.64 \times \text{List price} = \$544$$

$$0.64 \times B = \$544$$

$$0.64B = \$544$$

$$\frac{0.64B}{0.64} = \frac{\$544}{0.64} = \$850 \qquad \text{list price}$$

Check the answer.

$$
\begin{array}{ll}
\quad \$850 & \text{list price} \\
- \ \ 170 & (0.2 \times \$850) \\
\hline
\quad \$680 & \\
- \ \ 136 & (0.2 \times \$680) \\
\hline
\quad \$544 & \text{net cost}
\end{array}
$$

The list price of the rug is $850.  ∎

## EXAMPLE 4  *Solving for List Price*

Find the list price of a musical instrument having a net cost of $907.20 and a series discount of 10/30/20.

**SOLUTION**   Find the percent paid.

Therefore 0.504 of the list price is $907.20. Now use the basic percent equation.

$$R \times B = P$$

$$0.504 \times \text{List price} = \$907.20$$

$$0.504 \times B = \$907.20$$

$$0.504B = \$907.20$$

$$\frac{0.504B}{0.504} = \frac{\$907.20}{0.504} = \$1,800 \qquad \text{list price}$$

The list price of the instrument is $1,800. Check this answer as in the previous example.  ∎

PROBLEM-SOLVING HINT   Notice that Examples 3 and 4 are decrease problems similar to those shown in Chapter 3, Section 5. They are still base problems but may look different because the discount is now shown as a series of two or more discounts rather than a single percent decrease as in Chapter 3. If you need help refer to Section 3.5.  ■

OBJECTIVE **4** *Determine a single trade discount rate.*

| EXAMPLE 5  *Finding the Single Trade Discount Rate*

The list price of a compact disc player is $550. If the wholesaler offers the system at a net cost of $341, find the single trade discount rate being offered.

SOLUTION   Use the following formula.

$$\text{Percent paid} \times \text{List price} = \text{Net cost}$$

$$P \times L = N$$

$$P \times \$550 = \$341$$

$$\$550P = \$341$$

$$\frac{\cancel{550}P}{\cancel{550}} = \frac{341}{550} = 0.62 \text{ or } 62\% \qquad \text{percent paid}$$

Since 62% is paid, the discount offered is 38% (100% − 62% = 38%).

For an alternative approach, first find the amount of discount, or $550 − $341 = $209. Next, find the rate of discount by using the basic percent equation

$$R \times B = P$$

$$\underline{\hspace{2cm}} \% \text{ of List price is Discount}$$

$$\underline{\hspace{2cm}} \% \text{ of } \$550 = \$209$$

$$R \times \$550 = \$209$$

$$\$550R = \$209$$

$$\frac{\cancel{550}R}{\cancel{550}} = \frac{209}{550}$$

to find that

$$R = \frac{209}{550} = 0.38 = 38\%.$$

By either method, the discount is 38%.  ■

**OBJECTIVE 5** *Find the trade discount that must be added to match a competitor's price.*

**EXAMPLE 6** *Adding a Discount to Match a Competitor's Price*

S and B Distributors offered a 20% trade discount on small compressors list priced at $450. Find the trade discount that must be added to match a competitor's price of $342.

**SOLUTION**    First use the formula

$$P \times L = N$$

to find the single discount needed. The percent paid is found by multiplying together the complements of the 20% discount already given and the new, unknown discount, or

$$0.8 \times \text{Complement of discount} \times L = N.$$

$$0.8 \times d \times \$450 = \$342$$

$$\$360d = \$342$$

$$\frac{\cancel{360}d}{\cancel{360}} = \frac{342}{360}$$

$$d = 0.95 \text{ or } 95\%.$$

Therefore, 95% is the complement of the trade discount that must be added. The additional discount needed is 5% (100% − 95%). To match the competition, S and B Distributors must give a 20/5 series discount.    ■

# 8.2  EXERCISES

*Find the net cost equivalent and the percent form of the single discount equivalent for each of the following series discounts.*

| | | |
|---|---|---|
| **1.** 10/10 | **2.** 10/20 | **3.** 10/33⅓ |
| **4.** 10/50 | **5.** 20/20 | **6.** 20/20/20 |
| **7.** 20/20/10 | **8.** 15/5/10 | **9.** 25/10 |
| **10.** 30/37½ | **11.** 16⅔/10 | **12.** 30/25 |
| **13.** 10/10/20 | **14.** 20/20/10 | **15.** 55/40/10 |
| **16.** 10/30/10 | **17.** 40/25 | **18.** 5/5/5 |
| **19.** 20/12½ | **20.** 15/35 | **21.** 20/10/20/10 |
| **22.** 10/20/25/10 | **23.** 5/20/30/5 | **24.** 10/5/30/20 |

**25.** Using complements, show that the single discount equivalent of a 20/25/10 series discount is 46%. (See Objective 1.)

**26.** Suppose that you own a business and are offered a choice of a 10/20 trade discount or a 20/10 trade discount. Which do you prefer? Why? (See Objective 1.)

*Find the list price, given the net cost and the series discount.*

**27.** net cost, $648; trade discount, 10/20

**28.** net cost, $403.20; trade discount, 20/20

**29.** net cost, $279.30; trade discount, 40/5/30

**30.** net cost, $5,250; trade discount, $25/33\frac{1}{3}$

**31.** net cost, $1,313.28; trade discount, 5/10/20

**32.** net cost, $1,872.72; trade discount, 15/20/10

*Solve each of the following application problems in trade discount.*

**33.** Video Supply Center offers a series discount of 20/20/5 while Muz Music offers a series discount of 25/10/10. (a) Which is the higher discount? (b) Find the difference.

**34.** Jack Rowell is offered oak stair railing by The Turning Point for $1,370 less 30/10. Sierra Stair Company offers the same railing for $1,220 less 10/10. (a) Which offer is better? (b) How much does Rowell save by taking the better offer?

**35.** Irene's Plant Place paid a net price of $414.40 for a shipment of potted plants after a trade discount of 30/20 from the list price. Find the list price.

**36.** SJ's Nutrition Center received a shipment of vitamins, minerals, and diet supplements at a net cost of $1,125. This cost was the result of a trade discount of 25/20 from list price. Find the list price of this shipment.

**37.** All season radial tires, size P205/75R15, with a list price of $61.90 are offered to wholesalers with a series discount of 10/20/10. The same tire is offered to retailers with a series discount of 10/20. (a) Find the wholesalers price. (b) Find the retailers price. (c) Find the difference between the two prices.

**38.** A satellite dish is list priced at $1,995. The manufacturer offers a series discount of 25/20/10 to wholesalers and a 25/20 series discount to retailers. (a) What is the wholesaler's price? (b) What is the retailer's price? (c) What is the difference between the prices?

**39.** A portable generator with a list price of $295.95 is sold by a wholesaler at a net cost of $221.95. Find the single trade discount rate being offered. Round to the nearest tenth of a percent.

**40.** Truck Stuff offers a fiberglass truck-bed liner at a net cost of $180. If the list price of the bed liner is $281.25, find the single trade discount rate.

**41.** Capitol Alarm purchased a security alarm system at a net cost of $2,733.75 and a series discount of $10/10/12\frac{1}{2}$. Find the list price.

**42.** Find the list price of a 35-inch color television having a net cost of $898.56 and a series discount of 10/20/20.

**43.** An auto wholesaler offers a 10% trade discount on a case of oil priced at $27.60. A competitor offers the same oil at $23.60. What additional trade discount must be given to meet the competitor's price? Round to the nearest tenth of a percent.

**44.** A personal computer distributor has offered a computer system at a $1,450 list price less a 30% trade discount. Find the additional trade discount needed to meet a competitor's net price of $933.80.

**8.3**    **Cash Discounts: Ordinary Dating Method**

### OBJECTIVES

1  *Calculate net cost after discounts.*

2  *Use the ordinary dating methods.*

3  *Determine whether cash discounts are earned.*

4  *Use postdating when calculating cash discounts.*

5  *Determine the amount due when goods are returned.*

**OBJECTIVE 1** *Calculate net cost after discounts.*    **Cash discounts** are offered by sellers to encourage prompt payment by customers. Since businesses must often borrow money for their operation, the prompt receipt of cash payment from customers increases the efficiency of the business and decreases the need for borrowed money. Saving interest on borrowed funds is a main reason that a cash incentive is often given to customers. If effect, the seller is saying, "Pay me quickly and receive a discount."

To find the net cost when a cash discount is offered, begin with the list price and subtract any trade discounts. From this amount subtract the cash discount. Use the following formula.

$$\text{Net cost} = (\text{List price} - \text{Trade discount}) - \text{Cash discount}$$

If an invoice amount includes shipping and insurance charges, subtract these charges before a cash discount is taken. Then add them back to find the net cost after the cash discount is subtracted.

The type of cash discount appears on the invoice under "Terms," which can be found in the bottom right-hand corner of the Hershey Chocolate U.S.A. invoice in Figure 8.2. Many companies using automated billing systems state the exact amount of the cash discount at the bottom of the invoice, to eliminate all calculations on the part of the buyer. This Hershey invoice is an example of an invoice stating the exact amount of the cash discount. Not all businesses do this however, so it is important to know how to determine cash discounts.

There are many methods for determining cash discounts, but nearly all of these are based on the "ordinary dating method." The methods discussed in this section and the methods discussed in the next section, are the ones most commonly used today.

**OBJECTIVE 2** *Use the ordinary dating methods.*    The **ordinary dating method** of cash discount, for example, is expressed on an invoice as

2/10, n/30 or sometimes 2/10, net/30

and is read "two ten, net thirty." The first digit is the rate of discount (2%), the second digit is the number of days allowed to take the discount (10 days), and n/30 or net/30 is the total number of days given to pay the invoice in full, if the buyer does not use the cash discount. The 2% discount may be subtracted from the amount

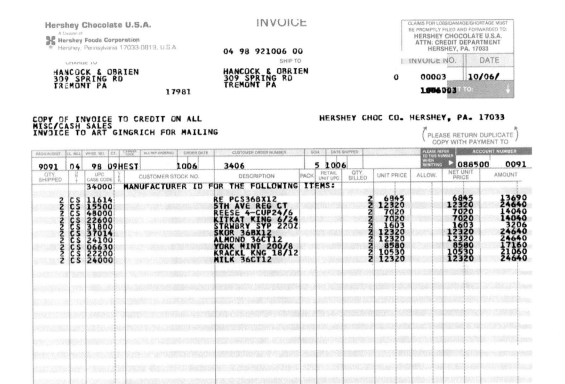

FIGURE **8.2**

*Source:* Reprinted by permission of Hershey Chocolate U.S.A., a division of Hershey Foods Corporation.

owed if the invoice is paid within 10 days from the date of the invoice. If payment is made between the 11th and 30th days from the invoice date, the entire amount of the invoice is due. After 30 days from the date of the invoice, the invoice is considered overdue and may be subject to a late charge.

To find the due date of an invoice, use the number of days in each month, given in Table 8.4.

TABLE 8.4　**The Number of Days in Each Month**

| **30-Day Months** | **31-Day Months** | | **Exception** |
|---|---|---|---|
| April | January | August | **February** |
| June | March | October | **(28 days normally; 29 days in leap year)** |
| September | May | December | |
| November | July | | |

**NOTE** Leap years occur every four years. They are the same as Summer Olympic years and presidential election years in the United States. If a year is evenly divisible by the number 4, it is a leap year. The years 2000 and 2004 are both leap years because they are evenly divisible by 4. This is the Gregorian Rule. However, all centenary years must be evenly divisible by 400 to be a leap year. The year 1600 was a leap year while 1700, 1800, and 1900 were not. Since the year 2000 is evenly divisible by 400, the year 2000 qualifies as a leap year.   ∎

**OBJECTIVE** **3** *Determine whether cash discounts are earned.*   Find the date that an invoice is due by counting from the next day after the date of the invoice. *The date of the invoice is never counted.* Another way to determine due dates is to add the given number of days to the starting date. For example, to determine 10 days from April 7, add the number of days to the date (7 + 10 = 17). The due date, or 10 days from April 7, is April 17.

When the discount date or net payment date falls in the next month, find the number of days remaining in the current month by subtracting the invoice date from the number of days in the month. Then find the number of days in the next month needed to equal the discount period or net payment period. For example, find 15 days from October 20 as follows.

$$
\begin{array}{ll}
31 & \text{days in October} \\
-20 & \text{the beginning date, October 20} \\
\hline
11 & \text{days remaining in October} \\
+\ 4 & \text{additional days needed in November to equal 15 days} \\
\hline
15 & \text{days}
\end{array}
$$

Finally, November 4 is 15 days from October 20.

### EXAMPLE 1 *Finding Cash Discount Dates*

A Hershey Chocolate invoice is dated January 2 and offers terms of 2/10, net 30. Find (a) the last date on which the 2% discount may be taken and (b) the net payment date.

**SOLUTION**

**(a)** Beginning with the invoice date, January 2, the last date for taking the discount is January 12 (2 + 10).

**(b)** The net payment date is February 1 (29 days remaining in January plus 1 day in February).   ∎

### EXAMPLE 2 *Finding the Amount Due on an Invoice*

An invoice received by Oaks Hardware for $840 is dated July 1 and offers terms of 2/10, n/30. If the invoice is paid on July 8 and the shipping and insurance charges, which were "FOB shipping point," are $18.70, find the total amount due.

**SOLUTION**   The invoice was paid 7 days after its date (8 − 1 = 7); therefore, the 2% cash discount may be taken. The discount is $840 × 0.02 = $16.80. The cash discount is subtracted from the invoice amount to determine the amount due.

$840 (invoice amount) − $16.80 (cash discount of 2%) = $823.20 (amount due)

The shipping and insurance charges are added to find the total amount due.

$823.20 (amount due) + $18.70 (shipping and insurance)

$$= \$841.90 \text{ (total amount due)} \quad \blacksquare$$

PROBLEM-SOLVING HINT   A cash discount is never taken on shipping and insurance charges. Be certain that shipping and insurance charges are excluded from the invoice amount before calculating the cash discount. Shipping and insurance charges must then be added back to find the total amount due.   ■

OBJECTIVE **4** *Use postdating when calculating cash discounts.*     In the ordinary dating method, the cash discount date and net payment date are both counted from the date of the invoice. Occasionally, the seller places a date later than the actual invoice date, sometimes labeling it ''as of.'' This is called **postdating**. Notice that the Levi Strauss invoice in Figure 8.3 is dated ''07/25 **AS OF** 08/01.'' The cash discount period and the net payment date are counted from 08/01 (August 1). This results in giving additional time for the purchaser to pay the invoice and receive the discount.

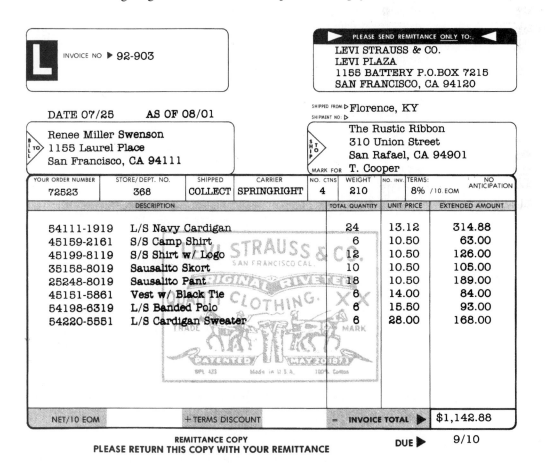

FIGURE 8.3

*Source:* Reprinted by permission of Levi Strauss & Co.

The date due (9/10) is the due date on the invoice. The "TERMS:" of 8%/10 EOM are explained in Section 8.4.

**EXAMPLE 3**   *Using Postdating "AS OF" with Invoices*

An invoice for some Australian glassware is dated October 21 AS OF November 1 with terms of 3/15, n/30. Find (a) the last date on which the cash discount may be taken and (b) the net payment date.

**SOLUTION**

**(a)** Beginning with the postdate (AS OF) of November 1, the last date for taking the discount is November 16 (1 + 15).

**(b)** The net payment date is December 1 (29 days remaining in November and 1 day in December).    ■

**NOTE**   Sometimes a sliding scale of cash discounts is offered. For example, with terms of 3/10, 2/20, 1/30, n/60, a discount of 3% is given if payment is made within 10 days, 2% if paid from the 11th through the 20th day, and 1% if paid from the 21st through the 30th day. The entire amount (net) must be paid no later than 60 days from the date of the invoice.   ■

**EXAMPLE 4**   *Determining Cash Discount Due Dates*

An invoice from Cellular Products is dated May 18 and offers terms of 4/10, 3/25, 1/40, n/60. Find (a) the three final dates for cash discounts and (b) the net payment date.

**SOLUTION**

**(a)** The three final cash discount dates are:

> 4% if paid by May 28 (10 days from May 18);
>
> 3% if paid by June 12 (25 days from May 18);
>
> 1% if paid by June 27 (40 days from May 18).

**(b)** The net payment date is July 17.    ■

**NOTE**   Never take more than one of the cash discounts. With all methods of giving cash discounts, if the net payment period is not given, the net payment due date is assumed to be 20 days beyond the cash discount period. After that date, the invoice is considered overdue. If either the final discount date or the net payment date is on a Sunday or holiday, the next business day is used. Many companies insist that payment is made when it is received. It is general practice, however, to consider payment made when it is mailed.   ■

**OBJECTIVE 5** *Determine the amount due when goods are returned.*    A buyer receiving incorrect or damaged merchandise may return the goods to the seller. The value of the **returned goods** must be subtracted from the amount of the invoice before calculating the cash discount.

| EXAMPLE 5  *Finding the Amount Due When Goods Are Returned*

An invoice from World Wide Web Services amounts to $380 is dated March 9 and offers terms of 4/10, net 30. If $75 of goods are returned and the invoice is paid on March 17, what amount is due?

SOLUTION    The invoice was paid 8 days after its date ($17 - 9 = 8$), so the 4% cash discount is taken. The discount is taken on $305.

$$\$380 \text{ (invoice amount)} - \$75 \text{ (goods returned)} = \$305 \text{ (goods retained)}$$

The cash discount is subtracted from the $305. Since $\$305 \times 0.04 = \$12.20$, the amount due is

$$\$305 \text{ (goods retained)} - \$12.20 \text{ (cash discount)} = \$292.80 \text{ (amount due)}. \quad ■$$

| 8.3   EXERCISES

*Find the final discount date and the net payment date for each of the following problems.*

| | Invoice Date | As of | Terms |
|---|---|---|---|
| 1. | Mar. 5 | | 3/10, n/30 |
| 2. | Jan. 14 | | 2/10, n/30 |
| 3. | Feb. 25 | Mar. 10 | 3/15, n/20 |
| 4. | Nov. 7 | Nov. 18 | 3/10, n/30 |
| 5. | Aug. 18 | | 4/10, n/60 |
| 6. | April 27 | | 2/10, n/30 |
| 7. | Jan. 14 | | 2/10, n/60 |
| 8. | Oct. 3 | | 3/10, net 15 |
| 9. | Dec. 7 | Jan. 5 | 5/15, n/60 |
| 10. | July 31 | Aug. 15 | 3/10, n/30 |

*Solve for the amount of discount and the amount due on each of the following invoices.*

| | Invoice Amount | Invoice Date | Terms | Shipping and Insurance | Goods Returned | Date Invoice Paid |
|---|---|---|---|---|---|---|
| 11. | $42.50 | Mar. 1 | 3/10, n/30 | | | Mar. 10 |
| 12. | $68.70 | Apr. 7 | 2/10, n/60 | | | Apr. 12 |
| 13. | $96.06 | Nov. 30 | Net 30 | $5.22 | | Dec. 20 |
| 14. | $148 | July 19 | 3/15, 1/25, n/60 | $7.45 | | Aug. 16 |
| 15. | $724 | Jan. 20 | 5/10, 2/20, n/30 | $38.14 | | Feb. 5 |

| | Invoice Amount | Invoice Date | Terms | Shipping and Insurance | Goods Returned | Date Invoice Paid |
|---|---|---|---|---|---|---|
| 16. | $1,282 | July 1 | 4/15, n/40 | $21.40 | | July 7 |
| 17. | $3,403 | Sept. 30 | 1/10, n/60 | | $125 | Oct. 10 |
| 18. | $162 | Jan. 15 | 2/15, net 30 | $8.18 | $12 | Jan. 23 |
| 19. | $975 | Oct. 12 | 2/10, n/30 | | $52 | Oct. 21 |
| 20. | $1,623.08 | Nov. 12 | 2/10, n/30 | $122.14 | $187 | Nov. 25 |

**21.** Describe the difference between a trade discount and a cash discount. Why are cash discounts offered? (See Objective 1.)

**22.** Using 2/10, n/30 as an example, explain what an ordinary cash discount means. (See Objective 2.)

*Solve each of the following application problems.*

**23.** Foothill Drilling Wholesalers offer cash discounts of 3/10, 2/15, net 30 to all customers. An invoice is dated August 22 amounting to $3,310.40 and is paid on September 5. Find the amount needed to pay the invoice.

**24.** A shipment of electrical supplies is received from the Lyskovo Electrotechnical Works (Nizhny Novgorod Region, Russia). The invoice is dated March 8, amounts to $6,824.58, and has terms of 2/15, 1/20 as of March 20. Find the amount needed to pay the invoice on April 2.

**25.** Agricultural Wholesale Products offers customers a trade discount of 10/20/5 on all products, with terms of net 30. Find the customers price for products with a total list price of $986 if the invoice was paid within 30 days.

**26.** Joe Nejad received an invoice for $586.12 for fishing tackle. The invoice was dated February 21, as of March 4, with terms of 4/10, 3/30, n/60. Find the total amount necessary to pay the invoice in full on March 22.

**27.** A $1\frac{1}{2}$-horsepower motor is list priced at $215.80 with trade discounts of 20/20 and terms of 4/15, n/30. If a retailer takes both of these discounts, find the net cost of the motor.

**28.** An invoice for $7,925 from Office Designers is dated May 15 and has cash terms of 6/20, 4/35, 2/60, n/90. Find the amount necessary to pay in full on July 10.

**29.** The list price of a popular brand of snowmobile is $5,190. If a dealer can obtain trade discounts of 10/20/30 and cash terms of 4/10, n/30, find the lowest possible net cost.

**30.** The list price of Road Thunder Speakers is $120. If the manufacturer offers trade discounts of 30/10 and terms of 3/15, n/30, find the net cost of the speakers assuming both discounts are taken.

**31.** Bayside Automotive Distributors offers auto parts stores a trade discount of 10/20/10 on all purchases, with terms of 3/10, n/30. If the total list price of an order is $3,215.80, find the retailers net cost if both discounts are earned.

**32.** Sheepskin seat covers are list priced at $79.90 with a trade discount of 10/10/25 and terms of 3/10, n/30. Find the net cost assuming that both discounts are earned.

**33.** An invoice from Rags Fashions is dated January 18 and offers terms of 6/10, 4/20, 1/30, n/50. Find (a) the three final discount dates and (b) the net payment date.

**34.** An invoice with terms of 4/15, 3/20, 1/30, n/60 is dated September 4. Find (a) the three final discount dates and (b) the net payment date.

**35.** Truck Stuff receives an invoice dated March 28 AS OF April 5 with terms of 4/20, n/30. Find (a) the final discount date and (b) the net payment date.

**36.** An invoice is dated May 20 AS OF June 5 with terms of 2/10, n/30. Find (a) the final discount date and (b) the net payment date.

**37.** Artistry Jewelry received an invoice for supplies amounting to $1,678.20. The invoice is dated May 18 AS OF June 15 and offers terms of 2/20, n/40. Find the amount necessary to pay in full on July 3 if $76.05 worth of supplies are returned.

**38.** The Fireside Shop received an invoice for hardware amounting to $218.80. The invoice is dated July 12 AS OF July 20 and offers terms of 3/20, n/60. Find the amount necessary to pay in full on August 3 if $24.30 worth of goods are returned.

**39.** An invoice received by Capital Appliance for repair parts amounts to $3,322.80. The invoice is dated August 22 AS OF September 10 and offers terms of 4/10, 2/20, n/30. Find the amount necessary to pay in full on September 26 if $152.80 worth of goods are returned.

**40.** An invoice received by Sydney's Baby Barn amounts of $380.50. The invoice is dated October 25 AS OF November 2 and offers terms of 3/15, n/30. Find the amount necessary to pay in full on November 18 if $56.50 worth of goods are returned.

**41.** How do you remember the number of days in each month of the year? List the months and the number of days in each.

**42.** Explain how ''AS OF'' dating (postdating) works. Why is it used? (See Objective 4.)

## 8.4 Cash Discounts: Other Dating Methods

**OBJECTIVES**

**1** *Solve cash discount problems with end-of-month dating.*

**2** *Use receipt-of-goods dating to solve cash discount problems.*

**3** *Use extra dating to solve cash discount problems.*

**4** *Determine credit given for partial payment of an invoice.*

Three other methods of cash discounts are often used in place of the ordinary dating method. Each method is shown here.

**OBJECTIVE** **1** *Solve cash discount problems with end-of-month dating.*

***End-of-Month and Proximo Dating.***   **End-of-month dating** and **proximo dating** abbreviated **EOM** and **prox.**, are both treated the same way. For example, both

3/10 EOM   and   3/10 prox.

mean that a 3% cash discount may be taken if payment is made within 10 days. However, the 10 days are counted from the end of the month in which the invoice is dated. For example, an invoice dated July 14 with terms of 3/10 EOM would have a discount date 10 days from the end of the month, or August 10.

Since this is a method of increasing the length of time during which a discount may be taken, it has become common business practice with EOM and prox. dating to add a month *when the date of an invoice is the twenty-sixth of the month or later.* For example, if an invoice is dated March 25 and the discount offered is 3/10 prox., the last date on which the discount may be taken is April 10. However, if the invoice is dated March 26 (or any later day in March) and the cash discount offered is 3/10 prox., then the last date on which the discount may be taken is May 10.

**PROBLEM-SOLVING HINT**   The practice of adding an extra month when the invoice is dated the 26th of a month or after is used *only* with the end-of-month (proximo) dating cash discount. If does *not* apply to any of the other cash discount methods.   ■

## EXAMPLE 1   *Using End-of-Month Dating*

If an invoice from Electric Distributors is dated April 6, with terms of 3/20 EOM, find (a) the final date on which the cash discount may be taken and (b) the net payment date.

**SOLUTION**

**(a)**  The discount date is May 20 (20 days after the end of April).

**(b)**  The net payment date is June 9 (20 days after the last discount date since the net payment date is not otherwise given).   ■

**NOTE**   With all methods of cash discounts, if the net payment period is not given, the net payment due date is assumed to be 20 days beyond the cash discount date.   ■

## EXAMPLE 2   *Understanding Proximo Dating*

Find the amount due on an invoice of $782 for some threaded fasteners which is dated August 3 if terms are 1/10 prox., and the invoice is paid on September 4.

**SOLUTION**   The last date on which the discount may be taken is September 10 (10 days after the end of August). September 4 is within the discount period, so the discount is earned. The 1% cash discount is computed on $782, the amount of the invoice. Subtract the discount, $7.82 ($782 × 0.01 = $7.82), from the invoice amount to find the amount due.

$782 (invoice amount) − $7.82 (cash discount) = $774.18 (amount due)   ■

**OBJECTIVE 2**  *Use receipt-of-goods dating to solve cash discount problems.*

*Receipt-of-Goods Dating.*   **Receipt-of-goods dating**, abbreviated **ROG**, offers discounts determined from the date the goods are actually received. This method is often used when shipping time is long. The invoice might arrive overnight by mail, but the goods may take several weeks. Under the ROG method of cash discount, the buyer is given time to receive and inspect the merchandise and then benefit from a cash discount. For example, the discount

3/15 ROG

allows a 3% cash discount if paid within 15 days from receipt of goods. If the invoice was dated March 5 and goods were received on April 7, the last date to take the 3% cash discount is April 22 (April 7 plus 15 days). The net payment date, since it is not stated, is 20 days after the last discount date, or May 12 (April 22 plus 20 days).

### EXAMPLE 3  *Using Receipt-of-Goods Dating*

Java City received an invoice dated December 12, with terms of 2/10 ROG. The goods were received on January 2. Find (a) the final date on which the cash discount may be taken and (b) the net payment date.

**SOLUTION**

**(a)** The discount date is January 12 (10 days after receipt of goods, January 2 + 10 days).

**(b)** The net payment date is February 1 (20 days after the last discount date).  ■

### EXAMPLE 4  *Working with ROG Dating*

Find the amount due on an invoice of $285, with terms of 3/10 ROG, if the invoice is dated June 8, goods are received on June 18, and the invoice is paid on June 30.

**SOLUTION**   The last date to take the 3% cash discount is June 28, 10 days after June 18. Since the invoice is paid on June 30, 2 days after the last discount date, no cash discount may be taken. The entire amount of the invoice must be paid.

$285 (invoice amount) − $0 (no discount) = $285 (amount due)  ■

**OBJECTIVE 3**  *Use extra dating to solve cash discount problems.*

**Extra Dating.**   **Extra dating**, abbreviated **extra, ex.,** or **x**, gives additional time to the buyer to take a cash discount. For example, the discount

2/10-50 extra   or   2/10-50 ex.   or   2/10-50 x

allows a 2% cash discount if paid within (10 + 50) or 60 days from the date of the invoice. The discount is written in this form rather than combining the 10 + 50 and writing 2/60 to show that the 50 days are *extra* or in addition to the normal 10 days offered.

There are several reasons for using extra dating. A supplier might extend the discount period during a slack season to generate more sales or perhaps to gain a competitive advantage. For example, Christmas merchandise might be offered with extra dating, allowing the buyer to take the cash discount after the holiday selling period.

### EXAMPLE 5  *Using Extra Dating*

An invoice for garden tools is dated May 17, with terms of 2/10-50 ex. Find (a) the final date on which the cash discount may be taken and (b) the net payment date.

### SOLUTION

**(a)** The discount date is July 16. (14 days remaining in May and 30 days in June total 44. Thus 16 more days are needed in July to total 60.)

**(b)** The net payment date is August 5 (20 days after the last discount date).    ■

## EXAMPLE 6  *Understanding Extra Dating*

An invoice from Rocky Mountaineers is dated August 5, amounts to $750, offers terms of 3/10-30 x, and is paid on September 12. Find the net payment.

**SOLUTION**    The last day to take the 3% cash discount is September 14 (August 5 + 40 days = September 14). Since the invoice is paid on September 12, the 3% discount may be taken. The 3% cash discount is computed on $750, the amount of the invoice.

$$3\% \times \$750 = 0.03 \times \$750 = \$22.50$$

The discount to be taken is $22.50. The cash discount is subtracted from the invoice amount to determine the amount of payment.

$$\$750 \text{ (invoice amount)} - \$22.50 \text{ (cash discount)} = \$727.50 \text{ (amount of payment)}$$
■

When customers pay invoices quickly, there is less need for a business to borrow money. In certain industries it is common to deduct interest that would have to be paid on borrowed money from the invoice amount. To do this, the company uses the current rate of interest and calculates the amount of interest over the remaining days on which the cash discount is allowable. This deduction, known as **anticipation**, is taken in addition to the cash discount earned. Anticipation involves the use of simple interest, which is discussed in Chapter 11.

**OBJECTIVE 4** *Determine credit given for partial payment of an invoice.*    Occasionally, a customer may pay only a portion of the total amount due on an invoice. If this **partial payment** is made within a discount period, the customer is entitled to a discount on the portion of the invoice which is paid.

If the terms of an invoice are 3%, 10 days, then only 97% (100% − 3%) of the invoice amount must be paid during the first 10 days. So, for each $0.97 paid, the customer is entitled to $1.00 of credit. When a partial payment is made, the credit given for the partial payment is found by dividing the partial payment by the complement of the cash discount percent. Then, to find the balance due, subtract the credit given from the invoice amount. The cash discount is found by subtracting the partial payment from the credit given.

## EXAMPLE 7  *Finding Credit for Partial Payment*

J and K Mustang Parts receives an invoice of $380, dated March 8, offers terms of 2/10 proximo. A partial payment of $150 is made on April 5. Find (a) the amount credited for the partial payment, (b) the balance due on the invoice, and (c) the cash discount earned.

### SOLUTION

**(a)** The cash discount is earned on the $150 partial payment made on April 5 (April 10 was the last discount date).

$$100\% - 2\% = 98\% = 0.98$$

$$\text{Amount paid} = 0.98 \times \text{Credit given}$$

$$\$150 = 0.98 \times C$$

$$\$150 = 0.98C$$

$$\frac{\$150}{0.98} = \frac{\cancel{0.98}C}{\cancel{0.98}}$$

$$\frac{\$150}{0.98} = C$$

$$C = \$153.06 \qquad \text{credit given (rounded)}$$

**(b)** Balance due = Invoice amount − Credit given

$$\text{Balance due} = \$380 - \$153.06$$

$$\text{Balance due} = \$226.94$$

**(c)** Cash discount = Credit given − Partial payment

$$\text{Cash discount} = \$153.06 - \$150$$

$$\text{Cash discount} = \$3.06 \qquad\qquad\blacksquare$$

---

**CALCULATOR APPROACH TO EXAMPLE 7**

A calculator solution to this example will include these three steps.

**(a)** First, find the amount of credit given.

150 $\boxed{\div}$ .98 $\boxed{=}$ 153.06 (rounded)

**(b)** Next, store the amount of credit and subtract this amount from the invoice amount to find the balance due.

$\boxed{\text{STO}}$ 380 $\boxed{-}$ $\boxed{\text{RCL}}$ $\boxed{=}$ 226.94 (rounded)

**(c)** Finally, subtract the partial payment from the amount of credit given to find the cash discount.

$\boxed{\text{RCL}}$ $\boxed{-}$ 150 $\boxed{=}$ 3.06 (rounded)

---

**NOTE** Cash discounts are important, and a business should make the effort to pay invoices early to earn the cash discount. In many cases the money saved through cash discounts has a great effect on the profitability of a business. Often companies will borrow money to enable them to take advantage of cash discounts. The mathematics of this type of loan is discussed in Chapter 11.1, **Basics of Simple Interest.** ∎

The cash discounts discussed here are normally not used when selling to foreign customers or purchasing from foreign suppliers. Instead, other types of discounts may be offered to reduce the price of goods sold to foreign buyers. These discounts may be given as allowances for tariffs paid (import duties) by the customer, reimbursement for shipping, and insurance paid by the customer or in the form of an advertising allowance.

## 8.4 EXERCISES

*Find the discount date and net payment date for each of the following (the net payment date is 20 days after the final discount date).*

| | Invoice Date | Terms | Date Goods Received |
|---|---|---|---|
| 1. | Mar. 3 | 2/15 EOM | Mar. 10 |
| 2. | June 8 | 4/20 ROG | Aug. 5 |
| 3. | Nov. 22 | 1/10-20 x | Dec. 1 |
| 4. | May 17 | 6/30 EOM | June 2 |
| 5. | April 12 | 3/15-50 x | April 29 |

| | Invoice Date | Terms | Date Goods Received |
|---|---|---|---|
| 6. | May 5 | 1/10 prox. | May 10 |
| 7. | June 26 | 2/10 EOM | July 6 |
| 8. | Sept. 27 | 3/15 prox. | Sept. 15 |
| 9. | July 6 | 2/20 ROG | Aug. 4 |
| 10. | Jan. 15 | 3/15 ROG | Feb. 5 |

*Solve for the amount of discount and the amount due on each of the following.*

| | Invoice Amount | Invoice Date | Terms | Date Goods Received | Date Invoice Paid |
|---|---|---|---|---|---|
| 11. | $42.50 | April 5 | 2/15 prox. | | May 12 |
| 12. | $328 | Nov. 16 | 2/10-20 x | | Dec. 20 |
| 13. | $194.04 | Aug. 22 | 5/10-60 ex. | | Nov. 5 |

| | Invoice Amount | Invoice Date | Terms | Date Goods Received | Date Invoice Paid |
|---|---|---|---|---|---|
| 14. | $9,240.40 | Nov. 23 | 1/20 ROG | Mar. 5 | Mar. 8 |
| 15. | $2,960 | Oct. 31 | 2/10 EOM | | Dec. 5 |
| 16. | $127.50 | Feb. 17 | 3/20 ROG | Mar. 19 | Apr. 10 |
| 17. | $4,220 | Oct. 4 | 4/15 prox. | | Nov. 10 |
| 18. | $256.50 | July 17 | 3/10-40 extra | | Sept. 2 |
| 19. | $12.38 | Mar. 29 | 2/15 ROG | April 15 | April 30 |
| 20. | $11,480 | April 6 | 2/15 prox. | | April 30 |
| 21. | $3,250.60 | Oct. 17 | 3/15-20 x | | Oct. 20 |
| 22. | $8,318 | June 9 | 3/20 EOM | | July 18 |
| 23. | $1,708.18 | Nov. 13 | 4/10 prox. | | Dec. 10 |
| 24. | $13,728.34 | April 6 | 2/10 ROG | April 28 | May 6 |

25. Quite often there is no mention of a net payment date on an invoice. Explain the common business practice when no net payment date is given. (See Objective 1.)

26. Describe why receipt-of-goods dating (ROG) is offered to customers. Use an example in your description. (See Objective 2.)

*Find the credit given and the balance due on the invoice after making the following partial payments.*

| | Invoice Amount | Invoice Date | Terms | Date Invoice Paid | Partial Payment |
|---|---|---|---|---|---|
| 27. | $1,575 | Nov. 7 | 5/15 EOM | Dec. 12 | $798 |
| 28. | $968 | May 2 | 4/15-20 x | June 5 | $360 |
| 29. | $1,750 | Aug. 12 | 5/10-30 x | Sept. 15 | $684 |
| 30. | $920 | Jan. 11 | 3/10, 2/15, n/30 | Jan. 23 | $450.80 |
| 31. | $160 | Dec. 8 | 3/10, n/30 | Dec. 15 | $97 |
| 32. | $8,120 | Oct. 4 | 4/20 prox. | Nov. 15 | $2,016 |

33. Write a short explanation of partial payment. Why would a company accept a partial payment? Why would a customer make a partial payment? (See Objective 4.)

34. Of all the different types of cash discounts presented in this section, which type seemed most interesting to you? Explain your reasons.

*Solve each of the following application problems in cash and trade discounts.*

35. An invoice received by Crafts and More is dated July 21 with terms of 3/10 EOM. Find (a) the final date on which the discount may be taken and (b) the net payment date.

**36.** An invoice from Pittsburgh Milling is dated March 4, with terms of 3/20 ROG, and the goods are received on April 8. Find (a) the final date on which the cash discount may be taken and (b) the net payment date.

**37.** An invoice from Carmichael Glass is dated November 11 with terms of 3/20 ROG, and the goods are received on December 3. Find (a) the final date on which the cash discount may be taken and (b) the net payment date.

**38.** An invoice received from the Stained Glass Exchange is dated June 16, with terms of 2/10 prox. Find (a) the final date on which the cash discount may be taken and (b) the net payment date.

**39.** Find the amount due on an invoice of $1,525 with terms of 1/20 ROG. The invoice is dated October 20, goods are received December 1, and the invoice is paid on December 20.

**40.** What payment should be made on an invoice dated July 30, amounting to $1,730 offering terms of 2/10-60 x, and paid October 4?

**41.** Big Tooth Blades, a power saw blade distributor, offers terms of 2/10-30 x to stimulate slow sales in the winter months. Oaks Hardware purchased $970.68 worth of saw blades and was offered the above terms. If the invoice was dated November 3, find (a) the final date on which the cash discount may be taken and (b) the amount paid if the discount was earned.

**42.** Christy La Pierre, a wholesaler of French cheeses, offers terms of 4/15-40 ex. to encourage the sales of her product. In a recent order, a retailer purchased $2,118.40 worth of French cheeses and was offered the above terms. If the invoice was dated January 10, find (a) the final date on which the cash discount may be taken and (b) the amount paid if the discount was earned.

**43.** A recent invoice for some playground equipment amounted to $4,358.50, was dated February 20, and offered terms of 2/20 ROG. If the equipment was received on March 20 and the invoice was paid on April 8, find the amount due.

**44.** Claudia Aldea purchased some copy paper and other supplies for her insurance office and was offered a cash discount of 2/10 EOM. The invoice amounted to $178.72 and was dated June 2. The forms were received 7 days later, and the invoice was paid on July 7. Find the amount necessary to pay the invoice in full.

**45.** An invoice amounting to $1,920 is dated July 23 by Lexington Foot Locker and offers cash terms of 6/30-120 x. If a partial payment of $940 is made on November 28, find (a) the credit given for the partial payment and (b) the balance due on the invoice.

**46.** Lamps For Less receives an invoice amounting to $5,832, with cash terms of 3/10 prox. and dated August 9. If a partial payment of $3,350 is made on August 15, find (a) the credit given for the partial payment and (b) the balance due on the invoice.

**47.** An invoice dated December 8 is received with a shipment of hockey equipment from Canada on April 18 of the following year. The list price of the equipment is $2,538, with allowed series discounts of 25/10/10. If cash terms of sale are 3/15 ROG, find the amount necessary to pay in full on April 21.

**48.** William Glen receives an invoice for some Waterford Crystal from Ireland amounting to $3,628.10 and dated May 17. The terms of the invoice are 5/20-90 x and the invoice is paid on September 2. Find the amount necessary to pay the invoice in full.

**49.** Michael Anderson Beauty Supplies offers series discounts of 15/10 with terms of 5/15-30 x. On an invoice dated June 4 for items list priced at $128, find the amount necessary to pay the invoice in full on June 18.

50. The Copy Corner receives an invoice amounting to $388.20, with terms of 8/10, n/30, and dated August 20 AS OF September 1. If a partial payment of $225 is made on September 8, find (a) the credit given for the partial payment and (b) the balance due on the invoice.

51. The Frozen Dessert Shop receives an invoice amounting to $526.80, with terms of 2/20 prox. and dated October 5. If a partial payment of $300 is made on November 12, find (a) the credit given for the partial payment and (b) the balance due on the invoice.

52. An invoice of $7,819.20 with terms of 4/10 prox. is received by Penny Carter Construction and is dated May 2. If a partial payment of $6,000 is made on May 8, find (a) the credit given for the partial payment and (b) the balance due on the invoice.

53. An invoice received by Chapman Appliance has terms of 3/15-30 x and is dated March 18. The amount of the invoice is $792.58, and a partial payment of $580 is made on April 24. Find (a) the credit given for the partial payment and (b) the balance due on the invoice.

54. Auto Detail Plus makes a partial payment of $220 on an invoice of $397.18. If the invoice is dated June 4 with terms of 5/15 prox. and the partial payment is made on July 10, find (a) the credit given for the partial payment and (b) the balance due on the invoice.

# Chapter 8 Quick Review

| TOPIC | APPROACH | EXAMPLE |
|---|---|---|
| **8.1 Trade discount and net cost** | First find the amount of the trade discount. Then use the formula:<br><br>Net cost = List price − Trade discount. | List price, $28; trade discount, 25%. Find the net cost.<br><br>$28 × 0.25 = $7<br><br>Net cost = $28 − $7 = $21 |
| **8.1 Complements with respect to 1** | The complement is the number that must be added to a given discount to get 1 or 100%. | Find the complement with respect to 1 for each of the following.<br><br>**(a)** $10\% + x = 100\%$<br>$x = 100\% - 10\%$<br>$x = 90\%$<br>**(b)** $12\frac{1}{2}\%$;<br>complement = 87.5%<br>**(c)** 50%;<br>complement = 50% |

| 8.1 | Complements and series discounts | The complement of a discount is the percent paid. Multiply the complements of the discounts in the series to get the net cost equivalent. | Series discount, 10/20/10. Find the net cost equivalent.<br><br>$\quad$ 10 $\;/\;$ 20 $\;/\;$ 10<br>$\quad$ ↓ $\quad\;$ ↓ $\quad\;$ ↓<br>$\quad$ 0.9 × 0.8 × 0.9 = 0.648 |

| 8.1 | Net cost equivalent (percent paid) and the net cost | Multiply the net cost equivalent (percent paid) by the list price to get the net cost.<br>Percent paid × List price = Net cost | List price, \$280; series discount 10/30/20 Find the net cost.<br><br>$\quad$ 10 $\;/\;$ 30 $\;/\;$ 20<br>$\quad$ ↓ $\quad\;$ ↓ $\quad\;$ ↓<br>$\quad$ 0.9 × 0.7 × 0.8 = 0.504 percent<br>$\hspace{10.5em}$ paid<br><br>0.504 × \$280 = \$141.12 |

| 8.2 | Single discount equivalent to a series discount | Often needed to compare one series discount to another, the single discount equivalent is found by subtracting the net cost equivalent from 1.<br>1 − Net cost equivalent = Single discount equivalent | What single discount is equivalent to a 10/20/20 series discount?<br><br>$\quad$ 10 $\;/\;$ 20 $\;/\;$ 20<br>$\quad$ ↓ $\quad\;$ ↓ $\quad\;$ ↓<br>$\quad$ 0.9 × 0.8 × 0.8 = 0.576<br><br>1 − 0.576 = 0.424 = 42.4% |

| 8.2 | Finding net cost using complements of individual discounts | To find the net cost, multiply the list price by the product of the complements of the individual discounts. | List price, \$510; series discount, 30/10/5. Find the net cost.<br><br>$\quad\quad$ 30 $\;/\;$ 10 $\;/\;$ 5<br>$\quad\quad$ ↓ $\quad\;$ ↓ $\quad\;$ ↓<br>\$510 × 0.7 × 0.9 × 0.95 =<br>$\hspace{5em}$ \$305.24 (rounded) |

| 8.2 | Finding list price if given the series discount and the net cost | First, find the net cost equivalent (percent paid), then use the formula to find the list price.<br><br>$\qquad P \times L = N$<br><br>Percent paid × List price = Net cost | Net cost, \$224; series discount, 20/20. Find list price.<br><br>$\quad\quad$ 20 $\;/\;$ 20<br>$\quad\quad$ ↓ $\quad\;$ ↓<br>$\quad\quad$ 0.8 × 0.8 = 0.64<br><br>0.64 × List price = \$224<br><br>$\qquad$ 0.64L = \$224<br><br>$\qquad\qquad$ L = \$350 |

**8.2 Determining the trade discount that must be added to meet a competitor's price**

First use the formula $P \times L = N$ to find the single discount needed. The answer is the complement of the discount that must be added; subtract it from 100% to get the discount.

List price $640; trade discount 25%. Find the trade discount that must be added to match the competitor's price of $432.

$$P \times L = N$$

$0.75 \times$ Complement of discount $\times L = N$

$$0.75 \times d \times \$640 = \$432$$

$$\$480d = \$432$$

$$d = 0.9 = 90\%$$

$$100\% - 90\% = 10\% \text{ additional}$$
discount

---

**8.3 Determining number of days and dates**

| 30 day months | 31 day months |
| --- | --- |
| April | All the rest |
| June | except February |
| September | with 28 days |
| November | |

Date, July 24. Find 10 days from date.

July $31 - 24 = 7$ remaining in July

$\quad$ 10 total number of days
$- \quad$ 7 days remaining in July
$\quad\quad$ 3 August—future date

---

**8.3 Ordinary dating and cash discounts**

With ordinary dating, count days from the date of the invoice. Remember:

$$\begin{array}{cccc} 2 & / \ 10, & n & / \ 30 \\ \downarrow & \downarrow \quad \downarrow & & \downarrow \\ \% & \text{days net} & & \text{days} \end{array}$$

Invoice amount $182; terms 2/10, n/30. Find cash discount and amount due.

Cash discount:
$\$182 \times 0.02 = \$3.64$

Amount due:
$\$182 - \$3.64 = \$178.36$

---

**8.3 Returned goods**

Subtract returned goods amount from invoice before calculating the cash discount.

Invoice amount, $95; returned goods, $15; terms, 3/15, n/30. Find amount due if discount is earned.

Cash discount:
$(\$95 - \$15) \times 0.03 = \$2.40$

Amount due:
$\$95 - \$15 - \$2.40 = \$77.60$

| | | |
|---|---|---|
| **8.4** **Cash discounts with end-of-month dating (EOM or proximo)** | Count the final discount date and the net date from the end of the month. If the invoice is dated the 26th or after, add the entire following month when determining the dates. If not stated, the net date is 20 days beyond the discount date. | Terms, 2/10 EOM; invoice date, Oct. 18. Find the final discount date and the net payment date.<br><br>Final discount date: November 10, which is 10 days from the end of October.<br><br>Net payment date: November 30, which is 20 days beyond the discount date. |
| **8.4** **Receipt-of-goods dating and cash discounts (ROG)** | Time is counted from the date goods are received to determine the final cash discount date and the net payment date. | Terms, 3/10 ROG; invoice date, March 8; goods received, May 10. Find the final discount date and the net payment date.<br><br>Final discount date: May 20 (May 10 + 10 days)<br><br>Net payment date: June 9 (May 20 + 20 days) |
| **8.4** **Extra dating and cash discounts** | Extra dating adds extra days to the usual cash discount period; for example, 3/10-20 x means 3/30. | Terms, 3/10-20 x; invoice date, January 8. Find the final discount date and the net payment date.<br><br>Final discount date: February 7 (23 days in January + 7 days in February = 30)<br><br>Net payment date: February 27 (February 7 + 20 days) |

**8.4 Partial payment credit**

When only a portion of an invoice amount is paid within the cash discount period, credit is given for the partial payment. Use the formula Amount paid = (1 − Discount rate) × Credit given.

Invoice, $400; terms, 2/10, n/30; invoice date, Oct. 10; partial payment of $200 on Oct. 15. Find credit given for partial payment and the balance due on the invoice.

$200 = (1 − 0.02) × Credit given

$200 = 0.98C

$204.08 (rounded) = C

$400 − $204.08 = $195.92 balance due

# Chapter 8 Review Exercises

*Find the trade discount and the net cost (invoice amount) for each of the following. Round to the nearest cent. [8.1]*

1. $260 less 10/20
2. $37 less 10/10/12½
3. $1,194 less 5/15/20
4. $1,620 less 20/25/15

*Find the net cost equivalent and the percent form of the single discount equivalent for each of the following series discounts. [8.2]*

5. 10/30
6. 5/10/20
7. 20/32½
8. 10/20/10/30

*Find the list price, given the net cost and the series discount. [8.2]*

9. Net cost, $361.50; trade discount, 10/20
10. Net cost, $1,050.74; trade discount, 15/20
11. Net cost, $328.70; trade discount, 10/20/15
12. Net cost, $1,289.40; trade discount, 5/20/25

*Find the final discount date and net payment date for each of the following. (The net payment date is 20 days after the final discount date.) [8.3 and 8.4]*

|     | Invoice Date | Terms | Date Goods Received |
|-----|--------------|-------|---------------------|
| 13. | Feb. 10 | 4/15 EOM | Feb. 16 |
| 14. | May 8 | 2/10 ROG | May 20 |
| 15. | Dec. 6 | 2/15 prox. | Jan. 15 |
| 16. | Oct. 20 | 2/20-40 extra | Oct. 31 |

*Solve for the amount of discount and the amount due on each of the following. [8.4]*

|     | Invoice Amount | Invoice Date | Terms | Shipping and Insurance | Date Goods Received | Date Invoice Paid |
|-----|----------------|--------------|-------|------------------------|---------------------|-------------------|
| 17. | $370.90 | June 14 | 2/10 ROG | $28.70 | June 22 | June 30 |
| 18. | $945.60 | May 9 | 3/15 proximo | | May 20 | June 12 |
| 19. | $875.50 | Feb. 20 | 4/15 EOM | $67.18 | Mar. 1 | Mar. 12 |
| 20. | $2,210.60 | Aug. 5 | 2/10-60 x | | Sept. 10 | Oct. 13 |

*Find the credit given and the balance due on the invoice after making the following partial payments. Round to the nearest cent. [8.4]*

|     | Invoice Amount | Invoice Date | Terms | Date Invoice Paid | Partial Payment |
|-----|----------------|--------------|-------|-------------------|-----------------|
| 21. | $660 | February 2 | 2/10, n/30 | February 10 | $300 |
| 22. | $5,310 | April 22 | 3/15 EOM | May 14 | $2,520 |
| 23. | $860 | July 23 | 1/10 prox. | August 5 | $500 |
| 24. | $3,850 | September 17 | 3/10-40 x | November 2 | $2,050 |

*Solve each of the following application problems in cash and trade discounts.*

**25.** The following invoice was paid on November 15. Find (a) the invoice total, (b) the amount that should be paid after the cash discount, and (c) the total amount due, including shipping and insurance. [8.1 and 8.3]

**HOLIDAY APPLIANCE REPAIR PARTS**

Terms: 2/10, 1/15, n/60                          November 6

| Quantity | Description | Unit Price | Extension Total |
|---|---|---|---|
| 16 | M-2 mixers | @   17.50 ea. | _____ |
| 8 | shelf brackets | @   3.25 ea. | _____ |
| 4 | blender, model L | @   12.65 ea. | _____ |
| 12 | bowls,  1 qt. stainless | @   3.15 ea. | _____ |
| | | Invoice Total | _____ |
| | | Cash Discount | _____ |
| | | Due after Cash Discount | _____ |
| | | Shipping and Insurance | $ 11.55 |
| | | Total Amount Due | _____ |

**26.** Fireside Shop offers chimney caps for $120 less 25/10. The same chimney cap is offered by Builders Supply for $111 less 25/5. Find (a) the firm that offers the lowest price and (b) the difference in price. [8.1]

**27.** Jon Zillioux Wheel Alignment purchased a new alignment rack at a net cost of $24,782 and a series discount of 10/5/20. Find the list price. [8.2]

**28.** Restaurant Distributing offers a commercial pasta maker for $980 with a trade discount of 25%. Find the trade discount that must be added to match a competitor's price of $661.50. [8.2]

**29.** An invoice amounting to $2,018 is dated September 18 and offers terms of 3/20 EOM. If $183 of goods are returned and the invoice is paid on October 18, what amount is due? [8.4]

**30.** Freitas Pneumatic Service receives an invoice dated April 22 for $1,854 with terms of 3/15 EOM. If the invoice is paid on May 12, find the amount necessary to pay the invoice in full. [8.4]

**31.** Chris Batchelor-Ayers receives an invoice amounting to $2,916 with cash terms of 3/10 prox. and dated June 7. If a partial payment of $1,666 is made on July 8, find (a) the credit given for the partial payment and (b) the balance due on the invoice. [8.4]

**32.** An invoice from Round Table Pizza Products amounts to $5,280, was dated November 1, and offers terms of 4/15 proximo. A partial payment of $1,800 is made on December 12. Find (a) the amount credited for the partial payment, (b) the balance due on the invoice, and (c) the cash discount earned. [8.4]

The Plescia Heat and Cool Company specializes in repairs and installation of heating and air conditioning units. In early October they order 15 heater blower motors which have a list price of $180 each, and 18 programmable thermostats which list at $98 per unit. The supplier of these parts offers trade discounts of 20/20 and charges for shipping.

The invoice for this order arrives a few days later, is dated October 20, has terms of 3/10 EOM, and shows a shipping charge of $118.80. Plescia Heat and Cool will need to know all of the following.

**(a)** The total amount of the invoice excluding shipping.

**(b)** The final discount date.

**(c)** The net payment date.

**(d)** The amount necessary to pay the invoice on November 8 including the shipping.

**(e)** Suppose that on November 8 the invoice is not paid in full, but a partial payment of $1,500 is made instead. Find the credit given for the partial payment and the balance due on the invoice including shipping.

# Markup

**9**

The success of a business depends on many things. One of the most important is the price that the business charges for its goods and services. Prices must be low enough to attract customers, yet high enough to cover all operating expenses and provide a profit.

The difference between the price a business pays for an item and the price at which the item is sold is called **markup**. For example, if a store buys a package of blank videotapes for $11 and sells it for $15, the markup is $4. There are two standard methods of calculating markup—as a percent of cost and as a percent of selling price. This chapter discusses these two methods, along with how to convert markups from one method to the other, and how to use markup to allow for spoilage.

## 9.1 Markup on Cost

**OBJECTIVES**

1. *Identify the terms used in selling.*
2. *Use the basic markup formula.*
3. *Calculate markup based on cost.*
4. *Apply percent to markup problems.*

**OBJECTIVE 1** *Identify the terms used in selling.*    The following terms are used in markup.

**Cost** is the price paid to the manufacturer or supplier after trade and cash discounts have been taken. Shipping and insurance charges are included in the cost. This is often called the **wholesale price**.

**Selling price** or **retail price** is the price at which merchandise is offered for sale to the public.

**Markup** or **margin** or **gross profit** is the difference between the cost and the selling price. These three terms are often used interchangeably.

**Operating expenses** (or **overhead**) include the many expenses of business operation, such as wages and salaries of employees, rent for buildings and equipment, utilities, insurance, and advertising. Even an expense item like postage can add up. Mailing costs average from 6.2% of operating expense for small companies to as

**Comparison of first-class postage rates of the U.S. and other countries (up to 1 ounce):**

Japan ................... 80 cents        Italy ..................... 46 cents
Germany ............. 64 cents        Netherlands ......... 46 cents
Denmark ............. 61 cents        Sweden ............... 42 cents
Switzerland ......... 60 cents        Great Britain ....... 39 cents
Austria ................ 54 cents        Australia .............. 35 cents
France ................. 52 cents        United States ....... 32 cents
Norway ............... 51 cents        Canada ................ 31 cents
Belgium .............. 47 cents

**History of U.S. postal rates since 1971**

May 16, 1971 ....... 8 cents
March 2, 1974 .... 10 cents
Dec. 31, 1975 ..... 13 cents
May 29, 1978 ..... 15 cents
March 22, 1981 .. 18 cents
Nov. 1, 1981 ....... 20 cents
Feb. 17, 1985 ...... 22 cents
April 3, 1988 ...... 25 cents
Feb. 3, 1991 ........ 29 cents
Jan. 1, 1995 ........ 32 cents

high as 9.2% for the largest companies. Notice at the side and above how postal rates have changed during the last quarter century and how postage rates vary around the world.

**Net profit (net earnings)** is the amount, if any, remaining for the business after the cost of goods and operating expenses have been paid. (Income tax for the business is computed on net profit.)

Most manufacturers, many wholesalers, and some retailers calculate markup as a percent of cost, called **markup on cost**. Manufacturers, who usually evaluate their inventories on the basis of cost, find this method to be most consistent with their business operations. Retailers, on the other hand, usually compute, **markup on selling price** since retailers compare most areas of their business operations to sales revenue. Such items as sales commissions, sales taxes, advertising, and other items of expense are expressed as a percent of sales. It is reasonable, then, for the retailer to express markup as percent of sales. Wholesalers, however, use either cost or selling price, so be sure to find out which is being used.

**OBJECTIVE 2** *Use the basic markup formula.*      Whether markup is based on cost or on selling price, the same basic **markup formula** is always used. This formula is as follows.

$$\text{Cost} + \text{Markup} = \text{Selling price}$$
$$C + M = S$$

The markup formula is illustrated in Figure 9.1.

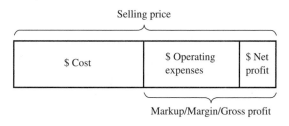

FIGURE 9.1

Most problems in markup give two of the items in the formula and ask for the third.

## EXAMPLE 1  *Using the Basic Markup Formula*

The Red Balloon Bookstore received some new children's books. Use the markup formula to determine the selling price, markup, and cost of the books in the following problems.

**(a)**        Cost = $3.50               **(b)**        Cost = $3.50

           Markup = $1.50                    Selling price = $5.00

       Selling price = _____                 Markup = _____

**(c)**        Markup = $1.50

       Selling price = $5.00

              Cost = _____

## SOLUTION

**(a)**        $C + M = S$             **(b)**       $C + M = S$

       $\$3.50 + \$1.50 = S$                 $\$3.50 + M = \$5.00$

              $\$5.00 = S$                    $M = \$5.00 - \$3.50$

                                               $M = \$1.50$

**(c)**      $C + M = S$

       $C + \$1.50 = \$5.00$

              $C = \$5.00 - \$1.50$

              $C = \$3.50$                                            ■

**OBJECTIVE 3  *Calculate markup based on cost.***        *Markup based on cost* is expressed as a percent of cost. As shown in the work with percent, *the base (that to which a number is being compared) is always 100%, so cost will have a value of 100%.* Markup and selling price will also have percent values found by comparing their dollar values to the dollar value of cost. Solve markup problems with the basic markup formula $C + M = S$ (Cost + Markup = Selling price).

**OBJECTIVE 4  *Apply percent to markup problems.***

## EXAMPLE 2  *Calculating Markup on Cost*

The manager of Kitchen Things purchased a pastry tool manufactured in France for $10 and will sell it for $15. Find the percent of markup based on cost.

**SOLUTION**    Use the markup formula

$$C + M = S$$

with $C = \$10$ and $S = \$15$.

$$\$10 + M = \$15$$

$$M = \$15 - \$10$$

$$M = \$5$$

The markup is $5. Now, find the percent of markup based on cost with the basic percent equation, $R \times B = P$. The base is the cost, or $10, and the markup is the part, or $5. Substituting these values into $R \times B = P$ gives

$$R \times B = P$$

$$R \times \$10 = \$5$$

$$\$10R = \$5$$

$$\frac{\cancel{10}R}{\cancel{10}} = \frac{5}{10}$$

$$R = 0.5 = 50\%.$$

The pastry tool costing $10 and selling for $15 has a 50% markup based on cost. ∎

---

*The calculator solution uses the parentheses to find the markup and then divides by the cost.

$$\boxed{(} \ 15 \ \boxed{-} \ 10 \ \boxed{)} \quad \boxed{\div} \ 10 \ \boxed{=} \ 0.5$$

**NOTE** The markup formula and the basic percent equation can be used for solving various types of problems involving markup, as shown in the next examples. ∎

## EXAMPLE 3 *Finding Cost When Cost is Base*

Olympic Sports and Leisure has a markup on a basketball of $14, which is 50% based on cost. Find the cost and the selling price.

**SOLUTION** The markup is 50% of the cost.

$$P = R \times B$$

$$M = 50\% \times C$$

$$M = 0.50C$$

---

*NOTE: All calculator solutions use a scientific calculator. Refer to Appendix A for scientific and financial calculator basics.

Since the markup is $14, substitute 14 for $M$.

$$\$14 = 0.50C$$

$$\frac{14}{0.50} = \frac{\cancel{0.50}C}{\cancel{0.50}}$$

$$28 = C$$

The cost of the basketball is $28.
   Now use the basic markup formula to find the selling price.

$$C + M = S$$

$$\$28 + \$14 = S$$

$$\$42 = S$$

The selling price of the basketball is $42.    ■

| EXAMPLE 4  *Finding the Markup and the Selling Price*

Find the markup and selling price for a Texas Instruments financial calculator assembled in Italy, if the cost is $23.60 and the markup is 25% of cost.

SOLUTION    Since the markup is 25% of cost,

$$M = 0.25(\$23.60)$$

$$M = \$5.90.$$

The markup is $5.90. Now use the markup formula, with $C = \$23.60$ and $M = \$5.90$.

$$C + M = S$$

$$\$23.60 + \$5.90 = S$$

$$\$29.50 = S$$

The selling price of the calculator is $29.50.    ■

CALCULATOR APPROACH
TO EXAMPLE 4

This calculator solution uses the percent add-on feature found on many calculators.

23.6 $\boxed{+}$ 25 $\boxed{\%}$ $\boxed{=}$ 29.5

| EXAMPLE 5  *Finding Cost When Cost Is Base*

Find the cost of a bracelet if the selling price is $112, which is 140% of the cost.

**SOLUTION** If the selling price is 140% of cost, then the markup must be 40% of cost. (The cost is always 100% when markup is based on cost.) This means

$$M = 0.4C.$$

Now use the basic formula.

$$C + M = S$$
$$C + 0.4C = \$112$$
$$1.4C = \$112$$
$$\frac{\cancel{1.4}C}{\cancel{1.4}} = \frac{\$112}{1.4}$$
$$C = \$80$$

The cost of the bracelet is $80. Check this: 0.40($80) = $32, and $80 + $32 = $112. ∎

## EXAMPLE 6 *Finding the Cost and the Markup*

The retail price of a 40-gallon gas water heater at Bechtold Plumbing is $195.75. If the markup is 35% of cost, find the cost and the markup.

**SOLUTION** Use the formula, with $M = 0.35C$.

$$C + M = S$$
$$C + 0.35C = \$195.75$$
$$1C + 0.35C = \$195.75$$
$$1.35C = \$195.75$$
$$\frac{\cancel{1.35}C}{\cancel{1.35}} = \frac{\$195.75}{1.35}$$
$$C = \$145$$

The cost of the water heater is $145.
    Now find markup.

$$C + M = S$$
$$\$145 + M = \$195.75$$
$$M = \$195.75 - \$145$$
$$M = \$50.75$$

The markup is $50.75. ∎

**NOTE** Remember, when calculating markup on cost, cost is always the base, 100%. ∎

# 9.1 EXERCISES

*Find the missing quantities. Round rates to the nearest tenth of a percent and money to the nearest cent.*

|     | Cost Price | Markup | % Markup on Cost | Selling Price |
|-----|------------|--------|------------------|---------------|
| 1.  | $6         | _____ | 30%             | _____       |
| 2.  | _____    | $3.60  | _____          | $21.60        |
| 3.  | $47        | $23.50 | _____          | _____       |
| 4.  | _____    | _____ | 100%            | $68.98        |
| 5.  | $158.70    | _____ | _____          | $198.50       |
| 6.  | _____    | $14.40 | 60%              | _____       |
| 7.  | _____    | $13.50 | _____          | $81           |
| 8.  | $7.75      | _____ | 28%             | _____       |
| 9.  | $210       | _____ | _____          | $328          |
| 10. | _____    | $25.25 | _____          | $73.80        |
| 11. | $495       | _____ | 27%             | _____       |
| 12. | _____    | _____ | 16%             | $90.83        |

✎ **13.** Markup may be calculated on cost or on selling price. Explain why most manufacturers prefer to use cost as base when calculating markup. (See Objective 1.)

✎ **14.** Write the basic markup formula. Define each term. (See Objective 2.)

*Solve each of the following application problems using cost as base. Round rates to the nearest tenth of a percent and money to the nearest cent.*

**15.** A telemarketing company pays $98.20 for an earring and necklace set and the markup is 35% of cost. Find the markup.

**16.** The cost of a dentist's handpiece is $560 and the markup is 25% of cost. Find the markup.

**17.** Orchard Supply sells garden sprayers at a price of $18.95. If markup is 38% of cost, find the cost.

**18.** Thermal Insulation Supplies sells bulk insulation at a price of $9.18 per bag. If the markup is 35% of cost, find the cost.

**19.** The cost of some hand tools imported from South Korea is $11.96 per set. The Tool Shed decides to use a markup of 25% on cost. Find the selling price of the tool set.

**20.** Water Sports purchases jet skis at a cost of $2,880 each. If its operating expenses are 25% of its cost, and it wishes to make a net profit of 15% of its cost, find the selling price.

**21.** What percent of markup on cost must be used if a wide screen (32-inch) Sony television costing $870 is sold for $1,024.60?

**22.** The Tower Market sells aspirin (100 tablet size) for $3.38 per bottle. If they pay $2.60 per bottle, find the markup percent on cost.

**23.** Patios Plus sold an outdoor lighting set for $119.95. If the markup on the set was $23.99, find (a) the cost, (b) the markup percent on cost, and (c) the selling price as a percent of cost.

**24.** Fleet Feet had a markup of $11.66 on some shoes that they sold for $55.66. Find (a) the cost, (b) the markup percent on cost, and (c) the selling price as a percent of cost.

**25.** Bismark Tool put a markup of 26% on cost on some parts for which they paid $4.50. Find (a) the selling price as a percent of cost, (b) the selling price, and (c) the markup.

**26.** A lighting manufacturer offers brass lamps at a selling price that is 175% of the cost. If the markup is $61.50, find (a) the markup percent on cost, (b) the cost, and (c) the selling price.

**27.** Nature Trails, a manufacturer of hiking equipment, prices lightweight hiking boots at $44.52, which is 127.2% of their cost. Find (a) the cost, (b) the markup as a percent of cost, and (c) the markup.

**28.** North Area Coins priced a proof coin at $868, which was 112% of cost. Find (a) the cost, (b) the markup as a percent of cost, and (c) the markup.

**29.** Welder's Supply purchases arc welding units for $3,860 each. The company has operating expenses of 22% of cost, and a net profit of 12% of cost. Find the selling price of each arc welding unit.

**30.** Olympic Sports and Leisure purchases mountain bikes at a cost of $280 each. If the company's operating expenses are 16% of cost, and a net profit of 7% of cost is desired, find the selling price of one mountain bike.

**31.** Bell Hardware has operating expenses of 18% of cost and desires a 17% net profit on cost. If the selling price of a tube of 20-year silicone caulk is $8.95, find the cost.

**32.** American Glass Company sells eight-foot sliding patio doors for $299.90. If their operating expenses are 15% of cost and their net profit is 15% of cost, find the cost.

---

## 9.2    Markup on Selling Price

**OBJECTIVES**

**1** Calculate markup based on selling price.

**2** Solve markup problems when selling price is base.

**3** Use the markup formula to solve markup problems.

**4** Determine percent markup on cost and the equivalent percent markup on selling price.

**5** Convert markup percent on cost to selling price.

**6** Convert markup percent on selling price to cost.

As mentioned in the previous section, wholesalers sometimes calculate markup based on cost and other times calculate markup based on selling price. Retailers use sales figures in almost all aspects of their business. Almost all expense and income amounts are calculated as a percent of sales. Therefore it is common for retailers to calculate markup based on selling price. In each case, markup will be given as ''on cost'' or ''on selling price.'' Remember that if markup is based on selling price, then selling price is the base. Since the base is 100%, selling price will have a value of 100%. This section discusses markup on selling price.

**OBJECTIVE** **1** *Calculate markup based on selling price.* The same basic markup formula is used with **markup on selling price**.

$$\text{Cost} + \text{Markup} = \text{Selling price}$$
$$C + M = S$$

**OBJECTIVE** **2** *Solve markup problems when selling price is base.*

**EXAMPLE 1** *Solving for Markup on Selling Price*

To remain competitive, the Sports Authority must sell a Rawlings split leather Little League baseball for $3.00. They pay $2.00 for the baseball and calculate markup on selling price. Find the amount of markup and the percent of markup on selling price.

**SOLUTION** First, solve for markup.

$$C + M = S$$
$$\$2 + M = \$3$$
$$M = \$3 - \$2$$
$$M = \$1$$

Now solve for percent of markup on selling price. Use the basic percent equation, $R \times B = P$. In this example, $P$ is the markup, or $1, and the base $B$ is the selling price, or $3. Substitute these values into $R \times B = P$, and solve the equation.

$$R \times \$3 = \$1$$
$$R = \frac{\$1}{\$3}$$
$$R = \frac{1}{3} = 0.333 \ldots = 33\frac{1}{3}\%$$

The percent of markup on selling price is $33\frac{1}{3}\%$. ■

**OBJECTIVE** **3** *Use the markup formula to solve markup problems.* As with problems where markup is based on cost, the basic formula $C + M = S$ may be used for all variations of markup problems when selling price is the base.

**EXAMPLE 2** *Finding Markup When Selling Price Is Given*

Find the markup on a bottle of vitamin E capsules if the selling price is $3.43 and the markup is 30% of selling price.

**SOLUTION**    Since the markup is 30% of the selling price,

$$M = 0.3S$$

or

$$M = 0.3(\$3.43) = \$1.03. \qquad \text{(rounded)}$$

The markup is $1.03.                                                              ∎

## EXAMPLE 3    *Finding Cost When Selling Price Is Base*

A bookstore employee knows that the 3-hole binders have a markup of $1.72 which is 35% based on selling price. Find the cost of the binders.

**SOLUTION**    Start by finding selling price and then subtract markup to find cost. Here $R = 35\%$ (the rate of markup) and $P = \$1.72$ (the markup). Use $R \times B = P$ as follows.

$$R \times B = P$$
$$35\% \times S = \$1.72$$
$$0.35S = \$1.72$$
$$S = \frac{\$1.72}{0.35}$$
$$S = \$4.91 \qquad \text{(rounded)}$$

The selling price is $4.91. Now solve for cost.

$$C + M = S$$
$$C + \$1.72 = \$4.91$$
$$C + \$1.72 - \$1.72 = \$4.91 - \$1.72$$
$$C = \$4.91 - \$1.72$$
$$C = \$3.19$$

The cost is $3.19.                                                              ∎

## EXAMPLE 4    *Finding the Selling Price and the Markup When Cost Is Given*

Find the selling price and the markup on a 9-volt battery if the cost is $1.50 and the markup is 25% of selling price.

**SOLUTION**    Use the formula $C + M = S$. Since the markup is 25% of the selling price, $M = 0.25S$.

$$\$1.50 + 0.25S = S$$

$$\$1.50 + 0.25S - 0.25S = 1S - 0.25S$$

$$\$1.50 = 1S - 0.25S$$

$$\$1.50 = 0.75S$$

$$\frac{1.50}{0.75} = \frac{\cancel{0.75}S}{\cancel{0.75}}$$

$$\$2 = S$$

The selling price is $2.

Now find the markup using the markup formula.

$$C + M = S$$

$$\$1.50 + M = \$2$$

$$M = \$2.00 - \$1.50$$

$$M = \$0.50$$

The markup is $0.50.                                                    ■

Markups vary widely from industry to industry and from business to business. This variation is a result of different costs of merchandise, operating costs, level of profit margin, and local competition. Table 9.1 shows average markups for different types of retail stores.

**OBJECTIVE** **4** *Determine percent markup on cost and the equivalent percent markup on selling price.*     Sometimes a markup based on cost must be compared to a markup based on selling price. Such a conversion might be necessary for a manufacturer who thinks in terms of cost, and who wants to understand a wholesaler or retail customer. Or perhaps a retailer or wholesaler might convert markup on selling

TABLE 9.1  **Average Markups for Retail Stores (Markup on Selling Price)**

| Type of Store | Markup | Type of Store | Markup |
|---|---|---|---|
| General merchandise stores | 29.97% | Furniture and home furnishings | 35.75% |
| Grocery stores | 22.05% | Drinking places | 52.49% |
| Other food stores | 27.31% | Eating places | 56.35% |
| Motor vehicle dealers (new) | 12.83% | Drug and proprietary stores | 30.81% |
| Gasoline service stations | 14.47% | Liquor stores | 20.19% |
| Other automotive dealers | 29.57% | Sporting goods and bicycle shops | 29.72% |
| Apparel and accessories | 37.64% | Gift, novelty, and souvenir shops | 41.86% |

*Source:* Sole Proprietorship Income Tax Returns, U.S. Treasury Dept., Internal Revenue Service, Statistics Division.

price to markup on cost to better understand the manufacturer. Make these comparisons by first computing the markup on cost, then computing the markup on selling price.

| EXAMPLE 5 *Determining Equivalent Markups*

A Eureka Bravo, The Boss, vacuum cleaner costs a retailer $84 and is sold for $105. Find the percent of markup on cost. Also, find the percent of markup on selling price.

**SOLUTION**    To solve for the percent markup on cost, use the formula $C + M = S$, with $C = \$84$ and $S = \$105$.

$$C + M = S$$

$$\$84 + M = \$105$$

$$M = \$105 - \$84$$

$$M = \$21$$

The markup is $21.
    Next, use the percent equation, $R \times B = P$, with $B = \$84$ (the cost, since markup is on cost) and $P = \$21$ (the markup).

$$R \times B = P$$

$$R \times \$84 = \$21$$

$$\$84R = \$21$$

$$R = \frac{21}{84}$$

$$R = 0.25 = 25\%$$

The markup on cost is 25%.
    To find the percent of markup on selling price, use the percent equation again. While $P$ is still $21, $B$ changes to $105 since the markup on selling price must be found. Substitute into the equation as follows.

$$R \times B = P$$

$$R \times \$105 = \$21$$

$$\$105R = \$21$$

$$R = \frac{21}{105}$$

$$R = 0.2 = 20\%$$

The markup on selling price is 20%. This example shows that a 25% markup on cost is equivalent to a 20% markup on selling price.    ■

NOTE   In Example 5 the markup on cost was determined first (25%). The problem was then reworked with the same dollar amounts but with the selling price as base. The result was 20%. This shows that a markup of 25% on cost is the same as a markup of 20% on selling price.   ■

**OBJECTIVE** **5** *Convert markup percent on cost to selling price.*     Another method for making markup comparisons is to use conversion formulas. No dollar amounts are needed for you to use these formulas. Only the percent of markup is needed. If you have markup percent on cost, you can convert the markup percent on cost to markup percent on selling price with the following formula.

$$\frac{\% \text{ of markup on}}{\text{selling price}} = \frac{\% \text{ of markup on cost}}{100\% + \% \text{ of markup on cost}}$$

Or, if $M_c$ represents markup on cost and $M_s$ represents markup on selling price,

$$M_s = \frac{M_c}{100\% + M_c}.$$

**EXAMPLE 6**   *Converting Markup on Cost to Markup on Selling Price*

Convert a markup of 25% on cost to its equivalent markup on selling price.

**SOLUTION**   Use the formula for converting markup on cost to markup on selling price:

$$\frac{M_c}{100\% + M_c} = M_s,$$

with $M_c = 25\%$.

$$\frac{25\%}{100\% + 25\%} = \frac{25\%}{125\%} = \frac{0.25}{1.25} = \frac{1}{5} = 20\%$$

As in Example 1, a markup of 25% on cost is equivalent to a markup of 20% on selling price.   ■

CALCULATOR APPROACH
TO EXAMPLE 6

The markup on cost (25%) is divided by 100% plus the markup on cost. The parentheses keys are used here.

25 %  ÷  ( 100 %  + 25 % )  = 0.2

**OBJECTIVE** **6** *Convert markup percent on selling price to cost.*     Convert markup percent on selling price to markup percent on cost with the following formula.

$$\begin{matrix} \% \text{ of markup} \\ \text{on cost} \end{matrix} = \frac{\% \text{ of markup on selling price}}{100\% - \% \text{ of markup on selling price}}$$

Or, if $M_c$ represents markup on cost and $M_s$ represents markup on selling price,

$$M_c = \frac{M_s}{100\% - M_s}.$$

**EXAMPLE 7** *Converting Markup on Selling Price to Markup on Cost*

Convert a markup of 20% on selling price to its equivalent markup on cost.

**SOLUTION**  Use the formula for converting markup on selling price to markup on cost:

$$\frac{M_s}{100\% - M_s} = M_c,$$

with $M_s = 20\%$.

$$\frac{20\%}{100\% - 20\%} = \frac{20\%}{80\%} = \frac{0.2}{0.8} = \frac{1}{4} = 25\%$$

A markup of 20% on selling price is equivalent to a markup of 25% on cost.    ■

**CALCULATOR APPROACH TO EXAMPLE 7**

The markup on selling price (20%) is divided by 100% minus the markup on selling price. The parentheses keys are used here.

20 $\boxed{\%}$ $\boxed{\div}$ $\boxed{(}$ 100 $\boxed{\%}$ $\boxed{-}$ 20 $\boxed{\%}$ $\boxed{)}$ $\boxed{=}$ 0.25

Table 9.2 shows common markup equivalents expressed as percents on cost and also on selling price.

TABLE 9.2  **Markup Equivalents**

| Markup on Cost | Markup on Selling Price |
|:---:|:---:|
| 20% | $16\frac{2}{3}\%$ |
| 25% | 20% |
| $33\frac{1}{3}\%$ | 25% |
| 50% | $33\frac{1}{3}\%$ |
| $66\frac{2}{3}\%$ | 40% |
| 75% | $42\frac{6}{7}\%$ |
| 100% | 50% |

## 9.2  EXERCISES

*Find the missing quantities. Round rates to the nearest tenth of a percent and money to the nearest cent.*

|  | Cost Price | Markup | % Markup on Selling Price | Selling Price |
|---|---|---|---|---|
| 1. | $16 | _____ | 20% | _____ |
| 2. | $40 | _____ | _____ | $58.50 |
| 3. | _____ | $112 | 46% | _____ |
| 4. | _____ | $72 | _____ | $189.50 |
| 5. | $18.60 | _____ | $66\frac{2}{3}$% | _____ |
| 6. | $17.28 | _____ | _____ | $29.95 |
| 7. | _____ | _____ | 35% | $71.32 |
| 8. | $178 | _____ | $33\frac{1}{3}$% | _____ |
| 9. | _____ | $42.18 | _____ | $120 |
| 10. | $193.15 | _____ | 42.5% | _____ |

*Find the missing quantities by first computing the markup on one base and then computing the markup on the other. Round rates to the nearest tenth of a percent and money to the nearest cent.*

|  | Cost | Markup | Selling Price | % Markup on Cost | % Markup on Selling Price |
|---|---|---|---|---|---|
| 11. | _____ | $57.50 | _____ | 25% | 20% |
| 12. | _____ | $0.23 | $0.73 | _____ | _____ |
| 13. | $13.80 | _____ | _____ | _____ | 38% |
| 14. | $33.75 | _____ | $67.50 | _____ | _____ |
| 15. | _____ | $300 | _____ | 40% | _____ |
| 16. | $5.15 | _____ | $15.45 | _____ | _____ |
| 17. | _____ | $78.48 | $436 | _____ | 18% |
| 18. | _____ | $480 | _____ | 25% | _____ |

*Find the equivalent markups on either cost or selling price using the appropriate formula. Round to the nearest tenth of a percent.*

|  | Markup on Cost | Markup on Selling Price |
|---|---|---|
| 19. | 25% | _____ |
| 20. | 100% | _____ |
| 21. | _____ | 26% |

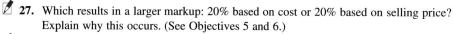

| | Markup on Cost | Markup on Selling Price |
|---|---|---|
| 22. | _____ | 15.3% |
| 23. | 50% | _____ |
| 24. | $33\frac{1}{3}\%$ | _____ |
| 25. | _____ | 40% |
| 26. | _____ | $16\frac{2}{3}\%$ |

27. Which results in a larger markup: 20% based on cost or 20% based on selling price? Explain why this occurs. (See Objectives 5 and 6.)

28. Show and explain the conditions that must exist in order to have a 100% markup on selling price. Is this possible? (See Objectives 5 and 6.)

*Solve each of the following application problems. Round rates to the nearest tenth of a percent and money to the nearest cent.*

29. The cost of a custom chrome spoked wheel is $42.30. If the markup is 40% on selling price, find the selling price.

30. An auto parts dealer pays $7.14 per dozen gallons of windshield washer fluid and the markup is 50% on selling price. Find the selling price per bottle.

31. Orchard Supply sells a yard mulcher for $492.80 and maintains a markup of 30% on selling price. Find the cost.

32. Olympic Sports and Leisure sells a home gymnasium package for $3,522 and maintains a markup of 35% on selling price. Find the cost.

33. If the cost of steel-belted tires, size P205/70R15, is $71.25 each and the markup is 35% on selling price, find the selling price.

34. Field and Stream Sports pays $20.80 for a fly rod and sells it for $32. Find the percent of markup on selling price.

35. Handmade floor tile from Belgium has a markup of 36% on the selling price. If the tile has a markup of $1.62 per tile, find (a) the selling price, (b) the cost, and (c) the cost as a percent of the selling price per tile.

36. Circuit City pays $73.76 for a Fontec cordless telephone. If the markup is 18% on selling price, find (a) the cost as a percent of selling price, (b) the selling price, and (c) the markup.

37. Best Products buys clock radios for $258 per dozen and has a gross profit of $7.74 per clock radio. Find the percent of gross profit based on selling price.

38. A retailer pays $87.36 per dozen for baseball hats and has a gross profit of $1.68 per hat. Find the percent of gross profit based on selling price.

39. The Workem's Store placed a selling price of $27.50 on slacks that cost 68% of the selling price. Find (a) the cost, (b) the markup, and (c) the markup as a percent of selling price.

40. Mervyns Department Store priced some Levi Docker shirts at $29.95. If the cost of the shirts was 58% of the selling price, find (a) the cost, (b) the markup, and (c) the markup as a percent of selling price.

41. Recyclable aluminum can be sold for $2,880 per ton (1 ton = 2,000 pounds). If Alcan Recycling Plant wants a 50% markup on selling price, (a) how much per pound can it

pay local residents for their recycled aluminum? (b) What is the equivalent markup percent on cost?

**42.** A retailer purchases silk flowers for $31.56 per dozen and sells them for $4.78 each. (a) Find his percent of markup on selling price. (b) What is the equivalent markup on cost?

**43.** White Water Supply purchased a job lot of 380 river rafts for $7,600. If they sold 158 of the rafts at $45 each, 74 at $35 each, 56 at $30 each, and the remainder at $25 each find (a) the total amount received for the rafts, (b) the total markup, (c) the markup percent on selling price, and (d) the equivalent markup percent on cost.

**44.** Dress for Success purchased 240 Italian silk ties for $2,280. They sold 162 ties at $25 each, 45 ties at $15 each, 20 ties at $10 each, and the remainder at $5 each. Find (a) the total amount received for the ties, (b) the total markup, (c) the markup percent on selling price, and (d) the equivalent markup percent on cost.

**45.** General Electric Parts Department sells ice cube maker repair kits for $27.90 each, which reflects a markup of 50% on selling price. Find (a) the cost and (b) the percent of markup on cost.

**46.** The Tinder Box Smoke Shop buys a special blend of pipe tobacco in ten-pound tins at a cost of $24 per tin. If the shop sells the tobacco for $1.20 per ounce, find (a) the markup on selling price, and (b) the equivalent markup on cost. (Hint: 1 pound = 16 ounces.)

**47.** A restaurant supplier sells coffee filters for $6.90 per box. If the cost of the filters is $4.80, find (a) the percent of markup on cost and (b) the equivalent percent of markup on selling price.

**48.** Home Base sells a 40-pound bag of Pax All-Purpose Fertilizer for $10.98. If the cost of the fertilizer is $7.32 per bag, find (a) the percent of markup on cost and (b) the equivalent percent of markup on selling price.

**49.** A discount store purchased touch-tone wall phones at a cost of $288 per dozen. If they need 20% of cost to cover operating expenses and 15% of cost for net profit, find (a) the selling price per phone and (b) the percent of markup on selling price.

**50.** The Bowlers Pro-Shop determines that operating expenses are 23% of selling price and desires a net profit of 12% of selling price. If the cost of a team shirt is $29.25, find (a) the selling price and (b) the percent of markup on cost.

**51.** Cycle City advertises mountain bikes for $199.90. If their cost is $2,100 per dozen, find (a) the markup per bicycle, (b) the percent of markup on selling price, and (c) the percent of markup on cost.

**52.** The Tool Shed advertises standard/metric socket sets (manufactured in the U.S.A.) for $39. If their cost is $351 per dozen sets, find (a) the markup per set, (b) the percent of markup on selling price, and (c) the percent of markup on cost.

## 9.3  Markup with Spoilage

### OBJECTIVES

**1** *Solve markup problems when items are unfit for sale.*

**2** *Solve markup problems when a certain percent of items are unsaleable.*

**3** *Calculate markup when a percent of the merchandise must be sold at a reduced price.*

**OBJECTIVE 1** *Solve markup problems when items are unfit for sale.* Merchandise that is perishable, becomes damaged or soiled, or is manufactured with a blemish, causes problems for many businesses. To a nursery or garden center, produce buyer, food processor, and clothing manufacturer, such problems are a common occurrence. These items that cannot be sold at the regular price, called **irregulars**, are often sold at a reduced price. In fact, such items may be **unsaleable** and represent a total loss. In either case, the markup applied to the items sold at regular price must allow for **spoilage** and damaged items. The result is that perfect items are sold at a higher price to make up for the unsold items, in a process called **markup with spoilage**.

---

**EXAMPLE 1** *Finding Selling Price with Spoilage*

Village Nursery purchases 105 5-gallon size juniper tams for $351. If a markup of 40% on selling price is necessary and 15 of the plants will be unfit for sale, find the selling price per plant.

**SOLUTION** First, find the total selling price of the plants using a 40% markup on selling price and a cost of $351.

$$C + M = S$$
$$C + 40\%S = S$$
$$\$351 + 0.4S = S$$
$$\$351 = 1.00S - 0.4S$$
$$\$351 = 0.6S$$
$$\frac{\$351}{0.6} = S$$
$$\$585 = S$$

The total selling price is $585. Now, divide the total selling price by the number of saleable plants to find the selling price per plant.

$$\frac{\$585}{105 \text{ purchased } - \text{ 15 unsaleable}} = \frac{585}{90} = \$6.50 \qquad \text{selling price per plant}$$

The juniper tams must be priced at $6.50 each to realize a markup of 40% on selling price and to allow for 15 plants that cannot be sold. ∎

**NOTE** Controlling loss due to spoilage is critical in business. As spoilage increases, profits will fall. These additional costs due to spoilage may be added to the price of the products sold but the resulting higher price may be too high and no longer competitive. ∎

**OBJECTIVE** **2** *Solve markup problems when a certain percent of items are unsaleable.*

| EXAMPLE 2 *Finding Selling Price When a Percent of Items Is Unsaleable*

The Muffin Mill bakes 60 dozen muffins at a cost of $2.16 per dozen. If a markup of 50% on selling price is needed and 5% of the muffins will not be sold and must be thrown away, find the selling price per dozen muffins.

**SOLUTION**    To begin, find the total cost of the muffins.

$$\text{Cost} = 60 \text{ dozen} \times \$2.16 = \$129.60$$

Now find the selling price, using a markup of 50% of selling price.

$$C + M = S$$
$$C + 50\%S = S$$
$$\$129.60 + 0.5S = S$$
$$\$129.60 = 1.00S - 0.5S$$
$$\$129.60 = 0.5S$$
$$\frac{\$129.60}{0.5} = S$$
$$\$259.20 = S$$

The total selling price is $259.20.
   Next, find the number of dozen muffins that will be sold. Since 5% will not be sold, 95% (100% − 5%) will be sold.

$$95\% \times 60 \text{ dozen} = 57 \qquad \text{dozen muffins sold}$$

The total selling price of $259.20 must be received from 57 dozen muffins.
   Find the selling price per dozen muffins by dividing the total selling price by the number of muffins sold.

$$\frac{\text{total selling price}}{\text{number saleable}} = \frac{\$259.20}{57} = \$4.55 \qquad \text{selling price per dozen (rounded)}$$

A selling price of $4.55 per dozen gives the desired markup of 50% on selling price while allowing for 5% of the muffins to be unsold.    ∎

**OBJECTIVE** **3** *Calculate markup when a percent of the merchandise must be sold at a reduced price.*

| EXAMPLE 3 *Finding Selling Price When Some Items Are Sold at a Reduced Price*

An athletic shoe manufacturer makes a walking shoe at a cost of $16.80 per pair. Based on past experience, 10% of the shoes will be defective and must be sold as irregulars for $24 per pair. If the manufacturer produces 1,000 pairs of shoes and desires a markup of 100% on cost, find the selling price per pair.

**SOLUTION**    First, find the cost of the total production.

$$1{,}000 \text{ pairs} \times \$16.80 = \$16{,}800 \qquad \text{total production cost}$$

The total selling price is

$$C + M = S$$
$$C + 100\%C = S$$
$$2C = S.$$

Since $C = \$16{,}800$ and $2C = S$, $2 \times \$16{,}800 = \$33{,}600$ is the total selling price of all shoes.

If 10% of the shoes will sell for $24 per pair, then the sales of irregulars will be

$$(0.10 \times 1{,}000) \times \$24 = 100 \times \$24$$
$$= \$2{,}400.$$

Calculate the selling price per pair of the regular priced shoe as shown.

$$\$33{,}600 - \$2{,}400 = \$31{,}200 \qquad \text{total sales of regulars}$$

$$\frac{\$31{,}200}{1{,}000 - 100} = \frac{31{,}200}{900} = \$34.67 \qquad \text{(rounded)}$$

A regular selling price of $34.67 will give the manufacturer a 100% markup on cost while allowing for 10% of the production to sell at $24 per pair.    ■

**CALCULATOR APPROACH TO EXAMPLE 3**

The calculator solution requires several steps. First, find the total selling price and place it in memory.

$$1000 \;\boxed{\times}\; 16.8 \;\boxed{\times}\; 2 \;\boxed{=}\; \boxed{\text{STO}}$$

Next, find the total amount received from the sale of irregulars.

$$.1 \;\boxed{\times}\; 1000 \;\boxed{\times}\; 24 \;\boxed{=}$$

Now, subtract the sales of irregulars from the total selling price.

$$\boxed{+/-} \;\boxed{+}\; \boxed{\text{RCL}} \;\boxed{=}$$

Finally, divide by the number of regular pairs.

$$\boxed{\div}\; 900 \;\boxed{=}\; 34.67$$

# 9.3 EXERCISES

*Find the selling price per item.*

| | Total Cost | Quantity Purchased | Number Unsaleable | % Markup on Selling Price | Selling Price per Item |
|---|---|---|---|---|---|
| 1. | $180 | 12 | 2 | 25% | _____ |
| 2. | $27 | 30 | 3 | 10% | _____ |
| 3. | $340 | 1 gr. | 8 | 20% | _____ |
| 4. | $189 | 4 doz. | 6 | 40% | _____ |
| 5. | $120 | 25 pr. | 5 pr. | $33\frac{1}{3}\%$ | _____ |
| 6. | $2,750 | 120 | 10 | 50% | _____ |
| 7. | $126 | 8 doz. | 6 | 15% | _____ |
| 8. | $2,025 | 250 pr. | 25 pr. | 25% | _____ |

*Find the missing quantities.*

| | Total Cost | Quantity Purchased | Percent Unsaleable | % Markup on Selling Price | Number to Sell | Selling Price per Item |
|---|---|---|---|---|---|---|
| 9. | $322 | 50 | 8% | 25% | _____ | _____ |
| 10. | $171 | 60 | 5% | 20% | _____ | _____ |
| 11. | $198 | 2 doz. | 25% | 50% | _____ | _____ |
| 12. | $162 | 20 cs. | 10% | 30% | _____ | _____ |
| 13. | $190 | 80 pr. | 5% | $33\frac{1}{3}\%$ | _____ | _____ |
| 14. | $8,750 | 100 | 30% | 15% | _____ | _____ |
| 15. | $25,200 | 2,000 gal. | 5% | 20% | _____ | _____ |
| 16. | $7,200 | 100 bbl. | 10% | 80% | _____ | _____ |

*Find the missing quantities. Markup is based on total cost.*

| | Total Cost | Quantity Purchased | Percent Sold at Reduced Price | % Markup on Total Cost | Number at Regular Price | Number at Reduced Price | Reduced Price | Regular Selling Price |
|---|---|---|---|---|---|---|---|---|
| 17. | $250 | 100 | 20% | 25% | _____ | _____ | $2.20 | _____ |
| 18. | $180 | 60 | 10% | 20% | _____ | _____ | $2.00 | _____ |
| 19. | $2,200 | 40 gal. | 15% | 35% | _____ | _____ | $50.00 | _____ |
| 20. | $270 | 90 pr. | 20% | 40% | _____ | _____ | $4.00 | _____ |

| | Total Cost | Quantity Purchased | Percent Sold at Reduced Price | % Markup on Total Cost | Number at Regular Price | Number at Reduced Price | Reduced Price | Regular Selling Price |
|---|---|---|---|---|---|---|---|---|
| 21. | $432 | 1 gr. | 25% | 25% | _____ | _____ | $2.50 | _____ |
| 22. | $3,000 | 600 | 10% | $33\frac{1}{3}\%$ | _____ | _____ | $5.00 | _____ |
| 23. | $2,800 | 1,000 pr. | 30% | 50% | _____ | _____ | $3.00 | _____ |
| 24. | $7,500 | 1,000 | 50% | 25% | _____ | _____ | $5.00 | _____ |

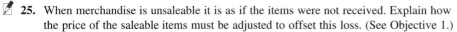

**25.** When merchandise is unsaleable it is as if the items were not received. Explain how the price of the saleable items must be adjusted to offset this loss. (See Objective 1.)

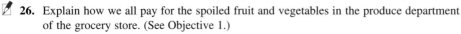

**26.** Explain how we all pay for the spoiled fruit and vegetables in the produce department of the grocery store. (See Objective 1.)

*Solve each of the following application problems.*

**27.** Country Produce knows that 20% of the strawberries purchased will spoil and must be thrown out. If they buy 200 baskets of strawberries for $0.24 per basket and want a markup of 50% on selling price, find the selling price per basket of strawberries.

**28.** The Bagel Factory baked 200 dozen bagels at a cost of $108. If 20 dozen bagels cannot be sold and the bakery needs a markup of $66\frac{2}{3}\%$ on selling price, find the selling price per dozen bagels.

**29.** Fowler Nursery purchases 75 mature palm trees for $511. If 2 of the palms are judged unfit for resale and the nursery desires to maintain a $33\frac{1}{3}\%$ markup on selling price, find the selling price for each palm.

**30.** Cost Plus Imports purchased 30 crates of candles from Mexico for a total cost of $237.60. Each crate contains 3 dozen candles. If 4 crates of the candles are sold at the reduced price of $0.25 per candle and Cost Plus Imports wants a markup of 100% on cost, find the regular price per candle.

**31.** Flower Sack purchased twelve gross of carnations at a cost of $128.60. If 25% of the carnations must be sold at $1.50 per dozen and a markup of 200% on cost is needed, find the regular selling price per dozen carnations.

**32.** Custom Caps buys 2,000 baseball hats at $2.50 per hat. If a markup of 50% on selling price is needed and 5% of the hats are unsaleable, find the selling price of each hat.

**33.** Bethel Metals finds that 20% of its stove shell castings are unsaleable. If the cost of manufacturing 55 stoves is $10,450 and they need a markup of 30% on cost, find the selling price per stove.

**34.** Transco Products knows that 4% of their manufactured transmission pan gaskets are rejects and cannot be sold. If the cost of manufacturing 5,000 gaskets is $3,168 and they need a markup of 200% on cost, find the selling price of each gasket.

**35.** Woolever Tire recaps tires at a cost of $11.50 per tire. Past experience shows that 12% of the recaps must be sold as blemishes for $15. If they recap 500 tires and a markup of 110% on cost is desired, find the regular selling price per tire.

**36.** Solano Tile manufactures roof tile at a cost of $42 per square. Past experience shows that 8% of a production run are irregulars and must be sold for $45 per square. If a production run of 10,000 squares is completed and they desire a markup of 80% on cost, find the selling price per square.

**37.** U.S. Publishing Company prints a book on sports memorabilia at a production cost of $10.80 per copy. They know that 20% of the production will be sold for $11.50 per copy. If they print 50,000 books and they want a markup of 50% on selling price, find the selling price per book. Round to the nearest cent.

**38.** Wallpaper Specialty Imports purchased 7,000 rolls of wallpaper manufactured in France at a cost of $6.30 per roll. Past experience shows that 25% of the wallpaper will have to be sold for $6.75 per roll. Find the selling price per roll if the store wants a markup of 50% on selling price.

# Chapter 9 Quick Review

| TOPIC | APPROACH | EXAMPLE |
|---|---|---|
| **9.1 Markup on cost** | Use Rate × Base = Part ($R \times B = P$) with Cost as Base (100%), Markup % as Rate, and Markup as Part. | Cost, $160; markup, 25% on cost. Find the markup. $R \times B = P$ $$0.25 \times \$160 = \$40$$ |
| **9.1 Calculating the percent of markup** | Use Cost + Markup = Selling price ($C + M = S$) and the basic percent equation $R \times B = P$. | Cost, $420; selling price, $546. Find the percent of markup based on cost. $C + M = S$ $$\$420 + M = \$546$$ $$M = \$126$$ $$R \times B = P$$ $$R \times \$420 = \$126$$ $$R = \frac{126}{420} = 0.3 = 30\%$$ |
| **9.1 Finding the cost and selling price** | Use $P = R \times B$ to solve for cost; then use $C + M = S$ to find selling price. | Markup, $56; markup on cost, 50%. Find cost and selling price. $P = R \times B$ $$\$56 = 0.5C$$ $$C = \frac{56}{0.5} = \$112 \quad \text{cost}$$ $$C + M = S$$ $$\$112 + \$56 = \$168 \quad \text{selling price}$$ |

| | | |
|---|---|---|
| **9.2   Markup on selling price** | Use Rate × Base = Part ($R \times B = P$) with Selling Price as Base (100%), Markup % as Rate, and Markup as Part. | Selling price, $6; markup, 25% on selling price. Find the markup.<br>$P = R \times B$<br><br>Markup = 25% × Selling price<br>$M = 0.25(\$6) = \$1.50$ |
| **9.2   Finding the cost** | Use the formulas $R \times B = P$ and $C + M = S$. | Markup, $87.50; markup on selling price, 35%. Find the cost.<br>First, use $R \times B = P$ to find selling price.<br><br>35% × Selling price = $87.50<br>$$0.35S = \$87.50$$<br>$$S = \$250$$<br><br>Now find cost.<br>$$C + M = S$$<br>$$C + \$87.50 = \$250$$<br>$$C = \$250 - \$87.50 = \$162.50 \text{ cost}$$ |
| **9.2   Calculating the selling price and the markup** | Use the formula $C + M = S$. | Cost, $150; markup, 25% of selling price. Find the selling price and the markup.<br>$C + M = S$<br><br>$\$150 + 0.25S = S$<br>$$\$150 = 0.75S$$<br>$$\$200 = S \quad \text{selling price}$$<br>$$C + M = S$$<br>$$\$150 + M = \$200$$<br>$$M = \$200 - \$150$$<br>$$= \$50$$ |

| | | | |
|---|---|---|---|
| **9.2 Converting markup on cost to markup on selling price** | Use the formula $$M_s = \frac{M_c}{100\% + M_c}.$$ | Markup on cost, 25%. Convert to markup on selling price. $$M_s = \frac{25\%}{100\% + 25\%}$$ $$= \frac{0.25}{1.25} = 0.2 = 20\%$$ | |

| | | |
|---|---|---|
| **9.2 Converting markup on selling price to markup on cost** | Use the formula $$M_c = \frac{M_s}{100\% - M_s}.$$ | Markup on selling price, 20%. Convert to markup on cost. $$M_c = \frac{20\%}{100\% - 20\%}$$ $$= \frac{0.2}{0.8} = 0.25 = 25\%$$ |

| | | |
|---|---|---|
| **9.3 Solving markup with spoilage or unsaleable items** | 1. Find total cost and selling price. <br> 2. Subtract total sales at reduced prices from total sales. <br> 3. Divide the remaining sales by the number of saleable units to get selling price per unit. | 60 doughnuts cost $0.15 each; 10 are not sold; 50% markup on selling price. Find selling price per doughnut. <br> Cost = 60 × $0.15 = $9 <br> $C + M = S$ <br> $9 + 0.5S = S$ <br> $9 = 0.5S$ <br> $18 = S$ <br> $18 ÷ 50 = $0.36 per doughnut |

# Chapter 9 Review Exercises

*Find the missing quantities. Round rates to the nearest tenth of a percent and money to the nearest cent. [9.1]*

| | Cost Price | Markup | % Markup on Cost | Selling Price |
|---|---|---|---|---|
| 1. | $15 | _____ | 20% | _____ |
| 2. | _____ | $13.30 | 35% | _____ |
| 3. | _____ | $73.50 | _____ | $220.50 |
| 4. | $108 | _____ | _____ | $153.90 |

*Find the missing quantities. Round rates to the nearest tenth of a percent and money to the nearest cent. [9.2]*

| | Cost Price | Markup | % Markup on Selling Price | Selling Price |
|---|---|---|---|---|
| 5. | $144.64 | _____ | 20% | _____ |
| 6. | _____ | $25 | _____ | $175 |
| 7. | _____ | $17.35 | $33\frac{1}{3}$% | _____ |
| 8. | $283.02 | $177.18 | _____ | _____ |

*Find the missing quantities by first computing the markup on one base and then computing the markup on the other. Round rates to the nearest tenth of a percent and money to the nearest cent. [9.2]*

| | Cost Price | Markup | Selling Price | % Markup on Cost | % Markup on Selling Price |
|---|---|---|---|---|---|
| 9. | _____ | $70.40 | _____ | 100% | 50% |
| 10. | $64.50 | _____ | $129 | _____ | _____ |
| 11. | _____ | $3.68 | $11.68 | _____ | _____ |
| 12. | _____ | $256.32 | _____ | 25% | _____ |

*Find the equivalent markups on either cost or selling price using the appropriate formula. Round to the nearest tenth of a percent. [9.2]*

| | % Markup on Cost | % Markup on Selling Price |
|---|---|---|
| 13. | _____ | 20% |
| 14. | 100% | _____ |
| 15. | _____ | 15.3% |
| 16. | 20% | _____ |

*Find the selling price per item. [9.3]*

| | Total Cost | Quantity Purchased | Number Unsaleable | % Markup on Selling Price | Selling Price per Item |
|---|---|---|---|---|---|
| 17. | $162 | 180 | 18 | 20% | _____ |
| 18. | $390 | 26 | 6 | 10% | _____ |

| | Total Cost | Quantity Purchased | Number Unsaleable | % Markup on Selling Price | Selling Price per Item |
|---|---|---|---|---|---|
| **19.** | $970 | 9 doz. | 6 | 30% | _____ |
| **20.** | $12,650 | 1,500 pr. | 150 pr. | 45% | _____ |

*Find the missing quantities. Markup is based on total cost. [9.3]*

| | Total Cost | Quantity Purchased | Percent Sold at Reduced Price | % Markup on Total Cost | Number at Regular Price | Number at Reduced Price | Reduced Price | Regular Selling Price Each |
|---|---|---|---|---|---|---|---|---|
| **21.** | $750 | 150 | 10% | 25% | _____ | _____ | $2.50 | _____ |
| **22.** | $135 | 90 pr. | 20% | 40% | _____ | _____ | $1.00 | _____ |
| **23.** | $1,728 | 2 gr. | 25% | 20% | _____ | _____ | $4.00 | _____ |
| **24.** | $2,800 | 1,000 pr. | 30% | 50% | _____ | _____ | $3.00 | _____ |

*Solve each of the following application problems on markup.*

**25.** Olympic Sports and Leisure buys jogging shorts manufactured in Taiwan for $97.50 per dozen pair. Find the selling price per pair if the retailer maintains a markup of 35% on selling price. [9.2]

**26.** Circuit City sells a dishwasher for $395. If the cost of the dishwasher is $334.75, find the markup as a percent of cost. [9.2]

**27.** A wholesaler purchased a carton of toothpaste at a cost of $25.65. If the markup is 15% on cost, find the markup. [9.1]

**28.** Wild Rivers offers an inflatable boat for $199.95. If the boats cost $1,943.52 per dozen, find (a) the markup, (b) the percent of markup on selling price, and (c) the percent of markup on cost. Round to the nearest tenth of a percent. [9.1 and 9.2]

**29.** Raleys Superstore bought 1,820 swimming pool blow-up toys for total cost of $10,010. The toys were sold as follows: 580 at $13.95 each, 635 at $9.95 each, 318 at $8.95 each, 122 at $7.95 each, and the balance at $5.00 each. Find (a) the total selling price of all the toys and (b) the markup as a percent of selling price (to the nearest whole percent). [9.2]

**30.** Fan Fever purchased 200 posters at a cost of $360. If 20% of the posters must be sold at $2 each and a markup of 100% on cost is needed, find the regular selling price of each poster. [9.3]

**31.** Office Depot pays $3.96 for a package of 20-pound paper and sells it for $4.95. Find (a) the percent of markup on selling price and (b) the percent of markup on cost. [9.2]

**32.** Fosters' Doughnuts bakes lemon squares at a cost of $1.93 per dozen. Markup on cost is 100% and 15% of the lemon squares will have to be sold at $2.40 per dozen. If Fosters bakes 180 dozen lemon squares, find the regular selling price per dozen. Round to the nearest cent. [9.3]

# Chapter 9 Summary Exercise

The Hallmark Shop buys 3,400 boxes of holiday greeting cards directly from the manufacturer. The list price of the cards is $4.95 per box, there is a trade discount of 30/10/20, and a cash discount of 5/10-40 x. The Hallmark Shop earns and receives both discounts.

The cards were sold as follows: 1,080 boxes at $3.95, 1,250 boxes at $2.95, 660 boxes at $2.50, 230 boxes at $2.00, and the remaining boxes were unsaleable.

To better manage greeting card sales next year, each of the following must be determined.

**(a)** The net cost of the greeting cards after trade and cash discounts.

**(b)** The total sales amount received from all the holiday greeting cards.

**(c)** The amount of net profit from the sales of the cards.

**(d)** The markup as a percent of selling price to the nearest whole percent.

**(e)** The equivalent percent of markup on cost to the nearest whole percent.

# Markdown and Inventory Control

Management spends a great deal of time controlling inventory. While on one hand the inventory must include the correct kinds and quantities of products to satisfy customers, it is equally important to control inventory to minimize any unsaleable or surplus merchandise. If inventory is too low, product choices may be limited and customers will go to other stores to do their shopping. However, if inventory is too high, merchandise may become dated while it sits on the shelves, tying up needed business capital. This chapter discusses some of the main ideas of inventory control.

## 10.1 Markdown

**OBJECTIVES**

1. *Calculate markdown and reduced price.*
2. *Calculate percent of markdown.*
3. *Find original selling price.*
4. *Identify the terms associated with loss.*
5. *Determine the breakeven point and operating loss.*
6. *Determine the amount of absolute loss and the percent of absolute loss.*
7. *Find the maximum percent of markdown to be given.*

Merchandise often does not sell at its marked price, for any of several reasons. The retailer may have ordered too much, or the merchandise may have become soiled or damaged, or perhaps only odd sizes and colors are left. Also, merchandise may not sell because of lower prices at other stores, seasonal changes, economic fluctuations,

**No Weather Is Good Weather**

Lingering Warm Weather Is Blamed
For Keeping Shoppers Out of Malls

*Changing Weather Should Mean
Mixed Nov. Retail Sales Reports*

Weather Puts Retail Sales on Ice in January

Retail Executives Blame
Weather for March Sales

Bad Weather Rains Out
Retail Apparel Sales in May

Weather Bashes Retail Biz

or changes in fashion. The newspaper headlines above show that low sales volume is even blamed on the weather.

**OBJECTIVE** **1** *Calculate markdown and reduced price.* When merchandise does not sell at its marked price, its price is often reduced. The difference between the original selling price and the reduced selling price is called the **markdown**, with the selling price after the markdown called **reduced price**, **sale price**, or **actual selling price**. The basic formula for markdown is as follows.

Reduced price = Original price − Markdown

**EXAMPLE 1** *Finding the Reduced Price*

Price-Cosco has marked down a Coleman Canoe. Find the reduced price if the original price was $480 and the markdown is 25%.

**SOLUTION** The markdown is 25% of $480, or 0.25 × $480 = $120. The reduced price is

$480 (original price) − $120 (markdown) = $360 (reduced price) ∎

*The calculator solution to this example uses the complement with respect to one of the 25% discount.

CALCULATOR APPROACH
TO EXAMPLE 1

$$480 \times (1 - .25) = 360$$

**OBJECTIVE** **2** *Calculate percent of markdown.*    The next example shows how to find a **percent** or **rate of markdown**.

**NOTE** The original selling price is always the base or 100% and the percent of markdown is always calculated on the original selling price.  ∎

| **EXAMPLE 2** *Calculating the Percent of Markdown*

The total inventory of Mother's Day cards has a retail value of $785. If the cards were sold at reduced prices that totaled $530, what is the percent of markdown on the original price?

**SOLUTION** First find the amount of the markdown.

$785 (original price) − $530 (reduced price) = $255 (markdown)

To solve for percent of markdown on original price, use the percent equation: Rate × Base = Part. The base is the original price of $785, the rate is unknown, and the part is the amount of markdown or $255.

$$R \times B = P$$
$$_____\% \times \$785 = \$255$$
$$R \times \$785 = \$255$$
$$\$785R = \$255$$
$$R = \frac{255}{785}$$
$$R = 0.3248 = 32\% \qquad \text{rounded to the nearest whole percent}$$

The cards were sold at a markdown of 32%.  ∎

*NOTE: All calculator solutions use a scientific calculator. Refer to Appendix A for scientific and financial calculator basics.

CALCULATOR APPROACH
TO EXAMPLE 2

In the calculator solution, the reduced price is subtracted from the original price using parentheses. This results in the markdown which is then divided by the original price.

( 785 − 530 ) ÷ 785 = 0.3248

**OBJECTIVE 3** *Find original selling price.*

**EXAMPLE 3**  *Finding the Original Price*

Find the original price if a child's rain coat is offered at the reduced price of $18 after a 40% markdown from the original price.

**SOLUTION**    After the 40% markdown, the reduced price represents 60% of the original price. Find the original price, which is the base.

$$R \times B = P$$
$$60\% \times B = \$18$$
$$0.6B = \$18$$
$$\frac{18}{0.6} = \$30$$

The original price of the rain coat was $30.    ■

**OBJECTIVE 4** *Identify the terms associated with loss.*    The amount of markdown must be large enough to sell the merchandise while providing as much profit as possible. Merchandise which is marked down will result in either a *reduced net profit*, *breaking even*, an *operating loss*, or an *absolute loss*. Figure 10.1 illustrates the meanings of these terms.

**Reduced net profit** results when the reduced price is still within the net profit range; that is, when it is greater than the total cost plus operating expenses.

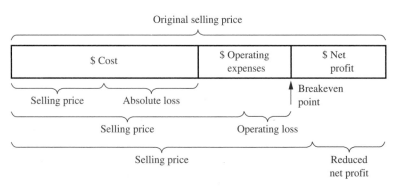

FIGURE 10.1

| | Cost | Operating Expense | Breakeven Point | Reduced Price | Operating Loss | Absolute Loss |
|---|---|---|---|---|---|---|
| **15.** | $50 | _____ | $66 | $44 | _____ | _____ |
| **16.** | $12.50 | _____ | $16.50 | $11 | _____ | _____ |
| **17.** | $310 | $75 | _____ | _____ | $135 | _____ |
| **18.** | $25 | $8 | _____ | _____ | $11 | _____ |
| **19.** | _____ | _____ | _____ | $25 | $14 | $4 |
| **20.** | _____ | _____ | _____ | $100 | $56 | $16 |

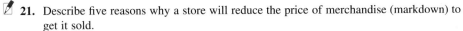

**21.** Describe five reasons why a store will reduce the price of merchandise (markdown) to get it sold.

**22.** As a result of a markdown, there are three possible results: reduced net profit, operating loss, and absolute loss. As a business owner, which would concern you the most? Explain. (See Objective 4.)

*Solve each of the following application problems. Round rates to the nearest whole percent and money to the nearest cent.*

**23.** A Whirlpool 18-cubic foot refrigerator is marked down $131.49, a reduction of 18%. Find the original price.

**24.** A General Electric 4-head VCR with remote is marked down 15% to $158.95. Find the original price.

**25.** After water damage, A and A Builders priced their entire stock of carpeting at $37,180. If the original price of the carpet was $68,500, find the percent of markdown on the original price.

**26.** World Electronics prices their entire inventory of last year's model videocassette recorders (VCRs) at $44,503. If the original price of these VCRs was $75,428, find the percent of markdown on the original price.

**27.** The Persian and Oriental Rug Gallery paid $2,211 for an imported rug from China. Their operating expenses are $33\frac{1}{3}$% of cost. If they sell the rug at a clearance price of $2,650, find the amount of profit or loss.

**28.** Ship Shape Shop has an end-of-season sale during which it sells a stationary bicycle for $265. If the cost was $198 and the operating expenses were 25% of cost, find the amount of profit or loss.

**29.** American Antique paid $153.49 for a fern stand. Their original selling price was $208.78 but this was marked down 46% in order to make room for incoming merchandise. If operating expenses are 14.9% of cost, find (a) the operating loss, (b) the absolute loss, and (c) the percent of absolute loss based on cost.

**30.** Pep Boys Automotive paid $208.50 for a pick-up truck bed liner. The original selling price was $291.90, but this was marked down 35%. If operating expenses are 28% of cost, find (a) the operating loss, (b) the absolute loss, and (c) the percent of absolute loss based on cost.

**31.** Photo Supply, a retailer, pays $190 for an enlarger. The store's operating expenses are 20% of cost and net profit is 15% of cost. Find (a) the selling price of the enlarger and (b) the maximum percent of markdown which may be given without taking an operating loss (round to the nearest whole percent).

**32.** A room air conditioner cost a retailer $278. The store's operating expenses are 30% of cost and net profit is 10% of cost. Find (a) the selling price of the air conditioner and (b) the maximum percent of markdown that may be given without taking an operating loss.

## 10.2    Average Inventory and Inventory Turnover

**OBJECTIVES**

**1**  *Determine average inventory.*

**2**  *Calculate stock turnover at retail.*

**3**  *Calculate stock turnover at cost.*

**4**  *Identify considerations in stock turnover.*

The average time needed for merchandise to sell is a common measure of the efficiency of a business. The number of times that the merchandise sells during a certain period of time is called the **inventory turnover** or the **stock turnover**. Businesses such as florist shops or produce departments have a very fast turnover of merchandise, perhaps just a few days. On the other hand, a furniture store will normally have a much slower turnover, perhaps several months.

If inventory is kept at a minimum level, less capital is needed to operate the business and the speed of selling the inventory is increased. In addition, the risk of having old and unsaleable merchandise is decreased. On the other hand, if the inventory is too low, sales may be lost due to poor selection and inadequate quantities of merchandise offered to the customer.

**OBJECTIVE 1** *Determine average inventory.*    Find stock turnover by first calculating the **average inventory**. The average inventory for a certain time period is found by adding the inventories taken during the time period and then dividing the total by the number of times that the inventory was taken.

**EXAMPLE 1** *Determining Average Inventory*

The inventory value at Olympic Sports and Leisure was $168,520 on April 1 and $143,240 on April 30. What was the average inventory?

**SOLUTION**    First, add the inventory values.

$$\begin{array}{ll} \$168,520 & \text{(April 1)} \\ + \$143,240 & \text{(April 30)} \\ \hline \$311,760 & \end{array}$$

Then divide by the number of times inventory was taken.

$$\frac{\$311,760}{2} = \$155,880$$

The average inventory was $155,880.    ■

| EXAMPLE 2 *Finding Average Inventory for the Quarter*

The retail value of inventory at Federal Drug was $22,615 on January 1, $18,321 on February 1, $26,718 on March 1, and $16,228 on March 31. Find the average inventory for the first quarter of the year.

**SOLUTION**    First add the inventories and then divide by the number of inventories taken.

$$\frac{\$22,615 + \$18,321 + \$26,718 + \$16,228}{4} = \$20,970.50$$

The average inventory for the first quarter of the year is $20,970.50.    ■

**NOTE**   In Example 2, inventory was taken four times to find the average inventory for the first quarter of the year. To find the average inventory for a period of time, an inventory must be taken at the beginning of the period and one final time at the end of the period. To find average inventory for a full year, it is common to find inventory on the first day of each month and on the last day of the last month. Average inventory is found by adding all these inventory amounts (13 of them) and then dividing by 13, the number of inventories taken. Methods of taking inventory and inventory valuation are discussed in the next section.    ■

**OBJECTIVE** **2** *Calculate stock turnover at retail.*      Most inventories are taken at retail because products or shelf locations are marked with the retail price and not the cost. Also, statistical averages are usually shown as average turnover at retail. Many businesses however, value inventory at cost. For this reason, stock turnover is found by either of these formulas.

$$\text{Turnover at retail} = \frac{\text{Retail sales}}{\text{Average inventory at retail}}$$

$$\text{Turnover at cost} = \frac{\text{Cost of goods sold}}{\text{Average inventory at cost}}$$

**OBJECTIVE** **3** *Calculate stock turnover at cost.*      Stock turnover may be identical by either method. The variation that often exists is caused by stolen merchandise (called *inventory shrinkage*) or merchandise which has been marked down or has become unsaleable. Normally, **turnover at retail** is slightly lower than **turnover at cost**. For this reason, many businesses prefer this more conservative figure.

| EXAMPLE 3 *Finding Stock Turnover at Retail*

During May, the Country Feed Store has sales of $32,032 and an average retail inventory of $9,856. Find the stock turnover at retail.

### SOLUTION

$$\text{Turnover at retail} = \frac{\text{Retail sales}}{\text{Average inventory at retail}} = \frac{\$32,032}{\$9,856} = 3.25$$

On the average, the store turned over its entire inventory 3.25 times during the month. ∎

### EXAMPLE 4    *Finding Stock Turnover at Cost*

If the Country Feed Store in Example 3 used a markup of 40% on selling price and if the cost of goods sold was $19,396, find the stock turnover on cost.

**SOLUTION**    Inventory at retail in the feed store was $9,856. Since markup is 40% on selling price, the cost is 60% of the inventory.

$$C = 0.6 \times \$9,856$$

$$C = \$5,913.60$$

Inventory value at cost is $5,913.60.

$$\text{Turnover at cost} = \frac{\text{Cost of goods sold}}{\text{Average inventory at cost}}$$

$$= \frac{\$19,396}{\$5,913.60} = 3.28 \text{ at cost (rounded)}.$$

The turnover on cost is 3.28. ∎

**NOTE**   In Example 4, the average inventory at cost needed to be calculated. To do this the average markup was used along with the cost of goods sold. Since the markup was 40% on selling price, the cost of goods sold was 60% of the selling price. ∎

**OBJECTIVE 4** *Identify considerations in stock turnover.*    Stock turnover is useful for comparison purposes only. Many trade organizations publish such operating statistics to permit businesses to compare their operation with the industry as a whole. In addition to this, management will compare turnover from period to period and from department to department.

A rapid stock turnover is usually given high priority by management. Some of the benefits are:

- capital invested in inventory is kept at a minimum. This allows additional funds to be used for special purchases and discounts;

- items in inventory are up-to-date, fresher, and are therefore less likely to be sold at a reduced price or loss;

- costly storage space and the other expenses of handling inventory can be minimized.

On the other hand, a high inventory turnover may cause problems which result in reduced profits:

- orders for smaller quantities of goods from wholesalers may result in losses of quantity discounts and thus incur additional processing, handling, and book-keeping expenses;
- items can be sold out which results in customer dissatisfaction.

Both inventory selection and inventory turnover are very important management decisions, and much attention is typically given to this part of the business.

## 10.2 EXERCISES

*Find the average inventory in each of the following.*

| Date | Inventory Amount at Retail |
|------|---------------------------|
| 1. September 1 | $8,479 |
|    September 30 | $11,685 |
| 2. January 1 | $24,880 |
|    July 1 | $32,750 |
|    December 31 | $28,620 |
| 3. July 1 | $18,300 |
|    October 1 | $26,580 |
|    December 31 | $23,139 |
| 4. January 31 | $69,480 |
|    April 30 | $55,860 |
|    July 31 | $80,715 |
|    October 31 | $88,050 |
|    January 31 | $63,975 |

| Date | Inventory Amount at Retail |
|------|---------------------------|
| 5. January 1 | $16,250 |
|    March 1 | $20,780 |
|    May 1 | $28,720 |
|    July 1 | $24,630 |
|    September 1 | $23,550 |
|    November 1 | $34,800 |
|    December 31 | $22,770 |
| 6. January 1 | $65,430 |
|    April 1 | $58,710 |
|    July 1 | $53,410 |
|    October 1 | $78,950 |
|    December 31 | $46,340 |

*Find the stock turnover at retail and at cost in each of the following. Round to the nearest hundredth.*

| | Average Inventory at Cost | Average Inventory at Retail | Cost of Goods Sold | Retail Sales |
|---|---|---|---|---|
| 7. | $17,830 | $35,390 | $50,394 | $99,450 |
| 8. | $15,140 | $24,080 | $67,408 | $106,193 |
| 9. | $22,390 | $32,730 | $178,687 | $259,876 |
| 10. | $30,280 | $48,160 | $134,816 | $212,386 |
| 11. | $26,400 | $42,660 | $270,600 | $437,260 |
| 12. | $72,120 | $138,460 | $259,123 | $487,379 |
| 13. | $180,600 | $256,700 | $846,336 | $1,196,222 |
| 14. | $411,580 | $780,600 | $1,905,668 | $3,559,536 |

📝 **15.** Identify three types of businesses that you think would have a high turnover. Identify three types of businesses that you think would have a low turnover.

📝 **16.** Which departments in a grocery store do you think have the highest turnover? Which ones have the lowest turnover?

*Solve each of the following application problems. Round stock turnover to the nearest hundredth.*

**17.** Sure Fit Upholstery took inventory at the first of each month for the full year. The sum of these inventories was $218,658. On December 31, inventory was again taken and amounted to $17,492. Find the average inventory for the year.

**18.** Inventory at retail at the Barn Stormers Bookstore was $9,716 on April 1, $11,884 on May 1, and $6,532 on June 1. Find the average inventory.

**19.** The Glass Works has an average inventory at cost of $15,730 and cost of goods sold for the same period is $85,412. Find the stock turnover at cost.

**20.** The Jumbo Market has an average canned fruit inventory of $2,320 at retail. Sales of canned fruit for the year were $98,669. Find the stock turnover at retail.

**21.** Capital Plating had an average inventory of $27,250 at retail. The cost of goods sold for the year was $103,400 and a markup of 40% on selling price was used. What was the turnover at cost?

**22.** The Associated Divers uses a markup of 30% on selling price. If their average inventory is $15,650 at retail and the cost of goods sold is $53,023, find the stock turnover at cost.

**23.** The cost of goods sold at Capitol Electric was $2,108,410. The following inventories were taken at cost: $208,180, $247,660, and $114,438. Find the stock turnover at cost.

**24.** Inventory at Harbortown Hobby and Sports was taken at retail value four times and found to be at $53,820, $49,510, $60,820, and $56,380. Sales during the same period were $252,077. Find the stock turnover at retail.

**25.** Posters and Cards had the following inventories at retail: $33,820, $46,240, $39,830, $52,040, and $48,700. If this business uses a 35% markup on cost and the cost of goods sold during this period was $136,450, find the turnover at cost.

**26.** Inventory at Clinton Floor Covering was taken at retail four different times and found to be $98,500, $135,820, $107,420, and $124,300. If the company uses a markup of 25% on cost and the cost of goods sold for this period was $305,920, find the inventory turnover at cost.

## 10.3   Valuation of Inventory

**OBJECTIVES**

1. Define perpetual inventory.
2. Understand uniform product codes (UPC).
3. Use specific identification to value inventory.
4. Use the weighted average method to value inventory.
5. Use the FIFO method to value inventory.
6. Use the LIFO method to value inventory.

**7** *Use the gross profit method to estimate inventory.*

**8** *Use the retail method to estimate inventory.*

OBJECTIVE **1** *Define perpetual inventory.* Placing a value on the merchandise that a firm has in stock is called **inventory valuation**. It is not always easy to place this value on each of the items in inventory. Many large companies keep a **perpetual inventory** by using a computer. As new items are received, the quantity, size, and cost of each are placed in the computer. Sales clerks enter product codes into the cash register (or uniform product codes are entered automatically with an optical scanner), and the computer processes the information. The result is an up to the moment or perpetual inventory value.

OBJECTIVE **2** *Understand uniform product codes (UPC).* **Uniform product codes (UPC)** are the stripes known as "bar codes" that appear on many items sold in stores. Each product and product size is assigned its own code number. These UPCs are a great help in keeping track of inventory.

A portion of a Cracker Jack box is reproduced here to show its product code. The UPC number on the wrapper is 4125723255. The check out clerk in a retail store passes the coded lines over an optical scanner. The numbers are picked up by a computer which recognizes the product by its code. The computer tells the cash register the price of the item. After all the items being purchased have passed over the scanner, the customer receives a detailed cash register receipt that gives a description of each item, the price of each item, and a total purchase price. This system provides more accurate inventory control and lower labor costs for the store.

Most businesses take a **physical inventory** (an actual count of each item in stock at a given time) at regular intervals. For example, inventory may be taken monthly, quarterly, semiannually, or just once a year. An inventory taken at regular time intervals is called a **periodic inventory**.

There are four major methods used for **inventory valuation**.

OBJECTIVE **3** *Use specific identification to value inventory.* The **specific identification method** of inventory valuation is useful where items are easily identified and costs do not fluctuate. If the number of items is large and the exact cost of each unit is not known, then it may be difficult or impossible to use this method of inventory. With specific identification, each item is cost-coded, either with numerals or a letter code. The cost may be included in a group of numbers written on the item or in a 10-letter code (where each letter is different).

For example, if a store uses the code SMALPROFIT, or

| 1 | 2 | 3 | 4 | 5 | 6 | 7 | 8 | 9 | 0 |
|---|---|---|---|---|---|---|---|---|---|
| S | M | A | L | P | R | O | F | I | T, |

then an item bearing the cost code ARF would have a cost of

$$\begin{array}{ccc} A & R & F \\ \downarrow & \downarrow & \downarrow, \\ 3 & 6 & 8 \end{array}$$

or $3.68. An item coded PMITT would have a cost of $529.00.

| EXAMPLE 1 | *Finding the Value of Inventory* |

Hoig's Marine has four fishing boats in stock. Cost codes indicate the following costs to the store.

| | |
|---|---|
| Model A | $2,718 |
| Model B | $2,571 |
| Model C | $3,498 |
| Model D | $3,974 |

Find the value of the fishing boat inventory.

**SOLUTION**     The value of the inventory is found by adding the costs of the four fishing boats.

| | | |
|---|---|---|
| Model A | $2,718 | |
| Model B | 2,571 | |
| Model C | 3,498 | |
| Model D | + 3,974 | |
| | $12,761 | total value of inventory ∎ |

**OBJECTIVE** **4** *Use the weighted average method to value inventory.*     Since the cost of many items changes over time, there may be several of the same items that were purchased at different costs. Because of this variation, there are several common methods used to value an inventory. One method, the **weighted average method**, values the items in an inventory at the average cost of buying them.

| EXAMPLE 2 | *Using Weighted Average (Average Cost) Inventory Valuation* |

Olympic Sports and Leisure made the following purchases of the Explorer External Frame backpack during the year.

| | |
|---|---|
| Beginning inventory | 20 backpacks at $70 |
| January | 50 backpacks at $80 |
| March | 100 backpacks at $90 |
| July | 60 backpacks at $85 |
| October | 40 backpacks at $75 |

At the end of the year there are 75 backpacks in inventory. Use the weighted average method to find the inventory value.

**SOLUTION**     Find the total cost of all the backpacks.

| | | |
|---|---|---|
| Beginning inventory | 20 × $70 = | $1,400 |
| January | 50 × $80 = | $4,000 |
| March | 100 × $90 = | $9,000 |
| July | 60 × $85 = | $5,100 |
| October | 40 × $75 = | $3,000 |
| Total | 270 | $22,500 |

Find the average cost per backpack by dividing this total cost by the number purchased. The average cost per backpack is

$$\frac{\$22,500}{270} = \$83.33 \text{ (rounded)}.$$

Since the average cost is $83.33 and 75 backpacks remain in inventory, the weighted average method gives the inventory value of the remaining backpacks as $83.33 × 75 = $6,249.75.  ∎

---

The calculator solution to this example has several steps. First, find the total number of backpacks purchased and place the total in memory.

$$20 \boxed{+} 50 \boxed{+} 100 \boxed{+} 60 \boxed{+} 40 \boxed{=} 270 \boxed{\text{STO}}$$

Next, find the total cost of all the backpacks purchased and divide by the number stored in memory. This gives the average cost per backpack.

**CALCULATOR APPROACH TO EXAMPLE 2**

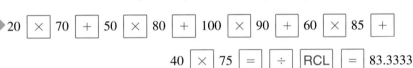

$$20 \boxed{\times} 70 \boxed{+} 50 \boxed{\times} 80 \boxed{+} 100 \boxed{\times} 90 \boxed{+} 60 \boxed{\times} 85 \boxed{+}$$

$$40 \boxed{\times} 75 \boxed{=} \boxed{\div} \boxed{\text{RCL}} \boxed{=} 83.3333$$

Finally, round the average cost to the nearest cent and multiply by the number of backpacks in inventory to get the weighted average inventory value.

$$83.33 \boxed{\times} 75 \boxed{=} 6249.75$$

---

**OBJECTIVE** **5** *Use the FIFO method to value inventory.*     The **first-in, first-out (FIFO) method** of inventory valuation assumes a natural flow of goods through the inventory: the first goods to arrive are the first goods to be sold, so, the last items purchased are the items remaining in inventory.

**EXAMPLE 3** *Using FIFO Inventory Valuation*

Use the FIFO method to find the inventory value of the 75 backpacks from Olympic Sports and Leisure in Example 2.

**SOLUTION**     With the FIFO method, the 75 remaining backpacks are assumed to consist of the 40 packbacks bought in October and 35 (75 − 40 = 35) backpacks from the previous purchase in July.
    The value of the inventory is.

| | | |
|---|---|---|
| October | 40 backpacks at $75 = $3,000 | value of last 40 |
| July | 35 backpacks at $85 = $2,975 | value of previous 35 |
| | 75 valued at          $5,975 | |

The value of the backpack inventory is $5,975 using the FIFO method.  ∎

**OBJECTIVE** **6** *Use the LIFO method to value inventory.*    The **last-in, first-out (LIFO) method** of inventory valuation assumes a flow of goods through the inventory that is just the opposite of the FIFO method. With LIFO, the goods remaining in inventory are the first goods purchased.

**EXAMPLE 4** *Using LIFO Inventory Valuation*

Use the LIFO method to value the 75 backpacks in inventory at Olympic Sports and Leisure (see Example 2).

**SOLUTION**    The calculation starts with the beginning inventory and moves through the year's purchases, resulting in 75 backpacks. The beginning inventory and January purchases come to 70 backpacks, so the cost of 5 more ($75 - 70 = 5$) backpacks from the March purchase is needed.

| | | |
|---|---|---|
| Beginning inventory | 20 backpacks at $70 = $1,400 | value of first 20 |
| January | 50 backpacks at $80 = $4,000 | value of next 50 |
| March | 5 backpacks at $90 = $450 | value of last 5 |
| Total | 75 valued at   $5,850 | |

The value of the backpack inventory is $5,850 using the LIFO method.    ■

Depending on the method of valuing inventories that is used, Olympic Sports and Leisure may show the inventory value of the 75 backpacks as follows.

| | |
|---|---|
| Average cost method | $6,249.75 |
| FIFO | $5,975 |
| LIFO | $5,850 |

The preferred inventory valuation method would be determined by Olympic Sports and Leisure, perhaps on the advice of an accountant. The comparison of inventory evaluation methods below would help them in selecting the method.

---

**COMPARING INVENTORY EVALUATION METHODS**

- When the market is stable, prices do not fluctuate. Since prices are not changing, all methods give the *same* inventory value.

- In a market where prices are rising and falling, each method gives a *different* inventory value.

- Weighted average costs tend to *smooth out* inventory values that might result from price fluctuations.

- The FIFO method results in an inventory value that most closely reflects the *current* replacement cost of inventory.

- The LIFO method results in the last cost of inventory being assigned to the cost of merchandise sold. This results in a *closer matching* of current costs with sales revenues.

**NOTE**  Accepted accounting practice insists that the method used to evaluate inventory be stated on the company financial statements.  ■

The large quantities and varied types of items that are often in inventory make it time-consuming and expensive to take an actual physical inventory. Where this is the case, a physical inventory may be taken only once or twice a year. However, the need to monitor the performance of the business throughout the year is extremely important. To do this, methods of approximating inventory value have been developed. Two common methods for doing this are the *gross profit method* and the *retail method*.

**OBJECTIVE  7**  *Use the gross profit method to estimate inventory.*     An estimate of inventory using the **gross profit method** is found as follows.

$$
\begin{array}{l}
\phantom{+}\text{Beginning inventory (at cost)} \\
+\ \text{Purchase (at cost)} \\
\hline
\phantom{+}\text{Merchandise available for sale (at cost)} \\
-\ \text{Cost of goods sold} \\
\hline
\phantom{+}\text{Ending inventory (at cost)}
\end{array}
$$

The beginning inventory and amount of purchases are taken from company records and the cost of goods sold is normally determined by applying the rate of markup to the amount of net sales.

**EXAMPLE 5**  *Estimating Inventory Value Using the Gross Profit Method*

Inventory on June 30 was $242,000. During the next three months, the company had purchases of $425,000 and net sales of $528,000. Use the gross profit method to estimate the value of the inventory on September 30 if the company uses a markup of 25% on selling price.

**SOLUTION**  First, find the cost of goods sold. Since markup is 25% of selling price, find cost.

$$C + M = S$$
$$C + 0.25S = S$$
$$C + 0.25S - 0.25S = S - 0.25S$$
$$C = S - 0.25S$$
$$C = 0.75S$$
$$C = 0.75 \times \$528{,}000 = \$396{,}000$$

The cost of goods sold is $396,000. Now use the gross profit method.

| | |
|---|---|
| $242,000 | beginning inventory (June 30) |
| + 425,000 | purchases |
| $667,000 | merchandise available for sale |
| − 396,000 | cost of goods sold |
| $271,000 | ending inventory (September 30) |

The estimated value of the inventory on September 30 is $271,000.    ■

**OBJECTIVE** **8** *Use the retail method to estimate inventory.*    The **retail method** of estimating inventory requires that a business keep records of all purchases at both cost and retail prices. The format for estimating inventory value at retail is the same as that used in estimating inventory using the gross profit method. The difference however, is that all amounts used are at retail. Inventory at retail is estimated as follows.

| |
|---|
| Beginning inventory (at retail) |
| + Purchases (at retail) |
| Merchandise available for sale (at retail) |
| − Net sales |
| Ending inventory (at retail) |

Notice that net sales are used in this method instead of cost of goods sold. Also, ending inventory value at retail must now be changed to an estimated value at cost. This is done by multiplying the ending inventory value at retail by a ratio determined by comparing the merchandise available for sale at cost to the merchandise available for sale at retail.

**EXAMPLE 6** *Estimating Inventory Value Using the Retail Method*

At one store, inventory on March 31 was valued at $9,000 at cost and $15,000 at retail. During the next three months, the company made purchases of $36,000 at cost, or $60,000 at retail, and had total sales of $54,000. Use the retail method to estimate the value of inventory at cost on June 30.

**SOLUTION**

| At Cost | At Retail | |
|---|---|---|
| $9,000 | $15,000 | beginning inventory |
| + 36,000 | + 60,000 | purchases |
| $45,000 | $75,000 | merchandise available for sale |
| | − 54,000 | net sales |
| | $21,000 | June 30 inventory (at retail) |

Now find the ratio of merchandise available for sale at cost to merchandise available for sale at retail.

$$\frac{\$45,000}{\$75,000} \quad \begin{array}{l} \text{merchandise available for sale at cost} \\ \text{merchandise available for sale at retail} \end{array}$$

Finally, the estimated inventory value at cost on June 30 is found by multiplying inventory at retail on June 30 by this ratio.

$$\$21,000 \times \frac{45,000}{75,000} = \$12,600 \text{ June 30 inventory (at cost)}$$

The retail method of estimating inventory value assumes that the ratio of the merchandise available for sale at cost to the merchandise available for sale at retail is the same as the ratio of the ending inventory at cost to ending inventory at retail. Both the gross profit method and the retail method of estimating inventories must be updated from time to time with physical inventories to assure accurate record keeping.    ■

## 10.3 EXERCISES

*Find the inventory value in each of the following using the specific identification method.*

| Description | Cost | | Description | Cost |
|---|---|---|---|---|
| 1. fair | $208 | 2. | economy | $1,215 |
| good | $274 | | standard | $1,509 |
| excellent | $345 | | luxury | $1,873 |
| | | | deluxe | $2,116 |
| 3. good | $79 | 4. | incomplete | $835 |
| excellent | $186 | | cheap | $972 |
| mint | $295 | | improved | $1,170 |
| | | | tolerable | $1,360 |

*Find the inventory values using (a) the weighted average method, (b) the FIFO method, and (c) the LIFO method for each of the following. Round to the nearest dollar.*

| Purchases | | Now in Inventory |
|---|---|---|
| 5. Beginning inventory: | 10 units at $8 | |
| June: | 25 units at $9 | |
| August: | 15 units at $10 | 20 units |
| 6. Beginning inventory: | 80 units at $14.50 | |
| July: | 50 units at $15.80 | |
| October: | 70 units at $13.90 | 90 units |
| 7. Beginning inventory: | 50 units at $30.50 | |
| March: | 70 units at $31.50 | |
| June: | 30 units at $33.25 | |
| August: | 40 units at $30.75 | 75 units |
| 8. Beginning inventory: | 700 units at $1.25 | |
| May: | 400 units at $1.75 | |
| August: | 500 units at $2.25 | |
| October: | 600 units at $3.00 | 720 units |

*Solve each of the following application problems. Round to the nearest dollar.*

9. Delta Power Tools had the following table saws in stock.

| Serial Number | Cost |
|---|---|
| 380612 | $275 |
| 793562 | $395 |
| 618751 | $227 |
| 245532 | $875 |
| 112079 | $704 |

Find the inventory value using the specific identification method.

10. Foothill Heat and Cool had the following refrigeration compressors in stock.

| Model Number | Cost |
|---|---|
| AC129 | $428 |
| AC428 | $715 |
| AC2207 | $526 |
| AC78C | $1,718 |
| AC3107 | $635 |

Use the specific identification method to find the inventory value.

11. Raley's Super Store made the following purchases of key ring flashlights made in Taiwan.

| | |
|---|---|
| Beginning inventory: | 24 units at $1.50 |
| June: | 40 units at $1.35 |
| August: | 48 units at $1.25 |
| November: | 18 units at $1.60 |

Inventory at the end of the year shows that 35 units remain. (a) Find the inventory value using the weighted average method. (b) Find the inventory value using the FIFO method. (c) Find the inventory value using the LIFO method.

12. The Graphic Hobby House made purchases of assorted colors of spray paint during the year as follows.

| | |
|---|---|
| Beginning inventory: | 200 cans at $1.10 |
| March: | 400 cans at $1.20 |
| May: | 700 cans at $1.00 |
| August: | 500 cans at $1.15 |
| November: | 300 cans at $1.30 |

At the end of the year, they had 450 cans of spray paint in stock. (a) Find the inventory value using the weighted average method. (b) Find the inventory value using the FIFO method. (c) Find the inventory value using the LIFO method.

13. B & B Appliance Repair made the following purchases of dishwasher pumps.

| | |
|---|---|
| Beginning inventory: | 200 units at $3.10 |
| July: | 250 units at $3.50 |
| August: | 300 units at $4.25 |
| October: | 280 units at $4.50 |

Inventory at the end of October shows that 320 units remain. (a) Find the inventory value using the weighted average method. (b) Find the inventory value using the FIFO method. (c) Find the inventory value using the LIFO method.

14. Marco Muffler Wholesalers made purchases of automobile mufflers throughout the year as follows.

| | |
|---|---|
| Beginning inventory: | 300 units at $21.60 |
| March: | 400 units at $24.00 |
| August: | 450 units at $24.30 |
| November: | 350 units at $22.50 |

An inventory at the end of December shows that 530 mufflers remain. (a) Find the inventory value using the weighted average method. (b) Find the inventory value using the FIFO method. (c) Find the inventory value using the LIFO method.

15. Central States Auto Wholesalers made the following purchases of antifreeze.

| | |
|---|---|
| Beginning inventory: | 350 cases at $8.25 |
| October: | 300 cases at $9.50 |
| November: | 360 cases at $11.45 |
| December: | 240 cases at $10.10 |

The January inventory found that there were 625 cases remaining. (a) Find the inventory value using the weighted average method. (b) Find the inventory value using the FIFO method. (c) Find the inventory value using the LIFO method.

16. Industrial Linen Supply made the following purchases of shop towels.

| | |
|---|---|
| Beginning inventory: | 650 towels at $3.80 |
| June: | 500 towels at $4.20 |
| September: | 450 towels at $3.95 |
| December: | 600 towels at $4.05 |

In January an inventory found that there were 775 towels remaining. (a) Find the inventory value using the weighted average method. (b) Find the inventory value using the FIFO method. (c) Find the inventory value using the LIFO method.

17. The inventory on December 31 at Safe Security Doors was $136,000 at cost. During the next 3 months, the company made purchases of $148,000 (cost) and had net sales of $236,000. Use the gross profit method to estimate the value of the inventory at cost on March 31 if the company uses a markup of 35% on selling price.

18. Happy Toys has an inventory of $52,000 at cost on June 30. Purchases during the next 3 months were $68,000 (cost) and net sales were $126,000. If the company uses a 40% markup on selling price, use the gross profit method to estimate the value of the inventory at cost on September 30.

19. The September 30 inventory at Liverpool Piano Repair was $43,750 at cost and $62,500 at retail. Purchases during the next 3 months were $51,600 at cost, $73,800 at retail, and net sales were $92,500. Use the retail method to estimate the value of inventory at cost on December 31.

20. Tower Video had an inventory of $54,000 at cost and $90,000 at retail on March 31. During the next 3 months, they made purchases of $216,000 at cost, $360,000 at retail, and had net sales of $324,000. Use the retail method to estimate the value of inventory at cost on June 30.

21. In your opinion, what are the benefits to a merchant who is using uniform product codes (UPC)? (See Objective 2.)

22. List the four inventory valuation methods discussed in this section. Explain how one of these methods is used to determine inventory value.

# Chapter 10 Quick Review

| TOPIC | APPROACH | EXAMPLE |
|---|---|---|
| **10.1  Percent of markdown** | Markdown is always a percent of the original price. Use the formula $$\frac{\text{Markdown}}{\text{percent}} = \frac{\text{Markdown amount}}{\text{Original price}}.$$ | Original price, $76; markdown, $19. Find the percent of markdown. $$\frac{\text{Markdown}}{\text{percent}} = \frac{19}{76}$$ $$= 0.25 = 25\%$$ |
| **10.1  Breakeven point** | Add cost to operating expenses to find the breakeven point. | Cost, $54; operating expenses, $16. Find the breakeven point. $54 + $16 = $70 breakeven point |
| **10.1  Operating loss** | When the reduced price is below the breakeven point, subtract the reduced price from the breakeven point to find the operating loss. | Breakeven point, $70; reduced price, $58. Find the operating loss. $70 − $58 = $12 operating loss |
| **10.1  Absolute loss (Gross loss)** | When the reduced price is below cost, subtract the reduced price from the cost to find the absolute loss. | Cost, $54; reduced price, $48. Find the absolute loss. $54 − $48 = $6 absolute loss |

| 10.2 | **Average inventory** | Take inventory two or more times; add the totals and divide by the number of inventories to get the average. | Inventories: $22,635, $24,692, and $18,796. Find the average inventory. $$\frac{\$22,635 + \$24,692 + \$18,796}{3}$$ $$= \frac{\$66,123}{3} = \$22,041 \text{ average inventory}$$ |
|---|---|---|---|
| 10.2 | **Turnover at retail** | Use the formula $$\text{Turnover} = \frac{\text{Retail sales}}{\text{Average inventory at retail}}.$$ | Sales, 78,496; average inventory at retail, $18,076. Find turnover at retail. $$\frac{\$78,496}{\$18,076}$$ $$= 4.34 \text{ at retail (rounded)}$$ |
| 10.2 | **Turnover at cost** | Use the formula $$\text{Turnover} = \frac{\text{Cost of goods sold}}{\text{Average inventory at cost}}.$$ | Cost of goods sold, $26,542; average inventory at cost, $6,592. Find turnover at cost. $$\frac{\$26,542}{\$6,592}$$ $$= 4.03 \text{ at cost (rounded)}$$ |
| 10.3 | **Specific identification to value inventory** | Cost code each item; add the costs to find total inventory. | Costs: item 1, $593; item 2, $614; item 3, $498. Find total value of inventory. $593 + $614 + $498 = $1,705 |
| 10.3 | **Weighted average method of inventory valuation** | This method values items in an inventory at the average cost of buying them. | Beginning inventory of 20 at $75; purchases of 15 at $80; 25 at $65; 18 at $70; 22 remain in inventory. Find the inventory value. $$20 \times \$75 = \$1,500$$ $$15 \times \$80 = \$1,200$$ $$25 \times \$65 = \$1,625$$ $$18 \times \$70 = \$1,260$$ Totals 78      $5,585 $$\frac{\$5,585}{78} = \$71.60 \text{ average cost}$$ $$\$71.60 \times 22 = \$1,575.20$$ |

| 10.3 | **First-in, first-out (FIFO) method of inventory valuation** | First items in are first sold. Inventory is based on cost of last items purchased. | Beginning inventory of 25 items at $40; purchase on Aug. 7, 30 items at $35; 35 remain in inventory. Find the inventory value. |
|------|------|------|------|

$$30 \times \$35 = \$1,050 \quad \text{(value of last 30)}$$
$$\underline{\ \ 5 \times \$40 = \ \ \$200} \quad \text{(value of previous 5)}$$
Totals 35 $\qquad\quad$ $1,250 $\quad$ value of inventory

| 10.3 | **Last-in, first-out (LIFO) method of inventory valuation** | The goods remaining in inventory are the first goods purchased. | Beginning inventory of 48 items at $20 each; purchase on May 9, 40 items at $25 each; 55 remain in inventory. Find the inventory value. |
|------|------|------|------|

$$48 \times \$20 = \ \ \$960 \quad \text{(value of first 48)}$$
$$\underline{\ \ 7 \times \$25 = \ \ \$175} \quad \text{(value of last 7)}$$
Totals 55 $\qquad\quad$ $1,135 $\quad$ value of inventory

# Chapter 10 Review Exercises

*Find the missing quantities. Round rates to the nearest whole percent and money to the nearest cent. [10.1]*

|    | Original Price | % Markdown | $ Markdown | Reduced Price |
|----|----------------|------------|------------|---------------|
| 1. | $27.50 | 40% | _____ | _____ |
| 2. | _____ | $33\frac{1}{3}\%$ | _____ | $10 |
| 3. | _____ | 50% | $2.70 | _____ |
| 4. | $2,340 | _____ | _____ | $1,755 |

*Complete the following. If there is no operating loss or absolute loss, write* none. *Use Figure 10.1 as a guide. [10.1]*

|    | Cost | Operating Expense | Breakeven Point | Reduced Price | Operating Loss | Absolute Loss |
|----|------|-------------------|-----------------|---------------|----------------|---------------|
| 5. | $75 | _____ | $99 | $66 | _____ | $9 |
| 6. | $160 | $40 | _____ | $186 | _____ | _____ |
| 7. | $78 | $22 | _____ | _____ | $30 | _____ |
| 8. | $5 | $1.25 | _____ | $5.50 | _____ | _____ |

*Find the average inventory in each of the following. [10.2]*

| Date | Inventory Amount at Retail |
|---|---|
| **9.** Beginning inventory: | $23,683 |
| March 31: | $31,615 |
| **11.** Beginning inventory: | $77,159 |
| April 1: | $67,305 |
| July 1: | $80,664 |
| October 1: | $95,229 |
| December 31: | $61,702 |

| Date | Inventory Amount at Retail |
|---|---|
| **10.** Beginning inventory: | $316,481 |
| July 1: | $432,185 |
| December 31: | $296,738 |
| **12.** Beginning inventory: | $36,502 |
| April 1: | $27,331 |
| July 1: | $28,709 |
| October 1: | $32,153 |
| December 31: | $39,604 |

*Find the stock turnover at retail and at cost in each of the following. Round to the nearest hundredth. [10.2]*

| | Average Inventory at Cost | Average Inventory at Retail | Cost of Goods Sold | Retail Sales |
|---|---|---|---|---|
| **13.** | $7,060 | $12,786 | $40,656 | $73,264 |
| **14.** | $22,390 | $32,730 | $178,687 | $259,876 |
| **15.** | $90,300 | $128,350 | $423,168 | $598,111 |
| **16.** | $102,895 | $195,150 | $476,417 | $889,884 |

*Find the inventory value in each of the following using the specific identification method. [10.2]*

| Description | Cost |
|---|---|
| **17.** small | $87 |
| medium | $136 |
| large | $205 |
| **19.** economy | $795 |
| standard | $850 |
| luxury | $915 |
| deluxe | $1,080 |

| Description | Cost |
|---|---|
| **18.** poor | $182 |
| fair | $276 |
| good | $355 |
| **20.** good | $1,283 |
| better | $1,398 |
| best | $1,564 |
| superb | $1,772 |

*Solving the following application problems.*

**21.** An industrial floor buffer originally priced at $1,850 is marked down to $1,332. Find the percent of markdown on the original price. [10.1]

22. A portable telephone costs a retailer $56. The store's operating expenses are 30% of cost and net profit is 10% of cost. Find (a) the selling price of the portable telephone and (b) the maximum percent of markdown that may be given without taking an operating loss. (Round to the nearest whole percent.) [10.1]

23. Red Cross Medical Supplies had an inventory of $58,664 on January 1, $73,815 on July 1, and $62,938 on December 31. Find the average inventory. [10.2]

24. The Leaded Glass Exchange has an average inventory of $2,820 at cost. If the cost of goods sold for the year was $30,375, find the stock turnover at cost. [10.2]

25. Inventory at a local store was taken at retail value four times and was found to be $53,820, $49,510, $60,820, and $56,380. Sales during the same period were $252,077. Find the stock turnover at retail. [10.3]

26. Thunder Manufacturing made the following purchases of rivet drums during the year: 25 at $135 each, 40 at $165 each, 15 at $108.50 each, and 30 at $142 each. An inventory shows that 45 rivet drums remain. (a) Find the inventory value using the weighted average method. (b) Find the inventory value using the FIFO method. (c) Find the value of the inventory using the LIFO method. [10.3]

27. The inventory on December 31 at Modern Clothiers was $118,000 at cost. During the next 3 months, the company made purchases of $186,000 (cost) and had net sales of $378,000. Use the gross profit method to estimate the value of the inventory at cost on March 31 if the company uses a markup of 50% on selling price. [10.3]

28. Tap Plastics had an inventory of $54,000 at cost and $90,000 at retail on June 30. During the next 3 months, they made purchases of $216,000 at cost, $360,000 at retail, and had net sales of $324,000. Use the retail method to estimate the value of the inventory at cost on September 30. [10.3]

# Chapter 10 Summary Exercise

McIntosh Pet Center purchased two dozen pet travel cages at a cost of $780. Operating expenses for the store are 25% of cost while total markup on this type of product is 35% of selling price. Only 6 of the cages sell at the original price and the owner decides to markdown the remaining cages. The price is reduced 25% and 6 more cages sell. The remaining 12 cages are marked down 50% of the original selling price and are finally sold.

(a) Find the original selling price of each cage.

(b) Find the total of the selling prices of all the cages.

(c) Find the operating loss.

(d) Find the absolute loss.

# Simple Interest

Some of the oldest documents in existence—clay tablets dating back almost 5,000 years—show the calculation of interest charges. **Interest**, a fee for borrowing money, is about as old as civilization itself.

The largest and financially most secure companies such as IBM and AT&T borrow at or near the most favorable interest rate for short-term loans, known as the **prime rate**. The prime rate is an important factor in determining the rates of interest paid to depositors on savings and the rates of interest charged to borrowers on loans. As you can see in Figure 11.1, prime rates fluctuate widely although they typically remain between 6% and 15%. Most short-term interest rates move up and down with the prime rate. For example, when the prime rate moves up, it will likely cost you more to finance a car. It is important to have a good understanding of interest since interest charges can represent a significant cost for both individuals and firms.

Two basic types of interest are in common use today: **simple interest** and **compound interest**. Simple interest is interest paid on only the principal. Compound interest is interest paid on both principal and past interest. This chapter discusses simple interest, and Chapter 13 covers compound interest.

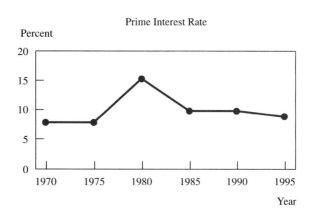

FIGURE 11.1

*Source:* Data taken from Federal Reserve Bulletin. "Federal Reserve Considers Hiking Interest Rates Again."

## 11.1   Basics of Simple Interest

### OBJECTIVES

1. *Find simple interest.*
2. *Find interest for less than a year.*
3. *Find principal if given rate and time.*
4. *Find rate if given principal and time.*
5. *Find time if given principal and rate.*

**Interest** is the price paid for borrowing money. Interest rates are usually expressed as a percent of the amount borrowed. For example, in some states, retail companies such as Sears, Wards, and Penney's charge up to 21% interest per year on money owed to them. The amount borrowed is called the **principal**. The percent of interest charged is called the **rate of interest**. The number of years or fraction of a year for which the loan is made is called the **time**.

**OBJECTIVE** 1 *Find simple interest.*     Simple interest, interest charged on the entire principal for the entire length of the loan, is found by the following formula which is simply a modification of the basic percent formula.

> The *simple interest I*, on a principal of *P* dollars at a rate of interest *R* percent per year for *T* years is given by
>
> $$I = PRT.$$
>
> The rate *R*, is expressed as a decimal or fraction, and time *T*, is expressed as the number of years, or the fraction of a year.

### EXAMPLE 1   *Finding Simple Interest*

Gilbert Construction Company must borrow $60,000 to build an 1,800 square-foot home. The owner, Susan Gilbert, is considering whether she should borrow the funds at (a) 8% for 1 year or (b) $8\frac{1}{2}\%$ for $1\frac{1}{2}$ years. Find the simple interest on both loans.

#### SOLUTION

**(a)** Use the formula $I = PRT$. Substitute $60,000 for *P*, 0.08 (the decimal form of 8%) for *R*, and 1 for *T*.

$$I = PRT$$
$$I = \$60,000 \times 0.08 \times 1$$
$$I = \$4,800 \text{ simple interest}$$

**(b)** Again use the simple interest formula; however, now use $R = 0.085$ ($8\frac{1}{2}\%$) and $T = 1.5$ ($1\frac{1}{2}$ years).

$$I = PRT$$

$$I = \$60,000 \times 0.085 \times 1.5$$

$$I = \$7,650 \text{ simple interest}$$

Gilbert chooses the 1-year loan since she believes that she can build and sell the home within 1 year.    ■

**NOTE** Simple interest is usually used for short-term loans, such as those for less than a year. It is important to remember that in the formula for simple interest, time is expressed *in years* or *parts of years*.    ■

**OBJECTIVE** **2** *Find interest for less than a year.*    Notice in part (a) of the next example how 9 months is written as $\frac{9}{12}$ of a year and in part (b) that 13 months (obviously more than 1 year) is written as $\frac{13}{12}$ or $1\frac{1}{12}$ of a year.

**EXAMPLE 2** *Finding Simple Interest Using Months*

Find the interest on a loan of $2,800 at 8% simple interest for a period of (a) 9 months and a period of (b) 13 months.

**SOLUTION**

**(a)** Since there are 12 months in a year, 9 months is $\frac{9}{12}$ or 0.75 of a year. Find the interest as follows.

$$I = PRT$$

$$I = \$2,800 \times 0.08 \times \frac{9}{12}$$

$$I = \$168$$

**(b)** Use $\frac{13}{12}$ to represent 13 months in terms of number of years.

$$I = PRT$$

$$I = \$2,800 \times 0.08 \times \frac{13}{12}$$

$$I = \$242.67$$    ■

---

**CALCULATOR APPROACH TO EXAMPLE 2**

*The calculator solution to part 2(a) of this example is to use the formula $I = PRT$ and multiply and divide in a chain calculation to find the interest.

2800 ⨯ .08 ⨯ 9 ÷ 12 = 168

---

*NOTE: All calculator solutions use a scientific calculator. Refer to Appendix A for scientific and financial calculator basics.

**OBJECTIVE** **3** *Find principal if given rate and time.*    Sometimes the amount of interest is known, but the principal, rate, or time must be found. Do this with the following modifications of the formula for simple interest.

$$I = PRT$$

$$\frac{I}{RT} = \frac{P\cancel{R}\cancel{T}}{\cancel{R}\cancel{T}} \qquad \text{Divide both sides by } RT.$$

$$\frac{I}{RT} = P \quad \text{or} \quad P = \frac{I}{RT}$$

Similarly, dividing both sides of $I = PRT$ by $PT$ gives the formula for $R$.

$$R = \frac{I}{PT}$$

And dividing both sides of $I = PRT$ by $PR$ gives the formula for $T$.

$$T = \frac{I}{PR}$$

**PROBLEM-SOLVING HINT**  Don't forget, for an annual interest rate, the time is always **in years**.  ■

**NOTE**  You do not have to remember all of these formulas. Just remember $I = PRT$ and use algebra to solve for the unknown.  ■

**EXAMPLE 3** *Finding the Principal*

Jean Videtto's mother wishes to invest enough money so that the interest on the investment, at 4%, will pay Jean's college tuition of $800 in 6 months. How much must be invested?

**SOLUTION**    Find the principal by dividing both sides of $I = PRT$ by $RT$.

$$P = \frac{I}{RT}$$

$$P = \frac{\$800}{0.04 \times \frac{6}{12}} \qquad \text{Substitute values for variables.}$$

$$P = \$40,000$$

A principal of $40,000 invested for 6 months at 4% will generate $800 in interest.  ■

**CALCULATOR APPROACH TO EXAMPLE 3**

For the calculator solution to this example, divide using the chain calculation.

800 ÷ ( .04 × 6 ÷ 12 ) = 40000

**OBJECTIVE 4** *Find rate if given principal and time.*     The next example shows how to find the interest rate if the principal and time are given.

### EXAMPLE 4 *Finding the Rate*

Jeff Guerrant took out a loan of $9,000 for 9 months for a used truck and had an interest charge of $540. What was the interest rate?

**SOLUTION**     Divide both sides of $I = PRT$ by $PT$ to get

$$R = \frac{I}{PT}$$

$$R = \frac{\$540}{\$9,000 \times \frac{9}{12}} \qquad \text{Substitute values for variables.}$$

$$R = 0.08.$$

The rate was 8%.     ∎

**NOTE**  In order to avoid rounding errors, it is important not to round off any calculations too soon when solving these types of problems.     ∎

**OBJECTIVE 5** *Find time if given principal and rate.*     The simple interest formula can also be used to find the time of a loan.

### EXAMPLE 5 *Finding the Time*

Eric Thomas, a loan officer at Midwest Bank, made a loan of $4,800 at 10%. How many months will it take to produce $280 in interest?

**SOLUTION**     Use $I = PRT$ and divide both sides by $PR$ to get

$$T \text{ (in years)} = \frac{I}{PR}.$$

We included "(in years)" to emphasize this important point—time is measured in years. Now substitute $280 for $I$, $4,800 for $P$, and 0.10 for $R$.

$$T \text{ (in years)} = \frac{\$280}{\$4,800 \times 0.10} \qquad \text{Substitute values for variables.}$$

$$T \text{ (in years)} = \frac{\$280}{\$480}$$

Writing $\frac{\$280}{\$480}$ in lowest terms gives

$$T \text{ (in years)} = \frac{7}{12} \text{ year,}$$

or 7 months.     ∎

**NOTE** In all the examples of this section the time has been expressed in years or months. Section 11.2 will deal with interest problems in which the time is expressed in days.  ■

## 11.1  EXERCISES

*Find the simple interest for each of the following. Round to the nearest cent.*

1. $3,400 at 9% for 1 year
2. $5,600 at 14% for $1\frac{1}{2}$ years
3. $860 at 9% for 6 months
4. $1,200 at 8% for 8 months
5. $8,250 at 13% for 15 months
6. $4,270 at 18% for 20 months
7. $9,874 at $7\frac{1}{8}$% for 11 months
8. $10,745 at $4\frac{5}{8}$% for 9 months
9. $74,986.15 at 12.23% for 5 months
10. $39,072.76 at 11.23% for 7 months

*Complete this chart. Round money to the nearest cent, rate to the nearest tenth of a percent, and time to the nearest month.*

| | Principal | Interest | Rate | Time in Months |
|---|---|---|---|---|
| 11. | $5,000 | _____ | 9% | 8 |
| 12. | $7,000 | _____ | 11% | 9 |
| 13. | _____ | $162.50 | 8% | 6 |
| 14. | _____ | $84 | 10% | 7 |
| 15. | $3,800 | $199.50 | _____ | 9 |
| 16. | $2,600 | $144.08 | _____ | 7 |
| 17. | $5,350 | $749 | 12% | _____ |
| 18. | $8,200 | $1,722 | 14% | _____ |

*Solve each application problem. Round money to the nearest cent, rate to the nearest tenth of a percent, and time to the nearest month.*

19. Find the principal on an 8-month loan producing $240 interest at 9.5%.
20. The interest on a 3-month, 8% loan is $19. Find the principal.
21. Find the principal if $245 in interest is due after 10 months at 7%.
22. What amount of principal produces $55 in interest after 1 month at 11%?
23. What time (in months) is necessary for a principal of $840 to produce $77 in interest at 10%?
24. How many months are necessary for $4,800 to produce $44 in interest at 11%?
25. Find the rate if a principal of $1,890 produces $138.60 in interest after 11 months.
26. A loan of $8,500 produces interest of $595 in 7 months. Find the rate.

27. Jackie Botts borrows $45,000 at 11.5% for 3 months in order to build a large swimming pool. Find the interest.

28. Boston Bank borrows $3,500,000 for 4 months at 10% interest. How much interest must they pay?

29. Doug Minder misses a payment on a loan. The payment is 4 months late. The penalty is 9% simple interest on a balance of $7,600. Find the penalty.

30. Trisha Martin bought a new car. To pay for the car, which was priced at $18,250, she gave $4,000 as a down payment and agreed to pay the balance in 5 months. Find the amount of interest charged if the interest rate is $10\frac{1}{4}$%.

31. The Green Care Company needs to borrow $7,000 to buy new lawn mowers. The firm wants to pay no more than $560 in interest. If the interest rate is 12%, what is the longest time for which the money may be borrowed?

32. The Mall Frame Shop wants to borrow $9,300 to remodel the front of the store. The least expensive interest rate they can find is 14%. Find the longest time for which the money may be borrowed if the firm can pay only $1,193.50 in interest.

33. Sam Casio deposits $5,400 in a savings account at the Friendly Savings and Loan Bank. When he withdraws his money 8 months later, he receives a check for $5,544. What rate of interest does the bank pay?

34. Dorothy Duerr invested $7,800 in an account that pays dividends monthly, based on simple interest. If Duerr has received a total of $276.25 over the past ten months, what rate of interest does the account pay?

35. A $2,000 loan was made for 3 months at 7% simple interest. A student calculates the interest due on the loan as follows:

$$I = \$2,000 \times 0.07 \times 3 = \$420.$$

Is this correct? If not, explain why not and state the correct answer. (See Objective 1.)

36. Are you willing to invest your own funds in an account paying 2% per year, for several years? Why or why not?

37. Lupe Garcia needs to borrow $3,200 for 8 months for an operation that she needs this month. She can choose between a credit union charging 10% or a loan company charging 18%. How much will she save by using the credit union?

38. You need to borrow $800 for 4 months and can go to a pawn shop charging 20% interest or to your uncle who will charge 12% interest. Find the difference in the interest charges.

39. An accounting firm wishes to borrow $6,800 for computer upgrades and they believe that they will only be able to repay a total of $7,276 in 6 months. What is the highest interest rate at which they can afford to borrow?

40. Your roommate wishes to borrow $7,875. She believes that she will be able to repay as much as $10,000 in 18 months after she graduates and has several months to save. Find the maximum interest rate she can afford. (Round to the nearest percent.)

41. Gladys' Dress Shop received an invoice for $2,543, with terms of 2/15, n/60. The store can borrow money at the bank at 12%. How much would be saved by borrowing money to take advantage of the cash discount?

42. Westside Pet Supplies received an invoice of $1,796, with terms 1/10, n/30. The store can borrow money at 14.5%. How much would the store save by borrowing money to take advantage of the cash discount?

## 11.2    Simple Interest for a Given Number of Days

**OBJECTIVES**

1  *Find the number of days from one date to another using a table.*

2  *Find the number of days from one date to another using the actual number of days.*

3  *Find exact and ordinary interest.*

The previous section showed how to find simple interest for loans of a given number of months or years. In this section, loans for a given *number of days* are discussed. In business, it is common for loans to be for a given number of days, such as "due in 90 days," or else to be due at some fixed date in the future, such as "due on April 17." You will find this topic useful if you own your own business or if you are involved in the finances of a business.

**OBJECTIVE** 1 *Find the number of days from one date to another using a table.*    There are two ways to find the number of days from one date to another. One way is by the use of Table 11.1. This table assigns a different number to each day of the year. For example, the number for June 11 is found by locating 11 at the left, and June across the top. You should find that June 11 is day 162. Also, December 29 is day 363. The number of days from June 11 to December 29 is found by subtracting.

$$
\begin{array}{lr}
\text{December 29 is day} & 363 \\
\text{June 11 is day} & -\,162 \quad \text{Subtract.} \\
\hline
& 201
\end{array}
$$

There are 201 days from June 11 to December 29. (Throughout this book, ignore leap years unless otherwise stated.)

**EXAMPLE 1** *Finding the Number of Days*

Bill Maxwell makes two loans on October 10. The first loan is due on (a) November 24 and the second loan is due on (b) January 8. Find the number of days of both loans.

**SOLUTION**

**(a)** October 10 is day 283 and November 24 is day 328.

$$
\begin{array}{lr}
\text{November 24 is day} & 328 \\
\text{October 10 is day} & -\,283 \quad \text{Subtract.} \\
\hline
& 45
\end{array}
$$

There are 45 days from October 10 to November 24.

**(b)** Since October 10 is in one year, and January 8 is in the next year, proceed as follows.

TABLE 11.1    **The Number of Each of the Days of the Year (Add 1 to each date after February 29 for a leap year)**

| Day of Month | Jan. | Feb. | March | April | May | June | July | Aug. | Sept. | Oct. | Nov. | Dec. | Day of Month |
|---|---|---|---|---|---|---|---|---|---|---|---|---|---|
| 1 | 1 | 32 | 60 | 91 | 121 | 152 | 182 | 213 | 244 | 274 | 305 | 335 | 1 |
| 2 | 2 | 33 | 61 | 92 | 122 | 153 | 183 | 214 | 245 | 275 | 306 | 336 | 2 |
| 3 | 3 | 34 | 62 | 93 | 123 | 154 | 184 | 215 | 246 | 276 | 307 | 337 | 3 |
| 4 | 4 | 35 | 63 | 94 | 124 | 155 | 185 | 216 | 247 | 277 | 308 | 338 | 4 |
| 5 | 5 | 36 | 64 | 95 | 125 | 156 | 186 | 217 | 248 | 278 | 309 | 339 | 5 |
| 6 | 6 | 37 | 65 | 96 | 126 | 157 | 187 | 218 | 249 | 279 | 310 | 340 | 6 |
| 7 | 7 | 38 | 66 | 97 | 127 | 158 | 188 | 219 | 250 | 280 | 311 | 341 | 7 |
| 8 | 8 | 39 | 67 | 98 | 128 | 159 | 189 | 220 | 251 | 281 | 312 | 342 | 8 |
| 9 | 9 | 40 | 68 | 99 | 129 | 160 | 190 | 221 | 252 | 282 | 313 | 343 | 9 |
| 10 | 10 | 41 | 69 | 100 | 130 | 161 | 191 | 222 | 253 | 283 | 314 | 344 | 10 |
| 11 | 11 | 42 | 70 | 101 | 131 | 162 | 192 | 223 | 254 | 284 | 315 | 345 | 11 |
| 12 | 12 | 43 | 71 | 102 | 132 | 163 | 193 | 224 | 255 | 285 | 316 | 346 | 12 |
| 13 | 13 | 44 | 72 | 103 | 133 | 164 | 194 | 225 | 256 | 286 | 317 | 347 | 13 |
| 14 | 14 | 45 | 73 | 104 | 134 | 165 | 195 | 226 | 257 | 287 | 318 | 348 | 14 |
| 15 | 15 | 46 | 74 | 105 | 135 | 166 | 196 | 227 | 258 | 288 | 319 | 349 | 15 |
| 16 | 16 | 47 | 75 | 106 | 136 | 167 | 197 | 228 | 259 | 289 | 320 | 350 | 16 |
| 17 | 17 | 48 | 76 | 107 | 137 | 168 | 198 | 229 | 260 | 290 | 321 | 351 | 17 |
| 18 | 18 | 49 | 77 | 108 | 138 | 169 | 199 | 230 | 261 | 291 | 322 | 352 | 18 |
| 19 | 19 | 50 | 78 | 109 | 139 | 170 | 200 | 231 | 262 | 292 | 323 | 353 | 19 |
| 20 | 20 | 51 | 79 | 110 | 140 | 171 | 201 | 232 | 263 | 293 | 324 | 354 | 20 |
| 21 | 21 | 52 | 80 | 111 | 141 | 172 | 202 | 233 | 264 | 294 | 325 | 355 | 21 |
| 22 | 22 | 53 | 81 | 112 | 142 | 173 | 203 | 234 | 265 | 295 | 326 | 356 | 22 |
| 23 | 23 | 54 | 82 | 113 | 143 | 174 | 204 | 235 | 266 | 296 | 327 | 357 | 23 |
| 24 | 24 | 55 | 83 | 114 | 144 | 175 | 205 | 236 | 267 | 297 | 328 | 358 | 24 |
| 25 | 25 | 56 | 84 | 115 | 145 | 176 | 206 | 237 | 268 | 298 | 329 | 359 | 25 |
| 26 | 26 | 57 | 85 | 116 | 146 | 177 | 207 | 238 | 269 | 299 | 330 | 360 | 26 |
| 27 | 27 | 58 | 86 | 117 | 147 | 178 | 208 | 239 | 270 | 300 | 331 | 361 | 27 |
| 28 | 28 | 59 | 87 | 118 | 148 | 179 | 209 | 240 | 271 | 301 | 332 | 362 | 28 |
| 29 | 29 | | 88 | 119 | 149 | 180 | 210 | 241 | 272 | 302 | 333 | 363 | 29 |
| 30 | 30 | | 89 | 120 | 150 | 181 | 211 | 242 | 273 | 303 | 334 | 364 | 30 |
| 31 | 31 | | 90 | | 151 | | 212 | 243 | | 304 | | 365 | 31 |

***Step 1***    Find the number of days from October 10 to the end of the year.

last day of the year is number          365
October 10 is day                      − 283          Subtract.
                                        ─────
                                          82

There are 82 days from October 10 to the end of the year.

***Step 2***    Find the number of days from the beginning of the year to January 8. From the table, we see that January 8 is the 8th day of the year.

***Step 3***    Add to get the **total** number of days.

| | | |
|---|---:|---|
| October 10 to the end of the year | 82 | |
| first of year to January 8 | + 8 | Add. |
| | 90 | |

There are 90 days from October 10 to January 8.     ■

**NOTE**    Using this method, you are not counting the day the loan was made, but you are counting the day the money was returned as a full day.    ■

**OBJECTIVE 2**    *Find the number of days from one date to another using the actual number of days.*    An alternate way of finding the number of days, useful when Table 11.1 is not available, is to use the actual number of days in each month, as shown in Table 11.2.

TABLE 11.2   **The Number of Days in Each Month**

| **31 Days** | | **30 Days** | **28 Days** |
|---|---|---|---|
| January | August | April | February |
| March | October | June | (29 days in leap year) |
| May | December | September | |
| July | | November | |

**EXAMPLE 2**   *Finding the Number of Days from One Date to Another Using Actual Days*

Find the number of days from (a) March 12 to June 7 and (b) November 4 to February 21.

**SOLUTION**

**(a)** Since March has 31 days, there are $31 - 12 = 19$ days left in March, then 30 days in April, 31 in May, and an additional 7 days in June for a total of

| | |
|---:|---|
| 19 | remaining in March |
| 30 | April |
| 31 | May |
| + 7 | June |
| 87 | days from March 12 to June 7. |

**(b)** Add.

$$
\begin{array}{rl}
26 & \text{remaining in November} \\
31 & \text{December} \\
31 & \text{January} \\
+\ 21 & \text{February} \\
\hline
109 &
\end{array}
$$

There are 109 days from November 4 to February 21. ∎

### EXAMPLE 3  *Finding Specific Dates*

Find the date that is 90 days from (a) March 25 and (b) November 7.

### SOLUTION

**(a)** From Table 11.1, March 25 is day 84. Add 90.

$$
\begin{array}{rl}
\text{March 25 is day} & 84 \\
+ & 90 \ \text{days} \\
\hline
& 174
\end{array}
$$

As shown in Table 11.1, day 174 is June 23, so 90 days from March 25 is June 23. Alternatively, work as follows.

$$
\begin{array}{lr}
\text{March 25 to end of month} & 6 \\
\text{April} & 30 \\
\text{May} & +\ 31 \\
\hline
& 67
\end{array}
$$

Since $90 - 67 = 23$, an additional 23 days in June are needed, giving June 23.

**(b)** November 7 is day 311. Add 90 days to get

$$
\begin{array}{r}
311 \\
+\ 90 \\
\hline
401.
\end{array}
$$

Since there are only 365 days in a year, subtract 365.

$$
\begin{array}{rl}
401 & \\
-\ 365 & \\
\hline
36 & \text{day of the following year}
\end{array}
$$

Day 36 of the following year is February 5, so that 90 days from November 7 is February 5 of the following year. ∎

In the formula for simple interest, time is always measured in years or parts of years. In the examples of the previous section, time was in months, with $T$ in the formula $I = PRT$ written as

$$
T = \frac{\text{Given number of months}}{12}.
$$

**OBJECTIVE 3** *Find exact and ordinary interest.*    Things are not so simple when the loan is given in days—there are two common methods for calculating simple interest for a given number of days: **exact interest**, and **ordinary** or **banker's interest**.

In the formula $I = PRT$, the fraction for time is found as follows.

Exact interest    $T = \dfrac{\text{Exact number of days in the loan}}{365}$

Ordinary or
banker's interest    $T = \dfrac{\text{Exact number of days in the loan}}{360}$

Government agencies and the Federal Reserve Bank use exact interest, as do many credit unions, while most banks and other financial institutions use ordinary interest. Ordinary interest may have been used originally because it is easier to calculate than exact interest. With the modern use of calculators and computers, however, ordinary interest is probably used today out of tradition and because it produces a greater amount of interest than does exact interest, as shown in the next example.

**EXAMPLE 4** *Finding Exact and Ordinary Interest*

Tyler Radio Shop borrowed $17,650 on May 12. The loan, at an interest rate of 13.5%, is due on August 27. Find the interest on the loan using (a) exact interest and (b) ordinary interest.

**SOLUTION**    Using the table or calculating the number of days in each month, there are 107 days from May 12 to August 27.

**(a)** The exact interest is found from $I = PRT$ with $P = \$17,650$, $R = 0.135$, and $T = \frac{107}{365}$. (Remember to use 365 as the denominator with exact interest.)

$$I = PRT$$

$$I = \$17,650 \times 0.135 \times \frac{107}{365}$$

$$I = \$698.50 \text{ (rounded)}$$

**(b)** Find ordinary interest with the same formula and values, except that $T = \frac{107}{360}$.

$$I = PRT$$

$$I = \$17,650 \times 0.135 \times \frac{107}{360}$$

$$I = \$708.21 \text{ (rounded)}$$

In this example, the ordinary interest is $708.21 - \$698.50 = \$9.71$ more than the exact interest.    ∎

The method for forming the *time fraction* used for $T$ in the formula $I = PRT$ is summarized as follows.

The *numerator* is the *exact number* of days of the loan.

The *denominator* is one of the following:
  *exact interest* assumes 365 days in a year and uses 365 as denominator.
  *Ordinary*, or *banker's*, *interest* assumes 360 days in a year and uses 360 as denominator.

For example, $T$ for a 60-day loan using banker's interest would be

$$T = \frac{60}{360} = \frac{1}{6}.$$

**NOTE** Throughout the balance of this book, assume ordinary, or banker's, interest unless stated otherwise. ■

## 11.2 EXERCISES

*Find the exact number of days from the first date to the second. (In Exercises 5–6, assume that the second month given is in the following year.)*

1. June 5 to October 15
2. January 3 to August 10
3. October 27 to December 2
4. July 12 to October 29
5. September 2 to March 17
6. July 24 to March 30

*Find the date that is the indicated number of days from the given date.*

7. 80 days from March 12
8. 45 days from July 28
9. 30 days from February 8
10. 90 days from November 18
11. 120 days from December 12
12. 150 days from November 1

*How much ordinary interest would you pay for each of the following? Round to the nearest cent.*

13. $850 at 8% for 60 days
14. $980 at $9\frac{1}{2}$% for 90 days
15. $3,250 at 12% for 150 days
16. $8,620 at 11.25% for 120 days
17. A loan of $1,250 at 11% made on May 9 and due August 25
18. A loan of $680.40 at 12% made on June 20 and due December 26
19. A loan of $1,520 at 10% made on February 27 and due August 5
20. A loan of $3,600 at 11% made on December 2 and due February 20

*Find the exact interest for each of the following. Round to the nearest cent.*

**21.** $1,200 at 9% for 75 days

**22.** $3,800 at $7\frac{3}{4}$% for 120 days

**23.** $4,600 at 13% for 60 days

**24.** $3,150 at 12.5% for 200 days

**25.** A loan of $6,500 at 7% made on July 12 and due on October 12

**26.** A loan of $8,120 at 9% made on January 30 and due May 20

**27.** A loan of $2,050 at 12% made on June 24 and due February 12 of the next year

**28.** A loan of $14,000 at 8% made on August 12 and due March 19 of the next year

**29.** Explain the difference between exact and ordinary interest. (See Objective 3.)

**30.** Explain why ordinary interest results in more interest than does exact interest. (See Objective 3.)

*Solve each of the following application problems using exact interest. Round to the nearest cent.*

**31.** Oscar Torres' property tax is due April 10. He doesn't pay until June 22. The county adds a penalty of 11% simple interest on his unpaid tax of $946.50. Find the penalty.

**32.** Bella Steinem misses an income tax payment. The payment was due June 15 and was paid September 7. The penalty is 14% simple interest on the unpaid tax of $4,600. Find the penalty.

**33.** Burns Construction borrows $56,000 on October 23 at 12% simple interest. Find the interest that must be paid on March 15.

**34.** Future Tech Inc. borrows $28,000 on November 9 for computer purchases and agrees to repay the 12% interest loan on March 30 of the following year. Find the interest.

*Solve each application problem using ordinary interest.*

**35.** Lisa Brink opened a security service. To pay for the building the firm uses, Brink borrowed $134,500 at the bank on March 3, agreeing to repay the money on December 12, at $11\frac{3}{8}$% interest. Find the interest she must pay.

**36.** On May 18, the Wilson Dude Ranch bought a supply of cowboy outfits for $11,270. The ranch agreed to pay for them on August 30, with $10\frac{1}{2}$% interest. Find the interest owed.

**37.** Gilbert Construction Company can borrow $80,000 for 120 days at 11% interest. In 1980, the same note would have been at a rate of 20%. Find the difference in the interest charges based on the two rates.

**38.** A construction company in Mexico City borrows 300,000 pesos for 90 days at an interest rate of 18%. The same loan would have been at a rate of 35% several years ago. Find the difference in the interest charges based on the two rates.

*In Exercises 39–42 find the (a) exact interest and (b) ordinary interest for each of the following. Then (c) find the amount by which the ordinary interest is larger.*

**39.** $24,000 at 10% for 90 days

**40.** $75,000 at 11% for 120 days

**41.** $145,000 at $9\frac{1}{2}$% for 240 days

**42.** $250,000 at $12\frac{1}{8}$% for 180 days

*Solve each of the following application problems.*

**43.** Classic Jewelry needs to borrow $160,000 to finance an inventory of jewelry for Christmas sales. The loan will be for 95 days at $9\frac{5}{8}$%. How much more would the interest be at a bank using ordinary interest than at one using exact interest?

**44.** Life Foods wants to borrow $120,000 to take advantage of a manufacturer's overstock and buy a large inventory of granola. The firm can sell the granola in 120 days, when it will pay off the loan. The interest rate is $13\frac{1}{2}$%. How much more would the firm pay at a bank using ordinary interest than at a bank using exact interest?

**45.** Blaine Trucking wishes to borrow $880,000 for new trucks on September 20 and plans to pay off the loan on May 1 of the following year. State Bank will lend them the funds at 9% based on exact interest calculations. First Bank will lend them the funds at $8\frac{7}{8}$% interest based on ordinary interest calculations. Which bank is asking for less interest? How much less?

**46.** A Canadian construction firm needs to borrow an additional $3,500,000 for 150 days to build a bridge linking Mexico to the United States. National Bank will lend them the funds at $10\frac{1}{2}$% simple interest based on exact interest calculations, and Laredo Bank will lend them the funds at $10\frac{5}{8}$% simple interest based on ordinary interest calculations. Which bank is asking for less interest? How much less?

 **Maturity Value**

### OBJECTIVES

**1** *Find maturity value.*

**2** *Find principal if given maturity value, time, and rate.*

**3** *Find rate if given principal, maturity value, and time.*

**4** *Find time if given maturity value, principal, and rate.*

Suppose you borrow $8,000 at 11% interest for 9 months. The interest you owe on the loan would be calculated as follows.

$$I = PRT$$

$$I = \$8,000 \times 0.11 \times \frac{9}{12}$$

$$I = \$660$$

**OBJECTIVE 1** *Find maturity value.* The total amount that must be repaid in 9 months is made up of the principal and the interest, or

$$\text{Principal} + \text{Interest} = \$8,000 + \$660 = \$8,660.$$

This amount, $8,660, is called the **maturity value** of the loan, and the date the loan is paid off is the **maturity date**. The formula for maturity value is as follows.

A loan with a principal of *P* dollars and interest of *I* dollars has a maturity value *M* given by

$$M = P + I.$$

**NOTE** The maturity value of a loan always exceeds the principal (the original loan amount). ∎

**EXAMPLE 1** *Finding Interest and Maturity Value*

Jane Flynn, a nurse, plans to open a home health-care business and borrows $15,000 for 9 months at $11\frac{1}{2}\%$ interest. Find the interest and the maturity value of the loan.

**SOLUTION**   Find the interest using $I = PRT$; here $P = \$15,000$, $R = 0.115$, and $T$ is $\frac{9}{12}$ of a year.

$$I = PRT$$

$$I = \$15,000 \times 0.115 \times \frac{9}{12}$$

$$I = \$1,293.75$$

Flynn must repay the $15,000 plus interest of $1,293.75.

$$M = P + I$$

$$M = \$15,000 + \$1,293.75$$

$$M = \$16,293.75$$

Nine months after receiving $15,000, Flynn must repay $16,293.75.    ∎

The formula for maturity value, $M = P + I$, can be written in a different way if *I* is replaced with *PRT* (since $I = PRT$).

$$M = P + I$$

$$M = P + PRT \qquad \text{Substitute } PRT \text{ for } I.$$

$$M = P(1 + RT) \qquad \text{Use the distributive property.}$$

Notice that $P(1 + RT) = P + PRT$ by the distributive property of algebra discussed in Chapter 2. Therefore, there are two formulas for maturity value.

The *maturity value*, *M*, of a principal of *P* dollars at a rate of interest *R* for *T* years is either

$$M = P + I,$$

or, since $I = PRT$,

$$M = P(1 + RT).$$

## EXAMPLE 2  *Finding Maturity Value*

Use the formula $M = P(1 + RT)$ to find the maturity value for a loan of $6,000 for 120 days at 9% interest.

**SOLUTION**  Substitute $6,000 for $P$, 0.09 for $R$, and $\frac{120}{360}$ for $T$ (since 120 days is $\frac{120}{360}$ of a year). The maturity value is

$$M = P(1 + RT)$$

$$M = \$6,000 \times \left[1 + \left(0.09 \times \frac{120}{360}\right)\right].$$

**NOTE**  Parentheses were placed around $0.09 \times \frac{120}{360}$ to emphasize that these numbers are multiplied as a first step.  ■

After multiplying 0.09 and $\frac{120}{360}$, add 1.

$$M = \$6,000 \times (1 + 0.03)$$

$$M = \$6,000 \times 1.03$$

$$M = \$6,180$$

The interest could be found by subtracting the principal from the maturity value.

$$I = \$6,180 - \$6,000 = \$180$$  ■

**CALCULATOR APPROACH TO EXAMPLE 2**

The calculator solution to this example uses parentheses on the calculator in place of the brackets.

6000 $\boxed{\times}$ $\boxed{(}$ 1 $\boxed{+}$ .09 $\boxed{\times}$ 120 $\boxed{\div}$ 360 $\boxed{)}$ $\boxed{=}$ 6180

Subtract the principal from $6,180 to obtain the interest.

6180 $\boxed{-}$ 6000 $\boxed{=}$ 180

**OBJECTIVE 2**  **Find principal if given maturity value, time, and rate.**  Sometimes the maturity value is given, and either the principal, rate, or time must be found. For example, given the maturity value, rate, and time, find principal as follows.

$$M = P(1 + RT)$$

$$\frac{M}{(1 + RT)} = \frac{P(1 + RT)}{(1 + RT)} \qquad \text{Divide both sides by } (1 + RT).$$

$$\frac{M}{(1 + RT)} = \frac{P\cancel{(1 + RT)}}{\cancel{(1 + RT)}} \qquad \text{Divide out common factors.}$$

$$\frac{M}{1 + RT} = P \quad \text{or} \quad P = \frac{M}{1 + RT}$$

| EXAMPLE 3  *Finding Principal Given Time, Rate, and Maturity Value*

Find the principal that would produce a maturity value of $1,530 in 4 months at 6% interest.

**SOLUTION**   Use the formula on the preceding page and substitute $1,530 for $M$, 0.06 for $R$, and $\frac{4}{12}$ for $T$.

$$P = \frac{M}{1 + RT}$$

$$P = \frac{\$1,530}{1 + (0.06 \times \frac{4}{12})}$$

As shown by the parentheses, first multiply 0.06 and $\frac{4}{12}$, and then add 1.

$$P = \frac{\$1,530}{1 + 0.02}$$

$$P = \frac{\$1,530}{1.02}$$

$$P = \$1,500$$

The principal is $1,500; the interest is $1,530 − $1,500 = $30.    ∎

---

**CALCULATOR APPROACH
TO EXAMPLE 3**

The calculator solution to this example uses parentheses for the entire denominator. The calculator will automatically do the chain calculations correctly.

1530  ÷  (  1  +  .06  ×  4  ÷  12  )  =  1500

---

**OBJECTIVE 3**  *Find rate if given principal, maturity value, and time.*    If the principal, maturity value, and time are given, the rate can be found as follows.

$$M = P(1 + RT)$$

$$M = P + PRT \qquad \text{Use the distributive property.}$$

$$M - P = PRT \qquad \text{Subtract } P \text{ from both sides.}$$

$$\frac{M - P}{PT} = \frac{\cancel{P}R\cancel{T}}{\cancel{P}\cancel{T}} \qquad \text{Divide both sides by } PT.$$

$$\frac{M - P}{PT} = R$$

| EXAMPLE 4  *Finding Rate Given Principal, Maturity Value, and Time*

Lin Pao invests a principal of $7,200 and receives a maturity value of $7,540 in 200 days. Find the interest rate.

**SOLUTION**   Use the formula above and substitute values.

$$R = \frac{M - P}{PT}$$

$$R = \frac{\$7{,}540 - \$7{,}200}{\$7{,}200 \times \frac{200}{360}}$$

$$R = 0.085 \quad \text{or} \quad 8.5\%$$

■

---

The calculator solution to this example uses parentheses for the numerator ($7,540 − $7,200) and for the denominator ($7,200 × $\frac{200}{360}$).

**CALCULATOR APPROACH TO EXAMPLE 4**

$\boxed{(}$  7540  $\boxed{-}$  7200  $\boxed{)}$  $\boxed{\div}$  $\boxed{(}$  7200  $\boxed{\times}$  200  $\boxed{\div}$  360  $\boxed{)}$

$\boxed{=}$  0.085

---

Since $I = M - P$,

$$R = \frac{M - P}{PT} = \frac{I}{PT}.$$

From Example 4, $M = P + I$ or $I = M - P = \$7{,}540 - \$7{,}200 = \$340$.

$$R = \frac{\$340}{\$7{,}200 \times \frac{200}{360}}$$

$$R = 0.085 \quad \text{or} \quad 8.5\%$$

**OBJECTIVE 4** *Find time if given maturity value, principal, and rate.*   The time can be determined in a manner similar to that above.

$$M = P(1 + RT)$$

$$M = P + PRT \qquad \text{Use the distributive property.}$$

$$M - P = PRT \qquad \text{Subtract } P \text{ from both sides.}$$

$$\frac{M - P}{PR} = \frac{PRT}{PR} \qquad \text{Divide both sides by } PR.$$

$$\frac{M - P}{PR} = T \text{ (in years)}$$

This gives a value for time $T$ in **years**. To convert to **days** multiply by 360; for example, $\frac{1}{2}$ of a year is $\frac{1}{2} \times 360 = 180$ days.

$$T \text{ (in days)} = \frac{M - P}{PR} \times 360$$

Since $I = M - P$, this is the same as

$$T \text{ (in days)} = \frac{I}{PR} \times 360.$$

### EXAMPLE 5  *Finding the Time in Days*

Neon Lights, Inc. borrowed $18,250 at $10\frac{1}{8}\%$ interest for the construction of new signs and agreed to repay $19,687.19. Find the time in days.

**SOLUTION**    Use the formula above and substitute values.

$$T = \frac{M - P}{PR} \times 360$$

$$T = \frac{\$19,687.19 - \$18,250}{\$18,250 \times 0.10125} \times 360$$

$$T = \frac{1,437.19}{1,847.81} \times 360$$

$$T = 280 \text{ days (rounded)} \qquad \blacksquare$$

---

The calculator solution to this example uses parentheses to set off both the numerator and the denominator. The calculator will then handle all chain calculations for you.

**CALCULATOR APPROACH TO EXAMPLE 5**

$$( \boxed{19687.19} \boxed{-} \boxed{18250} ) \boxed{\div} ( \boxed{18250} \boxed{\times} \boxed{.10125} )$$

$$\boxed{\times} \boxed{360} \boxed{=} \boxed{280}$$

---

**Summary Table of Formulas**

| Find | |
|------|--|
| Interest | $I = PRT$ |
| Maturity Value | $M = P(1 + RT)$ |
| Principal | $P = \dfrac{I}{RT} = \dfrac{M - P}{RT} = \dfrac{M}{1 + RT}$ |
| Rate | $R = \dfrac{I}{PT} = \dfrac{M - P}{PT}$ |
| Time | Time in years $= \dfrac{I}{PR} = \dfrac{M - P}{PR}$ |
| | Time in days $= \dfrac{I}{PR} \times 360 = \dfrac{M - P}{PR} \times 360$ |

# 11.3 EXERCISES

*Find the interest and the maturity value for each of the following loans. Round to the nearest cent.*

1. $2,400 at 12% for 8 months

2. $4,300 at $9\frac{1}{4}$% for 11 months

3. $5,800 at 8.5% for 140 days

4. $10,800 at $7\frac{3}{4}$% for 220 days

5. $8,640 at 10% for $1\frac{1}{4}$ years

6. $9,500 at 15% for $1\frac{1}{2}$ years

*Complete this chart. Round money to the nearest cent, rate to the nearest tenth of a percent, and time to the nearest day.*

|      | Principal | Interest    | Rate              | Time in Days | Maturity Value |
|------|-----------|-------------|-------------------|--------------|----------------|
| 7.   | $2,400    | _____  | 11%               | 80           | _____     |
| 8.   | $4,250    | _____  | $12\frac{1}{2}$%  | 90           | _____     |
| 9.   | $8,600    | $133.78     | 8%                | _____   | _____     |
| 10.  | $7,400    | $292.92     | $9\frac{1}{2}$%   | _____   | _____     |
| 11.  | $14,000   | $490        | _____        | 120          | _____     |
| 12.  | $12,800   | $544        | _____        | 180          | _____     |
| 13.  | _____ | _____ | $7\frac{7}{8}$%   | 200          | $17,117.50     |
| 14.  | _____ | _____ | 14%               | 205          | $38,870        |
| 15.  | _____ | $1,311.01   | 13.7%             | _____   | $33,811.01     |
| 16.  | _____ | $8,086.05   | 9.1%              | _____   | $89,086.05     |
| 17.  | $1,800    | _____  | 14%               | _____   | $1,926         |
| 18.  | $11,250   | _____  | 12.8%             | _____   | $11,710        |
| 19.  | _____ | $3,272.92  | _____        | 185          | $45,732.36     |
| 20.  | _____ | $1,963.33  | _____        | 76           | $76,963.33     |

*Solve the following application problems.*

21. José Garcia borrowed $12,000 for 140 days at $10\frac{1}{2}$% to add a hot tub and enclosure to his home. Find the interest and the maturity value.

22. Johnson Credit Union makes a loan to the city of Smallville for $82,500 at $11\frac{3}{8}$% for 240 days. Find the interest and the maturity value.

23. Bill Moyer borrows $4,500 at 11% to purchase a car for his college-bound daughter and agrees to repay $4,775. Find the time in days and the amount of interest.

24. Walt Wilson borrows $60,000 at 9% interest to expand his car dealership. He agrees to repay $61,800. Find the time in days and the amount of interest paid.

25. Martha Wheat borrowed $930 from her uncle and agreed to repay him $1,000 after 150 days. Find the interest rate to the nearest percent and the amount of interest.

**26.** Jenny Cronin borrows $46,000 to open a small health-food store. She agrees to repay $49,105 in 270 days. Find the interest rate and the amount of interest.

**27.** Bill Melton of Melton Motor Company agreed to repay $854,166.67 at 10% interest in 150 days. Find the principal and the interest.

**28.** Jill Phan borrowed some money to settle a lawsuit against her restaurant—a customer fell due to a puddle of water from the icemaker. The 180-day loan was at 9% interest and Phan must repay $44,412.50. Find the principal and the interest.

**29.** Explain how to calculate the annual interest rate, given the maturity value, principal, and number of days (term) of the loan. (See Objective 3.)

**30.** Using $I = PRT$ and $M = P + I$, explain the steps to derive the equation for principal given maturity value, rate, and time. (See Objective 2.)

# 11.4   Inflation and the Time Value of Money

**OBJECTIVES**

**1**  *Define inflation and the consumer price index.*

**2**  *Understand the time value of money.*

**3**  *Define present value and future value.*

**4**  *Calculate present and future values using simple interest.*

**5**  *Find present value for a given maturity value.*

**6**  *Find present value after a loan is made.*

Your grandfather and his family would have done *well* with an income of only $500 per month in 1950. Today, this amount will not go far in terms of taking care of a family. Five hundred dollars today will not purchase nearly as much in the year 2005 as it did in 1950. Why?

**OBJECTIVE 1** *Define inflation and the consumer price index.*   **Inflation** is the culprit. It results in a continuing rise in the general price level of goods and services. The effect of inflation can be seen by the increasing costs in a grocery store.

| Item | 1970 Price | Projected Price for the Year 2000 |
|------|-----------|------------------------------------|
| Loaf of bread | $0.24 | $1.50 |
| $\frac{1}{2}$ gal. of milk | $0.66 | $2.25 |
| 1 lb. of bacon | $0.95 | $2.50 |

Effectively, a dollar buys less in 2000 than it did in 1970; every year the dollar is worth less.

The **consumer price index (CPI)** is calculated by the government annually in the United States and is often referred to as the "cost of living index." Other countries calculate similar indexes. The CPI can be used to track inflation—it measures the average change in prices from one year to the next for a common bundle of goods and services bought by the average consumer on a regular basis. Figure 11.2 shows that the yearly inflation, as measured by the CPI index, differs substantially from year to year. Your local librarian can help you find recent CPI data. The CPI is discussed in more detail in Chapter 19.

Annual Inflation Rate
Based on Consumer Price Index

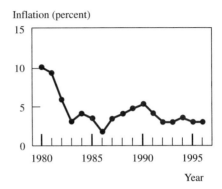

FIGURE 11.2

*Source:* U.S. Bureau of the Census.

## EXAMPLE 1  *Estimating the Effect of Inflation*

Inflation from one year to the next was 4.8% as measured by the CPI index. (a) Find the effect of the increase on a family with an annual income and budget of $19,800 (after taxes). (b) What is the overall effect if the family members only receive a 2% (after tax) increase in pay for the year?

### SOLUTION

**(a)** This is a percent problem. The cost of the goods and services that this family buys, if they buy the "common bundle of goods and services," went up by 4.8% as measured by the CPI, or by

$$0.048 \times \$19,800 = \$950.40.$$

Therefore, these same goods and services will cost the family

$$\$19,800 + \$950.40 = \$20,750.40 \text{ next year.}$$

**(b)** The family's income only went up 2% after taxes or by

$$0.02 \times \$19,800 = \$396.$$

Thus, their new income is $19,800 + $396 = $20,196. However, the cost of buying the same goods and services as they bought the previous year is $20,750.40. In effect, the family has lost $20,750.40 − $20,196 = $554.40 in purchasing power.  ∎

As shown in Example 1, inflation slowly erodes fixed incomes or incomes with a small annual increase built into them. Imagine the effect of loosing purchasing power every year for 10 years in a row. Inflation can erode people's purchasing power even as their annual salaries are increasing. Retired people are particularly concerned with inflation since they must live off of social security and the assets they have accumulated during their lifetime. Some retired people do not have ways of increasing their income to keep pace with inflation and must lower their standards of living substantially during their 10 to 30 or more years of retirement. Other retired people have investments such as stocks that help them stay ahead of inflation.

The Federal Government generally tries to keep inflation at moderate levels since inflation can be so harmful. When the economy becomes overheated and inflationary pressures increase, the Federal Reserve nudges interest rates upward which reduces borrowing slightly, slows the economy, and reduces inflationary pressures. Conversely, if inflation is low and the economy is growing very slowly or not at all, the Federal Reserve nudges interest rates downward, thereby stimulating the economy and creating more jobs. The Federal Reserve has been assigned the very difficult task of maintaining a growing and healthy economy with low levels of inflation.

**OBJECTIVE 2** *Understand the time value of money.*    Would you leave $1,000 on deposit with your bank for 2 years (in a savings account) and expect only $1,000 back when the money is returned? You would expect interest in addition to a return of your principal. The **time value of money** is the idea that the loaning of money to someone or to a firm has value, and that value is typically repaid by returning interest in addition to principal. It is interesting to note that the Islamic religion does not approve of interest. Banks in some Islamic countries take partial ownership of a company that they lend money to and share in profits until they have been repaid. The bank is not repaid in the event that there are no profits.

The time value of money is a *very important concept* in modern society. Regular investments of relatively small sums of money can result in large sums at later dates. For example, how would you like to turn $36,000 into $350,000? Invest $100 per month for 30 years, say from age 30 to age 60, at 12% interest compounded monthly. Application of the time value of money will help you send your children to college, purchase a home, and prepare for your own retirement. The time value of money is equally important to firms that invest to build factories, develop new technologies, or need capital for many other reasons.

**OBJECTIVE 3** *Define present value and future value.*    The principal amount that must be invested today to produce a given future amount is called the **present value**. The amount that this sum grows to at some future date is called the **future value**. We have been calculating the future value in the earlier sections of this chapter when we were calculating the maturity amount.

$$\text{Future value: } M = P(1 + RT)$$

We have also been calculating the present value in the earlier sections of this chapter when we were calculating the principal with the following form of the above equation.

$$\text{Present value: } P = \frac{M}{(1 + RT)}$$

**OBJECTIVE** **4** *Calculate present and future values using simple interest.*

| **EXAMPLE 2** *Finding Future Value*

Joan Waters invests her inheritance of $28,500 at $9\frac{1}{4}\%$ simple interest on May 30. Find the future value of this amount on February 4 of the following year to the nearest cent.

**SOLUTION** First find the number of days from May 30 to February 4 by finding the number of days from May 30 to the end of the year. Then find the number of days from the beginning of the year to February 4.

$$
\begin{array}{ll}
\text{The end of the year is day} & 365 \\
\text{May 30 is day} & -\,150 \\
\text{May 30 to end of year} & \overline{215}
\end{array}
$$

February 4 is day 35 of the next year. The total number of days is $215 + 35 = 250$ days. Now use the formula for the maturity value or future value using simple interest.

$$M = P(1 + RT)$$

$$M = \$28,500\left(1 + 0.0925 \times \frac{250}{360}\right)$$

$$M = \$30,330.73$$

The future value on February 4 is $30,330.73. ∎

| **EXAMPLE 3** *Finding Present Value*

Bob Jackson, the owner of Bob's Hardware & Paint, would like to purchase a new delivery truck in 15 months. He anticipates that the truck will cost $19,200. What present value must he invest today at 8% simple interest so that he has the needed future value in 15 months?

**SOLUTION** Use the following form of the simple interest formula.

$$P = \frac{M}{(1 + RT)}$$

$$P = \frac{\$19,200}{(1 + 0.08 \times \frac{15}{12})}$$

$$P = \frac{\$19,200}{(1 + 0.1)}$$

$$P = \frac{\$19,200}{1.1}$$

$$P = \$17,454.55$$

Jackson must invest a present value of $17,454.55 today at 8% in order to have a future value of $19,200 in 15 months. ∎

**CALCULATOR APPROACH
TO EXAMPLE 3**

For the calculator solution to this example, the denominator (1 + 0.08 × $\frac{15}{12}$) should be considered a single number. Set it apart using parentheses.

19200 ÷ ( 1 + .08 × 15 ÷ 12 ) = 17454.55

**OBJECTIVE 5** *Find present value for a given maturity value.*    Example 3 discussed the present value of the principal on a loan. More realistic problems would consider the present value of the *maturity value* (principal plus interest).

### EXAMPLE 4 *Finding Present Value on Date Loan Is Made*

Your loan of $450 is due to your Aunt Ruth in 9 months, with an interest rate of 12%. Find the present value of the loan on the day it is made if money has a time value of 10%.

**SOLUTION**    First find the maturity value for the loan, as explained earlier in this chapter.

$$M = P(1 + RT)$$

$$M = \$450\left[1 + \left(0.12 \times \frac{9}{12}\right)\right]$$

$$M = \$450(1 + 0.09)$$

$$M = \$450(1.09)$$

$$M = \$490.50$$

Now find the present value of this maturity value. The time, 9 months, is the same, but the interest rate is now 10%, instead of 12%. Use the present value formula.

$$P = \frac{M}{1 + RT}$$

$$P = \frac{\$490.50}{1 + (0.10 \times \frac{9}{12})} = \frac{\$490.50}{1 + 0.075} = \frac{490.50}{1.075} = \$456.28$$

On the day the loan is made, your Aunt Ruth should be willing to accept $456.28 in settlement of the debt. ∎

Figure 11.3 summarizes Example 4.

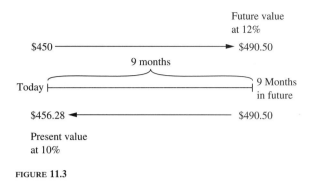

FIGURE **11.3**

**NOTE** In Example 4, an agreement was made to loan money at 12%. However, a change in interest rates caused the time value of money to change to 10%. If the time value of money was also 12%, then the present value and the principal would have been the same, or $450. ■

CALCULATOR APPROACH
TO EXAMPLE 4

For the calculator solution to this example, consider the quantity $[1 + (0.12 \times \frac{9}{12})]$ as a single number and set it apart using parentheses.

**OBJECTIVE** **6** ***Find present value after a loan is made.*** Sometime you may need to find the present value on some date after a loan is made, but before it is due. Such a step might be necessary, for example, in preparing a balance sheet—this would give the exact value of the loan on the date the balance sheet was prepared. (Balance sheets are explained in Chapter 17.) Also, a present value might be found before deciding to convert the loan to cash by discounting it at the bank (see Section 12.3).

**EXAMPLE 5** *Finding Present Value on a Date After Loan Is Made*

You make a loan of $6,500 to a business partner on May 13, for 90 days. The interest rate on the loan is 8%. After the loan is made, the general level of interest rates rises quickly so that the time value of money is 12%. Find the present value of the loan on June 26.

**SOLUTION** First find the maturity value of the loan. The principal is $6,500, the rate is 8%, and the time is 90 days, or $\frac{90}{360}$ year.

$$M = P(1 + RT)$$

$$M = \$6{,}500\left[1 + \left(0.08 \times \frac{90}{360}\right)\right]$$

$$M = \$6{,}500(1 + 0.02)$$

$$M = \$6{,}500(1.02)$$

$$M = \$6{,}630$$

The loan was made on May 13, for 90 days. The loan is due on August 11. As shown in Figure 11.4, the number of days from June 26 (the day for which the present value is desired) to August 11 is

|  |  |
|---:|---|
| 4 | days in June |
| 31 | days in July |
| + 11 | days in August |
| 46 | total days. |

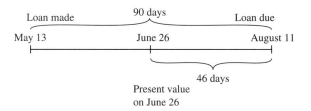

**FIGURE 11.4**

The total number of days could also be found by using Table 11.1.

To find the present value 46 days before the loan is paid off, use the formula for present value, with $M = \$6{,}630$, $R = 12\%$, and $T = \frac{46}{360}$ year.

$$P = \frac{M}{1 + RT}$$

$$P = \frac{\$6{,}630}{1 + (0.12 \times \frac{46}{360})}$$

$$P = \$6{,}529.88 \text{ (rounded)}$$

**NOTE** When time value of money and interest rate are different and when present value is found on a date after a loan is made, both the rate $R$ and the time fraction $T$ are different. ■

You should be willing to accept $6,529.88 on June 26 in full payment of the loan, both principal and interest. ■

**PROBLEM-SOLVING HINT** Since $\frac{46}{360}$ does not produce a terminating decimal, it is important that it not be rounded at an intermediate step. The calculation should be done in one step and the final answer rounded. ■

## 11.4 EXERCISES

*In the following problems, find the present value or future value, as indicated, to the nearest cent.*

| | Present Value | Interest Rate | Time | Future Value |
|---|---|---|---|---|
| 1. | $3,200 | 7% | 90 days | _____ |
| 2. | $4,800 | $7\frac{3}{4}$% | 120 days | _____ |
| 3. | $9,400 | 10% | 7 months | _____ |
| 4. | $6,800 | $12\frac{1}{2}$% | 9 months | _____ |
| 5. | $4,100 | $8\frac{3}{8}$% | $1\frac{1}{4}$ years | _____ |
| 6. | $7,400 | $10\frac{1}{4}$% | $1\frac{1}{2}$ years | _____ |
| 7. | _____ | 6% | 100 days | $2,440 |
| 8. | _____ | 9% | 180 days | $1,985.50 |
| 9. | _____ | $11\frac{1}{8}$% | 6 months | $8,867.25 |
| 10. | _____ | 12% | 11 months | $10,323 |
| 11. | _____ | $5\frac{7}{8}$% | $1\frac{1}{8}$ years | $9,275.02 |
| 12. | _____ | $7\frac{1}{4}$% | $1\frac{1}{2}$ years | $7,096 |

13. Explain the difference between the interest rate on a loan and the time value of money. (See Objective 4.)

14. Explain the difference between present value and future value. (See Objective 3.)

*Solve the following application problems.*

15. A bank made a loan to a contractor for $12,800 on June 17 at $9\frac{1}{2}$% simple interest. Find the future value of the loan that the bank would show on their financial statements on December 1.

16. Karl's Kameras loaned a supplier $28,300 on July 14 at 8% simple interest. Find the future value of the loan on March 15 of the following year.

17. Chase Bank loaned a large Canadian firm 8.5 million dollars (U.S.) at $9\frac{1}{2}$% simple interest for 90 days and simultaneously paid $6\frac{3}{4}$% interest for the same funds to their depositors. Find the difference between the interest earned by Chase Bank and the interest paid to their depositors.

18. A finance company carries an outstanding loan, to a bank on the east coast, of $875,000 at 10% simple interest. They simultaneously lend all $875,000 to individual customers at a rate of 18% simple interest. (a) Find the difference in interest earned and interest paid out on a daily basis, assuming 365 days in a year. (b) Without rounding the figure in part (a), find the difference between interest earned and interest paid out for a 365-day year.

**19.** A loan of $1,200 was made for 120 days at 9%. Find the present value of the loan on the day it was made if money is worth 6%.

**20.** Find the present value, on the date it was made, of a loan of $14,700 at 12% for 210 days if money is worth 10%.

**21.** A loan of $6,980 was made on May 24, for 214 days, at 11%. Find the present value of the loan on July 9, if the value of money is 10%.

**22.** On February 24, an 89-day loan of $980, at 12% is made. Find the present value of the loan on March 10, if the value of money is 10%.

**23.** On April 7, Plank Lumber Company borrowed $14,000 from a wholesaler. The loan was for 153 days at 12%. The firm came up with some extra cash, and decided to pay the loan off on July 20. If the value of money is 10%, find the amount it would take to pay off the loan.

**24.** McKeague Dairy has borrowed $7,600. The loan, made on September 11, is for 91 days at 10%. Find the amount necessary to pay off the loan on October 30, if the value of money is 12%.

**25.** A family with a spending budget of $26,500 receives an increase in wages of 3% in a year in which inflation was 4.5%. Find the net gain or loss in their purchasing power, ignoring taxes.

**26.** Ben Thomas spends $34,300 and receives a 6% raise in a year in which inflation was 2.5%. Ignoring taxes, find the net gain or loss in his purchasing power.

*In the following exercises, three different bids for a single item are given. Find the lowest bid by calculating the present value of each. Assume money has a value of 12%.*

**27.** $5,600 today, $5,800 in 150 days, $6,000 in 210 days

**28.** $41,250 today, $43,500 in 210 days, $45,000 in 300 days

**29.** Do you think that inflation will have a significant impact on your finances during your lifetime? Explain.

**30.** What effects can you foresee of a rapid increase in inflation from 6% to 10%?

# Chapter 11 Quick Review

| TOPIC | APPROACH | EXAMPLE |
|---|---|---|
| **11.1 Finding simple interest given time expressed in years** | Use formula $I = PRT$ with $R$ in decimal form and time in years. | Find the simple interest on $4,000 for $2\frac{1}{2}$ years at 8% per year. $$I = PRT$$ $$I = \$4,000 \times 0.08 \times 2.5$$ $$= \$800$$ |

| **11.1** | **Finding simple interest given time expressed in months** | Use $I = PRT$. Express time in years by dividing time in months by 12. | Find the simple interest on $1,200 for 15 months at 7% per year. $$I = PRT$$ $$I = \$1,200 \times 0.07 \times \frac{15}{12}$$ $$= \$1,200 \times 0.07 \times 1.25$$ $$= \$105$$ |
|---|---|---|---|
| **11.1** | **Determining principal given interest, rate, and time** | Use formula $$P = \frac{I}{RT}$$ with $R$ in decimal form and time in years. | Find the principal that would produce an interest of $150 in 8 months at 6%. $$P = \frac{I}{RT}$$ $$P = \frac{\$150}{0.06 \times \frac{8}{12}} = \$3,750$$ |
| **11.1** | **Finding rate given interest, principal, and time** | Use formula $R = \dfrac{I}{PT}$ with $T$ in years. | Find the rate on a $15,000 loan for 60 months if the interest was $6,750. $$R = \frac{I}{PT}$$ $$R = \frac{\$6,750}{\$15,000 \times \frac{60}{12}} = 0.09$$ $$= 9\%$$ |
| **11.1** | **Determining time given interest, principal, and rate** | Use formula $T = \dfrac{I}{PR}$ with $R$ in decimal form. | Find the time for a loan of $4,000 at 11% to produce $1,320 in interest. $$T = \frac{I}{PR}$$ $$T = \frac{\$1,320}{\$4,000 \times 0.11} = 3 \text{ yr.}$$ |
| **11.2** | **Finding the number of days from one date to another using a table** | Find the day corresponding to each date and subtract. | Find the number of days from February 15th to July 28th. July 28 is day    209 Feb. 15 is day −   46 ———— 163 |

| | | |
|---|---|---|
| **11.2 Determining the number of days from one date to another using the actual number of days in a month** | Add the actual number of days in each month or partial month from one date to the next. | Find the number of days from January 17th to April 15th. |

$$\begin{array}{rl} 14 & \text{remaining in January} \\ 28 & \text{February} \\ 31 & \text{March} \\ + 15 & \text{April} \\ \hline 88 & \end{array}$$

| | | |
|---|---|---|
| **11.2 Exact interest** | Use formula $I = PRT$ with $$T = \frac{\text{Time in days}}{365}.$$ | Find the exact interest on $600 at 8% for 120 days. $$I = PRT$$ $$I = \$600 \times 0.08 \times \frac{120}{365}$$ $$= \$15.78$$ |

| | | |
|---|---|---|
| **11.2 Ordinary interest** | Use formula $I = PRT$ with $$T = \frac{\text{Time in days}}{360}.$$ | Find the ordinary interest on $1,100 at 7% for 90 days. $$I = PRT$$ $$I = \$1,100 \times 0.07 \times \frac{90}{360}$$ $$= \$19.25$$ |

| | | |
|---|---|---|
| **11.3 Determining the maturity value of a loan, when principal, rate, and time are known** | Use formula $M = P(1 + RT)$ with $R$ in decimal form and $T$ in years. | Find the maturity value of a $2,500 loan that is made for 2 years at 6%. $$M = P(1 + RT)$$ $$M = \$2,500[1 + (0.06 \times 2)]$$ $$M = \$2,800$$ |

| | | |
|---|---|---|
| **11.3 Finding the principal when maturity value, rate, and time are known** | Use formula $$P = \frac{M}{1 + RT}$$ with $R$ in decimal form and $T$ in years. | Find the principal that would produce a maturity value of $1,500 in 9 months at 4%. $$P = \frac{M}{1 + RT}$$ $$P = \frac{\$1,500}{1 + (0.04 \times \frac{9}{12})}$$ $$= \$1,456.31 \text{ (rounded)}$$ |

| | | |
|---|---|---|
| **11.3** **Determining the time in days when maturity value, rate, and principal are known** | Use formula $$T = \frac{M - P}{PR} \times 360$$ to find time in days. | A principal of \$12,000 produces a maturity value of \$12,540 at a 6% rate. Find the time of the loan in days. $$T = \frac{M - P}{PR} \times 360$$ $$T =$$ $$\frac{\$12,540 - \$12,000}{\$12,000 \times 0.06} \times 360$$ $$T = 0.75 \times 360$$ $$T = 270 \text{ days}$$ |
| **11.3** **Finding rate given principal, maturity value, and time** | Use formula $$R = \frac{M - P}{PT} \text{ with}$$ time expressed in years. | A principal of \$8,400 produces a maturity value of \$8,596 in 210 days. Find the rate of interest. $$R = \frac{M - P}{PT}$$ $$R = \frac{\$8,596 - \$8,400}{\$8,400 \times \frac{210}{360}}$$ $$= 0.04$$ $$R = 4\%$$ |
| **11.3** **Finding time in days when principal, rate, and interest are known** | Use formula $$T = \frac{I}{PR} \times 360 \text{ with } R \text{ in decimal}$$ form. | Find the time in days that \$1,500 was invested at 8% if \$25 interest was earned. $$T = \frac{I}{PR} \times 360$$ $$T = \frac{\$25}{\$1,500 \times 0.08} \times 360$$ $$= 75 \text{ days}$$ |
| **11.4** **Finding the effect of inflation on the cost of living.** | Use the percent formula. | Find the increase in the cost of living for a family with a budget of \$23,800 in a year with 4% inflation. $$0.04 \times \$23,800 = \$952$$ They experience a \$952 increase in the cost of living. |

**11.4    Determining present value given maturity value, rate, and time**

Use formula

$$P = \frac{M}{1 + RT} \text{ with } R \text{ in decimal}$$

form and $T$ in years.

A debt of $8,000 must be paid in 9 months. Find the amount that could be deposited today at 9% interest so that enough money will be available.

$$P = \frac{M}{1 + RT}$$

$$P = \frac{\$8,000}{1 + (0.09 \times \frac{9}{12})}$$

$$= \$7,494.15$$

**11.4    Finding present value given rate and time value of money**

Use the formula
$M = P(1 + RT)$ with
$R$ in decimal form and time in years.
Then use the formula

$$P = \frac{M}{1 + RT} \text{ with}$$

$R$ = time value of money and $T$ in years.

A loan of $750 at 12% is due in 15 months. Find the present value of the loan if the time value of money is 9%.

$$M = P(1 + RT)$$

$$M = \$750 \times$$

$$\left[ 1 + \left( 0.12 \times \frac{15}{12} \right) \right]$$

$$= \$862.50$$

$$P = \frac{M}{1 + RT}$$

$$R = \frac{\$862.50}{1 + (0.09 \times \frac{15}{12})}$$

$$= \$775.28$$

**11.4    Finding present value after a loan is made**

Use formula $M = P(1 + RT)$ with $R$ in decimal form and $T$ in years.
Next, use the formula

$$P = \frac{M}{1 + RT} \text{ with}$$

$R$ = time value of money,

$T$ = number of days from present value date to due date.

An $8,000 loan is made on June 5 for 90 days at 9%. The time value of money is 11%. Find the present value of the loan on August 10.

$$M = P(1 + RT)$$

$$M = \$8,000 \times$$

$$\left[ 1 + \left( 0.09 \times \frac{90}{360} \right) \right]$$

$$= \$8,180$$

Now, find time in days.

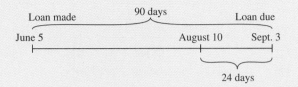

$$P = \frac{M}{1 + RT}$$

$$P = \frac{\$8,180}{1 + (0.11 \times \frac{24}{360})}$$

$$= \$8,120.45$$

# Chapter 11 Review Exercises

*Complete this table. Round money to the nearest cent, rate to the nearest tenth of a percent, and time to the nearest month.* [11.1]

|    | Interest   | Principal | Rate              | Time                    |
|----|-----------|-----------|-------------------|-------------------------|
| 1. | _____  | $4,600    | $9\frac{1}{4}\%$  | $1\frac{1}{2}$ years    |
| 2. | _____  | $5,800    | $10\frac{3}{4}\%$ | 16 months               |
| 3. | $696.80   | _____  | 12%               | 8 months                |
| 4. | $144      | _____  | 8%                | 9 months                |
| 5. | $810      | $12,000   | _____          | 9 months                |
| 6. | $750      | $8,000    | _____          | 15 months               |
| 7. | $540      | $12,000   | 6%                | _____                |
| 8. | $1,600    | $8,000    | 8%                | _____                |

*Find the number of days from the first date to the second.* [11.2]

**9.** April 15 to August 7

**10.** July 12 to November 4

*Find the exact interest for each of the following. Round to the nearest cent. [11.2]*

| | Interest | Principal | Rate | Time |
|---|---|---|---|---|
| 11. | _____ | $4,900 | $8\frac{3}{8}\%$ | 60 days |
| 12. | _____ | $8,400 | $9\frac{3}{4}\%$ | 150 days |
| 13. | _____ | $7,200 | 8% | From July 12 to November 30 |
| 14. | _____ | $6,800 | $7\frac{1}{2}\%$ | From February 4 to May 9 |

*Find the ordinary interest for each of the following. Round to the nearest cent. [11.2]*

| | Interest | Principal | Rate | Time |
|---|---|---|---|---|
| 15. | _____ | $7,400 | 7% | 30 days |
| 16. | _____ | $2,580 | 11% | 90 days |

*Complete the following table. Round money to the nearest cent, rate to the nearest tenth of a percent, and time to the nearest day. [11.3]*

| | Principal | Rate | Time | Interest |
|---|---|---|---|---|
| 17. | _____ | 12% | 75 days | $9 |
| 18. | _____ | 11% | 180 days | $340 |
| 19. | $6,000 | _____ | 60 days | $70 |
| 20. | $8,400 | _____ | 120 days | $231 |
| 21. | $7,800 | 9% | _____ | $78 |
| 22. | $4,900 | $10\frac{1}{8}\%$ | _____ | $124.03 |

*Complete the following table. Round money to the nearest cent and rate to the nearest tenth of a percent. [11.3]*

| | Maturity Value | Principal | Rate | Time |
|---|---|---|---|---|
| 23. | _____ | $6,800 | 9% | $1\frac{1}{2}$ years |
| 24. | _____ | $4,500 | $7\frac{1}{4}\%$ | 8 months |
| 25. | $12,180 | _____ | 9% | 60 days |
| 26. | $6,752.78 | _____ | 10% | 140 days |
| 27. | $8,120 | $8,000 | _____ | 60 days |
| 28. | $17,537.50 | $15,250 | _____ | 15 months |

*Find the present value of each of the following. Round to the nearest cent. [11.4]*

| | Present Value | Maturity Value | Rate | Time |
|---|---|---|---|---|
| **29.** | _____ | $2,000 | 9% | 150 days |
| **30.** | _____ | $12,000 | 12% | 100 days |

*Find the present value of the following loans on the day they are made. Round to the nearest cent. [11.4]*

| | Present Value | Principal Amount | Interest Rate of Loan | Length of Loan | Value of Money |
|---|---|---|---|---|---|
| **31.** | _____ | $5,000 | 10% | 9 months | 8% |
| **32.** | _____ | $20,000 | 7% | 15 months | 9% |

*Find the present value for the following loans on the indicated dates. Assume the value of money is 9%. Round to the nearest cent. [11.4]*

| | Present Value | Amount | Interest Rate of Loan | Length of Loan | Loan Made | Find Present Value on |
|---|---|---|---|---|---|---|
| **33.** | _____ | $800 | 10% | 60 days | Feb. 1 | March 15 |
| **34.** | _____ | $15,000 | 8% | 300 days | Apr. 1 | October 15 |

*Solve the following application problems. Round money to the nearest cent, rate to the nearest tenth of a percent, and time to the nearest day.*

**35.** Bob Jones borrows $4,200 at $7\frac{3}{4}$% for 220 days. Find the simple interest. [11.1]

**36.** Aikens Pest Control borrowed $14,200 and paid back $15,336 only 8 months later. Find the rate. [11.3]

**37.** A loan of $8,600 at a rate of $11\frac{1}{2}$% had a maturity value of $9,149.44. Find the term in days. [11.3]

**38.** An 8-month, 9% loan had a maturity value of $3,816. Find the amount originally borrowed. [11.3]

**39.** Collins Dairy has just bought new milking machines. The machines must be paid for with a single payment of $12,000 in 270 days. The firm has $11,200 that it can invest today. What rate of interest must it earn on this deposit to have the necessary $12,000? [11.2]

**40.** Quik Print is ordering a new $27,500 printing press. The seller of the press wants payment in 120 days. The print shop has $26,000 available for investment today. What rate of interest must it earn on this deposit to have the needed $27,500? [11.2]

**41.** How many days will it take for $17,600 to become $18,348 at 17% interest? [11.3]

**42.** Find the present value of a loan on the day it was made if the loan is for $9,100 at 11% for 85 days. Assume that money has a time value of 9.7%. [11.4]

**43.** A loan of $19,250 is made on October 15, at 12%. The loan is for 75 days. Find the present value of the loan on November 27 if money has a time value of 11.7%. [11.4]

**44.** Suppose a loan of $11,800 is made on July 12, for 153 days, at 9%. Find the present value of the loan on September 20, if money has a time value of 11%. [11.4]

**45.** Sherri Woods makes and spends $28,400 per year. She receives an increase in her annual salary of 6% during a year in which inflation is 3%. Ignoring taxes, find her net gain or loss in purchasing power. [11.4]

**46.** Bob and Jane Shaw have been spending their entire after-tax income of $46,850. Assume they receive no increase in their after-tax salary for a particular year during which inflation was 6%. Find the net gain or loss in their purchasing power. [11.4]

**47.** What would be the effect of a loss of $3,000 in yearly purchasing power? [11.4]

**48.** Which of the following would you prefer in a period with high inflation? (a) A salary of $25,000 per year with no raises for 10 years, or (b) a salary of $22,000 per year with annual raises, in each of the ten years, that slightly exceeds the rate of inflation. Explain. [11.4]

# Chapter 11 Summary Exercise

Oscar Risberg has the following simple interest loans, all due in the month of July. Complete the table by finding the interest and the maturity value due on each loan and the total payment due in July.

| Item | Principal | Rate | Term | Interest | Maturity Value |
|------|-----------|------|------|----------|----------------|
| Boat | $6,300 | 9% | 60 days | _____ | _____ |
| Dining table | $2,300 | 10% | 3 months | _____ | _____ |
| Trailer | $1,800 | 12% | 1 year | _____ | _____ |
| | | | Total | | _____ |

Risberg cannot afford to pay off all of these loans in July. Therefore, he makes an agreement with the bank to pay off the loans on the dining table and on the trailer. As a result, the bank agrees to refinance the principal and interest due on the boat which is due July 20, for another 90 days at 12%. Find the due date of the refinanced debt and the maturity value due at that time.

# Notes and
# Bank Discount

When an individual or business borrows money, written proof of the loan often takes the form of a **promissory note**. A promissory note is a legal and frequently transferable document in which one person or firm agrees to pay a stated amount of money, at a stated time and interest rate, to another. Banks typically require business owners to sign promissory notes when lending them money. Sometimes simple interest notes are used, while other times simple discount notes are used. Both types of notes are discussed in this chapter.

## 12.1  Simple Interest Notes

**OBJECTIVES**

1  *Identify the parts of a simple interest promissory note.*
2  *Find the due date of a note.*
3  *Find the face value, time, and rate of a note.*

An example of a promissory note is shown in Figure 12.1.

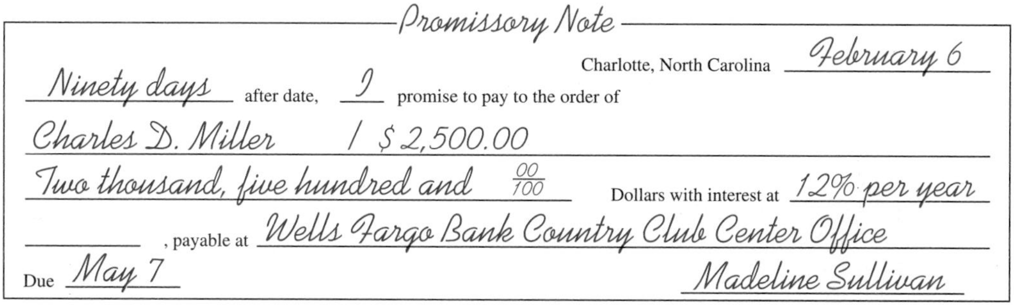

---

────── *Promissory Note* ──────

Charlotte, North Carolina  *February 6*

*Ninety days* ___ after date, *I* ___ promise to pay to the order of

*Charles D. Miller* / $2,500.00

*Two thousand, five hundred and* 00/100 ___ Dollars with interest at *12% per year*

___ , payable at *Wells Fargo Bank Country Club Center Office*

Due *May 7*  *Madeline Sullivan*

---

FIGURE 12.1

**OBJECTIVE** ▇1 *Identify the parts of a simple interest promissory note.*      The person borrowing the money is called the **maker** or **payer** of the note. The maker in the note in Figure 12.1 is Madeline Sullivan. The person who loaned the money, and who will receive the repayment, is called the **payee**. The payee in the note in Figure 12.1 is Charles D. Miller. The length of time until the note is due is the **term of the note**. The **face value**, or principal amount, of the note in Figure 12.1 is the amount written on the line in front of "Dollars," or $2,500. The interest rate on this same note is 12% per year. The phrase "per year" is very important—inclusion of the phrase eliminates arguments over the period for which the interest applies. The **maturity value** of the loan is the face value plus any interest that is due. Since the interest for this note is found by formulas for simple interest, this note is a **simple interest note**. Find the interest due on the 90-day (Feb. 6–May 7) loan in Figure 12.1 as follows.

$$\text{Interest} = \$2,500 \times 0.12 \times \frac{90}{360} = \$75$$

The maturity value of the loan is

$$
\begin{aligned}
\text{Maturity value} &= \text{Face value} + \text{Interest} \\
&= \$2,500 + \$75 \\
&= \$2,575.
\end{aligned}
$$

Madeline Sullivan must pay $2,575 to Charles D. Miller at the note's maturity, that is, 90 days after February 6.

The promissory note shown in Figure 12.1 contains all the information needed to calculate interest owed and maturity value. However, banks and other financial institutions use a more comprehensive note containing very detailed listings of necessary payment dates and amounts, as well as paragraphs describing the bank's rights in case of nonpayment of the note. A typical promissory note from a large bank is shown in Figure 12.2.

Many notes written by banks are secured by **collateral**. That is, the person borrowing the money must pledge assets that the bank can take in the event of nonpayment of the note. Typical collateral includes automobiles, stocks and bonds, real estate, or savings accounts. The collateral for the note in Figure 12.2 is real estate—in the event of nonpayment, the bank has the right to take a particular piece of property owned by the maker of the note, sell the property, and use the proceeds to pay off the note. (Any excess proceeds would be returned to the maker.)

**OBJECTIVE** ▇2 *Find the due date of a note.*      When the time on a promissory note is given in months, the loan is due on the same day of the month, after the given number of months has passed. For example, a four-month note made on May 25 would be due on the 25th, four months in the future. Since four months from May is September,

# FIXED RATE CONSUMER NOTE, DISCLOSURE AND SECURITY AGREEMENT

**BORROWER**

Joan Waters

**ADDRESS**
2705 4th St., Kansas City, MO

**IDENTIFICATION NO.** HA69724

**TELEPHONE NO.**

**CUSTOMER NUMBER** 3627014

**LOAN NUMBER** HA69724

| OFFICER INITIALS | INTEREST RATE | PRINCIPAL AMOUNT | FUNDING DATE | MATURITY DATE |
|---|---|---|---|---|
| GWS | 12% | $10,000 | 4/1 | 8/1 |

| ** ANNUAL PERCENTAGE RATE ** | ** FINANCE CHARGE ** | AMOUNT FINANCED | TOTAL OF PAYMENTS |
|---|---|---|---|
| THE COST OF THE CREDIT AS A YEARLY RATE. | THE DOLLAR AMOUNT THE CREDIT WILL COST. | THE AMOUNT OF CREDIT PROVIDED TO THE BORROWER OR ON BORROWER'S BEHALF. | THE AMOUNT BORROWER WILL HAVE PAID AFTER PAYMENTS HAVE BEEN MADE AS SCHEDULED. |
| 12% | $1957.04 | $10,000 | $11,957.04 |

| NUMBER OF PAYMENTS | AMOUNT OF PAYMENTS | WHEN PAYMENTS ARE DUE |
|---|---|---|
| 36 | $332.14 monthly | beginning April 11 |

**DEMAND FEATURE:** ☐ This Note has a demand feature.

**REQUIRED DEPOSIT ACCOUNT:** ☐ If checked, the Lender requires that Borrower maintain a deposit balance with Lender. The Annual Percentage Rate does not take into account required deposits.

**SECURITY:** A security interest has been granted in: ☐ Collateral securing other loans with Lender may also secure this loan; ☐ Any deposit accounts of Borrower with Lender; ☒ The goods or property being purchased; ☐ Other (describe): LOT 167, BILL MORRIS SURVEY

**FILING FEES:** $ _NONE_ In fees are being paid to public officials in order to research, perfect or release a security interest in the Collateral.

**PREPAYMENT:** If Borrower pays off early, Borrower ☐ may ☐ will not have to pay a penalty; ☐ may ☐ will not be charged a minimum finance charge; ☐ may ☐ will not be entitled to a refund of part of the finance charge.

**ITEMIZATION:** Borrower has the right to receive at this time an itemization of the Amount Financed. Borrower ☐ does ☐ does not want an itemization.

**LATE CHARGES:** If an installment is received more than _10_ days late, Borrower will be charged a late payment charge of: ☐ _____ % of the unpaid late payment charge of: ☒ _5_ % of the unpaid late installment or $ _15.00_ , whichever is ☒ greater ☐ less; as permitted by law.

**ASSUMPTION:** ☐ This loan may not be assumed on its original terms. ☐ This loan may be assumed on its original terms, subject to certain conditions.

See your contract documents for additional information about nonpayment, default, prepayment penalties and refunds and acceleration.          e means an estimate

FIGURE 12.2

the note would be due September 25. Other examples are shown in the following table.

| Date Made | Length of Loan | Due Date |
| --- | --- | --- |
| March 12 | 5 months | August 12 |
| April 24 | 7 months | November 24 |
| October 7 | 9 months | July 7 |
| January 31 | 3 months | April 30 |

**NOTE**  A loan made on January 31, for 3 months, would normally be due on April 31. However, there are only 30 days in April, so that the loan is due on April 30. Whenever a due date does not exist, such as February 30 or November 31, use the last day of the month (February 28 or November 30 in these examples).  ■

**EXAMPLE 1**  *Finding Due Date, Interest, and Maturity Value*

JoAnn's Hair Salon has two notes outstanding. The first is a loan made June 8 for 4 months at 9% with a face value of $2,800 and the second loan is dated June 30 for 8 months at $10\frac{1}{2}\%$ with a face value of $4,600. Find the due date, interest, and maturity value of (a) the first loan and (b) the second loan.

**SOLUTION**

(a)  Since 4 months from June 8 is October 8, the loan is due on October 8. Find the interest owed with the formula $I = PRT$. Substitute $2,800 for $P$, 0.09 for $R$, and $\frac{4}{12}$ for $T$.

$$I = PRT$$

$$I = \$2,800 \times 0.09 \times \frac{4}{12}$$

$$I = \$84$$

The interest on the loan is $84. Find the maturity value by adding principal and interest, with the formula $M = P + I$.

$$M = P + I$$

$$M = \$2,800 + \$84$$

$$M = \$2,884$$

The maturity value is $2,884; this amount must be paid on October 8.

(b)  Counting 8 months from June 30 produces February 30. Since February has only 28 days (if not a leap year), the note would be due on the last day of February, or February 28. Interest for 8 months is

$$I = \$4,600 \times 0.105 \times \frac{8}{12} = \$322$$

with maturity value

$$M = \$4,600 + \$322 = \$4,922.$$

A total of $4,922, representing both principal and interest, must be paid on February 28. ■

It is very common for the term of a promissory note to be expressed in days instead of months. For example, a loan might be signed on March 12, and be due in 90 days. To find the date due, use the exact number of days in a month. This can be done in either of two ways, as shown in Chapter 11.

One way is to look back at Table 11.1 which shows the number of each day. From the table, March 12 is the 71st day of the year. The loan is due 90 days after March 12. The number of the day on which the loan is due is

$$
\begin{array}{ll}
71 & \text{number of day loan is made} \\
\underline{+\ 90} & \text{number of days until due} \\
161 & \text{number of day loan is due.}
\end{array}
$$

From Table 11.1, day 161 is June 10. A 90-day loan made on March 12 is due on June 10.

As an alternate method, use the actual number of days in each month. The loan is made on March 12. Since March has 31 days, there are

$$
\begin{array}{l}
31 \\
\underline{-\ 12} \\
19
\end{array}
$$

or 19 more days in March. There are 30 days in April, and 31 in May. Find the total as follows.

$$
\begin{array}{ll}
19 & \text{rest of days in March} \\
30 & \text{days in April} \\
\underline{+\ 31} & \text{days in May} \\
80 &
\end{array}
$$

The loan is for 90 days, which is 10 more than 80, making the loan due on June 10. The following table shows several more examples.

| Date Made | Length of Loan | Due Date |
|-----------|----------------|----------|
| January 9 | 60 days | March 10 |
| May 28 | 120 days | September 25 |
| November 21 | 100 days | March 1 |
| October 9 | 180 days | April 7 |

**OBJECTIVE** **3** *Find the face value, time, and rate of a note.* The next examples show how to find the face value, time, or rate for a note. Each of these examples uses formulas from Chapter 11.

**NOTE** Face value for simple interest notes is the same as the principal $P$, that was used in Chapter 11. ■

| **EXAMPLE 2** *Finding Face Value and Interest*

Sheila Walker signed a 120-day note at 12% for funds she used for a vacation to Colorado. A single payment of $1,248 paid the note when it was due. Find the face value and interest for the note.

**SOLUTION** The payment of $1,248 is the maturity value of the note. The maturity value is found with the following formula from Chapter 11.

$$M = P(1 + RT)$$

Since $P$ is not known in this example, solve for $P$ by dividing both sides by $1 + RT$.

$$P = \frac{M}{1 + RT}$$

Now substitute $1,248 for $M$, 0.12 for $R$, and $\frac{120}{360}$ for $T$.

$$P = \frac{\$1,248}{1 + (0.12 \times \frac{120}{360})}$$

$$P = \frac{\$1,248}{1 + 0.04}$$

$$P = \frac{\$1,248}{1.04}$$

$$P = \$1,200$$

The face value of the note was $1,200; the interest charge was $1,248 − $1,200 = $48. ■

| **EXAMPLE 3** *Finding the Time of a Note*

A note is signed by the Movie Store, with a face value of $820. The interest rate is 10%, with a maturity value of $830.25. Find the time of the note, in days.

**SOLUTION** Recall the formula for time in days from Chapter 11.

$$T \text{ (in days)} = \frac{M - P}{PR} \times 360$$

Find the time by substituting $830.25 for *M*, $820 for *P*, and 0.10 for *R*.

$$T \text{ (in days)} = \frac{\$830.25 - \$820}{\$820 \times 0.10} \times 360$$

$$T \text{ (in days)} = \frac{\$10.25}{\$82} \times 360$$

$$T \text{ (in days)} = 0.125 \times 360$$

$$T \text{ (in days)} = 45 \text{ days}$$

The loan was for 45 days. The same time in days can also be found using the equation $T \text{ (in days)} = \dfrac{I}{PR} \times 360$ from Chapter 11.   ■

**NOTE**  A common error when solving for time (*T*) is forgetting to multiply by 360. When solving for time in Example 3, the number 0.125 ($\frac{1}{8}$) is the time in years. Multiplying by 360 gives the time in days.   ■

## EXAMPLE 4  *Finding the Rate of a Note*

Leslie Graham, owner of Creative Music, signed a note with a face value of $12,500 on April 12. She needed the funds to pay her income taxes. On August 30, a maturity value of $12,961.81 is to be repaid. Find the rate on the note.

**SOLUTION**  The interest on the loan is

$$\$12,961.81 - \$12,500 = \$461.81.$$

Find the rate by starting with the formula for simple interest, *I* = *PRT*, and dividing both sides by *PT*.

$$R = \frac{I}{PT}$$

Now use $461.81 for *I*, $12,500 for *P*, and $\frac{140}{360}$ for *T*, since there are 140 days from April 12 to August 30.

$$R = \frac{\$461.81}{\$12,500 \times \frac{140}{360}}$$

$$R = 9.5\% \text{ (rounded)}$$

The rate is 9.5%. The same rate can be found using the alternative form of the equation $R = \dfrac{M - P}{PT}$ found in Chapter 11.   ■

One expense that many people borrow money for is college. Figure 12.3 shows one estimate of the rising costs of just the tuition for a four-year college education. Some people use simple interest notes to help finance their college education.

College Costs on the Rise

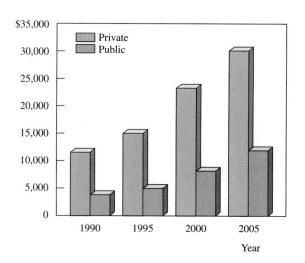

FIGURE **12.3**

*Source:* Griffin Financial News, Fall 1994.

## 12.1  EXERCISES

*Identify each of the following from the note below.*

1. maker
2. payer
3. payee
4. face value
5. term of loan
6. day loan made
7. day loan due
8. maturity value

---

**Promissory Note**

*Two Hundred and Ten Days* after date, *I* promise to pay to the order of

Denver, Colorado  *November 16*

*Julie Kern*                  / *$2,800.00*

*Two thousand, eight hundred and* $\frac{00}{100}$ Dollars with interest at  *10% per year*

_____ , payable at  *Crocker-Citizens Bank, Oak Park Branch*

Due *June 14*                          *Lupe Jones*

*Find the due date for each of the following.*

| Date Made | Term of Loan |
|---|---|
| 9. March 4 | 4 months |
| 10. July 28 | 8 months |
| 11. December 31 | 6 months |
| 12. May 31 | 4 months |
| 13. January 6 | 70 days |
| 14. September 14 | 125 days |
| 15. November 24 | 150 days |
| 16. December 8 | 160 days |

*Find the date due and the maturity value for each of the following. Use Table 11.1 on page 371 in your textbook. Round money to the nearest cent.*

| Date Made | Face Value | Term of Loan | Rate |
|---|---|---|---|
| 17. June 12 | $6,000 | 150 days | 9% |
| 18. February 28 | $3,500 | 240 days | 10% |
| 19. August 14 | $5,000 | 300 days | $8\frac{1}{2}\%$ |
| 20. October 20 | $4,500 | 180 days | 12% |

*Complete the following table. Round money to the nearest cent, time to the nearest day, and rate to the nearest tenth of a percent.*

| | Principal | Rate | Time | Maturity Value |
|---|---|---|---|---|
| 21. | _____ | 9% | 150 days | $16,600 |
| 22. | _____ | 6% | 80 days | $1,216 |
| 23. | $3,600 | 8% | _____ | $3,696 |
| 24. | $9,000 | 11% | _____ | $9,660 |
| 25. | $8,400 | _____ | 140 days | $8,759.33 |
| 26. | $9,500 | _____ | 180 days | $10,165 |
| 27. | $12,240 | $10\frac{1}{2}\%$ | 200 days | _____ |
| 28. | $15,000 | 9% | 150 days | _____ |

29. State and explain the different parts of a simple interest promissory note. (See Objective 1.)

30. Name at least five reasons why a small firm such as a bicycle or boat shop might need to borrow money.

*Solve each of the following application problems. Use Table 11.1 on page 371 in your text-book.*

**31.** Susan Eisenhammer and Pam Carlson manage the Nelison Real Estate Office. They bought a supply of "for sale" and "sold" signs by signing a 100-day, $8\frac{1}{4}$% note for $1,125 on October 1. Find (a) the due date and (b) the maturity value of the note.

**32.** Jill Sample's Ski House bought $15,900 worth of skis from Rossignol on September 19. The firm signed a 200-day, $11\frac{1}{2}$% note for the skis. Find (a) the due date and (b) the maturity value of the note.

**33.** Jones Fence Company signed a 9-month, 11% note on March 13 for $21,000. Find (a) the due date and (b) the maturity value.

**34.** Jane Reeves just became a veterinarian and needs $48,000 to start her small animal clinic. She borrows this amount at $12\frac{1}{8}$% for 8 months on a note dated March 31. Find (a) the due date and (b) the maturity value.

**35.** A 100-day note with an interest rate of 12% has a maturity value of $15,500. Find the face value.

**36.** A tire company gives a supplier a 72-day note, with interest of 9%. The maturity value of the note is $9,671. Find the face value of the note.

**37.** Susan Chong, an optometrist, signed a 7-month, 10% note with a maturity value of $23,812.50 due on July 7. Find (a) the date the loan was made and (b) the face value.

**38.** A physical therapist signed an 11-month, $9\frac{1}{2}$% note with a maturity value of $92,836.92 due on March 30. Find (a) the date the loan was made and (b) the face value.

**39.** West Stationery is getting ready to pay a note that is due. The interest rate is 12%, the face value is $4,000, and the interest is $120. Find the time (in days) of the note.

**40.** Lewin Scuba just paid the $7,536 maturity value on a note with a face value of $7,200. The interest rate was 8%. Find the time (in days) of the note.

**41.** The manager of the local electronics plant bought a security system for $12,000, paying for it with a 120-day note with a maturity value of $12,320. Find the interest rate she paid on the note.

**42.** Dunn Brothers Coffee Company signed a $17,000, 90-day note for a shipment of coffee. The maturity value of the note was $17,382.50. Find the interest rate paid.

## 12.2    Simple Discount Notes

**OBJECTIVES**

**1**  *Define simple discount notes.*

**2**  *Find bank discount and proceeds.*

**3**  *Calculate proceeds if given face value, discount rate, and time.*

**4**  *Distinguish between discount rates and interest rates.*

**5**  *Find effective interest rates.*

**6**  *Understand T-bills.*

**7**  *Find the face value that produces the desired proceeds.*

**8**  *Find discount rate, face value, or time.*

With the simple interest notes of the previous section, interest is based on the face value. The sum of the face value and the interest is the maturity value of the note.

**OBJECTIVE 1** *Define simple discount notes.* Another common type of note, called a **simple discount note**, has the interest deducted in advance from the face value, with only the difference given to the borrower. Such notes are sometimes called **interest-in-advance notes** since the interest is subtracted before any money is given to the borrower. In this section, we discuss simple discount notes; in the next section, simple discount notes and simple interest notes are compared.

Face value has a different meaning for simple discount notes than it does for the simple interest notes we just studied in Section 12.1. **For a simple discount note, the face value and the maturity value of the note are the same.** Therefore, the face value is the repayment amount at the end of the term of the loan. The amount the borrower receives at the beginning of the loan term is called the **proceeds**. The amount of interest charged, which is the difference between the face amount and the proceeds, is called the **bank discount**, or just the **discount**. A discount is just *interest deducted in advance*.

For example, suppose you sign a note for $2,000, and the bank charges a discount of $150. The proceeds, the amount you actually receive, is

$$\$2,000 - \$150 = \$1,850.$$

**NOTE** In this example, the maturity value of the note is $2,000, which is also the face value. This shows a key feature of simple discount notes—the face value and maturity value are the same. ∎

It is important to understand the difference between simple interest notes and simple discount notes.

> Simple *interest* is calculated on the *principal*, while simple *discount* is calculated on the *maturity value*.

**OBJECTIVE 2** *Find bank discount and proceeds.* The formula for finding bank discount is very similar to the formula for simple interest.

> The *discount B*, on a simple discount note with a maturity value (or face value) *M*, for *T* years at a discount rate *D* is
>
> $$B = MDT.$$
>
> The *proceeds*, *P*, are
>
> $$P = M - B.$$
>
> The **maturity value** or **face value**, *M*, is the sum of the discount and the proceeds.
>
> $$M = P + B$$

**NOTE**    Actually, the formula for simple interest, $I = PRT$, could be used with simple discount. However, the formula is written $B = MDT$ to emphasize that the loan is a *discount* loan.    ■

**EXAMPLE 1**    *Finding Discount and Proceeds*

Elizabeth Thornton signs an $8,800, 8-month note at the bank. The banker discounts the note at 12%. Find the amount of the discount and the proceeds.

**SOLUTION**    To find the discount, use the formula $B = MDT$. Here, $M =$ $8,800, $D = 12\%$, and $T = \frac{8}{12}$ year.

$$B = MDT$$

$$B = \$8,800 \times 0.12 \times \frac{8}{12}$$

$$B = \$704$$

The discount of $704 represents the interest charge on the loan. The proceeds are found by subtracting the discount from the face value, using the formula $P = M - B$.

$$\text{Proceeds} = \$8,800 - \$704 = \$8,096$$

Upon signing the note for $8,800, Thornton will be given $8,096. Then 8 months later, she must make a single payment of $8,800.    ■

In Example 1, the proceeds of $8,096 could be thought of as the present value at simple interest of $8,800 at 12% for 8 months. Similarly, the maturity value or face value of $8,800 can be thought of as the future value of $8,096 at 12% for 8 months.

**OBJECTIVE 3**    *Calculate proceeds if given face value, discount rate, and time.*    As given by the discount formula, the discount is $B = MDT$. If $P$ represents the proceeds, then $P$ is found by subtracting the bank discount from the face value, or

$$P = M - MDT.$$

The distributive property gives the formula for proceeds shown in the next box.

> The *proceeds*, $P$, for a simple discount note with a maturity value (or face value) $M$ for $T$ years at a discount rate $D$ is
>
> $$P = M - B$$
>
> or
>
> $$P = M(1 - DT).$$

**EXAMPLE 2**    *Finding Proceeds*

Adventure Travel borrows $25,000 for 90 days at a discount rate of $10\frac{1}{2}\%$ to help cover operating expenses. Find the proceeds.

**SOLUTION**   There are two ways to find the proceeds. One way would be to first use the formula $B = MDT$, find the discount, and then subtract the discount from the face value to find the proceeds. Doing this,

$$B = MDT$$

$$B = \$25,000 \times 0.105 \times \frac{90}{360} = \$656.25.$$

The proceeds are then

$$P = M - D = \$25,000 - \$656.25 = \$24,343.75.$$

As a second method for finding the proceeds, use the formula $P = M(1 - DT)$. Here, $M = \$25,000$, $D = 10\frac{1}{2}\%$, and $T = \frac{90}{360}$.

$$P = M(1 - DT)$$

$$P = \$25,000\left[1 - \left(0.105 \times \frac{90}{360}\right)\right]$$

Inside the brackets, be sure to first multiply 0.105 and $\frac{90}{360}$, and then subtract.

$$P = \$25,000(1 - 0.02625)$$

$$P = \$25,000(0.97375)$$

$$P = \$24,343.75$$

By this method, it is not necessary to find the bank discount.   ■

**NOTE**   It is important *not to round too soon* in these problems, in order to avoid rounding errors.   ■

---

**CALCULATOR APPROACH TO EXAMPLE 2**

*For the calculator solution to this example, think of the problem as

$$\$25,000\left(1 - 0.105 \times \frac{90}{360}\right)$$

and enter the parentheses accordingly.

25000 $\boxed{\times}$ $\boxed{(}$ 1 $\boxed{-}$ .105 $\boxed{\times}$ 90 $\boxed{\div}$ 360 $\boxed{)}$ $\boxed{=}$ 24343.75

---

**OBJECTIVE** **4** *Distinguish between discount rates and interest rates.*   A discount rate of 12% is not the same as an interest rate of 12%. The next example shows why.

**EXAMPLE 3**   *Comparing Discount Rates and Interest Rates*

Two different notes each have a face value of $7,500 and a time of 90 days. One has a simple interest rate of 12%, and the other has a discount rate of 12%.

---

*NOTE: All calculator solutions use a scientific calculator. Refer to Appendix A for scientific and financial calculator basics.

**(a)** Find the interest owed on each.

SOLUTION

| For the Simple Interest Note | For the Simple Discount Note |
|---|---|
| $I = PRT$ | $B = MDT$ |
| $I = \$7{,}500 \times 0.12 \times \dfrac{90}{360}$ | $B = \$7{,}500 \times 0.12 \times \dfrac{90}{360}$ |
| $I = \$225$ | $B = \$225$ |

In each case, the interest is $225.

**(b)** Find the amount *actually received* by the borrower in each case.

SOLUTION

| For the Simple Interest Note | For the Simple Discount Note |
|---|---|
| Principal = Face value | Proceeds = $M - B$ |
| = $7,500 | = $7,500 − $225 |
| | = $7,275 |

With the simple interest note, the borrower has the use of $7,500, but only $7,275 is available with the simple discount note. In each case, the interest charge is the same, $225, but more money is available with the simple interest note.

**(c)** Find the maturity value of each note.

SOLUTION

| For the Simple Interest Note | For the Simple Discount Note |
|---|---|
| $M = P + I$ | Maturity value = Face Value |
| = $7,500 + $225 | = $7,500 |
| = $7,725 | |

The differences between these two notes can be summarized as follows.

|  | Simple Interest | Simple Discount |
|---|---|---|
| Face value | $7,500 | $7,500 |
| Interest | $225 | $225 |
| Amount available to borrower | $7,500 | $7,275 |
| Maturity value | $7,725 | $7,500 |

Clearly, the simple interest note is better for the borrower.    ∎

**OBJECTIVE 5** *Find effective interest rates.*    Because of the possible confusion resulting from the different ways of calculating interest charges, the **Federal Truth in Lending Act** was passed in 1969. This act requires that all interest rates be given as comparable percents. While this law is discussed in more detail in Chapter 13, the next example shows how to get the simple interest rate corresponding to the given discount rate of Example 3.

| EXAMPLE 4 *Finding Rate of Interest for Discount Notes*

Find the rate of interest for the simple discount note in Example 3.

**SOLUTION**    The discount rate of 12% given in Example 3 is not the rate of interest, since the 12% applies to the maturity value of $7,500 and not to the proceeds of $7,275. Since the borrower received only $7,275, the interest rate must be found from this amount. Do this with the formula for simple interest, $I = PRT$. Here $I = $225$ (the discount), $P = $7,275$ (the proceeds), $T = \frac{90}{360}$ year, and $R$ must be found. Start with $I = PRT$, and divide both sides by $PT$.

$$R = \frac{I}{PT}$$

Then substitute the given numbers.

$$R = \frac{\$225}{\$7,275 \times \frac{90}{360}}$$

$$R = \frac{\$225}{\$1,818.75}$$

$$R = 0.1237 \quad \text{(rounded)}$$

The rate of interest is 12.37% rounded to the nearest hundredth of a percent. This rate is called the **effective rate of interest**, or the **true rate of interest**. By federal regulations, a person borrowing $7,500 for 90 days at a discount rate of 12% would have to be told that the **annual percentage rate** on the loan is 12.5% (instead of 12.37%, since the regulations require rounding up to the nearest quarter of a percent).    ∎

**OBJECTIVE** **6** *Understand T-bills.*    One common use of discount interest is that involved in the purchase of **U.S. Treasury bills** (often called just **T-bills**). The federal government uses T-bills to borrow money. T-bills are currently available with 13-week, 26-week, or 52-week maturity. An investor buys a T-bill at a price equal to the proceeds after the discount is subtracted. The investor then receives the full face value of the T-bill when it reaches maturity. Since T-bills are loans to the federal government, they are considered one of the safest of all possible investments.

**EXAMPLE 5** *Finding Facts About T-Bills*

An investor buys a $10,000 T-bill at a 4% discount rate for 26 weeks. Find (a) the purchase price of the T-bill, (b) the maturity value, (c) the interest earned, and (d) the effective rate of interest.

**SOLUTION**   $M = \$10,000; D = 0.04; T = \dfrac{26}{52}$

(a)  **Bank discount = Face value × Discount rate × Time**

$$= \$10,000 \times 0.04 \times \frac{26}{52}$$

$$= \$200$$

**Purchase price = Face value − Bank discount**

$$= \$10,000 - \$200$$

$$= \$9,800$$

(b)  **Maturity value = Face value**

$$= \$10,000$$

(c)  **Interest = Bank discount**

$$= \$200$$

(d)  **Effective rate** $= \dfrac{\textbf{Interest earned}}{\textbf{Purchase price × Time}}$

$$= \frac{\$200}{\$9,800 \times \frac{26}{52}}$$

$$= 0.0408$$

$$= 4.08\%$$   ∎

**OBJECTIVE** **7** *Find the face value that produces the desired proceeds.*    Normally a borrower wants to borrow a certain amount of money. The next example shows how to find the face value of a simple discount note so that the proceeds will be the amount needed by the borrower.

### EXAMPLE 6 *Finding Face Value that Produces Desired Proceeds*

Mike Collins needs $4,000 to repair his roof. Find the value of a note that will provide the $4,000 in proceeds if he plans to repay the note in 180 days and the bank charges a 15% discount rate.

**SOLUTION** Start with the formula $P = M(1 - DT)$. Since $M$ is not known, find a formula for $M$ by dividing both sides by $1 - DT$.

$$M = \frac{P}{1 - DT}$$

Replace $P$ with $4,000, $D$ with 0.15, and $T$ with $\frac{180}{360}$.

$$M = \frac{\$4,000}{(1 - 0.15 \times \frac{180}{360})}$$

$$M = \frac{\$4,000}{1 - 0.075}$$

$$M = \frac{4,000}{0.925}$$

$$M = \$4,324.32 \qquad \text{(rounded)}$$

Collins must sign a note with a face value of $4,324.32 (to the nearest cent) to get the $4,000 that he needs. ∎

---

**CALCULATOR APPROACH TO EXAMPLE 6**

The calculator solution to this example is

4000 $\div$ ( 1 $-$ .15 $\times$ 180 $\div$ 360 ) = 4324.32.

---

**OBJECTIVE 8** *Find discount rate, face value, or time.* Just as the formula for simple interest, $I = PRT$, can be solved for $P$, $R$, or $T$, the formula for discount, $B = MDT$, can be solved for $M$, $D$, or $T$. Do this as shown in the next example.

### EXAMPLE 7 *Finding Discount*

Sheila Watts borrowed proceeds of $4,480 to help with college expenses. Her 240-day note had a maturity value of $4,800. Find the discount rate.

**SOLUTION**    To find the discount rate, start with the formula $B = MDT$ and divide both sides by $MT$.

$$D = \frac{B}{MT}$$

The discount is

$$B = \$4,800 - \$4,480 = \$320;$$

also $M = \$4,800$ and $T = \frac{240}{360}$. Now find $D$.

$$D = \frac{\$320}{\$4,800 \times \frac{240}{360}}$$

$$D = \frac{\$320}{\$3,200}$$

$$D = 0.10$$

The discount rate is 10%.    ■

## 12.2    EXERCISES

*Find the discount and the proceeds. Round money to the nearest cent.*

|     | Maturity Value | Discount Rate | Time in Days |
| --- | --- | --- | --- |
| 1. | $2,800 | 10% | 60 |
| 2. | $4,500 | 16% | 90 |
| 3. | $6,200 | $14\frac{1}{4}\%$ | 180 |
| 4. | $15,500 | 12% | 200 |
| 5. | $8,400 | $9\frac{1}{2}\%$ | 30 |
| 6. | $9,800 | $8\frac{3}{4}\%$ | 50 |

*Find the due date and the proceeds for the following.*

|     | Maturity Value | Discount Rate | Date Made | Time in Days |
| --- | --- | --- | --- | --- |
| 7. | $4,200 | 10% | Sept. 10 | 60 |
| 8. | $5,400 | 12% | Mar. 25 | 90 |
| 9. | $12,000 | $9\frac{1}{2}\%$ | Aug. 21 | 180 |
| 10. | $8,500 | 14% | Nov. 12 | 240 |

*Complete this table.*

| | Maturity Value | Discount Rate | Date Made | Due Date | Time in Days | Discount | Proceeds |
|---|---|---|---|---|---|---|---|
| 11. | $16,000 | 9% | 5/11 | _____ | 90 | _____ | _____ |
| 12. | $8,275 | 7% | _____ | 9/10 | 120 | _____ | _____ |
| 13. | $14,400 | _____ | _____ | 1/4 | 150 | $660 | _____ |
| 14. | $8,200 | _____ | 2/9 | 5/10 | _____ | $205 | _____ |
| 15. | _____ | _____ | 11/12 | _____ | 90 | $108 | $7,092 |
| 16. | _____ | _____ | 11/4 | 6/2 | _____ | $1,176 | $24,024 |

*Solve each of the following application problems. Round rate to the nearest tenth of a percent and money to the nearest cent.*

17. The Early Learning Center signed a 240-day note at a discount rate of 9% with a face value of $12,000. Find the discount and the proceeds.

18. Find the discount and the proceeds on an $8,000 note for 90 days if the bank charges a 14% discount rate.

19. Walter Bates needed money to go on a business trip to Alaska and he signed a note for $6,000. At a $10\frac{1}{2}$% discount rate, the discount on the note was $210. Find the length of the loan in days.

20. Margaret Jones signs a $4,500 note at 12% simple discount to buy supplies for her catering company. Find the length of the loan in days if the discount is $135.

21. A 60-day note for $14,000 was signed. Given a discount of $291.67, find the discount rate.

22. A construction firm in Mexico signed a 200-day note with a U.S. bank for $850,000. Find the discount rate given proceeds of $793,333.33.

23. Jane Peters frequently travels to Hong Kong and needs to purchase a laptop computer costing $3,200. Given a discount rate of 10% and a 140-day term, find the maturity value of the loan.

24. Mary Gibb estimates that she needs $10,000 to finish her last year at college. She borrows the funds from her uncle for 12 months at a favorable 4% discount rate. Find the face value of the loan.

25. Marge Prullage signs a $4,200 note at the bank. The bank charges an 11% discount rate. Find the proceeds if the note is for 10 months. Find the effective interest rate charged by the bank.

26. Ed Foust goes to the bank and signs a note for $8,400. The bank charges a 7% discount rate. Find the proceeds and the effective rate charged by the bank if the note is for 8 months.

*Exercises 27 and 28 involve present value at simple interest, discussed in Section 11.4.*

27. Find the proceeds of a $4,000, 90-day note at an 8% discount rate. Find the present value of $4,000 in 90 days at 8% interest.

**28.** Find the proceeds of a $700 note for 180 days at a 10% discount rate. Find the present value of $700 in 180 days at 10% interest.

*The following exercises apply to U.S. Treasury bills. (Assume 52 weeks per year for each exercise, and round to the nearest hundredth of a percent.)*

**29.** An investor buys a $5,000 T-bill at a 4% discount for 13 weeks. Find each of the following: (a) the purchase price of the T-bill, (b) the maturity value, (c) the interest earned, and (d) the effective rate of interest.

**30.** Melissa Wilson buys a $100,000 T-bill at a 3.2% discount for 26 weeks. Find each of the following: (a) the purchase price of the T-bill, (b) the maturity value, (c) the interest earned, and (d) the effective rate of interest.

**31.** Explain the difference between simple interest notes and simple discount notes.

**32.** Compare the formulas for simple interest rate and simple discount rate. Define all variables for both and explain the difference between simple interest rate and simple discount rate. (See Objective 4.)

**33.** Find the current T-bill rate for 13-week, 26-week, and 52-week maturities.

**34.** Why do you think banks and large corporations sometimes own T-bills?

## 12.3   Comparing Simple Interest and Simple Discount

**OBJECTIVES**

**1**   *Compare the differences between simple interest and simple discount notes.*

**2**   *Convert between simple interest and simple discount rates.*

If you work in the finance area for a firm, or if you ever own your own business, you will see both simple interest and simple discount notes. We will compare these two types of notes in this section. Then we will discuss ways of comparing simple interest rates and simple discount rates.

First, let us list the key similarities between these two types of notes.

> The borrower receives a lump sum of money at the beginning of each type of note.
>
> Both types of notes are repaid with a single payment at the end of a stated period of time.
>
> This length of time is generally one year or less.

**OBJECTIVE 1   *Compare the differences between simple interest and simple discount notes.***
Table 12.1 compares these two types of notes.

TABLE 12.1   **A Comparison of Simple Interest and Simple Discount Notes**

| | **Variables Used for Simple Interest** | **Variables Used for Simple Discount** |
|---|---|---|
| | $I$ = Interest | $B$ = Discount |
| | $P$ = Principal (Face value) | $P$ = Proceeds (Amount received) |
| | $R$ = Rate of interest | $D$ = Discount rate |
| | $T$ = Time in years, or Fraction of a year | $T$ = Time in years, or Fraction of a year |
| | $M$ = Maturity value | $M$ = Maturity value (Face value) |

| | **Simple Interest** | **Simple Discount** |
|---|---|---|
| **Face value** | Stated on note, or $$P = \frac{M}{1 + RT}$$ | Same as Maturity value, or $$M = \frac{P}{1 - DT}$$ |
| **Interest charge** | $I = PRT$ | $B = MDT$ |
| **Maturity value** | $M = P + I$ or $M = P(1 + RT)$ | Same as face value, or $$M = \frac{P}{1 - DT}$$ |
| **Amount received by borrower** | Face value or principal | Proceeds: $P = M - B$ or $P = M(1 - DT)$ |
| **Identifying phrases** | Interest at a certain rate | Discounted at a certain rate |
| | Maturity value greater than face value | Proceeds |
| | Simple interest | Maturity value equal to face value |
| | | Simple discount rate |
| **True annual interest rate** | Same as stated rate, $R$ | Greater than stated rate, $D$ |

**OBJECTIVE** **2** *Convert between simple interest and simple discount rates.*   As shown earlier, a 15% simple interest rate is **NOT** the same as a 15% simple discount rate. The rest of this section shows formulas for conversion back and forth between simple interest rates and simple discount rates.

To find these formulas, start with the key formulas for simple interest and for simple discount.

|  **Simple Interest**  |  |  **Simple Discount**  |
|---|---|---|
| $M = P(1 + RT)$ | and | $P = M(1 - DT)$ |

Solve each of these formulas for $P$, the principal and proceeds respectively. This is the lump sum received by the borrower in both cases.

| **Simple Interest** | **Simple Discount** |
|---|---|
| $P = \dfrac{M}{1 + RT}$ | $P = M(1 - DT)$ |

Since each right-hand side is equal to $P$, the two right-hand sides must be equal to each other, or

$$\frac{M}{1 + RT} = M(1 - DT).$$

Divide both sides by $M$ to get

$$\frac{1}{1 + RT} = 1 - DT.$$

By going through several more algebraic steps, this equation can be solved first for $R$ and then for $D$, giving the results in the box.

> The simple interest rate $R$ and the simple discount rate $D$ are calculated by the formulas
>
> $$R = \frac{D}{1 - DT} \quad \text{and} \quad D = \frac{R}{1 + RT}$$
>
> where $T$ is time in years.

**NOTE**   The simple interest rate corresponding to a simple discount rate is also called the **effective rate of interest**. As these formulas show, the maturity value plays no part in converting between rates—only rate and time matter.   ■

**EXAMPLE 1**   *Converting Interest and Discount Rates*

The owner of Bass Boats, Inc. has two outstanding notes. (a) The first note is a 120-day simple discount note with a face value of $28,000 and a discount rate of 10%. Convert this rate to a simple interest (effective interest) rate. (b) The second note is a 160-day simple interest note with a face value of $85,000 and an interest rate of 12%. Find the corresponding simple discount rate.

**SOLUTION**

(a) Find $R$ with the following formula.

$$R = \frac{D}{1 - DT}$$

Note that the face value is not needed.
Here $D = 0.10$ and $T = \frac{120}{360}$.

$$R = \frac{0.10}{1 - (0.10 \times \frac{120}{360})} = \frac{0.1}{1 - 0.033333} = \frac{0.1}{0.966666} = 0.1034$$

rounding to the nearest hundredth of a percent. The corresponding simple interest rate is 10.34%.

**(b)** Find the simple discount rate that corresponds to a simple interest rate of 12% for 160 days. Use the following formula.

$$D = \frac{R}{1 + RT}$$

Note that the face value is not needed.

Replace $R$ with 0.12 and $T$ with $\frac{160}{360}$. Then

$$D = \frac{0.12}{1 + (0.12 \times \frac{160}{360})} = \frac{0.12}{1 + 0.053333} = \frac{0.12}{1.053333} = 0.1139$$

or 11.39%, rounded to the nearest hundredth of a percent. ∎

Notice that in both parts (a) and (b) in Example 1 above, the simple interest rate is larger than the simple discount rate. This is always the case when comparing the discount rate and interest rate of the same note.

CALCULATOR APPROACH
TO EXAMPLE 1

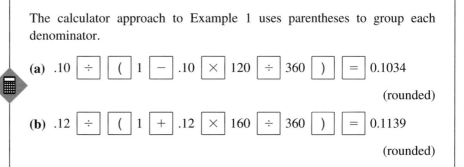

The calculator approach to Example 1 uses parentheses to group each denominator.

**(a)** .10 ÷ ( 1 − .10 × 120 ÷ 360 ) = 0.1034

(rounded)

**(b)** .12 ÷ ( 1 + .12 × 160 ÷ 360 ) = 0.1139

(rounded)

## 12.3  EXERCISES

*Find the simple interest rate that corresponds to the given discount rate for the given time. Round to the nearest hundredth of a percent.*

**1.** 8%, 90 days

**2.** 12%, 180 days

**3.** $14\frac{1}{4}$%, 200 days

**4.** $12\frac{1}{2}$%, 100 days

*Find the simple discount rate that corresponds to the given simple interest rate for the given time. Round to the nearest hundredth of a percent.*

**5.** 7%, 90 days

**6.** 8%, 240 days

**7.** 10%, 100 days

**8.** 9%, 180 days

**9.** Is the rate associated with simple discount notes the true annual interest rate? If not, explain why not and show how to calculate the true rate.

**10.** If you were offered a simple interest note at a rate of 12% and a simple discount note with a discount of 12%, which would you prefer? Why?

*Solve each of the following application problems.*

**11.** Sherri Johnson needs to borrow money for an operation for her invalid father. She can borrow at a 13% simple interest rate or at a 12.8% simple discount rate. If she needs the money for 90 days, which loan should she take?

**12.** Bill Walsh wants to borrow money to expand his business. One bank charges a 17% simple interest rate and a second bank charges a 16.4% simple discount rate. If he needs the money for 120 days, which loan should he take?

**13.** Joan Boston wishes to borrow exactly $4,500 for 180 days so that she can go on a Carribean cruise. How much less interest is paid with a 12% simple interest note compared to a 12% simple discount note?

**14.** Alamo Energy wishes to borrow exactly $900,000 for 9 months to drill three oil and gas wells. How much less interest is paid with a 14% simple interest note compared to a 14% simple discount note?

 **15.** Show the algebraic steps needed to solve $\dfrac{1}{1 + RT} = 1 - DT$   for $D$.

 **16.** Show the algebraic steps needed to solve $\dfrac{1}{1 + RT} = 1 - DT$   for $R$.

## 12.1   Discounting a Note

### OBJECTIVES

**1**   *Find the discount and the proceeds of a note.*

**2**   *Find the proceeds of a rediscounted note.*

Businesses often accept notes, either simple interest notes or simple discount notes, in place of immediate payment for goods or services. For example, a manufacturer of ski equipment may deliver goods to ski shops in October and may agree not to collect from the shops until April. To secure its payment, the manufacturer may request promissory notes from the ski shops receiving the goods.

As a result, the manufacturer may have a considerable amount of cash tied up in promissory notes that will not be paid until April. To get cash earlier, the manufacturer can sell the promissory notes to a bank. The bank will give the manufacturer the maturity value of the notes, less a fee charged by the bank for this service. This fee is called the **bank discount** or just **discount**. The process of receiving cash for a note is called **discounting a note**.

The amount of cash actually received by the manufacturer is called the **proceeds**. The bank then collects the maturity value from the maker of the note when it becomes due. Normally, such notes are sold with **recourse**. This means that if the maker of the note does not pay for some reason, the bank collects from the seller of the note. This protects the bank against loss.

**OBJECTIVE 1**   *Find the discount and the proceeds of a note.*    Use the following procedure to discount a note.

1. Find the maturity value of the original note (if necessary).
2. Find the discount period.
3. Find the discount using the formula $B = MDT$.
4. The proceeds are found by $P = M - B$.

This method is shown in the next examples.

## EXAMPLE 1 *Finding Proceeds*

Donna's Termite Service holds a 90-day simple interest note dated July 9 with a face value of $2,850 and interest of 10%. The firm wishes to convert the note to cash on August 19. Given a discount rate of 12%, find the proceeds to the company.

**SOLUTION**    Go through the four steps of discounting a note.

### DISCOUNTING A NOTE

***Step 1.*** First find the simple interest on the note.

$$\text{Interest} = \$2,850 \times 0.10 \times \frac{90}{360} = \$71.25$$

The **maturity value** of the note is

$$\$2,850 + \$71.25 = \$2,921.25.$$

***Step 2.*** Find the **discount period**, the number of days remaining before the note is due. The discount period is often found by a diagram as shown in Figure 12.4.

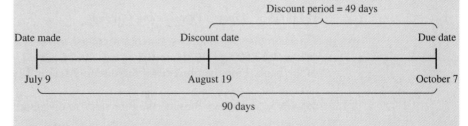

**FIGURE 12.4**

In this example, the date of the note is July 9, the note is discounted on August 19, and the due date is October 7 (July 9 + 90 days = October 7). August 19 to October 7 is 49 days, found as follows.

| | |
|---:|---|
| 12 | days left in August |
| 30 | days in September |
| + 7 | days until note is due in October |
| 49 | days discount period |

**Step 3.** Find the bank **discount**, using the formula $B = MDT$. Use the numbers in the example, including a discount rate of 12%.

$$B = \$2,921.25 \times 0.12 \times \frac{49}{360} = \$47.71$$

The bank discount is $47.71.

**Step 4.** Find the proceeds using the formula $P = M - B$.

$$P = \$2,921.25 - \$47.71 = \$2,873.54$$

The bank purchases the note on August 19 for $2,873.54 in cash paid to Donna's Termite Service. Then, on October 7 (the maturity date), the bank will collect $2,921.25 from the maker of the note.

In summary:

| Date | Transaction |
|------|-------------|
| July 9 | **Payer signs 90-day note in return for $2,850 cash or in return for $2,850 in services.** |
| August 19 | **Donna's Termite Service sells note to bank for $2,873.54.** |
| October 7 | **Bank receives $2,921.25 from payer.** |

&#9632;

**NOTE**  In discounting a note, the business gets less money but it will get the money sooner.  &#9632;

| **EXAMPLE 2**  *Finding Proceeds and Discount*

On February 27, Andrews Lincoln-Mercury receives a 150-day note with a face value of $3,500 at 8% interest per year. On March 27, the firm discounts the note at the bank. Find the proceeds if the discount rate is 12%.

**SOLUTION**    Again, go through the four steps in discounting a note.

**Step 1**  Find the interest and maturity value. Find the interest with the formula $I = PRT$.

$$\text{Interest} = \$3,500 \times 0.08 \times \frac{150}{360} = \$116.67$$

The interest on the note is $116.67. The maturity value is found with the formula $M = P + I$.

$$\text{Maturity value} = \$3,500 + \$116.67 = \$3,616.67$$

**Step 2**  Find the discount period using the diagram in Figure 12.5.

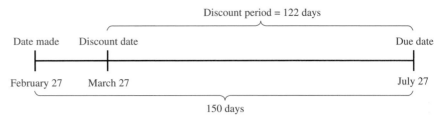

FIGURE 12.5

**PROBLEM-SOLVING HINT** Remember, the discount period is calculated from the *due date* of the loan, and not from the date the loan was made. ■

The discount period is 122 days.

**Step 3**  Find the bank discount, using the discount rate of 12%. Use the formula $B = MDT$.

$$\text{Discount} = \$3,616.67 \times 0.12 \times \frac{122}{360} = \$147.08$$

The discount is $147.08

**Step 4**  Find the proceeds.

$$P = M - B$$

$$P = \$3,616.67 - \$147.08 = \$3,469.59$$

Andrews receives $3,469.59 from the bank on March 27. ■

**OBJECTIVE 2**  *Find the proceeds of a rediscounted note.*  In the next example, a company borrows money from a bank by signing a simple discount note. The bank making the loan then sells the note to a large finance company. In this case, with the same note being discounted twice, the note is said to have been **rediscounted**. Notice in the example that the rate charged by the finance company to the bank is lower than the rate charged to the public. This is very common in transactions between large financial institutions, with the lower rate a sort of "wholesale" rate.

Even though the note in Example 3 is rediscounted, the steps used are basically the same as those used in earlier examples. The only difference is that since the original note was a simple discount note instead of a simple interest note, it is not necessary to solve for maturity value. The face value *is* the maturity value.

**EXAMPLE 3**  *Finding Proceeds of a Rediscounted Note*

Barbara Hanks, chief financial officer of Cole Springs Mattress, signed a 180-day note at the bank, with a face value of $140,000. The bank discounted the note at 12%. Then, 54 days after the note was signed, the bank rediscounted the note to Century Finance which charged an 8% discount. Find the proceeds Century Finance must pay to the bank.

**SOLUTION**    Go through the steps given for discounting a note.

**Step 1**    The maturity value of the note is $140,000.

**NOTE**    The fact that the bank charged a 12% discount rate plays no part in the problem since only the maturity value of the note is needed.    ■

**Step 2**    The discount period is $180 - 54 = 126$ days.

**Step 3**    The discount (at Century Finance) is

$$\text{Discount} = \$140,000 \times 0.08 \times \frac{126}{360} = \$3,920.$$

**Step 4**    The proceeds are

$$\$140,000 - \$3,920 = \$136,080.$$

This example can be summarized as follows: Cole Springs Mattress signs a note with a maturity value of $140,000. Then, 54 days after the note is signed, the bank rediscounts the note to Century Finance, receiving proceeds of $136,080. Finally, 180 days after signing the note and 126 days after the note was discounted, Cole Springs Mattress pays $140,000 to Century Finance.    ■

Not only notes are discounted. It is very common for a business to sell part of its accounts receivable (money owed to the business—see Section 17.3) to a financial institution. This process is called **factoring**, and the people who buy the accounts receivable are called **factors**. The calculations involved with factoring are the same as those discussed in this section.

## 12.4    EXERCISES

*Find the discount period for each of the following.*

| | Loan Made | Length of Loan | Date of Discount |
|---|---|---|---|
| 1. | February 20 | 90 days | March 30 |
| 2. | March 13 | 180 days | June 1 |
| 3. | August 4 | 220 days | January 12 |
| 4. | November 5 | 60 days | December 18 |

*Find the proceeds when each of the following simple discount notes are discounted.*

| | Maturity Value | Discount Period | Discount Rate |
|---|---|---|---|
| 5. | $4,800 | 90 days | $8\frac{1}{2}\%$ |
| 6. | $8,000 | 200 days | 9% |
| 7. | $15,000 | 180 days | 12% |
| 8. | $12,000 | 270 days | 14% |

*Each of the following simple interest notes was discounted at 12%. Find the discount period, the discount, and the proceeds for each.*

| | Loan Made | Face Value | Length of Loan | Simple Interest Rate | Discounted |
|---|---|---|---|---|---|
| 9. | January 9 | $3,500 | 120 days | 9% | March 9 |
| 10. | April 23 | $4,000 | 150 days | 7% | June 11 |
| 11. | July 10 | $2,000 | 72 days | 12% | August 2 |
| 12. | May 29 | $4,500 | 80 days | 8% | July 8 |
| 13. | September 18 | $10,000 | 220 days | 10% | February 4 |
| 14. | October 11 | $17,500 | 100 days | 11% | January 2 |

*Solve each of the following application problems.*

15. On May 10, Ace Plumbing accepted a 190-day, 10% interest note for $12,000 from a contractor in lieu of a cash payment. The note is discounted on July 26 at a 12% rate. Find (a) the discount period, (b) the discount, and (c) the proceeds to Ace Plumbing.

16. Home Health signed a $90,000 note at $11\frac{1}{2}$% interest for 180 days for electronic equipment, on October 1. On February 18 the note was sold to another firm at a discount rate of $12\frac{1}{2}$%. Find (a) the discount period, (b) the discount, and (c) the proceeds.

17. On April 18, Moline Foundry accepts a $4,500 note in settlement of a bill for goods purchased by a customer. The note is for 150 days at 10% interest. If Moline sells the note at a 14% discount rate 30 days after receipt, find (a) the bank discount and (b) the proceeds.

18. Cook and Daughters Farm Equipment Company accepts a $5,800, 14%, 100-day note for a small tractor. The note is dated May 12. On June 17, the firm discounts the note at the bank, at an 18% discount rate. Find (a) the bank discount and (b) the proceeds.

19. Eastside Bank accepted a $2,000 simple discount note from one of its customers. The note was for 90 days and was discounted at 16%. The bank then rediscounted the note at 12% to a second bank, 30 days before the maturity date of the note. Find each of the following: (a) the proceeds to the customer of Eastside Bank, (b) the proceeds to Eastside Bank when it sold the note, and (c) the actual amount of interest earned by Eastside Bank on the note.

20. Farmer's Bank accepted a $17,000 simple discount note from a customer. The note was for 120 days at an 11% discount rate. The bank then rediscounted the note at a second bank, at 8%, 15 days before the maturity date of the note. Find each of the following: (a) the proceeds to the customer of Farmer's Bank, (b) the proceeds to Farmer's Bank when it rediscounted the note, and (c) the actual amount of interest earned by Farmer's Bank on the note.

21. The Third National Bank owns a $2,400 simple discount note at 17%, made on November 9 and due on March 9 of the following year. On January 23, the bank rediscounts the note at 13%. Find each of the following: (a) the proceeds to the maker of the note, (b) the proceeds to the Third National Bank when it rediscounted the note, and (c) the actual amount of interest earned by the Third National Bank on the note.

22. On December 9, the Sunrise Bank accepted a $27,000 simple discount note from a customer. The note is at a discount rate of 16% and is due on March 9. On February 12, the bank rediscounted the note at 10%. Find each of the following: (a) the proceeds to the customer of Sunrise Bank, (b) the proceeds to Sunrise Bank when it rediscounted the note, and (c) the actual amount of interest earned by Sunrise Bank on the note.

23. Gilbert Construction Company signed a $78,000 simple interest note at 12% for 150 days with Union State Bank on November 20. On January 23, Union State Bank went bankrupt and sold all of their notes to National Bank effective 14 days later. Find the (a) maturity value of the note and (b) proceeds to Union State Bank given a discount rate of 13.5%.

24. Tina Klein bought a $10,000, 7.5%, 52-week T-bill on June 29 and sold it 26 weeks later at a discount rate of 8%. Find Tina's (a) purchase price for the T-bill, (b) the discount at time of sale, (c) the proceeds to Tina, and (d) her effective interest rate.

🖉 25. Explain the purpose of discounting a note. What does the discounting procedure cost the original holder of the note?

🖉 26. Explain why banks or other financial institutions may need to rediscount notes. (See Objective 2.)

# Chapter 12 Quick Review

| TOPIC | APPROACH | EXAMPLE |
|---|---|---|
| **12.1  Maturity value of a loan** | Use $I = PRT$ to find interest; then use $M = P + I$ to find maturity value. | A note with a face value of $1,200 is due in 60 days. The rate is 8%. Find the maturity value. |

$$I = PRT$$

$$I = \$1,200 \times 0.08$$

$$\times \frac{60}{360} = \$16$$

$$M = P + I$$

$$M = \$1,200 + \$16$$

$$= \$1,216$$

**12.1** **Finding the due date, interest, and maturity value of a note with the term in months**

1. Add the number of months to date of note to find due date.
2. Use $I = PRT$ to find interest.
3. Use $M = P + I$ to find maturity value.

Find due date, interest, and maturity value of a $1,500 loan made on February 15 for 7 months at 8%.

Due date is 7 months from February 15 which is September 15.

$$I = PRT$$

$$I = \$1{,}500 \times 0.08$$

$$\times \frac{7}{12} = \$70$$

$$M = P + I$$

$$M = \$1{,}500 + \$70$$

$$= \$1{,}570$$

**12.1** **Determining the face value of a note, given rate, time, and maturity value**

Use the formula

$$P = \frac{M}{1 + RT}.$$

A 90-day note has an interest rate of 9% and a maturity value of $1,431.50. Find the face value.

$$P = \frac{M}{1 + RT}$$

$$P = \frac{\$1{,}431.50}{1 + (0.09 \times \frac{90}{360})}$$

$$= \$1{,}400$$

**12.1** **Finding the time of a note in days given maturity value, face value, and interest rate**

Use $T = \dfrac{M - P}{PR} \times 360$ to find time in days. Alternatively, since $I = M - P$, use $T = \dfrac{I}{PR} \times 360$.

A note has a face value of $4,800, interest rate of 6%, and a maturity value of $5,000. Find the time of the note in days.

$$T = \frac{\$5{,}000 - \$4{,}800}{\$4{,}800 \times 0.06}$$

$$\times 360$$

$$T = 250 \text{ days}$$

| | | |
|---|---|---|
| **12.1** **Determining the rate of a note given the face value, time, and maturity value** | Use $R = \dfrac{M - P}{PT}$ to find the rate. Alternatively, since $I = M - P$, use $R = \dfrac{I}{PT}$. | A 240-day note has a face value of \$9,000 and a maturity value of \$9,300. Find the interest rate. $$R = \frac{\$9,300 - \$9,000}{\$9,000 \times \frac{240}{360}}$$ $$= 0.05$$ The rate is 5%. |

| | | |
|---|---|---|
| **12.2** **Finding the discount and proceeds of a simple discount note** | 1. Calculate bank discount ($B$) using the formula $B = MDT$ with $D =$ discount rate. 2. Calculate proceeds using the formula $P = M - B$. | Tom Jones borrows \$5,000 for 60 days at a discount rate of 9%. Find the bank discount and proceeds. $$B = MDT$$ $$= \$5,000 \times 0.09$$ $$\times \frac{60}{360} = \$75$$ $$P = M - B$$ $$= \$5,000 - \$75$$ $$= \$4,925$$ |

| | | |
|---|---|---|
| **12.2** **Determining the effective rate or true rate of interest given face value, time, and discount rate** | First, find the discount ($B$) using the formula $B = MDT$. Find the proceeds using the formula $P = M - B$. Calculate the true rate of interest from either $$R = \frac{M - P}{PT} \quad \text{or} \quad R = \frac{I}{PT}.$$ | A note has a face value of \$9,000, a time of 120 days, and a discount rate of 12%. Find the true rate of interest. $$B = MDT$$ $$= \$9,000 \times 0.12 \times \frac{120}{360}$$ $$= \$360$$ $$P = M - B$$ $$= \$9,000 - \$360$$ $$= \$8,640$$ $$R = \frac{I}{PT}$$ $$= \frac{\$360}{\$8,640 \times \frac{120}{360}} = 0.125$$ The effective rate is 12.5%. |

| | | |
|---|---|---|
| **12.2** **Finding the face value of a simple discount note** | Use the formula $M = \dfrac{P}{1 - DT}$ to find the face value $M$. | Find the face value of a note that will provide \$15,000 in proceeds if the note is repaid in 180 days and the bank charges a 7% discount rate.<br><br>$$M = \frac{P}{1 - DT}$$<br>$$= \frac{\$15,000}{1 - (0.07 \times \frac{180}{360})}$$<br>$$= \$15,544.04$$ |
| **12.2** **Determining the discount rate of a note given face value and proceeds** | Find the discount $(B)$ from the formula $B = M - P$. Find the rate from the formula $D = \dfrac{B}{MT}$. | A 90-day note has a face value of \$15,000 and proceeds of \$14,568.75. Find the discount rate.<br><br>$$B = M - P$$<br>$$B = \$15,000 - \$14,568.75$$<br>$$= \$431.25$$<br><br>$$D = \frac{B}{MT}$$<br>$$= \frac{\$431.25}{\$15,000 \times \frac{90}{360}} = 0.115$$<br><br>The discount rate is 11.5%. |
| **12.4** **Finding the proceeds to an individual or firm which discounts a note** | 1. Find $I$, the interest on the note, and add it to the face value to find the maturity value, $M$.<br>2. Find the discount period.<br>3. Find the bank discount using $B = MDT$.<br>4. Find the proceeds by using $P = M - B$. | Moe's Ice Cream converts a 9%, 150-day note dated March 1 with a face value of \$1,500 to cash on June 1. Assume a discount rate of 11% and find the proceeds.<br><br>$$I = \$1,500 \times 0.09$$<br>$$\times \frac{150}{360} = \$56.25$$<br><br>$$M = \$1,500 + \$56.25$$<br>$$= \$1,556.25$$ |

Find the discount period.

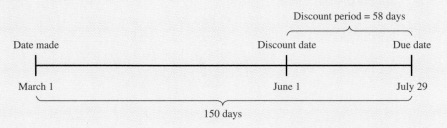

$$B = \$1,556.25 \times 0.11$$
$$\times \frac{58}{360} = \$27.58$$

$$P = \$1,556.25 - \$27.58$$
$$= \$1,528.67$$

The bank will pay $1,528.67 to Moe on June 1 and collect $1,556.25 on July 29 from the maker of the note.

# Chapter 12 Review Exercises

*Complete the following table for simple interest notes. [12.1]*

| | Face Value | Rate | Time | Interest | Maturity Value |
|---|---|---|---|---|---|
| 1. | $4,800 | 9% | 150 days | _____ | _____ |
| 2. | $3,000 | _____ | 90 days | $78.75 | _____ |
| 3. | $8,000 | 12% | _____ | $640 | _____ |
| 4. | _____ | 10% | 180 days | $615 | _____ |

*In the following, find the due date and the maturity value. [12.1]*

| | Date Made | Face Value | Term of Loan | Interest Rate | Date Due | Maturity Value |
|---|---|---|---|---|---|---|
| 5. | May 5 | $2,600 | 90 days | 8% | _____ | _____ |
| 6. | June 19 | $6,000 | 200 days | $12\frac{1}{2}\%$ | _____ | _____ |

*Find the discount and the proceeds for the following discounted notes. [12.2]*

| | Face Value | Discount Rate | Time | Discount | Proceeds |
|---|---|---|---|---|---|
| **7.** | $18,000 | 12% | 80 days | _____ | _____ |
| **8.** | $26,000 | $10\frac{1}{2}$% | 180 days | _____ | _____ |

*Each of the following simple interest notes was discounted 12%. Find the (a) discount period, (b) discount, and (c) proceeds for the following discounted notes. [12.4]*

| | Loan Made | Face Value | Length of Loan | Rate | Date of Discount |
|---|---|---|---|---|---|
| **9.** | September 4 | $12,000 | 150 days | 9% | October 25 |
| **10.** | December 20 | $8,500 | 120 days | $11\frac{1}{8}$% | February 28 |

*Find the true simple interest rate corresponding to each of the following simple discount rates. Round to the nearest hundredth of a percent. [12.3]*

| | Time | Discount Rate |
|---|---|---|
| **11.** | 90 days | 12% |
| **12.** | 170 days | 9% |

*Solve the following application problems. Round rates to the nearest hundredth of a percent, time to the nearest day, and money to the nearest cent.*

**13.** What simple discount rate corresponds to a simple interest rate of 12% on a 180-day note? [12.3]

**14.** Green Acres Pet Store borrowed $38,000 for 120 days at $11\frac{3}{4}$%. Find the maturity value. [12.1]

**15.** The note in problem 14 above was discounted 65 days before maturity at $12\frac{1}{2}$%. Find the discount. [12.2]

**16.** Benito Maintenance signed a $45,000 simple interest note for 200 days and was charged $2,250 in interest. Find the rate. [12.1]

**17.** A note for $9,800 at 10% simple interest generated $490 interest for the payee. Find the term of the loan. [12.1]

**18.** A borrower signed a note with a face value of $50,000 at a $9\frac{1}{2}$% discount rate and received $47,361.11. Find the term of the note. [12.2]

**19.** A businesswoman signed a 50-day discount note with a face value of $35,000 and proceeds of $34,319.44. Find the discount rate. [12.2]

20. A 90-day note has a loan amount of $12,000 and a maturity value of $12,330. Find the simple interest and simple discount rate of this note. [12.3]

21. Bill Bates needed money for a new automobile and signed a note for $15,000 at a simple discount rate of 12% and a term of 240 days. Find the effective rate of interest. [12.2]

22. On December 8, Joan Jones signed a 100-day, 10% discount note at First Bank for $14,000. First Bank sold the note to a finance company on February 12 at a $9\frac{1}{2}$% discount. Find the proceeds to First Bank. [12.4]

23. West Stables must pay a note given to one of its suppliers. The interest rate on the note is 8%, the face value is $12,300, and the interest is $410. Find the time of the note. [12.1]

24. Wilson Design must pay a note given to Capital Wholesale Yard Goods. Find the time of the note if the interest rate is 15%, the face value is $9,500, and the maturity value is $9,816.67. [12.1]

25. A company signed a $79,000, 120-day note for a shipment of goods. The maturity value of the note is $83,187. Find the rate of interest paid on the note. [12.1]

26. Mary Knabe borrowed $5,600 at an 11% discount rate for 120 days. Find the effective rate. [12.2]

27. Tom Watson Insurance accepted a 270-day, $8,000 note on May 25. The interest rate on the note is 15%. The note was then discounted at 12% on August 7. Find the proceeds. [12.4]

28. A note with a face value of $6,570 was discounted at 16%. If the discount was $788.40, find the length of the loan in days. [12.4]

29. Find the simple interest rate that corresponds to a simple discount rate of 17% for 45 days. [12.3]

30. A company signed an $81,000, 150-day note for a shipment of goods. The maturity value of the note is $86,062.50. Find the rate of interest paid on the note. [12.1]

31. On November 19, a firm accepts a $21,000, 150-day note with an interest rate of 15%. The firm discounts the note at 18% on February 2. Find the proceeds. [12.4]

32. Linda Youngman accepted a $16,000, 120-day note from a customer. The note had an interest rate of 9% and was accepted on May 12. The note was then discounted at 11% on July 20. Find the proceeds to Youngman. [12.4]

33. Colleen Elledge borrowed $17,500 at a 16% discount rate for 150 days. Find the equivalent simple interest rate. [12.2]

34. Diane Thompson needs $7,580 to buy a computer. She signs a simple discount note at the bank, which charges a 14% discount rate. If the note is for 120 days, find the face value of the note. [12.2]

35. The Florist Wholesale Shop accepted a 210-day, $6,420 note on December 12. Find the proceeds if the interest rate on the note is 12% and the note was discounted at 15% on January 19. [12.4]

**36.** Find the simple discount rate that corresponds to a simple interest rate of 15% on a 270-day note. [12.3]

**37.** Would you prefer a $15,000 note at 12% simple interest or one at 12% discount interest? Explain. [12.3]

**38.** Explain the differences between a simple interest note and a simple discount note. [12.3]

# Chapter 12 Summary Exercise

Walter's Card Shop signed a 180-day note at 9% on August 28 for $28,000 with State Bank in order to remodel the store. Unfortunately for State Bank, interest rates jumped up immediately to the point at which they must discount the note at 12% when selling to another bank.

**(a)** What was the original loan amount?

**(b)** Find the due date of the note.

**(c)** Find the maturity value of the note.

**(d)** Assume that State Bank has a policy which states that they will not sell a note for less than the original amount loaned. On what day will State Bank first be able to sell the note for more than the original loan amount?

(Hint: Part (d) can be solved by trial and error—by substituting successive dates into the formula until the discount amount is greater than or equal to the loan amount. Alternatively, the discount amount can be set equal to the simple interest and the equation solved for the number of days before the discount date that the note may be discounted. Check your answer.)

# 13

# Compound Interest

Simple interest is paid on the principal—not on any past interest. However, bank deposits and many other investments commonly earn **compound interest**. Compound interest is calculated on any interest previously credited (paid) to the account in addition to the original principal.

## 13.1 Compound Interest

**OBJECTIVES**

1  *Find compound interest and compound amount.*

2  *Determine the number of periods and rate per period.*

3  *Find values in the interest table.*

4  *Use the formula for compound interest to find the compound amount.*

5  *Find the effective rate of interest.*

**OBJECTIVE** 1 *Find compound interest and compound amount.* With **compound interest**, the interest is found by calculating the interest on all past interest as well as on the original principal. For example, suppose $1,000 is deposited in a mutual fund which we can assume pays 10% interest, with interest calculated at the end of each year. Let us find the amount of **compound interest** that will be earned in three years. At the end of the first year, interest is paid on the original deposit of $1,000. Using the formula for simple interest, $I = PRT$

$$\text{Interest} = \$1,000 \times 0.10 \times 1 = \$100.$$

At the end of the first year, the account contains

$$\text{Principal} + \text{Interest} = \$1,000 + \$100 = \$1,100.$$

The interest for the second year is paid on the original deposit plus the first year's interest.

$$\text{Interest} = \$1,100 \times 0.10 \times 1 = \$110$$

$$\text{Amount at end of second year} = \$1,100 + \$110 = \$1,210$$

The interest for the third year is paid on the amount at the end of the second year.

$$\text{Interest} = \$1,210 \times 0.10 \times 1 = \$121$$

$$\text{Amount at end of third year} = \$1,210 + \$121 = \$1,331$$

This amount, $1,331, the final amount on deposit at the end of the three year investment period, is called the **compound amount** or **future amount**, and symbolized with the letter, *M*.

**NOTE** The compound amount is also referred to as maturity value, or as future value. ■

The interest earned during the time of the investment is found by the following formula.

$$\text{Interest} = \text{Compound amount} - \text{Original principal}$$

In our example,

$$\text{Interest} = \$1,331 - \$1,000 = \$331.$$

**NOTE** As a comparison, the *simple* interest on $1,000 at 10% for 3 years is $300. The compound interest, therefore, is $31 more than the simple interest ($331 − $300). ■

The advantage of compound interest over simple interest increases greatly as the number of years increase as shown for a $1,000 investment earning 10% in Figure 13.1.

The process used for finding the compound amount can be simplified by multiplying the principal by the expression

**(1 + Rate)**

where rate is expressed as a decimal. This multiplication should be done as many times as the number of years in the problem. In the example above, the rate was 10%, or the decimal 0.10. The principal at the beginning of a year should be multiplied by $1 + 0.10 = 1.10$. Multiply by 1.10 three times to find the compound amount after three years. Work as follows.

| | |
|---|---|
| $1,000 | original principal |
| × 1.10 | 1 + rate as a decimal |
| $1,100 | amount after 1 year |
| × 1.10 | |
| $1,210 | amount after 2 years |
| × 1.10 | |
| $1,331 | amount after 3 years |

Compound Interest Versus Simple Interest
$1,000 Invested at 10%

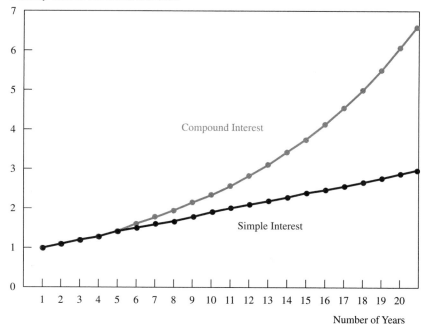

FIGURE 13.1

The total amount after 3 years is $1,331; as mentioned earlier, this sum is the compound amount, or the future amount.

The compound amount has been found by multiplying the principle of $1,000 by 1.10 a total of three times or

$$\$1,000 \times 1.10 \times 1.10 \times 1.10 = \$1,331.$$

In algebra, repeated multiplication with the same number is commonly written using exponents. An **exponent** is used to show how many times a number is used as a product. In this case, we have

exponent

$$\$1,000 \times 1.10 \times 1.10 \times 1.10 = \$1,000 \times (1.10)^3$$

or $\$1,000 (1.10)^3$.

**NOTE** The number 3 is the exponent and represents the number of years that the interest is calculated on an initial deposit of $1,000. ■

**OBJECTIVE** **2** *Determine the number of periods and rate per period.* Interest is often credited to an account more than once a year when calculating compound interest. The interest rate used to find the amount of interest credited at the end of each compounding period is the **nominal** or **stated** annual rate divided by the number of compounding periods in a year.

| Compounding Period | Interest Credited at the End of Each | Number of Times Interest Is Credited per Year | Number of Times Interest Would Be Credited over 5 Years |
|---|---|---|---|
| Annual | year | 1 | $5 \times 1 = 5$ |
| Semiannual | 6 months | 2 | $5 \times 2 = 10$ |
| Quarterly | quarter | 4 | $5 \times 4 = 20$ |
| Monthly | month | 12 | $5 \times 12 = 60$ |

**EXAMPLE 1** *Finding Number of Periods and Rate per Period*

**(a)** A bank pays interest of 8%, compounded semiannually. This means that semiannually, or twice a year, interest of $8\% \div 2 = 4\%$ is added to all money that has been on deposit for 6 months or more.

**(b)** An interest rate of 12% per year, compounded quarterly, means that every 3 months (quarterly), interest of $12\% \div 4 = 3\%$ is added to all money that has been on deposit for at least a quarter. ∎

**NOTE** In Example 1(a), the **period of compounding** is semiannual (every six months), while it is quarterly (every 3 months) in Example 1(b). ∎

The formula for compound interest is expressed using exponents.

If *P* dollars are deposited at a rate of interest *i* per period for *n* periods, then the *compound amount M*, or the final amount on deposit, is

$$M = P(1 + i)^n.$$

Interest earned is

$$I = M - P.$$

**NOTE** It is important to keep in mind that the interest rate for the formula is *per compounding period*, and not per year, and *n* is the number of *periods*, not the number of years. ∎

**EXAMPLE 2** *Finding Compound Interest*

A savings account at Northstar Bank in Canada pays 7% per year compounded semiannually. If you initially deposit $2,500, (a) find the compound amount after 2 years and (b) find the compound interest.

**SOLUTION**

**(a)** Every 6 months, $\frac{7\%}{2} = 3.5\%$ is added to all funds on deposit for 6 months or more. The number of 6 month periods in 2 years is 4. To find the compound amount, multiply $2,500 by $1 + 0.035$ a total of 4 times.

$$\$2,500 \times 1.035 \times 1.035 \times 1.035 \times 1.035 = \$2,868.81$$

Using exponents, the compound amount can be written as follows.

$$\$2{,}500(1 + 0.035)^4 \quad \text{or} \quad \$2{,}500(1.035)^4$$

**(b)** Interest = compound amount − original principal

$$= \quad \$2{,}868.81 - \$2{,}500$$

$$= \$368.81 \qquad \blacksquare$$

**OBJECTIVE** **3** *Find values in the interest table.*     The value of $(1 + i)^n$ can be found by direct calculation using scientific calculators or from tables. One such table is given in the compound interest column (column A) of the interest table in Appendix C.

| **EXAMPLE 3** *Using the Interest Table*

Find the following values in the compound interest table in Appendix C.

number of compounding periods

**(a)** $(1 + 5\%)^{12}$ or $(1 + 0.05)^{12} = (1.05)^{12}$

interest rate per compounding period

Find the 5% page of the interest table. Look in column A, for compound interest, and find 12 (or 12 periods) at the left side. You should find 1.79585633.

number of compounding periods

**(b)** $(1 + 8\%)^{27} = (1.08)^{27} = 7.98806147$

interest rate per compounding period

Find the 8% page. Then look in column A and find 27 at the left.     $\blacksquare$

---

*For the calculator solution to this example,

**(a)** the value of $(1.05)^{12}$ can be found as follows.

**CALCULATOR APPROACH**
**TO EXAMPLE 3**

$$1.05 \;\boxed{y^x}\; 12 \;\boxed{=}\; 1.795856326$$

**(b)** the value of $(1.08)^{27}$ is found as follows.

$$1.08 \;\boxed{y^x}\; 27 \;\boxed{=}\; 7.988061469$$

---

**NOTE**   some calculators have an $\boxed{a^x}$ or $\boxed{x^y}$ key instead of a $\boxed{y^x}$ key. All of these keys are used in the same way.     $\blacksquare$

**OBJECTIVE** **4** *Use the formula for compound interest to find the compound amount.*
The evaluation of $(1 + i)^n$ using tables or calculators can now be used to find the compound amount and interest.

---

*NOTE: All calculator solutions use a scientific calculator. Refer to Appendix A for scientific and financial calculator basics.

## EXAMPLE 4 *Finding Compound Interest*

John Smith inherits $15,000 which he deposits in a retirement account that pays interest compounded semiannually. How much will he have after 25 years if the funds grow (a) at 6%, (b) at 8%, and (c) at 10%?

**SOLUTION** In 25 years, there are $2 \times 25 = 50$ semiannual periods. The semiannual interest rates are (a) $\frac{6\%}{2} = 3\%$, (b) $\frac{8\%}{2} = 4\%$, and (c) $\frac{10\%}{2} = 5\%$. Using factors from the table (or use the formula):

**(a)** $\$15,000(1.03)^{50} = \$15,000 \times 4.38390602* = \$65,758.59$

**(b)** $\$15,000(1.04)^{50} = \$15,000 \times 7.10668335 = \$106,600.25$

**(c)** $\$15,000(1.05)^{50} = \$15,000 \times 11.46739979 = \$172,011$

Notice that relatively small differences in interest rates can add up to large differences in compound amount over time. ∎

**NOTE** Example 1 in Appendix A.2 shows how a financial calculator can be used to solve this same type of problem. ∎

**PROBLEM-SOLVING HINT** Simple interest rate calculations are usually indicated by phrases such as: simple interest, simple interest note, or discount rate. Compound interest rate calculations are usually indicated by phrases such as: compounded annually, 6% per quarter, or compounded daily. ∎

The more often interest is compounded, the more interest is earned. Use a financial calculator or a compound interest table more complete than the one in this text and use the compound interest formula to get the results shown in Table 13.1. (Leap years were ignored in finding daily interest.)

TABLE 13.1  **Interest on $1,000 at 12% per Year for 10 Years**

| Compounded | Interest |
|---|---|
| Not at all (simple interest) | $1,200.00 |
| Annually | $2,105.85 |
| Semiannually | $2,207.14 |
| Quarterly | $2,262.04 |
| Monthly | $2,300.39 |
| Daily | $2,319.46 |

*Some calculators will not take all these digits. With these, round to as many digits as will fit. This procedure may make answers vary by a few cents, especially on large sums of money.

As suggested by Table 13.1, it makes a big difference whether interest is compounded or not. Interest over the 10 years differs by $905.85 when simple interest is compared to interest compounded annually. However, increasing the frequency of compounding makes smaller and smaller differences in the amount of interest earned.

### EXAMPLE 5    *Finding Compound Amount*

Find the compound amount earned on a deposit, by Sarah Kline, of $6,000 for 3 years at (a) 12% compounded quarterly and (b) 12% compounded monthly.

### SOLUTION

**(a)** Interest compounded quarterly is compounded 4 times a year. In 3 years, there are $3 \times 4 = 12$ compounding periods. Interest of $\frac{12\%}{4} = 3\%$ is credited at the end of each quarter.

$$\$6,000(1.03)^{12} = \$6,000 \times 1.42576089 = \$8,554.57$$

**(b)** Interest compounded monthly is compounded 12 times a year. In 3 years, there are $3 \times 12 = 36$ compounding periods. Interest of $\frac{12\%}{12} = 1\%$ is credited at the end of each month.

$$\$6,000(1.01)^{36} = \$6,000 \times 1.43076878 = \$8,584.61 \qquad \blacksquare$$

**OBJECTIVE** **5** *Find the effective rate of interest.*    If interest is compounded *more often than annually*, then the actual rate of interest is greater than the nominal or stated rate of interest. For example, depositing $1,000 for 1 year at 12% compounded quarterly produces a compound amount of

$$M = \$1,000(1.12550881) \qquad \text{from the table}$$

$$M = \$1,125.51 \qquad \text{(to the nearest cent)}$$

The interest earned on this deposit is $125.51, which is 12.551% of the original deposit of $1,000. This amount of interest is the same as if the $1,000 were invested at simple interest of 12.551% for one year. Although the stated rate of interest was 12%, the actual increase in the investment was 12.551%, the **effective rate of interest**. It is important to know the effective rate of interest so that you can compare one loan to another, and know how much you are actually being charged.

**NOTE** The effective rate of interest is sometimes called the effective annual yield. $\qquad \blacksquare$

### EXAMPLE 6    *Finding the Effective Rate of Interest*

Find the effective rate corresponding to a nominal rate of 8% compounded semi-annually.

### SOLUTION    Look in Column A of the interest table for 4% and 2 periods (corresponding to $8\% \div 2 = 4\%$ per period and 2 semiannual periods in a year) or calculate

$$(1 + 0.04)^2.$$

You should find the number 1.08160000. This number means that $1 will increase to $1.08160000, an actual increase of 8.16%. The effective rate is 8.16%.   ∎

### FINDING THE EFFECTIVE RATE OF INTEREST

**Step 1.** Find the entry in column A of the interest table that corresponds to the proper rate per period and the proper number of periods.

**Step 2.** Subtract 1 from the number.

**Step 3.** Round to the nearest hundredth of a percent.

**PROBLEM-SOLVING HINT**   In Step 2, be sure to subtract 1 from the digits to the *left* of the decimal point.   ∎

**EXAMPLE 7**   *Finding the Effective Rate of Interest*

Bill Watson borrowed funds from a local pawn shop at 18% compounded monthly and used his car for collateral. Find the corresponding effective rate.

**SOLUTION**   Since 18% per year is $18\% \div 12 = 1\frac{1}{2}\%$ per month, look in column A of the interest table for $1\frac{1}{2}\%$ and 12 periods, finding 1.19561817. Then subtract 1.

$$
\begin{array}{ll}
1.19561817 & \text{number from the table} \\
-\,1.00000000 & \text{subtract 1} \\
\hline
0.19561817 &
\end{array}
$$

Rounding to the nearest hundredth of a percent gives an effective rate of 19.56%.   ∎

## 13.1 EXERCISES

*Find the compound amount and the amount of interest earned for each of the following. Round to the nearest cent. Do not use tables in Exercises 1–4.*

1. $12,000 at 8% compounded annually for 3 years
2. $8,500 at 6% compounded semiannually for $4\frac{1}{2}$ years
3. $6,000 at 12% compounded quarterly for 2 years
4. $9,200 at 15% compounded quarterly for $1\frac{1}{2}$ years

*Find the compound amount when the following deposits are made. Round to the nearest cent.*

5. $4,500 at 10% compounded annually for 20 years
6. $925 at 5% compounded annually for 12 years
7. $470 at 12% compounded semiannually for 9 years
8. $8,765.72 at 12% compounded monthly for 4 years

*Find the amount of interest earned by the following deposits.*

 **9.** $8,400 at 7% compounded annually for 8 years

**10.** $6,200 at 11% compounded annually for 5 years

**11.** $12,600 at 8% compounded quarterly for $4\frac{3}{4}$ years

**12.** $15,000 at 18% compounded monthly for $2\frac{5}{12}$ years

*Use column A of the interest table to find the simple interest and the interest compounded annually. Find the amount by which the compound interest is larger. Round to the nearest cent.*

| | Principal | Rate | Number of Years |
|---|---|---|---|
| **13.** | $1,000 | 6% | 5 |
| **14.** | $800 | 7% | 6 |
| **15.** | $7,908.42 | 5% | 8 |
| **16.** | $9,854.76 | 8% | 11 |

*Find the effective rate corresponding to each of the following nominal rates. Round to the nearest hundredth of a percent.*

**17.** 8% compounded quarterly

**18.** 10% compounded quarterly

**19.** 15% compounded monthly

**20.** 16% compounded monthly

*Solve each of the following application problems. Round to the nearest cent.*

**21.** Jane Gates invested $2,800 for $2\frac{1}{2}$ years at 12% interest. Find the compound amount if (a) the compounding is quarterly and (b) if the compounding is monthly.

**22.** Waters Electrical deposited $10,000 for 3 years at 10% interest. Find the compound amount if the compounding period is (a) semiannually and (b) quarterly.

**23.** Find the interest earned on $10,000 for 4 years at 6% compounded (a) yearly, (b) semiannually, (c) quarterly, and (d) monthly. (e) Find the simple interest.

**24.** Suppose $32,000 is deposited for 2 years at 10% interest. Find the interest earned on the deposit if the interest is compounded (a) yearly, (b) semiannually, (c) quarterly, and (d) monthly. (e) Find the simple interest.

**25.** Benjamin Moore loans $8,800 to the owner of a new restaurant. He will be repaid at the end of 4 years, with interest at 8% compounded semiannually. Find how much he will be repaid.

**26.** Glenda Wong deposits $8,270 in a bank that pays 12% interest, compounded semiannually. Find the amount she will have at the end of 5 years.

**27.** There are two banks in Citrus Heights. One pays interest of 4% compounded annually, and the other pays 4% compounded quarterly. If Stan deposits $10,000 in each bank, (a) how much will he have in each bank at the end of 3 years? (b) How much more would he have in the bank that paid more interest?

**28.** (a) Which yields more interest for Barker Aluminum: $5,000 at 12% simple interest for 7 years, or $4,000 at 12% interest compounded semiannually for 7 years? (b) How much more interest?

**29.** In order to guarantee a certain pension income, Mr. Watkins must have $125,000 in the bank 3 years from now. Suppose he deposits $80,000 today at 12% compounded monthly and leaves it there for 3 years. How much additional money would he then have to add to have the required amount?

**30.** To settle a government claim about the company's pension plan, West Hardware must have $275,000 in an account $2\frac{1}{2}$ years from now. Suppose $200,000 is deposited today at 12% interest compounded quarterly. How much additional money would have to be added in $2\frac{1}{2}$ years to have the necessary amount?

**31.** Maxine Bonn deposited $10,000 for 3 years at 10% compounded annually and simultaneously deposited $12,000 for 3 years at 9% compounded monthly. Find the sum of the two compounded amounts.

**32.** Deb Hulse deposited $1,200 for 1 year at 6% compounded semiannually and at the same time deposited $2,000 for 1 year at 6% compounded monthly. Find the sum of the two compounded amounts.

*Use either a scientific or financial calculator to solve the following for compound amount.*

**33.** $12,800 at 12.3% compounded annually for 3 years

**34.** $24,500 at 8.9% compounded semiannually for 2 years

**35.** $8,650 at 14.4% compounded quarterly for $4\frac{1}{2}$ years

**36.** $4,300 at 10.2% compounded monthly for $2\frac{1}{3}$ years

**37.** Explain the basic difference between simple interest and compound interest.

**38.** Does 8% simple interest for 1 year equal 8% compounded annually for one year? Explain.

**39.** Bill Baxter has $25,000 to invest for a year. He can lend it to his sister who has agreed to pay 10% simple interest for the year. Or, he can invest it with a bank at 8% compounded quarterly for a year. How much additional interest would the simple interest loan to his sister generate?

**40.** Citizens Bank has $850,000 to lend for 9 months. They can lend it to a local contractor at a simple interest rate of 12% or they can lend it to another bank which will pay 12% compounded monthly. How much additional interest would the compound interest loan to the bank generate?

## 13.2    Daily and Continuous Compounding

### OBJECTIVES

**1** *Define passbook account.*

**2** *Calculate interest compounded daily.*

**3** *Find compound interest for time deposit accounts.*

**4** *Determine the penalty for early withdrawal.*

**5** *Find compound amount with continuous compounding.*

**OBJECTIVE** **1** *Define passbook account.*    **Savings accounts** or **passbook accounts** meet the daily money needs of a person or business. Money may be deposited in or withdrawn from a passbook account anytime, with no penalty. Interest rates on savings accounts can vary from $2\frac{1}{2}\%$ to 6%—historically, a typical rate is $5\frac{1}{4}\%$. The Truth in Savings Act of 1991 resulted in **Regulation DD** which now requires that interest on savings accounts be paid based on the *exact number of days*, thus ordinary interest calculations (the 360 day year) *cannot* be used for savings accounts.

A savings account can be one of the safest places for money. Funds deposited in these accounts at most, but not all, banks are insured up to a certain amount by the federal government. Many credit unions and savings and loan associations offer similar insurance. Call your financial institution to determine if your funds are federally insured.

**OBJECTIVE** **2** *Calculate interest compounded daily.*    Interest in a passbook account is compound interest. It is common for banks to pay interest **compounded daily**—in this way, interest is credited for every day that the money is on deposit.

Money on deposit at the close of business earns interest for the day. However, the interest is not available to the depositer until the following morning. Therefore, if you deposit funds on March 30, you effectively earn 1 day's interest as of March 31 and you earn 2 day's interest as of April 1. You do not earn quarterly interest until after the close of business on *the last day* of the quarter. Therefore, the quarter's interest is not available to you until the morning of the first working day after the end of the quarter. Although interest may be compounded daily, it is normally *credited to an account either monthly or quarterly*.

The formula for daily compounding is exactly the same as the formula of the last section. However, because the annual interest rate must be divided by 365 (for daily compounding), the arithmetic can be very tedious. To avoid this, use a special table, such as Table 13.2, which gives the values of $(1 + i)^n$ for 1 to 90 days, as well as for 90, 91, and 92-day quarters, assuming $5\frac{1}{4}\%$ interest, compounded daily. The four quarters in a year begin on January 1, April 1, July 1, and October 1.

**NOTE** See Appendix A.2 for financial calculators that do not require the use of a table. ■

| **EXAMPLE 1** *Finding Interest Using Daily Compounding*

Shan Peters deposited $1,746 in a passbook account paying $5\frac{1}{4}\%$ interest, compounded daily, on July 9. He withdrew the money on August 17. Find the amount of interest he earned.

**SOLUTION**    August 17 is the 229th day of the year and July 9 is the 190th day of the year. The money is on deposit for

$$
\begin{array}{r}
229 \\
- 190 \\
\hline
39 \text{ days.}
\end{array}
$$

TABLE 13.2  **Values of $(1 + i)^n$ for $5\frac{1}{4}\%$**

| Interest Compounded Quarterly | | Interest Compounded Daily | | | | | |
|---|---|---|---|---|---|---|---|
| **Number of Days in Quarter** | **Value of $(1 + i)^n$** | **Number of Days $n$** | **Value of $(1 + i)^n$** | $n$ | **Value of $(1 + i)^n$** | $n$ | **Value of $(1 + i)^n$** |
| 90 | 1.013028415 | 1 | 1.000143836 | 31 | 1.004468538 | 61 | 1.008811940 |
| 91 | 1.013174124 | 2 | 1.000287692 | 32 | 1.004613016 | 62 | 1.008957043 |
| 92 | 1.013319855 | 3 | 1.000431569 | 33 | 1.004757515 | 63 | 1.009102167 |
| | | 4 | 1.000575467 | 34 | 1.004902035 | 64 | 1.009247312 |
| **Number of Days in Year** | **Value of $(1 + i)^n$** | 5 | 1.000719385 | 35 | 1.005046576 | 65 | 1.009392478 |
| | | 6 | 1.000863324 | 36 | 1.005191137 | 66 | 1.009537665 |
| 365 | 1.053898585 | 7 | 1.001007284 | 37 | 1.005335720 | 67 | 1.009682872 |
| 366 (Leap year) | 1.054050173 | 8 | 1.001151264 | 38 | 1.005480323 | 68 | 1.009828100 |
| | | 9 | 1.001295266 | 39 | 1.005624947 | 69 | 1.009973350 |
| | | 10 | 1.001439288 | 40 | 1.005769591 | 70 | 1.010118620 |
| | | 11 | 1.001583330 | 41 | 1.005914257 | 71 | 1.010263911 |
| | | 12 | 1.001727394 | 42 | 1.006058943 | 72 | 1.010409223 |
| | | 13 | 1.001871478 | 43 | 1.006203650 | 73 | 1.010554556 |
| | | 14 | 1.002015582 | 44 | 1.006348378 | 74 | 1.010699909 |
| | | 15 | 1.002159708 | 45 | 1.006493127 | 75 | 1.010845284 |
| | | 16 | 1.002303854 | 46 | 1.006637896 | 76 | 1.010990679 |
| | | 17 | 1.002448021 | 47 | 1.006782687 | 77 | 1.011136096 |
| | | 18 | 1.002592209 | 48 | 1.006927498 | 78 | 1.011281533 |
| | | 19 | 1.002736417 | 49 | 1.007072330 | 79 | 1.011426992 |
| | | 20 | 1.002880647 | 50 | 1.007217183 | 80 | 1.011572471 |
| | | 21 | 1.003024897 | 51 | 1.007362057 | 81 | 1.011717971 |
| | | 22 | 1.003169167 | 52 | 1.007506951 | 82 | 1.011863492 |
| | | 23 | 1.003313459 | 53 | 1.007651867 | 83 | 1.012009034 |
| | | 24 | 1.003457771 | 54 | 1.007796802 | 84 | 1.012154597 |
| | | 25 | 1.003602104 | 55 | 1.007941760 | 85 | 1.012300181 |
| | | 26 | 1.003746458 | 56 | 1.008086738 | 86 | 1.012445786 |
| | | 27 | 1.003890832 | 57 | 1.008231737 | 87 | 1.012591412 |
| | | 28 | 1.004035227 | 58 | 1.008376756 | 88 | 1.012737058 |
| | | 29 | 1.004179643 | 59 | 1.008521797 | 89 | 1.012882726 |
| | | 30 | 1.004324080 | 60 | 1.008666858 | 90 | 1.013028415 |

From Table 13.2, the number 1.005624947 corresponds to 39 days, so the compound amount is

$$\$1,746(1.005624947) = \$1,755.82.$$

The interest earned is

$$\$1,755.82 - \$1,746 = \$9.82. \qquad \blacksquare$$

**NOTE**   The number of days from July 9 to August 17 in Example 1 can also be found as follows. July has 31 days so there are $31 - 9 = 22$ days from July 9 to the end of the month. The 22 days in July plus the 17 days in August totals 39 days.   ∎

---

**CALCULATOR APPROACH TO EXAMPLE 1**

To solve this example using a calculator, first think of the problem as follows:

$$M = P(1 + i)^n = 1,746(1 + 0.0525 \div 365)^{39}.$$

Then, use parentheses where indicated.

$$( \quad 1 \quad + \quad .0525 \quad \div \quad 365 \quad ) \quad y^x \quad 39 \quad \times \quad 1746 \quad = \quad 1755.82$$

---

**EXAMPLE 2**  *Finding Quarterly Interest*

Melody Grath owns a catering business with $2,463 in a savings account paying $5\frac{1}{4}\%$ compounded daily on January 1. She deposits an additional $1,320 on February 18 and $804 on March 3. Find the total interest earned through the end of the quarter, that is, find the interest available to her on April 1.

**SOLUTION**   Treat each of the three amounts separately. The $2,463 was in the account for the entire 90-day quarter. Use the factor of 1.013028415 from Table 13.2.

$$\$2,463 \times 1.013028415 = \$2,495.09$$

A deposit of $1,320 was made on February 18. This amount is on deposit for $28 - 18 = 10$ days in February and 31 days in March and 1 day in April for a total of $10 + 31 + 1 = 42$ days. From the table, the compound amount is

$$\$1,320 \times 1.006058943 = \$1,328.$$

Finally, $804 was on deposit for $31 - 3 = 28$ days in March, plus 1 day in April, giving a compound amount of

$$\$804 \times 1.004179643 = \$807.36.$$

The total of the compound amount is

$$\$2,495.09 + \$1,328 + \$807.36 = \$4,630.45.$$

The total of the deposits is

$$\$2,463 + \$1,320 + \$804 = \$4,587.$$

The interest earned during the quarter is

$$\$4,630.45 - \$4,587 = \$43.45. \qquad \blacksquare$$

| EXAMPLE 3 *Finding Quarterly Interest*

The Great American Music Company had $11,350 in a savings account on July 1 at a bank that compounds interest on a daily basis at $5\frac{1}{4}\%$, but only credits interest to an account at the end of each quarter. The music company withdrew $5,000 on August 1 and withdrew the remaining $6,350 and closed the account on September 20. Find the interest earned for the quarter.

**SOLUTION** Since September 20 is day 263 of the year, and July 1 is day 182 of the year, $6,350 was on deposit for $263 - 182 = 81$ days. From Table 13.2, the compound amount is

$$\$6,350(1.011717971) = \$6,424.41.$$

The other $5,000 is on deposit from July 1 (day 182) to August 1 (day 213), or for $213 - 182 = 31$ days. Again, using Table 13.2

$$\$5,000(1.004468538) = \$5,022.34.$$

The interest earned for the quarter is

$$(\$6,424.41 + \$5,022.34) - \$11,350 = \$96.75. \qquad ■$$

---

For the calculator solution to this example, first find $6,350(1 + 0.0525 \div 365)^{81}$ and store the value in memory.

$$\boxed{(} \quad \boxed{1} \quad \boxed{+} \quad .0525 \quad \boxed{\div} \quad 365 \quad \boxed{)} \quad \boxed{y^x} \quad 81 \quad \boxed{\times} \quad 6350$$

$$\boxed{=} \quad 6424.41 \quad \boxed{\text{STO}}$$

**CALCULATOR APPROACH TO EXAMPLE 3**

Second, find $5,000(1 + .0525 \div 365)^{31}$.

$$\boxed{(} \quad \boxed{1} \quad \boxed{+} \quad .0525 \quad \boxed{\div} \quad 365 \quad \boxed{)} \quad \boxed{y^x} \quad 31 \quad \boxed{\times} \quad 5000 \quad \boxed{=} \quad 5022.34$$

Add this to the value stored in memory, then subtract the original amount in savings $11,350.

$$5022.34 \quad \boxed{+} \quad \boxed{\text{RCL}} \quad \boxed{-} \quad 11350 \quad \boxed{=} \quad 96.75$$

---

**OBJECTIVE** **3** *Find compound interest for time deposit accounts.* While passbook savings accounts are very useful for money needed for day-to-day living, the low interest rate paid by these accounts makes them undesirable for larger amounts of money, such as money being saved for retirement. These larger amounts are better off in a **time deposit account** where money must be left for a fixed period of time. For example, one local savings and loan pays $3\frac{1}{4}\%$ on money in a day-in and day-out passbook account, but pays 6% on money left with a **certificate of deposit** for 2 years. With a certificate of deposit (abbreviated CD), money must be left for some minimum time period, and a minimum amount of money must be deposited. Another popular certificate of deposit currently available pays interest depending on the interest rate paid by the U.S. government. While these CDs pay higher interest (as high as 6% or 8% at times) and require that money be left for only 6 months, a large minimum deposit (perhaps $10,000) may be required. A typical certificate of deposit is shown in Figure 13.2.

## NEW ENGLAND FEDERAL
### *Savings Bank*

### Certificate of Deposit

1. Account Summary
   Accountholder(s)   JOHN DOE

| Account Number | 123–45670 |
| Date of Issuance | JANUARY 23 |
| Maturity Date | JULY 23 |

| Principal Amount | Term | Nominal Rate / APR | Additional Deposits |
|---|---|---|---|
| $ 6,400.00 | 30 MONTHS | 4.08/4.50% | None |

2. **General**

   This is a Certificate of Deposit in the amount set forth above issued to the Accountholder(s) named above, by New England Federal Savings Bank.

3. **Account Renewal**

   Unless the Accountholder(s) has instructed the Bank not to renew this certificate of deposit, it will automatically and repeatedly be renewed at its maturity for an identical term and at the interest rate the Bank is then offering. Notice of maturity will be mailed to the Accountholder(s) at least 15 days prior to each maturity. The Bank reserves the right not to renew this certificate of deposit, but it must mail notice of such intention to the Accountholder(s) at least 15 days prior to maturity.

4. **Interest**

   This certificate of deposit shall earn interest at the rate set forth above. Such interest shall be compounded daily and credited monthly. During renewal terms, this certificate of deposit will earn interest at the rate the Bank is then offering. Interest earned during any term may be withdrawn during that term without penalty. Upon renewal, principal shall include interest earned (but not paid) during the prior term.

5. **Interest Checks** N/A

   The Accountholder(s) has authorized the Bank to pay interest on the following basis:
   □ Monthly    □ Quarterly    □ Semi Annually

6. **Withdrawal Penalty**

   In the event of any withdrawal of principal at any time prior to the maturity of this or any renewal term, the Accountholder(s) shall pay a penalty equal to three months' interest, (if the term of this certificate of deposit is equal to or less than one year), or six months' interest, (if the term of this certificate of deposit is greater than one year), on the amount withdrawn, at the rate being paid on this certificate of deposit at the time of withdrawal. If the Accountholder withdraws part or all of the balance of this certificate of deposit during the seven calendar days subsequent to the maturity of this or any renewal term, there will be no withdrawal penalty.

   Any withdrawal which reduces the balance of this certificate of deposit below $1,000 will be treated as a withdrawal of the remaining balance.

   No penalty will be charged for withdrawal following the death or adjudicated incompetence of the Accountholder.

   NEW ENGLAND FEDERAL SAVINGS BANK

   By _Sue Smith_
       Authorized Representative

FIGURE 13.2

TABLE 13.3   **Compound Interest for Time Deposit Accounts (Daily Compounding)**

| Number of Years | Interest Rate | | | |
| :---: | :---: | :---: | :---: | :---: |
| | 6% | 7% | 8% | 9% |
| 1 | 1.06183131 | 1.07250098 | 1.08327757 | 1.09416214 |
| 2 | 1.12748573 | 1.15025836 | 1.17349030 | 1.19719080 |
| 3 | 1.19719965 | 1.23365322 | 1.27121572 | 1.30992085 |
| 4 | 1.27122407 | 1.32309429 | 1.37707948 | 1.43326581 |
| 5 | 1.34982552 | 1.41901993 | 1.49175931 | 1.56822519 |
| 10 | 1.82202895 | 2.01361755 | 2.22534585 | 2.45933025 |

It is probably not a good idea to invest all of one's money in a certificate of deposit, since a penalty is charged for early withdrawal. At least some cash should be left in a passbook savings account (or perhaps in the money market accounts discussed later) for daily needs.

The higher interest paid by some certificates of deposit can be found using Table 13.3. (This table assumes daily compounding and 365 days per year.)

| EXAMPLE 4   *Finding Compound Amount and Interest on Time Deposits*

David Herren invests $20,000 in a certificate of deposit paying 8% compounded daily. Find the compound amount after 5 years. Also, find the interest earned.

SOLUTION    Look in Table 13.3 for 8% and 5 years, finding 1.49175931. Then

$$\text{Compound amount} = \$20,000(1.49175931)$$
$$= \$29,835.19.$$

Of this amount,

$$\$29,835.19 - \$20,000 = \$9,835.19$$

is interest.                                                                                    ■

NOTE    Many time deposits earn interest compounded monthly or quarterly rather than daily. In that event, calculate interest using the techniques of Section 13.1.    ■

OBJECTIVE **4** *Determine the penalty for early withdrawal.*    A depositor who agrees to leave money in an account for a certain period of time, but then withdraws it early, must pay a penalty. While it is not possible for the depositor to lose any of the *principal* involved as long as the institution is federally insured, it is very possible that all or part of the *interest* may be lost. The procedure for calculating this early withdrawal penalty is not standard. Many financial institutions use the following rules for calculating the **early withdrawal penalty**.

> ## CALCULATING THE EARLY WITHDRAWAL PENALTY
>
> 1. If money is withdrawn within 3 months of the deposit, *no interest* will be paid at all on the money withdrawn.
>
> 2. If money is withdrawn after 3 months but before the end of the term, then 3 months *is deducted from* the time the account has been open *and regular passbook interest is paid* on the account.

| EXAMPLE 5 *Finding Interest When Early Withdrawal Occurs*

Use the rules listed in the box to find the amount of interest earned on each of the following.

## SOLUTION

**(a)** On January 5, Raymond Hoyle deposited $5,000 in a 1-year certificate of deposit paying 6% compounded daily. He withdrew the money on March 12 of the same year.

   Since March 12 is within 3 months of January 5, no interest at all is earned. The bank will simply return the $5,000.

**(b)** Bob Kashir deposited $6,000 in a 4-year certificate of deposit paying 7% compounded daily. He withdrew the money 15 months later. The passbook rate at his bank is $5\frac{1}{4}\%$ compounded daily.

The money is withdrawn early, so 3 months interest is lost. The money was on deposit for 15 months, but only $15 - 3 = 12$ months interest will be paid. Also, interest will be paid at the passbook rates, $5\frac{1}{4}\%$ compounded daily, instead of the more generous 7% compounded daily. The compound amount is found using the factor for 365 days (assume it is not a leap year) at $5\frac{1}{4}\%$. From Table 13.2, this is 1.053898585.

$$\$6,000(1.053898585) = \$6,323.39$$

The interest is found by subtracting the initial deposit of $6,000 from $6,323.39.

$$\text{Interest} = \$6,323.39 - \$6,000 = \$323.39 \qquad \blacksquare$$

TABLE 13.4 **Sample IMMA Account Interest Rates**

| Effective Date of Rate | Interest Rate |
| --- | --- |
| 11/24 | 5.00% |
| 11/30 | 4.75% |
| 12/17 | 4.60% |
| 12/18 | 4.50% |
| 12/21 | 4.25% |

*Insured Money Market Accounts.*    Many savings institutions offer **insured money market accounts** (often called **IMMAs**). These accounts offer interest rates almost as high as those of certificates of deposit, while permitting funds to be withdrawn at any time. A typical IMMA account is insured by the federal government (up to a certain maximum), allows for balances as low as $2,500, pays interest rates within 1% or so of CDs, and allows for three checks or more per month to be written without charge. Unlike certificates of deposit, however, the interest rate may change weekly or even daily. As an example, Table 13.4 lists the interest rates paid during one 30-day period by a local bank on an IMMA account. Notice how often the rates changed.

Insured money market accounts were set up to compete with the money market funds offered by many stock brokerage and mutual fund firms—IMMAs offer competitive interest rates with the benefit of federal insurance.

TABLE 13.5  **Interest on $1,000 at 12% per Year for 10 Years**

| Frequency of Compounding | Number of Periods | Interest |
|---|---|---|
| Annually | 10 | $2,105.85 |
| Semiannually | 20 | $2,207.14 |
| Quarterly | 40 | $2,262.04 |
| Monthly | 120 | $2,300.39 |
| Daily | 3650 | $2,319.46 |
| Hourly | 87,600 | $2,320.09 |
| Every Minute | 5,256,000 | $2,320.11 |

**OBJECTIVE** **5** *Find compound amount with continuous compounding.*      In the first section of this chapter, we discussed annual, semiannual, quarterly, and monthly compounding. Then we saw daily compounding at the beginning of this section. There is no reason that interest could not be compounded more frequently, such as every hour or even every minute. Table 13.5, an extension of Table 13.1, shows the interest earned on $1,000 at 12% per year for 10 years, assuming various frequencies of compounding. (The results in this table were found with the formula $P(1 + i)^n$ and a financial calculator.)

Clearly, more frequent compounding results in more interest. However, after a while increasing the frequency of compounding makes less and less difference. For example, going from compounding daily to compounding every minute produces only 65 cents additional interest on $1,000 after 10 years.

It would be possible to extend Table 13.5 to include compounding every second, every half-second, or any desired small time interval. It would even be possible to think of compounding *every instant*. Compounding every instant is called **continuous compounding**. The formula for continuous compounding, given in the next box, uses the number *e*. The number *e* is approximately equal to 2.7182818. Some calculators have an $\boxed{e^x}$ button for working with this number.

> If *P* dollars is deposited at a rate of interest *i* per year and *compounded continuously* for *n* years, the compound interest *M* is
>
> $$M = Pe^{ni}.$$

Continuous compounding is used by some financial institutions and various government agencies.

**EXAMPLE 6**  *Finding the Compound Amount for Continuous Compounding*

Find the compound amount for the following deposits.

## SOLUTION

**(a)** $1,000 at 12% compounded continuously for 10 years

Use the formula in the box with $P = \$1,000$, $i = 0.12$, and $n = 10$. The compound amount is as follows.

$$M = Pe^{ni}$$

$$M = \$1,000e^{10(0.12)}$$

$$= \$1,000e^{1.2}$$

The value of $e^{1.2}$ is found in the table in Appendix B. Find 1.2 in the column labeled $x$ and read across to the number 3.32011692 in the column labeled $e^x$. Then

$$M = \$1,000(3.32011692) = \$3,320.12.$$

Of this amount,

$$\$3,320.12 - \$1,000 = \$2,320.12$$

is interest, only 1 cent more than when interest is compounded every minute, as shown in Table 13.5 in this section.

**(b)** $48,906.11 at 15% compounded continuously for 6 years (use Appendix B)

$$= \$48,906.11e^{6(0.15)}$$

$$= \$48,906.11e^{0.90}$$

$$= \$48,906.11(2.45960311)$$

$$= \$120,289.62.$$

The compound amount is $120,289.62, which includes $71,383.51 of interest.  ■

**NOTE**  The interest rates paid by banks in some years are quite low compared to the returns from other investments such as stocks. However, in other years the returns from banks may equal or even exceed returns from stocks.  ■

## 13.2  EXERCISES

*Find the interest earned by the following. Assume $5\frac{1}{4}$% interest compounded daily, and use the exact number of days.*

|    | Amount | Date Deposited | Date Withdrawn |
|----|--------|----------------|----------------|
| 1. | $1,200 | Jan. 1 | Mar. 3 |
| 2. | $2,400 | Mar. 10 | Apr. 8 |
| 3. | $4,800 | Aug. 3 | Oct. 12 |
| 4. | $3,600 | Apr. 15 | May 10 |

*Find the amount of deposit on the first day of the next quarter when the following sums are deposited as indicated. Assume $5\frac{1}{4}\%$ interest compounded daily.*

| | Amount | Date Deposited |
|---|---|---|
| 5. | $7,235.82 | Feb. 14 |
| 6. | $1,125.40 | Apr. 7 |
| 7. | $2,965.72 | July 1 |
| 8. | $4,031.46 | Apr. 1 |

*Find the compound amount for each of the following certificates of deposit. Assume daily compounding.*

| | Amount Deposited | Interest Rate | Time in Years |
|---|---|---|---|
| 9. | $5,000 | 6% | 2 |
| 10. | $8,500 | 9% | 5 |
| 11. | $14,000 | 7% | 3 |
| 12. | $3,000 | 8% | 4 |

*Find the amount of interest earned by the following certificates of deposit. Assume daily compounding and use Table 13.3.*

| | Amount Deposited | Interest Rate | Time in Years |
|---|---|---|---|
| 13. | $20,000 | 7% | 3 |
| 14. | $4,500 | 9% | 10 |
| 15. | $3,800 | 8% | 4 |
| 16. | $1,000 | 6% | 1 |

17. Explain the difference between passbook accounts, time deposit accounts, certificates of deposit, and insured money market accounts.

18. Which would you prefer on your own savings, semiannual compounding or continuous compounding? Why?

*Solve each of the following application problems. Assume $5\frac{1}{4}\%$ interest compounded daily. Round to the nearest cent.*

19. Teresa Tabor had $4,300 in her savings account on July 1. She then deposited $1,000 on July 30 and $500 on September 5. Find the balance in the account on October 1.

**20.** Vicki Phelps had $8,600 in her savings account on April 1. She then deposited $800 on May 5 and an additional $350 on June 20. Find the balance in the account on July 1.

**21.** Ace Tire Service has a savings account for spare cash. On the first day of a 90-day quarter the account contained $17,500. A withdrawal of $5,000 was made 21 days later, with a further withdrawal of $980 made 12 days before the end of the quarter. Find the interest earned during the quarter and the balance at the end of the quarter.

**22.** Office Supply maintains a savings account for the money it uses to pay income tax. On April 1, the account contained $61,200. A withdrawal of $9,616 was made on April 15, with an additional $20,000 withdrawn on June 15. Find the interest earned during the quarter and the balance at the end of the quarter. (Note that this quarter has 91 days.)

*For the following application problems on certificates of deposit, use the rules for finding the early withdrawal penalty as given in the text. Assume daily compounding of interest.*

**23.** Honey Watts deposited $4,500 in a 5-year time deposit account paying 8% interest. She withdrew the funds 65 days later. How much interest did she receive?

**24.** Jana Box deposited $6,000 in a 3-year account paying 6% interest but needed the money 2 months later and withdrew it. How much interest did she receive?

**25.** Emma Gilger placed $20,000 in a 10-year account paying 7% interest. The savings and loan where she placed her money pays a passbook rate of $5\frac{1}{4}$% compounded daily. She withdrew $5,000 of her money after 15 months. Find the interest that she earned on the $5,000.

**26.** Trish Hardison deposited $18,680 in a 4-year account paying 6% interest. The bank where she put the money pays a passbook rate of $5\frac{1}{4}$% compounded daily. She withdrew $2,000 after 15 months. Find the interest that she earned on the $2,000.

*Find the compound amount and the interest for the following deposits. Assume continuous compounding.*

| | Amount | Interest Rate | Time |
|---|---|---|---|
| **27.** | $2,000 | 9% | 3 years |
| **28.** | $1,200 | 8% | 11 years |
| **29.** | $4,100.70 | 8% | 9 months |
| **30.** | $1,900.63 | 9% | 8 months |

*Solve the following application problems.*

**31.** An Italian firm deposited $800,000 in a 2-year time deposit earning 6% compounded daily with a New York bank as partial collateral for a loan. At maturity, find (a) the compound amount and (b) the interest earned.

**32.** Joni Perez needs to borrow $20,000 to open a welding shop but the bank will not lend her the money. Joni's uncle agrees to put up collateral for the loan with a $20,000, 4-year certificate of deposit paying 7% compounded daily. This means that the bank will take all or part of his deposit if Joni should fail to repay the loan. Find (a) the compound amount earned by her uncle and (b) the interest earned if the funds remain at the bank for the full 4 years.

33. Pat Metzger can choose between two investments: one pays 10% compounded semiannually, and the other pays $9\frac{1}{2}$% compounded continuously. If she wants to deposit $17,000 for $1\frac{1}{2}$ years, which investment should she choose? How much extra interest will she earn by making the correct choice? (Hint: $e^{0.1425} = 1.15315308$.)

34. Gary Orr wishes to invest $62,904 from his company's pension plan. One investment offered 12% compounded quarterly, while another offers 11.75% compounded continuously. Which investment should he choose, if the money will be invested for 2 years? How much extra interest will he earn by making the proper choice? (Hint: $e^{0.235} = 1.26490877$.)

 35. Is it important to you for your bank to have insurance on your savings account? Why or why not?

 36. Go to your bank and find the current interest rates paid by them on savings accounts, IMMAs, and CDs.

## 13.3    Finding Time and Rate

**OBJECTIVES**

**1** *Determine time given compound interest.*

**2** *Determine rate.*

**3** *Use more than one table to solve interest problems.*

We saw in the previous chapter how to use the formula for simple interest, $I = PRT$, and find the value of any of the four variables when given the value of the other three. A similar thing can be done with the formula for compound interest, $M = P(1 + i)^n$.

While basic algebra was used to solve $I = PRT$, more advanced algebra is needed for $M = P(1 + i)^n$. This different procedure is required because of the exponent $n$ in the formula.

**OBJECTIVE 1** *Determine time given compound interest.*    The first two examples show how to find time for an investment.

**EXAMPLE 1** *Finding Time Given Compound Interest*

Suppose $1,500 is deposited at 10% compounded annually. How long will it take to have a compound amount of $2,415.77?

**SOLUTION**    Use the formula $M = P(1 + i)^n$, with $M = \$2,415.77$, $P = \$1,500$, and $i = 0.10$. The value of $n$ is unknown.

$$M = P(1 + i)^n$$

$$\$2,415.77 = \$1,500(1 + 0.10)^n$$

$$\$2,415.77 = \$1,500(1.10)^n$$

Divide both sides by $1,500.

$$\frac{\$2,415.77}{\$1,500} = (1.10)^n$$

Use a calculator to divide on the left side.

$$1.61051333 = (1.10)^n$$

Solving this equation would require advanced algebra. However, a good approximation can be found by looking down column A of the 10% page of the interest table in Appendix C. The number 1.61051000 in row 5 is very close to the number on the left side of the equation above. Since interest is compounded annually, the deposit was for 5 years.                                                                                                  ■

## EXAMPLE 2  *Finding Time*

Richard Buck needs $35,000 to start a computer repair business but only has $26,000. How long must he wait to start the business if he can earn 10% compounded quarterly?

**SOLUTION**   Interest of 10% per year is $\frac{10\%}{4}$ = 2.5% per quarter. Use the formula $M = P(1 + i)^n$ with $M$ = $35,000, $P$ = $26,000, and $i$ = 0.025.

$$\$35,000 = \$26,000(1 + 0.025)^n$$

Use a calculator to divide both sides by $26,000.

$$1.346153846 = (1.025)^n$$

Now look in column A of the $2\frac{1}{2}$% page of the interest table in Appendix C to find the number closest to 1.346153846. The closest number is 1.34488882 which corresponds to 12 quarters or 3 years.                                                                                           ■

## EXAMPLE 3  *Finding Time to Double*

Suppose the general level of inflation in the economy averages 4% per year. Find the number of years it would take for the general level of prices to double.

**SOLUTION**   To find the number of years it will take for $1 worth of goods and services to cost $2, solve for $n$ in the equation

$$2 = 1(1 + 4\%)^n$$

or

$$2 = 1(1 + 0.04)^n,$$

where $M$ = 2, $P$ = 1, and $i$ = 4%. This equation simplifies to

$$2 = (1.04)^n.$$

As in the previous examples, look down column A of the 4% page of the interest table to find the number closest to 2. The closest number is 2.02581652. This number corresponds to 18 periods, so to the nearest year, the general level of prices would double in 18 years.  ■

**NOTE**  Prices would double about every $7\frac{1}{2}$ years if inflation were 10%.  ■

**OBJECTIVE** **2** *Determine rate.*    The same method used for finding time can be used to find rate. Find rate by first looking in column A for the proper number of periods. Then look through several pages corresponding to different rates, as necessary.

| EXAMPLE 4  *Finding Rate*

One of your classmates needs to borrow $8,000 for 1 year. He has been offered a loan with interest compounded monthly and a compound amount of $9,287.08. Find the rate.

**SOLUTION**    Use the equation $M = P(1 + i)^n$, with $i$ unknown. Notice that $n$ is the number of compounding periods which is 12.

$$\$9,287.08 = \$8,000(1 + i)^{12}$$

Divide both sides by $8,000.

$$1.160885 = (1 + i)^{12}$$

Find the row for 12 periods in column A of the interest tables in Appendix C. Check this number in column A under different rates as necessary until you find the number closest to 1.160885. The closest number is 1.16075452 corresponding to an interest rate of $1\frac{1}{4}$% per month, or

$$1\frac{1}{4} \times 12 = 15\% \text{ per year.}$$    ■

**OBJECTIVE** **3** *Use more than one table to solve interest problems.*    Some problems require the use of more than one table, as in the next example.

| EXAMPLE 5  *Using More than One Table*

Jean King deposits $2,500 in an account paying 6% compounded quarterly. After 4 years the rate drops to 5% compounded semiannually. Find the amount in her account at the end of 7 years.

**SOLUTION**    First find the future value after 4 years. Look in column A of the interest rate table for $4 \times 4 = 16$ periods and $6\% \div 4 = 1.5\%$ interest to find 1.26898555.

$$\$2,500(1.26898555) = \$3,172.46$$

Now find the future value at the end of 7 years. Look in column A of the interest rate table for $2 \times 3 = 6$ periods and $5\% \div 2 = 2.5\%$ interest to find 1.15969342.

$$\$3,172.46(1.15969342) = \$3,679.08$$

King will have $3,679.08 in her account at the end of 7 years.  ■

# 13.3 EXERCISES

*Complete this table. Round time to the nearest period, interest to the nearest whole percent per year, and money to the nearest cent. (As review, some of these problems do not require the methods of this section.)*

| | Principal | Compound Amount | Interest Rate | Compounded | Time in Years |
|---|---|---|---|---|---|
| 1. | $4,500 | $5,898.58 | 7% | annually | _____ |
| 2. | $8,000 | $12,346.41 | $7\frac{1}{2}\%$ | annually | _____ |
| 3. | $3,600 | $4,824.34 | 10% | semiannually | _____ |
| 4. | $2,500 | $3,267.40 | 11% | semiannually | _____ |
| 5. | _____ | $11,082.73 | 8% | semiannually | 7 |
| 6. | _____ | $9,043.63 | 10% | quarterly | 6 |
| 7. | $12,000 | $15,149.72 | _____ | annually | 4 |
| 8. | $13,200 | $22,680.06 | _____ | annually | 8 |
| 9. | $8,500 | $13,403.64 | _____ | quarterly | $5\frac{3}{4}$ |
| 10. | $3,100 | $3,765.63 | _____ | monthly | $3\frac{1}{4}$ |

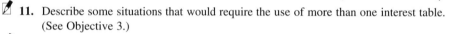

11. Describe some situations that would require the use of more than one interest table. (See Objective 3.)

12. Explain how to find the interest rate given principal, compound amount, compounding period, and time in years. (See Objective 2.)

*Solve the following application problems. Round as in Exercises 1–10.*

13. Elizabeth Loftin invests $12,000 in an account paying 8% per year compounded quarterly. Find the compound amount in (a) 4 years and in (b) 8 years.

14. Jim Pierce inherits $85,000 and places it in an account expected to yield 10% per year compounded semiannually. Find the compound amount in (a) 10 years and in (b) 25 years.

15. Roy Bledsoe deposits $46,000 in an account that has interest compounded semiannually. In $2\frac{1}{2}$ years the account contains $58,708.95. Find the interest rate paid.

16. Find the interest rate paid if a deposit of $35,200 becomes $61,723.41 in $4\frac{3}{4}$ years, with interest compounded quarterly.

17. A student loan of $5,200 at 9% compounded semiannually resulted in a maturity value of $5,934.06. Find the term or length of the loan.

18. A home construction loan of $80,000 at 12% compounded monthly resulted in a maturity value of $92,877.52. Find the term or length of the loan.

*Use the ideas of Example 3 in the text to answer the following questions. Find the time, to the nearest year, it would take for the general level of prices in the economy to double if the average annual inflation rate is as follows.*

19. $2\frac{1}{2}\%$

20. 3%

21. $3\frac{1}{2}\%$

22. 4%

**23.** Nationwide, demand for gasoline is increasing at a rate of about 2% per year. If it continues to increase at this rate indefinitely, find the number of years before the oil companies would need to double the supply of gasoline.

**24.** Assume that world population grows at a rate of $2\frac{1}{2}$% per year throughout the 21st century. Estimate the number of years it requires for world population to double. Approximately how many times would world population double during the 100 years?

*The remainder of these exercises may require the use of any of the tables presented so far in this chapter.*

**25.** Dawn Young deposits $10,000 at 8% compounded quarterly. Two years after she makes the first deposit, she adds another $20,000, also at 8%, compounded quarterly. What total amount will she have five years after her first deposit?

**26.** Jenny Toms deposits $10,000 in a bank account paying 8% compounded quarterly. After three years she deposits another $7,500, just as the bank changes its rate to 6% compounded semiannually. Find the total amount in her account after an additional two years.

*For exercises 27–30 use Table 13.3 for the certificates of deposit.*

**27.** Robert Jay deposits $4,200 in an account paying 8% per year compounded quarterly. After $3\frac{3}{4}$ years, the compound amount is used to buy a 3-year certificate of deposit paying 8%. What is the final amount, principal and interest, that Jay will have at the end of the $6\frac{3}{4}$-year period?

**28.** Daniel Jones buys a 10-year $24,000 certificate of deposit paying 9% compounded daily. After 10 years, the compound amount is placed in an account paying 12% per year, compounded quarterly. If the money is left in this account for an additional 15 months, find the final amount, principal and interest, that Jones will have.

**29.** Jean Sides has $11,000 in an account paying 10% compounded semiannually. After the money has been on deposit for 4 years, $5,000 is removed to buy a certificate of deposit paying 7% compounded daily for 3 years. (The remaining money stays at 10% compounded semiannually.) Find the total amount on deposit in both accounts, both principal and interest, after the 7 years.

**30.** Frank Sabas has $45,000 in an account paying 8% compounded quarterly. After $2\frac{1}{4}$ years, Sabas removes $20,000 and buys a 5-year certificate of deposit paying 6% compounded daily. (The remaining money continues to earn 8% compounded quarterly.) Find the total amount on deposit in both accounts, both principal and interest, after the $7\frac{1}{4}$ years.

 **Present Value at Compound Interest**

**OBJECTIVE**

**1** *Review the meaning of future value and present value.*

**2** *Find the present value.*

**OBJECTIVE 1** *Review the meaning of future value and present value.*      In Sections 13.1 and 13.2, compound interest calculations were used to find the maturity value or

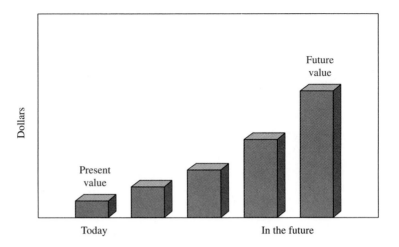

FIGURE **13.3**

**future value** (value at some future date) of an investment by using the formula $M = P(1 + i)^n$ or by using Appendix C. The initial deposit, interest rate, and term were given and future value was calculated.

In this section, the problem is reversed—the future value, interest rate, and term are given. The goal is to find the amount that must be deposited today to produce the desired future value at the specified future date. The amount that must be deposited today is called the **present value**; the amount to be accumulated at some specific future date is the **future value** (Figure 13.3).

**OBJECTIVE 2** *Find the present value.* Earlier, $P$ was used for **principal** which was the amount deposited at the beginning of the term. The phrase **present value** is often used instead of principal if the amount that must be deposited today is unknown. The letter $P$ will also be used for present value. Find $P$ as follows:

$$M = P(1 + i)^n$$

$$\frac{M}{(1 + i)^n} = \frac{P(1 + i)^n}{(1 + i)^n}$$

$$P = \frac{M}{(1 + i)^n} \qquad \text{Use this formula for present value.}$$

The present value, $P$, is found by dividing the compound amount, $M$, by $(1 + i)^n$. The values of $(1 + i)^n$ are given in column A of the interest table. Another way to solve this problem is to rewrite the formula as shown below and use column B of the interest table.

$$\frac{M}{(1 + i)^n} \quad \text{as} \quad M \cdot \frac{1}{(1 + i)^n}$$

In summary,

> the **present value**, $P$, of the future amount, $M$, at an interest rate of $i$ per period for $n$ periods is
>
> $$P = \frac{M}{(1 + i)^n} = M \cdot \frac{1}{(1 + i)^n}$$
>
> (Use column B of the interest table in Appendix C for the value of $\frac{1}{(1 + i)^n}$).

## EXAMPLE 1 *Finding Present Value*

Shannon Walker estimates that she will need $6,000 in 5 years in order to purchase a new, state-of-the-art, multimedia computer system, including software and a top quality color printer. What lump sum deposited today at 8% compounded annually will produce the needed $6,000?

**SOLUTION**  Use the formula in the box with $M = \$6{,}000$, $i = 8\%$, and $n = 5$.

$$P = M \cdot \frac{1}{(1 + i)^n}$$

$$P = \$6{,}000 \cdot \frac{1}{(1 + 0.08)^5}$$

$$P = \$6{,}000 \cdot \frac{1}{(1.08)^5}$$

Look on the 8% page of the interest table in Appendix C, in row 5, and the present value column to find that $\frac{1}{(1.08)^5} = 0.68058320$, and

$$P = \$6{,}000(0.68058320) = \$4{,}083.50.$$

A deposit of $4,083.50 today at 8% compounded annually will produce $6,000 in 5 years. Of this $6,000,

$$\$6{,}000 - \$4{,}083.50 = \$1{,}916.50$$

represents interest earned on the initial deposit of $4,083.50.  ∎

The same result could have been found by using the compound interest table, column A, and *dividing*. Looking up 8% and 5 periods in column A (or calculating $(1.08)^5$) gives 1.46932808. Now divide

$$P = \frac{\$6{,}000}{1.46932808} = \$4{,}083.50.$$

Here both methods gave the same answer. Sometimes the answers may differ by a few cents because of rounding error.

NOTE   For extremely large amounts of money, the method of *dividing* with a number from column A can be slightly more accurate.   ■

**CALCULATOR APPROACH
TO EXAMPLE 1**

The calculator solution to this example uses parentheses to set the denominator apart.

6000 $\boxed{\div}$ $\boxed{(}$ $\boxed{1}$ $\boxed{+}$ $\boxed{.08}$ $\boxed{)}$ $\boxed{y^x}$ $\boxed{5}$ $\boxed{=}$ 4083.50

The order of operations ensures that the denominator is raised to the 5th power before dividing into $6,000.

## EXAMPLE 2   *Finding Present Value*

Lin Roan, from Taiwan, will receive $16,000 in U.S. dollars in 9 years from a trust fund set up by his mother. Find the present value of this sum if money can be deposited at 6% compounded semiannually.

SOLUTION   In 9 years there are $2 \times 9 = 18$ semiannual periods. A rate of 6% per year is 3% each semiannual period. Look at the 3% page of the interest table in Appendix C, and find 18 periods in column B. You should see the number 0.58739461. The present value is

$$\$16,000(0.58739461) = \$9,398.31.$$

A deposit of $9,398.31 today, at 6% compounded semiannually, will produce $16,000 in 9 years.   ■

## EXAMPLE 3   *Finding Value of a Business*

Tom Fredrickson owns a men's clothing store worth $125,000. The business is doing well, with Fredrickson sure that the value of the business will increase at the rate of 16% per year, compounded semiannually, for the next 4 years. If he sells the business, he will invest the proceeds at 8% compounded quarterly. What sale price should he insist on?

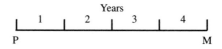

SOLUTION   This problem requires two steps. First decide on the future value of the business. This is done with the formula for compound amount, $M = P(1 + i)^n$. Here, $P = \$125,000$, $i = 16\% \div 2 = 8\%$, and $n = 4 \times 2 = 8$ periods.

$$M = \$125,000(1 + 8\%)^8$$

$$M = \$125,000(1.85093021) \qquad \text{Use column A.}$$

$$M = \$231,366.28$$

Now find the present value of this sum, assuming that money can be invested at 8% compounded quarterly. Use the formula

$$P = M \cdot \frac{1}{(1 + i)^n}$$

with $M = \$231,366.28$, $i = 8\% \div 4 = 2\%$, and $n = 4 \times 4 = 16$ periods.

$$P = \$231,366.28 \cdot \frac{1}{(1 + 0.02)^{16}}$$

$$P = \$231,366.28(0.72844581) \qquad \text{Use column B.}$$

$$P = \$168,537.80$$

Fredrickson should not sell the business for less than $168,537.80—an investment of this amount at 8% compounded quarterly for 4 years will produce the same future amount as the growth in the value of the business.    ∎

## 13.4   EXERCISES

*Find the present value and the amount of interest earned for each of the following. Round to the nearest cent.*

| | Amount Needed | Time | Interest | Compounded |
|---|---|---|---|---|
| 1. | $2,500 | 2 years | 7% | annually |
| 2. | $3,300 | 4 years | 11% | annually |
| 3. | $12,200 | $2\frac{1}{2}$ years | 12% | quarterly |
| 4. | $7,000 | $3\frac{1}{4}$ years | 10% | quarterly |
| 5. | $8,500 | 1 year | 12% | monthly |
| 6. | $1,400 | 2 years | 6% | monthly |

 7. Explain the difference between present value and future value. (See Objective 1.)

8. Outline the procedure for finding the present value of an investment using (a) column A of the interest table and (b) column B of the interest table. (See Objective 2.)

*Solve each of the following application problems.*

9. David Fontana Backpackers will need to buy some new pack mules in 5 years. These mules will cost a total of $5,000. What lump sum should the firm invest today at 7%, compounded annually, in order to be able to buy the mules? How much interest will be earned?

10. Management at Thomasina's Fabric Store feels that business conditions will require that it move into a larger store in 4 years. Moving will cost $46,200. What lump sum should be invested today at 15%, compounded semiannually, to yield $46,200? How much interest will be earned?

11. The retail meat industry is gradually becoming more automated. Halmost Meat Market feels that it will need to invest $37,500 in 4 years for new machinery. What lump sum must be invested today at 12%, compounded quarterly, so that the firm will have the necessary money?

12. A new *Encyclopedia of World Business* is being prepared that will cost $3,675 for all volumes. The encyclopedia will be available in 2 years. What lump sum should be invested by the Manhattan Business Library at 8%, compounded quarterly, so that the library will have enough to buy the new books?

13. Jose Martinez, an immigrant from Mexico, estimates that he needs $9,000 to start a small grocery store in 3 years. How much must he deposit today if his credit union will pay 8% compounded quarterly?

14. Mrs. Jones wants all of her grandchildren to go to college and decides to help financially. How much must she give to each child at birth if they are to have $10,000 on entering college 18 years later, assuming 6% interest compounded annually?

15. Assume that money can be invested at 8% compounded quarterly. Which is larger, $2,500 now or $3,800 in 5 years? (Hint: First find the present value of $3,800, then compare present values.)

16. Assume that money can be invested at 10% compounded semiannually. Which is larger, $3,000 now or $7,500 in 10 years? (Hint: First find the present value of $7,500, then compare present values.)

17. An investment of $30,000 earns interest of 10% compounded semiannually for $2\frac{1}{2}$ years. Find the future value of the investment. If money can be deposited at 8% compounded quarterly, find the present value of the investment.

18. Suppose $50,000 was invested in a business, with the value of the investment growing at 12% per year, compounded quarterly. Find the value of the investment in 5 years. Find the minimum sales price of the investment if money earns 9% per year, compounded annually.

19. A note is due in 3 years, with simple interest of 8%. The face value of the note is $35,000. Find the maturity value of the note. Find the minimum sale price of the note if money can be deposited at 10% compounded annually.

20. In 6 years, Susan Hessney must pay off a note with a face value of $12,000, and simple interest of 9% per year. Find the maturity value of the note. What should the holder of the note be willing to accept in complete payment today, if money can be invested at 6% per year compounded quarterly?

21. Jessie Jones believes her hair salon is worth $20,000 and estimates that its value will grow at 10% per year for the next 3 years. If she sells the business, the funds will be invested at 8% compounded quarterly. (a) Find the future value if she holds onto the business. (b) What price should she insist on now if she sells the business?

22. Andy Sargent figures his bike shop is worth $88,000 if sold today and that it will grow in value at 8% per year for the next 6 years. If he sells the business, the funds will be invested at 5% compounded semiannually. (a) Find the future value of the shop. (b) What price should he insist on at this time if he sells the business?

# Chapter 13 Quick Review

| TOPIC | APPROACH | EXAMPLE |
|-------|----------|---------|
| **13.1 Find the compound amount and the interest** | Determine the interest rate per period and the number of compounding periods. Use the formula $M = P(1 + i)^n$ and the interest table to calculate the compound amount. Then subtract the principal from the compound amount to obtain interest. | Find the compound amount and the interest if $1,200 is deposited at 12% compounded monthly for 4 years.<br><br>$i = \dfrac{0.12}{12} = 0.01$<br><br>$n = 4 \times 12 = 48$<br><br>$M = P(1 + i)^n$<br>$\quad = \$1,200(1.01)^{48}$<br>$\quad = \$1,200(1.61222608)$<br>$\quad = \$1,934.67$<br><br>$I = M - P$<br>$\quad = \$1,934.67 - \$1,200$<br>$\quad = \$734.67$ |
| **13.1 Determining the effective rate of interest** | Determine the value from column A of the interest table in Appendix C that corresponds to the rate and number of periods. Subtract 1 from this value and round as required. | Find the effective rate of interest to the nearest hundredth, if the annual rate is 8% compounded quarterly.<br><br>$i = \dfrac{0.08}{4} = 0.02; n = 4$<br><br>1.08243216 table value for $i = 2\%, n = 4$<br>$1.08243216 - 1.00000000$<br>$= 0.08243216$<br>The effective rate is 8.24%. |
| **13.2 Interest compounded daily** | Determine the number of days and then find the value of $(1 + i)^n$ from a table or calculator. Multiply this value by the principal to obtain compound amount. Subtract principal from compound amount to obtain interest. | $1,535 was deposited on September 5 in an account paying $5\frac{1}{4}\%$ and withdrawn on December 5. How much interest was earned?<br>There are 25 additional days in September, 31 days in October, 30 days in November, and 5 days in December. |

**469**

$$25 + 31 + 30 + 5$$
$$= 91 \text{ days}$$

Compound amount
$$= \$1,535(1.013174124)$$
$$= \$1,555.22$$

Interest
$$= \$1,555.22 - \$1,535$$
$$= \$20.22$$

---

**13.2  Finding the interest and balance when withdrawals are made**

Find the amount which earns interest for entire quarter and determine compound amount and interest on this sum. Then, find compound amount and interest for amount withdrawn. Find the final balance by adding the total interest to the original balance and subtracting the withdrawal.

Tom had $1,500 in his $5\frac{1}{4}$% savings account on October 1. He withdrew $450 on October 15. How much interest had he earned by January 1 and what was his final balance?
$1,500 - $450 = $1,050 earns interest for the entire 92-day quarter.

Compound amount
$$= \$1,050(1.013319855)$$
$$= \$1,063.99$$

Interest
$$= \$1,063.99 - \$1,050$$
$$= \$13.99$$

The withdrawn $450 earns interest for 14 days.

Compound amount
$$= \$450(1.002015582)$$
$$= \$450.91$$

Interest $= \$450.91 - \$450$
$$= \$0.91$$

Total interest
$$= \$13.99 + \$0.91$$
$$= \$14.90$$

Final balance
$$= \$1,500 + \$14.90 - \$450$$
$$= \$1,064.90$$

| 13.2 | **Finding the compound amount and interest earned on time deposits** | Use Table 13.3 to find the value corresponding to the rate and number of years. Next multiply table value by initial amount to obtain amount. Then subtract initial investment from compound amount to obtain interest. | Mike invests $15,000 in a certificate of deposit paying 7% compounded daily. Find the compound amount and interest after 4 years. |

Table value $= 1.32309429$

Compound amount
$$= \$15{,}000(1.32309429)$$
$$= \$19{,}846.41$$

Interest
$$= \$19{,}846.41 - \$15{,}000$$
$$= \$4{,}846.41$$

| 13.2 | **Finding the penalty for early withdrawal of funds from a time deposit account** | Determine the number of months for which interest will be paid. Find value in table for rate and time. Then multiply this by initial deposit to obtain compound amount. Find the interest by subtracting initial deposit from compound amount. | Tom deposited $5,000 in a 3-year CD paying 7% compounded daily. He withdrew the money 15 months later. The passbook rate at his bank is $5\frac{1}{4}\%$ compounded daily. Find the amount of interest earned. Tom will get the passbook rate for $15 - 3 = 12$ months, or 365 days. Passbook rate of $5\frac{1}{4}\%$ for 365 days gives a table value of 1.053898585 |

Compound amount
$$= \$5{,}000 \times 1.053898585$$
$$= \$5{,}269.49$$

Interest
$$= \$5{,}269.49 - \$5{,}000$$
$$= \$269.49$$

**13.2    Determining the interest and compound amount for continuous compounding**

Use the formula

$$M = Pe^{ni}.$$

Use table in Appendix C to find value of $e^{ni}$. Find interest from the formula

$$I = M - P.$$

Find the interest and compound amount for $2,000 at 6% compounded continuously for 8 years.

$$M = Pe^{ni}$$

$$M = \$2,000e^{(8)(0.06)}$$

$$= \$2,000e^{0.48}$$

$$= \$2,000(1.6160744)$$

$$= \$3,232.15$$

$$I = M - P$$

$$I = \$3,232.15 - \$2,000$$

$$= \$1,232.15$$

**13.3    Finding the time given interest rate, compound amount, and principal**

Substitute values for $M$, $P$, and $i$ in the formula $M = P(1 + i)^n$; then divide both sides by the value of $P$. Find the value in column A of the interest table (Appendix C) closest to the left-hand side of the equation for the correct value of $i$. The corresponding value of $n$ is the number of periods required to obtain the compound amount.

How long would it take for $1,800 at 9% compounded semiannually to become $7,361.97?

$$i = 9\% \div 2 = 4.5\%$$

$$M = P(1 + i)^n$$

$$\$7,361.97 = \$1,800(1.045)^n$$

$$4.0899833 = (1.045)^n$$

In column A of the 4.5% page the number 4.08998104 is *very close* to 4.0899833, so $n = 32$ and it would take 32 6-month periods or 16 years.

**13.3    Finding the rate, given principal, compound amount, and time**

Divide the compound amount by the principal. Use the row of the interest table that corresponds to the number of interest periods and find the value of column A closest to the quotient obtained above. Then find the interest rate per year.

A principal of $7,000 is deposited for 18 months with interest compounded monthly. Find the rate if the compound amount is $8,373.03.

$$M = P(1 + i)^n$$

$$\$8,373.03 = \$7,000(1 + i)^{18}$$

$$1.196147 = (1 + i)^{18}$$

Find the row for 18 periods in the interest table. Check the table until an entry closest to 1.196147 is found. The closest number is 1.19614748 per month or $1\% \times 12 = 12\%$ per year.

**13.4   Finding the present value of a future amount**

Use the formula

$$P = \frac{M}{(1 + i)^n} \text{ with}$$

$M =$ Future value;

$i =$ interest rate per period; and

$n =$ number of periods.

Substitute values for $i$, $n$, and $M$ and find the value of $\dfrac{1}{(1 + i)^n}$ from column B of the interest table.

What amount deposited today at 9% compounded monthly will produce $8,000 in 3 years?

$M = \$8,000$

$$i = \frac{9\%}{12} = 0.75\%$$

$n = 3 \times 12 = 36$

$$P = \frac{M}{(1 + i)^n}$$

$$= M \cdot \frac{1}{(1 + i)^n}$$

$P = \$8,000$

$$\times \frac{1}{(1 + 0.0075)^{36}}$$

$$P = \$8,000 \cdot \frac{1}{(1.0075)^{36}}$$

$P = \$8,000(0.76414896)$

$P = \$6,113.19$

# Chapter 13 Review Exercises

*Find the compound amount and the interest earned for each of the following. Round to the nearest cent. [13.1]*

1. $8,500 at 5% compounded annually for 5 years
2. $7,000 at 6% compounded semiannually for 4 years
3. $4,800 at 10% compounded quarterly for 3 years
4. $10,000 at 8% compounded quarterly for 2 years

**5.** $9,000 at 9% compounded monthly for $2\frac{1}{2}$ years

**6.** $12,000 at 6% compounded monthly for $3\frac{1}{4}$ years

*Find the effective rate of interest corresponding to the following nominal rates. Round to the nearest hundredth of a percent. [13.1]*

**7.** 6% compounded monthly

**8.** 8% compounded quarterly

**9.** 7% compounded semiannually

**10.** 9% compounded monthly

*Find the interest earned by the following. Assume $5\frac{1}{4}$% interest compounded daily. Round to the nearest cent. [13.2]*

| | Interest | Amount | Date Deposited | Date Withdrawn |
|---|---|---|---|---|
| **11.** | _____ | $1,400 | Jan. 7 | Mar. 3 |
| **12.** | _____ | $6,000 | May 20 | July 1 |
| **13.** | _____ | $3,020.80 | July 15 | Oct. 1 |

*Find the amount on deposit on the first day of the next quarter when the following sums are deposited as indicated. Assume $5\frac{1}{4}$% compounded daily. Round to the nearest cent. [13.2]*

| | Amount at End of Quarter | Amount | Date Deposited |
|---|---|---|---|
| **14.** | _____ | $3,500 | January 22 |
| **15.** | _____ | $7,200.35 | April 22 |
| **16.** | _____ | $7,178.75 | September 3 |

*Find the compound amount for each of the following certificates of deposit. Assume daily compounding. Round to the nearest cent. [13.2]*

| | Compound Amount | Amount Deposited | Interest Rate | Time in Years |
|---|---|---|---|---|
| **17.** | _____ | $4,000 | 7% | 3 |
| **18.** | _____ | $6,500 | 6% | 2 |
| **19.** | _____ | $8,800 | 8% | 4 |

*Find the compound amount and the interest for the following deposits. Assume continuous compounding. [13.2]*

| | Compound Amount | Interest | Amount | Interest Rate | Time |
|---|---|---|---|---|---|
| **20.** | _____ | _____ | $3,000 | 6% | 4 years |
| **21.** | _____ | _____ | $5,000 | 7% | 5 years |

*Complete the following table. Round time to the nearest period, interest to the nearest whole percent per year, and money to the nearest cent. [13.3]*

| | Principal | Compound Amount | Interest Rate | Compounded | Time in Years |
|---|---|---|---|---|---|
| **22.** | $7,500 | $10,203.50 | _____ | annually | 4 |
| **23.** | $8,600 | $11,566.04 | _____ | quarterly | 3 |
| **24.** | $7,500 | $9,914.25 | _____ | quarterly | $3\frac{1}{2}$ |
| **25.** | $6,000 | $7,986.00 | 10% | annually | _____ |
| **26.** | $8,400 | $10,357.20 | 6% | monthly | _____ |

*Find the present value for each of the following. Round to the nearest cent. Also find the interest earned. [13.4]*

| | Amount Needed | Time | Interest Rate | Compounded | Present Value | Interest Earned |
|---|---|---|---|---|---|---|
| **27.** | $2,800 | 2 years | 7% | annually | _____ | _____ |
| **28.** | $4,000 | 3 years | 9% | semiannually | _____ | _____ |
| **29.** | $6,000 | 5 years | 10% | quarterly | _____ | _____ |
| **30.** | $3,000 | 4 years | 6% | monthly | _____ | _____ |

*Solve the following application problems.*

**31.** The Train Company had $12,500 in a savings account on July 1 and deposited an additional $3,450 in the account on August 3. Find the balance on Ocober 1 assuming an interest rate of $5\frac{3}{4}$% compounded daily. [13.2]

**32.** Discount Auto Insurance had $1,800 in a savings account paying $5\frac{1}{4}$% compounded daily on January 1 and deposited an additional $2,300 in the account on March 10. Find the balance on April 1. [13.2]

**33.** Sam Cracker deposits $18,000 in an 8% certificate of deposit compounded daily for 10 years. Find the compound amount and the interest earned. [13.2]

**34.** Melissa Smith deposited $7,350 in an 8%, 2-year certificate of deposit with daily compounding. She took out the money 15 months later. What was the interest Melissa received if her bank has a passbook rate of $5\frac{1}{4}$% compounded daily? (Use the rules for finding the early withdrawal penalty as given in the text.) [13.2]

**35.** Wooden Desk Company will need $47,500 in 4 years for capital improvements. What lump sum should be invested today at 12% compounded monthly to yield $47,500? [13.4]

**36.** Computers, Inc. accepted a 2-year note for $12,540 in lieu of immediate payment for computer equipment sold to a local firm. Find (a) the maturity value given a rate of 10% compounded annually and (b) the present value of the note at 6% per year compounded semiannually. [13.4]

**37.** Jack Taylor invests $15,000 in an account paying 6% per year compounded annually. In how many years will the compound amount become $18,937.15? [13.3]

**38.** The consumption of electricity has increased historically at 6% per year. If it continued to increase at this rate indefinitely, find the number of years before the electric utilities would need to double the amount of generating capacity. [13.3]

# Chapter 13 Summary Exercise

Officers at Hard Rock Recording Company currently value the music company at $12,000,000 and believe that it will grow at 10% per year for the next 5 years. If they sell the company, the funds will be invested at a rate of 6% compounded semiannually. Round all answers to the nearest dollar.

**(a)** Find the future value of the music company.

**(b)** What price should they insist on today if they sell the company and they wish to have the same future value at the end of 5 years?

**(c)** Find the future value of Hard Rock Recording if it grows at 12% per year for 5 years.

**(d)** What price should they insist on today if they sell the company and they are convinced it will grow at 12% per year?

**(e)** Find the difference in the two estimates of the present value of the recording company.

**NOTE** Increasing the growth rate of the firm from 10% to 12% adds over one million dollars to the present value of the business. ■

# 14

# Annuities and Sinking Funds

The earlier work with simple and compound interest involved *lump sums*: a lump sum of money would be borrowed or deposited today, with the appropriate formulas used to find the maturity value or future value, respectively. However, in practical, day-to-day life, such lump sum payments are not as common as sequences of *periodic payments*. For example, few people prepare for their children's college education, or their own retirement, by making a lump sum deposit—most people must save for these events by periodic deposits.

## 14.1 Amount of an Annuity

**OBJECTIVES**

**1** *Identify the types of annuities.*

**2** *Find the amount of an annuity.*

**3** *Find the amount of an annuity payment.*

**4** *Find the number of payments.*

**5** *Find the amount of an annuity due.*

**6** *Understand an Individual Retirement Account (IRA).*

Suppose a small firm decides to accumulate money to buy a new truck. To do so, they make deposits of $1,500 at the end of each year for 6 years in an account paying 8% per year, compounded annually. Such a *sequence of equal payments* is called an **annuity**. (Many people think of an annuity only as a sequence of payments made by a life insurance company when a person retires, but this is only one special kind of annuity.)

The time between the payments of an annuity is the **payment period**, with the time from the beginning of the first payment period to the end of the last called the **term of the annuity**. The **amount of the annuity**, the final sum on deposit, is defined

**477**

as the sum of the compound amounts of all the payments, compounded to the end of the term.

**OBJECTIVE 1** *Identify the types of annuities.*     There are many kinds of annuities. An **annuity certain** has a specified beginning date and a specified ending date. The example of payments for 6 years is an annuity certain. Other examples would include the 48 monthly payments needed to pay off a car loan, or 18 annual payments into a college fund beginning at the birth of a child.

A **contingent annuity** has variable beginning or ending dates. For example, an insurance policy that pays a fixed amount per month beginning when a person is age 65 and lasting until that person's death has a variable ending date and is a contingent annuity. A person might prepare a will leaving a fixed annual sum to the surviving spouse for a fixed number of years, an example of a contingent annuity with a variable beginning date (because the annual payments do not start until the death of the person making the will). We will only discuss annuities certain in this book.

With an **ordinary annuity**, payments are made at the *end* of each period of time, while an **annuity due** has payments made at the *beginning* of each period.

Finally, a **simple annuity** has payment dates matching the compounding period. For example, an annuity with payments made quarterly and having interest compounded quarterly is a simple annuity, while an annuity with payments made quarterly and interest compounded daily is not a simple annuity. While there are formulas available for annuities that are not simple (see a textbook on mathematics of finance), we discuss only simple annuities in this book.

Let us return to the annuity mentioned at the beginning of this section—payments of $1,500 at the end of each year for 6 years in an account paying 8% per year compounded annually. By the definitions, this annuity is certain, ordinary, and simple. To find the amount of the annuity, or the final sum on deposit, find the sum of the compound amounts of all the payments compounded to the end of the term.

The first deposit of $1,500 will produce a compound amount of

$$\$1,500(1 + 0.8)^5 = \$1,500(1.08)^5$$

Use 5 as the exponent instead of 6 since the money is deposited at the *end* of the first year, and earns interest for only 5 years. The second payment of $1,500 will produce a compound amount of $\$1,500(1.08)^4$. Continuing in this way, the amount of the annuity is $\$1,500(1.08)^5 + \$1,500(1.08)^4 + \$1,500(1.08)^3 + \$1,500(1.08)^2 + \$1,500(1.08)^1 + \$1,500$. (The last payment earns no interest at all.) From column A of the interest table in Appendix C, this sum is

$$\$1,500(1.4693208) + \$1,500(1.36048896) + \$1,500(1.25971200)$$
$$+ \$1,500(1.16640000) + \$1,500(1.08000000) + \$1,500$$
$$= \$2,203.99 + \$2,040.73 + \$1,889.57 + \$1,749.60 + \$1,620 + \$1,500$$
$$= \$11,003.89.$$

The amount of the annuity is $11,003.89. Since 6 deposits of $1,500 each were made, the interest earned is

$$\$11,003.89 - (6 \times \$1,500) = \$2,003.89.$$

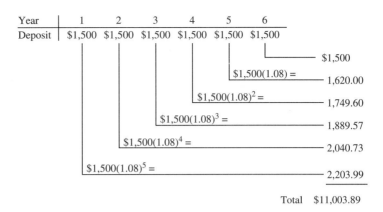

| Year | 1 | 2 | 3 | 4 | 5 | 6 |
|------|---|---|---|---|---|---|
| Deposit | $1,500 | $1,500 | $1,500 | $1,500 | $1,500 | $1,500 |

$1,500

$1,500(1.08) = \quad$ 1,620.00

$1,500(1.08)^2 = \quad$ 1,749.60

$1,500(1.08)^3 = \quad$ 1,889.57

$1,500(1.08)^4 = \quad$ 2,040.73

$1,500(1.08)^5 = \quad$ 2,203.99

Total  $11,003.89

**FIGURE 14.1**

Figure 14.1 shows each payment into the annuity and the compound amount of each payment.

**CALCULATOR APPROACH**

*The value for $1,500(1.08)^5$ from above can be found using a calculator as follows:

$$1.08 \boxed{y^x} \; 5 \; \boxed{\times} \; 1500 \; \boxed{=} \; 2203.99.$$

**OBJECTIVE 2** *Find the amount of an annuity.* This method for finding the amount of the annuity of $1,500 at the end of each year for 6 years was tedious. Using algebra, a formula for the amount of an annuity can be derived. This formula follows.

If a simple annuity is made up of payments of $R$ dollars at the end of each period for $n$ periods, at a rate of interest $i$ per period, then the amount of the annuity $S$, is

$$S = R\left[\frac{(1 + i)^n - 1}{i}\right].$$

The quantity in brackets is commonly written $s_{\overline{n}|i}$ (read "*s*-angle-*n*-at-*i*") so that

$$S = R \cdot s_{\overline{n}|i}.$$

The value of $s_{\overline{n}|i}$ for a specific $n$ and $i$ is found in Appendix C.

*NOTE: All calculator solutions use a scientific calculator. Refer to Appendix A for scientific and financial calculator basics.

For our annuity, $R = \$1,500$, $n = 6$, and $i = 0.08$. By the formula, the amount of the annuity is

$$S = R \cdot s_{\overline{n}|i}$$

$$S = \$1,500 \cdot s_{\overline{6}|0.08}$$

By the definition of the symbol $s_{\overline{6}|0.08}$

$$S = \$1,500 \left[ \frac{(1 + 0.08)^6 - 1}{0.08} \right]$$

$$S = \$1,500 \left[ \frac{(1.08)^6 - 1}{0.08} \right].$$

The value of $(1.08)^6$ can be found in column A of the interest table in Appendix C or by using a calculator as shown below. By either method,

$$S = \$1,500 \left( \frac{1.58687432 - 1}{0.08} \right)$$

$$S = \$1,500(7.33592900)$$

$$S = \$11,003.89,$$

exactly the same result found earlier.

---

**CALCULATOR APPROACH**

The expression $S = \$1,500 \left[ \dfrac{(1 + 0.08)^6 - 1}{0.08} \right]$ above can be evaluated using a calculator as follows:

1500 $\boxed{\times}$ $\boxed{(}$ $\boxed{(}$ 1 $\boxed{+}$ .08 $\boxed{)}$ $\boxed{y^x}$ 6 $\boxed{-}$ 1 $\boxed{)}$

$\boxed{\div}$ .08 $\boxed{=}$ 11003.89.

Notice that the numerator in the brackets is entered as $((1 + 0.08)^6 - 1)$ in order to maintain the order of operations.

---

To save time, tables of values of $s_{\overline{n}|i}$ have been calculated using the expression given above for the amount of an annuity for different values of $n$ and $i$. They appear in column $C$ of the interest table in Appendix C. Look in this table for 8% and 6 periods to find

$$s_{\overline{6}|0.08} = 7.33592904.$$

**NOTE** The number from the table is slightly different from the result found by using the formula. This variation is due to rounding. ∎

| EXAMPLE 1 *Finding the Amount of an Annuity*

Roberto Garcia, a soccer player from Argentina, believes that his playing career will last 7 years. To prepare for his future, he deposits $22,000 at the end of each year for 7 years in an account paying 10% compounded annually. How much will he have on deposit after 7 years?

**SOLUTION**    His payments form an ordinary annuity with $R = \$22,000$, $n = 7$, and $i = 0.10$. The amount of this annuity is

$$S = \$22,000 \left[ \frac{(1.10)^7 - 1}{0.10} \right] \text{ or using the tables,}$$

$$S = R \cdot s_{\overline{n}|i}$$

$$S = \$22,000 \cdot s_{\overline{7}|0.10}.$$

From column C of the interest table, the number in brackets, $s_{\overline{7}|0.10}$, is 9.48717100, so

$$S = \$22,000(9.48717100) = \$208,717.76.$$

Garcia deposits $22,000 per year for 7 years, for a total deposit of

$$7 \times \$22,000 = \$154,000.$$

Of the $208,717.76, which was the amount of his annuity, the difference

$$\$208,717.76 - \$154,000 = \$54,717.76$$

represents interest earned.                                              ∎

| EXAMPLE 2 *Finding the Amount of an Annuity*

At the birth of her grandson, Junella Smith decides to help pay for his college education. She commits to making deposits of $600 into an account at the end of each six months for 18 years. Smith has narrowed her choices to an annuity at a bank paying 6% compounded semiannually, a CD at a bank paying 5% compounded semiannually, or a savings account at a credit union paying approximately $3\frac{1}{2}\%$ compounded semiannually. (a) Find the amount of the annuity in each case (ignore taxes). (b) Which is preferred?

**SOLUTION**

**(a)** There are $2 \times 18 = 36$ semiannual periods in 18 years. The semiannual interest, value from Appendix C, and future amount is shown in the table below. In each case, the future amount is found using either $S = R \left[ \dfrac{(1 + i)^n - 1}{i} \right]$ or $S = R \cdot s_{\overline{n}|i}$ and table values where $R = \$600$, $n = 36$, and $i$ is the semiannual interest.

|  | Semiannual Interest | Value from Appendix C | Future Amount |
|---|---|---|---|
| **Annuity** | $\dfrac{6\%}{2} = 3\%$ | 63.27594427 | $37,965.57 |
| **CD** | $\dfrac{5\%}{2} = 2.5\%$ | 57.30141263 | $34,380.85 |
| **Savings account** | $\dfrac{3\frac{1}{2}\%}{2} = 1.75\%$ | 49.56612949 | $29,739.68 |

**(b)** The annuity with the insurance company is best as long as all three investment choices have equal risk in terms of loss due to reputation and past performance of companies. Notice that an increase in the interest rate from $3\frac{1}{2}\%$ to 6% results in the accumulation of an extra $8,225.89 in 18 years.     ∎

**NOTE**   Example 2 in Appendix A.2 shows how a financial calculator can be used to solve this same type of problem.     ∎

**OBJECTIVE** **3** *Find the amount of an annuity payment.*     Sometimes the lump sum that will be needed at some time in the future is known, and the amount of each payment into an annuity that will guarantee the availability of the necessary amount must be found.

**EXAMPLE 3** *Finding the Amount of an Annuity Payment*

Wolf Films needs to buy a new model video camera 3 years from now. The firm wants to deposit an equal amount at the end of each quarter for 3 years in order to accumulate enough money to pay for the camera. The camera will cost $2,400, and the bank pays 8% interest compounded quarterly. Find the amount of each of the 12 deposits to be made.

**SOLUTION**   This example describes an ordinary annuity with $S = $2,400$, $i = 2\%$ (8% ÷ 4 = 2%), and $n = 3 \times 4 = 12$ periods. The unknown here is the amount of each payment, $R$. Use the formula for the amount of an annuity.

$$\$2,400 = R \cdot s_{\overline{12}|0.02}$$

From column C of the interest table, with $n = 12$ and $i = 2\%$, find $s_{\overline{12}|0.02} = 13.41208973$, and

$$\$2,400 = R(13.41208973).$$

Dividing both sides by 13.41208973 gives

$$\$178.94 = R.$$

Each payment must be $178.94. (As we shall see in Section 3 of this chapter, these payments form a sinking fund.)     ∎

**PROBLEM-SOLVING HINT**   The value of $n$ is the number of compounding periods (*not years*) and $i$ is the interest per compounding period (*not interest per year*). So $n = 12$ and $i = 0.02$.   ■

**OBJECTIVE 4** *Find the number of payments.*   The next example shows how to find the number of periods necessary to accumulate a certain amount of money.

### EXAMPLE 1  *Finding the Number of Payments*

The Dunlaps want to purchase their first home and need $4,000 for a down payment. They can save $275 per quarter. If they deposit this amount in an account paying 3% interest compounded quarterly, how long will it be before they can purchase a home?

**SOLUTION**   Here the amount of the annuity is known, $S$, and $R$ is known, the amount of each payment, as is $i$, the interest rate per period. The unknown is $n$, the number of quarters for which deposits must be made. Start with the formula for the amount of an annuity.

$$S = R \cdot s_{\overline{n}|i}$$

Replace $S$ with $4,000, $R$ with $275, and $i$ with $3\% \div 4 = \frac{3}{4}\%$.

$$\$4,000 = \$275 \cdot s_{\overline{n}|0.0075}$$

Divide both sides by $275 to get the following.

$$14.54545455 = s_{\overline{n}|0.0075}$$

Go to the $\frac{3}{4}\%$ page in the interest table. Look down column C for the first number *larger* than 14.54545455. The first number that is larger is 14.70340370 which corresponds to 14 quarters. The family must save for 14 quarters or $3\frac{1}{2}$ years; at the end of this period of time they will have

$$\$275(14.70340370) = \$4,043.44.$$   ■

**NOTE**   The table value used is the one *larger* than the calculated value, not closest to it.   ■

**OBJECTIVE 5** *Find the amount of an annuity due.*   As mentioned earlier, with ordinary annuities, payments are made at the *end* of each time period. With **annuities due** the payments are made at the *beginning* of the time period. The difference between an annuity and an annuity due is subtle, but both are used in the financial services industry. The following charts may help you understand the *difference* between an ordinary annuity and an annuity due.

Ordinary annuity—payments at end of each period

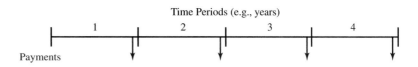

In an ordinary annuity, think of the payments being made in the last second of the last day of each period.

Annuity due—payments at beginning of each period

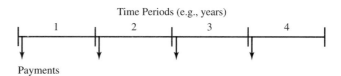

In an annuity due, think of the payments being made on the first second of the first day of each period. If you subtract one from each time period in the chart below, the annuity due above is the same as the following ordinary annuity, *except for* the extra, last payment in the ordinary annuity.

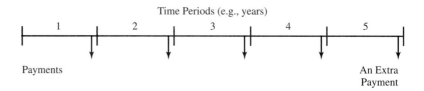

Therefore, the amount of an annuity due can be found using an ordinary annuity table and following the rule stated below.

> To find the amount of an annuity due, treat each payment as if it were made at the *end* of the *preceding* period. Then use column C of the interest table to find $s_{\overline{n}|i}$ for *one additional* period; to compensate for this, subtract the amount of one payment.

## EXAMPLE 5   *Finding the Amount of an Annuity Due*

Susan Ellwood is saving to buy a new boat. Find the amount of an annuity due if payments of $500 are made at the beginning of each quarter for 7 years, in an account paying 4% compounded quarterly.

SOLUTION    In 7 years, there are $4 \times 7 = 28$ quarterly periods. Use the $4\% \div 4 = 1\%$ page of the interest table. Look in row 29 (28 + 1) of column C of the table and find the number 33.45038766. Multiply this number by $500, the amount of each payment.

$$\$500(33.45038766) = \$16,725.19$$

Subtract the amount of one payment from this result.

$$\$16,725.19 - \$500 = \$16,225.19$$

The account will contain a total of $16,225.19 after 7 years.     ∎

**PROBLEM-SOLVING HINT**     When solving for the amount of an annuity due, be sure to add one *period* to the total number of annuity periods and then subtract one *payment* to find the total in the account.     ∎

**OBJECTIVE** **6** *Understand an Individual Retirement Account (IRA).*     If you work, you can probably reduce your current income taxes and build funds for retirement using an **Individual Retirement Account**, also called an **IRA**. IRA accounts permit money to be deposited each year. The deposits, in addition to interest earned, may be excluded from federal income taxes. At retirement, you will withdraw funds from the IRA and pay taxes at that time. Typically, the retired person has less income than before retirement and pays income tax at a lower rate. The maximum contribution for IRA accounts changes from time to time—be sure to ask for current limits when making a contribution to an IRA.

**EXAMPLE 6** *Finding the Value of an IRA*

At 27, Joann Gretz sets up an IRA with Merrill Lynch where she plans to deposit $2,000 at the end of each year until age 60. Find the amount of the annuity if she invests in (a) a treasury bill fund which has historically yielded 6% compounded annually versus (b) a stock fund which has historically yielded 10% compounded annually. Assume that future yields equal historical yields.

**SOLUTION**     Age 60 is $60 - 27 = 33$ years away.

**Treasury Bill Fund**
Look in column C of Appendix C with $n = 33$ and $i = 6\%$ to find 97.34316471.

$$\text{Amount} = \$2,000 \times 97.34316471 = \$194,686.33$$

**Stock Fund**
Look in column C of Appendix C with $n = 33$ and $i = 10\%$ to find 222.25154420.

$$\text{Amount} = \$2,000 \times 222.25154420 = \$444,503.09$$

Gretz can see the projected difference in the results of the treasury bill fund and the stock fund using the graph in Figure 14.2. On this basis, she decides to try to maximize return on investment in the future—however, she plans to do so without taking too much risk.     ∎

**EXAMPLE 7** *Saving for Retirement*

At age 20, Tom Jones begins saving for retirement by making end of year payments of $300 into an IRA account, until age 65 (a total of 45 years). Becky Smith doesn't

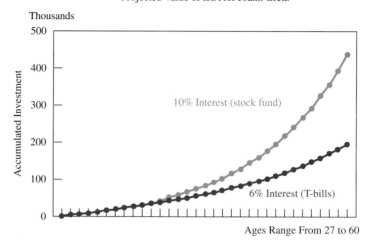

FIGURE 14.2

begin saving for retirement until age 40 at which time she deposits $800 at the end of each year until age 65 (a total of 25 years). Assume both funds earn 10% compounded annually and find the amount available at age 65 to both individuals.

**SOLUTION**    Tom Jones saves $300 at the end of each year for 45 years at 10% per year.

$$\text{Amount} = \$300 \times s_{\overline{45}|0.10} = \$300 \times 718.90483685$$
$$= \$215,671.45$$

Becky Smith saves $800 at the end of each year for 25 years at 10% per year.

$$\text{Amount} = \$800 \times s_{\overline{25}|0.10} = \$800 \times 98.34705943$$
$$= \$78,677.65$$

Smith only ends up with *about one-third* the amount that Jones ends up with, *even though* she makes payments of *more than twice* those of Jones.    ∎

**NOTE**    The last example shows that it is very important to begin saving early in life, but it is never too late to begin saving.    ∎

## 14.1    EXERCISES

*Find each of the following values using column C of the table in Appendix C.*

**1.** $s_{\overline{20}|0.055}$

**2.** $s_{\overline{30}|0.08}$

**3.** $s_{\overline{10}|0.09}$

**4.** $s_{\overline{50}|0.12}$

*Find the value of the following ordinary annuities. Interest is compounded annually. Find the total amount of interest earned.*

**5.**  $R = \$150$, $i = 0.05$, $n = 15$

**6.**  $R = \$200$, $i = 0.10$, $n = 20$

**7.**  $R = \$1,000$, $i = 0.08$, $n = 25$

**8.**  $R = \$60$, $i = 0.065$, $n = 40$

*Find the value of each of the following annuities and then find the total amount of interest earned.*

**9.**  $R = \$300$, 12% per year compounded quarterly for 4 years

**10.**  $R = \$250$, 8% per year compounded quarterly for 10 years

**11.**  $R = \$800$, 9% per year compounded monthly for 4 years

**12.**  $R = \$500$, 6% per year compounded monthly for 3 years

*Find the amount of each of the following annuities due. Assume that interest is compounded annually. Find the amount of interest earned.*

**13.**  $R = \$900$, $i = 0.07$, $n = 10$          **14.**  $R = \$1,400$, $i = 0.08$, $n = 10$

**15.**  $R = \$17,544$, $i = 0.08$, $n = 6$          **16.**  $R = \$64,715$, $i = 0.06$, $n = 12$

*Assume that you are able to invest $900 per year into an Individual Retirement Account. Find the amount accumulated after each of the time periods at each of the interest rates shown in the table.*

| | Annual Compounding Rate | | | | |
| --- | --- | --- | --- | --- | --- |
| | 5% | 7% | 9% | 11% | 13% |
| **10 years** | 17. _____ | 18. _____ | 19. _____ | 20. _____ | 21. _____ |
| **20 years** | 22. _____ | 23. _____ | 24. _____ | 25. _____ | 26. _____ |
| **30 years** | 27. _____ | 28. _____ | 29. _____ | 30. _____ | 31. _____ |

**32.** Explain the difference in the methods used to calculate the amount of an annuity versus the amount of an annuity due. (See Objectives 2 and 5.)

**33.** Explain the advantages of tax deferral and compounding of interest when investing in an IRA. (See Objective 6.)

**34.** Explain the difference between an annuity certain and a contingent annuity. (See Objective 1.)

*Find the amounts of each of the following annuities due. Find the amount of interest earned.*

**35.** payments of $200 made at the beginning of each quarter for 11 years at 6% compounded quarterly

**36.** $50 deposited at the beginning of each month for 4 years at 6% compounded monthly

**37.** $100 deposited at the beginning of each quarter for 9 years at 8% compounded quarterly

**38.** $1,500 deposited at the beginning of each semiannual period for 11 years at 14% compounded semiannually

*Find the periodic payment that will amount to the following sums under the given conditions.*

**39.** $S = \$10,000$, interest is 8% compounded annually, payments made at the end of each year for 12 years

**40.** $S = \$50,000$, interest is 7% compounded semiannually, payments made at the end of each semiannual period for 8 years

**41.** $S = \$50,000$, interest is 12% compounded quarterly, payments made at the end of each quarter for 8 years

**42.** $S = \$24,000$, interest is 9% compounded monthly, payments are made at the end of each month for $3\frac{1}{4}$ years

*Find the minimum number of payments that must be made to accumulate the given amount of money at the stated interest rate. Also, find the amount of the annuity.*

**43.** $9,500 needed, payments of $250 are made at the end of each quarter at 8% compounded quarterly

**44.** $21,000 needed, payments of $1,500 are made at the end of each 6-month period at 10% compounded semiannually

**45.** $40,000 needed, payments of $750 are made at the end of each month at 10% compounded monthly

**46.** $37,500 needed, payments of $1,250 are made at the end of each month at 12% compounded monthly

*Solve each of the following application problems.*

**47.** At the end of each quarter, the Thompsons invest $450 in an IRA earning 8% compounded quarterly. Find the amount of their annuity at the end of $3\frac{1}{2}$ years.

**48.** Sharon Stone deposits $2,000 at the end of each year in an account earning 10% compounded annually. Find the amount of the annuity after 25 years.

**49.** John Peters deposits $1,000 at the beginning of each semiannual period into a stock fund that is expected to earn 12% per year compounded semiannually. Find the amount of the annuity and total interest after $12\frac{1}{2}$ years.

**50.** Debbie Peebles invests $800 at the beginning of each quarter in a mutual fund that she expects will earn 8% per year compounded quarterly. Find the amount of the annuity and the total interest earned in 9 years.

**51.** Pam Parker deposits $2,435 at the beginning of each year for 8 years in an account paying 6% compounded annually. She then leaves that money alone, with no further deposits, for an additional 5 years. Find the final amount on deposit after the entire 13-year period. Find the total amount of interest earned.

**52.** Barb Silverman wants to buy an $18,000 car in 6 years. How much money must she deposit at the end of each quarter in an account paying 3% compounded quarterly, so that she will have enough to pay for her car?

**53.** Tom and Sandra Kip are trying to save $4,000 as the down payment on a new recreational vehicle. If they can deposit $125 at the end of each month in an account paying 4% compounded monthly, how long will it take them to accumulate the necessary amount? How much will they actually accumulate?

**54.** Western Motors needs $120,000 as a down payment on a new showroom. If the company deposits $10,000 at the end of each quarter at 5% compounded quarterly, how long will it take them to get the needed money? How much will the company actually have?

**55.** In order to put his daughter through college, Bill Thomas plans to invest $250 per quarter for 10 years in either (a) an annuity paying 8% compounded quarterly or (b) a CD yielding 6% compounded quarterly. Find the amount of the annuity for both choices.

**56.** The Crockers have decided to invest $1,500 at the end of each year for 12 years in a college fund for their twin grandsons. They can choose either (a) a mutual fund of domestic stocks expected to yield 10% per year or (b) a savings account expected to yield about 4% per year. Find the amount of the annuity in both cases.

## 14.2    Present Value of an Annuity

**OBJECTIVES**

**1**    *Calculate the present value of an annuity.*

**2**    *Use the formula for the present value of an annuity.*

**3**    *Find the equivalent cash price.*

The previous section discussed how to find the amount of an annuity after a series of equal, periodic payments. This section considers the present value of such an annuity. There are two ways to think of the **present value of an annuity**.

> **1.**    The *present value of an annuity* is a lump sum that can be deposited today that will amount to the same future amount as would the periodic *payments* of an annuity, (see Example 1 on page 491).
>
> **2.**    The present value of an annuity is a lump sum that could be deposited today so that equal periodic *withdrawals* could be made (see Example 2 on page 492).

**OBJECTIVE** **1** *Calculate the present value of an annuity.*    As an example of this second way of looking at the present value of an annuity, let us find the amount that *must be deposited today*, at 10% compounded annually, so that $1,500 could be removed *at the end of each year for 6 years.*

The amount that must be deposited today is the sum of the present values of each of the separate withdrawals. In other words, today's deposit must include the

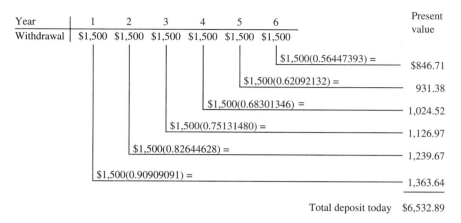

FIGURE 14.3

present value of the withdrawal to be made at the end of the first year. The present value in 1 year of $1,500 at 10% compounded annually is found by looking in column B of the interest table in Appendix C for 10% and 1 period, finding 0.90909091. The present value is

$$\$1,500(0.90909091) = \$1,363.64.$$

It is also necessary to deposit today the present value of the $1,500 to be withdrawn at the end of the second year. Again use column B of the interest table, this time with 10% and 2 periods, finding 0.82644628. The present value for the withdrawal at the end of the second year is

$$\$1,500(0.82644628) = \$1,239.67.$$

Continuing in this way for all six withdrawals gives the result shown in Figure 14.3.

A lump sum deposit today of $6,532.89 at 10% compounded annually would permit withdrawals of $1,500 at the end of each year for 6 years. Also, a lump sum deposit today of $6,532.89 left in an account for 6 years would produce *the same final total* as deposits of $1,500 at the end of each year for 6 years, with all deposits at 10% compounded annually.

**OBJECTIVE** **2** *Use the formula for the present value of an annuity.*    The formula for the present value of an annuity is as follows.

> The present value of an annuity $A$, of $R$ dollars at the end of each period for $n$ periods, at a rate of interest $i$ per period, is
>
> $$A = R\left[\frac{(1 + i)^n - 1}{i(1 + i)^n}\right].$$
>
> The expression in brackets is abbreviated $a_{\overline{n}|i}$, making the formula
>
> $$A = R \cdot a_{\overline{n}|i}.$$
>
> $a_{\overline{n}|i}$ is read as *a-angle-n-at-i.*

Values of $a_{\overline{n}|i}$ are given in column D of the interest table. We can use the table to check the problem given on the preceding page. Look on the 10% page, for 6 payments at 10%, finding the number 4.35526070. Then multiply, which gives

$$A = \$1{,}500(4.35526070) = \$6{,}532.89,$$

the same answer found earlier.

## EXAMPLE 1  *Finding the Present Value of an Annuity*

An annuity earning 6% compounded annually has payments of $1,500 at the end of each year, for 12 years. What lump sum deposited today at 6% compounded annually will result in the same future value (Figure 14.4)?

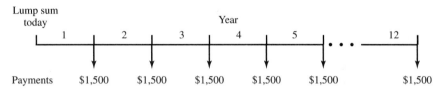

**FIGURE 14.4**

**SOLUTION**     Column D of the interest tables in Appendix C shows that $a_{\overline{12}|0.06} = 8.38384394$ ($n = 12$, $i = 0.06$).

$$\text{Present Value} = A = R \cdot a_{\overline{n}|i}$$

$$A = \$1{,}500 \cdot 8.38384394$$

$$A = \$12{,}575.77$$

A lump sum of $12,575.77 deposited today at 6% compounded annually will result in the same total after 12 years as year-end deposits of $1,500 for 12 years at 6%. This result can be checked by finding the future value of $12,575.77 for 12 years at 6%. Using column A of Appendix C, and the formula from Chapter 13 for compound amount $M$:

$$M = P(1 + i)^n$$

$$M = \$12{,}575.77 \cdot 2.01219647$$

$$M = \$25{,}304.92.$$

On the other hand, using the amount of an annuity which is column C of Appendix C, deposits of $1,500 at the end of each year for 12 years, at 6% produces the following.

$$S = R \cdot s_{\overline{n}|i}$$

$$S = R \cdot s_{\overline{12}|0.06}$$

$$S = \$1{,}500 \cdot 16.86994120$$

$$S = \$25{,}304.91$$

The difference of 1 cent is due to rounding.     ■

**NOTE**   There are two ways to produce $25,304.92 in 12 years at 6% compounded annually—a single deposit of $12,575.77 today, or payments of $1,500 at the end of each year for 12 years.   ■

## EXAMPLE 2   *Finding the Present Value*

Fred and Sara Gonzales recently divorced. As a part of the divorce settlement, Fred must pay Sara $2,000 at the end of each year for 10 years. If money can be deposited at 6% compounded annually, find the lump sum he could deposit today to have enough money, with principal and interest, to make the payments.

**SOLUTION**   Look under $n = 10$ and $i = 0.06$ in column $D$ of the interest tables to find $a_{\overline{10}|0.06} = 7.36008705$.

$$A = R \cdot a_{\overline{10}|0.06}$$
$$A = \$2,000 \cdot 7.36008705$$
$$A = \$14,720.17$$

A deposit of $14,720.17 today at 6% compounded annually is sufficient to make the 10 payments of $2,000 each. The difference between the sum of all payments, $10 \times \$2,000 = \$20,000$, and the amount deposited today is the interest.

$$\text{Interest} = 10 \times \$2,000 - \$14,720.17 = \$5,279.83 \qquad ■$$

**NOTE**   Although the $2,000 withdrawals are at the end of each year, the original deposit must be made at the beginning of year 1.   ■

## EXAMPLE 3   *Finding the Present Value*

An Australian engineering firm hires a new manager for their North American operations. The contract states that if the new manager works for 5 years, then he will receive a retirement benefit of $15,000 at the end of each semiannual period for 8 years. Find the lump sum the firm could deposit today to satisfy the retirement contract if funds can be invested at 10% compounded semiannually (Figure 14.5).

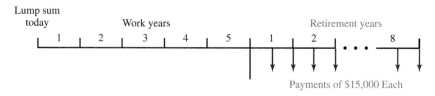

**FIGURE 14.5**

**SOLUTION**   First find the present value of an annuity with $2 \times 8 = 16$ periods at $= 5\%$ per compounding period. Use column D of the interest tables to find $a_{\overline{16}|0.05} = 10.83776956$.

$$A = R \cdot a_{\overline{16}|0.05}$$

$$A = \$15,000 \cdot 10.83776956$$

$$A = \$162,566.54$$

The firm needs $162,566.54 at the end of the 5-year work period to satisfy the retirement benefits.

They can meet this liability today by depositing the present value of $162,566.54 given 10% compounded semiannually over 5 years. Use column B of the interest tables with $n = 5 \times 2 = 10$ and $i = \frac{10\%}{2} = 5\%$ and the formula from Chapter 13 to find the following.

$$P = \frac{M}{(1 + i)^n} = M \frac{1}{(1 + i)^n}$$

$$P = \$162,566.54 \cdot 0.61391325$$

$$P = \$99,801.75$$

A lump sum of $99,801.75 deposited today will grow to $162,566.54 in 5 years which, with interest, is enough to make all 16 retirement payments of $15,000 each. ∎

## EXAMPLE 4 *Determining Retirement Income*

Bill Jones wishes to retire at age 65 and withdraw $25,000 per year until age 90. (a) If money earns 8% per year compounded annually, how much will he need at age 65? (b) If Jones starts an IRA at age 32 by depositing $2,000 per year in an account paying 8% per year compounded annually, will the IRA account contain enough money?

## SOLUTION

**(a)** The amount needed at age 65 is the present value of an annuity of $25,000 per year for $90 - 65 = 25$ years, with interest of 8% compounded annually. Use column D of the interest tables to find $a_{\overline{25}|0.08} = 10.67477619$.

$$A = R \cdot a_{\overline{n}|i}$$

$$A = \$25,000 \cdot 10.67477619$$

$$A = \$266,869.40$$

Jones will need $266,869.40 at age 65; this sum, at 8% compounded annually, will permit withdrawals of $25,000 per year until age 90.

**(b)** Jones makes payments of $2,000 at the end of each year for $65 - 32 = 33$ years, at 8% compounded annually. These payments form a regular annuity with $n = 33$ and $i = 0.08$. Use column C of the interest tables to find $s_{\overline{33}|0.08} = 145.95062044$.

$$S = R \cdot s_{\overline{n}|i}$$

$$S = \$2,000 \cdot 145.95062044$$

$$S = \$291,901.24$$

The value in the IRA account at age 65 ($291,901.24) exceeds the amount needed to fund 25 yearly withdrawals of $25,000 each ($266,869.40). Therefore, Jones will have more than enough.    ■

**NOTE**  Example 7 in Appendix A.2 shows how a financial calculator can be used to solve a similar problem.    ■

**OBJECTIVE** **3** *Find the equivalent cash price.*    As we have seen, two sums of money *can look quite different* and *yet be equivalent* because the sums of money are available at different periods of time. As in the next example, the present value of a future sum must be calculated to permit meaningful comparisons.

| **EXAMPLE 5**  *Finding Equivalent Cash Price*

Julia Smithers is an attorney trying to settle an estate. The estate owns a piece of property which is desired by two different developers. Developer A offers $140,000 in cash, today, for the land. Developer B offers $50,000 now as a down payment, with payments of $8,000 at the end of each quarter for 4 years. Money may be invested at 12% compounded quarterly. If Developer B offers a bank guarantee that the payment will be made, making each offer equally safe, which bid should the attorney accept?

**SOLUTION**    The bids can be compared only by finding the present value of the offer of Developer B. This offer is a down payment and an annuity of $8,000 at the end of each quarter for 4 years. The present value of this annuity is found with column D of the interest table, with $n = 4 \times 4 = 16$ periods, and, since money may be invested at 12% compounded quarterly, $i = 12\% \div 4 = 3\%$. The value of $R$ is $8,000.

$$A = R \cdot a_{\overline{n}|i}$$
$$= \$8,000 \cdot a_{\overline{16}|0.03}$$
$$= \$8,000(12.56110203)$$
$$= \$100,488.82$$

The present value of the annuity is $100,488.82. Since Developer B also offers a down payment of $50,000, the total cash price today of Developer B's offer is

$$\$50,000 + \$100,488.82 = \$150,488.82.$$

This amount, $150,488.82, is called the **equivalent cash price**. This exceeds the $140,000 offered by Developer A, so the attorney should accept the bid of Developer B.    ■

| **14.2**  **EXERCISES**

*Find each of the following values.*

**1.** $a_{\overline{12}|0.055}$

**2.** $a_{\overline{20}|0.09}$

**3.** $a_{\overline{15}|0.12}$

**4.** $a_{\overline{40}|0.06}$

*Find the present value of each of the following annuities. Round to the nearest cent.*

| | Amount per Payment | Payment at End of Each | No. of Years | Money Invested at |
|---|---|---|---|---|
| 5. | $1,500 | year | 6 | 7% compounded annually |
| 6. | $2,000 | year | 7 | 5% compounded annually |
| 7. | $800 | 6 months | 10 | 6% compounded semiannually |
| 8. | $650 | 6 months | 8 | 7% compounded semiannually |
| 9. | $400 | quarter | 5 | 8% compounded quarterly |
| 10. | $200 | month | $3\frac{1}{2}$ | 5% compounded monthly |

 **11.** Explain the difference between future value and present value of an annuity. Illustrate the difference with an example.

 **12.** An individual wins a state lottery that pays $50,000 a year for 20 years. Must the state have one million dollars to pay for this prize? If not, how can the state ensure that it has the necessary funds? (See Objective 1.)

*Solve each of the following application problems. Round to the nearest cent.*

**13.** The Johnsons recently settled a lawsuit. They are required to pay the plaintiff $10,000 per year for 18 years. What amount of money do they need to set aside today in an account earning 9% per year to fund these payments?

**14.** Tom and Kitty Wysong recently divorced and Ms. Wysong agreed to pay Mr. Wysong $8,000 every 6 months for 12 years since he had helped her through medical school. What amount should Ms. Wysong set aside today in an account earning 10% per year compounded semiannually in order to satisfy this obligation?

**15.** Tom Frederickson wants to buy a piece of property for a service station. The seller wants to receive $5,000 at the end of each year for the next 9 years. If Frederickson can invest money at 6% compounded annually, find the lump sum that he should deposit today so he will be able to make the annual payments.

**16.** "The Million Dollar Lottery" offers a first prize of $1,000,000 paid at the rate of $25,000 at the end of each 6-month period for 20 years. If the lottery officials can invest money at 10% compounded semiannually, find the lump sum they must deposit today so they will be able to make the semiannual payments.

**17.** What lump sum deposited today at 8% compounded semiannually would permit withdrawals of $1,200 at the end of each 6-month period for 7 years? How much interest is earned?

**18.** Find the amount that could be placed in a bank account today, at 8% compounded quarterly, to permit withdrawals of $1,000 at the end of each quarter for 5 years.

**19.** Lupé Garcia wishes to have a retirement income of $15,000 at the end of each year for 25 years. Find the amount she must accumulate if she can earn (a) 8% per year versus (b) 12% per year.

**20.** Kashundra Jones plans to make a lump sum deposit so that she can withdraw $12,000 at the end of each year for 10 years. Find this lump sum if the money earns (a) 10% per year versus (b) 13% per year.

21. To hire a new sales manager, Gladewater Ford must guarantee her an annual retirement bonus of $7,000 at the end of each year for 8 years, starting in 6 years. The firm can invest money at 12% compounded annually. Find the lump sum that will be necessary to guarantee the retirement payments. Find the amount that can be deposited today that will produce that lump sum.

22. The Coen's daughter will enter college in 5 years. At that time, they want her to be able to withdraw $2,000 at the end of each 6-month period for 4 years. The Coen's can invest money at 7% compounded semiannually. Find the lump sum that will be necessary to guarantee the payments while in college. Find the amount that can be deposited today that will produce that lump sum.

23. A small commercial building sells for a down payment of $11,000, and payments of $4,000 at the end of each semiannual period for 20 years. Find the equivalent cash price of the building, if money may be invested at 10% compounded semiannually.

24. A fishing boat is sold with a down payment of $21,000 and payments of $3,500 at the end of each quarter for $7\frac{1}{2}$ years. Find the equivalent cash price of the boat if money may be invested at 12% compounded quarterly.

*Based only on present value, which of the following bids should be accepted?*

25. $100,000 today, or $51,000 down and $8,000 at the end of each year for 12 years; money may be invested at 10% compounded annually

26. $140,000 today, or $86,000 down and $2,000 at the end of each month for 3 years; money may be invested at 12% compounded monthly

27. $2,500,000 today, or $1,250,000 down and $50,000 at the end of each quarter for 10 years; money may be invested at 16% compounded quarterly

28. $4,000,000 today, or $600,000 down and $300,000 at the end of each 6-month period for 8 years; money may be invested at 10% compounded semiannually

*Solve the following application problems.*

29. A manager for a commercial farmer plans to retire in 5 years and is to receive $10,000 at the end of each semiannual period for 15 years. Find the shortage in 5 years if the farmer deposits $12,000 at the end of each semiannual period. Assume 8% compounded semiannually.

30. Six years from now, a school district in North Carolina expects to pay $12,000 at the end of each quarter for 5 years for the purchase of personal computers. Find the shortage in 6 years if the school district deposits $5,000 at the end of each quarter. Assume 10% compounded quarterly.

31. George Joyce is terminally ill and expects to live 5 years. He has a daughter who will need $12,000 at the end of each year for 4 years beginning at the time of his death. Assume 8% per year and find the amount that must be deposited today to satisfy his daughter's needs.

32. Beatrice Rice plans to live in Europe for 3 years beginning in 10 years. Assume an interest rate of 9% per year and assume she needs $35,000 at the end of each year while in Europe. Find the lump sum that must be deposited today to satisfy this need.

# 14.3 Sinking Funds

## OBJECTIVES

**1** *Find the amount of a sinking fund payment.*

**2** *Set up a sinking fund table.*

Section 1 of this chapter showed how to find the amount of an annuity—the sum of money that will be in an account after making a series of equal periodic payments. Businesses often have a need to raise a certain amount of money at some fixed time in the future. In such a case, the problem is turned around. The businessperson knows how much money is needed in the future, and must find the amount of each periodic payment.

A **sinking fund** is a fund that is set up to receive these periodic payments. The periodic payments plus the interest on them produce the necessary lump sum needed in the future.

Sinking funds are set up to provide money to build new factories, buy equipment, and to purchase other companies. Also, many corporations and governmental agencies set up sinking funds to cover the face value of **bonds** that must be paid off at some time in the future.

A bond has many similarities to a promissory note—a bond is *a promise to pay* a fixed amount of money at some stated time in the future. Bonds and notes both pay simple, and not compound, interest. However, interest on a bond is often paid periodically, while interest on a note is usually paid only on the maturity date of the note. Bonds are normally issued only by large corporations and by governments, including cities, states, and the federal government. A typical U.S. government bond is shown in Figure 14.6.

This section discusses only the mechanics of setting up a sinking fund to pay off a bond when it is due. In Chapter 18 the investment aspect of bonds is discussed in detail.

FIGURE **14.6**

**OBJECTIVE** **1** *Find the amount of a sinking fund payment.*    The payments into a sinking fund are just the payments of an annuity. If $S$ is the amount that must be accumulated, $R$ is the amount of each periodic payment, $n$ is the number of periods, and $i$ is the interest rate per period, then

$$S = R \cdot s_{\overline{n}|i}.$$

For a sinking fund $S$, the amount needed, is known, and $R$, the amount of each periodic payment, is unknown. Divide both sides of the formula for $S$ by $s_{\overline{n}|i}$ to get

$$R = \frac{S}{s_{\overline{n}|i}}.$$

The amount of each payment $R$, into a *sinking fund* that must contain $S$ dollars after $n$ payments, with interest of $i$ per period, is

$$R = S \cdot \left( \frac{1}{s_{\overline{n}|i}} \right).$$

The right-hand side is read as capital $S$ times 1 divided by *s-angle-n-at-i*.

Values of $1 \div s_{\overline{n}|i}$ are given in column E of the interest table. (These values also can be found by dividing the corresponding numbers from column C into 1.)

**EXAMPLE 1** *Finding Periodic Payments*

KidsToys, Inc. sold $100,000 worth of bonds that must be paid off in 8 years. They now must set up a sinking fund to accumulate the necessary $100,000 to pay off their debt. Find the amount of each payment going into a sinking fund if the payments are made at the end of each year, and the fund earns 10% compounded annually.

**SOLUTION**    Look in column E of the interest table for 10% and 8 payments, finding 0.08744402. The amount of each payment is

$$R = S \cdot \left( \frac{1}{s_{\overline{n}|i}} \right)$$

$$R = \$100,000 \left( \frac{1}{s_{\overline{8}|0.10}} \right)$$

$$R = \$100,000(0.08744402)$$

$$R = \$8,744.40.$$

If the corporation deposits $8,744.40 at the end of each year for 8 years in an account paying 10% compounded annually, it will have the necessary $100,000.    ■

**NOTE**    The 10% interest rate in Example 1 is what the corporation *earns* on money it has deposited. The *interest that the corporation pays* to the people who bought the $100,000 in bonds plays no part in this calculation.    ■

OBJECTIVE **2** *Set up a sinking fund table.*      To keep track of the various payments into a sinking fund, accountants often make up a sinking fund table, as shown in Example 2.

| EXAMPLE 2 *Setting Up a Sinking Fund Table*

KidsToys, Inc. in Example 1 deposited $8,744.40 at the end of each year in a sinking fund that earned 10% compounded annually. Set up a sinking fund table for these deposits.

SOLUTION    The sinking fund account contains no money until the end of the first year, when a single deposit of $8,744.40 is made. Since the deposit is made at the end of the year, no interest is earned that year.

At the end of the second year, the account contains the original $8,744.40, plus the interest earned by this money. This interest is found by the formula for simple interest.

$$I = \$8,744.40(0.10)(1) = \$874.44$$

An additional deposit is also made at the end of the second year, so that the sinking fund then contains a total of

$$\$8,744.40 + \$874.44 + \$8,744.40 = \$18,363.24.$$

Continue this work to get the following sinking fund table. A spreadsheet package on a personal computer is an excellent tool to calculate sinking fund tables. Be sure to round interest to the nearest cent each time before completing each row of the table.                                                                   ■

**Sinking Fund Table**

| | Beginning of Period | | End of Period | |
|---|---|---|---|---|
| **Period** | **Accumulated Amount** | **Periodic Deposit** | **Interest Earned** | **Accumulated Amount** |
| 1 | $0 | $8,744.40 | $0 | $8,744.40 |
| 2 | 8,744.40 | 8,744.40 | 874.44 | 18,363.24 |
| 3 | 18,363.24 | 8,744.40 | 1,836.32 | 28,943.96 |
| 4 | 28,943.96 | 8,744.40 | 2,894.40 | 40,582.76 |
| 5 | 40,582.76 | 8,744.40 | 4,058.28 | 53,385.44 |
| 6 | 53,385.44 | 8,744.40 | 5,338.54 | 67,468.38 |
| 7 | 67,468.38 | 8,744.40 | 6,746.84 | 82,959.62 |
| 8 | 82,959.62 | 8,744.42 | 8,295.96 | 100,000.00 |

**NOTE**   In Example 2, the last payment differs by 2 cents due to rounding error. The accumulated amount must equal $100,000.   ■

In Example 1, a sinking fund was set up to pay off the principal due on some bonds. A sinking fund can be set up to pay off *both principal and interest* on a loan. The following example presents yet another application for a sinking fund in which funds are accumulated for a large purchase.

**EXAMPLE 3**   *Finding Periodic Payments and Interest Earned*

In 4 years, Ajax Coal Company plans to purchase a new, D11N Caterpillar tractor for their open pit coal mine. At 214,800 pounds, the tractor is so large that it must be disassembled before being moved from one location to another. It currently sells for $758,000 but the price is increasing at 6% per year compounded semiannually. Ajax decides to set up a sinking fund in order to buy the tractor. Find the amount of each payment into the fund, to the nearest dollar, if annual payments are made and the money is expected to earn 8% compounded annually.

**SOLUTION**   Use column A of the interest tables to find the value of $(1 + i)^n$ in the formula found in Chapter 13, or simply calculate it using your calculator.

$$M = P(1 + i)^n$$

$$M = \$758{,}000 \cdot 1.26677008$$

$$M = \$960{,}211.72$$

The sinking fund must produce enough to pay off this total. The required payment is found by using column E in the interest tables to find $\dfrac{1}{s_{\overline{4}|0.08}} = 0.22192080$.

$$R = S \cdot \frac{1}{s_{\overline{n}|i}}$$

$$R = \$960{,}211.72 \cdot 0.22192080$$

$$R = \$213{,}090.95$$

Payments of $213,090.95 at the end of each year into a sinking fund paying 8% per year compounded annually will produce enough to pay cash for the D11N in 4 years.   ■

**NOTE**   Two different rates are involved in Example 3: the price is increasing at 6% per year compounded semiannually, but deposits in the sinking fund earn 8% compounded annually. Such an **interest rate spread** is common. For example, banks use an interest rate spread between what they pay on funds on deposit and what they charge on loans to customers.   ■

# 14.3 EXERCISES

*Find each of the following values.*

**1.** $\dfrac{1}{s_{\overline{10}|0.06}}$

**2.** $\dfrac{1}{s_{\overline{20}|0.035}}$

**3.** $\dfrac{1}{s_{\overline{40}|0.09}}$

**4.** $\dfrac{1}{s_{\overline{30}|0.045}}$

*Find the amount of each payment to be made into a sinking fund so that the indicated amount will be present. Round to the nearest cent.*

**5.** $6,000, money earns $4\frac{1}{2}\%$ compounded annually, 6 annual payments

**6.** $4,850, money earns 7% compounded semiannually, 15 semiannual payments

**7.** $14,000, money earns 8% compounded quarterly, 20 quarterly payments

**8.** $28,000, money earns 10% compounded quarterly, 40 quarterly payments

**9.** Explain the purpose of a sinking fund.

**10.** Define the phrase *interest rate spread*. Why do interest rate spreads exist? (See Objective 2.)

*In Exercises 11–14, do the following. Find (a) the present value needed to fund the end of period retirement benefit using the interest rate given, and find (b) the end of period semi-annual payment needed to accumulate the value found in part (a) assuming regular invest-ments for 25 years in an account yielding 8% compounded semiannually.*

**11.** $10,000 per year for 25 years, 8% per year

**12.** $12,000 every 6 months for 25 years, 7% compounded semiannually

**13.** $8,000 per quarter for 10 years, 10% compounded quarterly

**14.** $10,000 per quarter for 12 years, 12% compounded quarterly

*Solve each of the following application problems. Round to the nearest cent.*

**15.** A hardware store needs $22,000 for a computerized inventory system. Assume payments are made at the end of each quarter for 3 years with interest at 8% compounded quarterly. Find the amount of each payment and the total amount of interest earned by the deposits.

**16.** In 3 years, a factory needs a new welding robot costing $150,000. Find the amount of each payment into a sinking fund. Assume payments are made at the end of each month and money earns 12% compounded monthly. Find the total amount of interest earned by the deposits.

**17.** Smith Dry Cleaning must buy a new cleaning machine in 9 years for $110,000. The firm desires to set up a sinking fund for this purpose. Find the payment into the fund at the end of each year if money in the fund earns 6% compounded annually.

**18.** Catriona Kaplan's Baby Beautiful Talent Agency needs $79,000 in 6 years. To accumulate the necessary funds, the company sets up a sinking fund with payments made into the fund quarterly. Find the payment into this fund if money in the fund earns 5% compounded quarterly.

19. A city sold $4,000,000 worth of bonds to pay for a new jail. To pay off the bonds when they mature in 8 years the city sets up a sinking fund. Find the amount of each payment into the fund if the city makes annual payments, and the money earns 6% compounded annually. Find the amount of interest earned by the deposits.

20. A small church-related college sold $1,480,000 in bonds to pay for an addition to the administration building. The bonds must be paid off in 15 years. To accumulate the money to pay off the bonds, the college sets up a sinking fund. If the college makes payments at the end of each 6 months and the money earns 10% compounded semiannually, find the amount of each payment into the fund. Find the amount of interest earned by the deposits.

21. Complete this sinking fund table for Example 3.

| | Beginning of Period | | End of Period | |
| --- | --- | --- | --- | --- |
| **Period** | **Accumulated Amount** | **Periodic Deposit** | **Interest Earned** | **Accumulated Amount** |
| 1 | $0 | $213,090.95 | $0 | $213,090.95 |
| 2 | $213,090.95 | $213,090.95 | _____ | _____ |
| 3 | _____ | _____ | _____ | _____ |
| 4 | _____ | _____ | _____ | _____ |

22. Complete this sinking fund table for Exercise 19 above.

| | Beginning of Period | | End of Period | |
| --- | --- | --- | --- | --- |
| **Period** | **Accumulated Amount** | **Periodic Deposit** | **Interest Earned** | **Accumulated Amount** |
| 1 | $0 | $404,143.76 | $0 | $404,143.76 |
| 2 | $404,143.76 | $404,143.76 | _____ | _____ |
| 3 | _____ | $404,143.76 | _____ | _____ |
| 4 | _____ | $404,143.76 | _____ | _____ |
| 5 | _____ | $404,143.76 | _____ | _____ |
| 6 | _____ | $404,143.76 | _____ | _____ |
| 7 | _____ | $404,143.76 | _____ | _____ |
| 8 | _____ | _____ | _____ | _____ |

23. HiTec Manufacturing plans to purchase a new telecommunications network in 3 years. The cost to do so today is $148,000 but the cost is increasing by 7% per year. Assume

they can earn 8% compounded semiannually. What amount should they deposit in a sinking fund at the end of each semiannual period to cover the expected expense?

24. Butternut Candies plans to automate their production process in 4 years. The cost to do so today is $280,000 but the cost is rising at 6% per year. Assume they can earn 10% compounded quarterly. What amount should they deposit in a sinking fund at the end of each quarter to cover the expected expense?

# Chapter 14 Quick Review

| TOPIC | APPROACH | EXAMPLE |
|---|---|---|
| **14.1 Finding the amount of an annuity** | Use $n$, the number of periods, and $i$, the interest rate per period, to find $s_{\overline{n}|i}$ in column C of the interest table in Appendix C. Find the amount $S$ from the formula $S = R \cdot s_{\overline{n}|i}$ with $R$ the periodic payment into the annuity. | Nick Pinto deposits $1,500 at the end of each year at 4% compounded annually. How much will Nick have at the end of 20 years? $$n = 20; \ i = 4\%$$ From the table, $$s_{\overline{20}|0.04} = 29.77807858$$ $$S = (\$1,500)(29.77807858)$$ $$= \$44,667.12.$$ |
| **14.1 Finding the amount of each payment into an annuity** | Determine the amount needed in the future $S$, the interest rate per period $i$, and the number of periods $n$. Use the interest table in Appendix C to find $s_{\overline{n}|i}$, then find $R$ from the formula $S = R \cdot s_{\overline{n}|i}$. | Find the amount of the periodic payment that will produce $18,000 if the interest is 6% compounded monthly and monthly payments are made for 4 years. $$S = \$18,000$$ $$n = 4 \times 12 = 48$$ $$i = 0.06 \div 12 = 0.005$$ $$s_{\overline{48}|0.005} = 54.09783222$$ $$S = R \cdot s_{\overline{n}|i}$$ $$\$18,000 = R(54.09783222)$$ $$\$332.73 = R$$ |

**14.1    Finding the number of payments**

Divide $S$, the amount of the annuity, by $R$, the amount of the payment. Find the page in Appendix C corresponding to the interest rate $i$. Look in column C for $S/R$ (or the first larger number) and find $n$ for this number.

George Gleine needs $5,000. He can put $210 per quarter into an account paying 4% compounded quarterly. How long will it take to accumulate the money?

$$s_{\overline{n}|0.01} = \frac{S}{R} = \frac{\$5,000}{\$210}$$

$$= 23.80952381$$

Closest table value is 24.47158598 so $n = 22$ quarters; $22 \div 4 = 5\frac{1}{2}$ years.

**14.1    Finding the amount of an annuity due**

Add 1 to the number of periods and use this as the value of $n$. Use $n$ and $i$, the interest rate per period, to find $s_{\overline{n}|i}$ in the interest table. To find the amount, use the formula

$$S = R \cdot s_{\overline{n}|i} - \text{one payment.}$$

Find the amount of an annuity due if payments of $700 are made at the beginning of each month for 3 years into an account paying 5% compounded monthly.

$$n = (12 \times 3) + 1 = 37$$

$$i = 5\% \div 12 = \frac{5}{12}\%$$

$$s_{\overline{37}|0.467} = 39.91480775$$

$$S = \$700(39.91480775) - \$700$$

$$= \$27,240.37$$

**14.1    Finding the amount of an IRA**

Use $n$, the number of periods, and $i$, the interest rate per period, to find $s_{\overline{n}|i}$ in column C of the interest table in Appendix C. Find the amount $S$ from the formula $S = R \cdot s_{\overline{n}|i}$ with $R$ the periodic payment into the annuity.

Deposits of $1,500 per year are made into an IRA account paying 10% per year. Find the accumulated amount in 30 years.

$$n = 30; \ i = 10\%$$

From the table,

$$s_{\overline{30}|0.10} = 164.49402269$$

$$S = \$1,500 \cdot 164.49402269$$

$$S = \$246,741.03$$

| 14.2 | **Finding the present value of an annuity** | Use the number of periods $n$, interest rate per period $i$, and column D of the interest table to find $a_{\overline{n}|i}$. Find the present value of the annuity $A$, using the formula $$A = R \cdot a_{\overline{n}|i}$$ with $R$ the payment per period. | What lump sum deposited today at 8% compounded annually will yield the same total as payments of $160 at the end of each year for 10 years? $$R = \$160; \; n = 10; \; i = 8\%$$ $$a_{\overline{10}|0.08} = 6.71008140$$ $$A = \$160(6.71008140)$$ $$= \$1,073.61$$ |

| 14.2 | **Finding equivalent cash price** | Use the number of periods $n$, interest rate per period $i$, and column D of the interest table to find $a_{\overline{n}|i}$. Find the present value using the formula $$A = R \cdot a_{\overline{n}|i}.$$ Add the value of $A$ to the down payment to obtain the equivalent cash value. | A buyer offers to purchase a business for $75,000 down and quarterly payments of $4,000 for 5 years. If money may be invested at 8% compounded quarterly, how much is the buyer actually offering? $$R = \$4,000$$ $$n = 4 \times 5 = 20$$ $$i = 8\% \div 4 = 2\%$$ $$a_{\overline{20}|0.02} = 16.3514334$$ $$A = \$4,000 \times 16.3514334$$ $$= \$65,405.73$$ Equivalent cash value $= \$75,000 + \$65,405.73 = \$140,405.7$ |

| 14.3 | **Determining the payment into a sinking fund** | Use the number of payments $n$, the interest rate period $i$, and column E of the interest table to find the value of $1 \div s_{\overline{n}|i}$. Use the formula $R = P \cdot \dfrac{1}{s_{\overline{n}|i}}$ to calculate payment. | A company must set up a sinking fund to accumulate $50,000 in 5 years. Find the amount of the payments if they are made at the end of each year and the fund earns 8%. $$n = 5; \; i = 0.05$$ $$\frac{1}{s_{\overline{n}|i}} = 0.17045645$$ $$R = \$50,000(0.17045645)$$ $$= \$8,522.82$$ |

**14.3  Setting up a sinking fund table**

Determine the payment $R$ and the interest at the end of each payment. Then add the previous total, next payment, and interest to find the accumulated amount. Repeat for each period.

A company wants to set up a sinking fund to accumulate $10,000 in 4 years. It wishes to make annual payments into the account, which pays 8% compounded annually. Set up a table.

$$n = 4; i = 0.08$$

$$s_{\overline{4}|0.08} = 0.22192080$$

$$R = \$10,000(0.22192080)$$

$$= \$2,219.21 \text{ (rounded)}$$

| | Beginning of Period | | End of Period | |
| --- | --- | --- | --- | --- |
| Period | Accumulated Amount | Periodic Deposit | Interest Earned | Accumulated Amount |
| 1 | $0 | $2,219.21 | $0 | $2,219.21 |
| 2 | 2,219.21 | 2,219.21 | 177.54 | 4,615.96 |
| 3 | 4,615.96 | 2,219.21 | 369.28 | 7,204.45 |
| 4 | 7,204.45 | 2,219.19 | 576.36 | 10,000.00 |

# Chapter 14 Review Exercises

*Find the amount of each of the following annuities. Round to the nearest cent. [14.1]*

1. $1,200 is deposited at the end of each year for 12 years, money earns 6% compounded annually

2. $4,500 is deposited at the end of each semiannual period for $4\frac{1}{2}$ years, money earns 5% compounded semiannually

3. $3,000 is deposited at the end of each quarter for $6\frac{3}{4}$ years, money earns 10% compounded quarterly

4. $1,000 is deposited at the end of each month for $3\frac{1}{2}$ years, money earns 9% compounded monthly

5. $18,000 is deposited at the beginning of each year for 7 years, money earns $6\frac{1}{2}$% compounded annually

6. $3,500 is deposited at the beginning of each quarter for $5\frac{1}{2}$ years, money earns 8% compounded quarterly

7. Willa Burke deposits $803.47 at the end of each quarter for $3\frac{3}{4}$ years, in an account paying 12% compounded quarterly. Find the final amount in the account. Find the amount of interest earned.

8. A firm of attorneys deposits $7,500 of profit sharing money at the end of each semiannual period for $7\frac{1}{2}$ years. Find the final amount in the account if the deposit earns 5% compounded semiannually. Find the amount of interest earned.

*Find the present value of each of the following ordinary annuities. Round to the nearest cent. [14.2]*

9. payments of $2,000 are made annually at $7\frac{1}{2}$% compounded annually for 10 years

10. payments of $800 are made semiannually at 8% compounded semiannually for $4\frac{1}{2}$ years

11. payments of $450 are made quarterly for $5\frac{1}{4}$ years at 6% compounded quarterly

12. payments of $125 are made monthly for $4\frac{1}{6}$ years at 10% compounded monthly

*Find the amount of each payment to be made to a sinking fund so that enough money will be available to pay off the indicated loan. Round to the nearest cent. [14.3]*

13. $10,000 loan, money earns 10% compounded annually, 7 annual payments

14. $42,000 loan, money earns 6% compounded quarterly, 26 quarterly payments

15. $100,000 loan, money earns 12% compounded semiannually, 9 semiannual payments

16. $35,000 loan, money earns 9% compounded monthly, 47 monthly payments

*Solve each of the following application problems. Round to the nearest cent.*

17. Bill Wild can save $600 at the end of each year in an account earning 10% per year. How many years are required for him to accumulate $100,000? [14.1]

18. Suzanne Waters wishes to have a retirement income of $45,000 at the end of each year for 20 years, beginning in 30 years. Assume that she can earn 12% compounded annually throughout this period of time. Find the lump sum needed to achieve this goal. [14.2]

19. In 3 years Ms. Thompson must pay a pledge of $7,500 to her college's building fund. What lump sum can she deposit today, at 10% compounded semiannually, so that she will have enough to pay the pledge? [14.2]

20. According to the terms of a divorce settlement, one spouse must pay the other a lump sum of $28,000 in 17 months. What lump sum can be invested today, at 6% compounded monthly, so that enough will be available for the payment? [14.2]

**21.** A-1 Plumbing needs $48,000 in 4 years to replace two trucks. Find the amount they must deposit at the end of each quarter in a fund earning 6% compounded quarterly. [14.3]

**22.** A power company needs to replace some large generators at an estimated cost of $680,000 in $5\frac{1}{2}$ years. They expect to receive a payment of $240,000 from another source at that time. Find the payment required at the end of each semiannual period to accumulate the remaining funds needed to purchase the generators. Assume they can earn 8% compounded semiannually. [14.3]

**23.** Hilda Worth invests $500 at the *beginning* of each semiannual period into an IRA account paying 10% compounded semiannually. Given that she is 30 years old, find the amount she will have accumulated at age 54. [14.1]

**24.** Koplan Kitchens plans to purchase some land for expansion purposes in 3 years. They anticipate payments at that time of $11,546.48 at the end of each quarter for 5 years. Find the present value of the payments assuming 10% compounded quarterly. Find the lump sum they must deposit today in an account earning 12% compounded monthly to satisfy the debt. [14.1]

*Prepare a sinking fund table for the following. [14.3]*

**25.** A firm sets up a sinking fund to pay off a $100,000 note due in 4 years. The firm makes annual payments into an account earning 9% compounded annually.

| | Beginning of Period | | | End of Period |
| --- | --- | --- | --- | --- |
| **Period** | **Accumulated Amount** | **Periodic Deposit** | **Interest Earned** | **Accumulated Amount** |
| 1 | $0 | $21,866.87 | $0 | $21,866.87 |
| 2 | _____ | _____ | _____ | _____ |
| 3 | _____ | _____ | _____ | _____ |
| 4 | _____ | _____ | _____ | _____ |

# Chapter 14 Summary Exercise

Jason and Kara Kline wish to achieve the following financial goals:

I) give $10,000 to one grandchild in 8 years;

II) give $12,000 to a second grandchild in 12 years; and

III) beginning in 16 years, receive a retirement income of $40,000 at the end of each year for 30 years.

**(a)** Use 9% per year and find the present value of financial goals I and II above (ignore taxes).

**(b)** They currently have $80,000 in savings that can be used for goals I and II. How much of the $80,000 remains after setting aside the present value of goals I and II calculated in part (a)?

**(c)** Find the future value in 16 years of the remaining portion of the $80,000 found in part (b).

**(d)** Find the lump sum needed in 16 years to fund financial goal III.

**(e)** Subtract the amount available in 16 years found in part (c) from the amount needed found in part (d). This is the additional amount needed by the Klines in 16 years to fund financial goal III.

**(f)** Find the amount they must save at the end of each year for the next 16 years to achieve the last of their financial goals.

# 15

# Business and Consumer Loans

It is almost impossible to pay cash for everything. Using the telephone, turning on the lights, or using running water involves credit. Many people buy on credit at the department store, use a credit card at the gas station, or buy cars or furniture on the installment plan. It is often necessary to borrow to pay taxes, medical expenses, or educational costs. Almost everyone borrows when buying a home.

In addition, most businesses, including banks, borrow money from time to time. The person or firm doing the lending is called the **lender** or **creditor**. The person or firm doing the borrowing is the **borrower** or **debtor**. Even governments borrow money as shown in Figure 15.1. Some of their debt is open-end credit but much of their debt is financed with bonds which are discussed in Section 18.3 on page 673.

Credit card companies typically set the interest rates and minimum payments without consulting the borrower. However, *you may be able to negotiate a lower interest rate* on your credit cards with the lenders. Contact the companies that hold your credit cards and try it, it may save you money! If they do not give you a good rate, shop around for a card with a lower interest rate and/or better terms. One of the authors of this text currently has a VISA card with an APR of 9.9% and a MasterCard with an APR of 18.15%. Neither card requires an annual fee and the MasterCard actually has higher minimum payment requirements. As you can see the rates may differ considerably from one company to another.

Years ago, consumer credit was offered as an additional service to attract more customers and increase total sales. Today, consumer credit is not merely a service to the customer; for many retail stores the interest or finance charge represents *a large portion* of company profit. This chapter examines the various methods used in determining interest charges.

There is a fundamental difference between the notes discussed in earlier sections and the loans discussed in this chapter. In the earlier situations, a sum of money was paid back, with interest, with a lump sum payment at some future date. In this chapter, the principal and interest are paid back in periodic payments.

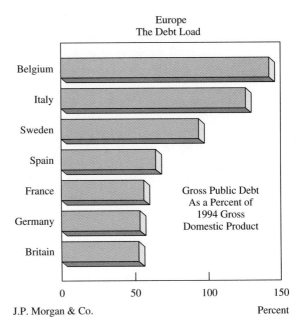

Europe
The Debt Load

FIGURE 15.1

*Source:* Reprinted from Jan. 30, 1995 issue of *Business Week* by special permission, copyright © 1995 by McGraw-Hill, Inc.

## 15.1 Open-End Credit

### OBJECTIVES

1 *Define open-end credit.*

2 *Understand revolving charge accounts and credit accounts.*

3 *Use the average daily balance method to calculate finance charges.*

4 *Define loan consolidation.*

OBJECTIVE 1 ***Define open-end credit.*** A common way of buying on credit, called **open-end credit**, has no fixed payments. The customer continues making payments until no outstanding balance is owed. With open-end credit, additional credit is often extended before the initial amount is paid off. Examples of open-end credit include most department store charge accounts and charge cards as well as MasterCard and VISA. Individuals are given a **credit limit** on these accounts that is based on income and other factors. They are then allowed to charge up to this amount.

OBJECTIVE 2 ***Understand revolving charge accounts and credit accounts.*** Individuals may open **charge accounts** at certain stores such as department stores. This allows the customer to make frequent purchases from that store, or chain of stores, during a month without having to pay cash or write a check. Such accounts are often never paid off. New purchases are continually being made, although a minimum amount must be paid each month. Since the account may never be paid off, it is called a **revolving charge account**.

**Credit cards** such as MasterCard and VISA also allow for many purchases during a month at numerous stores and restaurants. Sometimes there is an annual membership fee or a minimum monthly charge for the use of this service. A sample copy of a receipt signed by a customer using a credit card is shown in Figure 15.2. Many credit cards also allow you to get cash immediately although there may be an extra charge for this if you are at an automated teller machine (ATM). Whether you use an ATM, or even checks written on the credit card account, these are considered a cash advance and result in an immediate charge.

At the end of a billing period, the customer receives a statement of payments and purchases made. This statement typically takes one of two forms: **country club billing** provides a carbon copy of all original charge receipts, while **itemized billing**, becoming more and more common because of its lower cost to the credit card companies, provides an itemized listing of all charges, without copies of each individual charge. A typical itemized statement is shown in Figure 15.3.

Any charges beyond the cash price of an item are called **finance charges**. Finance charges include interest, credit life insurance, a time payment differential, and carrying charges. Many lenders charge **late fees** for payments that are received after the due date and **over the limit fees** in the event the debt exceeds the amount authorized by the issuer of the card. Both late fees and over the limit fees tend to be high, so it is best to avoid them if you can. Lenders also typically charge a late fee if the payment made is *less than the minimum payment* requested by the lender. They may even cancel the account if two successive payments are less than the minimum requested.

NOTE    Lenders may simply deny charges to an account that cause the debt to exceed previously established credit limits.    ■

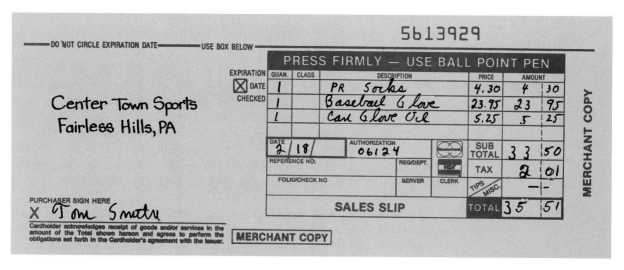

FIGURE 15.2

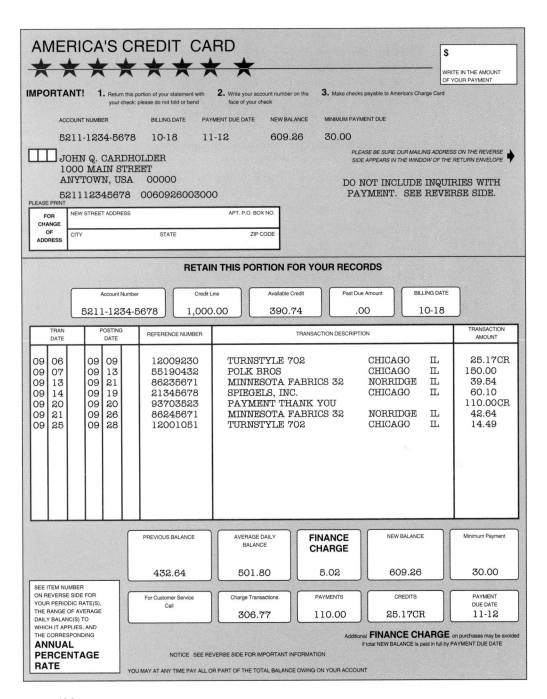

## AMERICA'S CREDIT CARD

★ ★ ★ ★ ★ ★ ★

$

WRITE IN THE AMOUNT
OF YOUR PAYMENT

**IMPORTANT!**　**1.** Return this portion of your statement with your check: please do not fold or bend　**2.** Write your account number on the face of your check　**3.** Make checks payable to America's Charge Card

| ACCOUNT NUMBER | BILLING DATE | PAYMENT DUE DATE | NEW BALANCE | MINIMUM PAYMENT DUE |
|---|---|---|---|---|
| 5211-1234-5678 | 10-18 | 11-12 | 609.26 | 30.00 |

JOHN Q. CARDHOLDER
1000 MAIN STREET
ANYTOWN, USA　00000

521112345678　0060926003000

PLEASE PRINT

PLEASE BE SURE OUR MAILING ADDRESS ON THE REVERSE
SIDE APPEARS IN THE WINDOW OF THE RETURN ENVELOPE ➤

DO NOT INCLUDE INQUIRIES WITH
PAYMENT.  SEE REVERSE SIDE.

| FOR CHANGE OF ADDRESS | NEW STREET ADDRESS | | APT. P.O. BOX NO. |
|---|---|---|---|
| | CITY | STATE | ZIP CODE |

### RETAIN THIS PORTION FOR YOUR RECORDS

| Account Number | Credit Line | Available Credit | Past Due Amount | BILLING DATE |
|---|---|---|---|---|
| 5211-1234-5678 | 1,000.00 | 390.74 | .00 | 10-18 |

| TRAN DATE | POSTING DATE | REFERENCE NUMBER | TRANSACTION DESCRIPTION | | | TRANSACTION AMOUNT |
|---|---|---|---|---|---|---|
| 09 06 | 09 09 | 12009230 | TURNSTYLE 702 | CHICAGO | IL | 25.17CR |
| 09 07 | 09 13 | 55190432 | POLK BROS | CHICAGO | IL | 150.00 |
| 09 13 | 09 21 | 86235671 | MINNESOTA FABRICS 32 | NORRIDGE | IL | 39.54 |
| 09 14 | 09 19 | 21345678 | SPIEGELS, INC. | CHICAGO | IL | 60.10 |
| 09 20 | 09 20 | 93703523 | PAYMENT THANK YOU | | | 110.00CR |
| 09 21 | 09 26 | 86245671 | MINNESOTA FABRICS 32 | NORRIDGE | IL | 42.64 |
| 09 25 | 09 28 | 12001051 | TURNSTYLE 702 | CHICAGO | IL | 14.49 |

| PREVIOUS BALANCE | AVERAGE DAILY BALANCE | **FINANCE CHARGE** | NEW BALANCE | Minimum Payment |
|---|---|---|---|---|
| 432.64 | 501.80 | 5.02 | 609.26 | 30.00 |

SEE ITEM NUMBER
ON REVERSE SIDE FOR
YOUR PERIODIC RATE(S),
THE RANGE OF AVERAGE
DAILY BALANC(S) TO
WHICH IT APPLIES, AND
THE CORRESPONDING
**ANNUAL
PERCENTAGE
RATE**

| For Customer Service Call | Charge Transactions | PAYMENTS | CREDITS | PAYMENT DUE DATE |
|---|---|---|---|---|
| | 306.77 | 110.00 | 25.17CR | 11-12 |

Additional **FINANCE CHARGE** on purchases may be avoided
if total NEW BALANCE is paid in full by PAYMENT DUE DATE

NOTICE  SEE REVERSE SIDE FOR IMPORTANT INFORMATION

YOU MAY AT ANY TIME PAY ALL OR PART OF THE TOTAL BALANCE OWING ON YOUR ACCOUNT

FIGURE 15.3

**OBJECTIVE** **3** *Use the average daily balance method to calculate finance charges.*    Finance charges on many open-ended accounts are zero as long as the borrower *pays the full amount owed each month*. An exception is on cash advances which result in a finance charge even if the balance is paid in full at the end of the month. Finance charges apply if balances are not paid in full, and they are usually calculated using the **average daily balance** method.

First, the balance owed on the account is found at the end of each day during a month or billing period. All of these amounts are added and the total divided by the number of days during the billing period. The result is the average daily balance of the account. The finance charge is then calculated on this amount.

### EXAMPLE 1   *Finding Average Daily Balance*

The activity in the MasterCard account of Kay Chamberlin for one billing period is shown in the following table. (a) Find the average daily balance on the next billing date of April 3, if the previous balance was $209.46. (b) Find the finance charge for the month if the monthly charge is $1\frac{1}{2}\%$ of the average daily balance. (c) Find the total amount due at the end of the billing period.

**SOLUTION**

**(a)**

| Transaction Description | | Transaction Amount |
| --- | --- | --- |
| Previous balance, $209.46 | | |
| March 3 | Billing date | |
| March 12 | Payment | $50.00CR* |
| March 17 | Clothes | $28.46 |
| March 20 | Mail order | $31.22 |
| April 1 | Auto parts | $59.10 |

*CR represents "credit."

At the close of business on March 3, the unpaid balance was $209.46. This balance was the same for 9 days until March 12, when it changed to

$$\$209.46 - \$50 = \$159.46.$$

This balance was the same for 5 days until March 17 when it became

$$\$159.46 + \$28.46 = \$187.92.$$

In 3 days, on March 20, the balance became

$$\$187.92 + \$31.22 = \$219.14,$$

which remained unchanged for 12 days, becoming

$$\$219.14 + \$59.10 = \$278.24$$

on April 1. The new billing date is April 3, so the unpaid balance was $278.24 for 2 days. These results are summarized in the following table.

| Date | Unpaid Balance | Number of Days Until Balance Changes |
|------|----------------|--------------------------------------|
| March 3 | $209.46 | 9 |
| March 12 | $159.46 | 5 |
| March 17 | $187.92 | 3 |
| March 20 | $219.14 | 12 |
| April 1 | $278.24 | 2 |
| | | 31  total number of days in billing period |

To find the average daily balance, weigh each unpaid balance according to the number of days for that balance, total the products, and then divide by the 31 days of this particular billing cycle. Do all this with the following shortcut procedure.

$$
\begin{aligned}
\$209.46 \times 9 &= \$1,885.14 \\
\$159.46 \times 5 &= 797.30 \\
\$187.92 \times 3 &= 563.76 \\
\$219.14 \times 12 &= 2,629.68 \\
\$278.24 \times 2 &= \underline{556.48} \\
&\ \ \$6,432.36
\end{aligned}
$$

(For example, $209.46 × 9 = $1,885.14 represents the sum of the average daily balances at the end of the day from March 3 through March 11.) Now divide the total by 31.

$$\frac{\$6,432.36}{31} = \$207.50 \text{ average daily balance (rounded)}$$

Chamberlin will pay a finance charge based on the average daily balance of $207.50.

CALCULATOR APPROACH
TO EXAMPLE 1

*The calculator solution to part (a) of this problem is as follows: multiply each unpaid balance times the respective number of days until the balance changes. Add these values together and divide by the number of days in the month (31 days).

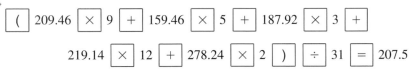

( 209.46 × 9 + 159.46 × 5 + 187.92 × 3 + 219.14 × 12 + 278.24 × 2 ) ÷ 31 = 207.5

*NOTE: All calculator solutions use a scientific calculator. Refer to Appendix A for scientific and calculator basics.

**(b)** Find the finance charge for the month by multiplying the monthly rate of $1\frac{1}{2}\%$ by the average daily balance.

$$\text{Finance charge} = 0.015 \times \$207.50 = \$3.11$$

The finance charge would be different for a month with a different average daily balance.

**(c)** The amount due at the end of the billing period is the previous balance minus any payments and credits plus any new charges including the finance charge.

| Previous Balance | Payment | Clothes | Mail Order | Auto Parts | Finance Charge |
|---|---|---|---|---|---|
| $209.46 − | $50 + | $28.46 + | $31.22 + | $59.10 + | $3.11 |

= $281.35                                                          ■

**PROBLEM-SOLVING HINT**    The billing period in Example 2 is 31 days. Some billing periods are 30 days. Be sure to use the correct number of days.    ■

**NOTE**    Not all billings for open-end accounts occur on the same day of the month.    ■

If finance charges are expressed on a per month basis, find the **annual percentage rate** by multiplying the monthly rate by 12, the number of months in a year. Table 15.1 shows typical monthly rates and the corresponding annual percentage rates.

TABLE 15.1    **Monthly Finance Charges and Corresponding Annual Percentage Rates**

| Quoted Monthly Finance Charge | Annual Percentage Rate |
|---|---|
| $\frac{1}{2}$ of 1% | 6% |
| $\frac{2}{3}$ of 1% | 8% |
| $\frac{3}{4}$ of 1% | 9% |
| $\frac{5}{6}$ of 1% | 10% |
| 1% | 12% |
| $1\frac{1}{4}\%$ | 15% |
| $1\frac{1}{2}\%$ | 18% |
| $1\frac{2}{3}\%$ | 20% |
| $1\frac{3}{4}\%$ | 21% |
| 2% | 24% |

**Objective** ☑ *Define loan consolidation.*  Credit can be so easy to obtain for stable, employed individuals in our society that it can be problematic—the headline shows that some people even use credit cards to pay for their education. Individuals with many, high interest revolving account loans sometimes **consolidate their loans** into one, lower interest loan, frequently with a longer term. This allows them to handle their monthly payments rather than defaulting on debt which ruins their credit history. Consolidating a loan may help someone afford the payments, but it does not extend the life of the items purchased which created the loans in the first place. Someone who consolidates loans, then makes additional loans, can develop serious financial problems.

# Credit cards giving students an education

*Source:* ''Credit cards giving students an education'' from *The Sacramento Bee*, August 25, 1994. Copyright © 1994 by The Sacramento Bee. Reprinted by permission.

## EXAMPLE 2 *Loan Consolidation*

Between auto loans, a home loan, and the revolving account loans shown below, teachers Bill and Cynthia Taylor have more debt than they can handle. They have gone to George Willis at Glaston Credit Union for help.

| Revolving Account | Debt | Annual Percentage Rate | Minimum Payment |
|---|---|---|---|
| Sears | $3,880.54 | 18% | $150 |
| Dillards | 1,620.13 | 16% | 50 |
| MasterCard | 3,140.65 | 14% | 100 |
| VISA | 4,920.98 | 20% | 135 |
| Totals | $13,562.30 | | $435 |

**SOLUTION**  George Willis (1) put the Taylors on a strict budget, (2) consolidated the revolving account debts into one, longer term low interest loan at the credit union, and (3) decreased the payment on one auto by refinancing it at a lower rate. In all, Willis reduced the Taylor's monthly payments by about $280 per month. The Taylors should be okay *as long as they stay on the budget*, do not make additional credit purchases, and pay off some of the debt. ■

Unfortunately, families sometimes owe so much on high interest credit card and automobile loans that they simply cannot handle the debt even by consolidating loans. In that event the family may either have to declare bankruptcy or perhaps *get second jobs*, pushing workloads up to perhaps 60 hours per week. Most financial planners suggest that it is best to *avoid high interest charges on credit cards*. This can be done by paying off credit card balances in full at the end of each monthly billing cycle.

In general, consider the following issues before borrowing:

1. Do I really need the item *now*, or can I delay the purchase until I have the cash to buy it?

2. What is the real cost, including cash price, sales tax, and finance charges, of purchasing this item?

3. Am I getting the best price for the item and best loan terms (such as interest rate and term of loan) possible or should I shop around for a better deal?

4. Can I truly afford the payments?

## 15.1 EXERCISES

*Find the finance charge for each of the following revolving charge accounts. Assume interest is calculated on the average daily balance of the account. (See Example 1.)*

|    | Average Daily Balance | Monthly Interest Rate |
|----|-----------------------|------------------------|
| 1. | $836.15 | 1.2% |
| 2. | $125.40 | $1\frac{1}{2}\%$ |
| 3. | $389.95 | $1\frac{1}{4}\%$ |
| 4. | $2,235.46 | 1.6% |

*Complete each of the following tables, showing the unpaid balance at the end of each month. Assume an interest rate of 1.7% per month on the unpaid balance.*

5.

| Month | Unpaid Balance at Beginning of Month | Finance Charge | Purchases During Month | Returns | Payment | Unpaid Balance at End of Month |
|-------|--------------------------------------|----------------|------------------------|---------|---------|--------------------------------|
| August | $822.91 | _____ | $155.01 | $38.11 | $100 | _____ |
| September | _____ | _____ | $208.75 | — | $75 | _____ |
| October | _____ | _____ | $56.30 | — | $90 | _____ |
| November | _____ | _____ | $190 | $83.57 | $150 | _____ |

**6.**

| Month | Unpaid Balance at Beginning of Month | Finance Charge | Purchases During Month | Returns | Payment | Unpaid Balance at End of Month |
|---|---|---|---|---|---|---|
| March | $1,522.83 | _____ | $308.13 | $74.88 | $250 | _____ |
| April | _____ | _____ | $488.35 | — | $350 | _____ |
| May | _____ | _____ | $134.99 | $18.12 | $175 | _____ |
| June | _____ | _____ | $157.72 | — | $190 | _____ |

*Find the average daily balance for each of the following credit card accounts. Assume one month between billing dates (using the proper number of days in the month). Then find the finance charge if interest is 1.5% per month on the average daily balance. (See Example 1.) Finally, find the balance at the end of the billing cycle.*

**7.** Previous balance $139.56
    September 12    Billing date
    September 20    Payment    $45
    September 21    Athletic shoes    $37.25

**8.** Previous balance $228.95
    January 27    Billing date
    February 9    Cheese    $11.08
    February 13    Returns    $26.54
    February 20    Payment    $29
    February 25    Repairs    $71.19

**9.** Previous balance $312.78
    June 11    Billing date
    June 15    Returns    $106.45
    June 20    Jewelry    $115.73
    June 24    Car rental    $74.19
    July 3    Payment    $115

**10.** Previous balance $355.72
    March 29    Billing date
    March 31    Returns    $209.53
    April 2    Auto parts    $28.76
    April 10    Gasoline    $14.80
    April 12    Returns    $63.54
    April 13    Returns    $11.71
    April 20    Payment    $72
    April 21    Flowers    $29.72

**11.** Previous balance $714.58
    August 17    Billing date
    August 21    Mail order    $26.94
    August 23    Returns    $25.41
    August 27    Beverages    $31.82
    August 31    Payment    $128
    September 9    Returns    $71.14
    September 11    Plane ticket    $110
    September 14    Cash advance    $100

**12.** Previous balance $412.42

| | | |
|---|---|---|
| March 10 | Billing date | |
| March 13 | Returns | $28.18 |
| March 15 | Gasoline | $16 |
| March 20 | Payment | $200 |
| April 3 | Restaurant | $28.45 |
| April 5 | Clothing | $86.80 |

*Solve the following application problems.*

**13.** Jerry Jasper owes $2,800.35 on a credit card that charges 1.5% on the average daily balance. (a) Find the monthly finance charge. (b) Find the finance charge if he can change the loan to a credit card that charges 1% on the average unpaid balance. (c) Find the savings.

**14.** Maria Estefan owes $4,509.66 on a credit card that charges 1.8% on the average daily balance. (a) Find the monthly finance charge. (b) Find the finance charge if she can change the loan to a credit card that charges 1% on the average unpaid balance. (c) Find the savings.

**15.** Explain how the average daily balance is determined. (See Objective 3.)

**16.** Explain how consolidating loans may be of some advantage to a credit card holder. What disadvantages can you think of? (See Objective 4.)

**17.** Assume your brother owes $1,200, $1,500, and $440 on credit cards charging 15%, 18%, and 12% respectively. What would you recommend to your brother? Why? (See Objective 4.)

**18.** Make a list of all of your debts and write down the payments, amount owed, and interest rates.

## 15.2    Installment Loans

### OBJECTIVES

1. *Define installment loan and annual percentage rate.*
2. *Find the total installment cost and finance charge.*
3. *Use a table to find the APR.*

**OBJECTIVE 1**  *Define installment loan and annual percentage rate.*    A loan is **amortized** if both principal and interest are paid off by a sequence of periodic payments. An example is the paying of $250 per month for 48 months on a car loan. This type of loan is called an **installment loan**. Installment loans are used for cars, boats, home improvements, furniture, and even for consolidating several smaller loans into one affordable payment. As seen in Figure 15.4, the use of installment loans has grown rapidly over the past 20 years.

Since the enactment of the **Federal Truth-in-Lending Act** (Regulation Z) in 1969, lenders must report their **finance charge** (the charge for credit) and their **annual percentage rate (APR)** on installment loans. The Truth-in-Lending law does *not* regulate interest rates or credit charges but merely requires a standardized and truthful report of what they are. Each individual state sets the allowable interest rates

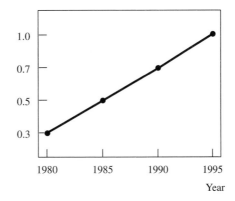

U.S. Installment Credit Outstanding
(in billions of dollars)

*Source:* Board of Governors of the Federal Reserve
System, Federal Reserve Bulletin.

**FIGURE 15.4**

and charges. Lenders normally give borrowers a document such as the one in Figure 15.5, showing all credit charges.

The APR represents the *true effective annual interest rate* for a loan and helps individuals distinguish interest charges on different loans. For example, interest charges of $120 paid at the end of 1 year on a $1,000 loan equates to 12% APR. However, $120 in interest charges on a 9-month loan of $1,000 has a much higher APR (16%). The **nominal**, or **stated rate**, can differ significantly from the APR, so lenders are *required to inform you* of the APR before you sign any credit agreement.

The charge for borrowing money or obtaining credit varies from source to source, just as the price for any other product or service varies. The amount of the credit charges paid by a borrower depends on the borrower's past credit record, present financial standing, amount of down payment, and other factors. However, some lenders charge more interest than others, so it pays to shop and make comparisons based on APR figures before borrowing.

**OBJECTIVE 2** *Find the total installment cost and finance charge.* Installment plans almost always require a **down payment**—a portion of the cash price paid at the time of purchase. (With a car, the trade-in often makes most or all of the down payment.) The **amount financed** is found by subtracting the down payment from the cash price.

Amount financed = Cash price − Down payment

For example, a $12,000 car with a $4,000 down payment would have an amount financed of

$12,000 − $4,000 = $8,000.

# Note and
# Disclosure Statement

| BORROWER NAME (Last – First – Middle Initial) AND ADDRESS (Street – City – State – Zip Code) | DATE | MEMBER NUMBER | NOTE NUMBER |
|---|---|---|---|

Smith, John Q.
10123 Fair Oaks Blvd.
Fair Oaks, CA 95628

| CONTRACT NUMBER | REFERENCE NUMBER | MATURITY DATE |
|---|---|---|
| 012-2719-6 | XXXXXXXXX | XXXXXXX |

In this agreement "you" and "your" mean each person who signs this agreement. The "credit union" means the credit union whose name appears above and anyone to whom the credit union transfers its rights under this agreement. The terms on the reverse side are part of this agreement. Boxes checked below apply to this agreement.

### TRUTH IN LENDING DISCLOSURE

| ANNUAL PERCENTAGE RATE The cost of your credit as a yearly rate. | FINANCE CHARGE The dollar amount the credit will cost you. | Amount Financed The amount of credit provided to you or on your behalf. | Total of Payments The amount you will have paid when you have made all payments as scheduled. | Prepayment: If you pay off early you will not have to pay a penalty. |
|---|---|---|---|---|
| 13.99% | $ 1,605.64 | $ 6,800.00 | $ 8,405.64 | e means an estimate |

| | Number of Payments | Amount of Payments | When Payments Are Due | Property Insurance: You may obtain property insurance from anyone you want that is acceptable to the credit union. |
|---|---|---|---|---|
| Your Payment Schedule will be: | 36 | $233.49 | monthly beginning May 15 | XXXXXXXXXXXXXXXXXXXXXXXXXXXXXXXXXXXX $ |

**Security:** Collateral securing other loans with the credit union will also secure this loan. You are giving a security interest in your shares and/or deposits in the credit union; and ☒ the goods/property being purchased; ☐ Other (Describe)

| Late Charge:    N/A | Filing Fees | Non-Filing Insurance |
|---|---|---|
| | $    N/A | $    N/A |

See your contract documents for any additional information about nonpayment, default, and any required repayment in full before the scheduled date.

### ITEMIZATION OF THE AMOUNT FINANCED

| ITEMIZATION OF AMOUNT FINANCED OF $ | AMOUNT GIVEN TO YOU DIRECTLY $ | AMOUNT PAID ON YOUR ACCOUNT  $ | PREPAID FINANCE CHARGE    $ |
|---|---|---|---|
| AMOUNT PAID TO OTHERS    $ | To | $ | To |
| ON YOUR BEHALF    $ | To | $ | To |

### NOTE AND SECURITY AGREEMENT    CONTINUED ON REVERSE SIDE

**Promise to Pay:** You promise to pay $ _____ to the credit union plus interest on the unpaid balance at _____ % per year until what you owe has been repaid.

**Collection Costs:**    You promise to pay all costs of collecting the amount you owe under this agreement including court costs and reasonable attorney fees.

| Security Offered: | MODEL | YEAR | I.D. NUMBER | | TYPE | VALUE |
|---|---|---|---|---|---|---|
| | Chevrolet Caprice | | 1NA1G1H96XE6811 | | | |

**Other (Describe):**

You Pledge Shares and/or Deposits of $ _____ in account number _____ Key No. _____ This Note is governed by the laws of **Illinois**

**SIGNATURE:** If you agree to make and be bound by the terms of this Note and Security Agreement sign below. *If you are not a borrower but an owner of the collateral for this loan, sign below and check the box for "Owner of Collateral". By doing so you agree your name only to the terms of the Security Agreement.*
**CAUTION: IT IS IMPORTANT THAT YOU THOROUGHLY READ THIS CONTRACT BEFORE YOU SIGN IT.**

| Borrower X | Date | (SEAL) | Borrower ☐ Owner of Collateral (other than a Borrower) X | Date | (SEAL) |
|---|---|---|---|---|---|
| Borrower ☐ Owner of Collateral (other than a Borrower) X | Date | (SEAL) | Witness X | Date | (SEAL) |

### CREDIT INSURANCE APPLICATION

"You" or "Your" means the member and the joint insured (if applicable).

Credit insurance **is voluntary and not required in order to obtain this loan.** You may select any insurer of your choice. You can get this insurance only if you check the "yes" box below and sign your name and write in the date. The rate you are charged for the insurance is subject to change. You will receive written notice before any increase goes into effect. You have the right to stop this insurance by notifying your credit union in writing. Your signature below means you agree that:

• If you elect insurance, you authorize the credit union to add the charges for insurance to your loan each month.

• You are eligible for disability insurance only if you are working for wages or profit for 25 hours a

week or more on the date of any advance. If you are not, that particular advance will not be insured until you return to work. If you are off work because of temporary layoff, strike or vacation, but soon to resume, you will be considered at work. Are you working for wages or profit for 25 hours a week or more? ☐ Yes ☐ No

• You are eligible for insurance up to the Maximum Age for Insurance. Insurance will stop when you reach that age.

**NOTE: THE LIFE AND DISABILITY INSURANCE CONTAINS CERTAIN BENEFIT EXCLUSIONS, INCLUDING A PRE-EXISTING CONDITION EXCLUSION. PLEASE REFER TO YOUR CERTIFICATE FOR DETAILS.**

| YOU ELECT THE FOLLOWING INSURANCE COVERAGE(S) | YES | NO | PREMIUM SCHEDULE | INSURANCE MAXIMUMS | | DISABILITY | LIFE |
|---|---|---|---|---|---|---|---|
| CREDIT DISABILITY | | X | $ | e | MONTHLY TOTAL BENEFIT | $   600 | N/A |
| | | | | | INSURABLE BALANCE PER LOAN ACCOUNT | $50,000 | N/A |
| | | | | | MAXIMUM AGE FOR INSURANCE | 66 | N/A |

If you are totally disabled for more than **30** days, then the Disability Benefit will begin with the **31st** day of disability.

| | | | SECONDARY (If you desire to name one) BENEFICIARY |
|---|---|---|---|

| DATE    April 3 | DATE OF BIRTH | DATE | DATE OF BIRTH |
|---|---|---|---|

| SIGNATURE OF BORROWER ELIGIBLE TO BE INSURED  (Be sure to check the boxes above.) | SIGNATURE OF JOINT INSURED (CO-BORROWER)  (Only required if JOINT CREDIT LIFE coverage is selected) | |
|---|---|---|
| X   *John Q. Smith* | X | N/A |

FIGURE 15.5

The **deferred payment price** or **total installment cost** is found by adding the cash price and the finance charge.

$$\text{Deferred payment price} = \text{Cash price} + \text{Finance charge}$$

Find the amount financed by first finding the **total installment cost** (another name for **deferred payment price**) and the **finance charge** on the loan. Do this with the following steps.

> ### FINDING AMOUNT FINANCED
>
> ***Step 1.*** Find the total installment cost.
>
> Total installment cost = Down payment and/or trade-in
> $\qquad\qquad\qquad$ + (Amount of each payment × Number of payments)
>
> ***Step 2.*** Find the finance charge.
>
> $\qquad\qquad$ Finance charge = Total installment cost − Cash price
>
> ***Step 3.*** Finally, find the amount financed.
>
> $\qquad\qquad$ Amount financed = Cash price − Down payment

**NOTE** Lenders frequently *allow the borrower to choose the day of the month* that installment payments are due. This allows the borrower to pay the bill after a payday, for example. ■

| **EXAMPLE 1** *Finding Total Installment Cost, Amount Financed, and Finance Charge*

Ed Chamski purchased a new Ford automobile at a total cost of $24,000. He was allowed $3,500 for his old trade-in and he also paid an additional $2,000 down. Chamski agreed to make 48 payments of $505.54 each. Find (a) the total installment cost, (b) finance charge, and (c) amount financed.

**SOLUTION**

**(a)** The total installment cost is found by adding the allowance for the trade-in, the cash down payment, and the product of the number of payments times the amount of each payment.

$$\begin{aligned}
\text{Total installment cost} &= \$3,500 + \$2,000 + 48 \times \$505.54 \\
&= \$3,500 + \$2,000 + \$24,265.92 \\
&= \$29,765.92
\end{aligned}$$

**(b)** The finance charge is the difference between the total installment cost and the cash price.

$$\begin{aligned}
\text{Finance charge} &= \$29,765.92 - \$24,000 \\
&= \$5,765.92
\end{aligned}$$

TABLE 15.2   Annual Percentage Rate Table for Monthly Payment Plans

| Number of Payments | Annual Percentage Rate (Finance Charge per $100 of Amount Financed) | | | | | | | | | | | | | | | |
|---|---|---|---|---|---|---|---|---|---|---|---|---|---|---|---|---|
| | 10.00% | 10.25% | 10.50% | 10.75% | 11.00% | 11.25% | 11.50% | 11.75% | 12.00% | 12.25% | 12.50% | 12.75% | 13.00% | 13.25% | 13.50% | 13.75% |
| 1 | 0.83 | 0.85 | 0.87 | 0.90 | 0.92 | 0.94 | 0.96 | 0.98 | 1.00 | 1.02 | 1.04 | 1.06 | 1.08 | 1.10 | 1.12 | 1.15 |
| 2 | 1.25 | 1.28 | 1.31 | 1.35 | 1.38 | 1.41 | 1.44 | 1.47 | 1.50 | 1.53 | 1.57 | 1.60 | 1.63 | 1.66 | 1.69 | 1.72 |
| 3 | 1.67 | 1.71 | 1.76 | 1.80 | 1.84 | 1.88 | 1.92 | 1.96 | 2.01 | 2.05 | 2.09 | 2.13 | 2.17 | 2.22 | 2.26 | 2.30 |
| 4 | 2.09 | 2.14 | 2.20 | 2.25 | 2.30 | 2.35 | 2.41 | 2.46 | 2.51 | 2.57 | 2.62 | 2.67 | 2.72 | 2.78 | 2.83 | 2.88 |
| 5 | 2.51 | 2.58 | 2.64 | 2.70 | 2.77 | 2.83 | 2.89 | 2.96 | 3.02 | 3.08 | 3.15 | 3.21 | 3.27 | 3.34 | 3.40 | 3.46 |
| 6 | 2.94 | 3.01 | 3.08 | 3.16 | 3.23 | 3.31 | 3.38 | 3.45 | 3.53 | 3.60 | 3.68 | 3.75 | 3.83 | 3.90 | 3.97 | 4.05 |
| 7 | 3.36 | 3.45 | 3.53 | 3.62 | 3.70 | 3.78 | 3.87 | 3.95 | 4.04 | 4.12 | 4.21 | 4.29 | 4.38 | 4.47 | 4.55 | 4.64 |
| 8 | 3.79 | 3.88 | 3.98 | 4.07 | 4.17 | 4.26 | 4.36 | 4.46 | 4.55 | 4.65 | 4.74 | 4.84 | 4.94 | 5.03 | 5.13 | 5.22 |
| 9 | 4.21 | 4.32 | 4.43 | 4.53 | 4.64 | 4.75 | 4.85 | 4.96 | 5.07 | 5.17 | 5.28 | 5.39 | 5.49 | 5.60 | 5.71 | 5.82 |
| 10 | 4.64 | 4.76 | 4.88 | 4.99 | 5.11 | 5.23 | 5.35 | 5.46 | 5.58 | 5.70 | 5.82 | 5.94 | 6.05 | 6.17 | 6.29 | 6.41 |
| 11 | 5.07 | 5.20 | 5.33 | 5.45 | 5.58 | 5.71 | 5.84 | 5.97 | 6.10 | 6.23 | 6.36 | 6.49 | 6.62 | 6.75 | 6.88 | 7.01 |
| 12 | 5.50 | 5.64 | 5.78 | 5.92 | 6.06 | 6.20 | 6.34 | 6.48 | 6.62 | 6.76 | 6.90 | 7.04 | 7.18 | 7.32 | 7.46 | 7.60 |
| 13 | 5.93 | 6.08 | 6.23 | 6.38 | 6.53 | 6.68 | 6.84 | 6.99 | 7.14 | 7.29 | 7.44 | 7.59 | 7.75 | 7.90 | 8.05 | 8.20 |
| 14 | 6.36 | 6.52 | 6.69 | 6.85 | 7.01 | 7.17 | 7.34 | 7.50 | 7.66 | 7.82 | 7.99 | 8.15 | 8.31 | 8.48 | 8.64 | 8.81 |
| 15 | 6.80 | 6.97 | 7.14 | 7.32 | 7.49 | 7.66 | 7.84 | 8.01 | 8.19 | 8.36 | 8.53 | 8.71 | 8.88 | 9.06 | 9.23 | 9.41 |
| 16 | 7.23 | 7.41 | 7.60 | 7.78 | 7.97 | 8.15 | 8.34 | 8.53 | 8.71 | 8.90 | 9.08 | 9.27 | 9.46 | 9.64 | 9.83 | 10.02 |
| 17 | 7.67 | 7.86 | 8.06 | 8.25 | 8.45 | 8.65 | 8.84 | 9.04 | 9.24 | 9.44 | 9.63 | 9.83 | 10.03 | 10.23 | 10.43 | 10.63 |
| 18 | 8.10 | 8.31 | 8.52 | 8.73 | 8.93 | 9.14 | 9.35 | 9.56 | 9.77 | 9.98 | 10.19 | 10.40 | 10.61 | 10.82 | 11.03 | 11.24 |
| 19 | 8.54 | 8.76 | 8.98 | 9.20 | 9.42 | 9.64 | 9.86 | 10.08 | 10.30 | 10.52 | 10.74 | 10.96 | 11.18 | 11.41 | 11.63 | 11.85 |
| 20 | 8.98 | 9.21 | 9.44 | 9.67 | 9.90 | 10.13 | 10.37 | 10.60 | 10.83 | 11.06 | 11.30 | 11.53 | 11.76 | 12.00 | 12.23 | 12.46 |
| 21 | 9.42 | 9.66 | 9.90 | 10.15 | 10.39 | 10.63 | 10.88 | 11.12 | 11.36 | 11.61 | 11.85 | 12.10 | 12.34 | 12.59 | 12.84 | 13.08 |
| 22 | 9.86 | 10.12 | 10.37 | 10.62 | 10.88 | 11.13 | 11.39 | 11.64 | 11.90 | 12.16 | 12.41 | 12.67 | 12.93 | 13.19 | 13.44 | 13.70 |
| 23 | 10.30 | 10.57 | 10.84 | 11.10 | 11.37 | 11.63 | 11.90 | 12.17 | 12.44 | 12.71 | 12.97 | 13.24 | 13.51 | 13.78 | 14.05 | 14.32 |
| 24 | 10.75 | 11.02 | 11.30 | 11.58 | 11.86 | 12.14 | 12.42 | 12.70 | 12.98 | 13.26 | 13.54 | 13.82 | 14.10 | 14.38 | 14.66 | 14.95 |
| 25 | 11.19 | 11.48 | 11.77 | 12.06 | 12.35 | 12.64 | 12.93 | 13.22 | 13.52 | 13.81 | 14.10 | 14.40 | 14.69 | 14.98 | 15.28 | 15.57 |
| 26 | 11.64 | 11.94 | 12.24 | 12.54 | 12.85 | 13.15 | 13.45 | 13.75 | 14.06 | 14.36 | 14.67 | 14.97 | 15.28 | 15.59 | 15.89 | 16.20 |
| 27 | 12.09 | 12.40 | 12.71 | 13.03 | 13.34 | 13.66 | 13.97 | 14.29 | 14.60 | 14.92 | 15.24 | 15.56 | 15.87 | 16.19 | 16.51 | 16.83 |
| 28 | 12.53 | 12.86 | 13.18 | 13.51 | 13.84 | 14.16 | 14.49 | 14.82 | 15.15 | 15.48 | 15.81 | 16.14 | 16.47 | 16.80 | 17.13 | 17.46 |
| 29 | 12.98 | 13.32 | 13.66 | 14.00 | 14.33 | 14.67 | 15.01 | 15.35 | 15.70 | 16.04 | 16.38 | 16.72 | 17.07 | 17.41 | 17.75 | 18.10 |
| 30 | 13.43 | 13.78 | 14.13 | 14.48 | 14.83 | 15.19 | 15.54 | 15.89 | 16.24 | 16.60 | 16.95 | 17.31 | 17.66 | 18.02 | 18.38 | 18.74 |

| | | | | | | | | | | | | | | | | |
|---|---|---|---|---|---|---|---|---|---|---|---|---|---|---|---|---|
| 31 | 13.89 | 14.25 | 14.61 | 14.97 | 15.33 | 15.70 | 16.06 | 16.43 | 16.79 | 17.16 | 17.53 | 17.90 | 18.27 | 18.63 | 19.00 | 19.38 |
| 32 | 14.34 | 14.71 | 15.09 | 15.46 | 15.84 | 16.21 | 16.59 | 16.97 | 17.35 | 17.73 | 18.11 | 18.49 | 18.87 | 19.25 | 19.63 | 20.02 |
| 33 | 14.79 | 15.18 | 15.57 | 15.95 | 16.34 | 16.73 | 17.12 | 17.51 | 17.90 | 18.29 | 18.69 | 19.08 | 19.47 | 19.87 | 20.26 | 20.66 |
| 34 | 15.25 | 15.65 | 16.05 | 16.44 | 16.85 | 17.25 | 17.65 | 18.05 | 18.46 | 18.86 | 19.27 | 19.67 | 20.08 | 20.49 | 20.90 | 21.31 |
| 35 | 15.70 | 16.11 | 16.53 | 16.94 | 17.35 | 17.77 | 18.18 | 18.60 | 19.01 | 19.43 | 19.85 | 20.27 | 20.69 | 21.11 | 21.53 | 21.95 |
| 36 | 16.16 | 16.58 | 17.01 | 17.43 | 17.86 | 18.29 | 18.71 | 19.14 | 19.57 | 20.00 | 20.43 | 20.87 | 21.30 | 21.73 | 22.17 | 22.60 |
| 37 | 16.62 | 17.06 | 17.49 | 17.93 | 18.37 | 18.81 | 19.25 | 19.69 | 20.13 | 20.58 | 21.02 | 21.46 | 21.91 | 22.36 | 22.81 | 23.25 |
| 38 | 17.08 | 17.53 | 17.98 | 18.43 | 18.88 | 19.33 | 19.78 | 20.24 | 20.69 | 21.15 | 21.61 | 22.07 | 22.52 | 22.99 | 23.45 | 23.91 |
| 39 | 17.54 | 18.00 | 18.46 | 18.93 | 19.39 | 19.86 | 20.32 | 20.79 | 21.26 | 21.73 | 22.20 | 22.67 | 23.14 | 23.61 | 24.09 | 24.56 |
| 40 | 18.00 | 18.48 | 18.95 | 19.43 | 19.90 | 20.38 | 20.86 | 21.34 | 21.82 | 22.30 | 22.79 | 23.27 | 23.76 | 24.25 | 24.73 | 25.22 |
| 41 | 18.47 | 18.95 | 19.44 | 19.93 | 20.42 | 20.91 | 21.40 | 21.89 | 22.39 | 22.88 | 23.38 | 23.88 | 24.38 | 24.88 | 25.38 | 25.88 |
| 42 | 18.93 | 19.43 | 19.93 | 20.43 | 20.93 | 21.44 | 21.94 | 22.45 | 22.96 | 23.47 | 23.98 | 24.49 | 25.00 | 25.51 | 26.03 | 26.55 |
| 43 | 19.40 | 19.91 | 20.42 | 20.94 | 21.45 | 21.97 | 22.49 | 23.01 | 23.53 | 24.05 | 24.57 | 25.10 | 25.62 | 26.15 | 26.68 | 27.21 |
| 44 | 19.86 | 20.39 | 20.91 | 21.44 | 21.97 | 22.50 | 23.03 | 23.57 | 24.10 | 24.64 | 25.17 | 25.71 | 26.25 | 26.79 | 27.33 | 27.88 |
| 45 | 20.33 | 20.87 | 21.41 | 21.95 | 22.49 | 23.03 | 23.58 | 24.12 | 24.67 | 25.22 | 25.77 | 26.32 | 26.88 | 27.43 | 27.99 | 28.55 |
| 46 | 20.80 | 21.35 | 21.90 | 22.46 | 23.01 | 23.57 | 24.13 | 24.69 | 25.25 | 25.81 | 26.37 | 26.94 | 27.51 | 28.08 | 28.65 | 29.22 |
| 47 | 21.27 | 21.83 | 22.40 | 22.97 | 23.53 | 24.10 | 24.68 | 25.25 | 25.82 | 26.40 | 26.98 | 27.56 | 28.14 | 28.72 | 29.31 | 29.89 |
| 48 | 21.74 | 22.32 | 22.90 | 23.48 | 24.06 | 24.64 | 25.23 | 25.81 | 26.40 | 26.99 | 27.58 | 28.18 | 28.77 | 29.37 | 29.97 | 30.57 |
| 49 | 22.21 | 22.80 | 23.39 | 23.99 | 24.58 | 25.18 | 25.78 | 26.38 | 26.98 | 27.59 | 28.19 | 28.80 | 29.41 | 30.02 | 30.63 | 31.24 |
| 50 | 22.69 | 23.29 | 23.89 | 24.50 | 25.11 | 25.72 | 26.33 | 26.95 | 27.56 | 28.18 | 28.80 | 29.42 | 30.04 | 30.67 | 31.29 | 31.92 |
| 51 | 23.16 | 23.78 | 24.40 | 25.02 | 25.64 | 26.26 | 26.89 | 27.52 | 28.15 | 28.78 | 29.41 | 30.05 | 30.68 | 31.32 | 31.96 | 32.60 |
| 52 | 23.64 | 24.27 | 24.90 | 25.53 | 26.17 | 26.81 | 27.45 | 28.09 | 28.73 | 29.38 | 30.02 | 30.67 | 31.32 | 31.98 | 32.63 | 33.29 |
| 53 | 24.11 | 24.76 | 25.40 | 26.05 | 26.70 | 27.35 | 28.00 | 28.66 | 29.32 | 29.98 | 30.64 | 31.30 | 31.97 | 32.63 | 33.30 | 33.97 |
| 54 | 24.59 | 25.25 | 25.91 | 26.57 | 27.23 | 27.90 | 28.56 | 29.23 | 29.91 | 30.58 | 31.25 | 31.93 | 32.61 | 33.29 | 33.98 | 34.66 |
| 55 | 25.07 | 25.74 | 26.41 | 27.09 | 27.77 | 28.44 | 29.13 | 29.81 | 30.50 | 31.18 | 31.87 | 32.56 | 33.26 | 33.95 | 34.65 | 35.35 |
| 56 | 25.55 | 26.23 | 26.92 | 27.61 | 28.30 | 28.99 | 29.69 | 30.39 | 31.09 | 31.79 | 32.49 | 33.20 | 33.91 | 34.62 | 35.33 | 36.04 |
| 57 | 26.03 | 26.73 | 27.43 | 28.13 | 28.84 | 29.54 | 30.25 | 30.97 | 31.68 | 32.39 | 33.11 | 33.83 | 34.56 | 35.28 | 36.01 | 36.74 |
| 58 | 26.51 | 27.23 | 27.94 | 28.66 | 29.37 | 30.10 | 30.82 | 31.55 | 32.27 | 33.00 | 33.74 | 34.47 | 35.21 | 35.95 | 36.69 | 37.43 |
| 59 | 27.00 | 27.72 | 28.45 | 29.18 | 29.91 | 30.65 | 31.39 | 32.13 | 32.87 | 33.61 | 34.36 | 35.11 | 35.86 | 36.62 | 37.37 | 38.13 |
| 60 | 27.48 | 28.22 | 28.96 | 29.71 | 30.45 | 31.20 | 31.96 | 32.71 | 33.47 | 34.23 | 34.99 | 35.75 | 36.52 | 37.29 | 38.06 | 38.83 |

TABLE 15.2 (continued) Annual Percentage Rate Table for Monthly Payment Plans

Annual Percentage Rate (Finance Charge per $100 of Amount Financed)

| Number of Payments | 14.00% | 14.25% | 14.50% | 14.75% | 15.00% | 15.25% | 15.50% | 15.75% | 16.00% | 16.25% | 16.50% | 16.75% | 17.00% | 17.25% | 17.50% | 17.75% |
|---|---|---|---|---|---|---|---|---|---|---|---|---|---|---|---|---|
| 1 | 1.17 | 1.19 | 1.21 | 1.23 | 1.25 | 1.27 | 1.29 | 1.31 | 1.33 | 1.35 | 1.37 | 1.40 | 1.42 | 1.44 | 1.46 | 1.48 |
| 2 | 1.75 | 1.78 | 1.82 | 1.85 | 1.88 | 1.91 | 1.94 | 1.97 | 2.00 | 2.04 | 2.07 | 2.10 | 2.13 | 2.16 | 2.19 | 2.22 |
| 3 | 2.34 | 2.38 | 2.43 | 2.47 | 2.51 | 2.55 | 2.59 | 2.64 | 2.68 | 2.72 | 2.76 | 2.80 | 2.85 | 2.89 | 2.93 | 2.97 |
| 4 | 2.93 | 2.99 | 3.04 | 3.09 | 3.14 | 3.20 | 3.25 | 3.30 | 3.36 | 3.41 | 3.46 | 3.51 | 3.57 | 3.62 | 3.67 | 3.73 |
| 5 | 3.53 | 3.59 | 3.65 | 3.72 | 3.78 | 3.84 | 3.91 | 3.97 | 4.04 | 4.10 | 4.16 | 4.23 | 4.29 | 4.35 | 4.42 | 4.48 |
| 6 | 4.12 | 4.20 | 4.27 | 4.35 | 4.42 | 4.49 | 4.57 | 4.64 | 4.72 | 4.79 | 4.87 | 4.94 | 5.02 | 5.09 | 5.17 | 5.24 |
| 7 | 4.72 | 4.81 | 4.89 | 4.98 | 5.06 | 5.15 | 5.23 | 5.32 | 5.40 | 5.49 | 5.58 | 5.66 | 5.75 | 5.83 | 5.92 | 6.00 |
| 8 | 5.32 | 5.42 | 5.51 | 5.61 | 5.71 | 5.80 | 5.90 | 6.00 | 6.09 | 6.19 | 6.29 | 6.38 | 6.48 | 6.58 | 6.67 | 6.77 |
| 9 | 5.92 | 6.03 | 6.14 | 6.25 | 6.35 | 6.46 | 6.57 | 6.68 | 6.78 | 6.89 | 7.00 | 7.11 | 7.22 | 7.32 | 7.43 | 7.54 |
| 10 | 6.53 | 6.65 | 6.77 | 6.88 | 7.00 | 7.12 | 7.24 | 7.36 | 7.48 | 7.60 | 7.72 | 7.84 | 7.96 | 8.08 | 8.19 | 8.31 |
| 11 | 7.14 | 7.27 | 7.40 | 7.53 | 7.66 | 7.79 | 7.92 | 8.05 | 8.18 | 8.31 | 8.44 | 8.57 | 8.70 | 8.83 | 8.96 | 9.09 |
| 12 | 7.74 | 7.89 | 8.03 | 8.17 | 8.31 | 8.45 | 8.59 | 8.74 | 8.88 | 9.02 | 9.16 | 9.30 | 9.45 | 9.59 | 9.73 | 9.87 |
| 13 | 8.36 | 8.51 | 8.66 | 8.81 | 8.97 | 9.12 | 9.27 | 9.43 | 9.58 | 9.73 | 9.89 | 10.04 | 10.20 | 10.35 | 10.50 | 10.66 |
| 14 | 8.97 | 9.13 | 9.30 | 9.46 | 9.63 | 9.79 | 9.96 | 10.12 | 10.29 | 10.45 | 10.62 | 10.78 | 10.95 | 11.11 | 11.28 | 11.45 |
| 15 | 9.59 | 9.76 | 9.94 | 10.11 | 10.29 | 10.47 | 10.64 | 10.82 | 11.00 | 11.17 | 11.35 | 11.53 | 11.71 | 11.88 | 12.06 | 12.24 |
| 16 | 10.20 | 10.39 | 10.58 | 10.77 | 10.95 | 11.14 | 11.33 | 11.52 | 11.71 | 11.90 | 12.09 | 12.28 | 12.46 | 12.65 | 12.84 | 13.03 |
| 17 | 10.82 | 11.02 | 11.22 | 11.42 | 11.62 | 11.82 | 12.02 | 12.22 | 12.42 | 12.62 | 12.83 | 13.03 | 13.23 | 13.43 | 13.63 | 13.83 |
| 18 | 11.45 | 11.66 | 11.87 | 12.08 | 12.29 | 12.50 | 12.72 | 12.93 | 13.14 | 13.35 | 13.57 | 13.78 | 13.99 | 14.21 | 14.42 | 14.64 |
| 19 | 12.07 | 12.30 | 12.52 | 12.74 | 12.97 | 13.19 | 13.41 | 13.64 | 13.86 | 14.09 | 14.31 | 14.54 | 14.76 | 14.99 | 15.22 | 15.44 |
| 20 | 12.70 | 12.93 | 13.17 | 13.41 | 13.64 | 13.88 | 14.11 | 14.35 | 14.59 | 14.82 | 15.06 | 15.30 | 15.54 | 15.77 | 16.01 | 16.25 |
| 21 | 13.33 | 13.58 | 13.82 | 14.07 | 14.32 | 14.57 | 14.82 | 15.06 | 15.31 | 15.56 | 15.81 | 16.06 | 16.31 | 16.56 | 16.81 | 17.07 |
| 22 | 13.96 | 14.22 | 14.48 | 14.74 | 15.00 | 15.26 | 15.52 | 15.78 | 16.04 | 16.30 | 16.57 | 16.83 | 17.09 | 17.36 | 17.62 | 17.88 |
| 23 | 14.59 | 14.87 | 15.14 | 15.41 | 15.68 | 15.96 | 16.23 | 16.50 | 16.78 | 17.05 | 17.32 | 17.60 | 17.88 | 18.15 | 18.43 | 18.70 |
| 24 | 15.23 | 15.51 | 15.80 | 16.08 | 16.37 | 16.65 | 16.94 | 17.22 | 17.51 | 17.80 | 18.09 | 18.37 | 18.66 | 18.95 | 19.24 | 19.53 |
| 25 | 15.87 | 16.17 | 16.46 | 16.76 | 17.06 | 17.35 | 17.65 | 17.95 | 18.25 | 18.55 | 18.85 | 19.15 | 19.45 | 19.75 | 20.05 | 20.36 |
| 26 | 16.51 | 16.82 | 17.13 | 17.44 | 17.75 | 18.06 | 18.37 | 18.68 | 18.99 | 19.30 | 19.62 | 19.93 | 20.24 | 20.56 | 20.87 | 21.19 |
| 27 | 17.15 | 17.47 | 17.80 | 18.12 | 18.44 | 18.76 | 19.09 | 19.41 | 19.74 | 20.06 | 20.39 | 20.71 | 21.04 | 21.37 | 21.69 | 22.02 |
| 28 | 17.80 | 18.13 | 18.47 | 18.80 | 19.14 | 19.47 | 19.81 | 20.15 | 20.48 | 20.82 | 21.16 | 21.50 | 21.84 | 22.18 | 22.52 | 22.86 |
| 29 | 18.45 | 18.79 | 19.14 | 19.49 | 19.83 | 20.18 | 20.53 | 20.88 | 21.23 | 21.58 | 21.94 | 22.29 | 22.64 | 22.99 | 23.35 | 23.70 |
| 30 | 19.10 | 19.45 | 19.81 | 20.17 | 20.54 | 20.90 | 21.26 | 21.62 | 21.99 | 22.35 | 22.72 | 23.08 | 23.45 | 23.81 | 24.18 | 24.55 |

| | | | | | | | | | | | | | | | |
|---|---|---|---|---|---|---|---|---|---|---|---|---|---|---|---|---|
| 31 | 19.75 | 20.12 | 20.49 | 20.87 | 21.24 | 21.61 | 21.99 | 22.37 | 22.74 | 23.12 | 23.50 | 23.88 | 24.26 | 24.64 | 25.02 | 25.40 |
| 32 | 20.40 | 20.79 | 21.17 | 21.56 | 21.95 | 22.33 | 22.72 | 23.11 | 23.50 | 23.89 | 24.28 | 24.68 | 25.07 | 25.46 | 25.86 | 26.25 |
| 33 | 21.06 | 21.46 | 21.85 | 22.25 | 22.65 | 23.06 | 23.46 | 23.86 | 24.26 | 24.67 | 25.07 | 25.48 | 25.88 | 26.29 | 26.70 | 27.11 |
| 34 | 21.72 | 22.13 | 22.54 | 22.95 | 23.37 | 23.78 | 24.19 | 24.61 | 25.03 | 25.44 | 25.86 | 26.28 | 26.70 | 27.12 | 27.54 | 27.97 |
| 35 | 22.38 | 22.80 | 23.23 | 23.65 | 24.08 | 24.51 | 24.94 | 25.36 | 25.79 | 26.23 | 26.66 | 27.09 | 27.52 | 27.96 | 28.39 | 28.83 |
| 36 | 23.04 | 23.48 | 23.92 | 24.35 | 24.80 | 25.24 | 25.68 | 26.12 | 26.57 | 27.01 | 27.46 | 27.90 | 28.35 | 28.80 | 29.25 | 29.70 |
| 37 | 23.70 | 24.16 | 24.61 | 25.06 | 25.51 | 25.97 | 26.42 | 26.88 | 27.34 | 27.80 | 28.26 | 28.72 | 29.18 | 29.64 | 30.10 | 30.57 |
| 38 | 24.37 | 24.84 | 25.30 | 25.77 | 26.24 | 26.70 | 27.17 | 27.64 | 28.11 | 28.59 | 29.06 | 29.53 | 30.01 | 30.49 | 30.96 | 31.44 |
| 39 | 25.04 | 25.52 | 26.00 | 26.48 | 26.96 | 27.44 | 27.92 | 28.41 | 28.89 | 29.38 | 29.87 | 30.36 | 30.85 | 31.34 | 31.83 | 32.32 |
| 40 | 25.71 | 26.20 | 26.70 | 27.19 | 27.69 | 28.18 | 28.68 | 29.18 | 29.68 | 30.18 | 30.68 | 31.18 | 31.68 | 32.19 | 32.69 | 33.20 |
| 41 | 26.39 | 26.89 | 27.40 | 27.91 | 28.41 | 28.92 | 29.44 | 29.95 | 30.46 | 30.97 | 31.49 | 32.01 | 32.52 | 33.04 | 33.56 | 34.08 |
| 42 | 27.06 | 27.58 | 28.10 | 28.62 | 29.15 | 29.67 | 30.19 | 30.72 | 31.25 | 31.78 | 32.31 | 32.84 | 33.37 | 33.90 | 34.44 | 34.97 |
| 43 | 27.74 | 28.27 | 28.81 | 29.34 | 29.88 | 30.42 | 30.96 | 31.50 | 32.04 | 32.58 | 33.13 | 33.67 | 34.22 | 34.76 | 35.31 | 35.86 |
| 44 | 28.42 | 28.97 | 29.52 | 30.07 | 30.62 | 31.17 | 31.72 | 32.28 | 32.83 | 33.39 | 33.95 | 34.51 | 35.07 | 35.63 | 36.19 | 36.76 |
| 45 | 29.11 | 29.67 | 30.23 | 30.79 | 31.36 | 31.92 | 32.49 | 33.06 | 33.63 | 34.20 | 34.77 | 35.35 | 35.92 | 36.50 | 37.08 | 37.66 |
| 46 | 29.79 | 30.36 | 30.94 | 31.52 | 32.10 | 32.68 | 33.26 | 33.84 | 34.43 | 35.01 | 35.60 | 36.19 | 36.78 | 37.37 | 37.96 | 38.56 |
| 47 | 30.48 | 31.07 | 31.66 | 32.25 | 32.84 | 33.44 | 34.03 | 34.63 | 35.23 | 35.83 | 36.43 | 37.04 | 37.64 | 38.25 | 38.86 | 39.46 |
| 48 | 31.17 | 31.77 | 32.37 | 32.98 | 33.59 | 34.20 | 34.81 | 35.42 | 36.03 | 36.65 | 37.27 | 37.88 | 38.50 | 39.13 | 39.75 | 40.37 |
| 49 | 31.86 | 32.48 | 33.09 | 33.71 | 34.34 | 34.96 | 35.59 | 36.21 | 36.84 | 37.47 | 38.10 | 38.74 | 39.37 | 40.01 | 40.65 | 41.29 |
| 50 | 32.55 | 33.18 | 33.82 | 34.45 | 35.09 | 35.73 | 36.37 | 37.01 | 37.65 | 38.30 | 38.94 | 39.59 | 40.24 | 40.89 | 41.55 | 42.20 |
| 51 | 33.25 | 33.89 | 34.54 | 35.19 | 35.84 | 36.49 | 37.15 | 37.81 | 38.46 | 39.12 | 39.79 | 40.45 | 41.11 | 41.78 | 42.45 | 43.12 |
| 52 | 33.95 | 34.61 | 35.27 | 35.93 | 36.60 | 37.27 | 37.94 | 38.61 | 39.28 | 39.96 | 40.63 | 41.31 | 41.99 | 42.67 | 43.36 | 44.04 |
| 53 | 34.65 | 35.32 | 36.00 | 36.68 | 37.36 | 38.04 | 38.72 | 39.41 | 40.10 | 40.79 | 41.48 | 42.17 | 42.87 | 43.57 | 44.27 | 44.97 |
| 54 | 35.35 | 36.04 | 36.73 | 37.42 | 38.12 | 38.82 | 39.52 | 40.22 | 40.92 | 41.63 | 42.33 | 43.04 | 43.75 | 44.47 | 45.18 | 45.90 |
| 55 | 36.05 | 36.76 | 37.46 | 38.17 | 38.88 | 39.60 | 40.31 | 41.03 | 41.74 | 42.47 | 43.19 | 43.91 | 44.64 | 45.37 | 46.10 | 46.83 |
| 56 | 36.76 | 37.48 | 38.20 | 38.92 | 39.65 | 40.38 | 41.11 | 41.84 | 42.57 | 43.31 | 44.05 | 44.79 | 45.53 | 46.27 | 47.02 | 47.77 |
| 57 | 37.47 | 38.20 | 38.94 | 39.68 | 40.42 | 41.16 | 41.91 | 42.65 | 43.40 | 44.15 | 44.91 | 45.66 | 46.42 | 47.18 | 47.94 | 48.71 |
| 58 | 38.18 | 38.93 | 39.68 | 40.43 | 41.19 | 41.95 | 42.71 | 43.47 | 44.23 | 45.00 | 45.77 | 46.54 | 47.32 | 48.09 | 48.87 | 49.65 |
| 59 | 38.89 | 39.66 | 40.42 | 41.19 | 41.96 | 42.74 | 43.51 | 44.29 | 45.07 | 45.85 | 46.64 | 47.42 | 48.21 | 49.01 | 49.80 | 50.60 |
| 60 | 39.61 | 40.39 | 41.17 | 41.95 | 42.74 | 43.53 | 44.32 | 45.11 | 45.91 | 46.71 | 47.51 | 48.31 | 49.12 | 49.92 | 50.73 | 51.55 |

**(c)** The amount financed is

$$\$24,000 - \$3,500 - \$2,000 = \$18,500. \qquad \blacksquare$$

**OBJECTIVE 3** *Use a table to find the APR.*          APR rates accurate enough to satisfy federal law can be found in the *Annual Percentage Rate Tables*, available from the nearest Federal Reserve Bank or the Board of Governors of the Federal Reserve System, Washington, DC 20551. Your local library may also have these data. The complete set of tables consists of two volumes. Volume I provides four tables for varying interest rates and time periods and Volume II includes irregular transactions and is used with Volume I. A portion of such a table is shown in Table 15.2 on pages 524– 527.

---

### FINDING ANNUAL PERCENTAGE RATE USING TABLE

**Step 1.** Divide the finance charge by the amount financed, and multiply by $100, that is,

$$\frac{\text{Finance charge}}{\text{Amount financed}} \times \$100$$

The result is the finance charge per $100 of the amount financed.

**Step 2.** Read down the left column of Table 15.2 to the proper number of payments. Go across to the number closest to the number found in Step 1. Read up the column to find the annual percentage rate.

---

The annual percentage rate found with this method is accurate to the nearest quarter of a percent, as required by federal law.

**EXAMPLE 2** *Finding Annual Percentage Rate*

In Example 1, a car costing $24,000 was financed at $505.54 per month for 48 months after a down payment of $5,500 including the value of the trade-in. The total finance charge was $5,765.92, and the amount financed was $18,500. Find the annual percentage rate.

**SOLUTION**     Divide the finance charge ($5,765.92) by the total amount financed ($18,500) and multiply by $100.

$$\frac{\$5,765.92}{\$18,500} \times \$100 = \$31.17$$

This gives the finance charge per $100 of amount financed.

Read down the left column of Table 15.2 to the line for 48 months (the *actual* number of monthly payments). Follow across to the right to find the number *closest to* $31.17, which is on the second page of the table. Here, find exactly $31.17. Read up this column of figures to find the annual percentage rate, 14%.

In this example, 14% is the annual percentage rate that must be disclosed to the buyer of the car, Ed Chamski. ■

**NOTE** The precise APR can be found using a financial calculator as shown in Example 5 in Appendix A.2.

## 15.2 EXERCISES

*Find the finance charge and the total installment cost for the following. (See Example 1.)*

| | Amount Financed | Down Payment | Cash Price | Number of Payments | Amount of Payment | Total Installment Cost | Finance Charge |
|---|---|---|---|---|---|---|---|
| 1. | $480 | $100 | $580 | 18 | $30 | _____ | _____ |
| 2. | $650 | $125 | $775 | 24 | $32 | _____ | _____ |
| 3. | $150 | none | $150 | 12 | $15 | _____ | _____ |
| 4. | $1,200 | none | $1,200 | 20 | $70 | _____ | _____ |
| 5. | $65 | $25 | $90 | 10 | $7.50 | _____ | _____ |
| 6. | $45.80 | none | $45.80 | 12 | $4.25 | _____ | _____ |

*Find the annual percentage rate using the Annual Percentage Rate Table. (See Example 2.)*

| | Amount Financed | Finance Charge | No. of Monthly Payments | APR |
|---|---|---|---|---|
| 7. | $287 | $29.23 | 18 | _____ |
| 8. | $345 | $24.62 | 12 | _____ |
| 9. | $442 | $28.68 | 14 | _____ |
| 10. | $4,690 | $1,237.22 | 48 | _____ |
| 11. | $145 | $13.25 | 18 | _____ |
| 12. | $650 | $73.45 | 24 | _____ |

13. Explain the difference between open-end credit and installment loans. (See Section 15.1 and Objective 1 of this section.)

14. Explain the difference between down payment, cash price, and total installment cost. (See Objective 2.)

*Solve the following application problems.*

15. Teri Murthy bought a set of speakers manufactured in Ontario, Canada for $375. She paid nothing down but agreed to payments of $33.16 per month for 12 months. Find the annual percentage rate for the loan.

16. On a 24-month loan of $1,500 payable in equal monthly installments, the Mouse House advertises only $169.50 interest. What is the annual percentage rate?

17. House Television and Appliance wants to advertise a table model color television for $400, with 25% down and monthly payments of only $39.75 per month for 8 months. They must also include the annual percentage rate in the ad. Find the annual percentage rate.

18. A department store has a sofa on sale for $900. A buyer paying 20% down may finance the balance by paying $34.75 per month for 2 years. Find the annual percentage rate that the store must include in its advertising.

19. A contractor in Mexico City purchases a computer system for 650,000 pesos. After making a down payment of 100,000 pesos he agrees to payments of 26,342.18 pesos per month for 24 months. Find (a) the total installment cost and (b) the annual percentage rate.

20. An electrical contractor in Hiroshima, Japan purchases a truck costing 2,700,000 yen. He makes a down payment of 1,000,000 yen and agrees to monthly payments of 54,855 yen for 36 months. Find (a) the total installment cost and (b) the annual percentage rate.

21. Dillon Sporting Goods borrows $180,000 to expand their store to include winter sporting supplies including skis and snowmobiles. They make no down payment but agree to monthly payments of $6,974.66 for 30 months. Find (a) the total installment cost and (b) the annual percentage rate.

22. Bob Zombo starts a small stereo store with $60,000 borrowed from his uncle. Zombo agrees to repay his uncle with 24 monthly payments of $2,880. Find (a) the total installment cost and (b) the annual percentage rate.

23. When would people be more likely to use installment loans rather than open-end credit? (Hint: Search your local newspaper for examples.)

24. Do installment loans or open-end credit loans tend to have higher interest rates? Document this with several examples of each type of loan.

## 15.3   Early Payoffs of Loans

### OBJECTIVES

**1**   Use the United States Rule when prepaying a loan.

**2**   Find the amount due on the maturity date using the United States Rule.

**3**   Use the Rule of 78 when prepaying a loan.

**OBJECTIVE 1   Use the United States Rule when prepaying a loan.**   It is fairly common for a loan, or part of a loan, to be paid off before it is due. There are several reasons for this: for instance, a person might come into some extra money or might be able to borrow money at a cheaper rate and pay off a more expensive loan. This section discusses how to handle these prepayments of a loan.

The first method is called the **United States Rule**. It is the method used by the U.S. government as well as most states and financial institutions. With the United States Rule, any payment is first applied to any interest owed, with the balance used to reduce the principal amount of the loan. The United States Rule is applied as follows.

> ## THE UNITED STATES RULE
>
> **Step 1.** Find the interest due from the date the loan was made until the date the partial payment is made. Use the formula $I = PRT$.
>
> **Step 2.** Subtract this interest from the amount of the payment.
>
> **Step 3.** Any difference is used to reduce the principal.
>
> **Step 4.** Additional partial payments are treated in the same way, always applying interest only to the balance after the last partial payment.
>
> **Step 5.** On the date the loan is due, any remaining principal, together with interest on this unpaid principal, is due.

**OBJECTIVE 2** *Find the amount due on the maturity date using the United States Rule.* If the partial payment is not large enough to pay the interest due, the payment is simply held until enough money is available to pay the interest due. This means that a partial payment smaller than the interest due offers no advantage to the borrower— the lender just holds the partial payment until enough money is available to pay the interest owed.

### EXAMPLE 1 *Finding the Amount Due*

Bill Thomas borrows $4,000 for 120 days on May 9 for a new multimedia personal computer. The loan has an interest rate of 10%. On June 17, a payment of $1,500 is made. Find the balance owed on the principal after the partial payment is made. If no additional payments are made, find the amount that will be due on the maturity date of the loan.

**SOLUTION** First find the interest due from May 9 until June 17. There are 22 + 17 = 39 days from May 9 until June 17. The interest is found from the formula $I = PRT$ (use ordinary time or 360 days).

$$I = \$4,000 \times 0.10 \times \frac{39}{360} = \$43.33 \qquad \text{interest due}$$

The payment made on June 17 was $1,500. Of this amount, $43.33 is applied to interest. The difference,

$$
\begin{array}{rl}
\$1,500.00 & \text{payment} \\
- \quad 43.33 & \text{interest due} \\
\hline
\$1,456.67 & \text{applied to reduction of principal}
\end{array}
$$

is applied to the reduction of the amount owed. The amount owed was $4,000; after June 17, it is

$$
\begin{array}{rl}
\$4,000.00 & \text{amount owed} \\
- \ 1,456.67 & \text{principal reduction} \\
\hline
\$2,543.33. & \text{balanced owed}
\end{array}
$$

The balance owed on the note is $2,543.33.

The note was originally for 120 days, with the partial payment paid after 39 days. This means that interest on the $2,543.33 will be charged only for $120 - 39 = 81$ days. The interest, still at 10%, is

$$I = \$2{,}543.33 \times 0.10 \times \frac{81}{360} = \$57.22.$$

If no additional partial payments are made,

| | |
|---|---|
| $2,543.33 | principal owed |
| + 57.22 | interest |
| $2,600.55 | total owed |

will be due on the maturity date of the note.  ■

In order to find the total interest paid when partial payments are made, the individual interest payments are added.

## EXAMPLE 2  *Finding Total Interest Paid*

A lawn furniture manufacturer signs a 140-day note on February 5. The note, for $45,600, is to a supplier of aluminum tubing for the furniture, and carries an interest rate of 12%. On March 19, the manufacturer receives an unexpected payment from one of its customers, and applies $16,000 toward the note. A further early payment permits a second $13,250 partial payment on April 23. Find the interest paid on the note and the amount paid on the due date of the note.

**SOLUTION**    The first partial payment was made on March 19, which is $23 + 19 = 42$ days after the loan is made. In 42 days, the interest on the note is

$$I = PRT$$

$$I = \$45{,}600 \times 0.12 \times \frac{42}{360} = \$638.40.$$

A partial payment of $16,000 was made on March 19. Of this amount, $638.40 is applied to interest.

| | |
|---|---|
| $16,000.00 | amount of payment |
| − 638.40 | interest owed |
| $15,361.60 | applied to principal |

After March 19, the balance on the loan is as follows.

| | |
|---|---|
| $45,600.00 | original amount of loan |
| − 15,361.60 | applied to principal |
| $30,238.40 | new amount owed |

After March 19, the balance on the note is $30,238.40. A second partial payment is made on April 23, which is $12 + 23 = 35$ days later. Interest on $30,238.40 for 35 days is

$$I = \$30{,}238.40 \times 0.12 \times \frac{35}{360} = \$352.78.$$

A payment of $13,250 is made on April 23. Of this, $352.78 applies to interest, leaving

$$\$13,250 - \$352.78 = \$12,897.22$$

to reduce the principal. After April 23, the principal is as follows.

| | |
|---|---|
| $30,238.40 | previous balance |
| − 12,897.22 | applied to principal |
| $17,341.18 | new principal |

The first partial payment was made 42 days after the note was signed, with the second payment made 35 days after that. The second payment was made $42 + 35 = 77$ days after the note was signed. Since the note was for 140 days, the note is due

$$140 - 77 = 63$$

days after the second partial payment. Interest on the new balance of $17,341.18 for 63 days is

$$I = \$17,341.18 \times 0.12 \times \frac{63}{360} = \$364.16.$$

On the date the loan matures, a total of

$$\$17,341.18 + \$364.16 = \$17,705.34$$

must be paid. The total interest paid over the life of the loan is

$$\$638.40 + \$352.78 + \$364.16 = \$1,355.34.$$

All this work can be summarized in the following table.

| Date Payment Made | Amount of Payment | Applied to Interest | Applied to Principal | Remaining Balance |
|---|---|---|---|---|
| March 19 | $16,000 | $638.40 | $15,361.60 | $30,238.40 |
| April 23 | 13,250 | 352.78 | 12,897.22 | 17,341.18 |
| Date of maturity (June 25) | 17,705.34 | 364.16 | 17,341.18 | 0 |
| Totals | | $1,355.34 | $45,600 | |

■

**OBJECTIVE** ■ 3 ■ *Use the Rule of 78 when prepaying a loan.*    A variation of the United States Rule, called the **Rule of 78**, is still used by many lenders. The Rule of 78 is sometimes called the **sum of the balances method** when the length of the contract is other than one year. This rule allows a lender to earn more of the finance charge during the early months of the loan compared to the United States Rule. Lenders typically use this rule to protect against early payoffs on **small loans**. Effectively, the lender will earn a higher rate of interest in the event of an early payoff under the Rule of 78 than under the United States Rule. Obviously, the Rule of 78 favors the lender in the event of an early payoff and not the borrower.

The Rule of 78 gets its name from a loan of 12 months—the sum of the months $1 + 2 + 3 + \cdots + 12 = 78$. The finance charge for the first month is $\frac{12}{78}$ of the total charge, with $\frac{11}{78}$ in the second month, $\frac{10}{78}$ in the third month, and $\frac{1}{78}$ in the final month. The Rule of 78 can be applied to loans with terms other than 12 months. For example, the sum of the months in a 6-month contract is $1 + 2 + 3 + 4 + 5 + 6 = 21$. The finance charge for the first month would be $\frac{6}{21}$, $\frac{5}{21}$ for the second month, and so on.

The **unearned interest** or interest not earned by the lender under the Rule of 78 for a loan of 12 months depends on the month in which the loan is paid off. If the loan is paid off at the end of 2 months, then the interest earned by the lender is $\frac{12}{78} + \frac{11}{78} = \frac{23}{78}$ of the finance charge. Thus, the interest not earned by the lender is

$$\left(1 - \frac{23}{78}\right) \quad \text{or equivalently} \quad \left(\frac{1}{78} + \frac{2}{78} + \cdots + \frac{10}{78}\right)$$

which is $\frac{55}{78}$ of the finance charges. The process is similar for loans of lengths *other than* 12 months.

> The unearned interest is given by
>
> $$U = F\left(\frac{N}{P}\right)\left(\frac{1 + N}{1 + P}\right)$$
>
> where $U$ = unearned interest, $F$ = finance charge, $N$ = number of payments remaining, and $P$ = total number of payments.

## EXAMPLE 3  *Finding Payoff Value*

Richard Buck borrowed $600, which he is paying back in 24 monthly payments of $29.50 each. With 9 payments remaining, he decides to repay the loan in full. Find (a) the amount of unearned finance charge and (b) the amount necessary to repay the loan in full.

### SOLUTION

(a)  Buck is scheduled to make 24 payments of $29.50 each, for a total repayment of

$$24 \times \$29.50 = \$708.$$

His finance charge is

$$\$708 - \$600 = \$108.$$

Find the amount of unearned interest as follows. The finance charge is $108, the scheduled number of payments is 24, and the loan is paid off with 9 payments left. Use the formula.

$$\text{Unearned interest} = \$108 \times \left(\frac{9}{24}\right) \times \frac{(1 + 9)}{(1 + 24)}$$

$$= \$108 \times \left(\frac{9 \times 10}{24 \times 25}\right)$$

$$= \$16.20$$

Paying off the loan 9 months early produces a savings of $16.20 in interest.

**(b)** When Buck decides to pay off the loan, he has 9 payments of $29.50 left. These payments total

$$9 \times \$29.50 = \$265.50.$$

By paying the loan early, Buck saves the unearned interest of $16.20, so

$$\$265.50 - \$16.20 = \$249.30$$

is needed to pay the loan in full. ∎

---

The calculator solution to Example 3 is to

**(a)** first think of the problem as $\dfrac{(108 \times 9 \times (1 + 9))}{(24 \times (1 + 24))}$, then solve.

**CALCULATOR APPROACH TO EXAMPLE 3**

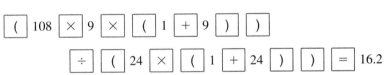

| ( | 108 | × | 9 | × | ( | 1 | + | 9 | ) | ) |

| ÷ | ( | 24 | × | ( | 1 | + | 24 | ) | ) | = | 16.2 |

**(b)** 9 | × | 29.5 | − | 16.2 | = | 249.3

---

## 15.3 EXERCISES

*Find the balance due on the maturity date of the following notes. Find the total amount of interest paid on the note. Use the United States Rule.*

| | Principal | Interest | Time in Days | Partial Payents |
|---|---|---|---|---|
| 1. | $4,500 | 9% | 90 | $1,000 on day 40 |
| 2. | $5,800 | 10% | 120 | $2,500 on day 60 |
| 3. | $8,500 | 12% | 150 | $5,000 on day 45 |
| 4. | $6,000 | $10\frac{1}{2}\%$ | 130 | $3,000 on day 100 |
| 5. | $10,000 | $8\frac{1}{4}\%$ | 180 | $6,000 on day 120 |
| 6. | $15,000 | $14\frac{1}{2}\%$ | 120 | $12,500 on day 70 |

*Each of the following loans is paid in full before their date of maturity. Find the amount of unearned interest. Use the Rule of 78.*

| | Finance Charge | Total Number of Payments | Remaining Number of Payments When Paid in Full |
|---|---|---|---|
| 7. | $975 | 48 | 30 |
| 8. | $325 | 36 | 6 |
| 9. | $174 | 18 | 5 |
| 10. | $325 | 24 | 22 |
| 11. | $3,653.82 | 48 | 9 |
| 12. | $3,085.54 | 60 | 15 |

13. Explain the concept of the United States Rule. When is the United States Rule likely to be applied? (See Objective 1.)

14. Explain the concept of the Rule of 78. When is the Rule of 78 likely to be applied? (See Objective 3.)

15. Why is it of no advantage to the borrower to make a partial payment smaller than the amount of interest due? What would the lender do with this payment? (See Objective 2.)

16. Do either the United States Rule or the Rule of 78 apply if no part of a loan is paid off before maturity? Explain. (See Objectives 1 and 3.)

*Solve the following application problems.*

17. The Main Street Frostee finances a remodeling program by giving the builder a note for $37,500. The note was made on September 14 and is due in 120 days. Interest on the note is 14.5%. On December 9, the firm makes a partial payment of $12,000. Find the amount due on the maturity date of the note and the amount of interest paid on the note using the United States Rule.

18. Bill's Banana Company borrowed $63,000 on May 7, signing a note due in 90 days and carrying 9.5% interest. On June 24, the company made a partial payment of $17,275. Find the amount due on the maturity date of the note and the amount of interest paid on the note using the United States Rule.

19. Sheila Goshorn decides to use her income tax refund to pay her travel agency loan in full. She finds that her 36-month loan includes $240 in interest and that she will be paying the loan in full with 21 months remaining. Calculate the amount of unearned interest using the Rule of 78.

20. George Duda has decided that making the small monthly payment on a 6-month loan is a nuisance. The total finance charge is only $34, and the loan is paid in full with 3 months remaining. Find the unearned interest using the Rule of 78.

21. Anne Kelly purchased a refrigerator on the "easy payment plan" with only $100 down and 18 equal monthly payments of $45.20. The total cash price of the refrigerator was $800. After making 6 monthly payments, she decided to pay the loan in full. Use the Rule of 78 and find (a) the amount of unearned interest and (b) the amount necessary to pay the loan in full.

**22.** A used car costs $8,850. After a down payment of $2,000, the balance is financed with 48 payments of $194.25 each. Suppose the loan is paid off with 15 payments left. Use the Rule of 78 and find (a) the amount of unearned interest and (b) the amount necessary to pay the loan in full.

**23.** To save on freight charges, Wholesale Paper orders large quantities of basic paper goods every 4 months. For their last order, the firm signed a note on February 18 that will mature on May 15. The face value of the note was $104,500, with interest of 11%. The firm made a partial payment of $38,000 on March 20, with a second partial payment of $27,200 on April 16. Find the amount due on the maturity date of the note and the amount of interest paid on the note using the United States Rule.

**24.** Mid-City Electronics bought new testing equipment, paying for it with a note for $32,000. The note was made on July 26 and is due on November 20. The interest rate is 13%. The firm made a partial payment of $6,000 on August 31, with a second partial payment of $11,700 on October 4. Find the amount due on the maturity date of the note and the amount of interest paid on the note using the United States Rule.

## 15.4  Personal Property Loans

**OBJECTIVES**

1. *Define personal property and real estate.*
2. *Use the formula for amortization to find payment.*
3. *Set up an amortization table.*
4. *Find monthly payments.*

**OBJECTIVE 1** *Define personal property and real estate.*   Items that can be moved from one location to another such as an automobile, a boat, or a stereo are called **personal property**. In contrast, buildings, land, and homes cannot be moved and are called **real estate** or **real property**. Personal property loans are discussed in this section and real estate loans are discussed in the next section.

As the headline suggests, people can end up with more debt than they can afford. In that event, individuals are sometimes forced to return personal property such as an automobile to the lender. When this happens, the property is said to be **repossessed** by the lender.

# Consumers Cautioned To Pay Up Debts Before Trouble

*Source:* Headline "Consumers Cautioned to Pay Up Debts Before Trouble" from *The Tyler-Courier-Times Telegraph*, January 8, 1995. Reprinted by permission.

**OBJECTIVE 2** *Use the formula for amortization to find payment.*   A loan is **amortized** if both the principal and interest are paid off by *a sequence of equal payments* made at regular intervals in time. One example of a loan that is amortized is a car loan with 48 equal monthly payments.

There is no loan and no need to make any payments for an item purchased with cash. However, many larger, more expensive items are purchased on credit and require a series of regular payments. The amount of each payment can be calculated using the formula, given in Section 14.2, for the present value $A$ of an annuity with payment $R$, interest rate per period $i$, and $n$ periods (the formula is repeated here).

$$A = R\left[\frac{(1 + i)^n - 1}{i(1 + i)^n}\right]$$

The unknown in Section 14.2 was the present value $A$. Now the present value (loan amount) is known along with the interest rate per compounding period and number of periods—the payment $R$ is the unknown. The equation above can be solved for $R$ and a scientific calculator can be used to calculate payments. Alternately, you can use the tables in Appendix C and solve the equation $A = R \cdot a_{\overline{n}|i}$ for $R$.

The periodic payment $R$, needed to amortize a loan of $A$ dollars, with interest of $i$ per period for $n$ periods, is

$$R = A\left(\frac{1}{a_{\overline{n}|i}}\right).$$

The notation $a_{\overline{n}|i}$ is read "$a$-angle–$n$-at-$i$." Values of $\dfrac{1}{a_{\overline{n}|i}}$ for different $n$'s and $i$'s can be found in column F of Appendix C. Thus, the periodic payment $R$ is found by multiplying the loan amount $A$ times a number taken from the table in Appendix C.

### EXAMPLE 1  *Finding Amortization Information*

Debbie Ross went to her company's credit union to apply for a $15,000 loan to remodel her home. A loan officer checked her credit and authorized a 36-month loan at 12% compounded monthly. Find (a) the monthly payment, (b) the portion of the first payment that is interest, (c) the balance due after 1 payment, and (d) the interest owed for the second month.

### SOLUTION

**(a)** Use $\dfrac{12\%}{12} = 1\%$ per period for $i$ and 36 periods for $n$ in the Amortization Table in Appendix C to find 0.03321431.

Payment $= \$15,000 \times 0.3321431 = \$498.21$ at the end of each month

**(b)** Interest for the month is found using the simple interest formula. One month is $\frac{1}{12}$ of a year which is used for $T$.

$$I = PRT$$

$$\text{Interest} = \$15,000 \times 0.12 \times \frac{1}{12} = \$150$$

The amount of the first payment that is applied to reduce the loan is

$$\$498.21 - \$150 = \$348.21.$$

**(c)** The debt after the first payment is

$$\$15,000 - \$348.21 = \$14,651.79.$$

**(d)** Interest owed for the second month is found using the loan balance after the first payment.

$$\text{Interest} = \$14,651.79 \times 0.12 \times \frac{1}{12} = \$146.52$$

A payment of $498.21 is made at the end of period 2 and a total of

$$\$498.21 - \$146.52 = \$351.69 \text{ is applied to the debt.} \qquad \blacksquare$$

**OBJECTIVE 3** *Set up an amortization table.* An **amortization table** or **schedule** shows the amount of each payment that goes to interest and to principal. It also shows the debt remaining after each payment. One excellent way to calculate an amortization table is to use a spreadsheet package on a personal computer. Sometimes, amortization tables are referred to as **loan repayment tables**.

**PROBLEM-SOLVING HINT** Be sure to round interest to the nearest cent each time before proceeding. ■

| **EXAMPLE 2** *Finding Payments, Interest, and Loan Balances*

A contractor agrees to pay $15,000 for a new computer system. This amount will be repaid in 3 years with semiannual payments at an interest rate of 8% compounded semiannually. Set up an amortization schedule for this loan.

**SOLUTION** An interest rate of $\dfrac{8\%}{2} = 4\%$ for $i$ is applied to the $3 \times 2 = 6$ semiannual payments. A payment of $2,861.43 is found using column F in Appendix C. Interest is calculated using $I = PRT$ with $P = $ the balance at the end of the previous period, $R = $ annual interest of 8%, and $T = \frac{1}{2}$ of a year.

| Payment Number | Amount of Payment | Interest for Period | Portion of Principal | Balance at End of Period |
|---|---|---|---|---|
| 0 | — | — | — | $15,000.00 |
| 1 | $2,861.43 | $600.00 | $2,261.43 | 12,738.57 |
| 2 | 2,861.43 | 509.54 | 2,351.89 | 10,386.68 |
| 3 | 2,861.43 | 415.47 | 2,445.96 | 7,940.72 |
| 4 | 2,861.43 | 317.63 | 2,543.80 | 5,396.92 |
| 5 | 2,861.43 | 215.88 | 2,645.55 | 2,751.37 |
| 6 | 2,861.42 | 110.05 | 2,751.37 | 0 |

■

NOTE As in the last example, the final payment will frequently vary slightly from the regular payments due to rounding errors. ■

OBJECTIVE **4** *Find monthly payments.* The Loan Payoff Table (Table 15.3) can also be used to find the monthly payment as an alternative to the Amortization Table. Determine the table value corresponding to the annual percentage rate (APR) and the number of monthly payments. Then find the monthly payment by multiplying the number from the table by the amount to be financed.

TABLE 15.3 **Loan Payoff Table**

| APR \ Months | 18 | 24 | 30 | 36 | 42 | 48 | 54 | 60 |
|---|---|---|---|---|---|---|---|---|
| 8% | 0.059138 | 0.045229 | 0.036887 | 0.031336 | 0.027376 | 0.024413 | 0.022113 | 0.020277 |
| 9% | 0.0596 | 0.045683 | 0.037347 | 0.0318 | 0.027845 | 0.024885 | 0.022589 | 0.020758 |
| 10% | 0.060056 | 0.046146 | 0.03781 | 0.032267 | 0.028317 | 0.025363 | 0.023072 | 0.021247 |
| 11% | 0.060516 | 0.046608 | 0.038277 | 0.032739 | 0.028793 | 0.025846 | 0.023561 | 0.021742 |
| 12% | 0.060984 | 0.047075 | 0.038747 | 0.033214 | 0.029276 | 0.026333 | 0.024057 | 0.022245 |
| 13% | 0.06145 | 0.047542 | 0.03922 | 0.033694 | 0.029762 | 0.026827 | 0.024557 | 0.022753 |
| 14% | 0.061917 | 0.048013 | 0.0397 | 0.034178 | 0.030252 | 0.027327 | 0.025065 | 0.023268 |
| 15% | 0.062383 | 0.048488 | 0.04018 | 0.034667 | 0.03075 | 0.027831 | 0.025578 | 0.02379 |
| 16% | 0.062855 | 0.048963 | 0.040663 | 0.035159 | 0.03125 | 0.02834 | 0.026096 | 0.024318 |
| 17% | 0.063328 | 0.049442 | 0.04115 | 0.035653 | 0.031755 | 0.028854 | 0.026620 | 0.024853 |
| 18% | 0.063806 | 0.049925 | 0.04164 | 0.036153 | 0.032264 | 0.029369 | 0.027152 | 0.025393 |
| 19% | 0.064283 | 0.050408 | 0.042133 | 0.036656 | 0.032779 | 0.0299 | 0.027687 | 0.02594 |
| 20% | 0.064761 | 0.050896 | 0.04263 | 0.037164 | 0.033298 | 0.030431 | 0.02823 | 0.026493 |
| 21% | 0.065244 | 0.051388 | 0.04313 | 0.037675 | 0.033821 | 0.030967 | 0.028776 | 0.027053 |

| EXAMPLE 3  *Finding Monthly Payments*

After a down payment, Linda Dean owes $8,700 on a Ford Taurus. She wishes to pay the loan off in 60 monthly payments. Find the amount of each payment and the finance charge, if the APR on her loan is 18%. Her interest rate is high because she has a poor credit history.

SOLUTION   Multiply the amount to be financed, $8,700, and the number from Table 15.3 for 60 months and 18%, 0.025393

$$\text{Payment} = (\$8{,}700)(0.025393) = \$220.92$$

The total amount repaid in 60 months is

$$60(\$220.92) = \$13{,}255.20.$$

The finance charge is

$$\$13{,}255.20 - \$8{,}700 = \$4{,}555.20. \qquad \blacksquare$$

## 15.4  EXERCISES

*Find each of the following.*

1. $\dfrac{1}{a_{\overline{20}|0.06}}$

2. $\dfrac{1}{a_{\overline{40}|0.075}}$

3. $\dfrac{1}{a_{\overline{36}|0.10}}$

4. $\dfrac{1}{a_{\overline{48}|0.12}}$

*Find the payment necessary to amortize each of the following loans. Use column F of the interest table in Appendix C and the formula of this section.*

| | Amount of Loan | Interest Rate | Payments Made | Number of Years | Payment |
|---|---|---|---|---|---|
| 5. | $1,200 | 10% | annually | 8 | _____ |
| 6. | $2,650 | 12% | annually | 10 | _____ |
| 7. | $4,500 | 8% | semiannually | $7\frac{1}{2}$ | _____ |
| 8. | $1,900 | 16% | semiannually | $4\frac{1}{2}$ | _____ |
| 9. | $96,000 | 8% | quarterly | $7\frac{3}{4}$ | _____ |
| 10. | $210,000 | 12% | quarterly | 8 | _____ |
| 11. | $4,876 | 12% | monthly | 3 | _____ |
| 12. | $7,325 | 18% | monthly | 4 | _____ |

*Use the Loan Payoff Table (Table 15.3) to find the monthly payment and finance charge for each loan.*

| | Amount Financed | Number of Months | APR | Monthly Payment | Finance Charge |
|---|---|---|---|---|---|
| 13. | $3,200 | 30 | 10% | _____ | _____ |
| 14. | $4,800 | 24 | 12% | _____ | _____ |
| 15. | $12,000 | 48 | 13% | _____ | _____ |
| 16. | $8,102 | 48 | 8% | _____ | _____ |

*Solve each of the following application problems.*

17. Chuck and Judy Nielson opened a restaurant at a cost of $340,000. They paid $40,000 of their own money and agreed to pay the remainder in quarterly payments over 7 years at 12% compounded quarterly. Find the quarterly payment and the total amount of interest paid over 7 years.

18. Oil Field Construction bought a piece of equipment for $57,000. They agreed to pay 10% down and pay off the rest with monthly payments for 36 months, at 18%. Their interest rate is high because the firm has a poor credit history. Find the amount of each monthly payment necessary to amortize the loan. Find the total amount of interest paid over 3 years.

19. An insurance firm pays $4,000 for a new printer for its computer. It amortizes the loan for the printer in 4 annual payments at 8%. Prepare an amortization schedule for this printer.

| Payment Number | Amount of Payment | Interest for Period | Portion to Principal | Principal at End of Period |
|---|---|---|---|---|
| 0 | — | — | — | $4,000.00 |
| 1 | _____ | _____ | _____ | _____ |
| 2 | _____ | _____ | _____ | _____ |
| 3 | _____ | _____ | _____ | _____ |
| 4 | _____ | _____ | _____ | _____ |

20. Long Haul Trucking purchases a used tractor for pulling large trailers on interstate highways at a cost of $72,000. They agree to pay for it with a loan that will be amortized over 9 annual payments at 8% interest. Prepare an amortization schedule for the truck.

| Payment Number | Amount of Payment | Interest for Period | Portion to Principal | Principal at End of Period |
|---|---|---|---|---|
| 0 | — | — | — | $72,000.00 |
| 1 | ___ | ___ | ___ | ___ |
| 2 | ___ | ___ | ___ | ___ |
| 3 | ___ | ___ | ___ | ___ |
| 4 | ___ | ___ | ___ | ___ |
| 5 | ___ | ___ | ___ | ___ |
| 6 | ___ | ___ | ___ | ___ |
| 7 | ___ | ___ | ___ | ___ |
| 8 | ___ | ___ | ___ | ___ |
| 9 | ___ | ___ | ___ | ___ |

*Solve the following application problems. Use the Loan Payoff Table.*

**21.** An accounting firm purchases 7 new computers for $3,500 each. They make a down payment of $10,000 and amortize the balance with monthly payments at 11% for 4 years. Prepare an amortization schedule showing the first 5 payments.

| Payment Number | Amount of Payment | Interest for Period | Portion to Principal | Principal at End of Period |
|---|---|---|---|---|
| 0 | — | — | — | $14,500.00 |
| 1 | ___ | ___ | ___ | ___ |
| 2 | ___ | ___ | ___ | ___ |
| 3 | ___ | ___ | ___ | ___ |
| 4 | ___ | ___ | ___ | ___ |
| 5 | ___ | ___ | ___ | ___ |

**22.** Denise Sullivan purchased $14,000 worth of law books and $7,200 worth of office furniture when she opened her law office. She paid $1,200 down and agreed to amortize the balance with monthly payments for 5 years at 12%. Prepare an amortization schedule for the first 5 payments.

| Payment Number | Amount of Payment | Interest for Period | Portion to Principal | Principal at End of Period |
|---|---|---|---|---|
| 0 | — | — | — | $20,000.00 |
| 1 | | | | |
| 2 | | | | |
| 3 | | | | |
| 4 | | | | |
| 5 | | | | |

**23.** Identify and explain three important items that you will see in an installment loan. (See Objectives 2 and 3.)

**24.** Explain how to construct a repayment schedule. (See Objective 3.)

*Prepare an amortization schedule for the following loans. Use a spreadsheet package on a computer if you have one available. Do not forget to round interest to the nearest cent each month before finding the portion of each payment that goes to principal.*

**25.** Tim Gates financed $8,000 on a used car at 12% for 15 months.

| Payment Number | Amount of Payment | Interest for Period | Portion to Principal | Principal at End of Period |
|---|---|---|---|---|
| 0 | — | — | — | $8,000.00 |
| 1 | | | | |
| 2 | | | | |
| 3 | | | | |
| ⋮ | ⋮ | ⋮ | ⋮ | ⋮ |
| 14 | | | | |
| 15 | | | | |

**26.** Caribbean Tours, Inc. financed $108,000 to set up a network link between their offices in Canada, the United States, and Mexico. They agree to repay the 10% loan with 16 quarterly payments.

| Payment Number | Amount of Payment | Interest for Period | Portion to Principal | Principal at End of Period |
|---|---|---|---|---|
| 0 | — | — | — | $108,000.00 |
| 1 | _____ | _____ | _____ | _____ |
| 2 | _____ | _____ | _____ | _____ |
| 3 | _____ | _____ | _____ | _____ |
| ⋮ | ⋮ | ⋮ | ⋮ | ⋮ |
| 15 | _____ | _____ | _____ | _____ |
| 16 | _____ | _____ | _____ | _____ |

## 15.5   Real Estate Loans

### OBJECTIVES

**1** *Determine monthly payments on a home.*

**2** *Prepare a repayment schedule.*

**3** *Define escrow accounts.*

**4** *Define fixed and variable rate loans.*

OBJECTIVE **1** *Determine monthly payments on a home.*    A home is *one of the most expensive purchases* made by the average person. The amount of the monthly payment is a major concern of prospective buyers. The size of this payment is found by the exact same methods and formulas used in Section 15.4, but because of the many different interest rates and repayment periods, special tables are often used. Figure 15.6 shows that 30-year mortgage rates have varied considerably depending on when you took out a home loan. In particular, rates were very high during 1980–1984. As shown in Figure 15.6, the 1990's saw rates that were more moderate.

The Real Estate Amortization Table (Table 15.4) shows the monthly payment necessary to repay a $1,000 loan for differing interest rates and lengths of repayment. Higher interest rates mean higher borrowing costs, as you can clearly see from the next example.

### EXAMPLE 1   *Finding Payments to Amortize a Loan*

After making a large down payment, a couple needs to borrow $56,280 for 30 years to purchase a home. (a) Find the monthly payment required at $9\frac{3}{4}\%$ and the sum of all payments over the 30-year period. (b) Find the monthly payment required at 8% and the sum of all payments. (c) Find the difference in the total costs.

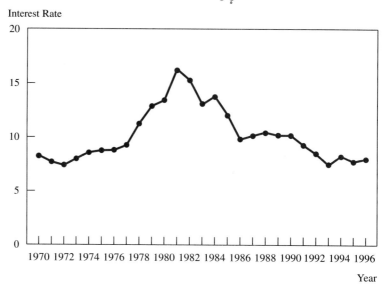

Mortgage Interest Rates
30-Year Mortgages

**FIGURE 15.6**

*Source:* Board of Governors of the Federal Reserve System, Federal Reserve Bulletin, 1996.

## Solution

(a) Use $9\frac{3}{4}\%$ and 30 years in the Real Estate Amortization Table to find $8.60 which is the payment needed to amortize $1,000 for 30 years at $9\frac{3}{4}\%$. Find the number of thousands in $56,280 by moving the decimal point three places to the left, resulting in 56,280.

$$\text{Payment} = 56.28 \times \$8.60 = \$484.01 \text{ per month}$$

Thirty years of monthly payments of $484.01 total

$$\$484.01 \times 12 \times 30 = \$174,243.60.$$

**TABLE 15.4  Amortization (Principal and Interest per Thousand Dollars)**

| Term in Years | 7% | $7\frac{1}{4}\%$ | $7\frac{1}{2}\%$ | $7\frac{3}{4}\%$ | 8% | $8\frac{1}{4}\%$ | $8\frac{1}{2}\%$ | $8\frac{3}{4}\%$ | 9% | $9\frac{1}{4}\%$ | $9\frac{1}{2}\%$ | $9\frac{3}{4}\%$ |
|---|---|---|---|---|---|---|---|---|---|---|---|---|
| 10 | 11.62 | 11.75 | 11.88 | 12.01 | 12.14 | 12.27 | 12.40 | 12.54 | 12.67 | 12.81 | 12.94 | 13.08 |
| 15 | 8.99 | 9.13 | 9.28 | 9.42 | 9.56 | 9.71 | 9.85 | 10.00 | 10.15 | 10.30 | 10.45 | 10.60 |
| 20 | 7.76 | 7.91 | 8.06 | 8.21 | 8.37 | 8.53 | 8.68 | 8.84 | 9.00 | 9.16 | 9.33 | 9.49 |
| 25 | 7.07 | 7.23 | 7.39 | 7.56 | 7.72 | 7.89 | 8.06 | 8.23 | 8.40 | 8.57 | 8.74 | 8.92 |
| 30 | 6.66 | 6.83 | 7.00 | 7.17 | 7.34 | 7.52 | 7.69 | 7.87 | 8.05 | 8.23 | 8.41 | 8.60 |

**(b)** Use 8% and 30 years in the table to find $7.34 which is the payment needed to amortize $1,000 for 30 years at 8%.

$$\text{Payment} = 56.28 \times \$7.34 = \$413.10 \text{ per month}$$

Thirty years of monthly payments total

$$\$413.10 \times 12 \times 30 = \$148,716.$$

**(c)** The difference in total costs is

$$\$174,243.60 - \$148,716 = \$25,527.60.$$

The lower interest rate results in a savings of more than $25,000 in interest charges over the 30-year period of time. ■

**PROBLEM-SOLVING HINT** Be sure to divide the loan amount by $1,000 before calculating the monthly payment. ■

For many years, mortgage payoffs of 25 or 30 years have been the most common. The last few years, however, have seen **accelerated mortgages**, with payoffs of 15 or 18 years. As the next example shows, interest savings can be substantial with these accelerated payoff periods.

**EXAMPLE 2** *Finding Total Interest Charges*

Leon and Fran Johnson need to borrow $84,500 to buy a condominium. Find the monthly payment at $8\frac{1}{4}$% and find total interest charges over the life of the mortgages for (a) 30 years and (b) 15 years.

**SOLUTION**

**(a)** Use $8\frac{1}{4}$% and 30 years in the Real Estate Amortization Table to find $7.52 and note that $84,500 has 84.5 thousands.

$$\text{Monthly Payment} = 84.5 \times \$7.52 = \$635.44$$

$$\text{Total 30-Year Cost} = \$635.44 \times 12 \times 30 = \$228,758.40$$

$$\text{Interest Charges} = \$228,758.40 - \$84,500 = \$144,258.40$$

**(b)** Use $8\frac{1}{4}$% and 15 years in the Real Estate Amortization Table to find $9.71.

$$\text{Monthly Payment} = 84.5 \times \$9.71 = \$820.50$$

$$\text{Total 15-Year Cost} = \$820.50 \times 12 \times 15 = \$147,690$$

$$\text{Interest Charges} = \$147,690 - \$84,500 = \$63,190$$

Cutting the period of the mortgage from 30 years to 15 year increases the monthly payment by $820.50 − $635.44 = $185.06. However, the total interest charge falls by $144,258.40 − $63,190 = $81,068.40.   ■

**NOTE**   The effect of different rates on a house payment is calculated with a financial calculator in Example 6 of Appendix A.2.   ■

### EXAMPLE 3   *Finding Loan Amount*

The Mocks wish to purchase the largest, nicest home they can but are limited to a monthly payment of $900 not including insurance and taxes. If the current mortgage rate is $8\frac{1}{2}\%$ and they would like a 20-year mortgage, what is the most they can finance?

**SOLUTION**   The relationship outlined in the first part of this section is:

$$\frac{\text{Number of Thousands}}{\text{of Debt}} \times \frac{\text{Factor from}}{\text{Table 15.4}} = \text{Monthly Payment.}$$

Previously the monthly payment was unknown. Now the payment ($900) and the factor from Table 15.4 (20 years, $8\frac{1}{2}\%$ interest yields a factor of 8.68) are known but the debt is unknown. Using algebra, the equation above can be solved for debt.

$$\frac{\text{Number of Thousands}}{\text{of Debt}} = \frac{\text{Monthly Payment}}{\text{Factor from Table 15.4}}$$

$$= \frac{\$900}{8.68}$$

$$= 103.687 \text{ (rounded)}$$

Therefore, they can afford a mortgage of $103,687.   ■

**OBJECTIVE** **2** *Prepare a repayment schedule.*    The interest on real estate loans is computed on *the decreasing balance* of the loan. Each equal monthly payment is first applied toward the interest for the previous month. The balance is then applied toward reduction of the amount owed. Payments in the *early years* of a real estate loan are mostly interest; only a small amount goes toward reducing the principal. The amount of interest gradually decreases each month, so that larger and larger amounts of the payment apply to the principal. During the last years of the loan, most of the monthly payment is applied toward the principal.

Many lenders supply an **amortization schedule** also called a **repayment schedule** or **loan reduction schedule** showing the amount of payments for interest, the amount for principal, and the principal balance for each month over the entire life of the loan. These calculations can be done by hand as shown in the next example, but they are commonly done on computers.

| EXAMPLE 4 *Preparing a Repayment Schedule*

Prepare a repayment schedule for the first 2 months on a loan of $60,000 at 8% interest for 30 years. The monthly payment on this loan is $440.40.

**SOLUTION**     Find the interest for the first month using the formula for simple interest.

$$I = PRT$$

$$\text{Interest} = \$60,000 \times 0.08 \times \frac{1}{12} = \$400$$

Subtract to find the amount of the first payment that reduces the debt.

$$\$440.40 - \$400 = \$40.40$$

Find the remaining debt after the first payment by subtracting.

$$\$60,000 - \$40.40 = \$59,959.60$$

Use the simple interest formula with the new loan balance to find the interest for month 2.

$$\text{Interest} = \$59,959.60 \times 0.08 \times \frac{1}{12} = \$399.73$$

Subtract to find the amount of the first payment that reduces the debt.

$$\$440.40 - \$399.73 = \$40.67$$

Find the remaining debt after the first payment by subtracting.

$$\$59,959.60 - \$40.67 = \$59,918.93$$

The following repayment schedule shows the first and second months of this loan.

**Repayment Schedule**

| Payment Number | Interest Payment | Principal Payment | Balance of Principal |
|:---:|:---:|:---:|:---:|
| 1 | $400.00 | $40.40 | $59,959.60 |
| 2 | $399.73 | $40.67 | $59,918.93 |

The Loan Reduction Schedule (Table 15.5) shows the interest payment, principal payment, and loan balance for the first 24 payments, payments numbered 256–270, and the last 6 payments of the loan in Example 4. Notice how slowly the Remaining Balance falls during the first 12 months. In fact, during the first 12 months a total of $4,781.83 is paid to interest and the Remaining Balance is reduced by only $502.97.

TABLE 15.5   **Loan Reduction Schedule***

| Payment Number | Interest Payment | Principal Payment | Remaining Balance | Payment Number | Interest Payment | Principal Payment | Remaining Balance |
|---|---|---|---|---|---|---|---|
| 1 | $400.00 | $40.40 | $59,959.60 | 256 | $220.50 | $219.90 | $32,854.74 |
| 2 | 399.73 | 40.67 | 59,918.93 | 257 | 219.03 | 221.37 | 32,633.37 |
| 3 | 399.46 | 40.94 | 59,877.99 | 258 | 217.55 | 222.85 | 32,410.53 |
| 4 | 399.19 | 41.21 | 59,836.78 | 259 | 216.07 | 224.33 | 32,186.20 |
| 5 | 398.91 | 41.49 | 59,795.29 | 260 | 214.57 | 225.83 | 31,960.37 |
| 6 | 398.64 | 41.76 | 59,753.53 | 261 | 213.07 | 227.33 | 31,733.04 |
| 7 | 398.36 | 42.04 | 59,711.49 | 262 | 211.55 | 228.85 | 31,504.19 |
| 8 | 398.08 | 42.32 | 59,669.17 | 263 | 210.03 | 230.37 | 31,273.82 |
| 9 | 397.79 | 42.61 | 59,626.56 | 264 | 208.49 | 231.91 | 31,041.91 |
| 10 | 397.51 | 42.89 | 59,583.67 | 265 | 206.95 | 233.45 | 30,808.46 |
| 11 | 397.22 | 43.18 | 59,540.49 | 266 | 205.39 | 235.01 | 30,573.45 |
| 12 | 396.94 | 43.46 | 59,497.03 | 267 | 203.82 | 236.58 | 30,336.87 |
| 13 | 396.65 | 43.75 | 59,453.28 | 268 | 202.24 | 238.16 | 30,098.72 |
| 14 | 396.36 | 44.04 | 59,409.24 | 269 | 200.66 | 239.74 | 29,858.98 |
| 15 | 396.06 | 44.34 | 59,364.90 | 270 | 199.06 | 241.34 | 29,617.64 |
| 16 | 395.77 | 44.63 | 59,320.27 | | | | |
| 17 | 395.47 | 44.93 | 59,275.34 | | | | |
| 18 | 395.17 | 45.23 | 59,230.11 | 355 | 15.87 | 424.53 | 1,955.31 |
| 19 | 394.87 | 45.53 | 59,184.58 | 356 | 13.04 | 427.36 | 1,527.95 |
| 20 | 394.56 | 45.84 | 59,138.74 | 357 | 10.19 | 430.21 | 1,097.74 |
| 21 | 394.26 | 46.14 | 59,092.60 | 358 | 7.32 | 433.08 | 664.66 |
| 22 | 393.95 | 46.45 | 59,046.15 | 359 | 4.43 | 435.97 | 228.69 |
| 23 | 393.64 | 46.76 | 58,999.39 | 360 | 1.52 | 228.69 | 0.00 |
| 24 | 393.33 | 47.07 | 58,952.32 | | | | |
| | | | | | $98,331.96 | $60,000 | |

*Interest rate 8%, loan amount $60,000, monthly principal and interest payment $440.40, term in years 30, total no. of payments 360.

The 257th payment is the first payment in which a larger amount goes to principal than to interest. The Remaining Balance drops below one-half of the original loan of $60,000 only after 269 payments (22 years, 5 months). In other words, it takes almost $22\frac{1}{2}$ years to cut the loan balance in half and then about $7\frac{1}{2}$ years more to pay off the other half of the loan. The final payment is $230.21.

**OBJECTIVE 3** *Define escrow accounts.*    Many lenders require **escrow accounts** (also called **impound accounts**) for people taking out a mortgage. With an escrow account, buyers pay $\frac{1}{12}$ of the total estimated property tax and insurance each month. The lender holds these funds until the taxes and insurance fall due and then pays the bills for the borrower. Many consumer groups oppose this practice, since the lender earns interest on the money while waiting for payments to come due. In fact, a few states require that interest be paid to the homeowner on escrow accounts on any homes located in those states.

## EXAMPLE 5 *Finding Total Monthly Payment*

George Willis arranged for a client to receive a $75,000 loan for 25 years at 8% to purchase a summer cabin. Annual insurance and taxes on the property are $654 and $1,329 respectively. Find the monthly payment.

**SOLUTION** Use the Real Estate Amortization Table to find $7.72. Add monthly insurance and taxes to the loan amortization.

$$\text{Payment} = 75 \times \$7.72 + \frac{\$654 + \$1,329}{12}$$
$$= \$579 + \$165.25$$
$$= \$744.25 \qquad \blacksquare$$

---

**CALCULATOR APPROACH TO EXAMPLE 5**

The calculator solution to this problem is to first, find the monthly payment on the principal by multiplying the number of thousands (75) times the number from the table. Add to this the monthly payment due to insurance and taxes.

75 ⊠ × ⊠ 7.72 ⊠ + ⊠ ⊠ ( ⊠ 654 ⊠ + ⊠ 1329 ⊠ ) ⊠ ⊠ ÷ ⊠ 12 ⊠ = ⊠ 744.25

---

**OBJECTIVE 4** *Define fixed and variable rate loans.* Home loans with fixed, stated interest rates are called **fixed rate loans**. These loans help borrowers during times of rising interest rates since monthly payments remain fixed. Conversely, fixed rate loans hurt lenders during times of rising interest rates. The lenders may have to pay higher interest rates on deposits than they receive on loans. This can result in large losses to the financial institutions.

As a result, many lenders now use **variable interest rate loans**, also called **adjustable rate mortgages**. The interest rates on these loans can vary up or down at stated periods over the life of the loan depending on the movement of interest rates in general. The monthly payments will change as interest rates are changed on the loan. Thus a borrower's monthly payment is not fixed for 15 or 30 years, but may go up or down every few years. In Canada and Britain, variable rate mortgages are the only ones available.

When filing an annual income tax return, a person with a real estate loan must decide whether to take the standard deduction or to itemize deductions. Both the interest paid on the loan and the property taxes may currently be used in itemizing deductions. If interest and taxes are itemized, the result is usually more than the standard deduction. The resulting tax savings *are often a major reason* to buy instead of rent. However, because of the standard deduction given to everyone, these deductions do not usually *result in a dollar-for-dollar gain*. While the tax advantages of owning are often praised greatly by zealous real estate sales people, don't forget that because of the standard deduction the savings *are often not as great as claimed* and, in any event, the savings may not show up until a refund is received next April, while the house payments begin immediately.

## 15.5 EXERCISES

*Use the Real Estate Amortization Table to find the monthly payment for the following loans.*

| | Amount of Loan | Interest Rate | Term of Loan | Monthly Payment |
|---|---|---|---|---|
| 1. | $82,000 | 9% | 30 years | _____ |
| 2. | $65,500 | $7\frac{3}{4}$% | 20 years | _____ |
| 3. | $112,800 | $8\frac{1}{2}$% | 15 years | _____ |
| 4. | $27,000 | 7% | 20 years | _____ |
| 5. | $96,500 | $9\frac{3}{4}$% | 15 years | _____ |
| 6. | $38,200 | $7\frac{1}{4}$% | 15 years | _____ |

7. Explain how different interest rates can make a large difference in interest charges over a 30-year loan. (See Objective 1.)

8. Explain why a 15-year loan at 8% results in significantly lower interest charges than does a 30-year loan at 8%. (See Objective 1.)

*Find the total monthly payment including taxes and insurance for the following loans. Round to the nearest cent.*

| | Amount of Loan | Interest Rate | Term of Loan | Annual Taxes | Annual Insurance | Monthly Payment |
|---|---|---|---|---|---|---|
| 9. | $88,000 | 9% | 25 years | $955 | $425 | _____ |
| 10. | $75,400 | $8\frac{1}{2}$% | 20 years | $1,177 | $520 | _____ |
| 11 | $58,600 | 8% | 30 years | $745 | $380 | _____ |
| 12. | $68,400 | 9% | 30 years | $1,256 | $350 | _____ |
| 13. | $91,580 | $8\frac{1}{4}$% | 25 years | $1,326 | $489 | _____ |
| 14. | $64,750 | $7\frac{3}{4}$% | 30 years | $1,101 | $342 | _____ |

*Solve the following application problems.*

15. John Forman wants to buy a home costing $62,500 with annual insurance and taxes of $450 and $1,345 respectively. He has $3,500 to pay down and plans to amortize the

balance at $8\frac{1}{4}\%$ for 30 years. Mr. Forman is qualified for a home loan as long as the total monthly payment does not exceed $600. Is he qualified for the loan?

**16.** Mr. and Mrs. Ariz wish to buy a condominium costing $95,000 with annual insurance and taxes of $680 and $2,278 respectively. They have $6,000 to pay down and plan to amortize the balance at 9% for 25 years. They are qualified for a home loan as long as the total monthly payment does not exceed $850. Are they qualified for the loan?

**17.** June and Bill Able borrow $122,500 at $7\frac{1}{2}\%$ for 15 years. Prepare a repayment schedule for the first two payments.

| Payment Number | Total Payment | Interest Payment | Principal Payment | Balance of Principal |
|:---:|:---:|:---:|:---:|:---:|
| 0 | — | — | — | $122,500.00 |
| 1 | _____ | _____ | _____ | _____ |
| 2 | _____ | _____ | _____ | _____ |

**18.** Tom Ajax purchases a home for his elderly mother. He finances $44,300 at $7\frac{1}{4}\%$ for 10 years. Prepare a repayment schedule for the first two payments.

| Payment Number | Total Payment | Interest Payment | Principal Payment | Balance of Principal |
|:---:|:---:|:---:|:---:|:---:|
| 0 | — | — | — | $44,300.00 |
| 1 | _____ | _____ | _____ | _____ |
| 2 | _____ | _____ | _____ | _____ |

**19.** Whitney Bank built a new building for the bank and amortized $9,500,000 for 10 years at 9%. Find the monthly payment and the sum of the interest charges.

**20.** Raul Aguinaga borrowed 8,000,000 pesos for 15 years at $9\frac{3}{4}\%$. Find the monthly payment and the sum of the interest charges.

**21.** Paul Shingle can afford a mortgage payment of $650 per month not including insurance and taxes. Given a 30-year loan with a rate of 9%, find the maximum mortgage (to the nearest thousand) that he can afford.

**22.** Jessie Baker can spend $780 per month not including insurance and taxes. Given a 15-year loan with a rate of $9\frac{1}{2}\%$, find the maximum mortgage (to the nearest hundred) that she can afford.

**23.** Take the amount you currently pay each month for rent and subtract $100 (for insurance and taxes). Use this amount to estimate the home loan you can afford to pay assuming an 8%, 30-year mortgage. Are there homes in your area selling for this amount?

**24.** Mortgage companies tend to require a 5% to 20% down payment, a good credit history, and a steady job before financing a home for you. First calculate 10% of the amount calculated in Exercise 23 (this approximates your required down payment). How long will it take you to save this amount if you can save $200 per month in a fund yielding 6% compounded monthly (ignore taxes)?

| TOPIC | APPROACH | EXAMPLE |
|---|---|---|
| **15.1 Finding the finance charge on a revolving charge account using the average daily balance method** | First find the unpaid balance on each day. Then add the daily unpaid balances and divide by the number of days in the billing period. Finally, calculate the finance charge by multiplying the average daily balance by the interest rate. | Previous balance, $115.45; November 1, Billing date; November 15, Payment of $35; November 22, Jacket $45. Find the finance charge if interest is 1% per month on the average daily balance. |

14 days at $115.45 = $1,616.30

7 days at ($115.45 − $35 = $80.45)

= $563.15

9 days at ($80.45 + $45 = $125.45)

= $1,129.05

14 + 7 + 9 = 30 days

$1,616.30 + $563.15
+ $1,129.05 = $3,308.50

$$\text{Average daily balance} = \frac{\$3,308.50}{30}$$

$$= \$110.28$$

Finance charge = $110.28 × 0.01

= $1.10

| **15.2 Finding the total installment cost, finance charge, and amount financed** | Total installment cost = Down payment + (Amount of each payment × Number of payments)<br>Finance charge =<br>  Total installment cost − Cash price<br>Amount financed =<br>  Cash price − Down payment | Joan Taylor bought a fur coat for $1,580. She put $350 down and then made 12 payments of $115 each. Find the total installment cost, the finance charge, and the amount financed. |

Total installment cost

= $350 + (12 × $115)

= $1,730

Finance charge = $1,730 − $1,580

= $150

Amount financed = $1,580 − $350

= $1,230

**15.2 Finding APR using a table**

1. Determine the finance charge per $100:

$$\frac{\text{Finance charge}}{\text{Amount financed}} \times \$100.$$

2. Find the number of payments in the leftmost column of Table 15.1; then go across to the number closest to the number found in Step 1 and read up to find APR.

Use the table to find the APR for the following example.

Finance charge = $1,500

Amount financed = $5,700

Finance charge per $100 =

$$\frac{1,500}{5,700} \times \$100 = \$26.32$$

Number of payments = 36; table value closest to $26.32 is $26.12; APR = 15.75%.

**15.3 United States Rule for repayment of loans**

First find interest from date of loan to date of partial payment. Then subtract interest from partial payment. Next reduce principal by any difference. Find additional interest from date of partial payment to next partial payment or maturity date and add this interest to unpaid principal.

Sam Spade signed a 120-day note for $3,000 at 11% on February 1. Sam made a partial payment of $1,200 on March 18. What is the amount due at maturity?

There are 27 + 18 = 45 days from February 1 to March 18.

$I = PRT$

$$I = \$3,000 \, (0.11)\left(\frac{45}{360}\right)$$

$$= \$41.25$$

$1,200 − $41.25 = $1,158.75 is applied to reduction of principal.

$3,000 − $1,158.75 = $1,841.25 is balance owed.

There are 120 − 45 = 75 days until maturity, so additional interest is

$$I = \$1,841.25 \, (0.11)\left(\frac{75}{360}\right)$$

$$= \$42.20.$$

Then $1,841.25 + $42.20 = $1,883.45 is due at maturity.

**15.3 Finding the unearned interest using the Rule of 78**

Find the unearned interest:

$$U = F\left(\frac{N}{P}\right)\left(\frac{1 + N}{1 + P}\right)$$

where

$U$ = unearned interest,

$F$ = finance charge,

$N$ = number of payments remaining, and

$P$ = total number of payments.

Then find the amount left to pay and subtract the unearned interest to find balance remaining.

Tom Fish borrows $1,500 which he is paying back in 36 monthly installments of $52.75 each. With 10 payments remaining he decides to pay the loan in full. Find the amount of unearned interest and the amount necessary to pay the loan in full.

Installment cost = 36 × $52.75
            = $1,899

Finance charge = $1,899 − $1,500
            = $399

Unearned Interest

$$= \$399 \times \frac{10}{36} \times \frac{(1 + 10)}{(1 + 36)}$$

$$= \$32.95$$

The 10 payments of $52.75 that are left amount to $52.75 × 10 = $527.50.

Balance = $527.50 − $32.95
        = $494.55

**15.4 Finding the periodic payment to amortize a loan**

Use the number of periods for the loan $n$, interest rate per period $i$, and column F of the interest table to find $1 \div a_{\overline{n}|i}$. Then use the formula

$$R = A \cdot \left(\frac{1}{a_{\overline{n}|i}}\right)$$

to calculate the payment.

Bob agrees to pay $12,000 for a car. The amount will be repaid in monthly payments over 3 years at an interest rate of 6%. Find the amount of each payment.

$$n = 12 \times 3 = 36$$

$$i = \frac{6\%}{12} = \frac{1}{2}\%$$

$$\frac{1}{a_{\overline{36}|0.005}} = 0.03042194$$

$$R = \$12,000 \times 0.03042194$$

$$R = \$365.06$$

**15.4   Setting up an amortization schedule**

Find the periodic payment $R$; then find the interest for the first period using $I = PRT$. Subtract $I$ from $R$ and reduce the original debt by this amount, $D$. Find the balance by subtracting the debt reduction $D$ from the original amount $A$. Repeat until original debt is amortized.

Teri Meyer borrows $1,800 for 2 years at 10%. She will repay this amount with semiannual payments. Set up an amortization schedule.

$$n = 4; \; i = \frac{10\%}{2} = 5\%$$

$$\frac{1}{a_{\overline{4}|0.05}} = 0.28201183$$

$$R = \$1,800$$
$$\times \; 0.28201183$$
$$= \$507.62$$

$$I = PRT$$
$$= \$1,800 \times 0.10 \times \frac{1}{2}$$
$$= \$90$$

$$D = R - I$$
$$= \$507.62 - \$90$$
$$= \$417.62$$

$$A - D = \$1,800 - \$417.62$$
$$= \$1,382.38$$

Continue to get table shown below.

| Payment Number | Amount of Payment | Interest for Period | Portion to Principal | Principal at End of Period |
|---|---|---|---|---|
| 0 | — | — | — | $1,800.00 |
| 1 | $507.62 | $90.00 | $417.62 | 1,382.38 |
| 2 | 507.62 | 69.12 | 438.50 | 943.88 |
| 3 | 507.62 | 47.19 | 460.43 | 483.45 |
| 4 | 507.62 | 24.17 | 483.45 | 0 |

**15.4    Finding monthly payments, total amount paid, and finance charge**

Multiply the amount to be financed by the number from Table 15.3. This is the periodic payment.
Find the total amount repaid by multiplying the periodic payment by the number of payments.
Subtract the amount financed from the total amount repaid to obtain the finance charge.

Nick owes $9,600 on a Ford Taurus. He wishes to pay the car off in 48 monthly payments. Find the amount of each payment and the finance charge if the APR on his loan is 12%.

$9,600 = amount financed

Table value (Table 15.3) for 48 payments and 12% is 0.026333

Payment = $9,600 × 0.026333
        = $252.80

Total amount repaid =
$252.80 × 48 = $12,134.40

Finance charge =
$12,134.40 − $9,600
              = $2,534.40

**15.5    Finding the amount of monthly mortgage payments and total interest charges over the life of a mortgage**

Use the number of years and the interest rate to find the amortization value per thousand dollars from Table 15.4. Then multiply the table value by the number of thousands in the principal to obtain monthly payment. Find total amount of payments and subtract original amount owed from total payments to obtain interest paid.

Lou and Rose buy a house at the shore. After a down payment, they owe $75,000. Find the monthly payment at $7\frac{3}{4}\%$ and the total charges over the life of a 25-year mortgage.

$$n = 25; i = 7\frac{3}{4}\%$$

Table Value (Table 15.4)
                    = 7.56
There are $\dfrac{\$75,000}{1,000} = 75$
thousands in $75,000.

Monthly payment = 75 × 7.56
                = $567
There are 25 × 12 =
                300 payments.

Total payments = 300 × $567
              = $170,100

Interest Paid = $170,100 − $75,000
              = $95,100

Find the finance charge for each of the following revolving charge accounts. Assume interest is calculated on the average daily balance of the account. [15.1]

|     | Average Daily Balance | Monthly Interest Rate |
| --- | --- | --- |
| 1. | $243 | $1\frac{1}{2}\%$ |
| 2. | $115.50 | $1\frac{1}{4}\%$ |
| 3. | $347.46 | 1.62% |

Find the average daily balance for each of the following credit card accounts. Assume one month between billing dates (using the proper number of days in the month). Then find the finance charge if interest is $1\frac{1}{2}\%$ per month on the average daily balance. Finally, find the amount due at the end of the billing cycle. [15.1]

4. Previous balance $634.25
   March 9   Billing date
   March 17  Payment       $125
   March 30  Lunch              $34.26

5. Previous balance $236.26
   July 10    Billing date
   July 15    Athletic shoes   $28.25
   July 20    Payment          $75
   July 31    Pillow cases     $35
   August 5   Returns          $24.36

Find the total cash price, total installment cost, and the finance charge for each of the following. [15.2]

|     | Amount Financed | Down Payment | Cash Price | Number of Payments | Amount of Payment | Total Installment Cost | Finance Charge |
| --- | --- | --- | --- | --- | --- | --- | --- |
| 6. | $1,200 | $350 | _____ | 15 | $86.55 | _____ | _____ |
| 7. | $3,800 | $800 | _____ | 20 | $212 | _____ | _____ |
| 8. | $6,500 | $1,500 | _____ | 36 | $225 | _____ | _____ |

*Find the annual percentage rate using the Annual Percentage Rate Table. [15.2]*

|     | Amount Financed | Finance Charge | Number of Monthly Payments |
| --- | --- | --- | --- |
| 9.  | $4,100 | $435 | 18 |
| 10. | $5,600 | $698 | 20 |
| 11. | $12,500 | $2,081.25 | 24 |
| 12. | $14,950 | $3,972.22 | 36 |

*Find the balance due on the maturity date and the total amount of interest on the following notes. Use the United States Rate. [15.3]*

|     | Principal | Interest | Time in Days | Partial Payments |
| --- | --- | --- | --- | --- |
| 13. | $8,000 | 8% | 90 days | $1,500 on day 24 |
| 14. | $9,000 | 12% | 120 days | $2,000 on day 40 |
| 15. | $6,000 | 11% | 120 days | $3,200 on day 30 $2,000 on day 90 |
| 16. | $9,000 | 9% | 90 days | $3,000 on day 30 $1,500 on day 45 |

*Find the amount of each payment needed to amortize each of the following loans. Round to the nearest cent. [15.4]*

17. $45,000 loan, repaid at 12% in 16 semiannual payments

18. $18,500 loan, repaid at 10% in 10 semiannual payments

19. $12,400 loan, repaid at 10% in 20 quarterly payments

20. $8,600 loan, repaid at 9% in 24 monthly payments

*Find the monthly payment and finance charge for each of the following loans using the Loan Payoff Table (Table 15.3). Round to the nearest cent. [15.4]*

21. $6,800 financed for 36 months at 13%

22. $7,500 financed for 42 months at 16%

23. $9,000 financed for 48 months at 14%

24. $15,000 financed for 30 months at 11%

*Find the monthly payment for each of the following real estate loans. [15.5]*

**25.** $80,000 loan at $7\frac{3}{4}$% for 25 years

**26.** $65,000 loan at $8\frac{1}{2}$% for 20 years

**27.** $100,000 loan at 8% for 15 years

**28.** $120,000 loan at $7\frac{1}{4}$% for 30 years

*Solve each of the following application problems.*

**29.** Sandmeyer Concrete Company was the maker of an 11% note for $5,600 dated June 20 for 150 days. The firm made partial payments of $1,330 on July 20 and $1,655 on September 3. (a) What payment is required when the note is due? (b) What was the total interest paid on the note? [15.2]

**30.** Debbie Blaisdell has a revolving charge at a department store. Her monthly statement contained the following information. [15.1]

| | | |
|---|---|---|
| 6–10 | Billing date; previous balance | $52.45 |
| 6–20 | Payment | $15   CR |
| 6–25 | Craft department | $17.40 |
| 7–2 | Shoe department | $23 |

Find the average daily balance on the next billing date of July 10. Then, find the finance charge if the interest is 1.5% per month on the average daily balance.

**31.** Ben Franklin purchased a one-year-old Ford Taurus with a cash price of $15,780 with a down payment of $2,780 and agrees to make 48 monthly payments of $332.84. Find the total installment cost and the annual percentage rate. [15.2]

**32.** Lee's Nursery bought a truck and financed $7,400 with 48 monthly payments of $228.14 each. Suppose the firm pays the loan off with 12 payments left. Find (a) the amount of unearned interest and (b) the amount necessary to pay off the loan. [15.2]

**33.** General Business Forms purchases a $145,000 commercial building, pays 25% down and finances the balance at $9\frac{3}{4}$% for 15 years. (a) Find the total monthly payment given taxes of $2,300 per year and insurance of $1,350 per year. (b) Assume that insurance and taxes do not increase and find the total cost of owning the building for 15 years (include the down payment). [15.5]

**34.** Jerome Watson, owner of Watson Welding, purchases a building for his business and makes a $25,000 down payment. He finances the balance of $122,500 for 20 years at 8%. (a) Find the total monthly payment given taxes of $3,200 per year and insurance of $1,275 per year. (b) Assume that insurance and taxes do not increase and find the total cost of owning the building for 20 years (include the down payment). [15.5]

Bob and Shun Roberts need to borrow $78,500 to purchase a home and are examining the effect of interest rates and length of amortization on monthly payments. Find the monthly amortization payment for each case in the table.

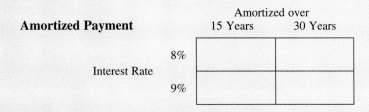

**Amortized Payment**

| | Amortized over | |
| --- | --- | --- |
| | 15 Years | 30 Years |
| Interest Rate 8% | | |
| 9% | | |

Find the total deferred payment price in each case (see Section 15.2), which would include their down payment of $8,722.

**Total Deferred Payment Price**

| | Amortized over | |
| --- | --- | --- |
| | 15 Years | 30 Years |
| Interest Rate 8% | | |
| 9% | | |

Annual taxes and insurance on the home will be $2,022 and $636 respectively. Both of these costs must be deposited in an escrow account held by the lender who will pay these bills when due. Find the total monthly payments including taxes and insurance.

**Total Monthly Payment**

| | Amortized over | |
| --- | --- | --- |
| | 15 Years | 30 Years |
| Interest Rate 8% | | |
| 9% | | |

The Roberts decide to go with a 15-year amortization at the best rate they can find in order to minimize the total amount they must pay, including interest.

# Depreciation

A business finds its net income (profit) by subtracting all expenses from the amount of money received by the business (revenues). Major expenses include the cost of goods sold, salaries, rent, and utilities. Other expenses include the cost of assets such as machines, buildings, and fixtures. These assets usually last several years, so it would not show the true income of the business if the entire cost of an asset were considered an expense in the year of purchase. Instead, a method called **depreciation** is used to spread the cost of the asset over the several years of its life. Depreciation is used with assets having a useful life of more than one year. The asset to be depreciated must have a predictable life: a computer system can be depreciated because its useful life can be estimated, but land cannot be depreciated because its life is indefinite.

Physical assets such as machinery, cars, or buildings are *tangible assets*. A tangible asset may be depreciated, as long as its useful life can be estimated.

The key terms used in depreciation are summarized as follows.

**Cost**, the basis for determining depreciation, is the total amount paid for the asset.

**Useful life** is the period of time for which the asset is expected to last in the business. The Internal Revenue Service (IRS) has guidelines as to the estimated life of assets used in a particular trade or business. However, useful life depends on the use of the asset, repair policy, replacement policy, obsolescence, and other factors.

**Salvage value** or **scrap value** (sometimes called **residual value**) is the estimated value of an asset when it is retired from service, traded in, disposed of, or exhausted. The term *scrap value* is sometimes used in place of *salvage value*, since an asset's value at the end of its useful life is often only its value as scrap. An asset may have a salvage value of zero or **no salvage value**.

**Accumulated depreciation** is the amount of depreciation taken so far, a running balance of depreciation to date.

**Book value** is the cost of an asset minus the total depreciation to date (cost minus accumulated depreciation). The book value at the end of an asset's life will be equal to the salvage value. Book value can never be less than salvage value.

Department
of the
Treasury

Internal
Revenue
Service

**Publication 534**
Cat. No. 15064O

# Depreciation

**For use in preparing returns**

*Source:* IRS.

Over the years, several methods of computing depreciation have been used, including *straight-line*, *declining-balance*, *sum-of-the-years'-digits*, and *units-of-production*. These methods are used in keeping company accounting records, and, in many states, for preparing state income tax returns. Assets purchased after 1981 are depreciated for federal tax returns with the accelerated cost recovery system or the modified accelerated cost recovery system, discussed later. The use of depreciation for federal income tax purposes is detailed in an Internal Revenue Service publication. The complete title of this publication is shown above.

A company need not use the same method of depreciation for all of its various assets. For example, the straight-line method of depreciation might be used on some assets and the declining-balance method on other assets. Furthermore, the depreciation method used in preparing a company's financial statement may be different from the method used in preparing income tax returns.

 ## Straight-Line Method

**OBJECTIVES**

1. *Use the straight-line method to find the annual depreciation.*
2. *Use the straight-line method to find the book value of an asset.*
3. *Determine the book value of an asset after several years.*
4. *Calculate the accumulated depreciation.*
5. *Use the straight-line method to prepare a depreciation schedule.*

**OBJECTIVE 1** *Use the straight-line method to find the annual depreciation.* The simplest method of depreciation, **straight-line depreciation**, assumes that assets lose an equal amount of value during each year of life. For example, suppose a heavy equipment trailer is purchased by Village Nursery and Landscaping at a cost of $4,700. The trailer has an estimated useful life of 8 years, and a salvage value of $700. Find the amount to be depreciated (**depreciable amount**) using the following formula.

> Amount to be depreciated = Cost − Salvage value

Here the amount to be depreciated over the 8-year period is figured as follows.

$$
\begin{array}{ll}
\$4,700 & \text{cost} \\
-\phantom{0}700 & \text{salvage value} \\
\hline
\$4,000 & \text{amount to be depreciated}
\end{array}
$$

With the straight-line method, an equal amount of depreciation is taken each year of the 8-year life of the trailer. The annual depreciation for this trailer is

$$\$4,000 \div 8 = \$500.$$

Or, use the following formula.

> The annual depreciation by the *straight-line method* for an item having a cost of $c$, a salvage value $s$, and a life of $n$ years, is $d$, where
>
> $$d = \frac{c - s}{n}.$$

Use the formula for the example by substituting $4,700 for $c$, $700 for $s$, and 8 for $n$.

$$d = \frac{\$4,700 - \$700}{8} = \frac{\$4,000}{8} = \$500$$

The annual straight-line depreciation is $500. Each year during the 8-year life of the trailer, $500 will be treated as an expense by the company owning the trailer. The annual depreciation of $500 is $\frac{1}{8}$ of the depreciable amount. The annual rate of depreciation is often given as a percent, in this case, $12\frac{1}{2}\%$ $\left(\frac{1}{8} = 12\frac{1}{2}\%\right)$.

**OBJECTIVE** **2** *Use the straight-line method to find the book value of an asset.*    The **book value**, or remaining value of an asset at the end of a year, is the original cost minus the depreciation up to and including that year (the **accumulated depreciation**). In the example, the book value at the end of the first year is $4,200.

$$
\begin{array}{ll}
\$4,700 & \text{cost} \\
-\phantom{0}500 & \text{first-year's depreciation} \\
\hline
\$4,200 & \text{book value at the end of the first year}
\end{array}
$$

Book value is found with the following formula.

> Book value = Cost − Accumulated depreciation

| EXAMPLE 1 *Finding First Year Depreciation and Book Value*

Dependable Insurance Company purchased a personal computer at a cost of $2,650. The estimated life of the computer is 5 years, with a salvage value of $350. Find the (a) annual rate of depreciation, (b) annual amount of depreciation, and (c) book value at the end of the first year.

## SOLUTION

**(a)** The annual rate of depreciation is 20%, since a 5-year life means $\frac{1}{5}$ or 20% per year.

**(b)** First find the depreciable amount.

$$
\begin{array}{ll}
\phantom{-}\$2,650 & \text{cost} \\
-\phantom{0}350 & \text{salvage value} \\
\hline
\phantom{-}\$2,300 & \text{depreciable amount}
\end{array}
$$

This $2,300 will be depreciated evenly over the 5-year life for an annual depreciation of $460 ($2,300 $\times$ 20% = $460, or $2,300 $\div$ 5 = $460). The annual depreciation can also be found by the formula

$$ d = \frac{c - s}{n}. $$

Substitute $2,650 for *c*, $350 for *s*, and 5 for *n*.

$$ d = \frac{\$2,650 - \$350}{5} = \frac{\$2,300}{5} = \$460 $$

The annual depreciation by the straight-line method is $460.

**(c)** Since the annual depreciation is $460, the book value at the end of the first year will be found as follows.

$$
\begin{array}{ll}
\phantom{-}\$2,650 & \text{cost} \\
-\phantom{0}460 & \text{first-year's depreciation} \\
\hline
\phantom{-}\$2,190 & \text{book value after 1 year}
\end{array}
$$

The book value of the personal computer after 1 year is $2,190.    ∎

---

**CALCULATOR APPROACH**
**TO EXAMPLE 1**

*To solve this example using a calculator, first use parentheses to find the depreciable amount. Next, divide to find depreciation. Finally, find the book value.

$$ (\boxed{2650} \;\boxed{-}\; \boxed{350}\;) \;\boxed{\div}\; \boxed{5} \;\boxed{=}\; 460 $$

$$ 2650 \;\boxed{-}\; 460 \;\boxed{=}\; 2190 $$

---

*NOTE: All calculator solutions use a scientific calculator. Refer to Appendix A for scientific and financial calculator basics.

If an asset has **no salvage value** at the end of the expected life, then the entire cost will be depreciated over the life of the asset. In Example 1, if the personal computer was expected to have no salvage value at the end of 5 years, the annual amount of depreciation would have been $530 (since $2,650 ÷ 5 = $530).

**NOTE** Find the book value at the end of any year by multiplying the annual amount of straight-line depreciation by the number of years and subtract this result, the depreciation to date, from the cost. ■

**OBJECTIVE 3** *Determine the book value of an asset after several years.*

| **EXAMPLE 2** *Finding the Book Value at the End of Any Year*

A lighted display case at the Bead Works costs $3,400 and has an estimated life of 10 years and a salvage value of $800. Find the book value at the end of 6 years.

**SOLUTION**    The annual rate of depreciation is 10% (10-year life leads to $\frac{1}{10}$ or 10%).

$$
\begin{array}{ll}
\$3,400 & \text{cost} \\
- \quad 800 & \text{salvage value} \\
\hline
\$2,600 & \text{depreciable amount}
\end{array}
$$

Since $2,600 is depreciated evenly over the 10-year life of the case, the annual depreciation is $260 ($2,600 × 10% = $260).

**OBJECTIVE 4** *Calculate the accumulated depreciation.*    The accumulated depreciation over the 6-year period is

$260 × 6 (years) = $1,560 accumulated depreciation (6 years).

Find the book value at the end of 6 years by subtracting the accumulated depreciation from the cost.

$$
\begin{array}{ll}
\$3,400 & \text{cost} \\
- \ 1,560 & \text{accumulated depreciation (6 years)} \\
\hline
\$1,840 & \text{book value at the end of 6 years}
\end{array}
$$

After 6 years, this display case would be carried "on the books" with a value of $1,840. ■

**NOTE** This book value helps the owner of a business estimate the value of the business. Although market value (the amount that a buyer is willing to pay) and book value are not necessarily the same, the book value may be important when the owner is borrowing money or trying to sell the business. ■

**OBJECTIVE 5** *Use the straight-line method to prepare a depreciation schedule.*    A **depreciation schedule** is often used to show the annual depreciation, accumulated depreciation, and book value over the useful life of an asset. As an aid in comparing the three methods of depreciation, the depreciation schedule of Example 3 and the schedules shown in the double-declining-balance method (see Section 16.2) and the sum-of-years'-digits method (see Section 16.3) use the same asset.

| EXAMPLE 3 *Preparing a Depreciation Schedule*

Village Nursery and Landscaping bought a new pickup truck for $14,000. It is estimated that the truck will have a useful life of 5 years, at which time it will have a salvage value (trade-in value) of $2,000. Prepare a depreciation schedule using the straight-line method of depreciation.

SOLUTION  The annual rate of depreciation is 20% (5-year life $= \frac{1}{5}$ per year $= 20\%$). Find the depreciable amount as follows.

$$\begin{array}{ll} \$14,000 & \text{cost} \\ -\;\;\;2,000 & \text{salvage value} \\ \hline \$12,000 & \text{depreciable amount} \end{array}$$

This $12,000 will be depreciated evenly over the 5-year life, giving an annual depreciation of $2,400 ($12,000 $\times$ 20% = $2,400).

This depreciation schedule includes a year zero to show the initial cost of the truck.

| Year | Computation | Amount of Depreciation | Accumulated Depreciation | Book Value |
|------|-------------|------------------------|--------------------------|------------|
| 0 | — | — | — | $14,000 |
| 1 | (20% × $12,000) | $2,400 | $2,400 | 11,600 |
| 2 | (20% × $12,000) | 2,400 | 4,800 | 9,200 |
| 3 | (20% × $12,000) | 2,400 | 7,200 | 6,800 |
| 4 | (20% × $12,000) | 2,400 | 9,600 | 4,400 |
| 5 | (20% × $12,000) | 2,400 | 12,000 | 2,000 |

The depreciation is $2,400 each year, the accumulated depreciation at the end of 5 years is equal to the depreciable amount, and the book value at the end of 5 years is equal to the salvage value. ∎

PROBLEM-SOLVING HINT  If the rate is a repeating decimal, use the fraction that is equivalent to the decimal. Instead of 33.3%, use the fraction $\frac{1}{3}$; instead of 16.7%, use the fraction $\frac{1}{6}$. ∎

# 16.1 EXERCISES

*Find the annual straight-line rate of depreciation, given each of the following estimated lives.*

**1.** 10 years      **2.** 4 years      **3.** 8 years      **4.** 5 years

**5.** 20 years      **6.** 25 years      **7.** 15 years      **8.** 30 years

**9.** 80 years      **10.** 40 years      **11.** 50 years      **12.** 100 years

*Find the annual amount of depreciation for each of the following, using the straight-line method.*

**13.** Cost:    $18,000
     Estimated life:    25 years
     Estimated scrap value:   none

**14.** Cost:    $3,400
     Estimated life:    4 years
     Estimated scrap value:   $800

**15.** Cost:    $120
     Estimated life:    3 years
     Estimated scrap value:   $30

**16.** Cost:    $8,100
     Estimated life:    6 years
     Estimated scrap value:   $750

**17.** Cost:    $4,200
     Estimated life:    5 years
     Estimated scrap value:   none

**18.** Cost:    $12,200
     Estimated life:    10 years
     Estimated scrap value:   $3,200

*Find the book value at the end of the first year for each of the following, using the straight-line method.*

**19.** Cost:    $3,200
     Estimated life:    8 years
     Estimated scrap value:   $400

**20.** Cost:    $35,000
     Estimated life:    10 years
     Estimated scrap value:   $2,500

**21.** Cost:    $1,600
     Estimated life:    10 years
     Estimated scrap value:   $400

**22.** Cost:    $17,000
     Estimated life:    15 years
     Estimated scrap value:   $1,700

*Find the book value at the end of 5 years for each of the following, using the straight-line method.*

**23.** Cost:    $4,800
     Estimated life:    10 years
     Estimated scrap value:   $750

**24.** Cost:    $16,000
     Estimated life:    20 years
     Estimated scrap value:   $2,000

**25.** Cost:    $80,000
     Estimated life:    50 years
     Estimated scrap value:   $10,000

**26.** Cost:    $660
     Estimated life:    8 years
     Estimated scrap value:   $100

**27.** Develop a single formula that will show how to find annual depreciation using the straight-line method of depreciation. (See Objective 1.)

**28.** Explain the procedure used to calculate depreciation when there is no salvage value. Why will the book value always be zero at the end of the asset's life?

*Solve each of the following application problems.*

**29.** Dallas Tool and Diecasting Company selects the straight-line method of depreciation for a lathe costing $12,000 with a 3-year life and an expected scrap value of $3,000. Prepare a depreciation schedule.

| Year | Computation | Amount of Depreciation | Accumulated Depreciation | Book Value |
|------|-------------|------------------------|--------------------------|------------|
| 0 | — | — | — | $12,000 |
| 1 | _____ | _____ | _____ | _____ |
| 2 | _____ | _____ | _____ | _____ |
| 3 | _____ | _____ | _____ | _____ |

**30.** Foxworthy Forest Products paid $25,600 for a $1\frac{1}{2}$-ton dual axle flatbed truck with an estimated life of 6 years and a salvage value of $7,000. Prepare a depreciation schedule using the straight-line method of depreciation.

| Year | Computation | Amount of Depreciation | Accumulated Depreciation | Book Value |
|------|-------------|------------------------|--------------------------|------------|
| 0 | — | — | — | $25,600 |
| 1 | _____ | _____ | _____ | _____ |
| 2 | _____ | _____ | _____ | _____ |
| 3 | _____ | _____ | _____ | _____ |
| 4 | _____ | _____ | _____ | _____ |
| 5 | _____ | _____ | _____ | _____ |
| 6 | _____ | _____ | _____ | _____ |

**31.** Shippers' Express paid $9,400 for office equipment with an estimated life of 6 years and a salvage value of $2,200. Prepare a depreciation schedule using the straight-line method of depreciation.

**32.** Macy's buys display counters for the cosmetics department at a cost of $15,600 and estimates that the life of the fixtures is 10 years, at which time they will have no salvage value. Prepare a depreciation schedule calculating depreciation by the straight-line method.

**33.** A Dutch petroleum company purchased a barge for $1,300,000. The estimated life is 20 years, at which time it will have a salvage value of $200,000. Use the straight-line method of depreciation to find the annual amount of depreciation. Find the book value at the end of 5 years.

**34.** A scaffold has a cost of $7,250, an estimated life of 8 years, and scrap value of $1,050. Find the annual depreciation and the book value at the end of 4 years using the straight-line method of depreciation.

**35.** A boat ramp has an estimated life of 20 years and no scrap value. If the ramp costs $75,800 and the straight-line method is used, find the annual depreciation and the book value after 9 years.

**36.** The packaging equipment line at Rainbow Bakery has a cost of $132,400, an estimated life of 10 years, and a salvage value of $35,000. Find the book value of the packaging equipment line after 8 years using the straight-line method of depreciation.

**37.** A bookcase costs $880, has an estimated life of 8 years, and has a scrap value of $160. Use the straight-line method of depreciation to find (a) the annual rate of depreciation, (b) the annual amount of depreciation, and (c) the book value at the end of the first year.

**38.** Levinson Supply purchased a new forklift for $12,500. The estimated life is 10 years, with a salvage value of $2,500. Use the straight-line method of depreciation to find (a) the annual rate of depreciation, (b) the annual amount of depreciation, (c) the book value at the end of 5 years, and (d) the accumulated depreciation at the end of 8 years.

## 16.2 Declining-Balance Method

**OBJECTIVES**

**1** *Compare the declining-balance methods.*

**2** *Find the declining-balance rate.*

**3** *Find depreciation and book value using the double-declining-balance method.*

**4** *Use the formula to find depreciation by the declining-balance method.*

**5** *Prepare a depreciation schedule using the declining-balance method.*

The straight-line method of depreciation assumes that the cost of an asset is spread equally and evenly over each year of its life. This assumption is not realistic for many assets. For example, a new car loses much more value during its first year of life than during its fifth year. Using straight-line depreciation for such assets would give a book value higher than the actual value of the asset.

Methods of accelerated depreciation are used to more accurately reflect the rate at which most assets actually lose value. **Accelerated depreciation** produces larger amounts of depreciation in the earlier years of the life of an asset and smaller amounts in the later years. The total amount of depreciation taken over the life of an asset is the same as with the straight-line method (the difference of cost and salvage value), but the distribution of the annual amounts is different.

One of the more common accelerated methods of depreciation is called the **declining-balance method;** with this method a *declining-balance rate* is first estab-lished. This rate is multiplied by the previous year's book value to get the current year's depreciation. *Since the book value declines from year to year, the annual depreciation will also decline;* this explains the method's name.

**OBJECTIVE 1** *Compare the declining-balance methods.*

### THREE COMMON DECLINING-BALANCE METHODS

**200% declining-balance method** or **double-declining-balance method.** With this method, 200% of the straight-line rate, or twice the straight-line rate, is used.

**150% declining-balance method.** With this method, $1\frac{1}{2}$ times the straight-line rate is used.

**125% declining-balance method.** With this method, $1\frac{1}{4}$ times the straight-line rate is used.

**OBJECTIVE 2** *Find the declining-balance rate.*    Calculate depreciation using the declining-balance method by first finding the straight-line rate of depreciation. Then adjust the straight-line rate to the desired declining-balance rate (200%, 150%, or 125% as desired). The following examples of declining-balance depreciation show the *200%* or *double-declining-balance method.*

**EXAMPLE 1** *Finding the 200% Declining-Balance Rate*

Find the straight-line rate and the double-declining-balance (200%) rate for each of the following years of life.

**SOLUTION**

| Years of Life | Straight-Line Rate | Double-Declining-Balance Rate |
|:---:|:---:|:---:|
| 3 | 33.33% $\left(\frac{1}{3}\right)$ | 66.67% $\left(\frac{2}{3}\right)$ |
| 4 | 25% | 50% |
| 5 | 20% | 40% |
| 8 | 12.5% | 25% |
| 10 | 10% | 20% |
| 20 | 5% | 10% |
| 25 | 4% | 8% |
| 50 | 2% | 4% |

**NOTE** Throughout the remainder of this chapter, money amounts will be rounded to the nearest dollar, a common practice when dealing with depreciation. The rounded value is then used in further calculations. ∎

**OBJECTIVE** **3** *Find depreciation and book value using the double-declining-balance method.*

**EXAMPLE 2** *Finding Depreciation and Book Value Using Double-Declining-Balance*

Northridge Golf and Country Club purchased a portable storage building for $8,100. It is expected to have a life of 10 years, at which time it will have no salvage value. Using the double-declining-balance method of depreciation, find the first and second years' depreciation and the book value at the end of the first and second year.

**SOLUTION** Start by finding the double-declining-balance rate; find this rate by doubling the straight-line rate. The straight-line rate for a life of 10 years is $\frac{1}{10}$, or 10%, and 10% doubled is 20%. The double-declining-balance rate (20%) is then multiplied by the book value, or in year 1 the *original cost*. The depreciation in year 1 is

$$\text{Original cost} \times \text{Double-declining rate}$$

or

$$\$8,100 \times 0.20 = \$1,620.$$

Depreciation in year 1 is $1,620. Therefore, the book value at the end of the first year is as follows.

$$
\begin{array}{ll}
\$8,100 & \text{cost} \\
-\ 1,620 & \text{depreciation to date} \\
\hline
\$6,480 & \text{book value at the end of the first year}
\end{array}
$$

The second year's depreciation is 20% of $6,480 (last year's book value or declining balance), or

$6,480 (declining balance) $\times 0.20 = \$1,296$ (depreciation in second year, rounded).

The book value at the end of the second year is $8,100 − $2,916 (depreciation year 1 and year 2) = $5,184. ∎

**OBJECTIVE** **4** *Use the formula to find depreciation by the declining-balance method.* Declining-balance depreciation can also be found with the following formula.

The annual depreciation, $d$, by the declining-balance method, is given by

$$d = r \times b$$

where $r$ is the declining-balance rate and $b$ is the book value in the previous year. (In year 1, $b$ is the original cost of the asset.)

**EXAMPLE 3** *Using a Formula to Find Depreciation and Book Value*

Minuteman Printing buys a new copy machine for $5,400. The expected life of the copy machine is 5 years, at which time it will have no salvage value. Using the double-declining-balance method of depreciation, find the first and second years' depreciation and the book value at the end of the first and second year.

**SOLUTION**    The straight-line depreciation rate for a 5-year life is 20%. The double-declining rate is 20% times 2, or 40%. The first year's depreciation is 40% of the declining balance or, in the first year, 40% of the cost. Use the formula, substituting 0.40 for $r$ and $5,400 for $b$.

$$d = r \times b$$
$$= 0.40 \times \$5,400 = \$2,160$$

The depreciation in the first year is $2,160. The book value at the end of the first year is as follows.

$$
\begin{array}{ll}
\$5,400 & \text{cost} \\
-\ 2,160 & \text{depreciation to date} \\
\hline
\$3,240 & \text{book value at the end of the first year}
\end{array}
$$

The second year's depreciation is 40% of $3,240 (last year's book value or declining balance) or, again with the formula,

$$d = r \times b$$
$$= 0.40 \times \$3,240 = \$1,296.$$

The depreciation in the second year is $1,296. At the end of the second year the book value is figured as shown.

$$
\begin{array}{ll}
\$5,400 & \text{cost} \\
-\ 3,456 & \text{depreciation to date } (\$2,160 + \$1,296 = \$3,456) \\
\hline
\$1,944 & \text{book value at the end of the second year} \quad \blacksquare
\end{array}
$$

**NOTE**    The total amount of depreciation taken over the life of the asset is the same using either the straight-line or the double-declining-balance methods of depreciation, but the distribution of the annual amounts is different.    ∎

**OBJECTIVE 5** *Prepare a depreciation schedule using the declining-balance method.* The next example shows a depreciation schedule for the same pickup truck used in Example 3 of Section 16.1. Here, the declining-balance method is used, where the same rate is used each year, and the rate is multiplied by the declining balance (last year's book value). This example shows that the amount of depreciation in a given year may have to be adjusted so that book value is never less than salvage value.

**EXAMPLE 4** *Preparing a Depreciation Schedule*

Village Nursery and Landscaping bought a new pickup truck at a cost of $14,000. It is estimated that the truck will have a useful life of 5 years, at which time it will have a salvage value (trade-in value) of $2,000. Prepare a depreciation schedule using the double-declining-balance method of depreciation.

**SOLUTION**　The annual rate of depreciation is 40% (20% straight-line × 2 = 40%). *Do not subtract salvage value from cost before calculating depreciation. In year 1, the full cost is used to calculate depreciation.*

| Year | Computation | Amount of Depreciation | Accumulated Depreciation | Book Value |
|---|---|---|---|---|
| 0 | — | — | — | $14,000 |
| 1 | (40% × $14,000) | $5,600 | $5,600 | 8,400 |
| 2 | (40% × $8,400) | 3,360 | 8,960 | 5,040 |
| 3 | (40% × $5,040) | 2,016 | 10,976 | 3,024 |
| 4 | | 1,024* | 12,000 | 2,000 |
| 5 | | 0 | 12,000 | 2,000 |

**NOTE**　The double-declining-balance method of depreciation allows rapid depreciation in early years but little or no depreciation in the later years of an asset's life. As mentioned, the total depreciation over the life of the asset is the same by all methods of depreciation. ■

## 16.2　EXERCISES

*Find the annual double-declining-balance (200% method) rate of depreciation, given each of the following estimated lives.*

**1.** 4 years
**2.** 8 years
**3.** 20 years
**4.** 25 years
**5.** 15 years
**6.** 5 years
**7.** 10 years
**8.** 30 years
**9.** 6 years
**10.** 40 years
**11.** 50 years
**12.** 100 years

*Find the first year's depreciation for each of the following, using the double-declining-balance method of depreciation.*

**13.** Cost: $14,000
　　Estimated life: 10 years
　　Estimated scrap value: $2,000

**14.** Cost: $120
　　Estimated life: 3 years
　　Estimated scrap value: $30

**15.** Cost: $10,500
　　Estimated life: 5 years
　　Estimated scrap value: $500

**16.** Cost: $38,000
　　Estimated life: 40 years
　　Estimated scrap value: $5,000

*Notice that in year 4, 40% of $3,024 is $1,210 (rounded). If this amount were subtracted from $3,024, the book value would drop below the salvage value of $2,000. Since book value can never be less than salvage value, only $1,024 of depreciation is taken in year 4, resulting in a book value equal to the salvage value. No further depreciation remains for year 5.

17. Cost:              $3,800
     Estimated life:          4 years
     Estimated scrap value:   none

18. Cost:              $1,140
     Estimated life:          6 years
     Estimated scrap value:   $350

*Find the book value at the end of the first year for each of the following, using the double-declining-balance method of depreciation. Round to the nearest dollar.*

19. Cost:              $4,200
     Estimated life:          10 years
     Estimated scrap value:   $1,000

20. Cost:              $2,500
     Estimated life:          6 years
     Estimated scrap value:   $400

21. Cost:              $1,620
     Estimated life:          8 years
     Estimated scrap value:   none

22. Cost:              $5,640
     Estimated life:          5 years
     Estimated scrap value:   $800

*Find the book value at the end of 3 years for each of the following, using the double-declining-balance method of depreciation. Round to the nearest dollar.*

23. Cost:              $16,200
     Estimated life:          8 years
     Estimated scrap value:   $1,500

24. Cost:              $8,500
     Estimated life:          10 years
     Estimated scrap value:   $1,100

25. Cost:              $6,000
     Estimated life:          3 years
     Estimated scrap value:   $750

26. Cost:              $75,000
     Estimated life:          50 years
     Estimated scrap value:   none

27. Another name for the double-declining-balance method of depreciation is the 200% method. Explain why the straight-line method of depreciation is often called the 100% method.

28. Explain why the amount of depreciation taken in the last year of an asset's life may be zero when using the double-declining-balance method of depreciation.

*Solve each of the following application problems. Round to the nearest dollar.*

29. Gold's Gym selects the double-declining-balance method of depreciation for some weight training equipment costing $14,400. If the estimated life of the equipment is 4 years and the salvage value is zero, prepare a depreciation schedule.

| Year | Computation | Amount of Depreciation | Accumulated Depreciation | Book Value |
|------|-------------|------------------------|--------------------------|------------|
| 0    | —           | —                      | —                        | $14,400    |
| 1    |             |                        |                          |            |
| 2    |             |                        |                          |            |
| 3    |             |                        |                          |            |
| 4    |             |                        |                          |            |

**30.** A pneumatic tire changer costing $1,680 has a 3-year life and a scrap value of $200. Prepare a depreciation schedule using the double-declining-balance method of depreciation.

| Year | Computation | Amount of Depreciation | Accumulated Depreciation | Book Value |
|------|-------------|------------------------|--------------------------|------------|
| 0 | — | — | — | $1,680 |
| 1 | _____ | _____ | _____ | _____ |
| 2 | _____ | _____ | _____ | _____ |
| 3 | _____ | _____ | _____ | _____ |

**31.** Neilo Lincoln-Mercury decides to use the double-declining-balance method of depreciation on a Barnes Electronic Analyzer that was acquired at a cost of $25,500. If the estimated life of the analyzer is 8 years and the estimated scrap value is $3,500, prepare a depreciation schedule.

**32.** Prepare a depreciation schedule for the installation of a conveyor system using the double-declining-balance method of depreciation. Cost = $14,000; estimated life = 5 years; estimated scrap value = $2,500.

**33.** John Walker, owner of the Carpet Solution, purchased some truck-mounted carpet-cleaning equipment at a cost of $8,200. The estimated life of the equipment is 8 years and the expected salvage value is $1,250. Use the double-declining-balance method of depreciation to find the depreciation in the third year.

**34.** A harbor boat costs $478,000 and has an estimated life of 10 years and a salvage value of $150,000. Find the depreciation in the second year using the double-declining-balance method of depreciation.

**35.** Nature's Products purchased a new juice extractor. The cost of the extractor is $1,090 and it has an estimated life of 5 years with no salvage value. Use the double-declining-balance method of depreciation to find the book value at the end of the third year.

**36.** Deborah Uliani purchased some communication equipment for her public relations firm at a cost of $19,700. She estimates the life of the equipment to be 8 years, at which time the salvage value will be $1,000. Use the double-declining-balance method of depreciation to find the book value at the end of 5 years.

**37.** West Construction purchased some power tools for the shop at a cost of $5,800. They have a life of 8 years and a scrap value of $1,000. Use the double-declining-balance method of depreciation to find (a) the annual rate of depreciation, (b) the amount of depreciation in the first year, (c) the accumulated depreciation at the end of the fifth year, and (d) the book value at the end of the fifth year.

**38.** Kay Schrudder bought some white boards for her reading clinic at a cost of $3,620. The estimated life of the white boards is 5 years, with a salvage value of $400. Use the double-declining-balance method of depreciation to find (a) the annual rate of depreciation, (b) the amount of depreciation in the first year, (c) the accumulated depreciation at the end of the third year, and (d) the book value at the end of the third year.

## 16.3 Sum-of-the-Years'-Digits Method

**OBJECTIVES**

1 *Understand the sum-of-the-years'-digits method.*

2 *Find the depreciation fractions for the sum-of-the-years'-digits method.*

3 *Use the formula to calculate the sum-of-the-years'-digits depreciation.*

4 *Prepare a depreciation schedule using the sum-of-the-years'-digits method.*

**OBJECTIVE** 1 *Understand the sum-of-the-years'-digits method.* The double-declining-balance method produces more depreciation than the straight-line method in the early years of an asset's life, and less in the later years. An alternate accelerated method, the **sum-of-the-years'-digits method**, produces results in-between; more than straight-line at the beginning and more than double-declining-balance at the end.

**OBJECTIVE** 2 *Find the depreciation fractions for the sum-of-the-years'-digits method.* The use of the sum-of-the-years'-digits method requires a **depreciation fraction**, instead of the depreciation rate used earlier. If this depreciation fraction, which decreases annually, is multiplied by the depreciable amount (cost minus salvage value) the result is the annual depreciation.

To find the depreciation fraction, first find the denominator, which remains constant for every year of the life of the asset. The denominator is the sum of all the years of the estimated life of the asset (sum-of-the-years'-digits). For example, if the life is 6 years, the denominator is 21 (since $1 + 2 + 3 + 4 + 5 + 6 = 21$). The numerator of the fraction changes each year, and represents the years of life remaining at the beginning of that year.

**EXAMPLE 1** *Finding the Depreciation Fraction*

Find the depreciation fraction for each year if the sum-of-the-years'-digits method of depreciation is to be used for an asset with a useful life of 6 years.

**SOLUTION** First determine the denominator of the depreciation fraction. The denominator is 21 ($1 + 2 + 3 + 4 + 5 + 6 = 21$). Next determine the numerator for each year. The number of years of life remaining at the beginning of any year is the numerator.

| Year | Depreciation Fraction |
|------|----------------------|
| 1 | $\dfrac{6}{21}$ |
| 2 | $\dfrac{5}{21}$ |
| 3 | $\dfrac{4}{21}$ |
| 4 | $\dfrac{3}{21}$ |
| 5 | $\dfrac{2}{21}$ |
| 6 | $\dfrac{1}{21}$ |
| 21   sum of the year's digits | $\dfrac{21}{21}$ |

As this table shows, by the sum-of-the-years'-digits method an asset having a life of 6 years is assumed to lose $\frac{6}{21}$ of its value the first year, $\frac{5}{21}$ the second year, and so on. The sum of the six fractions in the table is $\frac{21}{21}$, or 1, so that the entire depreciable amount is used over the 6-year life.     ■

**NOTE**   It is common not to write these fractions in lowest terms, so that the year in question can be seen.   ■

A fast method of finding the sum-of-the-years'-digits is to use the formula

$$\text{Sum-of-the-years'-digits} = \frac{n(n+1)}{2},$$

where $n$ is the estimated life of the asset.

For example, if the life is 6 years, 6 is multiplied by 6 plus 1, resulting in $6 \times 7$, or 42. Then 42 is divided by 2, giving 21, the same denominator used in Example 1. This method eliminates adding digits and is especially useful when the life of an asset is long.

**OBJECTIVE 3** *Use the formula to calculate the sum-of-the-years'-digits depreciation.* The depreciation fraction in any year is multiplied by the amount to be depreciated (as in the straight-line method) to calculate the amount of depreciation in any one year.

---

The formula for sum-of-the-years'-digits depreciation is

$$d = r \times (c - s),$$

where $r$ is the depreciation fraction, $c$ is the cost of the asset, and $s$ is the salvage value.

---

**EXAMPLE 2** *Finding Depreciation Using the Sum-of-the-Years'-Digits Method*

A Ditch Witch 1220 Trencher is purchased by Village Nursery and Landscaping at a cost of $8,200. It has a useful life of 8 years, and has an estimated salvage value of $1,000. Find the first and second years' depreciation using the sum-of-the-years'-digits method.

**SOLUTION**    The depreciation fraction has a denominator of 36 (or $1 + 2 + 3 + 4 + 5 + 6 + 7 + 8$). The numerator for the first year of useful life is 8. The first year fraction $\frac{8}{36}$ is multiplied by the depreciable amount, $7,200 ($8,200 cost − $1,000 salvage value). Substitute the proper numbers into the formula

$$d = r \times (c - s)$$

$$= \frac{8}{36} \times (\$8,200 - \$1,000)$$

$$= \frac{8}{36} \times \$7,200 = \$1,600$$

The first year's depreciation is $1,600.

The book value at the end of the first year is $8,200 (original cost) − $1,600 (first year's depreciation) = $6,600. For the second and succeeding years, always go back to the *original* depreciable amount and not to book value, as in the declining-balance method. The depreciation fraction for the second year, $\frac{7}{36}$, is multiplied by the original depreciable amount, $7,200 ($8,200 cost − $1,000 salvage value). This gives

$$\frac{7}{36} \times \$7,200 = \$1,400.$$

The second year's depreciation is $1,400. (In this example the depreciation for any year is always found by multiplying the appropriate fraction by $7,200.)   ∎

CALCULATOR APPROACH
TO EXAMPLE 2

The calculator solution to this example finds $\frac{1}{36}$ of the depreciation amount and stores the result $\boxed{\text{STO}}$ in memory. This amount is then recalled $\boxed{\text{RCL}}$ to find future depreciation amounts.

$$8200 \boxed{-} 1000 \boxed{=} \boxed{\div} 36 \boxed{=} \boxed{\text{STO}} \boxed{\times} 8 \boxed{=} 1600$$

$$\boxed{\text{RCL}} \boxed{\times} 7 \boxed{=} 1400$$

## EXAMPLE 3 *Finding Depreciation When There Is No Salvage Value*

City Saturn purchased an electronic smog analyzer for $9,000. Using the sum-of-the-years'-digits method of depreciation, find the first and second years' depreciation if the analyzer has an estimated life of 4 years and no salvage value.

**SOLUTION** The depreciation fraction has a denominator of 10 (or $4 + 3 + 2 + 1$). The numerator in the first year is 4. The first year depreciation fraction is $\frac{4}{10}$, which is multiplied by the amount to be depreciated, or $9,000 ($9,000 cost because there is no salvage value). Use the formula as follows.

$$d = r \times (c - s)$$
$$= \frac{4}{10} \times (\$9,000 - \$0)$$
$$= \frac{4}{10} \times \$9,000$$
$$= \$3,600$$

The first year's depreciation is $3,600.

The fraction for finding the depreciation in the second year is $\frac{3}{10}$, which is multiplied by the depreciable amount, or $9,000.

$$\frac{3}{10} \times \$9,000 = \$2,700$$

The second year's depreciation is $2,700. ∎

**OBJECTIVE** **4** *Prepare a depreciation schedule using the sum-of-the-years'-digits method.* For comparison, the next example uses the same pickup truck discussed in Sections 16.1 and 16.2.

## EXAMPLE 4 *Preparing a Depreciation Schedule*

Village Nursery and Landscaping bought a new pickup truck for $14,000. It is estimated that the truck will have a useful life of 5 years, at which time it will have a salvage value (trade-in value) of $2,000. Prepare a depreciation schedule using the sum-of-the-years'-digits method of depreciation.

**SOLUTION**    Using the formula on page 579 the depreciation fraction has a denominator of $(5 \times 6) \div 2$, or 15.

| Year | Computation | Amount of Depreciation | Accumulated Depreciation | Book Value |
|------|-------------|------------------------|--------------------------|------------|
| 0 | — | — | — | $14,000 |
| 1 | $\left(\frac{5}{15} \times \$12,000\right)$ | $4,000 | $4,000 | 10,000 |
| 2 | $\left(\frac{4}{15} \times \$12,000\right)$ | 3,200 | 7,200 | 6,800 |
| 3 | $\left(\frac{3}{15} \times \$12,000\right)$ | 2,400 | 9,600 | 4,400 |
| 4 | $\left(\frac{2}{15} \times \$12,000\right)$ | 1,600 | 11,200 | 2,800 |
| 5 | $\left(\frac{1}{15} \times \$12,000\right)$ | 800 | 12,000 | 2,000 |

∎

**NOTE**    The sum-of-the-years'-digits method of depreciation allows rapid depreciation in the early years of the asset's life and also provides some depreciation during the last years. With each of the depreciation methods, the total depreciation over the life of the asset is the same, but the distribution of the amount is different.    ∎

The three methods of depreciation can be compared visually by graphing the amounts of depreciation in each year and the book values at the end of each year. Figures 16.1 and 16.2 show the annual depreciation and book value for the pickup truck owned by Village Nursery and Landscaping.

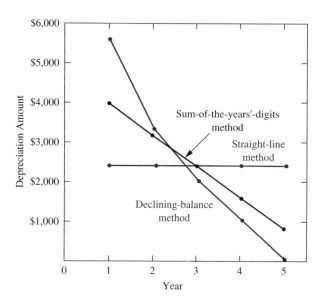

FIGURE 16.1   Comparison of depreciation on Village Nursery and Landscaping pickup truck using three depreciation methods

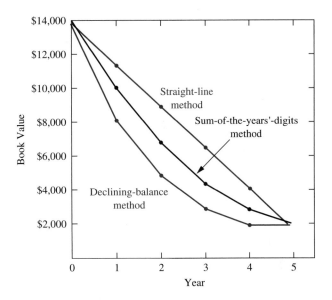

FIGURE 16.2 Comparison of book value on Village Nursery and Landscaping pickup truck using three depreciation methods

## CHOOSING A METHOD OF DEPRECIATION

While there is no simple way to decide which method of depreciation is preferable in a given case, the following considerations may help to arrive at an answer.

- Will a larger deduction in the first year or years help pay for the asset with the tax dollars saved?

- Is it expected that earnings during the first years will be larger than in the following years? Larger depreciation deductions help to reduce taxes.

- Will a steady deduction over the life of the asset be advantageous?

- Accelerated deductions in early years mean little or no deductions in later years.

- Is profit expected to increase in the coming years during the life of the asset? If this is the case, a steady deduction over the life of the asset will allow depreciation in later years.

- Will repair bills be more in later years? Since these are also deductions, they might offset lower depreciation amounts in later years.

## 16.3 EXERCISES

*Find the sum-of-the-years'-digits depreciation fraction for the first year given each of the following estimated lives.*

**1.** 5 years    **2.** 6 years    **3.** 3 years    **4.** 4 years

**5.** 7 years    **6.** 8 years    **7.** 10 years   **8.** 20 years

*Find the first year's depreciation for each of the following, using the sum-of-the-years'-digits method of depreciation.*

**9.** Cost: $1,800
Estimated life: 4 years
Estimated scrap value: $300

**10.** Cost: $3,800
Estimated life: 5 years
Estimated scrap value: $500

**11.** Cost: $60,000
Estimated life: 10 years
Estimated scrap value: $5,000

**12.** Cost: $1,440
Estimated life: 8 years
Estimated scrap value: none

**13.** Cost: $1,350
Estimated life: 3 years
Estimated scrap value: $150

**14.** Cost: $9,500
Estimated life: 8 years
Estimated scrap value: $1,400

*Find the book value at the end of the first year for each of the following, using the sum-of-the-years'-digits method of depreciation. Round to the nearest dollar.*

**15.** Cost: $9,500
Estimated life: 8 years
Estimated scrap value: $1,400

**16.** Cost: $4,000
Estimated life: 3 years
Estimated scrap value: $400

**17.** Cost: $5,000
Estimated life: 6 years
Estimated scrap value: $1,000

**18.** Cost: $15,650
Estimated life: 6 years
Estimated scrap value: $2,000

*Find the book value at the end of 3 years for each of the following, using the sum-of-the-years'-digits method of depreciation.*

**19.** Cost: $2,240
Estimated life: 6 years
Estimated scrap value: $350

**20.** Cost: $600
Estimated life: 5 years
Estimated scrap value: $150

**21.** Cost: $3,800
Estimated life: 4 years
Estimated scrap value: $300

**22.** Cost: $6,600
Estimated life: 5 years
Estimated scrap value: $1,500

**23.** Write a description of how the depreciation fraction is determined in any year of an asset's life when using the sum-of-the-years'-digits method of depreciation. (See Objective 2.)

**24.** If you were starting your own business, what type of business would it be? Which of the three depreciation methods, straight-line, double-declining-balance, or sum-of-the-years'-digits, would you decide to use? Why?

*Solve each of the following application problems. Round to the nearest dollar.*

**25.** Big Town Market has purchased a new freezer case at a cost of $10,800. The estimated life of the freezer case is 6 years, at which time the salvage value is estimated to be $2,400. Complete a depreciation schedule using the sum-of-the-years'-digits method of depreciation.

| Year | Computation | Amount of Depreciation | Accumulated Depreciation | Book Value |
|------|-------------|------------------------|--------------------------|------------|
| 0 | — | — | — | $10,800 |
| 1 | _____ | _____ | _____ | _____ |
| 2 | _____ | _____ | _____ | _____ |
| 3 | _____ | _____ | _____ | _____ |
| 4 | _____ | _____ | _____ | _____ |
| 5 | _____ | _____ | _____ | _____ |
| 6 | _____ | _____ | _____ | _____ |

**26.** Old South Restaurant has purchased a new steam table for $7,200. The expected life of the unit is 4 years, at which time the salvage value is estimated to be $1,200. Complete a depreciation schedule using the sum-of-the-years'-digits method of depreciation.

| Year | Computation | Amount of Depreciation | Accumulated Depreciation | Book Value |
|------|-------------|------------------------|--------------------------|------------|
| 0 | — | — | — | $7,200 |
| 1 | _____ | _____ | _____ | _____ |
| 2 | _____ | _____ | _____ | _____ |
| 3 | _____ | _____ | _____ | _____ |
| 4 | _____ | _____ | _____ | _____ |

**27.** Sunset Real Estate Company has purchased office furniture at a cost of $2,700. The estimated life of the furniture is 6 years, at which time the salvage value is estimated to be $600. Complete a depreciation schedule using the sum-of-the-years'-digits method of depreciation.

**28.** Prepare a depreciation schedule for the following fork lift, using the sum-of-the-years'-digits method of depreciation. Cost is $15,000, estimated life is 10 years, and estimated scrap value is $4,000.

**29.** Village Nursery and Landscaping purchased a new Ditch Witch 3500 at a cost of $32,000. The expected life of the unit is 8 years, and the salvage value is expected to be $5,000. Use the sum-of-the-years'-digits method of depreciation to determine the first year's depreciation.

**30.** Orangevale Rents uses the sum-of-the-years'-digits method of depreciation on all hospital rental equipment. If they purchase new hospital beds at a cost of $12,800 and estimate the life of the beds to be 10 years with no scrap value, find the book value at the end of the fourth year.

**31.** Electro-car, a light rail manufacturer, purchased a power-wheel and axle jig from a German manufacturer for $31,880. The jig has an expected life of 20 years and an estimated salvage value of $5,000. Find the book value at the end of the third year.

**32.** Find the depreciation in the third year for a solar collector, using the sum-of-the-years'-digits method of depreciation. Cost is $23,000, estimated life is 8 years, and estimated scrap value is $5,000.

**33.** The cost to install new carpeting at Norma's Art Studio is $6,360. It has a useful life of 5 years and no salvage value. Find (a) the first and (b) the second year's depreciation using the sum-of-the-years'-digits method.

**34.** Using the sum-of-the-years'-digits method of depreciation, find (a) the first and (b) the second year's depreciation for an asset that has a cost of $3,375, an estimated life of 5 years and no salvage value.

**35.** IN-N-OUT Burgers purchased a new deep fry unit at a cost of $12,420. The expected life of the unit is 8 years, with a scrap value of $1,800. Use the sum-of-the-years'-digits method of depreciation to find (a) the first year's depreciation fraction, (b) the amount of depreciation in the first year, (c) the accumulated depreciation at the end of the eighth year, and (d) the book value at the end of the fourth year.

**36.** Armour Drain bought a new sewer de-rooter for $6,725. The life of the machine is 10 years and the scrap value is $1,500. Use the sum-of-the-years'-digits method of depreciation to find (a) the first year's depreciation fraction, (b) the amount of depreciation in the first year, (c) the accumulated depreciation at the end of the tenth year, and (d) the book value at the end of the sixth year.

# Units-of-Production Method and Partial-Year Depreciation

## OBJECTIVES

**1**    *Describe the units-of-production method of depreciation.*

**2**    *Find the depreciation per unit.*

**3**    *Calculate annual depreciation by the units-of-production method.*

**4**    *Prepare a depreciation schedule using the units-of-production method.*

**5**    *Calculate partial-year depreciation by the straight-line method.*

**6**    *Calculate partial-year depreciation by the double-declining-balance method.*

**7**    *Calculate partial-year depreciation by the sum-of-the-years'-digits method.*

**OBJECTIVE 1**   *Describe the units-of-production method of depreciation.*    An asset often has a useful life given in terms of *units of production* or *units of output*, such as hours of use or miles of service. For example, an airliner or truck may have a useful life given as hours of air time or miles of travel. A steel press or stamping machine may have a life given as the total number of units that it can produce. With these assets, the **units-of-production method** of depreciation is used. Just as with the straight-line method of depreciation, a constant amount of depreciation is taken with the units-of-production method. With the straight-line method a constant amount of depreciation is taken each year, while the units-of-production method depreciates a constant amount per unit of use or production.

**OBJECTIVE 2**   *Find the depreciation per unit.*    With the units-of-production method, find the depreciation per unit with the following formula.

$$\text{Depreciation per unit} = \frac{\text{Depreciable amount}}{\text{Units of life}}$$

For example, suppose a stump chipper owned by Brent's Tree Service costs $15,000, has a salvage value of $3,000, and is expected to operate 700 hours. Find the depreciation per hour by dividing the depreciable amount by the number of hours of life.

The depreciable amount is $15,000 − $3,000 = $12,000. Use the formula to find the depreciation per unit.

$$\frac{\$12{,}000 \text{ depreciable amount}}{700 \text{ hours of life}} = \$17.14 \text{ (rounded) depreciation per hour}$$

**OBJECTIVE** **3** *Calculate annual depreciation by the units-of-production method.*     Multiply the depreciation per unit by the number of units produced during the year to find the annual depreciation.

**EXAMPLE 1** *Using Units-of-Production Depreciation*

North American Trucking purchased a new Kenworth truck for $95,000. The truck has a salvage value of $15,000 and an estimated life of 500,000 miles. Find the depreciation for a year in which the truck is driven 128,000 miles.

**SOLUTION**     First find the depreciable amount.

| | |
|---|---|
| $95,000 | cost |
| − 15,000 | scrap value |
| $80,000 | depreciable amount |

Next find the depreciation per unit.

$$\frac{\$80{,}000 \text{ depreciable amount}}{500{,}000 \text{ miles of life}} = \$0.16 \text{ depreciation per mile}$$

Multiply to find the depreciation for the year.

128,000 miles × $0.16 = $20,480 depreciation for the year.     ■

**CALCULATOR APPROACH TO EXAMPLE 1**

The calculator solution to this example uses parentheses to find the depreciable amount and then chain calculations to find the depreciation amount.

( 95000 − 15000 ) ÷ 500000 = × 128000 = 20480

| **EXAMPLE 2** *Preparing a Depreciation Schedule*

Watson Produce purchased a lettuce packing machine that costs $52,300, has an estimated salvage value of $4,000, and an expected life of 230,000 units. Prepare a depreciation schedule using the units-of-production method of depreciation. Use the following packaging schedule.

| | |
|---|---|
| Year 1 | 80,000 units |
| Year 2 | 50,000 units |
| Year 3 | 30,000 units |
| Year 4 | 40,000 units |
| Year 5 | 30,000 units |

**SOLUTION**    The depreciable amount is $48,300 (or $52,300 − $4,000). The depreciation per unit is

$$\frac{\$48,300}{230,000 \text{ units}} = \$0.21 \text{ per unit.}$$

The annual depreciation is found by multiplying the number of units packaged each year by the depreciation per unit.

| | | |
|---|---|---|
| Year 1 | 80,000 units × 0.21 = | $16,800 |
| Year 2 | 50,000 units × 0.21 = | $10,500 |
| Year 3 | 30,000 units × 0.21 = | $6,300 |
| Year 4 | 40,000 units × 0.21 = | $8,400 |
| Year 5 | 30,000 units × 0.21 = | $6,300 |
| Total | 230,000 units | $48,300    depreciable amount |

**OBJECTIVE 4** *Prepare a depreciation schedule using the units-of-production method.*
These results were used to help prepare the following depreciation schedule.

| Year | Computation | Depreciation | Accumulated Depreciation | Book Value |
|---|---|---|---|---|
| 0 | — | — | — | $52,300 |
| 1 | (80,000 × $0.21) | $16,800 | $16,800 | 35,500 |
| 2 | (50,000 × $0.21) | 10,500 | 27,300 | 25,000 |
| 3 | (30,000 × $0.21) | 6,300 | 33,600 | 18,700 |
| 4 | (40,000 × $0.21) | 8,400 | 42,000 | 10,300 |
| 5 | (30,000 × $0.21) | 6,300 | 48,300 | 4,000 |

**NOTE**    In Example 2, the book value at the end of year 5 ($4,000) is the amount of the salvage value. This is true because the total number of units of life (230,000) have been used up by the machine during the 5 years. The machine may continue in use producing more units; however, no additional depreciation may be taken.  ■

**OBJECTIVE 5** *Calculate partial-year depreciation by the straight-line method.*     So far, each of the examples in depreciation assumed that the depreciable asset was purchased at the beginning of a year. If the asset is purchased during the year, only a fraction of the first year's depreciation may be taken. For example, if an asset is acquired on June 1, only $\frac{7}{12}$ (since 7 months remain) of the first year's depreciation may be taken. For an asset acquired on April 1, only $\frac{9}{12}$ or $\frac{3}{4}$ of the first year's depreciation may be taken. If the asset is purchased at other than the beginning of the month, then count that month for depreciation if purchased on or before the 15th of the month. This **partial-year depreciation** is explained in the following examples.

Each of the methods of depreciation studied so far (except the units-of-production method) is affected differently by a partial year. The units-of-production method is not affected by the partial first year since actual use determines depreciation.

**EXAMPLE 3** *Finding Partial-Year Depreciation with Straight-Line*

A mountain bike display rack purchased on October 1 at a cost of $6,750 has an estimated salvage value of $750 and an expected life of 5 years. Using the straight-line method of depreciation, find the depreciation in the year of purchase.

**SOLUTION**     The depreciation for a full year is

$$\frac{\$6,750 - \$750}{5 \text{ years}} = \frac{\$6,000}{5} = \$1,200.$$

Since the purchase date is October 1, 3 months remain in the year. This means that only $\frac{3}{12}$ or $\frac{1}{4}$ of the $1,200 may be taken in the year of purchase.

$$\$1,200 \times \frac{1}{4} = \$300 \qquad \text{depreciation allowed in the year of purchase}$$

The next 4 years are depreciated at the full $1,200 per year and the last 9 months ($\frac{3}{4}$) of the fifth year has depreciation figured as follows.

$$\$1,200 \times \frac{3}{4} = \$900 \qquad \text{partial-year depreciation}$$

As before, the total depreciation over all the years is the depreciable amount, or $6,000.  ■

**OBJECTIVE 6** *Calculate partial-year depreciation by the double-declining-balance method.*

**EXAMPLE 4** *Finding Partial Year Depreciation with Double-Declining-Balance*

A boat dock with a life of 10 years is installed on April 12 at a cost of $18,000. If the double-declining-balance method is used, find the depreciation for the first partial year and the next full year.

**SOLUTION**   The double-declining-balance rate is 20% $\left(\frac{1}{10} \times 2 = \frac{2}{10} = \frac{1}{5} = 20\%\right)$. Calculate the first year's depreciation.

$$\$18,000 \times 0.2 = \$3,600 \qquad \text{depreciation first full year}$$

Now find the depreciation for 9 months or $\frac{3}{4}$ year. (Since April 12 is on or before April 15 count all of April.)

$$\$3,600 \times \frac{3}{4} = \$2,700 \qquad \text{partial-year depreciation}$$

The book value (declining balance) is \$15,300 (\$18,000 − \$2,700). Use this book value to find the first full year depreciation.

$$\$15,300 \text{ declining balance} \times 0.2 = \$3,060$$

The depreciation for the first full year is \$3,060. Depreciation for the following years would be calculated as usual. (Make sure that book value does not go below any scrap value.)   ■

**OBJECTIVE  7**  *Calculate partial-year depreciation by the sum-of-the-years'-digits method.*

| **EXAMPLE 5**  *Finding Partial-Year Depreciation with Sum-of-the-Years'-Digits*

An industrial air conditioning compressor is purchased on July 1 at a cost of \$3,800. It is estimated that the compressor will have a life of 4 years and a scrap value of \$600. Use the sum-of-the-years'-digits method to find the depreciation for each year of the life of the asset.

**SOLUTION**   The partial year here is $\frac{1}{2}$ (6 months). The depreciation fraction in year 1 is $\frac{4}{10}$ and the depreciable amount is \$3,200 (\$3,800 − \$600).

$$\frac{4}{10} \times \$3,200 = \$1,280 \qquad \text{depreciation year 1}$$

$$\$1,280 \times \frac{1}{2} = \$640 \qquad \text{partial-year depreciation}$$

Partial-year depreciation in the sum-of-the-years'-digits method requires depreciation in the first full year (year 2) to be the sum of the second half of depreciation in year 1 and the first half of depreciation in year 2. Depreciation in year 3 will be the sum of the second half of year two and the first half of year three and so on for the remaining life. See Figure 16.3.

**NOTE**   If an asset is purchased on or before the 15th of the month, then count that month for depreciation. However, if an asset is purchased on the 16th of the month or after, begin depreciation with the following month.   ■

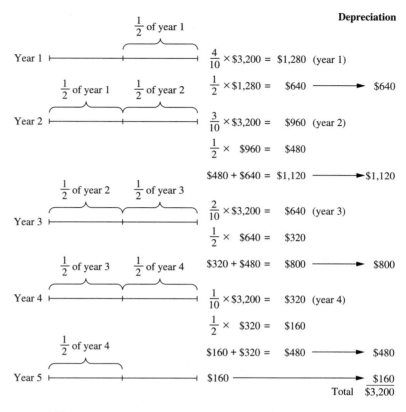

**Depreciation**

FIGURE **16.3**

## 16.4 EXERCISES

*Find the depreciation per unit in each of the following. Round to the nearest thousandth of a dollar.*

|    | Cost | Salvage Value | Estimated Life |
|----|------|---------------|----------------|
| 1. | $7,500 | $500 | 20,000 units |
| 2. | $5,000 | $400 | 10,000 units |
| 3. | $22,000 | $2,000 | 200,000 miles |
| 4. | $37,500 | $7,500 | 125,000 miles |
| 5. | $300,000 | $25,000 | 4,000 hours |
| 6. | $600,000 | $50,000 | 2,000 hours |
| 7. | $175,000 | $25,000 | 5,000 hours |
| 8. | $115,000 | $15,000 | 1,000,000 units |

*Find the annual amount of depreciation in each of the following.*

| | Depreciation per Unit | Units Produced | | | Depreciation per Unit | Units Produced |
|---|---|---|---|---|---|---|
| | | | | 10. | $0.15 | 380,000 |
| 9. | $0.04 | 42,000 | | 12. | $0.01 | 750,000 |
| 11. | $0.07 | 85,000 | | 14. | $0.032 | 73,000 |
| 13. | $0.185 | 15,000 | | 16. | $0.015 | 180,000 |
| 15. | $0.40 | 17,400 | | | | |

17. Describe the conditions under which the units-of-production method of depreciation is most applicable. (See Objective 1.)

18. Use an example of your own to demonstrate how the annual depreciation amount is found using the units-of-production method of depreciation. (See Objective 3.)

*Find the depreciation in the first partial year and the next full year for each of the following. Round to the nearest dollar.*

| | Cost | Salvage Value | Life | Depreciation Method | Date Acquired |
|---|---|---|---|---|---|
| 19. | $9,700 | $700 | 4 years | Straight-line | June 1 |
| 20. | $5,600 | $1,000 | 10 years | Straight-line | Oct. 1 |
| 21. | $20,000 | $1,000 | 20 years | Double-declining | Mar. 1 |
| 22. | $5,250 | $550 | 10 years | Double-declining | May 1 |
| 23. | $3,150 | none | 6 years | Sum-of-years'-digits | July 12 |
| 24. | $9,600 | $600 | 5 years | Sum-of-years'-digits | Sept. 10 |
| 25. | $6,300 | $900 | 8 years | Sum-of-years'-digits | Mar. 28 |
| 26. | $14,375 | $2,000 | 10 years | Sum-of-years'-digits | Apr. 19 |

*Solve each of the following application problems. Round to the nearest dollar.*

27. Dunkin Donuts purchased a new deep fryer at a cost of $6,800. The expected life is 5,000 hours of production, at which time it will have a salvage value of $500. Prepare a depreciation schedule, using the units-of-production method, given the following production: year 1: 1,350 hours; year 2: 1,820 hours; year 3: 730 hours; year 4: 1,100 hours.

| Year | Computation | Amount of Depreciation | Accumulated Depreciation | Book Value |
|---|---|---|---|---|
| 0 | — | — | — | $6,800 |
| 1 | | | | |
| 2 | | | | |
| 3 | | | | |
| 4 | | | | |

**28.** Jack Armstrong purchased a Kenworth truck at a cost of $87,000. He estimates that it is good for 300,000 miles and will have a salvage value of $15,000. Use the units-of-production method to prepare a depreciation schedule given the following production: year 1: 108,000 miles; year 2: 75,000 miles; year 3: 117,000 miles.

| Year | Computation | Amount of Depreciation | Accumulated Depreciation | Book Value |
|------|-------------|------------------------|--------------------------|------------|
| 0 | — | — | — | $87,000 |
| 1 | | | | |
| 2 | | | | |
| 3 | | | | |

**29.** A small soft drink bottler purchased an automatic filling and capping machine for $185,000. The machine has a scrap value of $30,000 and an estimated life of 20,000 hours. Find the depreciation for a year in which the machine was in operation 3,400 hours.

**30.** A cardboard crusher costs $13,800, has an estimated salvage value of $2,400, and has an expected life of 300,000 units. Find (a) the amount of depreciation each year and (b) the book value at the end of each year. Use the units-of-production method of depreciation given the following production schedule.

| | |
|---|---|
| Year 1 | 36,000 units |
| Year 2 | 42,000 units |
| Year 3 | 39,000 units |

**31.** A new irrigation system costs $78,000, has an estimated life of 10 years, and a scrap value of $5,000. If the straight-line method of depreciation is used and the system is purchased on October 1, find the first partial-year depreciation and the following full year's depreciation.

**32.** Perri-bilt Pools bought a backhoe for $38,900. The backhoe has a life of 7 years and a scrap value of $6,000. If the straight-line method of depreciation is used and the backhoe is purchased on March 1, find the first partial-year depreciation and the following full year's depreciation.

**33.** Tri-State Insurance Company purchased cellular phones for all outside sales people at a cost of $4,500. The phones were purchased on October 8, the estimated life of the phones is 5 years, and they are expected to have no salvage value. Use the double-declining-balance method of depreciation to find the first partial-year depreciation and the following full year's depreciation.

**34.** Action Paging Service purchased a $14,200 switching system on June 25. The estimated life of the system is 8 years and the salvage value is $3,000. Use the double-declining-balance method of depreciation to find the first partial-year's depreciation and the following full year's depreciation.

**35.** A warehouse has a new roof installed on June 27 at a cost of $44,400. The estimated life is 15 years and there is no scrap value. Use the sum-of-the-years'-digits to find the first partial-year's depreciation and the following full year's depreciation.

**36.** On September 14, Dr. Umeda purchased new furniture for his office. The cost of the furniture was $7,850, the salvage value is $500, and expected life is 6 years. Use the sum-of-the-years'-digits to find the first partial-year's depreciation and the following full year's depreciation.

**Modified Accelerated Cost Recovery System**

**OBJECTIVES**

1. *Understand the modified accelerated cost recovery system (MACRS).*
2. *Determine the recovery period of different types of property.*
3. *Find the depreciation rate given the recovery period and recovery year.*
4. *Use the MACRS method to find the amount of depreciation.*
5. *Prepare a depreciation schedule using the MACRS.*

**OBJECTIVE 1** *Understand the modified accelerated cost recovery system (MACRS).*   A depreciation method known as the **accelerated cost recovery system (ACRS)** originated as part of the Economic Recovery Tax Act of 1981. It was later modified by the Tax Equity and Fiscal Responsibility Act of 1982 and again by the Tax Reform Act of 1984. The Tax Reform Act of 1986 brought the most recent and significant overhaul to the accelerated cost recovery system (ACRS), and applies to all property placed in service after 1986. This new method is known as the **modified accelerated cost recovery system (MACRS)**. The result is that there are now three systems for computing depreciation for *federal tax purposes.*

1. The MACRS method of depreciation is used for all property placed in service after 1986.
2. The ACRS method of depreciation will continue to be used for all property placed in service from 1981 through 1986.
3. The straight-line, declining-balance, and sum-of-the-years'-digits methods continue to be used if the property was placed in service before 1981.

**NOTE** The units-of-production method of depreciation is still allowed under the MACRS.  ∎

Keep two things in mind about MACRS. First, the system is designed, really, for tax purposes (it is sometimes called the **income tax method**), and businesses often use some alternate method of depreciation (in addition to MACRS) for financial accounting purposes. Second, many states do not allow the modified accelerated cost recovery system of depreciation for finding state income tax liability. This means businesses must use the MACRS on the federal tax return and one of the previous methods on the state tax return.

**OBJECTIVE 2** *Determine the recovery period of different types of property.*   Under the modified accelerated cost recovery system, assets are placed in one of **nine recovery classes**, depending on whether the law assumes a 3-, 5-, 7-, 10-, 15-, 20-, 27.5-, 31.5-, or 39-year life for the asset. These lives, or **recovery periods**, are determined as follows.

| 3-year property | Tractor units for over-the-road use, any race horse that is over 2 years old, or any other horse that is over 12 years old |
| 5-year property | Automobiles, trucks, buses, computers and peripheral equipment, office machinery (typewriters, calculators), copiers, and research equipment |
| 7-year property | Office furniture and fixtures (desks, files), and any property not designated by law to be in any other class |
| 10-year property | Vessels, barges, tugs, and similar water transportation equipment |
| 15-year property | Wharves, roads, fences, and any municipal waste-water treatment plant |
| 20-year property | Certain farm buildings and municipal sewers |
| 27.5-year property | Residential rental real estate such as rental houses and apartments |
| 31.5-year property | Nonresidential rental real estate such as office buildings, stores, and warehouses if placed in service on or before May 12, 1993 |
| 39-year property | Nonresidential property placed in service after May 12, 1993 |

## EXAMPLE 1 *Finding the Recovery Period for Property*

Rancher's Supply owns the following assets. Determine the recovery period for each of them.

**(a)** a computer

**(b)** an industrial warehouse (after May 12, 1993)

**(c)** a pickup truck

**(d)** office furniture

**(e)** a farm building (storage shed)

SOLUTION   Use the list just given.

**(a)** 5 years

**(b)** 39 years

**(c)** 5 years

**(d)** 7 years

**(e)** 20 years                                                                          ∎

OBJECTIVE **3** *Find the depreciation rate given the recovery period and recovery year.*
With MACRS, salvage value is ignored, so that depreciation is based on the entire original cost of the asset. The depreciation rates are determined by applying the

double-declining-balance (200%) method to the 3-, 5-, 7-, and 10-year class properties, the 150% declining-balance method to the 15- and 20-year class properties, and the straight-line (100%) method to the 27.5-, 31.5-, and 39-year class properties. Since these calculations are repetitive and require additional knowledge, the Internal Revenue Service provides tables that show the depreciation rates expressed as percents. The rates are shown in Table 16.1. To determine the rate of depreciation for any year of life, find the recovery year in the left-hand column, and then read across to the allowable recovery period.

Notice that the number of recovery years is one greater than the class life of the property. This is because only a half year of depreciation is allowed for the first year that property is placed in service, regardless of when the property is placed in service during the year. This is known as the **half-year convention** and is used by most tax payers. A complete coverage of depreciation, including all depreciation tables, is included in the **Internal Revenue Service, Publication 534, Depreciation**, and may be obtained by contacting the IRS Forms Distribution Center. This publication (534) lists several items that the taxpayer or tax preparer might find useful and is shown below.

# Modified Accelerated Cost Recovery System (MACRS)

**Useful Items**
You may want to see:

**Publication**

☐ 225  **Farmer's Tax Guide**

☐ 463  **Travel, Entertainment, and Gift Expenses**

☐ 544  **Sales and Other Dispositions of Assets**

☐ 551  **Basis of Assets**

☐ 583  **Taxpayers Starting a Business**

☐ 587  **Business Use of Your Home**

☐ 917  **Business Use of a Car**

*Source:* IRS.

**PROBLEM-SOLVING HINT**  MACRS is the income tax method of depreciation and several important points should be remembered.

1. No salvage value is used.

2. The life of the asset is determined by using the recovery periods assigned to different types of property.

3. A depreciation rate is usually found for each year by referring to a MACRS Table of Depreciation Rates.  ■

TABLE 16.1   **MACRS Depreciation Rates**

| Recovery Year | Applicable Percent for the Class of Property | | | | | | | | |
|---|---|---|---|---|---|---|---|---|---|
| | 3-year | 5-year | 7-year | 10-year | 15-year | 20-year | 27.5-year | 31.5-year | 39-year |
| 1 | 33.33 | 20.00 | 14.29 | 10.00 | 5.00 | 3.750 | 1.818 | 1.587 | 2.568 |
| 2 | 44.45 | 32.00 | 24.49 | 18.00 | 9.50 | 7.219 | 3.636 | 3.175 | 2.564 |
| 3 | 14.81 | 19.20 | 17.49 | 14.40 | 8.55 | 6.677 | 3.636 | 3.175 | 2.564 |
| 4 | 7.41 | 11.52 | 12.49 | 11.52 | 7.70 | 6.177 | 3.636 | 3.175 | 2.564 |
| 5 | | 11.52 | 8.93 | 9.22 | 6.93 | 5.713 | 3.636 | 3.175 | 2.564 |
| 6 | | 5.76 | 8.92 | 7.37 | 6.23 | 5.285 | 3.636 | 3.175 | 2.564 |
| 7 | | | 8.93 | 6.55 | 5.90 | 4.888 | 3.636 | 3.175 | 2.564 |
| 8 | | | 4.46 | 6.55 | 5.90 | 4.522 | 3.636 | 3.175 | 2.564 |
| 9 | | | | 6.56 | 5.91 | 4.462 | 3.637 | 3.175 | 2.564 |
| 10 | | | | 6.55 | 5.90 | 4.461 | 3.636 | 3.174 | 2.564 |
| 11 | | | | 3.28 | 5.91 | 4.462 | 3.637 | 3.175 | 2.564 |
| 12 | | | | | 5.90 | 4.461 | 3.636 | 3.174 | 2.564 |
| 13 | | | | | 5.91 | 4.462 | 3.637 | 3.175 | 2.564 |
| 14 | | | | | 5.90 | 4.461 | 3.636 | 3.174 | 2.564 |
| 15 | | | | | 5.91 | 4.462 | 3.637 | 3.175 | 2.564 |
| 16 | | | | | 2.95 | 4.461 | 3.636 | 3.174 | 2.564 |
| 17 | | | | | | 4.462 | 3.637 | 3.175 | 2.564 |
| 18 | | | | | | 4.461 | 3.636 | 3.174 | 2.564 |
| 19 | | | | | | 4.462 | 3.637 | 3.175 | 2.564 |
| 20 | | | | | | 4.461 | 3.636 | 3.174 | 2.564 |
| 21 | | | | | | 2.231 | 3.637 | 3.175 | 2.564 |
| 22 | | | | | | | 3.636 | 3.174 | 2.564 |
| 23 | | | | | | | 3.637 | 3.175 | 2.564 |
| 24 | | | | | | | 3.636 | 3.174 | 2.564 |
| 25 | | | | | | | 3.637 | 3.175 | 2.564 |
| 26 | | | | | | | 3.636 | 3.174 | 2.564 |
| 27 | | | | | | | 3.637 | 3.175 | 2.564 |
| 28 | | | | | | | 3.636 | 3.174 | 2.564 |
| 29 | | | | | | | | 3.175 | 2.564 |
| 30 | | | | | | | | 3.174 | 2.564 |
| 31 | | | | | | | | 3.175 | 2.564 |
| 32 | | | | | | | | 3.174 | 2.564 |
| 33–39 | | | | | | | | | 2.564 |

| EXAMPLE 2 | *Finding the Rate of Depreciation with MACRS* |

Use Table 16.1 to find the rate of depreciation given the following recovery year and recovery period.

| Recovery Year | Recovery Period | | Recovery Year | Recovery Period |
|---|---|---|---|---|
| (a)  4 | 5-year | | (c)  3 | 10-year |
| (b)  2 | 3-year | | (d)  9 | 27.5-year |

SOLUTION

(a) 11.52%    (b) 44.45%    (c) 14.40%    (d) 3.637%                    ■

**OBJECTIVE 4** *Use the MACRS method to find the amount of depreciation.*        No salvage value is subtracted from the cost of property. Under the MACRS method, the depreciation rate multiplied by the original cost determines the depreciation amount.

Depreciation by the MACRS method is given by

$$d = r \times c$$

where $d$ is the depreciation for a rate $r$ (from Table 16.1) and an original cost $c$.

| EXAMPLE 3 | *Finding the Amount of Depreciation with MACRS* |

Village Nursery and Landscaping purchased a pickup truck. Find the amount of depreciation in the third year if the truck had a cost of $14,000.

SOLUTION    A pickup truck has a recovery period of 5 years. From Table 16.1, the depreciation rate in the third year of recovery of 5-year property is 19.20%. Multiply this rate by the full cost of the property to determine the amount of depreciation.

$$19.20\% \times \$14,000 = \$2,688$$

The amount of depreciation is $2,688.                    ■

**OBJECTIVE 5** *Prepare a depreciation schedule using the MACRS.*

| EXAMPLE 4 | *Preparing a Depreciation Schedule with MACRS* |

Omaha Insurance Company has purchased desks and chairs at a cost of $24,160. Prepare a depreciation schedule using the modified accelerated cost recovery system.

**SOLUTION** No salvage value is used with MACRS. Office desks and chairs have a 7-year recovery period. The annual depreciation rates for 7-year property from Table 16.1 are as follows.

| Recovery Year | Recovery Percent (Rate) |
|:---:|:---:|
| 1 | 14.29% |
| 2 | 24.49% |
| 3 | 17.49% |
| 4 | 12.49% |
| 5 | 8.93% |
| 6 | 8.92% |
| 7 | 8.93% |
| 8 | 4.46% |

Multiply the appropriate percents by $24,160 to get the results shown in the following depreciation schedule.

| Year | Computation | Amount of Depreciation | Accumulated Depreciation | Book Value |
|:---:|:---:|:---:|:---:|:---:|
| 0 | — | — | — | $24,160 |
| 1 | (14.29% × $24,160) | $3,452 | $3,452 | 20,708 |
| 2 | (24.49% × $24,160) | 5,917 | 9,369 | 14,791 |
| 3 | (17.49% × $24,160) | 4,226 | 13,595 | 10,565 |
| 4 | (12.49% × $24,160) | 3,018 | 16,613 | 7,547 |
| 5 | (8.93% × $24,160) | 2,157 | 18,770 | 5,390 |
| 6 | (8.92% × $24,160) | 2,155 | 20,925 | 3,235 |
| 7 | (8.93% × $24,160) | 2,157 | 23,082 | 1,078 |
| 8 | (4.46% × $24,160) | 1,078 | 24,160 | 0 |

■

The MACRS method of depreciation allows a rapid rate of investment recovery and at the same time results in a less complicated computation. By eliminating the necessity of estimating the life of an asset and the need for using a salvage value, the tables provide a more direct method of calculating depreciation.

# 16.5  EXERCISES

*Use Table 16.1 to find the recovery percent (rate) given the following recovery year and recovery period.*

| | Recovery Year | Recovery Period | | Recovery Year | Recovery Period |
|---|---|---|---|---|---|
| 1. | 1 | 10-year | 2. | 2 | 3-year |
| 3. | 1 | 5-year | 4. | 1 | 7-year |
| 5. | 3 | 10-year | 6. | 2 | 20-year |
| 7. | 14 | 27.5-year | 8. | 10 | 31.5-year |
| 9. | 6 | 5-year | 10. | 4 | 27.5-year |
| 11. | 14 | 39-year | 12. | 4 | 31.5-year |

*Find the first year's depreciation for each of the following, using the MACRS method of depreciation. Round to the nearest dollar.*

**13.** Cost:                     $10,750
Recovery period:   5 years

**14.** Cost:                     $1,270
Recovery period:   7 years

**15.** Cost:                     $9,680
Recovery period:   3 years

**16.** Cost:                     $72,300
Recovery period:   20 years

**17.** Cost:                     $48,000
Recovery period:   10 years

**18.** Cost:                     $786,400
Recovery period:   31.5 years

*Find the book value at the end of the first year for each of the following, using the MACRS method of depreciation. Round to the nearest dollar.*

**19.** Cost:                     $2,360
Recovery period:   3 years

**20.** Cost:                     $10,820
Recovery period:   15 years

**21.** Cost:                     $18,800
Recovery period:   10 years

**22.** Cost:                     $370,500
Recovery period:   31.5 years

*Find the book value at the end of 3 years for each of the following, using the MACRS method of depreciation. Round to the nearest dollar.*

**23.** Cost:                     $9,570
Recovery period:   5 years

**24.** Cost:                     $6,500
Recovery period:   3 years

**25.** Cost:                     $87,300
Recovery period:   27.5 years

**26.** Cost:                     $390,800
Recovery period:   31.5 years

**27.** The same business asset may be depreciated using two or more different methods. Explain why a business would do this. (See Objective 1.)

**28.** After learning about MACRS, what three features stand out to you as being unique to this method? (See Objective 3.)

*Solve the following application problems. Use the MACRS Depreciation Rates Table. Round to the nearest dollar.*

**29.** Rocking Horse Ranch purchased a race horse for $10,980. Prepare a depreciation schedule using the MACRS method of depreciation.

| Year | Computation | Amount of Depreciation | Accumulated Depreciation | Book Value |
|------|-------------|------------------------|--------------------------|------------|
| 0 | — | — | — | $10,980 |
| 1 | | | | |
| 2 | | | | |
| 3 | | | | |
| 4 | | | | |

**30.** Speedy Plumbers purchased a pickup truck at a cost of $14,000. Prepare a depreciation schedule using the MACRS method of depreciation.

| Year | Computation | Amount of Depreciation | Accumulated Depreciation | Book Value |
|------|-------------|------------------------|--------------------------|------------|
| 0 | — | — | — | $14,000 |
| 1 | | | | |
| 2 | | | | |
| 3 | | | | |
| 4 | | | | |
| 5 | | | | |
| 6 | | | | |

**31.** Gulf Drilling purchased a tugboat for $122,700. Prepare a depreciation schedule using the MACRS method of depreciation.

**32.** Andy Kirkpatrick purchased some residential rental real estate before May 12, 1993 for $415,000. Prepare a depreciation schedule for the first ten years using the MACRS method of depreciation. (31.5-year property)

**33.** Shirley Cicero purchased an apartment building for $285,000. Find the book value at the end of the tenth year using the MACRS method of depreciation.

**34.** Delta Dental purchased new office furniture at a cost of $13,800. Find the book value at the end of the fifth year using the MACRS method of depreciation.

**35.** Jim Bralley, the owner of Bralley's Bookkeeping, purchased an office building at a cost of $480,000. Find the amount of depreciation for each of the first five years using the MACRS method of depreciation. (39-year property)

**36.** Maretha Roseborough, owner of the Barnstormer Bookstore, bought a building to use for her business. The cost of the building was $220,000. Find the amount of depreciation each of the first five years using the MACRS method of depreciation. (39-year property)

# Chapter 16 Quick Review

| TOPIC | APPROACH | EXAMPLE |
|---|---|---|
| **16.1 Straight-line method of depreciation** | The depreciation is the same each year. Use the formula $$d = \frac{c - s}{n}$$ with $c$ = cost, $s$ = salvage value, and $n$ = life (in years). | Cost, $500; salvage value, $100; life, 8 years. Find the annual depreciation. $$d = \frac{\$500 - \$100}{8}$$ $$= \frac{\$400}{8} = \$50$$ |
| **16.1 Book value** | Book value is the value remaining at the end of the year. Cost minus accumulated depreciation equals book value. | Cost, $400; salvage value, $100; life, 3 years. Find the book value at the end of the first year. $$d = \frac{\$400 - \$100}{3}$$ $$= \frac{\$300}{3} = \$100$$ Book value = $400 − $100 = $300 |
| **16.2 Double-declining-balance rate** | First, find the straight-line rate, then adjust it as follows: 200%: multiply by 2 150%: multiply by $1\frac{1}{2}$ 125%: multiply by $1\frac{1}{4}$ | Life of an asset is 10 years. Find the double-declining-balance (200%) rate. 10 years $$= 10\% \left(\frac{1}{10}\right) \text{ straight-line}$$ $2 \times 10\% = 20\%$ |

| 16.2 | Double-declining-balance depreciation method | First, find the double-declining-balance rate; then use the formula $d = r \times b$ where $b$ is total cost in the first year and the declining-balance in the following years. | Cost, $1,400; life, 5 years. Find depreciation in years 1 and 2.<br>$2 \times 20\%$ (straight-line rate) $= 40\%$<br><br>Year 1:<br><br>Depreciation = $40\% \times \$1,400 = \$560$<br><br>Book Value = $\$1,400 - \$560 = \$840$<br><br>Year 2:<br><br>Depreciation = $40\% \times \$840 = \$336$ |
|---|---|---|---|

### 16.3 Sum-of-the-years'-digits depreciation fraction

Add the years' digits together to get the denominator. The numerator is the number of years of life remaining. The denominator shortcut is

$$\text{Sum-of-the-years'-digits} = \frac{n(n + 1)}{2}$$

Useful life is 4 years. Find the depreciation fraction for each year.

$$1 + 2 + 3 + 4 = 10$$

| Year | Depreciation Fraction |
|---|---|
| 1 | $\dfrac{4}{10}$ |
| 2 | $\dfrac{3}{10}$ |
| 3 | $\dfrac{2}{10}$ |
| 4 | $\dfrac{1}{10}$ |

### 16.3 Sum-of-the-years'-digits depreciation method

First find the depreciation fraction, and then use the formula

$$d = r \times (c - s).$$

Cost, $2,500; salvage value, $400; life, 6 years. Find depreciation in year 1.

$$\text{Depreciation fraction} = \frac{6}{21}$$

$$d = \frac{6}{21} \times (\$2,500 - \$400)$$

$$= \frac{6}{21} \times \$2,100 = \$600$$

**16.4**  **Units-of-production depreciation amount per unit**

Use the formula

$$\text{Depreciation per unit} = \frac{\text{Depreciable amount}}{\text{Units of life}}.$$

Cost $10,000; salvage value, $2,500; useful life, 15,000 units. Find depreciation per unit.

Depreciation per unit

$$= \frac{\$7,500 \text{ depreciable amount}}{15,000 \text{ units of life}}$$

$$= \$0.50$$

---

**16.4**  **Units-of-production depreciation method**

Multiply the depreciation per unit (hour) by the number of units (hours) of production.

In the preceding example: first year's production, 3,800 units. Find depreciation in year 1.

$$3,800 \times \$0.50 = \$1,900$$

---

**16.4**  **Partial-year depreciation**

If an asset is purchased during the year, take only a fraction of the year's depreciation.

Depreciable amount, $4,500; life, 5 years; date purchased, June 7. Find first partial-year depreciation by straight-line method.

$$7 \text{ months} = \frac{7}{12} \text{ year}$$

$$\frac{\$4,500}{5} \times \frac{7}{12} = \$525$$

---

**16.5**  **Modified accelerated cost recovery system (MACRS)**

Established in 1986 for federal tax. No salvage value. Recovery periods are:

| | |
|---|---|
| 3-year | 15-year |
| 5-year | 20-year |
| 7-year | 27.5-year |
| 10-year | 31.5-year |
| | 39-year |

Use the formula

$$d = r \times c$$

with rate from Table 16.1.

Cost, $4,850; recovery period, 5 years; recovery year, 3. Find the depreciation.
Find 5-year recovery period column at top of Table 16.1, and recovery year 3 in leftmost column; rate is 19.20%.

$$d = 19.20\% \times \$4,850$$
$$= \$931.20$$

*Find the annual straight-line and double-declining-balance rates (percents) of depreciation and the sum-of-the-years'-digits fractions in the first year for each of the following estimated lives. [16.1–16.3]*

**1.** 4 years

**2.** 5 years

**3.** 20 years

**4.** 10 years

**5.** 6 years

**6.** 8 years

*Use Table 16.1 to find the recovery percent (rate) given the following recovery year and recovery period. [16.5]*

| | Recovery Year | Recovery Period | | Recovery Year | Recovery Period |
|---|---|---|---|---|---|
| **7.** | 4 | 5-year | **8.** | 1 | 3-year |
| **9.** | 8 | 20-year | **10.** | 3 | 7-year |
| **11.** | 20 | 39-year | **12.** | 20 | 31.5-year |

*Solve the following application problems. Round to the nearest dollar if necessary.*

**13.** Cloverdale Creamery purchased an ice cream machine at a cost of $12,400. The machine has an estimated life of 10 years, and a scrap value of $3,000. Use the straight-line method of depreciation to find the annual depreciation. [16.1]

**14.** The dry cleaning machinery at Stopwatch Dry Cleaners costs $52,000, has an estimated life of 40 years, and an estimated scrap value of $8,000. Use the straight-line method of depreciation to find the book value of the machinery at the end of 10 years. [16.1]

**15.** Sunset Swimming pools purchased a dump truck for $38,000. If the estimated life of the dump truck is 8 years, find the book value at the end of 2 years using the double-declining-balance method of depreciation. [16.2]

**16.** Star Bushing Company bought some Belgian manufactured drill presses at a total cost of $18,500. The estimated life of the drill presses is 5 years, and there is no scrap value. Find the depreciation in the first year using the double-declining-balance method of depreciation. [16.2]

**17.** The Feather River Youth Camp has purchased a diesel generator for $8,250. Use the sum-of-the-years'-digits method of depreciation to determine the amount of depreciation to be taken during *each of the 4 years* on the diesel generator that has a 4-year life and scrap value of $1,500. [16.3]

**18.** Murray's Delicatessen purchased a new display case for $7,375. It has an estimated life of 10 years, and salvage value of $500. Use the sum-of-the-years'-digits method of depreciation to find the book value at the end of the third year. [16.3]

**19.** A grape press costs $11,000, has a scrap value of $2,500, and an estimated life of 5,000 hours. Use the units-of-production method to find the depreciation for a year in which the machine was in operation 900 hours. [16.4]

**20.** Table Fresh Foods purchased a machine to package their pre-sliced garden salads. The machine costs $20,100 and has an estimated life of 30,000 hours and a salvage value of $1,500. Use the units-of-production method of depreciation to find (a) the annual amount of depreciation and (b) the book value at the end of each year, given the following use information: year 1: 7,800 hours; year 2: 4,300 hours; year 3: 4,850 hours; year 4: 7,600 hours. [16.4]

**21.** The Fashion Express purchased new clothing racks at a cost of $22,400. Using the straight-line method of depreciation, a 5-year life, and a scrap value of $3,500, find the accumulated depreciation at the end of the fourth year. [16.1]

**22.** Using the sum-of-the-years'-digits method of depreciation, find the amount of depreciation to be charged off each year on a tour bus purchased by Bayside Tours. The bus has a cost of $85,000, an estimated life of 5 years, and a scrap value of $13,000. [16.3]

**23.** A recycled glass crusher costs $48,000, has an estimated life of 5 years, and a scrap value of $4,500. If the straight-line method of depreciation is used and the system is purchased on September 10, find the first partial-year depreciation. [16.4]

**24.** A parking lot is resurfaced on June 1 at a cost of $9,720. The estimated life is 8 years and there is no scrap value. Use the sum-of-the-years'-digits method to find the first partial-year depreciation and the following full year's depreciation. [16.4]

**25.** Instant Copy Service purchased a new copy system at a cost of $28,400 on June 19. The estimated life of the system is 10 years and the salvage value is $6,000. Use the double-declining-balance method of depreciation to find the first partial-year depreciation and the following full year's depreciation. [16.4]

**26.** Don Rosa, owner of Southeast Appliance Parts, has added paging and intercom features to the communication systems of his 4 stores at a cost of $2,800 per store. The estimated life of the systems is 10 years, with no expected salvage value. Using the sum-of-the-years'-digits method of depreciation, find the total book value of all the systems at the end of the third year. [16.3]

**27.** A job printer purchased an automatic composer at a cost of $15,000. If the estimated life of the composer is 8 years, find the book value at the end of 4 years, using the double-declining-balance method of depreciation. Assume no scrap value. [16.2]

**28.** Lumber and More Company buys 5 fork lifts at a cost of $14,825 each. The life of the fork lifts is estimated to be 10 years and the scrap value $3,000 each. Use the sum-of-the-years'-digits method of depreciation to find the total book value of all the fork lifts at the end of the fourth year. [16.3]

**29.** King's Table bought new dining room tables at a cost of $14,750. If the estimated life of the tables is 8 years, at which time they will be worthless, and the double-declining-balance method of depreciation is used, find the book value at the end of the third year. [16.2]

**30.** Use the MACRS method of depreciation to find the amount of depreciation to be taken during each of the 4 years on a $19,600 tractor that is 3-year property. [16.5]

**31.** Kathy Woodward purchased a new refrigeration system (7-year property) for her flower shop at a cost of $8,100. Find the amount of depreciation for each of the first five years using the MACRS method of depreciation. [16.5]

**32.** Blue Diamond Almond Growers paid $2,800,000 to build a new warehouse on or before May 12, 1993. The recovery period is 31.5 years. Use the MACRS method of depreciation to find the book value of the warehouse at the end of the fifth year. [16.5]

# Chapter 16 Summary Exercise

On June 24 the Natoma Coffee Company purchased a lighted outdoor sign at a cost of $45,500. The estimated life (recovery period) for the sign is 7 years, at which time it will have no salvage value. The company is looking at allowable depreciation methods and decides to prepare depreciation schedules for the sign using the straight-line, double-declining-balance, sum-of-the-years'-digits, and MACRS (income tax method) methods of depreciation. Using the depreciation schedules, the company wants to answer the following questions. Be certain that you use partial-year depreciation as you answer these questions for the Natoma Coffee Company.

**(a)** What is the depreciation in the first partial year and the following full year using the straight-line depreciation method?

**(b)** Using the double-declining-balance method of depreciation, what is the book value at the end of the third year?

**(c)** With the sum-of-the-years'-digits method of depreciation, what is the accumulated depreciation at the end of 3 years?

**(d)** Using the MACRS method of depreciation, what is the book value at the end of 5 years?

**(e)** What amount of depreciation will be taken in year 4 with each of these methods?

# 17

# Financial Statements and Ratios

A business owner or manager must keep careful records of the expenses and income of the business. Only by paying *careful attention* to income and expenses will an adequate net income be provided for the firm. Companies use bookkeepers to help keep track of the money coming in and going out, while accountants answer questions like "Why is this year's net income less than last year's?"; "How do our business expenses compare to those of similar firms?"; and "Have our expenses for overhead increased as a percent of sales?" This chapter discusses some of the methods used by accountants to answer these and other questions.

## 17.1 The Income Statement

**OBJECTIVES**

1. *Learn the terms used with income statements.*
2. *Understand the income statement of The Coca-Cola Company.*
3. *Complete an income statement.*

**OBJECTIVE** 1 *Learn the terms used with income statements.* An **income statement** is prepared for the management and owners of a business to summarize all income and expenses for a given period of time, such as a month or a year. As a first step, find the **gross sales**, the total amount of money received from customers for the goods or services sold by the firm. Then subtract the value of any **returns** from customers to arrive at **net sales**, the value of the goods and services bought and kept by customers. Use the following formula.

$$\text{Net sales} = \text{Gross sales} - \text{Returns}$$

After finding net sales, look at company records to find the **cost of goods sold**, the amount paid by the firm for the items sold to customers during the period of time covered by the income statement. Then subtract the cost of goods sold from the net sales to find the **gross profit**. Gross profit is often called **gross profit on sales**. The gross profit is the amount of money left over after the business pays for the goods it sells. This money is used to pay the expenses involved in running the business and anything remaining after expenses goes to either taxes or profit.

$$\text{Gross profit} = \text{Net sales} - \text{Cost of goods sold}$$

**Operating expenses** represent the amount paid by the firm in an attempt to sell its goods. Common expenses include rent, salaries and wages, advertising, utilities, losses from uncollectible accounts, and taxes on inventory and payroll. Operating expenses are sometimes called **overhead**. Finally, **net income before taxes** is the actual amount earned by the firm during the given time period.

$$\text{Net income before taxes} = \text{Gross profit} - \text{Operating expenses}$$

**Net income**, also called **net income after taxes**, is found by subtracting income taxes from net income before taxes.

$$\text{Net income} = \text{Net income before taxes} - \text{Income taxes}$$

Banks do not wish to lend money to firms that may not be able to repay the loans. As a result, a bank will usually want to see all of the values identified in this section so far, in addition to other data, before making a loan to a firm. The values introduced here are typically included in an income statement which we will now examine.

**OBJECTIVE 2** *Understand the income statement of The Coca-Cola Company.* A portion of The Coca-Cola Company's 1995 income statement is shown in Example 1. Shares of the company are publicly traded on the New York Stock Exchange under the symbol KO. Check the New York Stock Exchange page in your newspaper for a current stock price and dividend. The income statement is **consolidated** since it shows the total results of all of the subsidiary companies within The Coca-Cola Company.

**EXAMPLE 1** *Finding the Net Income*

The Coca-Cola Company had gross sales of approximately $18,018,000,000 during 1995. Assume no returns of merchandise, a cost of goods sold of $6,940,000,000, operating expenses of $6,750,000,000, and income taxes of $1,342,000,000. Find the net income after taxes for the year.

SOLUTION    Use the formulas in the boxes. For convenience, work with millions of dollars by first rounding each number to the nearest million.

$$\text{Net sales} = \text{Gross sales} - \text{Returns}$$
$$= \$18{,}018 - 0$$
$$= \$18{,}018 \text{ (in millions of dollars)}$$

Note that gross sales = net sales for The Coca-Cola Company because they have no returns of merchandise. Now find the gross profit.

$$\text{Gross profit} = \text{Net sales} - \text{Cost of goods sold}$$
$$= \$18{,}018 - \$6{,}940$$
$$= \$11{,}078 \text{ (in millions of dollars)}$$

The gross profit is used to pay expenses of running the business. Now find the net income before taxes.

$$\text{Net income before taxes} = \text{Gross profit} - \text{Operating expenses}$$
$$= \$11{,}078 - \$6{,}750$$
$$= \$4{,}328 \text{ (in millions of dollars)}$$

Finally, calculate the net income after income taxes.

$$\text{Net income after taxes} = \text{Net income before taxes} - \text{Income taxes}$$
$$= \$4{,}328 - \$1{,}342$$
$$= \$2{,}986 \text{ (in millions of dollars)}$$

In 1995, The Coca-Cola Company paid approximately $1,342,000,000 in income taxes and still had an after tax profit of $2,986,000,000. The results are summarized in the following income statement.

---

**The Coca-Cola Company and Subsidiaries**
**Consolidated Statements of Income**
**Year ended December 31, 1995 (millions of dollars)**

---

| | |
|---|---|
| Gross Sales | $18,018 |
| Returns | −      0 |
| Net Sales | $18,018 |
| Cost of Goods Sold | −  6,940 |
| Gross Profit | $11,078 |
| Operating Expenses | −  6,750 |
| Net Income before Taxes | $  4,328 |
| Income Taxes | −  1,342 |
| Net Income after Taxes | $  2,986 |

---

Check the results shown on the income statement with the following basic formula.

Cost of     Operating    Income    Net income

goods sold + expenses + taxes + after taxes = Net sales

$6,940    +    $6,750   + $1,342 +    $2,986    = $18,018

The income statement checks.                               ■

      The value of a company's stock is based on recent financial results in addition to perceived opportunities for the firm. As a publicly held corporation, The Coca-Cola Company *must publish* financial results. The stock price generally rises when company profits are rising and the stock price generally falls when company profits are falling. You can obtain The Coca-Cola Company's current financial statements mailed to you free of charge by calling their home office in Atlanta, Georgia. You can also get the financial statements of *any other* publicly held company free by calling their home office.

**OBJECTIVE** **3** *Complete an income statement.*      Example 1 gives the value for the cost of goods sold whereas this amount would normally need to be calculated. The cost of goods sold can be found using the formula below. **Initial inventory** is the at cost value of all goods on hand for sale at the beginning of the period and **ending inventory** is the at cost value of all goods on hand for sale at the end of the period.

Initial inventory (or Beginning inventory)

+ Cost of goods purchased during time period

+ Freight

− Ending inventory

Cost of goods sold

| **EXAMPLE 2**   *Preparing an Income Statement*

Josie's Clothing had gross sales of $159,000 during the past year, with returns of $9,000. Inventory on January 1 of last year was $47,000. A total of $104,000 worth of goods was purchased last year, with freight on the goods totaling $2,000. Inventory on December 31 of last year was $56,000. Wages paid to employees totaled $18,000. Rent was $9,000, advertising was $1,000, utilities totaled $2,000, and taxes on inventory and payroll totaled $4,000. Miscellaneous expenses totaled $6,000 and income taxes were $500. Complete an income statement for the store.

**SOLUTION**    Go through the steps that follow, which refer to the income statement in Figure 17.1.

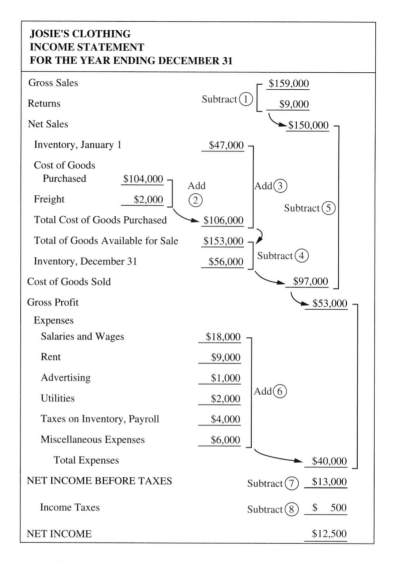

FIGURE 17.1

# WORKING THROUGH AN INCOME STATEMENT

***Step 1.*** Enter gross sales and sales returns. Subtract sales returns from gross sales to find net sales. Net sales in this example were $150,000.

***Step 2.*** Enter the cost of goods purchased and the freight. Add these two numbers.

***Step 3.*** Add the inventory on January 1 and the total cost of goods purchased.

**Step 4.** Subtract the inventory on December 31 from the result of step 3. This gives the cost of goods sold.

**Step 5.** Subtract the cost of goods sold from net sales, which were found in step 1. The result is the gross profit.

**Step 6.** Enter all expenses and add them to get the total expenses.

**Step 7.** Subtract the total expenses from the gross profit to find the net income before taxes.

**Step 8.** Subtract taxes from net income before taxes to find net income after taxes.

■

**NOTE** Be sure to check the results of your income statement by adding the cost of goods sold, expenses, net income before taxes, and taxes. This total should equal net sales.  ■

## 17.1 EXERCISES

*Find (a) the gross profit, (b) the net income before taxes, and (c) the net income after taxes for each firm.*

1. Last year, Toni's Hardware had a cost of goods sold of $623,234, operating expenses of $122,500, taxes of $21,800, and net sales of $840,090.

2. A bookstore in Ontario, Canada had net sales of $376,000, operating expenses of $36,000, a cost of goods sold of $294,000, and paid $6,800 in taxes.

*Find the cost of goods sold for the following firms.*

3. At Rainbow Paint, the inventory on January 1 was $263,400 with $343,500 worth of goods purchased during the year. Freight was $4,800 and the inventory on December 31 was $287,500.

4. Inventory at Southside Auto was $428,340 on January 1 and $387,708 on December 31. They paid freight of $8,400 during the year on purchases of $548,200.

5. Future Tech Computing had gross sales of $284,000 last year, with returns of $6,000. The inventory on January 1 was $58,000. A total of $232,000 worth of goods was purchased, with freight of $3,000. The inventory on December 31 was $69,000. Wages and salaries were $15,000, rent was $6,000, advertising was $2,000, utilities were $1,000, taxes on inventory and payroll totaled $3,000, miscellaneous expenses totaled $4,000, and income taxes amounted to $2,400. Complete the income statement on the following page.

**FUTURE TECH COMPUTING**
**INCOME STATEMENT**
**YEAR ENDING DECEMBER 31**

Gross Sales          _____

Returns          _____

Net Sales          _____

    Inventory, January 1      _____

    Cost of Goods
      Purchased      _____

    Freight      _____

    Total Cost of Goods Purchased      _____

    Total of Goods Available for Sale      _____

    Inventory, December 31      _____

Cost of Goods Sold      _____

Gross Profit      _____

    Expenses

      Salaries and Wages      _____

      Rent      _____

      Advertising      _____

      Utilities      _____

      Taxes on Inventory, Payroll      _____

      Miscellaneous Expenses      _____

        Total Expenses      _____

NET INCOME BEFORE TAXES      _____

    Income Taxes      _____

NET INCOME      ==========

**6.** New England Dental Supply is a regional wholesaler which had gross sales last year of $2,215,000. Returns totaled $26,000. Inventory on January 1 was $215,000. Goods purchased during the year totaled $1,123,000. Freight was $4,000. Inventory on December 31 was $265,000. Salaries and wages were $154,000, rent was $59,000, advertising was $11,000, utilities were $12,000, taxes on inventory and payroll totaled

$10,000, and miscellaneous expenses were $9,000. In addition, taxes for the year amounted to $287,400. Complete the following income statement for the firm.

**NEW ENGLAND DENTAL SUPPLY**
**INCOME STATEMENT**
**YEAR ENDING DECEMBER 31**

Gross Sales      _____

Returns      _____

Net Sales      _____

   Inventory, January 1    _____

   Cost of Goods
     Purchased    _____

   Freight    _____

   Total Cost of Goods Purchased    _____

   Total of Goods Available for Sale    _____

   Inventory, December 31    _____

Cost of Goods Sold    _____

Gross Profit    _____

   Expenses

    Salaries and Wages    _____

    Rent    _____

    Advertising    _____

    Utilities    _____

    Taxes on Inventory, Payroll    _____

    Miscellaneous Expenses    _____

      Total Expenses    _____

NET INCOME BEFORE TAXES    _____

   Income Taxes    _____

NET INCOME    _____

7. Kathy Gilmore owns her own small business consulting firm. She sells a service to her customers rather than goods, so that she has no inventory, no returns, no freight, and

no cost of goods purchased. Gross sales were $170,500, salaries and wages were $63,000, rent was $28,000, advertising was $12,000, utilities were $4,000, taxes on payroll were $3,800, and miscellaneous office expenses were $9,400. Complete the income statement for this firm given that income taxes were $6,800.

---

**KATHY GILMORE, CONSULTANT**
**INCOME STATEMENT**
**FOR THE YEAR ENDING DECEMBER 31**

| | | |
|---|---|---|
| Gross Sales | | _____ |
| Returns | | _____ |
| Net Sales | | _____ |
|   Inventory, January 1 | _____ | |
|   Cost of Goods | _____ | |
|     Purchased   _____ | | |
|   Freight   _____ | | |
|   Total Cost of Goods Purchased | _____ | |
|   Total of Goods Available for Sale | _____ | |
|   Inventory, December 31 | _____ | |
| Cost of Goods Sold | | _____ |
| Gross Profit | | _____ |
|   Expenses | | |
|     Salaries and Wages | _____ | |
|     Rent | _____ | |
|     Advertising | _____ | |
|     Utilities | _____ | |
|     Taxes on Inventory, Payroll | _____ | |
|     Miscellaneous Expenses | _____ | |
|       Total Expenses | | _____ |
| NET INCOME BEFORE TAXES | | _____ |
|   Income Taxes | | _____ |
| NET INCOME | | _____ |

  **8.** What are the different factors that control gross profit? Is it important for management to continue to watch their gross profit? Why? (See Objective 1.)

  **9.** Were you aware that The Coca-Cola Company paid over $1.3 billion in taxes in 1995? Obtain the financial statement of another large, publicly held company from your library or over the internet and find the income taxes that they have been paying.

**10.** Name several companies for which returns might not be insignificant as was the situation with The Coca-Cola Company.

**11.** Explain why a lender might like to see an income statement before making a loan. (See Objective 1.)

**12.** (a) Discuss the purpose of an income statement.
    (b) Outline the basic structure of an income statement. (See Objective 2.)

## 17.2   Analyzing the Income Statement

**OBJECTIVES**

  **1**   *Compare income statements using vertical analysis.*

  **2**   *Calculate percents of net sales.*

  **3**   *Compare an income statement with published charts.*

  **4**   *Prepare a horizontal analysis.*

By going through the steps presented in the previous section, a firm can find its net income for a given period of time. A question which might be asked is, "What happened to each part of the sales dollar?" The first step toward answering this question is to *list each of the important items* on the income statement as a percent of net sales, in a process called a **vertical analysis** of the income statement.

**OBJECTIVE** **1**   *Compare income statements using vertical analysis.*      A vertical analysis of an income statement is another application of the fundamental formula for percent from Chapter 3, $P = RB$. Since a percent is needed, the formula must be solved for the rate $R$, as in the next box.

In a vertical analysis, each item is found as a percent of net sales.

$$\left(R = \frac{P}{B}\right) \quad \text{or} \quad \left(R = \frac{\text{Particular item}}{\text{Net sales}}\right)$$

A comparison of the results for two different years can be made by calculating a vertical analysis for both years. This results in a **comparative income statement**.

**EXAMPLE 1**   *Performing a Vertical Analysis*

First perform a vertical analysis of the summary 1994 and 1995 income statements shown below for The Coca-Cola Company. Then construct a comparative income statement by showing the results in a table.

**The Coca-Cola Company and Subsidiaries**
**Consolidated Statements of Income (millions of dollars)**

| Year Ended December 31, | 1995 | 1994 |
|---|---|---|
| Gross Sales | $18,018 | $16,181 |
| Returns | − 0 | − 0 |
| Net Sales | $18,018 | $16,181 |
| Cost of Goods Sold | − 6,940 | − 6,168 |
| Gross Profit | $11,078 | $10,013 |
| Operating Expenses | − 6,750 | − 6,285 |
| Net Income before Taxes | $ 4,328 | $ 3,728 |
| Income Taxes | − 1,342 | − 1,174 |
| Net Income | $ 2,986 | $ 2,554 |

**SOLUTION**    Calculate each value in the column labeled 1995 as a percent of 1995 net sales. Also calculate each value in the column labeled 1994 as a percent of 1994 net sales, and round both to the nearest tenth of a percent.

**Comparative Income Statement**

| | 1995 | 1994 |
|---|---|---|
| Percent cost of goods sold | $\frac{\$6,940}{\$18,018} = 38.5\%$ | $\frac{\$6,168}{\$16,181} = 38.1\%$ |
| Percent gross profit | $\frac{\$11,078}{\$18,018} = 61.5\%$ | $\frac{\$10,013}{\$16,181} = 61.9\%$ |
| Percent operating expenses | $\frac{\$6,750}{\$18,018} = 37.5\%$ | $\frac{\$6,285}{\$16,181} = 38.8\%$ |
| Percent net income before taxes | $\frac{\$4,328}{\$18,018} = 24.0\%$ | $\frac{\$3,728}{\$16,181} = 23.0\%$ |
| Percent income taxes | $\frac{\$1,342}{\$18,018} = 7.4\%$ | $\frac{\$1,174}{\$16,181} = 7.3\%$ |
| Percent net income after taxes | $\frac{\$2,986}{\$18,018} = 16.6\%$ | $\frac{\$2,554}{\$16,181} = 15.8\%$ |

Note that the cost of goods sold increased slightly from 38.1% of net sales in 1994 to 38.5% in 1995. This is *not a good sign* since it suggests that the company may be facing increasing costs. However, they were able to decrease operating expenses from 38.8% of net sales in 1994 to 37.5% of net sales in 1995. As a result, net income after taxes increased from 15.8% of net sales in 1994 to 16.6% of net sales in 1995. In summary, The Coca-Cola Company was able to decrease expenses more than enough to overcome the slight increase in the cost of goods sold. As an investor, you might want to watch the cost of goods sold percent to see if it continues to grow in subsequent years.

**OBJECTIVE 2** *Calculate percents of net sales.*     The formula given in the previous section for checking income statements,

Cost of         Operating
goods sold + expenses + Income taxes + Net income after taxes = Net sales

is just as valid for percents as for dollar amounts. Use the information from Example 1 to verify that this is true for 1995 data. Notice that net sales equals gross sales for The Coca-Cola Company since they have no returns.

$$38.5\% + 37.5\% + 7.4\% + 16.6\% = 100\%$$

These figures may not always add to 100% due to rounding.

The next example shows how to calculate these percents when there are returns.

**EXAMPLE 2** *Finding Percents of Net Sales*

Write each of the following items as a percent of net sales. The salaries and wages for this firm are low because it is a small business and the owner currently is not taking any income out of the business.

| | | | |
|---|---|---|---|
| Gross sales | $209,000 | Salaries and wages | $11,000 |
| Returns | $9,000 | Rent | $6,000 |
| Cost of goods sold | $145,000 | Advertising | $11,000 |

**SOLUTION**    Use the formula for net sales, with gross sales = $209,000 and returns = $9,000.

$$\text{Net sales} = \text{Gross sales} - \text{Returns}$$
$$\text{Net sales} = \$209,000 - \$9,000 = \$200,000$$

Now find all the desired percents.

$$\text{Percent gross sales} = \frac{\$209,000}{\$200,000} = 104.5\%$$

**NOTE**  This percent is more than 100% because returns are included in it, but not in net sales.  ■

$$\text{Percent returns} = \frac{\$9,000}{\$200,000} = 4.5\%$$

$$\text{Percent cost of goods sold} = \frac{\$145,000}{\$200,000} = 72.5\%$$

$$\text{Percent salaries and wages} = \frac{\$11,000}{\$200,000} = 5.5\%$$

$$\text{Percent rent} = \frac{\$6,000}{\$200,000} = 3\%$$

$$\text{Percent advertising} = \frac{\$11,000}{\$200,000} = 5.5\%$$   ∎

**OBJECTIVE** **3** *Compare an income statement with published charts.*      Once the percent of net sales for each item on the income statement has been found, they can be compared to the percents for similar businesses. To do this, consult published charts which have the required data. One such chart is shown in Table 17.1. These charts are compiled by averaging statistics from many similar firms.

**EXAMPLE 3** *Compare Business Ratios*

Gina Burton wishes to compare the business ratios of her shoe store to industry averages. Figures from her store and industry averages for shoe stores are shown

TABLE 17.1   **Typical Percents**

| Type of Business | Cost of Goods | Gross Profit | Total Operating Expenses* | Net Income | Wages | Rent | Advertising |
|---|---|---|---|---|---|---|---|
| Supermarkets | 82.7% | 17.3% | 13.9% | 3.4% | 6.5% | 0.8% | 1.0% |
| Men's and women's apparel | 67.0% | 33.0% | 21.2% | 11.8% | 8.0% | 2.5% | 1.9% |
| Women's apparel | 64.8% | 35.2% | 23.4% | 11.7% | 7.9% | 4.9% | 1.8% |
| Shoes | 60.3% | 39.7% | 24.5% | 15.2% | 10.3% | 4.7% | 1.6% |
| Furniture | 68.9% | 31.2% | 21.7% | 9.6% | 9.5% | 1.8% | 2.5% |
| Appliances | 66.9% | 33.1% | 26.0% | 7.2% | 11.9% | 2.4% | 2.5% |
| Drugs | 67.9% | 32.1% | 23.5% | 8.6% | 12.3% | 2.4% | 1.4% |
| Restaurants | 48.4% | 51.6% | 43.7% | 7.9% | 26.4% | 2.8% | 1.4% |
| Service station | 76.8% | 23.2% | 16.9% | 6.3% | 8.5% | 2.3% | 0.5% |

*This column represents the total of all expenses involved in running the firm. Total operating expenses include, but are not limited to, wages, rent, and advertising.

below. Burton sees that her expenses are higher and her net income is lower than the industry averages. What might Ms. Burton do to decrease total expenses and increase net income?

|  | Cost of Goods | Gross Profit | Total Expense | Net Income | Wages | Rent | Advertising |
|---|---|---|---|---|---|---|---|
| **Burton's Shoes** | 58.2% | 41.8% | 28.3% | 13.5% | 11.7% | 5.6% | 2.8% |
| **Shoes (from chart)** | 60.3% | 39.7% | 24.5% | 15.2% | 10.3% | 4.7% | 1.6% |

**SOLUTION**    Burton's wages, rent, and advertising all seem to be above the averages. If she can decrease any of these, or increase total sales without increasing any of these, then her net income will improve. Perhaps she can reschedule some employees to reduce overtime or shift more work to lower wage employees. It may be that she can try to renegotiate her rent with her landlord, or purchase her own building and move the store. Perhaps she can get the same advertising exposure by changing her advertising strategy to one that costs less.

On the other hand, her store may never compare favorably with national averages. That is fine as long as she makes an adequate profit.    ■

**OBJECTIVE** **4** *Prepare a horizontal analysis.*    Another way to analyze an income statement is to prepare a **horizontal analysis**. A horizontal analysis finds percents of change (either increases or decreases) between the current time period *and a previous time period*. This comparison can expose *unusual changes* such as a rapid increase in expenses or decline in net sales or profits.

A horizontal analysis is done by finding the amount of any change from the previous year to the current year, both in dollars and as a percent. For example, the income statement for The Coca-Cola Company given earlier shows that net operating revenues increased from $16,181 (in millions) in 1994 to $18,018 (in millions) in 1995, an increase of $18,018 − $16,181 = $1,837 (in millions). Find the percent of increase by comparing the increase to 1994 sales.

$$\frac{\$1,837}{\$16,181} = 11.4\% \text{ (rounded)}$$

$$\text{Percent of change} = \frac{\text{Change}}{\text{Last year's amount}}$$

Always use last year as the base.

| EXAMPLE 4 *Performing a Horizontal Analysis*

Perform a horizontal analysis for the 1994 and 1995 income statements for The Coca-Cola Company shown in Example 1.

SOLUTION   Find the increase by subtracting the 1994 figure from the 1995 figure, then divide by the 1994 figure to find the percent increase and finally round to the nearest tenth of a percent.

**The Coca-Cola Company and Subsidiaries**
**Consolidated Statements of Income (millions of dollars)**

| Year Ending December 31, | 1995 | 1994 | Increase | Percent |
|---|---|---|---|---|
| Net sales | $18,018 | $16,181 | $1,837 | 11.4% |
| Gross profit | 11,078 | 10,013 | 1,065 | 10.6% |
| Net income before taxes | 4,328 | 3,728 | 600 | 16.1% |
| Net income after taxes | 2,986 | 2,554 | 432 | 16.9% |

Net sales increased by 11.4% from 1994 to 1995 which appears to be a potentially sustainable growth rate. A large growth rate probably cannot be maintained and a small growth rate suggests that the company's profits may never increase much above current levels. The Coca-Cola Company hopes to maintain a good growth rate of sales into the future:

1. by encouraging existing customers to consume more of their products, and
2. by finding new customers for their products in international markets such as China and Russia.

Growth in sales alone is not a complete indicator of the health of a firm—profits must also be examined. Notice that income after taxes increased 16.9% from 1994 to 1995 which is roughly in line with the 11.4% growth in net sales. It would appear that their strong increase in profits is coming from reduced expenses in addition to increased sales. Overall, the company seems to have done very well during 1994 and 1995. However, this is no guarantee that they will continue to do well in the future. ■

NOTE   Parentheses around a number means it is a negative number. For example, a net income of ($48,000) means the company lost $48,000. ■

## 17.2  EXERCISES

*Prepare a vertical analysis for each of the following firms. Round percents to the nearest tenth of a percent.*

1.  Last year, Toy Trains Incorporated had a cost of goods sold of $178,682, operating expenses of $96,104, and net sales of $312,240.

2.  Traver's Coin Shop, Inc. had net sales of $294,380, a cost of goods sold of $163,890, and operating expenses of $68,650.

*The following charts show some figures from the income statements of several companies. In each case, prepare a vertical analysis by expressing each item as a percent of net sales. Then write in the appropriate average percent from the table in the book.*

3.  **Capital Appliance Center**

|  | Amount | Percent | Percent from Table 17.1 |
|---|---|---|---|
| Net Sales | $900,000 | 100.0% | 100.0% |
| Cost of Goods Sold | 617,000 | _____ | _____ |
| Gross Profit | 283,000 | _____ | _____ |
| Wages | 108,900 | _____ | _____ |
| Rent | 20,700 | _____ | _____ |
| Advertising | 27,000 | _____ | _____ |
| Total Expenses | 216,000 | _____ | _____ |
| Net Income before Taxes | 67,000 | _____ | _____ |

4.  **Ellis Restaurant**

|  | Amount | Percent | Percent from Table 17.1 |
|---|---|---|---|
| Net Sales | $600,000 | 100.0% | 100.0% |
| Cost of Goods Sold | 280,000 | _____ | _____ |
| Gross Profit | 320,000 | _____ | _____ |
| Wages | 160,000 | _____ | _____ |
| Rent | 15,000 | _____ | _____ |
| Advertising | 8,000 | _____ | _____ |
| Total Expenses | 255,000 | _____ | _____ |
| Net Income before Taxes | 65,000 | _____ | _____ |

*Complete the following comparative income statement. Round percents to the nearest tenth of a percent.*

5.  **Best Tires, Inc.**
    **Comparative Income Statement**

|  | This Year | | Last Year | |
|---|---|---|---|---|
|  | **Amount** | **Percent** | **Amount** | **Percent** |
| Gross Sales | $1,856,000 | ——— | $1,692,000 | ——— |
| Returns | 6,000 | ——— | 12,000 | ——— |
| Net Sales | ——— | 100.0% | ——— | 100.0% |
| Cost of Goods Sold | 1,202,000 | ——— | 1,050,000 | ——— |
| Gross Profit | 648,000 | ——— | 630,000 | ——— |
| Wages | 152,000 | ——— | 148,000 | ——— |
| Rent | 82,000 | ——— | 78,000 | ——— |
| Advertising | 111,000 | ——— | 122,000 | ——— |
| Utilities | 32,000 | ——— | 17,000 | ——— |
| Taxes on Inv., Payroll | 17,000 | ——— | 18,000 | ——— |
| Miscellaneous Expenses | 62,000 | ——— | 58,000 | ——— |
| Total Expenses | 456,000 | ——— | 441,000 | ——— |
| Net Income | ——— | ——— | ——— | ——— |

*Complete the following horizontal analysis for Best Tires, Inc. comparative income statement given above. Round percents to the nearest tenth of a percent.*

6   **Best Tires, Inc.**
    **Comparative Income Statement**

|  |  |  | Increase or (Decrease) | |
|---|---|---|---|---|
|  | **This Year** | **Last Year** | **Amount** | **Percent** |
| Gross Sales | $1,856,000 | $1,692,000 | ——— | ——— |
| Returns | 6,000 | 12,000 | ——— | ——— |
| Net Sales | 1,850,000 | 1,680,000 | ——— | ——— |
| Cost of Goods Sold | 1,202,000 | 1,050,000 | ——— | ——— |
| Gross Profit | 648,000 | 630,000 | ——— | ——— |
| Wages | 152,000 | 148,000 | ——— | ——— |
| Rent | 82,000 | 78,000 | ——— | ——— |
| Advertising | 111,000 | 122,000 | ——— | ——— |
| Utilities | 32,000 | 17,000 | ——— | ——— |
| Taxes on Inv., Payroll | 17,000 | 18,000 | ——— | ——— |
| Miscellaneous Expenses | 62,000 | 58,000 | ——— | ——— |
| Net Income | 192,000 | 189,000 | ——— | ——— |

*The following tables give the percents for various items from the income statements of firms in various businesses. Complete these tables by including the appropriate percents from Table 17.1. Identify any areas that might require attention by management. Also list suggestions for improving any problem area.*

| Type of Store | Cost of Goods | Gross Profit | Total Operating Expenses | Net Income | Wages | Rent | Advertising |
|---|---|---|---|---|---|---|---|
| 7. Supermarkets | 84.5% | 15.5% | 14.4% | 1.1% | 6.4% | 2.1% | 0.9% |
| | | | | | | | |
| 8. Shoes | 60.5% | 39.5% | 24.3% | 15.2% | 10.4% | 4.8% | 1.5% |
| | | | | | | | |
| 9. Appliances | 66.4% | 33.6% | 28.9% | 4.7% | 14.0% | 2.3% | 2.6% |
| | | | | | | | |
| 10. Restaurant | 57.8% | 42.2% | 38.6% | 3.6% | 28.1% | 2.4% | 1.0% |
| | | | | | | | |

11. Compare a vertical analysis to a horizontal analysis. What are the strengths of each? (See Objectives 1 and 4.)

12. Explain the purpose of comparing percent of net sales on an income statement to percents for similar businesses. (See Objective 2.)

13. The average net income before taxes for supermarkets is 3.4%. Go to the supermarket where you normally shop and list 10 items that you normally buy and the price of each. Total these and find 3.4% of this total. Approximately what is the net income for the store for selling these 10 items?

14. When would you use a horizontal analysis and when would you use a vertical analysis?

## 17.3     The Balance Sheet

**OBJECTIVES**

**1**   *Identify the terms used with balance sheets.*

**2**   *Prepare a balance sheet.*

**3**   *Look at the balance sheet of The Coca-Cola Company*

An income statement summarizes the financial affairs of a business firm for a given period of time, such as a year. On the other hand, a **balance sheet** describes the financial condition of a firm *at one point in time*, such as the last day of a year. A balance sheet shows the worth of a business at a particular time by listing its **assets** which are the things it owns, such as property, equipment, and money owed to the business, as well as its **liabilities** which are amounts owed by the business to others. The difference of these two amounts gives the **owner's equity** in the business.

OBJECTIVE **1** *Identify the terms used with balance sheets.*    Both assets and liabilities are divided into two categories, **long-term** and **current (short-term)**. Long-term generally applies when the time involved is more than one year, whereas short term applies when the time involved is less than one year. The following items appear as assets on balance sheets.

*ASSETS:*
**Current assets**—cash or items that can be converted into cash within a short period of time such as a year

*Cash*—cash in checking and savings accounts

*Marketable securities*—stocks, bonds, and other securities that can quickly be converted to cash

*Accounts receivable*—funds owned by customers of the firm

*Notes receivable*—value of all notes owed to the firm

*Inventory*—cost of merchandise that the firm has for sale

**Plant and equipment**—assets that are expected to be used for more than one year (also called **fixed assets** or **plant assets**)

*Land*—book value of any land owned by the firm

*Buildings*—book value of any building owned by the firm

*Equipment*—book value of equipment, store fixtures, furniture, and similar items owned by the firm

The following items, which must be paid by the firm, appear as liabilities on balance sheets.

*LIABILITIES:*
**Current liabilities**—items that must be paid by the firm within a short period of time, usually one year

*Accounts payable*—amounts that must be paid to other firms

*Notes payable*—value of all notes owed by the firm

**Long-term liabilities**—items that will be paid after one year

*Mortgages payable*—total due on all mortgages

*Long-term notes payable*—total of all other debts of the firm

The difference between the total of all assets and the total of all liabilities is called the **owner's equity** in the firm. That is

$$\text{Owner's equity} = \text{Assets} - \text{Liabilities.}$$

Owner's equity is also called **proprietorship**, **net worth**, or, for a corporation, **stockholder's equity**. The formula for owner's equity is equivalent to the following *fundamental formula for accounting.*

$$\text{Assets} = \text{Liabilities} + \text{Owner's equity}$$

The fundamental formula for accounting makes intuitive sense. Your net worth is the value of all of your assets minus your debts.

**OBJECTIVE** **2** *Prepare a balance sheet.*    Now that all the terms have been defined, a balance sheet can be prepared.

| EXAMPLE 1 *Preparing a Balance Sheet*

The Farmersville Market lists its current cash assets as $8,000. Notes receivable total $11,000, accounts receivable total $15,000, and inventory is $51,000. Plant assets include land worth $24,000, buildings worth $22,000, and fixtures worth $18,000. Current liabilities include notes payable, which are $8,000, and accounts payable, which are $26,000. Mortgages total $39,000 and long-term notes payable total $24,000. Owner's equity is $52,000. Complete a balance sheet for the market, and use the fundamental formula for accounting to find owner's equity.

**SOLUTION**    To prepare a balance sheet, go through the following steps. Refer to the balance sheet in Figure 17.2.

### PREPARING A BALANCE SHEET

*Step 1.* Enter all current assets. On the balance sheet cash is $8,000, notes receivable are $11,000, accounts receivable are $15,000, and inventory is $51,000.

*Step 2.* Add the current assets. The total in the example is $85,000.

*Step 3.* Enter all plant assets. In the example, land is $24,000, buildings are $22,000, and fixtures are $18,000.

*Step 4.* Add the plant assets of step 3. In the example, the total is $64,000.

*Step 5.* Add the results from steps 2 and 4. This gives the total value of all assets owned by the firm. Total assets in the example are $149,000.

**FARMERSVILLE MARKET**
**BALANCE SHEET**
**FOR DECEMBER 31**

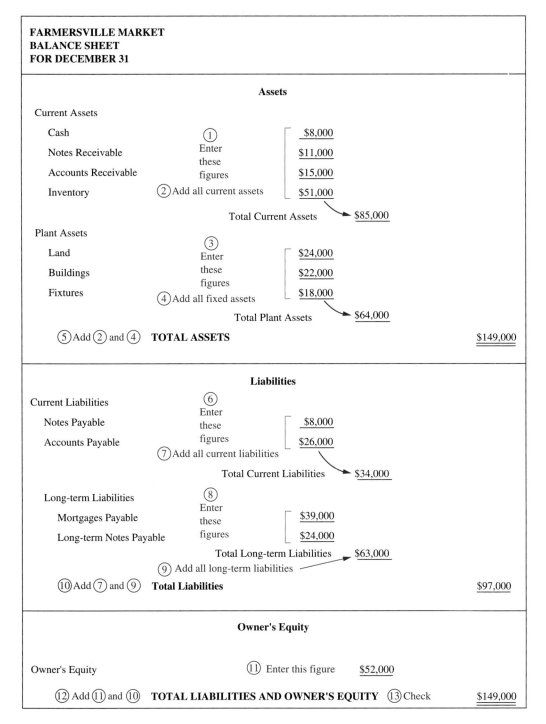

FIGURE 17.2

***Step 6.*** Enter all current liabilities. In the example, notes payable are $8,000 and accounts payable are $26,000.

***Step 7.*** Add all current liabilities. The sum in the example is $34,000.

***Step 8.*** Enter long-term liabilities. In the example, mortgages total $39,000, and long-term notes payable total $24,000.

***Step 9.*** Add all long-term liabilities. The sum in the example is $63,000.

***Step 10.*** Add the results of steps 7 and 9. This gives the total of all liabilities owed by the firm. The total liabilities in the example is $97,000.

***Step 11.*** Enter owner's equity. In the example, owner's equity is $52,000.

***Step 12.*** Add owner's equity to total liabilities. The total in the example is $97,000 + $52,000 = $149,000.

***Step 13.*** Use the fundamental formula of accounting:

$$\text{Assets} = \text{Liabilities} + \text{Owner's equity.}$$

In the example, assets = $149,000, liabilities = $97,000, and owner's equity = $52,000. To check, see that

$$\$149,000 = \$97,000 + \$52,000,$$

which is correct.    ∎

**PROBLEM-SOLVING HINT**    Always make sure that total assets equal *total liabilities plus owner's equity.*    ∎

**OBJECTIVE** **3** *Look at the balance sheet of The Coca-Cola Company.*

| **EXAMPLE 2** *Preparing a Balance Sheet*

The assets and liabilities of The Coca-Cola Company on December 31, 1995 follow (all figures are in millions of dollars): cash and marketable securities ($1,315), accounts receivable ($1,750), inventories ($1,117), other current assets ($1,268), subsidiaries and other assets ($4,311), land and buildings ($2,177), other assets ($3,103), accounts payable ($2,894), loans and notes payable ($2,371), other payables ($552), accrued taxes ($1,531), long-term debt ($1,141), and other liabilities ($1,160). Complete a balance sheet for The Coca-Cola Company. Recall that stockholder's equity = total assets − total liabilities.

**SOLUTION**

**Consolidated Balance Sheet**
**The Coca-Cola Company and Subsidiaries**
**December 31, 1995 (in millions of dollars)**

**Current Assets:**

| | | |
|---|---|---|
| Cash and marketable securities | $1,315 | |
| Accounts receivable | 1,750 | |
| Inventories | 1,117 | |
| Other current assets | 1,268 | |
| Total Current Assets | $5,450 | sum of all current assets |

**Other Assets:**

| | | |
|---|---|---|
| Subsidiaries and other assets | $4,311 | |
| Land and buildings | 2,177 | |
| Other assets | 3,103 | |
| Total Assets | $15,041 | sum of current assets plus all other assets |

**Current Liabilities:**

| | | |
|---|---|---|
| Accounts payable | $2,894 | |
| Loans and notes payable | 2,371 | |
| Other payables | 552 | |
| Accrued taxes | 1,531 | |
| Total Current Liabilities | $7,348 | sum of all current liabilities |

**Other Liabilities:**

| | | |
|---|---|---|
| Long-term debt | $1,141 | |
| Other liabilities | 1,160 | |
| Total Liabilities | $9,649 | sum of current liabilities plus all other liabilities |

| | | |
|---|---|---|
| **Stockholder's Equity** | **$5,392** | **Total Assets − Total Liabilities** |
| Total Liabilities & Equity | $15,041 | |

**NOTE** The sum of the liabilities and the stockholder's equity *must* equal the assets. ■

A balance sheet shows the position of a company at one point in time. The figures could be very different a week or a month later. For example, The Coca-Cola Company and Subsidiaries had approximately $1,315,000,000 in cash and marketable securities on December 31, 1995. This balance sheet does not provide any information about cash and marketable securities held on any date other than the specific day indicated above.

## 17.3 EXERCISES

*Complete the corresponding balance sheets for the following business firms.*

1. Palmer Electric has mortgages totaling $65,000. Its notes receivable are $28,000; land is $42,000; notes payable total $52,000; accounts payable total $42,000; buildings are

worth $35,000; cash is $21,000; inventory is $54,000; long-term notes payable are $9,000; fixtures are $9,000; and accounts receivable are $36,000. Use the fundamental formula of accounting to find owner's equity.

---

**PALMER ELECTRIC**
**BALANCE SHEET FOR DECEMBER 31**

|  | **Assets** |  |
|---|---|---|
| Current Assets |  |  |
| Cash | _____ |  |
| Notes Receivable | _____ |  |
| Accounts Receivable | _____ |  |
| Inventory | _____ |  |
| Total Current Assets |  | _____ |
| Plant Assets |  |  |
| Land | _____ |  |
| Buildings | _____ |  |
| Fixtures | _____ |  |
| Total Plant Assets |  | _____ |
| **TOTAL ASSETS** |  | _____ |

|  | **Liabilities** |  |
|---|---|---|
| Current Liabilities |  |  |
| Notes Payable | _____ |  |
| Accounts Payable | _____ |  |
| Total Current Liabilities |  | _____ |
| Long-term Liabilities |  |  |
| Mortgages Payable | _____ |  |
| Long-term Notes Payable | _____ |  |
| Total Long-term Liabilities |  | _____ |
| **Total Liabilities** |  | _____ |

|  | **Owner's Equity** |  |
|---|---|---|
| Owner's Equity | _____ |  |
| **TOTAL LIABILITIES AND OWNER'S EQUITY** |  | _____ |

---

**2.** A-1 Fence Company has land valued at $8,750. Its accounts payable total $49,230; notes receivable are $2,600; accounts receivable are $37,820; cash is $14,800; buildings are $21,930; notes payable are $3,780; long-term notes payable total $18,740;

mortgages total $26,330; inventory is $49,680; and fixtures are $16,820. Use the fundamental formula of accounting to find owner's equity.

---

**A-1 FENCE COMPANY**
**BALANCE SHEET FOR DECEMBER 31**

Assets

Current Assets

  Cash         _____

  Notes Receivable     _____

  Accounts Receivable   _____

  Inventory       _____

        Total Current Assets   _____

Plant Assets

  Land         _____

  Buildings       _____

  Fixtures       _____

        Total Plant Assets   _____

      **TOTAL ASSETS**   _____

Liabilities

Current Liabilities

  Notes Payable     _____

  Accounts Payable     _____

      Total Current Liabilities   _____

Long-term Liabilities

  Mortgages Payable   _____

  Long-term Notes Payable   _____

      Total Long-term Liabilities   _____

    **Total Liabilities**   _____

Owner's Equity

Owner's Equity   _____

  **TOTAL LIABILITIES AND OWNER'S EQUITY**   _____

---

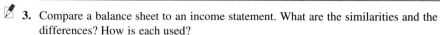 **3.** Compare a balance sheet to an income statement. What are the similarities and the differences? How is each used?

✎ **4.** Explain how the fundamental formula for accounting is used to check a balance sheet.
(See Objective 1.)

✎ **5.** Prepare a balance sheet for your own family or for your parents.

✎ **6.** Name several reasons The Coca-Cola Company might have to justify maintaining a
large amount of cash and marketable securities.

## 17.4   Analyzing the Balance Sheet; Financial Ratios

**OBJECTIVES**

**1**  *Compare balance sheets by vertical analysis.*

**2**  *Prepare a horizontal analysis.*

**3**  *Find the current ratio.*

**4**  *Find the acid-test ratio.*

**5**  *Find the ratio of net income after taxes to average owner's equity.*

**6**  *Find the accounts receivable turnover.*

**7**  *Find the average age of accounts receivable.*

**8**  *Find the debt-to-equity ratio.*

**OBJECTIVE 1** *Compare balance sheets by vertical analysis.*     A balance sheet can be analyzed in much the same way as an income statement. In a **vertical analysis**, each
item on the balance sheet is expressed as a percent of total assets. A **comparative
balance sheet** shows the vertical analysis for two different years. You may want to
look at a firm's comparative balance sheet before buying their stock or before accepting a job offer.

**EXAMPLE 1** *Comparing Balance Sheets*

First do a vertical analysis for both the 1994 and 1995 balance sheets for The Coca-
Cola Company by calculating each value as a percent of the total assets for the year.
Then compare the percents to identify changes from 1994 to 1995.

**SOLUTION**

**Comparative Analysis of Consolidated Balance Sheets
The Coca-Cola Company and Subsidiaries (in millions of dollars)**

| December 31, Assets | 1995 | | 1994 | |
|---|---|---|---|---|
| | Amount | Percent | Amount | Percent |
| **Current Assets:** | | | | |
| Cash and marketable securities | $1,315 | 8.7% | $1,531 | 11.0% |
| Accounts receivable | 1,750 | 11.6% | 1,525 | 11.0% |
| Inventories & other | 2,385 | 15.9% | 2,149 | 15.5% |
| Total Current Assets | $5,450 | 36.2% | $5,205 | 37.5% |

| December 31,<br>Assets | 1995 | | 1994 | |
|---|---|---|---|---|
| | Amount | Percent | Amount | Percent |
| **Property, Plant, and Equipment:** | | | | |
| Subsidiaries and other assets | $4,311 | 28.7% | $3,928 | 28.3% |
| Land and buildings | 2,177 | 14.5% | 2,035 | 14.7% |
| Other assets | 3,103 | 20.6% | 2,705 | 19.5% |
| Total Plant Assets | $9,591 | 63.8% | $8,668 | 62.5% |
| **TOTAL ASSETS** | $15,041 | 100.0% | $13,873 | 100.0% |
| **Liabilities** | Amount | Percent | Amount | Percent |
| **Current Liabilities:** | | | | |
| Accounts payable | $2,894 | 19.2% | $2,564 | 18.5% |
| Loans and notes payable | 2,371 | 15.8% | 2,048 | 14.8% |
| Other | 2,083 | 13.8% | 1,565 | 11.3% |
| Total Current Liabilities | $7,348 | 48.9% | $6,177 | 44.5% |
| **Other Liabilities** | | | | |
| Long-term debt | $1,141 | 7.6% | $1,426 | 10.3% |
| Other liabilities | 1,160 | 7.7% | 1,035 | 7.5% |
| Total Other Liabilities | $2,301 | 15.3% | $2,461 | 17.7% |
| **Stockholder's Equity** | $5,392 | 35.8% | $5,235 | 37.7% |
| **TOTAL LIABILITIES &<br>OWNER'S EQUITY** | $15,041 | 100.0% | $13,873 | 100.0% |

■

**NOTE**   Each value in the table above, including column subtotals, was divided by the respective value for total assets. Thus the amounts add up to the appropriate subtotal, which cannot be said for all of the percent figures.   ■

**PROBLEM-SOLVING HINT**   The tax year for The Coca-Cola Company ends on December 31. Other companies use tax years that end *on a different day of the year* such as April 30 or July 31.   ■

Most worrisome for the stock investor is the fact that current liabilities (liabilities that are expected to be paid within one year) *increased* from 44.5% of total assets in 1994 to 48.9% of total assets in 1995. This is a significant increase in short-term liabilities.

$7,348,000,000 − $6,177,000,000 = $1,171,000,000 increase in short-term debt

Although this is an important trend to watch, some relief can be found in the fact that *other liabilities decreased* from 17.7% of total assets in 1994 to 15.3% of total assets in 1995. It is also comforting to know that the company has $1,315,000,000 in cash and marketable securities suggesting that they can handle financial emergencies.

**OBJECTIVE** **2** *Prepare a horizontal analysis.*     Perform a **horizontal analysis** by finding the change, both in dollars and in percent, for each item on the balance sheet from one year to the next. As before, always use the *previous year* as a base when finding the percents.

| EXAMPLE 2  *Using Horizontal Analysis*

According to the balance sheet for The Coca-Cola Company, cash and marketable securities on December 31, 1995 was $1,315 (in millions) and $1,531 (in millions) on December 31, 1994. This represents a decrease in cash and marketable securities of $1,315 − $1,531 = ($216) in millions of dollars. The parentheses around the figure indicates that it is a negative number. The percent decrease is

$$\frac{(\$216)}{\$1,531} = (14.1\%).$$

In a similar way, complete a horizontal analysis of the current assets portion of The Coca-Cola Company's balance sheet.

**SOLUTION**     Calculating percents to the nearest tenth of a percent produces the following.

**Comparative Analysis of Consolidated Balance Sheets**
**The Coca-Cola Company and Subsidiaries (in millions of dollars)**

| | | | Increase or Decrease | |
|---|---|---|---|---|
| **Current Assets—December 31,** | **Amount 1995** | **Amount 1994** | **Amount** | **Percent** |
| **Cash and marketable securities** | $1,315 | $1,531 | ($216) | (14.1%) |
| **Accounts receivable** | 1,750 | 1,525 | 225 | 14.8% |
| **Inventories & other** | 2,385 | 2,149 | 236 | 11.0% |
| **Total Current Assets** | $5,450 | $5,205 | $245 | 4.7% |

Notice how clearly this shows the significant 14.1% decrease in cash and marketable securities in 1995 over 1994. ■

**OBJECTIVE** **3** *Find the current ratio.*     The **current ratio**, also known as **banker's ratio**, is found by dividing current assets by current liabilities.

$$\text{Current ratio} = \frac{\text{Current assets}}{\text{Current liabilities}}$$

| EXAMPLE 3  *Finding the Current Ratio*

According to the 1995 balance sheet for The Coca-Cola Company, current assets were $5,450 (in millions) and current liabilities were $7,348 (in millions). Find the current ratio.

**SOLUTION** Use the formula for current ratio.

$$\text{Current ratio} = \frac{\$5,450}{\$7,348} = 0.74$$

This ratio is often expressed as 0.74 to 1 or as 0.74:1. A common rule of thumb, not necessarily applicable to all businesses or at all times, is that the current ratio should be at least 2:1. A firm with a current ratio much less than 2:1 may have an increased risk of financial difficulty and may have difficulty borrowing money. This rule of thumb does not apply to The Coca-Cola Company since they are able to turn over their inventory so rapidly during the year. ■

One disadvantage of the current ratio is that inventory is included in current assets. In a period of financial difficulty, a firm might have trouble disposing of the inventory at a reasonable price. Some accountants feel that the "acid test" for a firm's financial health is to consider only **liquid assets**: assets that are either cash or that can be converted to cash quickly, such as securities and accounts and notes receivable.

**OBJECTIVE 4** *Find the acid-test ratio.* The **acid-test ratio**, also called the **quick ratio**, is defined as follows.

$$\text{Acid-test ratio} = \frac{\text{Liquid assets}}{\text{Current liabilities}}$$

**EXAMPLE 4** *Finding the Acid-Test Ratio*

Find the 1995 acid-test ratio for The Coca-Cola Company.

**SOLUTION** Liquid assets are made up of cash and marketable securities in addition to accounts receivables. Using data from the 1995 balance sheet:

Liquid assets = $1,315 + $1,750 = $3,065 (in millions).

Since current liabilities are $7,348, the acid-test ratio is

$$\frac{\$3,065}{\$7,348} = 0.42.$$

■

**NOTE** As a general rule, the acid-test ratio should be at least 1 to 1, with the idea that liquid assets are at least enough to cover current liabilities. Again, the rule of thumb does not apply to The Coca-Cola Company since they can turn their inventory over so rapidly during the year. ■

**OBJECTIVE** **5** *Find the ratio of net income after taxes to average owner's equity.* A company with a large amount of capital invested should have a higher net income than a company that has only a relatively small amount invested. To check on this, accountants often find the **ratio of net income after taxes to average owner's equity**. The average owner's equity is found by adding the owner's equity at the beginning and end of the year and dividing by 2.

$$\frac{\text{Average}}{\text{owner's equity}} = \frac{\text{Owner's equity at beginning} + \text{Owner's equity at end}}{2}$$

Then the ratio of net income after taxes to average owner's equity is found as follows.

$$\frac{\text{Ratio of net income}}{\text{after taxes to average}} = \frac{\text{Net income after taxes}}{\text{Average owner's equity}}$$

**NOTE** The ratio of net income after taxes to average owner's equity is also called "return on equity." ∎

**EXAMPLE 5** *Finding the Return on Average Equity*

Find the 1995 ratio of net income after taxes to average owner's equity for The Coca-Cola Company.

**SOLUTION** At the end of 1994 which is the same as the beginning of 1995, the firm had a stockholder's equity of $5,235 (in millions) and at the end of 1995 the stockholder's equity was $5,392 (in millions). The average owner's equity was

$$\frac{\$5,392 + \$5,235}{2} = \$5,313.5 \text{ (in millions)}.$$

Use of the net income after taxes for 1995 results in the following ratio of net income after taxes found on page 622 to average owner's equity.

$$\frac{\$2,986}{\$5,313.5} = 0.56$$

This ratio should be at least as much as the interest paid on savings accounts by banks. Otherwise the capital represented by these assets should be deposited in a bank account. After all, savings accounts of up to $100,000 are guaranteed by the federal government, while business profits are not. Increased risk should bring a higher return than that of risk-free savings accounts. Notice that this ratio for The Coca-Cola Company (56%) is considerably higher than savings account yields. ∎

**OBJECTIVE** **6** *Find the accounts receivable turnover.*    The accounts receivable of a firm represent credit sales—goods sold on credit and later billed to the customer. The **accounts receivable turnover** is an indication of how fast the firm is collecting its bills. If this ratio *starts to decline*, then the firm may well need to *be more aggressive* in collecting its receivables from customers. By collecting receivables promptly, the firm will need to borrow less money, thus cutting its interest charges.

To find the accounts receivable turnover ratio, first find the average accounts receivable.

$$\text{Average accounts receivable} =$$
$$\frac{\text{Accounts receivable at beginning} + \text{Accounts receivable at end}}{2}$$

Then,

$$\text{Accounts receivable turnover} = \frac{\text{Net sales}}{\text{Average accounts receivable}}$$

**EXAMPLE 6** *Finding the Accounts Receivable Turnover*

Find the accounts receivable turnover for The Coca-Cola Company for 1995.

**SOLUTION**    Accounts receivable at the end of 1994 were the same as those at the beginning of 1995 or $1,525. Accounts receivable at the end of 1995 were $1,750.

$$\text{Average accounts receivable} = \frac{\$1,525 + \$1,750}{2} = \$1,637.5 \text{ (in millions)}$$

From the income statement on page 622, net sales for 1995 were $18,018.

$$\text{Accounts receivable turnover} = \frac{\$18,018}{\$1,637.5} = 11$$

This ratio should be watched over time. If the ratio were to decline it could indicate some fundamental problems within the company.    ∎

**OBJECTIVE** **7** *Find the average age of accounts receivable.*    As mentioned, a firm must collect its accounts receivable promptly to minimize its own need to borrow money. To tell how well accounts are being collected, the firm can find the **average age of accounts receivable**, or the average number of days needed to collect its receivables. This is found by the formula

$$\text{Average age of accounts receivable} = \frac{365}{\text{Accounts receivable turnover}}$$

### EXAMPLE 7 *Finding the Average Age of Accounts Receivable*

Find the average age of accounts receivable for The Coca-Cola Company during 1995.

**SOLUTION** Divide 365 by the accounts receivable turnover found in Example 6.

$$\text{Average age of accounts receivable} = \frac{365}{11} = 33.2 \text{ days (rounded)}$$

Again, this ratio is one that should be watched over time. A decline in this ratio would suggest that the company is improving their collections of receivables. ■

**OBJECTIVE 8 *Find the debt-to-equity ratio.*** Companies borrow money to expand and take advantage of business opportunities. This is fine as long as total debt *does not* become excessive. One common measure used to see if debt is reasonable is the **debt-to-equity ratio** which is the ratio of all liabilities to all owner's equity.

$$\text{Debt-to-equity ratio} = \frac{\text{Current liabilities} + \text{Long-term liabilities}}{\text{Owner's equity}}$$

### EXAMPLE 8 *Finding the Debt-to-Equity Ratio*

Find the debt-to-equity ratio for The Coca-Cola Company at the end of 1995.

**SOLUTION** Divide the sum of the current liabilities and all other liabilities by the owner's equity.

$$\text{Debt-to-equity ratio} = \frac{\$7,348 + \$2,301}{\$5,392} = 1.8 \text{ or } 180\% \text{ (rounded)}$$

**NOTE** An acceptable level for debt-to-equity ratios varies drastically from industry to industry. For some, a ratio of 150% is reasonable, while for others a 25% ratio might make the firm's bankers nervous. Once again, this guideline does not apply to The Coca-Cola Company due to the amount of cash that the firm carries and the fact that their inventory is so **liquid** or quickly convertible to cash. ■

## 17.4  EXERCISES

*Complete the following.*

1. Complete the balance sheet for Grocery Warehouse. Round to the nearest tenth of a percent.

**GROCERY WAREHOUSE**
**COMPARATIVE BALANCE SHEET**

|  | Amount This Year | Percent This Year | Amount Last Year | Percent Last Year |
|---|---|---|---|---|
| **Assets** | | | | |
| Current Assets | | | | |
| Cash | $52,000 | _____ | $42,000 | _____ |
| Notes Receivable | $8,000 | _____ | $6,000 | _____ |
| Accounts Receivable | $148,000 | _____ | $120,000 | _____ |
| Inventory | $153,000 | _____ | $120,000 | _____ |
| Total Current Assets | _____ | _____ | _____ | _____ |
| | | | | |
| Plant Assets | | | | |
| Land | $10,000 | _____ | $8,000 | _____ |
| Buildings | $14,000 | _____ | $11,000 | _____ |
| Fixtures | $15,000 | _____ | $13,000 | _____ |
| Total Plant Assets | _____ | _____ | _____ | _____ |
| | | | | |
| TOTAL ASSETS | _____ | 100.0% | _____ | 100.0% |
| | | | | |
| **Liabilities** | | | | |
| | | | | |
| Current Liabilities | | | | |
| Accounts Payable | $3,000 | _____ | $4,000 | _____ |
| Notes Payable | $201,000 | _____ | $152,000 | _____ |
| Total Current Liabilities | _____ | _____ | _____ | _____ |
| | | | | |
| Long-term Liabilities | | | | |
| Mortgages Payable | $20,000 | _____ | $16,000 | _____ |
| Long-term Notes Payable | $58,000 | _____ | $42,000 | _____ |
| Total Long-term Liabilities | _____ | _____ | _____ | _____ |
| | | | | |
| Total Liabilities | _____ | _____ | _____ | _____ |
| | | | | |
| **Owner's Equity** | $118,000 | _____ | $106,000 | _____ |
| | | | | |
| TOTAL LIABILITIES AND OWNER'S EQUITY | _____ | _____ | _____ | _____ |

2. Complete the horizontal analysis for a portion of the balance sheet for Grocery Warehouse.

| GROCERY WAREHOUSE HORIZONTAL ANALYSIS | This Year | Last Year | Increase or (Decrease) Amount | Percent |
|---|---|---|---|---|
| **Assets** | | | | |
| Current Assets | | | | |
| Cash | $52,000 | $42,000 | _____ | _____ |
| Notes Receivable | $8,000 | $6,000 | _____ | _____ |
| Accounts Receivable | $148,000 | $120,000 | _____ | _____ |
| Inventory | $153,000 | $120,000 | _____ | _____ |
| Total Current Assets | $361,000 | $288,000 | _____ | _____ |
| Plant Assets | | | | |
| Land | $10,000 | $8,000 | _____ | _____ |
| Buildings | $14,000 | $11,000 | _____ | _____ |
| Fixtures | $15,000 | $13,000 | _____ | _____ |
| Total Plant Assets | $39,000 | $32,000 | _____ | _____ |
| TOTAL ASSETS | $400,000 | $320,000 | _____ | _____ |

*In Exercises 3–6, find the current ratio and the acid-test ratio. Round each ratio to the nearest hundredth.*

3. Grocery Warehouse, having the balance sheet on the previous page.

4. Kool Air Conditioning has current liabilities of $225,500; cash of $45,300; notes and accounts receivable total of $168,500; and inventory of $73,200.

5. Farm & Garden Implements has cash of $82,500; notes and accounts receivable total of $423,120; inventory of $268,300; and current liabilities of $360,020.

6. Best Music Shoppe has cash of $48,000; current liabilities total $72,500; notes and accounts receivable of $3,800; and inventory valued at $42,800.

*A portion of a comparative balance sheet is shown on the next page. First complete the chart, and then find the current ratio and the acid-test ratio for the indicated year. Round each ratio to the nearest hundredth.*

7. This year

8. Last year

|  | Amount This Year | Percent This Year | Amount Last Year | Percent Last Year |
|---|---|---|---|---|
| **Current assets** | | | | |
| Cash | $12,000 | _____ | $15,000 | _____ |
| Notes Receivable | 4,000 | _____ | 6,000 | _____ |
| Accounts Receivable | 22,000 | _____ | 18,000 | _____ |
| Inventory | 26,000 | _____ | 24,000 | _____ |
| **Total Current Assets** | 64,000 | 80.0% | 63,000 | 84.0% |
| **Total Plant and Equipment** | 16,000 | _____ | 12,000 | _____ |
| TOTAL ASSETS | _____ | 100.0% | _____ | 100.0% |
| **Total Current Liabilities** | $30,000 | _____ | $25,000 | _____ |

*Find the debt-to-equity ratio for each of the following firms. Round to the nearest hundredth.*

9. Grocery Warehouse from Exercises 1 and 3, for this year.

10. Kool Air Conditioning from Exercise 4; owner's equity of $140,000 and long-term liabilities of $123,500.

11. Farm & Garden Implements from Exercise 5; owner's equity of $420,000 and long-term debt of $325,000.

12. Best Music Shoppe from Exercise 6; owner's equity of $64,500 and long-term debt of $8,000.

13. Explain the different purposes of an income statement versus a balance sheet.

14. List three ratios that can be used to analyze a balance sheet and the purpose of each ratio.

*Find the ratio of net income after taxes to average owner's equity for the following firms. Round to the nearest tenth of a percent.*

15. The stockholders equity in TNA Airline, a small international airline that uses small airplanes to move freight to and from Mexico, is $845,000 at the beginning of the year and $928,500 at the end of the year. Net income after taxes for the year was $54,400.

16. TransCanada Pipe is an international company that does business both in Canada and in the United States. In thousands of dollars, owner's equity at the beginning of the year was $48,340 and $62,842 at the end of the year. Net income after taxes for the year was $6,838.

*Find the accounts receivable turnover rate and the average age of the accounts receivable for the following firms. Round each rate to the nearest tenth.*

17. Men's Factory Warehouse with accounts receivable at the beginning of the year of $320,000; accounts receivable at the end of the year $450,000; and net sales $6,500,000.

18. Plates and Plants Galore with accounts receivable at the beginning of the year of $110,000; accounts receivable at the end of the year $80,000; and net sales of $875,000.

19. Explain why the acid-test ratio is a better measure of the financial health of a firm than the current ratio. (See Objectives 3 and 4.)

20. Explain why increased risk requires a higher return on investment.

# Chapter 17 Quick Review

| TOPIC | APPROACH | EXAMPLE |
|---|---|---|
| **17.1 Gross profit, net income before taxes, and net income after taxes** | Gross profit = Net sales − Cost of goods sold<br><br>Net income before taxes = Gross profit − Operating expenses<br><br>Net income after taxes = Net income before taxes − income taxes | Cost of goods sold, $156,000; operating expenses, $35,000; net sales, $210,000; taxes, $4,000. Find gross profit, net income before taxes, and net income after taxes.<br><br>Gross profit<br>   = $210,000 − $156,000<br>   = $54,000<br><br>Net income before taxes<br>   = $54,000 − $35,000<br>   = $19,000<br><br>Net income after taxes<br>   = $19,000 − $4,000<br>   = $15,000 |

**17.2 Finding the percent of net sales of individual items**

Subtract returns from gross sales to determine net sales. Then divide the value of an item by net sales to obtain percent of net sales.

Express the following items for Mr. Bill's Appliance store as percents of net sales: gross sales, $340,000; returns, $15,000; cost of goods sold, $210,000; wages, $19,000; gross profit.

$$\text{Net sales} = \$340,000 - \$15,000$$
$$= \$325,000$$

$$\text{Gross profit} = \$325,000 - \$210,000$$
$$= \$115,000$$

$$\text{Percent gross sales} = \frac{\$340,000}{\$325,000}$$
$$= 104.6\%$$

$$\text{Percent returns} = \frac{\$15,000}{\$325,000}$$
$$= 4.6\%$$

Percent cost of goods sold
$$= \frac{\$210,000}{\$325,000}$$
$$= 65\%$$

Percent wages
$$= \frac{\$19,000}{\$325,000} = 5.8\%$$

$$\text{Percent gross profit} = \frac{\$115,000}{\$325,000}$$
$$= 35.4\%$$

**17.2 Comparing income statements to published charts**

In one chart, list the percents of net sales for each item from a published chart and a particular company.

Prepare a vertical analysis of Mr. Bill's Appliance Store.

| Cost of Goods | Gross Profit | Wages | |
|---|---|---|---|
| 65% | 35% | 5.8% | Mr. Bill's Appliances |
| 66.9% | 33.1% | 11.9% | (from chart) |

| 17.2 | **Preparing a horizontal analysis** | List last year's and this year's values for each item. Then calculate the amount of the increase or decrease for each item and express as percents. | The results of a horizontal analysis of the portion of a business is given. Calculate the % increases or decreases in each item. |

| | This Year | Last Year | Increase Amount | or | Decrease Percent |
|---|---|---|---|---|---|
| Gross Sales | $735,000 | $700,000 | $35,000 | | 5% |
| Returns | 5,000 | 10,000 | (5,000) | | (50%) |
| Net Sales | 730,000 | 690,000 | 40,000 | | 5.8% |
| Cost of Goods Sold | 530,000 | 540,000 | (10,000) | | (1.9%) |
| Gross Profit | 200,000 | 150,000 | 50,000 | | 33.3% |

| 17.3 | **Fundamental formula for accounting** | Assets = Liabilities + Owner's equity<br><br>or<br><br>Assets − Liabilities = Owner's equity | Pleasant Stay Hotels has assets of $3,420,500 and liabilities of $2,104,700. Find the owner's equity.<br><br>$3,420,500 − $2,104,700<br>$\qquad\qquad = \$1,315,800$ |

| 17.4 | **Current ratio; Acid-test ratio; Ratio of net income after taxes to the average owner's equity** | $\dfrac{\text{Current}}{\text{ratio}} = \dfrac{\text{Current assets}}{\text{Current liabilities}}$<br><br>$\dfrac{\text{Acid-test}}{\text{ratio}} = \dfrac{\text{Liquid assets}}{\text{Current liabilities}}$<br><br>$\text{Ratio} = \dfrac{\text{Net income after taxes}}{\text{Average owner's equity}}$ | The Circle Towne Agency has current assets of $250,000, current liabilities of $110,000, cash of $45,000, and accounts receivable of $80,000. The agency had owner's equity of $140,000 at the beginning of the year, and $180,000 at the end of the year. The net income after taxes was $25,000. Calculate the following ratios.<br><br>$\dfrac{\text{Current}}{\text{ratio}} = \dfrac{\$250,000}{\$110,000} = 2.27$<br><br>$\dfrac{\text{Acid-test}}{\text{ratio}} = \dfrac{\$45,000 + \$80,000}{\$110,000}$<br><br>$\qquad = 1.14$ |

$$\text{Average owner's equity} = \frac{\$140,000 + \$180,000}{2}$$

$$= \$160,000$$

Ratio of net income after taxes to average owner's equity is

$$\frac{\$25,000}{\$160,000} = 0.156 = 15.6\%$$

---

**17.4   Accounts receivable turnover;**

Accounts receivable turnover

$$= \frac{\text{Net sales}}{\text{Average accounts receivable}}$$

A firm has net sales of $793,750; accounts receivable of $50,000 at the beginning of the year; $75,000 at the end of the year; current liabilities of $15,000; long-term liabilities of $10,000; and owner's equity of $80,000. Find the accounts receivable turnover, the average age of accounts receivable, and the debt-to-equity ratio.

**Average age of accounts receivable**

Average age of accounts receivable

$$= \frac{365}{\text{Accounts receivable turnover}}$$

Average accounts receivable

$$= \frac{\$50,000 + \$75,000}{2}$$

$$= \$62,500$$

Accounts receivable turnover

$$= \frac{\$793,750}{\$62,500} = 12.7$$

Average age of accounts receivable

$$= \frac{365}{12.7} = 28.7 \text{ days}$$

**Debt-to-equity ratio**

Debt-to-equity ratio

$$= \frac{\text{Current liabilities} + \text{Long-term liabilities}}{\text{Owner's equity}}$$

Debt-to-equity ratio

$$= \frac{\$15,000 + \$10,000}{\$80,000}$$

$$= 0.31$$

*Find the gross profit and net income before taxes for each of the following. [17.1]*

| | Cost of Goods | Operating Expenses | Net Sales |
|---|---|---|---|
| 1. | $168,000 | $52,500 | $280,300 |
| 2. | $379,520 | $124,800 | $643,250 |
| 3. | $300,900 | $98,400 | $442,500 |
| 4. | $606,520 | $212,300 | $842,400 |

*Find the cost of goods sold for each of the following firms. [17.1]*

| | Initial Inventory | Cost of Goods Purchased | Freight | Final Inventory |
|---|---|---|---|---|
| 5. | $240,000 | $380,000 | $42,400 | $265,000 |
| 6. | $125,400 | $94,300 | $8,200 | $101,400 |
| 7. | $84,000 | $52,400 | $4,300 | $98,000 |
| 8. | $184,200 | $245,000 | $18,300 | $165,400 |

*Find the net income after taxes for each of the following. Then find the ratio of net income after taxes to average owner's equity. [17.1]*

9. BGI Waste Haulers has net sales of $943,080; no inventory and thus no cost of goods sold; total expenses of $798,400; average owner's equity of $580,000; and taxes of $42,600.

10. Big Rod's Auto Dealership has net sales of $8,453,200; cost of goods sold of $6,762,500; total expenses of $1,200,850; average owner's equity of $1,540,000; and taxes of $156,750.

*Complete the accompanying income statements for the following firms. [17.1]*

11. Lori's Boutique had gross sales of $175,000 last year, with returns of $8,000. The inventory on January 1 was $44,000. A total of $126,000 worth of goods was purchased with a freight of $2,000. The inventory on December 31 was $52,000. Salaries and wages were $9,000, rent was $4,000, advertising was

$1,500, utilities were $1,000, taxes on inventory and payroll totaled $2,000, and miscellaneous expenses totaled $3,000.

---

**LORI'S BOUTIQUE**
**INCOME STATEMENT**
**FOR THE YEAR ENDING DECEMBER 31**

| | | |
|---|---|---|
| Gross Sales | | _____ |
| Returns | | _____ |
| Net Sales | | _____ |
| Inventory, January 1 | _____ | |
| Cost of Goods Purchased | _____ | |
| Freight | _____ | |
| Total Cost of Goods Purchased | _____ | |
| Total of Goods Available for Sale | _____ | |
| Inventory, December 31 | _____ | |
| Cost of Goods Sold | | _____ |
| Gross Profit | | _____ |
| Expenses | | |
| Salaries and Wages | _____ | |
| Rent | _____ | |
| Advertising | _____ | |
| Utilities | _____ | |
| Taxes on Inventory, Payroll | _____ | |
| Miscellaneous Expenses | _____ | |
| Total Expenses | | _____ |
| NET INCOME BEFORE TAXES | | _____ |

---

**12.** The Guitar Warehouse had gross sales of $2,215,000 with returns of $26,000. The inventory on January 1 was $215,000. A total of $1,123,000 worth of goods was purchased with a freight of $4,000. The inventory on December 31 was $265,000. Salaries and wages were $154,000, rent was $59,000, advertising was $11,000, utilities were $12,000, taxes on inventory and payroll totaled $10,000, and miscellaneous expenses totaled $9,000. Income taxes for the year were $242,300.

---

**THE GUITAR WAREHOUSE**
**INCOME STATEMENT**
**FOR THE YEAR ENDING DECEMBER 31**

| | | |
|---|---|---|
| Gross Sales | _____ | |
| Returns | _____ | |
| Net Sales | | _____ |
| Inventory, January 1 | _____ | |
| Cost of Goods Purchased | _____ | |
| Freight | _____ | |
| Total Cost of Goods Purchased | _____ | |
| Total of Goods Available for Sale | _____ | |
| Inventory, December 31 | _____ | |
| Cost of Goods Sold | | _____ |
| Gross Profit | | _____ |
| Expenses | | |
| Salaries and Wages | _____ | |
| Rent | _____ | |
| Advertising | _____ | |
| Utilities | _____ | |
| Taxes on Inventory, Payroll | _____ | |
| Miscellaneous Expenses | _____ | |
| Total Expenses | | _____ |
| NET INCOME BEFORE TAXES | | ========== |
| Income Taxes | | _____ |
| NET INCOME | | ========== |

*Prepare a vertical analysis for each of the following firms. Round to the nearest tenth of a percent. [17.2]*

|  | Cost of Goods Sold | Operating Expenses | Net Sales |
|---|---|---|---|
| **13.** | $1,248,180 | $210,460 | $1,642,350 |
| **14.** | $420,850 | $168,600 | $678,800 |

*Complete the following chart. Express each item as a percent of net sales and then write in the appropriate average percent from Table 17.1. Round each percent to the nearest tenth of a percent. [17.2]*

**15. Andy's Steak House**

|  | Amount | Percent | Percent from Table 17.1 |
|---|---|---|---|
| Net Sales | $300,000 | 100% | 100% |
| Cost of Goods Sold | $125,000 | _____ | _____ |
| Gross Profit | $175,000 | _____ | _____ |
| Wages | $72,000 | _____ | _____ |
| Rent | $12,000 | _____ | _____ |
| Advertising | $5,700 | _____ | _____ |
| Total Expenses | $123,000 | _____ | _____ |
| Net Income | $52,000 | _____ | _____ |

*Complete the following balance sheet. [17.3]*

**16.** Gaskets, Inc. manufactures gaskets for gasoline engines. They have been under intense financial pressure recently due to foreign competition. The firm has notes payable of $410,000; accounts receivable of $460,000; cash is $240,000; long-term notes payable of $194,000; buildings worth $260,000; inventory of $225,000; fixtures are $48,000; notes receivable of $180,000; land worth $180,000; accounts payable of $882,000; and mortgages payable of $220,000. Use the fundamental formula of accounting to find owner's equity.

**GASKETS, INC.**
**BALANCE SHEET**
**FOR DECEMBER 31**

### Assets

Current Assets

   Cash _____

   Notes Receivable _____

   Accounts Receivable _____

   Inventory _____

           Total Current Assets _____

Plant Assets

   Land _____

   Buildings _____

   Fixtures _____

           Total Plant Assets _____

TOTAL ASSETS ═══════════

### Liabilities

Current Liabilities

   Notes Payable _____

   Accounts Payable _____

           Total Current Liabilities _____

Long-term Liabilities

   Mortgages Payable _____

   Long- term Notes Payable _____

           Total Long-term Liabilities _____

Total Liabilities _____

### Owner's Equity

Owner's Equity _____

_____

TOTAL LIABILITIES AND OWNER'S EQUITY ═══════════

*Calculate the current ratio, acid-test ratio, and debt-to-equity ratio for each of the following. Round to the nearest hundredth. [17.4]*

| | Current Assets | Current Liabilities | Long-Term Liabilities | Owner's Equity | Liquid Assets |
|---|---|---|---|---|---|
| **17.** | $342,000 | $260,000 | $140,000 | $225,000 | $120,000 |
| **18.** | $95,000 | $115,000 | $85,000 | $48,000 | $5,000 |
| **19.** | $160,000 | $205,000 | $0 | $185,000 | $145,000 |

*Find the accounts receivable turnover rate and the average age of the accounts receivable in each of the following firms. Round to the nearest tenth. [17.4]*

**20.** Accounts receivable at beginning of year    $145,300
      Accounts receivable at end of year        $162,500
      Net sales                               $864,300

**21.** Accounts receivable at beginning of year    $124,800
      Accounts receivable at end of year        $107,200
      Net sales                              $1,206,750

**22.** Complete the following comparative balance sheet. [17.4]

| | Amount This Year | Percent This Year | Amount Last Year | Percent Last Year |
|---|---|---|---|---|
| **Current assets** | | | | |
|    Cash | $28,000 | _____ | $22,000 | _____ |
|    Notes Receivable | $12,000 | _____ | $15,000 | _____ |
|    Accounts Receivable | $39,000 | _____ | $31,500 | _____ |
|    Inventory | $22,000 | _____ | $20,000 | _____ |
| **Total Current Assets** | $101,000 | _____ | $88,500 | _____ |
| **Total Plant and Equipment** | $48,000 | | $16,000 | |
| **TOTAL ASSETS** | _____ | _____ | _____ | _____ |
| **Total Current Liabilities** | $38,000 | _____ | $36,000 | _____ |

# Chapter 17 Summary Exercise

Kelli Birdsong needs to do a financial analysis of her music business. She has collected the following facts for last year.

| | |
|---|---|
| **Gross Sales** | **$212,000** |
| **Returns** | **$12,500** |
| **Inventory on January 1** | **$44,000** |
| **Cost of Goods Purchased** | **$75,000** |
| **Freight** | **$8,000** |
| **Inventory on December 31** | **$65,000** |
| **Salaries and Wages** | **$37,000** |
| **Rent** | **$12,000** |
| **Advertising** | **$2,000** |
| **Utilities** | **$3,000** |
| **Taxes on Inventory, Payroll** | **$7,000** |
| **Miscellaneous Expenses** | **$4,500** |

**(a)** Prepare an income statement.

**BIRDSONG MUSIC, INC.**
**INCOME STATEMENT**
**YEAR ENDING DECEMBER 31**

Gross Sales _____

Returns _____

Net Sales _____
  Inventory, January 1 _____
  Cost of Goods Purchased _____
  Freight _____
  Total Cost of Goods Purchased _____
  Total of Goods Available for Sale _____
  Inventory, December 31 _____

Cost of Goods Sold _____

Gross Profit _____
  Expenses
    Salaries and Wages _____
    Rent _____
    Advertising _____
    Utilities _____
    Taxes on Inventory, Payroll _____
    Miscellaneous Expenses _____
     Total Expenses _____

NET INCOME BFORE TAXES _____

**(b)** Express the following items as a percent of net sales.

Gross sales _____      Salaries and wages _____

Returns _____      Rent _____

Cost of goods sold _____      Utilities _____

**(c)** After the year is completed, Birdsong has $62,000 in cash, $2,500 in notes receivable, $8,200 in accounts receivable, and $65,000 in inventory. She has land worth $28,000, buildings valued at $84,000, and fixtures worth $13,500. She also has $16,800 in notes payable, $27,000 in accounts payable, mortgages for $15,000, long-term notes payable of $42,000, and owner's equity of $162,400. Prepare a balance sheet.

**BIRDSONG MUSIC, INC.**
**BALANCE SHEET**
**DECEMBER 31**

**Assets**

Current Assets

   Cash            _____

   Notes Receivable          _____

   Accounts Receivable          _____

   Inventory          _____

          Total Current Assets        _____

Plant Assets

   Land          _____

   Buildings          _____

   Fixtures          _____

          Total Plant Assets        _____

TOTAL ASSETS        ════════

**Liabilities**

Current Liabilities

   Notes Payable          _____

   Accounts Payable          _____

          Total Current Liabilities        _____

Long-term Liabilities

   Mortgages Payable          _____

   Long-term Notes Payable          _____

          Total Long-term Liabilities        _____

Total Liabilities        _____

**Owner's Equity**

Owner's Equity          _____

TOTAL LIABILITIES AND OWNER'S EQUITY        ════════

**(d)** Find the current ratio and the acid-test ratio for Birdsong's business. Do you think she has a strong operation? Explain your reasoning.

# Securities and Profit Distribution

As shown in the previous chapter, the net profit of a business is the amount left over after all the expenses and taxes involved in running the business are paid. Typically, a portion of any net profit is reinvested in the business, for labor-saving machinery, to build new plants, and so on. The rest of the net profit can then be distributed to the owners of the business. This chapter discusses the way the profits are distributed.

The distribution of profits depends on the way a company is formed. If a business is a **sole proprietorship**, that is, if it is owned by one person, then all the profits go to that person. Sole proprietorships are most common among the smallest businesses, such as a small retail store, restaurant, hair salon, and the like. With a typical sole proprietorship, there is no division of assets between personal assets and business assets, so that personal property could be **attached** (seized under court order) to pay debts associated with the business, while business assets could also be attached to pay personal debts.

A **partnership** is a business formed by two or more parties. Since partnerships involve the resources of several people, they are common for somewhat larger businesses, such as a small factory or perhaps a small chain of retail stores. Unless they have a prior agreement setting up a different method, profits in a partnership are divided equally among the partners.

Partnerships are often set up by individuals with different interests and abilities—one partner might actually run the business on a day-to-day basis, while the other partner makes a substantial financial investment but does not actively take part in the business. A partner who makes only a financial investment is called a **silent partner**.

The law often says that partners are responsible ''jointly and separately'' for partnership debts, which means that a partner with money may have to pay all debts of the partnership. The methods of dividing the profits in a partnership are discussed in Section 18.4.

To get around the problem of the lack of protection for personal assets, most larger businesses are set up as **corporations**. The people investing money in a corporation have **limited liability**—they can lose no more money than they have invested in the corporation. Distribution of profits in a corporation is discussed in the first section.

## 18.1   Distribution of Profits in a Corporation

**OBJECTIVES**

**1**   *Compare preferred and common stocks.*

**2**   *Distribute profits to shareholders and calculate dividend per share.*

**3**   *Find earnings per share.*

A corporation is set up with money, or **capital**, raised by selling shares of **stock**. A share of stock represents partial ownership in a corporation. If one million shares of stock are sold to establish a new firm, the owner of one share will hold 1/1,000,000 of the corporation. The ownership of stock is shown by **stock certificates**, such as the one shown in Figure 18.1, for a large publicly held corporation.

In most states, corporations are required to have an **annual meeting**. At this meeting, open to all owners of the stock (or **stockholders**), the management of the firm is open to questions from stockholders. The stockholders also elect a **board of directors**—a group of people who represent the stockholders. The board of directors hires the **executive officers** of the corporation, such as the president, vice presidents, and so on. The board of directors also typically authorize the distribution of some of the profits in the form of dividends. Dividends are covered in more detail later in this section.

FIGURE 18.1

**OBJECTIVE** **1** *Compare preferred and common stocks.*    Corporations normally issue two types of stock, **preferred stock** and **common stock**. As the name implies, preferred stock has certain rights over common stock. Owners of preferred stock must be paid dividends before any dividends can be paid to owners of common stock. In the case of bankruptcy of the corporation, owners of preferred stock must be paid off completely before common stock owners get any money. (Preferred stockholders receive no money, however, until all other debts of the corporation are paid.)

Each share of preferred stock has a **par value**—the amount printed on the stock certificate that must be paid to its owner before common stockholders receive any money. Each share also has a stated **dividend**, often given as a percent of par value. These dividends must be paid by the company to the preferred stockholders before any dividends can be paid to the common stockholders. (However, there is no guarantee that any dividends will be paid at all.)

Sometimes, preferred stock is given additional features to make it more attractive to potential buyers. For example, the stock may be **cumulative preferred stock**, which means that any dividends not paid in the past must be paid before common stockholders receive any money. The stock might also be **convertible preferred stock**, which means that one share is convertible into a stated number of shares of common stock at some future date.

Holders of preferred stock usually are not able to vote at the annual meeting of the corporation. Also, most preferred stock is **nonparticipating**, which means the corporation will never pay dividends above the stated rate. (Holders of **participating** preferred stock could share in any good success of the corporation by an increase in the dividend.)

**NOTE**    Common stock carries no guarantees—its holders are last in line when profits are distributed or when the corporation is dissolved. However, common stockholders are able to vote at the annual meeting. Common stock may or may not have a par value, but since nothing is guaranteed, par value for common stock is of little importance. ■

**OBJECTIVE** **2** *Distribute profits to shareholders and calculate dividend per share.*    The next examples show how the profits of a corporation might be distributed.

**EXAMPLE 1** *Calculating Dividend per Share*

Thornton Electronics had a net income of $1,200,000 last year. The board of directors decides to reinvest $500,000 in the business and distribute the remaining $700,000 to stockholders. The company has 40,000 shares of $100 par value, 6% preferred stock, and 350,000 shares of common stock. Find (a) the amount paid to holders of preferred stock, and (b) the amount per share given to holders of common stock.

**SOLUTION**

**(a)** Each share of preferred stock has a par value of $100, and pays a dividend of 6%. The dividend per share is

$$\text{Dividend per share} = \$100 \times 6\% = \$100 \times 0.06 = \$6$$

A dividend of $6 must be paid for each share of preferred stock. Since there are 40,000 shares of preferred, a total of

$$\$6 \times 40{,}000 = \$240{,}000$$

will be paid to owners of preferred shares.

**(b)** A total of $700,000 is available for stockholders, with $240,000 going to the owners of preferred shares, leaving

$$
\begin{array}{ll}
\$700{,}000 & \text{total} \\
-\ \ 240{,}000 & \text{to preferred} \\
\hline
\$460{,}000 &
\end{array}
$$

available for the common stockholders. There are 350,000 shares of common stock outstanding, with each share being paid a dividend of

$$\frac{\$460{,}000}{350{,}000} = \$1.31 \text{ per share.} \qquad \blacksquare$$

### EXAMPLE 2    *Finding Dividends*

Due to a steep drop in the price of oil, Alamo Energy paid no dividend last year. The company has done much better this year and the board of directors has set aside $175,000 for the payment of dividends. The company has outstanding 12,500 shares of cumulative preferred stock having par value of $50, with an 8% dividend. The company also has 40,000 shares of common stock. What dividend will be paid to the owners of each type of stock?

**SOLUTION**    The dividend per share of preferred stock is

$$\$50 \text{ par value} \times 8\% \text{ (dividend rate)} = \$4.$$

Dividends have not been paid for 2 years (last year and this year), so that each share of preferred stock must be paid

$$\$4 \text{ per share} \times 2 \text{ years} = \$8$$

before any dividends can be paid to holders of common stock. Since there are 12,500 shares of preferred stock outstanding, a total of

$$\$8 \times 12{,}500 = \$100{,}000$$

must be paid to the owners of the preferred stock. This leaves

$$
\begin{array}{ll}
\$175{,}000 & \text{total} \\
-\ \ 100{,}000 & \text{to owners of preferred} \\
\hline
\$75{,}000 &
\end{array}
$$

to be divided among owners of common stock. Since there are 40,000 shares of common stock, each share will be paid a dividend of

$$\frac{\$75{,}000}{40{,}000} = \$1.88 \text{ (rounded).} \qquad \blacksquare$$

**NOTE** In Example 2, the dividend for owners of preferred stock was paid for each of the last two years before any common stock dividends were paid. ■

**OBJECTIVE** **3** *Find earnings per share.* One way to measure the financial success of a corporation is by finding the **earnings per share** made by the corporation. Earnings per share is found with the following formula.

$$\text{Earnings per share} = \frac{\text{Net income} - \text{Dividends on preferred}}{\text{Number of shares of common outstanding}}$$

**EXAMPLE 3** *Finding Earnings per Share*

Bill Watson started a plumbing company in 1982 as a sole proprietorship. He took on a partner who remains with the company today as part owner. The business continued to grow rapidly and in 1995 the two partners incorporated the company under the name of Watson Plumbing.

The two then gave stock to their children and they have also allowed three of their key employees to earn bonuses paid in the stock of the company. The two founders hope to convince these key employees to remain with the firm.

**(a)** Watson Plumbing made $420,000 last year. They had 500,000 shares of common stock outstanding and no preferred stock.

$$\text{Earnings per share} = \frac{\$420,000 - 0}{500,000} = \$0.84 \text{ per share}$$

**(b)** This year, the company issued preferred stock and paid $85,000 in dividends to preferred shareholders out of a net income of $544,000. The earnings per share are

$$\text{Earnings per share} = \frac{\$544,000 - \$85,000}{500,000} = \$0.92 \text{ (rounded)}.$$

**(c)** Find Mr. Watson's total dividend income this year if he owns 300,000 shares of common stock and one-fourth of the preferred stock. The total dividend income is the sum of the dividends from common stock plus those from preferred stock.

$$(300,000 \times \$0.92) + \left(\frac{1}{4} \cdot \$85,000\right) = \$297,250$$

**(d)** Find Mr. Watson's total dividends in a bad year with no profits, no dividends on common stock, and only a $10,000 dividend to preferred stock owners.

$$\frac{1}{4} \cdot \$10,000 = \$2,500$$

■

## 18.1 EXERCISES

*Find the dividend that will be paid for each share of preferred stock and common stock.*

| | Common Stock (in shares) | Preferred Stock (in shares) | Total Dividends |
|---|---|---|---|
| 1. | 400,000 | none | $0 |
| 2. | 650,000 | none | $28,000 |
| 3. | 175,000 | 50,000, $10 par value, 3% | $40,000 |
| 4. | 200,000 | 30,000, $5 par value, 5% | $80,000 |
| 5. | 1,000,000 | 100,000, $1,000 par value, 2% | $2,000,000 |
| 6. | 500,000 | 40,000, $50 par value, 3% | $44,800 |

*Solve the following application problems.*

7. Reeves Animal Hospital had a net income of $320,000 last year. If $280,000 was reinvested in an expansion of the business, and the remainder was paid in dividends, find the dividend per share on the 400,000 shares of common stock outstanding.

8. Kennedy Imports had a net income of $3,500,000 last year. The board of directors decided to purchase another firm with $2,800,000 of the profits and pay the remainder out as dividends. Find the dividend for each of the company's 1,500,000 shares of common stock.

9. Topeka Forest Products has 300,000 shares of $10 par value, 10% preferred stock outstanding, and 1,800,000 shares of common stock. Find the dividend per share for the preferred and common stockholders if the board of directors set aside $2,400,000 for dividends.

10. The local Chevrolet dealer is a corporation with 1,000 shares of $200 par value, 11% preferred stock, and 5,000 common shares. Decide on the dividend per share for a total dividend of $39,500.

11. Northern Maine Paper Products has sold 25,000 shares of $40 par value, 4% preferred stock to help remodel its mill. It already had 300,000 shares of common stock. Find the dividend per share if the total profit is $850,000, and 35% was distributed to shareholders.

12. The Harris Furniture Company had a net income of $2,937,500 last year. The company decided to distribute 40% of this money to shareholders. Find the dividend per share if there are 50,000 shares of $100 par value, 10% preferred stock outstanding, and 300,000 shares of common stock.

13. Since the computer business is booming, a small new company has decided to pay no dividend for 3 years, and instead, reinvests the profits in expansion. During the fourth year, the board decides to pay a dividend of $2,675,000. Find the dividend per share if the company has outstanding 20,000 cumulative preferred shares of $100 par value, at 5%, and 450,000 common shares.

14. To pay for a new factory, Wilson Rubber Goods has paid no dividend for 2 years. Now, at the end of the third year, a dividend of $1,200,000 was declared. Find the dividend per share if the company has 10,000 cumulative preferred shares outstanding of $100 par value at 10%, and 400,000 common shares.

**15.** A corporation had net income of $7,000,000, has 1,200,000 common shares, and no preferred shares. Find the earnings per share.

**16.** Suppose a corporation with 750,000 common shares outstanding and no preferred shares had a net income of $2,350,000 last year. Find the earnings per share.

**17.** Far East Imports has 300,000 common shares, and 12,500 preferred shares, of $150 par value, 10%. The company last year had a net income of $1,500,000, with 45% of this going to shareholders. Find the earnings per share.

**18.** Boyle Cleaners had a net income of $600,000 last year, and distributed 55% to shareholders. The firm has 50,000 common shares, and 10,000 preferred shares, of $100 par value, 12%. Find the earnings per share.

**19.** Arckat has 250,000 shares of common stock and 40,000 shares of preferred stock ($50 par, 4%) outstanding. Net income last year and this year were respectively $680,000 and $765,000. The board of directors disbursed 40% of net income as dividends in both years. Find the dividend per share of common stock (a) last year and (b) this year. (c) Find the percent increase in the *earnings per share* of this year over last year.

**20.** Rhythm Recording Studio has 60,000 shares of $1,000 par value, 4% preferred stock. They also have 2,000,000 shares of common stock outstanding. This year the company increased their net income by 20% over last year's $4,300,000. In both years the board of directors authorized the payment of 60% of net income for payment of dividends. Find the dividend per share of common stock for (a) last year and (b) this year. (c) Find the percent increase in *earnings per share* of this year over last year.

**21.** Bill Baker owns a paving company with 1,000,000 shares of common stock. He wishes to help provide for his 6 grandchildren so he establishes 20,000 shares of preferred stock with a $100 par value, 8%, and donates the preferred stock to a trust for his grandchildren. Given a year with a net income of $620,000 and a payment of 30% of net income for dividends, find the dividend to be paid on behalf of *each* grandchild.

**22.** In Exercise 21, find the dividend to be paid on behalf of *each* grandchild if net income is $85,000, and 30% of net income is used for dividends.

**23.** Explain the difference between common stock and preferred stock. (See Objective 1.)

**24.** Explain the process used to calculate the dividend per share for cumulative preferred stock. Provide an example. (See Objective 2.)

## 18.2 Buying Stock

**OBJECTIVES**

**1** *Know the basics of stock ownership.*

**2** *Read stock tables.*

**3** *Find the commission for buying or selling stocks.*

**4** *Find the total price of a stock purchase.*

**5** *Find the current yield on a stock.*

**6** *Find the PE ratio of a stock.*

**7** *Define the Dow Jones Industrial Average.*

**8** *Define a mutual fund.*

**OBJECTIVE** **1** *Know the basics of stock ownership.*        As mentioned in the previous section, buying stock in a corporation makes the stockholder a part owner of the corporation. In return for the money a person invests in stock, he or she shares in any profits the company makes. Hopefully, the company will do well and prosper. If this happens, many other people will want the company's stock, and they will be willing to pay a good price for its shares. If this happens, the stockholders can sell at a profit.

On the other hand, if the company does not do well, then fewer people will want its stock and the price will fall. The price of the shares of most large, publicly held firms, is set by the law of supply and demand at institutions called *stock exchanges*. The largest stock exchange is the New York Stock Exchange, located on Wall Street in New York City. Many foreign countries including Japan, Taiwan, England, Canada, and Mexico have their own stock exchanges. One of the most widely circulated financial newspapers in the world is *The Wall Street Journal* which is published daily by Dow Jones & Company, Inc. This newspaper provides daily prices for stocks and bonds in several different markets. *The Wall Street Journal* also maintains a home page on the World Wide Web (Internet).

**THE WALL STREET JOURNAL.**

The public does not go directly to the exchange to buy and sell stock. Instead, members of the public buy their stock through **stockbrokers**, people who do have access to the exchanges. Stockbrokers charge a fee for buying or selling stock, as discussed below.

Most people buy stock in hopes of making a profit. Obviously, there is no way to know for sure which stocks will increase in value and which will decrease. Stockbrokers can give advice, but this advice is not guaranteed to produce a profit.

**OBJECTIVE** **2** *Read stock tables.*        Find the current price of a stock by looking in many daily local newspapers, or in *The Wall Street Journal*. A portion of the stock market page from *The Journal* is shown in Figure 18.2.

**NOTE**    In reading the stock table, the following should be noted.

1.    Price rises or declines of 5% or more are highlighted with boldface type.

2.    Up or down arrowheads next to a stock indicate a new 52-week high or low.

3.    Stocks with unusual volume activity are underlined.    ■

The first step in reading this table is to find the line corresponding to the company whose stock is of interest. Company names are usually abbreviated in newspapers. For example, Bell Atlantic is abbreviated BEL. Look in the stock tables to find the following information on Bell Atlantic.

## -B-B-B-

| 52 Weeks Hi | Lo | Stock | Sym | Div | Yld % | PE | Vol 100s | Hi | Lo | Close | Net Chg |
|---|---|---|---|---|---|---|---|---|---|---|---|
| 41⅛ | 26⅞ | ♣BeckmanInstr | BEC | .52 | 1.4 | 20 | 311 | 36⅞ | 36⅜ | 36½ | − ⅝ |
| 89⅛ | 55⅝ | BectonDksn | BDX | .92 | 1.1 | 21 | 1976 | 84½ | 82¾ | 83 | −1 |
| s 16 | 10½ | BedfdPrpty | BED | .96 | 7.4 | 31 | 567 | 13⅛ | 12¾ | 13 | − ⅛ |
| n 30⅞ | 21⅝ | BelcoOG | BOG | | ... | ... | 590 | 27¼ | 26⅜ | 27⅛ | − ⅜ |
| ▲ 33½ | 22¼ | ♣Belden | BWC | .20 | .6 | 18 | 594 | 34 | 32⅝ | 33¾ | + ¾ |
| 6⅞ | 2 | BeldngHeminwy | BHY | | ... | dd | 102 | 2¼ | 2⅛ | 2¼ | ... |
| 35⅛ | 18 | BellHowell | BHW | | ... | ... | 52 | 33¾ | 33½ | 33¾ | + ⅛ |
| 74⅞ | 52⅝ | ♣BellAtlantic | BEL | 2.88f | 4.6 | 14 | 4875 | 64⅝ | 62¾ | 62⅞ | −1¼ |
| 25⅝ | 18⅞ | ♣BellIndus | BI | stk | ... | 10 | 201 | 22⅛ | 21¾ | 21⅞ | ... |
| s 45⅞ | 29⅛ | BellSouth | BLS | 1.44 | 3.6 | 23 | 5931 | 41½ | 40⅜ | 40⅜ | − ¾ |
| s▲ 38⅞ | 28¾ | Belo AH A | BLC | .44f | 1.1 | 23 | 683 | 39½ | 38¾ | 39½ | + ¾ |
| 33½ | 24¾ | Bemis | BMS | .72 | 2.2 | 19 | 294 | 32⅜ | 31⅝ | 32⅜ | ... |
| ▲ 59⅛ | 42¼ | Beneficial | BNL | 1.88 | 3.2 | 14 | 575 | 59⅜ | 58⅝ | 59⅜ | + ⅞ |
| 68½ | 57½ | Beneficial pfA | | 4.50 | 7.0 | ... | z680 | 64 | 64 | 64 | −1½ |
| 38 | 31¾ | Beneficial pfV | | 2.50 | 6.9 | ... | 1 | 36 | 36 | 36 | + ¾ |
| 25⅛ | 18 | Benetton | BNG | .54e | 2.2 | ... | 13 | 24⅜ | 24 | 24⅜ | + ¼ |
| ⅞ | ⅜ | Benguet | BE | | ... | 63 | 826 | 11/16 | ⅝ | ⅝ | − 1/16 |
| n 28⅝ | 22⅜ | BergElec | BEI | | ... | ... | 654 | 28½ | 27¾ | 27¾ | − ¾ |
| 28¼ | 19¼ | BergnBruns | BBC | .48 | 1.8 | 16 | 1090 | 27⅜ | 26¾ | 26¾ | − ⅝ |
| 38000 | 22125 | BerkHathwy A | BRKA | | ... | 71 | z110 | 34400 | 34000 | 34000 | −100 |
| n 1220 | 1110 | BerkHathwy B | BRKB | | ... | ... | z4750 | 1150 | 1120 | 1125 | − 15 |
| 10⅞ | 9¼ | BrkshreRlty | BRI | .90 | 8.6 | 29 | 329 | 10⅝ | 10½ | 10½ | ... |
| ¾ | 5/16 | BrkshreRlty wt | | | ... | ... | 73 | ⅝ | 9/16 | 9/16 | − 1/16 |
| 19¼ | 14 | Berlitz | BTZ | | ... | 62 | 25 | 19¼ | 19¼ | 19¼ | ... |
| 12½ | 8¾ | BerryPete | BRY | .40 | 3.5 | 18 | 315 | 11⅝ | 11½ | 11½ | ... |
| 46⅞ | 27 | BestBuyCap pf | | 3.25 | 8.6 | ... | 50 | 37⅞ | 37⅜ | 37⅞ | + ½ |
| 30¼ | 12 | BestBuy | BBY | | ... | 19 | 4958 | 21½ | 21 | 21¼ | + ⅛ |
| 18¼ | 12⅝ | BethSteel | BS | | ... | 17 | 8063 | 13¼ | 12⅞ | 13 | − ⅛ |
| 55⅛ | 50⅞ | BethSteel pf | | 5.00 | 9.6 | ... | 26 | 52⅛ | 52 | 52 | − ⅛ |
| 28⅛ | 25½ | BethSteel pfB | | 2.50 | 9.3 | ... | 52 | 26⅞ | 26⅝ | 26⅞ | + ⅛ |
| 48 | 38¾ | BetzLab | BTL | 1.48 | 3.1 | 20 | 974 | 47⅞ | 47 | 47 | − ¾ |
| 14½ | 9 | ♣BeverlyEnt | BEV | | ... | dd | 6810 | 12⅜ | 12⅛ | 12⅛ | ... |
| n 19¼ | 10⅝ | BigFlower | BGF | | ... | ... | 148 | 13¾ | 13½ | 13½ | − ⅛ |
| 21 | 14½ | BndlyWest | BDY | .08 | .5 | 11 | 142 | 16¾ | 16½ | 16⅝ | − ⅛ |
| 22⅛ | 12⅝ | BiocraftLabs | BCL | | ... | dd | 68 | 21⅝ | 21½ | 21½ | − ¼ |
| 8¾ | 6⅜ | BioWhit | BWI | | ... | 30 | 34 | 8⅛ | 8 | 8 | ... |
| 21⅝ | 14 | BirmghamStl | BIR | .40 | 2.4 | 63 | 1026 | 16½ | 16 | 16⅜ | + ¼ |
| 40⅜ | 27½ | BlackDeck | BDK | .48 | 1.2 | 14 | 2105 | 39⅝ | 38¾ | 39⅝ | +1 |
| 26¼ | 19¾ | BlackHills | BKH | 1.38 | 5.7 | 13 | 62 | 24⅛ | 23⅞ | 24 | − ¼ |
| 9⅛ | 8 | BlkrkAdv | BAT | .62 | 7.8 | ... | 34 | 8⅛ | 8 | 8 | ... |
| 14⅞ | 13½ | BlkrkCal2008 | BFC | .77 | 5.5 | ... | 94 | 13⅞ | 13¾ | 13⅞ | ... |
| 15½ | 14⅛ | BlkrkFla2008 | BRF | .86 | 5.8 | ... | 57 | 14⅞ | 14¾ | 14⅞ | ... |
| 7½ | 5⅞ | BlkrkIncTr | BKT | .56 | 9.1 | ... | 3048 | 6¼ | 6 | 6⅛ | + ⅛ |
| 10⅜ | 9½ | BlkrkMuni | BMT | .62 | 6.1 | ... | 115 | 10¼ | 10⅛ | 10⅛ | − ⅛ |
| 14⅝ | 13 | BlkrkMuni2008 | BRM | .80a | 5.8 | ... | 142 | 13⅞ | 13¾ | 13¾ | − ⅛ |
| 13⅛ | 11⅜ | BlkrkInvQty | BKN | .79a | 6.6 | ... | 220 | 12⅛ | 12 | 12 | − ⅛ |
| 8¼ | 7⅛ | BlackRockInv | BQT | .60 | 7.9 | ... | 316 | 7⅝ | 7½ | 7⅝ | + ⅛ |
| 10⅝ | 9¾ | BlkrkMuniTr | BMN | .62a | 6.1 | ... | 418 | 10⅜ | 10⅛ | 10⅛ | ... |
| 15⅛ | 13⅞ | BlkrkNY2008 | BLN | .86 | 5.9 | ... | 91 | 14½ | 14⅜ | 14½ | ... |
| 10⅜ | 9¼ | BlkrkNoAm | BNA | .84 | 9.0 | ... | 1482 | 9½ | 9⅜ | 9⅜ | ... |
| 8¼ | 7⅛ | BlkrkStrat | BGT | .50 | 6.6 | ... | 836 | 7⅝ | 7½ | 7⅝ | + ⅛ |
| 9⅜ | 8⅜ | BlkrkTrgt | BTT | .58 | 6.6 | ... | 1088 | 8⅞ | 8¾ | 8 13/16 | − ⅛ |
| 9¾ | 8½ | Blkrk1998 | BBT | .50 | 5.4 | ... | 477 | 9¼ | 9⅛ | 9¼ | ... |
| 9 | 7¾ | Blkrk1999 | BNN | .40 | 4.8 | ... | 289 | 8½ | 8⅜ | 8⅜ | ... |
| 8⅜ | 7⅛ | Blkrk2001 | BLK | .45 | 6.0 | ... | 1166 | 7⅝ | 7½ | 7½ | ... |
| 25½ | 16½ | ♣BlanchHldg | EWB | .40 | 1.8 | 17 | 622 | 22 | 21⅞ | 22 | + ⅛ |
| 48⅞ | 31½ | BlockHR | HRB | 1.28 | 3.6 | 19 | 6423 | 35⅜ | 34¾ | 35⅛ | ... |
| s 35⅛ | 24½ | BlountInt A | BLTA | .44 | 1.4 | 12 | 87 | 32⅜ | 32 | 32¼ | − ⅛ |
| 25¾ | 12⅛ | BrownGp | BG | 1.00 | 6.1 | 92 | 202 | 16⅞ | 16⅜ | 16½ | − ⅜ |
| 42⅝ | 32¼ | ♣BrownFormn A | BFA | 1.04 | 2.5 | 18 | 4 | 41⅞ | 41½ | 41½ | − ¾ |
| 42½ | 31½ | ♣BrownFormn B | BFB | 1.04 | 2.5 | 18 | 216 | 41¾ | 40⅞ | 41⅜ | − ⅜ |
| 40⅝ | 27⅜ | BrownFer | BFI | .68 | 2.3 | 17 | 6011 | 30 | 29½ | 29⅝ | − ⅛ |
| n 39½ | 29¾ | BrownFer aces | BFE | 1.26p | ... | ... | 565 | 32¾ | 32½ | 32¾ | + ⅛ |
| 24⅞ | 16¼ | ♣Brunswick | BC | .50 | 2.4 | 15 | 1229 | 21⅛ | 20⅞ | 21 | + ⅛ |
| 23⅝ | 16 | BrushWell | BW | .40 | 2.1 | 16 | 180 | 19 | 18¾ | 19 | ... |
| n 27 | 19 | BuckeyeCell | BKI | | ... | ... | 138 | 26 | 25 | 25⅛ | − ⅞ |
| 39¾ | 30 | ♣BuckeyePtr | BPL | 3.00 | 7.9 | 9 | 272 | 38 | 37½ | 37¾ | − ⅛ |
| 32¾ | 13½ | BuenosAirEmb | BAE | .46e | 3.0 | ... | 746 | 15⅜ | 15⅛ | 15⅜ | + ⅛ |
| 21 | 9½ | BufetInd | GBI | | ... | ... | 496 | 19¼ | 18⅝ | 19¼ | + ¾ |
| 14⅜ | 9⅜ | BurlgtnCoat | BCF | | ... | 22 | 281 | 11⅝ | 11⅜ | 11½ | ... |
| 14¼ | 10⅛ | BurlgtnInd | BUR | | ... | 13 | 553 | 12⅞ | 12⅝ | 12¾ | ... |
| 88¾ | 58 | BurlNthSF | BNI | 1.20 | 1.4 | ... | 1880 | 87⅝ | 85½ | 86¼ | − ¾ |
| 17⅛ | 10 | BurlgtnResCl | BRU | 1.49e | 13.5 | ... | 192 | 11⅛ | 10⅞ | 11 | + ⅛ |
| 42¼ | 34⅞ | BurlgtnRes | BR | .55 | 1.5 | dd | 4244 | 38 | 36⅜ | 37⅝ | + ¾ |
| 14½ | 9½ | BurnhmPacif | BPP | 1.00 | 9.2 | dd | 244 | 10⅞ | 10¾ | 10⅞ | + ⅛ |
| 32¾ | 24½ | BushBoake | BOA | | ... | 16 | 308 | 25½ | 25⅛ | 25⅛ | − ⅛ |
| 34⅝ | 10¾ | BushInd | BSH | .10 | .3 | 20 | 202 | 32⅝ | 32⅛ | 32¼ | ... |

## -C-C-C-

| 52 Weeks Hi | Lo | Stock | Sym | Div | Yld % | PE | Vol 100s | Hi | Lo | Close | Net Chg |
|---|---|---|---|---|---|---|---|---|---|---|---|
| 22⅜ | 19 | CBL Assoc | CBL | 1.68f | 8.0 | 18 | 218 | 21¼ | 21 | 21⅛ | + ⅛ |
| 33¾ | 13½ | CDI | CDI | | ... | 94 | 151 | 30⅞ | 30¾ | 30⅞ | + ⅛ |
| 125½ | 72⅞ | CIGNA | CI | 3.20f | 2.8 | 62 | 2549 | 114¼ | 113⅜ | 113⅞ | + ⅞ |
| 8⅜ | 7⅜ | CIGNA High | HIS | .81a | 10.0 | ... | 306 | 8¼ | 8⅛ | 8⅛ | − ⅛ |
| 41¼ | 28¾ | ♣CIPSCO | CIP | 2.08f | 5.6 | 16 | 95 | 37¼ | 37⅛ | 37⅛ | − ⅜ |
| ▲ 23⅞ | 7⅛ | CKE Restr | CKR | .08 | .3 | 41 | 363 | 24⅜ | 23½ | 24⅛ | + ⅝ |
| 27½ | 23¾ | CL&P MIPS | | 2.33 | 9.3 | ... | 251 | 25¼ | 25⅛ | 25⅛ | ... |
| 59¼ | 40¼ | CMAC | CMT | .20 | .4 | 12 | 384 | 54 | 52½ | 53⅜ | +1 |
| 8¼ | 4¼ | ♣CMI Cp | CMX | | ... | 7 | 96 | 6¼ | 6 | 6⅛ | + ⅛ |
| 9¼ | 2⅞ | CML | CML | .10 | 2.3 | dd | 3692 | 4⅜ | 4⅛ | 4⅜ | + ⅛ |
| 31⅞ | 22⅞ | CMS Engy | CMS | .96 | 3.3 | 14 | 794 | 29½ | 29¼ | 29½ | + ⅛ |
| n 20 | 16⅛ | CMS Engy G | CPG | 1.12 | 6.1 | ... | 268 | 18¾ | 18¼ | 18½ | ... |
| 123¼ | 82½ | CNA Fnl | CNA | | ... | 7 | 202 | 100 | 99 | 99¾ | + ⅞ |
| 11⅛ | 9⅞ | CNA IncShrs | CNN | 1.00 | 9.8 | ... | 45 | 10⅜ | 10¼ | 10¼ | − ⅛ |
| 29½ | 25 | CNB Bncshr | BNK | .84b | 2.9 | 14 | 16 | 28⅝ | 28½ | 28½ | ... |
| 75½ | 57⅜ | CPC Int | CPC | 1.52 | 2.2 | 20 | 1843 | 69 | 68½ | 69 | + ¼ |
| 22⅛ | 14⅛ | CPI Cp | CPY | .56 | 3.2 | 15 | 226 | 17⅝ | 17¼ | 17⅝ | ... |
| 4 | 1¾ | CRI Liq | CFR | 2.20e | 117.3 | ... | 129 | 1⅞ | 1¾ | 1⅞ | + ⅛ |
| 25¾ | 15¾ | CSS Ind | CSS | | ... | 21 | 5 | 25⅝ | 25⅝ | 25⅝ | ... |
| s 53⅛ | 36 | CSX | CSX | 1.04 | 2.1 | 16 | 5569 | 50⅝ | 49⅜ | 49½ | − ¾ |
| 45 | 29¼ | CTS | CTS | .72f | 1.6 | 13 | 13 | 45 | 44½ | 44¾ | + ⅛ |
| s 39⅞ | 24¼ | CUC Int | CU | | ... | 44 | 5866 | 37¾ | 37⅜ | 37⅜ | − ⅜ |
| 11⅞ | 8⅞ | CV REIT | CVI | 1.08 | 9.8 | 9 | 36 | 11 | 10⅞ | 11 | + ⅛ |
| 18¾ | 11⅛ | CWM Mtg | CWM | 1.44f | 8.3 | 13 | 2074 | 17½ | 17 | 17¼ | − ⅛ |
| 25¼ | 19 | ♣CablWirels | CWP | .55e | 2.6 | ... | 1532 | 21⅛ | 20¾ | 20⅞ | − ⅛ |
| 87¾ | 48⅝ | CabltrnSys | CS | | ... | 36 | 5988 | 87⅛ | 83¾ | 83⅞ | −2⅝ |
| s 31⅝ | 20½ | Cabot Cp | CBT | .36 | 1.4 | 12 | 2079 | 27 | 26½ | 26⅝ | − ¼ |
| 17⅝ | 13 | CabotO&G | COG | .16 | .9 | dd | 682 | 17 | 16¾ | 17 | ... |
| 27⅜ | 25⅜ | Cadbury quips | A | 2.16 | 8.3 | ... | 160 | 26⅛ | 26 | 26⅛ | + ⅛ |
| 35⅜ | 28¼ | CadburySch | CSG | 1.61e | 5.3 | ... | 584 | 30⅝ | 30⅛ | 30½ | ... |
| s 56½ | 18⅝ | CadenceDsgn | CDN | | ... | 35 | 1294 | 55⅝ | 54⅞ | 55⅜ | + ⅛ |
| 18½ | 11½ | CalFedBcp | CAL | | ... | 11 | 542 | 17⅞ | 17½ | 17¾ | + ⅛ |
| 21⅛ | 2⅞ | Caldor | CLD | | ... | dd | 6958 | 3⅛ | 2⅞ | 2⅞ | − ⅛ |
| 27 | 15⅝ | CalEnergy | CE | | ... | 20 | 1009 | 26¼ | 25¾ | 26⅛ | + ⅛ |
| 13⅛ | 10¾ | CalgnCarb | CCC | .32 | 2.6 | 22 | 508 | 12⅜ | 12¼ | 12⅜ | ... |
| 23⅞ | 17⅛ | CaliRlty | CLI | 1.70 | 7.4 | 15 | 64 | 23⅛ | 22⅞ | 23 | − ⅛ |
| s 48 31/64 | 35 7/16 | CaliberSys | CBB | .72 | 1.8 | dd | 237 | 39¾ | 38⅞ | 39 | − ¼ |

FIGURE 18.2

*Source:* New York Stock Exchange, May 21, 1996. Reprinted by permission of *The Wall Street Journal*, © 1996 Dow Jones & Co., Inc. All Rights Reserved Worldwide.

| 52 Weeks Hi | Lo | Stock | Sym | Div | Yld % | PE | Vol 100s | Hi | Lo | Close | Net Chg |
|---|---|---|---|---|---|---|---|---|---|---|---|
| $74\frac{7}{8}$ | $52\frac{5}{8}$ | BellAtlantic | BEL | 2.88f | 4.6 | 14 | 4875 | $64\frac{5}{8}$ | $62\frac{3}{4}$ | $62\frac{7}{8}$ | $-1\frac{1}{4}$ |

The numbers $74\frac{7}{8}$ and $52\frac{5}{8}$ in front of the company's name show that $74\frac{7}{8}$ ($74.875) was the highest price the stock reached in the previous 52 weeks, while $52\frac{5}{8}$ ($52.625) was the lowest. After the name of the company and its symbol, find 2.88f, which means that the company pays $2.88 per year per share of stock as a dividend to the owners of the stock. Dividends typically go up when the company is doing well and down when business is bad. The symbol "f" after the 2.88 refers to a footnote indicating that the dividend was recently increased. The 4.6 in the next column is the current yield on the company's stock, in percent. The dividend of $2.88 per share is 4.6% of the current purchase price of the stock. After the 4.6 is 14, the price-earnings ratio, discussed later. Then comes 4875, the sales for the day in hundreds of shares. On the day reported, a total of

$$4{,}875 \times 100 = 487{,}500$$

shares of Bell Atlantic were sold. After 4875 comes a list of prices reached by the stock during the day. The first number, $64\frac{5}{8}$, was the highest price reached by the stock during the day, while $62\frac{3}{4}$ was the lowest. The next number, $62\frac{7}{8}$, says the stock closed at $62\frac{7}{8}$ ($62.875) at the end of the day. The last number is $-1\frac{1}{4}$, indicating that the stock price fell by $1\frac{1}{4}$ ($1.25) compared to the previous day.

**EXAMPLE 1** *Reading a Stock Table*

Use the stock table to find (a) the highest price for the last 52 weeks for the large insurance company CIGNA and (b) the dividend for Cabot Oil and Gas.

**(a)** The symbol for CIGNA is CI. Find the correct line in the stock table.

| 52 Weeks | | | | | Yld | | Vol | | | | Net |
| Hi | Lo | Stock | Sym | Div | % | PE | 100s | Hi | Lo | Close | Chg |
|---|---|---|---|---|---|---|---|---|---|---|---|
| $125\frac{1}{2}$ | $72\frac{7}{8}$ | CIGNA | CI | 3.2of | 2.8 | 62 | 2549 | $114\frac{1}{4}$ | $113\frac{3}{8}$ | $113\frac{7}{8}$ | $+\frac{7}{8}$ |

The highest price during the last 52 weeks was $125\frac{1}{2}$ or $125.50, the first number on the left.

**(b)** In the table, the dividend for Cabot Oil and Gas is given just after the company symbol, COG. The dividend is $0.16 per share per year. ■

The letters "pf" appear after some of the company names in the stock table. These letters represent "preferred stock," which was discussed in Section 18.1.

**EXAMPLE 2** *Reading a Stock Table*

Find the cost for 100 shares of Best Buy at the high price for the day.

**SOLUTION**   Find the total cost of a stock purchase by multiplying the price per share by the number of shares. From the stock table, the high price of Best Buy was $21\frac{1}{2}$ per share. First change $21\frac{1}{2}$ to the decimal 21.5, then multiply.

$$100 \times 21.5 = \$2{,}150$$

The cost of 100 shares of this stock is $2,150 (plus any broker's fee). ■

**OBJECTIVE 3** *Find the commission for buying or selling stocks.*   It is necessary to use a broker to buy or sell a stock. The broker has representatives at the exchange who will execute a buyer's order. (It is sometimes possible to buy stock directly from a bank, which might sell it with no sales charge.) The broker will charge a fee, or **commission**, for executing an order. Commission rates formerly were set by stock exchange rules and did not vary from broker to broker. Now, however, commissions are competitive and vary considerably among brokers.

In the last few years, several **discount brokers** have become popular. These brokers merely buy and sell stock and offer no additional services, such as research or recommendations on stocks to buy or sell.

The rates charged depend on whether the order is for a **round lot** of shares (multiples of 100) or an **odd lot** (fewer than 100 shares). Odd lot orders often involve an **odd-lot differential**, an extra charge of $\$\frac{1}{8}$, or 12.5 cents, a share. Typical expenses in buying and selling stock are as follows. (There is often a minimum commission charge.)

| **Buying Stock** | **Selling Stock** |
| --- | --- |
| **Broker's commission of** | **Broker's commission of** |
| **2.5% of purchase price** | **2.5% of selling price** |
| **plus** | **plus** |
| **Any odd-lot differential** | **Any odd-lot differential** |
| | **plus** |
| | **SEC fee (see below)** |
| | **plus** |
| | **Any transfer taxes (see below)** |

The SEC fee is set by the Securities and Exchange Commission, a federal government agency that regulates stock markets. The fee is currently 1 cent ($0.01) per $500 in value (or any fraction of $500). For example, to find the fee for a sale of $1,100, first divide $1,100 by $500.

$$\frac{\$1,100}{\$500} = 2.2$$

Since the fee is 1¢ per $500, or *fraction of $500*, round 2.2 *up* to 3. The fee is then $3 \times 1¢ = 3¢$.

**NOTE**  Some state and local governments charge a **transfer tax** when stock is sold. The amount of this tax would be subtracted by the broker before turning over the balance of the money to the seller.  ■

**OBJECTIVE** **4** ***Find the total price of a stock purchase.***    The next two examples show the total cost of a stock purchase and the cost of selling a stock.

**EXAMPLE 3** *Finding Total Cost of a Purchase*

Marie Wilson bought 75 shares of stock, paying $\$26\frac{3}{4}$ per share. Find her total cost for the purchase.

**SOLUTION**    The basic cost of the stock is found by multiplying the price per share and the number of shares.

$$\text{Price per share} \times \text{Number of shares} = \$26\frac{3}{4} \times 75$$
$$= \$26.75 \times 75$$
$$= \$2,006.25$$

The broker's commission is 2.5% of this amount, or

$$\text{Broker's commission} = 2.5\% \times \$2,006.25$$
$$= 0.025 \times \$2,006.25$$
$$= \$50.16.$$

Since Wilson bought 75 shares (and not a multiple of 100 shares), she must pay an odd-lot differential of $\$\frac{1}{8}$, or 12.5 cents, per share. For 75 shares, this odd-lot differential amounts to

$$75 \text{ shares} \times \$\frac{1}{8} \text{ per share} = \$9.38 \text{ (rounded)}.$$

The total cost of the shares of stock is

| | |
|---|---|
| $2,006.25 | basic cost |
| 50.16 | broker's commission |
| +    9.38 | odd-lot differential |
| $2,065.79. | |

■

### EXAMPLE 4    *Finding Total Cost of a Stock Sale*

Find the amount received by a person selling 700 shares of a stock at $\$63\frac{5}{8}$.

**SOLUTION**    The basic price of the stock is

$$700 \times \$63\frac{5}{8} = 700 \times \$63.625 = \$44,537.50.$$

Find the SEC fee as described. First,

$$\frac{\$44,537.50}{\$500} = 89.075.$$

Round 89.075 up to 90. The SEC fee is then

$$90 \times 1\cent = 90\cent \text{ (or } \$0.90).$$

The broker's commission is 2.5% of the basic price, or

$$0.025 \times \$44,537.50 = \$1,113.44.$$

Finally, the seller receives

$$
\begin{array}{ll}
\$44,537.50 & \text{basic price} \\
-\quad 1,113.44 & \text{broker's fee} \\
\hline
\$43,424.06 & \\
-\quad\quad\ 0.90 & \text{SEC fee} \\
\hline
\$43,423.16. &
\end{array}
$$

There is no odd-lot differential since the number of shares traded is a multiple of 100. ■

Most people buy stock because they hope that the price will go up. If the price does go up, the investor can then sell the stock at a profit. Some people, however, buy a stock because of the dividend that it pays. (A dividend is usually paid quarterly.)

While there is no certain way of choosing stocks that will go up, there are a couple of **stock ratios** that can be looked at when considering a stock purchase. Two useful ratios are the **current yield** and the **price-earnings ratio**.

OBJECTIVE **5** *Find the current yield on a stock.* The **current yield** on a stock is used to compare the dividends paid by stocks selling at different prices. Find current yield with the following formula.

$$
\text{Current yield} = \frac{\text{Annual dividend per share}}{\text{Current price per share}}
$$

This result usually is converted to a percent (rounded to the nearest tenth). The annual dividend rate and the current yield can be found in the stock tables in daily newspapers.

**EXAMPLE 5** *Finding Current Yield*

Find the current yield for each of the following stocks: (a) Beneficial with a dividend of $1.88 per share per year and (b) Caldor with no dividend.

**SOLUTION**

**(a)** The closing price of Beneficial, symbol BNL, was $59\frac{3}{8}$. Use the formula for current yield to get the following.

$$
\text{Current yield} = \frac{\$1.88}{\$59.375} = 3.2\% \text{ (rounded)}
$$

**(b)** The closing price of Caldor, symbol CLD, was $2\frac{7}{8}$. The following is found using the formula for current yield.

$$
\text{Current yield} = \frac{0}{\$2.875} = 0\%
$$

■

NOTE   A stock pays no dividend when the company has been going through bad times or is investing in research or new plants which promise a long-term payoff. Sometimes a small new company will pay no dividends during its early years, preferring to reinvest the money for long-term growth.   ■

OBJECTIVE **6**   *Find the PE ratio of a stock.*   One number that some people use to help decide which stock to buy is the **price-earnings ratio** (abbreviated **PE ratio**). This ratio is found with the following formula.

$$PE \text{ ratio} = \frac{\text{Price per share}}{\text{Annual net income per share}}$$

NOTE   Annual net income per share is the same thing as earnings per share discussed in Section 18.1.   ■

| EXAMPLE 6   *Finding the PE Ratio*

Find the PE ratio for the following stocks: (a) Nike, Inc., price per share $96.125, annual earnings per share $3.47 and (b) Sears, Roebuck and Company, price per share $49.875, annual earnings per share $3.51.

SOLUTION

**(a)**  Use the formula to get

$$PE \text{ ratio} = \frac{\$96.125}{\$3.47} = 27.7, \text{ or } 28 \text{ after rounding.}$$

**(b)**  $PE \text{ ratio} = \dfrac{\$49.875}{\$3.51} = 14.2, \text{ or } 14 \text{ after rounding.}$   ■

PROBLEM-SOLVING HINT   It is customary to round the PE ratio to the nearest whole number.   ■

Sometimes a low PE ratio may indicate that the stock is a ''sleeper'' which has not been found by other investors. On the other hand, a high PE ratio may indicate that the stock's price is too high; as other people notice this, the stock's price could fall.

Unfortunately, the PE ratio is not a perfect guide to future stock market behavior. The PE ratio may be low, not because the stock is an undervalued sleeper, but because investors correctly see a poor future for the company. A PE ratio may be high, not because the stock is overpriced, but because investors correctly feel that company earnings will increase over the next few years.

Many daily newspapers now give the PE ratio. If no PE ratio is given for a particular stock, most probably that company has lost money during the previous year.

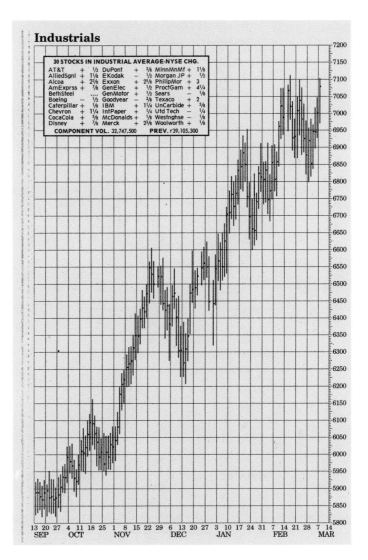

**Industrials**

| 30 STOCKS IN INDUSTRIAL AVERAGE-NYSE CHG. |
| --- |

| | | | | | | |
|---|---|---|---|---|---|---|
| AT&T | + ½ | DuPont | + ⅜ | MinnMnMf | + | 1⅛ |
| AlliedSgnl | + 1⅛ | EKodak | − ½ | Morgan JP | + | ½ |
| Alcoa | + 2⅜ | Exxon | + 2⅝ | PhillpMor | + | 3 |
| AmExprss | + ⅞ | GenElec | + ½ | ProctGam | + | 4¼ |
| BethSteel | .... | GenMotor | + ½ | Sears | − | ⅛ |
| Boeing | − ½ | Goodyear | − ⅜ | Texaco | + | 2 |
| Caterpillar | + ⅛ | IBM | + 1¼ | UnCarbide | + | ⅝ |
| Chevron | + 1¼ | IntPaper | + ¼ | Utd Tech | − | ¼ |
| CocaCola | + ⅝ | McDonalds | + ⅛ | Westnghse | − | ⅛ |
| Disney | + ⅞ | Merck | + 2⅜ | Woolworth | + | ⅛ |

COMPONENT VOL. 32,747,500   PREV. r39,105,300

FIGURE 18.3

*Source:* Dow Jones Industrial Average, March 11, 1997. Reprinted by permission of *The Wall Street Journal,* © 1997 Dow Jones & Co., Inc. All Rights Reserved Worldwide.

**OBJECTIVE** **7** *Define the Dow Jones Industrial Average.* The **Dow Jones Industrial Average** is frequently used as an indicator of overall trends in stock prices. Actually, Dow Jones & Company publishes several different averages. The one most commonly used refers to an average of the stock prices of 30 large industrial companies listed in Figure 18.3. It is the movement of this average that is typically quoted on television news and in the newspapers. As you can see in Figure 18.4, the Dow Jones Industrial Average has increased greatly over the past 90 years.

Dow Jones Industrial Average Performance Since 1900

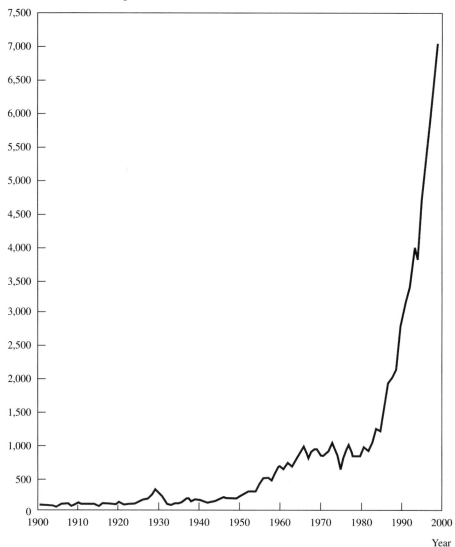

FIGURE 18.4

*Source:* Reprinted by permission of Dow Jones and Company.

**OBJECTIVE 8** *Define a mutual fund.*     Ownership of shares in a single company can be risky—the company may suffer poor financial results causing the stock price to fall. This risk can be reduced by simultaneously investing in the stocks of several different companies. One way of doing this is to invest with a mutual fund that buys stocks. A **mutual fund** that invests in stocks receives investment funds from many different investors and uses the money to purchase stock in several different companies. For example, a $1,000 investment in a typical mutual fund owning stock means that you own a very small piece of perhaps 100 different companies or more.

Over periods of many years, stocks have consistently provided a greater return on investment than savings accounts, certificates of deposit, or bonds. Most financial planners agree that stocks should be a part of any long-range retirement or investment plan.

## 18.2 EXERCISES

*Find each of the following from the stock table. Give money answers in whole dollars.*

1. High for the day for Brushwell
2. Low for the day for Berkshire Hathaway A
3. Closing price for Belden
4. Change from the previous day for Bergman Electric
5. 52-week high for Brunswick
6. 52-week low for CMAC
7. Dividend for Cabot Corporation
8. Dividend yield for Cadence Design
9. Volume for the day for H and R Block (Block HR)
10. Closing price for Bethlehem Steel

*Find the price for each of the following stock purchases. Ignore any broker's fees.*

| | Stock | Number of Shares | Transaction |
|---|---|---|---|
| 11. | CIGNA | 1,000 | close |
| 12. | Black and Decker | 100 | high |
| 13. | Benquet | 200 | low |
| 14. | Berkshire Hathaway B | 5 | close |
| 15. | Brunswick | 75 | low |
| 16. | Cadbury Schools | 300 | high |

*Find the price for each of the following stock purchases. Use the broker's charges given in the text. (Hint: In Exercises 23 and 24, the odd-lot differential is charged on only 40 shares.)*

17. 200 shares at $27\frac{5}{8}$
18. 700 shares at $19\frac{1}{8}$
19. 1,200 shares at $37\frac{3}{4}$
20. 1,400 shares at $16\frac{7}{8}$
21. 60 shares at $35\frac{5}{8}$
22. 90 shares at $53\frac{3}{4}$
23. 540 shares at $69\frac{1}{4}$
24. 740 shares at $32\frac{3}{8}$

*Find the amount received by the sellers of the following stocks. Use the broker's charges listed in the text.*

**25.** 300 shares at $30\frac{1}{2}$

**26.** 500 shares at $10\frac{1}{4}$

**27.** 100 shares at $40\frac{3}{4}$

**28.** 200 shares at $13\frac{7}{8}$

**29.** 830 shares at $52\frac{3}{4}$

**30.** 360 shares at $72\frac{1}{8}$

*Find the current yield for each of the following stocks. Round to the nearest tenth of a percent.*

| Stock | Current Price per Share | Annual Dividend |
|-------|------------------------|-----------------|
| **31. Nucor** | $55\frac{1}{8}$ | $0.32 |
| **32. Seagram** | $36\frac{1}{4}$ | $0.60 |
| **33. Ratheon** | $52\frac{1}{4}$ | $0.80 |
| **34. Office Depot** | $23\frac{7}{8}$ | $0 |
| **35. Travelers** | $62 | $0.90 |
| **36. Exxon** | $87\frac{1}{4}$ | $3.16 |

*Find the PE ratio for each of the following. Round all answers to the nearest whole number.*

| Stock | Price per Share | Net Income per Share |
|-------|-----------------|----------------------|
| **37. Caterpillar** | $67\frac{7}{8}$ | $5.85 |
| **38. Dupont** | $82\frac{7}{8}$ | $5.78 |
| **39. General Motors** | $56\frac{5}{8}$ | $5.45 |
| **40. Hilton** | $103\frac{3}{4}$ | $3.76 |

*Solve each of the following application problems. Exercises 43 and 44 require concepts from Chapter 14.*

**41.** Bill Moss bought 100 shares of Micron Technologies at $33 per share and 200 shares of Intel at $71 per share. Find the total amount paid if the broker's commission is 2.5%.

**42.** Theresa Tabor purchased 200 shares of Omnicare at $56\frac{7}{8}$ and 100 shares of Schwab at $23\frac{7}{8}$. Find the total amount paid if her broker charges 1.5%.

**43.** Toni Chavez is comparing two different investment alternatives for his $500 semiannual contribution to a retirement plan. Plan A uses certificates of deposits currently yielding 8% compounded semiannually. Plan B uses a global stock mutual fund with Merrill Lynch that has historically yielded 12% compounded semiannually. Find the amount of an annuity after 20 years of (a) Plan A and (b) Plan B. (c) Find the difference between the two.

**44.** Laurie Zimms is trying to decide whether she should place her quarterly $2,000 retirement account investment in a certificate of deposit yielding 6% compounded quarterly or in a stock mutual fund that has historically yielded 10% compounded quarterly. Find the amount of an annuity after 12 years using (a) the CDs and (b) the mutual fund. (c) Find the difference between the two.

**45.** Leslie Toombs purchased 250 shares of Microsoft at $105 per share and paid a 2% commission. She later sold the same stock at $118\frac{1}{4} but paid a 1.5% sales commission. Find her profit ignoring any dividends paid.

**46.** Bob Thomas bought 100 shares of Brunswick at $16 per share and paid a 2.5% sales commission. The company paid $0.50 per share in dividends during the period of time he owned the stock. Thomas then sold the stock at $22\frac{3}{8} per share and paid a 2% commission. Find Thomas' gain, including dividends, on this stock.

**47.** Explain current yield and the PE ratio. Why might investors be interested in these numbers? (See Objectives 5 and 6.)

**48.** What is a mutual fund? Name any particular mutual funds that you have read or heard about. (See Objective 8.)

## 18.3   Bonds

### OBJECTIVES

**1** *Know the basics of bonds.*

**2** *Read bond tables.*

**3** *Find the cost of bonds, including commission.*

**4** *Use mutual funds containing bonds for monthly income.*

A corporation can raise money by selling additional shares of stock. The purchasers of this stock become part owners of the business. However, company management may feel that the sale of additional stock would excessively dilute the ownership rights of current stockholders. If so, management might decide to raise money by borrowing.

**OBJECTIVE** **1** *Know the basics of bonds.*    For short-term money needs, a corporation might borrow from a bank or an insurance company. For longer term borrowing (such as 5 years or more), the corporation might borrow money from the public. The corporation borrows this money by selling **bonds**. A bond is a promise to repay the borrowed money at some specified time. The bond also promises to pay interest at a certain annual rate.

However, there is one type of bond, called a **zero coupon bond**, that does not pay annual interest—it only pays the face value at maturity. An example of a zero coupon bond is a bond bought for $600 in 1998 with no annual interest payments, but it pays the bondholder $1,000 at maturity in 2005. In this case, a present value of $600 would grow to $1,000 in 7 years resulting in a yield of just over 7.5%.

National governments, states and provinces, and some cities also issue bonds. Bonds issued by a state or local governmental authority are called **municipal bonds**.

| Bonds | Cur Yld | Vol | Close | Net Chg |
|---|---|---|---|---|
| Arvln 7½14 | cv | 35 | 103 | ... |
| Ashlnd 6¾14 | cv | 10 | 100½ | − ½ |
| AubrnHl 12⅜20f | ... | 4 | 145½ | + 2 |
| AutDt zr12 | ... | 89 | 50 | − 1½ |
| BkrHgh zr03 | ... | 3 | 67¼ | + ¼ |
| Bally 10s06f | cv | 5 | 104 | − ¼ |
| BarBks 10⅞03 | 9.2 | 5 | 118 | + 3 |
| Barnet 8½07 | 8.0 | 5 | 106⅛ | − ⅞ |
| BellPa 7⅛12 | 7.4 | 12 | 96⅞ | − ½ |
| BellsoT 6½00 | 6.5 | 50 | 100 | − ¼ |
| BellsoT 6½05 | 6.7 | 35 | 96⅜ | − ⅞ |
| BellsoT 5⅞09 | 6.5 | 77 | 90¼ | + ⅞ |
| BellsoT 8¼32 | 7.9 | 2 | 104⅛ | + ⅝ |
| BellsoT 7⅞32 | 7.8 | 10 | 101⅜ | + ⅜ |
| BellsoT 7½33 | 7.7 | 12 | 97⅞ | + ½ |
| BstBuy 8⅝00 | 8.8 | 73 | 98¼ | + ⅛ |
| BethSt 8.45s05 | 8.5 | 8 | 99 | − ⅞ |
| Bevrly 7⅝03 | cv | 25 | 93½ | + ½ |
| Bevrly 5½18 | cv | 10 | 104 | ... |
| Bluegrn 8¼12 | cv | 10 | 88½ | + ½ |
| Bordn 8⅜16 | 8.8 | 10 | 95 | − 1⅜ |
| BorgWS 9⅛03 | 9.4 | 20 | 97⅛ | + 1⅞ |
| CalEgy zr04 | ... | 35 | 97½ | + ⅞ |
| CarnCp 4½97 | cv | 1 | 164 | + 4 |
| CaterpInc 9s06 | 8.2 | 15 | 109⅛ | − 4 |
| CaterpInc 6s07 | 6.6 | 17 | 90½ | + 1¼ |
| ChsCp 6¾08 | 7.2 | 5 | 94⅛ | + ⅞ |
| CPoM 7¼12 | 7.6 | 20 | 96 | ... |
| Chiquta 10½04 | 10.2 | 22 | 102⅞ | − ½ |
| ChckFul 7s12 | cv | 5 | 84½ | − ½ |
| Chryslr 10.4s99 | 10.0 | 75 | 104⅜ | − ½ |
| Citicp 6½04t | 6.5 | 9 | 99½ | ... |
| Clardge 11¾02 | 12.7 | 305 | 92¾ | − 1⅝ |
| ClrkOil 9½04 | 9.2 | 190 | 103⅜ | − ⅝ |
| ClevEl 8¾05 | 8.7 | 35 | 100⅛ | + 1⅜ |
| ClevEl 8⅜11 | 9.1 | 31 | 91⅝ | − ¼ |
| ClevEl 8⅜12 | 9.2 | 100 | 91 | − 1 |
| Coastl 11¾cld | ... | 10 | 103 9/16 | + 1/32 |
| CompUSA 9½00 | 9.3 | 117 | 102½ | ... |
| ConrPer 6¾01 | cv | 5 | 110 | ... |
| ConrPer 6½02 | cv | 174 | 121 | + 1¾ |
| Consec 8⅛03 | 8.0 | 93 | 101¼ | + ⅛ |
| CnNG 5⅞98 | 5.9 | 10 | 99⅛ | + ¾ |
| ConNG 7¼15 | cv | 17 | 105¼ | + ¼ |
| CntlHm 10s06 | 10.1 | 10 | 99½ | + ½ |
| CoopIn 7.05s15 | cv | 24 | 106¾ | ... |
| DDL Elc 8½08 | cv | 4 | 76 | ... |
| DataGn 01 | cv | 10 | 102½ | + 1 |
| Datpnt 8⅞06f | cv | 14 | 49 | ... |
| DetEd 6s96 | 6.0 | 16 | 99 15/16 | ... |
| duPnt dc6s01 | 6.2 | 207 | 96½ | ... |
| DukePw 5⅜97 | 5.4 | 2 | 98 25/32 | − 23/32 |
| DukePw 7s00 | 7.0 | 3 | 100¼ | − 2½ |
| DukePw 7s05 | 7.0 | 2 | 99½ | − ½ |
| DukePw 6 08 | 6.9 | 25 | 93 | − 1¼ |
| DukePw 8¾21 | 8.4 | 50 | 104 | − 1⅝ |
| DukePw 8⅜21 | 8.2 | 5 | 102⅝ | + ⅜ |
| DukePw 7⅜23 | 7.7 | 5 | 96 | + ½ |
| DukePw 7⅞24 | 8.0 | 33 | 98⅞ | + ½ |
| Eckerd 9¼04 | 8.9 | 54 | 104⅛ | − ⅛ |
| ElanInt zr12 | ... | 34 | 67¾ | + ¾ |
| EthAln 8¾01 | 8.7 | 10 | 101 | − ¼ |

| Bonds | Cur Yld | Vol | Close | Net Chg |
|---|---|---|---|---|
| NETelTel 7⅞22 | 7.8 | 10 | 101 | + ¾ |
| NJBTl 7¼11 | 7.4 | 9 | 98½ | + ⅝ |
| NYTel 4⅝04 | 5.5 | 2 | 84½ | + ½ |
| NYTel 7¼24 | 7.8 | 20 | 93¼ | + ⅞ |
| NYTel 4⅞06 | 5.8 | 2 | 84⅜ | + ½ |
| NYTel 7½09 | 7.7 | 1 | 97½ | ... |
| NYTel 7⅜11 | 7.7 | 15 | 96¼ | − ¾ |
| NYTel 7⅞17 | 8.0 | 25 | 98⅛ | − ⅜ |
| NoPac 4s97r | 3.9 | 2 | 103⅜ | + 2⅛ |
| Novacr 5½2000 | cv | 25 | 88½ | − ½ |
| Nynex rp9.55s10 | ... | 87 | 87⅛ | − 1⅛ |
| OcciP 9⅝99 | 9.6 | 12 | 100 17/32 | + 3/16 |
| OffDep zr08 | ... | 5 | 60 | ... |
| Olsten 4⅞03 | ... | 14 | 126 | ... |
| Oryx 7½14 | cv | 67 | 90 | − ½ |
| OwnIll 10¼99 | 10.0 | 38 | 102⅜ | ... |
| OwnIll 10½02 | 10.1 | 25 | 103½ | − ⅞ |
| OwIll 11s03 | 10.3 | 5 | 107¼ | − 1¾ |
| OwnIll 9¾04 | 9.7 | 40 | 100¾ | − 1¾ |
| PacBell 7¼02 | 7.1 | 10 | 101⅝ | + ¼ |
| PacBell 6¼05 | 6.6 | 34 | 94⅝ | + ⅝ |
| PacBell 7⅛26 | 7.6 | 50 | 94 | + ¼ |
| PacBell 7½33 | 7.8 | 10 | 96 | + ¾ |
| PacTT 7¼08 | 7.3 | 21 | 99 | ... |
| ParCm 7s03A | 7.7 | 33 | 90⅞ | − ⅝ |
| ParkElc 5½06 | cv | 36 | 88 | ... |
| Pathmk zr03 | ... | 5 | 62⅞ | − ⅝ |
| PaylCsh 9⅛03 | 11.3 | 388 | 81⅛ | + ¼ |
| PennTr 9⅝05 | 11.4 | 272 | 84¾ | + ¼ |
| Pennzl 4¾03 | 4.4 | 36 | 107½ | + 1 |
| PhilEl 7¾23 | 7.9 | 20 | 97⅞ | + 1⅜ |
| PhilP 9s01 | 8.4 | 6 | 107½ | ... |
| Pier1 6⅞02 | cv | 30 | 130 | ... |
| PionFn 6½03 | cv | 58 | 102½ | ... |
| PogoP 8s05 | cv | 15 | 106 | + ⅝ |
| PotEl 5s02 | cv | 20 | 89 | − 1 |
| PotEl 7s18 | cv | 18 | 99¾ | − ¾ |
| Primark 8¾00 | 8.7 | 46 | 100½ | ... |
| PrmHsp 9¼06 | 9.6 | 40 | 96¾ | ... |
| PSEG 7⅝00 | 7.5 | 10 | 102 | − ⅜ |
| PSvEG 6⅛02 | 6.4 | 25 | 95½ | + ¼ |
| PSEG 8¾22 | 8.2 | 15 | 107¼ | + ¼ |
| PSEG 7½23 | 7.7 | 10 | 97⅜ | ... |
| PSvEG 7s24 | 7.8 | 25 | 89½ | + 1⅜ |
| PSEG 5s37 | 7.5 | 5 | 67 | ... |
| RJR Nb 8s00 | 8.0 | 10 | 99¾ | ... |
| RJR Nb 8s01 | 8.1 | 414 | 99 | + ⅛ |
| RJR Nb 8⅝02 | 8.6 | 69 | 100½ | + ½ |
| RJR Nb 7⅝03 | 8.1 | 107 | 94½ | − ⅛ |
| RJR Nb 8¾05 | 8.8 | 12 | 99¼ | + 1 |
| RJR Nb 8¾07 | 8.9 | 5 | 98¾ | + ¾ |
| RJR Nb 9¼13 | 9.3 | 101 | 99⅝ | + ⅜ |
| RJR Nb 8.3s99 | 8.1 | 3 | 102⅛ | + ⅛ |
| RJR Nb 8¾04 | 8.8 | 95 | 99⅜ | + ⅛ |
| Rallys 9⅞00 | 13.2 | 139 | 75⅛ | + ⅝ |
| RalsP 8⅝22 | 8.1 | 14 | 107 | − 1 |
| RegHS 6½03 | cv | 9 | 101 | + 2 |
| RelGrp 9s00 | 9.0 | 424 | 99⅞ | − ⅛ |
| RelGrp 9¾03 | 9.8 | 285 | 100 | ... |
| Revl 9½99 | 9.3 | 23 | 101⅝ | + ¾ |
| Roadmst 8s03 | cv | 102 | 68 | ... |
| RocInt 8⅜01 | 7.9 | 5 | 105¾ | + ½ |

FIGURE 18.5

*Source:* New York Exchange Bonds, May 21, 1996. Reprinted by permission of *The Wall Street Journal*, © 1996 Dow Jones & Co., Inc. All Rights Reserved Worldwide.

One advantage of municipal bonds is that the income from these bonds is usually *not* subject to federal income taxes, but may be subject to a state income tax.

Suppose a person buys a bond for $1,000 from Duke Power due in 2021 (see Figure 18.5). This bond is a promise to repay the $1,000 in the year 2021 and until then to pay interest of $8\frac{3}{4}\%$ per year. For this bond, the investor would receive annual interest payments of

$$\$1{,}000 \times 8\frac{3}{4}\% = \$1{,}000 \times 0.0875 = \$87.50.$$

In this example, $1,000 is the amount that the company promises to repay to the investor. This amount is called the **face value** or **par value** of the bond. Almost all corporations issue bonds with a par value of $1,000.

**OBJECTIVE 2** ***Read bond tables.*** The Duke Power bond will be redeemed by the company in 2021 for $1,000. Suppose, however, that the bond's owner needs money now.

The bond can be sold quickly through a bond dealer. However, the price for the bond is set, not by Duke Power, but by market conditions. To find the selling price of a bond, look in the "Corporate Bond" section of the daily newspaper. A portion of *The Wall Street Journal* corporate bond page is reproduced in Figure 18.5. For these Duke Power bonds, the table gives the following.

| Bonds | Cur Yld | Vol | Close | Net Chg |
|---|---|---|---|---|
| DukePw $8\frac{3}{4}$21 | 8.4 | 50 | 104 | $-1\frac{5}{8}$ |

After the name of the company, which may be abbreviated, comes $8\frac{3}{4}$21. The $8\frac{3}{4}$ says that the bonds pay $8\frac{3}{4}\%$ interest on their face value of $1,000, while 21 is an abbreviation for the year 2021. (An "s" indicates that interest is paid by the company every 6 months instead of annually.) The number 8.4 is the current yield. The 50 shows that 50 bonds with a face value of $1,000 each were sold that day. The next number gives the closing price of the bonds. The bond prices in the table represent *not dollar amounts but percents.* Here 104 says that the bond is selling at 104% of its par value of $1,000. An investor who sold these bonds at this price would receive

$$\$1,000 \times 104\% = \$1,000 \times 1.04 = \$1,040.$$

**NOTE** This selling price of $1,040 *is higher than* the face value of $1,000 since general interest rates are lower than the $8\frac{3}{4}\%$ of this bond. ■

| **EXAMPLE 1** *Finding the Selling Price of Bonds*

Find the current selling price of the following bonds: (a) Pacific Bell, $6\frac{1}{4}\%$ bonds of 2005, (b) Eckerd, $9\frac{1}{4}\%$ bonds of 2004, and (c) RJR Nabisco, $8\frac{3}{4}\%$ bonds of 2007.

**SOLUTION**

**(a)** The listing for Pacific Bell provides the following.

| Bonds | Cur Yld | Vol | Close | Net Chg |
|---|---|---|---|---|
| PacBell $6\frac{1}{4}$05 | 6.6 | 34 | $94\frac{5}{8}$ | $+\frac{5}{8}$ |

The price information for these bonds comes from the number $94\frac{5}{8}$. Notice that only 34 of these Pacific Bell bonds were sold that day. This number represents 34 bonds, not 34 hundreds as with stocks.

Since the price of these bonds for the day was $94\frac{5}{8}$, or $94\frac{5}{8}\%$ of par value, the selling price for one bond was

$$\$1,000 \times 94\frac{5}{8}\% = \$1,000 \times 0.94625 = \$946.25.$$

**(b)** Find the listing for Eckerd. The price for the day is given as $104\frac{1}{8}$, with one bond selling for

$$\$1,000 \times 104\frac{1}{8}\% = \$1,000 \times 1.04125 = \$1,041.25.$$

**(c)** The selling price of an RJR Nabisco $8\frac{3}{4}\%$ bond of 2007 is given in the bond table as $98\frac{3}{4}$. The selling price of one bond is

$$\$1,000 \times 98\frac{3}{4}\% = \$1,000 \times 0.9875 = \$987.50. \qquad \blacksquare$$

**OBJECTIVE 3** *Find the cost of bonds, including commission.*    Commissions charged on bond sales vary among brokers. A common charge is $5 per bond, either to buy or to sell.

| EXAMPLE 2 *Finding the Cost of Purchasing Bonds*

Find the charge to purchase 15 bonds of Borden, $8\frac{3}{8}\%$ of 2016. Use the closing price for the day and assume a sales charge of $5 per bond.

**SOLUTION**    From the bond table in Figure 18.5, the price is found to be 95, or 95%. The cost to buy one bond of $1,000 par value is

$$\$1,000 \times 95\% = \$1,000 \times 0.95 = \$950.$$

Fifteen of these bonds cost

$$15 \times \$950 = \$14,250.$$

Commission is $5 per bond, with a total commission of

$$15 \times \$5 = \$75.$$

The purchase price of the 15 bonds is

$$\$14,250 + \$75 = \$14,325. \qquad \blacksquare$$

Bonds are a debt; a corporation owes money to its bondholders. As such, bondholders have first claim, after bankruptcy lawyers, taxing authorities, and wage earners, on the assets of the corporation if it goes into bankruptcy. (Stockholders have the last claim.) Even so, bonds may pay off only a few cents on the dollar in the event of bankruptcy. Bondholders have lost substantial sums in recent bankruptcies. Some investors like to buy the bonds of bankrupt and troubled companies—such **junk bonds** have been known to pay off handsomely when and if a company regains its financial health. We might mention that bond salespeople do not like the term "junk bonds," they prefer "high-yield securities." Junk bonds are usually very risky and best left for professional investors.

**OBJECTIVE 4** *Use mutual funds containing bonds for monthly income.*    A mutual fund can invest in stocks, in bonds, or partially in stocks and partially in bonds. Typically, people and companies invest in stocks when they have a long period of time during which they are accumulating funds. They tend to invest in bonds when they need the income from their investments. Many financial planners suggest that people invest in both stocks and bonds throughout their adult lifetime—perhaps a higher percent of stocks when young and a higher percent of bonds when approaching retirement.

**EXAMPLE 3**   *Using a Bond Fund for Income*

Ada Clen needs income and is worried about investing her money in the bonds of a single company since that company might go bankrupt. Therefore she chooses to invest in a bond fund that invests in the bonds of many different companies and that currently yields 7% per year. Find the annual interest if she invests $75,000 in the bond fund.

**SOLUTION**   Use the formula for simple interest $I = PRT$.

$$\text{Annual interest} = \$75,000 \times 0.07 \times 1 = \$5,250 \text{ per year} \qquad \blacksquare$$

## 18.3   EXERCISES

*Find the following information from the bond table in Figure 18.5. Use the listing for Payless Cashways.*

1. Closing price
2. Number or bonds sold
3. Interest paid on the par value of the bonds, both as a percent and in dollars
4. Year when the bonds will be paid off by the company
5. Change since the previous day in the price of one bond
6. Price to buy 25 such bonds at the closing price with sales charges of $5 per bond

*Find the cost, including sales charges of $5 per bond, for each of the following transactions.*

| Bond | Number Purchased |
|---|---|
| 7. Chiquita Banana, $10\frac{1}{2}$% bonds of 2004 | 30 |
| 8. Pennzoil, $4\frac{3}{4}$% bonds of 2003 | 20 |
| 9. Revlon, $9\frac{1}{2}$% bonds of 1999 | 100 |
| 10. Cleveland Electric, $8\frac{3}{8}$% bonds of 2012 | 40 |
| 11. PacTT, $7\frac{1}{4}$% bonds of 2008 | 50 |
| 12. Ralston Purina, $8\frac{5}{8}$% bonds of 2022 | 10 |
| 13. PrmHsp, $9\frac{1}{4}$% bonds of 2006 | 25 |
| 14. Clark Oil, $9\frac{1}{2}$% bonds of 2004 | 35 |

🖊 **15.** Explain the purpose of bonds. (See Objective 1.)

🖊 **16.** Explain how to calculate the value of one bond at the closing price. (See Objective 2.)

*Solve each application problem. Assume sales commissions of $5 per bond. Use the table of bond prices in Figure 18.5, and don't forget the sales commission.*

**17.** Onita Fields purchased 20 bonds of Citicorp. Find the total cost.

**18.** Mary Dunlap bought 15 bonds of PSEG. Find the total cost.

**19.** Linda Cypert purchased 10 bonds of Payless Cashways and 10 bonds of Oryx. Find the total cost.

**20.** Jake Botswana bought 10 bonds of Pogo Producing and 15 bonds of Cooper Industries. Find the total cost.

**21.** A pension fund purchased 300 bonds of Payless Cashways. Find the (a) total cost and (b) annual interest.

**22.** A manager of a retirement fund purchased 400 bonds of Reliance Group, 9% due in 2000. Find (a) the total cost and (b) the annual interest.

**23.** A wealthy couple places $100,000 in a municipal bond fund which allows them to reduce their taxes. Find their tax free income from this investment if the fund earns $4\frac{1}{2}$% per year.

**24.** Helmut Schmidt places all $150,000 of his retirement funds in a mutual fund containing only high quality corporate bonds. Find his annual interest if the fund earns 8% per year.

**25.** Bob and Martha Jones recently divorced. As a part of the divorce settlement, Bob Jones agrees to pay Martha Jones $7,000 per year for several years. Find the number of Duke Power $7\frac{7}{8}$ bonds maturing in 2024 needed to provide this income—round any fractional number of bonds up to the next larger whole number. Find Mr. Jones' cost, including commissions, to buy these bonds at the closing price.

**26.** Joan Klein lost a lawsuit to Milton Freeman. As a result, she must make annual payments of $28,500 to Freeman for several years. Find the number of Bell South $8\frac{1}{4}$ bonds maturing in 2032 that Klein needs to provide for the required annual payment—round any fractional number of bonds up to the next larger whole number. Find Klein's cost, including commissions, to buy these bonds at the closing price.

## 18.4   Distribution of Profits and Losses in a Partnership

**OBJECTIVES**

**1** *Divide profits by equal shares.*

**2** *Divide profits by agreed ratio.*

**3** *Divide profits by original investment.*

**4** *Divide profits by salary and agreed ratio.*

**5** *Divide profits by interest on investment and agreed ratio.*

In a partnership, a business is owned by two or more people. These partners may have invested equal amounts of money to start the business, or one may have invested money while another invested specialized knowledge. The partners must agree on the relative amounts of money and time that will be invested in the business. They must also agree on the method by which any profits will be distributed. This section considers the various methods by which partnership profits may be distributed.

**OBJECTIVE** **1** *Divide profits by equal shares.*     The partners may simply agree to share all profits and losses equally. (In fact, if there is no formal agreement stating the terms under which profits are to be divided, most states require that profits be divided equally.)

**EXAMPLE 1** *Dividing Profits by Equal Shares*

Three partners opened a music store, and agreed to divide the profits equally. If the store produced profits of $69,000 in one year, each partner would get

$$\frac{1}{3} \times \$69,000 = \$23,000$$

as the annual share of the profits.                                                                 ■

**OBJECTIVE** **2** *Divide profits by agreed ratio.*     Partners may agree to divide the profits using some given rule. For example, two partners might agree that profits will be divided so that 60% goes to one partner and 40% to the other. Profit divisions are sometimes given as a ratio; this division could be written 60:40, or in a reduced form, 3:2, with profits said to be divided in an **agreed ratio**.

**EXAMPLE 2** *Dividing Profits by Agreed Ratio*

Three partners divide the profits from a business in the ratio 2:3:5. How would profits of $47,500 be divided?

**SOLUTION**    The ratio 2:3:5 says that the profit should be divided into $2 + 3 + 5 = 10$ equal shares. The first partner gets 2 of these 10 shares, or

$$\frac{2}{10} \times \$47,500 = \$9,500.$$

The second partner gets 3 of the 10 equal shares, or

$$\frac{3}{10} \times \$47,500 = \$14,250.$$

Finally, the third partner gets 5 shares, or

$$\frac{5}{10} \times \$47,500 = \$23,750.$$

To check, the sum of the three shares, $9,500 + $14,250 + $23,750, is the total profit, or $47,500.                                                                 ■

**OBJECTIVE** **3** *Divide profits by original investment.*     A common way of dividing the profits is on the basis of the **original investments** made by each partner. The fraction of the total original investment supplied by each partner is used to find the fraction of the profit that each partner receives.

| **EXAMPLE 3** *Dividing Profits by Original Investment*

Bob Huffman and Gary White form a partnership to drill for oil. Huffman contributes $80,000 and White contributes $40,000. They sign an agreement which says that each partner will lose the money each invested if they drill a dry hole, and that any profits will be distributed based on the original investment. If they discover an oil field and sell it for $600,000, find the share received by each.

**SOLUTION**   The total amount contributed to start the venture was

$$\$80,000 + \$40,000 = \$120,000.$$

Of this total, Huffman contributed

$$\frac{\$80,000}{\$120,000} = \frac{2}{3}$$

and White contributed $\frac{1}{3}$. Therefore, Huffman is entitled to $\frac{2}{3}$ of the price received for the oil field, or

$$\frac{2}{3} \times \$600,000 = \$400,000$$

and White is entitled to

$$\frac{1}{3} \times \$600,000 = \$200,000.$$                                       ■

**NOTE**   Each partner's fraction or percent of the total investment must be determined before the profit distribution is calculated.   ■

| **EXAMPLE 4** *Dividing Losses by Original Investment*

Suppose the oil company in Example 3 had a loss of $40,000 the first year. Find the share of the loss that each partner must pay.

**SOLUTION**   Just as partners share profits, they may be called on to share loses. In this case, Huffman must pay $\frac{2}{3}$ of the loss, or

$$\frac{2}{3} \times \$40,000 = (\$26,666.67)$$

and White must pay $\frac{1}{3}$ of the loss.

Losses are usually indicated with parentheses.

$$\frac{1}{3} \times \$40,000 = (\$13,333.33)$$                                       ■

**OBJECTIVE** **4** *Divide profits by salary and agreed ratio.*        Sometimes one partner contributes money to get a business started, while a second partner contributes money and also operates the business on a daily basis. In such a case, the partner operating the business may be paid a salary out of profits, with any additional profits divided in some agreed-upon ratio, called dividing profits by **salary and agreed ratio**. As mentioned in the introduction to this chapter, a partner who makes only a financial investment, but takes no part in running the business, is a **silent partner**.

**EXAMPLE 5** *Dividing Profits by Salary and Original Investment*

Ben Walker has managed a restaurant for 8 years and would open his own restaurant except that he does not have enough money. He finally decides to form a partnership with Herma Gonzalez to open a restaurant that will be managed by Walker at an annual salary of $18,000. Walker invests $20,000 and Gonzalez invests $60,000. They agree to divide any profits based on the original investment. Find the amount each partner would receive from a profit of $70,000.

**SOLUTION**    The first $18,000 is used for Walker's salary.

$$
\begin{array}{ll}
\$70,000 & \text{profit} \\
-\ \ \underline{18,000} & \text{salary} \\
\$52,000 & \text{profit to be divided}
\end{array}
$$

Walker would also receive

$$\frac{1}{4} \times \$52,000 = \$13,000$$

and Gonzalez would receive

$$\frac{3}{4} \times \$52,000 = \$39,000.$$

Thus Walker receives $18,000 + $13,000 = $31,000 and Gonzalez receives $39,000. ■

**OBJECTIVE 5** *Divide profits by interest on investment and agreed ratio.*    Sometimes one partner will put up a large share of the money necessary to start a firm, while other partners may actually operate the firm. In such a case, an agreement to divide profits by **interest on investment and agreed ratio** may be reached by which the partner putting up the money gets interest on the investment before any further division of profits.

**EXAMPLE 6** *Dividing Profits by Interest and Agreed Ratio*

Laura Cameron, Jay Davis, and Donna Friedman opened a tool rental business. Cameron contributed $250,000 to the opening of the business, which will be operated by Davis and Friedman. The partners agree that Cameron will first receive a 10% return on her investment before any further division of profits. Additional profits will be divided in the ratio 1:2:2. Find the amount that each partner would receive from a profit of $75,000.

**SOLUTION**    Cameron is first paid a 10% return on her investment of $250,000. This amounts to

$$\$250,000 \times 10\% = \$250,000 \times 0.10 = \$25,000.$$

This leaves an additional

$$
\begin{array}{rl}
\$75,000 & \text{total profit} \\
-\ \ 25,000 & \text{amount to Cameron} \\
\hline
\$50,000 &
\end{array}
$$

to be divided. The additional profit of $50,000 is to be divided in the ratio $1:2:2$ respectively. First divide this amount into $1 + 2 + 2 = 5$ equal shares. Cameron gets 1 of these 5 shares, or

$$\frac{1}{5} \times \$50,000 = \$10,000.$$

Davis and Friedman each get 2 of the 5 shares, or

$$\frac{2}{5} \times \$50,000 = \$20,000.$$

In summary, Cameron gets the following amount.

$$
\begin{array}{rl}
\$25,000 & \text{return on investment} \\
+\ \ 10,000 & \text{share of profit} \\
\hline
\$35,000 & \text{total}
\end{array}
$$

Both Davis and Friedman get $20,000.                            ■

**NOTE**  The return on investment is paid first and then the remaining profit is divided among the partners.  ■

### EXAMPLE 7  *Dividing Losses by Agreed Rates*

Suppose the tool rental business in Example 6 had a profit of only $15,000. What would be the distribution of this amount?

**SOLUTION**    The partners agreed to give Cameron a 10% return, or $25,000. The profits were only $15,000, leaving a loss of $10,000.

$$
\begin{array}{r}
\$25,000 \\
-\ \ 15,000 \\
\hline
(\$10,000)
\end{array}
$$

This loss of $10,000 will be shared in the ratio $1:2:2$, just as were the profits. Cameron's share of the loss is

$$\frac{1}{5} \times \$10,000 = (\$2,000)$$

while the share of both Davis and Friedman is

Losses are shown in parentheses.

$$\frac{2}{5} \times \$10,000 = (\$4,000)$$

Cameron gets $25,000, minus her share of the loss.

| | |
|---|---|
| $25,000 | due to Cameron |
| − 2,000 | her share of loss |
| $23,000 | actually received by Cameron |

Both Davis and Friedman must each *contribute* $4,000 toward the loss. The $23,000 that Cameron actually receives is made up as follows.

| | |
|---|---|
| $15,000 | profit |
| 4,000 | from Davis |
| + 4,000 | from Friedman |
| $23,000 | total to Cameron |

**NOTE** Cameron does absorb her share of the loss by accepting $23,000 instead of the $25,000 return on investment initially agreed upon. ■

## 18.4 EXERCISES

*Divide the following profits. Round all answers to the nearest dollar.*

| | Partners | Investment | Method | Profits |
|---|---|---|---|---|
| **1.** | 1<br>2 | $25,000<br>$30,000 | **Equal shares** | **$42,000** |
| **2.** | 1<br>2<br>3 | $10,000<br>$15,000<br>$15,000 | **Ratio 1:2:2** | **$80,000** |
| **3.** | 1<br>2 | $80,000<br>$20,000 | **Ratio of investment** | **$46,000** |
| **4.** | 1<br>2<br>3 | $20,000<br>$20,000<br>$5,000 | **$22,000 salary to partner 3;<br>balance divided 3:3:2** | **$72,000** |
| **5.** | 1<br>2 | $40,000<br>$10,000 | **12% return to partner 1;<br>balance in ratio 3:2** | **$25,000** |
| **6.** | 1<br>2<br>3 | $40,000<br>$60,000<br>$50,000 | **10% return to partner 2;<br>balance in ratio of<br>investment** | **$111,000** |
| **7.** | 1<br>2<br>3 | $20,000<br>$15,000<br>$40,000 | **$10,000 salary to partner 1;<br>$12,000 salary to partner 2;<br>balance in ratio of<br>investment** | **$22,000** |
| **8.** | 1<br>2<br>3<br>4 | $40,000<br>$40,000<br>$5,000<br>$35,000 | **$20,000 salary to partner 3;<br>10% return to partners 1<br>and 2; balance divided<br>2:2:1:2** | **$133,000** |

*Solve the following application problems.*

9. Two partners make a profit of $2,800 on a duplex they own. Find the amount of profit each gets if they have no agreement for dividing profits.

10. A firm with five surgeons has agreed to split the profits equally. Find the profit to each if the firm has a profit of $1,400,000 one year.

11. Three attorneys contribute $10,000, $40,000, and $50,000 respectively to start a land venture. Find the share that each gets if the profit is $120,000 and profits are divided in the ratio of the original investments.

12. Kathy Bates and Marion Tomlin have started a new florist shop. Bates contributed $25,000 to the firm and Tomlin contributed $15,000. Find the division of a profit of $30,000 if profits are divided in the ratio of the original investments.

13. Four partners have agreed to divide profits in the ratio $3:5:7:9$. Find the division of a profit of $180,000.

14. Suppose the partners in Exercise 13 have a loss of $96,000. How much of the loss would be paid by each partner?

15. Mary Finch and Pete Renz have started a new travel agency. Finch will run the agency. She gets a $15,000 salary, with any additional profits distributed in the ratio $1:4$. Find the distribution of a profit of $57,000.

16. Beth, Maureen, and Patty have started a new bookstore to be run by Maureen. Maureen will get a salary of $17,000, with any additional profits divided in the ratio $3:1:2$. Find the division of a profit of $53,000.

17. Bob Coker has invested $80,000 in a new hardware store. His partner, Will Toms, will actually run the store. The partners agree that Coker will get a 10% return on his investment, with any additional profits divided in the ratio $1:3$. Find the division of a profit of (a) $60,000 and (b) $6,000.

18. Wilma Dickson has invested $350,000 in a small electronics plant, to be run by her partner, John Ardery. They agree that she will receive a 10% return on her investment, and that any additional profits will be divided in the ratio $2:3$. Divide a profit of (a) $90,000 and (b) $30,000.

19. Three partners invest $15,000, $25,000, and $30,000 in a business. The partners agree that partner 1 will receive a 10% return on investment, with partner 2 receiving a salary of $12,000. Any additional profits will be divided in the ratio of the original investments. Divide a profit of $110,000.

20. A plumbing wholesale business has three partners. Partner 1 invested $50,000 in the business, and is given a 10% return on investment. Partner 2 invested $75,000, and earns a 6% return on investment, plus a salary of $21,000. Partner 3 invested $100,000 and earns a 12% return on investment. Any additional profits are divided in the ratio $2:1:2$. Divide a profit of $180,000.

21. State the approach used to divide profits among 3 partners if partner 1 gets a fixed salary and the remaining profits are divided according to a ratio of $2:3:2$. (See Objective 4.)

22. Explain the difference between the distribution of profits and loses in a partnership versus those in a corporation.

## 18.5     Distribution of Overhead

**OBJECTIVES**

**1**  *Allocate overhead by floor space.*

**2**  *Allocate overhead by sales value.*

**3**  *Allocate overhead by number of employees.*

Businesses have many expenses in addition to the cost of the materials and labor that are actually used to make a product. Rent on the factory building must be paid, insurance premiums and executive salaries must be paid, office supplies must be ordered, and so on. These general expenses, which cannot be avoided but which do not go directly for the production of goods and services, are called **overhead**. The cost of an office computer would come under overhead, while the cost of sheet metal used to actually make a product would not.

A company can usually decide on the total overhead expenses fairly quickly; however, a problem often comes up in dividing the overhead among the various products or lines of business in a company. This is one area in which **cost accounting** is used. Various methods are used by different firms to divide overhead. The choice of a method often depends on industry practice.

In any case, the **allocation of overhead** is usually done by forming a ratio of each product or department to the total firm. There are several ways of forming this ratio.

**OBJECTIVE 1**  *Allocate overhead by floor space.*     Overhead can be allocated by department according to the **floor space** used by each department of the company.

**EXAMPLE 1**  *Allocating Overhead by Floor Space*

Clover Printing has three departments, with floor space as shown.

| Department | Floor Space |
|---|---|
| Magazine printing | 50,000 square feet |
| Book printing | 30,000 square feet |
| Catalog printing | 20,000 square feet |
| Total | 100,000 square feet |

Allocate an overhead of $275,000.

**SOLUTION**    The magazine printing department has a floor space of 50,000 square feet out of a total of 100,000 square feet. Therefore, this department is allocated

$$\frac{50,000}{100,000} = \frac{1}{2}$$

of the overhead, or

$$\frac{1}{2} \times \$275,000 = \$137,500.$$

When finding the expenses of this department, the company accountants would assign an overhead expense of $137,500 for the department.

The book printing department uses

$$\frac{30,000}{100,000} = \frac{3}{10}$$

of the floor space, and so would be allocated $\frac{3}{10}$ of the overhead, or

$$\frac{3}{10} \times \$275,000 = \$82,500.$$

Finally, catalog printing would be allocated

$$\frac{20,000}{100,000} = \frac{1}{5}$$

of the overhead, or

$$\frac{1}{5} \times \$275,000 = \$55,000.$$    ■

**NOTE**    Check your answer by adding the individual departmental allocations. This sum should equal the total overhead.    ■

**OBJECTIVE** **2** *Allocate overhead by sales value.*    It is common to allocate overhead according to the **sales value** of each department or product, as shown in the next example.

| **EXAMPLE 2**    *Allocating Overhead by Sales Value*

Bales Manufacturing produces four products, with monthly production and value as shown.

| Product | Production | Value of Each |
|---|---|---|
| Wheelbarrows | 2,500 | $40 |
| Ladders | 5,000 | 25 |
| Shovels | 6,000 | 10 |
| Hammers | 25,000 | 3 |

Allocate an overhead of $50,000.

**SOLUTION**    First find the total value of each item.

| Product | Production | Value of Each | Total Value |
|---|---|---|---|
| Wheelbarrows | 2,500 | $40 | 2,500 × $40 = $100,000 |
| Ladders | 5,000 | 25 | 5,000 ×   25 =   125,000 |
| Shovels | 6,000 | 10 | 6,000 ×   10 =     60,000 |
| Hammers | 25,000 | 3 | 25,000 ×     3 =     75,000 |
| | | | Total   $360,000 |

Wheelbarrows amounted to $100,000 of the total value of $360,000. Therefore, the fraction

$$\frac{\$100,000}{\$360,000} = \frac{5}{18}$$

of the total overhead must be applied to wheelbarrows. The total overhead is $50,000, so

$$\frac{5}{18} \times \$50,000 = \$13,888.89$$

must be applied to wheelbarrows. Also,

$$\frac{\$125,000}{\$360,000} \times \$50,000 = \frac{25}{72} \times \$50,000 = \$17,361.11$$

of overhead will be applied to ladders, and

$$\frac{\$60,000}{\$360,000} \times \$50,000 = \frac{1}{6} \times \$50,000 = \$8,333.33$$

to shovels. Finally,

$$\frac{\$75,000}{\$360,000} \times \$50,000 = \$10,416.67$$

is applied to hammers. Check that the sum of the various allocated overheads is the total overhead of $50,000.    ■

**OBJECTIVE 3** *Allocate overhead by number of employees.*    Overhead can also be allocated by the number of employees associated with a department or product.

**EXAMPLE 3** *Allocating Overhead by Number of Employees*

A small factory that produces gear boxes has an overhead charge of $380,000. Allocate this overhead expense based on the number of employees.

**SOLUTION**    Allocate this expense based on a ratio of the number of employees in the department to the total number of employees.

| Department | Number of Employees | Ratio of Employees | Overhead of Department |
|---|---|---|---|
| Machining | 11 | $\dfrac{11}{31}$ | $\dfrac{11}{31} \times \$380,000 = \$134,838.71$ |
| Welding | 5 | $\dfrac{5}{31}$ | $\dfrac{5}{31} \times \$380,000 = \phantom{0}61,290.32$ |
| Assembly | 15 | $\dfrac{15}{31}$ | $\dfrac{15}{31} \times \$380,000 = \underline{\phantom{0}183,870.97}$ |
| | Total    31 | | $380,000 |

■

## 18.5  EXERCISES

*Allocate overhead as indicated. Round to the nearest dollar.*

**1.**

| Department | Floor Space |
|---|---|
| A | 5,000 square feet |
| B | 7,000 square feet |
| C | 8,000 square feet |

Overhead: $440,000

**2.**

| Department | Floor Space |
|---|---|
| A | 32,000 square feet |
| B | 57,000 square feet |
| C | 11,000 square feet |

Overhead: $280,000

**13.** Dayton Auto Parts allocates its $360,000 overhead by the floor space used by each department. Allocate the overhead for the following departments.

| Department | Floor Space |
|---|---|
| Hoses | 2,000 square feet |
| Carburetors | 8,000 square feet |
| Water pumps | 6,000 square feet |
| Fuel pumps | 9,000 square feet |
| Gaskets | 1,000 square feet |
| Filters | 4,000 square feet |

**14.** Savon Office and School Supplies wishes to allocate its $110,000 overhead among its various departments by floor space. Allocate the overhead for the following departments.

| Department | Floor Space |
|---|---|
| Typing paper | 750 square feet |
| Copy machine paper | 600 square feet |
| Copy machines | 1,000 square feet |
| Office furniture | 1,500 square feet |
| Filing cabinets | 500 square feet |
| Calculators | 650 square feet |

**15.** Salvage Lumber wishes to allocate its overhead of $68,000 by the sales value of each product. Allocate overhead for the following products.

| Product | Number Produced | Value per Unit |
|---|---|---|
| Construction 2 × 4's | 150 | $200 |
| Plywood | 200 | $400 |
| Veneers | 100 | $600 |
| Wood chips | 500 | $75 |
| Furniture wood | 300 | $150 |

**16.** Allocate the $8,732 monthly overhead of Victor Meats by sales value of products, using the information in this chart.

| Product | Number Produced | Value per Unit |
|---|---|---|
| Beef | 10 | $800 |
| Lamb | 7 | $300 |
| Pork | 5 | $750 |
| Chicken | 14 | $120 |
| Sausage | 12 | $150 |
| Luncheon meats | 15 | $300 |

**17.** Allocate a weekly overhead of $4,500 for Chalet Manufacturing according to the number of employees per department. Use the information in the following chart.

| Department | Number of Employees |
|---|---|
| Office | 20 |
| Sales | 35 |
| Manufacturing | 75 |
| Finishing | 12 |
| Shipping | 8 |

**18.** Drug Research, Inc. wishes to allocate a weekly overhead of $11,400 among its departments according to the number of employees per department. Use the following chart.

| Department | Number of Employees |
|---|---|
| Headache remedies | 15 |
| Pain killer | 20 |
| Cold remedies | 20 |
| Foot powder | 5 |
| Eye wash | 8 |
| Skin lotion | 8 |

**19.** Define the term *overhead*. List at least three expenses that would be included in overhead. (See Objective 1.)

**20.** Compare and contrast the three ways of allocating overhead that were discussed in this section. Give circumstances under which each of the three might be appropriate. (See Objectives 1–3.)

# Chapter 18 Quick Review

| TOPIC | APPROACH | EXAMPLE |
|---|---|---|
| **18.1 Determining the amounts paid to holders of preferred and common stock** | To find total paid to owners of preferred stock, multiply par value by dividend rate to obtain dividend per share, then multiply by number of shares. To find the dividend paid to owners of common stock, subtract total paid to owners of preferred stock from total available to stockholders, then divide by number of shares of common stock. | A company distributes $750,000 to stockholders. It has 15,000 shares of $100 par value 4% preferred stock and 150,000 shares of common stock. Find (a) amount paid to holders of preferred stock and (b) amount per share to holders of common stock. <br><br> **(a)** Dividend per share $= \$100 \times 0.04 = \$4$ <br><br> Total to preferred $= \$4 \times 15,000$ $= \$60,000$ <br><br> **(b)** Dividend to common $$= \frac{\$750,000 - \$60,000}{150,000}$$ $= \$4.60$ |
| **18.1 Finding earnings per share** | Subtract dividends on preferred stock from net income, then divide by the number of shares of common stock outstanding. | A company made $500,000 last year. The company has 750,000 shares of common stock outstanding and paid $75,000 to owners of preferred stock. Find the earnings per share. <br><br> $$EPS = \frac{\$500,000 - \$75,000}{750,000}$$ $= \$0.57$ |
| **18.2 Reading the stock table** | Locate the stock involved and determine the various quantities required. <br><br> Stock table entry follows. | Use the stock table to find the following information for Black and Decker (BlackDeck): dividend; high for day; low for day; total sales; yearly high; yearly low. |

| 52 Weeks Hi | Lo | Stock | Sym | Div. | Yld % | PE | Vols 100s | Hi | Lo | Close | Net Chg |
|---|---|---|---|---|---|---|---|---|---|---|---|
| $40\frac{3}{8}$ | $27\frac{1}{2}$ | BlackDeck | BDK | .48 | 1.2 | 14 | 2105 | $39\frac{5}{8}$ | $38\frac{3}{4}$ | $39\frac{5}{8}$ | +1 |

Dividend is $0.48; high is $39\frac{5}{8}$ or $39.625; low is $38\frac{3}{4}$ or $38.75; total sales are 210,500; yearly high is $40\frac{3}{8}$ or $40.375; yearly low is $27\frac{1}{2}$ or $27.50; and net change is +1 or +$1.

---

**18.2  Finding the current yield on a stock**

$$\text{Current yield} = \frac{\text{Annual dividend}}{\text{Current price}}$$

Find the current yield for IBM if the purchase price is $112\frac{1}{8}$ per share and the annual dividend is $1.40.

$$\text{Current Yield} = \frac{\$1.40}{\$112.125}$$
$$= 0.012 = 1.2\%$$

---

**18.2  Selling shares of a stock**

Find the basic price of the stock from the table. Subtract the SEC fee and the broker's commission from the basic price of the stock.

Find the amount received by a person selling 500 shares of a stock at $53\frac{3}{8}$.

Basic price = 500 × $53.375
$$= \$26,687.50$$

SEC fee: $26,687.50 ÷ $500
$$= 54 \text{ (rounded)}$$

SEC fee = 54 × $0.01
$$= \$0.54$$

Broker's commission
= 0.025 × $26,687.50
= $667.19

Seller's proceeds
= $26,687.50 − $667.19 − $0.5
= $26,019.77

---

**18.2  Finding the price to earnings ratio (PE ratio)**

To find the price to earnings ratio use the formula:

$$\frac{\text{PE}}{\text{ratio}} = \frac{\text{Price per share}}{\text{Annual net income per share}}.$$

Price per share, $42.50; annual net income per share, $2.75.

$$\text{PE ratio} = \frac{\$42.50}{\$2.75} = 15.45$$

| 18.3 | **Determining the cost of purchasing bonds** | Locate the bond in the table, then multiply the price of the bond by 1,000 and the number of bonds purchased. Then, add $5 per bond to the total cost. | Find the cost, including sales charges, of 20 Oryx bonds. $20 \times (1,000 \times 0.90) + (20 \times \$5) = \$18,100$ |
|---|---|---|---|
| 18.3 | **Determining the amount received from the sale of bonds** | Locate the bond in the table, then multiply the price of the bond by 1,000 and the number of bonds sold. Subtract $5 per bond from the total selling price. | Find the amount received from the sale of 15 Pennzoil bonds. $15 \times (1,000 \times 1.075) - (15 \times \$5) = \$16,050$ |
| 18.3 | **Find the annual income from a mutual fund containing bonds** | Multiply the amount invested in the fund by the yield rate. | Find the annual income from $120,000 invested in a bond fund yielding $7\frac{1}{2}\%$. $\$120,000 \times 0.075 = \$9,000$ |

**18.4  Dividing profits in a partnership**

Use one of the following methods to determine each partner's ratio of the profits:
Equal shares
Agreed ratio
Original investment
Salary and agreed ratio
Interest on investment and agreed ratio
Multiply total profits by each partner's ratio.

Divide profits of $75,000 among 3 investors by original investment if each partner invests the following amount.

| Partner | Investment |
|---|---|
| 1 | $12,000 |
| 2 | $15,000 |
| 3 | $18,000 |

Total initial investment
$= \$12,000 + \$15,000 + \$18,000$
$= \$45,000$

Ratios for each partner:

1. $\dfrac{12,000}{45,000} = \dfrac{4}{15}$

2. $\dfrac{15,000}{45,000} = \dfrac{1}{3}$

3. $\dfrac{18,000}{45,000} = \dfrac{2}{5}$

Profit for each partner:

1. $\dfrac{4}{15}(\$75,000) = \$20,000$

2. $\dfrac{1}{3}(\$75,000) = \$25,000$

3. $\dfrac{2}{5}(\$75,000) = \$30,000$

**18.5   Allocating overhead by floor space**

Determine the percent of floor space each department occupies. Multiply the percent by the amount of overhead to be allocated.

| Department | Floor Space |
|---|---|
| Printing | 40,000 sq. ft. |
| Cutting | 25,000 sq. ft. |
| Binding | 55,000 sq. ft. |

Allocate $330,000 overhead.

$$\text{Printing: } \frac{40,000}{120,000} \times \$330,000$$
$$= \$110,000$$

$$\text{Cutting: } \frac{25,000}{120,000} \times \$330,000$$
$$= \$68,750$$

$$\text{Binding: } \frac{55,000}{120,000} \times \$330,000$$
$$= \$151,250$$

**18.5   Allocating overhead by sales value**

Determine the percent of sales for each department.
Multiply this percent by the amount of overhead to be allocated.

Allocate $120,000 overhead.

| Product | Number Produced | Value of Each |
|---|---|---|
| A | 5,000 | $12 |
| B | 8,000 | 5 |
| C | 10,000 | 10 |

Total Value = (5,000)($12) + (8,000)($5) + (10,000)($10) = $200,000

$$\text{A: } \frac{(5,000)(\$12)}{\$200,000} \times \$120,000$$
$$= \$36,000$$

$$\text{B: } \frac{(8,000)(\$5)}{\$200,000} \times \$120,000$$
$$= \$24,000$$

$$\text{C: } \frac{(10,000)(\$10)}{\$200,000} \times \$120,000$$
$$= \$60,000$$

**18.5 Allocating overhead by number of employees**

Determine the ratio of employees in the department to total number of employees.
Multiply this ratio by the amount of overhead to be allocated.

Allocate $15,000 overhead.

| Department | Number of Employees |
|---|---|
| 1 | 5 |
| 2 | 6 |
| 3 | 9 |
| Total | 20 |

1. $\dfrac{5}{20} \times \$15,000 = \$3,750$

2. $\dfrac{6}{20} \times \$15,000 = \$4,500$

3. $\dfrac{9}{20} \times \$15,000 = \$6,750$

# Chapter 18 Review Exercises

*In each of the following find (a) the amount paid to holders of preferred stock and (b) the amount per share to holders of common stock. [18.1]*

| | Net Income | Reinvested Funds | Par Value | Rate | Number of Preferred Stockholders | Number of Common Stockholders |
|---|---|---|---|---|---|---|
| 1. | $1,250,000 | $500,000 | $100 | 9% | 10,000 | 150,000 |
| 2. | $2,375,000 | $750,000 | $150 | 8% | 15,000 | 200,000 |
| 3. | $2,640,000 | $425,000 | $125 | 7% | 22,750 | 750,000 |

*In each of the following, find the earnings per share. [18.1]*

| | Net Income | Dividends on Preferred Stock | Number of Shares of Common Stock |
|---|---|---|---|
| 4. | $725,000 | $0 | 100,000 |
| 5. | $1,425,000 | $675,000 | 275,000 |
| 6. | $2,750,000 | $900,000 | 500,000 |

*Use the stock table to find each of the following. Give money answers to the nearest thousandth of a dollar. [18.2]*

**7.** High for the day for CIPSCO

**8.** Low for the day for BushInd

**9.** Closing price for CBL Associates

**10.** Change from the previous day for Best Buy

**11.** Dividend for Biocraft Labs

**12.** Sales for the day for Bemis

**13.** Yield for CTS

**14.** 52-week high for Belden

**15.** 52-week low for Berkshire Hathaway A

*Find the price for each of the following stock purchases. Ignore any broker's fees. [18.2]*

| Stock | Number of Shares | Transaction |
|---|---|---|
| **16. CV REIT** | 100 | close |
| **17. Cabot Corp.** | 200 | high |
| **18. Big Flower** | 1,000 | low |

*Find the price for each of the following stock purchases. Use the broker's fees in the text. [18.2]*

**19.** 200 shares at $41\frac{5}{8}$

**20.** 340 shares at $73\frac{1}{8}$

*Find the current yield for the following. Round to the nearest tenth of a percent. [18.2]*

**21.** CMS Energy at $\$29\frac{1}{2}$ per share and a dividend of $0.96

**22.** Belo at $\$38\frac{3}{4}$ per share and a dividend of $0.44

*Find the PE ratio for each of the following. Round all answers to the nearest whole number. [18.2]*

**23.** CNB Bankshares at $\$28\frac{1}{2}$ with a net income per share of $2.11

**24.** Buckeye Petroleum at $\$37\frac{3}{4}$ with a net income per share of $4.10

Use the bond table to find each of the following. Use the listing for New York Telephone $7\frac{3}{8}$ 11. [18.3]

**25.** Closing price

**26.** Number of bonds sold

**27.** Year when the bonds will be paid off by the company

**28.** Change since the previous day in the price of one bond

**29.** Price to buy 30 such bonds at the closing price, with sales charges of $5 per bond.

**30.** Interest paid on the par value of the bonds, both as a percent and in dollars

Find the cost, including sales charges of $5 per bond, for each of the following. [18.3]

| Bond | | Number Purchased |
|---|---|---|
| **31. PrmHsp** | $9\frac{1}{4}$% of 2006 | 10 |
| **32. PaylCsh** | $9\frac{1}{8}$% of 2003 | 25 |

In Problems 33–35, divide the profits based on the indicated method. Round all answers to the nearest dollar. [18.4]

| | Partners | Investment | Method | Profits |
|---|---|---|---|---|
| **33.** | 1 | $8,500 | Equal shares | $48,000 |
| | 2 | $7,000 | | |
| | 3 | $10,500 | | |
| **34.** | 1 | $16,000 | Ratio 2:3 | $120,000 |
| | 2 | $25,000 | | |
| **35.** | 1 | $9,000 | Ratio of | $90,000 |
| | 2 | $12,000 | investment | |

In problems 36–38, allocate the overhead to each department of the company. Round to the nearest dollar. [18.5]

| **36.** | Department | Floor Space |
|---|---|---|
| | A | 3,000 square feet |
| | B | 5,000 square feet |
| | C | 4,000 square feet |

**Overhead: $100,000**

**37.**

| Product | Number Produced | Value of Each |
|---------|-----------------|---------------|
| 1 | 8,000 | $12 |
| 2 | 40,000 | 6 |
| 3 | 20,000 | 9 |

**Overhead: $125,000**

**38.**

| Department | Number of Employees |
|------------|---------------------|
| A | 70 |
| B | 55 |
| C | 45 |
| D | 60 |

**Overhead: $85,000**

*Solve each of the following application problems.*

**39.** Ralph Toombs invested his retirement funds of $225,000 in a bond fund currently paying $8\frac{1}{4}\%$. Find his annual income. [18.3]

**40.** George and Wanda Joyce invested their life's savings of $320,000 in a bond fund. If the fund charged them a 1% sales commission, find the annual income if the fund is currently paying $7\frac{5}{8}\%$. [18.3]

# Chapter 18 Summary Exercise

Dougherty Educational Services, Inc. was formed several years ago with an investment of $15,000 from Trish Shields, $10,000 from Katie Abbot and $25,000 from Beth Dougherty. Every $1 of their initial contribution resulted in the purchase of 2 shares of common stock. They also sold 10,000 preferred shares of $50 par value at 8% to other investors. Last year the firm had a net income after taxes of $250,000 and the board of directors allocated 45% of net income to the shareholders.

**(a)** Find the number of common shares of stock owned by Shields, Abbot, and Dougherty.

**(b)** Find the dividend per share.

**(c)** Shields, Abbot, and Dougherty respectively earn salaries of $32,000, $40,000 and $48,000. Find the sum of salary plus dividend for each of the three.

**(d)** Twenty-five percent of the net income after dividends is paid to a profit sharing plan which invests in a mutual fund containing both stocks and bonds. Recently the fund has yielded 12%. Find the contribution to the pension plan and one year's return on this investment assuming the current yield continues.

**(e)** An overhead of $142,000 has to be allocated to 3 departments of the company based on the following number of employees.

| Dept | No. of Employees |
| --- | --- |
| Math | 7 |
| English | 5 |
| Reading | 4 |

Find the allocation to each department. Round to the nearest dollar.

**(f)** Would the profits represent a good return on their original investment if they formed the firm 5 years ago? If the company had been formed 30 years ago, would they be better off if they had placed their original investments in the stock market?

# 19 Business Statistics

The word **statistics** comes from words that mean *state numbers*, or data gathered by the government such as numbers of births, deaths, etc. Today the word *statistics* is used in a much broader sense to include data from business, economics, and many other fields. Statistics is a powerful and commonly used tool in business. For example, the Japanese depended on a technique called statistical process control (SPC) to improve the quality of the production from their factories as they emerged from the ruins of World War II. Today, many companies use statistics on a regular basis. In this chapter, only a few of the basic ideas of statistics are introduced. We encourage you to take a class in statistics at your college if you wish to know more about this important subject.

 **19.1 Frequency Distributions and Graphs**

### OBJECTIVES

1. *Construct a frequency distribution.*
2. *Make a bar graph.*
3. *Make a line graph.*
4. *Make a circle graph.*

**OBJECTIVE 1 Construct a frequency distribution.** It can be difficult to interpret or find patterns in a large group of numbers called **raw data**. One way of analyzing the numbers is to organize them into a table that shows the frequency of occurrence of the various numbers. This type of table is called a **frequency distribution**.

**EXAMPLE 1** *Constructing a Frequency Distribution*

One year ago, Bill Parker started his own insurance agency called National Insurance Agency. Parker is analyzing his personal telephone call activity over the past 50 weeks. The number of sales calls he made for each of the weeks is given below.

Read down the columns, beginning with the left column, for successive weeks of the year.

| | | | | | | | | | |
|---|---|---|---|---|---|---|---|---|---|
| 75 | 65 | 40 | 50 | 45 | 30 | 30 | 35 | 45 | 25 |
| 75 | 70 | 60 | 55 | 30 | 25 | 44 | 30 | 35 | 30 |
| 75 | 70 | 50 | 30 | 50 | 20 | 30 | 30 | 20 | 25 |
| 60 | 62 | 45 | 45 | 48 | 40 | 35 | 25 | 20 | 25 |
| 75 | 45 | 50 | 40 | 35 | 40 | 40 | 30 | 27 | 40 |

Construct a table that shows each possible number of sales calls (Table 19.1). Then go through the original data and place a tally mark ( | ) next to each corresponding value, thereby creating a frequency distribution table.

   This frequency distribution shows that the most common number of sales calls in a week was 30. In 9 of the weeks shown, Mr. Parker made 30 sales calls.     ■

   The frequency distribution given in the last example contains a great deal of information—perhaps too much to digest. It can be simplified by combining the number of sales calls into groups. In order to define the groups, divide the range of values into 5 to 10 *equal sized* groupings. Then *count the number* of occurrences in each group. In this case, we chose the groups shown in Table 19.2.

**NOTE**   The number of classes in the left column of the table above is arbitrary and usually varies between 5 and 15.     ■

| EXAMPLE 2   *Analyzing a Frequency Distribution*

Based on the data from the National Insurance Agency in Example 1, answer the following questions.

**(a)**  During how many weeks were fewer than 30 calls made?

**(b)**  During how many weeks were 40 or more calls made?

TABLE **19.1**

| Number of Sales Calls | Tally | Frequency | Number of Sales Calls | Tally | Frequency |
|---|---|---|---|---|---|
| 20 | ||| | 3 | 48 | | | 1 |
| 25 | ⊬⊬⊤ | 5 | 50 | |||| | 4 |
| 27 | | | 1 | 55 | | | 1 |
| 30 | ⊬⊬⊤ |||| | 9 | 60 | || | 2 |
| 35 | |||| | 4 | 62 | | | 1 |
| 40 | ⊬⊬⊤ | | 6 | 65 | | | 1 |
| 44 | | | 1 | 70 | || | 2 |
| 45 | ⊬⊬⊤ | 5 | 75 | |||| | 4 |

TABLE 19.2 **Grouped Data**

| Number of Sales Calls (Class) | Frequency (Number of Weeks) |
|:---:|:---:|
| 20–29 | 9 |
| 30–39 | 13 |
| 40–49 | 13 |
| 50–59 | 5 |
| 60–69 | 4 |
| 70–79 | 6 |

**SOLUTION**

(a) The first class in the grouped data table above (20–29) is the number of weeks during which fewer than 30 calls were made. Therefore, Mr. Parker made fewer than 30 calls, 9 weeks out of the 50 shown.

(b) The last four classes in the grouped data table above is the number of weeks during which 40 or more calls were made.

$$13 + 5 + 4 + 6 = 28 \text{ weeks of the 50 weeks} \qquad \blacksquare$$

**OBJECTIVE 2** *Make a bar graph.* The next step in analyzing this information is to use it to make a graph. In statistics, a **graph** is a visual presentation of numerical data. One of the most common graphs is a **bar graph**, where the height of a bar represents the frequency of a particular value. A bar graph for the data in Example 1 is shown in Figure 19.1.

**NOTE** Many of the graphs shown in this chapter can be *quickly* and *easily* done using a spreadsheet software package on a personal computer. ■

The information from the grouped data is shown in Figure 19.2. This bar graph shows that both the 30–39 and 40–49 calls per week occurred most frequently—they were tied at 13 weeks each.

**OBJECTIVE 3** *Make a line graph.* Bar graphs show which numbers occurred, and how many times, but do not necessarily show the order in which the numbers occurred. To discover any trends that may have developed, draw a **line graph** (Figure 19.3).

**EXAMPLE 3** *Drawing a Line Graph*

Show the progression of Mr. Parker's sales call activity through the year using a line graph. Do this by totaling the first 5 weeks (first column) of data in Example 1 for the first data point. Similarly, total the second 5 weeks (second column) of data for the next data point and so on.

Sales Call Data for the Past 50 Weeks

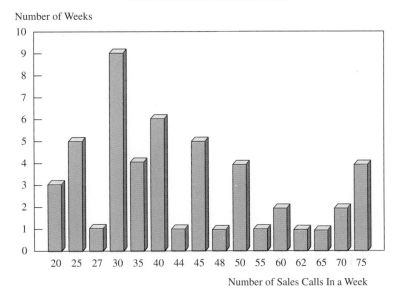

FIGURE **19.1**

Sales Call Data for the Past 50 Weeks (Grouped Data)

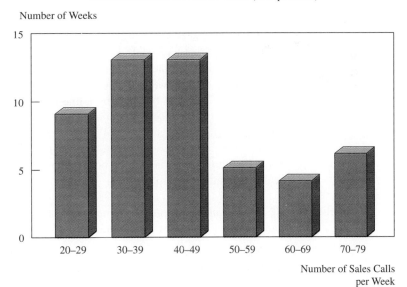

FIGURE **19.2**

**SOLUTION**   The total for the first five weeks is 360 (75 + 75 + 75 + 60 + 75), the total for the second five weeks is 312 (65 + 70 + 70 + 62 + 45), and so on. The 10 data points corresponding to successive 5-week periods are: 360, 312, 245, 220, 208, 155, 179, 150, 147, and 145. The data are shown in the following line graph.

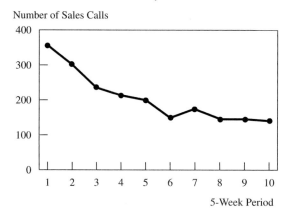

Sales Call Data for Past 50 Weeks
Broken Down by 5-Week Periods

**FIGURE 19.3**

Mr. Parker was not aware that his sales call activity had fallen *so dramatically* during the course of his first year in business. In fact, average sales contacts for the sixth through the tenth 5-week period are only one-half (approximately) of sales contacts during the first 5-week period. He has decided to increase his effort at contacting new customers since his agency is not growing as fast as he would like.                                                        ■

One advantage of line graphs is that two or more sets of data can be shown on the same graph. For example, suppose the managers of a company called Eastside Tire Sales want to compare total sales, profits, and overhead. Assume that they have extracted the data shown in Table 19.3 from their historical records.

Separate lines can be made on a line graph for each category so that necessary comparisons can be made. A graph such as this is called a **comparative line graph** (Figure 19.4).

**NOTE** Including zero on one or both scales of a line graph *may help* the viewer understand and relate to the data.    ■

**OBJECTIVE** ◼**4** *Make a circle graph.*       Suppose a sales manager for Novel Recording Company makes a record of the expenses involved in keeping a sales force on the road.

**TABLE 19.3**

| Year | Total Sales | Overhead | Profit |
|------|-------------|----------|--------|
| 1995 | $740,000 | $205,000 | $83,000 |
| 1996 | $860,000 | $251,000 | $102,000 |
| 1997 | $810,000 | $247,000 | $21,000 |
| 1998 | $1,040,000 | $302,000 | $146,000 |

Eastside Tire Sales

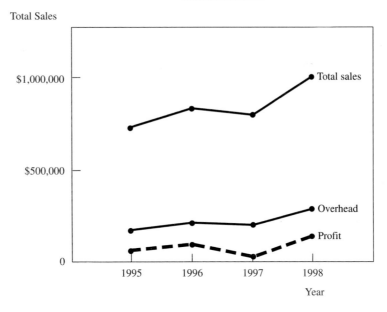

FIGURE **19.4**

After finding the total expense, she could convert each expense into a percent of the total, with the results in Table 19.4.

**NOTE** The percents should total 100%.  ■

The sales manager can show these percents by using a **circle graph**. Every circle *has 360 degrees* (written 360°). The 360° represents the total expenses. Since entertainment is 10% of the total expense, she used

$$360° \times 10\% = 360° \times 0.10 = 36°$$

TABLE **19.4**

| Item | Percent of Total |
|---|---|
| Car and plane | 30% |
| Lodging | 25% |
| Food | 15% |
| Entertainment | 10% |
| Sales meetings | 10% |
| Other | 10% |

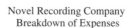

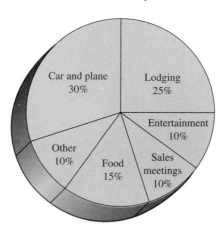

FIGURE 19.5

to represent her entertainment expense. Since lodging is 25% of the total expenses, she used

$$360° \times 25\% = 90°$$

to represent lodging. After she found the degrees that represent each of her expenses, she drew the circle graph shown in Figure 19.5.

Circle graphs are used to show comparisons when the one item represents a small portion compared to another. In the circle graph shown here, an item representing 1% of the total could be drawn as a small but noticeable slice; such a small item would hardly show up in a line graph.

**EXAMPLE 4** *Interpreting a Circle Graph*

Based on the circle graph of expenses, answer the following questions.

**(a)** What percent of expenses was spent on Travel and Entertainment?

**(b)** What percent of expenses was spent on Food and Lodging?

**SOLUTION**

**(a)**  Travel is              30%   (car and plane)
        Entertainment is   $\underline{+\ 10\%}$
        Total spent          40%

**(b)**  Food is              15%
        Lodging is       $\underline{+\ 25\%}$
        Total spent         40%                               ■

An example of both a bar graph and a circle graph recently found in a newspaper is shown in Figure 19.6. These data show the country of origin of students from other countries, who come to the United States to study at colleges and universities.

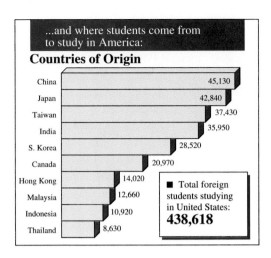

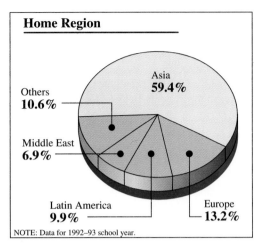

FIGURE **19.6**

*Source:* Copyright © 1995 by the Los Angeles Times.
Reprinted by permission.

## 19.1 EXERCISES

*Solve the following application problems using the information provided.*

*For Exercises 1 and 2, the following graph shows annual sales for two different furniture stores for each of the past few years.*

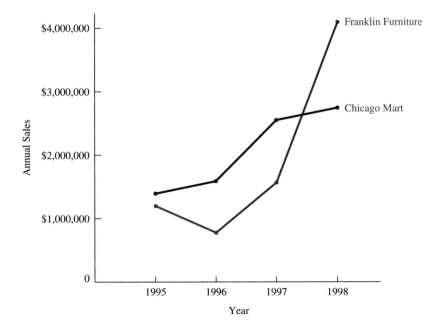

1. Estimate annual sales for Chicago Mart in each of the following years: (a) 1998, (b) 1997, and (c) 1996.

2. Estimate annual sales for Franklin Furniture in each of the following years: (a) 1998, (b) 1997, and (c) 1996.

3. The following set of data shows the number of college units completed by 30 of the employees of the Franklin Bank.

| | | | | | | | |
|---|---|---|---|---|---|---|---|
| 74 | 133 | 4 | 127 | 20 | 30 | 4 | 64 |
| 103 | 27 | 139 | 118 | 138 | 121 | 140 | 119 |
| 149 | 132 | 64 | 141 | 130 | 76 | 12 | |
| 42 | 50 | 95 | 56 | 65 | 104 | 88 | |

Use these numbers to complete the following table.

| | Number of Units | Frequency |
|---|---|---|
| (a) | 0–24 | _____ |
| (b) | 25–49 | _____ |
| (c) | 50–74 | _____ |
| (d) | 75–99 | _____ |
| (e) | 100–124 | _____ |
| (f) | 125–149 | _____ |

(g) Make a line graph using the frequencies that you found.

 4. Compare bar graphs, line graphs, and circle graphs. (See Objectives 1–3.)

5. Explain the purpose of a comparative line graph. (See Objective 3.)

6. The following numbers show the percent scores of 80 students on a marketing test.

79 60 74 59 55 98 61 67 83 71 69 56 84 93 63 60 68 51 73 54
71 46 63 66 69 42 75 62 71 77 50 88 76 93 48 70 39 76 95 57
78 65 87 57 78 91 82 73 94 48 63 94 82 54 89 64 77 94 72 69
87 65 62 81 63 66 65 49 45 51 51 56 67 88 81 70 81 54 66 87

Use these data to complete the following table.

| | Score | Frequency |
|---|---|---|
| (a) | 30–39% | _____ |
| (b) | 40–49% | _____ |
| (c) | 50–59% | _____ |
| (d) | 60–69% | _____ |
| (e) | 70–79% | _____ |
| (f) | 80–89% | _____ |
| (g) | 90–99% | _____ |

(h) Make a bar graph showing the results in the table above.

(i) How many students scored less than 60 on the exam?

(j) How many students scored 70 or higher?

**(k)** How many students scored from 60 to 89?

**(l)** How many students scored from 50 to 69?

**7.** The following graph is used to estimate the acreage covered by a farm implement per hour, when its width and speed of travel are known. For example, a $7\frac{1}{2}$ foot (90-inch) mower blade moving 4 miles per hour would cover about $3\frac{5}{8}$ acres per hour. This is found by going across the graph from the working width (90 inches) to the diagonal line for speed (4 mph), then down to the bottom to find acreage per hour.

**(a)** What is the acreage per hour for a 36-inch implement moving $2\frac{1}{2}$ miles per hour?

**(b)** What is the acreage per hour for an 8-foot-wide combine moving 4 miles per hour?

**(c)** How fast must a tractor pull a 48-inch plow in order to plow one acre per hour?

**(d)** How wide a spray pattern is needed in order to spray $4\frac{1}{2}$ acres per hour at a speed of $4\frac{1}{2}$ miles per hour?

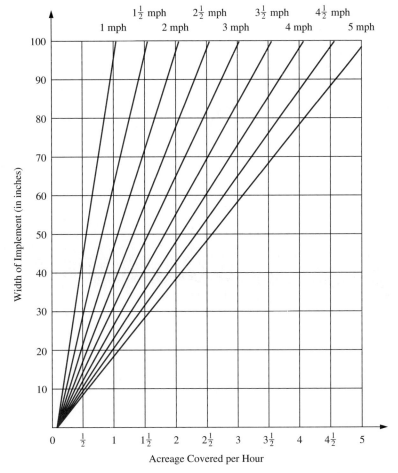

**8.** The comparative line graph shows the change in average weight (in pounds) for a recent 20-year period for various categories of American adults. Find the change in weight for each of the following groups of people.

**(a)** Men aged 20–24 who are 5 feet 10 inches tall (Hint: first find 5' 10" on the horizontal line in the center of the graph.)

**(b)** Women aged 40–49 whose height is 5 feet 8 inches

**(c)** 5-foot-tall women aged 20–24

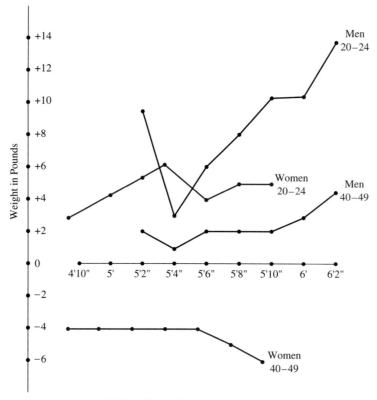

20-Year Change in Average Weight of Americans

**9.** In today's business environment it is important for administrative and office support professionals to possess computer skills. A recent survey asked the question of employers: "What does your company use as the primary method for evaluating a job candidate's software proficiency?" Draw a circle graph using the data.

|                         |      |
|-------------------------|------|
| The interview only      | 47%  |
| Reference checking      | 26%  |
| A test on a computer    | 8%   |
| Other                   | 19%  |
|                         | 100% |

**10.** The Social Security Administration recently found that the average retired couple has the following source of retirement income. Show the data in a circle graph.

|                  |      |
|------------------|------|
| Social Security  | 40%  |
| Personal assets  | 21%  |
| Earnings         | 17%  |
| Pensions         | 19%  |
| Other            | 3%   |
|                  | 100% |

**11.** A family kept track of its expenses for a year, with the following results. Draw a circle graph for this distribution.

| Item | Percent of Total |
|------|------------------|
| **Housing** | **30%** |
| **Food** | **21%** |
| **Automobile** | **14%** |
| **Clothing** | **10%** |
| **Medical** | **5%** |
| **Savings** | **8%** |
| **Other** | **12%** |

**12.** In Exercise 11, what percent did the family spend on food and housing?

**13.** In Exercise 11, what percent did the family spend on automobile and medical?

**14.** Interest rates in the United States have changed considerably during this century, creating an environment that either nourishes business growth and associated stock market rallies or stunts their growth. Use the data in the line chart to answer the questions that follow.

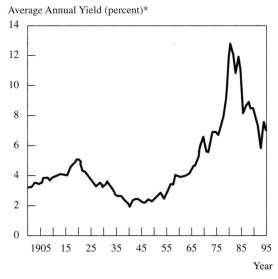

Average Annual Yield (percent)*

*1900-1919, average long-term corporate bonds; 1920-1995, average ten-year Treasury bonds.*

*Sources:* From WORTH Magazine, May 1996, p. 80. Reprinted with permission.

**(a)** Find the average annual yield in 1925.

**(b)** Over what range did interest rates fluctuate between 1905 and 1965?

**(c)** Over what range have interest rates fluctuated since 1965?

**(d)** Approximate the percent increase in interest rates from 1941 (World War II) to 1980.

**15.** A survey of banks has shown the following average salaries for some of their employees. Use the data to answer the questions that follow.

Average Annual Salaries (x $1,000)

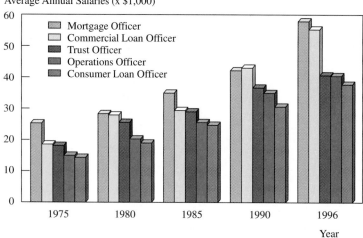

*Sources:* Reprinted with permission from the 1996 Robert Half and Accountemps Salary Guide.

**(a)** Find the average annual salary of a consumer loan officer in 1990 and 1996. Then find the percent increase in 1996 over 1990.

**(b)** Find the average 1996 annual salary of a mortgage officer and the difference between this salary and that of the consumer loan officer using 1996 data.

**(c)** Find the average annual salary of a trust officer in 1975 and in 1996.

# 19.2    The Mean

**OBJECTIVES**

**1**  *Understand the difference between population and sample.*

**2**  *Find the mean of a set of data.*

**3**  *Find a weighted mean.*

**4**  *Find the mean for grouped data.*

**OBJECTIVE 1  *Understand the difference between population and sample.***    In statistics, it is important to distinguish between the concepts of population and sample. **Population** is the entire group being studied, whereas **sample** is a portion of the entire group. Samples should be chosen randomly, meaning that no one individual in the population is more likely to be chosen than is another.

An administrator, for example, might be interested in the grade point average (GPA) of all freshmen at a community college. The GPA of the *entire population* of freshmen can be obtained but this might be time consuming to compile. Or, if an estimate of the GPA is adequate, the administrator can randomly choose a sample of perhaps 50 freshmen and find their grade point averages. The administrator might then *assume* that the grade point average of *this sample of students* is close to that of the entire population of all freshmen.

**OBJECTIVE 2** *Find the mean of a set of data.*     Businesses are often faced with the problem of analyzing a mass of raw data. Reports come in from many different branches of a company, or salespeople may send in a large number of expense claims, for example. In analyzing all the data, one of the first things to look for is a **measure of central tendency**—a single number that is designed to represent the entire list of numbers. One such measure of central tendency is the **mean**, which is just the common **average** of everyday life.

For example, suppose the sales of carnations at Tom's Flower Shop for each of the days last week were

$$\$86, \$103, \$118, \$117, \$126, \$158, \text{ and } \$149.$$

To find a single number that is representative of this list, use the following formula.

$$\text{Mean} = \frac{\text{Sum of all values}}{\text{Number of values}}$$

For Tom's Flower Shop, the mean is

$$\text{Mean} = \frac{\$86 + \$103 + \$118 + \$117 + \$126 + \$158 + \$149}{7}$$

$$= \frac{\$857}{7}$$

$$= \$122.43 \qquad \text{rounded to the nearest cent.}$$

**EXAMPLE 1** *Finding the Mean*

A factory that manufactures air conditioners is making a forecast for the second quarter of this year. (a) First, find the average monthly sales for the months of the second quarter of last year (April—2,600 units; May—2,825 units; June—2,906 units). (b) Assume sales are growing at 4% per year. Now increase the monthly average found in part (a) by 4%. This is the number of units they plan to produce in each month of the second quarter of this year.

**SOLUTION**

**(a)** The average or mean is the sum of the 3 months of sales divided by 3.

$$\text{Mean} = \frac{2,600 + 2,825 + 2,906}{3} = 2,777 \text{ units}$$

**(b)** Increase this monthly average by 4% to incorporate growth, i.e., use 100% for the original plus 4% for the growth or, 104%.

$$\text{Forecast} = 2{,}777 \times 1.04$$
$$= 2{,}888 \text{ units} \quad \text{(rounded)}$$

Thus, they plan to produce 2,888 units in April, May, and June of this year. ■

**OBJECTIVE 3** *Find a weighted mean.*    Table 19.5 shows a frequency distribution of annual salaries received by the management employees of a medium-sized corporation.

TABLE 19.5 **Sample Salaries of Management Employees**

As the table shows, 27 management employees were paid $32,000 each, 16 were paid $40,000 each, and so on. The average salary paid to these employees cannot be found by just adding the salaries, since different salaries are earned by different numbers of employees. To find the mean of the salaries, it is necessary to first multiply each annual salary by the number of employees receiving that salary. This process produces a **weighted mean**, where each number (a salary here) is "weighted" by multiplying it by the number of times it occurs.

| Salary | Number of Managers (Frequency) |
|---|---|
| $32,000 | 27 |
| 40,000 | 16 |
| 50,000 | 11 |
| 72,000 | 6 |
| 90,000 | 4 |
| 96,000 | 4 |
| 110,000 | 3 |
| 160,000 | 2 |
| 296,000 | 1 |

| Salary | Number of Managers | Salary × Number of Managers |
|---|---|---|
| $32,000 | 27 | $864,000 |
| 40,000 | 16 | 640,000 |
| 50,000 | 11 | 550,000 |
| 72,000 | 6 | 432,000 |
| 90,000 | 4 | 360,000 |
| 96,000 | 4 | 384,000 |
| 110,000 | 3 | 330,000 |
| 160,000 | 2 | 320,000 |
| 296,000 | 1 | 296,000 |
| Totals | 74 | $4,176,000 |

By adding the numbers in the "Number of Managers" column, find that the corporation has a total of 74 management employees. Find the mean by dividing the total of all salaries, $4,176,000, by the total number of employees, 74.

$$\text{Mean salary} = \frac{\$4{,}176{,}000}{74} = \$56{,}432 \quad \text{(rounded)}$$

The mean salary of a management employee is $56,432.

As you can see in the next example, weighted means are also used to find grade point averages.

**EXAMPLE 2** *Finding Grade Point Average*

Find the grade point average for the following student. Assume A = 4, B = 3, C = 2, D = 1, and F = 0.

## SOLUTION

| Course | Units | Grade | Grade × Units |
|---|---|---|---|
| Business Mathematics | 3 | A (= 4) | 4 × 3 = 12 |
| Retailing | 4 | C (= 2) | 2 × 4 = 8 |
| English | 3 | B (= 3) | 3 × 3 = 9 |
| Computer Science | 2 | A (= 4) | 4 × 2 = 8 |
| Lab for Computer Science | 2 | D (= 1) | 1 × 2 = 2 |
| | Totals 14 | | 39 |

The grade point average for this student is

$$\frac{39}{14} = 2.79.$$ ∎

**NOTE** It is common to round a grade point average to the nearest hundredth. ∎

**OBJECTIVE** **4** *Find the mean for grouped data.* The mean can also be found for data that has been grouped into a frequency distribution. To do so, find the midpoint of each interval, or class. This midpoint is found by averaging the highest and lowest numbers that can go into a class. For example, the midpoint of **class mark** of the interval 100–109 is the mean of 100 and 109.

$$\text{Class midpoint} = \frac{100 + 109}{2} = \frac{209}{2} = 104.5$$

**NOTE** The intervals in a frequency table should not overlap with one another. ∎

**EXAMPLE 3** *Finding the Mean for Grouped Data*

A researcher surveyed a number of farmers on their use of a particular brand of fertilizer. Although the recommended usage is 135 pounds per acre, she found that the usage varied from that. Find the mean for the frequency distribution shown.

| Intervals | Frequency |
|---|---|
| 100–109 | 9 |
| 110–119 | 12 |
| 120–129 | 17 |
| 130–139 | 28 |
| 140–149 | 21 |
| 150–159 | 16 |
| 160–169 | 4 |

**SOLUTION**  Begin by finding the class mark for each class of fertilizer use. As explained, the class mark or midpoint of the first class is 104.5, while the midpoint of the second class is

$$\frac{110 + 119}{2} = \frac{229}{2} = 114.5.$$

Find the other midpoints in a similar way. Then multiply the frequencies and the class marks, giving the column at the right (labeled "Frequency $\times$ Class Mark"). Next, find the totals in the "Frequency" column and the "Frequency $\times$ Class Mark" column.

| Intervals | Frequency | Class Mark | Frequency $\times$ Class Mark |
|---|---|---|---|
| 100–109 | 9 | 104.5 | 9 $\times$ 104.5 =     940.5 |
| 110–119 | 12 | 114.5 | 12 $\times$ 114.5 =  1,374.0 |
| 120–129 | 17 | 124.5 | 17 $\times$ 124.5 =  2,116.5 |
| 130–139 | 28 | 134.5 | 28 $\times$ 134.5 =  3,766.0 |
| 140–149 | 21 | 144.5 | 21 $\times$ 144.5 =  3,034.5 |
| 150–159 | 16 | 154.5 | 16 $\times$ 154.5 =  2,472.0 |
| 160–169 | 4 | 164.5 | 4 $\times$ 164.5 =     658.0 |
| Totals | 107 | | 14,361.5 |

Finally, the mean is the quotient of these totals, or

$$\text{Mean} = \frac{14,361.5}{107} = 134.2 \quad \text{(to the nearest tenth).}$$

The mean usage rate of 134.2 pounds per acre is close to the recommended usage rate of 135 pounds per acre.  ∎

**NOTE**  When a set of data is divided up into classes, it is no longer possible to tell where in a class a particular item falls. For this reason, *a mean found from grouped data is only approximate*, although in most cases the approximation to the true mean is very good.  ∎

## 19.2  EXERCISES

*Find the mean for each of the following sets of data. Round to the nearest tenth.*

**1.** 24, 24, 26, 30

**2.** 60, 65, 67, 62, 59, 58, 70

**3.** 3,800, 3,625, 3,904, 3,296, 3,400, 3,650, 3,822, 4,020

**4.** 10.3, 11.7, 12.4, 8.6, 9.9, 12.1, 13.2, 10.8, 9.6, 8.8

*Round to the nearest whole number in Exercises 5–10.*

5. Five different head of cattle weighed 720 pounds, 685 pounds, 665 pounds, 710 pounds, and 704 pounds. Find the mean weight.

6. The yield of milk at a dairy, for four successive days, was 410 gallons, 440 gallons, 520 gallons, and 423 gallons. Find the mean.

7. The seven people at Hein Securities earned commissions last year of $32,750, $49,811, $12,092, $17,583, $27,854, $98,253, and $37,584. Find the mean commission.

8. Life insurance sold last year by the six new agents of National Insurance Agency totaled $294,000, $580,000, $722,000, $463,000, $814,000, and $1,785,000. Find the mean total of life insurance sold.

9. Last year, the value of the new cars sold by the eight salespeople at The Autoplex was $385,000, $495,000, $873,000, $1,210,000, $611,000, $802,000, $173,000, and $708,000. Find the mean value of the cars.

10. Telesales employs nine people to make telephone calls to sell magazines. Last year, these people produced total sales of $492,811, $763,455, $901,852, $179,806, $244,193, $382,574, $591,873, $1,003,058, and $473,902. Find the mean sales per employee.

*Find the weighted mean for each of the following. Round to the nearest tenth.*

11.

| Value | Frequency |
|-------|-----------|
| 4 | 4 |
| 6 | 4 |
| 9 | 1 |
| 12 | 3 |

12.

| Value | Frequency |
|-------|-----------|
| 10 | 8 |
| 12 | 5 |
| 15 | 1 |
| 18 | 1 |

13.

| Value | Frequency |
|-------|-----------|
| 125 | 6 |
| 130 | 4 |
| 150 | 5 |
| 190 | 3 |
| 220 | 2 |
| 230 | 5 |

14.

| Value | Frequency |
|-------|-----------|
| 25 | 1 |
| 26 | 2 |
| 29 | 5 |
| 30 | 4 |
| 32 | 3 |
| 33 | 5 |

 15. Explain the difference between population and sample. (See Objective 1.)

 16. What is the purpose of a weighted mean? Give an example of where it is used. (See Objective 3.)

*In the following problems, find the mean salary for the employees. Round to the nearest thousand dollars.*

| 17. Salary | Number of Employees | | 18. Salary | Number of Employees |
|---|---|---|---|---|
| $18,000 | 8 | | $15,000 | 8 |
| $21,000 | 10 | | $20,000 | 15 |
| $28,000 | 8 | | $22,000 | 13 |
| $29,000 | 6 | | $25,000 | 9 |
| $38,000 | 4 | | $30,000 | 4 |
| $41,000 | 3 | | $42,000 | 3 |
| $53,000 | 2 | | $57,000 | 2 |
| $162,000 | 1 | | $260,000 | 1 |

*Find the grade point average for each of the following students. Assume $A = 4$, $B = 3$, $C = 2$, $D = 1$, and $F = 0$. Round to the nearest hundredth.*

| 19. Units | Grade | | 20. Units | Grade |
|---|---|---|---|---|
| 4 | D | | 3 | A |
| 2 | A | | 3 | B |
| 3 | C | | 4 | B |
| 1 | F | | 2 | C |
| 3 | D | | 4 | D |

*Find the mean for the following grouped data. Round to the nearest tenth.*

| 21. Interval | Frequency | | 22. Interval | Frequency |
|---|---|---|---|---|
| 50–59 | 15 | | 320–339 | 7 |
| 60–69 | 20 | | 340–359 | 9 |
| 70–79 | 21 | | 360–379 | 12 |
| 80–89 | 27 | | 380–399 | 11 |
| 90–99 | 18 | | 400–419 | 6 |
| 100–109 | 2 | | 420–439 | 5 |

| 23. Interval | Frequency |
|:---:|:---:|
| 25–49 | 18 |
| 50–74 | 15 |
| 75–99 | 30 |
| 100–124 | 18 |
| 125–149 | 32 |
| 150–174 | 14 |
| 175–199 | 7 |

| 24. Interval | Frequency |
|:---:|:---:|
| 150–154 | 4 |
| 155–159 | 7 |
| 160–164 | 9 |
| 165–169 | 12 |
| 170–174 | 16 |
| 175–179 | 8 |
| 180–184 | 3 |

*Solve the following application problems.*

25. The final grade in a history class is the average of three tests taken during the semester. Wanda Kroll made 74% and 68% on the first two tests. Find the minimum score she can make on the third test and still have a 70% average.

26. A platform used to wash the outside of windows on tall buildings was built to hold 3 180-pound workers. A company has a 190-pound worker and a 200-pound worker and is looking to hire a third worker to work on this platform. What weight restriction should they place on the third worker?

## 19.3 The Median and the Mode

### OBJECTIVES

**1** Find the median of a set of data.

**2** Find the mode of a set of data.

**3** Find the median and the mode of data in a frequency table.

In everyday life, the word "average" usually refers to the mean. However, there are two other "averages" in common use, the *median* and the *mode*. Median and mode are discussed in this section.

Suppose the owner of a small company pays five employees annual salaries of

$$\$12,500, \$13,000, \$13,200, \$14,000, \text{ and } \$15,000.$$

The average, or mean, salary paid to the employees is

$$\text{Mean} = \frac{\$12,500 + \$13,000 + \$13,200 + \$14,000 + \$15,000}{5}$$

$$= \frac{\$67,700}{5} = \$13,540.$$

Now suppose that the employees go on strike and demand a raise. To get public support, they appear on television to talk about their low salaries, which average only $13,540 per year.

The television station sends a reporter to interview the owner of the company. Before the interviewer arrives, the owner decides to find the average salary of *all employees*, including the five on strike, plus his own. To do this, he adds the five salaries given on the previous page, plus his salary of $127,000. This gives an average of

$$\text{Mean} = \frac{\$12,500 + \$13,000 + \$13,200 + \$14,000 + \$15,000 + \$127,000}{6}$$

$$= \frac{\$194,700}{6} = \$32,450.$$

When the television reporter arrives, the owner is prepared to state that there is no reason for the employees to be on strike, since they have an average salary of $32,450.

There are two points to this story. First, both averages are correct, depending on what is being measured. *This shows how easily statistics can be manipulated.* Second, *the mean is often a poor indicator of the "middle" of a list of numbers.* In fact, when the mean was computed by the owner, it was greater than 5 of the 6 employees' salaries. The mean may be greatly affected by extreme values, such as the owner's salary of $127,000.

OBJECTIVE **1** *Find the median of a set of data.*   To avoid such a misleading result when using the mean, use a different measure of the "middle" of a list of numbers, the **median**. As a general rule, the median divides a list of numbers in half: one-half of the numbers lie at or above the median and one half lie at or below the median.

Since the median divides a list of numbers in half, the first step in finding a median is to rewrite the list of numbers as an **ordered array**, with the numbers going from *smallest to largest.* For example, the list of numbers 9, 6, 11, 17, 14, 12, 8 would be written in order as the ordered array

$$6, \ 8, \ 9, \ 11, \ 12, \ 14, \ 17.$$

The median is found from the ordered array as explained in the following box. Notice that the procedure for finding the median depends on whether the number of numbers in the list is *even* or *odd.*

> If the ordered array has an *odd* number of numbers, divide the number of numbers by 2. The next higher whole number gives the *location* of the median.
>
> If the ordered array has an *even* number of numbers, there is no single middle number. Find the median by first dividing the number of numbers by 2. The median is the average (mean) of the number in this position and the number in the next higher position.

Example 1 shows lists of numbers having an *odd* number of numbers; Example 2 shows an *even* number of numbers.

**EXAMPLE 1**   *Finding the Median*

Find the median for the annual salaries of the 5 employees introduced earlier in this section ($12,500, $13,000, $13,200, $14,000, and $15,000).

SOLUTION    First, make sure to list the numbers from smallest to largest.

$12,500, $13,000, $13,200, $14,000, $15,000

There are 5 numbers in the list. Divide 5 by 2 to get $\frac{5}{2} = 2.5$. The *next higher number* is 3 so that the median is the third number or $13,200. Two numbers are larger than $13,200 and two are smaller.    ∎

### EXAMPLE 2  *Finding the Median*

Find the median of the salaries of the employer and the 5 employees introduced earlier in this section ($127,000, $12,500, $13,000, $13,200, $14,000, and $15,000).

SOLUTION    First arrange the numbers from smallest to largest.

$12,500, $13,000, $13,200, $14,000, $15,000, $127,000

There are 6 numbers (an even number of numbers) in the list. Divide 6 by 2 to get 3. The median is the *mean of the numbers in the third and fourth positions.*

$$\text{median} = \frac{\$13,200 + \$14,000}{2} = \$13,600$$    ∎

The median of this set of numbers is $13,600 and the mean is $32,450. The median is probably a better measure of central tendency for this set of numbers than is the mean, which is distorted by one large number, i.e., $127,000.

OBJECTIVE **2** *Find the mode of a set of data.*    The last important statistical measure of central tendency is called the **mode**. The mode is the number which occurs *the most often.* For example, if ten students earned the following scores on a business law examination

74, 81, 39, 74, 82, 80, 100, 92, 74, 85,

then the mode is 74, since more students obtained this score than any other. (It is not necessary to form an ordered array when looking for the mode.)

### EXAMPLE 3  *Finding the Mode*

Find the mode for each of the following sets of data: (a) 51, 32, 49, 73, 49, 90; (b) 482, 485, 483, 485, 487, 487, 489; and (c) 10,708; 11,519; 10,972; 12,546; 13,905; 12,182.

SOLUTION

(a) The number 49 occurs more often than any other number. Therefore, 49 is the mode.

(b) Here 485 and 487 both occur twice. This data set has *two* modes. Such sets are sometimes called **bimodal**.

(c) No number here occurs more than once. This data set has no mode.    ∎

The mean, median, and mode are different ways of locating the middle or center of a list of numbers. Each of these three ways is a measure of central tendency.

**OBJECTIVE** **3** *Find the median and the mode of data in a frequency table.*    The same basic ideas of median and mode are applied as shown in the next example.

**EXAMPLE 4** *Finding the Mean, Median, and Mode*

The diameter of a part coming out of a machining process is measured regularly. The diameters vary some as shown in the frequency table. Find the (a) mean, (b) median, and (c) mode.

| Diameter (inches) | Frequency |
|---|---|
| 0.720–0.729 | 3 |
| 0.730–0.739 | 12 |
| 0.740–0.749 | 8 |
| 0.750–0.759 | 9 |
| 0.760–0.769 | 2 |

**SOLUTION**

(a) The weighted mean is found using the technique shown in the previous section. The class mark for the first class is

$$\frac{0.720 + 0.729}{2} = 0.7245$$

and so on for the other classes.

| Class Mark | Frequency × Class Mark |
|---|---|
| 0.7245 | 3 × 0.7245 =  2.1735 |
| 0.7345 | 12 × 0.7345 =  8.814 |
| 0.7445 | 8 × 0.7445 =  5.956 |
| 0.7545 | 9 × 0.7545 =  6.7905 |
| 0.7645 | 2 × 0.7645 =  1.529 |
| **Totals**  34 | 25.263 |

The group average is

$$\frac{25.263}{34} = 0.743 \qquad \text{(rounded)}.$$

(b) There are 34, or an even number, of numbers. Divide 34 by 2 to get 17. Thus the seventeenth and eighteenth numbers from the smallest are averaged to find the median. The numbers have already been arranged from smallest to largest in the table. Three numbers fall in the first class (0.720–0.729) and 15 numbers fall in the first and second classes combined (0.720–0.729 and 0.730–0.739). The seventeenth and eighteenth numbers fall in the third class (0.740–0.749).

Assume that the seventeenth and eighteenth both have values at the class mark of 0.7445. The median is the average of these two class marks.

$$\frac{0.7445 + 0.7445}{2} = 0.7445$$

**(c)** The mode is the number that occurs most often. Assuming that the numbers in each class fall at the class mark, the second class (0.730–0.739) has the most observations. The mode is 0.7345.

Thus, we have the following.

mean = 0.743    median = 0.7445    mode = 0.7345    ∎

## 19.3 EXERCISES

*Find the median for each of the following sets of data.*

**1.** 60, 54, 35, 21, 19

**2.** 104, 121, 130, 130, 107, 112, 115

**3.** 95, 98, 75, 81

**4.** 6.8, 9.7, 5.2, 6.0, 6.8, 6.3

**5.** 0.81, 0.82, 0.86, 0.84

**6.** 900, 860, 840, 880, 920, 940

*Find the mode or modes for each of the following sets of data.*

**7.** 4, 7, 3, 7, 9, 2, 5

**8.** 12, 13, 10, 13, 14, 13

**9.** 65, 60, 68, 72, 56, 70, 85

**10.** 180, 195, 162, 173, 184, 195, 186, 170

**11.** 6, 4, 8, 4, 6, 9, 3, 2

**12.** 5.8, 5.6, 5.8, 5.5, 5.3, 5.4, 5.6, 5.2

 **13.** When is the median a better average to use than the mean to describe a set of data? (See Objective 1.)

 **14.** Compare mean, median, and mode. (See Objectives 1–3.)

*Solve the following application problems.*

**15.** A chemistry student working on a lab experiment copied the following meter readings into a notebook.

3, 4, 5, 2, 3, 2, 2, 30, 3

Use these numbers to find the mean and the median.

**16.** The student in Exercise 15 later found that the measurement of 30 was incorrect. He removed this number from the list leaving 3, 4, 5, 2, 3, 2, 2, 3. Find the mean and median.

**17.** If you want to avoid a single extreme value having a large effect on the average, would you use the mean or the median? Explain.

18. Suppose you own a hat shop and can only order hats in one size. You look at last year's sales to decide on the size to order. Should you find the mean, median, or mode for these sales? Explain.

*Find the mean, median, and mode for the following grouped data sets. Round to the nearest tenth.*

| 19. Interval | Frequency |
|---|---|
| 100–109 | 10 |
| 110–119 | 12 |
| 120–129 | 8 |
| 130–139 | 2 |

| 20. Interval | Frequency |
|---|---|
| 10–14 | 2 |
| 15–19 | 1 |
| 20–24 | 5 |
| 25–29 | 7 |

*Solve the following application problems.*

21. A biochemical company tries to place exactly 3 pounds of a particular enzyme in each bag that they produce. However, a tolerance of ±0.1 pounds is considered acceptable. A recent sample of 56 bags of enzyme showed the following.

| Pounds of Enzyme | Frequency |
|---|---|
| below 2.86 | 0 |
| 2.86–2.95 | 3 |
| 2.96–3.05 | 48 |
| 3.06–3.15 | 5 |
| over 3.15 | 0 |

Find the weighted mean. Based on the data available, does the company appear to have a successful bagging operation?

22. A robot designed to drill a hole to a depth of 1.5 centimeters in a block of steel is being tested with the following results.

| Depth of Hole (centimeters) | Frequency |
|---|---|
| below 1.26 | 0 |
| 1.26–1.35 | 1 |
| 1.36–1.45 | 18 |
| 1.46–1.55 | 20 |
| over 1.55 | 0 |

Find the weighted mean. Does the robot appear to be working as desired?

# 19.4   Standard Deviation

TABLE 19.6   **Comparison of Distributions A and B**

| | A | B |
|---|---|---|
| | 5 | 1 |
| | 6 | 2 |
| | 7 | 7 |
| | 8 | 12 |
| | 9 | 13 |
| **Mean** | 7 | 7 |
| **Median** | 7 | 7 |

## OBJECTIVES

**1**   *Find the range for a set of data.*

**2**   *Find the standard deviation.*

**3**   *Use the normal curve to estimate data.*

The mean is a good indicator of the middle, or central tendency, of a set of data values, but *it does not give the whole story* about the data. To see why, compare distribution A with distribution B in Table 19.6.

Both distributions of numbers have the same mean (and the same median also), but beyond that they are quite different. In the first, 7 is a fairly typical value; but in the second, most of the values differ quite a bit from 7. To show this difference requires some measure of the **dispersion**, or spread, of the data.

**OBJECTIVE** **1**   *Find the range for a set of data.*     Two of the most common measures of dispersion, the **range** and the **standard deviation**, are discussed here.

The range for a set of data is defined as the *difference between the largest value and the smallest value in the set*. In distribution A in Table 19.6, the largest value is 9 and the smallest is 5. The range is

$$\text{Highest} - \text{Lowest} = \text{Range}$$

$$9 - 5 = 4.$$

In distribution B, the range is

$$13 - 1 = 12.$$

The range can be misleading if it is interpreted unwisely. For example, suppose three executives rate two employees, Mark and Myrna, on five different jobs, as shown in the following table.

| Job | Mark | Myrna |
|---|---|---|
| 1 | 28 | 27 |
| 2 | 22 | 27 |
| 3 | 21 | 28 |
| 4 | 26 | 6 |
| 5 | 18 | 27 |
| **Mean** | 23 | 23 |
| **Median** | 22 | 27 |
| **Range** | 10 | 22 |

By looking at the range for each person, we might be tempted to conclude that Mark is a more consistent worker than Myrna. However, by checking more closely, we might decide that Myrna is actually more consistent with the exception of one very poor score, which is probably due to some special circumstance. Myrna's median score is not affected much by the single low score and is more typical of her performance as a whole than is her mean score.

One of the most useful measures of dispersion, the standard deviation, is based on *deviation from the mean* of the data. To find how much each value deviates from the mean, first find the mean, and then subtract the mean from each data value.

| EXAMPLE 1   *Finding Deviations from the Mean*

Find the deviations from the mean for the data values

$$32, 41, 47, 53, 57.$$

SOLUTION    Add these numbers and divide by 5. *The mean is 46.* To find the deviations from the mean, subtract 46 from each data value. (Subtracting 46 from a smaller number produces a negative result.)

| Data value | 32 | 41 | 47 | 53 | 57 |
|---|---|---|---|---|---|
| **Deviation** | **−14** | **−5** | **1** | **7** | **11** |

∎

NOTE    To check the work in Example 1, add the deviations. The sum of the deviations for a set of data is always 0, as long as the mean was not rounded.    ∎

OBJECTIVE **2**  *Find the standard deviation.*      To find the measure of dispersion, it might be tempting to find the mean of the deviations. However, this number always turns out to be 0 no matter how much the dispersion in the data is, because the positive deviations simply cancel out the negative ones.

Get around this problem of adding positive and negative numbers by *squaring* each deviation. (The square of a negative number is positive.) Take Example 1 one step further.

| Data value | 32 | 41 | 47 | 53 | 57 |
|---|---|---|---|---|---|
| Deviation from mean | −14 | −5 | 1 | 7 | 11 |
| **Square of deviation** | **196** | **25** | **1** | **49** | **121** |

We can now define the **standard deviation**: it is *the square root of the mean of the squares of the deviation.* The square root of a number $n$ is written $\sqrt{n}$. It is the number that when multiplied by itself equals $n$. Thus, $\sqrt{144} = 12$ since $12 \times 12 = 144$, $\sqrt{1} = 1$ since $1 \times 1 = 1$, and so on. Therefore, the standard deviation is defined to be

$$\sqrt{\frac{\text{the sum of the squared deviations from the mean}}{\text{the number of observations}}}.$$

Continuing the example on the preceding page we have the following, where *s* is used for standard deviation:

$$s = \sqrt{\frac{196 + 25 + 1 + 49 + 121}{5}}$$

$$= \sqrt{\frac{392}{5}}$$

$$= \sqrt{78.4}$$

$$= 8.9 \quad \text{(rounded to the nearest tenth)}.$$

---

**CALCULATOR APPROACH TO EXAMPLE 1**

*The calculator solution to this problem is as follows.

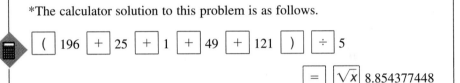

( 196 + 25 + 1 + 49 + 121 ) ÷ 5

= √x̄ 8.854377448

---

The algebraic expression for the standard deviation is

$$s = \sqrt{\frac{\Sigma d^2}{n}},$$

where $d$ = a deviation from the mean, $n$ is *the number of data points in the group of numbers* and the Greek letter $\Sigma$ (sigma) represents a "sum of."

---

**NOTE** Some calculators have statistical function keys that can be used to calculate means and standard deviations—check your calculator manual to see if your calculator has these keys. ■

**EXAMPLE 2** *Finding Standard Deviation*

Find the standard deviation of the values

$$7, 9, 18, 22, 27, 29, 32, 40.$$

**SOLUTION**

**Step 1**  Find the mean of the values.

$$\frac{7 + 9 + 18 + 22 + 27 + 29 + 32 + 40}{8} = 23$$

---

*NOTE: All calculator solutions use a scientific calculator. Refer to Appendix A for scientific and financial calculator basics.

***Step 2*** Find the deviations from the mean.

| Data values | 7 | 9 | 18 | 22 | 27 | 29 | 32 | 40 |
|---|---|---|---|---|---|---|---|---|
| Deviations | −16 | −14 | −5 | −1 | 4 | 6 | 9 | 17 |

***Step 3*** Square each deviation.

Squares of deviations: 256  196  25  1  16  36  81  289

These numbers are the $d^2$ values in the formula.

***Step 4*** Find the sum of the $d^2$ values.

$$\Sigma d^2 = 256 + 196 + 25 + 1 + 16 + 36 + 81 + 289 = 900$$

Now divide $\Sigma d^2$ by $n$, which is 8 in this example.

$$\frac{\Sigma d^2}{n} = \frac{900}{8} = 112.5$$

***Step 5*** Take the square root of the answer in Step 4. The standard deviation of the given list of numbers is

$$s = \sqrt{112.5} = 10.6. \qquad \blacksquare$$

**NOTE** The **variance**, which is used in some textbooks, is the square of the standard deviation.

$$\text{Variance} = (\text{Standard deviation})^2$$

Similarly, the standard deviation is the square root of the variance.

$$\text{Standard deviation} = \sqrt{\text{Variance}} \qquad \blacksquare$$

**OBJECTIVE** **3** *Use the normal curve to estimate data.*       Soft drink bottlers such as The Coca-Cola Company wish to deliver a quality product to their customers. Of course, a primary measure of quality is taste. The level of liquid placed in each container during the bottling process *affects* the level of carbonation which, in turn, *influences* taste. Thus, these bottlers try to put a very specific amount of the liquid drink into each container. Some even X-ray each bottle as it *rapidly* moves down the production line in order to make sure that the amount of liquid is "close enough."

If the bottling process is working well, the amount of liquid in successive containers *will be centered* around the desired amount. Further, there will be very few containers with a fluid level that is either too low or too high. (This problem continues in Example 3.) Experience has shown that the output in this case (or in similar situations) can be described using the **normal curve** which is shown in Figure 19.7.

It turns out that if a group of data is very closely approximated by a normal curve, approximately 68% of the data will lie *within 1 standard deviation* of the mean or between (mean − one standard deviation) and (mean + one standard

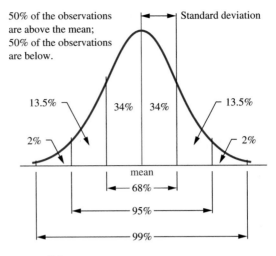

FIGURE 19.7

deviation). Approximately 95% of the data will lie within 2 standard deviations of the mean; and about 99% will lie within 3 standard deviations of the mean.

## EXAMPLE 3  *Using the Normal Distribution*

A worker uses statistics to look at the quality, in terms of fluid level in the containers, of 300 containers of a beverage bottled at his workstation. Suppose that the fluid level in the containers is approximated by the normal curve with a mean of 6 inches and a standard deviation of 0.04 inches. (a) Find the mean minus 3 standard deviations and the mean plus three standard deviations. (b) Use Figure 19.7 to find the number of containers out of the 300 that are expected to fall within the two limits found in part (a).

## SOLUTION

**(a)** Mean $-$ 3 standard deviations $= 6 - (3 \cdot 0.04) = 5.88$ inches
Mean $+$ 3 standard deviations $= 6 + (3 \cdot 0.04) = 6.12$ inches

**(b)** Simply add the percents within 3 standard deviations of the mean in Figure 19.7 to find the total percent of the containers that should fall within the limits found in (a) above.

$$2\% + 13.5\% + 34\% + 34\% + 13.5\% + 2\% = 99\%$$

Now multiply this percent times the 300 containers to find the number of containers that should fall within the limits found in (a).

$$99\% \text{ of } 300 = 0.99 \cdot 300 = 297 \text{ containers} \qquad ■$$

**NOTE**  Workers from all over the world have been trained in statistics so that they can monitor the quality of their own work.  ■

# 19.4  EXERCISES

*Find the mean and standard deviation for each set of data. Round answers to the nearest tenth.*

**1.** 8, 10, 12, 10

**2.** 15, 20, 17, 18, 22

**3.** 20, 22, 23, 18, 21, 22

**4.** 120, 118, 109, 115, 112, 110

**5.** 55, 58, 54, 52, 51, 59, 58, 60

**6.** 7.5, 7.3, 7.2, 7.5, 7.8, 7.1, 7.4, 8.0, 7.2, 7.6

*Find the range for each set of data.*

**7.** 6, 12, 10, 9, 19, 24

**8.** 10, 15, 12, 17, 21, 13

**9.** 500, 274, 361, 295, 112

**10.** 10.3, 7.4, 8.1, 6.5, 9.7

**11.** When can the range of a set of numbers be misleading? (See Objective 1.)

**12.** Explain how to interpret the standard deviation. (See Objective 2.)

*The weight of 200 bags of chemical is measured. Not all bags have exactly the same weight due to the production process. However, the results can be approximated by a normal curve with a mean of 80 pounds and a standard deviation of 0.5 pounds. Use the following graph to find the number of bags weighing as indicated in Exercises 13–20.*

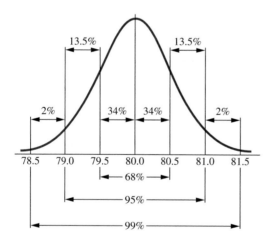

**13.** More than 80 pounds

**14.** More than 79.5 pounds

**15.** Between 79.5 and 80.5 pounds

**16.** Between 79 and 81 pounds

**17.** Between 80.5 and 81 pounds

**18.** Between 79.5 and 81 pounds

**19.** Within 1 pound of the mean

**20.** More than $1\frac{1}{2}$ pounds away from the mean

*Personal computer sales at PC Outlet have recently averaged 120 per month with a standard deviation of 20. Use the graph of the normal curve used for Exercises 13–20 to help the manager estimate the chances of next months sales falling into each of the following categories.*

**21.** Less than 80

**22.** More than 160

**23.** Between 80 and 160

**24.** Between 100 and 140

*On standard IQ tests, the mean is* 100, *with a standard deviation of* 15. *The results are very close to fitting a normal curve. Suppose an IQ test is given to a very large group of people. Find the percent of people whose IQ score is:*

**25.** More than 100

**26.** Less than 100

**27.** Greater than 115

**28.** Between 85 and 115

**29.** Between 70 and 130

**30.** Between 55 and 145

**31.** Less than 55

**32.** More than 145

*After a 30,000 mile road test, the wear on a particular brand of tire averaged 0.2 inches with a standard deviation of 0.015 inches. The tire wear fits a normal curve closely. What percent of the tire wear is:*

**33.** 0.185 inches or more?

**34.** Less than 0.185 inches?

**35.** 0.23 inches or less?

**36.** More than 0.23 inches?

*At one factory, production line workers can assemble a certain computer component with a mean time of* 47.6 *minutes, and a standard deviation of* 2.7 *minutes. The times are very closely approximated by a normal curve. What percent of the times are:*

**37.** At least 44.9 minutes?

**38.** No more than 44.9 minutes?

**39.** No more than 53 minutes?

**40.** At least 53 minutes?

**41.** Between 44.9 minutes and 50.3 minutes?

**42.** Between 42.2 minutes and 53 minutes?

**43.** The time required to handle a claim by one claim adjuster at an insurance company is approximated by the normal curve with mean 12.5 minutes and standard deviation 2.2 minutes. Out of 200 claims, how many would you expect to take more than 19.1 minutes?

**44.** A machine automatically inflates automobile tires at a factory. Results can be approximated by a normal curve with mean 30.8 pounds per square inch (psi) with a standard deviation of 0.4 psi. Find the number of tires, out of 2,000 filled, that will likely have less than 30 psi.

## 19.5 Index Numbers

### OBJECTIVES

**1** *Find the price relative.*

**2** *Use the Consumer Price Index to compare costs.*

**OBJECTIVE** **1** *Find the price relative.* A house that cost $55,000 ten years ago now sells for $115,000. Ten years ago, a gallon of gasoline cost $1.15; today it costs $1.60.

Both items increased in price. To find out which increased more in percent, find the *price relative* for each item. A **price relative** is the quotient of the current price and the price in some past year with the quotient multiplied by 100. The past year is called the **base year**. The formula for the price relative is as follows.

$$\text{Price relative} = \frac{\text{Price this year}}{\text{Price in base year}} \times 100$$

## EXAMPLE 1 *Finding the Price Relative*

**(a)** Using the prices just given, the price relative for the house is

$$\text{Price relative} = \frac{\$115,000}{\$55,000} \times 100 = 209.1 \quad \text{(rounded)}.$$

The price of the house today is 209.1% of its price ten years ago. Note that a price relative is really just a percent—it gives the percent that this year's price is of the price in the base year.

**(b)** The price relative for gasoline, using the prices given is

$$\text{Price relative} = \frac{\$1.60}{\$1.15} \times 100 = 139.1 \quad \text{(rounded)}.$$

The price of gasoline this year is 139.1% of its price ten years ago. ∎

Compare the price relatives of Example 1 to find that the price of the house has increased at a faster rate than that of gasoline.

## EXAMPLE 2 *Finding the Price Relative*

The price of a particular computer chip dropped from $1,100 two years ago *to $220 today*. The price relative is

$$\frac{\$220}{\$1,100} \times 100 = 20.$$

The computer chip sells today for 20% of its previous selling price. This example shows that a price relative can be less than 100; this occurs when the price of an item *drops* over time. A few things go down in price over the years *but most go up in price* with time. In particular, almost all price relatives are over 100 during inflationary periods. ∎

**NOTE** The price relative gives a way of comparing the two prices and showing a percent increase. ∎

TABLE 19.7   **Urban Prices Index***

|  | Chicago | Dallas | Los Angeles-Long Beach | New York-New Jersey | Philadelphia |
|---|---|---|---|---|---|
| **All items** | 148.6 | 141.2 | 152.3 | 158.2 | 154.6 |
| **Food and beverages** | 147.0 | 142.2 | 148.5 | 151.9 | 142.7 |
| **Housing** | 144.8 | 129.0 | 151.0 | 159.9 | 155.1 |
| **Apparel and upkeep** | 131.0 | 148.2 | 129.6 | 126.2 | 105.8 |
| **Transportation** | 130.3 | 134.5 | 140.5 | 141.8 | 144.0 |
| **Medical** | 213.2 | 205.6 | 215.2 | 217.6 | 223.9 |
| **Entertainment** | 160.0 | 147.1 | 137.2 | 154.0 | 160.3 |

*All figures are expressed as a percent of the 1987 base of 100.

**OBJECTIVE 2** *Use the Consumer Price Index to compare costs.*     The **Consumer Price Index**, published by the Bureau of Labor Statistics, gives good examples of price relatives. The Bureau keeps track of the costs of a great many items in different cities throughout the country, and publishes its findings monthly. A recent portion of the report for one month is included in Table 19.7.

The numbers in this table represent price relatives, with a base year of 1987. For example, in Chicago the cost of food and beverages is now 147% of the cost in 1987, or, in other words, it now costs $147 to buy the food and beverages that could have been bought with $100 in 1987. As a further example, medical care that cost $100 in Philadelphia in 1987 now costs $223.90, and so on.

The price relatives in Table 19.7 can only be used to compare prices for the given city—they *cannot* be used for comparisons between cities. For example, the cost of housing in Los Angeles is now 151% of what it was in 1987, while the cost of housing in Chicago is now 144.8% of what it was in 1987. However, it cannot be said that housing in Los Angeles is more expensive than in Chicago from the data in the table, only that housing costs have increased at a faster rate in Los Angeles. It is possible that housing in Los Angeles was less expensive to begin with, so that even with a greater percent increase, it is still less expensive than Chicago.

## EXAMPLE 3   *Using the CPI*

Suppose that a specific surgical operation cost $3,200 in Dallas in 1987. Estimate its cost today.

**SOLUTION**   From Table 19.7, medical costs in Dallas today are 205.6% of what they were in 1987. A $3,200 operation in 1987 should cost about

$$\$3,200 \times 2.056 = \$6,579.20,$$

or approximately $6,600 today.     ∎

## 19.5  EXERCISES

*Find the price relatives for the following items. Round to the nearest tenth.*

| Item | Price Then | Price Now |
|------|-----------|-----------|
| 1.  Rent | $225 per month | $375 per month |
| 2.  Refrigerator | $815 | $1,050 |
| 3.  Computer | $3,800 | $2,800 |
| 4.  Jeans | $25 per pair | $40 per pair |
| 5.  Natural gas | $1.25 per thousand cubic feet | $2.10 per thousand cubic feet |
| 6.  House | $60,000 | $95,000 |

*Use the Urban Prices Index in Table 19.7 to complete the following chart.*

| Urban Area | Item | $100 Worth in 1987 Will Cost Today |
|-----------|------|-----------------------------------|
| 7.  Philadelphia | Food and beverages | _____ |
| 8.  Chicago | Transportation | _____ |
| 9.  New York-New Jersey | Medical | _____ |
| 10.  Los Angeles | Entertainment | _____ |
| 11.  Dallas | All items | _____ |
| 12.  New York-New Jersey | Apparel and upkeep | _____ |

*Solve the following application problems.*

13. Suppose a house near New York costs $180,000 in 1987. Estimate its cost today. Round to the nearest $1,000.

14. Estimate the cost today of a medical operation in Chicago that cost $1,850 in 1987. Round to the nearest $500.

15. A family of five in Dallas spent an average of $7,200 on food and beverages in 1987. Estimate to the nearest $100 what a family of five would spend today.

16. A family in Philadelphia budgeted $28,000 for all expenditures other than taxes and vacations in 1987. Find the amount they would need to budget today to the nearest $100.

17. Which expense item increased most rapidly over the past ten years?

18. In which area in Table 19.7 did prices rise most rapidly over the past ten years?

| TOPIC | APPROACH | EXAMPLE |
|---|---|---|

**19.1 Constructing a frequency distribution from raw data**

1. Construct a table listing each value, and the number of times this value occurs.
2. For a distribution with grouped data, combine the data into classes.

For the following data, construct a frequency distribution:

12, 15, 15, 14, 13, 20, 10, 12, 11, 9, 10, 12, 17, 20, 16, 17, 14, 18, 19, 13.

| Data | Tally | Frequency |
|---|---|---|
| 9 | \| | 1 |
| 10 | \|\| | 2 |
| 11 | \| | 1 |
| 12 | \|\|\| | 3 |
| 13 | \|\| | 2 |
| 14 | \|\| | 2 |
| 15 | \|\| | 2 |
| 16 | \| | 1 |
| 17 | \|\| | 2 |
| 18 | \| | 1 |
| 19 | \| | 1 |
| 20 | \|\| | 2 |

| Classes | Frequency |
|---|---|
| 9–11 | 4 |
| 12–14 | 7 |
| 15–17 | 5 |
| 18–20 | 4 |

**19.1    Constructing a bar graph from a frequency distribution**

Draw a bar for each class using the frequency of the class as the height of the bar.

Construct a bar graph from the frequency distribution of the previous example.

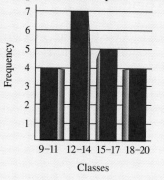

**19.1    Constructing a line graph**

1. Plot each year on the horizontal axis.
2. For each year, find the values for that year and plot a point for each value.
3. Connect all points with straight lines.

Construct a line graph for the following data.

| Year | Value |
|------|-------|
| 1995 | $850,000 |
| 1996 | $920,000 |
| 1997 | $875,000 |
| 1998 | $975,000 |

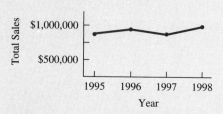

**19.1    Constructing a circle graph**

1. Determine the percent of the total for each item.
2. Find the number of degrees represented by each percent.
3. Draw the circle.

Construct a circle graph for the following expenses.

| Item | Amount | Percent |
|------|--------|---------|
| Car | $200 | 20% |
| Lodging | 300 | 30% |
| Food | 250 | 25% |
| Entertainment | 150 | 15% |
| Other | 100 | 10% |

Multiply each percent by 360°.

Car: $360° \times 0.2 = 72°$

Lodging: $360° \times 0.3 = 108°$

Food: $360° \times 0.25 = 90°$

Entertainment: $360° \times 0.15 = 54°$

Other: $360° \times 0.1 = 36°$

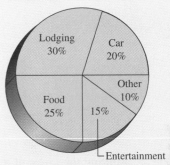

| 19.2 **Finding the mean of a set of data** | Divide the sum of the data by the number of data. | The test scores for Pat Phelan in her Business Math course were 85, 76, 93, 91, 78, 82, 87, and 85. Find Phelan's test average. |

Mean =

$$\frac{85 + 76 + 93 + 91 + 78 + 82 + 87 + 85}{8}$$

$$= \frac{677}{8} = 84.63$$

**19.2 Finding the weighted mean**

1. Multiply frequency by value.
2. Add all products obtained in Step 1.
3. Divide the sum in Step 2 by the total number of data.

| No. of School Age Children | Frequency |
|:---:|:---:|
| 0 | 12 |
| 1 | 6 |
| 2 | 7 |
| 3 | 3 |
| 4 | 2 |
| **Total families** | **30** |

Find the mean number of school age children per family.

| No. | Frequency | No. × Frequency |
|-----|-----------|-----------------|
| 0 | 12 | 0 |
| 1 | 6 | 6 |
| 2 | 7 | 14 |
| 3 | 3 | 9 |
| 4 | 2 | 8 |
| | | 37 |

$$\text{Mean} = \frac{37}{30} = 1.23$$

## 19.2 Finding the mean of a frequency distribution

1. Determine the class mark (the midpoint) for each class.
2. Multiply the class mark by the frequency of each class.
3. Add all the products obtained in Step 2.

Find the mean.

| Intervals | Frequency |
|-----------|-----------|
| 3–5 | 2 |
| 6–8 | 10 |
| 9–11 | 12 |
| 12–14 | 9 |
| 15–17 | 7 |

| Intervals | Freq. | Class Mark | Frequency × Class Mark |
|-----------|-------|------------|------------------------|
| 3–5 | 2 | 4 | 8 |
| 6–8 | 10 | 7 | 70 |
| 9–11 | 12 | 10 | 120 |
| 12–14 | 9 | 13 | 117 |
| 15–17 | 7 | 16 | 112 |
| | 40 | | 427 |

$$\text{Mean} = \frac{427}{40} = 10.68$$

| 19.3 | **Finding the median of a set of data** | 1. Arrange the data from lowest to highest. <br> 2. The median is the middle value or the average of the middle values. | Find the median for Pat Phelan's grades from an earlier example. <br> The data arranged from lowest to highest is 76, 78, 82, 85, 85, 87, 91, and 93. <br> The average of the middle two values is $\dfrac{85 + 85}{2} = 85$. |
|------|------|------|------|
| 19.3 | **Determining the mode of a set of data** | The mode is the most frequently occurring value. | Find the mode for Phelan's grades in the previous example. <br> 85 occurs most frequently (twice). |
| 19.3 | **Finding the median of a frequency distribution** | The median is the class mark associated with the middle number or with the average of the middle numbers. | <table><tr><th>Intervals</th><th>Frequency</th></tr><tr><td>10–19</td><td>5</td></tr><tr><td>20–29</td><td>8</td></tr><tr><td>30–39</td><td>2</td></tr></table> Divide 15 by 2 to find 7.5. Thus, the class mark associated with the eighth value from the smallest, or 24.5, is the median. |
| 19.3 | **Finding the mode of a frequency distribution** | The mode is the class mark of the class with the highest frequency. | <table><tr><th>Intervals</th><th>Frequency</th></tr><tr><td>10–19</td><td>5</td></tr><tr><td>20–29</td><td>8</td></tr><tr><td>30–39</td><td>2</td></tr></table> The second class has the highest frequency. The mode is the associated class mark of 24.5. |
| 19.4 | **Finding the range of a set of data** | Range = Highest − Lowest | Find the range of the values 7, 6, 10, 7, 9, 5, 2, 8, and 9. <br> Range = Highest − Lowest <br> $= 10 - 2 = 8$ |

## 19.4    Finding the standard deviation

1. Determine the mean of the data.
2. Subtract the mean from each value to obtain individual deviations, $d$.
3. Square each deviation.
4. Sum all the squared deviations.
5. Divide the sum by the number of data.
6. Take the square root of the number obtained in Step 5.

Find the standard deviation of the values, 7, 6, 10, 7, 9, 5, 2, 8, and 9.

Mean =

$$\frac{7 + 6 + 10 + 7 + 9 + 5 + 2 + 8 + 9}{9}$$

$$= 7$$

| Data Value | Deviation $d$ | Deviation Squared, $d^2$ |
|---|---|---|
| 7 | 0 | 0 |
| 6 | −1 | 1 |
| 10 | 3 | 9 |
| 7 | 0 | 0 |
| 9 | 2 | 4 |
| 5 | −2 | 4 |
| 2 | −5 | 25 |
| 8 | 1 | 1 |
| 9 | 2 | 4 |

$$\frac{\Sigma d^2}{n} = \frac{48}{9} = 5.33$$

$$s = \sqrt{5.33} = 2.31$$

## 19.5    Finding the price relative

Divide the price this year by the price in a base year and multiply by 100.

A car cost $16,000 ten years ago. It now costs $22,500. Find the price relative for the car.

Price Relative

$$= \frac{\text{Price this year}}{\text{Price in base year}} \times 100$$

$$= \frac{\$22,500}{\$16,000} \times 100 = 140.6$$

**19.5 Finding cost today using the Consumer Price Index (CPI)**

Multiply CPI by cost in base year to estimate current cost.

A typical house in Philadelphia cost $88,000 in 1987.

Estimate its cost today.

Cost today = $88,000 × 155.1%
= $88,000 × 1.551
= $136,488

## Chapter 19 Review Exercises

*Construct frequency distributions for the sets of data in problems 1 and 2. Use the table provided. [19.1]*

| | Number | Frequency |
|---|---|---|
| | 1–3 | _____ |
| | 4–6 | _____ |
| | 7–9 | _____ |
| | 10–12 | _____ |
| | 13–15 | _____ |

**1.**

| | | | | |
|---|---|---|---|---|
| 2 | 5 | 8 | 6 | 7 |
| 9 | 8 | 8 | 7 | 8 |
| 3 | 15 | 8 | 10 | 12 |
| 13 | 3 | 4 | 6 | 14 |
| 10 | 11 | 8 | 15 | 9 |
| 4 | 2 | 13 | 11 | 8 |

| | Number | Frequency |
|---|---|---|
| | 15–19 | _____ |
| | 20–24 | _____ |
| | 25–29 | _____ |
| | 30–34 | _____ |
| | 35–39 | _____ |
| | 40–44 | _____ |
| | 45–49 | _____ |
| | 50–54 | _____ |

**2.**

| | | | | | | | |
|---|---|---|---|---|---|---|---|
| 27 | 23 | 22 | 38 | 43 | 24 | 35 | 24 |
| 26 | 28 | 18 | 20 | 25 | 23 | 22 | 37 |
| 52 | 31 | 30 | 41 | 45 | 29 | 27 | 28 |
| 43 | 29 | 28 | 27 | 25 | 29 | 28 | 29 |
| 18 | 26 | 33 | 25 | 27 | 25 | 34 | 32 |
| 36 | 22 | 32 | 33 | 21 | 23 | 24 | 18 |
| 48 | 23 | 16 | 38 | 26 | 21 | 23 | |

*Solve problems 3–6 using the information provided. [19.1]*

**3.** Construct a bar graph for the data of Exercise 1.

**4.** Construct a bar graph for the data of Exercise 2.

**5.** Construct a circle graph for the following data.

| Region | Frequency |
| --- | --- |
| Northeast | 49,519 |
| Midwest | 58,953 |
| South | 79,539 |
| West | 45,970 |

**6.** Construct a circle graph for the following. [19.1]

| Item | Number |
| --- | --- |
| 1 | 1,080 |
| 2 | 390 |
| 3 | 360 |
| 4 | 270 |
| 5 | 60 |

*Calculate the mean, median, and mode for the following sets of data. Round answers to the nearest tenth. [19.2–19.3]*

**7.** 10, 12, 12, 11, 13
**8.** 85, 80, 82, 82, 88, 90, 92
**9.** 21, 20, 20, 18, 21, 19, 21, 22
**10.** 42, 44, 41, 44, 45, 44
**11.** 8, 7, 6, 6, 7, 7, 5, 9
**12.** 2.5, 2.4, 2.4, 2.3, 2.4, 2.6, 2.0, 2.2

*Calculate the mean for the frequency distribution given in problems 13 and 14. Round answers to the nearest tenth. [19.2]*

| **13. Intervals** | **Frequency** | | **14. Intervals** | **Frequency** |
| --- | --- | --- | --- | --- |
| 10–14 | 6 | | 0–4 | 10 |
| 15–19 | 3 | | 5–9 | 8 |
| 20–24 | 5 | | 10–14 | 15 |
| 25–29 | 7 | | 15–19 | 8 |
| 30–34 | 5 | | 20–24 | 4 |
| 35–39 | 9 | | | |

*Calculate the median and the mode for the frequency distribution given in problems 15 and 16. [19.3]*

| 15. Intervals | Frequency |
|---|---|
| 1–5 | 20 |
| 6–10 | 12 |
| 11–15 | 14 |
| 16–20 | 10 |
| 21–25 | 5 |

| 16. Intervals | Frequency |
|---|---|
| 50–59 | 3 |
| 60–69 | 5 |
| 70–79 | 18 |
| 80–89 | 12 |
| 90–99 | 4 |

*Find the range and standard deviation for problems 17–20. Round answers to the nearest hundredth. [19.4]*

**17.** 3, 6, 2, 4, 4, 11

**18.** 5, 7, 12, 10, 7, 12, 18

**19.** 82, 86, 78, 74, 65

**20.** 150, 145, 130, 120, 162, 158

*Find the price relative for problems 21–24. Round to the nearest tenth. [19.5]*

| Item | Price in Base Year | Price in Current Year |
|---|---|---|
| 21. Automobile | $22,500 | $32,300 |
| 22. Television | $250 | $410 |
| 23. Shovel | $22 | $38 |
| 24. Lawn mower | $185 | $300 |

*Solve the following application problems.*

**25.** The Dallas Chamber of Commerce advertised in 1987 that a family of 5 could live comfortably in their community with an income of $33,500 per year. Estimate the amount that a family of 5 would need today to live as comfortably to the nearest $100. [19.5]

**26.** The thickness of an alloy coating on a military weapon can be approximated by a normal curve with mean 7.2 millimeters and standard deviation 0.08 millimeters. Find the percent of items expected to have a coating thicker than 7.12 millimeters. [19.4]

**27.** Okba Asad, the owner of Current's Restaurant, has monitored weekly sales for the past 6 weeks.

| Week | Sales | Week | Sales |
|------|-------|------|-------|
| 1 | $4,227 | 4 | $5,009 |
| 2 | $4,806 | 5 | $4,198 |
| 3 | $4,559 | 6 | $5,126 |

Plot these data in a line graph. Do sales appear to be increasing or can you tell from the data given? [19.1]

**28.** Sean Baker wishes to calculate his grade point average for the semester he just completed. (A = 4.0, B = 3.0, C = 2.0, D = 1.0, and F = 0.0)

| Course | Semester Hours | Grade |
|--------|----------------|-------|
| Chemistry | 4 | D |
| History | 3 | B |
| English Literature | 3 | B |
| Music Appreciation | 3 | A |

Also, find his grade point average if he had been unable to pull his chemistry grade up from the F he had in the course before the final exam. [19.2]

**29.** The average house price in a resort area in Colorado increased from $110,000 in 1990 to $195,000 today. Find the price relative. Use this value to estimate the cost today of a small home that sold in the resort area for $90,000 in 1990. [19.5]

# Chapter 19 Summary Exercise

The following 20 values give the weekly earnings of the part-time employees at a college bookstore.

$125   $121   $127   $123   $144
$132   $148   $128   $128   $136
$136   $142   $136   $130   $131
$133   $135   $139   $135   $130

**(a)** Use these numbers to complete the following table.

| Salary | Number of Salespeople |
|--------|-----------------------|
| $120–$124 | _____ |
| $125–$129 | _____ |
| $130–$134 | _____ |
| $135–$139 | _____ |
| $140–$144 | _____ |
| $145–$149 | _____ |

**(b)** Use the numbers in the above table to draw a bar graph.

**(c)** Calculate the mean, median, and mode for the weekly salaries of the salespeople.

**(d)** Estimate the mean part-time wage in 7 years if the current year is the base year and if the urban price index in 7 years is 140.7.

**(e)** Find the standard deviation of the wages of the part-time employees.

**(f)** Assume that the wages of the part-time employees can be approximated by the normal distribution with the mean found in part (c) and the standard deviation found in part (e). Find the percent of the part-time employees that would be expected to earn over $146.47 in a given week.

# Calculator Basics

**Calculators** are among the more popular inventions of the last three decades. Each year better calculators are developed and costs drop. The first all-transistor desktop calculator was introduced to the market in 1966; it weighed 55 pounds, cost $2,500, and was slow. Today, these same calculations are performed quite well on a calculator costing less than $10. And today's $200 pocket calculators have more ability to solve problems than some of the early computers.

Many colleges allow students to use calculators in business mathematics courses. Some courses require calculator use. Many types of calculators are available, from the inexpensive basic calculator to the more complex **scientific**, **financial**, and **graphing** calculators.

In the first section we discuss the common scientific calculator including percent key, reciprocal key, exponent keys, square root key, memory function, order of operations, and parentheses keys. In the second section, the financial calculator with its associated financial keys is discussed.

NOTE  The various calculator models differ significantly—*use the booklet that came with your calculator* for specifics about that calculator if your answers differ from those in this section.  ■

## A.1  Scientific Calculators

**OBJECTIVES**

1  *Learn the basic calculator keys.*

2  *Understand the* C *,* CE *, and* ON/C *keys.*

3  *Understand the floating decimal point.*

4  *Use the* % *and* 1/x *keys.*

5  *Use the* $y^x$ *and* $\sqrt{\phantom{x}}$ *keys.*

6  *Use the* $a^{b/c}$ *key.*

**A-1**

> **7** *Solve problems with negative numbers.*
> **8** *Use the calculator memory function.*
> **9** *Solve chain calculations using order of operations.*
> **10** *Use the parentheses keys.*
> **11** *Use the calculator for problem solution.*

**OBJECTIVE** **1** *Learn the basic calculator keys.* Most calculators use **algebraic logic**. Some problems can be solved by entering number and function keys in the same order as you would solve a problem by hand; others require a knowledge of the order of operations when entering the problem.

**EXAMPLE 1** *Using the Basic Keys*

**(a)** 12 + 25    **(b)** 456 ÷ 24

**SOLUTION**

**(a)** The problem 12 + 25 would be entered as

$$12 \boxed{+} 25 \boxed{=}$$

and 37 would appear as the answer.

**(b)** Enter 456 ÷ 24 as

$$456 \boxed{÷} 24 \boxed{=}$$

and 19 appears as the answer.    ■

**OBJECTIVE** **2** *Understand the* $\boxed{C}$, $\boxed{CE}$, *and* $\boxed{ON/C}$ *keys.* All calculators have a $\boxed{C}$ key. Pressing this key erases everything in most calculators and prepares them for a new problem. Some calculators have a $\boxed{CE}$ key. Pressing this key erases only the number displayed, thus allowing for correction of a mistake without having to start the problem over. Many calculators combine the $\boxed{C}$ key and $\boxed{CE}$ key and use an $\boxed{ON/C}$ key. This key turns the calculator on and is also used to erase the calculator display. If the $\boxed{ON/C}$ is pressed after the $\boxed{=}$, or after one of the operation keys ($\boxed{+}$, $\boxed{-}$, $\boxed{\times}$, $\boxed{÷}$), everything in the calculator is erased. If the wrong operation key is pressed, simply press the correct key and the error is corrected. For example, in 7 $\boxed{+}$ $\boxed{-}$ 3 $\boxed{=}$ 4, pressing the $\boxed{-}$ key cancels out the previous $\boxed{+}$ key entry.

**NOTE**  Be sure to look at the directions that come with your calculator in terms of clearing the memory.  ■

**OBJECTIVE** **3** *Understand the floating decimal point.*    Most calculators have a **floating decimal** which locates the decimal point in the final result.

| **EXAMPLE 2** *Calculating with Decimal Numbers*

A contractor purchased 55.75 square yards of vinyl floor covering, at $18.99 per square yard. Find her total cost.

**SOLUTION**    Proceed as follows.

$$55.75 \boxed{\times} 18.99 \boxed{=} 1058.6925$$

The decimal point is automatically placed in the answer. Since money answers are usually rounded to the nearest cent, the answer is $1,058.69.  ■

In using a machine with a floating decimal, enter the decimal point as needed. For example, enter $47 as

$$47$$

with no decimal point, but enter $0.95 as follows.

$$\boxed{\cdot} \; 95$$

One problem utilizing a floating decimal is shown by the following example.

| **EXAMPLE 3** *Placing the Decimal Point in Money Answers*

Add $21.38 and $1.22.

**SOLUTION**

$$21.38 \boxed{+} 1.22 \boxed{=} = 22.6$$

The final 0 is left off. Remember that the problem deals with dollars and cents, and write the answer as $22.60.  ■

**OBJECTIVE** **4** *Use the* $\boxed{\%}$ *and* $\boxed{1/x}$ *keys.*    The $\boxed{\%}$ key moves the decimal point two places to the left when used following multiplication or division.

| **EXAMPLE 4** *Using the* $\boxed{\%}$ *Key*

Find 8% of $4,205.

**SOLUTION**

$$4205 \;\boxed{\times}\; 8 \;\boxed{\%}\; \boxed{=}\; 336.4 = \$336.40 \qquad \blacksquare$$

The $\boxed{1/x}$ key replaces a number with the reciprocal of that number.

| **EXAMPLE 5**  *Using the* $\boxed{1/x}$ *Key*

Find the inverse or reciprocal of 40.

**SOLUTION**

$$40 \;\boxed{1/x}\; 0.025 \qquad \blacksquare$$

**OBJECTIVE** $\boxed{5}$ *Use the* $\boxed{y^x}$ *and* $\boxed{\sqrt{\;}}$ *keys.*    The product of $3 \times 3$ can be written as:

$$3^2.$$

The exponent (2 in this case) shows how many times the base is multiplied by itself (multiply 3 times itself). The $\boxed{y^x}$ key raises a base to a power; be sure to enter the base first followed by the exponent.

| **EXAMPLE 6**  *Using the* $\boxed{y^x}$ *Key*

Find $5^3$.

**SOLUTION**

$$5 \;\boxed{y^x}\; 3 \;\boxed{=}\; 125$$

Since $3^2 = 9$, the number 3 is called the **square root** of 9. Square roots of numbers are written with the symbol $\sqrt{\;}$.

$$\sqrt{9} = 3$$

| **EXAMPLE 7**  *Using the* $\boxed{\sqrt{\;}}$ *Key*

Find each square root.

**(a)** $\sqrt{144}$    **(b)** $\sqrt{20}$

**Solution**

**(a)** Using the calculator, enter

$$144 \;\boxed{\sqrt{\;}}$$

and 12 appears in the display. The square root of 144 is 12.

**(b)** The square root of 20 is

$$20 \;\boxed{\sqrt{\;}}\; 4.4721360$$

which may be rounded to the desired position.    ■

**OBJECTIVE** **6** *Use the* $\boxed{a^{b/c}}$ *key.*    Many calculators have an $\boxed{a^{b/c}}$ key that can be used for problems containing fractions and mixed numbers. A mixed number is a number with both a whole number and a fraction such as $7\frac{3}{4}$ which equals $7 + \frac{3}{4}$. The rules for adding, subtracting, multiplying, and dividing both fractions and mixed numbers are given in Chapter 1. Here, we simply show how these operations are done on a calculator.

**EXAMPLE 8** *Using the* $\boxed{a^{b/c}}$ *Key with Fractions*

Solve the following.

**(a)** $\dfrac{6}{11} + \dfrac{3}{4}$

**(b)** $\dfrac{3}{8} \div \dfrac{5}{6}$

**Solution**

**(a)** $6 \;\boxed{a^{b/c}}\; 11 \;\boxed{+}\; 3 \;\boxed{a^{b/c}}\; 4 \;\boxed{=}\; 1\dfrac{13}{44}$

**(b)** $3 \;\boxed{a^{b/c}}\; 8 \;\boxed{\div}\; 5 \;\boxed{a^{b/c}}\; 6 \;\boxed{=}\; \dfrac{9}{20}$    ■

**NOTE**    The calculator automatically reduces fractions for you.    ■

**EXAMPLE 9** *Using the* $\boxed{a^{b/c}}$ *Key*

Solve the following.

**(a)** $4\dfrac{7}{8} \div 3\dfrac{4}{7}$

**(b)** $\dfrac{5}{3} \div 27.5$

**(c)** $65.3 \times 6\dfrac{3}{4}$

SOLUTION

(a) $4 \boxed{a^{b/c}} 7 \boxed{a^{b/c}} 8 \boxed{\div} 3 \boxed{a^{b/c}} 4 \boxed{a^{b/c}} 7 \boxed{=} 1\frac{73}{200}$

(b) $5 \boxed{a^{b/c}} 3 \boxed{\div} 27.5 \boxed{=} 0.060606061$

(c) $65.3 \boxed{\times} 6 \boxed{a^{b/c}} 3 \boxed{a^{b/c}} 4 \boxed{=} 440.775$ ■

**OBJECTIVE** **7** *Solve problems with negative numbers.* There are several calculations in business that result in a **negative number** or **deficit amount**.

| EXAMPLE 10 *Working with Negative Numbers*

The amount in the advertising account last month was \$4,800 while \$5,200 was actually spent. Find the balance remaining in the advertising account.

SOLUTION    Enter the numbers in the calculator.

$$4800 \boxed{-} 5200 \boxed{=} -400$$

The minus sign in front of the 400 indicates that there is a deficit or negative amount. This value can be written as −\$400 or sometimes as (\$400) which indicates a negative amount. Some calculators place the minus after the number, or as 400−. ■

Negative numbers may be entered into the calculator by using the $\boxed{-}$ before entering the number. For example, if \$3,000 is now added to the advertising account in Example 10, the new balance is calculated as follows.

$$\boxed{-} 400 \boxed{+} 3000 \boxed{=} 2600$$

The new account balance is \$2,600.

The $\boxed{+/-}$ key can be used to change the sign of a number that has already been entered. For example, $520 \boxed{+/-}$ changes +520 to −520.

**OBJECTIVE** **8** *Use the calculator memory function.* Many calculators feature memory keys, which are a sort of electronic scratch paper. These **memory keys** are used to store intermediate steps in a calculation. On some calculators, a key labeled $\boxed{M}$ or $\boxed{STO}$ is used to store the numbers in the display, with $\boxed{MR}$ or $\boxed{RCL}$ used to recall the numbers from memory.

Other calculators have $\boxed{M+}$ and $\boxed{M-}$ keys. The $\boxed{M+}$ key adds the number displayed to the number already in memory. For example, if the memory contains the number 0 at the beginning of a problem, and the calculator display contains the number 29.4, then pushing $\boxed{M+}$ will cause 29.4 to be stored in the memory (the result of adding 0 and 29.4). If 57.8 is then entered into the display, pushing $\boxed{\text{M+}}$ will cause

$$29.4 + 57.8 = 87.2$$

to be stored. If 11.9 is then entered into the display, with $\boxed{\text{M−}}$ pushed, the memory will contain

$$87.2 - 11.9 = 75.3.$$

The $\boxed{\text{MR}}$ key is used to recall the number in memory as needed, with $\boxed{\text{MC}}$ used to clear the memory. (Always clear the memory before starting a problem—not doing so is a very common error.)

Scientific calculators typically have one or more storage registers in which to store numbers. These memory keys are usually labeled as $\boxed{\text{STO}}$ for store and $\boxed{\text{RCL}}$ for recall. For example, 32.5 can be stored in register 1 by

$$32.5 \;\boxed{\text{STO}}\; 1$$

or it can be stored in memory register 2 by 32.5 $\boxed{\text{STO}}$ 2 and so forth. Values are retrieved from a particular memory register by using the $\boxed{\text{RCL}}$ key followed by the number of the register. For example, $\boxed{\text{RCL}}$ 2 recalls the contents of memory register 2.

With a scientific calculator, a number stays in memory until it is replaced by another number or until the memory is cleared. The contents of the memory are saved even when the calculator is turned off.

| EXAMPLE 11   *Using the Memory Registers*

An elevator repairperson counted the number of people entering an elevator and also measured the weight of each group of people. Find the average weight per person.

| Number of People | Total Weight |
|:---:|:---:|
| 6 | 839 pounds |
| 8 | 1,184 pounds |
| 4 | 640 pounds |

SOLUTION    First find the weight of all three groups and store in memory register 1.

$$839 \;\boxed{+}\; 1184 \;\boxed{+}\; 640 \;\boxed{=}\; 2663 \;\boxed{\text{STO}}\; 1$$

Then find the total number of people.

$$6 \boxed{+} 8 \boxed{+} 4 \boxed{=} 18$$

Finally, divide the contents of memory register 1 by the 18 people.

$$\boxed{\text{RCL}} \ 1 \boxed{\div} 18 \boxed{=} \ 147.94444 \ \text{pounds}$$

This value can be rounded as needed.    ■

**OBJECTIVE 9** *Solve chain calculations using order of operations.*    Long calculations involving several operations (adding, subtracting, multiplying, and dividing) must be done in a specific sequence called the **order of operations** and are called **chain calculations**. The logic of the following order of operations is built into most scientific calculators and can help us work problems without having to store a lot of intermediate values.

### SOLVING CHAIN CALCULATIONS

1.  Do all operations inside parentheses first.
2.  Simplify any expressions with exponents (squares) and find any square roots.
3.  Multiply and divide from left to right.
4.  Add and subtract from left to right.

**EXAMPLE 12** *Using the Order of Operations*

Solve the following.

**(a)** $3 + 7 \times 9\frac{3}{4}$    **(b)** $42.1 \times 5 - 90 \div 4$

**SOLUTION**    The calculator automatically keeps track of the order of operations for us.

**(a)** $3 \boxed{+} 7 \boxed{\times} 9 \boxed{a^{b/c}} 3 \boxed{a^{b/c}} 4 \boxed{=} 71\frac{1}{4}$

**(b)** $42.1 \boxed{\times} 5 \boxed{-} 90 \boxed{\div} 4 \boxed{=} 188$    ■

**OBJECTIVE 10** *Use the parentheses keys.*    The parentheses keys can be used to help establish the order of operations in a more complex chain calculation. For example, $\dfrac{4}{5+7}$ can be written as $\dfrac{4}{(5+7)}$ which can be solved as

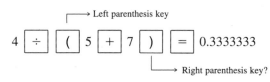

$$4 \boxed{\div} \boxed{(} 5 \boxed{+} 7 \boxed{)} \boxed{=} 0.3333333$$

**EXAMPLE 13** *Using Parentheses*

Solve the following problem.

$$\frac{16 \div 2.5}{39.2 - 29.8 \times 0.6}$$

**SOLUTION**　Think of this problem as follows.

$$\frac{(16 \div 2.5)}{(39.2 - 29.8 \times 0.6)}$$

Using parentheses to set off the numerator and denominator will help you minimize errors.

$$( \boxed{16} \boxed{\div} \boxed{2.5} ) \boxed{\div} ( \boxed{39.2} \boxed{-} \boxed{29.8} \boxed{\times} \boxed{0.6} ) \boxed{=} \boxed{0.3001876}　■$$

**OBJECTIVE** **11** *Use the calculator for problem solution.*

**EXAMPLE 14** *Finding Sale Price*

A compact disc player with an original price of $560 is on sale at 10% off. Find the sale price.

**SOLUTION**　If the discount from the original price is 10%, then the sale price is 100% − 10% of the original price.

$$\boxed{560} \boxed{\times} ( \boxed{100} \boxed{-} \boxed{10} ) \boxed{\%} \boxed{=} \boxed{504}　■$$

On some calculators the following key strokes will also work:

$$\boxed{560} \boxed{-} \boxed{10} \boxed{\%} \boxed{=} \boxed{504}.$$

**EXAMPLE 15** *Applying Calculator Use to Problem Solving*

A home buyer borrows $86,400 at 10% for 30 years. The monthly payment on the loan is $8.78 per $1,000 borrowed. Annual taxes are $780, and fire insurance is $453 a year. Find the total monthly payment including taxes and insurance.

**SOLUTION**　The monthly payment is the *sum* of the monthly payment on the loan plus monthly taxes plus monthly fire insurance costs. The monthly payment on the loan is the number of thousands in the loan (86.4) times the monthly payment per $1,000 borrowed (8.78).

Monthly taxes

$$\boxed{86400} \boxed{\div} \boxed{1000} \boxed{\times} \boxed{8.78} \boxed{+} \boxed{780} \boxed{\div} \boxed{12} \boxed{+} \boxed{453} \boxed{\div} \boxed{12} \boxed{=} \boxed{861.342}$$

Monthly fire insurance

To the nearest cent, this amount rounds to $861.34.

# A.1 EXERCISES

*Solve each of the following problems on a calculator. Round each answer to the nearest hundredth.*

**1.**  384.92
407.61
351.14
+  27.93

**2.**  85.76
21.94
+ 39.89

**3.**  6,850
321
+ 4,207

**4.**  781.42
304.59
+ 261.35

**5.**  4,270.41
−   365.09

**6.**  3,000.07
−    48.12

**7.**  384.96
− 129.72

**8.**  $36.84 - 12.17$

**9.**  365
× 43

**10.**  27.51
×  1.18

**11.**  $3.7 \times 8.4$

**12.**  $62.5 \times 81$

**13.**  $\dfrac{375.4}{10.6}$

**14.**  $\dfrac{9,625}{400}$

**15.**  $96.7 \div 3.5$

**16.**  $103.7 \div 0.35$

*Solve each of the following chain calculations. Round each answer to the nearest hundredth.*

**17.**  $\dfrac{9 \times 9}{2 \times 5}$

**18.**  $\dfrac{15 \times 8 \times 3}{11 \times 7 \times 4}$

**19.**  $\dfrac{87 \times 24 \times 47.2}{13.6 \times 12.8}$

**20.**  $\dfrac{2 \times (3 + 4)}{6 + 10}$

**21.**  $\dfrac{2 \times 3 + 4}{6 + 10}$

**22.**  $\dfrac{4,200 \times 0.12 \times 90}{365}$

**23.**  $\dfrac{640 - 0.6 \times 12}{17.5 + 3.2}$

**24.**  $\dfrac{16 \times 18 - 0.4 \div 2}{95.4 \times 3 - 0.8}$

**25.**  $\dfrac{14^2 - 3.6 \times 6}{95.2 \div 0.5}$

**26.**  $\dfrac{9^2 + 3.8 \div 2}{14 + 7.5}$

*Solve each of the following problems. Reduce any fractions to lowest terms or round to the nearest hundredth.*

**27.**  $7\dfrac{5}{8} \div \left(1 + \dfrac{3}{8}\right)$

**28.**  $\left(5\dfrac{1}{4}\right)^2 \times 3.65$

**29.**  $\left(\dfrac{3}{4} \div \dfrac{5}{8}\right)^3 \div 3\dfrac{1}{2}$

**30.**  $\sqrt{6} \times \dfrac{3^2 + 2\frac{1}{2}}{7 \times \frac{5}{6}}$

**31.**  Describe in your own words the order of operations to be used when solving chain calculations. (See Objective 9.)

**32.**  Explain how the parentheses keys are used when solving chain calculations. (See Objective 9.)

*Solve each of the following application problems on a calculator. Round each answer to the nearest cent.*

**33.** Bucks County Community College Bookstore bought 397 copies of a computer science book at a net cost of $23.86 each; 125 copies of an accounting book at $28.74 each; and 740 copies of a real estate text at $21.76 each. Find the total paid by the bookstore.

**34.** To find the monthly interest due on a certain home mortgage, multiply the mortgage balance by 0.007292. Find the monthly interest on a mortgage having a balance of $95,830.

**35.** Find the monthly interest on a mortgage having a balance of $113,720. (See Exercise 34.)

**36.** Judy Martinez needs to file her expense account claims. She spent 5 nights at the Macon Holiday Inn at $47.46 per night, 4 nights at the Charlotte Sheraton at $51.62 per night, and rented a car for 7.6 days at $29.95 per day. She drove the car 916 miles with a charge of $0.24 per mile. Find her total expenses.

**37.** In Virginia City, the sales tax is 6.5%. Find the tax on each of the following items: (a) a new car costing $17,908.43 and (b) an office word processor costing $1,463.58.

**38.** Marja Strutz bought a new commercial fishing boat equipped for sardine fishing at a cost of $78,250. Additional safety equipment was needed at a cost of $4,820 and sales tax of $7\frac{1}{4}\%$ was due on the boat and safety equipment. In addition she was charged a licensing fee of $1,135 and a Coast Guard registration fee of $428. Strutz will pay $\frac{1}{3}$ of the total cost as a down payment and will borrow the balance. How much will she borrow?

**39.** Ben Fick bought a home for $80,000. He paid $8,000 down and agreed to make payments of $528.31 each month for 30 years. By how much does the down payment and the sum of the monthly payments exceed the purchase price?

**40.** Linda Smelt purchased a 32-unit apartment house for $620,000. She made a down payment of $150,000 which she had inherited from her parents and agreed to make monthly payments of $5,050 for 15 years. By how much does the sum of her down payment and all monthly payments exceed the original purchase price?

**41.** Ben Hurd wishes to open a small repair shop but only has $32,400 in cash. He estimates that he will need $15,000 for equipment, $2,800 for the first month's rent on a building, and about $28,000 operating expenses until the business is profitable. How much additional funding does he need?

**42.** Koplan Kitchens wishes to expand their retail store. In order to do so, they must first purchase the $26,000 lot next door to them; they then anticipate $120,000 construction costs plus an additional $28,500 for additional inventory. They have $50,000 in cash and must borrow the balance from a bank. How much must they borrow?

 **Financial Calculators**

### OBJECTIVES

**1** *Learn the basic conventions used with cash flows.*

**2** *Learn the basic financial keys.*

**3** *Understand which keys to use for a particular problem.*

**4** *Use the financial calculator to solve financial problems.*

**Financial calculators** are calculators with added features that allow you to make certain compound interest calculations quickly and accurately. These calculators are commonly used by people in business. Financial calculators differ from one another—*be sure to use the booklet that came with your financial calculator* for specific information about that calculator.

**OBJECTIVE 1** *Learn the basic conventions used with cash flows.* There is a need to logically separate inflows of cash (cash received) from outflows of cash (cash paid out). The following convention is commonly used for this purpose, and will be used throughout this appendix.

1. Infows of cash (cash received) are positive.

2. Outflows of cash (cash paid out) are negative.

For example, assume you are making regular investments into an account. Your payments are outflows of cash and should be considered negative numbers. The future value of your savings will eventually be returned to you as an inflow of cash, thereby as a positive number.

**OBJECTIVE 2** *Learn the basic financial keys.* **Financial calculators** have special functions that allow the user to solve financial problems involving time, interest rates, and money. Many of the compound interest problems presented in this text can be solved using a financial calculator. Most financial calculators have financial keys similar to those shown below.

$$\boxed{n} \quad \boxed{i} \quad \boxed{PV} \quad \boxed{PMT} \quad \boxed{FV}$$

These keys represent the following functions:

$\boxed{n}$ —The number of compounding periods

$\boxed{i}$ —The interest rate *per compounding period*

$\boxed{PV}$ —Present value—the value in *today's* dollars

$\boxed{PMT}$ —The amount of a level payment (e.g., $625 per month); this is used for annuity type problems.

$\boxed{FV}$ —Future value—the value at *some future date*

**NOTE** Different financial calculators look and work somewhat differently from one another. You *must look at the instruction book* that came with your calculator to determine how the keys are used with that particular calculator. ■

You will find that different financial calculators will sometimes give slightly different answers to the same problems due to rounding.

**OBJECTIVE 3** *Understand which keys to use for a particular problem.* Most simple financial problems require only four of the five financial keys described above. Both the number of compounding periods $\boxed{n}$ and the interest rate per compounding period $\boxed{i}$ are needed for each financial problem—these two keys will always be used. Which two of the remaining three financial keys ($\boxed{PV}$, $\boxed{PMT}$, and $\boxed{FV}$) are used depends on the particular problem. Using the convention described above, one of these values will be negative and one will be positive. The process of solving a financial problem is to enter values for the three variables that are known, then press the key for the unknown, fourth variable.

For example, if you wish to know the future value of a series of known, equal payments, enter the specific values for $\boxed{n}$, $\boxed{i}$, and $\boxed{PMT}$. Then press $\boxed{FV}$ for the result. Or, if you wish to know how long it will take for an investment to grow to some specific value at a given interest rate, enter values for $\boxed{PV}$, $\boxed{i}$, and $\boxed{FV}$. Then press $\boxed{n}$ to find the required number of compounding periods.

**NOTE** Be sure to enter a cash inflow as a positive number or a cash outflow as a negative number. Also be sure to clear all values from the memory of your calculator before working a problem.  ■

**OBJECTIVE** **4** *Use the financial calculator to solve financial problems.*

### EXAMPLE 1 *Given n, i, and PV Find FV*

Mr. Willis invests $1,000 in an account paying 8% compounded quarterly. Find the future value in $1\frac{1}{2}$ years.

**SOLUTION** The present value of $1,000 (a cash outflow entered as a negative number) is compounded at 2% per quarter (8% ÷ 4 = 2%) for 6 quarters ($1\frac{1}{2} \times 4 = 6$). Enter values for $\boxed{PV}$, $\boxed{i}$, and $\boxed{n}$.

$$-1,000 \; \boxed{PV} \; 2 \; \boxed{i} \; 6 \; \boxed{n}$$

Then press $\boxed{FV}$ to find the compound amount at the end of 6 quarters.

$$\boxed{FV} \; 1126.16 \text{ which is the future value.} \qquad ■$$

### EXAMPLE 2 *Given n, i, and PMT Find FV*

Joan Jones plans to invest $100 at the end of each month in a mutual fund that she believes will grow at 12% per year compounded monthly. Find the future value at her retirement in 20 years.

**SOLUTION** Two hundred forty payments (12 × 20 = 240) of $100 each (cash outflows entered as a negative number) are made into an account earning 1% per month (12% ÷ 12 = 1%). Enter values for $\boxed{n}$, $\boxed{PMT}$, and $\boxed{i}$.

$$240 \; \boxed{n} \; -100 \; \boxed{PMT} \; 1 \; \boxed{i}$$

Press FV for the result.

> FV  98925.54 which is the future value.    ■

**NOTE**  The order in which data are entered into the calculator does not matter—just remember to press the financial key for the unknown value last.  ■

Any one of the four values used to solve a particular financial problem can be unknown. Look at the next three examples in which the number of compounding periods $n$ , the payment amount PMT , and the interest rate per compounding period $i$ , respectively, are unknown.

**EXAMPLE 3**  *Given i, PMT, and FV Find n*

Mr. Trebor needs $140,000 for a new farm tractor. He can invest $8,000 at the end of each month in an account paying 6% per year compounded monthly. How many monthly payments are needed?

**SOLUTION**  The $8,000 monthly payment (cash outflow) will grow at 0.5% per compounding period (6% ÷ 12 = 0.5%) until a future value of $140,000 (cash inflow at a future date) is accumulated. Enter values for PMT , $i$ , and FV .

> −8000 PMT  .5 $i$  140000 FV

Press $n$ to determine the number of payments.

> $n$  17 monthly payments of $8,000 each are needed.

Actually, 17 payments of $8,000 each in an account earning 0.5% per month will grow to slightly more than $140,000:

> −8000 PMT  .5 $i$  17 $n$ .

Press FV to determine the future value.

> FV  141578.41 which is the future value.

The seventeenth payment would only need to be

$$\$8,000 - (\$141,578.41 - \$140,000) = \$6,421.59$$

in order to accumulate exactly $140,000.    ■

**EXAMPLE 4**  *Given n, i, and FV Find PMT*

Jane Abel wishes to have $1,000,000 at her retirement in 40 years. Find the payment she must make at the end of each quarter into an account earning 10% compounded quarterly to attain her goal.

**SOLUTION**   One hundred sixty payments (40 × 4 = 160) are made into an account earning 2.5% per quarter (10% ÷ 4 = 2.5%) until a future value of $1,000,000 (cash inflow at a future date) is accumulated. Enter values for $\boxed{n}$, $\boxed{i}$, and $\boxed{\text{FV}}$.

$$160 \;\boxed{n}\; 2.5 \;\boxed{i}\; 1000000 \;\boxed{\text{FV}}$$

Press $\boxed{\text{PMT}}$ for the quarterly payment:

$$\boxed{\text{PMT}} \; -\,490.41 \text{ which is the required quarterly payment of cash.}$$

One hundred sixty payments of $490.41 at the end of each quarter in an account earning 10% compounded quarterly will grow to $1,000,000.   ∎

## EXAMPLE 5   *Given n, PV, and FV Find i*

Tom Fernandez bought 200 shares of stock in an oil company at $33$\frac{1}{2}$ per share. Exactly three years later he sold the stock at $41$\frac{1}{4}$ per share. Find the annual interest rate, rounded to the nearest tenth of a percent, that Mr. Fernandez earned on this investment assuming the company paid no dividends.

**SOLUTION**   In 3 years, the per share price increased from a present value of $33.50 ($33$\frac{1}{2}$) to a future value of $41.25 ($41$\frac{1}{4}$). The purchase of the stock is a cash outflow and the eventual sale of the stock is a cash inflow. It is not necessary to multiply the stock price times the number of shares—the interest rate indicating the return on the investment is the same whether 1 share or 200 shares are used. Enter values for $\boxed{n}$, $\boxed{\text{PV}}$, and $\boxed{\text{FV}}$.

$$3 \;\boxed{n}\; -33.50 \;\boxed{\text{PV}}\; 41.25 \;\boxed{\text{FV}}$$

Press $\boxed{i}$ for the annual interest rate:

$$\boxed{i} \; 7.18\% \text{ or about 7.2\% per year.}$$

Mr. Fernandez's return on his original investment compounded at 7.2% per year.   ∎

Interest rates can have a great influence on both individuals and businesses. Individuals borrow for homes, cars, and other personal items whereas firms borrow to buy real estate, expand operations, or cover operating expenses. A small difference in interest rates can make a large difference in costs over time as shown in the next example.

## EXAMPLE 6   *Compare Monthly House Payments*

John and Leticia Adams wish to borrow $62,000 on a 30-year home loan. Find the monthly payment at interest rates of (a) 8% and (b) 9%. Show (c) the monthly savings at the lower rate and (d) the total savings in monthly payments over the 30 years.

### Solution

**(a)** Enter a present value of $62,000 (cash inflow) with 360 compounding periods (30 × 12 = 360) and a rate of 0.666667% per month (8% ÷ 12 = 0.666667, rounded) and press $\boxed{\text{PMT}}$ to find the monthly payment.

$$62000 \;\boxed{\text{PV}}\; 360 \;\boxed{n}\; .666667 \;\boxed{i}$$

$\boxed{\text{PMT}}$ − 454.93 is the monthly payment at 8% per year, rounded to the nearest cent.

**(b)** Enter the values again using the new interest rate of 0.75% (9% ÷ 12 = 0.75%).

$$62000 \;\boxed{\text{PV}}\; 360 \;\boxed{n}\; .75 \;\boxed{i}$$

$\boxed{\text{PMT}}$ −498.87 is the monthly payment at 9% per year, again, rounded to the nearest cent.

**(c)** The difference in the monthly payments is

$$\$498.87 - \$454.93 = \$43.94.$$

**(d)** The total difference saved over 30 years (30 × 12 = 360 payments) is

$$\$43.94 \times 360 \text{ payments} = \$15,818.40.$$

The lower interest rate will reduce the Adam's mortgage payments by a total of $15,818.40 over 30 years. ∎

### | EXAMPLE 7  *Retirement Planning*

Courtney and Nathan Wright plan to retire in 25 years and need $3,500 per month for 20 years.

**(a)** Find the amount needed at retirement to fund the monthly retirement payments assuming the annuity earns 9% compounded monthly while payments are being made.

**(b)** Find the amount of the quarterly payment they must make for the next 25 years to accumulate the necessary funds, assuming earnings of 12% compounded quarterly during the accumulation period.

### Solution

**(a)** The accumulated funds at the end of 25 years is, at their retirement, a present value that must generate a cash inflow to the Wrights of $3,500 per month for 240 months (20 × 12 = 240) assuming earnings of 0.75% per month (9% ÷ 12 = 0.75%). Enter values for $\boxed{n}$, $\boxed{i}$, and $\boxed{\text{PMT}}$.

$$240 \;\boxed{n}\; .75 \;\boxed{i}\; 3500 \;\boxed{\text{PMT}}$$

Press $\boxed{PV}$ to find the amount needed at the end of 25 years:

$\boxed{PV}$ 389007.34 is the amount they must accumulate.

**(b)** The Wrights have 25 years of quarterly payments (100 payments that are cash outflows) in an account earning 3% per quarter (12% ÷ 4 = 3%) to accumulate a future value of $389,007.34. The question is one of what quarterly payment is required. Enter values for $\boxed{n}$, $\boxed{i}$, and $\boxed{FV}$.

100 $\boxed{n}$ 3 $\boxed{i}$ 389007.34 $\boxed{FV}$

Press $\boxed{PMT}$ to find the quarterly payment needed:

$\boxed{PMT}$ −640.57 is the required quarterly payment.

Thus, the Wrights must make 100 end of quarter deposits of $640.57 each into an account earning 3% per quarter in order to subsequently receive 20 years of payments of $3,500 per month, assuming 9% per year during the time that payments are made. ■

## A.2 EXERCISES

*Solve the following problems for the missing quantity using a financial calculator. Round dollar answers to the nearest hundredth, interest rates to the nearest hundredth of a percent, and number of compounding periods to the nearest whole number. Assume that any payments are made at the end of the period.*

|     | *n* | *i* | PV | PMT | FV |
|-----|-----|-----|-----|-----|-----|
| 1.  | 10  | 8%  | $3,500 | — | _____ |
| 2.  | 8   | 1.5% | $6,400 | — | _____ |
| 3.  | 10  | 3%  | _____ | — | $12,000 |
| 4.  | 16  | 4%  | _____ | — | $8,200 |
| 5.  | 7   | 8%  | — | $300 | _____ |
| 6.  | 25  | 2%  | — | $1,000 | _____ |
| 7.  | 30  | _____ | — | $319.67 | $12,000 |
| 8.  | 50  | _____ | — | $4,718.99 | $285,000 |
| 9.  | 360 | 1%  | $83,500 | _____ | — |
| 10. | 180 | 0.5% | $125,000 | _____ | — |
| 11. | _____ | 4% | $85,383 | $5,600 | — |
| 12. | _____ | 2% | $3,822 | $100 | — |

*Solve each of the following application problems.*

13. Milton Smyth placed $20,000 in a 3-year certificate of deposit earning 6% compounded quarterly. Find the future value at the end of the 3 years.

14. At the end of each month, Tina Ramirez has $50 per month taken out of her paycheck and invested in an account paying 0.5% per month. Find the future value at the end of 14 years.

15. Mr. and Mrs. Thrash borrowed $86,500 on a 30-year home loan at 9% per year. Find the monthly payment.

16. Terrance Walker wishes to have $20,000 in 10 years when his son begins college. What payment must he make at the end of each quarter in an investment earning 10% compounded quarterly?

17. The Daily Gazette needs $340,000 for new printing presses. They can invest $12,000 per month in an account paying 0.8% per month. Find the number of payments that must be paid before reaching their goal. Round to the nearest whole number.

18. Mr. and Mrs. Peters wish to build their dream home and must borrow $110,000 on a 30-year mortgage to do so. Find the highest acceptable annual interest rate, to the nearest tenth of a percent, if they can not afford a monthly payment above $845.

19. A farmer purchases a tractor costing $345,000 with 25% down and monthly payments at 1% per month for 5 years. Find the monthly payment.

20. A technical school purchases 25 state-of-the-art computers at a cost of $2,300 each. They pay 20% down and finance the balance at 0.8% per month for 3 years. Find the monthly payment.

# Powers of $e$

| $x$ | $e^x$ | $x$ | $e^x$ | $x$ | $e^x$ | $x$ | $e^x$ | $x$ | $e^x$ |
|------|------------|------|------------|------|------------|------|------------|------|-------------|
| 0.00 | 1.00000000 | 0.55 | 1.73325302 | 1.10 | 3.00416602 | 1.65 | 5.20697983 | 2.20 | 9.02501350 |
| 0.01 | 1.01005017 | 0.56 | 1.75067250 | 1.11 | 3.03435839 | 1.66 | 5.25931084 | 2.21 | 9.11571639 |
| 0.02 | 1.02020134 | 0.57 | 1.76826705 | 1.12 | 3.06485420 | 1.67 | 5.31216780 | 2.22 | 9.20733087 |
| 0.03 | 1.03045453 | 0.58 | 1.78603843 | 1.13 | 3.09565650 | 1.68 | 5.36555597 | 2.23 | 9.29986608 |
| 0.04 | 1.04081077 | 0.59 | 1.80398842 | 1.14 | 3.12676837 | 1.69 | 5.41948071 | 2.24 | 9.39333129 |
| 0.05 | 1.05127110 | 0.60 | 1.82211880 | 1.15 | 3.15819291 | 1.70 | 5.47394739 | 2.25 | 9.48773584 |
| 0.06 | 1.06183655 | 0.61 | 1.84043140 | 1.16 | 3.18993328 | 1.71 | 5.52896148 | 2.26 | 9.58308917 |
| 0.07 | 1.07250818 | 0.62 | 1.85892804 | 1.17 | 3.22199264 | 1.72 | 5.58452846 | 2.27 | 9.67940081 |
| 0.08 | 1.08328707 | 0.63 | 1.87761058 | 1.18 | 3.25437420 | 1.73 | 5.64065391 | 2.28 | 9.77668041 |
| 0.09 | 1.09417428 | 0.64 | 1.89648088 | 1.19 | 3.28708121 | 1.74 | 5.69734342 | 2.29 | 9.87493768 |
| 0.10 | 1.10517092 | 0.65 | 1.91554083 | 1.20 | 3.32011692 | 1.75 | 5.75460268 | 2.30 | 9.97418245 |
| 0.11 | 1.11627807 | 0.66 | 1.93479233 | 1.21 | 3.35348465 | 1.76 | 5.81243739 | 2.31 | 10.07442466 |
| 0.12 | 1.12749685 | 0.67 | 1.95423732 | 1.22 | 3.38718773 | 1.77 | 5.87085336 | 2.32 | 10.17567431 |
| 0.13 | 1.13882838 | 0.68 | 1.97387773 | 1.23 | 3.42122954 | 1.78 | 5.92985642 | 2.33 | 10.27794153 |
| 0.14 | 1.15027380 | 0.69 | 1.99371553 | 1.24 | 3.45561346 | 1.79 | 5.98945247 | 2.34 | 10.38123656 |
| 0.15 | 1.16183424 | 0.70 | 2.01375271 | 1.25 | 3.49034296 | 1.80 | 6.04964746 | 2.35 | 10.48556972 |
| 0.16 | 1.17351087 | 0.71 | 2.03399126 | 1.26 | 3.52542149 | 1.81 | 6.11044743 | 2.36 | 10.59095145 |
| 0.17 | 1.18530485 | 0.72 | 2.05443321 | 1.27 | 3.56085256 | 1.82 | 6.17185845 | 2.37 | 10.69739228 |
| 0.18 | 1.19721736 | 0.73 | 2.07508061 | 1.28 | 3.59663973 | 1.83 | 6.23388666 | 2.38 | 10.80490286 |
| 0.19 | 1.20924960 | 0.74 | 2.09593551 | 1.29 | 3.63278656 | 1.84 | 6.29653826 | 2.39 | 10.91349394 |
| 0.20 | 1.22140276 | 0.75 | 2.11700002 | 1.30 | 3.66929667 | 1.85 | 6.35981952 | 2.40 | 11.02317638 |
| 0.21 | 1.23367806 | 0.76 | 2.13827622 | 1.31 | 3.70617371 | 1.86 | 6.42373677 | 2.41 | 11.13396115 |
| 0.22 | 1.24607673 | 0.77 | 2.15976625 | 1.32 | 3.74342138 | 1.87 | 6.48829640 | 2.42 | 11.24585931 |
| 0.23 | 1.25860001 | 0.78 | 2.18147227 | 1.33 | 3.78104339 | 1.88 | 6.55350486 | 2.43 | 11.35888208 |
| 0.24 | 1.27124915 | 0.79 | 2.20339643 | 1.34 | 3.81904351 | 1.89 | 6.61936868 | 2.44 | 11.47304074 |
| 0.25 | 1.28402542 | 0.80 | 2.22554093 | 1.35 | 3.85742553 | 1.90 | 6.68589444 | 2.45 | 11.58834672 |
| 0.26 | 1.29693009 | 0.81 | 2.24790799 | 1.36 | 3.89619330 | 1.91 | 6.75308880 | 2.46 | 11.70481154 |
| 0.27 | 1.30996445 | 0.82 | 2.27049984 | 1.37 | 3.93535070 | 1.92 | 6.82095847 | 2.47 | 11.82244685 |
| 0.28 | 1.32312981 | 0.83 | 2.29331874 | 1.38 | 3.97490163 | 1.93 | 6.88951024 | 2.48 | 11.94126442 |
| 0.29 | 1.33642749 | 0.84 | 2.31636698 | 1.39 | 4.01485005 | 1.94 | 6.95875097 | 2.49 | 12.06127612 |
| 0.30 | 1.34985881 | 0.85 | 2.33964685 | 1.40 | 4.05519997 | 1.95 | 7.02868758 | 2.50 | 12.18249396 |
| 0.31 | 1.36342135 | 0.86 | 2.36316069 | 1.41 | 4.09595540 | 1.96 | 7.09932707 | 2.51 | 12.30493006 |
| 0.32 | 1.37712776 | 0.87 | 2.38691085 | 1.42 | 4.13712044 | 1.97 | 7.17067649 | 2.52 | 12.42859666 |
| 0.33 | 1.39096813 | 0.88 | 2.41089971 | 1.43 | 4.17869919 | 1.98 | 7.24274299 | 2.53 | 12.55350614 |
| 0.34 | 1.40494759 | 0.89 | 2.43512965 | 1.44 | 4.22069582 | 1.99 | 7.31553376 | 2.54 | 12.67967097 |
| 0.35 | 1.41906755 | 0.90 | 2.45960311 | 1.45 | 4.26311452 | 2.00 | 7.38905610 | 2.55 | 12.80710378 |
| 0.36 | 1.43332941 | 0.91 | 2.48432253 | 1.46 | 4.30595953 | 2.01 | 7.46331735 | 2.56 | 12.93581732 |
| 0.37 | 1.44773461 | 0.92 | 2.50929039 | 1.47 | 4.34923514 | 2.02 | 7.53832493 | 2.57 | 13.06582444 |
| 0.38 | 1.46228459 | 0.93 | 2.53450918 | 1.48 | 4.39294568 | 2.03 | 7.61408636 | 2.58 | 13.19713816 |
| 0.39 | 1.47698079 | 0.94 | 2.55998142 | 1.49 | 4.43709552 | 2.04 | 7.69060920 | 2.59 | 13.32977160 |
| 0.40 | 1.49182470 | 0.95 | 2.58570966 | 1.50 | 4.48168907 | 2.05 | 7.76790111 | 2.60 | 13.46373804 |
| 0.41 | 1.50681779 | 0.96 | 2.61169647 | 1.51 | 4.52673079 | 2.06 | 7.84596981 | 2.61 | 13.59905085 |
| 0.42 | 1.52196156 | 0.97 | 2.63794446 | 1.52 | 4.57222520 | 2.07 | 7.92482312 | 2.62 | 13.73572359 |
| 0.43 | 1.53725752 | 0.98 | 2.66445624 | 1.53 | 4.61817682 | 2.08 | 8.00446891 | 2.63 | 13.87376990 |
| 0.44 | 1.55270722 | 0.99 | 2.69123447 | 1.54 | 4.66459027 | 2.09 | 8.08491516 | 2.64 | 14.01320361 |
| 0.45 | 1.56831219 | 1.00 | 2.71828183 | 1.55 | 4.71147018 | 2.10 | 8.16616991 | 2.65 | 14.15403865 |
| 0.46 | 1.58407398 | 1.01 | 2.74560102 | 1.56 | 4.75882125 | 2.11 | 8.24824128 | 2.66 | 14.29628910 |
| 0.47 | 1.59999419 | 1.02 | 2.77319476 | 1.57 | 4.80664819 | 2.12 | 8.33113749 | 2.67 | 14.43996919 |
| 0.48 | 1.61607440 | 1.03 | 2.80106583 | 1.58 | 4.85495581 | 2.13 | 8.41486681 | 2.68 | 14.58509330 |
| 0.49 | 1.63231622 | 1.04 | 2.82921701 | 1.59 | 4.90374893 | 2.14 | 8.49943763 | 2.69 | 14.73167592 |
| 0.50 | 1.64872127 | 1.05 | 2.85765112 | 1.60 | 4.95303242 | 2.15 | 8.58485840 | 2.70 | 14.87973172 |
| 0.51 | 1.66529119 | 1.06 | 2.88637099 | 1.61 | 5.00281123 | 2.16 | 8.67113766 | 2.71 | 15.02927551 |
| 0.52 | 1.68202765 | 1.07 | 2.91537950 | 1.62 | 5.05309032 | 2.17 | 8.75823404 | 2.72 | 15.18032224 |
| 0.53 | 1.69893231 | 1.08 | 2.94467955 | 1.63 | 5.10387472 | 2.18 | 8.84630626 | 2.73 | 15.33288702 |
| 0.54 | 1.71600686 | 1.09 | 2.97427407 | 1.64 | 5.15516951 | 2.19 | 8.93521311 | 2.74 | 15.48698510 |

# Interest Tables

| Rate $\frac{1}{3}\%$ | A Compound Interest | B Present Value | C Amount of Annuity | D Present Value of Annuity | E Sinking Fund | F Amortization |
|---|---|---|---|---|---|---|
| $n$ | $(1 + i)^n$ | $\dfrac{1}{(1 + i)^n}$ | $s_{\overline{n}\rceil i}$ | $a_{\overline{n}\rceil i}$ | $\dfrac{1}{s_{\overline{n}\rceil i}}$ | $\dfrac{1}{a_{\overline{n}\rceil i}}$ |
| 1 | 1.00333333 | 0.99667774 | 1.00000000 | 0.99667774 | 1.00000000 | 1.00333333 |
| 2 | 1.00667778 | 0.99336652 | 2.00333333 | 1.99004426 | 0.49916805 | 0.50250139 |
| 3 | 1.01003337 | 0.99006630 | 3.01001111 | 2.98011056 | 0.33222469 | 0.33555802 |
| 4 | 1.01340015 | 0.98677704 | 4.02004448 | 3.96688760 | 0.24875347 | 0.25208680 |
| 5 | 1.01677815 | 0.98349871 | 5.03344463 | 4.95038631 | 0.19867110 | 0.20200444 |
| 6 | 1.02016741 | 0.98023127 | 6.05022278 | 5.93061759 | 0.16528317 | 0.16861650 |
| 7 | 1.02356797 | 0.97697469 | 7.07039019 | 6.90759228 | 0.14143491 | 0.14476824 |
| 8 | 1.02697986 | 0.97372893 | 8.09395816 | 7.88132121 | 0.12354895 | 0.12688228 |
| 9 | 1.03040313 | 0.97049395 | 9.12093802 | 8.85181516 | 0.10963785 | 0.11297118 |
| 10 | 1.03383780 | 0.96726972 | 10.15134114 | 9.81908487 | 0.09850915 | 0.10184248 |
| 11 | 1.03728393 | 0.96405620 | 11.18517895 | 10.78314107 | 0.08940402 | 0.09273736 |
| 12 | 1.04074154 | 0.96085335 | 12.22246288 | 11.74399442 | 0.08181657 | 0.08514990 |
| 13 | 1.04421068 | 0.95766115 | 13.26320442 | 12.70165557 | 0.07539656 | 0.07872989 |
| 14 | 1.04769138 | 0.95447955 | 14.30741510 | 13.65613512 | 0.06989383 | 0.07322716 |
| 15 | 1.05118369 | 0.95130852 | 15.35510648 | 14.60744364 | 0.06512491 | 0.06845825 |
| 16 | 1.05468763 | 0.94814803 | 16.40629017 | 15.55559167 | 0.06095223 | 0.06428557 |
| 17 | 1.05820326 | 0.94499803 | 17.46097781 | 16.50058970 | 0.05727056 | 0.06060389 |
| 18 | 1.06173060 | 0.94185851 | 18.51918107 | 17.44244821 | 0.05399807 | 0.05733140 |
| 19 | 1.06526971 | 0.93872941 | 19.58091167 | 18.38117762 | 0.05107015 | 0.05440348 |
| 20 | 1.06882060 | 0.93561071 | 20.64618137 | 19.31678832 | 0.04843511 | 0.05176844 |
| 21 | 1.07238334 | 0.93250236 | 21.71500198 | 20.24929069 | 0.04605111 | 0.04938445 |
| 22 | 1.07595795 | 0.92940435 | 22.78738532 | 21.17869504 | 0.04388393 | 0.04721726 |
| 23 | 1.07954448 | 0.92631663 | 23.86334327 | 22.10501167 | 0.04190528 | 0.04523861 |
| 24 | 1.08314296 | 0.92323916 | 24.94288775 | 23.02825083 | 0.04009159 | 0.04342492 |
| 25 | 1.08675344 | 0.92017192 | 26.02603071 | 23.94842275 | 0.03842307 | 0.04175640 |
| 26 | 1.09037595 | 0.91711487 | 27.11278414 | 24.86553763 | 0.03688297 | 0.04021630 |
| 27 | 1.09401053 | 0.91406798 | 28.20316009 | 25.77960561 | 0.03545702 | 0.03879035 |
| 28 | 1.09765724 | 0.91103121 | 29.29717062 | 26.69063682 | 0.03413299 | 0.03746632 |
| 29 | 1.10131609 | 0.90800453 | 30.39482786 | 27.59864135 | 0.03290033 | 0.03623367 |
| 30 | 1.10498715 | 0.90498790 | 31.49614395 | 28.50362925 | 0.03174992 | 0.03508325 |
| 31 | 1.10867044 | 0.90198130 | 32.60113110 | 29.40561055 | 0.03067378 | 0.03400712 |
| 32 | 1.11236601 | 0.89898468 | 33.70980154 | 30.30459523 | 0.02966496 | 0.03299830 |
| 33 | 1.11607389 | 0.89599802 | 34.82216754 | 31.20059325 | 0.02871734 | 0.03205067 |
| 34 | 1.11979414 | 0.89302128 | 35.93824143 | 32.09361454 | 0.02782551 | 0.03115885 |
| 35 | 1.12352679 | 0.89005444 | 37.05803557 | 32.98366898 | 0.02698470 | 0.03031803 |
| 36 | 1.12727187 | 0.88709745 | 38.18156236 | 33.87076642 | 0.02619065 | 0.02952399 |
| 37 | 1.13102945 | 0.88415028 | 39.30883423 | 34.75491670 | 0.02543957 | 0.02877291 |
| 38 | 1.13479955 | 0.88121290 | 40.43986368 | 35.63612960 | 0.02472808 | 0.02806141 |
| 39 | 1.13858221 | 0.87828528 | 41.57466322 | 36.51441488 | 0.02405311 | 0.02738644 |
| 40 | 1.14237748 | 0.87536739 | 42.71324543 | 37.38978228 | 0.02341194 | 0.02674527 |
| 41 | 1.14618541 | 0.87245920 | 43.85562292 | 38.26224147 | 0.02280209 | 0.02613543 |
| 42 | 1.15000603 | 0.86956066 | 45.00180833 | 39.13180213 | 0.02222133 | 0.02555466 |
| 43 | 1.15383938 | 0.86667175 | 46.15181436 | 39.99847389 | 0.02166762 | 0.02500095 |
| 44 | 1.15768551 | 0.86379245 | 47.30565374 | 40.86226633 | 0.02113912 | 0.02447246 |
| 45 | 1.16154446 | 0.86092270 | 48.46333925 | 41.72318903 | 0.02063415 | 0.02396749 |
| 46 | 1.16541628 | 0.85806249 | 49.62488371 | 42.58125153 | 0.02015118 | 0.02348451 |
| 47 | 1.16930100 | 0.85521179 | 50.79029999 | 43.43646332 | 0.01968880 | 0.02302213 |
| 48 | 1.17319867 | 0.85237055 | 51.95960099 | 44.28883387 | 0.01924572 | 0.02257905 |
| 49 | 1.17710933 | 0.84953876 | 53.13279966 | 45.13837263 | 0.01882077 | 0.02215410 |
| 50 | 1.18103303 | 0.84671637 | 54.30990899 | 45.98508900 | 0.01841285 | 0.02174618 |

| Rate $\frac{5}{12}\%$ | A Compound Interest | B Present Value | C Amount of Annuity | D Present Value of Annuity | E Sinking Fund | F Amortization |
|---|---|---|---|---|---|---|
| $n$ | $(1 + i)^n$ | $\dfrac{1}{(1 + i)^n}$ | $s_{\overline{n}\rvert i}$ | $a_{\overline{n}\rvert i}$ | $\dfrac{1}{s_{\overline{n}\rvert i}}$ | $\dfrac{1}{a_{\overline{n}\rvert i}}$ |
| 1 | 1.00416667 | 0.99585062 | 1.00000000 | 0.99585062 | 1.00000000 | 1.00416667 |
| 2 | 1.00835069 | 0.99171846 | 2.00416667 | 1.98756908 | 0.49896050 | 0.50312717 |
| 3 | 1.01255216 | 0.98760345 | 3.01251736 | 2.97517253 | 0.33194829 | 0.33611496 |
| 4 | 1.01677112 | 0.98350551 | 4.02506952 | 3.95867804 | 0.24844291 | 0.25260958 |
| 5 | 1.02100767 | 0.97942457 | 5.01484064 | 4.93810261 | 0.19834026 | 0.20250693 |
| 6 | 1.02526187 | 0.97536057 | 6.06284831 | 5.91346318 | 0.16493898 | 0.16910564 |
| 7 | 1.02953379 | 0.97131343 | 7.08811018 | 6.88477661 | 0.14108133 | 0.14524800 |
| 8 | 1.03382352 | 0.96728308 | 8.11764397 | 7.85205970 | 0.12318845 | 0.12735512 |
| 9 | 1.03813111 | 0.96326946 | 9.15146749 | 8.81532916 | 0.10927209 | 0.11343876 |
| 10 | 1.04245666 | 0.95927249 | 10.18959860 | 9.77460165 | 0.09813929 | 0.10230596 |
| 11 | 1.04680023 | 0.95529211 | 11.23205526 | 10.72989376 | 0.08903090 | 0.09319757 |
| 12 | 1.05116190 | 0.95132824 | 12.27885549 | 11.68122200 | 0.08144082 | 0.08560748 |
| 13 | 1.05554174 | 0.94738082 | 13.33001739 | 12.62860283 | 0.07501866 | 0.07918532 |
| 14 | 1.05993983 | 0.94344978 | 14.38555913 | 13.57205261 | 0.06951416 | 0.07368082 |
| 15 | 1.06435625 | 0.93953505 | 15.44549896 | 14.51158766 | 0.06474378 | 0.06891045 |
| 16 | 1.06879106 | 0.93563657 | 16.50985520 | 15.44722422 | 0.06056988 | 0.06473655 |
| 17 | 1.07324436 | 0.93175426 | 17.57864627 | 16.37897848 | 0.05688720 | 0.06105387 |
| 18 | 1.07771621 | 0.92788806 | 18.65189063 | 17.30686654 | 0.05361387 | 0.05778053 |
| 19 | 1.08220670 | 0.92403790 | 19.72960684 | 18.23090443 | 0.05068525 | 0.05485191 |
| 20 | 1.08671589 | 0.92020372 | 20.81181353 | 19.15110815 | 0.04804963 | 0.05221630 |
| 21 | 1.09124387 | 0.91638544 | 21.89852942 | 20.06749359 | 0.04566517 | 0.04983183 |
| 22 | 1.09579072 | 0.91258301 | 22.98977330 | 20.98007661 | 0.04349760 | 0.04766427 |
| 23 | 1.10035652 | 0.90879636 | 24.08556402 | 21.88887297 | 0.04151865 | 0.04568531 |
| 24 | 1.10494134 | 0.90502542 | 25.18592053 | 22.79389839 | 0.03970472 | 0.04387139 |
| 25 | 1.10954526 | 0.90127013 | 26.29086187 | 23.69516853 | 0.03803603 | 0.04220270 |
| 26 | 1.11416836 | 0.89753042 | 27.40040713 | 24.59269895 | 0.03649581 | 0.04066247 |
| 27 | 1.11881073 | 0.89380623 | 28.51457549 | 25.48650517 | 0.03506978 | 0.03923645 |
| 28 | 1.12347244 | 0.89009749 | 29.63338622 | 26.37660266 | 0.03374572 | 0.03791239 |
| 29 | 1.12815358 | 0.88640414 | 30.75685866 | 27.26300680 | 0.03251307 | 0.03667974 |
| 30 | 1.13285422 | 0.88272611 | 31.88501224 | 28.14573291 | 0.03136270 | 0.03552936 |
| 31 | 1.13757444 | 0.87906335 | 33.01786646 | 29.02479626 | 0.03028663 | 0.03445330 |
| 32 | 1.14231434 | 0.87541578 | 34.15544090 | 29.90021205 | 0.02927791 | 0.03344458 |
| 33 | 1.14707398 | 0.87178335 | 35.29775524 | 30.77199540 | 0.02833041 | 0.03249708 |
| 34 | 1.15185346 | 0.86816599 | 36.44482922 | 31.64016139 | 0.02743873 | 0.03160540 |
| 35 | 1.15665284 | 0.86456365 | 37.59668268 | 32.50472504 | 0.02659809 | 0.03076476 |
| 36 | 1.16147223 | 0.86097624 | 38.75333552 | 33.36570128 | 0.02580423 | 0.02997090 |
| 37 | 1.16631170 | 0.85740373 | 39.91480775 | 34.22310501 | 0.02505336 | 0.02922003 |
| 38 | 1.17117133 | 0.85384604 | 41.08111945 | 35.07695105 | 0.02434208 | 0.02850875 |
| 39 | 1.17605121 | 0.85030311 | 42.25229078 | 35.92725416 | 0.02366736 | 0.02783402 |
| 40 | 1.18095142 | 0.84677488 | 43.42834199 | 36.77402904 | 0.02302644 | 0.02719310 |
| 41 | 1.18587206 | 0.84326129 | 44.60929342 | 37.61729033 | 0.02241685 | 0.02658352 |
| 42 | 1.19081319 | 0.83976228 | 45.79516547 | 38.45705261 | 0.02183637 | 0.02600303 |
| 43 | 1.19577491 | 0.83627779 | 46.98597866 | 39.29333040 | 0.02128295 | 0.02544961 |
| 44 | 1.20075731 | 0.83280776 | 48.18175357 | 40.12613816 | 0.02075474 | 0.02492141 |
| 45 | 1.20576046 | 0.82935212 | 49.38251088 | 40.95549028 | 0.02025008 | 0.02441675 |
| 46 | 1.21078446 | 0.82591083 | 50.58827134 | 41.78140111 | 0.01976743 | 0.02393409 |
| 47 | 1.21582940 | 0.82248381 | 51.79905581 | 42.60388492 | 0.01930537 | 0.02347204 |
| 48 | 1.22089536 | 0.81907102 | 53.01488521 | 43.42295594 | 0.01886263 | 0.02302929 |
| 49 | 1.22598242 | 0.81567238 | 54.23578056 | 44.23862832 | 0.01843801 | 0.02260468 |
| 50 | 1.23109068 | 0.81228785 | 55.46176298 | 45.05091617 | 0.01803044 | 0.02219711 |

| Rate $\frac{1}{2}\%$ | A Compound Interest | B Present Value | C Amount of Annuity | D Present Value of Annuity | E Sinking Fund | F Amortization |
|---|---|---|---|---|---|---|
| $n$ | $(1 + i)^n$ | $\dfrac{1}{(1 + i)^n}$ | $s_{\overline{n}|i}$ | $a_{\overline{n}|i}$ | $\dfrac{1}{s_{\overline{n}|i}}$ | $\dfrac{1}{a_{\overline{n}|i}}$ |
| 1 | 1.00500000 | 0.99502488 | 1.00000000 | 0.99502488 | 1.00000000 | 1.00500000 |
| 2 | 1.01002500 | 0.99007450 | 2.00500000 | 1.98509938 | 0.49875312 | 0.50375312 |
| 3 | 1.01507513 | 0.98514876 | 3.01502500 | 2.97024814 | 0.33167221 | 0.33667221 |
| 4 | 1.02015050 | 0.98024752 | 4.03010012 | 3.95049566 | 0.24813279 | 0.25313279 |
| 5 | 1.02525125 | 0.97537067 | 5.05025063 | 4.92586633 | 0.19800997 | 0.20300997 |
| 6 | 1.03037751 | 0.97051808 | 6.07550188 | 5.89638441 | 0.16459546 | 0.16959546 |
| 7 | 1.03552940 | 0.96568963 | 7.10587939 | 6.86207404 | 0.14072854 | 0.14572854 |
| 8 | 1.04070704 | 0.96088520 | 8.14140879 | 7.82295924 | 0.12282886 | 0.12782886 |
| 9 | 1.04591058 | 0.95610468 | 9.18211583 | 8.77906392 | 0.10890736 | 0.11390736 |
| 10 | 1.05114013 | 0.95134794 | 10.22802641 | 9.73041186 | 0.09777057 | 0.10277057 |
| 11 | 1.05639583 | 0.94661487 | 11.27916654 | 10.67702673 | 0.08865903 | 0.09365903 |
| 12 | 1.06167781 | 0.94190534 | 12.33556237 | 11.61893207 | 0.08106643 | 0.08606643 |
| 13 | 1.06698620 | 0.93721924 | 13.39724018 | 12.55615131 | 0.07464224 | 0.07964224 |
| 14 | 1.07232113 | 0.93255646 | 14.46422639 | 13.48870777 | 0.06913609 | 0.07413609 |
| 15 | 1.07768274 | 0.92791688 | 15.53654752 | 14.41662465 | 0.06436436 | 0.06936436 |
| 16 | 1.08307115 | 0.92330037 | 16.61423026 | 15.33992502 | 0.06018937 | 0.06518937 |
| 17 | 1.08848651 | 0.91870684 | 17.69730141 | 16.25863186 | 0.05650579 | 0.06150579 |
| 18 | 1.09392894 | 0.91413616 | 18.78578791 | 17.17276802 | 0.05323173 | 0.05823173 |
| 19 | 1.09939858 | 0.90958822 | 19.87971685 | 18.08235624 | 0.05030253 | 0.05530253 |
| 20 | 1.10489558 | 0.90506290 | 20.97911544 | 18.98741915 | 0.04766645 | 0.05266645 |
| 21 | 1.11042006 | 0.90056010 | 22.08401101 | 19.88797925 | 0.04528163 | 0.05028163 |
| 22 | 1.11597216 | 0.89607971 | 23.19443107 | 20.78405896 | 0.04311380 | 0.04811380 |
| 23 | 1.12155202 | 0.89162160 | 24.31040322 | 21.67568055 | 0.04113465 | 0.04613465 |
| 24 | 1.12715978 | 0.88718567 | 25.43195524 | 22.56286622 | 0.03932061 | 0.04432061 |
| 25 | 1.13279558 | 0.88277181 | 26.55911502 | 23.44563803 | 0.03765186 | 0.04265186 |
| 26 | 1.13845955 | 0.87837991 | 27.69191059 | 24.32401794 | 0.03611163 | 0.04111163 |
| 27 | 1.14415185 | 0.87400986 | 28.83037015 | 25.19802780 | 0.03468565 | 0.03968565 |
| 28 | 1.14987261 | 0.86966155 | 29.97452200 | 26.06768936 | 0.03336167 | 0.03836167 |
| 29 | 1.15562197 | 0.86533488 | 31.12439461 | 26.93302423 | 0.03212914 | 0.03712914 |
| 30 | 1.16140008 | 0.86102973 | 32.28001658 | 27.79405397 | 0.03097892 | 0.03597892 |
| 31 | 1.16720708 | 0.85674600 | 33.44141666 | 28.65079997 | 0.02990304 | 0.03490304 |
| 32 | 1.17304312 | 0.85248358 | 34.60862375 | 29.50328355 | 0.02889453 | 0.03389453 |
| 33 | 1.17890833 | 0.84824237 | 35.78166686 | 30.35152592 | 0.02794727 | 0.03294727 |
| 34 | 1.18480288 | 0.84402226 | 36.96057520 | 31.19554818 | 0.02705586 | 0.03205586 |
| 35 | 1.19072689 | 0.83982314 | 38.14537807 | 32.03537132 | 0.02621550 | 0.03121550 |
| 36 | 1.19668052 | 0.83564492 | 39.33610496 | 32.87101624 | 0.02542194 | 0.03042194 |
| 37 | 1.20266393 | 0.83148748 | 40.53278549 | 33.70250372 | 0.02467133 | 0.02967139 |
| 38 | 1.20867725 | 0.82735073 | 41.73544942 | 34.52985445 | 0.02396045 | 0.02896045 |
| 39 | 1.21472063 | 0.82323455 | 42.94412666 | 35.35308900 | 0.02328607 | 0.02828607 |
| 40 | 1.22079424 | 0.81913886 | 44.15884730 | 36.17222786 | 0.02264552 | 0.02764552 |
| 41 | 1.22689821 | 0.81506354 | 45.37964153 | 36.98729141 | 0.02203631 | 0.02703631 |
| 42 | 1.23303270 | 0.81100850 | 46.60653974 | 37.79829991 | 0.02145622 | 0.02645622 |
| 43 | 1.23919786 | 0.80697363 | 47.83957244 | 38.60527354 | 0.02090320 | 0.02590320 |
| 44 | 1.24539385 | 0.80295884 | 49.07877030 | 39.40823238 | 0.02037541 | 0.02537541 |
| 45 | 1.25162082 | 0.79896402 | 50.32416415 | 40.20719640 | 0.01987117 | 0.02487117 |
| 46 | 1.25787892 | 0.79498907 | 51.57578497 | 41.00218547 | 0.01938894 | 0.02438894 |
| 47 | 1.26416832 | 0.79103390 | 52.83366390 | 41.79321937 | 0.01892733 | 0.02392733 |
| 48 | 1.27048916 | 0.78709841 | 54.09783222 | 42.58031778 | 0.01848503 | 0.02348503 |
| 49 | 1.27684161 | 0.78318250 | 55.36832138 | 43.36350028 | 0.01806087 | 0.02306087 |
| 50 | 1.28322581 | 0.77928607 | 56.64516299 | 44.14278635 | 0.01765376 | 0.02265376 |

| Rate $\frac{3}{4}\%$ | A Compound Interest | B Present Value | C Amount of Annuity | D Present Value of Annuity | E Sinking Fund | F Amortization |
|---|---|---|---|---|---|---|
| $n$ | $(1 + i)^n$ | $\dfrac{1}{(1 + i)^n}$ | $s_{\overline{n}\rceil i}$ | $a_{\overline{n}\rceil i}$ | $\dfrac{1}{s_{\overline{n}\rceil i}}$ | $\dfrac{1}{a_{\overline{n}\rceil i}}$ |
| 1 | 1.00750000 | 0.99255583 | 1.00000000 | 0.99255583 | 1.00000000 | 1.00750000 |
| 2 | 1.01505625 | 0.98516708 | 2.00750000 | 1.97772291 | 0.49813200 | 0.50563200 |
| 3 | 1.02266917 | 0.97783333 | 3.02255625 | 2.95555624 | 0.33084579 | 0.33834579 |
| 4 | 1.03033919 | 0.97055417 | 4.04522542 | 3.92611041 | 0.24720501 | 0.25470501 |
| 5 | 1.03806673 | 0.96332920 | 5.07556461 | 4.88943961 | 0.19702242 | 0.20452242 |
| 6 | 1.04585224 | 0.95615802 | 6.11363135 | 5.84559763 | 0.16356891 | 0.17106891 |
| 7 | 1.05369613 | 0.94904022 | 7.15948358 | 6.79463785 | 0.13967488 | 0.14717488 |
| 8 | 1.06159885 | 0.94197540 | 8.21317971 | 7.73661325 | 0.12175552 | 0.12925552 |
| 9 | 1.06956084 | 0.93496318 | 9.27477856 | 8.67157642 | 0.10781929 | 0.11531929 |
| 10 | 1.07758255 | 0.92800315 | 10.34433940 | 9.59957958 | 0.09667123 | 0.10417123 |
| 11 | 1.08566441 | 0.92109494 | 11.42192194 | 10.52067452 | 0.08755094 | 0.09505094 |
| 12 | 1.09380690 | 0.91423815 | 12.50758636 | 11.43491267 | 0.07995148 | 0.08745148 |
| 13 | 1.10201045 | 0.90743241 | 13.60139325 | 12.34234508 | 0.07352188 | 0.08102188 |
| 14 | 1.11027553 | 0.90067733 | 14.70340370 | 13.24302242 | 0.06801146 | 0.07551146 |
| 15 | 1.11860259 | 0.89397254 | 15.81367923 | 14.13699495 | 0.06323639 | 0.07073639 |
| 16 | 1.12699211 | 0.88731766 | 16.93228183 | 15.02431261 | 0.05905879 | 0.06655879 |
| 17 | 1.13544455 | 0.88071231 | 18.05927394 | 15.90502492 | 0.05537321 | 0.06287321 |
| 18 | 1.14396039 | 0.87415614 | 19.19471849 | 16.77918107 | 0.05209766 | 0.05959766 |
| 19 | 1.15254009 | 0.86764878 | 20.33867888 | 17.64682984 | 0.04916740 | 0.05666740 |
| 20 | 1.16118414 | 0.86118985 | 21.49121897 | 18.50801969 | 0.04653063 | 0.05403063 |
| 21 | 1.16989302 | 0.85477901 | 22.65240312 | 19.36279870 | 0.04414543 | 0.05164543 |
| 22 | 1.17866722 | 0.84841589 | 23.82229614 | 20.21121459 | 0.04197748 | 0.04947748 |
| 23 | 1.18750723 | 0.84210014 | 25.00096336 | 21.05331473 | 0.03999846 | 0.04749846 |
| 24 | 1.19641353 | 0.83583140 | 26.18847059 | 21.88914614 | 0.03818474 | 0.04568474 |
| 25 | 1.20538663 | 0.82960933 | 27.38488412 | 22.71875547 | 0.03651650 | 0.04401650 |
| 26 | 1.21442703 | 0.82343358 | 28.59027075 | 23.54218905 | 0.03497693 | 0.04247693 |
| 27 | 1.22353523 | 0.81730380 | 29.80469778 | 24.35949286 | 0.03355176 | 0.04105176 |
| 28 | 1.23271175 | 0.81121966 | 31.02823301 | 25.17071251 | 0.03222871 | 0.03972871 |
| 29 | 1.24195709 | 0.80518080 | 32.26094476 | 25.97589331 | 0.03099723 | 0.03849723 |
| 30 | 1.25127176 | 0.79918690 | 33.50290184 | 26.77508021 | 0.02984816 | 0.03734816 |
| 31 | 1.26065630 | 0.79323762 | 34.75417361 | 27.56831783 | 0.02877352 | 0.03627352 |
| 32 | 1.27011122 | 0.78733262 | 36.01482991 | 28.35565045 | 0.02776634 | 0.03526634 |
| 33 | 1.27963706 | 0.78147158 | 37.28494113 | 29.13712203 | 0.02682048 | 0.03432048 |
| 34 | 1.28923434 | 0.77565418 | 38.56457819 | 29.91277621 | 0.02593053 | 0.03343053 |
| 35 | 1.29890359 | 0.76988008 | 39.85381253 | 30.68265629 | 0.02509170 | 0.03259170 |
| 36 | 1.30864537 | 0.76414896 | 41.15271612 | 31.44680525 | 0.02429973 | 0.03179973 |
| 37 | 1.31846021 | 0.75846051 | 42.46136149 | 32.20526576 | 0.02355082 | 0.03105082 |
| 38 | 1.32834866 | 0.75281440 | 43.77982170 | 32.95808016 | 0.02284157 | 0.03034157 |
| 39 | 1.33831128 | 0.74721032 | 45.10817037 | 33.70529048 | 0.02216893 | 0.02966893 |
| 40 | 1.34834861 | 0.74164796 | 46.44648164 | 34.44693844 | 0.02153016 | 0.02903016 |
| 41 | 1.35846123 | 0.73612701 | 47.79483026 | 35.18306545 | 0.02092276 | 0.02842276 |
| 42 | 1.36864969 | 0.73064716 | 49.15329148 | 35.91371260 | 0.02034452 | 0.02784452 |
| 43 | 1.37891456 | 0.72520809 | 50.52194117 | 36.63892070 | 0.01979338 | 0.02729338 |
| 44 | 1.38925642 | 0.71980952 | 51.90085573 | 37.35873022 | 0.01926751 | 0.02676751 |
| 45 | 1.39967584 | 0.71445114 | 53.29011215 | 38.07318136 | 0.01876521 | 0.02626521 |
| 46 | 1.41017341 | 0.70913264 | 54.68978799 | 38.78231401 | 0.01828495 | 0.02578495 |
| 47 | 1.42074971 | 0.70385374 | 56.09996140 | 39.48616775 | 0.01782532 | 0.02532532 |
| 48 | 1.43140533 | 0.69861414 | 57.52071111 | 40.18478189 | 0.01738504 | 0.02488504 |
| 49 | 1.44214087 | 0.69341353 | 58.95211644 | 40.87819542 | 0.01696292 | 0.02446292 |
| 50 | 1.45295693 | 0.68825165 | 60.39425732 | 41.56644707 | 0.01655787 | 0.02405787 |

| Rate $\frac{5}{6}$% | A Compound Interest | B Present Value | C Amount of Annuity | D Present Value of Annuity | E Sinking Fund | F Amortization |
|---|---|---|---|---|---|---|
| $n$ | $(1 + i)^n$ | $\dfrac{1}{(1 + i)^n}$ | $s_{\overline{n}|i}$ | $a_{\overline{n}|i}$ | $\dfrac{1}{s_{\overline{n}|i}}$ | $\dfrac{1}{a_{\overline{n}|i}}$ |
| 1 | 1.00833333 | 0.99173554 | 1.00000000 | 0.99173554 | 1.00000000 | 1.00833333 |
| 2 | 1.01673611 | 0.98353938 | 2.00833333 | 1.97527491 | 0.49792531 | 0.50625864 |
| 3 | 1.02520891 | 0.97541095 | 3.02506944 | 2.95068586 | 0.33057092 | 0.33890426 |
| 4 | 1.03375232 | 0.96734970 | 4.05027836 | 3.91803557 | 0.24689661 | 0.25522994 |
| 5 | 1.04236692 | 0.95935508 | 5.08403068 | 4.87739065 | 0.19669433 | 0.20502766 |
| 6 | 1.05105331 | 0.95142652 | 6.12639760 | 5.82881717 | 0.16322806 | 0.17156139 |
| 7 | 1.05981209 | 0.94356349 | 7.17745091 | 6.77238066 | 0.13932523 | 0.14765856 |
| 8 | 1.06864386 | 0.93576545 | 8.23726300 | 7.70814611 | 0.12139955 | 0.12973288 |
| 9 | 1.07754922 | 0.92803185 | 9.30590686 | 8.63617796 | 0.10745863 | 0.11579196 |
| 10 | 1.08652880 | 0.92036217 | 10.38345608 | 9.55654013 | 0.09630705 | 0.10464038 |
| 11 | 1.09558321 | 0.91275587 | 11.46998489 | 10.46929600 | 0.08718407 | 0.09551741 |
| 12 | 1.10471307 | 0.90521243 | 12.56556809 | 11.37450843 | 0.07958255 | 0.08791589 |
| 13 | 1.11391901 | 0.89773134 | 13.67028116 | 12.27223976 | 0.07315138 | 0.08148472 |
| 14 | 1.12320167 | 0.89031207 | 14.78420017 | 13.16255183 | 0.06763978 | 0.07597311 |
| 15 | 1.13256168 | 0.88295412 | 15.90740184 | 14.04550595 | 0.06286382 | 0.07119715 |
| 16 | 1.14199970 | 0.87565698 | 17.03996352 | 14.92116292 | 0.05868557 | 0.06701890 |
| 17 | 1.15151636 | 0.86842014 | 18.18196322 | 15.78958306 | 0.05499956 | 0.06333289 |
| 18 | 1.16111233 | 0.86124312 | 19.33347958 | 16.65082618 | 0.05172375 | 0.06005708 |
| 19 | 1.17078827 | 0.85412540 | 20.49459191 | 17.50495158 | 0.04879336 | 0.05712669 |
| 20 | 1.18054483 | 0.84706652 | 21.66538017 | 18.35201810 | 0.04615659 | 0.05448992 |
| 21 | 1.19038271 | 0.84006597 | 22.84592501 | 19.19208406 | 0.04377148 | 0.05210482 |
| 22 | 1.20030256 | 0.83312327 | 24.03630772 | 20.02520734 | 0.04160373 | 0.04993706 |
| 23 | 1.21030509 | 0.82623796 | 25.23661028 | 20.85144529 | 0.03962497 | 0.04795831 |
| 24 | 1.22039096 | 0.81940954 | 26.44691537 | 21.67085483 | 0.03781159 | 0.04614493 |
| 25 | 1.23056089 | 0.81263756 | 27.66730633 | 22.48349240 | 0.03614374 | 0.04447708 |
| 26 | 1.24081556 | 0.80592155 | 28.89786721 | 23.28941395 | 0.03460463 | 0.04293796 |
| 27 | 1.25115569 | 0.79926104 | 30.13868277 | 24.08867499 | 0.03317995 | 0.04151328 |
| 28 | 1.26158199 | 0.79265558 | 31.38983846 | 24.88133057 | 0.03185744 | 0.04019078 |
| 29 | 1.27209517 | 0.78610471 | 32.65142045 | 25.66743527 | 0.03062654 | 0.03895987 |
| 30 | 1.28269596 | 0.77960797 | 33.92351562 | 26.44704325 | 0.02947808 | 0.03781141 |
| 31 | 1.29338510 | 0.77316493 | 35.20621158 | 27.22020818 | 0.02840408 | 0.03673741 |
| 32 | 1.30416331 | 0.76677514 | 36.49959668 | 27.98698332 | 0.02739756 | 0.03573090 |
| 33 | 1.31503133 | 0.76043815 | 37.80375999 | 28.74742147 | 0.02645240 | 0.03478573 |
| 34 | 1.35298993 | 0.75415354 | 39.11879132 | 29.50157501 | 0.02556316 | 0.03389650 |
| 35 | 1.33703984 | 0.74792087 | 40.44478125 | 30.24949588 | 0.02472507 | 0.03305840 |
| 36 | 1.34818184 | 0.74173970 | 41.78182109 | 30.99123559 | 0.02393385 | 0.03226719 |
| 37 | 1.35941669 | 0.73560962 | 43.13000293 | 31.72684521 | 0.02318572 | 0.03151905 |
| 38 | 1.37074516 | 0.72953020 | 44.48941962 | 32.45637541 | 0.02247725 | 0.03081059 |
| 39 | 1.38216804 | 0.72350103 | 45.86016479 | 33.17987644 | 0.02180542 | 0.03013875 |
| 40 | 1.39368611 | 0.71752168 | 47.24233283 | 33.89739813 | 0.02116746 | 0.02950079 |
| 41 | 1.40530016 | 0.71159175 | 48.63601893 | 34.60898988 | 0.02056089 | 0.02889423 |
| 42 | 1.41701099 | 0.70571083 | 50.04131909 | 35.31470070 | 0.01998349 | 0.02831682 |
| 43 | 1.42881942 | 0.69987851 | 51.45833008 | 36.01457921 | 0.01943320 | 0.02776653 |
| 44 | 1.44072625 | 0.69409439 | 52.88714950 | 36.70867360 | 0.01890818 | 0.02724152 |
| 45 | 1.45273230 | 0.68835807 | 54.32787575 | 37.39703167 | 0.01840676 | 0.02674009 |
| 46 | 1.46483840 | 0.68266916 | 55.78060805 | 38.07970083 | 0.01792738 | 0.02626071 |
| 47 | 1.47704539 | 0.67702727 | 57.24544645 | 38.75672809 | 0.01746864 | 0.02580197 |
| 48 | 1.48935410 | 0.67143200 | 58.72249183 | 39.42816009 | 0.01702925 | 0.02536258 |
| 49 | 1.50176538 | 0.66588297 | 60.21184593 | 40.09404307 | 0.01660803 | 0.02494136 |
| 50 | 1.51428009 | 0.66037981 | 61.71361131 | 40.75442288 | 0.01620388 | 0.02453721 |

| Rate 1% | A Compound Interest | B Present Value | C Amount of Annuity | D Present Value of Annuity | E Sinking Fund | F Amortization |
|---|---|---|---|---|---|---|
| $n$ | $(1 + i)^n$ | $\dfrac{1}{(1 + i)^n}$ | $s_{\overline{n}\vert i}$ | $a_{\overline{n}\vert i}$ | $\dfrac{1}{s_{\overline{n}\vert i}}$ | $\dfrac{1}{a_{\overline{n}\vert i}}$ |
| 1 | 1.01000000 | 0.99009901 | 1.00000000 | 0.99009901 | 1.00000000 | 1.01000000 |
| 2 | 1.02010000 | 0.98029605 | 2.01000000 | 1.97039506 | 0.49751244 | 0.50751244 |
| 3 | 1.03030100 | 0.97059015 | 3.03010000 | 2.94098521 | 0.33002211 | 0.34002211 |
| 4 | 1.04060401 | 0.96098034 | 4.06040100 | 3.90196555 | 0.24628109 | 0.25628109 |
| 5 | 1.05101005 | 0.95146569 | 5.10100501 | 4.85343124 | 0.19603980 | 0.20603980 |
| 6 | 1.06152015 | 0.94204524 | 6.15201506 | 5.79547647 | 0.16254837 | 0.17254837 |
| 7 | 1.07213535 | 0.93271805 | 7.21353521 | 6.72819453 | 0.13862828 | 0.14862828 |
| 8 | 1.08285671 | 0.92348322 | 8.28567056 | 7.65167775 | 0.12069029 | 0.13069029 |
| 9 | 1.09368527 | 0.91433982 | 9.36852727 | 8.56601758 | 0.10674036 | 0.11674036 |
| 10 | 1.10462213 | 0.90528695 | 10.46221254 | 9.47130453 | 0.09558208 | 0.10558208 |
| 11 | 1.11566835 | 0.89632372 | 11.56683467 | 10.36762825 | 0.08645408 | 0.09645408 |
| 12 | 1.12682503 | 0.88744923 | 12.68250301 | 11.25507747 | 0.07884879 | 0.08884879 |
| 13 | 1.13809328 | 0.87866260 | 13.80932804 | 12.13374007 | 0.07241482 | 0.08241482 |
| 14 | 1.14947421 | 0.86996297 | 14.94742132 | 13.00370304 | 0.06690117 | 0.07690117 |
| 15 | 1.16096896 | 0.86134947 | 16.09689554 | 13.86505252 | 0.06212378 | 0.07212378 |
| 16 | 1.17257864 | 0.85282126 | 17.25786449 | 14.71787378 | 0.05794460 | 0.06794460 |
| 17 | 1.18430443 | 0.84437749 | 18.43044314 | 15.56225127 | 0.05425806 | 0.06425806 |
| 18 | 1.19614748 | 0.83601731 | 19.61474757 | 16.39826858 | 0.05098205 | 0.06098205 |
| 19 | 1.20810895 | 0.82773992 | 20.81089504 | 17.22600850 | 0.04805175 | 0.05805175 |
| 20 | 1.22019004 | 0.81954447 | 22.01900399 | 18.04555297 | 0.04541531 | 0.05541531 |
| 21 | 1.23239194 | 0.81143017 | 23.23919403 | 18.85698313 | 0.04303075 | 0.05303075 |
| 22 | 1.24471586 | 0.80339621 | 24.47158598 | 19.66037934 | 0.04086372 | 0.05086372 |
| 23 | 1.25716302 | 0.79544179 | 25.71630183 | 20.45582113 | 0.03888584 | 0.04888584 |
| 24 | 1.26973465 | 0.78756613 | 26.97346485 | 21.24338726 | 0.03707347 | 0.04707347 |
| 25 | 1.28243200 | 0.77976844 | 28.24319950 | 22.02315570 | 0.03540675 | 0.04540675 |
| 26 | 1.29525631 | 0.77204796 | 29.52563150 | 22.79520366 | 0.03386888 | 0.04386888 |
| 27 | 1.30820888 | 0.76440392 | 30.82088781 | 23.55960759 | 0.03244553 | 0.04244553 |
| 28 | 1.32129097 | 0.75683557 | 32.12909669 | 24.31644316 | 0.03112444 | 0.04112444 |
| 29 | 1.33450388 | 0.74934215 | 33.45038766 | 25.06578530 | 0.02989502 | 0.03989502 |
| 30 | 1.34784892 | 0.74192292 | 34.78489153 | 25.80770822 | 0.02874811 | 0.03874811 |
| 31 | 1.36132740 | 0.73457715 | 36.13274045 | 26.54228537 | 0.02767573 | 0.03767573 |
| 32 | 1.37494068 | 0.72730411 | 37.49406785 | 27.26958947 | 0.02667089 | 0.03667089 |
| 33 | 1.38869009 | 0.72010307 | 38.86900853 | 27.98969255 | 0.02575744 | 0.03572744 |
| 34 | 1.40257699 | 0.71297334 | 40.25769862 | 28.70266589 | 0.02483997 | 0.03483997 |
| 35 | 1.41660276 | 0.70591420 | 41.66027560 | 29.40853009 | 0.02400368 | 0.03400368 |
| 36 | 1.43076878 | 0.69892495 | 43.07687836 | 30.10750504 | 0.02321431 | 0.03321431 |
| 37 | 1.44507647 | 0.69200490 | 44.05764714 | 30.79950994 | 0.02246805 | 0.03246805 |
| 38 | 1.45952724 | 0.68515337 | 45.95272361 | 31.48466330 | 0.02176150 | 0.03176150 |
| 39 | 1.47412251 | 0.67836967 | 47.41225085 | 32.16303298 | 0.02109160 | 0.03109160 |
| 40 | 1.48886373 | 0.67165314 | 48.88637336 | 32.83468611 | 0.02045560 | 0.03045560 |
| 41 | 1.50375237 | 0.66500311 | 50.37523709 | 33.49968922 | 0.01985102 | 0.02985102 |
| 42 | 1.51878989 | 0.65841892 | 51.87898946 | 34.15810814 | 0.01927563 | 0.02927563 |
| 43 | 1.53397779 | 0.65189992 | 53.39777936 | 34.81000806 | 0.01872737 | 0.02872737 |
| 44 | 1.54931757 | 0.64544546 | 54.93175715 | 35.45545352 | 0.01820441 | 0.02820441 |
| 45 | 1.56481075 | 0.63905492 | 56.48107472 | 36.09450844 | 0.01770505 | 0.02770505 |
| 46 | 1.58045885 | 0.63272764 | 58.04588547 | 36.72723608 | 0.01722775 | 0.02722775 |
| 47 | 1.59626344 | 0.62646301 | 59.62634432 | 37.35369909 | 0.01677111 | 0.02677111 |
| 48 | 1.61222608 | 0.62026041 | 61.22260777 | 37.97395949 | 0.01633384 | 0.02633384 |
| 49 | 1.62834834 | 0.61411921 | 62.83483385 | 38.58807871 | 0.01591474 | 0.02591474 |
| 50 | 1.64463182 | 0.60803882 | 64.46318218 | 39.19611753 | 0.01551273 | 0.02551273 |

| Rate $1\frac{1}{4}\%$ | A Compound Interest | B Present Value | C Amount of Annuity | D Present Value of Annuity | E Sinking Fund | F Amortization |
|---|---|---|---|---|---|---|
| $n$ | $(1+i)^n$ | $\dfrac{1}{(1+i)^n}$ | $s_{\overline{n}|i}$ | $a_{\overline{n}|i}$ | $\dfrac{1}{s_{\overline{n}|i}}$ | $\dfrac{1}{a_{\overline{n}|i}}$ |
| 1 | 1.01250000 | 0.98765432 | 1.00000000 | 0.98765432 | 1.00000000 | 1.01250000 |
| 2 | 1.02515625 | 0.97546106 | 2.01250000 | 1.96311538 | 0.49689441 | 0.50939441 |
| 3 | 1.03797070 | 0.96341833 | 3.03765625 | 2.92653371 | 0.32920117 | 0.34170117 |
| 4 | 1.05094534 | 0.95152428 | 4.07562695 | 3.87805798 | 0.24536102 | 0.25786102 |
| 5 | 1.06408215 | 0.93977706 | 5.12657229 | 4.81783504 | 0.19506211 | 0.20756211 |
| 6 | 1.07738318 | 0.92817488 | 6.19065444 | 5.74600992 | 0.16153381 | 0.17403381 |
| 7 | 1.09085047 | 0.91671593 | 7.26803762 | 6.66272585 | 0.13758872 | 0.15008872 |
| 8 | 1.10448610 | 0.90539845 | 8.35888809 | 7.56812429 | 0.11963314 | 0.13213314 |
| 9 | 1.11829218 | 0.89422069 | 9.46337420 | 8.46234498 | 0.10567055 | 0.11817055 |
| 10 | 1.13227083 | 0.88318093 | 10.58166637 | 9.34552591 | 0.09450307 | 0.10700307 |
| 11 | 1.14642422 | 0.87227746 | 11.71393720 | 10.21780337 | 0.08536839 | 0.09786839 |
| 12 | 1.16075452 | 0.86150860 | 12.86036142 | 11.07931197 | 0.07775831 | 0.09025831 |
| 13 | 1.17526395 | 0.85087269 | 14.02111594 | 11.93018466 | 0.07132100 | 0.08382100 |
| 14 | 1.18995475 | 0.84036809 | 15.19637988 | 12.77055275 | 0.06580515 | 0.07830515 |
| 15 | 1.20482918 | 0.82999318 | 16.38633463 | 13.60054592 | 0.06102646 | 0.07352646 |
| 16 | 1.21988955 | 0.81974635 | 17.59116382 | 14.42029227 | 0.05684672 | 0.06934672 |
| 17 | 1.23513817 | 0.80962602 | 18.81105336 | 15.22991829 | 0.05316023 | 0.06566023 |
| 18 | 1.250557739 | 0.79963064 | 20.04619153 | 16.02954893 | 0.04988479 | 0.06238479 |
| 19 | 1.26620961 | 0.78975866 | 21.29676893 | 16.81930759 | 0.04695548 | 0.05945548 |
| 20 | 1.28203723 | 0.78000855 | 22.56297854 | 17.59931613 | 0.04432039 | 0.05682039 |
| 21 | 1.29806270 | 0.77037881 | 23.84501577 | 18.36969495 | 0.04193749 | 0.05443749 |
| 22 | 1.31428848 | 0.76086796 | 25.14307847 | 19.13056291 | 0.03977238 | 0.05227238 |
| 23 | 1.33071709 | 0.75147453 | 26.45736695 | 19.88203744 | 0.03779666 | 0.05029666 |
| 24 | 1.34735105 | 0.74219707 | 27.78808403 | 20.62423451 | 0.03598665 | 0.04848665 |
| 25 | 1.36419294 | 0.73303414 | 29.13543508 | 21.35726865 | 0.03432247 | 0.04682247 |
| 26 | 1.38124535 | 0.72398434 | 30.49962802 | 22.08125299 | 0.03278729 | 0.04528729 |
| 27 | 1.39851092 | 0.71504626 | 31.88087337 | 22.79629925 | 0.03136677 | 0.04386677 |
| 28 | 1.41599230 | 0.70621853 | 33.27938429 | 23.50251778 | 0.03004863 | 0.04254863 |
| 29 | 1.43369221 | 0.69749978 | 34.69537659 | 24.20001756 | 0.02882228 | 0.04132228 |
| 30 | 1.45161336 | 0.68888867 | 36.12906880 | 24.88890623 | 0.02767854 | 0.04017854 |
| 31 | 1.46975853 | 0.68038387 | 37.58068216 | 25.56929010 | 0.02660942 | 0.03910942 |
| 32 | 1.48813051 | 0.67198407 | 39.05044069 | 26.24127418 | 0.02560791 | 0.03810791 |
| 33 | 1.50673214 | 0.66368797 | 40.53857120 | 26.90496215 | 0.02466786 | 0.03716786 |
| 34 | 1.52556629 | 0.65549429 | 42.04530334 | 27.56045644 | 0.02378387 | 0.03628387 |
| 35 | 1.54463587 | 0.64740177 | 43.57086963 | 28.20785822 | 0.02295111 | 0.03545111 |
| 36 | 1.56394382 | 0.63940916 | 45.11550550 | 28.84726737 | 0.02216533 | 0.03466533 |
| 37 | 1.58349312 | 0.63151522 | 46.67944932 | 29.47878259 | 0.02142270 | 0.03392270 |
| 38 | 1.60328678 | 0.62371873 | 48.26294243 | 30.10250133 | 0.02071983 | 0.03321983 |
| 39 | 1.62332787 | 0.61601850 | 49.86622921 | 30.71851983 | 0.02005365 | 0.03255365 |
| 40 | 1.64361946 | 0.60841334 | 51.48955708 | 31.32693316 | 0.01942141 | 0.03192141 |
| 41 | 1.66416471 | 0.60090206 | 53.13317654 | 31.92783522 | 0.01882063 | 0.03132063 |
| 42 | 1.68496677 | 0.59348352 | 54.79734125 | 32.52131874 | 0.01824906 | 0.03074906 |
| 43 | 1.70602885 | 0.58615656 | 56.48230801 | 33.10747530 | 0.01770466 | 0.03020466 |
| 44 | 1.72735421 | 0.57892006 | 58.18833687 | 33.68639536 | 0.01718557 | 0.02968557 |
| 45 | 1.74894614 | 0.57177290 | 59.91569108 | 34.25816825 | 0.01669012 | 0.02919012 |
| 46 | 1.77080797 | 0.56471397 | 61.66463721 | 34.82288222 | 0.01621675 | 0.02871675 |
| 47 | 1.79294306 | 0.55774219 | 63.43544518 | 35.38064224 | 0.01576406 | 0.02826406 |
| 48 | 1.81535485 | 0.55085649 | 65.22838824 | 35.93148091 | 0.01533075 | 0.02783075 |
| 49 | 1.83804679 | 0.54405579 | 67.04374310 | 36.47553670 | 0.01491563 | 0.02741563 |
| 50 | 1.86102237 | 0.53733905 | 68.88178989 | 37.01287575 | 0.01451763 | 0.02701763 |

| Rate $1\frac{1}{2}\%$ | A Compound Interest | B Present Value | C Amount of Annuity | D Present Value of Annuity | E Sinking Fund | F Amortization |
|---|---|---|---|---|---|---|
| $n$ | $(1 + i)^n$ | $\dfrac{1}{(1 + i)^n}$ | $s_{\overline{n}|i}$ | $a_{\overline{n}|i}$ | $\dfrac{1}{s_{\overline{n}|i}}$ | $\dfrac{1}{a_{\overline{n}|i}}$ |
| 1 | 1.01500000 | 0.98522167 | 1.00000000 | 0.98522167 | 1.00000000 | 1.01500000 |
| 2 | 1.03022500 | 0.97066175 | 2.01500000 | 1.95588342 | 0.49627792 | 0.51127792 |
| 3 | 1.04567838 | 0.95631699 | 3.04522500 | 2.91220042 | 0.32838296 | 0.34338296 |
| 4 | 1.06136355 | 0.94218423 | 4.09090337 | 3.85438465 | 0.24444479 | 0.25944479 |
| 5 | 1.07728400 | 0.92826033 | 5.15226693 | 4.78264497 | 0.19408932 | 0.20908932 |
| 6 | 1.09344326 | 0.91454219 | 6.22955093 | 5.69718717 | 0.16052521 | 0.17552521 |
| 7 | 1.10984491 | 0.90102679 | 7.32299419 | 6.59821396 | 0.13655616 | 0.15155616 |
| 8 | 1.12649259 | 0.88771112 | 8.43283911 | 7.48592508 | 0.11858402 | 0.13358402 |
| 9 | 1.14338998 | 0.87459224 | 9.55933169 | 8.36051732 | 0.10460982 | 0.11960982 |
| 10 | 1.16054083 | 0.86166723 | 10.70272167 | 9.22218455 | 0.09343418 | 0.10843418 |
| 11 | 1.17794894 | 0.84893323 | 11.86326249 | 10.07111779 | 0.08429384 | 0.09929384 |
| 12 | 1.19561817 | 0.83638742 | 13.04121143 | 10.90750521 | 0.07667999 | 0.09167999 |
| 13 | 1.21355244 | 0.82402702 | 14.23682960 | 11.73153222 | 0.07024036 | 0.08524036 |
| 14 | 1.23175573 | 0.81184928 | 15.45038205 | 12.54338150 | 0.06472332 | 0.07972332 |
| 15 | 1.25023207 | 0.79985150 | 16.68213778 | 13.34323301 | 0.05994436 | 0.07494436 |
| 16 | 1.26898555 | 0.78803104 | 17.93236984 | 14.13126405 | 0.05576508 | 0.07076508 |
| 17 | 1.28802033 | 0.77638526 | 19.20135539 | 14.90764931 | 0.05207966 | 0.06707966 |
| 18 | 1.30734064 | 0.76491159 | 20.48937572 | 15.67256089 | 0.04880578 | 0.06380578 |
| 19 | 1.32695075 | 0.75360747 | 21.79671636 | 16.42616837 | 0.04587847 | 0.06087847 |
| 20 | 1.34685501 | 0.74247042 | 23.12366710 | 17.16863879 | 0.04324574 | 0.05824574 |
| 21 | 1.36705783 | 0.73149795 | 24.47052211 | 17.90013673 | 0.04086550 | 0.05586550 |
| 22 | 1.38756370 | 0.72068763 | 25.83757994 | 18.62082437 | 0.03870332 | 0.05370332 |
| 23 | 1.40837715 | 0.71003708 | 27.22514364 | 19.33086145 | 0.03673075 | 0.05173075 |
| 24 | 1.42950281 | 0.69954392 | 28.63352080 | 20.03040537 | 0.03492410 | 0.04992410 |
| 25 | 1.45094535 | 0.68920583 | 30.06302361 | 20.71961120 | 0.03326345 | 0.04826345 |
| 26 | 1.47270953 | 0.67902052 | 31.51396896 | 21.39863172 | 0.03173196 | 0.04673196 |
| 27 | 1.49480018 | 0.66898574 | 32.98667850 | 22.06761746 | 0.03031527 | 0.04531527 |
| 28 | 1.51722218 | 0.65909925 | 34.48147867 | 22.72671671 | 0.02900108 | 0.04400108 |
| 29 | 1.53998051 | 0.64935887 | 35.99870085 | 23.37607558 | 0.02777878 | 0.04277878 |
| 30 | 1.56308022 | 0.63976243 | 37.53868137 | 24.01583801 | 0.02663919 | 0.04163919 |
| 31 | 1.58652642 | 0.63030781 | 39.10176159 | 24.64614582 | 0.02557430 | 0.04057430 |
| 32 | 1.61032432 | 0.62099292 | 40.68828801 | 25.26713874 | 0.02457710 | 0.03957710 |
| 33 | 1.63447918 | 0.61181568 | 42.29861233 | 25.87895442 | 0.02364144 | 0.03864144 |
| 34 | 1.65899637 | 0.60277407 | 43.93309152 | 26.48172849 | 0.02276189 | 0.03776189 |
| 35 | 1.68388132 | 0.59386608 | 45.59208789 | 27.07559458 | 0.02193363 | 0.03693363 |
| 36 | 1.70913954 | 0.58508974 | 47.27596921 | 27.66068431 | 0.02115240 | 0.03615240 |
| 37 | 1.73477663 | 0.57644309 | 48.98510874 | 28.23712740 | 0.02041437 | 0.03541437 |
| 38 | 1.76079828 | 0.56792423 | 50.71988538 | 28.80505163 | 0.01971613 | 0.03471613 |
| 39 | 1.78721025 | 0.55953126 | 52.48068366 | 29.36458288 | 0.01905463 | 0.03405463 |
| 40 | 1.81401841 | 0.55126232 | 54.26789391 | 29.91584520 | 0.01842710 | 0.03342710 |
| 41 | 1.84122868 | 0.54311559 | 56.08191232 | 30.45896079 | 0.01783106 | 0.03283106 |
| 42 | 1.86884712 | 0.53508925 | 57.92314100 | 30.99405004 | 0.01726426 | 0.03226426 |
| 43 | 1.89687982 | 0.52718153 | 59.79198812 | 31.52123157 | 0.01672465 | 0.03172465 |
| 44 | 1.92533302 | 0.51939067 | 61.68886794 | 32.04062223 | 0.01621038 | 0.03121038 |
| 45 | 1.95421301 | 0.51171494 | 63.61420096 | 32.55233718 | 0.01571976 | 0.03071976 |
| 46 | 1.98352621 | 0.50415265 | 65.56841398 | 33.05648983 | 0.01525125 | 0.03025125 |
| 47 | 2.01327910 | 0.49670212 | 67.55194018 | 33.55319195 | 0.01480342 | 0.02980342 |
| 48 | 2.04347829 | 0.48936170 | 69.56521929 | 34.04255365 | 0.01437500 | 0.02937500 |
| 49 | 2.07413046 | 0.48212975 | 71.60869758 | 34.52468339 | 0.01396478 | 0.02896478 |
| 50 | 2.10524242 | 0.47500468 | 73.68282804 | 34.99968807 | 0.01357168 | 0.02857168 |

| Rate $1\frac{3}{4}\%$ | A<br>Compound<br>Interest | B<br>Present<br>Value | C<br>Amount of<br>Annuity | D<br>Present Value<br>of Annuity | E<br>Sinking<br>Fund | F<br>Amortization |
|---|---|---|---|---|---|---|
| $n$ | $(1 + i)^n$ | $\dfrac{1}{(1 + i)^n}$ | $s_{\overline{n}\rceil i}$ | $a_{\overline{n}\rceil i}$ | $\dfrac{1}{s_{\overline{n}\rceil i}}$ | $\dfrac{1}{a_{\overline{n}\rceil i}}$ |
| 1 | 1.01750000 | 0.98280098 | 1.00000000 | 0.98280098 | 1.00000000 | 1.01750000 |
| 2 | 1.03530625 | 0.96589777 | 2.01750000 | 1.94869875 | 0.49566295 | 0.51316295 |
| 3 | 1.05342411 | 0.94928528 | 3.05280625 | 2.89798403 | 0.32756746 | 0.34506746 |
| 4 | 1.07185903 | 0.93295851 | 4.10623036 | 3.83094254 | 0.24353237 | 0.26103237 |
| 5 | 1.09061656 | 0.91691254 | 5.17808939 | 4.74785508 | 0.19312142 | 0.21062142 |
| 6 | 1.10970235 | 0.90114254 | 6.26870596 | 5.64899762 | 0.15952256 | 0.17702256 |
| 7 | 1.12912215 | 0.88564378 | 7.37840831 | 6.53464139 | 0.13553059 | 0.15303059 |
| 8 | 1.14888178 | 0.87041157 | 8.50753045 | 7.40505297 | 0.11754292 | 0.13504292 |
| 9 | 1.16898721 | 0.85544135 | 9.65641224 | 8.26049432 | 0.10355813 | 0.12105813 |
| 10 | 1.18944449 | 0.84072860 | 10.82539945 | 9.10122291 | 0.09237534 | 0.10987534 |
| 11 | 1.21025977 | 0.82626889 | 12.01484394 | 9.92749181 | 0.08323038 | 0.10073038 |
| 12 | 1.23143931 | 0.81205788 | 13.22510371 | 10.73954969 | 0.07561377 | 0.09311377 |
| 13 | 1.25298950 | 0.79809128 | 14.45654303 | 11.53764097 | 0.06917283 | 0.08667283 |
| 14 | 1.27491682 | 0.78436490 | 15.70953253 | 12.32200587 | 0.06365562 | 0.08115562 |
| 15 | 1.29722786 | 0.77087459 | 16.98444935 | 13.09288046 | 0.05887739 | 0.07637739 |
| 16 | 1.31992935 | 0.75761631 | 18.28167721 | 13.85049677 | 0.05469958 | 0.07219958 |
| 17 | 1.34302811 | 0.74458605 | 19.60160656 | 14.59508282 | 0.05101623 | 0.06851623 |
| 18 | 1.36653111 | 0.73177990 | 20.94463468 | 15.32686272 | 0.04774492 | 0.06524492 |
| 19 | 1.39044540 | 0.71919401 | 22.31116578 | 16.04605673 | 0.04482061 | 0.06232061 |
| 20 | 1.41477820 | 0.70682458 | 23.70161119 | 16.75288130 | 0.04219122 | 0.05969122 |
| 21 | 1.43953681 | 0.69466789 | 25.11638938 | 17.44754919 | 0.03981464 | 0.05731464 |
| 22 | 1.46472871 | 0.68272028 | 26.55592620 | 18.13026948 | 0.03765638 | 0.05515638 |
| 23 | 1.49036146 | 0.67097817 | 28.02065490 | 18.80124764 | 0.03568796 | 0.05318796 |
| 24 | 1.51644279 | 0.65943800 | 29.51101637 | 19.46068565 | 0.03388565 | 0.05138565 |
| 25 | 1.54298054 | 0.64809632 | 31.02745915 | 20.10878196 | 0.03222952 | 0.04972952 |
| 26 | 1.56998269 | 0.63694970 | 32.57043969 | 20.74573166 | 0.03070269 | 0.04820269 |
| 27 | 1.59745739 | 0.62599479 | 34.14042238 | 21.37172644 | 0.02929079 | 0.04679079 |
| 28 | 1.62541290 | 0.61522829 | 35.73787977 | 21.98695474 | 0.02798151 | 0.04548151 |
| 29 | 1.65385762 | 0.60464697 | 37.36329267 | 22.59160171 | 0.02676424 | 0.04426424 |
| 30 | 1.68280013 | 0.59424764 | 39.01715029 | 23.18584934 | 0.02562975 | 0.04312975 |
| 31 | 1.71224913 | 0.58402716 | 40.69995042 | 23.76987650 | 0.02457005 | 0.04207005 |
| 32 | 1.74221349 | 0.57398247 | 42.41219955 | 24.34385897 | 0.02357812 | 0.04107812 |
| 33 | 1.77270223 | 0.56411053 | 44.15441305 | 24.90796951 | 0.02264779 | 0.04014779 |
| 34 | 1.80372452 | 0.55440839 | 45.92711527 | 25.46237789 | 0.02177363 | 0.03927363 |
| 35 | 1.83528970 | 0.54487311 | 47.73083979 | 26.00725100 | 0.02095082 | 0.03845082 |
| 36 | 1.86740727 | 0.53550183 | 49.56612949 | 26.54275283 | 0.02017507 | 0.03767507 |
| 37 | 1.90008689 | 0.52629172 | 51.43353675 | 27.06904455 | 0.01944257 | 0.03694257 |
| 38 | 1.93333841 | 0.51724002 | 53.33362365 | 27.58628457 | 0.01874990 | 0.03624990 |
| 39 | 1.96717184 | 0.50834400 | 55.26696206 | 28.09462857 | 0.01809399 | 0.03559399 |
| 40 | 2.00159734 | 0.49960098 | 57.23413390 | 28.59422955 | 0.01747209 | 0.03497209 |
| 41 | 2.03662530 | 0.49100834 | 59.23573124 | 29.08523789 | 0.01688170 | 0.03438170 |
| 42 | 2.07226624 | 0.48256348 | 61.27235654 | 29.56780136 | 0.01632057 | 0.03382057 |
| 43 | 2.10853090 | 0.47426386 | 63.34462278 | 30.04206522 | 0.01578666 | 0.03328666 |
| 44 | 2.14543019 | 0.46610699 | 65.45315367 | 30.50817221 | 0.01527810 | 0.03277810 |
| 45 | 2.18297522 | 0.45809040 | 67.59858386 | 30.96626261 | 0.01479321 | 0.03229321 |
| 46 | 2.22117728 | 0.45021170 | 69.78155908 | 31.41647431 | 0.01433043 | 0.03183043 |
| 47 | 2.26004789 | 0.44246850 | 72.00273637 | 31.85894281 | 0.01388836 | 0.03138836 |
| 48 | 2.29959872 | 0.43485848 | 74.26278425 | 32.29380129 | 0.01346569 | 0.03096569 |
| 49 | 2.33984170 | 0.42737934 | 76.56238298 | 32.72118063 | 0.01306124 | 0.03056124 |
| 50 | 2.38078893 | 0.42002883 | 78.90222468 | 33.14120946 | 0.01267391 | 0.03017391 |

| Rate 2% | A Compound Interest | B Present Value | C Amount of Annuity | D Present Value of Annuity | E Sinking Fund | F Amortization |
|---|---|---|---|---|---|---|
| $n$ | $(1 + i)^n$ | $\dfrac{1}{(1 + i)^n}$ | $s_{\overline{n}\rvert i}$ | $a_{\overline{n}\rvert i}$ | $\dfrac{1}{s_{\overline{n}\rvert i}}$ | $\dfrac{1}{a_{\overline{n}\rvert i}}$ |
| 1 | 1.02000000 | 0.98039216 | 1.00000000 | 0.98039216 | 1.00000000 | 1.02000000 |
| 2 | 1.04040000 | 0.96116878 | 2.02000000 | 1.94156094 | 0.49504950 | 0.51504950 |
| 3 | 1.06120800 | 0.94232233 | 3.06040000 | 2.88388327 | 0.32675467 | 0.34675467 |
| 4 | 1.08243216 | 0.92384543 | 4.12160800 | 3.80772870 | 0.24262375 | 0.26262375 |
| 5 | 1.10408080 | 0.90573081 | 5.20404016 | 4.71345951 | 0.19215839 | 0.21215839 |
| 6 | 1.12616242 | 0.88797138 | 6.30812096 | 5.60143089 | 0.15852581 | 0.17852581 |
| 7 | 1.14868567 | 0.87056018 | 7.43428338 | 6.47199107 | 0.13451196 | 0.15451196 |
| 8 | 1.17165938 | 0.85349037 | 8.58296905 | 7.32548144 | 0.11650980 | 0.13650980 |
| 9 | 1.19509257 | 0.83675527 | 9.75462843 | 8.16223671 | 0.10251544 | 0.12251544 |
| 10 | 1.21899442 | 0.82034830 | 10.94972100 | 8.98258501 | 0.09132653 | 0.11132653 |
| 11 | 1.24337431 | 0.80426304 | 12.16871542 | 9.78684805 | 0.08217794 | 0.10217794 |
| 12 | 1.26824179 | 0.78849318 | 13.41208973 | 10.57534122 | 0.07455960 | 0.09455960 |
| 13 | 1.29360663 | 0.77303253 | 14.68033152 | 11.34837375 | 0.06811835 | 0.08811835 |
| 14 | 1.31947876 | 0.75787502 | 15.97393815 | 12.10624877 | 0.06260197 | 0.08260197 |
| 15 | 1.34586834 | 0.74301473 | 17.29341692 | 12.84926350 | 0.05782547 | 0.07782547 |
| 16 | 1.37278571 | 0.72844581 | 18.63928525 | 13.57770931 | 0.05365013 | 0.07365013 |
| 17 | 1.40024142 | 0.71416256 | 20.01207096 | 14.29187188 | 0.04996984 | 0.06996984 |
| 18 | 1.42824625 | 0.70015937 | 21.41231238 | 14.99203125 | 0.04670210 | 0.06670210 |
| 19 | 1.45681117 | 0.68643076 | 22.84055863 | 15.67846201 | 0.04378177 | 0.06378177 |
| 20 | 1.48594740 | 0.67297133 | 24.29736980 | 16.35143334 | 0.04115672 | 0.06115672 |
| 21 | 1.51566634 | 0.65977582 | 25.78331719 | 17.01120916 | 0.03878477 | 0.05878477 |
| 22 | 1.54597967 | 0.64683904 | 27.29898354 | 17.65804820 | 0.03663140 | 0.05663140 |
| 23 | 1.57689926 | 0.63415592 | 28.84496321 | 18.29220412 | 0.03466810 | 0.05466810 |
| 24 | 1.60843725 | 0.62172149 | 30.42186247 | 18.91392560 | 0.03287110 | 0.05287110 |
| 25 | 1.64060599 | 0.60953087 | 32.03029972 | 19.52345647 | 0.03122044 | 0.05122044 |
| 26 | 1.67341811 | 0.59757928 | 33.67090572 | 20.12103576 | 0.02969923 | 0.04969923 |
| 27 | 1.70688648 | 0.58586204 | 35.34432383 | 20.70689780 | 0.02829309 | 0.04829309 |
| 28 | 1.74102421 | 0.57437455 | 37.05121031 | 21.28127236 | 0.02698967 | 0.04698967 |
| 29 | 1.77584469 | 0.56311231 | 38.79223451 | 21.84438466 | 0.02577836 | 0.04577836 |
| 30 | 1.81136158 | 0.55207089 | 40.56807921 | 22.39645555 | 0.02464992 | 0.04464992 |
| 31 | 1.84758882 | 0.54124597 | 42.37944079 | 22.93770152 | 0.02359635 | 0.04359635 |
| 32 | 1.88454059 | 0.53063330 | 44.22702961 | 23.46833482 | 0.02261061 | 0.04261061 |
| 33 | 1.92223140 | 0.52022873 | 46.11157020 | 23.98856355 | 0.02168653 | 0.04168653 |
| 34 | 1.96067603 | 0.51002817 | 48.03380160 | 24.49859172 | 0.02081867 | 0.04081867 |
| 35 | 1.99988955 | 0.50002761 | 49.99447763 | 24.99861933 | 0.02000221 | 0.04000221 |
| 36 | 2.03988734 | 0.49022315 | 51.99436719 | 25.48884248 | 0.01923285 | 0.03923285 |
| 37 | 2.08068509 | 0.48061093 | 54.03425453 | 25.96945341 | 0.01850678 | 0.03850678 |
| 38 | 2.12229879 | 0.47118719 | 56.11493962 | 26.44064060 | 0.01782057 | 0.03782057 |
| 39 | 2.16474477 | 0.46194822 | 58.23723841 | 26.90258883 | 0.01717114 | 0.03717114 |
| 40 | 2.20803966 | 0.45289042 | 60.40198318 | 27.35547924 | 0.01655575 | 0.03655575 |
| 41 | 2.25220046 | 0.44401021 | 62.61002284 | 27.79948945 | 0.01597188 | 0.03597188 |
| 42 | 2.29724447 | 0.43530413 | 64.86222330 | 28.23479358 | 0.01541729 | 0.03541729 |
| 43 | 2.34318936 | 0.42676875 | 67.15946777 | 28.66156233 | 0.01488993 | 0.03488993 |
| 44 | 2.39005314 | 0.41840074 | 69.50265712 | 29.07996307 | 0.01438794 | 0.03438794 |
| 45 | 2.43785421 | 0.41019680 | 71.89271027 | 29.49015987 | 0.01390962 | 0.03390962 |
| 46 | 2.48661129 | 0.40215373 | 74.33056447 | 29.89231360 | 0.01345342 | 0.03345342 |
| 47 | 2.53634352 | 0.39426836 | 76.81717576 | 30.28658196 | 0.01301792 | 0.03301792 |
| 48 | 2.58707039 | 0.38653761 | 79.35351927 | 30.67311957 | 0.01260184 | 0.03260184 |
| 49 | 2.63881179 | 0.37895844 | 81.94058966 | 31.05207801 | 0.01220396 | 0.03220396 |
| 50 | 2.69158803 | 0.37152788 | 84.57940145 | 31.42360589 | 0.01182321 | 0.03182321 |

| Rate $2\frac{1}{2}\%$ | A Compound Interest | B Present Value | C Amount of Annuity | D Present Value of Annuity | E Sinking Fund | F Amortization |
|---|---|---|---|---|---|---|
| $n$ | $(1 + i)^n$ | $\dfrac{1}{(1 + i)^n}$ | $s_{\overline{n}|i}$ | $a_{\overline{n}|i}$ | $\dfrac{1}{s_{\overline{n}|i}}$ | $\dfrac{1}{a_{\overline{n}|i}}$ |
| 1 | 1.02500000 | 0.97560976 | 1.00000000 | 0.97560976 | 1.00000000 | 1.02500000 |
| 2 | 1.05062500 | 0.95181440 | 2.02500000 | 1.92742415 | 0.49382716 | 0.51882716 |
| 3 | 1.07689063 | 0.92859941 | 3.07562500 | 2.85602356 | 0.32513717 | 0.35013717 |
| 4 | 1.10381289 | 0.90595064 | 4.15251562 | 3.76197421 | 0.24081788 | 0.26581788 |
| 5 | 1.13140821 | 0.88385429 | 5.25632852 | 4.64582850 | 0.19024686 | 0.21524686 |
| 6 | 1.15969342 | 0.86229687 | 6.38773673 | 5.50812536 | 0.15654997 | 0.18154997 |
| 7 | 1.18868575 | 0.84126524 | 7.54753015 | 6.34939060 | 0.13249543 | 0.15749543 |
| 8 | 1.21840290 | 0.82074657 | 8.73611590 | 7.17013717 | 0.11446735 | 0.13946735 |
| 9 | 1.24886297 | 0.80072836 | 9.95451880 | 7.97086553 | 0.10045689 | 0.12545689 |
| 10 | 1.28008454 | 0.78119840 | 11.20338177 | 8.75206393 | 0.08925876 | 0.11425876 |
| 11 | 1.31208666 | 0.76214478 | 12.48346631 | 9.51420871 | 0.08010596 | 0.10510596 |
| 12 | 1.34488882 | 0.74355589 | 13.79555297 | 10.25776460 | 0.07248713 | 0.09748713 |
| 13 | 1.37851104 | 0.72542038 | 15.14044179 | 10.98318497 | 0.06604827 | 0.09104827 |
| 14 | 1.41297382 | 0.70772720 | 16.51895284 | 11.69091217 | 0.06053652 | 0.08553652 |
| 15 | 1.44829817 | 0.69046556 | 17.93192666 | 12.38137773 | 0.05576646 | 0.08076646 |
| 16 | 1.48450562 | 0.67362493 | 19.38022483 | 13.05500266 | 0.05159899 | 0.07659899 |
| 17 | 1.52161826 | 0.65719506 | 20.86473045 | 13.71219772 | 0.04792777 | 0.07292777 |
| 18 | 1.55965872 | 0.64116591 | 22.38634871 | 14.35336363 | 0.04467008 | 0.06967008 |
| 19 | 1.59865019 | 0.62552772 | 23.94600743 | 14.97889134 | 0.04176062 | 0.06676062 |
| 20 | 1.63861644 | 0.61027094 | 25.54465761 | 15.58916229 | 0.03914713 | 0.06414713 |
| 21 | 1.67958185 | 0.59538629 | 27.18327405 | 16.18454857 | 0.03678733 | 0.06178733 |
| 22 | 1.72157140 | 0.58086467 | 28.86285590 | 16.76541324 | 0.03464661 | 0.05964661 |
| 23 | 1.76461068 | 0.56669724 | 30.58442730 | 17.33211048 | 0.03269638 | 0.05769638 |
| 24 | 1.80872595 | 0.55287535 | 32.34903798 | 17.88498583 | 0.03091282 | 0.05591282 |
| 25 | 1.85394410 | 0.53939059 | 34.15776393 | 18.42437642 | 0.02927592 | 0.05427592 |
| 26 | 1.90029270 | 0.52623472 | 36.01170803 | 18.95061114 | 0.02776875 | 0.05276875 |
| 27 | 1.94780002 | 0.51339973 | 37.91200073 | 19.46401087 | 0.02637687 | 0.05137687 |
| 28 | 1.99649502 | 0.50087778 | 39.85980075 | 19.96488866 | 0.02508793 | 0.05008793 |
| 29 | 2.04640739 | 0.48866125 | 41.85629577 | 20.45354991 | 0.02389127 | 0.04889127 |
| 30 | 2.09756758 | 0.47674269 | 43.90270316 | 20.93029259 | 0.02277764 | 0.04777764 |
| 31 | 2.15000677 | 0.46511481 | 46.00027074 | 21.39540741 | 0.02173900 | 0.04673900 |
| 32 | 2.20375694 | 0.45377055 | 48.15027751 | 21.84917796 | 0.02076831 | 0.04576831 |
| 33 | 2.25885086 | 0.44270298 | 50.35403445 | 22.29188094 | 0.01985938 | 0.04485938 |
| 34 | 2.31532213 | 0.43190534 | 52.61288531 | 22.72378628 | 0.01900675 | 0.04400675 |
| 35 | 2.37320519 | 0.42137107 | 54.92820744 | 23.14515734 | 0.01820558 | 0.04320558 |
| 36 | 2.43253532 | 0.41109372 | 57.30141263 | 23.55625107 | 0.01745158 | 0.04245158 |
| 37 | 2.49334870 | 0.40106705 | 59.73394794 | 23.95731812 | 0.01674090 | 0.04174090 |
| 38 | 2.55568242 | 0.39128492 | 62.22729664 | 24.34860304 | 0.01607012 | 0.04107012 |
| 39 | 2.61957448 | 0.38174139 | 64.78297906 | 24.73034443 | 0.01543615 | 0.04043615 |
| 40 | 2.68506384 | 0.37243062 | 67.40255354 | 25.10277505 | 0.01483623 | 0.03983623 |
| 41 | 2.75219043 | 0.36334695 | 70.08761737 | 25.46612200 | 0.01426786 | 0.03926786 |
| 42 | 2.82099520 | 0.35448483 | 72.83980781 | 25.82060683 | 0.01372876 | 0.03872876 |
| 43 | 2.89152008 | 0.34583886 | 75.66080300 | 26.16644569 | 0.01321688 | 0.03821688 |
| 44 | 2.96380808 | 0.33740376 | 78.55232308 | 26.50384945 | 0.01273037 | 0.03773037 |
| 45 | 3.03790328 | 0.32917440 | 81.51613116 | 26.83302386 | 0.01226751 | 0.03726751 |
| 46 | 3.11385086 | 0.32114576 | 84.55403443 | 27.15416962 | 0.01182676 | 0.03682676 |
| 47 | 3.19169713 | 0.31331294 | 87.66788530 | 27.46748255 | 0.01140669 | 0.03640669 |
| 48 | 3.27148956 | 0.30567116 | 90.85958243 | 27.77315371 | 0.01100599 | 0.03600599 |
| 49 | 3.35327680 | 0.29821576 | 94.13107199 | 28.07136947 | 0.01062348 | 0.03562348 |
| 50 | 3.43710872 | 0.29094221 | 97.48434879 | 28.36231168 | 0.01025806 | 0.03525806 |

| Rate 3% | A Compound Interest | B Present Value | C Amount of Annuity | D Present Value of Annuity | E Sinking Fund | F Amortization |
|---|---|---|---|---|---|---|
| $n$ | $(1 + i)^n$ | $\dfrac{1}{(1 + i)^n}$ | $s_{\overline{n}|i}$ | $a_{\overline{n}|i}$ | $\dfrac{1}{s_{\overline{n}|i}}$ | $\dfrac{1}{a_{\overline{n}|i}}$ |
| 1 | 1.03000000 | 0.97087379 | 1.00000000 | 0.97087379 | 1.00000000 | 1.03000000 |
| 2 | 1.06090000 | 0.94259591 | 2.03000000 | 1.91346970 | 0.49261084 | 0.52261084 |
| 3 | 1.09272700 | 0.91514166 | 3.09090000 | 2.82861135 | 0.32353036 | 0.35353036 |
| 4 | 1.12550881 | 0.88848705 | 4.18362700 | 3.71709840 | 0.23902705 | 0.26902705 |
| 5 | 1.15927407 | 0.86260878 | 5.30913581 | 4.57970719 | 0.18835457 | 0.21835457 |
| 6 | 1.19405230 | 0.83748426 | 6.46840988 | 5.41719144 | 0.15459750 | 0.18459750 |
| 7 | 1.22987387 | 0.81309151 | 7.66246218 | 6.23028296 | 0.13050635 | 0.16050635 |
| 8 | 1.26677008 | 0.78940923 | 8.89233605 | 7.01969219 | 0.11245639 | 0.14245639 |
| 9 | 1.30477318 | 0.76641673 | 10.15910613 | 7.78610892 | 0.09843386 | 0.12843386 |
| 10 | 1.34391638 | 0.74409391 | 11.46387931 | 8.53020284 | 0.08723051 | 0.11723051 |
| 11 | 1.38423387 | 0.72242128 | 12.80779569 | 9.25262411 | 0.07807745 | 0.10807745 |
| 12 | 1.42576089 | 0.70137988 | 14.19202956 | 9.95400399 | 0.07046209 | 0.10046209 |
| 13 | 1.46853371 | 0.68095134 | 15.61779045 | 10.63495533 | 0.06402954 | 0.09402954 |
| 14 | 1.51258972 | 0.66111781 | 17.08632416 | 11.29607314 | 0.05852634 | 0.08852634 |
| 15 | 1.55796742 | 0.64186195 | 18.59891389 | 11.93793509 | 0.05376658 | 0.08376658 |
| 16 | 1.60470644 | 0.62316694 | 20.15688130 | 12.56110203 | 0.04961085 | 0.07961085 |
| 17 | 1.65284763 | 0.60501645 | 21.76158774 | 13.16611847 | 0.04595253 | 0.07595253 |
| 18 | 1.70243306 | 0.58739461 | 23.41443537 | 13.75351308 | 0.04270870 | 0.07270870 |
| 19 | 1.75350605 | 0.57028603 | 25.11686844 | 14.32379911 | 0.03981388 | 0.06981388 |
| 20 | 1.80611123 | 0.55367575 | 26.87037449 | 14.87747486 | 0.03721571 | 0.06721571 |
| 21 | 1.86029457 | 0.53754928 | 28.67648572 | 15.41502414 | 0.03487178 | 0.06487178 |
| 22 | 1.91610341 | 0.52189250 | 30.53678030 | 15.93691664 | 0.03274739 | 0.06274739 |
| 23 | 1.97358651 | 0.50669175 | 32.45288370 | 16.44360839 | 0.03081390 | 0.06081390 |
| 24 | 2.03279411 | 0.49193374 | 34.42647022 | 16.93554212 | 0.02904742 | 0.05904742 |
| 25 | 2.09377793 | 0.47760557 | 36.45926432 | 17.41314769 | 0.02742787 | 0.05742787 |
| 26 | 2.15659127 | 0.46369473 | 38.55304225 | 17.87684242 | 0.02593829 | 0.05593829 |
| 27 | 2.22128901 | 0.45018906 | 40.70963352 | 18.32703147 | 0.02456421 | 0.05456421 |
| 28 | 2.28792768 | 0.43707675 | 42.93092252 | 18.76410823 | 0.02329323 | 0.05329323 |
| 29 | 2.35656551 | 0.42434636 | 45.21885020 | 19.18845459 | 0.02211467 | 0.05211467 |
| 30 | 2.42726247 | 0.41198676 | 47.57541571 | 19.60044135 | 0.02101926 | 0.05101926 |
| 31 | 2.50008035 | 0.39998715 | 50.00267818 | 20.00042849 | 0.01999893 | 0.04999893 |
| 32 | 2.57508276 | 0.38833703 | 52.50275852 | 20.38876553 | 0.01904662 | 0.04904662 |
| 33 | 2.65233524 | 0.37702625 | 55.07784128 | 20.76579178 | 0.01815612 | 0.04815612 |
| 34 | 2.73190530 | 0.36604490 | 57.73017652 | 21.13183668 | 0.01732196 | 0.04732196 |
| 35 | 2.81386245 | 0.35538340 | 60.46208181 | 21.48722007 | 0.01653929 | 0.04653929 |
| 36 | 2.89827833 | 0.34503243 | 63.27594427 | 21.83225250 | 0.01580379 | 0.04580379 |
| 37 | 2.98522668 | 0.33498294 | 66.17422259 | 22.16723544 | 0.01511162 | 0.04511162 |
| 38 | 3.07478348 | 0.32522615 | 69.15944927 | 22.49246159 | 0.01445934 | 0.04445934 |
| 39 | 3.16702698 | 0.31575355 | 72.23423275 | 22.80821513 | 0.01384385 | 0.04384385 |
| 40 | 3.26203779 | 0.30655684 | 75.40125973 | 23.11477197 | 0.01326238 | 0.04326238 |
| 41 | 3.35989893 | 0.29762800 | 78.66329753 | 23.41239997 | 0.01271241 | 0.04271241 |
| 42 | 3.46069589 | 0.28895922 | 82.02319645 | 23.70135920 | 0.01219167 | 0.04219167 |
| 43 | 3.56451677 | 0.28054294 | 85.48389234 | 23.98190213 | 0.01169811 | 0.04169811 |
| 44 | 3.67145227 | 0.27237178 | 89.04840911 | 24.25427392 | 0.01122985 | 0.04122985 |
| 45 | 3.78159584 | 0.26443862 | 92.71986139 | 24.51871254 | 0.01078518 | 0.04078518 |
| 46 | 3.89504372 | 0.25673653 | 96.50145723 | 24.77544907 | 0.01036254 | 0.04036254 |
| 47 | 4.01189503 | 0.24925876 | 100.39650095 | 25.02470783 | 0.00996051 | 0.03996051 |
| 48 | 4.13225188 | 0.24199880 | 104.40839598 | 25.26670664 | 0.00957777 | 0.03957777 |
| 49 | 4.25621944 | 0.23495029 | 108.54064785 | 25.50165693 | 0.00921314 | 0.03921314 |
| 50 | 4.38390602 | 0.22810708 | 112.79686729 | 25.72976401 | 0.00886549 | 0.03886549 |

| Rate 3½% | A<br>Compound<br>Interest | B<br>Present<br>Value | C<br>Amount of<br>Annuity | D<br>Present Value<br>of Annuity | E<br>Sinking<br>Fund | F<br>Amortization |
|---|---|---|---|---|---|---|
| $n$ | $(1 + i)^n$ | $\dfrac{1}{(1 + i)^n}$ | $s_{\overline{n}|i}$ | $a_{\overline{n}|i}$ | $\dfrac{1}{s_{\overline{n}|i}}$ | $\dfrac{1}{a_{\overline{n}|i}}$ |
| 1 | 1.03500000 | 0.96618357 | 1.00000000 | 0.96618357 | 1.00000000 | 1.03500000 |
| 2 | 1.07122500 | 0.93351070 | 2.03500000 | 1.89969428 | 0.49140049 | 0.52640049 |
| 3 | 1.10871788 | 0.90194271 | 3.10622500 | 2.80163698 | 0.32193418 | 0.35693418 |
| 4 | 1.14752300 | 0.87144223 | 4.21494287 | 3.67307921 | 0.23725114 | 0.27225114 |
| 5 | 1.18768631 | 0.84197317 | 5.36246588 | 4.51505238 | 0.18648137 | 0.22148137 |
| 6 | 1.22925533 | 0.81350064 | 6.55015218 | 5.32855302 | 0.15266821 | 0.18766821 |
| 7 | 1.27227926 | 0.78599096 | 7.77940751 | 6.11454398 | 0.12854449 | 0.16354449 |
| 8 | 1.31680904 | 0.75941156 | 9.05168677 | 6.87395554 | 0.11047665 | 0.14547665 |
| 9 | 1.36289735 | 0.73373097 | 10.36849581 | 7.60768651 | 0.09644601 | 0.13144601 |
| 10 | 1.41059876 | 0.70891881 | 11.73139316 | 8.31660532 | 0.08524137 | 0.12024137 |
| 11 | 1.45996972 | 0.68494571 | 13.14199192 | 9.00155104 | 0.07609197 | 0.11109197 |
| 12 | 1.51106866 | 0.66178330 | 14.60196164 | 9.66333433 | 0.06848395 | 0.10348395 |
| 13 | 1.56395606 | 0.63940415 | 16.11303030 | 10.30273849 | 0.06206157 | 0.09706157 |
| 14 | 1.61869452 | 0.61778179 | 17.67698636 | 10.92052028 | 0.05657073 | 0.09157073 |
| 15 | 1.67534883 | 0.59689062 | 19.29568088 | 11.51741090 | 0.05182507 | 0.08682507 |
| 16 | 1.73398604 | 0.57670591 | 20.97102971 | 12.09411681 | 0.04768483 | 0.08268483 |
| 17 | 1.79467555 | 0.55720378 | 22.70501575 | 12.65132059 | 0.04404313 | 0.07904313 |
| 18 | 1.85748920 | 0.53836114 | 24.49969130 | 13.18968173 | 0.04081684 | 0.07581684 |
| 19 | 1.92250132 | 0.52015569 | 26.35718050 | 13.70983742 | 0.03794033 | 0.07294033 |
| 20 | 1.98978886 | 0.50256588 | 28.27968181 | 14.21240330 | 0.03536108 | 0.07036108 |
| 21 | 2.05943147 | 0.48557090 | 30.26947068 | 14.69797420 | 0.03303659 | 0.06803659 |
| 22 | 2.13151158 | 0.46915063 | 32.32890215 | 15.16712484 | 0.03093207 | 0.06593207 |
| 23 | 2.20611448 | 0.45328563 | 34.46041373 | 15.62041047 | 0.02901880 | 0.06401880 |
| 24 | 2.28332849 | 0.43795713 | 36.66652821 | 16.05836760 | 0.02727283 | 0.06227283 |
| 25 | 2.36324498 | 0.42314699 | 38.94985669 | 16.48151459 | 0.02567404 | 0.06067404 |
| 26 | 2.44595856 | 0.40883767 | 41.31310168 | 16.89035226 | 0.02420540 | 0.05920540 |
| 27 | 2.53156711 | 0.39501224 | 43.75906024 | 17.28536451 | 0.02285241 | 0.05785241 |
| 28 | 2.62017196 | 0.38165434 | 46.29062734 | 17.66701885 | 0.02160265 | 0.05660265 |
| 29 | 2.71187798 | 0.36874815 | 48.91079930 | 18.03576700 | 0.02044538 | 0.05544538 |
| 30 | 2.80679370 | 0.35627841 | 51.62267728 | 18.39204541 | 0.01937133 | 0.05437133 |
| 31 | 2.90503148 | 0.34423035 | 54.42947098 | 18.73627576 | 0.01837240 | 0.05337240 |
| 32 | 3.00670759 | 0.33258971 | 57.33450247 | 19.06886547 | 0.01744150 | 0.05244150 |
| 33 | 3.11194235 | 0.32134271 | 60.34121005 | 19.39020818 | 0.01657242 | 0.05157242 |
| 34 | 3.22086033 | 0.31047605 | 63.45315240 | 19.70068423 | 0.01575966 | 0.05075966 |
| 35 | 3.33359045 | 0.29997686 | 66.67401274 | 20.00066110 | 0.01499835 | 0.04999835 |
| 36 | 3.45026611 | 0.28983272 | 70.00760318 | 20.29049381 | 0.01428416 | 0.04928416 |
| 37 | 3.57102543 | 0.28003161 | 73.45786930 | 20.57052542 | 0.01361325 | 0.04861325 |
| 38 | 3.69601132 | 0.27056194 | 77.02889472 | 20.84108736 | 0.01298214 | 0.04798214 |
| 39 | 3.82537171 | 0.26141250 | 80.72490604 | 21.10249987 | 0.01238775 | 0.04738775 |
| 40 | 3.95925972 | 0.25257247 | 84.55027775 | 21.35507234 | 0.01182728 | 0.04682728 |
| 41 | 4.09783381 | 0.24403137 | 88.50953747 | 21.59910371 | 0.01129822 | 0.04629822 |
| 42 | 4.24125799 | 0.23577910 | 92.60737128 | 21.83488281 | 0.01079828 | 0.04579828 |
| 43 | 4.38970202 | 0.22780590 | 96.84862928 | 22.06268870 | 0.01032539 | 0.04532539 |
| 44 | 4.54334160 | 0.22010231 | 101.23833130 | 22.28279102 | 0.00987768 | 0.04487768 |
| 45 | 4.70235855 | 0.21265924 | 105.78167290 | 22.49545026 | 0.00945343 | 0.04445343 |
| 46 | 4.86694110 | 0.20546787 | 110.48403145 | 22.70091813 | 0.00905108 | 0.04405108 |
| 47 | 5.03728404 | 0.19851968 | 115.35097255 | 22.89943780 | 0.00866919 | 0.04366919 |
| 48 | 5.21358898 | 0.19180645 | 120.38825659 | 23.09124425 | 0.00830646 | 0.04330646 |
| 49 | 5.39606459 | 0.18532024 | 125.60184557 | 23.27656450 | 0.00796167 | 0.04296167 |
| 50 | 5.58492686 | 0.17905337 | 130.99791016 | 23.45561787 | 0.00763371 | 0.04263371 |

| Rate $3\frac{3}{4}$% | A Compound Interest | B Present Value | C Amount of Annuity | D Present Value of Annuity | E Sinking Fund | F Amortization |
|---|---|---|---|---|---|---|
| $n$ | $(1 + i)^n$ | $\dfrac{1}{(1 + i)^n}$ | $s_{\overline{n}|i}$ | $a_{\overline{n}|i}$ | $\dfrac{1}{s_{\overline{n}|i}}$ | $\dfrac{1}{a_{\overline{n}|i}}$ |
| 1 | 1.03750000 | 0.96385542 | 1.00000000 | 0.96385542 | 1.00000000 | 1.03750000 |
| 2 | 1.07640625 | 0.92901727 | 2.03750000 | 1.89287270 | 0.49079755 | 0.52829755 |
| 3 | 1.11677148 | 0.89543834 | 3.11390625 | 2.78831103 | 0.32114005 | 0.35864005 |
| 4 | 1.15865042 | 0.86307310 | 4.23067773 | 3.65138413 | 0.23636875 | 0.27386875 |
| 5 | 1.20209981 | 0.83187768 | 5.38932815 | 4.48326181 | 0.18555189 | 0.22305189 |
| 6 | 1.24717855 | 0.80180981 | 6.59142796 | 5.28507162 | 0.15171219 | 0.18921219 |
| 7 | 1.29394774 | 0.77282874 | 7.83860650 | 6.05790036 | 0.12757370 | 0.16507370 |
| 8 | 1.34247078 | 0.74489517 | 9.13255425 | 6.80279553 | 0.10949839 | 0.14699839 |
| 9 | 1.39281344 | 0.71797125 | 10.47502503 | 7.52076677 | 0.09546517 | 0.13296517 |
| 10 | 1.44504394 | 0.69202048 | 11.86783847 | 8.21278725 | 0.08426134 | 0.12176134 |
| 11 | 1.49923309 | 0.66700769 | 13.31288241 | 8.87979494 | 0.07511521 | 0.11261521 |
| 12 | 1.55545433 | 0.64289898 | 14.81211550 | 9.52269392 | 0.06751230 | 0.10501230 |
| 13 | 1.61378387 | 0.61966167 | 16.36756983 | 10.14235558 | 0.06109642 | 0.09859642 |
| 14 | 1.67430076 | 0.59726426 | 17.98135370 | 10.73961984 | 0.05561317 | 0.09311317 |
| 15 | 1.73708704 | 0.57567639 | 19.65565447 | 11.31529623 | 0.05087595 | 0.08837595 |
| 16 | 1.80222781 | 0.55486881 | 21.39274151 | 11.87016504 | 0.04674483 | 0.08424483 |
| 17 | 1.86981135 | 0.53481331 | 23.19496932 | 12.40497835 | 0.04311280 | 0.08061280 |
| 18 | 1.93992927 | 0.51548271 | 25.06478067 | 12.92046106 | 0.03989662 | 0.07739662 |
| 19 | 2.01267662 | 0.49685080 | 27.00470994 | 13.41731187 | 0.03703058 | 0.07453058 |
| 20 | 2.08815200 | 0.47889234 | 29.01738656 | 13.89620421 | 0.03446210 | 0.07196210 |
| 21 | 2.16645770 | 0.46158298 | 31.10553856 | 14.35778719 | 0.03214862 | 0.06964862 |
| 22 | 2.24769986 | 0.44489926 | 33.27199626 | 14.80268645 | 0.03005531 | 0.06755531 |
| 23 | 2.33198860 | 0.42881856 | 35.51969612 | 15.23150501 | 0.02815339 | 0.06565339 |
| 24 | 2.41943818 | 0.41331910 | 37.85168472 | 15.64482411 | 0.02641890 | 0.06391890 |
| 25 | 2.51016711 | 0.39837985 | 40.27112290 | 16.04320396 | 0.02483169 | 0.06233169 |
| 26 | 2.60429838 | 0.38398058 | 42.78129001 | 16.42718454 | 0.02337470 | 0.06087470 |
| 27 | 2.70195956 | 0.37010176 | 45.38558838 | 16.79728630 | 0.02203343 | 0.05953343 |
| 28 | 2.80328305 | 0.35672459 | 48.08754794 | 17.15401089 | 0.02079540 | 0.05829540 |
| 29 | 2.90840616 | 0.34383093 | 50.89083099 | 17.49784183 | 0.01964991 | 0.05714991 |
| 30 | 3.01747139 | 0.33140331 | 53.79923715 | 17.82924513 | 0.01858762 | 0.05608762 |
| 31 | 3.13062657 | 0.31942487 | 56.81670855 | 18.14867001 | 0.01760046 | 0.05510046 |
| 32 | 3.24802507 | 0.30787940 | 59.94733512 | 18.45654941 | 0.01668131 | 0.05418131 |
| 33 | 3.36982601 | 0.29675123 | 63.19536019 | 18.75330063 | 0.01582395 | 0.05332395 |
| 34 | 3.49619448 | 0.28602528 | 66.56518619 | 19.03932591 | 0.01502287 | 0.05252287 |
| 35 | 3.62730178 | 0.27568702 | 70.06138067 | 19.31501293 | 0.01427320 | 0.05177320 |
| 36 | 3.76332559 | 0.26572242 | 73.68868245 | 19.58073535 | 0.01357060 | 0.05107060 |
| 37 | 3.90445030 | 0.25611800 | 77.45200804 | 19.83685335 | 0.01291122 | 0.05041122 |
| 38 | 4.05086719 | 0.24686072 | 81.35645834 | 20.08371407 | 0.01229159 | 0.04979159 |
| 39 | 4.20277471 | 0.23793805 | 85.40732553 | 20.32165212 | 0.01170860 | 0.04920860 |
| 40 | 4.36037876 | 0.22933788 | 89.61010024 | 20.55098999 | 0.01115946 | 0.04865946 |
| 41 | 4.52389296 | 0.22104855 | 93.97047900 | 20.77203855 | 0.01064164 | 0.04814164 |
| 42 | 4.69353895 | 0.21305885 | 98.49437196 | 20.98509739 | 0.01015286 | 0.04765286 |
| 43 | 4.86954666 | 0.20535793 | 103.18791091 | 21.19045532 | 0.00969106 | 0.04719106 |
| 44 | 5.05215466 | 0.19793535 | 108.05745757 | 21.38833067 | 0.00925434 | 0.04675434 |
| 45 | 5.24161046 | 0.19078106 | 113.10961223 | 21.57917173 | 0.00884098 | 0.04634098 |
| 46 | 5.43817085 | 0.18388536 | 118.35122269 | 21.76305709 | 0.00844943 | 0.04594943 |
| 47 | 5.64210226 | 0.17723890 | 123.78939354 | 21.94029599 | 0.00807824 | 0.04557824 |
| 48 | 5.85368109 | 0.17083268 | 129.43149579 | 22.11112866 | 0.00772609 | 0.04522609 |
| 49 | 6.07319413 | 0.16465800 | 135.28517689 | 22.27578666 | 0.00739179 | 0.04489179 |
| 50 | 6.30093891 | 0.15870651 | 141.35837102 | 22.43449317 | 0.00707422 | 0.04457422 |

| Rate 4% | A<br>Compound<br>Interest | B<br>Present<br>Value | C<br>Amount of<br>Annuity | D<br>Present Value<br>of Annuity | E<br>Sinking<br>Fund | F<br><br>Amortization |
|---|---|---|---|---|---|---|
| $n$ | $(1 + i)^n$ | $\dfrac{1}{(1 + i)^n}$ | $s_{\overline{n}\|i}$ | $a_{\overline{n}\|i}$ | $\dfrac{1}{s_{\overline{n}\|i}}$ | $\dfrac{1}{a_{\overline{n}\|i}}$ |
| 1 | 1.04000000 | 0.96153846 | 1.00000000 | 0.96153846 | 1.00000000 | 1.04000000 |
| 2 | 1.08160000 | 0.92455621 | 2.04000000 | 1.88609467 | 0.49019608 | 0.53019608 |
| 3 | 1.12486400 | 0.88899636 | 3.12160000 | 2.77509103 | 0.32034854 | 0.36034854 |
| 4 | 1.16985856 | 0.85480419 | 4.24646400 | 3.62989522 | 0.23549005 | 0.27549005 |
| 5 | 1.21665290 | 0.82192711 | 5.41632256 | 4.45182233 | 0.18462711 | 0.22462711 |
| 6 | 1.26531902 | 0.79031453 | 6.63297546 | 5.24213686 | 0.15076190 | 0.19076190 |
| 7 | 1.31593178 | 0.75991781 | 7.89829448 | 6.00205467 | 0.12660961 | 0.16660961 |
| 8 | 1.36856905 | 0.73069021 | 9.21422626 | 6.73274487 | 0.10852783 | 0.14852783 |
| 9 | 1.42331181 | 0.70258674 | 10.58279531 | 7.43533161 | 0.09449299 | 0.13449299 |
| 10 | 1.48024428 | 0.67556417 | 12.00610712 | 8.11089578 | 0.08329094 | 0.12329094 |
| 11 | 1.53945406 | 0.64958093 | 13.48635141 | 8.76047671 | 0.07414904 | 0.11414904 |
| 12 | 1.60103222 | 0.62459705 | 15.02580546 | 9.38507376 | 0.06655217 | 0.10655217 |
| 13 | 1.66507351 | 0.60057409 | 16.62683768 | 9.98564785 | 0.06014373 | 0.10014373 |
| 14 | 1.73167645 | 0.57747508 | 18.29191119 | 10.56312293 | 0.05466897 | 0.09466897 |
| 15 | 1.80094351 | 0.55526450 | 20.02358764 | 11.11838743 | 0.04994110 | 0.08994110 |
| 16 | 1.87298125 | 0.53390818 | 21.82453114 | 11.65229561 | 0.04582000 | 0.08582000 |
| 17 | 1.94790050 | 0.51337325 | 23.69751239 | 12.16566885 | 0.04219852 | 0.08219852 |
| 18 | 2.02581652 | 0.49362812 | 25.64541288 | 12.65929697 | 0.03899333 | 0.07899333 |
| 19 | 2.10684918 | 0.47464242 | 27.67122940 | 13.13393940 | 0.03613862 | 0.07613862 |
| 20 | 2.19112314 | 0.45638695 | 29.77807858 | 13.59032634 | 0.03358175 | 0.07358175 |
| 21 | 2.27876807 | 0.43883360 | 31.96920172 | 14.02915995 | 0.03128011 | 0.07128011 |
| 22 | 2.36991879 | 0.42195539 | 34.24796979 | 14.45111533 | 0.02919881 | 0.06919881 |
| 23 | 2.46471554 | 0.40572633 | 36.61788858 | 14.85684167 | 0.02730906 | 0.06730906 |
| 24 | 2.56330416 | 0.39012147 | 39.08260412 | 15.24696314 | 0.02558683 | 0.06558683 |
| 25 | 2.66583633 | 0.37511680 | 41.64590829 | 15.62207994 | 0.02401196 | 0.06401196 |
| 26 | 2.77246978 | 0.36068923 | 44.31174462 | 15.98276918 | 0.02256738 | 0.06256738 |
| 27 | 2.88336858 | 0.34681657 | 47.08421440 | 16.32958575 | 0.02123854 | 0.06123854 |
| 28 | 2.99870332 | 0.33347747 | 49.96758298 | 16.66306322 | 0.02001298 | 0.06001298 |
| 29 | 3.11865145 | 0.32065141 | 52.96628630 | 16.98371463 | 0.01887993 | 0.05887993 |
| 30 | 3.24339751 | 0.30831867 | 56.08493775 | 17.29203330 | 0.01783010 | 0.05783010 |
| 31 | 3.37313341 | 0.29646026 | 59.32833526 | 17.58849356 | 0.01685535 | 0.05685535 |
| 32 | 3.50805875 | 0.28505794 | 62.70146867 | 17.87355150 | 0.01594859 | 0.05594859 |
| 33 | 3.64838110 | 0.27409417 | 66.20952742 | 18.14764567 | 0.01510357 | 0.05510357 |
| 34 | 3.79431634 | 0.26355209 | 69.85790851 | 18.41119776 | 0.01431477 | 0.05431477 |
| 35 | 3.94608899 | 0.25341547 | 73.65222486 | 18.66461323 | 0.01357732 | 0.05357732 |
| 36 | 4.10393255 | 0.24366872 | 77.59831385 | 18.90828195 | 0.01288688 | 0.05288688 |
| 37 | 4.26808986 | 0.23429685 | 81.70224640 | 19.14257880 | 0.01223957 | 0.05223957 |
| 38 | 4.43881345 | 0.22528543 | 85.97033626 | 19.36786423 | 0.01163192 | 0.05163192 |
| 39 | 4.61636599 | 0.21662061 | 90.40914971 | 19.58448484 | 0.01106083 | 0.05106083 |
| 40 | 4.80102063 | 0.20828904 | 95.02551570 | 19.79277388 | 0.01052349 | 0.05052349 |
| 41 | 4.99306145 | 0.20027793 | 99.82653633 | 19.99305181 | 0.01001738 | 0.05001738 |
| 42 | 5.19278391 | 0.19257493 | 104.81959778 | 20.18562674 | 0.00954020 | 0.04954020 |
| 43 | 5.40049527 | 0.18516820 | 110.01238169 | 20.37079494 | 0.00908989 | 0.04908989 |
| 44 | 5.61651508 | 0.17804635 | 115.41287696 | 20.54884129 | 0.00866454 | 0.04866454 |
| 45 | 5.84117568 | 0.17119841 | 121.02939204 | 20.72003970 | 0.00826246 | 0.04826246 |
| 46 | 6.07482271 | 0.16461386 | 126.87056772 | 20.88465356 | 0.00788205 | 0.04788205 |
| 47 | 6.31781562 | 0.15828256 | 132.94539043 | 21.04293612 | 0.00752189 | 0.04752189 |
| 48 | 6.57052824 | 0.15219476 | 139.26320604 | 21.19513088 | 0.00718065 | 0.04718065 |
| 49 | 6.83334937 | 0.14634112 | 145.83373429 | 21.34147200 | 0.00685712 | 0.04685712 |
| 50 | 7.10668335 | 0.14071262 | 152.66708366 | 21.48218462 | 0.00655020 | 0.04655020 |

| Rate $4\frac{1}{2}\%$ $n$ | A Compound Interest $(1 + i)^n$ | B Present Value $\dfrac{1}{(1 + i)^n}$ | C Amount of Annuity $s_{\overline{n}\mid i}$ | D Present Value of Annuity $a_{\overline{n}\mid i}$ | E Sinking Fund $\dfrac{1}{s_{\overline{n}\mid i}}$ | F Amortization $\dfrac{1}{a_{\overline{n}\mid i}}$ |
|---|---|---|---|---|---|---|
| 1 | 1.04500000 | 0.95693780 | 1.00000000 | 0.95693780 | 1.00000000 | 1.04500000 |
| 2 | 1.09202500 | 0.91572995 | 2.04500000 | 1.87266775 | 0.48899756 | 0.53399756 |
| 3 | 1.14116613 | 0.87629660 | 3.13702500 | 2.74896435 | 0.31877336 | 0.36377336 |
| 4 | 1.19251860 | 0.83856134 | 4.27819112 | 3.58752570 | 0.23374365 | 0.27874365 |
| 5 | 1.24618194 | 0.80245105 | 5.47070973 | 4.38997674 | 0.18279164 | 0.22779164 |
| 6 | 1.30226012 | 0.76789574 | 6.71689166 | 5.15787248 | 0.14887839 | 0.19387839 |
| 7 | 1.36086183 | 0.73482846 | 8.01915179 | 5.89270094 | 0.12470147 | 0.16970147 |
| 8 | 1.42210061 | 0.70318513 | 9.38001362 | 6.59588607 | 0.10660965 | 0.15160965 |
| 9 | 1.48609514 | 0.67290443 | 10.80211423 | 7.26879050 | 0.09257447 | 0.13757447 |
| 10 | 1.55296942 | 0.64392768 | 12.28820937 | 7.91271818 | 0.08137882 | 0.12637882 |
| 11 | 1.62285305 | 0.61619874 | 13.84117879 | 8.52891692 | 0.07224818 | 0.11724818 |
| 12 | 1.69588143 | 0.58966386 | 15.46403184 | 9.11858078 | 0.06466619 | 0.10966619 |
| 13 | 1.77219610 | 0.56427164 | 17.15991327 | 9.68285242 | 0.05827535 | 0.10327535 |
| 14 | 1.85194492 | 0.53997286 | 18.93210937 | 10.22282528 | 0.05282032 | 0.09782032 |
| 15 | 1.93528244 | 0.51672044 | 20.78405429 | 10.73954573 | 0.04811381 | 0.09311381 |
| 16 | 2.02237015 | 0.49446932 | 22.71933673 | 11.23401505 | 0.04401537 | 0.08901537 |
| 17 | 2.11337681 | 0.47317639 | 24.74170689 | 11.70719143 | 0.04041758 | 0.08541758 |
| 18 | 2.20847877 | 0.45280037 | 26.85508370 | 12.15999180 | 0.03723690 | 0.08223690 |
| 19 | 2.30786031 | 0.43330179 | 29.06356246 | 12.59329359 | 0.03440734 | 0.07940734 |
| 20 | 2.41171402 | 0.41464286 | 31.37142277 | 13.00793645 | 0.03187614 | 0.07687614 |
| 21 | 2.52024116 | 0.39678743 | 33.78313680 | 13.40472388 | 0.02960057 | 0.07460057 |
| 22 | 2.63365201 | 0.37970089 | 36.30337795 | 13.78442476 | 0.02754565 | 0.07254565 |
| 23 | 2.75216635 | 0.36335013 | 38.93702996 | 14.14777489 | 0.02568249 | 0.07068249 |
| 24 | 2.87601383 | 0.34770347 | 41.68919631 | 14.49547837 | 0.02398703 | 0.06898703 |
| 25 | 3.00543446 | 0.33273060 | 44.56521015 | 14.82820896 | 0.02243903 | 0.06743903 |
| 26 | 3.14067901 | 0.31840248 | 47.57064460 | 15.14661145 | 0.02102137 | 0.06602137 |
| 27 | 3.28200956 | 0.30469137 | 50.71132361 | 15.45130282 | 0.01971946 | 0.06471946 |
| 28 | 3.42969999 | 0.29157069 | 53.99333317 | 15.74287351 | 0.01852081 | 0.06352081 |
| 29 | 3.58403649 | 0.27901502 | 57.42303316 | 16.02188853 | 0.01741461 | 0.06241461 |
| 30 | 3.74531813 | 0.26700002 | 61.00706966 | 16.28888854 | 0.01639154 | 0.06139154 |
| 31 | 3.91385745 | 0.25550241 | 64.75238779 | 16.54439095 | 0.01544345 | 0.06044345 |
| 32 | 4.08998104 | 0.24449991 | 68.66624524 | 16.78889086 | 0.01456320 | 0.05956320 |
| 33 | 4.27403018 | 0.23397121 | 72.75622628 | 17.02286207 | 0.01374453 | 0.05874453 |
| 34 | 4.46636154 | 0.22389589 | 77.03025646 | 17.24675796 | 0.01298191 | 0.05798191 |
| 35 | 4.66734781 | 0.21425444 | 81.49661800 | 17.46101240 | 0.01227045 | 0.05727045 |
| 36 | 4.87737846 | 0.20502817 | 86.16396581 | 17.66604058 | 0.01160578 | 0.05660578 |
| 37 | 5.09686049 | 0.19619921 | 91.04134427 | 17.86223979 | 0.01098402 | 0.05598402 |
| 38 | 5.32621921 | 0.18775044 | 96.13820476 | 18.04999023 | 0.01040169 | 0.05540169 |
| 39 | 5.56589908 | 0.17966549 | 101.46442398 | 18.22965572 | 0.00985567 | 0.05485567 |
| 40 | 5.81636454 | 0.17192870 | 107.03032306 | 18.40158442 | 0.00934315 | 0.05434315 |
| 41 | 6.07810094 | 0.16452507 | 112.84668760 | 18.56610949 | 0.00886158 | 0.05386158 |
| 42 | 6.35161548 | 0.15744026 | 118.92478854 | 18.72354975 | 0.00840868 | 0.05340868 |
| 43 | 6.63743818 | 0.15066054 | 125.27640402 | 18.87421029 | 0.00798235 | 0.05298235 |
| 44 | 6.93612290 | 0.14417276 | 131.91384220 | 19.01838305 | 0.00758071 | 0.05258071 |
| 45 | 7.24824843 | 0.13796437 | 138.84996510 | 19.15634742 | 0.00720202 | 0.05220202 |
| 46 | 7.57441961 | 0.13202332 | 146.09821353 | 19.28837074 | 0.00684471 | 0.05184471 |
| 47 | 7.91526849 | 0.12633810 | 153.67263314 | 19.41470884 | 0.00650734 | 0.05150734 |
| 48 | 8.27145557 | 0.12089771 | 161.58790163 | 19.53560654 | 0.00618858 | 0.05118858 |
| 49 | 8.64367107 | 0.11569158 | 169.85935720 | 19.65129813 | 0.00588722 | 0.05088722 |
| 50 | 9.03263627 | 0.11070965 | 178.50302828 | 19.76200778 | 0.00560215 | 0.05060215 |

| Rate 5% | A<br>Compound<br>Interest | B<br>Present<br>Value | C<br>Amount of<br>Annuity | D<br>Present Value<br>of Annuity | E<br>Sinking<br>Fund | F<br>Amortization |
|---|---|---|---|---|---|---|
| $n$ | $(1 + i)^n$ | $\dfrac{1}{(1 + i)^n}$ | $s_{\overline{n}\|i}$ | $a_{\overline{n}\|i}$ | $\dfrac{1}{s_{\overline{n}\|i}}$ | $\dfrac{1}{a_{\overline{n}\|i}}$ |
| 1 | 1.05000000 | 0.95238095 | 1.00000000 | 0.95238095 | 1.00000000 | 1.05000000 |
| 2 | 1.10250000 | 0.90702948 | 2.05000000 | 1.85941043 | 0.48780488 | 0.53780488 |
| 3 | 1.15762500 | 0.86383760 | 3.15250000 | 2.72324803 | 0.31720856 | 0.36720856 |
| 4 | 1.21550625 | 0.82270247 | 4.31012500 | 3.54595050 | 0.23201183 | 0.28201183 |
| 5 | 1.27628156 | 0.78352617 | 5.52563125 | 4.32947667 | 0.18097480 | 0.23097480 |
| 6 | 1.34009564 | 0.74621540 | 6.80191281 | 5.07569207 | 0.14701747 | 0.19701747 |
| 7 | 1.40710042 | 0.71068133 | 8.14200845 | 5.78637340 | 0.12281982 | 0.17281982 |
| 8 | 1.47745544 | 0.67683936 | 9.54910888 | 6.46321276 | 0.10472181 | 0.15472181 |
| 9 | 1.55132822 | 0.64460892 | 11.02656432 | 7.10782168 | 0.09069008 | 0.14069008 |
| 10 | 1.62889463 | 0.61391325 | 12.57789254 | 7.72173493 | 0.07950457 | 0.12950457 |
| 11 | 1.71033936 | 0.58467929 | 14.20678716 | 8.30641422 | 0.07038889 | 0.12038889 |
| 12 | 1.79585633 | 0.55683742 | 15.91712652 | 8.86325164 | 0.06282541 | 0.11282541 |
| 13 | 1.88564914 | 0.53032135 | 17.71298285 | 9.39357299 | 0.05645577 | 0.10645577 |
| 14 | 1.97993160 | 0.50506795 | 19.59863199 | 9.89864094 | 0.05102397 | 0.10102397 |
| 15 | 2.07892818 | 0.48101710 | 21.57856359 | 10.37965804 | 0.04634229 | 0.09634229 |
| 16 | 2.18287459 | 0.45811152 | 23.65749177 | 10.83776956 | 0.04226991 | 0.09226991 |
| 17 | 2.29201832 | 0.43629669 | 25.84036636 | 11.27406625 | 0.03869914 | 0.08869914 |
| 18 | 2.40661923 | 0.41552065 | 28.13238467 | 11.68958690 | 0.03554622 | 0.08554622 |
| 19 | 2.52695020 | 0.39573396 | 30.53900391 | 12.08532086 | 0.03274501 | 0.08274501 |
| 20 | 2.65329771 | 0.37688948 | 33.06595410 | 12.46221034 | 0.03024259 | 0.08024259 |
| 21 | 2.78596259 | 0.35894236 | 35.71925181 | 12.82115271 | 0.02799611 | 0.07799611 |
| 22 | 2.92526072 | 0.34184987 | 38.50521440 | 13.16300258 | 0.02597051 | 0.07597051 |
| 23 | 3.07152376 | 0.32557131 | 41.43047512 | 13.48857388 | 0.02413682 | 0.07413682 |
| 24 | 3.22509994 | 0.31006791 | 44.50199887 | 13.79864179 | 0.02247090 | 0.07247090 |
| 25 | 3.38635494 | 0.29530277 | 47.72709882 | 14.09394457 | 0.02095246 | 0.07095246 |
| 26 | 3.55567269 | 0.28124073 | 51.11345376 | 14.37518530 | 0.01956432 | 0.06956432 |
| 27 | 3.73345632 | 0.26784832 | 54.66912645 | 14.64303362 | 0.01829186 | 0.06829186 |
| 28 | 3.92012914 | 0.25509364 | 58.40258277 | 14.89812726 | 0.01712253 | 0.06712253 |
| 29 | 4.11613560 | 0.24294632 | 62.32271191 | 15.14107358 | 0.01604551 | 0.06604551 |
| 30 | 4.32194238 | 0.23137745 | 66.43884750 | 15.37245103 | 0.01505144 | 0.06505144 |
| 31 | 4.53803949 | 0.22035947 | 70.76078988 | 15.59281050 | 0.01413212 | 0.06413212 |
| 32 | 4.76494147 | 0.20986617 | 75.29882937 | 15.80267667 | 0.01328042 | 0.06328042 |
| 33 | 5.00318854 | 0.19978254 | 80.06377084 | 16.00254921 | 0.01249004 | 0.06249004 |
| 34 | 5.25334797 | 0.19035480 | 85.06695938 | 16.19290401 | 0.01175545 | 0.06175545 |
| 35 | 5.51601537 | 0.18129029 | 90.32030735 | 16.37419429 | 0.01107171 | 0.06107171 |
| 36 | 5.79181614 | 0.17265741 | 95.83632272 | 16.54685171 | 0.01043446 | 0.06043446 |
| 37 | 6.08140694 | 0.16443563 | 101.62813886 | 16.71128734 | 0.00983979 | 0.05983979 |
| 38 | 6.38547729 | 0.15660536 | 107.70954580 | 16.86789271 | 0.00928423 | 0.05928423 |
| 39 | 6.70475115 | 0.14914797 | 114.09502309 | 17.01704067 | 0.00876462 | 0.05876462 |
| 40 | 7.03998871 | 0.14204568 | 120.79977424 | 17.15908635 | 0.00827816 | 0.05827816 |
| 41 | 7.39198815 | 0.13528160 | 127.83976295 | 17.29436796 | 0.00782229 | 0.05782229 |
| 42 | 7.76158756 | 0.12883962 | 135.23175110 | 17.42320758 | 0.00739471 | 0.05739471 |
| 43 | 8.14966693 | 0.12270440 | 142.99333866 | 17.54591198 | 0.00699333 | 0.05699333 |
| 44 | 8.55715028 | 0.11686133 | 151.14300559 | 17.66277331 | 0.00661625 | 0.05661625 |
| 45 | 8.98500779 | 0.11129651 | 159.70015587 | 17.77406982 | 0.00626173 | 0.05626173 |
| 46 | 9.43425818 | 0.10599668 | 168.68516366 | 17.88006650 | 0.00592820 | 0.05592820 |
| 47 | 9.90597109 | 0.10094921 | 178.11942185 | 17.98101571 | 0.00561421 | 0.05561421 |
| 48 | 10.40126965 | 0.09614211 | 188.02539294 | 18.07715782 | 0.00531843 | 0.05531843 |
| 49 | 10.92133313 | 0.09156391 | 198.42666259 | 18.16872173 | 0.00503965 | 0.05503965 |
| 50 | 11.46739979 | 0.08720373 | 209.34799572 | 18.25592546 | 0.00477674 | 0.05477674 |

| Rate $5\frac{1}{2}\%$ | A Compound Interest | B Present Value | C Amount of Annuity | D Present Value of Annuity | E Sinking Fund | F Amortization |
|---|---|---|---|---|---|---|
| $n$ | $(1 + i)^n$ | $\dfrac{1}{(1 + i)^n}$ | $s_{\overline{n}|i}$ | $a_{\overline{n}|i}$ | $\dfrac{1}{s_{\overline{n}|i}}$ | $\dfrac{1}{a_{\overline{n}|i}}$ |
| 1 | 1.05500000 | 0.94786730 | 1.00000000 | 0.94786730 | 1.00000000 | 1.05500000 |
| 2 | 1.11302500 | 0.89845242 | 2.05500000 | 1.84631971 | 0.48661800 | 0.54161800 |
| 3 | 1.17424138 | 0.85161366 | 3.16802500 | 2.69793338 | 0.31565407 | 0.37065407 |
| 4 | 1.23882465 | 0.80721674 | 4.34226637 | 3.50515012 | 0.23029449 | 0.28529449 |
| 5 | 1.30696001 | 0.76513435 | 5.58109103 | 4.27028448 | 0.17917644 | 0.23417644 |
| 6 | 1.37884281 | 0.72524583 | 6.88805103 | 4.99553031 | 0.14517895 | 0.20017895 |
| 7 | 1.45467916 | 0.68743681 | 8.26689384 | 5.68296712 | 0.12096442 | 0.17596442 |
| 8 | 1.53468651 | 0.65159887 | 9.72157300 | 6.33456599 | 0.10286401 | 0.15786401 |
| 9 | 1.61909427 | 0.61762926 | 11.25625951 | 6.95219525 | 0.08883946 | 0.14383946 |
| 10 | 1.70814446 | 0.58543058 | 12.87535379 | 7.53762583 | 0.07766777 | 0.13266777 |
| 11 | 1.80209240 | 0.55491050 | 14.58349825 | 8.09253633 | 0.06857065 | 0.12357065 |
| 12 | 1.90120749 | 0.52598152 | 16.38559065 | 8.61851785 | 0.06102923 | 0.11602923 |
| 13 | 2.00577390 | 0.49856068 | 18.28679814 | 9.11707853 | 0.05468426 | 0.10968426 |
| 14 | 2.11609146 | 0.47256937 | 20.29257203 | 9.58964790 | 0.04927912 | 0.10427912 |
| 15 | 2.23247649 | 0.44793305 | 22.40866350 | 10.03758094 | 0.04462560 | 0.09962560 |
| 16 | 2.35526270 | 0.42458109 | 24.64113999 | 10.46216203 | 0.04058254 | 0.09558254 |
| 17 | 2.48480215 | 0.40244653 | 26.99640269 | 10.86460856 | 0.03704197 | 0.09204197 |
| 18 | 2.62146627 | 0.38146590 | 29.48120483 | 11.24607447 | 0.03391992 | 0.08891992 |
| 19 | 2.76564691 | 0.36157906 | 32.10267110 | 11.60765352 | 0.03115006 | 0.08615006 |
| 20 | 2.91775749 | 0.34272896 | 34.86831801 | 11.95038248 | 0.02867933 | 0.08367933 |
| 21 | 3.07823415 | 0.32486158 | 37.78607550 | 12.27524406 | 0.02646478 | 0.08146478 |
| 22 | 3.24753703 | 0.30792567 | 40.86430965 | 12.58316973 | 0.02447123 | 0.07947123 |
| 23 | 3.42615157 | 0.29187267 | 44.11184669 | 12.87504239 | 0.02266965 | 0.07766965 |
| 24 | 3.61458990 | 0.27665656 | 47.53799825 | 13.15169895 | 0.02103580 | 0.07603580 |
| 25 | 3.81339235 | 0.26223370 | 51.15258816 | 13.41393266 | 0.01954935 | 0.07454935 |
| 26 | 4.02312893 | 0.24856275 | 54.96598051 | 13.66249541 | 0.01819307 | 0.07319307 |
| 27 | 4.24440102 | 0.23560450 | 58.98910943 | 13.89809991 | 0.01695228 | 0.07195228 |
| 28 | 4.47784307 | 0.22332181 | 63.23351045 | 14.12142172 | 0.01581440 | 0.07081440 |
| 29 | 4.72412444 | 0.21167944 | 67.71135353 | 14.33310116 | 0.01476857 | 0.06976857 |
| 30 | 4.98395129 | 0.20064402 | 72.43547797 | 14.53374517 | 0.01380539 | 0.06880539 |
| 31 | 5.25806861 | 0.19018390 | 77.41942926 | 14.72392907 | 0.01291665 | 0.06791665 |
| 32 | 5.54726238 | 0.18026910 | 82.67749787 | 14.90419817 | 0.01209519 | 0.06709519 |
| 33 | 5.85236181 | 0.17087119 | 88.22476025 | 15.07506936 | 0.01133469 | 0.06633469 |
| 34 | 6.17424171 | 0.16196321 | 94.07712207 | 15.23703257 | 0.01062958 | 0.06562958 |
| 35 | 6.51382501 | 0.15351963 | 100.25136378 | 15.39055220 | 0.00997493 | 0.06497493 |
| 36 | 6.87208538 | 0.14551624 | 106.76518879 | 15.53606843 | 0.00936635 | 0.06436635 |
| 37 | 7.25005008 | 0.13793008 | 113.63727417 | 15.67399851 | 0.00879993 | 0.06379993 |
| 38 | 7.64880283 | 0.13073941 | 120.88732425 | 15.80473793 | 0.00827217 | 0.06327217 |
| 39 | 8.06948699 | 0.12392362 | 128.53612708 | 15.92866154 | 0.00777991 | 0.06277991 |
| 40 | 8.51330877 | 0.11746314 | 136.60561407 | 16.04612469 | 0.00732034 | 0.06232034 |
| 41 | 8.98154076 | 0.11133947 | 145.11892285 | 16.15746416 | 0.00689090 | 0.06189090 |
| 42 | 9.47552550 | 0.10553504 | 154.10046360 | 16.26299920 | 0.00648927 | 0.06148927 |
| 43 | 9.99667940 | 0.10003322 | 163.57598910 | 16.36303242 | 0.00611337 | 0.06111337 |
| 44 | 10.54649677 | 0.09481822 | 173.57266850 | 16.45785063 | 0.00576128 | 0.06076128 |
| 45 | 11.12655409 | 0.08987509 | 184.11916527 | 16.54772572 | 0.00543127 | 0.06043127 |
| 46 | 11.73851456 | 0.08518965 | 195.24571936 | 16.63291537 | 0.00512175 | 0.06012175 |
| 47 | 12.38413287 | 0.08074849 | 206.98423392 | 16.71366386 | 0.00483129 | 0.05983129 |
| 48 | 13.06526017 | 0.07653885 | 219.36836679 | 16.79020271 | 0.00455854 | 0.05955854 |
| 49 | 13.78384948 | 0.07254867 | 232.43362696 | 16.86275139 | 0.00430230 | 0.05930230 |
| 50 | 14.54196120 | 0.06876652 | 246.21747645 | 16.93151790 | 0.00406145 | 0.05906145 |

| Rate 6% | A Compound Interest | B Present Value | C Amount of Annuity | D Present Value of Annuity | E Sinking Fund | F Amortization |
|---|---|---|---|---|---|---|
| $n$ | $(1 + i)^n$ | $\dfrac{1}{(1 + i)^n}$ | $s_{\overline{n}\rvert i}$ | $a_{\overline{n}\rvert i}$ | $\dfrac{1}{s_{\overline{n}\rvert i}}$ | $\dfrac{1}{a_{\overline{n}\rvert i}}$ |
| 1 | 1.06000000 | 0.94339623 | 1.00000000 | 0.94339623 | 1.00000000 | 1.06000000 |
| 2 | 1.12360000 | 0.88999644 | 2.06000000 | 1.83339267 | 0.48543689 | 0.54543689 |
| 3 | 1.19101600 | 0.83961928 | 3.18360000 | 2.67301195 | 0.31410981 | 0.37410981 |
| 4 | 1.26247696 | 0.79209366 | 4.37461600 | 3.46510561 | 0.22859149 | 0.28859149 |
| 5 | 1.33822558 | 0.74725817 | 5.63709296 | 4.21236379 | 0.17739640 | 0.23739640 |
| 6 | 1.41851911 | 0.70496054 | 6.97531854 | 4.91732433 | 0.14336263 | 0.20336263 |
| 7 | 1.50363026 | 0.66505711 | 8.39383765 | 5.58238144 | 0.11913502 | 0.17913502 |
| 8 | 1.59384807 | 0.62741237 | 9.89746791 | 6.20979381 | 0.10103594 | 0.16103594 |
| 9 | 1.68947896 | 0.59189846 | 11.49131598 | 6.80169227 | 0.08702224 | 0.14702224 |
| 10 | 1.79084770 | 0.55839478 | 13.18079494 | 7.36008705 | 0.07586796 | 0.13586796 |
| 11 | 1.89829856 | 0.52678753 | 14.97164264 | 7.88687458 | 0.06679294 | 0.12679294 |
| 12 | 2.01219647 | 0.49696936 | 16.86994120 | 8.38384394 | 0.05927703 | 0.11927703 |
| 13 | 2.13292826 | 0.46883902 | 18.88213767 | 8.85268296 | 0.05296011 | 0.11296011 |
| 14 | 2.26090396 | 0.44230096 | 21.01506593 | 9.29498393 | 0.04758491 | 0.10758491 |
| 15 | 2.39655819 | 0.41726506 | 23.27596988 | 9.71224899 | 0.04296276 | 0.10296276 |
| 16 | 2.54035168 | 0.39364628 | 25.67252808 | 10.10589527 | 0.03895214 | 0.09895214 |
| 17 | 2.69277279 | 0.37136442 | 28.21287976 | 10.47725969 | 0.03544480 | 0.09544480 |
| 18 | 2.85433915 | 0.35034379 | 30.90565255 | 10.82760348 | 0.03235654 | 0.09235654 |
| 19 | 3.02559950 | 0.33051301 | 33.75999170 | 11.15811649 | 0.02962086 | 0.08962086 |
| 20 | 3.20713547 | 0.31180473 | 36.78559120 | 11.46992122 | 0.02718456 | 0.08718456 |
| 21 | 3.39956360 | 0.29415540 | 39.99272668 | 11.76407662 | 0.02500455 | 0.08500455 |
| 22 | 3.60353742 | 0.27750510 | 43.39229028 | 12.04158172 | 0.02304557 | 0.08304557 |
| 23 | 3.81974966 | 0.26179726 | 46.99582769 | 12.30337898 | 0.02127848 | 0.08127848 |
| 24 | 4.04893464 | 0.24697855 | 50.81557735 | 12.55035753 | 0.01967900 | 0.07967900 |
| 25 | 4.29187072 | 0.23299863 | 54.86451200 | 12.78335616 | 0.01822672 | 0.07822672 |
| 26 | 4.54938296 | 0.21981003 | 59.15638272 | 13.00316619 | 0.01690435 | 0.07690435 |
| 27 | 4.82234594 | 0.20736795 | 63.70576568 | 13.21053414 | 0.01569717 | 0.07569717 |
| 28 | 5.11168670 | 0.19563014 | 68.52811162 | 13.40616428 | 0.01459255 | 0.07459255 |
| 29 | 5.41838790 | 0.18455674 | 73.63979832 | 13.59072102 | 0.01357961 | 0.07357961 |
| 30 | 5.74349117 | 0.17411013 | 79.05818622 | 13.76483115 | 0.01264891 | 0.07264891 |
| 31 | 6.08810064 | 0.16425484 | 84.80167739 | 13.92908599 | 0.01179222 | 0.07179222 |
| 32 | 6.45338668 | 0.15495740 | 90.88977803 | 14.08404339 | 0.01100234 | 0.07100234 |
| 33 | 6.84058988 | 0.14618622 | 97.34316471 | 14.23022961 | 0.01027293 | 0.07027293 |
| 34 | 7.25102528 | 0.13791153 | 104.18375460 | 14.36814114 | 0.00959843 | 0.06959843 |
| 35 | 7.68608679 | 0.13010522 | 111.43477987 | 14.49824636 | 0.00897386 | 0.06897386 |
| 36 | 8.14725200 | 0.12274077 | 119.12086666 | 14.62098713 | 0.00839483 | 0.06839483 |
| 37 | 8.63608712 | 0.11579318 | 127.26811866 | 14.73678031 | 0.00785743 | 0.06785743 |
| 38 | 9.15425235 | 0.10923885 | 135.90420578 | 14.84601916 | 0.00735812 | 0.06735812 |
| 39 | 9.70350749 | 0.10305552 | 145.05845813 | 14.94907468 | 0.00689377 | 0.06689377 |
| 40 | 10.28571794 | 0.09722219 | 154.76196562 | 15.04629687 | 0.00646154 | 0.06646154 |
| 41 | 10.90286101 | 0.09171905 | 165.04768356 | 15.13801592 | 0.00605886 | 0.06605886 |
| 42 | 11.55703267 | 0.08652740 | 175.95054457 | 15.22454332 | 0.00568342 | 0.06568342 |
| 43 | 12.25045463 | 0.08162962 | 187.50757724 | 15.30617294 | 0.00533312 | 0.06533312 |
| 44 | 12.98548191 | 0.07700908 | 199.75803188 | 15.38318202 | 0.00500606 | 0.06500606 |
| 45 | 13.76461083 | 0.07265007 | 212.74351379 | 15.45583209 | 0.00470050 | 0.06470050 |
| 46 | 14.59048748 | 0.06853781 | 226.50812462 | 15.52436990 | 0.00441485 | 0.06441485 |
| 47 | 15.46591673 | 0.06465831 | 241.09861210 | 15.58902821 | 0.00414768 | 0.06414768 |
| 48 | 16.39387173 | 0.06099840 | 256.56452882 | 15.65002661 | 0.00389765 | 0.06389765 |
| 49 | 17.37750403 | 0.05754566 | 272.95840055 | 15.70757227 | 0.00366356 | 0.06366356 |
| 50 | 18.42015427 | 0.05428836 | 290.33590458 | 15.76186064 | 0.00344429 | 0.06344429 |

| Rate $6\frac{1}{2}\%$ | A Compound Interest | B Present Value | C Amount of Annuity | D Present Value of Annuity | E Sinking Fund | F Amortization |
|---|---|---|---|---|---|---|
| $n$ | $(1 + i)^n$ | $\dfrac{1}{(1 + i)^n}$ | $s_{\overline{n}\rceil i}$ | $a_{\overline{n}\rceil i}$ | $\dfrac{1}{s_{\overline{n}\rceil i}}$ | $\dfrac{1}{a_{\overline{n}\rceil i}}$ |
| 1 | 1.06500000 | 0.93896714 | 1.00000000 | 0.93896714 | 1.00000000 | 1.06500000 |
| 2 | 1.13422500 | 0.88165928 | 2.06500000 | 1.82062642 | 0.48426150 | 0.54926150 |
| 3 | 1.20794963 | 0.82784909 | 3.19922500 | 2.64847551 | 0.31257570 | 0.37757570 |
| 4 | 1.28646635 | 0.77732309 | 4.40717462 | 3.42579860 | 0.22690274 | 0.29190274 |
| 5 | 1.37008666 | 0.72988084 | 5.69364098 | 4.15567944 | 0.17563454 | 0.24063454 |
| 6 | 1.45914230 | 0.68533412 | 7.06372764 | 4.84101356 | 0.14156831 | 0.20656831 |
| 7 | 1.55398655 | 0.64350621 | 8.52286994 | 5.48451977 | 0.11733137 | 0.18233137 |
| 8 | 1.65499567 | 0.60423119 | 10.07685648 | 6.08875096 | 0.09923730 | 0.16423730 |
| 9 | 1.76257039 | 0.56735323 | 11.73185215 | 6.65610419 | 0.08523803 | 0.15023803 |
| 10 | 1.87713747 | 0.53272604 | 13.49442254 | 7.18883022 | 0.07410469 | 0.13910469 |
| 11 | 1.99915140 | 0.50021224 | 15.37156001 | 7.68904246 | 0.06505521 | 0.13005521 |
| 12 | 2.12909624 | 0.46968285 | 17.37071141 | 8.15872532 | 0.05756817 | 0.12256817 |
| 13 | 2.26748750 | 0.44101676 | 19.49980765 | 8.59974208 | 0.05128256 | 0.11628256 |
| 14 | 2.41487418 | 0.41410025 | 21.76729515 | 9.01384233 | 0.04594048 | 0.11094048 |
| 15 | 2.57184101 | 0.38882652 | 24.18216933 | 9.40266885 | 0.04135278 | 0.10635278 |
| 16 | 2.73901067 | 0.36509533 | 26.75401034 | 9.76776418 | 0.03737757 | 0.10237757 |
| 17 | 2.91704637 | 0.34281251 | 29.49302101 | 10.11057670 | 0.03390633 | 0.09890633 |
| 18 | 3.10655438 | 0.32188969 | 32.41006738 | 10.43246638 | 0.03085461 | 0.09585461 |
| 19 | 3.30858691 | 0.30224384 | 35.51672176 | 10.73471022 | 0.02815575 | 0.09315575 |
| 20 | 3.52364506 | 0.28379703 | 38.82530867 | 11.01850725 | 0.02575640 | 0.09075640 |
| 21 | 3.75268199 | 0.26647608 | 42.34895373 | 11.28498333 | 0.02361333 | 0.08861333 |
| 22 | 3.99660632 | 0.25021228 | 46.10163573 | 11.53519562 | 0.02169120 | 0.08669120 |
| 23 | 4.25638573 | 0.23494111 | 50.09824205 | 11.77013673 | 0.01996078 | 0.08496078 |
| 24 | 4.53305081 | 0.22060198 | 54.35462778 | 11.99073871 | 0.01839770 | 0.08339770 |
| 25 | 4.82769911 | 0.20713801 | 58.88767859 | 12.19787673 | 0.01698148 | 0.08198148 |
| 26 | 5.14149955 | 0.19449579 | 63.71537769 | 12.39237251 | 0.01569480 | 0.08069480 |
| 27 | 5.47569702 | 0.18262515 | 68.85687725 | 12.57499766 | 0.01452288 | 0.07952288 |
| 28 | 5.83161733 | 0.17147902 | 74.33257427 | 12.74647668 | 0.01345305 | 0.07845305 |
| 29 | 6.21067245 | 0.16101316 | 80.16419159 | 12.90748984 | 0.01247440 | 0.07747440 |
| 30 | 6.61436616 | 0.15118607 | 86.37486405 | 13.05867591 | 0.01157744 | 0.07657744 |
| 31 | 7.04429996 | 0.14195875 | 92.98923021 | 13.20063465 | 0.01075393 | 0.07575393 |
| 32 | 7.50217946 | 0.13329460 | 100.03353017 | 13.33392925 | 0.00999665 | 0.07499665 |
| 33 | 7.98982113 | 0.12515925 | 107.53570963 | 13.45908850 | 0.00929924 | 0.07429924 |
| 34 | 8.50915950 | 0.11752042 | 115.52553076 | 13.57660892 | 0.00865610 | 0.07365610 |
| 35 | 9.06225487 | 0.11034781 | 124.03469026 | 13.68695673 | 0.00806226 | 0.07306226 |
| 36 | 9.65130143 | 0.10361297 | 133.09694513 | 13.79056970 | 0.00751332 | 0.07251332 |
| 37 | 10.27863603 | 0.09728917 | 142.74824656 | 13.88785887 | 0.00700534 | 0.07200534 |
| 38 | 10.94674737 | 0.09135134 | 153.02688259 | 13.97921021 | 0.00653480 | 0.07153480 |
| 39 | 11.65828595 | 0.08577590 | 163.97362996 | 14.06498611 | 0.00609854 | 0.07109854 |
| 40 | 12.41607453 | 0.08054075 | 175.63191590 | 14.14552687 | 0.00569373 | 0.07069373 |
| 41 | 13.22311938 | 0.07562512 | 188.04799044 | 14.22115199 | 0.00531779 | 0.07031779 |
| 42 | 14.08262214 | 0.07100950 | 201.27110981 | 14.29216149 | 0.00496842 | 0.06996842 |
| 43 | 14.99799258 | 0.06667559 | 215.35373195 | 14.35883708 | 0.00464352 | 0.06964352 |
| 44 | 15.97286209 | 0.06260619 | 230.35172453 | 14.42144327 | 0.00434119 | 0.06934119 |
| 45 | 17.01109813 | 0.05878515 | 246.32458662 | 14.48022842 | 0.00405968 | 0.06905968 |
| 46 | 18.11681951 | 0.05519733 | 263.33568475 | 14.53542575 | 0.00379743 | 0.06879743 |
| 47 | 19.29441278 | 0.05182848 | 281.45250426 | 14.58725422 | 0.00355300 | 0.06855300 |
| 48 | 20.54854961 | 0.04866524 | 300.74691704 | 14.63591946 | 0.00332505 | 0.06832505 |
| 49 | 21.88420533 | 0.04569506 | 321.29546665 | 14.68161451 | 0.00311240 | 0.06811240 |
| 50 | 23.30667868 | 0.04290616 | 343.17967198 | 14.72452067 | 0.00291393 | 0.06791393 |

| Rate 7% | A Compound Interest | B Present Value | C Amount of Annuity | D Present Value of Annuity | E Sinking Fund | F Amortization |
|---|---|---|---|---|---|---|
| $n$ | $(1 + i)^n$ | $\dfrac{1}{(1 + i)^n}$ | $s_{\overline{n}|i}$ | $a_{\overline{n}|i}$ | $\dfrac{1}{s_{\overline{n}|i}}$ | $\dfrac{1}{a_{\overline{n}|i}}$ |
| 1 | 1.07000000 | 0.93457944 | 1.00000000 | 0.93457944 | 1.00000000 | 1.00000000 |
| 2 | 1.14490000 | 0.87343873 | 2.07000000 | 1.80801817 | 0.48309179 | 0.55309179 |
| 3 | 1.22504300 | 0.81629788 | 3.21490000 | 2.62431604 | 0.31105167 | 0.38105167 |
| 4 | 1.31079601 | 0.76289521 | 4.43994300 | 3.38721126 | 0.22522812 | 0.29522812 |
| 5 | 1.40255173 | 0.71298618 | 5.75073901 | 4.10019744 | 0.17389069 | 0.24389069 |
| 6 | 1.50073035 | 0.66634222 | 7.15329074 | 4.76653966 | 0.13979580 | 0.20979580 |
| 7 | 1.60578148 | 0.62274974 | 8.65402109 | 5.38928940 | 0.11555322 | 0.18555322 |
| 8 | 1.71818618 | 0.58200910 | 10.25980257 | 5.97129851 | 0.09746776 | 0.16746776 |
| 9 | 1.83845921 | 0.54393374 | 11.97798875 | 6.51523225 | 0.08348647 | 0.15348647 |
| 10 | 1.96715136 | 0.50834929 | 13.81644796 | 7.02358154 | 0.07237750 | 0.14237750 |
| 11 | 2.10485195 | 0.47509280 | 15.78359932 | 7.49867434 | 0.06335690 | 0.13335690 |
| 12 | 2.25219159 | 0.44401196 | 17.88845127 | 7.94268630 | 0.05590199 | 0.12590199 |
| 13 | 2.40984500 | 0.41496445 | 20.14064286 | 8.35765074 | 0.04965085 | 0.11965085 |
| 14 | 2.57853415 | 0.38781724 | 22.55048786 | 8.74546799 | 0.04434494 | 0.11434494 |
| 15 | 2.75903154 | 0.36244602 | 25.12902201 | 9.10791401 | 0.03979462 | 0.10979462 |
| 16 | 2.95216375 | 0.33873460 | 27.88805355 | 9.44664860 | 0.03585765 | 0.10585765 |
| 17 | 3.15881521 | 0.31657439 | 30.84021730 | 9.76322299 | 0.03242519 | 0.10242519 |
| 18 | 3.37993228 | 0.29586392 | 33.99903251 | 10.05908691 | 0.02941260 | 0.09941260 |
| 19 | 3.61652754 | 0.27650833 | 37.37896479 | 10.33559524 | 0.02675301 | 0.09675301 |
| 20 | 3.86968446 | 0.25841900 | 40.99549232 | 10.59401425 | 0.02439293 | 0.09439293 |
| 21 | 4.14056237 | 0.24151309 | 44.86517678 | 10.83552733 | 0.02228900 | 0.09228900 |
| 22 | 4.43040174 | 0.22571317 | 49.00573916 | 11.06124050 | 0.02040577 | 0.09040577 |
| 23 | 4.74052986 | 0.21094688 | 53.43614090 | 11.27218738 | 0.01871393 | 0.08871393 |
| 24 | 5.07236695 | 0.19714662 | 58.17667076 | 11.46933400 | 0.01718902 | 0.08718902 |
| 25 | 5.42743264 | 0.18424918 | 63.24903772 | 11.65358318 | 0.01581052 | 0.08581052 |
| 26 | 5.80735292 | 0.17219549 | 68.67647036 | 11.82577867 | 0.01456103 | 0.08456103 |
| 27 | 6.21386763 | 0.16093037 | 74.48382328 | 11.98670904 | 0.01342573 | 0.08342573 |
| 28 | 6.64883836 | 0.15040221 | 80.69769091 | 12.13711125 | 0.01239193 | 0.08239193 |
| 29 | 7.11425705 | 0.14056282 | 87.34652927 | 12.27767407 | 0.01144865 | 0.08144865 |
| 30 | 7.61225504 | 0.13136712 | 94.46078632 | 12.40904118 | 0.01058640 | 0.08058640 |
| 31 | 8.14511290 | 0.12277301 | 102.07304137 | 12.53181419 | 0.00979691 | 0.07979691 |
| 32 | 8.71527080 | 0.11474113 | 110.21815426 | 12.64655532 | 0.00907292 | 0.07907292 |
| 33 | 9.32533975 | 0.10723470 | 118.93342506 | 12.75379002 | 0.00840807 | 0.07840807 |
| 34 | 9.97811354 | 0.10021934 | 128.25876481 | 12.85400936 | 0.00779674 | 0.07779674 |
| 35 | 10.67658148 | 0.09366294 | 138.23687835 | 12.94767230 | 0.00723396 | 0.07723396 |
| 36 | 11.42394219 | 0.08753546 | 148.91345984 | 13.03520776 | 0.00671531 | 0.07671531 |
| 37 | 12.22361814 | 0.08180884 | 160.33740202 | 13.11701660 | 0.00623685 | 0.07623685 |
| 38 | 13.07927141 | 0.07645686 | 172.56102017 | 13.19347345 | 0.00579505 | 0.07579505 |
| 39 | 13.99442041 | 0.07145501 | 185.64029158 | 13.26492846 | 0.00538676 | 0.07538676 |
| 40 | 14.97445784 | 0.06678038 | 199.63511199 | 13.33170884 | 0.00500914 | 0.07500914 |
| 41 | 16.02266989 | 0.06241157 | 214.60956983 | 13.39412041 | 0.00465962 | 0.07465962 |
| 42 | 17.14425678 | 0.05832857 | 230.63223972 | 13.45244898 | 0.00433591 | 0.07433591 |
| 43 | 18.34435475 | 0.05451268 | 247.77649650 | 13.50696167 | 0.00403590 | 0.07403590 |
| 44 | 19.62845959 | 0.05094643 | 266.12085125 | 13.55790810 | 0.00375769 | 0.07375769 |
| 45 | 21.00245176 | 0.04761349 | 285.74931084 | 13.60552159 | 0.00349957 | 0.07349957 |
| 46 | 22.47262338 | 0.04449859 | 306.75176260 | 13.65002018 | 0.00325996 | 0.07325996 |
| 47 | 24.04570702 | 0.04158747 | 329.22438598 | 13.69160764 | 0.00303744 | 0.07303744 |
| 48 | 25.72890651 | 0.03886679 | 353.27009300 | 13.73047443 | 0.00283070 | 0.07283070 |
| 49 | 27.52992997 | 0.03632410 | 378.99899951 | 13.76679853 | 0.00263853 | 0.07263853 |
| 50 | 29.45702506 | 0.03394776 | 406.52892947 | 13.80074629 | 0.00245985 | 0.07245985 |

| Rate $7\frac{1}{2}\%$ | A Compound Interest | B Present Value | C Amount of Annuity | D Present Value of Annuity | E Sinking Fund | F Amortization |
|---|---|---|---|---|---|---|
| $n$ | $(1 + i)^n$ | $\dfrac{1}{(1 + i)^n}$ | $s_{\overline{n}\|i}$ | $a_{\overline{n}\|i}$ | $\dfrac{1}{s_{\overline{n}\|i}}$ | $\dfrac{1}{a_{\overline{n}\|i}}$ |
| 1 | 1.07500000 | 0.93023256 | 1.00000000 | 0.93023256 | 1.00000000 | 1.07500000 |
| 2 | 1.15562500 | 0.86533261 | 2.07500000 | 1.79556517 | 0.48192771 | 0.55692771 |
| 3 | 1.24229688 | 0.80496057 | 3.23062500 | 2.60052574 | 0.30953763 | 0.38453763 |
| 4 | 1.33546914 | 0.74880053 | 4.47292187 | 3.34932627 | 0.22356751 | 0.29856751 |
| 5 | 1.43562933 | 0.69655863 | 5.80839102 | 4.04588490 | 0.17216472 | 0.24716472 |
| 6 | 1.54330153 | 0.64796152 | 7.24402034 | 4.69384642 | 0.13804489 | 0.21304489 |
| 7 | 1.65904914 | 0.60275490 | 8.78732187 | 5.29660132 | 0.11380032 | 0.18880032 |
| 8 | 1.78347783 | 0.56070223 | 10.44637101 | 5.85730355 | 0.09572702 | 0.17072702 |
| 9 | 1.91723866 | 0.52158347 | 12.22984883 | 6.37888703 | 0.08176716 | 0.15676716 |
| 10 | 2.06103156 | 0.48519393 | 14.14708750 | 6.86408096 | 0.07068593 | 0.14568593 |
| 11 | 2.21560893 | 0.45134319 | 16.20811906 | 7.31542415 | 0.06169747 | 0.13669747 |
| 12 | 2.38177960 | 0.41985413 | 18.42372799 | 7.73527827 | 0.05427783 | 0.12927783 |
| 13 | 2.56041307 | 0.39056198 | 20.80550759 | 8.12584026 | 0.04806420 | 0.12306420 |
| 14 | 2.75244405 | 0.36331347 | 23.36592066 | 8.48915373 | 0.04279737 | 0.11779737 |
| 15 | 2.95887735 | 0.33796602 | 26.11836470 | 8.82711975 | 0.03828724 | 0.11328724 |
| 16 | 3.18079315 | 0.31438699 | 29.07724206 | 9.14150674 | 0.03439116 | 0.10939116 |
| 17 | 3.41935264 | 0.29245302 | 32.25803521 | 9.43395976 | 0.03100003 | 0.10600003 |
| 18 | 3.67580409 | 0.27204932 | 35.67738785 | 9.70600908 | 0.02802896 | 0.10302896 |
| 19 | 3.95148940 | 0.25306913 | 39.35319194 | 9.95907821 | 0.02541090 | 0.10041090 |
| 20 | 4.24785110 | 0.23541315 | 43.30468134 | 10.19449136 | 0.02309219 | 0.09809219 |
| 21 | 4.56643993 | 0.21898897 | 47.55253244 | 10.41348033 | 0.02102937 | 0.09602937 |
| 22 | 4.90892293 | 0.20371067 | 52.11897237 | 10.61719101 | 0.01918687 | 0.09418687 |
| 23 | 5.27709215 | 0.18949830 | 57.02789530 | 10.80668931 | 0.01753528 | 0.09253528 |
| 24 | 5.67287406 | 0.17627749 | 62.30498744 | 10.98296680 | 0.01605008 | 0.09105008 |
| 25 | 6.09833961 | 0.16397906 | 67.97786150 | 11.14694586 | 0.01471067 | 0.08971067 |
| 26 | 6.55571508 | 0.15253866 | 74.07620112 | 11.29948452 | 0.01349961 | 0.08849961 |
| 27 | 7.04739371 | 0.14189643 | 80.63191620 | 11.44138095 | 0.01240204 | 0.08740204 |
| 28 | 7.57594824 | 0.13199668 | 87.67930991 | 11.57337763 | 0.01140520 | 0.08640520 |
| 29 | 8.14414436 | 0.12278761 | 95.25525816 | 11.69616524 | 0.01049811 | 0.08549811 |
| 30 | 8.75495519 | 0.11422103 | 103.39940252 | 11.81038627 | 0.00967124 | 0.08467124 |
| 31 | 9.41157683 | 0.10625212 | 112.15435771 | 11.91663839 | 0.00891628 | 0.08391628 |
| 32 | 10.11744509 | 0.09883918 | 121.56593454 | 12.01547757 | 0.00822599 | 0.08322599 |
| 33 | 10.87625347 | 0.09194343 | 131.68337963 | 12.10742099 | 0.00759397 | 0.08259397 |
| 34 | 11.69197248 | 0.08552877 | 142.55963310 | 12.19294976 | 0.00701461 | 0.08201461 |
| 35 | 12.56887042 | 0.07956164 | 154.25160558 | 12.27251141 | 0.00648291 | 0.08148291 |
| 36 | 13.51153570 | 0.07401083 | 166.82047600 | 12.34652224 | 0.00599447 | 0.08099447 |
| 37 | 14.52490088 | 0.06884729 | 180.33201170 | 12.41536952 | 0.00554533 | 0.08054533 |
| 38 | 15.61426844 | 0.06404399 | 194.85691258 | 12.47941351 | 0.00513197 | 0.08013197 |
| 39 | 16.78533858 | 0.05957580 | 210.47118102 | 12.53898931 | 0.00475124 | 0.07975124 |
| 40 | 18.04423897 | 0.05541935 | 227.25651960 | 12.59440866 | 0.00440031 | 0.07940031 |
| 41 | 19.39755689 | 0.05155288 | 245.30075857 | 12.64596155 | 0.00407663 | 0.07907663 |
| 42 | 20.85237366 | 0.04795617 | 264.69831546 | 12.69391772 | 0.00377789 | 0.07877789 |
| 43 | 22.41630168 | 0.04461039 | 285.55068912 | 12.73852811 | 0.00350201 | 0.07850201 |
| 44 | 24.09752431 | 0.04149804 | 307.96699080 | 12.78002615 | 0.00324710 | 0.07824710 |
| 45 | 25.90483863 | 0.03860283 | 332.06451511 | 12.81862898 | 0.00301146 | 0.07801146 |
| 46 | 27.84770153 | 0.03590961 | 357.96935375 | 12.85453858 | 0.00279354 | 0.07779354 |
| 47 | 29.93627915 | 0.03340428 | 385.81705528 | 12.88794287 | 0.00259190 | 0.07759190 |
| 48 | 32.18150008 | 0.03107375 | 415.75333442 | 12.91901662 | 0.00240527 | 0.07740527 |
| 49 | 34.59511259 | 0.02890582 | 447.93483451 | 12.94792244 | 0.00223247 | 0.07723247 |
| 50 | 37.18974603 | 0.02688913 | 482.52994709 | 12.97481157 | 0.00207241 | 0.07707241 |

| Rate 8% | A Compound Interest | B Present Value | C Amount of Annuity | D Present Value of Annuity | E Sinking Fund | F Amortization |
|---|---|---|---|---|---|---|
| $n$ | $(1 + i)^n$ | $\dfrac{1}{(1 + i)^n}$ | $s_{\overline{n}\rvert i}$ | $a_{\overline{n}\rvert i}$ | $\dfrac{1}{s_{\overline{n}\rvert i}}$ | $\dfrac{1}{a_{\overline{n}\rvert i}}$ |
| 1 | 1.08000000 | 0.92592593 | 1.00000000 | 0.92592593 | 1.00000000 | 1.08000000 |
| 2 | 1.16640000 | 0.85733882 | 2.08000000 | 1.78326475 | 0.48076923 | 0.56076923 |
| 3 | 1.25971200 | 0.79383224 | 3.24640000 | 2.57709699 | 0.30803351 | 0.38803351 |
| 4 | 1.36048896 | 0.73502985 | 4.50611200 | 3.31212684 | 0.22192080 | 0.30192080 |
| 5 | 1.46932808 | 0.68058320 | 5.86660096 | 3.99271004 | 0.17045645 | 0.25045645 |
| 6 | 1.58687432 | 0.63016963 | 7.33592904 | 4.62287966 | 0.13631539 | 0.21631539 |
| 7 | 1.71382427 | 0.58349040 | 8.92280336 | 5.20637006 | 0.11207240 | 0.19207240 |
| 8 | 0.85093021 | 0.54026888 | 10.63662763 | 5.74663894 | 0.09401476 | 0.17401476 |
| 9 | 1.99900463 | 0.50024897 | 12.48755784 | 6.24688791 | 0.08007971 | 0.16007971 |
| 10 | 2.15892500 | 0.46319349 | 14.48656247 | 6.71008140 | 0.06902949 | 0.14902949 |
| 11 | 2.33163900 | 0.42888286 | 16.64548746 | 7.13896426 | 0.06007634 | 0.14007634 |
| 12 | 2.51817012 | 0.39711376 | 18.97712646 | 7.53607802 | 0.05269502 | 0.13269502 |
| 13 | 2.71962373 | 0.36769792 | 21.49529658 | 7.90377594 | 0.04652181 | 0.12652181 |
| 14 | 2.93719362 | 0.34046104 | 24.21492030 | 8.24423698 | 0.04129685 | 0.12129685 |
| 15 | 3.17216911 | 0.31524170 | 27.15211393 | 8.55947869 | 0.03682954 | 0.11682954 |
| 16 | 3.42594264 | 0.29189047 | 30.32428304 | 8.85136916 | 0.03297687 | 0.11297687 |
| 17 | 3.70001805 | 0.27026895 | 33.75022569 | 9.12163811 | 0.02962943 | 0.10962943 |
| 18 | 3.99601950 | 0.25024903 | 37.45024374 | 9.37188714 | 0.02670210 | 0.10670210 |
| 19 | 4.31570106 | 0.23171206 | 41.44626324 | 9.60359920 | 0.02412763 | 0.10412763 |
| 20 | 4.66095714 | 0.21454821 | 45.76196430 | 9.81814741 | 0.02185221 | 0.10185221 |
| 21 | 5.03383372 | 0.19865575 | 50.42292144 | 10.01680316 | 0.01983225 | 0.09983225 |
| 22 | 5.43654041 | 0.18394051 | 55.45675516 | 10.20074366 | 0.01803207 | 0.09803207 |
| 23 | 5.87146365 | 0.17031528 | 60.89329557 | 10.37105895 | 0.01642217 | 0.09642217 |
| 24 | 6.34118074 | 0.15769934 | 66.76475922 | 10.52875828 | 0.01497796 | 0.09497796 |
| 25 | 6.84847520 | 0.14601790 | 73.10593995 | 10.67477619 | 0.01367878 | 0.09367878 |
| 26 | 7.39635321 | 0.13520176 | 79.95441515 | 10.80997795 | 0.01250713 | 0.09250713 |
| 27 | 7.98806147 | 0.12518682 | 87.35076836 | 10.93516477 | 0.01144810 | 0.09144810 |
| 28 | 8.62710639 | 0.11591372 | 95.33882983 | 11.05107849 | 0.01048891 | 0.09048891 |
| 29 | 9.31727490 | 0.10732752 | 103.96593622 | 11.15840601 | 0.00961854 | 0.08961854 |
| 30 | 10.06265689 | 0.09937733 | 113.28321111 | 11.25778334 | 0.00882743 | 0.08882743 |
| 31 | 10.86766944 | 0.09201605 | 123.34586800 | 11.34979939 | 0.00810728 | 0.08810728 |
| 32 | 11.73708300 | 0.08520005 | 134.21353744 | 11.43499944 | 0.00745081 | 0.08745081 |
| 33 | 12.67604964 | 0.07888893 | 145.95062044 | 11.51388837 | 0.00685163 | 0.08685163 |
| 34 | 13.69013361 | 0.07304531 | 158.62667007 | 11.58693367 | 0.00630411 | 0.08630411 |
| 35 | 14.78534429 | 0.06763454 | 172.31680368 | 11.65456822 | 0.00580326 | 0.08580326 |
| 36 | 15.96817184 | 0.06262458 | 187.10214797 | 11.71719279 | 0.00534467 | 0.08534467 |
| 37 | 17.24562558 | 0.05798572 | 203.07031981 | 11.77517851 | 0.00492440 | 0.08492440 |
| 38 | 18.62527563 | 0.05369048 | 220.31594540 | 11.82886899 | 0.00453894 | 0.08453894 |
| 39 | 20.11529768 | 0.04971341 | 238.94122103 | 11.87858240 | 0.00418513 | 0.08418513 |
| 40 | 21.72452150 | 0.04603093 | 259.05651871 | 11.92461333 | 0.00386016 | 0.08386016 |
| 41 | 23.46248322 | 0.04262123 | 280.78104021 | 11.96723457 | 0.00356149 | 0.08356149 |
| 42 | 25.33948187 | 0.03946411 | 304.24352342 | 12.00669867 | 0.00328684 | 0.08328684 |
| 43 | 27.36664042 | 0.03654084 | 329.58300530 | 12.04323951 | 0.00303414 | 0.08303414 |
| 44 | 29.55597166 | 0.03383411 | 356.94964572 | 12.07707362 | 0.00280152 | 0.08280152 |
| 45 | 31.92044939 | 0.03132788 | 386.50561738 | 12.10840150 | 0.00258728 | 0.08258728 |
| 46 | 34.47408534 | 0.02900730 | 418.42606677 | 12.13740880 | 0.00238991 | 0.08238991 |
| 47 | 37.23201217 | 0.02685861 | 452.90015211 | 12.16426741 | 0.00220799 | 0.08220799 |
| 48 | 40.21057314 | 0.02486908 | 490.13216428 | 12.18913649 | 0.00204027 | 0.08204027 |
| 49 | 43.42741899 | 0.02302693 | 530.34273742 | 12.21216341 | 0.00188557 | 0.08188557 |
| 50 | 46.90161251 | 0.02132123 | 573.77015642 | 12.23348464 | 0.00174286 | 0.08174286 |

| Rate 9% | A Compound Interest | B Present Value | C Amount of Annuity | D Present Value of Annuity | E Sinking Fund | F Amortization |
|---|---|---|---|---|---|---|
| $n$ | $(1 + i)^n$ | $\dfrac{1}{(1 + i)^n}$ | $s_{\overline{n}|i}$ | $a_{\overline{n}|i}$ | $\dfrac{1}{s_{\overline{n}|i}}$ | $\dfrac{1}{a_{\overline{n}|i}}$ |
| 1 | 1.09000000 | 0.91743119 | 1.00000000 | 0.91743119 | 1.00000000 | 1.09000000 |
| 2 | 1.18810000 | 0.84167999 | 2.09000000 | 1.75911119 | 0.47846890 | 0.56846890 |
| 3 | 1.29502900 | 0.77218348 | 3.27810000 | 2.53129467 | 0.30505476 | 0.39505476 |
| 4 | 1.41158161 | 0.70842521 | 4.57312900 | 3.23971988 | 0.21866866 | 0.30866866 |
| 5 | 1.53862395 | 0.64993139 | 5.98471061 | 3.88965126 | 0.16709246 | 0.25709246 |
| 6 | 1.67710011 | 0.59626733 | 7.52333456 | 4.48591859 | 0.13291978 | 0.22291978 |
| 7 | 1.82803912 | 0.54703424 | 9.20043468 | 5.03295284 | 0.10869052 | 0.19869052 |
| 8 | 1.99256264 | 0.50186628 | 11.02847380 | 5.53481911 | 0.09067438 | 0.18067438 |
| 9 | 2.17189328 | 0.46042778 | 13.02103644 | 5.99524689 | 0.07679880 | 0.16679880 |
| 10 | 2.36736367 | 0.42241081 | 15.19292972 | 6.41765770 | 0.06582009 | 0.15582009 |
| 11 | 2.58042641 | 0.38753285 | 17.56029339 | 6.80519055 | 0.05694666 | 0.14694666 |
| 12 | 2.81266478 | 0.35553473 | 20.14071980 | 7.16072528 | 0.04965066 | 0.13965066 |
| 13 | 3.06580461 | 0.32617865 | 22.95338458 | 7.48690392 | 0.04356656 | 0.13356656 |
| 14 | 3.34172703 | 0.29924647 | 26.01918919 | 7.78615039 | 0.03843317 | 0.12843317 |
| 15 | 3.64248246 | 0.27453804 | 29.36091622 | 8.06068843 | 0.03405888 | 0.12405888 |
| 16 | 3.97030588 | 0.25186976 | 33.00339868 | 8.31255819 | 0.03029991 | 0.12029991 |
| 17 | 4.32763341 | 0.23107318 | 36.97370456 | 8.54363137 | 0.02704625 | 0.11704625 |
| 18 | 4.71712042 | 0.21199374 | 41.30133797 | 8.75562511 | 0.02421229 | 0.11421229 |
| 19 | 5.14166125 | 0.19448967 | 46.01845839 | 8.95011478 | 0.02173041 | 0.11173041 |
| 20 | 5.60441077 | 0.17843089 | 51.16011964 | 9.12854567 | 0.01954648 | 0.10954648 |
| 21 | 6.10880774 | 0.16369806 | 56.76453041 | 9.29224373 | 0.01761663 | 0.10761663 |
| 22 | 6.65860043 | 0.15018171 | 62.87333815 | 9.44242544 | 0.01590499 | 0.10590499 |
| 23 | 7.25787447 | 0.13778139 | 69.53193858 | 9.58020683 | 0.01438188 | 0.10438188 |
| 24 | 7.91108317 | 0.12640494 | 76.78981305 | 9.70661177 | 0.01302256 | 0.10302256 |
| 25 | 8.62308066 | 0.11596784 | 84.70089623 | 9.82257960 | 0.01180625 | 0.10180625 |
| 26 | 9.39915792 | 0.10639251 | 93.32397689 | 9.92897211 | 0.01071536 | 0.10071536 |
| 27 | 10.24508213 | 0.09760781 | 102.72313481 | 10.02657992 | 0.00973491 | 0.09973491 |
| 28 | 11.16713952 | 0.08954845 | 112.96821694 | 10.11612837 | 0.00885205 | 0.09885205 |
| 29 | 12.17218208 | 0.08215454 | 124.13535646 | 10.19828291 | 0.00805572 | 0.09805572 |
| 30 | 13.26767847 | 0.07537114 | 136.30753855 | 10.27365404 | 0.00733635 | 0.09733635 |
| 31 | 14.46176953 | 0.06914783 | 149.57521702 | 10.34280187 | 0.00668560 | 0.09668560 |
| 32 | 15.76332879 | 0.06343838 | 164.03698655 | 10.40624025 | 0.00609619 | 0.09609619 |
| 33 | 17.18202838 | 0.05820035 | 179.80031534 | 10.46444060 | 0.00556173 | 0.09556173 |
| 34 | 18.72841093 | 0.05339481 | 196.98234372 | 10.51783541 | 0.00507660 | 0.09507660 |
| 35 | 20.41396792 | 0.04898607 | 215.71075465 | 10.56682148 | 0.00463584 | 0.09463584 |
| 36 | 22.25122503 | 0.04494135 | 236.12472257 | 10.61176282 | 0.00423505 | 0.09423505 |
| 37 | 24.25383528 | 0.04123059 | 258.37594760 | 10.65299342 | 0.00387033 | 0.09387033 |
| 38 | 26.43668046 | 0.03782623 | 282.62978288 | 10.69081965 | 0.00353820 | 0.09353820 |
| 39 | 28.81598170 | 0.03470296 | 309.06646334 | 10.72552261 | 0.00323555 | 0.09323555 |
| 40 | 31.40942005 | 0.03183758 | 337.88244504 | 10.75736020 | 0.00295961 | 0.09295961 |
| 41 | 34.23626789 | 0.02920879 | 369.29186510 | 10.78656899 | 0.00270789 | 0.09270789 |
| 42 | 37.31753197 | 0.02679706 | 403.52813296 | 10.81336604 | 0.00247814 | 0.09247814 |
| 43 | 40.67610984 | 0.02458446 | 440.84566492 | 10.83795050 | 0.00226837 | 0.09226837 |
| 44 | 44.33695973 | 0.02255455 | 481.52177477 | 10.86050504 | 0.00207675 | 0.09207675 |
| 45 | 48.32728610 | 0.02069224 | 525.85873450 | 10.88119729 | 0.00190165 | 0.09190165 |
| 46 | 52.67674185 | 0.01898371 | 574.18602060 | 10.90018100 | 0.00174160 | 0.09174160 |
| 47 | 57.41764862 | 0.01741625 | 626.86276245 | 10.91759725 | 0.00159525 | 0.09159525 |
| 48 | 62.58523700 | 0.01597821 | 684.28041107 | 10.93357546 | 0.00146139 | 0.09146139 |
| 49 | 68.21790833 | 0.01465891 | 746.86564807 | 10.94823436 | 0.00133893 | 0.09133893 |
| 50 | 74.35752008 | 0.01344854 | 815.08355640 | 10.96168290 | 0.00122687 | 0.09122687 |

| Rate 10% | A<br>Compound<br>Interest | B<br>Present<br>Value | C<br>Amount of<br>Annuity | D<br>Present Value<br>of Annuity | E<br>Sinking<br>Fund | F<br>Amortization |
|---|---|---|---|---|---|---|
| $n$ | $(1+i)^n$ | $\dfrac{1}{(1+i)^n}$ | $s_{\overline{n}\vert i}$ | $a_{\overline{n}\vert i}$ | $\dfrac{1}{s_{\overline{n}\vert i}}$ | $\dfrac{1}{a_{\overline{n}\vert i}}$ |
| 1 | 1.10000000 | 0.90909091 | 1.00000000 | 0.90909091 | 1.00000000 | 1.10000000 |
| 2 | 1.21000000 | 0.82644628 | 2.10000000 | 1.73553719 | 0.47619048 | 0.57619048 |
| 3 | 1.33100000 | 0.75131480 | 3.31000000 | 2.48685199 | 0.30211480 | 0.40211480 |
| 4 | 1.46410000 | 0.68301346 | 4.64100000 | 3.16986545 | 0.21547080 | 0.31547080 |
| 5 | 1.61051000 | 0.62092132 | 6.10510000 | 3.79078677 | 0.16379748 | 0.26379748 |
| 6 | 1.77156100 | 0.56447393 | 7.71561000 | 4.35526070 | 0.12960738 | 0.22960738 |
| 7 | 1.94871710 | 0.51315812 | 9.48717100 | 4.86841882 | 0.10540550 | 0.20540550 |
| 8 | 2.14358881 | 0.46650738 | 11.43588810 | 5.33492620 | 0.08744402 | 0.18744402 |
| 9 | 2.35794769 | 0.42409762 | 13.57947691 | 5.75902382 | 0.07364054 | 0.17364054 |
| 10 | 2.59374246 | 0.38554329 | 15.93742460 | 6.14456711 | 0.06274539 | 0.16274539 |
| 11 | 2.85311671 | 0.35049390 | 18.53116706 | 6.49506101 | 0.05396314 | 0.15396314 |
| 12 | 3.13842838 | 0.31863082 | 21.38428377 | 6.81369182 | 0.04676332 | 0.14676332 |
| 13 | 3.45227121 | 0.28966438 | 24.52271214 | 7.10335620 | 0.04077852 | 0.14077852 |
| 14 | 3.79749834 | 0.26333125 | 27.97498336 | 7.36668746 | 0.03574622 | 0.13574622 |
| 15 | 4.17724817 | 0.23939205 | 31.77248169 | 7.60607951 | 0.03147378 | 0.13147378 |
| 16 | 4.59497299 | 0.21762914 | 35.94972986 | 7.82370864 | 0.02781662 | 0.12781662 |
| 17 | 5.05447028 | 0.19784467 | 40.54470285 | 8.02155331 | 0.02466413 | 0.12466413 |
| 18 | 5.55991731 | 0.17985879 | 45.59917313 | 8.20141210 | 0.02193022 | 0.12193022 |
| 19 | 6.11590904 | 0.16350799 | 51.15909045 | 8.36492009 | 0.01954687 | 0.11954687 |
| 20 | 6.72749995 | 0.14864363 | 57.27499949 | 8.51356372 | 0.01745962 | 0.11745962 |
| 21 | 7.40024994 | 0.13513057 | 64.00249944 | 8.64869429 | 0.01562439 | 0.11562439 |
| 22 | 8.14027494 | 0.12284597 | 71.40274939 | 8.77154026 | 0.04100506 | 0.11400506 |
| 23 | 8.95430243 | 0.11167816 | 79.54302433 | 8.88321842 | 0.01257181 | 0.11257181 |
| 24 | 9.84973268 | 0.10152560 | 88.49732676 | 8.98474402 | 0.01129978 | 0.11129978 |
| 25 | 10.83470594 | 0.09229600 | 98.34705943 | 9.07704002 | 0.01016807 | 0.11016807 |
| 26 | 11.91817654 | 0.08390545 | 109.18176538 | 9.16094547 | 0.00915904 | 0.10915904 |
| 27 | 13.10999419 | 0.07627768 | 121.09994191 | 9.23722316 | 0.00825764 | 0.10825764 |
| 28 | 14.42099361 | 0.06934335 | 134.20993611 | 9.30656651 | 0.00745101 | 0.10745101 |
| 29 | 15.86309297 | 0.06303941 | 148.63092972 | 9.36960591 | 0.00672807 | 0.10672807 |
| 30 | 17.44940227 | 0.05730855 | 164.49402269 | 9.42691447 | 0.00607925 | 0.10607925 |
| 31 | 19.19434250 | 0.05209868 | 181.94342496 | 9.47901315 | 0.00549621 | 0.10549621 |
| 32 | 21.11377675 | 0.04736244 | 201.13776745 | 9.52637559 | 0.00497172 | 0.10497172 |
| 33 | 23.22515442 | 0.04305676 | 222.25154420 | 9.56943236 | 0.00449941 | 0.10449941 |
| 34 | 25.54766986 | 0.03914251 | 245.47669862 | 9.60857487 | 0.00407371 | 0.10407371 |
| 35 | 28.10243685 | 0.03558410 | 271.02436848 | 9.64415897 | 0.00368971 | 0.10368971 |
| 36 | 30.91268053 | 0.03234918 | 299.12680533 | 9.67650816 | 0.00334306 | 0.10334306 |
| 37 | 34.00394859 | 0.02940835 | 330.03948586 | 9.70591651 | 0.00302994 | 0.10302994 |
| 38 | 37.40434344 | 0.02673486 | 364.04343445 | 9.73265137 | 0.00274692 | 0.10274692 |
| 39 | 41.14477779 | 0.02430442 | 401.44777789 | 9.75695579 | 0.00249098 | 0.10249098 |
| 40 | 45.25925557 | 0.02209493 | 442.59255568 | 9.77905072 | 0.00225941 | 0.10225941 |
| 41 | 49.78518112 | 0.02008630 | 487.85181125 | 9.79913702 | 0.00204980 | 0.10204980 |
| 42 | 54.76369924 | 0.01826027 | 537.63699237 | 9.81739729 | 0.00185999 | 0.10185999 |
| 43 | 60.24006916 | 0.01660025 | 592.40069161 | 9.83399753 | 0.00168805 | 0.10168805 |
| 44 | 66.26407608 | 0.01509113 | 652.64076077 | 9.84908867 | 0.00153224 | 0.10153224 |
| 45 | 72.89048369 | 0.01371921 | 718.90483685 | 9.86280788 | 0.00139100 | 0.10139100 |
| 46 | 80.17953205 | 0.01247201 | 791.79532054 | 9.87527989 | 0.00126295 | 0.10126295 |
| 47 | 88.19748526 | 0.01133819 | 871.97485259 | 9.88661808 | 0.00114682 | 0.10114682 |
| 48 | 97.01723378 | 0.01030745 | 960.17233785 | 9.89692553 | 0.00104148 | 0.10104148 |
| 49 | 106.71895716 | 0.00937041 | 1057.18957163 | 9.90629594 | 0.00094590 | 0.10094590 |
| 50 | 117.39085288 | 0.00851855 | 1163.90852880 | 9.91481449 | 0.00085917 | 0.10085917 |

| Rate 11% | A<br>Compound<br>Interest | B<br>Present<br>Value | C<br>Amount of<br>Annuity | D<br>Present Value<br>of Annuity | E<br>Sinking<br>Fund | F<br>Amortization |
|---|---|---|---|---|---|---|
| $n$ | $(1 + i)^n$ | $\dfrac{1}{(1 + i)^n}$ | $s_{\overline{n}\mid i}$ | $a_{\overline{n}\mid i}$ | $\dfrac{1}{s_{\overline{n}\mid i}}$ | $\dfrac{1}{a_{\overline{n}\mid i}}$ |
| 1 | 1.11000000 | 0.90090090 | 1.00000000 | 0.90090090 | 1.00000000 | 1.11000000 |
| 2 | 1.23210000 | 0.81162243 | 2.11000000 | 1.71252333 | 0.47393365 | 0.58393365 |
| 3 | 1.36763100 | 0.73119138 | 3.34210000 | 2.44371472 | 0.29921307 | 0.40921307 |
| 4 | 1.51807041 | 0.65873097 | 4.70973100 | 3.10244569 | 0.21232635 | 0.32232635 |
| 5 | 1.68505816 | 0.59345133 | 6.22780141 | 3.69589702 | 0.16057031 | 0.27057031 |
| 6 | 1.87041455 | 0.53464084 | 7.91285957 | 4.23053785 | 0.12637656 | 0.23637656 |
| 7 | 2.07616015 | 0.48165841 | 9.78327412 | 4.71219626 | 0.10221527 | 0.21221527 |
| 8 | 2.30453777 | 0.43392650 | 11.85943427 | 5.14612276 | 0.08432105 | 0.19432105 |
| 9 | 2.55803692 | 0.39092477 | 14.16397204 | 5.53704753 | 0.07060166 | 0.18060166 |
| 10 | 2.83942099 | 0.35218448 | 16.72200896 | 5.88923201 | 0.05980143 | 0.16980143 |
| 11 | 3.15175729 | 0.31728331 | 19.56142995 | 6.20651533 | 0.05112101 | 0.16112101 |
| 12 | 3.49845060 | 0.28584082 | 22.71318724 | 6.49235615 | 0.04402729 | 0.15402729 |
| 13 | 3.88328016 | 0.25751426 | 26.21163784 | 6.74987040 | 0.03815099 | 0.14815099 |
| 14 | 4.31044098 | 0.23199482 | 30.09491800 | 6.98186523 | 0.03322820 | 0.14322820 |
| 15 | 4.78458949 | 0.20900435 | 34.40535898 | 7.19086958 | 0.02906524 | 0.13906524 |
| 16 | 5.31089433 | 0.18829220 | 39.18994847 | 7.37916178 | 0.02551675 | 0.13551675 |
| 17 | 5.89509271 | 0.16963262 | 44.50084281 | 7.54879440 | 0.02247148 | 0.13247148 |
| 18 | 6.54355291 | 0.15282218 | 50.39593551 | 7.70161657 | 0.01984287 | 0.12984287 |
| 19 | 7.26334373 | 0.13767764 | 56.93948842 | 7.83929421 | 0.01756250 | 0.12756250 |
| 20 | 8.06231154 | 0.12403391 | 64.20283215 | 7.96332812 | 0.01557564 | 0.12557564 |
| 21 | 8.94916581 | 0.11174226 | 72.26514368 | 8.07507038 | 0.01383793 | 0.12383793 |
| 22 | 9.93357404 | 0.10066870 | 81.21430949 | 8.17573908 | 0.01231310 | 0.12231310 |
| 23 | 11.02626719 | 0.09069252 | 91.14788353 | 8.26643160 | 0.01097118 | 0.12097118 |
| 24 | 12.23915658 | 0.08170498 | 102.17415072 | 8.34813658 | 0.00978721 | 0.11978721 |
| 25 | 13.58546380 | 0.07360809 | 114.41330730 | 8.42174466 | 0.00874024 | 0.11874024 |
| 26 | 15.07986482 | 0.06631359 | 127.99877110 | 8.48805826 | 0.00781258 | 0.11781258 |
| 27 | 16.73864995 | 0.05974197 | 143.07863592 | 8.54780023 | 0.00698916 | 0.11698916 |
| 28 | 18.57990145 | 0.05382160 | 159.81728587 | 8.60162183 | 0.00625715 | 0.11625715 |
| 29 | 20.62369061 | 0.04848793 | 178.39718732 | 8.65010976 | 0.00560547 | 0.11560547 |
| 30 | 22.89229657 | 0.04368282 | 199.02087793 | 8.69379257 | 0.00502460 | 0.11502460 |
| 31 | 25.41044919 | 0.03935389 | 221.91317450 | 8.73314646 | 0.00450627 | 0.11450627 |
| 32 | 28.20559861 | 0.03545395 | 247.32362369 | 8.76860042 | 0.00404329 | 0.11404329 |
| 33 | 31.30821445 | 0.03194050 | 275.52922230 | 8.80054092 | 0.00362938 | 0.11362938 |
| 34 | 34.75211804 | 0.02877522 | 306.83743675 | 8.82931614 | 0.00325905 | 0.11325905 |
| 35 | 38.57485103 | 0.02592363 | 341.58955480 | 8.85523977 | 0.00292749 | 0.11292749 |
| 36 | 42.81808464 | 0.02335462 | 380.16440582 | 8.87859438 | 0.00263044 | 0.11263044 |
| 37 | 47.52807395 | 0.02104020 | 422.98249046 | 8.89963458 | 0.00236416 | 0.11236416 |
| 38 | 52.75616209 | 0.01895513 | 470.51056441 | 8.91858971 | 0.00212535 | 0.11212535 |
| 39 | 58.55933991 | 0.01707670 | 523.26672650 | 8.93566641 | 0.00191107 | 0.11191107 |
| 40 | 65.00086731 | 0.01538441 | 581.82606641 | 8.95105082 | 0.00171873 | 0.11171873 |
| 41 | 72.15096271 | 0.01385983 | 646.82693372 | 8.96491065 | 0.00154601 | 0.11154601 |
| 42 | 80.08756861 | 0.01248633 | 718.97789643 | 8.97739698 | 0.00139086 | 0.11139086 |
| 43 | 88.89720115 | 0.01124895 | 799.06546504 | 8.98864593 | 0.00125146 | 0.11125146 |
| 44 | 98.67589328 | 0.01013419 | 887.96266619 | 8.99878011 | 0.00112617 | 0.11112617 |
| 45 | 109.53024154 | 0.00912990 | 986.63855947 | 9.00791001 | 0.00101354 | 0.11101354 |
| 46 | 121.57856811 | 0.00822513 | 1096.16880101 | 9.01613515 | 0.00091227 | 0.11091227 |
| 47 | 134.95221060 | 0.00741003 | 1217.74736912 | 9.02354518 | 0.00082119 | 0.11082119 |
| 48 | 149.79695377 | 0.00667570 | 1352.69957973 | 9.03022088 | 0.00073926 | 0.11073926 |
| 49 | 166.27461868 | 0.00601415 | 1502.49653350 | 9.03623503 | 0.00066556 | 0.11066556 |
| 50 | 184.56482674 | 0.00541815 | 1668.77115218 | 9.04165318 | 0.00059924 | 0.11059924 |

| Rate 12% | A<br>Compound<br>Interest | B<br>Present<br>Value | C<br>Amount of<br>Annuity | D<br>Present Value<br>of Annuity | E<br>Sinking<br>Fund | F<br><br>Amortization |
|---|---|---|---|---|---|---|
| $n$ | $(1+i)^n$ | $\dfrac{1}{(1+i)^n}$ | $s_{\overline{n}|i}$ | $a_{\overline{n}|i}$ | $\dfrac{1}{s_{\overline{n}|i}}$ | $\dfrac{1}{a_{\overline{n}|i}}$ |
| 1 | 1.12000000 | 0.89285714 | 1.00000000 | 0.89285714 | 1.00000000 | 1.12000000 |
| 2 | 1.25440000 | 0.79719388 | 2.12000000 | 1.69005102 | 0.47169811 | 0.59169811 |
| 3 | 1.40492800 | 0.71178025 | 3.37440000 | 2.40183127 | 0.29634898 | 0.41634898 |
| 4 | 1.57351936 | 0.63551808 | 4.77932800 | 3.03734935 | 0.20923444 | 0.32923444 |
| 5 | 1.76234168 | 0.56742686 | 6.35284736 | 3.60477620 | 0.15740973 | 0.27740973 |
| 6 | 1.97382269 | 0.50663112 | 8.11518904 | 4.11140732 | 0.12322572 | 0.24322572 |
| 7 | 2.21068141 | 0.45234922 | 10.08901173 | 4.56375654 | 0.09911774 | 0.21911774 |
| 8 | 2.47596318 | 0.40388323 | 12.29969314 | 4.96763977 | 0.08130284 | 0.20130284 |
| 9 | 2.77307876 | 0.36061002 | 14.77565631 | 5.32824979 | 0.06767889 | 0.18767889 |
| 10 | 3.10584821 | 0.32197324 | 17.54873507 | 5.65022303 | 0.05698416 | 0.17698416 |
| 11 | 3.47854999 | 0.28747610 | 20.65458328 | 5.93769913 | 0.04841540 | 0.16841540 |
| 12 | 3.89597599 | 0.25667509 | 24.13313327 | 6.19437423 | 0.04143681 | 0.16143681 |
| 13 | 4.36349311 | 0.22917419 | 28.02910926 | 6.42354842 | 0.03567720 | 0.15567720 |
| 14 | 4.88711229 | 0.20461981 | 32.39260238 | 6.62816823 | 0.03087125 | 0.15087125 |
| 15 | 5.47356576 | 0.18269626 | 37.27971466 | 6.81086449 | 0.02682424 | 0.14682424 |
| 16 | 6.13039365 | 0.16312166 | 42.75328042 | 6.97398615 | 0.02339002 | 0.14339002 |
| 17 | 6.86604098 | 0.14564434 | 48.88367407 | 7.11963049 | 0.02045673 | 0.14045673 |
| 18 | 7.68996580 | 0.13003959 | 55.74971496 | 7.24967008 | 0.01793731 | 0.13793731 |
| 19 | 8.61276169 | 0.11610678 | 63.43968075 | 7.36577686 | 0.01576300 | 0.13576300 |
| 20 | 9.64629309 | 0.10366677 | 72.05244244 | 7.46944362 | 0.01387878 | 0.13387878 |
| 21 | 10.80384826 | 0.09255961 | 81.69873554 | 7.56200324 | 0.01224009 | 0.13224009 |
| 22 | 12.10031006 | 0.08264251 | 92.50258380 | 7.64464575 | 0.01081051 | 0.13081051 |
| 23 | 13.55234726 | 0.07378796 | 104.60289386 | 7.71843370 | 0.00955996 | 0.12955996 |
| 24 | 15.17862893 | 0.06588210 | 118.15524112 | 7.78431581 | 0.00846344 | 0.12846344 |
| 25 | 17.00006441 | 0.05882331 | 133.33387006 | 7.84313911 | 0.00749997 | 0.12749997 |
| 26 | 19.04007214 | 0.05252081 | 150.33393446 | 7.89565992 | 0.00665186 | 0.12665186 |
| 27 | 21.32488079 | 0.04689358 | 169.37400660 | 7.94255350 | 0.00590409 | 0.12590409 |
| 28 | 23.88386649 | 0.04186927 | 190.69888739 | 7.98442277 | 0.00524387 | 0.12524387 |
| 29 | 26.74993047 | 0.03738327 | 214.58275388 | 8.02180604 | 0.00466021 | 0.12466021 |
| 30 | 29.95992212 | 0.03337792 | 241.33268434 | 8.05518397 | 0.00414366 | 0.12414366 |
| 31 | 33.55511278 | 0.02980172 | 271.29260646 | 8.08498569 | 0.00368606 | 0.12368606 |
| 32 | 37.58172631 | 0.02660868 | 304.84771924 | 8.11159436 | 0.00328033 | 0.12328033 |
| 33 | 42.09153347 | 0.02375775 | 342.42944555 | 8.13535211 | 0.00292031 | 0.12292031 |
| 34 | 47.14251748 | 0.02121227 | 384.52097901 | 8.15656438 | 0.00260064 | 0.12260064 |
| 35 | 52.79961958 | 0.01893953 | 431.66349649 | 8.17550391 | 0.00231662 | 0.12231662 |
| 36 | 59.13557393 | 0.01691029 | 484.46311607 | 8.19241421 | 0.00206414 | 0.12206414 |
| 37 | 66.23184280 | 0.01509848 | 543.59869000 | 8.20751269 | 0.00183959 | 0.12183959 |
| 38 | 74.17966394 | 0.01348078 | 609.83053280 | 8.22099347 | 0.00163980 | 0.12163980 |
| 39 | 83.08122361 | 0.01203641 | 684.01019674 | 8.23302988 | 0.00146197 | 0.12146197 |
| 40 | 93.05097044 | 0.01074680 | 767.09142034 | 8.24377668 | 0.00130363 | 0.12130363 |
| 41 | 104.21708689 | 0.00959536 | 860.14239079 | 8.25337204 | 0.00116260 | 0.12116260 |
| 42 | 116.72313732 | 0.00856728 | 964.35947768 | 8.26193932 | 0.00103696 | 0.12103696 |
| 43 | 130.72991380 | 0.00764936 | 1081.08261500 | 8.26958868 | 0.00092500 | 0.12092500 |
| 44 | 146.41750346 | 0.00682978 | 1211.81252880 | 8.27641846 | 0.00082521 | 0.12082521 |
| 45 | 163.98760387 | 0.00609802 | 1358.23003226 | 8.28251648 | 0.00073625 | 0.12073625 |
| 46 | 183.66611634 | 0.00544466 | 1522.21763613 | 8.28796115 | 0.00065694 | 0.12065694 |
| 47 | 205.70605030 | 0.00486131 | 1705.88375247 | 8.29282245 | 0.00058621 | 0.12058621 |
| 48 | 230.39077633 | 0.00434045 | 1911.58980276 | 8.29716290 | 0.00052312 | 0.12052312 |
| 49 | 258.03766949 | 0.00387540 | 2142.98057909 | 8.30103831 | 0.00046686 | 0.12046686 |
| 50 | 289.00218983 | 0.00346018 | 2400.01824858 | 8.30449849 | 0.00041666 | 0.12041666 |

| Rate 13% | A<br>Compound<br>Interest | B<br>Present<br>Value | C<br>Amount of<br>Annuity | D<br>Present Value<br>of Annuity | E<br>Sinking<br>Fund | F<br>Amortization |
|---|---|---|---|---|---|---|
| $n$ | $(1 + i)^n$ | $\dfrac{1}{(1 + i)^n}$ | $s_{\overline{n}\vert i}$ | $a_{\overline{n}\vert i}$ | $\dfrac{1}{s_{\overline{n}\vert i}}$ | $\dfrac{1}{a_{\overline{n}\vert i}}$ |
| 1 | 1.13000000 | 0.88495575 | 1.00000000 | 0.88495575 | 1.00000000 | 1.13000000 |
| 2 | 1.27690000 | 0.78314668 | 2.13000000 | 1.66810244 | 0.46948357 | 0.59948357 |
| 3 | 1.44289700 | 0.69305016 | 3.40690000 | 2.36115260 | 0.29352197 | 0.42352197 |
| 4 | 1.63047361 | 0.61331873 | 4.84979700 | 2.97447133 | 0.20619420 | 0.33619420 |
| 5 | 1.84243518 | 0.54275994 | 6.48027061 | 3.51723126 | 0.15431454 | 0.28431454 |
| 6 | 2.08195175 | 0.48031853 | 8.32270579 | 3.99754979 | 0.12015323 | 0.25015323 |
| 7 | 2.35260548 | 0.42506064 | 10.40465754 | 4.42261043 | 0.09611080 | 0.22611080 |
| 8 | 2.65844419 | 0.37615986 | 12.75726302 | 4.79877029 | 0.07838672 | 0.20838672 |
| 9 | 3.00404194 | 0.33288483 | 15.41570722 | 5.13165513 | 0.06486890 | 0.19486890 |
| 10 | 3.39456739 | 0.29458835 | 18.41974915 | 5.42624348 | 0.05428956 | 0.18428956 |
| 11 | 3.83586115 | 0.26069765 | 21.81431654 | 5.68694113 | 0.04584145 | 0.17584145 |
| 12 | 4.33452310 | 0.23070589 | 25.65017769 | 5.91764702 | 0.03898608 | 0.16898608 |
| 13 | 4.89801110 | 0.20416450 | 29.98470079 | 6.12181152 | 0.03335034 | 0.16335034 |
| 14 | 5.53475255 | 0.18067655 | 34.88271190 | 6.30248807 | 0.02866750 | 0.15866750 |
| 15 | 6.25427038 | 0.15989075 | 40.41746444 | 6.46237882 | 0.02474178 | 0.15474178 |
| 16 | 7.06732553 | 0.14149624 | 46.67173482 | 6.60387506 | 0.02142624 | 0.15142624 |
| 17 | 7.98607785 | 0.12521791 | 53.73906035 | 6.72909298 | 0.01860844 | 0.14860844 |
| 18 | 9.02426797 | 0.11081231 | 61.72513819 | 6.83990529 | 0.01620085 | 0.14620085 |
| 19 | 10.19742280 | 0.09806399 | 70.74940616 | 6.93796928 | 0.01413439 | 0.14413439 |
| 20 | 11.52308776 | 0.08678229 | 80.94682896 | 7.02475158 | 0.01235379 | 0.14235379 |
| 21 | 13.02108917 | 0.07679849 | 92.46991672 | 7.10155007 | 0.01081433 | 0.14081433 |
| 22 | 14.71383077 | 0.06796327 | 105.49100590 | 7.16951334 | 0.00947948 | 0.13947948 |
| 23 | 16.62662877 | 0.06014448 | 120.20483667 | 7.22965782 | 0.00831913 | 0.13831913 |
| 24 | 18.78809051 | 0.05322521 | 136.83146543 | 7.28288303 | 0.00730826 | 0.13730826 |
| 25 | 21.23054227 | 0.04710195 | 155.61955594 | 7.32998498 | 0.00642593 | 0.13642593 |
| 26 | 23.99051277 | 0.04168314 | 176.85009821 | 7.37166812 | 0.00565451 | 0.13565451 |
| 27 | 27.10927943 | 0.03688774 | 200.84061098 | 7.40855586 | 0.00497907 | 0.13497907 |
| 28 | 30.63348575 | 0.03264402 | 227.94989040 | 7.44119988 | 0.00438693 | 0.13438693 |
| 29 | 34.61583890 | 0.02888851 | 258.58337616 | 7.47008839 | 0.00386722 | 0.13386722 |
| 30 | 39.11589796 | 0.02556505 | 293.19921506 | 7.49565344 | 0.00341065 | 0.13341065 |
| 31 | 44.20096469 | 0.02262394 | 332.31511301 | 7.51827738 | 0.00300919 | 0.13300919 |
| 32 | 49.94709010 | 0.02002119 | 376.51607771 | 7.53829857 | 0.00265593 | 0.13265593 |
| 33 | 56.44021181 | 0.01771786 | 426.46316781 | 7.55601643 | 0.00234487 | 0.13234487 |
| 34 | 63.77743935 | 0.01567953 | 482.90337962 | 7.57169596 | 0.00207081 | 0.13207081 |
| 35 | 72.06850647 | 0.01387569 | 546.68081897 | 7.58557164 | 0.00182922 | 0.13182922 |
| 36 | 81.43741231 | 0.01227937 | 618.74932544 | 7.59785101 | 0.00161616 | 0.13161616 |
| 37 | 92.02427591 | 0.01086670 | 700.18673775 | 7.60871771 | 0.00142819 | 0.13142819 |
| 38 | 103.98743178 | 0.00961655 | 792.21101365 | 7.61833426 | 0.00126229 | 0.13126229 |
| 39 | 117.50579791 | 0.00851022 | 896.19844543 | 7.62684447 | 0.00111582 | 0.13111582 |
| 40 | 132.78155163 | 0.00753117 | 1013.70424333 | 7.63437564 | 0.00098648 | 0.13098648 |
| 41 | 150.04315335 | 0.00666475 | 1146.48579497 | 7.64104039 | 0.00087223 | 0.13087223 |
| 42 | 169.54876328 | 0.00589801 | 1296.52894831 | 7.64693840 | 0.00077129 | 0.13077129 |
| 43 | 191.59010251 | 0.00521948 | 1466.07771159 | 7.65215787 | 0.00068209 | 0.13068209 |
| 44 | 216.49261583 | 0.00461901 | 1657.66781410 | 7.65677688 | 0.00060326 | 0.13060326 |
| 45 | 244.64140189 | 0.00408762 | 1874.16462994 | 7.66086450 | 0.00053357 | 0.13053357 |
| 46 | 276.44478414 | 0.00361736 | 2118.80603183 | 7.66448185 | 0.00047196 | 0.13047196 |
| 47 | 312.38260608 | 0.00320120 | 2395.25081596 | 7.66768306 | 0.00041749 | 0.13041749 |
| 48 | 352.99234487 | 0.00283292 | 2707.63342204 | 7.67051598 | 0.00036933 | 0.13036933 |
| 49 | 398.88134970 | 0.00250701 | 3060.62576691 | 7.67302299 | 0.00032673 | 0.13032673 |
| 50 | 450.73592516 | 0.00221859 | 3459.50711660 | 7.67524158 | 0.00028906 | 0.13028906 |

# Answers to Selected Exercises

## CHAPTER 1

### Section 1.1 (page 10)

**1.** $\frac{5}{2}$ **3.** $\frac{17}{4}$ **5.** $\frac{183}{8}$ **7.** $\frac{101}{8}$ **9.** $\frac{3}{4}$ **11.** $\frac{8}{15}$ **13.** $\frac{9}{10}$ **15.** $\frac{4}{5}$ **17.** $\frac{11}{12}$ **19.** $\frac{8}{15}$ **21.** $2\frac{4}{7}$ **23.** $3\frac{4}{5}$ **25.** $1\frac{3}{11}$ **27.** $1\frac{2}{5}$ **29.** $1\frac{15}{16}$
**31.** $2\frac{17}{32}$ **35.** $\frac{2}{3}$ **37.** $\frac{17}{20}$ **39.** $1\frac{7}{60}$ **41.** $\frac{19}{22}$ **43.** $1\frac{23}{36}$ **45.** $2\frac{5}{24}$ **47.** $57\frac{6}{7}$ **49.** $80\frac{3}{4}$ **51.** $71\frac{3}{4}$ **53.** 187 **55.** $\frac{1}{2}$ **57.** $\frac{1}{2}$ **59.** $\frac{17}{48}$
**61.** $\frac{1}{3}$ **63.** $11\frac{5}{12}$ **65.** $3\frac{11}{24}$ **67.** $9\frac{5}{24}$ **69.** $6\frac{1}{4}$ **75.** $\frac{47}{60}$ in. **77.** $\frac{19}{24}$ of the debt **79.** $\frac{3}{16}$ in. **81.** 30 in. **83.** $342\frac{17}{24}$ acres
**85.** 50 cases **87.** $10\frac{7}{12}$ **89.** $\$118\frac{5}{8}$

### Section 1.2 (page 21)

**1.** $\frac{1}{2}$ **3.** $\frac{4}{7}$ **5.** $4\frac{1}{2}$ **7.** 69 **9.** $4\frac{7}{12}$ **11.** 90 **13.** $\frac{3}{4}$ **15.** $\frac{5}{8}$ **17.** $1\frac{1}{2}$ **19.** $\frac{2}{3}$ **21.** $3\frac{1}{3}$ **23.** $4\frac{4}{5}$ **27.** $\$2,070$ **29.** $\$1,341$
**31.** $\$1,828$ **33.** $\frac{1}{2}$ **35.** $\frac{6}{25}$ **37.** $\frac{81}{100}$ **39.** $\frac{7}{8}$ **41.** $\frac{3}{80}$ **43.** $\frac{3}{16}$ **45.** 32.6; 32.61 **47.** 0.1; 0.08 **49.** 8.6; 8.64
**51.** 59.0; 58.96 **53.** 0.5 **55.** 0.625 **57.** 0.167 **59.** 0.813 **61.** 0.88 **63.** 0.010 **69.** 13 yd. **71.** 600 shares
**73.** 12 homes **75.** $21\frac{7}{8}$ oz. **77.** 471 rolls **79.** 56 gal.

### Chapter 1 Review Exercises (page 26)

**1.** $\frac{3}{5}$ **2.** $\frac{1}{2}$ **3.** $\frac{1}{3}$ **4.** $\frac{1}{2}$ **5.** $\frac{9}{10}$ **6.** $\frac{7}{11}$ **7.** $\frac{1}{50}$ **8.** $\frac{3}{8}$ **9.** $7\frac{1}{2}$ **10.** $4\frac{2}{3}$ **11.** $1\frac{7}{12}$ **12.** $7\frac{6}{7}$ **13.** $2\frac{2}{3}$ **14.** $8\frac{1}{6}$ **15.** $8\frac{1}{16}$ **16.** $3\frac{1}{32}$
**17.** $\frac{5}{8}$ **18.** $\frac{7}{8}$ **19.** $\frac{1}{2}$ **20.** $\frac{1}{12}$ **21.** $71\frac{5}{6}$ **22.** $91\frac{5}{6}$ **23.** $4\frac{1}{4}$ **24.** $81\frac{1}{16}$ **25.** $34\frac{11}{24}$ lb. **26.** $8\frac{5}{8}$ hr. **27.** $22\frac{1}{2}$ hr. **28.** $24\frac{1}{8}$ lb.
**29.** $319\frac{1}{2}$ ft. **30.** $54\frac{11}{24}$ lb. **31.** $\frac{21}{32}$ **32.** $\frac{7}{40}$ **33.** $1\frac{2}{3}$ **34.** 16 **35.** $13\frac{17}{24}$ **36.** $2\frac{2}{9}$ **37.** $20\frac{5}{6}$ **38.** $6\frac{1}{6}$ **39.** 18 bags
**40.** $152\frac{4}{9}$ oz. **41.** $42\frac{1}{2}$ acres **42.** $\$405.38$ **43.** 108 units **44.** $\frac{1}{12}$ of the total profit **45.** $\frac{3}{4}$ **46.** $\frac{5}{8}$ **47.** $\frac{93}{100}$ **48.** $\frac{1}{200}$
**49.** 34.3; 34.32 **50.** 861.5; 861.55 **51.** 0.4; 0.35 **52.** 8.0; 8.03 **53.** 7.0; 6.97 **54.** 0.4; 0.43 **55.** 1.0; 0.96
**56.** 71.2; 71.25 **57.** 0.875 **58.** 0.111 **59.** 0.833 **60.** 0.438

### Chapter 1 Summary Exercise (page 28)

**(a)** $\$1,031.25$ **(b)** $\$1,121.25$ **(c)** $\$1,625$ **(d)** $\$1,535$ **(e)** $\$413.75$

## CHAPTER 2

### Section 2.1 (page 35)

**1.** 30 **3.** 27 **5.** 6 **7.** 4.2 **9.** 12 **11.** 2 **13.** 2.1 **15.** 5.9 **17.** 0.8 **19.** 400 **21.** 294 **23.** 7 **25.** 12 **27.** 25 **29.** $\frac{5}{6}$
**31.** $\frac{5}{36}$ **33.** 4 **35.** 8 **37.** 1.75 **39.** $1\frac{4}{15}$ **41.** $\frac{2}{3}$ **43.** 1 **45.** 3.5 **47.** 13 **49.** 2 **51.** 5 **53.** 7 **55.** 10 **57.** $\frac{16}{19}$ **59.** $\frac{2}{3}$
**61.** $1\frac{1}{6}$ **63.** 2.1 **65.** 0.8

### Section 2.2 (page 40)

**1.** $16 + x$ **3.** $8 + x$ **5.** $x - 4$ **7.** $x - \frac{1}{3}$ **9.** $3x$ **11.** $\frac{3}{5}x$ **13.** $9/x$ **15.** $16/x$ **17.** $2.1(4 + x)$ **19.** $7(x - 3)$ **21.** $3,000x$
**23.** $472 - x$ **25.** $73 - x$ **27.** $172/x$ **29.** $21 - x$ **31.** $4\frac{1}{3}$ **33.** 2 **35.** 1 **37.** $1\frac{3}{7}$ **39.** $\$4,150$ **41.** 146 **43.** $\$20,500$
**45.** 42—deluxe; 63—economy **47.** $\$3,937.50$—announcers; $\$6,562.50$—all other employees **49.** $\$15,000$; $\$52,500$
**51.** 28—new; 35—exp. **53.** 81—Altimas; 39—Sentras

**Section 2.3 (page 47)**

**1.** 504  **3.** 3,183.60  **5.** 0.0625  **7.** 14  **9.** 0.08  **11.** 576  **13.** 749.86  **15.** 7.5  **17.** 7  **19.** 24,000  **21.** $\dfrac{A}{L}$  **23.** $\dfrac{V}{LW}$

**25.** $\dfrac{m}{(1 + i)^n}$  **27.** $\dfrac{A - P}{P}$  **29.** $\dfrac{m - P}{mT}$  **31.** $\dfrac{2A}{(b + B)}$  **33.** $\dfrac{m}{e^{ni}}$  **35.** \$9.50  **37.** \$105  **39. (a)** \$194.56  **(b)** \$213.88

**(c)** \$229.42  **41.** \$1,200  **43.** \$48  **45.** \$90,000  **47.** \$390  **49.** 13%  **51.** 4 yr.  **53.** \$4,000  **55.** \$4,500

**Section 2.4 (page 54)**

**1.** $\frac{25}{3}$  **3.** $\frac{7}{18}$  **5.** $\frac{4}{3}$  **7.** $\frac{3,750}{1}$  **9.** $\frac{225}{1}$  **11.** 8/5  **13.** 1/6  **15.** 4/15  **17.** 9/2  **19.** T  **21.** T  **23.** F  **25.** F  **27.** F  **29.** F
**31.** T  **33.** T  **35.** F  **37.** T  **39.** 12  **41.** 245  **43.** 105  **45.** $3\frac{1}{2}$  **47.** 24  **49.** 8  **53.** 2,100 gal.  **55.** 25,000 people
**57.** \$96  **59.** 36 yd.  **61.** 1,020 mi.  **63.** \$33.75  **65.** \$24,000  **67.** 1,475 mi.  **69.** 3,500,000 cu. m.

**Chapter 2 Review Exercises (page 58)**

**1.** 16.5  **2.** $17\frac{1}{4}$  **3.** 4  **4.** $5\frac{1}{4}$  **5.** 252  **6.** 136  **7.** 56  **8.** $13\frac{1}{2}$  **9.** 7  **10.** $1\frac{2}{3}$  **11.** 21  **12.** 3.6  **13.** $5x$  **14.** $\frac{1}{2}x$
**15.** $x + 6x$  **16.** $5x - 11$  **17.** $3x + 7$  **18.** \$29,652  **19.** \$20,000  **20.** \$108—water; \$432—phone  **21.** 76
**22.** 70—child; 30—adult  **23.** \$4,000  **24.** \$3,250  **25.** \$8,200 (rounded)  **26.** $\dfrac{M - P}{PR}$  **27.** $\frac{9}{5}C + 32$  **28.** $\dfrac{R - D}{RD}$
**29.** 4/3  **30.** 18/1  **31.** 20/1  **32.** 12/5  **33.** 8/3  **34.** 4  **35.** $6\frac{3}{4}$  **36.** $4\frac{1}{2}$  **37.** 27  **38.** 24  **39.** 250 are defective
**40.** 1,333 parts  **41.** \$17.50  **42.** 105  **43.** \$57,000  **44.** \$139.50  **45.** 25

**Chapter 2 Summary Exercise (page 60)**

**(a)** \$6,100  **(b)** Profit = \$3.18N − \$6,100  **(c)** 1,919 books  **(d)** The owner would probably receive less salary.
**(e)** 2,705 books (2,704 books won't quite give them the profit they desire)

# CHAPTER 3

**Section 3.1 (page 65)**

**1.** 50%  **3.** 72%  **5.** 140%  **7.** 37.5%  **9.** 375.1%  **11.** 0.25%  **13.** 0.15%  **15.** 712%  **17.** 25%  **19.** 10%  **21.** 60%
**23.** 37.5%  **25.** 12.5%  **27.** 0.5%  **29.** 87.5%  **31.** 6%  **33.** 0.15  **35.** 0.75  **37.** 0.006  **39.** 0.0025  **41.** 2.1
**43.** 2.006  **45.** 3.508  **47.** 0.0007  **53.** 0.75; 75%  **55.** $\frac{3}{20}$; 15%  **57.** $\frac{1}{4}$; 25%  **59.** 6.125; 612.5%  **61.** $7\frac{1}{4}$; 725%
**63.** $\frac{1}{400}$; 0.25%  **65.** 0.333 (rounded); $33\frac{1}{3}$%  **67.** $\frac{3}{400}$; 0.0075  **69.** $\frac{1}{40}$; 2.5%  **71.** $3\frac{3}{4}$; 3.75  **73.** $23\frac{41}{50}$; 2382%
**75.** $\frac{3}{8}$; 0.375

**Section 3.2 (page 71)**

**1.** 52 adults  **3.** \$244.35  **5.** 4.8 ft.  **7.** 10,185 mi.  **9.** 182 crates  **11.** 148.44 yd.  **13.** \$5,366.65  **15.** \$6.50
**19.** \$19.80  **21.** \$645  **23.** 2,024 shoppers  **25.** 46 seniors  **27. (a)** 39% female
**(b)** 2.318 million or 2,318,000 workers  **29.** \$632.50  **31.** 2,156 products  **33.** \$19,952.90  **35.** \$51,844.20
**37.** \$510,390  **39.** \$5,958

**Section 3.3 (page 76)**

**1.** 2.650  **3.** 187.5  **5.** 2,000  **7.** 2,400  **9.** 22,000  **11.** 20,000  **13.** \$90,320  **15.** 1,750  **17.** 312,500  **19.** 65,400
**21.** 40,000  **25.** 94 students  **27.** 7,761 students  **29.** \$2,800  **31.** \$1,000 million or \$1,000,000,000  **33.** \$23,124
**35.** \$185,500

*Supplementary Exercises: Base and Part (page 78)*
**1.** 150,000 employees   **3.** $288,150   **5.** 478,175 Mustangs   **7.** $93.9 million   **9.** $18,600   **11.** 836 drivers   **13.** $23

*Section 3.4 (page 83)*
**1.** 40   **3.** 150   **5.** 28.3   **7.** 9.3   **9.** 5.0   **11.** 5.9   **13.** 102.5   **15.** 17.6   **17.** 27.8   **21.** 5.6%   **23.** 65.9%   **25.** 8.7%
**27.** 233.3%   **29.** 9.1%

*Supplementary Exercises: Rate, Base, and Part (page 84)*
**1.** 0.6 million patients   **3.** 4.9%   **5.** 16,910 economy hotels and motels   **7.** 5,000,000 cars   **9.** $396.05   **11.** 24%
**13.** 470,844 workers   **15.** 24.4%   **17.** 12.5%   **19.** 5.5%   **21.** 960 candy bars   **23.** $8,823   **25.** 23.6%
**27.** 5,742 deaths   **29.** 20%

*Section 3.5 (page 92)*
**1.** $256   **3.** $27.91   **5.** $20   **7.** $854.50   **11.** $150,500   **13.** $86.2 million   **15.** 160 ft.   **17.** $253.60   **19.** $118,080
**21.** $58.9 billion   **23.** $3,864   **25.** 39,000 items   **27.** 51.2 million acres   **29.** 20,000 students
**31.** $31.6 million or $31,600,000   **33.** 6,564 homes

*Chapter 3 Review Exercises (page 97)*
**1.** 140 customers   **2.** 7 trucks   **3.** 1,100 shippers   **4.** 2.5%   **5.** $3.75   **6.** $\frac{4}{25}$   **7.** 960 loads   **8.** $\frac{5}{8}$   **9.** 8.5%   **10.** $\frac{1}{200}$
**11.** $1.43   **12.** 224,000 units   **13.** 42 middle managers   **14.** 248.0 million people   **15. (a)** 11%   **(b)** $4,488   **16.** 68%
**17.** $1,450   **18.** 1,200 backpacks   **19.** 22.5%   **20.** 1.2 million permits   **21.** 125%   **22.** 12.5 oz.   **23.** 97,757 copies
**24.** $39,840   **25.** 23.8%   **26.** 0.7%   **27.** $53,302,307.80   **28.** $1.365 billion   **29.** 933.3%   **30.** 54.4%   **31.** 1.1%
**32.** 1,800,000 tourists   **33.** 91,757 units   **34.** 148,507 units   **35.** $240,000   **36.** 97 units

*Chapter 3 Summary Exercise (page 99)*
$6; 0%; $4; $1,620; $9; −65%; $10; $12

# CHAPTER 4

*Section 4.1 (page 109)*
**1.** $17.30   **3.** $20   **5.** $17.10   **7.** $21.90
**9.** Feb. 11; $380.71; Victoria Beltrano; travel; 3,971.28; 79.26; 4,050.54; 380.71; 3,669.83
**11.** Dec. 4; $37.52; Enid Power; utilities; 1,126.73; 1,126.73; 37.52; 1,089.21
**17.** May 8; $39.12; County Clerk; license; 5,972.89; 752.18; 23.32; 6,748.39; 39.12; 6,709.27
**19.** 1,379.41; 1,230.41; 1,348.14; 1,278.34; 1,608.20; 2,026.50; 1,916.74; 1,302.62; 1,270.44; 1,791.39
**21.** 3,709.32; 3,590.92; 3,877.24; 3,797.24; 2,811.02; 2,435.52; 3,637.34; 2,901.66; 2,677.72; 3,175.73; 3,097.49

*Section 4.2 (page 115)*
**1. (a)** $1,245.20   **(b)** $60.21   **(c)** $1,184.99   **(d)** $59.25   **(e)** $1,125.74   **3. (a)** $1,591.44   **(b)** $189.39
**(c)** $1,402.05   **(d)** $56.08   **(e)** $1,345.97   **5. (a)** $1,064.72   **(b)** $72.83   **(c)** $991.89   **(d)** $29.76   **(e)** $962.13

*Section 4.3 (page 124)*
**1.** $4,228.50   **3.** $7,690.62   **5.** $18,314.72   **7.** $6,967.88   **9.** $7,498.20   **11.** $4,496.01   **17.** $6,728.20

*Chapter 4 Review Exercises (page 128)*
**1.** $14.70 **2.** $19 **3.** $10.20 **4.** $9,517.70 **5.** $9,831.34 **6.** $19,415.20 **7.** $1,595.36 **8.** $207.69 **9.** $1,387.67
**10.** $55.51 **11.** $1,332.16 **12.** $6,043.16 **13.** $8,992.02 **14.** $1,267.21

*Chapter 4 Summary Exercise (page 131)*
**(a)** $6,101.69 **(b)** $5,888.13 **(c)** $9,810.36 **(d)** $4,882.58 **(e)** $5,188.69

# CHAPTER 5

*Section 5.1 (page 141)*
**1.** 40; 0; $11.10 **3.** 38.75; 0; $9.78 **5.** 40; 5.25; $17.22 **7.** $296; $0; $296 **9.** $252.65; $0; $252.65
**11.** $459.20; $90.41; $549.61 **13.** $12.15; $309.83; $0; $309.83 **15.** $10.80; $288; $48.60; $336.60
**17.** $13.77; $367.20; $58.52; $425.72 **19.** 51; 11; $3.40; $346.80; $37.40; $384.20
**21.** 50.25; 10.25; $4.30; $432.15; $44.08; $476.23 **23.** 50.25; 10.25; $5.10; $512.55; $52.28; $564.83
**25.** 35; 6; $8.31; $193.90; $49.86; $243.76 **27.** 39.5; 3.75; $10.05; $264.65; $37.69; $302.34
**29.** 39.75; 3.5; $15.30; $405.45; $53.55; $459 **33.** $496; $557.33; $1,074.67; $12,896
**35.** $426; $923; $1,846; $22,152 **37.** $501.92; $1,003.85; $2,175; $26,100 **39.** $618.46; $1,236.92; $1,340; $32,160
**41.** $415; $830; $899.17; $1,798.33 **43.** $832 **45.** $487.70 **47.** $703.08 **49.** $384.80 **51.** $335.40 **53.** $793.80
**55.** $925.16 **57. (a)** $840 **(b)** $910 **(c)** $1,820 **(d)** $21,840

*Section 5.2 (page 149)*
**1.** $208.16 **3.** $421.65 **5.** $1,941.75 **7.** $433.37 **9.** $1,405 **11.** $688.40 **13.** $748 **15.** $2,136
**19.** $3,800; $190; $530 **21.** $4,085; $245.10; $245.10 **23.** $9,530; $285.90; $285.90 **25.** $2,897; $144.85; $354.85
**27.** $577 **29.** $6,214 **31. (a)** $2,495 **(b)** $1,695 **33.** $412.14

*Section 5.3 (page 155)*
**1.** 326; $254.28 **3.** 451; $338.25 **5.** 665; $452.20 **7.** 588; $270.48 **9.** 670; $522.60 **11.** $71.70 **13.** $123.78
**15.** $86.62 **17.** $92.06 **19.** $145.12 **21.** $156 **23.** $260.19 **25.** $254.90 **27.** $198 **29.** $274.80 **31.** $439.52
**33.** $503.80 **35.** $322.57 **37.** $340.73 **41.** $580 **43.** $624.25 **45.** $373.05

*Section 5.4 (page 163)*
**1.** $14.03; $3.24 **3.** $54.65; $12.61 **5.** $23.95; $5.53 **7.** $59.55; $13.74 **9.** $138.37 **11.** $278.10 **13.** $11.72
**15.** $368.80; $76.07; $444.87; $28.92; $6.67; $4.45 **17.** $412; $61.80; $473.80; $30.80; $7.11; $4.74
**19.** $204; $38.25; $242.25; $15.75; $3.63; $2.42 **21.** $249.60; $63.18; $312.78; $20.33; $4.69; $3.13
**23. (a)** $25.24 **(b)** $5.82 **25. (a)** $100.30 **(b)** $23.15 **(c)** $15.43 **27.** $4,002.22; $923.59
**29.** $4,526.23; $1,044.51 **31.** $3,039.99; $701.54

*Section 5.5 (page 172)*
**1.** $177 **3.** $59 **5.** $97 **7.** $90 **9.** $32 **11.** $2.03 **13.** $19.57 **15.** $7.28 **17.** $8.13; $27.14; $6.26; $376.05
**19.** $166.03; $99.59; $22.98; $1,243.58 **21.** $278.07; $155.07; $35.79; $1,916.81
**23.** $323.87; $256.24; $59.13; $3,302.88 **25.** $48.32; $46.19; $10.66; $605.39 **27.** $117.45; $46.50; $10.73; $540.66
**29.** $766.14; $345.32; $79.69; $4,121.44 **31.** $42.76; $28.03; $6.47; $353.99 **35.** $493.76 **37.** $476.18
**39.** $3,545.13

*Section 5.6 (page 180)*
**1.** $1,186.04 **3.** $2,794.05 **5.** $2,261.05 **7.** $9,996.25 **9.** $1,289.96 **11.** $13,354.58 **13.** $13,092.06
**15.** $18,155.85 **19.** $3,508.50 **21.** $1,925.79 **23. (a)** $1,120 **(b)** $69.44 **25. (a)** $1,600 **(b)** $99.20

*Chapter 5 Review Exercises (page 185)*
**1.** 40; 8.5; $482.14 **2.** 40; 8; $442 **3.** 38.25; 0; $283.05 **4.** 40; 17.25; $447.95
**5.** $821.60; $890.07; $1,780.13; $21,361.60 **6.** $530; $1,148.33; $2,296.67; $27,560
**7.** $346.15; $692.31; $750; $1,500 **8.** $403.85; $807.69; $1,750; $21,000 **9.** $760 **10.** $427.50 **11.** $2,090.34
**12.** $1,696.40 **13.** $242.75 **14.** $134 **15.** $1,725 **16.** $465 **17.** $600 **18.** $265.02 **19. (a)** $406.25 **(b)** $93.75
**20. (a)** $227.50 **(b)** $93.75 **21.** $24 **22.** $149 **23.** $159 **24.** $57 **25.** $120 **26.** $70 **27.** $1,434.09
**28.** $401.26 **29.** $525.77 **30.** $2,035.22 **31.** $9,590.63 **32. (a)** $33.44 **(b)** $7.72 **(c)** $5.14
**33. (a)** $65.08 **(b)** $32.85 **34.** $5,451.25 **35. (a)** $3,044.24 **(b)** $702.52 **36. (a)** $4,490.08 **(b)** $1,036.17
**37. (a)** $913 **(b)** $56.61 **38. (a)** $2,140 **(b)** $132.68

*Chapter 5 Summary Exercise (page 189)*
**(a)** $560 **(b)** $252 **(c)** $812 **(d)** $52.78 **(e)** $12.18 **(f)** $144.52 **(g)** $8.12 **(h)** $60.94 **(i)** $306.46

# CHAPTER 6

*Section 6.1 (page 195)*
**1.** $0.90; $1.50; $17.40 **3.** $2.15; $1.43; $51.28 **5.** $8.68; $14.85; $197.03 **7.** $57.55; $98.66; $978.39
**9.** $1,837.50; $504; $31,741.50 **11.** $45.80; $48.09 **13.** $157.50; $163.80 **15.** $330; $351.45
**17.** $1,276.80; $1,340.64 **19.** $32; $2.24 **21.** $520.30; $31.22 **23.** $19.76; $0.84 **25.** $315; $18.90
**27.** $2,753.05; $192.71 **31. (a)** $7.19 **(b)** $13.18 **(c)** $140.17 **33.** $380 **35.** $2,490 **37.** $49.44
**39. (a)** $108 **(b)** $6.48 **41.** $201.35 **43.** $37,828.75

*Section 6.2 (page 202)*
**1.** $11,200 **3.** $109,500 **5.** $325,125 **7.** 12% **9.** 8% **11.** 3% **13.** 5.6; $5.60; $56 **15.** $2.41; $24.10; 24.1
**17.** 7.08; $70.80; 70.8 **21.** $5,861.60 **23.** $47,498.22 **25.** $915 **27.** 5.8 **29.** $6,273 **31.** $5.25 **33.** $236,800
**35.** 3.15% **37.** $6,295.08 **39.** $200,925 **41. (a)** The second county **(b)** $75.24 **43.** 8.4% **45.** $2,500

*Section 6.3 (page 216)*
**1.** $20,600 **3.** $21,710 **5.** $39,031 **7.** $13,750; $2,062.50 **9.** $14,401; $2,160.15 **11.** $42,350; $6,788
**13.** $33,800; $6,428.50 **15.** $62,024; $14,495.44 **17.** $39,832; $6,082.96 **19.** $910.50 refund **21.** $194.30 refund
**23.** $765.66 due **27.** $3,889.20 **29.** $4,089.94 **31.** $301.95 **33.** $7,676.44 **35.** $3,475.65

*Chapter 6 Review Exercises (page 221)*
**1.** $23.61; $47.21; $542.92 **2.** $3.67; $10.08; $105.43 **3.** $825; $660; $17,985 **4.** $24.22; $52.16; $422.34 **5.** $567
**6.** $142 **7.** $280 **8.** $350 **9.** $326 **10.** $170 **11.** $279 **12.** $414 **13.** 4.06; $40.60; 40.6 **14.** 2.7; $2.70; $27
**15.** $1.27; $12.70; 12.7 **16.** 1.95; $1.95; 19.5 **17.** $13,632 **18.** $18.50 per $1,000 **19.** $46,500 **20.** 2.8%
**21.** $96,200 **22.** $2,797.20 **23.** $25,364; $4,066.42 **24.** $38,741; $5,811.15 **25.** $26,972; $4,045.80
**26.** $42,202; $8,781.06 **27.** 2.2% **28.** $194.88 **29.** $15,701.97 **30.** $6,488.40 **31.** $3,967.30 **32.** $7,286.96
**33.** $2,026.40 due **34.** $37.10 due **35.** $2,148.10 refund **36.** $608.40 due

*Chapter 6 Summary Exercise (page 223)*

**(a)** Anderson: $3,143,664; Bentonville: $3,488,706   **(b)** Anderson: $785,916; Bentonville: $697,741.20

**(c)** Anderson: $25,149.31; Bentonville: $20,583.37   **(d)** Anderson: $8,395,157.10; Bentonville: $3,694,539.70

**(e)** Anderson   **(f)** Answers will vary.

# CHAPTER 7

*Section 7.1 (page 233)*

**1.** $2,400   **3.** $1,097   **5.** $9,299   **7.** $8,973   **9.** $162   **11.** $228.90   **13.** $828.85   **15.** $243

**17. (a)** $1,125   **(b)** $225   **19. (a)** $780   **(b)** $1,092   **21. (a)** $2,654   **(b)** $2,654   **23.** $17,800   **25.** $1,134.55

**27.** $36,500   **29.** $12,554.95   **31.** $60,000; $20,000   **33.** $292,500; $260,000; $97,500   **35. (a)** $30,000

**(b)** A: $20,000; B: $10,000   **(c)** $10,000   **37. (a)** $12,500   **(b)** 1: $7,500; 2: $5,000   **(c)** $7,500   **39.** $2,620

**41.** $2,616   **43.** $1,057.50   **45.** $412.50   **47.** $1,557.50   **49. (a)** $1,134   **(b)** $810   **53. (a)** $19,936.71

**(b)** $2,563.29   **55. (a)** $30,681.82   **(b)** $14,318.18   **59. (a)** $17,273   **(b)** $34,545   **(c)** $24,182

**61. (a)** $375,000   **(b)** A: $281,250; B: $93,750   **63. (a)** $75,000   **(b)** 1: $41,667; 2: $20,833; 3: $12,500

*Section 7.2 (page 245)*

**1.** $467   **3.** $551   **5.** $535   **7.** $682   **9.** $748   **11.** $356   **15.** $737.15   **17.** $1,321.25   **19. (a)** $15,000   **(b)** $3,500

**21. (a)** $1,628   **(b)** $6,936   **(c)** $100,000   **(d)** $15,250   **23. (a)** $60,000   **(b)** $10,250

*Section 7.3 (page 257)*

**1.** renewable term $89.10; $45.44; $23.17; $8.09   **3.** 20–pay life $1,303.60; $664.84; $338.94; $118.37

**5.** whole life $509.40; $259.79; $132.44; $46.25   **7.** universal life $51.10; $26.06; $13.29; $4.64

**9.** renewable term $116.50; $59.42; $30.29; $10.58   **11.** whole-life $1,836.10; $936.41; $477.39; $166.72

**13.** whole life $3,175; $1,619.25; $825.50; $288.29   **17.** $15,500   **19.** $30,000   **21.** $196,800   **23.** 23 yr. 315 days

**25.** $289   **27.** 18   **29.** $160.20   **31. (a)** $384   **(b)** $50,000   **33.** $173.91   **35.** $221.94   **37. (a)** $330.48

**(b)** $168.48   **(c)** $58.84   **(d)** $660.96; $673.92; $706.08   **39. (a)** $5,660   **(b)** $11,580   **(c)** 23 yr. 315 days

**41.** $149,500   **43. (a)** $211.50   **(b)** approx. 20 yr.   **(c)** $115.75   **(d)** $109.50   **45. (a)** $345.50   **(b)** 18 yr.   **(c)** $297

**(d)** $286.50

*Chapter 7 Review Exercises (page 264)*

**1.** $2,529   **2.** $4,983   **3.** $434   **4.** $1,028   **5.** $382.20   **6.** $525.80   **7.** $222.90   **8.** $1,007.30

**9. (a)** $410   **(b)** $820   **10. (a)** $1,424   **(b)** $712   **11. (a)** $1,230   **(b)** $246   **12. (a)** $464   **(b)** $2,320

**13.** $39,473.68   **14.** $72,689.19   **15.** $2,731.66   **16.** $35,707.69   **17.** $742   **18.** $587.45   **19.** $887.60   **20.** $643

**21.** $2,281.30   **22.** $246   **23.** $133.50   **24.** $192   **25. (A)** $120,000   **(B)** $80,000   **(C)** $40,000   **26. (a)** $125,762

**(b)** 1: $80,030; 2: $45,732   **27. (a)** $25,000   **(b)** $9,000   **28. (a)** $15,000   **(b)** $0   **29. (a)** $40,000   **(b)** $36,800

**30. (a)** $494.70   **(b)** $252.20   **(c)** $88.08   **(d)** $989.40; $1,008.80; $1,056.96   **31.** $67,500   **32. (a)** $11,320

**(b)** $23,160   **(c)** 23 yr. 315 days   **33. (a)** $552.80   **(b)** about 12 yr.   **(c)** $475.20   **(d)** $392.80   **34. (a)** $231.20

**(b)** about 18 yr.   **(c)** $185.20   **(d)** $179.60

*Chapter 7 Summary Exercise (page 266)*

**(a)** $39,940.40   **(b)** $370.39   **(c)** $40,310.79   **(d)** $1,389.21

# Chapter 8

### Section 8.1 (page 275)

**1.** foot **3.** sack **5.** great gross **7.** case **9.** drum **11.** cost per thousand **13.** gallon **15.** cash on delivery
**17.** $54.00; $57.00; $64.80; $28.40; $297.00; $501.20; $524.95 **21.** 0.72 **23.** 0.8075 **25.** 0.75 **27.** 0.4025
**29.** 0.532 **31.** 0.576 **33.** $346.80 **35.** $5.56 **37.** $532 **39.** $384.75 **41.** $11.81 **43.** $640 **49.** $424.04
**51. (a)** 20/15 **(b)** $1.02 **53.** $16,416 **55.** $33.84 **57.** $189 **59. (a)** $274.02 **(b)** $18.27

### Section 8.2 (page 282)

**1.** 0.81, 19% **3.** 0.6, 40% **5.** 0.64, 36% **7.** 0.576, 42.4% **9.** 0.675, 32.5% **11.** 0.75, 25% **13.** 0.648, 35.2%
**15.** 0.243, 75.7% **17.** 0.45, 55% **19.** 0.7, 30% **21.** 0.5184, 48.16% **23.** 0.5054, 49.46% **27.** $900 **29.** $700
**31.** $1,920 **33. (a)** 25/10/10 **(b)** 0.0005 or 0.05% **35.** $740 **37. (a)** $40.11 **(b)** $44.57 **(c)** $4.46 **39.** 25.0%
**41.** $3,857.14 **43.** 5.0%

### Section 8.3 (page 289)

**1.** Mar. 15; Apr. 4 **3.** Mar. 25; Mar. 30 **5.** Aug. 28; Oct. 17 **7.** Jan. 24; Mar. 15 **9.** Jan. 20; Mar. 6
**11.** $1.28; $41.22 **13.** $0; $101.28 **15.** $14.48; $747.66 **17.** $32.78; $3,245.22 **19.** $18.46; $904.54 **23.** $3,244.19
**25.** $674.42 **27.** $132.59 **29.** $2,511.13 **31.** $2,021.32 **33. (a)** Jan. 28, Feb. 7, Feb. 17 **(b)** Mar. 9
**35. (a)** Apr. 25 **(b)** May 5 **37.** $1,570.11 **39.** $3,106.60

### Section 8.4 (page 296)

**1.** Apr. 15; May 5 **3.** Dec. 22; Jan. 11 **5.** June 16; July 6 **7.** Aug. 10; Aug. 30 **9.** Aug. 24; Sept. 13
**11.** $0.85; $41.65 **13.** $0; $194.04 **15.** $59.20; $2,900.80 **17.** $168.80; $4,051.20 **19.** $0.25; $12.13
**21.** $97.52; $3,153.08 **23.** $68.33; $1,639.85 **27.** $840; $735 **29.** $720; $1,030 **31.** $100; $60
**35. (a)** Aug. 10 **(b)** Aug. 30 **37. (a)** Dec. 23 **(b)** Jan. 12 **39.** $1,509.75 **41. (a)** Dec. 13 **(b)** $951.27
**43.** $4,271.33 **45. (a)** $1,000 **(b)** $920 **47.** $1,495.58 **49.** $93.02 **51. (a)** $306.12 **(b)** $220.68
**53. (a)** $597.94 **(b)** $194.64

### Chapter 8 Review Exercises (page 303)

**1.** $72.80; $187.20 **2.** $10.78; $26.22 **3.** $422.68; $771.32 **4.** $793.80; $826.20 **5.** 0.63; 37% **6.** 0.684; 31.6%
**7.** 0.54; 46% **8.** 0.4536; 54.64% **9.** $502.08 **10.** $1,545.21 **11.** $537.09 **12.** $2,262.11 **13.** Mar. 15; Apr. 4
**14.** May 30; June 19 **15.** Jan. 15; Feb. 4 **16.** Dec. 19; Jan. 8 **17.** $7.42; $392.18 **18.** $28.37; $917.23
**19.** $35.02; $907.66 **20.** $44.21; $2,166.39 **21.** $306.12; $353.88 **22.** $2,597.94; $2,712.06 **23.** $505.05; $354.95
**24.** $2,113.40; $1,736.60 **25. (a)** $394.40 **(b)** $386.51 **(c)** $398.06 **26. (a)** Builders Supply **(b)** $1.91
**27.** $36,230.99 **28.** 10% **29.** $1,779.95 **30.** $1,798.38 **31. (a)** $1,717.53 **(b)** $1,198.47
**32. (a)** $1,875 **(b)** $3,405 **(c)** $75

### Chapter 8 Summary Exercise (page 306)

**(a)** $2,856.96 **(b)** Nov. 10 **(c)** Nov. 30 **(d)** $2,890.05 **(e)** $1,546.39; $1,429.37

# Chapter 9

*Section 9.1 (page 313)*

**1.** $1.80; $7.80  **3.** 50%; $70.50  **5.** $39.80; 25.1%  **7.** $67.50; 20%  **9.** $118; 56.2%  **11.** $133.65; $628.65
**15.** $34.37  **17.** $13.73  **19.** $14.95  **21.** 17.8%  **23. (a)** $95.96  **(b)** 25%  **(c)** 125%  **25. (a)** 126%  **(b)** $5.67
**(c)** $1.17  **27. (a)** $35  **(b)** 27.2%  **(c)** $9.52  **29.** $5,172.40  **31.** $6.63

*Section 9.2 (page 321)*

**1.** $4; $20  **3.** $131.48; $243.48  **5.** $37.20; $55.80  **7.** $46.36; $24.96  **9.** $77.82; 35.2%  **11.** $230; $287.50
**13.** $8.46; $22.26; 61.3%  **15.** $750; $1,050; 28.6%  **17.** $357.52; 22%  **19.** 20%  **21.** 35.1%  **23.** 33.3% or $33\frac{1}{3}$%
**25.** 66.7% or $66\frac{2}{3}$%  **29.** $70.50  **31.** $344.96  **33.** $109.62  **35. (a)** $4.50  **(b)** $2.88  **(c)** 64%  **37.** 26.5%
**39. (a)** $18.70  **(b)** $8.80  **(c)** 32%  **41. (a)** $0.72  **(b)** 100%  **43. (a)** $13,680  **(b)** $6,080  **(c)** 44.4%  **(d)** 80%
**45. (a)** $13.95  **(b)** 100%  **47. (a)** 43.8%  **(b)** 30.4%  **49. (a)** $32.40  **(b)** 25.9%  **51. (a)** $24.90  **(b)** 12.5%
**(c)** 14.2%

*Section 9.3 (page 327)*

**1.** $24  **3.** $3.13  **5.** $9  **7.** $1.65  **9.** $9.33  **11.** $22  **13.** $3.75  **15.** $16.58  **17.** 80; 20; $3.36  **19.** 34; 6; $78.53
**21.** 108; 36; $4.17  **23.** 700; 300; $4.71  **27.** $0.60  **29.** $10.50  **31.** $3.07  **33.** $308.75  **35.** $25.40  **37.** $24.13

*Chapter 9 Review Exercises (page 331)*

**1.** $3; $18  **2.** $38; $51.30  **3.** $147; 50%  **4.** $45.90; 42.5%  **5.** $36.16; $180.80  **6.** $150; 14.3%  **7.** $34.70; $52.05
**8.** 38.5%; $460.20  **9.** $70.40; $140.80  **10.** $64.50; 100%; 50%  **11.** $8; 46%; 31.5%
**12.** $1,025.28; $1,281.60; 20%  **13.** 25%  **14.** 50%  **15.** 18%  **16.** $16\frac{2}{3}$%  **17.** $1.25  **18.** $21.67  **19.** $13.59
**20.** $17.04  **21.** 135; 15; $6.67  **22.** 72 pr.; 18 pr.; $2.38  **23.** 216; 72; $8.27  **24.** 700; 300; $4.71  **25.** $12.50
**26.** 18%  **27.** $3.85  **28. (a)** $37.99  **(b)** 19.0%  **(c)** 23.5%  **29. (a)** $19,050.25  **(b)** 47%  **30.** $4
**31. (a)** 20%  **(b)** 25%  **32.** $4.12

*Chapter 9 Summary Exercise (page 334)*

**(a)** $8,058.20  **(b)** $10,063.50  **(c)** $2,005.30  **(d)** 20%  **(e)** 25%

# Chapter 10

*Section 10.1 (page 342)*

**1.** 25%; $645  **3.** 45%; $13.86  **5.** $5,350; $1,070  **7.** $2.70; $1.62  **9.** $18.30; $18.30  **11.** $857; 20%
**13.** $50; $10; none  **15.** $16; $22; $6  **17.** $385; $250; $60  **19.** $29; $10; $39  **23.** $730.50  **25.** 46%
**27.** $298 operating loss  **29. (a)** $63.62 operating loss  **(b)** $40.75 absolute loss  **(c)** 27%  **31. (a)** $256.50  **(b)** 11%

*Section 10.2 (page 347)*

**1.** $10,082  **3.** $22,673  **5.** $24,500  **7.** 2.81, 2.83  **9.** 7.94, 7.98  **11.** 10.25, 10.25  **13.** 4.66, 4.69  **17.** $18,165.38
**19.** 5.43  **21.** 6.32  **23.** 11.09  **25.** 4.17

*Section 10.3 (page 355)*

**1.** $827  **3.** $560  **5. (a)** $182  **(b)** $195  **(c)** $170  **7. (a)** $2,352  **(b)** $2,385  **(c)** $2,313  **9.** $2,476
**11. (a)** $48  **(b)** $50  **(c)** $51  **13. (a)** $1,252  **(b)** $1,430  **(c)** $1,040  **15. (a)** $6,142  **(b)** $6,784  **(c)** $5,500
**17.** $130,600  **19.** $30,641

*Chapter 10 Review Exercises (page 360)*

**1.** $11; $16.50  **2.** $15; $5  **3.** $5.40; $2.70  **4.** 25%; $585  **5.** $24; $33; $9  **6.** $200; $14; none  **7.** $100; $70; $8
**8.** $6.25; $0.75; none  **9.** $27,649  **10.** $348,468  **11.** $76,411.80  **12.** $32,859.80  **13.** 5.73; 5.76  **14.** 7.94; 7.98
**15.** 4.66; 4.69  **16.** 4.56; 4.63  **17.** $428  **18.** $813  **19.** $3,640  **20.** $6,017  **21.** 28%  **22. (a)** $78.40  **(b)** 7%
**23.** $65,139  **24.** 10.77  **25.** 4.57  **26. (a)** $6,489.20  **(b)** $5,887.50  **(c)** $6,675  **27.** $115,000  **28.** $75,600

*Chapter 10 Summary Exercise (page 362)*
**(a)** $50  **(b)** $825  **(c)** $150  **(d)** None

# CHAPTER 11

*Section 11.1 (page 368)*

**1.** $306  **3.** $38.70  **5.** $1,340.63  **7.** $644.90  **9.** $3,821.17  **11.** $300  **13.** $4,062.50  **15.** 7%  **17.** 14
**19.** $3,789.47  **21.** $4,200  **23.** 11  **25.** 8%  **27.** $1,293.75  **29.** $228  **31.** 0.667 yr. or 8 mo.  **33.** 4%  **37.** $170.67
**39.** 14%  **41.** $13.48

*Section 11.2 (page 375)*

**1.** 132  **3.** 36  **5.** 196  **7.** May 31  **9.** Mar. 10  **11.** Apr. 11  **13.** $11.33  **15.** $162.50  **17.** $41.25  **19.** $67.13
**21.** $22.19  **23.** $98.30  **25.** $114.68  **27.** $157.04  **31.** $20.82  **33.** $2,632.77  **35.** $12,069.51  **37.** $2,400
**39. (a)** $591.78  **(b)** $600  **(c)** $8.22  **41. (a)** $9,057.53  **(b)** $9,183.33  **(c)** $125.80  **43.** $55.67
**45.** First Bank; $9.34

*Section 11.3 (page 383)*

**1.** $192; $2,592  **3.** $191.72; $5,991.72  **5.** $1,080; $9,720  **7.** $58.67; $2,458.67  **9.** 70; $8,733.78
**11.** $10\frac{1}{2}$%; $14,490  **13.** $16,400; $717.50  **15.** $32,500; 106  **17.** $126; 180  **19.** $42,459.44; 15%
**21.** $490; $12,490  **23.** 200 days; $275  **25.** 18%; $70  **27.** $820,000; $34,166.67

*Section 11.4 (page 391)*

**1.** $3,256  **3.** $9,948.33  **5.** $4,529.22  **7.** $2,400  **9.** $8,400  **11.** $8,700  **15.** $13,364.09  **17.** $58,437.50
**19.** $1,211.76  **21.** $7,104.85  **23.** $14,516.42  **25.** $397.50 loss  **27.** $5,800 in 150 days

*Chapter 11 Review Exercises (page 397)*

**1.** $638.25  **2.** $831.33  **3.** $8,710  **4.** $2,400  **5.** 9%  **6.** 7.5%  **7.** 9 months  **8.** 30 months  **9.** 114 days
**10.** 115 days  **11.** $67.46  **12.** $336.58  **13.** $222.51  **14.** $131.34  **15.** $43.17  **16.** $70.95  **17.** $360
**18.** $6,181.82  **19.** 7%  **20.** $8\frac{1}{4}$%  **21.** 40 days  **22.** 90 days  **23.** $7,718  **24.** $4,717.50  **25.** $12,000  **26.** $6,500
**27.** 9%  **28.** 12%  **29.** $1,927.71  **30.** $11,612.90  **31.** $5,070.75  **32.** $19,550.56  **33.** $809.69  **34.** $15,598.34
**35.** $198.92  **36.** 12%  **37.** 200 days  **38.** $3,600  **39.** 9.5%  **40.** 17.3%  **41.** 90 days  **42.** $9,127.31
**43.** $19,528.16  **44.** $11,948.33  **45.** $852 gain  **46.** $2,811 loss

**Chapter 11 Summary Exercise (page 400)**
$94.50; $6,394.50; $57.50; $2,357.50; $216; $2,016; $10,768; October 18; $6,586.34

# Chapter 12

**Section 12.1 (page 408)**
**1.** Lupe Jones **3.** Julie Kern **5.** 210 days **7.** June 14 of the following year **9.** July 4 **11.** June 30 **13.** March 17
**15.** April 23 **17.** Nov. 9; $6,225 **19.** June 10; $5,354.17 **21.** $16,000 **23.** 120 days **25.** 11% **27.** $12,954
**31.** (a) Jan. 9 (b) $1,150.78 **33.** (a) Dec. 13 (b) $22,732.50 **35.** $15,000 **37.** (a) December 7 of the prior year
(b) $22,500 **39.** 90 **41.** 8%

**Section 12.2 (page 418)**
**1.** $46.67; $2,753.33 **3.** $441.75; $5,758.25 **5.** $66.50; $8,333.50 **7.** Nov. 9; $4,130 **9.** Feb. 17; $11,430
**11.** 8/9; $360; $15,640 **13.** 11%; 8/7; $13,740 **15.** $7,200; 6%; 2/10 **17.** $720; $11,280 **19.** 120 days **21.** $12\frac{1}{2}$%
**23.** $3,329.48 **25.** $3,815; 12.1% **27.** $3,920; $3,921.57 **29.** (a) $4,950 (b) $5,000 (c) $50 (d) 4.04%

**Section 12.3 (page 423)**
**1.** 8.16% **3.** 15.48% **5.** 6.88% **7.** 9.73% **11.** 13% simple interest **13.** $17.23

**Section 12.4 (page 428)**
**1.** 52 days **3.** 59 days **5.** $4,698 **7.** $14,100 **9.** 61 days; $73.30; $3,531.70 **11.** 49 days; $33.45; $2,014.55
**13.** 81 days; $286.50; $10,324.61 **15.** (a) 113 days (b) $475.86 (c) $12,157.47 **17.** (a) $218.75 (b) $4,468.75
**19.** (a) $1,920 (b) $1,980 (c) $60 **21.** (a) $2,264 (b) $2,361 (c) $97 **23.** (a) $81,900 (b) $79,688.70

**Chapter 12 Review Exercises (page 434)**
**1.** $180; $4,980 **2.** $10\frac{1}{2}$%; $3,078.75 **3.** 240 days; $8,640 **4.** $12,300; $12,915 **5.** August 3; $2,652
**6.** January 5; $6,416.67 **7.** $480; $17,520 **8.** $1,365; $24,635 **9.** (a) 99 days (b) $410.85 (c) $12,039.15
**10.** (a) 50 days (b) $146.92 (c) $8,668.29 **11.** 12.37% **12.** 9.40% **13.** 11.32% **14.** $39,488.33 **15.** $891.23
**16.** 9% **17.** 180 days **18.** 200 days **19.** 14% **20.** 11%; 10.71% **21.** 13.04% **22.** $13,874.39 **23.** 150 days
**24.** 80 days **25.** 15.9% **26.** 11.42% **27.** $8,318.53 **28.** 270 days **29.** 17.37% **30.** 15% **31.** $21,475.78
**32.** $16,223.19 **33.** 17.14% **34.** $7,951.05 **35.** $6,377.09 **36.** 13.48%

**Chapter 12 Summary Exercise (page 437)**
(a) $28,000 (b) February 24 (c) $29,260 (d) October 18

# Chapter 13

**Section 13.1 (page 445)**
**1.** $15,116.54; $3,116.54 **3.** $7,600.62; $1,600.62 **5.** $30,273.75 **7.** $1,341.54 **9.** $6,032.76 **11.** $5,755.82
**13.** $300; $338.23; $38.23 **15.** $3,163.37; $3,775.92; $612.55 **17.** 8.24% **19.** 16.08% **21.** (a) $3,762.97
(b) $3,773.98 **23.** (a) $2,624.77 (b) $2,667.70 (c) $2,689.86 (d) $2,704.89 (e) $2,400 **25.** $12,043.41
**27.** (a) $11,248.64; $11,268.25 (b) $19.61 **29.** $10,538.50 **31.** $29,013.74 **33.** $18,127.97 **35.** $16,349.02
**39.** $439.20

*Section 13.2 (page 456)*

**1.** $10.57  **3.** $48.57  **5.** $7,283.85  **7.** $3,005.22  **9.** $5,637.43  **11.** $17,271.15  **13.** $4,673.06  **15.** $1,432.90
**19.** $5,868.25  **21.** $176.27; $11,696.27  **23.** 0  **25.** $269.49  **27.** $2,619.93; $619.93  **29.** $4,354.27; $253.57
**31. (a)** $901,988.58  **(b)** $101,988.58  **33.** 10% compounded semiannually; $76.03


*Section 13.3 (page 462)*

**1.** 4  **3.** 3  **5.** $6,400  **7.** 6%  **9.** 8%  **13. (a)** $16,473.43  **(b)** $22,614.49  **15.** 10%  **17.** $1\frac{1}{2}$ yr.  **19.** 28 yr.
**21.** 20 yr.  **23.** 35 yr.  **25.** $40,224.31  **27.** $7,185.73  **29.** $21,247.04


*Section 13.4 (page 467)*

**1.** $2,183.60; $316.40  **3.** $9,077.95; $3,122.05  **5.** $7,543.32; $956.68  **9.** $3,564.93; $1,435.07  **11.** $23,368.76
**13.** $7,096.44  **15.** $3,800 in 5 yr.  **17.** $38,288.45; $31,409.86  **19.** $43,400; $32,607.06  **21. (a)** $26,620
**(b)** $20,989.69


*Chapter 13 Review Exercises (page 473)*

**1.** $10,848.39; $2,348.39  **2.** $8,867.39; $1,867.39  **3.** $6,455.47; $1,655.47  **4.** $11,716.59; $1,716.59
**5.** $11,261.45; $2,261.45  **6.** $14,576.65; $2,576.65  **7.** 6.17%  **8.** 8.24%  **9.** 7.12%  **10.** 9.38%  **11.** $11.12
**12.** $36.35  **13.** $34.08  **14.** $3,534.91  **15.** $7,273.21  **16.** $7,207.72  **17.** $4,934.61  **18.** $7,328.66  **19.** $12,118.30
**20.** $3,813.75; $813.75  **21.** $7,095.34; $2,095.34  **22.** 8%  **23.** 10%  **24.** 8%  **25.** 3  **26.** $3\frac{1}{2}$
**27.** $2,445.63; $354.37  **28.** $3,071.58; $928.42  **29.** $3,661.63; $2,338.37  **30.** $2,361.30; $638.70  **31.** $16,145.90
**32.** $4,130.74  **33.** $40,056.23; $22,056.23  **34.** $396.15  **35.** $29,462.37  **36. (a)** $15,173.40  **(b)** $13,481.37  **37.** 4
**38.** approx. 12


*Chapter 13 Summary Exercise (page 476)*

**(a)** $19,326,120  **(b)** $14,380,448  **(c)** $21,148,100  **(d)** $15,736,173  **(e)** $1,355,725


# CHAPTER 14

*Section 14.1 (page 486)*

**1.** 34.86831801  **3.** 15.19292972  **5.** $3,236.78; $986.78  **7.** $73,105.94; $48,105.94  **9.** $6,047.06; $1,247.06
**11.** $46,016.57; $7,616.57  **13.** $13,305.24; $4,305.24  **15.** $138,997.66; $33,733.66  **17.** $11,320.10  **19.** $13,673.64
**21.** $16,577.77  **23.** $36,895.94  **25.** $57,782.55  **27.** $59,794.96  **29.** $122,676.78  **31.** $263,879.29
**35.** $12,522.84; $3,722.84  **37.** $5,303.43; $1,703.43  **39.** $526.95  **41.** $952.33  **43.** 29; $9,698.06
**45.** 45; $40,745.91  **47.** $7,188.27  **49.** $58,156.38; $33,156.38  **51.** $34,186.78; $14,706.78
**53.** 31 months; $4,075.14  **55. (a)** $15,100.50  **(b)** $13,566.97


*Section 14.2 (page 494)*

**1.** 8.61851785  **3.** 6.81086449  **5.** $7,149.81  **7.** $11,901.98  **9.** $6,540.57  **13.** $87,556.25  **15.** $34,008.46
**17.** $12,675.75; $4,124.25  **19. (a)** $160,121.64  **(b)** $117,647.09  **21.** $34,773.48; $17,617.33  **23.** $79,636.35
**25.** Second offer  **27.** First offer  **29.** $28,847.04  **31.** $27,050.13

*Section 14.3 (page 501)*
**1.** 0.07586796  **3.** 0.00295961  **5.** $893.27  **7.** $576.19  **11.** (a) $106,747.76; (b) $699.22
**13.** (a) $200,822.20; (b) $1,315.43  **15.** $1,640.31; $2,316.28  **17.** $9,572.45  **19.** $404,143.76; $766,849.92
**21.** $17,047.28; $443,229.18; $443,229.18; $213,090.95; $35,458.33; $691,778.46; $691,778.46; $213,090.98;
$55,342.28; $960,211.72  **23.** $27,334.09

*Chapter 14 Review Exercises (page 506)*
**1.** $20,243.93  **2.** $44,795.33  **3.** $113,736  **4.** $49,153.29  **5.** $163,383.42  **6.** $97,457.37  **7.** $14,943.67; $2,891.62
**8.** $134,489.45; $21,989.45  **9.** $13,728.16  **10.** $5,948.27  **11.** $8,055.06  **12.** $5,094.30  **13.** $1,054.06
**14.** $1,332.74  **15.** $8,702.22  **16.** $623.89  **17.** 31 yr.  **18.** $11,219.15  **19.** $5,596.62  **20.** $25,723.79
**21.** $2,676.72  **22.** $32,625.58  **23.** $98,713.33  **24.** $179,999.95; $125,806.46

**25.**

|  | Beginning of Period |  | End of Period |  |
| Period | Accumulated Amount | Periodic Deposit | Interest Earned | Accumulated Amount |
| --- | --- | --- | --- | --- |
| 1 | $0 | $21,866.87 | $0 | $21,866.87 |
| 2 | 21,866.87 | 21,866.87 | 1,968.02 | 45,701.76 |
| 3 | 45,701.76 | 21,866.87 | 4,113.16 | 71,681.79 |
| 4 | 71,681.79 | 21,866.85 | 6,451.36 | 100,000.00 |

*Chapter 14 Summary Exercise (page 508)*
**(a)** $5,018.66; $4,266.42  **(b)** $70,714.92  **(c)** $280,759.86  **(d)** $410,946.16  **(e)** $130,186.30  **(f)** $3,944.63

# CHAPTER 15

*Section 15.1 (page 518)*
**1.** $10.03  **3.** $4.87  **5.** $13.99; $853.80; $853.80; $14.51; $1,002.06; $1,002.06; $17.04; $985.40; $985.40;
$16.75; $958.58  **7.** $132.64; $1.99; $133.80  **9.** $312.91; $4.69; $285.94  **11.** $681.52; $10.22; $769.01
**13.** (a) $42.01  (b) $28  (c) $14.01

*Section 15.2 (page 529)*
**1.** $640; $60  **3.** $180; $30  **5.** $100; $10  **7.** 12.50%  **9.** 10.25%  **11.** 11.25%  **15.** 11%  **17.** 15.75%
**19.** (a) 732,212.32 pesos  (b) 13.75%  **21.** (a) $209,239.80  (b) 12%

*Section 15.3 (page 535)*
**1.** $3,589.31; $89.31  **3.** $3,754.46; $254.46  **5.** $4,333.78; $333.78  **7.** $385.52  **9.** $15.26  **11.** $139.81
**17.** $27,165.96; $1,665.96  **19.** $83.24  **21.** (a) $51.82  (b) $490.58  **23.** $41,176.11; $1,876.11

**1.** 0.08718456  **3.** 0.10334306  **5.** $224.93  **7.** $404.73  **9.** $4,185.25  **11.** $161.95  **13.** $120.99; $429.70
**15.** $321.92; $3,452.16  **17.** $15,987.97; $147,663.16

**19.**

| Payment Number | Amount of Payment | Interest for Period | Portion to Principal | Principal at End of Period |
|:---:|:---:|:---:|:---:|:---:|
| 0 | — | — | — | $4,000.00 |
| 1 | $1,207.68 | $320.00 | $887.68 | 3,112.32 |
| 2 | 1,207.68 | 248.99 | 958.69 | 2,153.63 |
| 3 | 1,207.68 | 172.29 | 1,035.39 | 1,118.24 |
| 4 | 1,207.70 | 89.46 | 1,118.24 | 0 |

**21.**

| Payment Number | Amount of Payment | Interest for Period | Portion to Principal | Principal at End of Period |
|:---:|:---:|:---:|:---:|:---:|
| 0 | — | — | — | $14,500.00 |
| 1 | $374.77 | $132.92 | $241.85 | 14,258.15 |
| 2 | 374.77 | 130.70 | 244.07 | 14,014.08 |
| 3 | 374.77 | 128.46 | 246.31 | 13,767.77 |
| 4 | 374.77 | 126.20 | 248.57 | 13,519.20 |
| 5 | 374.77 | 123.93 | 250.84 | 13,268.36 |

**25.**

| Payment Number | Amount of Payment | Interest for Period | Portion to Principal | Principal at End of Period |
|:---:|:---:|:---:|:---:|:---:|
| 0 | — | — | — | $8,000.00 |
| 1 | $576.99 | $80.00 | $496.99 | 7,503.01 |
| 2 | 576.99 | 75.03 | 501.96 | 7,001.05 |
| 3 | 576.99 | 70.01 | 506.98 | 6,494.07 |
| ⋮ | ⋮ | ⋮ | ⋮ | ⋮ |
| 12 | 576.99 | 22.51 | 554.48 | 1,696.92 |
| 13 | 576.99 | 16.97 | 560.02 | 1,136.90 |
| 14 | 576.99 | 11.37 | 565.62 | 571.28 |
| 15 | 576.99 | 5.71 | 571.28 | 0.00 |

*Section 15.5 (page 552)*
**1.** $660.10  **3.** $1,111.08  **5.** $1,022.90  **9.** $854.20  **11.** $523.87  **13.** $873.82  **15.** Yes, qualified

| 17. Payment Number | Total Payment | Interest Payment | Principal Payment | Balance of Principal |
|---|---|---|---|---|
| **0** | — | — | — | **$122,500.00** |
| **1** | **$1,136.80** | **$765.63** | **$371.17** | 122,128.83 |
| **2** | 1,136.80 | 763.31 | 373.49 | 121,755.34 |

**19.** $120,365; $4,943,800  **21.** $81,000

*Chapter 15 Review Exercises (page 559)*
**1.** $3.65  **2.** $1.44  **3.** $5.63  **4.** $552.56; $8.29; $551.80  **5.** $216.51; $3.25; $203.40  **6.** $1,550; $1,648.25; $98.25
**7.** $4,600; $5,040; $440  **8.** $8,000; $9,600; $1,600  **9.** 13%  **10.** 13.75%  **11.** 15.25%  **12.** 16%
**13.** $6,638.63; $138.63  **14.** $7,309.87; $309.87  **15.** $915.66; $115.66  **16.** $4,641.89; $141.89  **17.** $4,452.85
**18.** $2,395.83  **19.** $795.42  **20.** $392.89  **21.** $229.12; $1,448.32  **22.** $234.38; $2,343.96  **23.** $245.94; $2,805.12
**24.** $574.16; $2,224.80  **25.** $604.80  **26.** $564.20  **27.** $956  **28.** $819.60  **29. (a)** $2,788.22  **(b)** $173.22
**30.** $57.28; $0.86  **31.** $18,756.32; 10.50%  **32. (a)** $235.51  **(b)** $2,502.17  **33. (a)** $1,456.92  **(b)** $298,495.60
**34. (a)** $1,398.24  **(b)** $360,577.60

*Chapter 15 Summary Exercise (page 562)*
$750.46; $576.19; $796.78; $631.93; $143,804.80; $216,150.40; $152,142.40; $236,216.80; $971.96; $797.69;
$1,018.28; $853.43

# CHAPTER 16

*Section 16.1 (page 569)*
**1.** 10%  **3.** 12.5%  **5.** 5%  **7.** $6\frac{2}{3}$%  **9.** 1.25%  **11.** 2%  **13.** $720  **15.** $30  **17.** $840  **19.** $2,850  **21.** $1,480
**23.** $2,775  **25.** $73,000
**29.** Year 1: ($\frac{1}{3} \times$ $9,000), $3,000, $3,000, $9,000; Year 2: ($\frac{1}{3} \times$ $9,000), $3,000, $6,000, $6,000; Year 3: ($\frac{1}{3} \times$ $9,000),
$3,000, $9,000, $3,000  **31.** Book values: $8,200; $7,000; $5,800; $4,600; $3,400; $2,200
**33.** $55,000 depreciation; $1,025,000  **35.** $3,790; $41,690  **37. (a)** $12\frac{1}{2}$%  **(b)** $90  **(c)** $790

*Section 16.2 (page 575)*
**1.** 50%  **3.** 10%  **5.** $13\frac{1}{3}$%  **7.** 20%  **9.** $33\frac{1}{3}$%  **11.** 4%  **13.** $2,800  **15.** $4,200  **17.** $1,900  **19.** $3,360  **21.** $1,215
**23.** $6,834  **25.** $750
**29.** Year 1: (50% $\times$ $14,400), $7,200, $7,200, $7,200; Year 2: (50% $\times$ $7,200), $3,600, $10,800, $3,600;
Year 3: (50% $\times$ $3,600), $1,800, $12,600, $1,800; Year 4: $1,800 to depreciate to 0 scrap value, $14,400; $0
**31.** Book values: $19,125; $14,344; $10,758; $8,068; $6,051; $4,538; $3,500; $3,500  **33.** $1,153  **35.** $235
**37. (a)** 25%  **(b)** $1,450  **(c)** $4,425  **(d)** $1,375

*Section 16.3 (page 583)*

**1.** 5/15  **3.** 3/6  **5.** 7/28  **7.** 10/55  **9.** $600  **11.** $10,000  **13.** $600  **15.** $7,700  **17.** $3,857  **19.** $890  **21.** $650
**25.** Year 1: ($\frac{6}{21}$ × $8,400), $2,400, $2,400, $8,400; Year 2: ($\frac{5}{21}$ × $8,400), $2,000, $4,400, $6,400;
Year 3: ($\frac{4}{21}$ × $8,400), $1,600, $6,000, $4,800; Year 4: ($\frac{3}{21}$ × $8,400), $1,200, $7,200, $3,600; Year 5: ($\frac{2}{21}$ × $8,400),
$800, $8,000, $2,800; Year 6: ($\frac{1}{21}$ × $8,400), $400, $8,400, $2,400
**27.** Book values: $2,100; $1,600; $1,200; $900; $700; $600  **29.** $6,000  **31.** $24,584  **33. (a)** $2,120  **(b)** $1,696
**35. (a)** $\frac{8}{36}$  **(b)** $2,360  **(c)** $10,620  **(d)** $4,750


*Section 16.4 (page 591)*

**1.** $0.35  **3.** $0.10  **5.** $68.75  **7.** $30  **9.** $1,680  **11.** $5,950  **13.** $2,775  **15.** $6,960  **19.** $1,313; $2,250
**21.** $1,667; $2,000  **23.** $450; $825  **25.** $900; $1,088
**27.** Year 1: (1,350 × $1.26), $1,701, $1,701, $5,099; Year 2: (1,820 × $1.26), $2,293, $3,994, $2,806;
Year 3: (730 × $1.26), $920, $4,914, $1,886; Year 4: (1,100 × $1.26), $1,386, $6,300, $500  **29.** $26,350
**31.** $1,825; $7,300  **33.** $450; $1,620  **35.** $2,775; $5,365


*Section 16.5 (page 600)*

**1.** 10%  **3.** 20%  **5.** 14.4%  **7.** 3.636%  **9.** 5.76%  **11.** 2.564%  **13.** $2,150  **15.** $3,226  **17.** $4,800  **19.** $1,573
**21.** $16,920  **23.** $2,756  **25.** $79,364
**29.** Year 1: (33.33% × $10,980), $3,660, $3,660, $7,320; Year 2: (44.45% × $10,980), $4,881, $8,541, $2,439;
Year 3: (14.81% × $10,980), $1,626, $10,167, $813; Year 4: (7.41% × $10,980), $813 due to rounding in prior years,
$10,980, $0
**31.** Book values: $110,430; $88,344; $70,675; $56,540; $45,227; $36,184; $28,147; $20,110; $12,061; $4,024; $0
**33.** $186,550  **35.** $12,326; $12,307; $12,307; $12,307; $12,307


*Chapter 16 Review Exercises (page 605)*

**1.** 25%; 50%; 4/10  **2.** 20%; 40%; 5/15  **3.** 5%; 10%; 20/210  **4.** 10%; 20%; 10/55  **5.** $16\frac{2}{3}$%; $33\frac{1}{3}$%; 6/21
**6.** $12\frac{1}{2}$%; 25%; 8/36  **7.** 11.52%  **8.** 33.33%  **9.** 4.522%  **10.** 17.49%  **11.** 2.564%  **12.** 3.174%  **13.** $940
**14.** $41,000  **15.** $21,375  **16.** $7,400  **17.** Year 1: $2,700; Year 2: $2,025; Year 3: $1,350; Year 4: $675  **18.** $4,000
**19.** $1,530  **20. (a)** Year 1: $4,836; Year 2: $2,666; Year 3: $3,007; Year 4: $4,712
**(b)** Year 1: $15,264; Year 2: $12,598; Year 3: $9,591; Year 4: $4,879  **21.** $15,120
**22.** $24,000; $19,200; $14,400; $9,600; $4,800  **23.** $2,900  **24.** $1,260; $2,003  **25.** $2,840; $5,112  **26.** $5,702
**27.** $4,746  **28.** $37,575  **29.** $6,222  **30.** $6,533; $8,712; $2,903; $1,452  **31.** $1,157; $1,984; $1,417; $1,012; $723
**32.** $2,399,964


*Chapter 16 Summary Exercise (page 607)*

**(a)** $3,250 first partial year; $6,500 next full year  **(b)** $19,898 book value 3 years  **(c)** $25,189 depreciation in 3 years
**(d)** $10,151 book value 5 years
**(e)** $6,500 straight-line; $5,685 double-declining-balance; $7,313 sum-of-the-years'-digits; $5,683 MACRS

# CHAPTER 17

*Section 17.1 (page 613)*

**1. (a)** $216,856  **(b)** $94,356  **(c)** $72,556  **3.** $324,200

**5.**

| FUTURE TECH COMPUTING<br>INCOME STATEMENT<br>YEAR ENDING DECEMBER 31 | | |
|---|---|---|
| Gross Sales | $284,000 | |
| Returns | $6,000 | |
| Net Sales | | $278,000 |
| Inventory, January 1 | $58,000 | |
| Cost of Goods<br>Purchased | $232,000 | |
| Freight | $3,000 | |
| Total Cost of Goods Purchased | $235,000 | |
| Total of Goods Available for Sale | $293,000 | |
| Inventory, December 31 | $69,000 | |
| Cost of Goods Sold | | $224,000 |
| Gross Profit | | $54,000 |
| Expenses | | |
| Salaries and Wages | $15,000 | |
| Rent | $6,000 | |
| Advertising | $2,000 | |
| Utilities | $1,000 | |
| Taxes on Inventory, Payroll | $3,000 | |
| Miscellaneous Expenses | $4,000 | |
| Total Expenses | | $31,000 |
| NET INCOME BEFORE TAXES | | $23,000 |
| Income Taxes | | $2,400 |
| NET INCOME | | $20,600 |

7.

| KATHY GILMORE, CONSULTANT<br>INCOME STATEMENT<br>FOR THE YEAR ENDING DECEMBER 31 | | |
|---|---|---|
| Gross Sales | | $ 170,500 | |
| Returns | | $ 7,000 | |
| Net Sales | | | $ 170,500 |
| Inventory, January 1 | $ 22,000 | | |
| Cost of Goods Purchased | $ 125,000 | | |
| Freight | $ 5,000 | | |
| Total Cost of Goods Purchased | $ 130,000 | | |
| Total of Goods Available for Sale | $ 152,000 | | |
| Inventory, December 31 | $ 26,000 | | |
| Cost of Goods Sold | | $ 126,000 | |
| Gross Profit | | | $ 170,500 |
| Expenses | | | |
| Salaries and Wages | $ 63,000 | | |
| Rent | $ 28,000 | | |
| Advertising | $ 12,000 | | |
| Utilities | $ 4,000 | | |
| Taxes on Inventory, Payroll | $ 3,800 | | |
| Miscellaneous Expenses | $ 9,400 | | |
| Total Expenses | | | $ 120,200 |
| NET INCOME BEFORE TAXES | | | $ 50,300 |
| Income Taxes | | | $ 6,800 |
| NET INCOME | | | $ 43,500 |

**Section 17.2 *(page 623)***

**1.** 57.2%; 30.8%

**3.** **Capital Appliance Center**

|  | Amount | Percent | Percent from Table 17.1 |
|---|---|---|---|
| Net Sales | $900,000 | 100% | 100.0% |
| Cost of Goods Sold | $617,000 | 68.6% | 66.9% |
| Gross Profit | $283,000 | 31.4% | 33.1% |
| Wages | $108,900 | 12.1% | 11.9% |
| Rent | $20,700 | 2.3% | 2.4% |
| Advertising | $27,000 | 3% | 2.5% |
| Total Expenses | $216,000 | 24% | 26% |
| Net Income before taxes | $67,000 | 7.4% | 7.2% |

**5.** **Best Tires, Inc.**
**Comparative Income Statement**

|  | This Year | | Last Year | |
|---|---|---|---|---|
|  | Amount | Percent | Amount | Percent |
| Gross Sales | $1,856,000 | 100.3% | $1,692,000 | 100.7% |
| Returns | 6,000 | 0.3% | 12,000 | 0.7% |
| Net Sales | 1,850,000 | 100.0% | 1,680,000 | 100.0% |
| Cost of Goods Sold | 1,202,000 | 65.0% | 1,050,000 | 62.5% |
| Gross Profit | 648,000 | 35.0% | 630,000 | 37.5% |
| Wages | 152,000 | 8.2% | 148,000 | 8.8% |
| Rent | 82,000 | 4.4% | 78,000 | 4.6% |
| Advertising | 111,000 | 6.0% | 122,000 | 7.3% |
| Utilities | 32,000 | 1.7% | 17,000 | 1.0% |
| Taxes on Inv., Payroll | 17,000 | 0.9% | 18,000 | 1.1% |
| Miscellaneous Expenses | 62,000 | 3.4% | 58,000 | 3.5% |
| Total Expenses | 456,000 | 24.6% | 441,000 | 26.3% |
| Net Income | 192,000 | 10.4% | 189,000 | 11.3% |

| | Type of Store | Cost of Goods | Gross Profit | Total Operating Expenses | Net Income | Wages | Rent | Advertising |
|---|---|---|---|---|---|---|---|---|
| 7. | Supermarkets | 84.5% | 15.5% | 14.4% | 1.1% | 6.4% | 2.1% | 0.9% |
| | Net income too low; Rent is high | 82.7% | 17.3% | 13.9% | 3.4% | 6.5% | 0.8% | 1.0% |
| 9. | Appliances | 66.4% | 33.6% | 28.9% | 4.7% | 14.0% | 2.3% | 2.6% |
| | Net income too low; Wages are high | 66.9% | 33.1% | 26.0% | 7.2% | 11.9% | 2.4% | 2.5% |

*Section 17.3 (page 630)*

1.

| PALMER ELECTRIC BALANCE SHEET FOR DECEMBER 31 |
|---|

**Assets**

Current Assets

| Cash | $21,000 | |
|---|---|---|
| Notes Receivable | $28,000 | |
| Accounts Receivable | $36,000 | |
| Inventory | $54,000 | |
| Total Current Assets | | $139,000 |

Plant Assets

| Land | $42,000 | |
|---|---|---|
| Buildings | $35,000 | |
| Fixtures | $9,000 | |
| Total Plant Assets | | $86,000 |
| TOTAL ASSETS | | $225,000 |

**Liabilities**

Current Liabilities

| Notes Payable | $52,000 | |
|---|---|---|
| Accounts Payable | $42,000 | |
| Total Current Liabilities | | $94,000 |

Long-term Liabilities

| Mortgages Payable | $65,000 | |
|---|---|---|
| Long-term Notes Payable | $9,000 | |
| Total Long-term Liabilities | | $74,000 |
| Total Liabilities | | $168,000 |

**Owner's Equity**

| Owner's Equity | $57,000 | |
|---|---|---|
| TOTAL LIABILITIES AND OWNER'S EQUITY | | $225,000 |

*Section 17.4 (page 640)*

1.

**GROCERY WAREHOUSE**
**COMPARATIVE BALANCE SHEET**

| | Amount This Year | Percent This Year | Amount Last Year | Percent Last Year |
|---|---|---|---|---|
| **Assets** | | | | |
| Current Assets | | | | |
| Cash | $52,000 | 13.0% | $42,000 | 13.1% |
| Notes Receivable | $8,000 | 2.0% | $6,000 | 1.9% |
| Accounts Receivable | $148,000 | 37.0% | $120,000 | 37.5% |
| Inventory | $153,000 | 38.3% | $120,000 | 37.5% |
| Total Current Assets | $361,000 | 90.3% | $288,000 | 90.0% |
| Plant Assets | | | | |
| Land | $10,000 | 2.5% | $8,000 | 2.5% |
| Buildings | $14,000 | 3.5% | $11,000 | 3.4% |
| Fixtures | $15,000 | 3.8% | $13,000 | 4.1% |
| Total Plant Assets | $39,000 | 9.8% | $32,000 | 10.0% |
| TOTAL ASSETS | $400,000 | 100.0% | $320,000 | 100.0% |
| **Liabilities** | | | | |
| Current Liabilities | | | | |
| Accounts Payable | $3,000 | 0.8% | $4,000 | 1.3% |
| Notes Payable | $201,000 | 50.3% | $152,000 | 47.5% |
| Total Current Liabilities | $204,000 | 51.0% | $156,000 | 48.8% |
| Long-term Liabilities | | | | |
| Mortgages Payable | $20,000 | 5.0% | $16,000 | 5.0% |
| Long-term Notes Payable | $58,000 | 14.5% | $42,000 | 13.1% |
| Total Long-term Liabilities | $78,000 | 19.5% | $58,000 | 18.1% |
| Total Liabilities | $282,000 | 70.5% | $214,000 | 66.9% |
| **Owner's Equity** | $118,000 | 29.5% | $106,000 | 33.1% |
| TOTAL LIABILITIES AND OWNER'S EQUITY | $400,000 | 100.0% | $320,000 | 100.0% |

**3.** 1.77; 1.02 **5.** 2.15; 1.40 **7.** 2.13; 1.27 **9.** 2.39 **11.** 1.63 **15.** 6.1% **17.** 16.9 times; 21.6 days

*Chapter 17 Review Exercises (page 647)*

**1.** $112,300; $59,800   **2.** $263,730; $138,930   **3.** $141,600; $43,200   **4.** $235,880; $23,580   **5.** $397,400
**6.** $126,500   **7.** $42,700   **8.** $282,100   **9.** $102,080; 17.6%   **10.** $333,100; 21.6%

**11.**

**LORI'S BOUTIQUE**
**INCOME STATEMENT**
**FOR THE YEAR ENDING DECEMBER 31**

| | | | |
|---|---|---|---|
| Gross Sales | | $175,000 | |
| Returns | | $8,000 | |
| Net Sales | | $167,000 | |
| Inventory, January 1 | $44,000 | | |
| Cost of Goods Purchased | $126,000 | | |
| Freight | $2,000 | | |
| Total Cost of Goods Purchased | $128,000 | | |
| Total of Goods Available for Sale | $172,000 | | |
| Inventory, December 31 | $52,000 | | |
| Cost of Goods Sold | | $120,000 | |
| Gross Profit | | | $47,000 |
| Expenses | | | |
| Salaries and Wages | $9,000 | | |
| Rent | $4,000 | | |
| Advertising | $1,500 | | |
| Utilities | $1,000 | | |
| Taxes on Inventory, Payroll | $2,000 | | |
| Miscellaneous Expenses | $3,000 | | |
| Total Expenses | | | $20,500 |
| **NET INCOME BEFORE TAXES** | | | $26,500 |

**12.**

| THE GUITAR WAREHOUSE |||
|---|---|---|
| **INCOME STATEMENT** |||
| **FOR THE YEAR ENDING DECEMBER 31** |||

| | | | |
|---|---|---|---|
| Gross Sales | | $2,215,000 | |
| Returns | | $26,000 | |
| Net Sales | | | $2,189,000 |
| Inventory, January 1 | $215,000 | | |
| Cost of Goods Purchased | $1,123,000 | | |
| Freight | $4,000 | | |
| Total Cost of Goods Purchased | $1,127,000 | | |
| Total of Goods Available for Sale | $1,342,000 | | |
| Inventory, December 31 | $265,000 | | |
| Cost of Goods Sold | | | $1,077,000 |
| Gross Profit | | | $1,112,000 |
| Expenses | | | |
| Salaries and Wages | $154,000 | | |
| Rent | $59,000 | | |
| Advertising | $11,000 | | |
| Utilities | $12,000 | | |
| Taxes on Inventory, Payroll | $10,000 | | |
| Miscellaneous Expenses | $9,000 | | |
| Total Expenses | | | $255,000 |
| **NET INCOME BEFORE TAXES** | | | $857,000 |
| **Income Taxes** | | | $242,300 |
| **NET INCOME** | | | $614,700 |

**13.** 76%; 12.8%  **14.** 62%; 24.8%

**15. Andy's Steak House**

|  | Amount | Percent | Percent from Table 17.1 |
|---|---|---|---|
| Net Sales | $300,000 | 100% | 100% |
| Cost of Goods Sold | $125,000 | 41.7% | 48.4% |
| Gross Profit | $175,000 | 58.3% | 51.6% |
| Wages | $72,000 | 24.0% | 26.4% |
| Rent | $12,000 | 4.0% | 2.8% |
| Advertising | $5,700 | 1.9% | 1.4% |
| Total Expenses | $123,000 | 41.0% | 43.7% |
| Net Income | $52,000 | 17.3% | 7.9% |

**16.**

**GASKETS, INC.**
**BALANCE SHEET**
**FOR DECEMBER 31**

### Assets

Current Assets

| | | |
|---|---|---|
| Cash | $240,000 | |
| Notes Receivable | $180,000 | |
| Accounts Receivable | $460,000 | |
| Inventory | $225,000 | |
| Total Current Assets | | $1,105,000 |

Plant Assets

| | | |
|---|---|---|
| Land | $180,000 | |
| Buildings | $260,000 | |
| Fixtures | $48,000 | |
| Total Plant Assets | | $488,000 |
| TOTAL ASSETS | | $1,593,000 |

### Liabilities

Current Liabilities

| | | |
|---|---|---|
| Notes Payable | $410,000 | |
| Accounts Payable | $882,000 | |
| Total Current Liabilities | | $1,292,000 |

Long-term Liabilities

| | | |
|---|---|---|
| Mortgages Payable | $220,000 | |
| Long- term Notes Payable | $194,000 | |
| Total Long-term Liabilities | | $414 ,000 |
| Total Liabilities | | $1,706,000 |

### Owner's Equity

| | | |
|---|---|---|
| Owner's Equity | ($113,000) | |
| TOTAL LIABILITIES AND OWNER'S EQUITY | | $1,593,000 |

**17.** 1.32; 0.46; 1.78   **18.** 0.83; 0.04; 4.17   **19.** 0.78; 0.71; 1.11   **20.** 5.6; 65.2 days   **21.** 10.4; 35.1 days

**22.**

|  | Amount This Year | Percent This Year | Amount Last Year | Percent Last Year |
|---|---|---|---|---|
| **Current assets** | | | | |
| Cash | $28,000 | 18.8% | $22,000 | 21.1% |
| Notes Receivable | $12,000 | 8.1% | $15,000 | 14.4% |
| Accounts Receivable | $39,000 | 26.2% | $31,500 | 30.1% |
| Inventory | $22,000 | 14.8% | $20,000 | 19.1% |
| **Total Current Assets** | $101,000 | 67.8% | $88,500 | 84.7% |
| **Total Plant and Equipment** | $48,000 | 32.2% | $16,000 | 15.3% |
| **TOTAL ASSETS** | $149,000 | 100.0% | $104,500 | 100.0% |
| **Total Current Liabilities** | $38,000 | 25.5% | $36,000 | 34.4% |

*Chapter 17 Summary Exercise (page 652)*

**(a)**

**BIRDSONG MUSIC, INC.**
**INCOME STATEMENT**
**YEAR ENDING DECEMBER 31**

| | | | |
|---|---|---|---|
| Gross Sales | | | $212,000 |
| Returns | | | $12,500 |
| Net Sales | | | $199,500 |
| Inventory, January 1 | | $44,000 | |
| Cost of Goods Purchased | $75,000 | | |
| Freight | $8,000 | | |
| Total Cost of Goods Purchased | | $83,000 | |
| Total of Goods Available for Sale | | $127,000 | |
| Inventory, December 31 | | $65,000 | |
| Cost of Goods Sold | | | $62,000 |
| Gross Profit | | | $137,500 |
| Expenses | | | |
| Salaries and Wages | | $37,000 | |
| Rent | | $12,000 | |
| Advertising | | $2,000 | |
| Utilities | | $3,000 | |
| Taxes on Inventory, Payroll | | $7,000 | |
| Miscellaneous Expenses | | $4,500 | |
| Total Expenses | | | $65,500 |
| NET INCOME BEFORE TAXES | | | $72,000 |

**(b)**  106%; 18.5%; 6.3%; 6%; 31.1%; 1.5%

**(c)**

| BIRDSONG MUSIC, INC. |
| BALANCE SHEET |
| DECEMBER 31 |

### Assets

Current Assets

|  |  |  |
|---|---|---|
| Cash | $62,000 | |
| Notes Receivable | $2,500 | |
| Accounts Receivable | $8,200 | |
| Inventory | $65,000 | |
| Total Current Assets | | $137,700 |

Plant Assets

|  |  |  |
|---|---|---|
| Land | $28,000 | |
| Buildings | $84,000 | |
| Fixtures | $13,500 | |
| Total Plant Assets | | $125,500 |
| TOTAL ASSETS | | | $263,200 |

### Liabilities

Current Liabilities

|  |  |  |
|---|---|---|
| Notes Payable | $16,800 | |
| Accounts Payable | $27,000 | |
| Total Current Liabilities | | $43,800 |

Long-term Liabilities

|  |  |  |
|---|---|---|
| Mortgages Payable | $15,000 | |
| Long-term Notes Payable | $42,000 | |
| Total Long-term Liabilities | | $57,000 |
| Total Liabilities | | | $100,800 |

### Owner's Equity

|  |  |  |
|---|---|---|
| Owner's Equity | $162,400 | |
| TOTAL LIABILITIES AND OWNER'S EQUITY | | | $263,200 |

**(d)**  3.14; 1.66; yes

# Chapter 18

*Section 18.1 (page 660)*
**1.** $0; $0   **3.** $0.30; $0.14   **5.** $20; $0   **7.** $0.10   **9.** $1; $1.17   **11.** $1.60; $0.86   **13.** $20; $5.06   **15.** $5.83
**17.** $4.38   **19. (a)** $0.77   **(b)** $0.90   **(c)** 14.2%   **21.** $26,666.67

*Section 18.2 (page 671)*
**1.** $19   **3.** $33$\frac{3}{4}$ or $33.75   **5.** $24$\frac{7}{8}$ or $24.875   **7.** $0.36   **9.** 642,300 shares   **11.** $113,875   **13.** $125   **15.** $1,565.63
**17.** $5,663.13   **19.** $46,432.50   **21.** $2,198.44   **23.** $38,334.88   **25.** $8,921.06   **27.** $3,973.04   **29.** $42,683.31
**31.** 0.6%   **33.** 1.5%   **35.** 1.5%   **37.** 12   **39.** 10   **41.** $17,937.50   **43. (a)** $47,512.76   **(b)** $77,380.98
**(c)** $29,868.22   **45.** $2,330.96

*Section 18.3 (page 677)*
**1.** $811.25   **3.** $91.25   **5.** $2.50   **7.** $31,012.50   **9.** $102,125   **11.** $49,750   **13.** $24,312.50   **17.** $20,000
**19.** $17,212.50   **21.** $244,875; $27,375   **23.** $4,500   **25.** 89 bonds; $88,443.75

*Section 18.4 (page 683)*
**1.** $21,000 each   **3.** $36,800 for 1; $9,200 for 2   **5.** $16,920 for 1; $8,080 for 2
**7.** $10,000 for 1; $12,000 for 2; 0 for 3   **9.** $1,400   **11.** $12,000 for 1; $48,000 for 2; $60,000 for 3
**13.** $22,500; $37,500; $52,500; $67,500   **15.** $23,400 for Finch; $33,600 for Renz
**17. (a)** $21,000 for Coker; $39,000 for Toms   **(b)** $7,500 for Coker; $1,500 by Toms to Coker
**19.** $22,179 to 1; $46,464 to 2; $41,357 to 3

*Section 18.5 (page 688)*
**1.** $110,000; $154,000; $176,000   **3.** $18,000; $27,000; $30,000; $45,000   **5.** $64,615; $37,692; $37,692
**7.** $9,739; $20,870; $2,087; $15,304   **9.** $352,500; $352,500; $235,000   **11.** $190,476; $228,571; $266,667; $114,286
**13.** $24,000; $96,000; $72,000; $108,000; $12,000; $48,000   **15.** $8,079; $21,545; $16,158; $10,099; $12,119
**17.** $600; $1,050; $2,250; $360; $240

*Chapter 18 Review Exercises (page 697)*
**1. (a)** $9   **(b)** $4.40   **2. (a)** $12   **(b)** $7.23   **3. (a)** $8.75   **(b)** $2.69   **4.** $7.25   **5.** $2.73   **6.** $3.70
**7.** 37$\frac{1}{4}$ or $37.25   **8.** 32$\frac{1}{8}$ or $32.125   **9.** 21$\frac{1}{8}$ or $21.125   **10.** +$\frac{1}{8}$ or +$0.125   **11.** $0   **12.** 29,400   **13.** 1.6%
**14.** 33$\frac{1}{2}$ or $33.50   **15.** $22,125   **16.** $1,100   **17.** $5,400   **18.** $13,500   **19.** $8,533.13   **20.** $25,489.06   **21.** 3.3%
**22.** 1.1%   **23.** 14   **24.** 9   **25.** $962.50   **26.** 15   **27.** 2011   **28.** −$0.75   **29.** $29,025   **30.** 7$\frac{3}{8}$% or $73.75   **31.** $9,725
**32.** $20,406.25   **33.** $16,000   **34.** $48,000 to 1; $72,000 to 2   **35.** $38,571 to 1; $51,429 to 2
**36.** $25,000; $41,667; $33,333   **37.** $23,255.81; $58,139.53; $43,604.65   **38.** $25,870; $20,326; $16,630; $22,174
**39.** $18,562.50   **40.** $24,156

*Chapter 18 Summary Exercise (page 700)*
**(a)** 30,000; 20,000; 50,000   **(b)** $4 preferred; $0.73 common   **(c)** $53,900; $54,600; $84,500   **(d)** $34,375; $4,125
**(e)** Math—$62,125; English—$44,375; Reading—$35,500   **(f)** yes; probably not

# CHAPTER 19

*Section 19.1 (page 709)*

**1. (a)** approx. $2,800,000 **(b)** approx. $2,500,000 **(c)** approx. $1,600,000 **3. (a)** 4 **(b)** 3 **(c)** 6 **(d)** 3 **(e)** 5
**(f)** 9

**(g)**

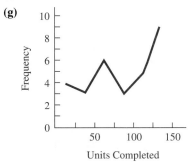

**7. (a)** almost 1 acre **(b)** almost $3\frac{7}{8}$ acre **(c)** 2 mph **(d)** 99 in.

**9.**

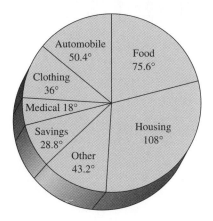

**11.** 108°; 75.6°; 50.4°; 36°; 18°; 28.8°; 43.2°

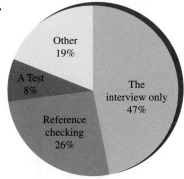

**13.** 19% **15. (a)** $30,000; $38,000; 27% **(b)** $57,000; $19,000 **(c)** $18,000; $41,000

*Section 19.2 (page 718)*

**1.** 26  **3.** 3,689.6  **5.** 697 lb.  **7.** $39,418  **9.** $657,125  **11.** 7.1  **13.** 167.2  **17.** $31,000  **19.** 1.62  **21.** 76.3
**23.** 105.8  **25.** Weigh no more than 150 pounds

*Section 19.3 (page 725)*

**1.** 35  **3.** 88  **5.** 0.83  **7.** 7  **9.** None  **11.** 4 and 6  **15.** 6; 3  **17.** Median  **19.** 115.1; 114.5; 114.5
**21.** 3.00 lb. (rounded); probably so

*Section 19.4 (page 732)*

**1.** 10; 1.4  **3.** 21; 1.6  **5.** 55.9; 3.1  **7.** 18  **9.** 388  **13.** 100  **15.** 136  **17.** 27  **19.** 136  **21.** 2.5%  **23.** 95%
**25.** 50%  **27.** 16%  **29.** 95%  **31.** $\frac{1}{2}$%  **33.** 84%  **35.** 97.5%  **37.** 84%  **39.** 97.5%  **41.** 68%  **43.** 1 claim

*Section 19.5 (page 736)*

**1.** 166.7  **3.** 73.7  **5.** 168  **7.** $142.70  **9.** $217.60  **11.** $141.20  **13.** $288,000  **15.** $10,200  **17.** Medical

*Chapter 19 Review Exercises (page 743)*

**1.** 4; 5; 11; 5; 5  **2.** 4; 14; 19; 7; 5; 3; 2; 1

**3.**

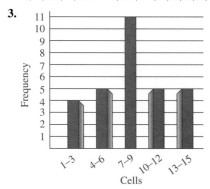

**4.**

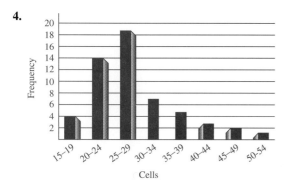

# Glossary

For further information on any of these terms, see the index.

**absolute** or **gross loss** The loss resulting when the selling price is less than the cost.

**accelerated cost recovery system (ACRS)** The method of depreciation required on all federal income tax returns for property acquired after January 1, 1981 and before 1986.

**accelerated depreciation** Depreciation which has a rate greater than a straight-line rate of depreciation. For example, declining balance, sum-of-the-year's-digits, or ACRS.

**accelerated mortgages** Home mortgages that are paid off faster than the typical 30 years for most home mortgages.

**accidental death benefit** Coverage which pays an additional death benefit if the insured dies as the result of an accident.

**accounts payable** Funds owed by a firm that must be paid within a short period of time such as a year or less.

**accounts receivable** Funds owed to a firm, by customers, that must be paid within a short period of time such as a year or less.

**accounts receivable turnover** Net sales divided by average accounts receivable.

**accumulated depreciation** A running balance or total of the depreciation to date on an asset.

**acid-test ratio** The ratio of current assets and current liabilities. Also called quick ratio.

**actual selling price** *See* Reduced price.

**actuary** A person who determines insurance premiums.

**adjustable rate mortgage** *See* variable rate loan.

**adjusted bank balance** This number represents the current checking account balance.

**adjusted gross income (AGI)** The sum total of all income received from wages, salaries, interest, and dividends less any adjustments to income such as sick pay and moving expenses.

**adult operator** A driver of a motor vehicle over a certain age, usually 25 years of age or older.

**agreed ratio** Partners of a business divide the profits using some given rule. These profit divisions are sometimes given as a ratio.

**algebraic logic** The logic used by most electronic calculators.

**allocation of overhead** Dividing the overhead among the various products or lines of business of a company.

**amortization schedule** A table showing the equal payment necessary to pay off a loan for a specific amount of money including interest, for a specific amount of time. Also called a repayment schedule.

**amortized** When principal and interest are paid by a sequence of equal payments (on a loan).

**amount financed** The difference of the cash price of an item and the down payment.

**amount of an annuity** The sum of the compound amounts of all the periodic payments into an annuity, compounded to the end of the term.

**annual meeting** A meeting open to all owners of stock where the management of the firm is open to questions from stockholders, and where the board of directors is elected.

**annual percentage rate** A rate of interest that must be stated for each loan, by federal regulation. This annual percentage rate is designed to help consumers compare interest rates. This is the true or effective rate of interest.

**annuity** Periodic payments of a given, fixed amount of money.

**annuity certain** An annuity with a fixed beginning date and a fixed ending date.

**annuity due** An annuity with payments made at the beginning of a time period.

**anticipation** The seller's offer of interest for early payment of an invoice, in addition to a cash discount.

**AS OF** An invoice which is postdated ''AS OF'' a future date.

**assessed** The procedure whereby a local official, called the assessor, makes an estimate of the fair market value of property.

**assessed valuation** The value for property tax purposes set by the tax assessor on a piece of property.

**assessment rate** A certain percent used in an area to determine assessed valuation.

**assets** Items of value owned by a firm.

**attached** A seizure of property by court order.

**automated teller machine (ATM)** A machine allowing 24-hour banking.

**average** *See* Mean.

**average age of accounts receivable** One year (365 days) divided by accounts receivable turnover rate.

**average daily balance** A method of calculating the balance owed on a revolving charge account. With this method, the balance on the account is found at the end of each day in the month and the total is divided by the number of days in the month.

**average daily balance method** A method of calculating the finance charge on a revolving charge account by using the average balance at the end of each day during a month.

**average inventory** Determined by dividing the sum of all inventories taken by the number of times inventory was taken.

**bad check** A check that is not honored because there are insufficient funds in the checking account.

**balanced** Agreement reached between the bank statement amount and the depositor's checkbook balance.

**balance brought forward** The amount left in a checking account after previous checks written have been subtracted; the current balance.

**balance sheet** A summary of the financial condition of a firm at one point in time.

**bank discount** *See* Discount.

**bank statement** A list of all charges and deposits made against and to a checking account, usually sent out monthly by the bank.

**bank statement balance** This is the checking account balance appearing on the front of the bank statement.

**banker's interest** *See* Ordinary interest.

**banker's ratio** *See* Current ratio.

**bar graph** A graph that uses bars to show data.

**base** In the number $3^2$, the number 3 is the base. *See* Exponent. The starting point or reference point or that to which something is being compared.

**base year** A previous year against which something is being compared.

**basic percent equation** Rate $\times$ Base = Part or $R \times B = P$.

**beneficiary** The person receiving insurance benefits upon the occurrence of a certain event.

**bimodal** A set of data in which two numbers occur equally often.

**blank endorsement** The endorsement of a check with a signature alone.

**board of directors** A group of people who represent the stockholders.

**bodily injury insurance** Another name for liability insurance.

**bond** A promise by a corporation or government to pay a certain fixed amount of money at a certain time in the future.

**book value** The cost of an asset minus any depreciation to date.

**borrow** Taking a number from one column of numbers in a problem in order to make a larger number in the column to which the borrowed number is added.

**breakeven point** The cost of an item plus the operating expenses associated with the item. Above this amount a profit is made, below it, a loss is incurred.

**business checking account** The type of checking account used by businesses.

**business owner's package policy** A business insurance policy insuring many additional perils beyond fire.

**cancellation** A process used to simplify multiplication and division of fractions using a modification of the method of writing fractions in lowest terms.

**cancellation rate** Another name for short-term rate.

**capital** The amount of money originally invested in a firm.

**carrier** The insurance company. Also known as the insurer.

**cash discount** A discount offered by the seller allowing the buyer to take a discount if payment is made within a specified period of time.

**cash settlement option** Life insurance benefits which are paid in cash.

**cash value** The value in cash remaining after a policy holder has canceled or borrowed against a life insurance policy.

**cashier's check** A check written by the financial institution itself and having the full faith and backing of the institution.

**certificate of deposit** Money placed in a time deposit account.

**chain calculation** A long sequence of calculations.

**chain discount** Involves two or more individual discounts.

**charge accounts** An account that allows an individual to charge purchases at a specific store.

**chargeback** A fee charged to a production employee for a rejected item of production.

**check register** A single page record of checks written and deposits made to a checking account.

**checks outstanding** Checks written that have not reached and cleared the bank as of the statement date.

**check stub** A stub attached to the check and retained for keeping a record of checks written.

**circle graph** A circle broken up into various parts, based on percentages of 360°.

**classes** The intervals of a frequency distribution.

**class frequency** The frequency of values for each class.

**class mark** The midpoint of an interval.

**C.O.D.** A shipping term meaning *cash on delivery*.

**coefficient** A number used to multiply a variable.

**coinsurance clause** A fire insurance clause which places part of the risk of fire loss upon the insured.

**collateral** Goods pledged as security for a loan—in the event that a loan is not paid off, the collateral can be seized by the lender and sold to pay the debt.

**collision insurance** A form of automobile insurance that pays for repairs to the insured's car in case of an accident.

**commission** A fee paid to an employee for transacting a piece of business or performing a service. A charge for buying or selling stock.

**common denominator** A number that all the denominators of a fraction problem divide into evenly.

**common stock** Ordinary capital stock not sharing the privileges of preferred stock.

**companion** or **spouse insurance** This lets the insured add a companion or spouse to a policy, resulting in both being insured.

**comparative income statement** Preparation of a vertical analysis for two or more years in order to compare incomes or balance sheet items for each year analyzed.

**comparative line graph** One graph which shows how several different things relate.

**compensatory time (comp time)** Time off given an employee to compensate for overtime previously worked.

**complement** The number which must be added to a given discount to get 1 or 100%.

**compound amount** The final amount, both principal and interest, after money is deposited at compound interest.

**compound interest** Interest computed on both principal and interest.

**compounded daily** Interest is paid for every day that money is on deposit in a savings account.

**comprehensive insurance** A form of automobile insurance that pays for damage to the insured's car caused by fire, theft, vandalism, and so on.

**consumer** The ultimate user of a product or service, the public.

**Consumer Price Index** A monthly publication by the federal government showing the change in the cost of living.

**contingent annuity** An annuity with a variable beginning or ending date.

**continuous compounding** An account offering continuous compounding features interest compounded every instant.

**convertible preferred stock** One share is convertible into a stated number of shares of common stock at some date.

**corporation** A form of business organization offering limited liability to shareholders—no more money may be lost than has been invested.

**cost** The price paid to a supplier after trade and cash discounts have been taken. This price includes transportation and insurance charges. The amount paid for a depreciable asset. This is the amount used to determine depreciation.

**cost of goods sold** The amount paid by a firm for the goods it sold during the time period covered by an income statement.

**country club billing** A type of billing received on revolving charge plans in which actual carbon copies of charges are returned.

**credit cards** Cards that allow an individual to make charges at several different businesses such as retail stores and restaurants.

**credit limit** The limit on the amount an individual can charge.

**credit union share draft accounts** A credit union account that may be used as a checking account.

**cross-products** In the proportion $\frac{a}{b} = \frac{c}{d}$, the crossproducts are *ad* and *bc*.

**cumulative preferred stock** Stock requiring that any dividends not paid in the past must be paid before common stockholders receive any money.

**current assets** Cash or items that can be converted into cash within a given period of time, such as a year.

**current balance** *See* Adjusted bank balance.

**current (short-term) liabilities** Those items which must be paid by a firm within a given period of time, such as a year.

**current ratio** The quotient of current assets and current liabilities. Also called banker's ratio.

**current yield** The annual dividend per share of stock divided by the current price per share.

**debit card** A bank card used at a point of sale terminal. The amount of the purchase is instantly subtracted from the customer's account and credit is given to the seller's account.

**debt-to-equity ratio** All liabilities divided by owner's equity.

**decimal** A number written with a decimal point, such as 4.3 or 7.22.

**decimal equivalent of a fraction** The decimal fraction that is equal to a proper fraction. For example, $\frac{1}{2} = 0.5$, $\frac{3}{8} = 0.375$.

**decimal number** A fraction with a denominator that is a power of ten, which is written with a decimal point, such as 4.3 or 7.22.

**decimal point** The starting point in the decimal system (.).

**declining-balance depreciation** An accelerated depreciation method.

**declining-balance method** A method of depreciation using a declining balance rate.

**(200%) declining-balance method** An accelerated method of depreciation using twice or 200% of the straight-line rate. Also called double-declining-balance method.

**(150%) declining-balance method** An accelerated method of depreciation using one and one-half or 150% of the straight-line rate.

**(125%) declining-balance method** An accelerated method of depreciation using one and one-fourth or 125% of the straight-line rate.

**decrease problem** Often called a difference problem; the part equals the base minus some portion of the base. Usually the base must be found.

**decreasing term insurance** A form of life insurance in which the insured pays a fixed premium until age 60 or 65 with the amount of life insurance decreasing periodically.

**deductible** The amount of the deductible is paid by the insured with the balance of the loss being paid by the insurance company.

**deductions** Amounts that are subtracted from the gross earnings of an employee to arrive at the amount of money the employee actually receives, net pay.

**deferred payment price** The cash price of an item, plus any finance charge.

**deficit number** *See* Negative number.

**denominator** The number below the line in a fraction. For example, in the fraction $\frac{7}{9}$, 9 is the denominator.

**deposit slip (deposit ticket)** The form used for making a bank savings or checking account deposit.

**depreciable amount** The amount to be depreciated over the life of the asset.

**depreciation** A method used to spread the value of an asset over the several years of its life.

**depreciation fraction** The fraction used with sum-of-the-years'-digits depreciation. The numerator is the year and the denominator is the sum of the years of life of the asset.

**depreciation schedule** A schedule or table showing the depreciation rate, amount of depreciation, book value, and accumulated depreciation for each year of an asset's life.

**destination** The city or town where goods or merchandise are being shipped.

**differential-piece rate** A piece rate designed to pay a greater amount for each unit of production as the number of units produced is increased.

**discount** An amount subtracted from the price of a product or service which helps the buyer purchase at a lower cost and increase profits. The amount of interest charged on a note. Also called a bank discount.

**discount broker** A stockbroker who charges less than full price for buying and selling stocks.

**discount note** A note where interest is deducted in advance.

**discount period** The period of time in the discounting process.

**discounting a note** The holder of a note sometimes sells the note to a bank before its maturity date. This gives cash to the holder earlier than otherwise.

**dispersion** Spread of data.

**distributive property** A property of algebra that says a number on the outside of the parentheses should be multiplied times each term inside the parentheses.

**dividends** Money paid by a company to the holders of a stock.

**docking** Same meaning as chargeback.

**double-declining-balance method** *See* (200%) declining-balance method.

**double-time** Twice the regular hourly rate. A premium often paid for working holidays and Sunday.

**Dow Jones Industrial Average** A commonly quoted average of the stock prices of 30 large industrial, publicly held corporations.

**down payment** An amount paid when an item is bought.

**draw** An amount paid by an employer to salespeople at regular intervals. This is often paid against future income.

**drawing account** An account from which a salesperson can receive payment against future commissions.

**duplicate statement** A duplicate of a checking account statement issued by the bank.

**early withdrawal penalty** A fine or amount of money charged by the lending institution for withdrawal of money earlier than the time agreed upon by the depositor and the institution. These penalties apply only to interest, not to principal.

**earnings per share** The difference of the net income of a corporation and any dividends on preferred shares, divided by the number of common shares outstanding.

**effective rate of interest** The simple interest rate corresponding to a given discount rate. Also called true rate of interest. The actual percent of interest earned during a year.

**electronic banking** The use of electronic technology in banking. Such services as direct deposits, ATM cards, debit cards, and home and business banking are all a part of electronic banking.

**Employer's Quarterly Federal Tax Return** The form (Form 941) is sent to the IRS along with quarterly payments of FICA and withholding tax.

**ending inventory** The value at cost of inventory at the end of a period.

**end-of-month dating (EOM)** In cash discounts, the time period beginning at the end of the month the invoice is dated. Proximo and prox. have the same meaning.

**endowment policy** A form of life insurance guaranteeing the payment of a fixed amount of money to a given individual whether or not the insured person lives.

**equal shares** Partners in a business share all profits equally.

**equation** A statement that says two expressions are equal.

**equivalent cash price** A single amount today equal to the present value of an annuity.

**escrow account** An account maintained by real estate lenders and used to pay taxes and insurance. Also called an impound account.

**exact interest** Simple interest calculated using 365 days in a year.

**excise tax** A tax charged on specific items which are purchased. Tobacco, alcoholic beverages, and gasoline have an excise tax.

**executive officers** President, vice president, and so on, of a corporation.

**exponent** In the number $3^2$ the small number 2 is the exponent. It says to multiply 3 by itself. A number that tells how many times a number is used in a product. For example, $3^2 = 3 \times 3 = 9$.

**extended term insurance** The nonforfeiture option which gives the insured term insurance for a fixed number of years and days.

**extension total** On an invoice, the product of the number of items times the unit price.

**extra dating (extra, ex., or x)** Extra time allowed in determining the net payment date of a cash discount.

**face value** The amount shown on the face of a note. *See* Par value.

**face value of the policy** The amount of an insurance policy.

**factor** A person who buys accounts receivable of a firm (accounts receivable represent money owed to the firm).

**factoring** The term for when a business sells part of its accounts receivable to a financial institution.

**Fair Labor Standards Act** A federal law setting work conditions and standards of employee treatment.

**fair market value** The price for which a piece of property could reasonably be expected to be sold in the market.

**FAS (free alongside ship)** Free alongside the ship on the loading dock with all freight charges to that point paid by the shipper.

**Federal Insurance Contributions Act (FICA)** A federal act requiring that a specified amount of money be collected from the paycheck of almost all nongovernmental employees, which is used by the federal government to pay pensions, survivors benefits, and disability.

**Federal Truth in Lending Act** An act passed in 1969 which requires that all interest rates be given as comparable percents.

**Federal Truth-in-Lending Law in 1969 (Regulation Z)** A federal law passed in 1969 that establishes uniform methods of disclosing information on finance charges and interest rates.

**Federal Unemployment Tax Act (FUTA)** A federal act covering unemployment insurance.

**finance charges** Charges paid to obtain credit.

**first-in, first-out method (FIFO)** Inventory valuation method following the flow of goods, first-in, first-out.

**fixed amount annuity** A settlement option which pays a fixed amount per month to life insurance beneficiaries.

**fixed assets** *See* Plant and equipment assets.

**fixed period annuity** A settlement option for life insurance beneficiaries paying a sum of money for a fixed period of time.

**fixed rate loan** A home loan made at a fixed rate of interest for a fixed period of time.

**floating decimal point** A feature on electronic calculators that locates the decimal point in the answer.

**floor space** Overhead is sometimes allocated among lines of business based on the amount of floor space used by each line.

**FOB (free on board)** Free on board shipping point means that the buyer pays for shipping. Free on board destination means that the seller pays for shipping.

**formula** A rule showing how quantities are related.

**fraction** Used to indicate a part of a whole. For example, $\frac{3}{4}$ means that the whole is divided into 4 parts and we are considering 3 of them.

**frequency distribution table** A table showing the number of times one or more events occur.

**future value** The amount an investment grows to at some future date.

**graph** A visual presentation of numeric data.

**gross earnings** The total amount of money earned by an employee before any deductions are taken.

**gross loss** *See* Absolute loss.

**gross profit** The difference between the amount received from customers for goods and what the firm paid for the goods.

**gross profit method** A method used to estimate inventory value at cost which utilizes cost amounts.

**gross sales** The total amount of money received from customers for the goods or services sold by the firm.

**group insurance plans** An insurance plan which includes a group of people employed by the same company or belonging to the same organization.

**grouped data** Items combined into groups (taken from a table) to simplify information for more immediate comprehension.

**guaranteed conversion privilege** This provision allows the insured to convert term insurance to ordinary or variable life insurance without physical examination.

**half-year convention** Under MACRS, property placed in service or disposed of is allowed one-half year of depreciation.

**home banking** A system that allows the customer to do banking from the home or business using the telephone and computer.

**homeowner's policy** A policy for homeowners providing fire, theft, and vandalism protection.

**horizontal analysis** Prepared by finding the amount of any change from last year to current year, both in dollars and as a percent.

**hourly wage** A rate of pay expressed as so much per hour. *See* Time rate.

**impound account** *See* Escrow account.

**improper fraction** A fraction with a numerator larger than or equal to the denominator. For example, $\frac{7}{5}$ is an improper fraction; $\frac{1}{9}$ is not.

**incentive rate** A payment system based on the amount of work completed.

**income statement** A summary of all the income and expenses involved in running a business for a given period of time.

**income tax method** *See* Accelerated cost recovery system (MACRS).

**income tax withholding** Federal income tax withheld from gross earnings by the employer.

**increase problem** Often called an amount problem; the part equals the base plus some portion of the base, resulting in a new value. Usually the base must be found.

**Individual Retirement Account (IRA)** An account that permits an individual to establish a retirement plan and to deduct any contributions to the account.

**inflation** The increase over time in the price levels of goods and services.

**initial inventory** The value at cost of inventory at the beginning of a period.

**installment loan** A loan paid off in a series of equal payments made at equal periods of time. Car loans are examples of installment loans.

**insufficient funds (NSF)** Not enough funds in a checking account for the bank to honor the check.

**insured** A person or business that has purchased insurance. Also known as the policyholder.

**insured money market accounts (IMMAs)** Accounts which are insured up to a certain maximum by the federal government, and which offer a higher rate than passbook accounts.

**insurer** The insurance company.

**interest** A charge paid for borrowing money or a fee received for lending money.

**interest-in-advance note** *See* Simple discount note.

**interest on investment and agreed ratio** Sometimes one partner will put up a large share of money to start a firm, while other partners operate it. The partner putting up the larger share of money gets interest on the investment before any further division of profits.

**interest rate spread** The difference between the interest rate charged on loans and that paid on deposits.

**inventory** The value of all goods on hand for sale.

**inventory turnover** The number of times each year that the average inventory is sold, also called stock turnover.

**inventory valuation** Determining the value of merchandise in stock. Four common methods are specific identification, weighted average cost, FIFO, and LIFO.

**invoice** A document which helps businesses keep track of sales and purchases.

**invoice total** The total amount owed on an invoice.

**irregulars** Items that are blemished or have flaws and must be sold at a reduced price.

**itemized billing** A method of credit card billing in which purchases are listed, along with payments, with no actual receipts returned to the user.

**junk bonds** Bonds of bankrupt or troubled companies.

**last-in, first-out method (LIFO)** Inventory valuation method following the flow of goods, last-in, first-out.

**late fees** Fees charged by lenders for late payments.

**least common denominator** The smallest whole number that all the denominators of two or more fractions evenly divide into.

**left side** In the equation $4x = 28$, the left side is $4x$.

**liabilities** Expenses which must be paid by a firm.

**liability** or **bodily injury insurance** Coverage which provides protection from suit by an injured party.

**like fractions** Two fractions that have the same denominator.

**limited liability** No more money can be lost than has been invested.

**limited payment life insurance** A form of life insurance in which premiums are paid for only a certain fixed number of years.

**line graph** A graph that uses a line to show data.

**liquid assets** Cash or items which can be converted to cash quickly.

**liquidity** A firm is liquid if it has the ability to pay its bills as they come due.

**list price** The suggested retail price or final consumer price given by the manufacturer or supplier.

**loan payoff table** A table used to decide on the payment that will amortize a loan.

**long-term liabilities** Those items which will be paid after one year.

**lowest terms** A fraction is written in lowest terms when no number except the number 1 divides evenly into both the numerator and denominator of the fraction.

**luxury tax** A name sometimes given to excise tax.

**maintenance charge per month** A flat charge for maintaining a checking account.

**maker** The person borrowing the money on a note.

**manufacturer** The assembler of component parts or finished products.

**markdown** A reduction from the original selling price. It may be expressed as a dollar amount or as a percent of the original selling price.

**marketable securities** Stocks, bonds, and other securities that can be converted quickly to cash.

**marketing channels** The path or steps that goods take from manufacturer to consumer.

**markup (margin or gross profit)** The difference between the cost and the selling price.

**markup conversion formula** A formula used to convert markup from one base to the other base.

**markup formula** The formula used when working with markup. Cost + Markup = Selling price.

**markup on cost** Markup that is calculated as a percent of cost.

**markup on selling price** Markup that is calculated as a percent of selling price.

**markup with spoilage** The calculation of markup including deduction for spoiled or unsaleable merchandise.

**MasterCard** A credit card plan.

**mathematics of buying** The mathematics involving trade and cash discounts.

**maturity date** The date a loan is due.

**maturity value** The total amount, principal, and interest, that must be repaid when a loan is paid off. It equals face value plus interest.

**mean** The sum of all the numbers divided by the number of numbers.

**measure of central tendency** A number that tries to estimate the middle of a set of data. Measures of central tendency include the mean, median, and mode.

**median** The middle number in an ordered array.

**medical insurance** Insurance providing medical protection in the event of accident or injury.

**medicare tax** Part of the social security tax (FICA) until 1991. Since 1991 medicare tax has been collected separately.

**memory keys** A feature on electronic calculators which allows answers to be stored for future use and recalled.

**merchant batch header ticket** A form used to deposit credit card sales in a business checking account.

**middlemen** Those along the marketing channels, such as wholesalers, brokers, and retailers.

**mill** A mill is one-tenth of a cent or one-thousandth of a dollar.

**mixed number** The sum of a fraction and a whole number. For example, $1\frac{1}{5}$ or $2\frac{5}{9}$ are mixed numbers.

**mode** The most common number in a list of numbers.

**modified accelerated cost recovery system (MACRS)** The Tax Reform Act of 1986 replaces the ACRS with the MACRS.

**money order** An instrument which is purchased and used in place of cash. It is usually preferred over a personal or business check.

**mortality table** A table showing statistics on life expectancy, survival, and death rates.

**multiple carriers** More than one insurance company sharing in an insurable risk.

**mutual company** An insurance company owned by the policyholders who receive a dividend.

**mutual fund** Typically receives money from many different small investors and reinvests the funds in stocks and/or bonds.

**negative number (deficit number)** A number which is less than zero; a negative balance or deficit. For example, −$800 or ($800).

**net cost** The cost or price after allowable discounts have been taken.

**net cost equivalent** or **percent paid** The decimal number derived from the product of the complements of the trade discounts. This number may be multiplied by the list price to find the net cost (price).

**net income** The difference between gross profit and operating expenses.

**net pay** The amount of money actually received by an employee after deductions are taken from gross pay.

**net profit** (or **net earnings**) The difference between gross margin and expenses. After the cost of goods and operating expenses are subtracted from total sales, the remainder is net profit.

**net sales** The value of goods bought by customers after subtracting goods returned.

**net worth** Same as owner's equity.

**no-fault insurance** Motor vehicle insurance which pays directly to the insured no matter who causes the accident.

**nominal rate** *See* Stated rate.

**noncustomer check cashing** A service that allows an individual who is not a bank customer to cash a check upon payment of a fee.

**nonforfeiture options** Options available to the insured when canceling the insurance policy.

**nonparticipating** A form of stock which will never pay dividends above the stated rate.

**nonparticipating policy** The type of life insurance policy issued by a stock insurance company.

**nonsmoker's discount** A discount given to nonsmokers because they are better insurance risks.

**nonsufficient funds (NSF)** Not enough funds in a checking account for the bank to honor the check.

**normal curve** The bell-shaped curve commonly used in statistics.

**notary service** A service that provides notarization, which is required on certain business documents and transfers.

**NOW account** This account uses a ''Negotiable Order of Withdrawal,'' which works and looks like a check.

**numerator** The number above the line in a fraction. For example, in the fraction $\frac{5}{8}$, 5 is the numerator.

**odd lot** Fewer than 100 shares of stock.

**odd-lot differential** An additional charge for buying or selling stocks when the number of shares is not a multiple of 100.

**open-end credit** An account that is not paid off in a fixed period of time; MasterCard and VISA accounts are examples of open-end credit.

**operating expenses** (or **overhead**) Expenses of operating a business. Wages, salaries, rent, utilities, and advertising are examples of operating expenses.

**operating loss** The loss resulting when the selling price is less than the breakeven point.

**order of operations** The rules determining which calculations must be done first in chain calculations.

**ordered array** An arrangement of a list of numbers from smallest to largest.

**ordinary annuity** An annuity with payments made at the end of a given period of time.

**ordinary dating method** A method for calculating the discount date and the net payment date. Days are counted from the date of the invoice.

**ordinary interest** Simple interest calculated assuming 360 days in a year. Also called banker's interest.

**ordinary life insurance** (Whole life insurance, straight life insurance) A form of life insurance in which the insured pays a constant premium until death or retirement, whichever occurs sooner. Upon retirement, monthly pay-

ments are made by the company to the insured until the death of the insured.

**original investment** Partners divide profits of a business on the basis of original investments by each partner.

**overdraft** This occurs when a customer writes a check for which there are insufficient funds in the account.

**overdraft protection** The bank service of honoring checks written on an account which has insufficient funds.

**overhead** *See* Operating expenses.

**override** A commission received by a sales supervisor or department head based on total sales of the sales group or department.

**overtime** The number of hours worked by an employee in excess of 40 hours per week, or 8 hours per day.

**overtime premium method** Payment of overtime as a premium. All hours worked are paid at regular rate. Overtime hours are paid at $\frac{1}{2}$ rate. Gross earnings are the sum of these.

**owner's equity** The difference between assets and liabilities. Also called proprietorship or net worth.

**paid-up insurance** A nonforfeiture option which provides paid-up insurance of a certain amount.

**par value** The amount printed on a stock certificate; usually the price at which a share of stock is first offered to the public.

**part** The result of multiplying the base times the rate.

**partial payment** A payment which is less than the total owed on an invoice; a cash discount may be earned.

**partial-year depreciation** The amount of depreciation that is determined for the asset during a period less than one year.

**participating** A type of stock that could be affected by an increase in the dividend.

**participating policy** The type of life insurance policy issued by a mutual insurance company.

**partnership** A business formed by two or more people.

**passbook account** A bank account used for day-in and day-out deposits of money. These accounts usually have the lowest interest rates of any accounts, but have no penalties when money is withdrawn.

**pay period** The time period for which an employee is paid.

**payee** The person who loans the money and will receive payment on a note.

**payer** *See* Maker.

**payment period** The time between the payments into an annuity.

**payments for life** A life insurance settlement option which pays an annuity for life.

**payments for life with a guaranteed number of years** A life insurance settlement option which pays a certain amount per month for the life of the insured but guarantees a certain length of time in the event that the insured dies before this guaranteed time period.

**payroll ledger** A chart showing all payroll information.

**per debit charge** A charge per check. Usually continues regardless of the number of checks written.

**percent** A percent is one hundredth. For example, 2 percent means 2 parts of a hundred.

**percent** or **rate of markdown** The markdown expressed as a percent of original price.

**percentage method of withholding** Used to determine federal withholding tax. This method does not require several pages of tables needed with the wage bracket method.

**percent formula** The basic percent formula is $P = B \times R$, or Part = Base $\times$ Rate.

**percent key** The electronic calculator key $\boxed{\%}$ which moves the decimal point two places to the left when used following multiplication or division.

**peril insurance** Insurance which pays upon a loss by the insured.

**period of compounding** Amount of time between the addition of interest to a deposit or loan.

**periodic inventory** A physical inventory taken at regular intervals.

**periodic payments** A series of payments made at regular intervals in time.

**perpetual inventory** A continuous inventory system normally utilizing a computer.

**personal checking account** The type of checking account used by individuals.

**personal exemption** Each taxpayer currently gets a deduction for each dependent, including the taxpayer.

**personal identification number (PIN)** A special code that must be entered when using an ATM card or a debit card.

**personal income tax** A type of tax charged by states and the federal government to individuals. The tax is based on income.

**personal property** That property which is not real property such as furnishings, appliances, cars, trucks, clothing, boats, and money.

**physical inventory** An actual physical count of each item in stock at a given time.

**piecework rate** A method of pay by which an employee receives so much money per item completed.

**plant assets** *See* Plant and equipment assets.

**plant and equipment assets** Items owned by a firm which will not be converted to cash within a year. Also called fixed assets or plant assets.

**policy** A contract between an insured and an insurance company.

**policy fee** An annual fee charged by insurance companies to cover the cost of processing the policy.

**policyholder** A person or business that has purchased insurance. Also known as the insured.

**population** The entire group being studied.

**postdating** Dating in the future; on an invoice "AS OF" dating.

**preferred stock** Stock which pays dividends before common stockholders receive any dividends.

**premium** The amount of money charged for an insurance policy.

**premium factor** A factor used to convert annual premiums to either semiannual, quarterly, or monthly premiums of an insurance policy.

**premium payment** An additional payment for extra service.

**premium rate** A higher amount of pay given for additional hours worked or additional units produced.

**present value** An amount that can be invested today to produce a given amount in the future.

**present value of an annuity** (1) The lump sum that can be deposited today that will amount to the same final total as would the periodic payment of an annuity. (2) A lump sum that could be deposited today so that equal periodic withdrawals could be made.

**price-earnings ratio (PE ratio)** The price per share of stock divided by the annual earnings per share of the stock.

**price relative** The quotient of the current price and the price in some past year with the quotient multiplied by 100.

**prime number** A number divisible without remainder only by itself or 1 (such as 7 or 13).

**prime rate** The interest rate at which large, financially secure corporations borrow money.

**principal** An amount of money either borrowed, loaned, or deposited. The initial amount of money deposited.

**proceeds** The amount of money the borrower receives after subtracting the discount from the face value of a note.

**promissory note** A document in which one person agrees to pay money to another person, a certain amount of time in the future, and at a certain rate of interest.

**proper fraction** A fraction in which the numerator is smaller than the denominator. For example, $\frac{2}{3}$ is a proper fraction; $\frac{9}{5}$ is not.

**property damage insurance** A type of automobile insurance that pays for damages caused to the property of others.

**property tax rate** For property, the tax rate is found by dividing total amount needed by total assessed value.

**proportion** A proportion says that two ratios are equal.

**proprietorship** *See* Owner's equity.

**proximo dating** In cash discounts, the time period beginning at the end of the month the invoice is dated. End-of-month dating (EOM) and "prox." have the same meaning.

**Publication 534** The Internal Revenue Service publication which gives a complete coverage of depreciation.

**purchase invoice** The invoice or document received by the purchaser of goods or services from the seller.

**quick ratio** *See* Acid-test ratio.

**quota bonus** A plan which pays a bonus to an employee after reaching a quota.

**range** The difference between the largest value and the smallest value in a set of numbers.

**rate** A number followed by "%" or "percent."

**rate of interest** The percent of interest charged for one year.

**ratio** A quotient of two quantities.

**ratio of net income after taxes to average owner's equity** Net income divided by average owner's equity.

**raw data** A set of data before analysis.

**real property** All land, buildings, and other improvements attached to the land.

**receipt of goods dating (ROG)** In cash discounts, time is counted from the date that goods are received.

**reciprocal** The result of interchanging the numerator and denominator of a fraction.

**reconciliation** The process of checking a bank statement against the depositor's own personal records.

**recourse** Merchants sometimes sell debts that are owed them. If the person owing the money is unavailable and the bank buying the debt has recourse to the merchant—the merchant is liable for the debt.

**recovery class** The class into which property is placed under MACRS (3-, 5-, 7- 10-, 15-, 20-, 27.5-, 31.5-, or 39-year class).

**recovery period** The number of years over which the cost of an asset is recovered using the MACRS.

**rediscounting** The process in which one financial institution discounts a note at a second institution.

**reduced net profit** This occurs when a markdown decreases the selling price to a point which is still above the breakeven point.

**reduced price** The selling price after subtracting the markdown, also called sale price and actual selling price.

**Regulation DD** A federal law requiring that interest paid on funds in savings accounts be paid based on the exact number of days.

**Regulation Z** *See* Federal Truth in Lending Act.

**repayment schedule** *See* Amortization schedule.

**repeating decimal** A decimal which repeats one or more digits without ending. A bar is often placed over the repeating digit(s). For example, .3$\overline{33}$ and .16$\overline{16}$ are both repeating decimals.

**repossess** The act by a lender of taking back ownership of an item when payments have not been made.

**restricted endorsement** Endorsement of a check so that only the person or company given the check may cash it.

**retail method** A method used to estimate inventory value at cost which utilizes both cost and retail amounts.

**retailer** A firm that sells directly to the consumer.

**returned deposit item** The return to the bank of an item which has been deposited, due to any number of irregularities.

**returned goods** Merchandise returned due to incorrect shipment or damage.

**returns** The total value of all goods returned by customers.

**revolving charge account** *See* Open-end credit.

**right side** In the equation $4x = 28$, the right side is 28.

**round lot** Multiple of 100 shares of stock.

**rounded decimals** Decimals reduced to a number with fewer decimals.

**Rule of 78** A method of calculating interest charges that need not be paid because the loan was paid off earlier than planned.

**rules for divisibility** Rules which help determine whether a number is evenly divisible by another number.

**salary** A fixed amount of money per pay period.

**salary and agreed ratio** Same as agreed ratio, except that a salary may be allowed to one partner or the other in addition to the profit division.

**salary plus commission** A commission is paid as a premium in addition to salary.

**sale price** *See* Reduced price.

**sales invoice** The invoice or document retained by the seller of goods or services, a copy of which is sent to the purchaser.

**sales quota** An expected level of production. A premium may be paid for surpassing quota.

**sales tax** A tax placed on sales to the final consumer. The tax is collected by the state, county, or local government.

**sales value** Value of sales for each department of a company.

**salvage value** or **scrap value** The value of an asset at the end of its useful life. For depreciation purposes, this is often an estimate.

**sample** A portion of the entire population being studied.

**savings account** *See* Passbook account.

**SDI (State Disability Insurance) deduction** The deduction for a state disability insurance program.

**self-employed individuals** Individuals who work for themselves instead of for the government or a company owned by someone else.

**selling price** The price at which merchandise is offered for sale to the public. The cost of an item plus its markup.

**series discount** *See* Chain discount.

**settlement options** Methods of receiving life insurance benefits in addition to a cash payment.

**shift-differential** A premium paid for working a less desirable shift, such as swing shift or graveyard shift.

**shipping point** The location from which merchandise is shipped by the seller to the buyer.

**short-term** or **cancellation rate** A rate used when charging for short-term policies and the refunds given when policies are canceled by the policyholder.

**silent partner** A partner who invests in a partnership, but takes no part in running it.

**simple annuity** An annuity with payment dates matching the compounding period.

**simple discount note** A note whose interest is deducted in advance from the face value, with only the difference given to the borrower.

**simple interest** Interest computed only on the principal.

**simple interest notes** Notes on which interest is found by formulas for simple interest.

**single discount** A discount expressed as a single percent and not as a series or chain discount.

**single discount equivalent to a series discount** A series or chain discount which is expressed as a single discount.

**sinking fund** A fund set up to receive equal periodic payments in order to pay off an obligation at some fixed time in the future.

**sliding-scale commission** A graduated commission plan giving a higher rate to top producing salespeople.

**SMP** The abbreviation for a special multi-perils policy. This policy gives additional insurance coverage to businesses. *See* Business owner's package policy.

**Social Security** *See* Federal Insurance Contributions Act (FICA).

**sole proprietorship** A business owned by one person.

**solution** A number that can replace a variable in an equation and result in a true statement.

**special endorsement** An endorsement to a specific payee.

**specific identification method** Inventory valuation method which identifies the cost of each individual item.

**split-shift premium** A premium paid for working a split shift. For example, an employee who is on 4 hours, off 4 hours, and then on 4 hours.

**spoilage** Merchandise which becomes unsaleable. Usually considered when calculating markup.

**square root** The square root $(\sqrt{\ })$ of a number is a number when multiplied by itself equals that number. The square root of 9, $\sqrt{9}$, is 3, since $3 \times 3 = 9$.

**square root key** The electronic calculator key  which calculates the square root of the number on the calculator.

**standard deduction** A deduction used to reduce taxable income for taxpayers who do not itemize their deductions.

**standard deviation** A measurement of the dispersion of a set of data.

**state withholding** State income tax withheld from gross earnings by the employer.

**stated rate** The rate of interest quoted by a bank, also called the nominal rate.

**statistics** Data and/or the analysis of data.

**stock** A share of stock represents partial ownership of a corporation.

**stock certificates** Documentation of stock ownership.

**stock company** An insurance company owned by stockholders. No dividend is paid to policyholders.

**stock exchange** A place or mechanism at or through which stocks can be bought and sold.

**stock ratio** Numbers used to compare stocks—typically the current yield and the PE ratio.

**stock turnover** *See* Inventory turnover.

**stockbroker** A person who buys and sells stock for the public.

**stockholders** The owners of a corporation.

**stockholders' equity** The difference between a corporation's assets and liabilities.

**stop payment order** A request that the bank not pay on a check previously written.

**straight commission** A fixed amount or percent for each unit of work. Earnings are based on performance alone.

**straight life insurance** Another name for ordinary or whole life insurance.

**straight-line depreciation** A depreciation method where depreciation is spread evenly over the life of the asset.

**substitution** Replacing the variable in an equation by the solution; substitution is used to check a solution.

**suicide clause** A clause which excludes suicide as an insurable cause of death (usually for the first two years of the policy).

**sum-of-the-years' digits method** An accelerated depreciation method using a depreciation fraction.

**T-bills** *See* U.S. Treasury bills.

**tax rate schedule** A schedule which shows the individual tax rates for tax filing status.

**taxable income** Adjusted gross income, minus exemptions, minus deductions.

**telephone transfer** The transfer of funds with a verbal request over the telephone.

**term** A single letter, a single number, or the product of a number and a letter.

**term insurance** A form of insurance providing protection for a fixed length of time.

**term of an annuity** The time from the beginning of the first payment into an annuity until the end of the last payment.

**term of the note** The length of time until a note is due.

**time** The number of years or fraction of a year for which the loan is made.

**time-and-a-half rate** Many employees are paid $1\frac{1}{2}$ times the normal rate of pay for any hours worked in excess of 40 hours per week, or 8 hours per day.

**time card** A card that is helpful in preparing the payroll. The time card includes such information as the dates of the pay period, the employee's name, and the number of hours worked.

**time deposit account** A savings account in which the depositor agrees to leave money for a certain period of time.

**time rate** Earnings based on hours worked, not work accomplished.

**time value of money,** or **value of money** The average interest rate for which money is loaned at a given time.

**total installment cost** Find the total installment cost by multiplying the amount of each payment on a loan and the number of payments; then add any down payment.

**total invoice amount** The sum of all the extension totals on an invoice.

**trade discount** The discount offered to businesses. This discount is expressed either as a single discount (such as 25%) or a series discount (such as 20/10) and is subtracted from the list price.

**transfer tax** A tax charged by some cities and states on the purchase or sale of stock.

**true rate of interest** *See* Effective rate of interest.

**turnover at cost** Found by the following formula.

$$\frac{\text{Cost of goods sold}}{\text{Amount of inventory at cost}}$$

**turnover at retail** Found by the following formula.

$$\frac{\text{Retail sales}}{\text{Average inventory at retail}}$$

**1099 form** This form is sent out by banks, savings and loans, and other financial institutions and shows interest, stock dividends, and other miscellaneous income.

**underinsured motorist insurance** Insurance coverage which covers the insured when involved in an accident with a driver who is underinsured. Coverage for bodily injury above the amounts of insurance carried by the underinsured driver.

**underwriter** An insurance company employee who determines the risk factors involved in the occurrence of various insurable losses. This helps determine the insurance premium.

**unearned interest** The amount of interest not owed when a loan is paid off early.

**unemployment insurance tax** A tax paid by employers. The money is used to pay unemployment benefits to qualified unemployed workers.

**uniform product codes (UPC)** Bar codes found on each product in most stores; used for efficient inventory control by stores. It also provides greater accuracy and perhaps faster service to the customer.

**uninsured motorist insurance** Insurance coverage which covers the insured when involved in an accident with a driver who is not insured.

**units-of-production method** A depreciation method using the units produced to determine depreciation allowance.

**United States Rule** A method of handling partial loan payoffs; any payment is first applied to the interest owed on the loan, with any balance then used to reduce the principal amount of the loan.

**universal life insurance** Allows the insured to vary the amount of premium and type of protection depending on changing insurance needs.

**unlike fractions** Fractions having different denominators.

**unpaid balance** The balance outstanding on a revolving charge account at the end of a billing period.

**unpaid balance method** A method of calculating the finance charge on a revolving charge account by using the balance at the end of the previous month.

**unsaleable items** Merchandise which cannot be sold. Usually considered when calculating markup.

**useful life** The estimated life of an asset. The IRS gives guidelines of useful life for depreciation purposes.

**U.S. Treasury bills** A loan of money to the United States government. Treasury bills (or T-bills) are a very safe way to invest money.

**variable** A letter that represents a number.

**variable commission** A rate of commission that depends on the total amount of the sales, with the rate increasing as sales increase.

**variable life insurance** Provides life insurance protection and allows the insured to select investment funds to invest the balance of the premium.

**variable rate loan** A home loan made at an interest rate that varies with market conditions.

**variance** The square of the standard deviation.

**vertical analysis** The process of listing each of the important items on an income statement as a percent of total net sales or each item on a balance sheet as a percent of total assets.

**VISA** A credit card plan.

**wage bracket method of withholding** Used to determine federal withholding tax. This method requires several pages of tables.

**waiver of premium clause** Allows insurance to continue without payment of premium when insured becomes disabled.

**weighted average method** Inventory valuation method where the cost of all purchases during a time period is divided by the number of units purchased.

**weighted mean** A mean calculated by using weights, so that each number is multiplied by its frequency.

**whole life insurance (Ordinary or straight life insurance)** A form of life insurance in which the insured pays a constant premium until death or retirement, whichever occurs sooner. Upon retirement, monthly payments are made by the company to the insured until the death of the insured.

**wholesaler** The middleman; purchases from manufacturers or other wholesalers and sells to retailers.

**wire transfer** The instant electronic transfer of funds from one account to another.

**withholding allowance** These allowances, for employees, their spouses and dependents, determine the amount of withholding tax taken from gross earnings.

**worker's compensation insurance** Insurance which provides payments to an employee who is unable to work due to a job related injury or illness.

**W-2 forms** The wage and tax statement given to the employee each year by the employer.

**youthful operator** A driver of a motor vehicle under a certain age, usually 25 years of age or younger.

**zero coupon bond** A bond that does not pay annual interest, rather it only pays the face value of the bond at maturity.

# Index

| | |
|---|---|
| **Comparing Simple Interest and Simple Discount Rates** | The simple interest rate $R$ and the simple discount rate $D$ are calculated by the formulas $$R = \frac{D}{1 - DT} \quad \text{and} \quad D = \frac{R}{1 + RT},$$ where $T$ is time in years. |
| **Compound Interest** | If $P$ dollars are deposited at a rate of interest $i$ per period for $n$ periods, then the *compound amount M*, or the final amount on deposit, is $$M = P(1 + i)^n.$$ The interest earned $I$ is $$I = M - P.$$ (Use column A of the interest table.) |
| **Present Value at Compound Interest** | The *present value P* of the future amount $M$ at an interest rate of $i$ per period for $n$ periods is $$P = \frac{M}{(1 + i)^n}. \qquad \text{(Use column B of the interest table.)}$$ |
| **Unearned Interest** | The *unearned interest* is given by $U = F\left(\dfrac{N}{P}\right)\left(\dfrac{1 + N}{1 + P}\right)$ where: $U$ = Unearned interest $\qquad$ $N$ = Number of payments remaining $\phantom{where: }F$ = Finance charge $\qquad\quad$ $P$ = Total number of payments |
| **Annuities, Sinking Funds, and Amortization** | **Lump Sums.** A lump sum is deposited today; to find the *compound amount* in the future, use the formula $M = P(1 + i)^n$ and column A of the interest table in Appendix C. To find the lump sum which is the *present value* today of a known amount in the future, use $P = \dfrac{M}{(1 + i)^n}$ and column B. **Making Periodic Payments.** To find the *amount of an annuity* when periodic payments are made for a fixed period of time, use $S = R \cdot s_{\overline{n}|i}$ and column C. To find the amount that could be deposited today that would be equivalent to a series of periodic payments, find the *present value of an annuity* by using the formula $A = R \cdot a_{\overline{n}|i}$ and column D. **Find Periodic Payments.** To find the periodic payment that must be made to produce some fixed total in the future, use the formula for a *sinking fund*, $$R = S\left(\frac{1}{s_{\overline{n}|i}}\right), \text{ and column E.}$$ The periodic payment that will pay off, or amortize, a loan is given by $$R = A\left(\frac{1}{a_{\overline{n}|i}}\right) \text{ and column F.}$$ |